Child Support Guidelines in Canada, 2024

Julien D. Payne
Marilyn A. Payne

UNIVERSITY OF TORONTO PRESS
Toronto Buffalo London

Irwin Law
An imprint of University of Toronto Press
Toronto Buffalo London
utorontopress.com
Printed and bound by CPI Group (UK) Ltd, Croydon, CR0 4YY

ISBN 978-1-5522-1742-9 (paper) ISBN 978-1-5522-1743-6 (PDF)

THE MATERIAL IN THIS BOOK IS CURRENT TO 14 FEBRUARY 2024.

Library and Archives Canada Cataloguing in Publication

Payne, Julien D.
Child Support Guidelines in Canada / Julien D. Payne and Marilyn A. Payne

Published: Toronto
Every 3 years

[1st ed. (2004–)]
ISSN 1922-0138
ISBN 978-1-55221-466-4 (2017 edition)

1. Child support—Law and legislation—Canada I. Payne, Julien D. II. Title

KE602.P29 346.7101

Cover design: Val Cooke
Cover image: iStock.com/marigold_88

We wish to acknowledge the land on which the University of Toronto Press operates. This land is the traditional territory of the Wendat, the Anishnaabeg, the Haudenosaunee, the Métis, and the Mississaugas of the Credit First Nation.

University of Toronto Press acknowledges the financial support of the Government of Canada and the Ontario Arts Council, an agency of the Government of Ontario, for its publishing activities.

Canada Council for the Arts Conseil des Arts du Canada

ONTARIO ARTS COUNCIL
CONSEIL DES ARTS DE L'ONTARIO
an Ontario government agency
un organisme du gouvernement de l'Ontario

Funded by the Government of Canada Financé par le gouvernement du Canada Canada

DEDICATION

In memoriam to Dr Arthur Barlow, a former lecturer at King's College, London, who was truly both a gentleman and a scholar.

Summary Table of Contents

PREFACE *xix*

ACKNOWLEDGEMENTS *xxi*

CHAPTER 1: **Criteria and Objectives of Child Support** *1*

CHAPTER 2: **Jurisdiction** *18*

CHAPTER 3: **Definitions of "Child of the Marriage"; Adult Children; Obligation of *De Facto* Parent** *33*

CHAPTER 4: **Determination of Income; Disclosure of Income** *117*

CHAPTER 5: **Special or Extraordinary Expenses** *278*

CHAPTER 6: **Split and Shared Parenting Time Arrangements** *335*

CHAPTER 7: **Undue Hardship** *370*

CHAPTER 8: **Impact of Child Support on Spousal Support** *406*

CHAPTER 9: **Low- and High-Income Earners; Annual Income over $150,000** *412*

CHAPTER 10: **Effect of Order or Agreement or Other Arrangement That Benefits Child; Consent Orders** *425*

CHAPTER 11: **Form and Types of Order** *446*

CHAPTER 12: **Effect, Registration, and Enforcement of Child Support Orders** *513*

CHAPTER 13: **Variation, Rescission, or Suspension of Child Support Orders** *547*

CHAPTER 14: **Evidence; Procedure; Costs** *596*

CHAPTER 15: **Appeals** *656*

TABLE OF CASES *667*

ABOUT THE AUTHORS *771*

Detailed Table of Contents

PREFACE *xix*

ACKNOWLEDGEMENTS *xxi*

CAVEAT *xxv*

CHAPTER 1
CRITERIA AND OBJECTIVES OF CHILD SUPPORT *1*

A. Introduction *1*

B. Relevance of Income Tax *2*

C. Statutory Provisions Regulating Child Support *5*

D. The *Federal Child Support Guidelines* *6*

1) Coming into Force *6*
2) Terminology *6*
3) Objectives of *Federal Child Support Guidelines* *7*
4) Obligor's Income Model of *Federal Child Support Guidelines* *7*

E. Application of *Federal Child Support Guidelines*; Provincial Legislation *8*

1) Orders Governed by *Federal Child Support Guidelines* *8*
2) Provincial Guidelines *9*
3) Extramarital Children; Disputed Paternity *10*

F. Presumptive Rule; Provincial and Territorial Tables *11*

G. Applicable Provincial or Territorial Table *14*

H. Fixed Table Amount; Judicial Discretion; Condition, Means, Needs, and Other Circumstances *14*

1) Definition of "Condition" of Spouses and Child *15*
2) Definition of "Means" *16*
3) Definition of "Other Circumstances" *17*

CHAPTER 2

JURISDICTION *18*

A. Judicial Jurisdiction over Applications for Child Support on or after Divorce *18*

B. Evidence; Practice and Procedure *19*

C. Legislative Authority of Parliament *20*

D. *Canadian Charter of Rights and Freedoms* *20*

E. Competing Jurisdictions under Provincial and Federal Legislation *20*

F. Time of Original Application *24*

G. Dismissal of Divorce Petition *24*

H. Status of Applicant; Payment to Child *24*

I. Third-Party Payments *30*

J. Advance Payments; Post-dated Cheques; Electronic Transfers *31*

K. Child Residing Outside Canada *32*

L. Effect of Death *32*

CHAPTER 3

DEFINITIONS OF "CHILD OF THE MARRIAGE"; ADULT CHILDREN; OBLIGATION OF *DE FACTO* PARENT *33*

A. Relevant Statutory Provisions *33*

B. Effect of Differing Criteria under Federal and Provincial Legislation *36*

C. Applicable Criteria under *Divorce Act* and *Federal Child Support Guidelines* Respecting Children under and Over the Provincial Age of Majority *38*

D. Child's Illness or Disability; Respective Obligations of Parents and State *39*

E. Post-Secondary Education or Training *46*

F. Children over Age of Majority: Section 3(2) of Guidelines *61*

G. Unemployment; Scope of "Other Cause" *78*

H. Withdrawal from Parental Charge *79*

I. Reversion to Former Status of Child of the Marriage *83*

J. Persons Standing in Place of Parents *85*

1) Legal Requirements *85*
2) Termination of Relationship *96*
3) Respective Obligations of Biological or Adoptive Parents and of Persons Standing in the Place of Parents; Joint and Several Liability *97*
4) Independent Actions between Sequential Parents *109*

K. Conduct *111*

CHAPTER 4

DETERMINATION OF INCOME; DISCLOSURE OF INCOME 117

A. Whose Income? 117

B. Written Agreement as to Annual Income 117

C. Determination of Annual Income; Use of CRA T1 General Form; Statutory Adjustments 118

1) General Observations 118
2) Basic Steps for Determining Income 119
3) Section 16 and Schedule III Adjustments 122
   a) Federal and Provincial Government Benefits; Canada Child Benefit and GST Credits 126
   b) Employment Expenses 126
   c) Social Assistance Benefits 129
   d) Dividend Income 129
   e) Capital Gains 133
   f) Non-Arm's-Length Payments 134
   g) Fiscal Year-End Adjustments 135
   h) Capital Cost Allowances on Real Property 135
   i) Partnership Income 136
   j) Stock Options 136
   k) Union Dues 142
   l) Spousal Support Payments 142
   m) Child Support Payments 143
4) Personal and Business Expenses and Losses 145
5) Commission Income; Bonuses; Stock Options; Severance Packages 146
6) Problems with Self-Employed Parents 148
7) Student Loans 150
8) Future Commissions 150
9) Exclusions from Income 151
10) RRSPs; Pensions 152
11) Work Done but Unbilled 154
12) Trust Funds 155
13) Seasonal Employment 155
14) Damages; Structured Settlements 155
15) Foster Parent's Allowance 156

D. Most Current Information to Be Used 156

E. Pattern of Income 162

F. Income of Shareholder, Director, or Officer of Corporation; Adjustment of Corporation's Pre-tax Income 170

G. Imputing Income 190

1) Listed Circumstances under Section 19 of Guidelines 190
2) Non-Exhaustive List under Section 19 of Guidelines 191
3) Evidence 193
4) Earning Capacity; Intentional Underemployment or Unemployment 196

5) Unreported Income; Underground Economy 213
6) Vocational Assessment 214
7) Forgivable Loans; Family Gifts 214
8) Income Tax Concessions 215
9) Failure to Make Financial Disclosure 217
10) Lifestyle 218
11) Investments; Financial Management 219
12) Bank Records 220
13) Income Splitting 220
14) Capital Assets 221
15) Diversion of Income 221
16) Unreasonable Expenses; Capital Cost Allowances; Optional Inventory Adjustments 221
17) Barter Arrangements 230
18) Casual Earnings 230
19) Underutilized Assets 230
20) Cohabitant's or Spouse's Income 231
21) Shareholder Loans 232
22) Personal Injuries Settlement 235
23) Overtime 235
24) Free or Subsidized Accommodation 236
25) Income from Illegal Activity 238
26) Foster Care Allowances 238
27) Legal Fees 239
28) Interim Orders 239
29) Applications to Vary 239
30) Appeals 240

H. Child's Access to Income 240

I. Income of Non-Resident Spouse; Currency Exchange Rate 241

J. Social Assistance 242

K. Income Information 245

L. Ongoing Disclosure 259

M. Non-disclosure of Income or Assets or of Material Change of Circumstances 262

N. Disclosure by Third Parties or Non-parties 263

O. Sanctions for Non-disclosure 273

P. Financial Statements and Budgets 276

CHAPTER 5
SPECIAL OR EXTRAORDINARY EXPENSES 278

A. Distinctions between Ordinary and Extraordinary Expenses; Definition of Extraordinary Expenses 278

B. Exhaustive List of Designated Expenses; Definition of "Means" 290

C. Sharing of Expenses as Guiding Principle; Effect of Spousal Support 295

D. Subsidies; Tax Deductions or Credits *300*
E. Particulars of Expense to Be Specified in Order *303*
F. Add-Ons or Set-Offs *303*
G. Direct and Hidden Costs of Primary Caregiving Parent *304*
H. Periodic or Lump Sum Payments *304*
I. Child Care Expenses *304*
J. Medical and Dental Insurance; Medical, Dental, or Health-Related Expenses *311*
K. Extraordinary Educational Expenses; Private School *315*
L. Expenses for Post-Secondary Education *320*
M. Extraordinary Expenses for Extracurricular Activities *326*

CHAPTER 6
SPLIT AND SHARED PARENTING TIME ARRANGEMENTS *335*

A. Section 8 of the Guidelines: Split Parenting Time Due to Separation of Siblings *335*
B. Section 9 of the Guidelines: Shared Parenting Time; 40 Percent Rule *338*
1) Basic Provisions of Section 9 of the Guidelines *338*
2) The 40 Percent Rule *338*
3) Shared Parenting Time under Section 9 of the *Federal Child Support Guidelines*—SCC Definitive Ruling on Relevant Criteria *347*
4) Increased Costs: Section 9(b) of the Guidelines *354*
a) Judicial Discretion to Deviate from Set-Off Under Section 9(c) of Guidelines *355*
5) Reasons for Decision *358*
6) Mixed Parenting Time Arrangements and Blended Families *359*
7) Section 7 and Other Expenses *362*
8) Evidence *362*
9) Negative Aspects of Section 9 of the Guidelines *363*
10) Canada Child Benefit; Eligible Dependant Tax Credit *364*
11) Variation Orders *366*
12) Provincial Guidelines *368*
13) Conclusion *369*

CHAPTER 7
UNDUE HARDSHIP *370*

A. General Observations *370*
B. Stringent Criterion of Undue Hardship *377*
C. Circumstances That May Cause Undue Hardship *379*
D. Family Debts or Employment Expenses *382*
E. Unusually High Expenses in Relation to Exercising Parenting Time with a Child; Payment of Child Support to Non-Primary Caregiving Parent *384*
F. Duty under Court Order or Separation Agreement to Support Any Person *390*

G. Legal Duty to Support Any Child Other Than a Child of the Marriage; Sequential Families *391*

H. Legal Duty to Support a Sick or Disabled Person *395*

I. Reasonable Time to Overcome Hardship *395*

J. Judicial Discretion in Cases of Undue Hardship Circumscribed by Comparison of Standard of Living in Respective Households *396*

K. Reasons for Deviation from Norm to Be Judicially Recorded *404*

L. Section 7 Expenses *404*

M. Shared Parenting Time *405*

CHAPTER 8

IMPACT OF CHILD SUPPORT ON SPOUSAL SUPPORT *406*

A. Priority of Child Support over Spousal Support; Effect of Child Support Order on Assessment of Spousal Support *406*

B. Implications of Child Care during Marriage and after Divorce on Spousal Support Entitlement *410*

CHAPTER 9

LOW- AND HIGH-INCOME EARNERS; ANNUAL INCOME OVER $150,000 *412*

A. Low-Income Earners *412*

B. Annual Income over $150,000 *413*

C. High-Income Spouse or Former Spouse with Short Career *423*

CHAPTER 10

EFFECT OF ORDER OR AGREEMENT OR OTHER ARRANGEMENT THAT BENEFITS CHILD; CONSENT ORDERS *425*

A. Advantages and Limitations of Parental Settlements *425*

B. Relevant Statutory Provisions *428*

C. Meaning of "Special Provisions" and "Inequitable" under Sections 15.1(5) and 17(6.2) of *Divorce Act* *429*

D. Ambit of Judicial Discretion *432*

E. Court Records *439*

F. Consent Orders *439*

G. Provincial Legislation and Guidelines *440*

H. Artificial Insemination *445*

CHAPTER 11

FORM AND TYPES OF ORDER *446*

A. Diverse Types of Order *446*

B. Interim Orders 447

1) Types of Interim Order 447
2) Effect of Reconciliation on Interim Order 447
3) Effect of Divorce on Interim Order 448
4) Relationship Between Federal Divorce Legislation and Provincial/Territorial Legislation 448
5) Relevance of Ultimate Entitlement; Definition of "Child of the Marriage" 448
6) Application of *Federal Child Support Guidelines* 449
7) Interim-Interim Orders; Adjournments 450
8) Effect of Delay 451
9) Voluntary Payments 451
10) Graduated Payments 451
11) Fixed-Term Orders 451
12) Interim Spousal Support; Interim Child Support 452
13) Retroactive Interim Orders 452
14) Subsequent Adjustment of Interim Order 453
15) Interim and Permanent Orders; Effect of Delay Before Trial 454
16) Right to Be Heard; Adjournments 455
17) Variation of Interim Orders 455
18) Appeals of Interim Orders 458

C. Periodic and Lump Sum Payments 459

1) Section 11 of Guidelines 459
2) Limits on Judicial Discretion 459
3) Consent Orders for Lump Sum in Lieu of Periodic Child Support 460
4) Lump Sums in Addition to Periodic Sums to Reflect Bonuses 461
5) Undue Hardship May Trigger Lump Sum 461
6) Lump Sum by Instalments 461
7) Lump Sum Interim Orders 461
8) Lump Sum Capitalization of Periodic Support 461
9) Periodic Support as the Norm 462
10) Lump Sum Contribution to Section 7 Expenses 463
11) Lump Sum Settlements 464
12) Reimbursement of Lump Sum 464
13) Lump Sum Retroactive Child Support 464
14) Lump Sum on Death of Parent 464
15) Variation of Lump Sum Orders 465

D. Orders to Pay and Secure Support 465

1) Section 12 of Guidelines 465
2) Orders to Pay and/or Secure Support 466
3) Diverse Types of Security 466
4) Justification for Orders to Secure Support Payments 470
5) Variation of Security 470
6) Remission to Trial Division by Appellate Court 471
7) Order to Restrain Disposition of Assets; Mareva Injunction 471

E. Division of Property; Possession of Matrimonial Home 472

F. Information to Be Specified in Order 473

G. Avoidance of Combined Orders for Child Support and Spousal Support 474

H. Commencement and Duration of Orders; Effect of Reconciliation 475

1) Normal Commencement Date 475
2) Fixed-Term and Review Orders 475
3) Duration of Order 475
4) Stay of Order 477
5) Future Child Support 477
6) Effect of Spousal Reconciliation 477
7) Effect of Obligor's Death 478

I. Terms and Conditions 480

1) Section 15.1(4) of *Divorce Act* 480
2) Speculative and Anticipated Future Contingencies 480
3) Registered Education Savings Plan 483
4) Retroactive Adjustment of Child Support Based on Subsequent Income Tax Returns; Ongoing Financial Disclosure 483
5) Control over Child Support Payments 484
6) Parenting 484
7) "Step Down" Provisions 485

J. Cost of Living Indexation 485

K. Retroactive Permanent and Variation Orders; Appeals 486

1) Retroactivity under Sections 15.1 and 17 of *Divorce Act* 486
2) Interim Orders 486
3) Diversity of Judicial Approaches 487
4) Enumerated Factors Relating to Retroactivity 489
5) Variation Orders 507
6) Types of Retroactive Order 507
7) Effect of Successful Appeal 508
8) Need for Application 508
9) Retroactive Orders under Shared Parenting Arrangements 508
10) Effect of Bankruptcy 509
11) Effect of Income Tax Reassessment 509
12) Significance of Separation Agreement or Minutes of Settlement 509
13) Retroactive Section 7 Expenses 510
14) Interest 511
15) Retroactive Child Support Orders After Adulthood 511
16) Jurisdiction of Provincial Court 511
17) Recalculation of Child Support Where Change in Income During the Year 512

CHAPTER 12
EFFECT, REGISTRATION, AND ENFORCEMENT OF CHILD SUPPORT ORDERS 513

A. Definition of "Court" 513

B. National Effect of Corollary Orders 514

C. Enforcement and Variation Distinguished 514
D. Enforcement under Provincial Laws 517
E. Burden of Proof; Failure to Attend 517
F. Federal Enforcement Legislation 517
G. Garnishment; Attachment; Execution 518
H. Enforcement by Provincial Agencies 520
I. Suspension of Driving Licence 527
J. Crown's Priority as Tax Collector; Other Creditors 528
K. Committal for Contempt; Receivership 529
L. Order or Agreement; Election of Remedy 534
M. Enforcement of Support Arrears Against Bankrupt Defaulter 534
N. Fraudulent Conveyances and Preferences 534
O. *Locus Standi* of Child 535
P. Child No Longer a Child of the Marriage 535
Q. Enforcement, Suspension, and Remission of Arrears 535
R. Enforcement by Provincial Court 537
S. Enforcement of Separation Agreement 537
T. Set-Off 538
U. Interest 540
V. Piercing the Corporate Veil 541
W. Division of Matrimonial Property 542
X. Effect of Death 542
Y. Stay of Enforcement 542
Z. Effect of Reconciliation 543
AA. Laches; Limitation of Actions 543
BB. Assignment of Orders 544
CC. Fixing of Arrears; Payment by Instalments 545
DD. Support Deduction Orders 546
EE. Preservation Orders 546
FF. Registration Against Land 546

CHAPTER 13
VARIATION, RESCISSION, OR SUSPENSION OF CHILD SUPPORT ORDERS 547

A. Relevant Statutory and Regulatory Provisions 547
B. Jurisdiction 550
C. Transfer of Proceeding to Another Province 550
D. Appropriate Judicial District; Change of Venue 550

E. Effect of Appeal 551
F. Enforcement and Variation Distinguished under Provincial Legislation 551
G. Status of Applicant; Effect of Default 551
H. Interim Variation of Permanent Orders 552
I. Future Contingencies 556
J. Change of Circumstances; Onus of Proof 556
K. Variation of Amount of Child Support Made under Applicable Table 560
L. Variation where Amount of Child Support Not under Provincial or Territorial Table 561
M. Variation of Orders Pre-dating Implementation of Guidelines 567
N. Adjournments; Stay of Variation Proceeding 569
O. Increase of Special or Extraordinary Expenses 569
P. Reduction of Child Support; Termination of Employment 569
Q. Effect of Remarriage or Unmarried Cohabitation with Third Party 571
R. Suspension of Orders 571
1) Suspension of Child Support as a Sanction for Denial of Parenting Time 572
S. Remission of Arrears 573
1) General Review 573
2) Remission of Child Support Arrears: Response of the Supreme Court of Canada in *Colucci v Colucci* 583
T. Overpayment 586
U. Variation of Consent Orders 590
V. Variation under Provincial Legislation 591
W. Variation Pending Appeal 591
X. Types of Order 592
Y. Effect of Death 592
Z. Automatic Annual Variation 593

CHAPTER 14
EVIDENCE; PROCEDURE; COSTS 596

A. Credibility 596
B. Proof of Paternity; Blood Tests and DNA Tests; Artificial Insemination 599
C. Written Interrogatories 601
D. Affidavits 602
E. Admissions 604
F. Notice; Inadequacy of Information; Non-Attendance 604
G. Formal Motion or Application Required; Telephone Application 606

H. Pleadings *606*

I. Amendment of Pleadings *608*

J. Striking Out of Pleadings *611*

K. Adjournments *616*

L. Duty to Make Full Disclosure *618*

M. Discovery *619*

N. Disclosure by Third Parties *620*

O. Exclusion of Party from Hearing *621*

P. Right to Cross-Examine and Give Evidence *621*

Q. Right to Be Heard; Allegations of Judicial Bias *622*

R. A Stay of Proceedings for Non-Compliance with a Subsisting Order or Other Cause *623*

S. Directing Trial of An Issue *624*

T. Joinder and Consolidation of Actions; Adding of Parties *624*

U. Judicial Reconsideration Before and After Formal Entry of Judgment; Reopening of Case *627*

V. Variation Proceeding *630*

W. Masters; Registrars *631*

X. Computer Programs *631*

Y. Plea of Undue Hardship *631*

Z. Pre-Trials *632*

AA. Summary Judgment *632*

BB. Rescission of Orders *632*

CC. Expert Opinions *633*

DD. Judicial Notice *634*

EE. Dispute Resolution Processes *635*

FF. Undertakings *636*

GG. Hearsay Evidence *636*

HH. Self-Represented Litigants *636*

II. Judicial Discretion Over Costs *640*

JJ. Costs On Solicitor and Client Basis; Special or Increased Costs *642*

KK. Fixed Costs *646*

LL. Security for Costs *646*

MM. Interim Costs and Disbursements *650*

NN. Public Officials *653*

OO. Enforcement of Costs; Bankruptcy *654*

PP. Tax Deduction of Legal Fees *655*

CHAPTER 15
APPEALS *656*

A. Definition of "Appellate Court" *656*

B. General Observations *656*

C. Restrictions on Status Appeals *657*

D. Restrictions on Corollary Order Appeals *657*

E. Role and Powers of Appellate Court *660*

F. Interim Orders *662*

G. Denial of Appeal; Motion to Dismiss Appeal; Reinstatement of Appeal *662*

H. Effect of Appeal *663*

I. Stay of Order Pending Appeal *664*

J. Absence or Delay of Reasons for Judgment *664*

K. Fresh Evidence *665*

L. Appeals to the Supreme Court of Canada *666*

TABLE OF CASES *667*

ABOUT THE AUTHORS *771*

Preface

The objectives underlying this edition of *Child Support Guidelines in Canada* are to provide a comprehensive analysis of the caselaw, to produce order out of chaos, and to provide a quick and efficient means for readers to gain access to pertinent information on all aspects of the *Federal Child Support Guidelines* and corresponding provincial guidelines. This book is a "meat-and-potatoes" analysis that is written primarily for practising lawyers and judges who serve in the trenches of family warfare. The author's role is perceived as that of an ana lyst, not that of an advocate engaged in social engineering. The book describes what judges have said and done without engaging in any socio-economic evaluation of the *Federal Child Support Guidelines*. This is a companion volume to Payne & Payne, *Canadian Family Law* (Irwin Law).

Acknowledgements

As with previous editions, the research and word-processing costs of this edition of *Child Support Guidelines in Canada, 2022* have been financed by Danreb Inc, a private corporation that engages in legal research and publications and in social policy and management consulting. The authors wish to acknowledge their access to relevant judicial decisions with neutral citations through their regular use of CanLII.

The authors thank Jeff Miller for his co-operation in facilitating this publication and arranging for the in-house preparation of a comprehensive case list. The authors much appreciate the efforts of Lesley Steeve, Dale Clarry, Heather Raven, and others who discharged editorial responsibilities in their usual efficient manner.

There comes a time in an author's life when he (for those who don't know me, I am a male) should look back and acknowledge with gratitude the contribution that others have made to the development of one's career. First and foremost, I want to thank my late parents, Kathleen Mary Payne and Frederick Payne. For the rest of this piece, I shall avoid the word "late." If the people I mention continue to influence what I do, then it is unfair to refer to them as late. In any event, I am not always sure whether some of them are still on the tree of life. Some people have the same thoughts about me. I derive my commitment and dedication from my mother. When my mother was in business with my father, she was the initiator of change. She had an uncanny ability to anticipate changes in market forces. For those who have followed my career, which probably means only me, I always took pride in being the first off the mark. It didn't always work out. In the mid-1980s, I submitted an article entitled "The Mediation of Family Disputes" to the *Canadian Bar Review* and to the *Irish Jurist*. They both declined to publish it because it had nothing to do with law. How times have changed. Not to be defeated, I published the paper in *Payne's Divorce and Family Law Digest* at pages 1861–67 (Richard De Boo Publishers, 1984). My publishers had no choice if they wanted to continue to use my services as a digester of cases. But, looking back beyond that point to the beginning of my writing and law reform careers, I owe a great deal to Tony Palmer, of Burroughs Company Limited, who invited me to write the second edition of the then bible in Canadian family law, namely, *Power on Divorce*. After the publication of the second edition in 1964, I was recognized as an authority on Canadian family law by legal practitioners, a remarkable feat for a thirty-year-old academic. What was that: "Those who can't do, teach"? I knew more about evidence, procedure, and costs in family law at that time than any living Canadian — and it was all attributable to that giant in the field, W Kent Power, who was too ill to write his own second edition. I earned forty cents per hour rewriting his book, but it opened the door to my passion for family law and its reform.

In the early 1960s, I enjoyed my initial foray into family law reform by serving as a research associate with the Ontario Law Reform Commission. I wrote papers on topics such as judicial separation, alimony, the *Deserted Wives and Children's Maintenance Act*, legitimacy, evidence, and procedure. For the historians and law reformers among you, copies of these and other of my research publications are freely available online, courtesy of ResearchGate. In 1966–1967, I submitted a Brief on Marriage and Divorce to The Special Joint Committee of the Senate and House of Commons on Divorce (Canada) (The Roebuck/Cameron Committee). Rejecting any predisposition towards humility, I can truly say that my brief to this committee bears a remarkable similarity to the actual provisions of the *Divorce Act* of 1968. From 1972–1975, I served as the Director of the Family Law Project undertaken by the Law Reform Commission of Canada, whose report contributed significantly to the *Divorce Act, 1985*, thereby laying the foundation for my next book on Canadian divorce law, *Payne's Commentaries on The Divorce Act, 1985*, which ultimately culminated in *Payne on Divorce*, 4th edition (Carswell, 1996). Both before and after the passage of the *Divorce Act, 1985*, I was requested by Glenn Rivard, former General Counsel for the Family, Children and Youth Section of the Department of Justice, Canada, to undertake research relating to spousal support and child support rights and obligations. My earlier consultations led to the implementation of diverse policy objectives as the basis of spousal support orders on or after divorce to replace the predominant emphasis placed on rehabilitative spousal support orders by the Law Reform Commission of Canada in its Report on Family Law in March 1976: see sections 15.2(6) and 17(7) of the *Divorce Act*, 1985; and see Julien D Payne, "Policy Objectives of Private Law Spousal Support Rights and Obligations" in Katherine Connell-Thouez & Bartha Maria Knoppers, *Contemporary Trends in Family Law: A National Perspective* (Toronto: Carswell Legal Publications, 1984); see further, *Income Support Systems for Family Dependants on Marriage Breakdown: An Examination of Fundamental Policy Questions: Part V. Nature and Purpose of Spousal Support*, a research project undertaken by Professor Julien D Payne on behalf of the Alberta Institute of Law Research and Reform, 5 June 1982; see also Julien David Payne, *A Review of Spousal and Child Support Under the Domestic Relations Act* of Alberta [Part 5 of 15], Nature and Purpose of Spousal Support, 8 October 1991, online, Julien David Payne — ResearchGate. In September 1988, I prepared a very detailed report for the Department of Justice, Canada, on *Spousal and Child Support*, which proposed the appointment of a special committee to consider the desirability of introducing fixed child support schedules. The implementation of the *Federal Child Support Guidelines* in 1996 annihilated my detailed chapter on child support in the fourth edition of *Payne on Divorce*, thus paving the way for diverse editions of *Payne and Payne on Child Support Guidelines in Canada*, which first appeared on Quicklaw as an electronic book in July 1997. Oh, I should mention that I also co-authored *Payne's Digests on Family Law* from 1968 to 1999 and a Family Law E-Letter for Canadian judges every three weeks from October 2000 until May 2016. Looking back, I estimate that I have read and digested well over 50,000 cases since 1968. After being unceremoniously transmitted into mandatory retirement by the Faculty of Law at the University of Ottawa in 1999, I took up an appointment as the Law Foundation Chair at the University of Saskatchewan College of Law from July 1999 until January 2001. Since then I have added to my "post-retirement" publications by co-authoring *Canadian Family Law*, now in its ninth edition, and *Child Support Guidelines in Canada*, now in its eighth hardcopy edition, in addition to preparing the aforementioned E-Letter for the National Judicial Institute. So much for mandatory retirement! Well, that just about summarizes my rise to fame as a family law author and zealous activist in reforming Canada's family law, without identifying many of those who helped me along the way in my career. So, let me list them.

First, there is Marilyn, my wife. Not only does she do the typing/word processing of my publications and our joint publications; she is the only person in the world who can tell me I'm wrong and avoid my paranoid response thereto. Frequent citation in the law reports generates a narcissistic disposition that lends itself to the perception that one is rarely wrong. It's quite amazing how much authority I wield outside of the home, whereas in the home I rank well behind Abby, our chocolate brown Labrador, now that Zoey, our black lab, has gone to doggie heaven. Thank you, Zoey, for all the good times. And welcome aboard, Abby, the friendliest dog in Canada.

Let me now turn to some other people who influenced my thinking during my early career. Thank you, Dr Sheila Kessler, for introducing me to the practice of mediation in the 1970s, and to OJ Coogler for his seminal work, *Structured Mediation in Divorce Settlement: A Handbook for Marital Mediators* (Lexington Books, 1978). You taught me well. Thank you to the Association of Family and Conciliation Courts, particularly Meyer (Mike) Elkin, for keeping me holistic. Thank you, Paul Bohannan, professor of Anthropology at Northwestern University. I never met you, but your chapter titled "The Six Stations of Divorce," which was published in *Divorce and After* (Doubleday & Company, 1971), laid the foundation for my lifelong involvement in promoting diverse systems of family conflict management and family dispute resolution processes that accommodate the multi-faceted aspects of divorce and family breakdown. It was a short chapter but it has had an immense and ongoing impact on my thinking, my publications, and my frequent contributions to family law reform and family dispute resolution in Canada.

In consequence of my serving as the Director of the Family Law Project undertaken by the Law Reform Commission of Canada from 1972 to 1975, I have been described as the architect of Unified Family Courts and no-fault divorce in Canada: see full text of Julien D Payne, "A Conceptual Analysis of Unified Family Courts," 31 December 1973, Law Reform Commission of Canada, online: https://archive.org/stream/conceptualanalysoopayn/conceptualanalysoopayn_djvu.txt. I am, of course, prepared to take all of the credit and none of the blame. But, in fact, the Family Law Project was a team effort, with Professor Terry Wuester of the University of Saskatchewan and Professor Murray Fraser of Dalhousie University being my major co-conspirators, and Drs Herman (Bobby) Hahlo and Richard (Dick) Gosse providing invaluable input. Useful contributions were also made by Francois Chretien, Hugh Silverman Barbara Hough, Ron Fritz, and by Leslie Katz who prepared an outstanding analysis of the ambit of federal and provincial legislative jurisdiction in family law matters in Canada. However, we would have achieved nothing without the vigilant and unqualified support of Justice Patrick Hartt, chairman of the Law Reform Commission, and of Professor JW (Hans) Mohr, the two commissioners assigned to the Family Law Project. We had disagreements within the commission but, for the most part, we won the war.

I also need to express my appreciation to my long-time friend, Justice Claire L'Heureux-Dubé, formerly of the Supreme Court of Canada. She cited my writings profusely but we were friends long before that. I always assert that there is no correlation between the two. We just happened to be on the same wavelength.

I also want to thank Dave Adamson, Mike Brady, and Carl Leahy, who kept me sane by taking me away from family law for seven days during the first week in November. I venture to think that we consumed more liquor during that week than we did during the rest of the year. Maybe that's why we rarely saw any deer.

Well, that's it, folks. As for the future, I will continue to write for as long as I have a single reader. And, at my age, I have to repeatedly read what I have written in order to stay on point. So I'll always have at least one reader. It's been a blast and in the words of Yogi Berra: "It ain't over till it's over." In 2014, I celebrated the fiftieth anniversary of the publication of my first book. And in 2019, I celebrated the publication of my fiftieth book. (Yes, every new edition is counted as a book.) I can't afford to quit writing. Marilyn needs the money.

Julien D Payne, CM, KC, LLD, LSM, FRSC
President, Danreb Inc
(Management and Social Policy Consultants and Legal Education Specialists)

CAVEAT

There is a danger in taking too much from a judgment by deriving broad general rules, tests, or propositions from the resolution of a particular dispute. Reasons for judgment must be read with a critical mind in light of the applicable legal and factual backgrounds: *MacDonald v MacDonald*, [2002] BCJ No 121 (CA), citing *Bell v Klein* (No 3) (1954), 13 WWR 193 (BCCA).

This publication is distributed on the basis that the authors, copyright holder, and pub lisher are not engaged in rendering legal, accounting, or other professional advice. If legal advice or other expert assistance is required, the services of a competent professional should be sought. The analysis contained herein should not be construed as being either official or unofficial policy of any governmental body.

CHAPTER 1

Criteria and Objectives of Child Support

A. INTRODUCTION

Before the implementation of the *Federal Child Support Guidelines* in Canada on 1 May 1997, empirical data in Canada indicate that a divorced primary caregiving parent was unlikely to receive more than 20 percent of the net income of the paying spouse and parent as spousal and/or child support. It is not surprising, therefore, that single mothers and their children represented a disproportionate percentage of the poverty classes. This societal problem, which has not been confined to Canada, led to the implementation of mandatory child support guidelines in England, Australia, New Zealand, the United States, as well as in Canada. The Guidelines are premised on objectively based numerical indicators of the specific amount of child support that an individual should normally pay by agreement or court order on marriage breakdown or divorce or to a single parent. As of 1 May 1997, child support rights and obligations under the *Divorce Act* underwent a radical change. The previous child support regime applying under the *Divorce Act*, which was premised on the exercise of an unfettered judicial discretion, was rejected by the government as unpredictable, inconsistent, costly, and unfair to children.[1] Recognition of these limitations of the judicial discretionary regime led to major research studies being undertaken by the Federal/Provincial/Territorial Family Law Committee for several years prior to the legislative and regulatory changes. These studies produced changes in the following key areas. First, child support paid under orders or agreements made on or after 1 May 1997 is no longer taxed as income to the recipient, nor is it tax deductible by the payor. Second, the *Federal Child Support Guidelines* provide fixed table amounts of monthly child support that help parents, lawyers, and judges to set fair and consistent child support in divorce cases. The table amounts take the new tax rules into account. Fixed schedules for the determination of child support can promote (1) simple and inexpensive administrative procedures for assessing the amount of child support; (2) consistency of amounts in comparable family situations; and (3) higher child support payments that more

1 *MGH v KLDH*, 2020 NBCA 46.

realistically reflect the actual costs of raising children. They are unlikely, however, to resolve the economic crises of separation and divorce for women and children. The war on poverty requires more than piecemeal reform of child support rights and obligations, although the Guidelines may reduce the economic plight of primary caregiving parents to some degree.

B. RELEVANCE OF INCOME TAX[2]

Prior to 1 May 1997, periodic child support payments made pursuant to a court order or written agreement after marriage breakdown were deductible from the taxable income of the payor under sections 60(b), 60(c), and 60.1 of the *Income Tax Act*[3] and were taxable as income in the hands of the payee under sections 56(1)(b) and (c), provided that such payments were made to the primary caregiving parent and not to the children directly.[4] As of 1 May 1997, Canada shifted to an income tax system whereby the payor no longer receives a deduction for payments made and the receiving parent no longer pays tax on child support received under any new order or agreement or pursuant to any variation made after 30 April 1997 of a pre-existing order or agreement.[5]

The new tax rules do not apply to orders or agreements made before 1 May 1997 unless (a) a court order or agreement made on or after 1 May 1997 changes the amount of child support payable under an existing agreement or court order; (b) the court order or agreement specifically provides that the new tax rules apply to payments made after a specified date, which cannot be earlier than 30 April 1997; or (c) the payor and the recipient have both signed and filed a form with the Canada Revenue Agency stating that the new tax rules apply to payments made after a specified date that cannot be earlier than 30 April 1997.[6] The tax changes do not apply to periodic spousal support payments, which continue to be deductible from the income of the payor and constitute taxable income in the hands of the payee.[7]

Before 1 May 1997, lawyers and courts sometimes arranged or ordered a global amount of spousal and child support without apportioning the amount payable to each category of dependant. Such global amounts were commonly used by lawyers and courts when dealing with interim support. This practice should be abandoned as a consequence of the new tax

---

2 And see David Kitai, "A Game Changer for Family Law," *Law Times*, 28 February 2020. This brief analysis discusses the impact of Ontario's Childcare Access and Relief from Expenses (CARE) tax credit on child support and spousal support.

3 RSC 1985 (5th Supp), c 1.

4 *Thibaudeau v Canada (Minister of National Revenue)*, [1995] 2 SCR 627.

5 *Del Puppo v Del Puppo*, [1999] BCJ No 1722 (SC); *Hilchie v Hilchie*, [1997] NSJ No 353 (Fam Ct); *Acorn v DeRoche*, [1997] PEIJ No 82 (TD). But see *Fung-Sunter v Fabian*, [1998] BCJ No 861 (SC), citing Revenue Canada Pamphlet on Support Payments, P102(E) Rev 97 at 19.

6 *Fontaine v Fontaine*, [2000] BCJ No 366 (CA); *Gordon-Tennant v Gordon-Tennant*, [1997] OJ No 3436 (Gen Div); *Richard v Richard*, [1999] SJ No 348 (QB) (unintended income tax consequences of amended agreement found to constitute sufficient reason to grant order for child support in accordance with the *Federal Child Support Guidelines*); compare *Schipper v Maher*, [2002] MJ No 319 (QB) (retroactive variation of child support arrears that accrued before and after implementation of *Federal Child Support Guidelines*). See also *Warbinek v Canada*, 2008 FCA 276, citing *Holbrook v Canada*, 2007 FCA 145; *Chadwick v Canada*, 2013 FCA 181.

7 *Williams v Williams*, [1997] BCJ No 2091 (SC); see also *SAJM v DDM*, [1999] MJ No 118 (CA) (trial judge's order for reduction in amount of spousal support not justified, having regard to financial disparity between old and new orders).

rules respecting child support because an amount in a written agreement or court order that is not identified as being solely for the support of a spouse will be treated as child support for income tax purposes. Similarly, where a written agreement or court order provides that certain expenses are to be paid directly to a third party, such as mortgage payments, any such expenses that are not clearly identified as being solely for the benefit of the recipient spouse will be treated as child support. Furthermore, where the total spousal and child support payments made in a year are less than the total amount required for the year under a written agreement or court order, the payments will first be considered to be child support for income tax purposes.

Because of the different tax treatment applicable to periodic child support and periodic spousal support after 1 May 1997, the question arises whether separated and divorced spouses can arrange their affairs so as to attract the tax consequences that are most beneficial to them.[8] In cases where the payor is in a higher tax bracket than the payee or the payee has no taxable income, it may be mutually advantageous for the spouses or former spouses to trade off child support against spousal support and thereby take advantage of the tax deduction/inclusion principles that continue to apply to periodic spousal support payable under a written agreement after marriage breakdown. It is uncertain how far any degree of flexibility and choice is currently possible under Canadian law. In several tax cases arising in other contexts, the language of a separation agreement has been regarded as important, but not decisive, for purposes of the *Income Tax Act*. Furthermore, in family law cases, it has been held that it is improper to order spousal support under the guise of child support. The amount of child support should be fixed, having regard to the benefits, direct and indirect, that will result to the child. It may include an amount that will defray the additional expense a primary caregiving parent has in caring for a child but should not include an amount to defray the personal expenses of the primary caregiving parent.[9]

The financial consequences that are personal to the primary caregiving parent, in that they arise from the limitations and demands of parenting, are relevant, however, to a determination of the right to and amount of *spousal* support under sections 15.2(4), 15.2(6), 17(4.1), and 17(7)(b) of the *Divorce Act*. In addition, in pre-divorce situations, lawyers and courts must not lose sight of section 11(1)(b) of the *Divorce Act*, which imposes a duty on the court to satisfy itself that reasonable arrangements have been made for the support of any children of the marriage and, if such arrangements have not been made, to stay the granting of divorce until such arrangements are made. If any hurdles arising under this section can be overcome and the Canada Revenue Agency does not successfully contest a specific designation of periodic payments as spousal support, the *Federal Child Support Guidelines* may leave the door open to negotiated settlements that deviate from the Guidelines by trading off child support against spousal support and property entitlements. This possibility might be inferred from section 15.1(5) of the *Divorce Act*, which empowers a court to order an amount of child support that is different from the amount that would be determined in accordance with the applicable Guidelines,[10] if the court is satisfied (a) that special provisions in an order,

---

8 See *Armstrong v Armstrong*, 2010 BCSC 1686.

9 *Richardson v Richardson*, [1987] 1 SCR 857.

10 This provision does not necessarily justify an order for no child support. It simply empowers a court to award a different amount of child support than would otherwise be ordered under the applicable Guidelines.

judgment, or written agreement respecting the financial obligations of the spouses, or the division or transfer of their property, directly or indirectly benefit a child, or that special provisions have otherwise been made for the benefit of a child, and (b) that the application of the applicable Guidelines would result in an amount of child support that is inequitable given those special provisions.[11]

In addition, section 15.1(7) of the *Divorce Act* permits orders for child support to be made in an amount that is different from the amount that would be determined in accordance with the applicable Guidelines on the consent of both spouses, if the court is satisfied that reasonable arrangements have been made for the support of the child to whom the order relates.

Child care expenses have been provided by way of a spousal support order instead of pursuant to section 7 of the *Federal Child Support Guidelines* where an income tax advantage thereby ensued for the payor and no disadvantage was sustained by the non-tax-paying recipient. Section 15.3 of the *Divorce Act* has been held to be no impediment to such an order.[12]

The right to claim the eligible dependant tax credit (formerly known as the "equivalent to spouse" tax credit),[13] GST credit, and child care expenses under the *Income Tax Act* is dependent on the claimant living separate and apart from his spouse by reason of the breakdown of marriage.[14] It is possible for spouses to live separate and apart even when residing under the same roof.[15] It is an abuse of the judicial process for parents to present a draft consent order for judicial approval where the proffered order is inconsistent with the evidence and has been framed to artificially attract the "equivalent to spouse" credit under the *Income Tax Act*.[16] The "equivalent to spouse" tax credit under section 118(1)(b) of the *Income Tax Act* is not available to a single parent of adult children who are pursuing post-secondary education or training programs.[17]

Shared parenting time arrangements and shared child-related expenses may affect eligibility for the "equivalent to spouse" credit under the *Income Tax Act*.[18]

The Canada Child Benefit program, which replaces the Canada Child Tax Benefit, National Child Benefit, and Universal Child Care Benefit, provides a tax-free monthly payment to eligible parents to help them with the cost of raising children under eighteen years of age.[19] Section 122.6 of the *Income Tax Act* provides for the payment of the Canada Child Benefit to an "eligible individual." To meet the definition of this term, section 122.6 provides that a person must reside in Canada with the child[20] and must be the parent who "primarily

---

11 *McGrath v McGrath*, [2001] BCJ No 1555 (SC); *MGH v KLDH*, 2020 NBCA 46; *Russell v Russell*, 2012 NSSC 258; *Da Silva v Da Silva*, [2004] OJ No 1976 (SCJ); see also *Marks v Marks*, [2000] AJ No 1247 at paras 70–72 (QB).

12 *Grant v Grant*, [2001] NSJ No 100 (SC).

13 See *Brown v Brown*, 2020 BCCA 53 at paras 72–83.

14 *Parmar v Canada*, [2007] TCJ No 465.

15 *Roby v Canada*, [2001] TCJ No 801.

16 *Swainson v Swainson*, [2001] YJ No 129 (SC) (judicial refusal to sign draft order; divorce stayed pursuant to s 11(1)(b) of *Divorce Act*).

17 *Hickson v Canada*, [2001] TCJ No 344.

18 And see Chapter 6, Section B(10): "Canada Child Benefit; Eligible Dependant Tax Credit."

19 See Chapter 5, Section D: "Subsidies; Tax Deductions or Credits."

20 *Song v Canada*, 2009 FCA 278; *Perlman v Canada*, 2010 TCC 658; *Fatima v Canada*, 2012 TCC 49; *Vegh v Canada*, 2012 TCC 95; *Goldstein v Canada*, 2013 TCC 165. See also *Jhanji v Canada*, 2014 TCC 126.

fulfils the responsibility for the care and upbringing of the [child]."[21] The Canada Child Benefit and the GST/HST tax credit each have a requirement that the taxpayer be a resident of Canada during the base taxation year. A person is resident in the country where he or she, in the settled routine of life, regularly, normally, or customarily lives, as opposed to the place where the person unusually, casually, or intermittently stays.[22]

C. STATUTORY PROVISIONS REGULATING CHILD SUPPORT

Section 26.1(2) of the *Divorce Act*, as amended by SC 1997, c 1, provides that "[t]he Guidelines shall be based on the principle that spouses have a joint financial obligation to maintain the children of the marriage in accordance with their relative abilities to contribute to the performance of that obligation." Section 26.1(2) of the *Divorce Act* must be read in conjunction with section 3(1)(a) of the *Federal Child Support Guidelines*, which provides that the applicable provincial or territorial table determines the amount of child support to be paid except in circumstances where sections 3 to 10 provide to the contrary. In cases where the basic table amount of child support is deemed payable, the court looks only to the income of the obligor and the number of children of the marriage who are entitled to support because the children will inevitably share the standard of living enjoyed in the primary caregiving parent's household.[23] A judicial discretion to deviate from the Guidelines arises under section 3(2) with respect to children over the age of majority, under section 4(b)(ii) with respect to obligors with annual incomes in excess of $150,000, under section 5 where a spouse stands in the place of a parent, under section 7, which empowers a court to grant designated special or extraordinary expenses, under section 9 in cases of shared parenting, and under section 10 in cases of undue hardship.

Sections 15.1 and 17 of the *Divorce Act* set out the basic provisions respecting original and variation applications for child support orders but more detailed substantive criteria respecting orders for child support are to be found in the *Federal Child Support Guidelines*

These Guidelines have the force of law pursuant to section 26.1 of the *Divorce Act*, which empowers the Governor in Council (that is, the Cabinet) to establish guidelines respecting the making of orders for child support. The implementation of substantive guidelines by means of regulations instead of statutory provisions has the advantage of facilitating amendments and revisions if problems arise that demand early attention.

Section 2(5) of the *Divorce Act* expressly allows the Governor in Council to provide for the application of provincial child support guidelines on or after divorce. By virtue of section 2(5) of the *Divorce Act*, an Order-in-Council authorizes Quebec to apply its own provincial *Child Support Guidelines* to divorcing spouses resident in that province, thereby promoting consistency with the Guidelines applicable to residents in that province who seek child support

---

21 *Fraser v Canada*, [2010] TCJ No 9 (TCC) (eligibility for Canada Child Benefit and GST credit considered); *Nadalin v Canada*, 2012 TCC 48. As to apportionment of the parental entitlement to the Canada Child Benefit in shared parenting situations, see *Friesen v The Queen*, 2022 TCC 53, which is reviewed in detail in Chapter 6, Section B(10): "Canada Child Benefit; Eligible Dependant Tax Credit."

22 *Goldstein v Canada*, 2013 TCC 165.

23 *Auer v Auer*, 2024 SCC 36; *Premi v Khodeir*, [2009] OJ No 3365 (SCJ); see Section D(4), below in this chapter. And see *Colucci v Colucci*, 2021 SCC 24 at para 34.

pursuant to provincial legislation. In some instances, especially those involving shared parenting, the amount available under the *Quebec Child Support Guidelines* is much lower than would be available to divorcing spouses, if one of them resided outside Quebec. In *Droit de la famille—139*,[24] the trial judge found that such differential treatment of divorced spouses resident in Quebec constituted an infringement of the right to equality under section 15(1) of the *Canadian Charter of Rights and Freedoms* but she concluded that the concept of cooperative federalism entitled Quebec to pursue its own family policy and the infringement was, therefore, found to be justified under section 1 of the *Charter*. The Quebec Court of Appeal held that the trial judge erred in finding that section 15(1) of the *Charter* had been infringed. It reasoned that whereas race, national or ethnic origin, colour, religion, sex, age, and mental or physical disability are enumerated grounds in section 15(1) of the *Charter*, the residence of the appellants in the circumstances of this case could not be treated as an analogous ground because it was not "a personal characteristic that is unchangeable or changeable only at an unacceptable cost in terms of personal identity." The appellate court further observed that Quebec's requested designation under section 2(5) of the *Divorce Act*, which enables it to apply the same child support guidelines to all parents in Quebec regardless of their marital status, represents a legitimate policy choice that reflects cooperative federalism and negates any suggestion of prejudice or stereotyping. And this is consistent with the observations of the Supreme Court of Canada in *DBS v SRG; LJW v TAR; Henry v Henry; Hiemstra v Hiemstra*.[25] As a result, the trial judge was found to have erred in concluding that the designation under section 2(5) of the *Divorce Act* infringed section 15(1) of the *Charter*, and it was unnecessary for the Quebec Court of Appeal to address section 1 of the *Charter*.

The *Federal Child Support Guidelines*, not the *Quebec Child Support Guidelines*, apply where the obligor is resident outside Quebec.[26]

D. THE *FEDERAL CHILD SUPPORT GUIDELINES*

1) Coming into Force

The *Federal Child Support Guidelines* came into force on 1 May 1997.[27]

2) Terminology

The expression "*Federal Child Support Guidelines*" refers to the entire contents of SOR/97-175, 8 April 1997, as amended from time to time. Accordingly, it includes the provincial and territorial tables that set out fixed amounts of child support as well as detailed rules to be applied by the courts in the assessment of child support. The word "guidelines" is often wrongly used to signify the "table" amount of support payable under the *Federal Child Support Guidelines* or their provincial counterparts.[28]

---

24 2013 QCCA 15, leave to appeal to SCC refused (*sub nom HC v PN*), [2013] SCCA No 113.
25 [2006] 2 SCR 231 at para 52.
26 *OM v AK*, [2000] QJ No 3224 (CS); *Droit de la famille—092181*, 2009 QCCS 4122.
27 SOR/97-175, s 27; see *Hughes v Hughes*, [1997] NSJ No 445 (CA).
28 *Keefe v Randall*, [2005] NSJ No 264 (SC).

The term "guidelines," which was borrowed from foreign jurisdictions, is misleading because it implies that they are advisory and that the courts have a residual discretion to override them. That is neither the case under the *Federal Child Support Guidelines* in Canada nor under corresponding provincial child support guidelines.[29] In cases that fall subject to the *Divorce Act*, the court is required to fix the amount of child support in accordance with the applicable provincial or territorial table except where the *Divorce Act* or Guidelines otherwise provide.[30] The *Federal Child Support Guidelines* in Canada have accordingly been characterized in the marginal note to section 3 of the Guidelines as establishing a "presumptive rule."

3) Objectives of *Federal Child Support Guidelines*

The objectives of the *Federal Child Support Guidelines* are expressly defined as follows:

(a) to establish a fair standard of support for children that ensures that they continue to benefit from the financial means of both spouses after separation;
(b) to reduce conflict and tension between spouses by making the calculation of child support more objective;
(c) to improve the efficiency of the legal process by giving courts and spouses guidance in setting the levels of child support orders and encouraging settlement; and
(d) to ensure consistent treatment of spouses and children who are in similar circumstances.[32]

The aforementioned objectives should be promoted in the interpretation and application of the substantive provisions of the *Federal Child Support Guidelines*.[33]

It has been judicially asserted that "[i]t is proving to be a vain hope that the introduction of the *Federal Child Support Guidelines* would make the task of setting child support easier and hence lead to settlements. If anything, fresh areas for dispute have arisen and certain aspects are at least as difficult and contentious as before."[34] Subject to the inhibiting factor of legal costs, this assertion is undoubtedly true in the many situations wherein the Guidelines confer a discretion on the court. However, families of modest means have secured an advantage under the Guidelines where the amount of child support is confined to the applicable provincial or territorial table amount.[35]

4) Obligor's Income Model of *Federal Child Support Guidelines*

Although the Governor in Council may endorse comprehensive guidelines established by the provinces under section 2(4) of the *Divorce Act*, the *Federal Child Support Guidelines* are premised on an obligor's income model of child support, variations of which exist in fifteen American states. An obligor must pay the table amount of child support set out in

29 *Lucia v Martin*, [1998] BCJ No 1798 (SC).
30 *HS v PW*, 2016 NLCA 67.
31 *Ibid.*
32 SOR/97-175, s 1.
33 *Shiels v Shiels*, [1997] BCJ No 1924 (SC); *Hoover v Hoover*, [1997] NWTJ No 43 (SC). And see *Colucci v Colucci*, 2021 SCC 24.
34 *Crick v Crick*, [1997] BCJ No 2222 (SC), Warren J.
35 *Tauber v Tauber*, [1999] OJ No 359 (Gen Div).

the Guidelines based upon his annual gross income as determined by the Guidelines. It is immaterial that the table amount and allowable section 7 expenses, when added to the recipient's income and resources, create a surplus for the recipient in his or her monthly budget.[36] The table amount is mandatory, subject only to specified exemptions provided in the Act and the Guidelines.[37] The rationale for the obligor's income model is that the primary caregiving parent inevitably contributes financial and other resources to the welfare of the child and any financial contribution from the other parent will typically be used to improve the child's circumstances.[38] By focusing on the obligor's income, the *Federal Child Support Guidelines* de-emphasize the traditional reliance that was placed on unrealistic spousal and child expense claims and on child care budgets filed under the former child support regime.[39]

The supposed attraction of the obligor's income model is its relative simplicity when compared to the Income Shares Model or the Melson Formula Model in the United States.[40] However, the inherent simplicity of the obligor's income model should not be exaggerated in an era of readily available computer software programs. Furthermore, the alleged simplicity may be belied by the manner in which Canadian courts have exercised their discretion to deviate from the applicable provincial or territorial table amount of child support pursuant to sections 15.1(5) to 15.1(8) and 17(6.2) to 17(6.5) of the *Divorce Act* and sections 4, 5, 7, 8, 9, and 10 of the *Federal Child Support Guidelines*. The obligor's income model has attracted criticism on the basis that it pays insufficient attention to the income of the primary caregiving parent with respect to the fixed amounts specified in the applicable provincial or territorial tables. It is noteworthy that Quebec has developed its own child support guidelines based on an Income Shares Model.

In *Premi v Khodeir*,[41] constitutional challenges to the obligor's income model under section 26.1(2) of the *Divorce Act* and sections 2(b) and 15(1) of the *Canadian Charter of Rights and Freedoms* were judicially rejected.

E. APPLICATION OF *FEDERAL CHILD SUPPORT GUIDELINES*; PROVINCIAL LEGISLATION

1) Orders Governed by *Federal Child Support Guidelines*

The *Federal Child Support Guidelines* not only apply to original permanent orders for child support under the *Divorce Act*; they also apply, with such modifications as the circumstances require, to interim orders, variation orders, interjurisdictional orders, and to the administrative calculation or recalculation of child support.

36 *HAK v TJW*, 2011 SKQB 68.

37 *PLC v CG*, 2020 ABQB 211, citing *Ewing v Ewing*, 2009 ABCA 227 at para 42.

38 *Auer v Auer*, 2024 SCC 36; *Fibke v Fibke*, [1999] AJ No 172 (QB); *Premi v Khodeir*, [2009] OJ No 3365 (SCJ). See also Government of Canada, *Budget 1996: The New Child Support Package* at 13.

39 *CHR v EBC*, [1997] AJ No 561 (QB); *Francis v Baker*, [1998] OJ No 924 (CA).

40 See Laura W Morgan, *Child Support Guidelines: Interpretation and Application*, loose-leaf (New York: Aspen Law and Business, 1996–) §1.03.

41 [2009] OJ No 3365 (SCJ); see also *Auer v Auer*, 2024 SCC 36.

2) Provincial Guidelines

The *Federal Child Support Guidelines* are not directly applicable to child support proceed ings instituted pursuant to provincial or territorial statute. Alberta, British Columbia,[42] New Brunswick, Newfoundland and Labrador, the Northwest Territories,[43] Nova Scotia,[44] Ontario, Prince Edward Island,[45] and Saskatchewan have all adopted or slightly modified the *Federal Child Support Guidelines* for application in child support proceedings initiated pursuant to provincial legislation. Quebec adopted its own guidelines on 1 May 1997.[46]

In Ontario, the *Uniform Federal and Provincial Child Support Guidelines Act, 1997*, came into force on 1 December 1997. As its name indicates, it seeks to establish uniformity concerning the application of federal and provincial guidelines in proceedings under the *Divorce Act*[48] and under the Ontario *Family Law Act*.[49]

The *Federal Child Support Guidelines* were adopted in Saskatchewan pursuant to *The Family Maintenance Act, 1997*,[50] which came into effect on 1 May 1997.

As of 1 May 1998, orders made pursuant to New Brunswick's *Family Services Act* must comply with the *Federal Child Support Guidelines*.[51] New Brunswick adopted the *Federal Child Support Guidelines* with two minor amendments relating to the time for filing income information and the amount of income information required on consent.

Manitoba implemented child support guidelines as of 1 June 1998 when *The Family Maintenance Act*, which establishes a statutory framework, and the *Child Support Guide lines Regulation* thereunder, came into effect. The *Manitoba Child Support Guidelines* apply to claims for child support under *The Family Maintenance Act*[52] or, where both parties are resident in Manitoba, under the *Divorce Act*.[53] The *Federal Child Support Guidelines*, not the *Manitoba Child Support Guidelines*, apply where the respondent is habitually resident outside Manitoba.[54] The Manitoba legislation resembles the *Divorce Act* child support provi sions. In addition, the Manitoba legislation contains provisions requiring parents to provide financial disclosure on request, without the need for a court application for support having first been made. Non-compliance may result in a fine of up to $5,000 in addition to any other

---

42 *Arcinas v Stanley*, [1999] BCJ No 1388 (SC).
43 *Wilson v Eronchi*, [2000] NWTJ No 3 (SC).
44 *Reid v Faubert*, 2019 NSCA 42.
45 *Koren v Blum*, [2000] PEIJ No 121 (CA).
46 See *Colucci v Colucci*, 2021 SCC 24 at para 35.
47 SO 1997, c 20.
48 RSC 1985 (2d Supp), c 3, as amended by SC 1997, c 1.
49 RSO 1990, c F3.
50 SS 1990–91, c F-6.1, as amended by SS 1997, c 3 and the regulations thereunder; *LDB v CWG*, [1997] SJ No 626 (QB).
51 See *An Act to Amend the Family Services Act*, SNB 1997; *Child Support Guidelines Regulation*, Regulation 98-197.
52 *Zdan v Zdan*, [2001] MJ No 450 (QB).
53 *Bates v Welcher*, [2001] MJ No 93 (CA); *Nesbitt v Nesbitt*, [2001] MJ No 291 (CA) (subtle differences exist with respect to the judicial imputation of income under the Manitoba guidelines and the federal guidelines).
54 *Sharpe v Sharpe*, [2001] MJ No 406 (QB).

penalties. The *Manitoba Child Support Guidelines Regulation* essentially replicates the *Federal Child Support Guidelines*, although there are some differences.[55]

The *Federal Child Support Guidelines* apply to both original and variation applications respecting child support under *The Family Maintenance Act of Saskatchewan*. Although the provisions of this Act respecting the threshold and the application of the *Federal Child Support Guidelines* to variation applications are not as clear as those in the *Divorce Act*, the provincial legislature obviously intended the Guidelines to apply to variation applications as well as to initial applications and the threshold in either case is a change of circumstances as defined in the Guidelines.[56]

Effective 1 October 2005, Alberta implemented provincial *Child Support Guidelines* to be applied where child support is sought pursuant to provincial statute. Prior to that date, Alberta courts applied the *Federal Child Support Guidelines* as a yardstick for determining the amount of child support to be paid and no distinction was drawn between the children of non-cohabiting unmarried parents and the children of divorcing or divorced parents.[57]

A person who voluntarily consents to serve and is appointed private guardian of a child under the *Child Welfare Act* (Alberta) has a legal responsibility to financially contribute to the needs of the child and cannot look to the biological father of the child to exclusively assume the burden of child support after the mother's death. Although the *Federal Child Support Guidelines* technically apply to child support orders on or after divorce, they provide a useful guide whenever two parties are responsible for the maintenance of a child.[58]

3) Extramarital Children; Disputed Paternity

It would be illogical, unjust, and contrary to public policy, as well as constitutionally questionable in light of the *Charter of Rights and Freedoms*, to draw distinctions in determining the level of child support payable according to whether the child was born as a consequence of a casual encounter, a common law relationship, or a marriage.[59] There are many occasions where courts have found fathers liable to pay child support, even though the mother decided to get pregnant or not to abort a pregnancy in contravention of the father's wishes.[60] There may be situations, however, where a court might decline to make an order in the exercise of its discretion under provincial statute. The use of a sperm donation bank might be one such situation. Courts must, nevertheless, be cautious about refusing an order for child support, even in the presence of parental contracts or agreements.[61]

---

55 See *Bates v Welcher*, [2001] MJ No 93 (CA).

56 *Katzer v Egeland*, [1997] SJ No 672 (QB) (variation proceeding). As to original orders, see *Hryhoriw v D'Lugos*, [1997] SJ No 636 (QB).

57 *Cavanaugh v Ziegler*, [1998] AJ No 1423 (CA); *DBS v SRG*, [2005] AJ No 2 (CA).

58 *WRA (Next friend of) v GFA*, [2001] AJ No 1472 (QB) (pre-Guidelines child support found too excessive in amount; father ordered to pay applicable table amount of child support under *Federal Child Support Guidelines*).

59 *Cavanaugh v Ziegler*, [1998] AJ No 1423 (CA); *PT v RB*, [2004] AJ No 803 (CA); *ABC v XYZ*, [2004] AJ No 1231 (QB); *DBS v SRG*, [2005] AJ No 2 (CA); *MDA v MS*, [2008] NBJ No 498 (QB); *DL v FK*, [1998] NWTJ No 42 (SC); compare *Hill v Davis*, [2006] NSJ No 331 (SC).

60 *Keller v MacDonald*, [1998] AJ No 1294 (QB).

61 *Ibid*.

A father is not absolved from his child support obligation by the mother's assertion that she would take steps to avoid a pregnancy[62] or that she was unable to bear children.[63] Liability for child support may be imposed even if pregnancy resulted from a brief sexual encounter and the father has been uninvolved since the child's birth.[64]

Where a mother brings an application against the alleged father of a child for a paternity test and child support, but the mother was living with her husband at the time of the child's conception, thereby raising a statutory presumption that the husband is the father, no order should be made that might affect the husband's relationship with the child until the husband has been added as a party to the proceedings.[65]

Where a child is born after the cessation of matrimonial cohabitation and an order for blood tests has been ordered to resolve disputed paternity, the respondent may be directed to assume the cost of the tests, subject to a right to be reimbursed if he is excluded as a father by the tests.[66]

Judicial opinion in Ontario is divided on the threshold that must be met before a court grants leave for blood tests where paternity is disputed in a proceeding for child support. In *FG v FG*,[67] it was held that the applicant must rebut the presumption of paternity before testing will be ordered. In *DH v DW*,[68] it was found to be sufficient that the applicant shows that there is a real issue to be tried on the question of paternity. The former test puts the applicant in an impossible position and it would appear more appropriate to ensure that the issue be determined on the best evidence available where a real issue of parentage is raised.

A court may order financial disclosure, notwithstanding a dispute as to a child's paternity.

A court may refuse to order retroactive support for an extramarital child before the date of the application where the obligor was unaware of paternity until that time.[71]

F. PRESUMPTIVE RULE; PROVINCIAL AND TERRITORIAL TABLES

The *Federal Child Support Guidelines* have replaced the former judicial discretionary regime that regulated child support applications under the *Divorce Act*. The word "guidelines" is a misnomer insofar as the *Federal Child Support Guidelines* establish a system of fixed child support payments. Section 3 of the *Federal Child Support Guidelines* creates a presumptive rule whereby, unless otherwise provided by the *Divorce Act* or under the Guidelines, the amount of a child support order for children under the age of majority is (a) the amount set out in the applicable table, according to the number of children under the age of majority to whom the order relates and the income of the spouse or former spouse against whom the

---

62 *New Brunswick (Minister of Income Assistance) v Hodnett*, [1995] NBJ No 323, 14 RFL (4th) 138 at 139–40 (QB).

63 *Miller v Ufoegbune*, [2000] OJ No 3979 (SCJ).

64 *Janfield v Foote*, [1999] AJ No 1355 (QB).

65 *C(S) v W(R)* (1996), 23 RFL (4th) 7 (BCCA).

66 *M(CF) v M(MF)* (1996), 23 RFL (4th) 55 (NBQB).

67 (1991), 32 RFL (3d) 252 (Ont Ct Gen Div).

68 [1992] OJ No 1737 (Gen Div).

69 *FB v LB*, [2000] OJ No 3833 (SCJ).

70 *BMH v LH*, [1997] MJ No 493 (QB).

71 *Lakusta v Hrytsay*, [1998] AJ No 969 (QB).

order is sought; and (b) the amount, if any, determined under section 7 of the Guidelines for special or extraordinary expenses.[72] The use of the word "may" in section 15.1(1) of the *Divorce Act* does not justify a court denying an application of child support simply because of the strained financial circumstances of a parent.[73] The fixed amount under the applicable provincial table is based on the obligor's presumed ability to pay, with the amount having been predetermined by statistical and general averages. Judicial deviation from the prescribed amount payable under the Guidelines is permissible only in a specifically prescribed range of circumstances.[74] The presumptive amount of support payable under section 3 of the Guidelines specifically applies to "the number of children to whom the order relates." There is no jurisdiction to reduce the table amount payable for those children because the obligor has an obligation to support children from a second family, unless the circumstances give rise to a finding of undue hardship within the meaning of section 10 of the Guidelines. The two families cannot be treated as a single unit for the purpose of determining and averaging out the applicable table amount of child support.[75] If section 3 of the Guidelines had been intended to base the amounts payable on the total number of the obligor's children, the language of the section would have stated this.[76] The table amounts remain presumptive where an obligor is responsible for children from different relationships.[77]

The capacity of an obligor to pay the basic amount of child support prescribed by the applicable provincial or territorial table will be presumed, subject to any right of set-off that may arise with respect to expenses incurred by the obligor that fall within section 7 of the *Federal Child Support Guidelines* and subject also to the potential application of the undue hardship provisions of section 10 of the Guidelines or the applicability of the split or shared parenting time provisions under sections 8 and 9 of the Guidelines.[78]

Schedule I of the *Federal Child Support Guidelines* sets out separate tables of fixed child support payments for each province and territory. The amounts vary from one province or territory to another because of differences in provincial or territorial income tax rates. Periodic adjustments to the provincial and territorial tables are envisaged when significant changes occur in federal, provincial, or territorial tax rates. The provincial and territorial tables prescribe the amount of monthly child support payments for each province and territory in accordance with the annual income of the spouse ordered to pay child support and the number of children for whom support will be paid.

Although the child support payments are prescribed on a monthly basis, a court may presumably order such payments to be made weekly, fortnightly, or on some other basis

72 *Federal Child Support Guidelines*, SOR/97-175, s 3(1); *MSD obo NC v AL*, 2022 NBQB 21; *HS v PW*, 2016 NLCA 67; *Merritt v Merritt*, [1999] OJ No 1732 (SCJ); *Bates v Bates*, [2000] OJ No 2269 (CA); *Birss v Birss*, [2000] OJ No 3692 (Div Ct); *DBB v DMB*, 2017 SKCA 59; compare *AG v LS*, [2006] AJ No 1308 (CA).

73 *Lindholm v Lindholm*, [1999] BCJ No 1704 (SC); *MSD obo NC v AL*, 2022 NBQB 21; *Antonishyn v Boucher*, 2011 SKQB 147.

74 *Covin v Covin*, 2021 NBQB 228; *Birss v Birss*, [2000] OJ No 3692 (Div Ct); *Travis v Travis*, 2010 SKCA 83 (mother not entitled to set off cost of children's frequent meals against her table amount of child support).

75 *ML v RSE*, [2006] AJ No 642 (CA); *Ewing v Malette*, 2009 ABCA 128; *Meuser v Meuser*, [1998] BCJ No 2808 (CA); *WL v NDH*, 2014 NBQB 214; *Locke v Goulding*, 2012 NLCA 8; *Soleimani v Melendez*, 2019 ONSC 36.

76 *Meuser v Meuser*, [1998] BCJ No 2808 (CA).

77 *Davis v Davis*, 2013 NBQB 115.

78 *MSD obo NC v AL*, 2022 NBQB 21.

pursuant to the provisions of section 15.1(4) of the *Divorce Act*. There is a minimum level of income, currently $12,000 per annum, below which no amount of child support is payable. Annual income is set out in the tables at intervals of $1,000. Monthly amounts of child support are determined by selecting the appropriate category of annual income and adding to the basic allocation a supplementary amount that is calculated by using the given percentage for income above the lowest value within that category of income. Fixed monthly child support amounts are set for incomes up to $150,000 per year. Separate tables are provided for one to six children or more. Special provisions under section 4 of the *Federal Child Support Guidelines* provide the basis for determining the amount of monthly child support payments for obligors with annual incomes over $150,000.[80]

The amounts in the tables are based on economic studies of average spending on children in families at different income levels in Canada. The formula sets support amounts to reflect average expenditures on children by a parent with a particular number of children and level of income. The calculation is based on the obligor's income. The formula uses the basic personal deduction from income tax to recognize personal expenses and takes other federal and provincial or territorial income taxes and credits into account. Federal child tax benefits and GST credits for children are excluded from the calculation. At lower income levels, the formula sets the amounts to take into account the combined impact of taxes and child support payments on the obligor's limited disposable income.[81]

It may seem anomalous for the provincial and territorial tables to ignore the payee's income because one of the stated objectives[82] of the *Federal Child Support Guidelines* is to ensure that children benefit from the financial means of both parents. Furthermore, section 26.1(2) of the *Divorce Act*[83] stipulates that the Guidelines shall be based on the principle that spouses have a joint financial obligation to maintain the children of the marriage in accordance with their relative abilities to contribute to the performance of that obligation. However, the underlying assumption is that children's lifestyle automatically reflects the income of the primary caregiving parent. In other words, children always enjoy the same standard of living as the primary caregiving parent by virtue of living in the same household. Consequently, the obligor's contribution can be set independently and the child will benefit from any increase in that parent's income.[84]

Payment of the applicable table amount of basic child support pursuant to section 3(1) of the Guidelines is not subject to any reduction where the child under the age of majority earns an income while attending high school[85] or the child is subsequently enrolled in a boarding school.[86]

---

79 *RWL v LB*, 2012 BCSC 457; *TAF v MWB*, 2013 MBQB 213.

80 See Chapter 9, Section B.

81 For a detailed explanation of the formula used to produce the child support tables, see Department of Justice, *Formula for the Table of Amounts Contained in the Federal Child Support Guidelines: A Technical Report* (Research Report, CSR-1997-1E) (Ottawa: DOJ, 1997).

82 *Federal Child Support Guidelines*, SOR/97-175, s 1(a).

83 RSC 1985 (2d Supp), c 3, as amended by SC 1997, c 1.

84 *Auer v Auer*, 2024 SCC 36; *Williams v Williams*, [1997] NWTJ No 49 (SC); see also *Cavanaugh v Ziegler*, [1998] AJ No 1423 (CA); *Premi v Khodeir*, [2009] OJ No 3365 (SCJ) (*Charter* challenge dismissed).

85 *Penney v Boland*, [1999] NJ No 71 (UFC).

86 *Steward v Ferguson*, 2018 BCCA 158.

G. APPLICABLE PROVINCIAL OR TERRITORIAL TABLE

If the spouse or former spouse against whom an original or variation order for child support is sought resides in Canada at the time of the application or at the time of the calculation or recalculation of the amount pursuant to section 25.1 of the *Divorce Act*, the table for the province or territory where that spouse or former spouse habitually resides is the applicable table for determining the prescribed monthly amount of child support.[87] Where an obligor resides six months of the year in one province and the other six months in another province, the applicable table under the *Federal Child Support Guidelines* will be determined by reference to his or her provincial residence for income tax purposes.[88] If the spouse or former spouse against whom an original or variation order for child support is sought resides outside of Canada at the time of the application or the calculation or recalculation of the amount pursuant to section 25.1 of the *Divorce Act*, or if the residence of that spouse is unknown, the applicable table is the table for the province where the recipient spouse habitually resides.[89]

Where the court is satisfied that the province in which the spouse or former spouse against whom an original or variation order for child support is sought has changed since the time of the application or will change in the near future after determination of the amount of support, the applicable table is that of the new province.[90]

Where the obligor's province of residence is unclear because of the nature of his or her employment, child support may be assessed pursuant to section 3(3)(b) of the *Federal Child Support Guidelines* in accordance with the table for the province wherein the primary caregiving spouse and child habitually resided.[91]

H. FIXED TABLE AMOUNT; JUDICIAL DISCRETION; CONDITION, MEANS, NEEDS, AND OTHER CIRCUMSTANCES

Provincial and territorial tables under the *Federal Child Support Guidelines* fix child support payments based on the obligor's income and the number of children of the marriage to whom a support obligation is owed. The judicial discretion to deviate from the presumptive rule under section 3(1) of the *Federal Child Support Guidelines* is strictly limited and clearly specified. The court may depart from the applicable provincial table amount under the Guidelines only under sections 15.1(5) to 15.1(8) and 17(6.2) to 17(6.5) of the *Divorce Act*,

---

87 *Federal Child Support Guidelines*, SOR/97-175,s 3(3)(a)(i), as amended by SOR/2020-247; *Riad v Riad*, [2002] AJ No 1338 (CA); *EAL v HMG*, 2010 BCSC 6892; *JLL v VLL*, 2017 NBQB 76; *Pomroy v Greene*, [2000] NJ No 38 (UFC); *Reid v Faubert*, 2019 NSCA 42; *Williams v Steinwand*, 2017 NWTSC 50; *Barrett v Mychasiw*, [2001] OJ No 2023 (SCJ) (different tables applicable in inter-provincial split parenting time arrangements); *Dunn v Dunn*, 2011 ONSC 6899; *Duncan v Mokelki*, [2008] SJ No 663 (QB). Compare *Timoshchenko v Timoshchenko*, 2012 ABQB 200 at para 44 (application under *Alberta Child Support Guidelines* with respect to child resident in Ukraine).

88 *St Amour v St Amour*, [1997] NSJ No 363 (TD).

89 *Federal Child Support Guidelines*, SOR/97-175, s 3(3)(b), as amended by SOR/2020-247; *Assinck v Assinck*, [1998] OJ No 875 (Gen Div).

90 *Federal Child Support Guidelines*, SOR/97-175, s 3(3)(a)(ii), as amended by SOR/2020-247; see *Tack v Fournier*, [1998] MJ No 596 (QB); *BC v AM*, 2014 NBQB 77; *Martens v Martens*, [2009] SJ No 180 (QB); compare *Riad v Riad*, [2002] AJ No 1338 (CA); *AD v TD*, [1998] QJ No 724 (CS).

91 *Butzelaar v Butzelaar*, [1998] SJ No 741 (QB).

or under sections 3(2), 4, 5, 7, 8, 9, or 10 of the Guidelines.[92] Under these various sections, the court is granted a discretion that is structured by the language of the particular section.

Deviation from the tables is permissible in cases which involve children over the age of majority,[93] obligors with an income over $150,000,[94] special and extraordinary expenses, shared parenting time,[96] or undue hardship.[97] Deviation from the applicable provincial or territorial table amount of child support is also permissible under sections 15.1(5) to 15.1(8) and 17(6.2) to 17(6.5) of the *Divorce Act*.[98] The right of children to support in accordance with the provisions of the *Federal Child Support Guidelines* is not foreclosed or fettered by the applicant mother's acknowledgement at the time of her divorce that reasonable arrangements had been made for the support of the children.[99] In these situations as well as in variation proceedings that fall subject to section 14(b) of the *Federal Child Support Guidelines*, the condition, means, needs, or other circumstances of the spouses and child must be considered.[100]

The presumptive rule under section 3(1) of the *Federal Child Support Guidelines* does not apply to a spouse standing in the place of a parent, in respect of whom section 5 of the Guidelines confers a broad discretion on the court to assess such an amount of child support as the court considers appropriate, having regard to the section 3(1) of the *Federal Child Support Guidelines*. It also has no application to parenting arrangements falling within the ambit of section 9 of the Guidelines.[101]

Absent a finding of undue hardship under section 10 of the Guidelines, a court has no discretion to adjust the applicable table amount of child support to reflect the fact that the primary caregiving parent has additional expenses because of the other parent's non-involvement with the child.[102] A court may average out the monthly payments of child support to reflect the obligor's seasonal employment.[103]

1) Definition of "Condition" of Spouses and Child

The "condition" of the spouses has been defined to include their age, health, needs, obligations, dependants, and the station in life of the parties.[104]

---

92 *Bates v Bates*, [2000] OJ No 2269 (CA); *OM v AK*, [2000] QJ No 3224 (CS); see also *Locke v Goulding* 2012 NLCA 8; *HS v PW*, 2016 NLCA 67.

93 *Federal Child Support Guidelines*, s 3(2); see also *Rémillard v Rémillard*, 2014 MBCA 101 at paras 64–66.

94 *Federal Child Support Guidelines*, s 4; see also *Rémillard v Rémillard*, 2014 MBCA 101; and see Chapter 9, Section B.

95 *Federal Child Support Guidelines*, s 7.

96 *Ibid*, s 9(2).

97 *Ibid*, s 10.

98 See Chapter 10.

99 *Nielsen v Nielsen*, 2006 BCCA 436.

100 See *Willick v Willick*, [1994] 3 SCR 670, 6 RFL (4th) 161 (child support); *Park v Park*, [1999] OJ No 5078 (SCJ).

101 *Contino v Leonelli-Contino*, [2005] 3 SCR 217.

102 *MDL v CR*, [2004] SJ No 326 (QB).

103 *Cooling v Noye*, [1999] PEIJ No 46 (SC).

104 *Moge v Moge*, [1992] 3 SCR 813; *Robichaud v Robichaud* (1988), 17 RFL (3d) 285 (BCCA); *Robichaud v Robichaud* (1992), 124 NBR (2d) 332 (QB); see also *Day v Day* (1994), 129 NSR (2d) 169 (TD).

2) Definition of "Means"

The word "means" includes all pecuniary resources, capital assets, income from capital assets or from employment earning capacity and any other source from which gains or benefits are received, together with, in certain circumstances, money that a person does not have in possession but that is available to such person.[105] In determining what support, if any, should be paid, the court should consider the income earning capacity of each spouse, their income from investments, and their net worth generally.[106] The same sections of the Guidelines also require the court to consider the "needs" of each spouse, thus allaying any notion that "means" are to be accorded paramountcy in determining the right to, amount, and duration of support.[107]

An obligor's unmarried cohabitational relationship with a third party may increase the ability to pay child support by reason of the unmarried cohabitant's responsibility to contribute to their common household income, thereby increasing the disposable income of the obligor who enjoys the economies of shared accommodation.[108] Income may be attributed to a spouse who has substantial capital assets that are not, but could become, income producing.[109] Although interest on a capital investment should be considered in determining the means of the spouse,[110] the allowance for interest income may take account of the cycle of interest over time, and instead of simply reflecting the interest rate at the precise time when the order is made.[111]

"Means" within the meaning of section 15(5) of the *Divorce Act* includes both income and unrealized earning capacity.[112] In determining whether there is an earning potential that can reasonably be attributed to a spouse, the court will have regard to such considerations as age, health, qualifications, and employment prospects in the local community or elsewhere.[113]

A fluctuating income and the inherent insecurity of the obligor's income source is a factor to be considered in determining the amount of support to be ordered.[114]

---

105 *Strang v Strang*, [1992] 2 SCR 112; *Leskun v Leskun*, [2006] 1 SCR 920; *Wallberg v Wallberg* (1994), 8 RFL 372 (BCCA); *Brockie v Brockie* (1987), 5 RFL (3d) 440 (Man QB), aff'd (1987), 8 RFL (3d) 302 (Man CA); *Robichaud v Robichaud* (1992), 124 NBR (2d) 332 (QB); *Butler v Butler* (1980), 27 Nfld & PEIR 1 at 3 (Nfld UFC); *Adie v Adie* (1994), 7 RFL (4th) 54 (NSTD); *Dick v Dick* (1993), 46 RFL (3d) 219 (Ont Ct Gen Div) (inclusion of MP's tax-free benefits in determining income); *Osborne v Osborne* (1973), 14 RFL 61 at 68–70 (Sask QB), var'd (1974), 23 RFL 358 (Sask CA); *Wittke v Wittke* (1974), 16 RFL 349 at 360–63 (Sask QB).

106 *Melnychuk v Melnychuk* (1995), 16 RFL (4th) 366 (Sask QB).

107 *Waterman v Waterman* (1995), 16 RFL (4th) 10 (Nfld CA).

108 *Irving v Irving* (1994), 153 AR 337 (QB); *Chevalier v Chevalier* (1993), 128 NSR (2d) 112 (TD); *Underwood v Underwood* (1994), 113 DLR (4th) 571 (Ont Ct Gen Div) (50 percent of household expenses attributed to new common law spouse despite that individual's lesser income).

109 *Bodor v Bodor* (1988), 12 RFL (3d) 425 (Alta QB); *Buick v Buick* (1988), 12 RFL (3d) 402 (Ont Dist Ct).

110 *Ross v Ross* (1995), 16 RFL (4th) 1 (NBCA).

111 *Vlahovic v Vlahovic* (1991), 37 RFL (3d) 247 (BCCA).

112 *Kollinger v Kollinger* (1995), 14 RFL (4th) 363 at 365 (Man CA), Twaddle JA, in a separate but concurring judgment.

113 *Muirhead v Muirhead* (1995), 14 RFL (4th) 276 (BCCA).

114 *Waterman v Waterman* (1995), 16 RFL (4th) 10 (Nfld CA).

3) Definition of "Other Circumstances"

It is impossible to catalogue all the "other circumstances" of the parties that might be deemed relevant under the Guidelines, although it has been stated that the circumstances must be "so nearly touching the matter in issue as to be such that a judicial mind ought to regard it as a proper thing to be taken into consideration."[115] "Other circumstances" may include the "likelihood of remarriage, cessation of employment, possibility of inheritance and many other unforeseen events."[116] "Other circumstances" may also include a deficiency in English language skills, the state of the employment market, a lack of professional qualifications, an innate shortage of skills, a shortfall of ambition and motivation, and mismanagement of funds.[117]

---

115 *Rogers v Rogers* (1962), 3 FLR 398 at 402 (NSWSC).

116 *Brockie v Brockie* (1987), 5 RFL (3d) 440 (Man QB), aff'd (1987), 8 RFL (3d) 302 (Man CA); *Butler v Butler* (1980), 27 Nfld & PEIR 1 (Nfld UFC); *Day v Day* (1994), 129 NSR (2d) 169 (TD).

117 See *Bodor v Bodor* (1988), 12 RFL (3d) 425 (Alta QB); *Klaudi v Klaudi* (1990), 25 RFL (3d) 134 (Ont HCJ); *Droit de la famille—620*, [1989] RDF 224 (Que CA); *Doncaster v Doncaster* (1991), 31 RFL (3d) 235 (Sask QB).

CHAPTER 2

Jurisdiction

A. JUDICIAL JURISDICTION OVER APPLICATIONS FOR CHILD SUPPORT ON OR AFTER DIVORCE

Sections 3, 4, 5, 6, 6.1, 6.2, and 6.3 of the *Divorce Act* define the jurisdictional competence of a court to entertain an original application for a child support order on or after divorce or an application to vary an existing child support order.[1] Subject to the discretionary powers of transfer conferred by section 6 of the *Divorce Act*, which applies where the proceedings include an application for an order for the exercise of parenting time or parental decision-

1 See Julien D Payne & Marilyn A Payne, *Canadian Family Law*, 10th ed (Toronto: Irwin Law, 2024) ch 7. As to interjurisdictional support orders, see ss 18–19 of the *Divorce Act*; see also ss 28–29.5 of the *Divorce Act* whereby the provisions of the *Convention of 23 November 2007 on the International Recovery of Child Support and Other Forms of Family Maintenance* (2007 Hague Child Support Convention) have the force of law in Canada insofar as they relate to subjects that fall within the legislative competence of Parliament. As to the implementation of the *Convention of 19 October 1996 on Jurisdiction, Applicable Law, Recognition, Enforcement and Co-operation in Respect of Parental Responsibility and Measures for the Protection of Children*, see the *Divorce Act*, ss 30–41. And see John-Paul E Boyd, "A Brief Overview of Bill C-78, An Act to Amend the Divorce Act and Related Legislation; Part 2: Amendments Relating to Interjurisdictional Agreements and Treaties" (June 2018), online: Canadian Research Institute For Law and the Family https://afccontario.ca/wp-content/uploads/2018/06/Boyd-Overview-of-Bill-C78-Pt-2-June-2018.pdf; Department of Justice, Canada, "The *Divorce Act* Changes Explained: Part II," online: Department of Justice, Canada www.justice.gc.ca/eng/fl-df/cfl-mdf/dace-clde/index.html. The 2007 Hague Child Support Convention came into force for Canada and applies to the provinces of Manitoba and Ontario on 1 February 2024, and to British Columbia on 1 March 2024. It is expected that the Convention will be progressively implemented in other provinces and territories in Canada: see Department of Justice, Canada, "Enforcement of Child and Spousal Support Payments between Provinces, Territories and Countries," online: www.justice.gc.ca/eng/fl-df/enforce-execution/enforce-execut.html. See also Ontario Family Responsibility Office (FRO) website and the Hague Conference on Private International Law website, subheading "Child Support," online: HCCH.net; and see Andina van Isschot & Annick Boulay, "Strengthening Family Justice Services: Recent Changes to the *Family Orders and Agreements Enforcement Assistance Act* and Canada's Implementation of the 2007 Hague Child Support Convention," County of Carleton Law Association, 33rd Annual Institute of Family Law, 5 April 2024, Montebello, Quebec.

making responsibility, the primary basis for the exercise of jurisdiction under the Act is the "habitual residence" of either spouse within the province wherein the proceedings are com menced.[2] Section 6(1)of the *Divorce Act* stipulates that if an application for an order for the exercise of parenting time or parental decision-making responsibility under section 16.1 of the *Divorce Act* is made in a divorce proceeding or corollary relief proceeding to a court in a province and the child of the marriage in respect of whom the order is sought is habitually resident in another province, the court may, on application by a spouse or former spouse or on its own motion, transfer the proceeding to a court in that other province. And section 6(2) provides that if an application for a variation order in respect of a parenting order is made in a variation proceeding to a court in a province and the child of the marriage in respect of whom the variation order is sought is habitually resident in another province, the court may, on application by a former spouse or on its own motion, transfer the variation proceeding to a court in that other province. Where a court issuing a divorce has not adjudicated the issue of child support, provincial legislation is a valid means of seeking a child support remedy.

B. EVIDENCE; PRACTICE AND PROCEDURE

Although the Parliament of Canada has exclusive legislative authority over the substantive law of divorce under section 91(26) of the *Constitution Act, 1867*,[4] control over the applicable laws of evidence and over matters of practice and procedure are delegated to the provinces by sections 23 and 25 of the *Divorce Act*.

The definition of "court" in section 2(1) of the *Divorce Act* renders it permissible for the Lieutenant Governor in Council of a province to designate a Unified Family Court that is presided over by federally appointed judges as a court of competent jurisdiction for all purposes of the *Divorce Act*.[5] In addition, the definition of "appellate court" in section 2(1), coupled with the provisions of sections 21(6) and 25(3), enable the provinces to determine the appropriate court for hearing appeals and the procedures to be applied in that court. The composition of the appellate court may vary according to whether the appeal relates to an interim order or a permanent order for corollary relief.

Section 26 of the *Divorce Act* reserves a power in the Governor in Council to override provincial rules of practice and procedure by making federal regulations for carrying out the purposes of the Act. Pursuant to this section, the *Federal Child Support Guidelines* were implemented on 1 May 1997 and revised in 2006 and 2011. For the most part, however, the exercise of power under section 26 of the *Divorce Act* does not unduly interfere with prov incial rules of practice and procedure.

---

2 See Julien D Payne & Marilyn A Payne, *Canadian Family Law*, 10th ed (Toronto: Irwin Law, 2024) ch 7.

3 *Cheng v Liu*, 2017 ONCA 104 at para 43, Hourigan JA; see also *Souhaibb v Javed*, 2023 BCSC 584; *Krause v Bougrine*, 2022 ONCA 161.

4 (UK), 30 & 31 Vict, c 3.

5 See *Gal v Gal*, [2002] OJ No 2937 (Div Ct); see Section H, below in this chapter.

C. LEGISLATIVE AUTHORITY OF PARLIAMENT

The provisions of the *Divorce Act* respecting spousal and child support fall within the legislative authority of the Parliament of Canada.[6] An order directing a divorced father to pay child support is inconsistent with a subsequent step-parental adoption order and is terminated thereby.[7]

D. *CANADIAN CHARTER OF RIGHTS AND FREEDOMS*

The *Federal Child Support Guidelines* are not *ultra vires* under section 26.1 of the *Divorce Act*,[8] nor do they violate the obligor's rights under section 2(b) or section 15(1) of the *Canadian Charter of Rights and Freedoms* or under section 1(a) of the *Canadian Bill of Rights*.[9] A constitutional challenge of the *Federal Child Support Guidelines* on the basis that they are beyond the legislative authority of Parliament and are inconsistent with the *Canadian Charter of Rights and Freedoms* cannot be pursued by divorced biological parents independently of proceedings in which they are personally engaged.[10]

The *Divorce Act* does not contravene section 15(1) of the *Canadian Charter of Rights and Freedoms* so far as extramarital children are concerned.[11]

An argument based on the equality provisions of section 15 of the *Canadian Charter of Rights and Freedoms* is inappropriate to a determination of the amount of support, which necessitates a balancing of need and ability to pay.[12] While it is undoubtedly true that parents with disabilities have crucial expenses that able-bodied parents do not, the undue hardship section of the *Federal Child Support Guidelines* empowers courts to take these kinds of factors into account in determining the amount payable. Accordingly, there is no substantial differential under the Guidelines between persons with disabilities and those without such as to constitute a contravention of section 15 of the *Canadian Charter of Rights and Freedoms*.[13]

E. COMPETING JURISDICTIONS UNDER PROVINCIAL AND FEDERAL LEGISLATION

An order for child support made pursuant to provincial statute will survive divorce where the divorce judgment is silent on the matter of support.[14] In Ontario, section 36(3) of the

---

6 See *Jackson v Jackson*, [1973] SCR 205 (child support); *Zacks v Zacks*, [1973] SCR 891 (spousal support); compare *Rothgiesser v Rothgiesser* (2000), 46 OR (3d) 577 (CA).

7 *Kunkel v Kunkel* (1994), 2 RFL (4th) 1 (Alta CA).

8 *Auer v Auer*, 2022 ABCA 375.

9 *Auer v Auer*, 2022 ABCA 375; *Premi v Khodeir*, [2009] OJ No 3365 (SCJ). See also *Brown v Canada (Attorney General)*, 2019 YKSC 21.

10 *Zeyha v Canada (Attorney General)*, [2004] SJ No 721 (CA).

11 *Massingham-Pearce v Konkulus* (1995), 13 RFL (4th) 313 (Alta QB).

12 Part I of the *Constitution Act, 1982*, being Schedule B to the *Canada Act 1982* (UK), 1982, c 11. See *Hommel v Hommel* (1985), 71 NSR (2d) 85 at 90 (TD).

13 *Dyck v Highton*, [2003] SJ No 600 (QB).

14 *Badakhshan v Moradi* (1993), 127 NSR (2d) 75 (Fam Ct); *Coutts v Coutts* (1995), 14 RFL (4th) 234 (Sask QB).

Family Law Act[15] specifically provides that an order for support made pursuant to this Act continues in force according to its terms where the question of support is not adjudicated in the divorce proceedings.[16]

The power of a court to vary an order for child support under section 17 of the *Divorce Act* does not vest the court with the power to vary support orders made under provincial statute.[17] However, a pre-existing order for child support under provincial statute does not preclude a successful subsequent application for child support under section 15.1 of the *Divorce Act,* which does not require proof of a change of circumstances since the granting of the order under the provincial statute.[18]

Where the issue of child support is expressly reserved in a divorce judgment, the Provincial Court of Alberta lacks the jurisdiction to subsequently order child support in a proceeding instituted pursuant to provincial legislation.[19]

There is no operational incompatibility between the child support provisions of the *Divorce Act* and those of the British Columbia *Family Law Act,* even though the latter statute imposes more extensive obligations on a step-parent. If the court encounters an obstacle in making an order for child support under the *Divorce Act,* an order may be granted pursuant to the *Family Law Act.*[20]

Where an Ontario divorce judgment is silent on the issue of corollary financial relief, an application for child support after the divorce is an original application that falls subject to section 15.1 of the *Divorce Act.* An alternative means of obtaining child support also exists by way of an application under section 33 of the Ontario *Family Law Act.*[21]

Where a divorce judgment is silent on support and a pre-existing child support order under provincial statute has terminated on the child's attainment of the age of majority, an order for child support can be made under the *Divorce Act* to provide for the college education of the child who is still a "child of the marriage" within the meaning of subsection 2(1) of the *Divorce Act.*[22]

The respondent's residence in the province suffices to confer jurisdiction on an Ontario court to entertain an application for child support under the Ontario *Family Law Act* and the *Ontario Child Support Guidelines,* but an Ontario court may decline to exercise jurisdiction when an order for child support has been previously granted in a foreign jurisdiction that provides a more convenient forum. Where there is little or no connection between Ontario and the subject matter of the dispute, jurisdiction should not be assumed by an Ontario court merely because the applicant's legal rights in Ontario are superior to those in the foreign jurisdiction.[23]

---

15 RSO 1990, c F3.

16 *Osterlund-Lenahan v Lenahan,* 2014 ONSC 7074.

17 *Champion v Champion* (1994), 2 RFL (4th) 455 (PEITD); *Tweel v Tweel* (1994), 7 RFL (4th) 204 (PEITD).

18 *Schaff v Schaff* (1997), 30 RFL (4th) 63 (BCCA); *Lewkoski v Lewkoski,* [1998] OJ No 1736 (SCJ).

19 *TRS v DGS,* [2001] AJ No 1311 (QB).

20 *Slattery v Slattery* (1993), 48 RFL (3d) 38 (BCSC); compare *Ruiterman v Ruiterman* (1994), 5 RFL (4th) 192 (BCSC). See also *Souhaibb v Javed,* 2023 BCSC 584; *Cheng v Liu,* 2017 ONCA 104. The BC *Family Relations Act* has now been superseded by the *Family Law Act,* SBC 2011, c 25.

21 *Barrett v Mychasiw,* [2001] OJ No 2023 (SCJ); *French v MacKenzie,* [2003] OJ No 1786 (SCJ).

22 *Edwards v Edwards* (1994), 7 RFL (4th) 105 (BCSC).

23 *Kasprzyk v Burks,* [2005] OJ No 289 (SCJ); *Prichichi v Prichichi,* [2005] OJ No 1979 (SCJ).

An order made pursuant to a provincial statute does not preclude support being subsequently granted by way of corollary relief under the *Divorce Act*.[24]

Where there are concurrent proceedings under a provincial statute and the *Divorce Act*,[25] any potential conflict of jurisdiction should be resolved by a stay of the proceedings under the provincial legislation unless urgency or fairness warrant the continuation of those proceedings.[26]

An application for support under the Ontario *Family Law Act*[27] may only be stayed pursuant to section 36(1) of the Act, if it has not been adjudicated by way of an interim-interim order, an interim order, or a final order prior to the commencement of the divorce proceeding.[28]

In a divorce proceeding, the Ontario Superior Court of Justice has jurisdiction under section 36(2) of the Ontario *Family Law Act* to deal with arrears of support that have accrued under a previous order of the Provincial Court.[29]

A joinder of support proceedings under a provincial statute and under the *Divorce Act* may be appropriate to prevent duplication of effort and unnecessary expense.[30] Where an application for child support under the *Divorce Act* is joined with a contemporaneous application under a provincial statute, the petitioner must choose and cannot have an order under both statutes.[31] Where a divorce judgment is silent on the matter of child support, an original application for such relief may be brought under either the *Divorce Act* or relevant provincial legislation, but an order must be made under one — not both — of the statutes.[32] A decision within the context of the *Divorce Act* not to grant child support constitutes an order and any subsequent application respecting child support should be brought under that Act and not pursuant to provincial statute.[33] A court, including one presided over by a provincially appointed judge, has jurisdiction to entertain a claim for child support under provincial statute where the parent's divorce judgment was silent on the issue; the doctrine of paramountcy does not apply in these circumstances.[34] An application for a child support order in the Ontario

---

24 See *Delaney v Delaney* (1995), 11 RFL (4th) 155 (BCCA); *Strickland v Strickland* (1991), 32 RFL (3d) 179 (NSCA); *Mascarenhas v Mascarenhas*, [1999] OJ No 37 (SCJ) (existing order under *Family Law Act* rescinded pursuant to application of doctrine of paramountcy); *Andrews v Andrews* (1986), 60 Nfld & PEIR 20 (PEICA); *Robbins v Robbins* (1975), 20 RFL 327 (Sask QB).

25 RSC 1985 (2d Supp), c 3.

26 See *Ferguson v Ferguson* (1983), 33 RFL (2d) 322 (NBQB); *Re Tuz* (1975), 25 RFL 87 (Ont CA); compare *Gomes v Gomes* (1985), 47 RFL (2d) 83 (BCSC); *Slattery v Slattery* (1993), 48 RFL (3d) 38 (BCSC); and see *Lyttle v Lyttle* (1992), 41 RFL (3d) 422 (Ont Ct Gen Div) (application by adult child under *Family Law Act*, RSO 1990, c F3). As to the judicial lifting of a stay in proceedings, see *Jordan v La Russa*, 2021 ONSC 7049 (parenting dispute).

27 RSO 1990, c F3.

28 *Mongrain v Mongrain* (1986), 1 RFL (3d) 330 (Ont HCJ); compare *Strong v Strong* (1987), 5 RFL (3d) 209 (Ont HCJ); *Lovett v Lovett* (1982), 26 RFL (2d) 194 (Ont Co Ct), subsequent proceedings (1983), 31 RFL (2d) 109 (Ont HCJ).

29 *Blake v Blake*, [2000] OJ No 2670 (SCJ).

30 *Bombier v Bombier* (1984), 42 RFL (2d) 93 at 97 (Ont Master); see also *Lovett v Lovett* (1983), 31 RFL (2d) 109 (Ont HCJ).

31 *Beatty v Beatty*, [1997] BCJ No 995 (CA).

32 *Evans v Evans*, [1987] BCJ No 67 (SC); compare *Foster v Foster*, [1994] NBJ No 167 (QB).

33 *Duncan v Duncan*, [1999] NBJ No 144 (QB).

34 *Melwood v Melwood*, [1998] AJ No 1435 (Prov Ct); *Ward v Spear*, [1999] OJ No 1795 (Prov Div).

Superior Court of Justice is not precluded by a prior separation agreement that could have been registered and thereafter enforced or varied by the Ontario Court of Justice pursuant to sections 35 and 37 of the Ontario *Family Law Act.* There is no need for the Ontario Superior Court of Justice to exercise its *parens patriae* jurisdiction under these circumstances.[35]

A subsisting order for child support granted to a parent in previous divorce proceedings precludes the child from personally pursuing an application for support under provincial legislation.[36]

A parenting order granted by the British Columbia Supreme Court in divorce proceedings does not oust the jurisdiction of the Provincial Court of British Columbia to determine a subsequent application for child support where the divorce judgment is silent on that issue. The Supreme Court of British Columbia has jurisdiction to order child support under the *Divorce Act* even though the Provincial Court has already granted an order pursuant to the *Family Relations Act*,[38] but the Supreme Court has no jurisdiction to vary the pre-existing order under the provincial statute pursuant to an application for variation brought in divorce proceedings.[39] The Supreme Court of British Columbia may enforce a written agreement providing for child support where that agreement has been filed with the Provincial Court but only the Provincial Court may vary or rescind it.[40] Concurrent jurisdiction vests over support applications in the Supreme Court of British Columbia and the Provincial Court pursuant to the *Family Law Act*, but neither court should interfere with the orders of the other court where concurrent jurisdiction exists.[41]

Where child support has been granted in divorce proceedings by the Supreme Court of Ontario in accordance with an existing order of the Provincial Court (Family Division), the Supreme Court of Ontario has no jurisdiction to direct that any motion to vary the order shall be adjudicated by or referred to the Provincial Court (Family Division).[42] A claim against a step-parent for child support cannot be entertained by the Ontario Court (Provincial Division) when a similar claim was previously before the Ontario Court (General Division).[43]

A child may be entitled to apply to vary a combined order for spousal and child support granted pursuant to provincial statute, where a subsequent divorce judgment is silent on the issue of child support except for providing that "other party may apply" for support and maintenance.[44]

Caselaw makes clear that there is no operational incompatibility between the *Divorce Act* and provincial family law legislation. Child support can be claimed under provincial legislation following a divorce.[45] The doctrine of paramountcy must be applied with common

35 *Reyes v Rollo*, [2001] OJ No 5110 (SCJ).

36 *Kulchyski v Kulchyski* (1996), 22 RFL (4th) 261 (Ont Ct Gen Div); *Skolney v Herman*, [2008] SJ No 73 (QB); see also *Parker v Tinline*, 2012 SKQB 313 (application under *The Inter-jurisdictional Support Orders Act* SS 2002, c I-10.03).

37 *GTW v AMK*, [2006] BCJ No 124 (Prov Ct).

38 See now the *Family Law Act*, SBC 2011, c 25.

39 *Schaff v Schaff* (1997), 30 RFL (4th) 63 (BCCA).

40 *Smith v Smith*, [2000] BCJ No 206 (SC).

41 *Ekland v Sangsari* (1996), 24 RFL (4th) 119 at 122 (BCCA), Southin JA.

42 *Knott (Jacob) v Jacob* (1986), 2 RFL (3d) 255 (Ont Prov Ct).

43 *Mohr v Baxter*, [1999] OJ No 1541 (Prov Div).

44 *S(T) v P(T)* (1996), 23 RFL (4th) 333 (Nfld Prov Ct).

45 *Cheng v Liu*, 2017 ONCA 104 at para 48, Hourigan JA.

sense so as to prevent the denial of a proper remedy to a child whose economic welfare warrants judicial intervention. An application for child support brought by the child's next friend against the father under the Ontario *Family Law Act* is not precluded by a previous order for child support granted to the mother pursuant to the *Divorce Act*, where the child was subsequently abandoned by the mother and was living with the applicant.[46]

In the context of the doctrine of federal paramountcy, the effects of a divorce judgment may be exhausted by the passage of time, in which event recourse may be had to provincial law, which may be better placed to address the applicant's motion for a variation order.[47]

F. TIME OF ORIGINAL APPLICATION

Pursuant to sections 3(1), 4, and 15.1 of the *Divorce Act*, an original application for interim or permanent child support may be pursued at the time of the divorce proceeding or subsequent to the granting of the divorce judgment.[48]

G. DISMISSAL OF DIVORCE PETITION

Dismissal of the divorce petition precludes a claim for child support under the *Divorce Act*, but such relief may be available where an alternative claim has been brought under provincial statute.[49] Where a prayer for corollary relief is contained in a petition for divorce that is withdrawn, the court does not have jurisdiction to grant the corollary relief requested unless the spouse claiming it can bring the matter before the court in another matter at the same time as the divorce proceeding.[50] It is for this reason that lawyers normally include in a divorce petition alternative claims for relief under provincial statute.

An application for child support under the Alberta *Family Law Act*[51] is an action *in personam* and jurisdiction can be exercised based on the defendant's submission by agreement or attornment, his ordinary residence in the jurisdiction, or a real and substantial connection between the subject matter of the action and the forum,[52] but the court may also be required to determine whether it is the *forum conveniens*.[53]

H. STATUS OF APPLICANT; PAYMENT TO CHILD

An application[54] for interim or permanent child support may be made by either or both spouses or former spouses pursuant to section15.1(1) of the *Divorce Act*. These sections

46 *VB (Next friend of) v DB*, [1998] OJ No 4814 (Gen Div).

47 *MN v NP*, [1999] QJ No 5524 (CS).

48 *Fortune v Fortune* (1987), 51 Man R (2d) 127 (QB). See also *Edwards v Edwards* (1994), 97 BCLR (2d) 177 (SC).

49 *Huber v Huber*, [1999] OJ No 4400 (SCJ).

50 *Cook v Cook* (1980), 30 Nfld & PEIR 42 (Nfld TD).

51 SA 2003, c F-4.5.

52 *AG v LS*, 2006 ABCA 311; *Matty v Rammasoot*, 2014 ABQB 2.

53 *Timoshchenko v Timoshchenko*, 2012 ABQB 200 (jurisdiction declined); compare *Matty v Rammasoot*, 2014 ABQB 2.

54 As to the appointment of *amici curiae* to represent each of the unrepresented parents in a complex child support proceeding, see *Morwald-Benevides v Benevides*, 2015 ONSC 7290.

apparently permit a joint application by the spouses or former spouses. The same is true under section 17(1)(a), which provides for the prospective or retroactive variation, rescission, or suspension of a support order.[55] Pursuant to sections 15.1(4) and 17(3) of the *Divorce Act* a court may impose such terms, conditions, or restrictions in connection with the order as it thinks fit and just.

The *Divorce Act* does not give a child of the marriage any standing to apply for interim or permanent support in a divorce proceeding instituted by a parent[56] or to apply to enforce or vary a child support order,[57] although it seems an unnecessary burden to impose on a parent where the child in respect of whom support is sought is an adult who is not living with either parent.[58] Non-spouses do not have standing to apply for child support orders under the *Divorce Act* and *Federal Child Support Guidelines.* An adult "child of the marriage" lacks the status to bring an application to vary a child support order obtained by a parent, even though both parents had previously agreed that periodic payments would be made directly to the child.[59]

Under the *Divorce Act*, 1968,[60] the court occasionally acted on its own initiative and ordered the payment of child support, notwithstanding that it was not requested or desired by the primary caregiving parent.[61] It is questionable whether such jurisdiction can now be exercised in view of section 15.1(1) of the *Divorce Act,* which defines the jurisdiction of the court "on application by either or both spouses." However, some courts have concluded that child support may be ordered in the exercise of the *parens patriae* jurisdiction.[62] While a child of the marriage has no standing to bring an application for child support under the *Divorce Act* does not follow that a court has no jurisdiction to order child support to be paid directly to the child on the application of either or both spouses or former spouses. There is no prohibition against such orders in either the *Divorce Act* or the *Federal Child Support Guidelines.* Furthermore, as stated previously, sections 15.1(4) and 17(3) of the *Divorce Act* specifically empower the court to impose such terms, conditions, and restrictions on its child support order as it deems fit and just. These provisions are sufficiently wide to permit a court to order direct

---

55 *Guiotto v Guiotto*, [2001] BCJ No 1032 (SC).

56 *Levesque v Levesque* (1994), 4 RFL (4th) 375 (Alta CA); *GG v JTG*, 2013 ABQB 726; *MV v DV*, [2005] NBJ No 505 (QB); *Garbers v Garbers* (1993), 48 RFL (3d) 217 (Ont UFC) (variation application by adult child); see also *Mierins v Mierins*, 9 RFL 396 (Ont SC), citing *Tapson v Tapson* (1970), 2 RFL 305 (Ont CA); *Skolney v Herman*, [2008] SJ No 73 (QB); compare *Lyttle v Lyttle* (1992), 41 RFL (3d) 422 (Ont Prov Div) (application by adult child under *Family Law Act*, RSO 1990, c F3); *Miller v Mitchell*, 2013 ONSC 7021 at para 17.

57 *Otto v Between*, [1996] OJ No 4786 (Gen Div); *Jivraj v Jivraj*, 2010 ONSC 4949; *Campbell v Chapple*, [2004] NWTJ No 42 (SC); *SB v RB*, [2000] QJ No 3298 (CS); *Skolney v Herman*, [2008] SJ No 73 (QB) As to the nature of the child's right to support, see *GG v JTG*, 2013 ABQB 726 wherein the litigation representative for the children unsuccessfully sought to have the children intervene in their parents' proceedings involving child support.

58 *Levesque v Levesque* (1994), 4 RFL (4th) 375 at 401 (Alta CA); *VS v DMS*, 2016 BCSC 1346.

59 *Wahl v Wahl*, [2000] AJ No 29 (QB).

60 SC 1967–68, c 24.

61 *Hansford v Hansford* (1973), 9 RFL 233 (Ont HCJ); *Dowden v Dowden* (1980), 29 Nfld & PEIR 165 (Nfld TD).

62 See *Hansen v Hansen* (1995), 13 RFL (4th) 335 at 337 (Ont Ct Gen Div) (variation of consent order for child support is not dependent on change of circumstances); *Boyer v Bradley* (1995), 15 RFL (4th) 33 (Ont Ct Gen Div) (interim variation of child support order). See also *Dixon v Dixon* (1995), 13 RFL (4th) 160 (Alta QB); *Re Kuehn* (1976), 2 BCLR 97 (SC); see *contra Harris v Harris* (1978), 90 DLR (3d) 699 (BCSC) (no inherent equitable jurisdiction over child support).

payments of support to an adult child in exceptional situations where such a course of action is considered appropriate. In the words of Jackson JA in *Burzminski v Burzminski*,[63] "[w]hile a decision to pay child support, directly to the child, is not the norm, a court has a discretion to make such an order." It should not be forgotten that "child support, is the right of the child."[64] And in *Bourque v Janzen*, Dufour J of the Saskatchewan Court of Queen's Bench stated that "[t]he theme that runs throughout is that the support should only be paid directly to the child where the payee incurs no expenses in relation to maintaining a home for the child (e.g., where the child attends university in another city and is not expected to regularly return to live with the payee)."[65] On occasion, the jurisdiction to make such orders has been denied: see *Adams v Adams*[66] and *MV v DV*,[67] both of which cite the brief judgment of the New Brunswick Court of Appeal in *LeBlanc v LeBlanc*.[68] It is noteworthy that *LeBlanc* pre-dates the implementation of the *Federal Child Support Guidelines* and accompanying changes to the *Income Tax Act* that render post-Guidelines child support orders payable in after-tax dollars.

Under the pre-Guidelines regime, an order for the payment of periodic child support to the primary caregiving parent would result in those payments being deductible from the payor's income and included in the recipient's taxable income. But these consequences would be negated by an order that provided for direct payments of support to the child instead of the primary caregiving parent. In contrast, under the current Guidelines regime, it is immaterial from an income tax standpoint whether the support is payable directly to the child or to the primary caregiving parent. In either event, it is payable in after-tax dollars and free of income tax liabilities in the hands of the recipient. It is perhaps not surprising, therefore, that the question of a court's jurisdiction, if any, to order child support payments to be made directly to the child did not attract much attention from Canadian courts under the pre-Guidelines regime but has done so in the post-Guidelines era.

Quite independently of income tax considerations, the decision of the New Brunswick Court of Appeal in *LeBlanc v LeBlanc* has not been followed in other provinces. Furthermore, the New Brunswick Court of Appeal in *Glaspy v Glaspy*[69] has itself now concluded that, although such cases are not numerous, there is judicial authority that supports the notion that child support payments may be ordered to be made directly to an adult child who is attending university away from home. Even if a court may order that the child support should be paid directly to the child,[70] such an order should not be made where the obligor's past conduct manifests financial control and manipulation,[71] where undue friction would

---

63 2010 SKCA 16 at para 19; *Ghremida v Elgahwas*, 2023 SKCA 23 at para 32.

64 *DBS v SRG*, 2006 SCC 37 at para 38, Bastarache J; *Richardson v Richardson*, [1987] 1 SCR 857, [1987] SCJ No 30 at para 14, Wilson J. Compare *GG v JTG*, 2013 ABQB 726.

65 2012 SKQB 458 at para 24; see also *Youle v Galloway*, 2018 SKQB 211 at para 81. And see *Miller v Miller*, 2019 NSSC 28.

66 [1998] NBJ No 15 (QB).

67 [2005] NBJ No 505 (QB). See also *Mitchell v Mitchell*, 2011 ONSC 7015.

68 (1982), 42 NBR (2d) 639 (CA). But see now *Glaspy v Glaspy*, 2011 NBCA 101.

69 2011 NBCA 101; see also *TTB v PHD*, 2014 NBQB 164; *Comeau v Newman*, 2021 NBQB 197. Compare *GFW v JLR*, 2012 BCCA 245 (support arrears not discharged by direct payments to adult child).

70 *Kazoleas v Kazoleas*, [1997] AJ No 820 (QB) (order that payment be made directly to seventeen-year-old child); *Colonval v Munson*, [1998] BCJ No 1178 (SC); *Bell v Bell*, 2011 BCSC 212; *Lu v Sun*, [2005] NSJ No 314 (CA); *Oczkowski v New*, 2011 ONSC 3932; *Burzminski v Burzminski (Lewis)*, 2010 SKCA 16.

71 *Owen v Owen*, 2011 BCSC 1284.

thereby be caused,[72] where the child's entitlement to student loans may be detrimentally affected,[73] or where the applicable provincial table amount of support is ordered for two or more children, only one of whom is an adult child attending college.[74] A court may refuse to order that payments be made directly to an adult child where there is no evidence that the child favours this[75] and the only reason raised is the payor's animosity to his or her divorced spouse.[76] A court should not order support payments to be made directly to a child whose money management skills are open to question.[77] Where the children reside with the primary caregiving parent who provides their basic needs, a court should not order child support payments to be made directly to the children, unless the primary caregiving parent consents or there are exceptional circumstances, such as the actual inability of the primary caregiving parent to handle finances.[78] A court may also refuse to order payments to be made to an adult child where this would contravene the terms of a separation agreement.[79] A court may order child support to be paid directly to the child during the months that he or she attends an out-of-town post-secondary institution but require the payments to be made to the parent during the summer months when the child is living with that parent.[80] Payments directly to the child may be ordered where it might be beneficial to the relationship between the payor and the child.[81] Although payments for an adult child attending college may be ordered to be made to the child directly,[82] the court may direct that the payor shall not establish per sonal contact without the child's consent.[83] Where a parent is ordered to pay the applicable provincial table amount of support in addition to a contribution to an adult child's costs of post-secondary education under section 7 of the *Federal Child Support Guidelines*, the court may direct that the table amount shall be paid to the parent with whom the child is living, but that the contribution to the costs of post-secondary education shall be paid directly to the child.[84] In *Douglas v Douglas*,[85] Sherr J of the Ontario Court of Justice ordered a significant portion of the arrears of child support to be paid directly to the adult child to reimburse her for substantial student loans that she had incurred.

Where child support is ordered to be paid to the primary caregiving parent, the obligor is not entitled to make payments to the child instead or to purchase things for the child in

---

72 *Sherlock v Sherlock*, [1998] BCJ No 116 (SC).

73 *McKinley v McKinley*, 2011 NBQB 260.

74 *Walls v Walls*, [1998] NBJ No 246 (QB).

75 *Sherlock v Sherlock*, [1999] BCJ No 1856 (SC) (child averse to direct payment); *Johnson v Johnson*, [2002] OJ No 3298 (SCJ).

76 *Potter v Graham*, [2004] AJ No 1133 (QB); *Barry v Wilson*, [1990] NBJ No 902, 29 RFL (3d) 42 at 48 (QB).

77 *Sherlock v Sherlock*, [1998] BCJ No 116 (SC); *Johnson v Johnson*, [2002] OJ No 3298 (SCJ).

78 *Tobias v Tobias*, [2000] AJ No 346 (QB); *Rozen v Rozen*, [2001] BCJ No 1633 (SC); *Morgan v Morgan*, [2006] BCJ No 1795 (SC); *Marshall v Marshall*, [1998] NSJ No 311 (SC); *Thompson v Thompson*, [1998] NSJ No 501 (SC). See also *PG v DDG*, 2017 BCSC 724.

79 *PHH v NRY*, 2015 BCSC 320.

80 *Longlitz v Longlitz*, 2012 BCSC 130; *MacEachern v MacLeod*, 2014 NSSC 238.

81 *Danyluk v Danyluk*, [2008] AJ No 509 (QB); *Mathusz v Carew*, 2011 NLTD(F) 28.

82 *Wakeford v Wakeford*, 2011 ABQB 106; *Bell v Bell*, 2011 BCSC 212; *Chapple v Campbell*, [2005] MJ No 323 (QB); *Wilkins v Wilkins*, [1998] NBJ No 325 (QB); *Tracey v Clarke*, [1998] NJ No 236 (SC) (hometown university); *Oczkowski v New*, 2011 ONSC 3932; *Burzminski v Burzminski (Lewis)*, 2010 SKCA 16.

83 *Wesemann v Wesemann*, [1999] BCJ No 1387 (SC).

84 *Rieder v Jenei*, [2006] BCJ No 176 (SC); *Armaz v Van Erp*, [2000] OJ No 1544 (SCJ).

85 2013 ONCJ 242.

partial discharge of the support obligation.[86] Without the agreement of the payee parent, a child support obligor cannot discharge arrears of child support by making payments directly to the child.[87]

Provincial legislation determines whether a child has the capacity to institute an application for support pursuant to provincial *Child Support Guidelines*.[88] A divorce judgment that is silent on the issue of child support does not preclude a child from bringing an application for support pursuant to provincial statute.[89]

Section 50 of the Alberta *Family Law Act* provides that the court may make an order requiring a parent to provide support for his or her child on application by the child and the court may order a parent to pay child support either to a guardian of a child or to a person who has the care and control of a child. A grandparent may seek child support thereunder for the period when the child was living with her but an order for retroactive child support may be denied.[90] The Director of Maintenance Enforcement has standing where a child support order has been registered with that office, but no right of subrogation exists in relation to Assured Income for the Severely Handicapped (AISH) payments made by the provincial government with respect to a severely disabled adult child.[91]

The Minister under the *BC Benefits (Income Assistance) Act* has standing to pursue a child support claim on behalf of a parent receiving income assistance where an assignment has been made in accordance with sections 78 and 79 of the Act. The assignment confers authority on the Minister to ensure that the proper level of child support is paid and the parent in receipt of income assistance has no authority to consent to a lower amount than that payable under the provincial *Child Support Guidelines*.[92] The Minister under the *BC Benefits (Income Assistance) Act* has standing to apply for an increase in child support by way of a variation order where income assistance is being provided and the original consent order for child support has been assigned to the Minister in accordance with section 24.1(1) of the Act and section 79 of the *Income Assistance Regulation*.[93]

Pursuant to section 149(b) of the British Columbia *Family Law Act*, "a child or a person acting on behalf of the child" may apply for an order for support. To have standing to make an application, however, the applicant must have a connection or interest in the children's welfare.[94]

A child under the age of provincial majority who is living with neither parent is entitled to apply by his guardian *ad litem* for child support to be paid by either or both of his parents pursuant to the *Family Law Act* (Newfoundland). The amount ordered to be paid may be reduced below the applicable table amount of support on the ground that concurrent

---

86 *Haisman v Haisman*, [1994] AJ No 553 (CA).

87 *Tobias v Meadley*, 2011 BCCA 472; *GFW v JLR*, 2012 BCCA 245.

88 *VS v DMS*, 2016 BCSC 1346 at para 8, citing s 149 of the *Family Law Act*, SBC 2011, c 25.

89 *S(T) v P(T)* (1996), 23 RFL (4th) 333 (Nfld Prov Ct); compare *Pope v Pope* (1995), 12 RFL (4th) 391 (Nfld UFC). As to the appointment of a litigation guardian for a minor, see *CMM v DGC*, 2014 ONSC 567.

90 *Cloutier v Cloutier*, 2012 ABQB 336.

91 *Buzon v Buzon*, [1999] AJ No 371 (QB).

92 *British Columbia (Minister under the BC Benefits (Income Assistance) Act) v Dent*, [2000] BCJ No 2035 (SC).

93 BC Reg 75/97; *Ward v Hanes*, [2000] BCJ No 2372 (SC).

94 *Kasper v Mundy* (1993), 81 BCLR (2d) 256 (SC); *Mohammed v Murtaza*, 2010 BCSC 177.

support obligations owed to other children create undue hardship for the parent within the meaning of section 10 of the *Federal Child Support Guidelines*.[95]

An adult child may seek child support from both parents pursuant to the *Maintenance and Custody Act* (Nova Scotia), notwithstanding that the *Nova Scotia Child Maintenance Guidelines* are modelled on the *Federal Child Support Guidelines* and make no special accom modation for a child bringing the application. There is nothing inherently inappropriate with a child recovering the full table amount of child support from each parent. Although the authors of the provincial guidelines may not have addressed their minds to the prospect of a child receiving the full table amount from each parent, neither the Act nor the Guidelines seem to leave any option to a court to deviate from the tables in the ordinary course of events. Where the child has attained the age of majority, however, section 3(2)(b) of the Guidelines may be applied so as to apportion the child support obligation between the parents after due account is taken of the adult child's own ability to contribute to his or her expenses.[96]

In *Winnipeg Child and Family Services (Northwest Area) v G(DF)*,[97] the Supreme Court of Canada concluded that neither the common law nor the civil law of Quebec recognizes an unborn child as a legal person with rights. Any right or interest the fetus may have remains inchoate and incomplete until birth. However, provincial legislation may confer legal rights on an unborn child. Although sections 11 and 23 of the *Maintenance and Custody Act* (Nova Scotia) entitle a pregnant mother to apply for lying-in expenses and child support, no similar right is conferred on the father of the child.[98]

The next friend of a mentally unstable person may be entitled to pursue an application for child support to be paid to the *de facto* custodian of the child as a trustee for the child.

Adult children, who are pursuing post-secondary education, may apply for support against both parents under the Ontario *Family Law Act* and the provincial guidelines. On an application by an adult child for support under the Ontario *Family Law Act*, judicial deviation from the provincial table amount of support under the *Ontario Child Support Guidelines* is permissible where the child is living with neither parent.[101]

An aunt who has assumed the parenting responsibility for her nephew has standing to apply for child support as a "parent" within the meaning of section 1(1) of the Ontario *Family Law Act*, whereby "parent" includes "a person who has demonstrated a settled intention to treat a child as a child of his or her family."[102]

---

95 *Stratton (Guardian ad litem of) v Gullage*, [2001] NJ No 332 (Prov Ct).

96 *JDF v HMF*, [2001] NSJ No 456 (Fam Ct) (judicial refusal to order either parent to pay the applicable table amount of child support where the child, who would attain the age of majority within a few weeks after the judgment, was capable of meeting the majority of her necessary expenses; existing support order whereby each parent to pay $70 per month left unchanged except for minor modifications).

97 [1997] 3 SCR 925.

98 *RDM v EEK*, [2002] NSJ No 332 (Fam Ct).

99 See *Robbins v Robbins* (1986), 43 Man R (2d) 53 (QB) (application under *Family Maintenance Act*, CCSM c F20); *Sullivan v Sullivan* (1986), 2 RFL (3d) 251 at 252–53 (Ont Dist Ct).

100 *Midena v Collette*, [2000] OJ No 4429 (Ct J). As to the appointment of a litigation guardian for a minor, see *CMM v DGC*, 2015 ONSC 2447 (Div Ct).

101 *Lynch v Lynch*, [1999] OJ No 4559 (SCJ) (interim order granted to reflect adult child's needs as established by proposed budget).

102 *Perovic v Nagtzaam*, [2001] OJ No 3462 (Ct J).

A biological father, who assumes primary care of his children on their mother's death, has standing under section 33(2) of the *Family Law Act* (Ontario) to bring an application for child support against the stepfather of the children.[103]

Rule 7.04(2) of the Ontario *Rules of Procedure*, which came into force on 3 April 1995, empowers the court to authorize the Children's Lawyer, formerly the Official Guardian, or some other proper person to act as a child's legal representative where, in the opinion of the court, the interests of a minor who is not a party require separate representation. It does not follow that the interests of justice and that of the children will be compromised if they lack representation on an appeal relating to the form and amount of child support.[104] The structure of the *Child Support Guidelines* and the *Family Responsibility and Support Arrears Enforcement Act* do not contemplate an order for the payment of support directly to an adult child without parental consent and a joint withdrawal of the support order from the support deduction system.[105]

A grandparent, with whom the father has placed one of the children of the marriage, may apply for an order for child support against the father under *The Family Maintenance Act, 1997* (Saskatchewan). The child's conduct and the reason for the child's placement in the grandparent's home is irrelevant and, in the absence of undue hardship, the father's obligation to pay the full table amount of support to the grandparent for the child in her care is unaffected by his concurrent obligation to pay the full table amount of support to the mother for the two children in her care.[106] A mother's application for child support against the father may be dismissed where the child is living with her aunt and the mother is making very little contribution towards the child's support.[107]

I. THIRD-PARTY PAYMENTS

A court may order that child support payments be made directly to the primary caregiving parent or to a third person[108] or through the court[109] or a designated agency,[110] such as a provincial support enforcement service.[111] A court order for support under the *Ontario Child Support Guidelines* is not precluded by a court order denying parenting time to the father

---

103 *Symons v Taylor*, [2000] OJ No 2703 (SCJ) (apportionment of liability between biological parent and step-parent effectuated on the notional basis that the deceased mother of the children was the applicant and the biological father and step-parent were the respondents).

104 *Gordon v Solmon* (1995), 16 RFL (4th) 403 (Ont CA).

105 *Surette v Surette*, [2000] OJ No 675 (SCJ).

106 *Abell v Abell*, [2003] SJ No 576 (QB) (father held entitled to add the mother as a party to the proceeding under s 27 of *The Family Maintenance Act* (Saskatchewan) but did not do so in this case).

107 *Cougan v Piche*, [2004] SJ No 587 (QB) (mother at liberty to re-apply for prospective child support if child returned to live with her).

108 *Sollis v Sollis*, [2003] BCJ No 1643 (SC) (s 7 expenses); see also *Brock v Sorger*, 2015 ONSC 7478. And see *Miller v White*, 2018 PECA 11 (interim order for third-party payments in lieu of interim child support payments).

109 *Adams v Adams*, [1998] NBJ No 15 (QB).

110 See *Smith v Smith* (1986), 4 RFL (3d) 210 (Ont Fam Ct) (application under *Family Law Act*, SO 1986, c 4). As to the assignment of orders, see *Divorce Act*, s 20.1.

111 *Faulkner v Faulkner*, [1997] AJ No 730 (QB); *McKinley v McKinley*, 2011 NBQB 260; *Turple v Turple*, 2011 NSSC 150; *Nugent v Nugent*, 2011 NLTD(F) 4; *Hare v Kendall*, [1997] NSJ No 310 (TD); *Crawford v Crawford*, [1998] OJ No 3894 (Prov Div); *Bruce v Kelly*, [2001] PEIJ No 53 (SC).

nor by the mother's fear of the father where payments can be made through the Director of the Family Responsibility Office and the whereabouts of the mother and children would not be disclosed.[112]

Child support payments made pursuant to an order of the court are usually within the exclusive control and management of the primary caregiving parent. Although there is no guarantee that the parent will expend the payments received for the benefit of the child, courts are reluctant to impose terms and conditions that would circumscribe the discretionary authority of the parent. It is irrelevant to the obligor's duty to support a child that the primary caregiving parent may spend the money on items that the obligor parent does not approve of. There is a presumption that the primary caregiving parent or the parent with day-to-day care of the child will act prudently with respect to spending child support payments in the best interests of the child. An interruption in the flow of child support pending an in-depth review of the primary caregiving parent's financial affairs is not in a child's best interests.[113]

A court may order a parent to pay a child's tuition expenses directly to the post-secondary institution in light of the child's past failure to disclose his academic record to the paying parent.[114]

J. ADVANCE PAYMENTS; POST-DATED CHEQUES; ELECTRONIC TRANSFERS

A self-employed parent with cash flow problems that have resulted in late payments may be ordered to pay child support a month in advance in order to alleviate the problem.[115]

A court may direct that child support payments be arranged by a series of post-dated cheques.[116] Alternatively, the court may order child support to be payable by means of electronic transfer by the payor[117] or his or her employer[118] to the payee's account. A court may grant an order whereby child support is to be paid by way of post-dated cheques in favour of the Maintenance Enforcement Program for direct deposit thereafter in the primary caregiving parent's account.[119] In fixing arrears of child support, a court may refuse to set off payments made to the primary caregiving parent where the child support order directed payments to be made through the office of the provincial Director of Maintenance Enforcement. Such payments may be treated as gifts, rather than set off against the

---

112 *Attwood v Sharma*, [2000] OJ No 1129 (SCJ), wherein *Close v Close* (1999), 50 RFL (4th) 342 (NBQB) was not followed.

113 *McIvor v McIvor*, [1997] BCJ No 1666 (SC).

114 *Polson v Polson*, [2000] BCJ No 2050 (SC).

115 *Dagg v Pereira*, [2000] OJ No 4450 (SCJ).

116 *Potter v Graham*, [2004] AJ No 1133 (QB); *S v S*, [1999] BCJ No 1043 (SC) (recipient parent entitled to elect payment of child support through Family Maintenance Enforcement Program or by way of post-dated cheques to be provided in advance for each year); *Dicks v Dicks*, [2001] NSJ No 302 (SC); *DeBora v DeBora*, [2003] OJ No 575 (SCJ) (post-dated cheques or direct bank deposit); *Clark v Taylor* [2004] NWTJ No 5 (SC).

117 *Volken v Volken*, [2001] BCJ No 1344 (SC); *Turple v Turple*, 2011 NSSC 150; *RL v BI*, [1997] QJ No 4450 (CS).

118 *Clark v Taylor*, [2004] NWTJ No 5 (SC).

119 *Veinotte v Veinotte*, [1999] NSJ No 327 (Fam Ct); *Haxton v Haxton*, [2002] NSJ No 229 (SC).

outstanding support arrears.[120] Insistence on post-dated cheques or direct bank deposits is a useful practice for lawyers to adopt in negotiating settlements; enforcement problems may be thereby eliminated.

Post-dated cheques for child support are not available as of right. Provincial employees are not entitled to demand post-dated cheques for future monthly payments of child support as a condition precedent to the reinstatement of a defaulter's licence after his discharge of all outstanding arrears.[121]

K. CHILD RESIDING OUTSIDE CANADA

An application for child support may be brought in the Supreme Court of British Columbia pursuant to the *Divorce Act* against a former spouse who habitually resides in British Columbia, even though the children reside outside of Canada.[122]

L. EFFECT OF DEATH

An application for child support is not terminated by the respondent's death after commencement of the proceeding. Relief is available under the Ontario *Family Law Act*, even if a claim for corollary financial relief under the *Divorce Act* terminates on the respondent's death. Where adult children are entitled to support to facilitate their post-secondary education, section 3(2)(b) of the *Child Support Guidelines* permits a court to deviate from the presumptive rule in favour of the applicable table amount of monthly support plus allowable expenses under section 7 of the Guidelines, if the court finds the application of the presumptive rule to be inappropriate. Consequently, the court may order the deceased's estate to pay lump sum child support in accordance with section 11 of the Guidelines. In assessing the amount to be allocated where the deceased parent's estate is modest, the court must take account of the priority to be accorded to the federal Crown with respect to the deceased's income tax liabilities. Otherwise, the child support obligation takes priority over the deceased's liability to ordinary creditors and the declared beneficiaries of the deceased's estate.[123]

An adult child pursuing a PhD may be entitled to periodic support out of her deceased father's estate pursuant to Part V of the Ontario *Succession Law Reform Act*, but the adult child's claim for an additional lump sum to apply to her student loan indebtedness may be denied where the deceased had only a modest estate and left a widow after a sixteen-year marriage.[124]

---

120 *KMH v MRN*, [2001] NSJ No 262 (Fam Ct).

121 *Mainwaring v Alberta*, [1998] AJ No 105, 48 RFL (4th) 171 (QB) (action for damages).

122 *MG v AF*, [2003] BCJ No 1196 (SC).

123 *Hillock v Hillock*, [2001] OJ No 3837 (SCJ).

124 *Sheffiel-Lambros v Sheffiel*, [2005] OJ No 697 (SCJ).

CHAPTER 3

Definitions of "Child of the Marriage"; Adult Children; Obligation of *De Facto* Parent

A. RELEVANT STATUTORY PROVISIONS

The definitions of "child of the marriage" in sections 2(1) and 2(2) of the *Divorce Act*[1] read as follows:

> **Definitions**
>
> 2(1) In this Act, . . .
>
> **child of the marriage** means a child of two spouses or former spouses who, at the material time,
>
> (a) is under the age of majority and who has not withdrawn from their charge, or
>
> (b) is the age of majority or over and under their charge but unable, by reason of illness, disability or other cause, to withdraw from their charge or to obtain the necessaries of life.
>
> . . .
>
> **Child of the marriage**
>
> (2) For the purposes of the definition **child of the marriage** in subsection (1), a child of two spouses or former spouses includes:
>
> (a) any child for whom they both stand in the place of parents; and
>
> (b) any child of whom one is the parent and for whom the other stands in the place of a parent.

The age of majority in respect of a child means the age of majority as determined by the laws of a province where the child resides. The age of majority is eighteen years of age in six provinces, namely, Alberta, Manitoba, Ontario, Prince Edward Island, Quebec, and Saskatchewan, and nineteen years of age in four provinces and the three territories, namely, British Columbia,[2] New Brunswick, Newfoundland and Labrador, Northwest Territories, Nova Scotia,

---

1 RSC 1985 (2d Supp), c 3, as amended by RSC 1985 (2d Supp), c 27, SC 1990, c 18, SC 1993, c 8, SC 1997, c 1. See also Maxine M Kerr, "Child Support for Adult Children" (2023) 41 CFLQ 315–90.

2 *MacLean v Mio*, 2019 BCSC 375.

3 *Homann v Briscoe*, 2020 NSSC 52.

Nunavut, and Yukon.[4] The applicable legislation for determining whether a child has reached the provincial age of majority is that of the province in which the child habitually resided during the relevant period.[5]

An analysis of whether a child is unable to withdraw from a parent's "charge" focuses on whether the child remains financially dependent on the parent.[6] A child is usually considered to have withdrawn from parental charge when he or she has sufficient income to meet his or her own financial needs.[7] A child who attains the provincial age of majority while attending school may cease to be eligible for child support by virtue of concurrent employment that provides the child with sufficient income to enable her to withdraw from her parents' care and to be independent had she chosen to do so.[8] The proper time for determining whether a person stands in the place of a parent within the meaning of the definition of "child of the marriage" under section 2(2) of the *Divorce Act* is during the marriage when the family functioned as a unit.[9]

Section 2(1) of the *Divorce Act*, above, defines a "child of the marriage" and deals with the entitlement to support. The *Federal Child Support Guidelines* do not deal with entitlement; they only deal with the amount of support.[10]

For the purpose of applying the definition of "child of the marriage" in section 2(1) of the *Divorce Act*, the age of majority in respect of a child means the age of majority as determined by the laws of a province where the child habitually resides, or, if the child resides outside of Canada, eighteen years of age.[11] A child under the age of majority is presumptively a child of the marriage.[12] The burden falls on the parent to prove on a balance of probabilities that the child has withdrawn from his parents' charge.[13] The fact that a child under the age of majority has voluntarily left her parent's home does not, of itself, signify that the child is no longer eligible for support as a "child of the marriage" within the meaning of section 2(1) of the *Divorce Act*[14] but a child under the age of majority who is financially self-sufficient ceases to be a child of the marriage within the meaning of section 2(1) of the *Divorce Act*.[15] It appears that any child under the provincial age of majority satisfies the definition of "child of the marriage" under section 2(1) of the *Divorce Act*, if that child is in fact financially dependent on his or her parents. The child's capacity to withdraw from their parents' charge and unwillingness

---

4 See *DS v WDG*, 2016 BCSC 1345 at para 37.

5 *Pakozdi v Pakozdi*, 2016 BCSC 2428.

6 *VS v DMS*, 2016 BCSC 1346; *Shelley v Russell*, 2012 ONSC 920.

7 *Chaulk v Avery*, 2009 NLTD 185; *AWH v CGS*, [2007] NSJ No 262 (QB).

8 *Smith v Smith*, 2020 ABQB 775.

9 *Chartier v Chartier*, [1999] 1 SCR 242; *DBS v SRG; LJW v TAR; Henry v Henry; Hiemstra v Hiemstra*, [2006] 2 SCR 231; *NP v IV*, 2013 BCSC 1323; *Friday v Friday*, 2013 ONSC 1931.

10 *Sherlow v Zubko*, [1999] AJ No 644 (QB).

11 *Divorce Act*, s 2(1) (definition of "age of majority"); see *Boisvert v Boisvert*, [2000] AJ No 1393 (QB); *RJM v EM*, 2015 BCSC 414; *Charbonneau v Charboneau*, 2010 ONSC 3883.

12 *Sappier v Francis*, 2013 NBQB 168.

13 *Sharma v Sharma*, 2022 MBQB 27; *JAM v SAJ*, 2014 NSSC 2; *DBB v DMB*, 2017 SKCA 59.

14 *Kallen v Michaud*, 2010 MBQB 151. Compare *JLT v KLH*, 2011 BCSC 560 at paras 25–26. See also *Matechuk v Kopp (Yaworenko)*, 2020 SKQB 196.

15 *Stockall v Stockall*, 2020 ABQB 229; *MacLean v Mio*, 2019 BCSC 375 at para 44; *Homann v Briscoe*, 2020 NSSC 52.

to do so appears to be irrelevant to the statutory definition.[16] A child under the provincial age of majority may cease to be eligible for child support as a "child of the marriage" within the meaning of section 2(1) of the *Divorce Act*, if the child has been living with her twenty-year-old boyfriend for seventeen months, has no intention of returning to the home of either parent, and is no longer dependent on her parents for financial support.[17]

Children under the provincial age of majority who are financially dependent while they continue with their schooling satisfy the definition of "children of the marriage" under section 2(1) of the *Divorce Act* even though they are alienated from the parent who is called upon to pay child support.[18] Special circumstances are required for a child under the provincial age of majority to be considered to have withdrawn from the charge of their parents. These circumstances could include a period of travel and work to another country or a lengthy period of incarceration, but not every child under majority who is living away from their parents will be considered to have withdrawn from their parent's charge, especially if a parent continues to provide financial and emotional support.[19] A divorcing or divorced spouse may be ordered to pay support in respect of an adult child who is unable to achieve self-sufficiency by reason of "illness, disability, or other cause."[20] The mere fact that an adult child lacks the ability to withdraw from parental charge or to obtain the necessaries of life is not determinative of the child's eligibility for support; the inability must be shown on the evidence to have arisen or to continue by reason of an illness, disability, or other cause recognized by the *Divorce Act*

The pursuit of post-secondary education may constitute "other cause" under the definition of "child of the marriage" in section 2(1) of the *Divorce Act* but each case is fact specific. In determining whether the pursuit of education is a valid reason for continued dependence, a court must consider two complex and value-laden questions. The first is whether, considering all of the child's circumstances, the child's educational pursuits are reasonable. If so, the court must next consider whether it is appropriate that the pursuits be financed by the parents.[23]

---

16 *Boisvert v Boisvert*, [2000] AJ No 1393 (QB); *Longhurst v Longhurst*, [2004] BCJ No 1637 (SC); *Thompson v Ducharme*, [2004] MJ No 129 (CA); *HS v PW*, 2018 NLSC 65; *Thomas v Thomas*, 2012 NSSC 440; *Wouters v Wouters*, 2008 NWTSC 61; *Frim v Brasseur*, [2001] OJ No 4384 (SCJ); *Garinger v Thompson* [2006] SJ No 36 (QB); compare *Wigmore v Wigmore*, [2004] PEIJ No 49 (TD); *Ladissa v Ladissa*, [2005] OJ No 276 (CA). Compare *Bachynski v Cale*, 2019 SKQB 176 (application under *The Family Maintenance Act, 1997*, SS 1997, c. F-6.2).

17 *Chaulk v Avery*, 2009 NLTD 185; *Wouters v Wouters*, 2013 NWTSC 9.

18 *VMH v JH*, 2020 ABQB 156; *Marsh v Marsh*, [2006] BCJ No 615 (CA); *Prittie v Dorey*, 2010 BCSC 1923.

19 *JCW v JKRW*, 2024 BCSC 139 at para 36, Matthews J.

20 *Divorce Act*, s 2(1) (definition of "child of the marriage"); *Rebenchuk v Rebenchuk*, 2007 MBCA 22; *Sherlow v Zubko*, [1999] AJ No 644 (QB). See also *Dumont v Dumont*, 2017 BCSC 668 (application under the BC *Family Law Act*, SBC 2011, c 25). And see Rose Branton, "Exploring Child Support for Adult Children: The Need for a Broader Conception of 'Other Cause'" (2018) 37 *Canadian Family Law Quarterly* 139.

21 *Ethier v Skrudland*, 2011 SKCA 17; *Blanchard v Blanchard*, 2019 ABCA 53; *LCR v IJER*, 2019 SKQB 229. See also *Marthinsen v Marthinsen*, 2020 BCSC 619; *LLM v DRM*, 2022 BSSC 143.

22 *Montalto v Montalto*, 2011 ABQB 574; *JCW v JKRW*, 2024 BCSC 139; *Rebenchuk v Rebenchuk*, 2007 MBCA 22; *MD v PD*, 2023 NBKB 202; *Hawco v Myers*, [2005] NJ No 378 (CA); *MacLennan v MacLennan*, [2003] NSJ No 15 (CA); *Edwards v Edwards*, 2021 ONSC 1550; *Cusack v Cusack*, [1999] PEIJ No 90 (SC); *MacLennan v MacLennan*, 2021 SKCA 132; see Section E, below in this chapter.

23 *Bobyn v Bobyn*, 2014 BCSC 1441 at para 41, Donegan J, citing *Nordeen v Nordeen*, 2013 BCCA 178; *Lu v Yao*, 2019 BCSC 652.

An adult child who is enrolled as a full-time student in high school may be found to be a "child of the marriage" within the meaning of section 2(1) of the *Divorce Act*, notwithstanding a "spotty" academic record and prior poor attendance record, where the child is currently maintaining a passing average.[24]

A divorcing or divorced spouse can be ordered to pay child support, even though he or she is not the biological parent of the child, if he or she has acted as a parent towards the child.[25]

A court may direct the trial of an issue as to whether a child falls within the definition of a "child of the marriage" where existing affidavit material is insufficient to resolve the issue.[26]

Pursuant to section 55 of the Alberta *Family Law Act*, a child support order is terminated by the adoption of the child but this does not affect arrears of child support that accrued prior to such termination.[27] A step-parental adoption terminates the ties between the child and his biological father and precludes an order for child support being made against the biological father.[28] The child support obligations of an adoptive parent in Saskatchewan correspond to the obligations of a natural parent.[29] The child support obligation of a biological parent arising pursuant to *The Family Maintenance Act* (Saskatchewan) does not survive the adoption of the child by a third party. The same is true where the biological parent's support obligation arose pursuant to the *Divorce Act*. The fact that provincial adoption legislation terminates rights under the *Divorce Act* does not raise any concerns under the doctrine of paramountcy.[30]

B. EFFECT OF DIFFERING CRITERIA UNDER FEDERAL AND PROVINCIAL LEGISLATION

The fact that different age cut-offs and standards apply to the statutory regulation of child support under federal and provincial legislation does not violate section 15 of the *Canadian Charter of Rights and Freedoms*.[31]

The *Divorce Act* and the *Family Law Act* (BC) establish different legal criteria for determining whether a step-parent is liable for child support.[32]

As of 6 December 2000, the *Family Services Act* of New Brunswick was amended to empower a court to order interim or permanent support for a child over the age of provincial majority, which is nineteen years of age, "who is unable to withdraw from the charge of his

---

24 *PGB v JLT*, [2000] AJ No 1408 (QB). See also *Sharma v Sharma*, 2022 MBQB 27; *Matechuk v Kopp (Yaworenko)*, 2020 SKQB 196, citing *MMG v KJT*, 2006 SKQB 41.

25 See Section J, below in this chapter.

26 *Laroque v Misling*, [1998] NWTJ No 18 (SC); *Akert v Akert*, [2000] SJ No 269 (QB).

27 *Re SNL*, [2005] AJ No 1845 (QB); compare *Rideout v Woodman*, 2016 NSSC 205 (proposal to adopt).

28 *Zien v Woida*, [2003] BCJ No 1864 (SC) (application for child support dismissed; alternative basis for dismissal found in the child's consent to the adoption coupled with the child's estrangement from his father over the preceding ten years).

29 *Marud v Marud*, [1999] SJ No 478 (QB).

30 *Reiss v Reiss*, [2001] SJ No 37 (QB); see also *Brennan v Brennan*, 2010 ABQB 221.

31 *Penner v Danbrook* (1992), 39 RFL (3d) 286 (Sask CA), leave to appeal to SCC refused (1993), 44 RFL (3d) 85 (note) (SCC).

32 See Section J, below in this chapter.

or her parents or to obtain the necessaries of life by reason of illness, disability, pursuit of reasonable education or other cause."[33]

Most provinces impose child support obligations on step-parents or persons who stand in the place of parents or persons who have demonstrated a settled intention to treat a non-biological child as a member of their family. The *Family Maintenance Act* of Nova Scotia includes no such provision but this gap in the provincial legislation is not sufficient, in itself, to justify the judicial exercise of the court's *parens patriae* jurisdiction.[34] In order for a child support obligation to arise pursuant to the *Family Property and Support Act* (Yukon),[35] the obligor must be either a biological or an adoptive parent of the child.[36]

In determining whether a husband "has demonstrated a settled intention to treat [his wife's child] as a child of his family" within the meaning of section 1 of the Ontario *Family Law Act*, similar criteria should be applied as those that are applied to the definition of "child of the marriage" under section 2(1) of the *Divorce Act*. Otherwise, the finality of a decision under the Ontario *Family Law Act* could be undermined because the "loser" could take proceedings under the *Divorce Act* in the hope of obtaining a contrary ruling. The duration of the step-parent/stepchild relationship is a factor to be considered under section 1 of the Ontario *Family Law Act*, but duration is secondary to the quality of the relationship. A relatively high threshold should be imposed so as to differentiate between a step-parent who shows affection to his stepchildren and a step-parent who assumes the role of the natural parent.

In *Coates v Watson*,[38] Sullivan J of the Ontario Court of Justice determined that section 31 of the Ontario *Family Law Act* discriminated against adult disabled children of unmarried parents on the basis of parental marital status, disability, and sex, contrary to section 15 of the *Canadian Charter of Rights and Freedoms* in that such children who did not attend school full-time were ineligible for child support. Consequently, Sullivan J, borrowing from the language of the *Divorce Act*, read into section 31 of the *Family Law Act* that the word "child" means a child who (a) is under the age of majority and who has not withdrawn from their charge, or (b) is the age of majority or over and under their charge but unable, by reason of illness, disability, or other cause, to withdraw from their charge or to obtain the necessaries of life. Subsequent to the decision in *Coates v Watson*, the Ontario legislature introduced statutory changes, and as of 1 January 2018, section 31(1)(c) of the Ontario *Family Law Act* provides that every parent has an obligation to provide support, to the extent that the parent is capable of doing so, for his or her unmarried child who is unable by reason of illness, disability, or other cause to withdraw from the charge of his or her parents.[39] Similarly, in Alberta, in *Ryan v Pitchers*,[40] the mother of an adult disabled child challenged the constitutionality of the definition of "child" in section 46(b) and in particular section 46(b) (ii) of the Alberta *Family Law Act*, which disentitled her daughter to child support because she had reached the age of majority and was not in full-time attendance at school. The mother

33 *Pollock v Rioux*, [2004] NBJ No 467 (CA).
34 *Baker v Peterson*, [2001] NSJ No 52 (SC).
35 RSY 2002, c 83.
36 *RSAO v RB*, [2005] YJ No 49 (SC).
37 *Neil v Neil*, [2002] OJ No 3003 (SCJ).
38 2017 ONCJ 454.
39 See *Stronger, Fairer Ontario Act (Budget Measures), 2017*, SO 2017, c 34, Sch 15, s 1.
40 2019 ABQB 19.

successfully argued that the definition of child infringed on her disabled adult child's right to equal protection and equal benefit of the law guaranteed by section 15(1) of the *Charter*. As in Ontario, the definition of "child" in section 46(b) of the *Family Law Act* was amended in December 2018 so as to allow courts to order child support for disabled adult children.[41]

C. APPLICABLE CRITERIA UNDER *DIVORCE ACT* AND *FEDERAL CHILD SUPPORT GUIDELINES* RESPECTING CHILDREN UNDER AND OVER THE PROVINCIAL AGE OF MAJORITY

A court may order support for a child under the age of majority who has not withdrawn from his or her parents' charge or for any child over the age of majority who is unable to withdraw from his or her parents' charge or obtain the necessaries of life by reason of "illness, disability or other cause."[42] The fact that there are funds available from other sources, including the state or a settlement does not necessarily signify that an adult child is no longer a child of the marriage.[43] "Necessaries of life" have traditionally included shelter, food, clothing, household equipment, and medical treatment, but section 2(1) of the *Divorce Act* should not be narrowly construed as meaning bare necessities, such as food and shelter.[44] It will vary with the specific applicant considering their reasonable expectations.[45] The phrase is sufficiently broad to encompass a reasonable program of education that will prepare an adult child to function effectively in an increasingly technological society.[46] The words "or other cause" are not to be construed *ejusdem generis* with the preceding words "illness, disability."[47] An order for the support of an adult child will not be made unless there is sufficient evidence to establish that such an order is justified.[48] Each case is determined on its own facts and all of the circumstances must be considered in determining whether a child remains a child of the marriage.[49]

With the implementation of the *Federal Child Support Guidelines* on 1 May 1997, a court has the jurisdiction to determine the amount of support for a child who is of the age of majority or over in accordance with the Guidelines applicable to a child under the age of majority or, if the court considers that approach to be inappropriate, the court may fix an amount that it considers appropriate, having regard to the condition, means, needs, and other circumstances of the child and the financial ability of each spouse to contribute to the support of the child.[50]

---

41 See Bill 28, the *Family Statutes Amendment Act, 2018*, SA 2018, c 18.

42 See *Divorce Act*, s 2(1); *Briard v Briard*, 2010 BCCA 431; *PER v CAR*, 2018 BCSC 339; *Locke v Goulding*, 2021 NLSC 8; *Welsh v Welsh*, [1998] OJ No 4550 (Gen Div); see also *Mirzahi v Sana*, 2022 ABQB 313; *Simpson v Lockman*, 2012 MBQB 216 (application under *Family Maintenance Act*, CCSM c F20); *DBB v DMB*, 2017 SKCA 59.

43 *Locke v Goulding*, 2021 NLSC 8.

44 *Briard v Briard*, 2010 BCCA 431; *Glenn v Glenn*, 2018 BCSC 2.

45 *Lougheed v Lougheed*, 2007 BCCA 396 at paras 23 and 25; *Glenn v Glenn*, 2018 BCSC 2.

46 *Barber v Barber* (1995), 18 RFL (4th) 282 (Nfld SC); see also *Oleksiewicz v Oleksiewicz*, 2017 BCSC 228.

47 *Jackson v Jackson*, [1973] SCR 205; *Keen v Keen* (1990), 30 RFL (3d) 172 (Sask QB); compare *Matthews v Matthews* (1988), 11 RFL (3d) 431 (Nfld TD).

48 *Passarello v Passarello*, [1998] OJ No 2792 (Gen Div).

49 *Pelletier v Richard*, 2021 NBQB 77 at paras 51–52; *DMH v CMM*, 2011 SKQB 104; *Montalto v Montalto*, 2011 ABQB 574.

50 SOR/97-175, s 3(2).

D. CHILD'S ILLNESS OR DISABILITY; RESPECTIVE OBLIGATIONS OF PARENTS AND STATE

A child over the provincial age of majority who is unable to work due to illness or disability may be eligible for support as a "child of the marriage" within the meaning of section 2(1) of the *Divorce Act*.[51] In *Carpenter v March*,[52] Handrigan J of the Family Division of the New foundland and Labrador Supreme Court provided the following list of relevant principles that may assist courts in determining when an adult child with disabilities is entitled to support pursuant to the *Divorce Act* and the *Federal Child Support Guidelines*:

- A child over the provincial age of majority who is unable to work due to illness or disability may be a "child of the marriage" within the meaning of section 2(1) of the *Divorce Act*.
- The onus of proving that an adult child remains a "child of the marriage" is on the parent making the claim.
- State-subsidized financial assistance does not relieve parents of their child support obligations.
- Child support set under section 3(2)(b) of the Guidelines for an adult child who is still a "child of the marriage" because of illness or disability may take into account subsidies and other disability benefits the adult child or the parent receives from the province, such as subsidized housing and respite care.[53]
- A disabled adult child may be entitled to child support if the child receives a monthly disability payment, even if the child stays in a foster home five nights a week.
- Proof of an adult child's disability alone does not justify a child support order if there is no indication that the disability prevents the child from being gainfully employed — evi dence of financial dependence is required.[54]
- It may be premature to limit the duration of support for a disabled adult child at the time when the child support order is made.
- Parental responsibility to support a permanently disabled child may last for the rest of the child's life.

Important factors in determining whether an adult child is a child of the marriage are employability and the extent of the disability when determining whether that individual is able to obtain the necessaries of life.[55] A time limited support order for an adult child

---

51 *Ripley v Ripley* (1991), 30 RFL (3d) 41 (BCCA); *Magne v Magne* (1990), 26 RFL (3d) 364 (Man QB); *Pitcher v Pitcher*, 2013 NLTD(F) 11; *Hill v Davis*, [2005] NSJ No 274 (CA) (application under *Maintenance and Custody Act* (NS)); *Gilkinson v Nichols*, 2023 ONSC 1504; *Nkwazi v Nkwazi*, 2014 SKCA 61.

52 2012 NLTD(F) 11 at para 7. For a brief review of general principles relating to support entitlement for adult children based on illness or disability, see also *Weber v Weber*, 2020 ONSC 4098 at paras 63–68. And see *Steidinger v Morrell*, 2013 MBQB 143; *Shipowick v Shipowick*, 2016 MBQB 124; *CG v TL*, 2024 NLCA 1; *Laramie v Laramie*, 2018 ONSC 4740; *DBB v DMB*, 2017 SKCA 59. And see Christine Dobby, "Whose Responsibility? Disabled Adult 'Children of the Marriage' Under the *Divorce Act* and the Canadian Social Welfare State" (2005) 20 *Windsor Review of Legal and Social Issues* 41.

53 See *Jensen v Jensen*, 2018 BCSC 283; *LEM v DMI*, 2019 BCSC 796 at para 18; *Locke v Goulding*, 2021 NLSC 8.

54 See *Galbraith v Galbraith*, 2018 SKQB 157; *Birnie v Birnie*, 2019 SKQB 303.

55 *TAP v JTP*, 2014 BCSC 2265.

is inappropriate where the child's future ability to "withdraw from parental charge" is unpredictable.[56] An adult child with a disability may be found to be a "child of the marriage" within the meaning of section 2(1) of the *Divorce Act*, but the amount of monthly support payable pursuant to section 3(2)(b) of the *Federal Child Support Guidelines* may take account of the parent's receipt of a provincial subsidy for the disabled adult child.[57] Section 3(2)(b) of the *Federal Child Support Guidelines* empowers a court to deny a primary caregiving parent's application for the support of an adult disabled child where the other parent is responsible for unusually high expenses in relation to exercising parenting time with the child, and disability benefits by way of subsidized housing, and diverse services, including respite care, are provided free of charge by the province.[58] Proof of an adult child's disability does not itself justify a child support order where there is no evidence that the disability prevents the child from obtaining gainful employment; evidence of financial dependence is required.[59] Cogent evidence must be provided by the parent requesting support about the nature and extent of the child's disability or illness, and the manner and extent to which this disability or illness is impacting on the child's ability to obtain the necessities of life on their own. Bald statements from a parent that the child suffers certain disabilities or illnesses with nothing more will not suffice.[60] Disability in and of itself does not, without more, ground entitlement to child support for an adult child. A court requires credible and trustworthy evidence that the adult child has a disability, is under the charge of the claimant parent, and is unable to withdraw from that parent's charge due to inability to manage daily living on their own without that parent's consistent care, monitoring, and support, or is unable, due to the disability, to obtain the necessaries of life.[61] With regard to a child who has health issues, relevant caselaw in British Columbia stands for the following principles:

a) Even if a child is living independently or semi-independently, if a parent is supplying the necessities of life due to the child's inability to earn a subsistence living because of the health issue, the child may remain a child of the marriage.
b) The factors listed by Master Joyce in *Farden v. Farden* may not be of as much assistance where disability is the reason or a reason for the child to not withdraw from parental care.
c) Two important factors to consider in determining whether an adult child with disabilities is unable to obtain the necessaries of life are the child's employability and the extent of the child's disability.

---

56 *Hill v Davis*, [2005] NSJ No 274 (CA).

57 *Grimes v Grimes*, [2002] AJ No 981 (QB); *Briard v Briard*, 2010 BCCA 431; *PER v CAR*, 2018 BCSC 339; *Willms v Willms*, 2019 BCSC 1944; *Felts v Silvestre*, 2021 BCSC 523; *SAD v MA*, 2019 NBQB 85; *Senos v Karcz*, 2014 ONCA 459; *Morden v Kelly*, 2019 ONSC 4620; *Da Silva v Kelly*, 2022 ONSC 1402; *Klette v Leland*, 2014 SKCA 122; see also *Brown v Rowe*, 2016 ONSC 5153; *Rémillard v Rémillard*, 2014 MBCA 101 at paras 64–66; *DBB v DMB*, 2017 SKCA 59. Compare *CM v GM*, 2019 NBQB 182.

58 *Dougherty v Humbel*, [2000] BCJ No 2323 (SCJ).

59 *Romanyshyn v Romanyshyn*, [2000] BCJ No 328 (SC) (application for child support adjourned pending professional assessment of allegedly autistic child's ability to obtain gainful employment and economic self-sufficiency); *Hartshorne v Hartshorne*, 2010 BCCA 327; *Crawford v Crawford*, [1999] NBJ No 173 (NBCA); *Scott v Scott*, [2004] NBJ No 468 (CA); *Szitas v Szitas*, 2012 ONSC 1548.

60 *Szitas v Szitas*, *ibid*. See also *Willis v Nagy*, 2023 BCSC 1493

61 *Jefic v Jefic (Grujicic)*, 2022 ONSC 7240 at para 72, Madsen J.

d) Where the child lives at home and is impaired by a serious disability such that their ability to generate income is negligible, the appropriate measure to consider need is section 3(2)(a) of the *Federal Child Support Guidelines.*
e) A child who is disabled and is completing post-secondary studies slowly and may not be able to complete them, should not be "denied the life-enriching satisfaction of the pursuit of that study".
f) Formal expert opinion evidence on medical issues and disability is not required. The evidence that establishes disability can including the evidence of a parent and the evidence of a child together with medical evidence, and relatively recent medical evidence is preferred.[62]

As d'Entremont J of the New Brunswick Court of Queen's Bench (Family Division) observed in *Pelletier v Richard,* "evidence that an adult child has a disability does not imply that an award of child support will be made for that person's benefit. There needs to be proof that the disability in question prevents the individual from finding employment. As well, there needs to be proof of dependency.[63] A court may refuse to order a parent or step-parent to pay child support, where the court is satisfied that reasonable arrangements are already in place to meet an adult disabled child's needs in that government allowances and benefits accommodate the child's basic needs and respite services.[64] A high functioning adult child with Down syndrome, who is in receipt of provincial assistance and a modest income from part-time employment, is not a "child of the marriage" within the meaning of section 2(1) of the *Divorce Act,* where the financial resources available to the adult child are sufficient to enable her to obtain the necessaries of life while living apart from either parent. The fact that the mother provides some day-to-day guidance on certain matters does not signify that the child is unable to withdraw from parental charge.[65] In *Krangle (Guardian ad litem of) v Brisco,*[66] McLachlin CJ of the Supreme Court of Canada addressed the issue of a dis abled adult child's withdrawal from the charge of his parents in the context of an action for damages for medical malpractice. She observed that the relevant statutory amendments "were not aimed at shifting the burden of caring for adult children from the state to parents, but rather with ensuring that in situations where one parent is charged with the care of an adult disabled child, the other parent is obliged to assist." A similar approach is tenable when interpreting federal or provincial legislation dealing with the support of adult disabled children.[67] A parent has no legal duty to support an adult child with learning disabilities in an unsuccessful attempt by that child to achieve an unrealistic professional goal.[68] The parental support obligation should be balanced against the need for an adult disabled child

62 *JCW v JKRW,* 2024 BCSC 139 at para 41, Matthews J.
63 2021 NBQB 77 at para 50.
64 *Jorgenson v Jorgenson,* [2003] NSJ No 292 (SC); *Hill v Davis,* [2006] NSJ No 331 (SC).
65 *REL v MLSB,* [2008] BCJ No 969 (SC); *Hanson v Hanson,* [2003] SJ No 514 (QB); see also *Hill v Davis* [2006] NSJ No 331 (SC).
66 [2002] 1 SCR 205 at para 35.
67 *Briard v Briard,* 2010 BCCA 431; *PER v CAR,* 2018 BCSC 339; *Hill v Davis,* [2006] NSJ No 331 (SC); *Senos v Karcz,* 2014 ONCA 459; *Hanson v Hanson,* [2003] SJ No 514 (QB).
68 *Long v Long,* [2001] BCJ No 2943 (SC).

to assume responsibility for his or her own future.[69] By the exercise of its statutory discretion under section 3(2)(b) or section 7 of the *Federal Child Support Guidelines*, a court may find it appropriate to segregate support for a disabled adult child from the applicable table amount of support allocated to other children of the marriage.[70] Where an adult child is not able to withdraw from the charge of their parents — such that they remain a child of the marriage — but are in receipt of government disability benefits, child support should be determined under section 3(2)(b) of the Guidelines.[71] State subsidized financial assistance for special needs adult children does not necessarily absolve parents of their child support obligation but disability payments may be taken into account under section 3(2)(b) of the *Federal Child Support Guidelines*.[72] In some cases, the subsidies will be sufficient to eliminate or significantly reduce child support otherwise payable.[73] In other cases, the table amount of child support may be unaffected.[74] However, an adult child with a disability, which does not preclude certain types of employment, may not be a "child of the marriage."[75] Child support orders under section 3(2)(b) of the Guidelines may take account of the extraordinary burden undertaken by one parent in the care of an adult disabled child where it is necessary to do justice between the parties.[76]

Payments from a structured settlement, which do not cover all of the expenses incurred by a parent with whom an adult disabled child is living, do not preclude a finding that the adult child is a "child of the marriage" within the meaning of section 2(1) of the *Divorce Act*, but the payments made under the structured settlement may render the table amount of child support inappropriate and result in a reduced amount of child support being granted pursuant to section 3(2) of the *Federal Child Support Guidelines*.[77]

An adult child suffering from schizophrenia ceases to be a "child of the marriage" within the meaning of section 2(1) of the *Divorce Act* where he or she has a successful university

---

69 *Graham v Graham*, [1998] BCJ No 2436 (SC) (order for support of employed adult child with disability to terminate after one more year in the absence of any evidence of the pursuit of further education or training); see also *Gamey v Gamey*, [2000] MJ No 304 (QB); *Hill v Davis*, [2006] NSJ No 331 (SC). And see *LMG v REG*, 2020 ONSC 2825 (adult child with chosen lifestyle of drug use and alcohol abuse while living with his mother).

70 *Van Harten v Van Harten*, [1998] OJ No 1299 (Gen Div).

71 *James v James*, 2022 BCSC 1402.

72 *McIver v McIver*, 2010 ABCA 155; *BGM v PGM*, 2013 ABQB 67; *Werenka v Werenka*, 2021 ABQB 789; *Briard v Briard*, 2010 BCCA 431; *Jensen v Jensen*, 2018 BCSC 283; *LEM v DMI*, 2019 BCSC 796 at para 18; *James v James*, 2022 BCSC 1402; *Rémillard v Rémillard*, 2014 MBCA 101 at paras 64–66; *Pitcher v Pitcher*, 2013 NLTD(F) 11; *SAD v MA*, 2019 NBQB 85; *CM v GM*, 2020 NBCA 17; *Senos v Karcz*, 2014 ONCA 459; *Laramie v Laramie*, 2018 ONSC 4740; *Morden v Kelly*, 2019 ONSC 4620 at para 63; *AT v CMK*, [1999] QJ No 2530 (CS); *Klette v Leland*, 2014 SKCA 122; *DBB v DMB*, 2017 SKCA 59. See also *Droit de la famille — 19819*, 2019 QCCA 830. See also Stephanie Dickson & Melanie Battaglia, "Child Support for Adult Children with a Disability: The Impact of ODSP, the Disability Tax Credit, RDSP and RESP" (2022) 40 CFLQ 169.

73 See *Werenka v Werenka*, 2021 ABQB 789; *CRL v SLL*, 2019 BCSC 2103.

74 *Willms v Willms*, 2019 BCSC 1944; *Misner v Misner*, 2010 ONSC 2284; *DBB v DMB*, 2017 SKCA 59.

75 *Hartshorne v Hartshorne*, 2010 BCCA 327; *Tingley v Tingley* (1993), 49 RFL (3d) 87 (NBQB); compare *Harrington v Harrington* (1981), 22 RFL (2d) 40 (Ont CA).

76 *James v James*, 2022 BCSC 1402.

77 *CG v TL*, 2024 NLCA 1.

record and can find suitable employment, if allowed to do so by the parent with whom the child resides.[78]

An adult child with emotional problems, who is completing Grade 10, may be a "child of the marriage" within the meaning of section 2 of the *Divorce Act* and entitled to child support.[79] Child support may be denied with respect to an adult child with unresolved medical or addiction problems, where the child is not dependent on either parent for the necessities of life.[80] Addiction is a disease, but courts will not condone chronic financial dependence for addicts who are unwilling to seek rehabilitation. An adult addicted child who has squandered opportunities for rehabilitation and the attainment of economic self-sufficiency is not entitled to call on a high income parent for support beyond the reasonable amount already being voluntarily provided.[81] An adult child with a drug abuse problem may be found to be a "child of the marriage" within the meaning of section 2(1) of the *Divorce Act* for the purpose of determining the father's ongoing court-ordered child support obligation for several months following the adult child's release from a youth detention centre on the condition that he reside with his mother.[82]

An adult child with special needs does not satisfy the definition of "child of the marriage" in section 2(1) of the *Divorce Act* if the adult child receives a monthly payment from a structured settlement sufficient to meet the child's needs.[83]

The onus of proving that an adult child remains a "child of the marriage" in that she is under her parents' charge and unable by reason of disability to withdraw from their charge or to obtain the necessaries of life falls on the parent asserting the claim.[84] Where this onus is discharged, the court may order the applicable table amount of child support, notwithstanding that the payor receives an income that is near the poverty line. If a parent earns an income above the minimum threshold established by the Guidelines, there is a presumed ability to pay the applicable table amount of child support.[85] A court may conclude that it is premature to determine how long child support must be paid. There may come a point where the adult child should reside in a state-subsidized group home or the child may achieve a sufficient degree of independence through some other means, but a court should not cut off child support where the adult child is reasonably striving to acquire skills that will enable her to withdraw from her parent's charge.[86]

Section 3(2)(b) of the *Federal Child Support Guidelines* empowers a court to decline to order the table amount of support for a disabled adult child in receipt of social assistance

---

78 *Lisevich v Lisevich*, [1998] AJ No 777 (QB).

79 *Young v Young*, [1999] NSJ No 63 (SC).

80 *Wood v Wood*, [1997] BCJ No 1501 (SC); *O'Kane v O'Kane*, 2013 ONSC 1617.

81 *RWG v SIG*, [2002] SJ No 231 (QB), aff'd (*sub nom Gilroy v Gilroy*), [2003] SJ No 250 (CA). See also *LMG v REG*, 2020 ONSC 2825 (adult child with chosen lifestyle of drug use and alcohol abuse while living with his mother).

82 *AEL v JDL*, [2002] AJ No 441 (QB) (retroactive variation to reflect father's increased annual income denied in light of the attendant circumstances, including the date of the mother's formal commencement of her application to vary the existing order). See also *Flynn v Daoust*, 2012 MBQB 295.

83 *Matheson v Matheson*, [2003] OJ No 3857 (SCJ).

84 *Lerner v Lerner*, 2013 BCSC 239; *Forrest v Aerin*, 2022 BCCA 184; *Gagnon v Gagnon*, 2012 NSSC 407; *Marsh v Jashewski*, 2011 ONSC 3793; *HNML v CPJL*, 2010 SKQB 456; *DBB v DMB*, 2017 SKCA 59.

85 *Nolte v Nolte*, [2001] SJ No 362 (QB).

86 *Ibid.*

which meets his basic needs while he resides with his mother, but the court may find it appropriate to order the father to pay the lion's share of additional expenses incurred for the disabled child's extracurricular activities.[87]

In *Nolan v Nolan*,[88] a forty-year-old disabled child was found to be a "child of the marriage" within the meaning of section 2(1) of the *Divorce Act*, but child support was denied because the court was not satisfied that the mother, with whom the child was living, suffered a regular shortfall in meeting his monthly expenses, having regard to the contribution of her cohabitant to the household expenses and the adult child's receipt of a disability pension. Judicial regard was also paid to the limited incomes of the two parents. An adult child with severe learning disabilities that preclude her from providing herself with necessaries of life may be entitled to an interim child support order under the *Divorce Act*, pending determination of her entitlement to receive a disability pension under the Ontario Disability Support Plan and the submission of supplementary affidavit evidence setting out the efforts made to obtain employment that her doctor believed her capable of undertaking. Eligibility for child support is not excluded because the adult child has a child of her own who is being cared for in part by the adult child's mother with whom they were both living. However, the table amount of child support may be inappropriate within the meaning of section 3(2)(b) of the *Federal Child Support Guidelines* where the adult child can meet some of her living costs out of a lump sum rehabilitation payment received as a result of an automobile accident.[89]

A father cannot contract out of his child support obligation owed to his twenty-one-year-old mentally challenged daughter who requires twenty-four-hour care. Pending the child's placement in a group home, a partnership approach may be essential that requires both parents to tend to their adult child's needs, both financial and otherwise, and the Ministry of Community and Social Services to underwrite the financial shortfall faced by the mother after receiving the Guidelines amount of child support from the father.[90]

A disabled adult child, who is unable to withdraw from the support of her parents because governmental facilities are unavailable, is entitled to ongoing support as a "child of the marriage" within the meaning of section 2(1) of the *Divorce Act*. Section 3(2)(b) of the *Federal Child Support Guidelines* empowers the court to deviate from the table amount of child support where that amount is inappropriate and thus enables the court to take account of funding provided for the adult child by governmental agencies or a court-ordered settlement for personal injuries.[91] Where both the parents wish to keep their child outside of the *Adult Protection Act* system, the court, being faced with few options, may order the father to provide ongoing support in the event that he does not exercise the parenting time prescribed by the court. The adult child's parental support entitlement does not exonerate the government from living up to the society's reasonable expectation that adequate assistance be provided for adult disabled children. Consequently, if any of the money allocated by the province for respite care should be terminated due to the father's court-ordered obligation

87 *Phillips v Phillips*, [2005] SJ No 350 (QB); see also *Kosowan v Vanderstap*, 2016 SKCA 149.

88 [2005] BCJ No 2864 (SC). See also *CM v GM*, 2020 NBCA 17.

89 *Racicot v Racicot*, [2003] OJ No 4666 (SCJ).

90 *King v Sutherland*, [2004] OJ No 3569 (SCJ).

91 *Steidinger v Morrell*, 2013 MBQB 143; *Carpenter v March*, 2012 NLTD(F) 11; *Locke v Goulding*, 2021 NLSC 8.

to pay supplementary respite costs, either parent may be entitled to apply for variation of the current order.[92] The Family Court of Nova Scotia has jurisdiction to impose terms and conditions on a plan proposed by the Minister of Health for a vulnerable adult. In assessing the terms and conditions most conducive to the adult's welfare under section 12 and his or her best interests under section 9(3)(c) of the *Adult Protection Act*, the court is, of course, obliged to consider the availability of services and the minister's capacity to provide them but, having made the decision to take responsibility for the adult, the state is obliged to develop a plan in that adult's best interests and the Family Court may attach reasonable terms and conditions to the minister's proposal.[93]

In *Harris v Harris*,[94] both the father and mother had been ordered to pay $300 per month to support their child who was then two months short of his nineteenth birthday. After the child reached the provincial age of majority, the father applied to terminate his court-ordered child support obligation. The application was dismissed on the basis that the child's financial deficit had increased since the original order and he was therefore entitled to ongoing support after attaining his majority. In dismissing the father's application, the presiding judge observed that the father must establish the threshold condition of a material change of circumstances pursuant to section 17 of the *Divorce Act*. Since the adult child was no more capable of supporting himself than he was at the time of the original order, the father had failed to establish a material change.

A provincial financial subsidy payable to or for the benefit of an adult disabled child is an important consideration in determining the appropriate amount of child support, if any, to be paid by a parent in a proceeding for child support under the *Family Maintenance Act 1997* (Saskatchewan).[95] Section 7(2) of the Act, which provides that a court shall not take into account any provincial financial subsidy, applies only to subsidies payable to a dependent spouse; section 7(2) has no application in a child support proceeding.[96]

The onus falls on the applicant to prove that an adult child is entitled to support as a "child of the marriage" within the meaning of section 2(1) of the *Divorce Act*.[97] A superior court of law has inherent jurisdiction to order an adult child to submit to neuropsychological assessment, which bears directly upon the issue of whether the adult child remains a "child of the marriage" within the meaning of the *Divorce Act* due to a disability, but such jurisdiction should be exercised sparingly and only in clear cases.[98] A non-party adult child may be required to provide financial information, such as income tax returns, to his parents in the context of a child support application.[99]

---

92 *Bird v Ritcey*, [2004] NSJ No 514 (SC).

93 *Nova Scotia (Minister of Health) v JJ*, [2005] SCJ No 13.

94 [2006] NSJ No 257 (CA).

95 SS 1997, c F-6.2.

96 *Hanson v Hanson*, [2001] SJ No 560 (QB) (payor entitled to judgment for overpayment of child support); see also *Riddell v Blackburn*, [2003] SJ No 53 (QB). Compare *Hill v Davis*, [2005] NSJ No 274 (CA).

97 *Winofsky v Winofsky*, 2012 BCSC 433; *JLL v VLL*, 2017 NBQB 76; *Gagnon v Gagnon*, 2012 NSSC 407; *HNML v CPJL*, 2010 SKQB 456.

98 *HNML v CPJL*, *ibid.*

99 *Burzminski v Burzminski*, 2010 SKCA 16; see also *HNML v CPJL*, 2010 SKQB 456.

E. POST-SECONDARY EDUCATION OR TRAINING

The definition of "child of the marriage" in section 2(1) of the *Divorce Act* and the definition of "child" in section 35.1 of *The Family Maintenance Act* (Manitoba), pursuant to which parents may be ordered to support their adult children who are pursuing post-secondary education, do not contravene section 15 of the *Canadian Charter of Rights and Freedoms.*[100] The *Divorce Act* does not purport to regulate the support obligations owed to the children of intact families and the proper exercise of plenary powers granted to the Parliament of Canada by section 91(26) of the Constitution is not subject to *Charter* scrutiny. Furthermore, section 36(1) of *The Family Maintenance Act* (Manitoba) imposes a general obligation on parents to support their adult children who are pursuing a reasonable program of post-secondary education. This obligation is not confined to separated parents; it also applies to the parents of children in intact families. Accordingly, it is not open to a parent to contend that the aforementioned statutory definitions impose a liability on a separated or divorced spouse that does not exist for children in intact families.[101]

It is not the serious pursuit of education itself that determines whether an adult child is unable to withdraw from the charge of his or her parents under the definition of "child of the marriage" in section 2(1) of the *Divorce Act*. Rather, the heart of the inquiry appears to be the extent of the financial independence/dependence of the child because of the pursuit of that education.[102] Post-secondary education and training programs that entitle an adult child to support can be extremely varied.[103] A court has broad discretionary powers under sections 15.1 and 17 of the *Divorce Act* to determine whether child support should be ordered to facilitate post-secondary vocational[104] or college education. Judicial opinion has been inconclusive on the question of whether the pursuit of a sports career falls within the ambit of "other cause" in the definition of "child of the marriage" under section 2(1) of the *Divorce Act*.[105] When dealing with children engaged in sporting or cultural activities in the hope of making it a career, the court should have regard to the aptitude of the child and the probability, if any, of the child attaining that goal.[106] If the child's goal is realistic, there is no reason why courts should distinguish between a sporting or cultural career, and a business career

---

100 See Chapter 5, Section L.

101 *Rebenchuk v Rebenchuk*, [2005] MJ No 201 (QB) (*Charter* challenge dismissed as untenable); see also *Michie v Michie*, [1997] SJ No 668 (QB).

102 *Hamdan v Hamdan*, 2012 NBQB 331, Walsh J; *TTB v PHD*, 2014 NBQB 164; *S CA v S CO*, 2022 NBBR 238.

103 *Kusnir v Kusnir*, [2001] OJ No 3491 (Ct J); *TTB v PHD*, 2014 NBQB 164.

104 *Pircio v Sarno*, [2003] BCJ No 977 (SC); *Hannigan v Hannigan*, [2003] BCJ No 2278 (SC) (plumbing apprentice); *Pearse v Pearse*, 2010 BCSC 117 (hairstyling program); *Newman v Tibbetts*, [2004] NBJ No 72 (QB) (cosmetology program); *Ryan v Ryan*, 2010 NSCA 2 (hairstyling apprentice); *Blake v Blake* (1994), 121 Nfld & PEIR 263 (PEITD) (post-secondary education includes technical college); *Van Wynsberghe v Van Wynsberghe*, [1997] OJ No 2566 (Gen Div) (film school); *McCabe v MacInnis*, [2000] PEIJ No 61 (SC).

105 See *Pink v Pink* (1991), 31 RFL (3d) 233 (Man CA) (child support denied where children on football scholarships and benefits thereof highly speculative); *Hutchinson v Hutchinson*, [1996] MJ No 549 (QB); *Strand v Strand* (1995), 12 RFL (4th) 188 (Sask QB); *Sapergia v Larner* (1995), 15 RFL (4th) 389 (Sask QB); *Nunn v McLeod*, [1999] SJ No 168 (QB); compare *Krueger v Tunison*, [1999] SJ No 482 (QB) (adult child taking correspondence course in Grade 12 while pursuing sporting aspirations with view to obtaining university athletic scholarship). See also *Hnidy v Hnidy*, 2017 SKCA 44, citing *Ethier v Skrudland*, 2011 SKCA 17.

106 *Kohan v Kohan*, 2016 ABCA 125.

or a career in a learned profession.[107] However, many children have sporting and cultural aspirations, but few will realize them. An adult child who is a gifted athlete pursuing legitimate career aspirations may, nevertheless, be found to be a "child of the marriage" within the meaning of section 2(1) of the *Divorce Act*. Pursuit of a career in sports or entertainment may be akin to the pursuit of higher education and may constitute an acceptable "other cause" under the *Divorce Act* that entitles an adult child to support, but the applicant must satisfy the court of the relationship between the adult child's aspirations and his or her achievement of economic independence.[108] The relationship between sports training and an adult child's career development and eventual economic independence is not self-evident and does not lend itself to the application of judicial notice.[109]

Support may be ordered in favour of a child over the age of majority who is unable to achieve financial self-sufficiency by reason of his or her attendance at school[110] or college for the purpose of completing such education as is necessary to equip the child for life in the future.[111] There is a need for careful inquiry and evidentiary underpinnings before issues of fact and law can be determined in the context of whether an adult child attending university is a "child of the marriage" entitled to support and, if so, in what amount.[112]

Although adult children are generally entitled to receive support while pursuing full-time post-secondary education, these types of cases are fact specific and require relevant evidence to be adduced.[113] An adult child who is pursuing university studies may be ineligible for child support or only eligible for a reduced amount where she can meet her own expenses out of earned income and an educational trust established by her parents.[114]

Parents are responsible for assisting their adult children to pursue post-secondary education that will equip them for employment. There is a corresponding responsibility on the children to select an appropriate program to which they can apply their talents and abilities. The parental obligation to pay child support continues as long as progress is being made in preparing the children for economic self-sufficiency, although adult children are expected to contribute to their own expenses by means of their employment income.[115] A child over the provincial age of majority who is working towards realistic educational and employment

---

107 *Dagenais v Blais*, 2010 ABQB 324.

108 *Olson v Olson*, [2003] AJ No 230 (CA); *Kohan v Kohan*, 2016 ABCA 125 (singing career); *KNH v JPB*, 2019 ABQB 511 (ballet); *CAW v KCS*, 2018 BCSC 298; *Campbell v Campbell*, 2022 ONSC 5816; *Hnidy v Hnidy* 2017 SKCA 44; compare *Willock v Willock*, [2005] BCJ No 2664 (SC). See also *BM v PM*, 2019 SKQB 36.

109 *Olson v Olson*, [2003] AJ No 230 (CA).

110 *GF v EF*, [1999] AJ No 1104 (Prov Ct) (application under *Domestic Relations Act*; adult child in full-time attendance at secondary school entitled to support).

111 *Jackson v Jackson*, [1973] SCR 205; *S CA v S CO*, 2022 NBBR 238. For a useful summary of the law respecting an adult child's entitlement to child support, see *Harrison v Vargek* (2002), 28 RFL (5th) 176 at paras 26–35 (Man QB); *VanSickle v VanSickle*, 2012 ONSC 7340.

112 *Erickson v Erickson*, [2007] NSJ No 483 (SC); *Meister v Meister*, [1998] SJ No 849 (QB) (leave to re-apply on proper material).

113 *TTB v PHD*, 2014 NBQB 164; *Fair v Jones*, [1999] NWTJ No 17 (SC); see also *Wahl v Wahl*, [2000] AJ No 29 (QB); *Sharma v Sharma*, 2022 MBQB 27.

114 *Leis v Leis*, 2014 ABCA 36; *Buller v Rosen*, [2003] BCJ No 1686 (SC); *S CA v S CO*, 2022 NBBR 238; *Lewi v Lewi*, [2006] OJ No 1847 (CA); *Fearon v Tzeng Fearon*, 2021 ONSC 7545; *Minish v Timmons*, 2021 ONSC 7622.

115 *Trueman v Trueman*, [2001] AJ No 1272 (QB); *DWM v MAB*, 2012 NBQB 146; *Hiebert v Hiebert*, [2007] SJ No 569 (QB).

goals in seeking to complete high school with a view to seeking admission to university should not be denied child support where a prior failure to obtain academic credits resulted from physical and psychological difficulties. Such a child, who is maximizing opportunities that will foster improved health, should be encouraged in his endeavours and not penalized for the disabilities.[116] An adult child with a learning disability may attend school or college to better himself and need not live at home in order to satisfy the statutory definition of "child of the marriage." Attendance on a full-time basis is not a prerequisite nor does limited earning capacity preclude such a status where the adult child can overcome the disability, and it would be unfair for him or her to be confined to menial employment when other opportunities are available. To facilitate the adult child's further education, a parent may be ordered to contribute a designated percentage of the child's tuition fees in addition to paying the applicable table amount of basic child support.[117] A child with health problems may be deemed to be in "full time" attendance at university for the purpose of applying section 31 of the Ontario *Family Law Act*, even though the child is not carrying the full course load of an able-bodied student.[118] As Hoegg JA of the Newfoundland and Labrador Court of Appeal observed in the context of provincial legislation:

> [23] What is pursuit of reasonable education involves considering all of the circumstances at play in a case, including the *Farden* and *Menegaldo* factors, as they relate to the adult child in issue. The "adult child" in section 37(7) of the *FLA* is not necessarily the healthy adult child with a part-time job, perfect full-time attendance, and high academic standing. Rather, that adult child is the particular child in issue, whose health, personal characteristics, abilities, and living circumstances inform what is pursuit of reasonable education in his or her case. A rigid requirement that nothing short of enrollment in five courses each semester of the year would fail to recognize the realities of the human condition, and therefore set too high a bar. In this regard I refer to *Sullivan v. Sullivan* (1999), 1999 CanLII 14997 (ON SC), 50 R.F.L. (4th) 326 (Ont. Div. Ct.) in which a trial judge's award of child support to a 22-year-old unwell child engaged in a part-time course of study was upheld. Although *Sullivan* was based on Ontario legislation that is differently worded than section 37 of the *FLA*, it is apparent from the decision that the court was motivated to an appropriate result in consideration of the child's illness and inability to undertake full-time studies.[119]

The definition of "child of the marriage" is not one of age but a question of dependence and the guiding principle is one of reasonableness.[120] An adult child who has no definite

116 *Crawford v Crawford*, [1998] OJ No 885 (Gen Div).

117 *Collins v Collins*, [1998] AJ No 417 (QB); see also *Oswald v Oswald*, [2001] MJ No 73 (QB); *Welsh v Welsh*, [1998] OJ No 4550 (Gen Div); *Aaston v Alm*, [2000] SJ No 383 (QB).

118 *Sullivan v Sullivan*, [1999] OJ No 3973 (Div Ct) (interim order for child support varied on appeal to take account of pension payable to child that enabled child to contribute towards expenses); see also *Winsor v Winsor*, 2017 NLCA 54; *Richardson v Richardson*, [2002] OJ No 2463 (SCJ) (interim order).

119 *Winsor v Winsor*, 2017 NLCA 54 at para 23. See also *Mirzahi v Sana*, 2022 ABQB 313; *Trecroce v Chorney*, 2023 ONSC 96.

120 *McKinnon v McKinnon*, [1998] AJ No 85 (QB); *Wahl v Wahl*, [2000] AJ No 29 (QB); *Harrison v Vargek*, [2002] MJ No 155 (QB); *S CA v S CO*, 2022 NBBR 238; *Ivany v Ivany* (1996), 24 RFL (4th) 289 (Nfld SC); *Martell v Height* (1994), 3 RFL (4th) 104 (NSCA); *Kusnir v Kusnir*, [2001] OJ No 3491 (Ct J); *Willie v Willie*, [2000] SJ No 750 (QB).

educational plans[121] and has made no effort to find employment is not a child of the marriage entitled to support.[122] An adult child is not entitled to call on a parent to subsidize the cost of further university studies where the adult child has not availed himself of previous opportunities and has shown no aptitude for a proposed new field of study.[123] An adult child's attendance at school, college, or university is not in itself sufficient to bring the child within the statutory definition of "child of the marriage" under section 2(1) of the *Divorce Act*, unless such attendance renders the child unable to withdraw from the charge of the parents or to obtain the necessaries of life.[124]

Once a child attains the age of majority, the child is no longer presumptively entitled to support.[125] The onus falls on the applicant to prove that an adult child who is pursuing post-secondary education is entitled to support as a "child of the marriage" within the meaning of section 2(1) of the *Divorce Act*.[126] Relevant factors include the age of the child, his or her academic achievements, the ability to profit from further education, inexperience, lack of job training, the possibility of securing employment having regard to the standard of education already achieved and the state of the labour market, and the capacity of the parents to bear the costs of a college education for a child who evinces an aptitude therefor.[127] Additional factors include: whether the child is a full-time or part-time student, whether the child is eligible for student loans or other financial assistance, whether the child has reasonable career plans, the ability of the child to contribute to his or her own support through part-time employment,[128] parental plans for the child's education, particularly those made during cohabitation, and at least in the case of a mature child who has reached the age of majority, whether or not the child has unilaterally terminated his or her relationship with the parent from whom child support is sought.[129] These non-exhaustive factors provide signposts but

---

121 *Chalmers v Chalmers*, [1997] AJ No 433 (QB); *Cennon v Cennon*, [1999] SJ No 504 (QB).

122 *Vokey v Vokey* (1991), 35 RFL (3d) 458 (Man QB); *Giorno v Giorno* (1992), 39 RFL (3d) 345 (NSCA).

123 *RWG v SIG*, [2002] SJ No 231 (QB).

124 *Durose v Durose*, [1996] BCJ No 420 (SC); *Ciardullo v Ciardullo* (1995), 15 RFL (4th) 121 (BCSC); *S CA v S CO*, 2022 NBBR 238; *Jarzebinski v Jarzebinski*, [2004] OJ No 4595 (SCJ); *Nitkin v Nitkin*, [2006] OJ No 2769 (SCJ); *Hildebrandt v Rossmo*, [1997] SJ No 630 (QB).

125 *TS v GC*, 2013 NBQB 358; *CC v KK*, 2020 PESC 16.

126 *Olson v Olson*, [2003] AJ No 230 (CA); *SLF v JWF*, 2016 ABQB 635; *Nitchie v Nitchie*, 2014 BCSC 468; *JLL v VLL*, 2017 NBQB 76; *Edwards v Edwards*, 2015 NLTD(G) 165; *MacLennan v MacLennan*, [2003] NSJ No 15 (CA); *Fair v Jones*, [1999] NWTJ No 17 (SC); *Edwards v Edwards*, 2021 ONSC 1550; *Geran v Geran*, 2011 SKCA 55; *Stephens v Stephens*, 2019 SKQB 114.

127 *Holland v Holland*, [2007] AJ No 1350 (QB); *Rainey v Rainey*, [2003] BCJ No 481 (SC); *Peterson v Farrer*, [2010] NBJ No 189 (QB); *Douglas v Campbell*, [2006] NSJ No 350 (SC); *CC v KK*, 2020 PESC 16; *Bradley v Zaba*, [1996] SJ No 5 (CA); *Geran v Geran*, 2011 SKCA 55 at para 21.

128 See *BLP v DAP*, 2014 ABQB 89.

129 *Olson v Olson* (2003), 320 AR 379 (CA); *Damphouse v Damphouse*, 2020 ABQB 101; *TDM v JDM*, 2020 ABQB 353; *Arnault v Arnault*, 2022 ABQB 176; *Mirzahi v Sana*, 2022 ABQB 313; *Betts v Chisholm*, 2023 ABCA 55; *Farden v Farden* (1993), 48 RFL (3d) 60 (BCSC); *Darlington v Darlington*, [1997] BCJ No 2534 (CA); *Dring v Gheyle*, 2018 BCCA 435; *Forrest v Aerin*, 2022 BCCA 184; *Deng v Zhang*, 2022 BCCA 271; *SAM v JAB*, 2023 BCSC 2110; *Sidhu v Chima*, 2020 BCSC 768; *LF v RB*, 2021 BCSC 464; *Rebenchuk v Rebenchuk*, 2007 MBCA 22; *Doerksen v Houlahan*, 2012 MBQB 110; *Sharma v Sharma*, 2022 MBQB 27; *PRR v JCG*, 2013 NBQB 405; *Green v Green*, [2005] NJ No 165 (CA); *Winsor v Winsor*, 2017 NLCA 54; *Mulders v Mulders*, 2014 NWTSC 50; *Nafar-Ross v Raahemi*, 2018 ONSC 3054; *Easton v Coxhead*, 2018 ONSC 4784; *Bradley v Zaba*, [1996] SJ No 5 (CA); *Olszewski v Willick*, 2009 SKCA 133; *Geran v Geran* 2011 SKCA 55; *Vantomme v Vantomme*, 2014 SKQB 227; *GTF v KLF*, 2009 YKSC 72. Compare *Chartier v Chartier*, [1999] 1 SCR 242; and see Section K, below in this chapter.

each case is unique and fact driven and the signposts are not exhaustive or weighted.[130] It is not necessary to adduce evidence on all of the aforementioned factors in order to prove that a child falls within the statutory definition of a "child of the marriage" within the meaning of section 2(1) of the *Divorce Act*.[131] A broad range of factors will be considered in determining whether an adult child is a "child of the marriage" and individual factors will vary in importance according to the circumstances of the particular case.[132]

Although relevant authorities have developed lengthy lists of factors relevant to determining whether an adult child remains a "child of the marriage" for support purposes,[133] such lists, helpful though they are, must not be used in place of the language of the statute nor should they be invoked to impose a burden on parents to call evidence about the obvious or on judges to address non-issues in their reasons for judgment. Judges are entitled to draw reasonable, common sense inferences from the proven facts and may take into account notorious facts such as, that post-secondary education is expensive, well paid part-time employment for full-time students is scarce, and the demands of a full-time course load limit the time available for part-time work.[134] Where the evidence of an adult child's intention to return to university is inconclusive, a conditional order may provide a pragmatic response that can avoid delay and additional costs, but such an order should provide a limited time frame within which the adult child must resume his or her full-time university studies.[135] A conditional order that is declared subject to review may also be appropriate for the purpose of determining whether adult children are making progress in their academic endeavours sufficient to consider their educational plans to be realistic and reasonable. If not, the support obligor may be relieved from payment of some or all of his child support obligation.[136]

It has been asserted that, while an estranged relationship between an adult child and the paying parent may not justify the immediate denial or reduction of child support, the child may ultimately be called upon to bear the consequence of persisting in the estrangement and that consequence may be cessation of child support.[137] This approach has been judicially

---

130 *MV v DV*, [2005] NBJ No 505 (QB); see also *Dorey v Dorey*, 2011 ABCA 192; *RJM v EM*, 2015 BCSC 414; *Shelley v Russell*, 2012 ONSC 920.

131 *Dorey v Dorey*, 2011 ABCA 192; *Lalonde v Lalonde*, 2016 ABQB 600; *Darlington v Darlington*, [1997] BCJ No 2534 (CA); *Geboers v Geboers*, 2018 BCSC 181; *Green v Green*, [2005] NJ No 165 (CA); *MacLennan v MacLennan*, [2003] NSJ No 15 (CA); *Gagnier v Gagnier*, [2002] OJ No 2183 (SCJ).

132 *WPN v BJN*, [2005] BCJ No 12 (CA); *CAMT v APGT*, 2011 BCSC 1456.

133 See, for example, *Farden v Farden* (1993), 48 RFL (3d) 60 (BCSC); *Rebenchuk v Rebenchuk*, 2007 MBCA 22; *Dove v MacIntyre*, 2021 NSSC 1; *Aubert v Cipriani*, 2015 ONSC 6103; *Geran v Geran*, 2011 SKCA 55; *Friesen v Braun*, 2020 SKQB 253.

134 *MacLennan v MacLennan*, [2003] NSJ No 15 (CA). See also *RJM v EM*, 2015 BCSC 414; *DWM v MAB*, 2012 NBQB 146; *Galbraith v Galbraith*, 2014 NSSC 337; *Osman v ElKadi*, 2015 ONSC 1124; *Brooke v Hertz*, 2008 SKQB 461.

135 *MacLennan v MacLennan*, [2003] NSJ No 15 (CA); see also *Rebenchuk v Rebenchuk* (2007), 35 RFL (6th) 239 (Man CA).

136 *TTB v PHD*, 2014 NBQB 164, Morrison J.

137 *Fraser v Jones* (1995), 17 RFL (4th) 218 at 224 (Sask QB), cited with approval in *Khoee-Solomonescu v Solomonescu*, [1997] OJ No 4876 (Gen Div). See also *Mirzahi v Sana*, 2022 ABQB 313 at para 50; *Marsland v Gibb*, [2000] BCJ No 558 (SC) (complete rejection of father by child from age of eleven; order for support terminated on child's attaining adulthood, even though child pursuing post-secondary education); *O'Connell v McIndoe*, [2000] BCJ No 1311 (SC) (application deemed premature while child still under the provincial age of majority); *Lawrence v Mortensen*, [2000] OJ No 1578 (SCJ) (order granted

questioned in circumstances of long-term estrangement on the basis that it is unfair to place such a burden on the child, when the responsibility for cementing a meaningful relationship with the child lay with both parents.[138] It is clear from the cases that the quality of the parent/child relationship is rarely determinative,[139] unless the circumstances are extremely grave. An appellate court will not lightly disturb an application judge's determination that an adult child is entitled to ongoing child support while she is undertaking full-time university studies, notwithstanding the estrangement of the adult child from the payor parent, where the application judge has reviewed all of the surrounding circumstances in determining that "the adult child is unable by reason of . . . pursuit of reasonable education to withdraw from the parent's charge or to obtain the necessities of life" within the meaning of section 37(7)(a) of the *Family Law Act* (Newfoundland and Labrador).[141] However, the breakdown of the parent/child relationship may be of the utmost importance in the establishment of conditions whereby the paying parent will be provided with all relevant financial information, any change of address, copies of transcripts of marks, together with periodic reports on the child's academic progress.[142] In order to foster better communication and information sharing, a court may recommend counselling for the estranged parent and child.[143] A further consideration is whether the child could have reasonably expected one or both of the parents to have continued to furnish support if the marriage had not broken down.[144] Complete rejection of a support paying father by his adult children may justify limitations being imposed on the father's child support obligation. An all-or-nothing response may be found inappropriate. Consequently, a father may be ordered to provide continued support to his adult children while they pursue their first post-secondary degree but not thereafter.[145]

A court may compel an adult child who is benefitting from a child support order to provide certain information respecting health issues or educational pursuits to the paying parent, even though the child is not a party to the proceedings.[146] The decision to place mandatory disclosure-type conditions on a child support order is discretionary, and when crafting such orders, courts must be aware of the competing interests that must be balanced.[147]

---

for payment of substantial arrears of child support but order for prospective child support payments denied); *Brooke v Hertz*, 2008 SKQB 461.

138 *JK v SD*, [1999] QJ No 4155 (CS); And see Section K, below in this chapter.

139 *Wahl v Wahl*, [2000] AJ No 29 (QB); *O'Donnell v O'Donnell*, 2011 NBQB 56; *Nitkin v Nitkin*, [2006] OJ No 2769 (SCJ); see also *Fernquist v Garland*, [2005] SJ No 747 (QB). And see *Urquhart v Loane*, 2016 PECA 15. Compare *Oleksiewicz v Oleksiewicz*, 2017 BCSC 228.

140 *CLD v RJB*, 2019 ABQB 852 at para 26; *Pepin v Jung*, [2003] OJ No 1779 (SCJ); *Rebenchuk v Rebenchuk* 2007 MBCA 22; *Brooke v Hertz*, 2008 SKQB 461.

141 RSNL 1990, c F-2. See *Green v Green*, [2005] NJ No 165 (CA).

142 *Wahl v Wahl*, [2000] AJ No 29 (QB); *Ciardullo v Ciardullo* (1995), 15 RFL (4th) 121 (BCSC); *Block v Baltimore*, [2000] MJ No 132 (QB); *MV v DV*, [2005] NBJ No 505 (QB); *Hill v Davis*, [2006] NSJ No 331 (SC); *Rosenberg v Rosenberg*, [2003] OJ No 2962 (SCJ); compare *Matwijiw v Matwijiw*, [2004] OJ No 1887 (SCJ).

143 *Khoee-Solomonescu v Solomonescu*, [1997] OJ No 4876 (Gen Div).

144 *Montalto v Montalto*, 2011 ABQB 574; *Rogge v Rogge* (1991), 37 RFL (3d) 108 at 110 (Man QB); *Trottier v Bradley*, [1999] MJ No 227 (CA); *Bradley v Zaba*, [1996] SJ No 5 (CA); *Peterson v Peterson*, 2011 SKQB 365.

145 *Johnson v Johnson*, [2004] OJ No 3567 (SCJ) (oldest child, having already graduated, not entitled to support while pursuing postgraduate degree); compare *Easton v Coxhead*, 2018 ONSC 4784; *Urquhart v Loane* 2016 PECA 15 at para 24.

146 *DBB v DMB*, 2017 SKCA 59 at para 143, citing *Burzminski v Burzminski*, 2010 SKCA 16.

147 *DBB v DMB*, 2017 SKCA 59 at para 148, Herauf JA.

It is not essential that the child live with either parent;[148] conversely, a child may be in need of support notwithstanding that the child is residing with one of the parents while pursuing post-secondary education.[149] Full-time post-secondary education may qualify a child as "a child of the marriage" who is entitled to support, even if it is undertaken by means of correspondence courses[150] or spread over more than the normal time period for completion of the program.[151] Children who defer their studies or pursue part-time studies because of financial considerations should not be penalized for their diligence.[152] Post-secondary education that is pursued on a part-time basis by an adult child with a clear career plan may entitle the child to support, where his or her income from employment is insufficient to enable the child to fully withdraw from the charge of his or her parents.[153] If a parent is obligated to contribute to the support of an adult child who is pursuing post-secondary education on a part-time basis, there is a corresponding obligation on the child to complete the education as expeditiously as possible and to contribute as much as is reasonable to his or her living and education costs.[154]

The fact that a child earns a part-time or summer income while enrolled in a post-secondary institution does not preclude that child from being a "child of the marriage," provided the amount earned is insufficient to allow him or her to withdraw from the charge of the parents.[155] Adult children cease to be "children of the marriage" under section 2(1) of the *Divorce Act*, where they are financially self-sufficient as a result of part-time employment, which is not inconsistent with their pursuit of further education.[156] The availability of student loans does not necessarily negate or reduce the obligation of parents to support a dependent child who is attending university,[157] although it may do so where the parents are of limited means.[158] The issue to determine is what is fit and just.[159] Adult children have an obligation to make a reasonable contribution to their own living and university expenses,[160] but they are not expected to mortgage their futures by assuming large student loans where their parents can

---

148 *Bates v Bates* (1995), 10 RFL (4th) 261 (Alta CA); *MV v DV*, [2005] NBJ No 505 (QB); *Sapergia v Sapergia*, [1998] SJ No 877 (QB); *Carrier v Carrier*, 2008 SKQB 439.

149 *Auld v Auld* (1994), 5 RFL (4th) 132 (PEITD); compare *Van Wynsberghe v Van Wynsberghe*, [1997] OJ No 2566 (Gen Div).

150 *Kirkpatrick v Kendall*, [1997] SJ No 212 (QB); see also *Krueger v Tunison*, [1999] SJ No 482 (QB) (Grade 12).

151 *Kapounek v Brown*, [2000] OJ No 1301 (SCJ).

152 *Rebenchuk v Rebenchuk*, 2007 MBCA 22; *Rumpel v Wills*, 2010 SKQB 397.

153 *Kovich v Kreut*, [1998] BCJ No 2586 (SC); *Sherlock v Sherlock*, [1999] BCJ No 1856 (SC) (monthly amount of support for two children fixed on sliding scale according to the number of courses taken).

154 *Sherlock v Sherlock*, *ibid.*

155 *Hannigan v Hannigan*, [2003] BCJ No 2278 (SC); *Mondoux v Mondoux* (1994), 152 NBR (2d) 259 (QB); *Westcott v Westcott*, [1997] OJ No 3060 (Gen Div); *McCabe v MacInnis*, [2000] PEIJ No 61 (SC); *Nunn v McLeod*, [1999] SJ No 168 (QB) (short *viva voce* hearing ordered to ascertain adult child's needs in light of his own earning capacity); *Hamel v Hamel*, [2001] SJ No 692 (CA).

156 *Saper v Silverman*, [2002] MJ No 215 (CA); *Hamdan v Hamdan*, 2012 NBQB 331.

157 *WPN v BJN*, [2005] BCJ No 12 (CA); *YHB v JPB*, 2014 BCSC 618; *Rebenchuk v Rebenchuk*, 2007 MBCA 22; *Selig v Smith*, 2008 NSCA 54; *Thompson v Thompson* (1988), 13 RFL (3d) 372 (Ont Div Ct); *Smith v Smith*, 2010 SKQB 2; compare *Molloy v Molloy*, [2001] YJ No 142 (SC).

158 *Klotz v Klotz*, [1999] BCJ No 148 (SC); *Boundford v Jacobs*, [2006] NJ No 199 (SC); *Nelson v Nelson* (2005), 14 RFL (6th) 26 at para 35 (NSSC); *Young v Rodgers*, [2000] OJ No 4564 (SCJ).

159 *Brooke v Hertz*, 2008 SKQB 461; see also *Williams v Wallace*, 2017 ABQB 421; *Sutherland v Schlamp*, 2014 SKQB 34 at paras 57–58.

160 *Evanow v Lannon*, 2018 BCCA 208; *Sutherland v Schlamp*, 2014 SKQB 34.

well afford to pay. The extent to which adult children should be required to obtain student loans while pursuing post-secondary education depends on the attendant circumstances including the financial circumstances of their parents. Adult children should not normally be required to work part-time while attending university if this would have a negative impact on their anticipated academic performance. They must be allowed time to relax and regenerate their batteries as well as enjoy and benefit from the university experience as a whole.[161] The fact that a commercial loan has been obtained from a credit union because the adult child is ineligible for a government student loan does not preclude it from being taken into account in determining the ability of the child to contribute towards her own support. In determining whether the adult child should be expected to borrow money to underwrite some of the costs of her post-secondary education, the court may have regard to what would have happened if the family had remained intact. The court may also take account of the spiralling costs of university education and must also have regard to the financial ability of the parents to contribute to their adult child's post-secondary education costs. A parent will not be ordered to pay more towards an adult child's section 7 post-secondary education expenses than he or she can reasonably afford after account is taken of a concurrent obligation to pay the basic table amount of child support.[162] Middle-class parents have an obligation to help their children obtain their first university degree if the children are bright and have performed well at the secondary school level. Where the parental incomes are not great, the court may have regard to their assets and their financial prospects based on their earning capacity. Although parents are not required to sell capital assets or go into so much debt that they will never recover, parents are expected to make sacrifices in order to assist their children with a university education.[164] While a parent is expected to make some sacrifices to assist his or her children with their education, a parent is not required to live a life of complete austerity in order to do so, particularly in relation to a graduate degree. Nor should a parent be required to jeopardize his or her financial security in retirement.[165] Parents should not have to face the prospect of little or nothing to live on in their old age as a result of funding an adult child's education.[166] As stated by Brown J of the British Columbia Supreme Court in *BLS v EJS*:

> 33 As provided by s. 3(2) of the *Guidelines*, the financial ability of each spouse to contribute to the support of the child is the prominent practical consideration. The higher the parental income and the marital standard of living, the greater the call on the parent's resources, assuming the child is entitled to support. The lower the parental income and the marital standard of living, the lesser the call on them. Entitlement to parental support arises when all the circumstances, considered in their totality, justify it.
>
> 34 Additional considerations seen in 3(2) of the *Guidelines* include the child's conditions, needs and circumstances, which would include their place of residence.

---

161 *Ross v Dunphy*, 2009 NBQB 281; *Rebenchuk v Rebenchuk*, 2007 MBCA 22; *MacDonald v MacDonald*, [2001] NSJ No 498 (SC); *Coghill v Coghill*, [2006] OJ No 2602 (SCJ).

162 *Beutler v Maki*, [2005] SJ No 562 (QB).

163 *Midena v Collette*, [2000] OJ No 4429 (Ct J). See also *RJC v RJJ*, [2006] BCJ No 2150 (SC); *AWH v CGS* [2007] NSJ No 262 (SC).

164 *JCR v JJR*, 2006 BCSC 1422 at para 20; *Tusnady v Tusnady*, 2010 BCSC 1310.

165 *SLF v JWF*, 2016 ABQB 635, citing *Bola v Bola*, 2014 BCSC 861.

166 *Bola v Bola*, 2014 BCSC 861.

> 35 These principles and considerations obligate the child and the parent seeking support to produce transcripts and other academic records, grant and scholarship applications, employment records, a budget setting out proposed necessary and reasonable expenses, and any other documents that show the child cannot financially manage independent their parent's support.[167]

A child who pursues university education and is also employed to the extent that educational and living expenses are capable of being met by the student is not generally considered to be a "child of the marriage" within the meaning of section 2(1) of the *Divorce Act*.[168] An order to pay support for a child pursuing a college education may be suspended for a period during which the child has a work placement that generates sufficient income for the child's support and may be revived on termination of that placement until the college program is completed.[169]

Whether child support should be ordered to finance a child's post-secondary education is ultimately dependent upon the circumstances of the particular case.[170] That which generosity or affection might motivate a parent to pay for a child's support is one thing; that which the law ought to compel is another.[171] It has been stated that "however laudable the standards these young people have set for themselves, there must surely come a time when the cost of such preparation is beyond parental duty."[172] A court must be careful not to be carried away with claims on behalf of a would-be "hanger on" in perpetuity, such as the perennial student.[173] The legislation was not intended to allow the children of divorced parents to pursue an unlimited number of degrees at their parents' expense.[174] The governing principle in determining whether child support should be paid is reasonableness.[175] There is no arbitrary cut-off of support for adult children who are serious students but have failures in their academic record. A court must consider all the attendant circumstances, including their age, education, and employment potential.[176] A temporary absence from educational studies does not inevitably mean that the child is no longer a "child of the marriage," although that status and the consequential right to child support may be lost if the child leaves school

167 2014 BCSC 1549; see also *CLD v RJB*, 2019 ABQB 852 at para 26; *Heubach v Heubach*, 2011 ONSC 1057 at para 38; *Smith v Smith*, 2010 SKQB 2 at para 39.

168 *Hamdan v Hamdan*, 2012 NBQB 331; *Kidson v Techentin* (1994), 129 NSR (2d) 228 (Fam Ct); compare *Farrus v Farrus*, [2000] AJ No 680 (QB) (adult child not required to maximize summer earnings by shift work in order to eliminate need for support where the summer employment selected was reasonable in light of the child's career goals and cultural activities).

169 *McLean v McLean*, [1997] OJ No 5315 (Gen Div).

170 *Jackson v Jackson*, [1973] SCR 205; *Wahl v Wahl*, [2000] AJ No 29 (QB); *Nitchie v Nitchie*, 2014 BCSC 468; *Rebenchuk v Rebenchuk*, 2007 MBCA 22; *McGregor v McGregor* (1994), 3 RFL (4th) 343 (NBCA); *TTB v PHD*, 2014 NBQB 164; *Shelley v Russell*, 2012 ONSC 920; *Borland v Borland*, 2019 SKQB 220.

171 *Garrow v Garrow*, [1997] BCJ No 1818 (SC); *Cole v Cole*, [2008] NSJ No 263 (SC); *DL v MB*, 2010 NBQB 33; *Borland v Borland*, 2019 SKQB 220.

172 *Ferguson v Ferguson* (1970), 1 RFL 387 at 396–97 (Man QB), Wilson J.

173 *Yaschuk v Logan* (1992), 39 RFL (3d) 417 at 438 (NSCA), Chipman JA; *Welsh v Welsh*, [1998] OJ No 4550 (Gen Div).

174 *Andersen v Andersen*, [1997] BCJ No 2496 (SC); *Poyntz Estate v Poyntz*, [1998] OJ No 1024 (Gen Div).

175 *Ivany v Ivany* (1996), 24 RFL (4th) 289 (Nfld SC); *MacMillan v Layden*, [2002] NJ No 156 (SC); *El Gahwas v Ghremida*, 2020 SKQB 311; *Ghremida v Elgahwas*, 2023 SKCA 23 at para 20.

176 *TTB v PHD*, 2014 NBQB 164; *Ivany v Ivany* (1996), 24 RFL (4th) 289; *Seburn v Seburn*, [2001] OJ No 1467 (SCJ).

and becomes self-supporting.[177] A period of grace may be appropriate before post-secondary education starts or after it ends because some children may not gain admission immedi ately after graduation or they may require upgrading. And some children may not find jobs immediately on graduation from their post-secondary education and require some time to become self-sufficient.[178] There is no presumed period of grace pending entry into work force; the relevant circumstances will dictate whether a *limited* extension of child support is warranted and the onus is on the claimant to establish dependency.[179] An appellate court may refuse to interfere with a trial judge's finding that a child falls within the definition of "child of the marriage," even though the parent/child relationship was acrimonious and the child's career plans were uncertain, where the trial court judgment was structured to afford the child a period of grace in which to finalize future plans.[180] The ability of the child to con tribute to his or her own support is a factor parents living together would take into account, and so should the court.[181] However, parents cannot consensually abrogate their natural or adopted child's legitimate right to support while pursuing a post-secondary education. Where the issue is litigated, the court should require evidence relating to the reasonableness of the adult child's plans and objective criteria should be furnished with respect to the child's future employability.[183] The post-secondary education of an older sibling can provide the benchmark against which the reasonableness of another child's post-secondary expenses can be measured.[184] A court may refuse to accede to an adult child's request to attend university on a year-round basis rather than on the more typical pattern of fall and spring terms, where no particular reason is given for this preference and such a plan would inevitably reduce, if not eliminate, the adult child's capacity to contribute towards her expenses and would increase the father's contribution.[185]

The failure of an adult child to obtain exemplary grades in his or her university studies is not a sufficient basis in itself to justify a finding that the child is no longer a "child of the marriage" within the meaning of section 2(1) of the *Divorce Act*, where the evidence does not support allegations that the child is taking advantage of the situation and is not serious in his or her studies.[186] The failure to complete each step in the educational program on schedule is not necessarily indicative of a lack of seriousness on the child's part and courts are often prepared to show considerable latitude when the educational program will take longer than is normal.[187] The parental support obligation is, nevertheless, premised on the child's application of time, talents, and abilities to course work, not on mere attendance at university. Consequently, an order for child support may be terminated retroactively where

---

177 *Pearce v Pearce*, [1999] BCJ No 2278 (SC).

178 *LRP v BJP*, 2013 ABQB 685 at para 54; *KKS v JSS*, 2019 BCSC 136 at para 28.

179 *Aquila v Aquila*, 2016 MBCA 33 at para 31, Mainella JA.

180 *Cador v Chichak*, [2000] AJ No 24 (QB).

181 *Newman v Thompson* (1997), 30 RFL (4th) 143 (Man CA).

182 *Bosse v Bosse* (1996), 19 RFL (4th) 54 (NBQB).

183 *Davids v Davids*, [1998] OJ No 2859 (Gen Div).

184 *Khoury v Khoury* (1994), 149 NBR (2d) 1 (QB); *Diotallevi v Diotallevi* (1982), 27 RFL (2d) 400 (Ont HCJ); *Warsh v Warsh*, 2012 ONSC 6903.

185 *DMR v AR*, [2006] BCJ No 42 (SC).

186 *Budyk v Sol*, [1998] MJ No 252 (CA).

187 *Kusnir v Kusnir*, [2001] OJ No 3491 (Ct J).

an adult child was enrolled in university but his academic achievement was so abysmal as to require withdrawal from the university.[188] A child attending a post-secondary educational institution may be entitled to change his or her educational program without loss of child support.[189] Courts must be cautious about drawing artificial distinctions based on the number or types of degrees or certificates.[190] Academically qualified children with reasonable expectations of undertaking post-secondary education will normally receive support to permit their completion of an undergraduate university degree or college diploma as long as the parents have the means to pay.[191] The parental support obligation does not necessarily extend to postgraduate or professional education or training,[192] although it may do so in appropriate circumstances.[193] There is no authority for the proposition that a parent must support a child seeking postgraduate qualifications. Each case must be decided on its own facts.[194] The goal of assisting children to become marketable in today's world does not necessarily require parents to provide support to enable their children to attain their highest level of achievement at the expense of the parents' need to provide for their own self-sufficiency upon retirement.[195] There is no fixed rule whereby the child support obligation terminates when an adult child obtains his or her first degree or certificate, nor is there any rule whereby an adult child may prolong his or her post-secondary education beyond what is reasonably necessary.[196] Adult children may be entitled to complete their current programs, whereafter an assessment will have to be made as to whether they remain "children of the marriage" who are entitled to further support.[197] Section 31 of the Ontario *Family Law Act* does not circumscribe the child support obligation by reference to the length or type of the full-time program of education being pursued by an adult child, but common sense and fairness frequently end the child support obligation upon or shortly after the child's completion of the first undergraduate degree or diploma. Section 31 was never intended to subsidize perpetual

---

188 *Lariviere v Lariviere*, [2001] AJ No 251 (QB).

189 *Kluczny v Kluczny*, [1999] AJ No 1420 (QB); *Krupa v Krupa*, 2010 BCSC 1400; *McGinn v McGinn*, [2006] OJ No 461 (SCJ).

190 *DWM v MAB*, 2012 NBQB 146 at para 15; *GES v FC*, 2012 NBQB 165.

191 *Achkewich v Achkewich*, [1998] AJ No 383 (QB); *Rebenchuk v Rebenchuk*, 2007 MBCA 22; *Kavanagh v Kavanagh*, [1999] NJ No 358 (SC); *Blaschuk v Bridgewater*, [2005] OJ No 3324 (SCJ); *Holizki v Reeves*, [1997] SJ No 746 (QB).

192 *Marshall v Marshall*, [2000] AJ No 347 (QB); *Williams v Wallace*, 2017 ABQB 421; *Daye v Ekkebus*, [2008] BCJ No 529 (SC); *Smith v Smith* (1990), 27 RFL (3d) 32 (Man CA); *McGregor v McGregor* (1994), 3 RFL (4th) 343 (NBCA); *Yaschuk v Logan* (1992), 39 RFL (3d) 417 (NSCA); *Osterlund-Lenahan v Lenahan*, 2014 ONSC 7074; *Makdissi v Masson*, 2017 ONSC 6498; see also *Guhl v Guhl*, [2008] SJ No 818 (QB) (rebuttable presumption that child support will not be provided to underwrite postgraduate degree).

193 *Zhang v Lin*, 2010 ABQB 420; *WPN v BJN*, [2005] BCJ No 12 (CA); *Joffres v Joffres*, 2014 BCSC 1778; *Newman v Thompson* (1997), 30 RFL (4th) 143 (Man CA); *Jamieson v Jamieson* (1995), 14 RFL (4th) 354 (NBCA); *O'Keefe v Clarke* (1994), 7 RFL (4th) 398 (Nfld UFC); *Martell v Height* (1994), 3 RFL (4th) 104 (NSCA); *Dove v MacIntyre*, 2021 NSSC 1; *Allooloo v Allooloo*, [1999] NWTJ No 48 (SC); *Easton v Coxhead*, 2018 ONSC 4784; *CU v MR*, [1997] QJ No 3289 (CS); *Vantomme v Vantomme*, 2014 SKQB 227.

194 *Jonasson v Jonasson*, [1998] BCJ No 726 (SC); *Rebenchuk v Rebenchuk*, 2007 MBCA 22; *Lee v Lee*, 2009 NSSC 121; *Davids v Davids*, [1998] OJ No 2859 (Gen Div); *CU v MR*, [1998] QJ No 3443 (CS).

195 *Hill v Davis*, [2006] NSJ No 331 (SC).

196 *DWM v MAB*, 2012 NBQB 146; *Penn v Penn*, 2014 ONSC 6321; compare *Mulders v Mulders*, 2014 NWTSC 50 at para 24.

197 *Monaghan v Monaghan*, [2002] OJ No 4168 (SCJ).

students.[198] A distinction can be drawn between the criteria under the *Divorce Act* and those under the Ontario *Family Law Act* with respect to parental obligations to support adult children. Under the *Divorce Act*, dependency is the key criterion. Under the Ontario statute, full-time enrolment in school and a continuing element of parental control are the keys to entitlement. Financial dependence is, nevertheless, perceived as one factor indicative of parental control. Where post-secondary education for their children has been a top priority of the parents who have supported their son or daughter into the second semester of his Master's program, a benchmark may have been thereby established that entitles their daughter to pursue a Master's degree in clinical psychology, which equips her for immediate entry into the workforce. The parental support obligation may not extend to the daughter's pursuit of a PhD degree, however, when no compelling reason is shown why she should not go into practice and pursue a PhD when she herself had saved enough money to meet this expense.

On an application for support to enable an adult child to pursue post-secondary education, the age of the child is not determinative, neither is the number of years that the child has already pursued post-secondary education, nor is the fact that the child does not have a good relationship with the parent against whom an order for child support is being sought; taken cumulatively, however, together with the financial circumstances of the parents, child support may be denied to an adult child who has already spent several years attending university and who has never pursued gainful employment for any length of time.[200] An adult child is expected to financially contribute to his or her higher education costs and cannot expend earned income on luxuries and then look at his or her parent to meet future educational costs.[201] There is no arbitrary cut-off point based on age or academic achievement,[202] although the onus of proving a child's continued dependence grows heavier as these increase.[203] At one time, courts were reluctant to extend support beyond a first degree; however, this is no longer the case.[204] The reasonableness of a child's plans and the reasonable expectation of the parents are factors to be taken into account. Neither the Guidelines nor the caselaw obliges parents to fund all of the cost of a child's education. Even with reasonable contribution from a child, a parent's contribution is still subject to the means or ability to pay of a parent.[205]

Cases are rare in which support is ordered to be paid for a child over the age of twenty-five or twenty-six.[206] There must be some degree of congruency between the financial circumstances of the family and the educational plans of the child.[207] As a general rule, parents of a *bona fide* adult student remain financially responsible until the child has reached a level of education commensurate with his or her demonstrated abilities that fits the child for entry

198 *Blaschuk v Bridgewater*, [2005] OJ No 3324 (SCJ).

199 *Oates v Oates*, [2004] OJ No 2984 (SCJ).

200 *Minski v Minski*, [2002] SJ No 773 (QB).

201 *Morissette v Ball*, [2000] OJ No 73 (SCJ). Compare *El Gahwas v Ghremida*, 2020 SKQB 311.

202 *Newman v Thompson* (1997), 30 RFL (4th) 143 (Man CA); *Jamieson v Jamieson*, [1995] NBJ No 342 (CA); *Martell v Height* (1994), 3 RFL (4th) 104 (NSCA); *Penn v Penn*, 2014 ONSC 6321; *Vantomme v Vantomme* 2014 SKQB 227.

203 *McArthur v McArthur*, [1998] AJ No 1522 (QB); *RYW v DWW*, 2013 BCSC 472; *Douglas v Campbell*, [2006] NSJ No 350 (SC); *Penn v Penn*, 2014 ONSC 6321.

204 *Haist v Haist*, 2010 ONSC 1283; *Penn v Penn*, 2014 ONSC 6321.

205 *Vantomme v Vantomme*, 2014 SKQB 227 at para 56, McIntyre J.

206 *Noseworthy v Noseworthy*, [2008] OJ No 2703 (SCJ).

207 *RYW v DWW*, 2013 BCSC 472; *Bari v Nassr*, 2015 ONSC 4318.

level employment in an appropriate field within a reasonable period of time. In making this determination, the court must be aware of prevailing socio-economic conditions wherein an undergraduate degree no longer assures economic self-sufficiency,[208] although this awareness must be tempered by the realization that the majority of children find their place in the world without the benefit of any post-secondary education.[209] There is no automatic rule that a child is no longer a child of the marriage once a first university degree is completed.[210] Although in the past some courts hesitated to grant support beyond a first degree, that is no longer the case.[211] While parents of significant means may be ordered to pay support for a second degree, support for a second degree is very much subject to the parents' ability to pay.[212] Whatever course of study is chosen by the child, the length of time for which the parent will be required by law to support that course of study will depend on the reasonableness of the choice and the means and needs of the child and parent.[213] The obligation of a parent is to support the child to a level of education "commensurate with the abilities [he or] she has demonstrated."[214] If a child attends an out-of-town[215] or an extra-provincial university, the parent seeking child support must justify the increased expenses thereby incurred.[216] An adult child may be called upon to make a greater contribution to post-secondary education costs if various options are available and the child's choice comes with a higher price tag than other possibilities.[217]

A court can take judicial notice of the costs of a Canadian university program for the purpose of responding to a budget setting out the costs of the child attending a foreign university and in order to lower the claim to the amount that it would cost were the child to attend at a Canadian university.[218] When adult children embark on a post-secondary educational program that is far more costly than other career paths, there is a positive obligation on the children or a parent seeking child support on their behalf to enter into meaningful discussions with the other parent who is expected to contribute towards the costs; in the absence of such discussions, that parent should not be expected to provide a blank cheque.[219] An order for parental contribution to an adult child's costs of attending an expensive first-year program at a foreign university may be justified by the child's reasonable expectation that the parents would meet these costs and by the impossibility of the child's making alternative plans for the current academic year. The child may be judicially expected to make other plans after

208 *Greenham v Woodfine Greenham*, 2015 NLTD(F) 2; *Martell v Height* (1994), 3 RFL (4th) 104 (NSCA); *MacLennan v MacLennan*, [2003] NSJ No 15 (CA); *Morissette v Ball*, [2000] OJ No 73 (SCJ); *Riley v Riley*, [2009] SJ No 142 (QB); see also *Chutter v Chutter*, 2016 BCSC 2407.

209 *Jonasson v Jonasson*, [1998] BCJ No 726 (SC).

210 *Beninger v Beninger*, 2010 BCSC 1509.

211 *LePine v LePine*, 2015 ONSC 7341.

212 *Decaen v Decaen*, 2013 ONCA 218 at para 58, citing *WPN v BJN*, 2005 BCCA 7.

213 *RYW v DWW*, 2013 BCSC 472; *Smith v Smith* (1990), 27 RFL (3d) 32 (Man CA); *Jamieson v Jamieson* (1995), 14 RFL (4th) 354 (NBCA); *Warsh v Warsh*, 2012 ONSC 6903; *Head v Head*, 2010 SKQB 25.

214 *Carmichael v Kiggins*, 2010 ABQB 78, citing *Martell v Height* (1994), 3 RFL (4th) 104 (NSCA).

215 *Bickerton v Bickerton*, [2004] BCJ No 2635 (SC); *Bauer v Bauer*, [2009] OJ No 135 (SCJ).

216 *Tusnady v Tusnady*, 2010 BCSC 1310; *Bitterman v Weaver*, [2002] NBJ No 42 (QB); *Bird v Ritcey*, [2004] NSJ No 514 (SC); *Penn v Penn*, 2014 ONSC 6321; *Fergusson v Kurylo*, [2005] SJ No 166, 264 Sask R 119 (QB). See also *Nafar-Ross v Raahemi*, 2018 ONSC 3054.

217 *Menegaldo v Menegaldo*, 2012 ONSC 2915.

218 *Lo v Lo*, 2011 ONSC 7663.

219 *Daicar-Gendron v Gendron*, [2004] BCJ No 2005 (SC).

completing the first-year program where the separated parents will be unable to meet the costs beyond the first year.[220] Support may be denied where the applicant fails to present to the court a detailed educational plan, supported by evidence as to how that plan will be executed and the role support would play under such a plan.[221] It may be desirable for the adult child to provide an affidavit setting out his or her income, assets, and need.[222] It may also be reasonable for both parents to be apprised regularly of information relating to the child's marks and progress at a post-secondary institution in order to assess the child's further education and employment prospects. Achievement or lack thereof in a chosen course of study should be the subject of an ongoing review process by both parents and the child.[223] court may grant child support that is conditional upon the child maintaining passing grades in all courses and may require that all results be made available to the paying parent.[224] Like their parents, adult children must adjust to the economic consequences of marriage breakdown and divorce by formulating plans that are reasonable and directed to their eventual self-sufficiency.[225] A parent is not relieved of the obligation to support an adult child pursuing post-secondary education or training at an accredited institution merely because the parent disapproves of the child's career choice.[226] A child support order relating to adult children attending university may be unnecessary during the summer,[227] but a reduction of support for summer months spent at home may be inappropriate where their income from employment is insufficient to provide for their room and board and incidental living expenses.[228]

Financial dependence is the key criterion for entitlement to child support under the *Divorce Act* where the child is over the provincial age of majority.[229] The family's expectations concerning higher education and the degree to which the parents are involved in deciding on the course of education to be pursued are relevant factors for consideration in the court's determination whether support for post-secondary education should be payable. Caselaw generally imposes an obligation on middle-class parents to assist their children with their first undergraduate degree, while recognizing a concomitant obligation on the adult child to contribute towards their expenses. The guiding principle is that each parent should contribute towards the post-secondary education expenses in proportion to their respective incomes after the adult child's contribution has been deducted.[230] In calculating post-secondary expenses under section 7 of the *Federal Child Support Guidelines*, the court must avoid duplicating expenses for food, clothing, telephone, and residence costs, which are subsumed under the applicable table amount of child support that is ordered. The court may direct adult children to provide both parents with a proposed budget for each academic

---

220 *Flikerski v Flikerski*, [2001] OJ No 2964 (SCJ).

221 *Brown v Brown* (1993), 45 RFL (3d) 444 (BCSC); *Davids v Davids*, [1998] OJ No 2859 (Gen Div).

222 *Jonasson v Jonasson*, [1998] BCJ No 726 (SC).

223 *Ciardullo v Ciardullo* (1995), 15 RFL (4th) 121 (BCSC); *Davids v Davids*, [1998] OJ No 2859 (Gen Div).

224 *Brown v Brown* (1993), 45 RFL (3d) 444 (BCSC); *Kusnir v Kusnir*, [2001] OJ No 3491 (Ct J); *MB v NS*, [2001] QJ No 3039 (CS).

225 *Davids v Davids*, [1998] OJ No 2859 (Gen Div).

226 *Evans v Evans*, [1998] SJ No 91 (QB).

227 *Achkewich v Achkewich*, [1998] AJ No 383 (QB).

228 *Comeau v Comeau*, [1997] NSJ No 409 (TD).

229 *Vantomme v Vantomme*, 2014 SKQB 227 at para 49.

230 *Selig v Smith*, 2008 NSCA 54, [2008] NSJ No 250.

year, such budget to include summer and part-time earnings, a copy of the child's income tax returns, and proof of application for and responses to any realistically available loans or scholarships. The court may also direct each adult child to provide receipts or estimates of the cost of tuition, books, computers, and software programs where applicable, and other required fees. Parents should not be legally obligated to support their adult children indefinitely. Either the date on which the first degree is received or the date when the child reaches the age of twenty-five, when independent borrowing is more readily available, is a reasonable cut-off point in most cases where the parents cannot agree.[231]

A payor who is aware his adult child is not attending an agreed program of education cannot later seek a retroactive reduction in the amount of child support.[232]

A court is not bound by a university's suggested budget in fixing the amount of support payable under the *Federal Child Support Guidelines*.[233]

An adult child with a scholarly bent may be entitled to live off campus in order to maintain and improve high academic performance. Student residences are not always ideal, even though they may be available at a reduced cost.[234]

An adult child, who continues to be financially dependent on her mother and whose post-secondary education has been interrupted by illness, may be entitled to support out of the estate of her deceased father so that she will be able to resume full-time studies.[235] In some cases, the court will order a parent to resume paying child support after lengthy interruptions in the child's studies.[236] Courts have also recognized "transition periods" while an adult child is preparing for the next stage in her life.[237] An adult child may require a reasonable period of time to become financially independent after finishing school and attaining the age of majority, but once that reasonable time has elapsed the child will cease to be a "child of the marriage" within the meaning of section 2(1) of the *Divorce Act*.[238] A delay in an adult child's enrolment in community college constitutes no bar to ongoing child support where a reasonable explanation exists because of the family's extra-provincial relocation and the adult child's upgrading of her qualifications.[239] When an adult child has completed his post-secondary education, it is not unreasonable to expect that it may take a little time for that child to secure employment.[240] A distinction must be drawn in this context between an adult child's eligibility for support under the Ontario *Family Law Act* and under the *Divorce Act*. Section 31(1) of the Ontario *Family Law Act* ties eligibility to enrolment in a full-time program of education. While it may be a hardship for the residential parent alone to support a newly graduated and unemployed child, the court has no jurisdiction under the Ontario

---

231 *McCrae v McCrae*, [2005] OJ No 50 (SCJ).

232 *Bain v Bain* (1994), 7 RFL (4th) 451 (Man QB).

233 *Lidster v Lidster*, [2000] BCJ No 1017 (SC).

234 *Midena v Collette*, [2000] OJ No 4429 (Ct J).

235 *Hillock v Hillock*, [2001] OJ No 3837 (SCJ).

236 *Rotondi v Rotondi*, 2014 ONSC 1520.

237 *Westergard v Buttress*, 2012 BCCA 38; *Edwards v Edwards*, 2021 ONSC 1550; see also *Cervi v McDonald*, 2021 ONSC 1843.

238 *Ibid*; *Harder v Harder*, 2003 SKQB 286.

239 *Malcolm v Chabot*, [2004] SJ No 817 (QB) (hiatus over the summer months found insufficient reason to terminate child support obligation of the father); see also *Mirzahi v Sana*, 2022 ABQB 313.

240 *Hartshorne v Hartshorne*, 2010 BCCA 327; *Jackson v Jackson*, 2021 ONSC 2614, citing *SP v RP*, 2011 ONCA 336.

Family Law Act to order the other parent to pay transitional child support until the adult child finds employment.[241]

F. CHILDREN OVER AGE OF MAJORITY: SECTION 3(2) OF GUIDELINES

Section 3(2) of the *Federal Child Support Guidelines* provides that, unless otherwise provided under the Guidelines, where a child who is entitled to support is the age of majority or over, the amount of the child support order is (a) the amount determined by applying the Guidelines as if the child were under the age of majority; or (b) if the court considers that approach to be inappropriate, the amount that it considers appropriate, having regard to the condition, means, needs, and other circumstances of the child and the financial ability of each spouse to contribute to the support of the child.[242]

Section 3(2) applies only to children who are over the age of majority.[243] The court cannot deviate from section 3(1) of the Guidelines, whereby support for a child under the age of majority is presumptively the table amount plus any add-ons under section 7, simply because a child is approaching the age of majority. Where a child is enrolled in a university program while still under the age of majority but soon will attain that age, the presumptive rule whereby child support is fixed at the applicable table amount plus any allowable section 7 expenses for post-secondary education must be applied while the child is still under the age of majority;[244] thereafter, section 3(2) of the Guidelines empowers the court to deviate from the presumptive rule where its application is deemed inappropriate.[245] A court cannot deviate from the presumptive rule respecting the table amount of child support and allowable section 7 expenses under section 3(1) of the Guidelines where the child is under the provincial age of majority, unless the attendant circumstances trigger the discretionary jurisdiction of the court under the Guidelines with respect to split or shared parenting time, undue hardship, or if the paying parent's annual income exceeds $150,000. The court cannot refuse to apply the presumptive rule by invoking section 3(2)(b) of the Guidelines, which applies to adult children, even if the parents are agreeable because the child will be pursuing his post-secondary education away from home.[246] When applying the presumptive rule with respect to a child under the age of majority who is attending an out-of-town university, the order for the payment of section 7 expenses pertaining to the child's post-secondary education must avoid double recovery for accommodation and food expenses that are already

241 *Trevisanutto v Crnkovic*, [2005] OJ No 2276 (SCJ); compare *Haist v Haist*, 2010 ONSC 1283. And see *Berger v Berger*, 2016 ONCA 884, citing *Aubert v Cipriani*, 2015 ONSC 6103.

242 For a succinct summary of the application of section 3(2) of the Guidelines to adult children pursuing post-secondary education, see *Coghill v Coghill*, [2006] OJ No 2602 (SCJ).

243 *Hodgson v Hodgson*, 2014 BCSC 1372; *Beissner v Matheusik*, 2015 BCCA 308.

244 *Buckhold v Buckhold*, [2006] BCJ No 2755 (CA); *Beissner v Matheusik*, 2015 BCCA 308; *Hosseini v Kazemi*, 2021 BCSC 1938; *Lu v Sun*, [2005] NSJ No 314 (CA); *Bury v Beaton*, 2012 NSSC 37; *Rotella v Rotella*, [2006] OJ No 208 (SCJ); *MacDonald v Rasmussen*, [2000] SJ No 660 (QB); *JC v SAW*, 2013 YKSC 1.

245 *Longlitz v Longlitz*, 2012 BCSC 130; *Beissner v Matheusik*, 2015 BCCA 308; *Hosseini v Kazemi*, 2021 BCSC 1938.

246 *Callahan v Callahan*, [2002] NJ No 117 (SC); compare *MacNeil v MacNeil*, 2012 NSSC 345.

included in the table amount of child support ordered.[247] When an adult child is attending university away from home, courts do not normally order the table amount of support; instead, they resort to the means and needs approach applicable to adult children under section 3(2)(b) of the *Federal Child Support Guidelines*.[248] The table amount of child support is usually inappropriate when an adult child attends university out-of-town and only returns home during the summer and school breaks. Although each case must be examined on its own facts, a court may order the full table amount in the months the child is living at home with a lesser amount when the child is away at school.[249]

What is appropriate or inappropriate under section 3(2) of the *Federal Child Support Guidelines* must be determined on a case-by-case basis;[250] there are no hard-and-fast rules.[251] A spouse who seeks to exclude the application of section 3(2)(a) of the Guidelines to a child of the age of majority or over has the onus of proving that such application would be inappropriate.[252] The fact that an adult child has some employment income does not itself signify that the table amount is inappropriate,[253] but to make a determination the court must examine the child's means and needs as well as the financial circumstances of the parents.[254] This onus is not discharged simply because an adult child earns a modest income and receives benefits from a registered educational scholarship plan, although these factors may be appropriate for consideration when dealing with the child's post-secondary education expenses under section 7(e) of the *Federal Child Support Guidelines*.[255]

The fact that the adult children enjoy a higher lifestyle than that of the payor does not necessarily justify judicial deviation from the presumptive rule.[256]

The initial approach under section 3(2) of the Guidelines involves a determination of the applicable table amount, together with such amounts for special or extraordinary expenses as may be justified under section 7 of the Guidelines. Only when the court considers that approach inappropriate can the court invoke the broader discretionary jurisdiction that is exercisable under section 3(2) of the Guidelines, having regard to the condition, means, needs, and other circumstances of the child, and the financial ability of each spouse to contribute

---

247 *Lu v Sun*, [2005] NSJ No 314 (CA); *Bury v Beaton*, 2012 NSSC 37; see also *PRM v BJM*, 2012 BCSC 1795 at paras 114–15.

248 *MT v JS*, 2020 BCSC 203; *Mastin v Mastin*, 2019 NSSC 248; *Easton v Coxhead*, 2018 ONSC 4784; *Trecroce v Chorney*, 2023 ONSC 96; compare *Birch v Birch*, 2010 ONSC 2915; *Caravello v Wickett*, 2011 ONSC 3702.

249 See *Proctor v Klammer*, 2023 ONSC 5279 at para 10; compare *MT v JS*, 2023 BCCA 64.

250 *Sherlow v Zubko*, [1999] AJ No 644 (QB); *Rebenchuk v Rebenchuk*, 2007 MBCA 22; *Collins v Collins*, 2010 NLTD(F) 15; *Radford v Radford*, 2010 SKQB 157.

251 *Van Der Voort v Keating*, [2006] NSJ No 9 (SC); *Simmons v Wilcox*, [2001] OJ No 2923 (SCJ) (father with annual income of $100,000 not entitled to contribution from mother with annual income of $27,252).

252 *Sherlow v Zubko*, [1999] AJ No 644 (QB); *Glen v Glen*, [1997] BCJ No 2806 (SC); *Rebenchuk v Rebenchuk*, 2007 MBCA 22; *Sharma v Sharma*, 2022 MBQB 27; *Cook v Cook*, 2016 NBQB 55; *Penney v Boland*, [1999] NJ No 71 (UFC); *MacLennan v MacLennan*, [2003] NSJ No 15 (CA); *Birch v Birch*, 2010 ONSC 2915; *Nkwazi v Nkwazi*, 2014 SKCA 61. Compare *Canada v Canada-Somers*, 2008 MBCA 59; *Hansen v Roy*, [2009] OJ No 282 at paras 134–35 (SCJ). And see *WPN v BJN*, [2005] BCJ No 12 (CA).

253 *Radford v Radford*, 2010 SKQB 157.

254 *Jordan v Jordan*, [2005] SJ No 168 (QB) (adjournment granted to allow relevant information to be provided).

255 *Penney v Boland*, [1999] NJ No 71 (UFC); *Kusnir v Kusnir*, [2001] OJ No 3491 (Ct J); *Katerynych v Hamel*, [2004] SJ No 329 (QB).

256 *Oswald v Oswald*, [2001] MJ No 73 (QB).

to the support of the child.[257] The words "inappropriate approach" in section 3(2)(b) of the Guidelines may be interpreted as signifying an unreasonable amount of child support. If section 3(2)(b) of the Guidelines is triggered, the court must undertake the budget driven approach that was in vogue before implementation of the Guidelines.[258]

The judicial flexibility conferred by section 3(2) of the Guidelines is justified by the generally different situations of adult children and of children under the age of majority. The language of section 3(2)(b) of the Guidelines does not inform courts how they are to determine whether the table amount of support is inappropriate, although such a conclusion has been perceived as the exception rather than the rule.[259] The amount of child support ordered pursuant to section 3(2) may be higher or lower than the table amount, depending upon the circumstances,[260] such as the additional costs attributable to an adult child's reasonable pursuit of post-secondary education at an out-of-town university, or the ability of the child to contribute to his or her own living and university expenses.[261]

There is insufficient judicial consistency of approach to lay down any hard-and-fast rules with respect to adult children who are pursuing university studies while living at home or away from home. Helpful guidance has been furnished, however, by the following analysis of Martinson J of the Supreme Court of British Columbia in *Wesemann v Wesemann*.[262] The law relating to adult children involves a four-step process. The court must first determine whether an adult child falls within the definition of a "child of the marriage" under section 2(1) of the *Divorce Act*. Secondly, the court must determine whether the approach of applying the Guidelines as if the child were under the age of majority is challenged. If not, the court shall apply the same criteria as those applicable to children under the age of majority. Thirdly, if this approach is challenged, the court must determine whether the challenger has satisfied the burden of proving that it is inappropriate. If not, the usual guidelines apply. Fourthly, if the usual guidelines approach is proven to be inappropriate, the court must decide what amount is appropriate, having regard to the condition, means, needs, and other circumstances of the child and the financial ability of each parent to contribute to the support of the child. Where it is appropriate to apply the same approach under the Guidelines to adult children as that applied to children under the age of provincial majority, this can result in an order for the applicable table amount or an order for the applicable table amount and

---

257 *SDB v PW*, [1998] NSJ No 565 (Fam Ct); *Hiebert v Hiebert*, [2007] SJ No 569 (QB).

258 *Welsh v Welsh*, [1998] OJ No 4550 (Gen Div).

259 *Rebenchuk v Rebenchuk*, 2007 MBCA 22, citing *Lewi v Lewi*, [2006] OJ No 1847 at para 129 (CA); *Sharma v Sharma*, 2022 MBQB 27.

260 *Whitley v Whitley*, [1997] BCJ No 3116 (SC); see also *Wambolt v Wambolt*, [2008] NBJ No 63 (SC) (disabled parent relieved of child support obligation); compare *Hunchak v Anton*, 2016 SKCA 44.

261 *Whitley v Whitley*, [1997] BCJ No 3116 (SC); *Flemming v Flemming*, [2009] OJ No 566 (Div Ct); *Rudulier v Rudulier*, [1999] SJ No 366 (QB).

262 [1999] BCJ No 1387 (SC); see also *Montalto v Montalto*, 2011 ABQB 574; *Gron v Gron*, 2021 BCSC 1375; *Hosseini v Kazemi*, 2021 BCSC 1938; *JCW v JKRW*, 2024 BCSC 139; *Rebenchuk v Rebenchuk*, 2007 MBCA 22; *Winstanley v Winstanley*, 2016 MBCA 17; *Swerid v Swerid*, 2022 MBQB 94; *Pollock v Rioux* [2004] NBJ No 467 (CA); *Mathusz v Carew*, 2011 NLTD(F) 28; *MacEachern v MacLeod*, 2014 NSSC 238; *Edwards v Edwards*, 2018 ONSC 6869; *Laramie v Laramie*, 2018 ONSC 4740; *Urquhart v Loane*, 2016 PECA 15; *Wionzek v Magyar*, 2013 SKQB 194, citing *Geran v Geran*, 2011 SKCA 55 at para 21; *HAP v DBC*, 2015 YKSC 4. Compare *WPN v BJN*, [2005] BCJ No 12 (CA), *De Beck v De Beck*, 2012 BCCA 465, and *McClement v McClement*, 2017 BCCA 416, discussed below in the text.

an additional amount under section 7 of the Guidelines for the expenses of post-secondary education. Justice Martinson suggests a third alternative whereby an order could be made under section 7 of the Guidelines without any table amount, but this suggestion negates the significance of the word "and" that links paragraphs (a) and (b) in section 3(1) of the Guidelines. This third alternative would be available, however, by recourse to section 3(2)(b) of the Guidelines in circumstances where the concurrent allocation of the applicable table amount is inappropriate.[263] Section 3(2) of the Guidelines does not inform a court how to determine whether or not the usual guidelines approach is appropriate. The usual guidelines approach is based on certain factors that normally apply to children under the age of majority, namely, they reside with one or both parents, are not earning an income, and are financially dependent on their parents. The closer the circumstances of an adult child are to those upon which the usual guidelines approach is based, the less likely it is that the usual guidelines approach will be found inappropriate. The opposite is also true. Children over the age of majority may reside away from home and/or earn a significant income, or they may have access to government grants or other resources.[264] In these circumstances, the adult child's expenses will be quite different from those of a typical child under the age of majority. And as Caldwell JA of the Saskatchewan Court of Appeal pointed out in *Wetsch v Kuski*,[265] the application of section 3(2)(a) of the Guidelines will be inappropriate where a payor parent has established that a basic assumption underpinning the table amounts has been displaced, in which case section 3(2)(b) of the Guidelines should be applied. In exercising the discretion to move away from the usual approach under the Guidelines, a court will find it helpful to consider (1) the reasonable needs of the child; (2) the ability and opportunity of the child to contribute to those needs; and (3) the ability of the parents to contribute to those needs. The reasonable needs of the child has two aspects, namely (1) the child's needs for accommodation, food, clothing, and miscellaneous expenses; and (2) the child's actual post-secondary expenses. Children have an obligation to make a reasonable contribution to their own post-secondary education or training. This does not signify that all of a child's income should be applied to the costs of the child's further education. A child should be entitled to some personal benefit from the fruits of his or her labours.[266] It is not appropriate to require a child to pursue part-time employment during the academic year where that would interfere with the child's academic progress,[267] nor should the availability of student loans automatically require the child to obtain such loans. Student loans are not to be equated with bursaries, grants, or scholarships. A student loan delays the payment of expenses, rather than defraying them. After considering the ability of both parents to contribute to an adult child's reasonable needs,

---

263 See *JABD v RAB*, 2012 PESC 6. See also *CM v GM*, 2020 NBCA 17 at para 25.

264 See *Jensen v Jensen*, 2018 BCSC 283; *Erdman v Erdman*, 2024 BCSC 119; *Wetsch v Kuski*, 2017 SKCA 77; see also *Mastin v Mastin*, 2019 NSSC 248.

265 *Wetsch v Kuski*, 2017 SKCA 77 at para 58; see also *MacLennan v MacLennan*, 2021 SKCA 132.

266 *Montalto v Montalto*, 2011 ABQB 574; *Wesemann v Wesemann*, [1999] BCJ No 1387 (SC); *Winsemann v Donaldson*, 2007 BCSC 1322; *Matwichuk v Stephenson*, 2007 BCSC 1589; *Rebenchuk v Rebenchuk*, 2007 MBCA 22; *Greenham v Woodfine Greenham*, 2015 NLTD(F) 2; *Lee v Lee*, 2009 NSSC 121; *Coghill v Coghill*, [2006] OJ No 2602 (SCJ); *Jahn-Cartwright v Cartwright*, 2010 ONSC 923; *Marsh v Jashewski*, 2011 ONSC 3793; compare *Fernquist v Garland*, [2005] SJ No 747 (QB).

267 *Coghill v Coghill*, [2006] OJ No 2602 (SCJ); *Jahn-Cartwright v Cartwright*, 2010 ONSC 923.

the court may choose to apportion the parental contributions in accordance with section 7 of the Guidelines.[268]

After reviewing relevant caselaw, including *Wesemann v Wesemann*, the British Columbia Court of Appeal, in *WPN v BJN*,[269] concluded that, even when a party has not challenged the appropriateness of applying the presumptive rule pursuant to section 3(2)(a) of the Guidelines, it is open to the court to find the application of the presumptive rule to be inappropriate on the facts of the particular case,[270] in which event the court should apply section 3(2)(b) of the Guidelines and order an appropriate amount of child support having regard to the condition, means, needs, and other circumstances of the child and the financial ability of each parent to contribute to the support of the child. Given a reasonable expectation that an adult child will contribute to his or her own expenses and the fact that the table amount is based solely on the obligor's income and can take no account of the child's contribution, Levine JA of the British Columbia Court of Appeal stated that, in principle, support for an adult child who is in attendance at a post-secondary institution should generally be determined under section 3(2)(b) of the Guidelines.[271] The British Columbia Court of Appeal further concluded that concurrent orders may be made under section 3(2)(b) and section 7 of the Guidelines[272] and suggested that a separation agreement providing for specific expenses might lead to such an approach. In cases where an adult child is attending a post-secondary institution while living at home with one of the parents, it makes a good deal of sense to allocate the table amount of child support to the parent who is providing a home for the child and to take account of the adult child's income from summer or part-time employment in determining the adult child's contribution to his or her post-secondary education expenses under section 7(2) of the *Federal Child Support Guidelines*.[273] Such an approach will be inappropriate, however, where the adult child's income substantially exceeds the post-secondary expenses and the adult child can reasonably be expected to contribute to the residential parent's costs.[274] In *De Beck v De Beck*,[275] Smith JA of the British Columbia Court of Appeal qualified the observations of Levine JA, in *WPN v BJN*, above, by stating that

---

268 *Wesemann v Wesemann*, [1999] BCJ No 1387 (SC); *Jordan v Stewart*, 2013 ONSC 902; *da Silva v Moreira*, 2020 ONSC 5167; *Jackson v Jackson*, 2021 ONSC 2614; compare *Fernquist v Garland*, [2005] SJ No 747 (QB).

269 [2005] BCJ No 12 (CA). See also *Beissner v Matheusik*, 2015 BCCA 308; *Cole v Cole*, 2016 BCSC 716; *Mohamed v Martone*, 2019 BCSC 38; *Rebenchuk v Rebenchuk*, 2007 MBCA 22; *Park v Thompson*, 2005 CanLII 14132 (CA); *Lewi v Lewi*, [2006] OJ No 1847 (CA); *Minish v Timmons*, 2021 ONSC 7622; *EAM v SHM*, 2018 PESC 19; *Royko v Royko*, 2008 SKQB 112, [2008] SJ No 155 (QB). Compare *De Beck v De Beck*, 2012 BCCA 465 at paras 54–58; *Pollock v Rioux*, [2004] NBJ No 467 (CA); *Simon v Adey*, 2012 NBCA 63; *LPS v MSF*, 2015 NBCA 23; *TMR v SMS*, 2019 NBQB 40; *Wionzek v Magyar*, 2013 SKQB 194.

270 See *Cole v Cole*, 2016 BCSC 716.

271 *Cole v Cole*, 2016 BCSC 716. See, to like effect, *Hojnik v Hojnik*, 2010 ABCA 192; *Rebenchuk v Rebenchuk* 2007 MBCA 22; *Price v Holman-Price*, 2014 NLTD(F) 30; *Park v Thompson*, 2005 CanLII 14132 (CA); *Lewi v Lewi*, [2006] OJ No1847 (CA); *EAM v SHM*, 2018 PESC 19, citing *Urquhart v Loane*, 2016 PECA 15; *Geran v Geran*, 2011 SKCA 55. Compare *De Beck v De Beck*, 2012 BCCA 465 at para 56; *Pollock v Rioux*, [2004] NBJ No 467 (CA), discussed in text below.

272 See also *Cole v Cole*, 2016 BCSC 716.

273 See *Leis v Leis*, 2014 ABCA 36.

274 *Meyer v Content*, 2014 ONSC 6001.

275 *De Beck v De Beck*, 2012 BCCA 465; see also *Lerner v Lerner*, 2013 BCSC 239 at paras 43–44; *PG v DDG* 2017 BCSC 724; *Nicholl v Nicholl*, 2020 BCCA 173.

[j]ust as the absence of a challenge to the "usual *Guidelines* approach" under s. 3(2)(a) should not preclude a consideration of s. 3(2)(b), similarly the fact that an adult child is attending a post-secondary institution while living at home should not in my view foreclose a consideration of the approach under s. 3(2)(a). In each case, the choice between applying s. 3(2)(a) and s. 3(2)(b) will be a discretionary one that will be governed by the circumstances of that case.

Summarizing the current position, Harris JA of the British Court of Appeal in *McClement v McClement*, observed:

[12] In sum, the choice between the two sections is discretionary and determined by the particular circumstances of each case and there is no specific requirement formally to challenge relying on s. 3(2)(a) before a judge can consider whether it is inappropriate to apply that subsection rather than s. 3(2)(b) and or vice versa. The view taken by this Court is that the burden of proof rests with each party in the ordinary manner to persuade the court which of the two sections is the appropriate one to apply in the particular circumstances before the court. There are of course factors that tend to support the appropriateness of relying on one section rather than another and which guide the exercise of a judge's discretion. For example, the more closely the circumstances of the adult child resemble those of a minor child living at home, the less likely it is that the approach found in s. 3(2)(a) will be determined to be inappropriate. Each case will depend on its facts.[276]

There is caselaw in Nova Scotia asserting that the table amount of support is inappropriate for an adult child who attends a post-secondary educational institution away from home because there is no sharing of common expenses in the parent's household and double-accounting for such expenses as food and accommodation must be avoided.[277] In *Hagen v Rankin*,[278] the Saskatchewan Court of Appeal pointed out that a court should not allocate the table amount of support under the Guidelines to a parent with whom an adult child is living while pursuing post-secondary education, if the child is reasonably capable of making a significant contribution towards his or her own support. Judicial deviation from the presumptive rule in favour of the table amount, which arises from the combined operation of sections 3(1) and 3(2)(a) of the Guidelines, is appropriate under section 3(2)(b) of the Guidelines where the actual means and needs of the child warrant a lower amount of support than the normal table amount. And, as is pointed out in the judgment of the Saskatchewan Court of Appeal in *Geran v Geran*,[279] when children attend university away from home, courts do not normally resort to the table amount but to the means and needs approach set out in section 3(2)(b) of the *Federal Child Support Guidelines*.

276 2017 BCCA 416 at para 12; see also *Briggs v Kasdorf*, 2020 BCSC 1702; *LF v RB*, 2021 BCSC 464; *Erdman v Erdman*, 2024 BCSC 119.

277 *HBC v CEM* (2002), 208 NSR (2d) 97 at para 14 (Fam Ct); *Everill v Everill*, [2005] NSJ No 37 (SC); compare *Van Der Voort v Keating*, [2006] NSJ No 9 (SC); *RM v AM*, 2018 BCSC 318.

278 [2002] SJ No 15 (CA); see also *Geran v Geran*, 2011 SKCA 55; *CC v KK*, 2020 PESC 16.

279 2011 SKCA 55. See also *Damphouse v Damphouse*, 2020 ABQB 101 at para 54, citing *Wahl v Wahl*, 2000 ABQB 10; *WPN v BJN*, [2005] BCJ No 12 (CA); *MT v JS*, 2020 BCSC 203; *Rebenchuk v Rebenchuk*, 2007 MBCA 22; *Lewi v Lewi*, [2006] OJ No 1847 (CA); *Coghill v Coghill*, [2006] OJ No 2602 (SCJ); compare *Pollock v Rioux*, [2004] NBJ No 467 (CA); *Simon v Adey*, 2012 NBCA 63; *TMR v SMS*, 2019 NBQB 40; *BM v PM*, 2019 SKQB 36.

In quantifying support for an adult child who is pursuing a reasonable program of post-secondary education, section 113(2)(b) of the *Family Services Act* (New Brunswick) confers discretionary authority on a trial court to depart from the presumptive rule in favour of the applicable table amount of child support, if it finds that "amount" to be inappropriate having regard to the condition, means, needs, and other circumstances of the child and the financial ability of each parent to contribute to the support of the child. Section 3(2) of the *Federal Child Support Guidelines*, on the other hand, confers a discretionary judicial power to deviate from the presumptive rule in favour of the table amount when the court considers that "approach" to be inappropriate. The terminological differences between section 113(2)(b) of the *Family Services Act* and section 3(2) of the *Federal Child Support Guidelines* are insignificant. In *Pollock v Rioux*,[280] Richard JA of the New Brunswick Court of Appeal articulated the following criteria for determining the issue of ongoing support for an adult child who is unable to withdraw from the charge of her or his parents by reason of legitimate post-secondary educational pursuits:

> Thus, in the usual case, the analytical framework for the determination of support consistent with s. 113(2)(*b*) of the *Family Services Act*, s. 3(2) of the *Guidelines* and the principles set out in *Francis v. Baker*, for a child who is at or over the age of majority but who is still eligible for support pursuant to the *Family Services Act*, is as follows:
>
> 1. There is a presumption that support for an eligible child at or over the age of majority will be determined pursuant to s. 3(1) of the *Guidelines*—that is the table amount plus any amount determined under s. 7.
> 2. If the application of the presumptive rule is challenged, the presumption can be rebutted by either the claimant or the parent against whom the order is sought by clear and compelling evidence that the approach set out in s. 3(1) of the *Guidelines* is inappropriate—that is unsuitable for the determination of the support.
> 3. If the approach set out in s. 3(1) of the *Guidelines* is found to be appropriate, the court must determine the amount of support pursuant to that approach.
> 4. There is a presumption that the amount established pursuant to s. 3(1) of the *Guidelines* is appropriate but, like the other presumption, it can be rebutted by clear and compelling evidence that it is unsuitable.
> 5. If either the approach or the amount is shown to be inappropriate, the court must determine the amount that "it considers appropriate, having regard to the condition, means, needs and other circumstances of the child and the financial ability of each parent to contribute to the support of the child."

This framework set out is consistent with the four-step procedure set out above by Martinson J in *Wesemann v Wesemann*. In responding to counsel's submission in *Simon v Addy* that New Brunswick should endorse the practice of other provincial appellate courts by holding the presumption in favour of the table amount to be effectively rebutted when the adult child is living away from home while pursuing post-secondary education, the New Brunswick Court of Appeal disagreed, stating that "[i]t is incumbent upon the motion judge

280 2004 NBCA 98 at para 40. Compare *TMR v SMS*, 2019 NBQB 40. See also *Leis v Leis*, 2014 ABCA 36; *Mulders v Mulders*, 2014 NWTSC 50; *MEL v PRH*, 2018 NBQB 224; *CM v GM*, 2020 NBCA 17.

281 2012 NBCA 63; see also *LPS v MSF*, 2015 NBCA 23.

to conduct an analysis using the framework articulated above, and reach a determination based on the facts of the case. It may be that the result of the analysis is a determination the Guidelines amount is inappropriate, but that is by no means a certain outcome."

The following principles set out in *Francis v Baker*[282] in the context of section 4 of the *Federal Child Support Guidelines* apply equally to an analysis of section 3(2) of the Guidelines. The word "inappropriate" must be broadly defined to mean "unsuitable" rather than "inadequate"; consequently, courts may either increase or reduce the amount specified in the tables. In addition, there must be clear and compelling evidence that the table amount of child support is inappropriate.[283] Where no challenge to the application of the table amount has been presented, the presumptive rule must be applied and judicial deviation from the applicable table amount constitutes a reversible error on an appeal. After determining the applicable table amount, the court must determine what amount, if any, should be allocated under section 7 of the Guidelines to meet the adult child's university expenses. Given that the adult child's room and board expenses are already covered by the applicable table amount of child support, the section 7 expenses for the child's post-secondary education will be limited to expenses for tuition, books and supplies, education-related transportation costs, and other incidental expenses relating to the university program. Where these expenses are less than the amount that the adult child can personally pay through summer employment, part-time employment, and student loans, no order will be granted under section 7 of the Guidelines.[284] In *Menegaldo v Menegaldo*,[285] Chappel J of the Ontario Superior Court of Justice set out the following summary of various approaches taken by the courts as to how child support should be determined in cases involving children who attend school away from home for all or a part of the year:

1. In some cases, the courts have determined that the appropriate approach is to calculate the actual costs of providing for the needs of the child during the entire year, factoring in a contribution towards the costs to the recipient of maintaining a residence for the child to return home to on weekends and during the summer, and apportioning the amount between the parents after taking into account the appropriate amount that the child should contribute. Other courts have adopted the same approach, without adding in an amount for the cost to the recipient of maintaining a home base for the children.
2. Some courts have made what can be described as "bifurcated orders," ordering the *Table* amount for the period of time when the child is residing with the recipient, and directing the parents to each pay a share of the child's total expenses for the remaining months of the school year, including both living expenses and education expenses, reduced by the appropriate amount of the child's contribution.
3. Other courts have adopted the approach set out in subsection 2 above, with the exception that they have also factored in the recipient parent's costs of maintaining a residence for the child to return home to during the summer and for holidays.

---

282 [1999] 3 SCR 250.

283 See *Klette v Leland*, 2014 SKCA 122.

284 *Pollock v Rioux*, [2004] NBJ No 467 (CA); *GES v FC*, 2012 NBQB 165; see also *MEL v PRH*, 2018 NBQB 224; *TMR v SMS*, 2019 NBQB 40.

285 2012 ONSC 2915 at para 176. See also *VanSickle v VanSickle*, 2012 ONSC 7340; *Almeida v Malek-Gilani*, 2018 ONSC 5699.

4. The trial judge in *Lewi* adopted the approach outlined in subsection 2 above, with the exception that she pro-rated the total *Table* amount payable for the period of time the child would be residing with the recipient during the year over the course of twelve months. The Ontario Court of Appeal in *Lewi* determined that this approach would have been appropriate if it had been taken globally pursuant to section 3(2)(b) rather than as a two step analysis involving the determination of an appropriate *Table* amount and then a section 7 analysis, as the trial judge had done. It is significant, however, that the court commented that this approach may not be the most appropriate from the perspective of the recipient, in that it fails to recognize the ongoing costs to the recipient of maintaining a home for the child to return to during the summers and other holiday periods. Thus, the court endorsed the possibility that where the full *Table* amount of child support is ordered for the time that a child is at home while attending post secondary education, it may be appropriate for the recipient to also receive not only a contribution towards the child's expenses during the school year but also a contribution towards the cost of maintaining their own residence as a home base for the child.
5. In other cases, the courts have ordered the *Table* amount for the months when the child is home during the summer, a specified percentage of the *Table* amount each month for the months when the child is away at school for the recipient to cover the child's living needs, and a proportion of the child's education expenses (i.e. tuition, residence, books and supplies).

The applicable table amount of support for an adult child pursuing post-secondary education or training may be deemed inappropriate because of the obligor's ill health and reduced income[286] or the child's ability to make a financial contribution.[287]

In addressing section 3(2)(b) of the *Federal Child Support Guidelines*, the court should consider (1) pre-break-up plans; (2) necessity; (3) effort and aptitude; and (4) ability to pay. The question whether it is necessary for the child to attend an out-of-town post-secondary institution ultimately depends on the facts of the case. In the context of necessity, the court may also address particular expenses. While the acquisition of a computer may be found to be necessary, the court may limit the parental contribution towards the child's transportation costs between the university and his hometown.[288]

The ability of an adult child to cover the expenses of attending university with a student loan does not mean that the child has withdrawn from parental charge.[289] Such a child may still be a "child of the marriage" within the meaning of section 2(1) of the *Divorce Act* who is entitled to support. Where an application for child support specifically seeks assistance relating to the post-secondary education expenses, the court may conclude that it is inappro priate to determine support on the basis of section 3(2)(a) of the *Federal Child Support Guidelines*, whereby support would be calculated in accordance with the applicable provin cial table, with further consideration being given to the post-secondary education expenses

---

286 *Clark v Clark*, [1997] NBJ No 432 (QB).

287 *Hojnik v Hojnik*, 2010 ABCA 192; *Peters v Peters*, [2002] NSJ No 413 (SC); *Higgins v Higgins*, [2001] OJ No 3011 (SCJ); *Hagen v Rankin*, [2002] SJ No 15 (CA); *Geran v Geran*, 2011 SKCA 55; *Kozak v Moore*, 2020 SKQB 22.

288 *MacPherson v MacPherson*, [2005] OJ No 3448 (SCJ).

289 *Chapple v Campbell*, [2005] MJ No 323 (QB).

pursuant to sections 7(1)(e) and 7(2). That approach being deemed inappropriate, section 3(2)(b) provides that support shall be assessed in the amount that the court considers appropriate, having regard to the condition, means, needs, and other circumstances of the child and the financial ability of each spouse to contribute to the support of the child. Where the means of the parents are limited and the expenses are substantial, the court may conclude that there shall be some combination of contribution by the child and each parent, having regard to scholarships, bursaries, and savings of the child. Once a determination has been made that child support is to be addressed under section 3(2)(b) of the *Federal Child Support Guidelines*, it has been held that the entirety of the analysis, including with respect to post-secondary expenses, should be conducted under section 3(2)(b). However, the court may draw on the principles set out in section 7 of the *Federal Child Support Guidelines* and may find it helpful to do so.[290] Given the difference in wording between section 3(2)(b) and section 7(2) of the *Federal Child Support Guidelines*, section 3(2)(b) does not necessarily require that the parental contribution be shared in proportion to their respective incomes, even if each parent must contribute according to his or her financial ability to do so. In determining the respective contribution of each parent, the court may consider the fact that one parent will be providing a home for the child during those months that the child is not in attendance at university,[291] although it is open to the court to address these costs by an order for the payment of the applicable provincial table amount for those months of the academic year that adult children live at home with one of the parents.[292]

The fact that an adult child is earning income is relevant but not determinative of the question whether it would be inappropriate to apply the provisions of section 3(2)(a) of the Guidelines because it is necessary to consider the desirability of allowing the child to receive some personal benefit from the fruits of his or her labours. Additional factors to be considered in determining the question include the relative means and financial abilities of the parents to contribute to the support of the child and the reasonableness of the child being wholly or partly supported while pursuing a college education.[293] If section 3(1)(a) of the Guidelines is deemed applicable, the basic amount of child support fixed by the applicable provincial table cannot be reduced to reflect the child's ability to contribute to his or her own support, but any supplementary amount ordered pursuant to section 7 of the Guidelines will be determined having regard to the guiding principle set out in section 7(2), whereby the expense is shared by the spouses in proportion to their respective incomes after deducting from the expense the contribution, if any, from the child.[294] Judicial determination of a parent's "ability . . . to contribute to the support of the child" within the meaning of section 3(2)(b) of the Guidelines may take account of that parent's reduced household

290 *Easton v Coxhead*, 2018 ONSC 4784 at para 81, Madsen J.

291 *Karhoffer v Karhoffer*, [2002] BCJ No 2550 (SC); *Michie v Michie*, [1997] SJ No 668 (QB); compare *Johnson v Johnson*, [1998] BCJ No 1080 (SC). See also *Wilkins v Wilkins*, [1998] NBJ No 325 (QB) (deviation from proportionate sharing because of parental debt load); *Erickson v Erickson*, [1999] NSJ No 159 (SC) (parent with whom child residing unable to contribute to university expenses other than by way of providing accommodation and food; non-resident parent to bear full responsibility).

292 *Lavdovsky v Lavdovsky*, [1998] BCJ No 1952 (SC); *Davis v Davis*, [1999] BCJ No 1832 (SC); *Simpson v Palma*, [1998] SJ No 581 (QB); compare *Green v Green*, [2005] NJ No 165 at paras 32–36 (CA).

293 *Ibid*; *Chapple v Campbell*, [2005] MJ No 323 (QB).

294 *Ibid.*

costs arising from the presumed contribution of his or her present spouse to their common household expenses.[295] The inquiry involves determining what the parents can reasonably be expected to contribute towards their children's post-secondary education; it is not just an exercise of apportioning what may be reasonable expenses. In determining a parent's ability to pay, the court may take note of the amount of table support that would have been ordered if section 3(2)(a) had been applied. Although the table amount is not determinative of the ability to pay, it is one of the circumstances to be taken into account.[296] Where more than one child is pursuing post-secondary education, the court should examine each child's situation independently in light of their particular expenses and the ability of each child to contribute towards his or her expenses.[297] In determining the parental contributions to the adult child's living and university expenses pursuant to section 3(2)(b) of the Guidelines, there is no guiding principle similar to that under section 7(2) of the Guidelines whereby a proportionate sharing will be ordered in accordance with the respective parental incomes, but the application of such a principle makes sense when section 3(2)(b) of the Guidelines is read in conjunction with section 1(a) of the Guidelines, which stipulates that one of the objectives of the Guidelines is "to establish a fair standard of support for children that ensures that they continue to benefit from the financial means of both spouses after separation."[298]

A court is more likely to order the applicable table amount of support with respect to an adult child attending university, where that child is pursuing his or her studies while living at home with a parent and any other siblings.[299] In addition to ordering the table amount of basic child support in these circumstances, the court may order a contribution towards tuition, books, and incidental expenses pursuant to section 7 of the Guidelines,[300] unless the child can be reasonably expected to meet these expenses.[301] A court should not simply pro rate allowable section 7 expenses based on the annual income of each parent; it should also pay some attention to the financial ability of each parent to contribute to the expenses. The table amount of support under the *Federal Child Support Guidelines* may be deemed inappropriate for an adult child attending a hometown university, where the child is capable of contributing to his or her own support from earned income.[303] The Guidelines may, nevertheless, provide a useful standard of comparison to determine the proper amount of child support to be paid pursuant to section 3(2) of the Guidelines, having regard to the condition, means, needs, and other circumstances of the child and the ability of each parent to contribute to the support of the child.[304] Where an adult child resides with neither parent during his or her out-of-town post-secondary education or training, thereby incurring separate living

295 *MacDonald v Rasmussen*, [2000] SJ No 660 (QB).

296 *Ibid.*

297 *Ibid.*

298 *Power v Hunt*, [2000] NJ No 315 (UFC); *Taylor v Taylor*, [2002] NJ No 52 (SC); see also *Greenham v Woodfine Greenham*, 2015 NLTD(F) 2; *Higgins v Higgins*, [2001] OJ No 3011 (SCJ).

299 *Sherlow v Zubko*, [1999] AJ No 644 (QB) (child support to be reviewed if children pursued post-secondary education away from home); *Glen v Glen* (1998), 34 RFL (4th) 105 (BCSC); *Lewi v Lewi*, [2006] OJ No 1847 (CA); *Radford v Radford*, 2010 SKQB 157.

300 *Ibid.*

301 *Mills v Mills*, [1999] SJ No 177 (QB).

302 *Donald v Brown*, [2005] SJ No 692 (QB).

303 *Hagen v Rankin*, [2002] SJ No 15 (CA); *Geran v Geran*, 2011 SKCA 55; *Kozak v Moore*, 2020 SKQB 22.

304 *Phillipchuk v Phillipchuk*, [1999] AJ No 438 (QB).

expenses such as shelter and utilities, and the child can contribute towards his or her own living expenses and educational expenses, a court will be more inclined to apply section 3(2)(b) of the Guidelines in assessing the parental contribution to the child's support.[305] A court may refrain from ordering the table amount of child support and simply order that the cost of the adult child's education be shared proportionately among the child and both parties in accordance with section 7 of the Guidelines.[306] Where the presumptive rule in favour of the table amount is found inappropriate, the court may take a practical approach by ordering lump sum payments to coincide with the adult child's need to pay tuition, book, and residence fees. In determining the appropriate amount of child support to be paid, the court may devise a formula to avoid the need for re-litigation and in so doing may take account of the potential ability of the child to contribute towards his own expenses.[307] Although the table amount of child support is usually inappropriate where one of several children of the marriage is attending an out-of-town university, a parent may reasonably expect the child to attend the hometown university if the desired course of study is offered there, in which event the table amount of child support may be deemed appropriate. Special expenses associated with the university program may be the subject of a supplemental order under section 7 of the Guidelines.[308] In some cases, courts have required parents seeking child support for children attending out-of-town universities to justify the increased expenses incurred.[309] Courts do not normally question the legitimacy of residential costs for children whose career goals can only be met away from home. If the choice to reside away from home is optional and offers no advantages, the adult child may be called upon to contribute a greater portion of the costs of her post-secondary education.[310] If a child wishes to pursue studies away from home, reasonable evidence should be offered to justify that course of action, for example, evidence that the chosen university offers a program that better accommodates the child's anticipated career path than the hometown university.[311] A parent may be relieved from fully subsidizing the increased costs of the child's attendance at a foreign university where attendance at a Canadian university would have been significantly less costly and the parent was not consulted prior to the decision being taken.[312]

A court may refuse to apply section 3(2)(b) of the *Federal Child Support Guidelines* where the parents have negotiated a separation agreement that reflects the presumptive

---

305 *Wahl v Wahl*, [2000] AJ No 29 (QB); *LB v PAV*, 2008 ABQB 623; *WPN v BJN*, [2005] BCJ No 12 (CA); *Wilkins v Wilkins*, [1998] NBJ No 325 (QB); *Sacrey v Sacrey*, [2008] NJ No 392 (UFC); *Coghill v Coghill*, [2006] OJ No 2602 (SCJ); *Park v Thompson*, 2005 CanLII 14132 (CA); *F (ML) v B (IE)*, 2021 ONSC 3522; *Krueger v Tunison*, [1999] SJ No 482 (QB).)

306 *Whitley v Whitley*, [1997] BCJ No 3116 (SC); *Johnson v Johnson*, [1998] BCJ No 1080 (SC).

307 *Watts v Willie*, [2004] BCJ No 1824 (SC).

308 *Woods v Woods*, [1998] SJ No 687 (QB); see also *Degagne v Sargeant*, [1999] AJ No 506 (CA) (very little justification for child attending out-of-town university with consequential travel and accommodation costs when similar program was available locally but appellate court refused to interfere with the order that was of only one year's duration); *Corsano v Simms*, [2002] NSJ No 440 (CA); compare *Kluczny v Kluczny*, [1999] AJ No 1420 (QB) (parent's personal travelling expenses disallowed). And see *BM v PM*, 2019 SKQB 36.

309 *Krupa v Krupa*, 2010 BCSC 1400.

310 *Rebenchuk v Rebenchuk*, 2007 MBCA 22.

311 *Friday v Friday*, 2013 ONSC 1931; *Krueger v Tunison*, [1999] SJ No 482 (QB); *Fergusson v Kurylo*, [2005] SJ No 166 (QB).

312 *Carr v Wilson*, [2005] BCJ No 2353 (SC); *Van Vroenhoven v Van Vroenhoven*, [2009] OJ No 995 (SCJ).

rule set out in section 3(1) of the Guidelines in favour of the applicable table amount of child support and allowable section 7 expenses under the Guidelines. Judicial disturbance of the scheme of child support agreed to by the parents is not justified without a serious reason. Section 3(2)(b) of the *Federal Child Support Guidelines* will normally be applied to an adult child who attends an out-of-town university, but an exception may be made where the parties have addressed this issue in a prior agreement that was sanctioned by the court.[314]

The applicable provincial table amounts for several children reflect economies of scale but only where the children are living under one roof. Economies of scale do not apply where one child is living at home but a second child spends most of the year away from home while attending college. In these circumstances, a needs and means approach to the assessment of support for the child attending college may be more appropriate than an order for the provincial table amount.[315] Where one child is over the age of majority and a second child is under the age of majority, section 3 of the Guidelines empowers the court to compartmentalize child support but a court should avoid separate orders for the two children that would generate an inequitable result for the payor. Whether the court determines the amount of support for the child under the age of majority before or after determining the amount of support payable for the child over the age of majority, the result should be the same.[316]

An adult child is expected to contribute towards his own university and living costs by means of student loans, scholarships, bursaries, summer employment, part-time employment during the academic year, and/or savings. In determining the extent to which the child should maximize his summer earnings, the court may take account of the relationship between the summer employment and the adult child's chosen field of university study. The economic impact of parental remarriage or entry into a common law relationship may be considered in determining an apportionment of the child's post-secondary education and living expenses.[318] It is appropriate that recourse be had to RESP funds before looking to other sources of support for post-secondary education expenses.[319]

The applicant and child may be judicially required to keep the payor parent fully informed about the child's educational progress and expenses and about the child's employment income and student loans.[320] The court may order that a parent be provided with copies of the child's academic transcripts and with proof of continuing enrolment in a post-secondary educational institution.[321]

If the applicable provincial table amount is deemed appropriate for a child attending college, it will be necessary to exclude the residence, meals, and other costs that are subsumed in the table amount from any supplementary order for post-secondary expenses under section 7

313 *Etienne v Etienne*, [2002] OJ No 4220 (SCJ).

314 *CMP v PEP*, [1999] AJ No 1478 (QB); *MacPherson v MacPherson*, [2005] OJ No 3448 (SCJ).

315 *Blair v Blair*, [1997] OJ No 4949 (Gen Div); *Samson v Samson*, [2003] NJ No 289 (SC); *Urquhart v Loane*, 2016 PECA 15; compare *Burzminski v Burzminski (Lewis)*, 2010 SKCA 16.

316 *Foster v Foster*, [2000] OJ No 4006 (SCJ); see also *Burzminski v Burzminski (Lewis)*, 2010 SKCA 16.

317 *MacPherson v MacPherson*, [2005] OJ No 3448 (SCJ).

318 *Ibid.*

319 *Crisp v Crisp*, 2012 ONSC 521.

320 *MacPherson v MacPherson*, [2005] OJ No 3448 (SCJ); see also *Kusnir v Kusnir*, [2001] OJ No 3491 (Ct J); *SB v RB*, [2000] QJ No 3298 (CS).

321 *Woods v Woods*, [1998] SJ No 687 (QB); *Kusnir v Kusnir*, [2001] OJ No 3491 (CS).

of the *Federal Child Support Guidelines*.[322] Given the impossibility of breaking down the table amount into specific components, any adjustment of the supplementary order to take account of the food costs will involve a high degree of judicial discretion.[323] Clothing expenses, spending money, and personal expenses should be excluded from allowable section 7 expenses because they are covered by the applicable table amount of child support and, unlike food costs, are movable and not dependent on "economy of scale" that underlies the applicable table amount of child support.[324] Double counting must also be avoided if the court addresses the issue of out-of-town college expenses before determining the potential application of the monthly table amount of child support established by the Guidelines.[325] In the absence of evidence of any marginal costs incurred by the parent with whom the children live when they are not attending college, the court may conclude that it is appropriate to supplement the special college expenses by an order providing for the payment of the applicable provincial table amount of child support for those months that the children live at home. The court may further conclude that, rather than changing the monthly amount payable, an average monthly amount shall be payable throughout the year.[326] The provincial table amount of child support for two children may be appropriate where the older child has attained the age of majority but is also living with the parent while attending college.[327]

In assessing a child's personal capacity to contribute to his own post-secondary education, a court may take account of trust funds beneficially owned by the child,[328] even though the child does not have unfettered control over the trust asset.[329] Both sections 3(2)(b) and 7 of the *Federal Child Support Guidelines* require the court to consider whether children over the age of majority are able to make a contribution to their post-secondary education out of capital assets. Although a court lacks jurisdiction to compel adult children to expend trust funds to underwrite the costs of their post-secondary education, the amount of support payable by a parent may be reduced to reflect the children's ability to use their trust funds or a reasonable portion thereof as a contribution towards the costs of their post-secondary education. The term "means," which appears in both sections 3(2)(b) and 7 of the Guidelines, includes both capital assets and income and requires the means of the children as well as those of the parents to be considered in determining the parental contributions towards the costs of the post-secondary education of adult children.[330] There is no provision in the Guidelines that implies that children over the age of majority should contribute all their capital assets towards their post-secondary education before their parents will be required

322 *Degagne v Sargeant*, [1999] AJ No 506 (CA); *BM v ALG*, 2014 NSSC 443; *Blair v Blair*, [1997] OJ No 4949 (Gen Div).

323 *Bruce v Kelly*, [2002] PEIJ No 43 (SC).

324 *Callahan v Callahan*, [2002] NJ No 117 (SC).

325 *Comeau v Newman*, 2021 NBQB 197.

326 *Moss v Moss*, [1997] NJ No 299 (SC). See also *Arsenault v Arsenault*, [1998] NBJ No 401 (QB). Compare *Carbonneau v Carbonneau*, [1998] SJ No 82 (QB), wherein a monthly allocation for accommodation and weekends at home was ordered during the college year in addition to the regular table amount during the summer months.

327 *Miller v McClement*, [1997] SJ No 761 (QB).

328 *Dort v Dort*, 2009 NSSC 372; *Merritt v Merritt*, [1999] OJ No 1732 (SCJ); *Lewi v Lewi*, [2006] OJ No 1847 (CA); *Fearon v Tzeng Fearon*, 2021 ONSC 7545.

329 *Hamoline v Hamoline*, 2014 SKQB 316.

330 *Sharma v Sharma*, 2022 MBQB 27 at para 123, citing *Leskun v Leskun*, 2006 SCC 25.

to provide support, or that such children should not have to make any contribution out of their capital. As a general rule, however, the amount of child support that a parent is ordered to pay should be determined in the expectation that a child with means, such as independent assets, will contribute something from those means towards his or her post-secondary education. The extent of the contribution expected depends on the circumstances of the case. Neither section 3(2)(b) nor section 7 of the Guidelines contains any indication whatsoever of the level of contribution an adult child with capital should be expected to make to his or her post-secondary education expenses. There is no standard formula. Under both provisions, the question is largely a matter of discretion for the trial judge.[331]

Children have a substantial responsibility to contribute towards their own post-secondary education by maximizing their income through scholarships, bursaries, student loans, and summer employment. This does not mean that all of a child's income should necessarily be applied to the costs of the child's further education. The court should consider whether the child should be entitled to some personal benefit from the fruits of his or her labours. If children do not contribute from any of these sources, it may be appropriate to impute a reasonable contribution to them comparable to what they could have provided from any of these sources.[333] Grants, scholarships, and bursaries are generally treated as a reduction of the education expense as they involve a net transfer of resources to the child without any obligation of repayment.[334] Student loans should not be equated with income available to the child. Unlike a bursary, grant, or scholarship, which is designed to defray a student's expenses, a student loan merely delays payment of certain expenses.[335] Courts are disinclined to saddle adult children with onerous debt when the parents have the necessary means to pay for their post-secondary education.[336] Student loans and income from part-time employment may, nevertheless, become of critical importance where the parent from whom support is sought is of limited means.[337] The fundamental issue to be addressed is one of reasonableness, having regard to the attendant circumstances, especially the present and prospective financial circumstances of the child and her parents. The extent to which an adult child can reasonably be expected to contribute to her living or post-secondary education expenses through loans or otherwise should be determined by seeking to achieve a fair balance between the child's

---

331 *Lewi v Lewi*, [2006] OJ No 1847 (CA) (trust funds); see also *Fearon v Tzeng Fearon*, 2021 ONSC 7545; *Minish v Timmons*, 2021 ONSC 7622. For an excellent detailed summary of the principles espoused in *Lewi v Lewi*, see *Durso v Mascherin*, 2013 ONSC 6522 at para 48, Chappel J. See also *LB v PAV*, 2008 ABQB 623; *Dunn v Dunn*, 2013 NLTD(F) 7; *KJ v VP*, 2008 SKQB 489.

332 *MS v DMA*, 2011 NBQB 79; *Samson v Samson*, [2003] NJ No 289 (SC); *Selig v Smith*, 2008 NSCA 54; *Roth v Roth*, 2010 ONSC 2532; *Zaba v Bradley* (1996), 137 Sask R 295 (CA); *Zaba v Bradley* (1996), 140 Sask R 297 at 300 (QB), Archambault J; *Hagen v Rankin*, [2002] SJ No 15 (CA); *Geran v Geran*, 2011 SKCA 55.

333 *Samson v Samson*, [2003] NJ No 289 (SC).

334 *MS v DMA*, 2011 NBQB 79, citing *Roth v Roth*, 2010 ONSC 2532.

335 *Palmer v Palmer*, [1998] BCJ No 2092 (SC); *Winstanley v Winstanley*, 2016 MBCA 17; *Armstrong v Armstrong*, [1999] OJ No 2614 (SCJ); compare *Tusnady v Tusnady*, 2010 BCSC 1310; *Bundus v Bundus* [1999] SJ No 715 (QB).

336 *Young v Young*, 2012 BCSC 1727; *Stephan v Cunningham*, 2016 ABCA 177; *Rebenchuk v Rebenchuk*, 2007 MBCA 22; *MS v DMA*, 2011 NBQB 79; *Selig v Smith*, [2008] NSJ No 250 (CA); *Lacroix v D'Aoust* 2011 ONSC 5586; *Fournier v Meyers*, 2014 SKQB 283.

337 *Lee v Chung*, 2011 BCSC 404; *Symonds v Symonds*, 2009 NSSC 26; *Roth v Roth*, 2010 ONSC 2532; *Chyz v Prystupa*, [2008] SJ No 580 (QB).

means and capabilities and those of the parents.[338] The following questions are apposite in determining the relative needs, abilities, resources, debts, and obligations of the parent and the adult child: (1) Is the parent's cash flow sufficient to fund all or part of the adult child's education needs without jeopardizing the parent's reasonable standard of living or ability to service his or her obligations? (2) What are the likely future financial positions of the parent and adult child upon the latter's completion of his or her studies? Will the parent's long-term standard of living be adversely affected? How soon might the adult child be expected to retire a student loan? (3) Will the parent have to borrow funds to provide support for the adult child and, if so, what are the consequences to the parent in comparison to those of an adult child who has access to a student loan? (4) What are the relative ages and work life expectancy of the parent and the adult child? (5) What time is remaining before the adult child can be expected to gain material earnings from his or her education? In the final analysis, if the adult child lacks the ability to provide for herself or himself and the payment of child support would prejudice the parent more than a student loan would prejudice the adult child, then the adult child is required to secure available student loans and use such other resources at his or her disposal to cover the cost of post-secondary education before looking to the parent for support.[339]

Courts have a very broad discretion in determining how to balance the many competing considerations relevant to determining the respective responsibilities of the parents and the child to cover the post-secondary education costs of an adult child still considered to be a child of the marriage for the purpose of the *Federal Child Support Guidelines*. Relevant cases indicate that there is a growing trend to impose one-third to one-half of the responsibility on the adult child, to be met by part-time employment, scholarships, or student loans, depending on the talents and choices of the child, and the balance on the parents, proportional to their respective incomes. However, this is far from invariable; it depends on the incomes and circumstances of the parties.[340]

An adult child is not expected to work part-time during the college year, where it might interfere with his or her ability to pass the course.[341]

The income of an adult child that has already been spent may be excluded from the assessment of the appropriate amount of support that will enable the child to pursue post-secondary education, but realistic prospects of future income may be taken into account.[342]

---

338 *Stephan v Cunningham*, 2016 ABCA 177; *Ashlie v Ashlie*, 2010 BCSC 1101; see also *Ross v Dunphy*, 2009 NBQB 281; *Selig v Smith*, [2008] NSJ No 250 (CA); *Menegaldo v Menegaldo*, 2012 ONSC 2915; *Brook v Hertz*, 2008 SKQB 700.

339 *Fernquist v Garland*, [2005] SJ No 747 (QB); *Sundararajan v Periasamy*, 2021 SKQB 148 at paras 30–31; see also *D'Ovidio v Clement*, 2013 ONSC 5002 at para 32; compare *Krzak v Erixon*, 2008 SKQB 468, citing *Chyz v Prystupa*, 2008 SKQB 247.

340 *Dunn v Dunn*, 2013 NLTD(F) 7 at para 41; *Easton v Coxhead*, 2018 ONSC 4784; *Fleming v Boyachek*, 2011 SKCA 11; *Firkola v Firkola*, 2017 SKQB 31; *Youle v Galloway*, 2018 SKQB 211; compare *Semancik v Saunders*, 2011 BCCA 264; see also *Werenka v Werenka*, 2021 ABQB 1023; *Wiewiora v Wiewiora*, 2014 MBQB 218; *Corby v Corby*, 2015 ONSC 2700; *Perez v Chiris*, 2021 ONSC 101. And see *F (ML) v B (IE)*, 2021 ONSC 3522 at paras 63–69.

341 *Palmer v Palmer*, [1998] BCJ No 2092 (SC); *Rebenchuk v Rebenchuk*, 2007 MBCA 22; *Coghill v Coghill*, [2006] OJ No 2602 (SCJ).

342 *Brockman v Ofukany*, [1998] SJ No 650 (QB).

Tax credits for tuition costs should be factored into the equation where an order is sought under section 3(2)(b) or section 7 of the *Federal Child Support Guidelines*.[343]

Where a child is over the age of majority and a court concludes that it is inappropriate to order the applicable table amount of child support, section 13 of the *Federal Child Support Guidelines* requires the amount determined as appropriate to be specified in the order.

The provisions of section 3(2)(b) of the *Federal Child Support Guidelines* may be applied to deny support to an adult child whose needs are fully met by financial subsidies received under Alberta's program of Assured Income for the Severely Handicapped.[344]

Pursuant to the discretion conferred by section 3(2)(b) of the *Federal Child Support Guidelines*, a court may order the applicable table amount of child support to be paid during the summer months, if the adult child returns home from an out-of-town university at the end of the academic year.[345] Whether the applicable table amount of child support is appropriate may depend on the adult child's capacity to contribute to his or her own living expenses out of income earned from employment during the summer. It may be more appropriate, however, to allocate any such income to the adult child's out-of-town expenses incurred while attending university, because the applicable table amount will vary according to whether there are other siblings at home and a proper accounting is more likely to be made, if the child's income is used for the purpose of reducing the parental contributions to the child's out-of-town university expenses. Support should not be denied to adult students during the summer months, if their summer income is used to meet educational and living expenses during the academic year.[346] In addition to calculating the support payable for an adult child during the summer months and making that amount payable over twelve months, the court may order that a further sum be paid to the recipient parent each month towards the cost of maintaining the home to which the child would return.[347]

Where an adult child is pursuing university studies but spending weekends, summer, and other vacations at the mother's home and virtually all university expenses are met out of the child's earnings and student loans, the father may be ordered to make a monthly contribution to meet the mother's overhead costs where she is unable to make any contribution from her income after due allowance is made for her personal financial needs in order to ensure her economic self-sufficiency.[348]

In determining the ability of a parent to contribute to the adult child's expenses pursuant to section 3(2)(b) or section 7 of the *Federal Child Support Guidelines*, third-party spousal income or obligations are relevant.[349]

---

343 *Menegaldo v Menegaldo*, 2012 ONSC 2915 at para 181; *Krueger v Tunison*, [1999] SJ No 482 (QB); *McConnell v McConnell*, [2002] SJ No 117 (QB).

344 *Buzon v Buzon*, [1999] AJ No 371 (QB).

345 *Erdman v Erdman*, 2024 BCSC 119; *Gagnier v Gagnier*, [2002] OJ No 2183 (SCJ); *Bond v Bond*, [2007] OJ No 3677 (Div Ct); *Blonski v Blonski*, 2010 ONSC 2552; *Bundus v Bundus*, [1999] SJ No 715 (QB).

346 *Rebenchuk v Rebenchuk*, 2007 MBCA 22; see also *Montalto v Montalto*, 2011 ABQB 574 at para 20, citing *SIB v MDB*, 2009 ABQB 612.

347 *Craig v Niro*, 2022 ONSC 5178 at para 56.

348 *Kapogianes v Kapogianes*, [2000] OJ No 2572 (SCJ) (father to pay full amount of mother's increased overhead costs for adult child in addition to applicable table amount of support for younger child).

349 *JWF v JAT*, [2003] NSJ No 226 (Fam Ct). Compare Chapter 5, Section C.

G. UNEMPLOYMENT; SCOPE OF "OTHER CAUSE"

Some courts have held that a child's inability to obtain employment, which does not result from illness or disability but from restrictions on job availability, falls outside the meaning of "other cause" in section 2(2) of the *Divorce Act*. Given this interpretation, parents cannot be ordered to support a child who cannot withdraw from the charge of his or her parents or provide himself or herself with the necessities of life because of the state of the labour market. Other courts have opted for a broader interpretation of "other cause" and have ordered child support in cases where the economic climate makes it impossible for a diligent child to find employment and become self-supporting.

In *Gartner v Gartner*,[350] Cowan CJTD of the Nova Scotia Supreme Court stated:

> It seems to me that it was not the intention of the *Divorce Act* that parents should be required to support a child who is not ill or not disabled, and who can withdraw himself from the parents' charge and can provide himself with the necessities of life, except that he cannot, in the present state of the labour market, find suitable work.

This approach has been endorsed by the Appellate Division of the Supreme Court of Nova Scotia and by several trial courts in other provinces, although it has been considered appropriate to grant a period of grace to unemployed children before support is terminated.[351]

In *Baker v Baker*,[352] Berger J of the Alberta Court of Queen's Bench rejected the reasoning in *Gartner v Gartner* because of the unfair burden such an approach placed on the primary caregiving parent, stating:

> The reasoning in *Gartner* fails, in my opinion, to address the reality of unemployment and its impact on the spouse who has no choice but to support her unemployed child. It is little comfort to her that but for the sorry state of the economy the child *could* be expected to be self-supporting. The fact is that the child *cannot* provide for herself and that one parent *is* supporting the child.
>
> . . . If the other parent has the resources to contribute, then he has a legal obligation to do so arising from s. 15 of the Act.
>
> There is no justifiable reason to differentiate between a child who cannot provide for himself because he is in school, and a child who cannot provide for himself because the economic situation makes it impossible to obtain a job.

A similar conclusion was reached in *Bruehler v Bruehler*[353] wherein Hutcheon JA of the British Columbia Court of Appeal declined to follow *Gartner v Gartner* and concluded that the words "other cause" are sufficiently wide to include a state of economic depression in the province that renders young people unable to obtain employment and thus provide themselves with the necessaries of life. Such orders are typically transitional, rather than

350 (1978), 5 RFL (2d) 270 at 274 (NSTD). See also *Cook v Cook*, 2016 NBQB 55 at paras 59–61.

351 See *Sproule v Sproule* (1986), 2 RFL (3d) 54 (NSCA); see also *Smith v Smith* (1987), 12 RFL (3d) 50 (BCSC); *LN v TMN*, 2015 NBQB 155; *Matthews v Matthews* (1988), 11 RFL (3d) 431 (Nfld TD); *Grail v Grail* (1990), 27 RFL (3d) 317 (Ont Master), aff'd (1990), 30 RFL (3d) 454 (Ont Ct Gen Div); *Taylor v Taylor*, [1999] SJ No 732 (QB).

352 (1994), 2 RFL (4th) 147 at 155–56 (Alta QB).

353 (1985), 49 RFL (2d) 44 (BCCA).

long-term.[354] In *McAdam v McAdam*,[355] Duncan J of the Manitoba Court of Queen's Bench concluded that the words "other cause" in section 2(2) of the *Divorce Act* should be interpreted to include an inability to obtain employment where the child has made a diligent attempt to find employment and the inability to do so renders the child unable to withdraw from the charge of the parents. But adult children are not entitled to remain at home, unemployed and dependent upon a parent for support, without seeking gainful employment. If none is available locally, they may have to find employment elsewhere.[356]

An adult child who is capable of self-support from low paying employment may be disentitled to support unless he or she reverts to the status of a "child of the marriage" by future enrolment in a college program.[357] While rejecting a parent's request for ongoing periodic support until an adult child finds suitable employment, a court may grant a transitional order for a brief period of time to afford the child a reasonable opportunity to find employment.

A parent's formal commitment to support a child who would not otherwise be a child of the marriage may render that child eligible for support. However, the amount of support may be reduced from that which a child of the marriage would ordinarily receive.[359]

H. WITHDRAWAL FROM PARENTAL CHARGE

A child will be considered to have withdrawn from his or her parents' charge[360] when he or she leaves home with sufficient income to financially meet his or her basic needs.[361] An adult child must be unable to withdraw from his or her parents' charge or to obtain the necessaries of life by reason of illness, disability, or other cause in order to be eligible for child support as a "child of the marriage" within the meaning of section 2(1) of the *Divorce Act*. A healthy and able adult child who has no definite plans to obtain any further education or training and who has made no real effort to find employment is not a "child of the marriage" entitled to support.[362] Once a child who is the subject of an existing support order reaches the age of majority, there is no continuing presumption of child support entitlement in the absence of evidence that such support remains statutorily required under the *Divorce Act*. Nevertheless, an existing support order does not automatically expire upon the child attaining the age of majority; the question is not one of age, but of dependency. A parent who seeks to vary a support order by reason that the child is no longer a "child of the marriage" has the onus of bringing an application to that effect and of establishing that the child has attained the age of majority, but this usually requires nothing more than proof that the child has reached the

354 *CLB v BTC*, [2006] BCJ No 3112 (SC); see also *Aquila v Aquila*, 2016 MBCA 33 at para 31 (no presumed period of grace pending entry into workforce); compare *KKS v JSS*, 2019 BCSC 136 at para 28. And see *KMR v* IWR, 2020 ABQB 77 at paras 38–45, Jerke J, citing *Brear v Brear*, 2019 ABCA 419 and Rose Branton, "Exploring Child Support for Adult Children: The Need for a Broader Conception of 'Other Cause'" (2018) 37 CFLQ 139.

355 (1994), 8 RFL (4th) 252 at 255–56 (Man QB).

356 *Thorp v Thorp*, [2002] BCJ No 2826 (SC).

357 *Cram v Cram*, [1999] BCJ No 2518 (SC).

358 *Hrabluik v Hrabluik*, [1999] MJ No 472 (QB); compare *Callahan v Brett*, [2000] NJ No 354 (SC).

359 *Parsons v Parsons* (1994), 9 RFL (4th) 437 (Alta QB).

360 As to children under the age of majority, see text relating to note 5, above in this chapter.

361 *Gagnon v Gagnon*, 2012 NSSC 407 at para 5, MacDonald J.

362 *Ethier v Skrudland*, 2011 SKCA 17; see also *DBB v DMB*, 2017 SKCA 59.

provincial age of majority and the child's plans for the future have not been made known to the supporting parent.[363]

An adult child who is financially dependent on his or her parents while completing school is a "child of the marriage" within the meaning of section 2(1) of the *Divorce Act* and, therefore, is eligible for support under the *Federal Child Support Guidelines*.[364] An adult child who has experienced learning difficulties does not lose her status as a "child of the marriage" under section 2(1) of the *Divorce Act* in consequence of her temporary withdrawal from school while awaiting an opportunity to complete her high school diploma.[365]

An adult child who does not attend school on a full-time basis because of post-traumatic stress disorder associated with family violence is entitled to ongoing support as a "child of the marriage" within the meaning of section 2(1) of the *Divorce Act*.[366]

The voluntary withdrawal of a child from either parent's home does not necessarily preclude a finding that the child is a "child of the marriage" within the meaning of section 2(1) of the *Divorce Act*. Children live away from their parents' homes for a variety of reasons without withdrawing from the charge of their parents in the sense that the parents have a continuing obligation for their support.[367] Conversely, a child may reside with one or other of the parents and still have withdrawn from their charge.[368] An adult child who is financially independent is not a "child of the marriage" within the meaning of section 2(1) of the *Divorce Act*, even though he or she still lives with one of the parents.[369] Each case must be examined in light of its own circumstances.[370]

Whether a child remains in the charge of one or other parent and is thus entitled to support is a question of fact and the court must draw the line where it thinks fit and proper having regard to the condition, means, needs, and other circumstances of the child and its parents. A child under the age of majority is entitled to continued financial assistance from the parents unless the evidence demonstrates that the child has withdrawn from parental charge. The fact that the child is not living with either parent is not determinative; the test is whether the child is independent in the sense that no financial assistance or parental guidance is necessary.[371] A pregnant child living with the prospective father of her child may be entitled to child support from her parents in order to finish her high school education.[372]

---

363 *Smith v Smith*, 2008 SKCA 141; *Ethier v Skrudland*, 2011 SKCA 17; *Kosowan v Vanderstat*, 2016 SKCA 149. See also *LIP v LHB*, 2013 MBQB 37 (minor child incarcerated); *Pitcher v Pitcher*, 2013 NLTD(F) 11 (child with development disorder).

364 *Stebner v Stebner*, [2005] AJ No 392 (QB); *Wood v Wood*, [2005] BCJ No 910 (SC); *Garinger v Thompson*, [2006] SJ No 36 (QB).

365 *Tughan v Tughan*, [2003] OJ No 2656 (SCJ) (adult child's modest earnings from employment taken into account pursuant to s 3(2)(b) of *Federal Child Support Guidelines* in fixing arrears of child support).

366 *GD c GD*, [2003] QJ No 10303 (CS).

367 *Pound v Pound* (1987), 6 RFL (3d) 231 (BCCA); see also *Saccary v Spencer*, 2022 BCSC 1151.

368 See *Derkach v Derkach* (1989), 22 RFL (3d) 423 (Man QB); *Depeel v Abramyk*, [1997] SJ No 749 (QB).

369 *Leonard v Leonard* (1996), 29 RFL (4th) 237 (NWTSC).

370 *LIP v LHB*, 2013 MBQB 37.

371 *Laurie v Barre*, 2009 MBQB 284; *Kosowan v Vanderstat*, 2016 SKCA 149; compare *Chaulk v Avery*, 2009 NLTD 185.

372 *MR v SRR*, [2000] BCJ No 1954 (SC).

If a child marries[373] or chooses to enjoy an independent lifestyle, such a child may be found to have withdrawn from the charge of both parents so as to be disentitled to the status of a "child of the marriage" for the purpose of child support.[374] A parent is not obligated to pay support for a child who has withdrawn from parental control and voluntarily adopted an independent lifestyle.[375] An adult child, who is a single mother and in full-time attendance at school, may be eligible for child support as a "child of the marriage" within the meaning of section 2(1) of the *Divorce Act*.[376] An adult child who is a single parent may cease to fall within the definition of a "child of the marriage" if she is not pursuing further education and, in such a case, the father of the adult child is not legally obliged to support her and the grandchild.[377] A pregnant child who is living with her mother has been deemed to be a "child of the marriage" within the meaning of section 2(1) of the *Divorce Act*, pending anticipated pursuit of university studies at the commencement of the academic year.[378] A child support order requires that the child for whom support is sought be in the "charge" of the applicant parent. This presupposes that the applicant parent has assumed a degree of responsibility for the care and support of the child.[379] A child who attends school or university and is unable to provide for herself or himself may be entitled to support even though the child resides with a boyfriend[380] or girlfriend[381] or with an older sibling[382] or grandparent[383] rather than with either parent. A parent is not relieved of his or her child support responsibility in circum stances where the child remains a dependant but lives with or receives financial assistance from a non-parental family member, such as a grandparent.[384] An adult child's "common-law relationship" while attending university does not warrant the termination of child support where the adult child remains economically dependent on her parents. An adult child does not cease to be a "child of the marriage" within the meaning of section 2(1) of the *Divorce*

373 *Poohkay v Poohkay* (1997), 33 RFL (4th) 140 (Alta CA); *AAC v MAB*, [2006] NSJ No 169 (SC); *Stoangi v Petersen*, [2006] OJ No 2902 (SCJ) (common law relationship); *Ashman v Ashman*, [2009] OJ No 3310 (SCJ) (application under *Family Law Act*).

374 *Schultz v Schultz*, [1998] AJ No 245 (QB); *Hamilton v Hamilton*, 2010 BCSC 844; *Chaulk v Avery*, 2009 NLTD 185; *Pothier v Pothier*, [2001] NSJ No 489 (SC); *Merasty v Merasty*, [2000] SJ No 341 (QB) (*viva voce* hearing directed to determine whether daughter had withdrawn from parental charge by establishing an independent lifestyle before obtaining the age of majority); *Molloy v Molloy*, [2001] YJ No 142 (SC).

375 *Edwards v Watt* (1993), 123 NSR (2d) 210 (TD); *Wieland v Wieland* (1994), 3 RFL (4th) 56 (Ont Ct Gen Div); *Holmes v Holmes* (1991), 96 Nfld & PEIR 281 (PEITD); compare *Auld v Auld* (1994), 5 RFL (4th) 132 (PEITD).

376 *Reidy v Reidy*, [2005] OJ No 5152 (SCJ).

377 *Budden v Budden*, [2001] BCJ No 269 (SC); *PC v SV*, 2022 ABKB 644; *Walsh v Walsh* (1988), 16 RFL (3d) 1 (NBCA).

378 *Bragg v Bragg*, [2000] NJ No 14 (UFC); see also *Gervais v Tongue*, [2000] OJ No 529 (SCJ); *Sandor v Sandor*, [2004] OJ No 2741 (SCJ).

379 *Murray v Murray*, [1997] SJ No 175 (QB).

380 *Thompson v Thompson*, 2010 MBQB 7; *Tarrant v Tarrant*, [2005] NJ No 212 (SC); *Van Der Voort v Keating*, [2006] NSJ No 9 (SC); *Bast v Dyck*, [1997] SJ No 174 (QB); compare *Hrechka v Andries*, [2003] MJ No 114 (QB); *Ritchie v Ritchie*, [2003] SJ No 326 (CA).

381 *Robertson v Hibbs*, [1997] BCJ No 1305 (SC); *Lafleur v Donoghue*, [2005] OJ No 5416 (SCJ); compare *Geddes v Svendsen*, [1997] NSJ No 565 (Fam Ct).

382 *Jonasson v Evans*, [1997] SJ No 71 (QB).

383 *Dufault v Dufault*, 2009 BCSC 1220.

384 *TG v SG*, 2019 ONSC 4662.

Act when the economic realities that she faces while pursuing post-secondary education are no different from what they would be if she were not living in a conjugal relationship.[385]

An adult child who withdraws from a parent's home is not disentitled to child support while pursuing post-secondary education merely because he or she is currently sharing household expenses with a common law partner.[386] In *Karol v Karol*,[387] Wilkinson J, as she then was, undertakes a review of the caselaw and identifies the following factors as relevant in determining the impact of an adult child's common law relationship upon his or her eligibility for child support to meet the costs of post-secondary education:

> [para 19] Similarly, the fact that Sharla resides in a common-law relationship does not automatically disqualify her for support. A review of the case law shows mixed results, depending on a number of factors including the child's age, whether the parents approved the relationship, how long the common-law relationship has lasted, and whether the common-law partner is working full-time or part-time or attending school and without income. Other considerations are how long the child has been in school, how much the child has been able to contribute from other sources, and whether the parents would provide assistance in any event, whether ordered to or not. Another relevant consideration is whether the parents had provided any financial assistance at all towards the child's post-secondary training and, if so, for how long.

A child with a drinking or drug problem who is under the age of majority but no longer living with either parent is eligible for child support under the *Divorce Act* where the child is unable to provide himself or herself with the necessaries of life. In these circumstances, it may be inappropriate for the court to order periodic support payments to be made directly to the child, in which event the court may order the payments to be made to the mother when she continues to have a close relationship with the child.[388]

Where a child has been incarcerated and there is no evidence that a parent either voluntarily contributes to the support of the child or is required by law to contribute to the support of the child, the child must be regarded as having withdrawn from the charge of that parent for the purpose of determining child support.[389] Section 31(2) of the Ontario *Family Law Act* provides that the child support obligation owed by a parent does not extend to a child who is sixteen years of age or older if that child has "withdrawn from parental control." Such a withdrawal presupposes a free choice of the child to cut the family ties.[390] The question of whether a child over the age of sixteen has withdrawn from parental control, or has been forced to leave the parents' home is, in all cases, fact specific.[391] The parent who seeks to avoid paying child support to an adult child pursuant to section 31(2) of the Ontario *Family Law*

---

385 *Crowdis v Crowdis*, [2003] SJ No 371 (QB). Compare *Rothenburg v Rothenburg*, [2003] OJ No 1551 (SCJ); *Ritchie v Ritchie*, [2003] SJ No 326 (CA); *Karol v Karol*, [2005] SJ No 349 (QB).

386 *Fisher v Rogers*, 2012 ONSC 669; compare *Broaders v Broaders*, 2014 NLTD(F) 13.

387 [2005] SJ No 349 at para 19 (QB); see also *BFL v KRL*, 2018 PESC 1.

388 *JJDC v SLC*, [1996] OJ No 3501 (Gen Div).

389 *MA v FA*, 2013 BCSC 1077. See also *LIP v LHB*, 2013 MBQB 37; *Clewlow v Clewlow*, [2004] OJ No 3468 (SCJ); *Fincham v Fincham*, 2017 ONSC 4279. Compare *Allard v Allard*, [1999] OJ No 3535 (SCJ).

390 *Ball v Broger*, [2010] OJ No 5824 (Ct J).

391 *Juneau v Latreille*, 2011 ONSC 6424 (child living with friend's parents entitled to interim support).

Act, based on the child's repudiation of the relationship, bears the onus of proving that fact. Where the child has been forced out of the family home and has no means of supporting himself, child support may be granted to the child's aunt who has undertaken the parenting role. A retroactive order that pre-dates the application may be appropriate in light of the father's initial undertaking, which was later withdrawn, to pay periodic support for the child.

A maternal grandmother, who provides a home for her grandchildren, may fall within the definition of "parent" under section 1 of the Ontario *Family Law Act*, but her application for child support should be dismissed where the children are over sixteen years of age and both of the separated parents are willing to provide a home for the children who voluntarily "withdrew from parental control" within the meaning of section 31(2) of the Ontario *Family Law Act*.[394]

The provisions of sections 57–59, 61, and 63(1) of the *Child and Family Services Act*[395] signify that a Crown ward is no longer in the charge of her parents, even though she remains their child. The fact that one of the parents has liberal parenting time with the child and continues to play an active role in the disabled child's life does not negate the primary responsibility for the child's parenting care and support that has been vested in the government by virtue of the Crown wardship order. While both parents may have a moral responsibility to provide financial assistance for their disabled child, a parent who incurs expenses for the child has no right to seek child support from the other parent pursuant to the *Divorce Act* and the *Federal Child Support Guidelines*. It is the role of the Children's Aid Society to seek support from either parent pursuant to section 60 of the *Child and Family Services Act*, if it chooses to do so.[396]

I. REVERSION TO FORMER STATUS OF CHILD OF THE MARRIAGE

If a child has ceased to be a child of the marriage by reason of having achieved self-sufficiency, the question may arise whether that child can regain his or her lost status. Some courts have been reluctant to order support when a child has withdrawn from school or college but thereafter seeks to resume his or her education, although there is nothing in the *Divorce Act* to suggest that a child may not move from being a child of the marriage to being outside that category and thereafter within it again.[397] An adult child who has ceased to be a "child of the marriage" under the *Divorce Act* and the *Federal Child Support Guidelines* may regain that lost status by reason of the pursuit of further education or a finding of illness or disability that prevents them from becoming financially independent,[398] but the door to reinstatement

---

392 *Friday v Friday*, 2013 ONSC 1931; *Rotondi v Rotondi*, 2014 ONSC 1520.

393 *Perovic v Nagtzaam*, [2001] OJ No 3462 (Ct J).

394 *Belanger v Belanger*, [2005] OJ No 3033 (SCJ).

395 RSO 1990, c C11.

396 *Seabrook v Major*, [2005] OJ No 3085 (Div Ct).

397 *Stocchero v Stocchero* (1997), 29 RFL (4th) 223 (Alta CA); *Horvath v Horvath*, [2000] MJ No 428 (CA); *Aquila v Aquila*, 2016 MBCA 33; *Sharma v Sharma*, 2022 MBQB 27; *Lockerby v Lockerby*, 2017 NSCA 26; *Geran v Geran*, 2011 SKCA 55.

398 *De Beck v De Beck*, 2012 BCCA 465; *JT v CT*, 2013 BCSC 28; *NDS v JAS*, 2020 BCSC 1034; *Forrest v Aerin* 2022 BCCA 184 at para 110; *JCW v JKRW*, 2024 BCSC 139 at para 39; *Prince v Soenen*, 2015 MBQB 31; *Ross v Dunphy*, 2009 NBQB 281; *Nelson v Nelson*, [2005] NSJ No 18 (SC); *Leonard v Leonard* (1996), 29 RFL (4th) 237 (NWTSC); *Edwards v Edwards*, 2021 ONSC 1550; *McCabe v MacInnis*, [2000] PEIJ No 61

of dependent status for support purposes is not open forever.[399] In determining whether the status has been regained, each fact situation must be analyzed carefully and the timelines between the time when the child lost that status and the time when an application is made respecting the resumption of the status must be considered fully.[400] A hiatus of one year in a child's pursuit of education constitutes no bar to an order for future child support where the child thereafter diligently seeks to remedy past academic failures.[401] In the words of Charney J, of the Ontario Superior Court of Justice, in *Edwards v Edwards*:

> [37] There are many cases in which courts have found that a child taking a "gap year" before starting post-secondary studies, or a brief hiatus from an educational program, may nonetheless remain a "child of the marriage" ...
>
> [38] Other cases have held that a child may require a "modest transition period" after completion of an educational program to search for employment.
>
> [39] Apart from these brief periods, however, and in the absence of "illness or other disability", courts generally require attendance at school for an adult child to maintain his or her dependant status....
>
> [41] The loss of dependent status is not necessarily permanent. Once lost, dependant status may be regained.[402]

Each case rests on its own facts and each child's circumstances may need to be individually addressed.[403] Past failure in the pursuit of higher education does not necessarily preclude ongoing child support on the child's resumption of post-secondary education.[404] Whether the status of being "a child of the marriage" has been regained is a question of fact that may be determined by whether the educational program and the resources of the parent render such a course realistic. When the child in respect of whom support is brought has already been provided with the means to be independent and the parent against whom support is sought has assumed new obligations to a second family, a court may conclude that the parent should not be called upon to support an adult child's pursuit of postgraduate professional training.[405]

(SC); *Geran v Geran*, 2011 SKCA 55. See also *Mirzahi v Sana*, 2022 ABQB 313 at paras 92–93; *Dove v MacIntyre*, 2021 NSSC 1.

399 *Harrison v Vargek*, [2002] MJ No 155 (QB); *Geran v Geran*, 2011 SKCA 55; see also *Aubert v Cipriani*, 2015 ONSC 6103 (application under *Family Law Act*, RSO 1990, c F-3).

400 *Lawless v Asaro*, [2003] OJ No 2522 (SCJ).

401 *Erb v Erb*, [2003] OJ No 1527 (SCJ); see also *Geboers v Geboers*, 2018 BCSC 181; *Cervi v McDonald*, 2021 ONSC 1843.

402 *Edwards v Edwards*, 2021 ONSC 1550 at paras 37–39 and 41; see also *Fraser v Jacobsen-Fraser*, 2021 ABQB 955; *Gilkinson v Nichols*, 2023 ONSC 1504 at para 39.

403 *Harrison v Vargek*, [2002] MJ No 155 (QB).

404 *Brandner v Brandner*, [2002] BCJ No 1398 (CA); *Goundrey-Beskau v Beskau*, 2015 BCSC 168; *Sharma v Sharma*, 2022 MBQB 27; *MacDonald v Rasmussen*, [2000] SJ No 660 (QB).

405 *Jonasson v Jonasson*, [1998] BCJ No 726 (SC).

J. PERSONS STANDING IN PLACE OF PARENTS

1) Legal Requirements

Pursuant to section 2(2) of the *Divorce Act*, the phrase "child of the marriage" is not confined to the common offspring of the spouses. The definition of "child of the marriage" is satisfied where both or either of the spouses or former spouses stands in the place of parents.[406] spouse stands in the place of a parent when that spouse manifests an intention of placing himself or herself in a situation ordinarily occupied by the biological parent. Judicial opinion is divided on the question whether the requisite intention can exist when a husband who is alleged to be standing in the place of the parent erroneously believes that he is the father of the child.[407] In *Peters v Graham*,[408] Boudreau J of the Nova Scotia Supreme Court concluded that a husband, who unknowingly stands in the place of a parent to his wife's children because he erroneously believes that he is their biological father, may be ordered to support the children but the amount of support to be paid may be reduced pursuant to section 5 of the *Federal Child Support Guidelines* in light of the concurrent obligations owed by the children's biological father and the wife's "common law spouse" who currently stands in the place of a parent to the children.

While financial contribution toward the support of a child is a material consideration, it is not decisive in determining whether the contributor stands in the place of a parent. Evidence of financial support may simply be indicative of kindness and compassion and is insufficient in itself to justify a finding that a spouse stands in the place of a parent where there is no evidence of any relationship akin to that of parent and child.[409] Such a status implies an intention on the part of the person alleged to stand in the place of a parent to fulfill the office and duty of a parent in both a practical and legal sense.[410] Courts may look to a number of objective factors for the purpose of determining intention. For example, they may consider the duration of the relationship, the age of the children, whether psychological parenting has taken place, day-to-day care of the children, involvement in vital activities such as the child's education or discipline, how the child and the person in question acknow

---

406 See Carol Rogerson, "The Child Support Obligations of Step-Parents" (2001) 18 *Canadian Journal of Family Law* 9; Nicholas Bala, "Who Is a 'Parent'? 'Standing in the Place of a Parent' and Section 5 of the *Child Support Guidelines*" in The Law Society of Upper Canada, *Special Lectures 2006: Family Law* (Toronto: Irwin Law, 2007) 71.

407 See, for example, *Allen v Allen*, 1999 CanLII 6749 (BCSC); *Aksugyuk v Aksugyuk* (1975), 17 RFL 224 (NWTSC); *RC v CW*, [2003] OJ No 3755 (SCJ); *TW v SL*, 2017 SKQB 45; compare *EZ v PZ*, 2017 BCSC 375; *GNP v LAG*, 2001 NSSC 165; *Day v Weir*, 2014 ONSC 5975. And see *RR v DLK*, [2005] OJ No 5591 (SCJ) (action for damages dismissed where the evidence did not support a finding of deceit or negligence); *Saunders v Vargas*, 2018 ONSC 1892; *Unger v Scott*, 2023 ABKB 500.

408 [2001] NSJ No 452 (SC); see also *Day v Weir*, 2014 ONSC 5975. Compare *SS v PS*, 2012 ABCA 163. See also *PP v DD*, 2017 ONCA 180 (no action for damages available to father in fraud or negligence against mother who falsely assured him that she was using contraceptive pill). And see *DL v EC*, 2023 ONCA 494 (application under the Ontario *Succession Law Reform Act*).

409 *Fournier v Fournier*, [1997] BCJ No 2299 (SC); *Henderson v Henderson*, [1999] BCJ No 2938 (SC); *Fair v Jones*, [1999] NWTJ No 17 (SC). Compare *Hearn v Bacque*, [2006] OJ No 2385 (SCJ). See also *VLM v RDM*, 2010 NBQB 412; *Hyatt v Ralph*, 2015 ONSC 580 (application under the *Family Law Act*, RSO 1990, c F-3); *Laframboise v Laframboise*, 2015 ONSC 1752.

410 *Wuzinski v Wuzinski* (1987), 10 RFL (3d) 420 (Man QB); *Andrews v Andrews* (1992), 38 RFL (3d) 200 (Sask CA).

ledge each other in their daily roles, as well as any financial contribution to the children.[411] In *Chartier v Chartier*, Bastarache J, speaking for the Supreme Court of Canada as a whole, observed:

> Whether a person stands in the place of a parent must take into account all factors relevant to that determination, viewed objectively. What must be determined is the nature of the relationship. The *Divorce Act* makes no mention of formal expressions of intent. The focus on voluntariness and intention in *Carignan*, above, was dependent on the common law approach discussed earlier. It was wrong. The Court must determine the nature of the relationship by looking at a number of factors, among which is intention. Intention will not only be expressed formally. The court must also infer intention from actions, and take into consideration that even expressed intentions may sometimes change. The actual fact of forming a new family is a key factor in drawing an inference that the step-parent treats the child as a member of his or her family, i.e., a child of the marriage.[412] The relevant factors in defining the parental relationship include, but are not limited to, whether the child participates in the extended family in the same way as would a biological child; whether the person provides financially for the child (depending on ability to pay); whether the person disciplines the child as a parent; whether the person represents to the child, the family, the world, either explicitly or implicitly, that he or she is responsible as a parent to the child; the nature or existence of the child's relationship with the absent biological parent. The manifestation of the intention of the step-parent cannot be qualified as to duration, or be otherwise made conditional or qualified, even if this intention is manifested expressly. Once it is shown that the child is to be considered, in fact, a "child of the marriage," the obligations of the step-parent towards him or her are the same as those relative to a child born of the marriage with regard to the application of the *Divorce Act*. The step-parent, at this point, does not only incur obligations. He or she also acquires certain rights, such as the right to apply eventually for [a parenting order] under s. 16(1) of the *Divorce Act*.
>
> Nevertheless, not every adult-child relationship will be determined to be one where the adult stands in the place of a parent. Every case must be determined on its own facts and it must be established from the evidence that the adult acted so as to stand in the place of a parent to the child.
>
> Huband J.A., in *Carignan, supra*, expressed the concern that individuals may be reluctant to be generous toward children for fear that their generosity will give rise to parental obligations. I do not share those concerns. The nature of a parental relationship is complex and includes more than financial support. People do not enter into parental relationships with the view that they will be terminated.[413]

---

411 *Varga v Varga*, [2009] BCJ No 626 (SC); *Motuzas v Yarnell*, [1997] MJ No 520 (QB); *BP v AT*, 2013 NBQB 309; *Laframboise v Laframboise*, 2015 ONSC 1752; *MML v PMF*, [2005] SJ No 514 (QB).

412 *Sullivan v Struck*, 2015 BCCA 521.

413 [1999] 1 SCR 242 at paras 39–41. See also *MDG v GDG*, 2013 ABCA 49; *Friesen v Friesen*, 2020 ABQB 103; *DCD v RJPC*, 2014 BCSC 2420; *Charan v Charan*, 2018 BCSC 1537; *KLB v SWB*, 2021 BCSC 1437; *Moynihan v Nakano*, 2022 BCSC 2186; *SLS v RJP*, 2023 MBKB 69; *MS v CS*, 2009 NBCA 66; *BKWR v NVR*, 2023 NBKB 17; *Ball v Murray*, 2008 NLTD 176; *Dunleavy v Comeau*, 2019 ONSC 4535; *Julien v Julien*, 2021 ONSC 8435; *Cui v Liwanpo*, 2022 ONSC 4549; *McGuire v Bator*, 2022 ONCA 431; *Udalaya v Amfoubalela*, 2018 PECA 16; *CNC v WJM*, 2018 PESC 45; *SLL v DBL*, 2022 SKKB 277; *LBM v RDE*, 2016 YKSC 4.

But a court is not limited to an examination of the factors as set out in *Chartier*.[414] Professor Carol Rogerson in her article, "The Child Support Obligations of Step Parents,"[415] provides a list of additional factors that can be considered by a court, including minimal involvement by a biological parent, deliberate behaviour to exclude the biological parent, reference to the stepfather as "Dad" and changes in a child's surname, a good relationship between the child and the step-parent, joint participation in family activities, the birth of one or more children to the spouses during their relationship, adoption proceedings or discussions, and the exercise of parenting time after separation. She also identifies several factors that tend to demonstrate an individual has not stood in the place of a parent, including a poor relationship between the child and step-parent prior to separation, the children are older when the spousal relationship begins, an involved biological parent, and the fact that the potential payor is a stepmother rather than a stepfather.[416]

The above criteria are to be viewed as a whole and differences in the treatment of biological and non-biological children may be insufficient to negate a finding that a spouse stands in the place of a parent to the non-biological child within the meaning of section 2(1) of the *Divorce Act*.[417]

The relevant factors listed in *Chartier v Chartier*, discussed above, as indicative of a parental relationship do not represent an exclusive list, nor is it necessary to establish that all the listed factors are present in a particular case. The fact that a husband has not been a good step-parent or that he may have been an excessive disciplinarian does not preclude a finding that he stood in the place of a parent to his wife's children, where he performed most of the functions normally performed by a parent. Furthermore, absence for extended periods from the family home for employment-related purposes does not preclude such a finding.

The child's perceptions of the relationship may be relevant but are not determinative. Children often resent step-parents but that does not negate the existence of a parent/child relationship that has developed. Animosity between the child and a step-parent does not preclude a finding that the latter stood in the place of a parent.[419]

The judgment in *Chartier v Chartier* leaves open the question whether a person can or should be deemed to stand in the place of a parent in circumstances where both biological parents continue to play a significant role in their child's life. This question was examined by Campbell J of the Supreme Court of Nova Scotia in *Cook v Cook*.[420] He concluded that Parliament endorsed the use of the words "in the place of" to indicate that parental status, with its concomitant child support obligations and the right to apply for [a parenting order], would arise only when a person has "substantially replaced the biological parent with respect to the various needs of the [child]." Justice Campbell acknowledged that the judgment of the

---

414 *Chartier v Chartier*, [1999] 1 SCR 242 at para 39; *Bodner v Huckerby*, 2013 SKQB 89.

415 (2001) 18 *Canadian Journal of Family Law* 9.

416 Cited in *Proulx v Proulx*, [2009] OJ No 1680 (SCJ) see also *Pitt v Mouland*, 2015 NWTSC 4.

417 *Peacock v Peacock*, [1999] NBJ No 313 (QB).

418 *RM v PM*, [2000] NJ No 180 (SC).

419 *Millar v Millar*, [2001] BCJ No 1803 (SC), citing *Chartier v Chartier*, [1999] 1 SCR 242.

420 [2000] NSJ No 19 (SC); see also *Maher v Maher*, [2001] BCJ No 1912 (SC); *BP v AT*, 2013 NBQB 309; *Hodder v Hodder*, [2007] NJ No 402 (SC); *Pitt v Mouland*, 2015 NWTSC 4; *Neil v Neil*, [2002] OJ No 3003 (SCJ); *Lewcock v Natali-Lewcock*, [2001] OJ No 2051 (SCJ); *CNC v WJM*, 2018 PESC 45. Compare *Hearn v Bacque*, [2006] OJ No 2385 (SCJ).

Supreme Court of Canada "clearly implies that both the biological parent and the step-parent can be required to pay support in appropriate circumstances" and that there are circumstances where concurrent payments would be appropriate, as for example, where the biological parent is paying inadequate support and the step-parent has provided "financial, emotional and physical support and guidance over a sufficient period of time in substitution for the natural parent."

In *Widdis v Widdis*,[421] McIntyre J of the Saskatchewan Court of Queen's Bench rejected *Cook v Cook* by concluding that a step-parent may stand in the place of a parent even though that parent still plays a role in the child's life, but the role of the parent may be relevant to a determination of the amount of support to be paid by the step-parent in the exercise of the judicial discretion conferred by section 5 of the *Federal Child Support Guidelines*. In *Swindler v Belanger*,[422] the Saskatchewan Court of Appeal held that a stepfather, who stood in the place of a parent to his wife's child from a previous relationship, was not entitled to withdraw from that relationship and thus avoid his child support obligation simply because the biological parents of the child renewed their relationship after the mother's separation from the stepfather. In fixing the amount of child support payable by the stepfather, however, section 5 of the *Federal Child Support Guidelines* was applied to reduce the amount of support payable in respect of the stepchild even though the biological father of the child earned no income.

It remains to be seen whether the aforementioned high threshold in *Cook v Cook*, discussed above, for imposing child support obligations on a step-parent will ultimately be perceived as reflecting the sentiments of the Supreme Court of Canada in *Chartier v Chartier*, wherein Bastarache J stated:

> [para 41] . . . I share the view expressed by Beaulieu J. in *Siddall, supra*, at p. 337:
>
> > It is important to examine the motive behind a person's generosity towards the children of the person they wish to be involved with or are involved with in a relationship. In many cases children are used as pawns by men and, on occasion, women who desire the attention of the children's parent and once the relationship between the adults fail, the children are abandoned. This is not to be encouraged. If requiring men to continue their relationship, financially and emotionally with the children is a discouragement of generosity then, perhaps such generosity should be discouraged. This type of generosity which leaves children feeling rejected and shattered once a relationship between the adults sours is not beneficial to society in general and the children, in particular. After all, it is the court's obligation to look out for the best interests of the children. In too many of these situations the ultimate result is that the child is a mere object used to accommodate a person's selfish and personal interests as long as the relationship is satisfying and gratifying. As soon as things sour and become less comfortable, the person can leave, abandoning both the parent and child, without any legal repercussions . . . It is important to encourage the type of relationship that includes commitment, not superficial generosity. If relationships

---

421 [2000] SJ No 614 (QB); see also *Sullivan v Struck*, 2015 BCCA 521; *Hearn v Bacque*, [2006] OJ No 2385 (SCJ); *Molnar v Bruton*, 2013 SKQB 301.

422 [2005] SJ No 709 (CA); see also *Woodrow v Lepoudre*, 2022 SKQB 143. Compare *Delorey v Callahan*, 2009 NSSC 387.

are more difficult for a person to extricate him- or herself from then, perhaps, more children will be spared the trauma of rejection, bruised self-image and loss of financial support to which they have become accustomed.[423]

Both before and after the implementation of the *Federal Child Support Guidelines* on 1 May 1997, several courts have shared the concerns expressed by Campbell J in *Cook v Cook* above, and have been disinclined to impose long-term child support obligations on cohabit ants who assume parental responsibilities during a relatively brief relationship with the child's primary caregiving parent.[424] However, it should not be overlooked that the parties in *Chartier v Chartier*[425] lived together in premarital cohabitation and marital cohabitation for an aggregate period of less than three years and the marriage itself lasted only fifteen months.

The uncertainties that continue to exist after *Chartier v Chartier* have been explained by a Saskatchewan legal practitioner in the following words:

> In summary, although the *Chartier* case has outlined the principles which should be applied in determining whether or not a person stands in the place of a parent, it is still not clear how those principles will be applied to future cases. The result will depend very much on the amount of evidence and how this evidence is presented to the court. It may also depend on the judge's own beliefs whether a high or low threshold test should be applied. The finding will be in the judge's discretion and will likely not be subject to an appeal providing the principles as set out in the *Chartier* case have been applied.[426]

A spouse's subjective feelings[427] and motivation[428] are not relevant where his or her objective behaviour has manifested an intention to treat the child as a member of his or her family. Contractual covenants do not suffice to negate child support obligations that would otherwise ensue from the parent/child relationship.[429] In an age when individuals establish sequential short relationships with several partners, courts should be cautious before finding that a person stands in the place of a parent to his or her partner's child.[430] Whether such a relationship exists turns on the step-parent's conduct, not on the child's conduct.[431] The

---

423 [1999] 1 SCR 242 at para 41.

424 For pre-Guidelines cases, see, for example, *Weichholz v Weichholz* (1987), 81 AR 236 (QB); *Gavigan v Gavigan* (1990), 30 RFL (3d) 314 (Alta QB); *M(CF) v M(MF)* (1996), 23 RFL (4th) 55 (NBQB); *Sloat v Sloat* (1990), 102 NBR (2d) 390 (QB). For post-Guidelines cases, see *Maher v Maher*, [2001] BCJ No 1912 (SC); *Collins v Collins*, 2008 NLUFC 31, [2008] NJ No 296; *Li v Wu*, 2020 ONSC 7329; *Prowse-Myers v Myers*, [2004] SJ No 212 (QB); and see Section J(3), below in this chapter.

425 [1999] 1 SCR 242.

426 Marcia E Jackson, "Multiple Parents" (Paper presented to Saskatchewan Legal Education Society Inc, University of Saskatchewan College of Law and Law Foundation of Saskatchewan, Family Law Conference: *Economic and Parenting Consequences of Separation and Divorce*, Saskatoon, 31 March and 1 April 2000) tab "Multiple Parents" at 5–6.

427 *Cassar-Fleming v Fleming* (1996), 20 RFL (4th) 201 (Ont Ct Gen Div).

428 *F(RL) v F(S)* (1996), 26 RFL (4th) 392 (Ont Ct Gen Div) (application under *Family Law Act*).

429 *Chartier v Chartier*, [1999] 1 SCR 242; *Richardson v Richardson*, [1987] 1 SCR 857.

430 *Wuzinski v Wuzinski* (1987), 10 RFL (3d) 420 (Man QB).

431 *Miller v Miller* (1988), 13 RFL (3d) 80 (Ont HCJ). See also *Burns v Burns* (1994), 158 AR 153 (QB) (child support order against step-parent who admitted he stood in parental relationship to the child). Compare *Guidry v Guidry* (1994), 153 NBR (2d) 125 (QB) (child found not to be a "child of the marriage" because she never addressed the step-parent as her father and made no attempt to contact him after the separation).

conduct of a husband during a two-year marriage with intermittent cohabitation may be insufficient to demonstrate a "settled" intention to treat a child as a child of his family.[432] An extremely brief matrimonial cohabitation may also preclude a finding that the husband stands in the place of a parent to the wife's child.[433]

A stepfather has no obligation to support his stepchild under Nova Scotia provincial legislation and no such obligation can be imposed by section 5 of the *Nova Scotia Child Support Guidelines*.[434] If the Guidelines purport to create an obligation that is inconsistent with the legislation, the Guidelines may be viewed as *ultra vires* the enabling legislation.[435] Although a stepfather has no legal obligation to support his stepchild under Nova Scotia provincial law, he cannot challenge a consent order that provides such support after a breakdown occurs in the relationship between the stepfather and the stepchild. A consent order is not based upon a conditional or optional consent that permits the step-parent to unilaterally terminate the obligation previously assumed.[436]

Most provinces and territories have adopted a statutory definition of "child" that substantially corresponds to the definition set out in section 2(2) of the federal divorce legislation. In Manitoba, section 1 of *The Family Maintenance Act*[437] stipulates that the term child "includes a child to whom a person stands *in loco parentis*." In New Brunswick, section 1 of the *Family Services Act*[438] provides that "'child' includes ... (d) a child to whom a person stands *in loco parentis*, if that person's spouse is a parent of the child" and "'parent' ... includes ... a person with whom the child habitually resides who has demonstrated a settled intention to treat the child as a child of his or her family." In applying these definitions, a judicial distinction has been drawn between a person who maintains a positive and affectionate relationship with the children as a consequence of a relationship with the children's mother and a person who assumes a parental role with respect to the children.[439] In Newfoundland and Labrador,[440] the Northwest Territories,[441] Ontario,[442] Prince Edward Island,[443] Saskatchewan,[444] and Yukon,[445] the definitions of "child" and/or "parent" include "a child whom a person has demonstrated a settled intention to treat as a child of his or her family," but they expressly exclude a foster child placed with the family for valuable consideration. Alberta's *Family Law Act*,[446] deals with children *in loco parentis* in section 48 as follows:

---

432 *Sloat v Sloat* (1990), 102 NBR (2d) 390 (QB); see also *Gavigan v Gavigan* (1990), 30 RFL (3d) 314 (Alta QB).

433 *Weichholz v Weichholz* (1987), 81 AR 236 (QB); compare *Millward v Millward*, [2003] OJ No 1517 (SCJ).

434 *Casey v Chute*, 2010 NSFC 8, citing *Reed v Smith* (1988), 86 NSR (2d) 72 (CA).

435 *MAB v TLB*, [2002] NSJ No 192 (Fam Ct).

436 *LGP v JRH*, [2003] NSJ No 218 (SC).

437 RSM 1987, c F-20, s 1, as amended by SM 1997, c 56, s 2. As to the obligation of other "parents," see *ibid*, s 36.

438 SNB 1980, c F-2.2, as amended.

439 *Hachey v Dempster*, [2003] NBJ No 124 (QB), applying *Cook v Cook*, [2000] 182 NSR (2d) 299 (SC); *Morton v May*, [2004] NBJ No 254 (QB); see also *WAF v WF*, 2011 NBQB 319.

440 *Family Law Act*, RS Nfld 1990, c F-2, ss 2(1)(a) and 2(1)(d) (definitions of "child" and "parent"); *Ball v Murray*, 2008 NLTD 176.

441 *Children's Law Act*, SNWT 1997, c 14, s 57 (definition of "parent").

442 *Family Law Act*, RSO 1990, c F3, s 1(1) (definitions of "child" and "parent").

443 *Family Law Act*, SPEI 1995, c 12, s 1(1)(a) (definitions of "child" and "parent").

444 *The Family Maintenance Act, 1997*, SS 1997, c F-6.2, s 2 (definition of "parent").

445 *Family Property and Support Act*, RSY 1986, c 63, s 1 (definitions of "child" and "parent").

446 SA 2003, c F-4.5.

48 (1) A person is standing in the place of a parent if the person

(a) is the spouse of the mother or father of the child or is or was in a relationship of interdependence of some permanence with the mother or father of the child, and

(b) has demonstrated a settled intention to treat the child as the person's own child.

(2) In determining whether a person has demonstrated a settled intention to treat the child as the person's own child, the court may consider any or all of the following factors:

(a) the child's age;

(b) the duration of the child's relationship with the person;

(c) the nature of the child's relationship with the person, including

  (1) the child's perception of the person as a parental figure,

  (2) the extent to which the person is involved in the child's care, discipline, education and recreational activities, and

  (3) any continuing contact or attempts at contact between the person and the child if the person is living separate and apart from the child's father or mother;

(d) whether the person has considered

  (1) applying for guardianship of the child,

  (2) adopting the child, or

  (3) changing the child's surname to that person's surname;

(e) whether the person has provided direct or indirect financial support for the child;

(f) the nature of the child's relationship with any other parent of the child;

(g) any other factor that the court considers relevant.

As Graesser J of the Alberta Court of Queen's Bench observed in *Green v Green*, "[i]t would be surprising if a person might be in *loco parentis* to a child under the *Divorce Act* and not under the *Family Law Act*, or *vice versa*, although the treatment of children so found under each act appears different."[447]

The test of whether a person "stands in the place of a parent" within the meaning of section 2(2) of the *Divorce Act* or "has demonstrated a settled intention to treat a child as a child of his or her family" within the meaning of section 1(1) of the Ontario *Family Law Act* is essentially the same.[448] These statutory definitions require the applicant who seeks a child support order to provide evidence that the respondent voluntarily and unconditionally assumed a parental role. There must be proof of a permanent or indefinite unconditional commitment to stand in the place of a parent. The court must distinguish situations in which a clear, loving relationship was formed with the child from those situations where the respondent demonstrated only helpfulness and kindness while living with the child's parent. It is not the length of the respondent's relationship with the child that governs but whether the respondent treated the child as his or her own while living with the child's biological parent. The intention of the respondent is to be determined objectively from

447 *Green v Green*, 2011 ABQB 476 at para 29; see also *Shirley v Shirley*, 2007 ABCA 281; *SS v PS*, 2012 ABCA 163.

448 *Kincaid v Arsenault*, [2002] OJ No 1516 (SCJ); *Lamb v Copeland*, 2015 ONSC 3547 (application under *Family Law Act*, RSO 1990, c F-3).

the attendant circumstances.[449] *Chartier v Chartier*[450] identifies several relevant factors for consideration in determining the respondent's intention. It is the cumulative acts and the circumstances under which they are carried out that enable the court to determine whether the respondent's conduct reflects an intention to create a parent/child relationship.[451]

In those provinces wherein the governing statute provides that an application for child support may be brought against a person other than the biological or adoptive parent who has "demonstrated a settled intention to treat the child as a child of his or her family," the term "settled" denotes quality and not duration. What is required is a state of mind consciously formed and firmly established. The brevity of the intention is not itself decisive, but the conduct of a person during a relatively brief cohabitation may be insufficient to demonstrate the requisite intention.[452] In the context of the Ontario *Family Law Act*, the following factors have been identified as relevant:

(i) the length of the relationship;
(ii) the age of the child at the time of the relationship;
(iii) the contact of the child with the non-residential parent;
(iv) any financial contribution to the child's welfare;
(v) how the child views the alleged parent and how the alleged parent views the child;
(vi) how the child and the adult address each other;
(vii) the role, if any, of the adult in the child's education, discipline or recreation;
(viii) how the members of the household present themselves to the public; and
(ix) whether the parties considered a step-parent adoption.[453]

A child who is unwilling to abide by the rules of the step-parental household and who withdraws to live with her boyfriend and subsequently in separate accommodation while she pursues university studies may be found to have voluntarily "withdrawn from parental control" within the meaning of section 31(2) of the Ontario *Family Law Act* and may consequently be disentitled to a step-parental child support order.[454] The definition of "parent" under various provincial statutes has been judicially interpreted to include a wide range of

449 *Azougarh v Maliakkal*, 2010 ONCJ 610.
450 [1999] 1 SCR 242.
451 *Dovicin v Dovicin*, [2002] OJ No 5339 (SCJ).
452 *M(CF) v M(MF)* (1996), 23 RFL (4th) 55 (NBQB); *LN v NL*, [2002] OJ No 1082 (SCJ).
453 *Parker v Wagner*, [2002] OJ No 1581 (SCJ). Compare s 48(2) of the Alberta *Family Law Act*, SA 2003, c F-4.5.
454 *Dovicin v Dovicin*, [2002] OJ No 5339 (SCJ); compare *Erb v Erb*, [2003] OJ No 1527 (SCJ).

persons, including biological parents, adoptive parents,[455] step-parents,[456] unmarried hetero sexual cohabitants,[457] same-sex cohabitants,[458] aunts,[459] and grandparents.[460]

British Columbia deviates from the provincial/territorial norm by imposing a child sup port obligation on a "step-parent" in addition to the biological and adoptive parents, but the step-parental obligation is qualified by temporal considerations. Section 147(4) of the *Family Law Act*[461] provides that a child's step-parent does not have to provide support for the child unless the step-parent contributed to the support of the child for at least one year and a pro ceeding for an order for support has been started within one year after the step-parent last contributed to the support of the child.[462] The step-parent's duty is secondary to that of the stepchild's natural parents to provide financial support.[463] The statutory obligation imposed on a step-parent to support a child under the British Columbia *Family Law Act* is not condi tioned on the step-parent standing in the place of a parent to the child. Instead, it is based on a contribution to the support of the child for not less than one year. A partial but significant contribution will suffice.[464] Expenditures by the step-parent on behalf of the stepchild that are trivial in nature or are sporadic or in the character of gestures of occasional generosity or kindness may not qualify as contributions that attract a duty to support.[465] Section 147(4) of the British Columbia *Family Law Act* does not impose a requirement of a one-year period of consecutive support before ongoing parental obligations can be imposed on a step-parent. A brief interruption in an otherwise long step-parental relationship does not preclude an order for child support against the step-parent. The amount payable by the step-parent may be reduced by the amount actually paid[466] by the biological parent pursuant to exercise of judicial discretion under section 5 of the *Federal Child Support Guidelines*. An additional adjustment may also be appropriate by way of a set-off under section 8 of the Guidelines, having regard to split parenting of the two children.[467] The British Columbia *Family Law Act* applies to a wider variety of circumstances than the *Divorce Act*, but the primary interest underlying both statutes is to provide for the children's needs. A step-parent's assumption

455 *Marud v Marud*, [1999] SJ No 478 (QB).

456 *Hryhoruk v Hryhoruk*, [1994] BCJ No 103 (BCCA).

457 *Doe v Alberta*, 2007 ABCA 50; *Spence v Boyd*, [1999] BCJ No 2612 (SC); *Watch v Watch*, [1999] SJ No 490 (QB).

458 *Re LKF*, [1999] BCJ No 819 (Prov Ct); see also *Re LKF*, [1998] BCJ No 3186 (Prov Ct) (successive same-sex relationships; contributions of second partner found too trivial and sporadic to meet statutory requirement); *Spence v Boyd*, [1999] BCJ No 2612 (SC); *Murphy v Laurence*, [2002] OJ No 1368 (SCJ); *NA v CMW*, [2003] OJ No 1780 (SCJ); *M(DE) v S(HJ)* (1996), 25 RFL (4th) 264 (Sask QB).

459 *Perovic v Nagtzaam*, [2001] OJ No 3462 (Ct J); *PAH v RBH*, [2001] OJ No 5748 (SCJ) (each parent ordered to pay the applicable table amount of child support based on his or her income, where the aunt had assumed the responsibility for the children's upbringing).

460 *Cheng v Cheng* (1996), 21 RFL (4th) 58 (Ont CA); *Mitchell v Mitchell*, [1998] SJ No 404 (QB) (factual foundation must be established that grandparents demonstrated the requisite settled intention to treat the child as their own); see also *SAL v KH*, 2011 SKQB 397; and see *Fein v Fein*, [2001] OJ No 4554 (SCJ) (action for damages against grandparents).

461 SBC 2011, c 25.

462 *DCD v RJPC*, 2014 BCSC 2420; *Duffy v Boisvert*, 2017 BCSC 500; *Charan v Charan*, 2018 BCSC 1537.

463 *Ibid.*

464 *Hryhoruk v Hryhoruk*, [1994] BCJ No 103 (CA).

465 *DCD v RJPC*, 2014 BCSC 2420.

466 *EMLF v SLS*, 2009 BCSC 1242.

467 *SEH v SRM*, [1999] BCJ No 1458 (SC).

of new family responsibilities does not entitle him to unilaterally terminate the pre-existing step-parental relationship and thereby evade pre-existing child support obligations to the children of a former spouse.[468]

An applicant must establish, on objective evidence, a *prima facie* case that a respondent stood in the place of a parent before support will be ordered by way of interim relief.[469] An interim order for child support under provincial legislation or the *Divorce Act* should be refused where the evidence is contradictory as to whether a spouse made a significant contribution to the child's financial support or stood in the place of a parent.[470] Where affidavit evidence is inconclusive, the issue is best dealt with by a trial judge who can order retroactive support if entitlement is proven.[471] Caution is appropriate on an application for interim child support because, if it transpires at trial that there was no entitlement, it may be impractical to order any repayment.[472] Although a *prima facie* case may suffice for an interim order, a permanent order should rarely be made in chambers or even special chambers when the facts are contested.[473]

The Latin phrase "*in loco parentis*" in section 36(4) of the *The Family Maintenance Act* (Manitoba) has the same meaning as the phrase "stands in the place of a parent" in section 2(2) of the *Divorce Act*. Although section 36 of *The Family Maintenance Act* (Manitoba) limits the child support obligation of an alternative parent to the degree by which the biological parent fails to discharge his responsibilities, this limitation relates to the financial obligation and does not relate to the definition of the phrase *in loco parentis*. A person stands *in loco parentis* to a child when that person takes the place of a parent and this is a question of fact to be determined by the circumstances of the particular case. A person who participates in the care of a non-biological child and exercises all the responsibility and privileges ordinarily exercised by a parent will be found to stand *in loco parentis* to the child for the purpose of determining any child support obligation. Once the relationship exists, it cannot be terminated by the unilateral action of the person who stood *in loco parentis* to the child.[474] Although section 36(4) of *The Family Maintenance Act* (Manitoba) expressly declares that the obligation of a person who stands *in loco parentis* to a child is secondary to that of the child's biological parents, such a person will not be relieved from paying the full amount of child support based on his or her income under the *Manitoba Child Support Guidelines*, where the biological parent has no income or earning capacity or it is unrealistic to expect the primary caregiving parent to look to the other biological parent for support.[475] However, a court may refuse to order a stepfather to pay any child support where the biological father

468 *Dutrisac v Ulm*, [2000] BCJ No 1078 (CA).

469 *Green v Green*, 2011 ABQB 476; *Pitt v Mouland*, 2015 NWTSC 4 (judicial direction for trial of an issue); *Dunleavy v Comeau*, 2019 ONSC 4535; *Li v Wu*, 2020 ONSC 7329; *SLL v DBL*, 2022 SKKB 277.

470 *Hardy v Hardy*, [1998] BCJ No 1182 (SC); *Williamson v Williamson* (1991), 31 RFL (3d) 378 (NBQB); *Cote v Cote*, [1995] OJ No 807 (Ct J); *Pangborn v Elash*, [1999] SJ No 786 (QB).

471 *McFarland v McFarland* (1995), 18 RFL (4th) 59 (Ont Ct Gen Div).

472 *Segal v Segal* (1988), 14 RFL (3d) 453 (Man QB). Compare *Juneau v Latreille*, 2011 ONSC 6424 at para 24, citing *Ball v Broger*, 2010 ONCJ 1557.

473 *Green v Green*, 2011 ABQB 476.

474 *Thierman v Tymchuk*, 2021 ABQB 902; *Monkman v Beaulieu*, [2003] MJ No 24 (CA); *Phelan v Verni*, 2013 ONSC 2893.

475 *Monkman v Beaulieu*, [2003] MJ No 24 (CA); *Mraovic v Mraovic*, [2003] MJ No 457 (QB).

had already been ordered to pay child support and the child's needs would be fully met if the mother discharged her statutory child support obligation instead of having the child sacrifice his schooling by working long hours to maintain his mother's selfish lifestyle. A retroactive child support order may also be deemed inappropriate on the basis that it would impose an unreasonable and unfair burden on the stepfather, while generating a windfall for the mother and providing no real benefit to the child.[476]

Pursuant to sections 8 and 9 of the *Maintenance and Custody Act*, RSNS 1989, c 160, a parent or guardian of a child under the age of majority is under an obligation to maintain that child. In *Skinner v Cullen*,[477] the grandmother of a child and her married partner became joint guardians of the grandchild by court order after they assumed responsibility for him due to protection concerns. The grandmother and her spouse separated eighteen months later. Justice Gass ordered the *de facto* grandfather, as a continuing guardian of the child, to pay the table amount of child support based on his annual income. The biological mother and father were named in the style of cause but no steps were taken to procure their response or attendance. Justice Gass observed that it would be open to either the grandmother or the grandfather to pursue a contribution to the child's support from the biological parents, but this did not absolve them from their own maintenance obligations under the *Maintenance and Custody Act*.

Similar criteria apply under the *Divorce Act* and the Ontario *Family Law Act* when deter mining whether a person stands in the place of a parent or demonstrates a settled intention to treat the child as a member of the family.[478]

The naming of the husband and wife as parents of a child in a foreign birth certificate may be insufficient to warrant a finding that the husband was the biological or adoptive father of the child. Furthermore, the husband's sponsorship of a child for purposes of Canadian immigration does not trigger a child support obligation under the *Divorce Act* or the Ontario *Family Law Act* where the husband has never stood in the place of a parent to the child or demonstrated a settled intention to treat the child as a member of his family.[479]

A person living in a lesbian relationship with another person who has been granted the primary care of children may be shown to have demonstrated a settled intention to treat those children as children of her family within the meaning of section 2(j)(iii) of *The Family Maintenance Act, 1997* (Saskatchewan) so as to incur a liability to pay court-ordered child support.[480] Although the list is not closed, the following factors have been identified as tending to establish that a respondent has demonstrated a settled intention to treat a child as his or her own within the meaning of section 2(j)(iii) of *The Family Maintenance Act, 1997* (Saskatchewan):

(i) changing the child's name to that of the respondent;
(ii) discussing the possibility of adopting the child;
(iii) the child's reference to the respondent as "Dad" or "Mom";

---

476 *Deimuth v Fortin*, [2003] MJ No 60 (QB).
477 2009 NSSC 200.
478 *Andela v Jovetic*, 2011 ONSC 892.
479 *Bhullar v Bhullar*, [2001] OJ No 3034 (SCJ).
480 *M(DE) v S(HJ)* (1996), 25 RFL (4th) 264 (Sask QB).

(iv) the child's perception of the respondent as a father or mother figure;
(v) the age of the child;
(vi) the duration of the child's relationship with the respondent;
(vii) whether the respondent participates in disciplining the child;
(viii) whether the respondent provided financial support for the child;
(ix) whether the application is for interim or final support;
(x) whether there has been any intention to terminate the relationship;
(xi) whether the child has a relationship with the absent biological parent;
(xii) whether any other person is obligated to support the child;
(xiii) whether the respondent spends time personally with the child;
(xiv) whether the respondent has ever sought parenting time with the child; and
(xv) the nature of the post separation conduct of the applicant or the respondent, such as a denial by the applicant of parenting time with the child by the respondent.[481]

The factors listed in paragraphs (x) and (xv), above, may require review in light of the subsequent ruling in *Chartier v Chartier*— albeit in the context of the *Divorce Act*— that the appropriate time for determining the existence of a parent/child relationship is during cohabitation, not on its termination. Grandparents may fall within the definition of "parent" in section 2(j) of *The Family Maintenance Act, 1997* (Saskatchewan) but a factual foundation must be established before a support order will be granted.[482] There is no common law right to child support. Any such right can only arise pursuant to statutory authority. Pursuant to section 3 of *The Family Maintenance Act, 1997* (Saskatchewan), to which the definition of "parent" in section 2 applies, a person who has demonstrated a settled intention to treat a child of his former unmarried cohabitant as a member of his family may be ordered to pay maintenance for that child. However, section 4 of *The Family Maintenance Act, 1997* governs applications for the maintenance of children who are eighteen years or older and it includes its own definition of "parent" in section 4(1), which precludes the court from ordering a step-parent to pay maintenance for a stepchild who is eighteen years or older.[483]

2) Termination of Relationship

The appropriate time for determining whether a person stands in the place of a parent for the purpose of ascertaining child support rights and obligations under the *Divorce Act* or under provincial statute is the time when the parties were cohabiting as a family unit.[484] A person who has established an enduring parent/child relationship during spousal cohabitation cannot be permitted to escape the statutory child support obligations that flow from

481 *Major v Major*, [1998] SJ No 835 (QB) (relationship found to be that of a caring adult, rather than that of a person standing in the place of a parent); see also *SLL v DBL*, 2022 SKKB 277.

482 *Mitchell v Mitchell*, [1998] SJ No 404 (QB); *SAL v KH*, 2011 SKQB 397. See also *Snow v Snow*, 2013 ABQB 146.

483 *Kretchmer v Baran*, 2010 SKQB 63; *SDP v LMT*, 2016 SKQB 48.

484 *Chartier v Chartier*, [1999] 1 SCR 242; *Friesen v Friesen*, 2020 ABQB 103; *H(UV) v H(MW)*, 2008 BCCA 177; *Sullivan v Struck*, 2015 BCCA 521; *M(CF) v M(MF)* (1996), 23 RFL (4th) 55 (NBQB) (application under *Family Services Act*); *LMA v PH*, 2014 ONSC 1707; *Udalava v Amfoubalela*, 2018 PECA 16; *Swindler v Belanger*, [2005] SJ No 709 (CA); *SLL v DBL*, 2022 SKKB 277.

that relationship simply by a unilateral abandonment of the relationship after the separation of the spouses.[485]

Although a person who has stood in the place of a parent cannot unilaterally sever the relationship and thereby avoid the child support obligation, the question arises whether a parent can or should be required to support a child who is instrumental in severing the parent/child relationship. In *Cox v Cox*,[486] Adams J of the Newfoundland Unified Family Court concluded on the basis of *Chartier v Chartier* that the obligation to support a child is not discharged even if the child is responsible for severing the parent/child relationship. However, there are several judicial decisions, the earliest ones of which pre-dated the judgment of the Supreme Court of Canada in *Chartier v Chartier*, in which judges observed that where support is claimed for an adult child pursuing post-secondary education, it may be relevant for the court to consider whether or not the child has unilaterally terminated his or her relationship with the parent from whom child support is sought.[487] In *Ollinger v Ollinger*, Sandomirski J of the Saskatchewan Court of Queen's Bench held that standing in the place of a parent is not static and such a relationship, with its attendant rights and obligations, can cease when a stepchild of sufficient maturity unilaterally withdraws from the step-parent or where there is a bilateral or mutual withdrawal from each other.

Variation of a step-parental child support order may be justified where the child establishes stronger links to the biological father and the stepfather no longer stands in the place of a parent to the child.[489]

3) Respective Obligations of Biological or Adoptive Parents and of Persons Standing in the Place of Parents; Joint and Several Liability

Where the spouse against whom a child support order is sought stands in the place of a parent for a child, the amount of a child support order is, in respect of that spouse, such amount as the court considers appropriate, having regard to the *Federal Child Support Guidelines* and any other parent's legal duty to support the child.[490] This does not signify that the court should simply look at the amount payable under the Guidelines by the person who stands in the place of a parent and simply subtract the amount of the natural parent's obligation. Courts have employed a variety of techniques, such as time limited support, apportionment, percentages, and top ups to fix the amount of child support payable by the step-parent and

---

485 *Chartier v Chartier*, [1999] 1 SCR 242; *Thierman v Tymchuk*, 2021 ABQB 902; *KLB v SWB*, 2021 BCSC 1437

486 [1999] NJ No 242 (UFC); see also *Necemer v Necemer*, [1999] BCJ No 3023 (SC); *Lamarche v Crevier*, [2000] OJ No 45 (SCJ).

487 See, for example, *Wahl v Wahl*, [2000] AJ No 29 (QB); *Farden v Farden* (1993), 48 RFL (3d) 60 (BCSC); *Darlington v Darlington*, [1997] BCJ No 2534 (CA); *Swaine v Swaine*, [1996] NSJ No 553 (TD); *LMA v PH*, 2014 ONSC 1707; *Rudulier v Rudulier*, [1999] SJ No 366 (QB); but see *Necemer v Necemer*, [1999] BCJ No 3023 (SC). See also *Hamel v Hamel*, [2001] SJ No 692 (CA) (issue left unresolved). And see Section K below in this chapter.

488 2006 SKQB 433.

489 *Ewan v Emrick*, [2000] SJ No 742 (QB).

490 *Federal Child Support Guidelines*, SOR/97-175, s 5. And see Nicholas Bala, "Child Support Obligations of Stepparents in Canada: 'Standing in the Place of a Parent' & the C.S.G s. 5" (2023) 42 CFLQ 197.

the reasons employed by the courts vary.[491] A court has discretionary jurisdiction under section 5 of the *Federal Child Support Guidelines* to determine the liability of a step-parent in light of the obligations of the natural parents. Diverse factors may be considered by the court[492] but sorting out the extent of the obligation ought not to operate to the detriment of children.[493] A court may decline to reduce the amount of child support payable by a step-parent or a person who stood in the place of a parent where there is no evidence of any child support being paid by the biological parent[494] or where paternity is not proven.[495] A failure to locate the biological parent does not justify shifting the child support obligation to the provincial taxpayers.[496] There is no fixed formula or criterion whereby biological parents have the primary obligation to support their children or whereby a step-parent is only responsible for child support for the number of years or months that the step-parent has lived with the child. Parliament requires the courts to determine what is "appropriate" in each particular case.[497] There is no presumption that a person who stands in the place of a parent to a child should pay the table amount of child support but such an order is appropriate where the father is obligated to pay child support and has failed to do so. In granting such an order, the court may direct the mother to inform the "stepfather" of future payments received from the biological father.[498] The obligation of a natural parent to contribute toward the support of his or her child is simply a factor that may result in the reduction of the amount that a person standing in the place of a parent to the child may be called upon to pay.[499] In determining the amount of child support to be paid by a spouse who stands in the place of a parent to the other spouse's child, section 5 of the *Federal Child Support Guidelines* confers a discretion on the court to determine such amount as the court deems appropriate, having regard to the Guidelines and any other parent's duty to support the child. The court may consider circumstances other than the duty of another parent. The small amount of child support payable by the biological parent and the prospect of default by the biological parent are both factors to be considered in assessing the amount to be paid by the step-parent.[500] In addition to the payment of the applicable table amount of child support, a step-parent may

---

491 *LMA v PH*, 2014 ONSC 1707 at para 159, Horkins J; see also *Woodrow v Lepoudre*, 2022 SKQB 143 at paras 28–31 (order for ongoing financial disclosure in lieu of time limited support).

492 *H(UV) v H(MW)*, 2008 BCCA 177; see also *McBride v McBride*, [2001] NWTJ No 69 (SC); *O'Connor v O'Connor*, [1999] OJ No 362 (Gen Div); *Widdis v Widdis*, [2000] SJ No 614 (QB).

493 *Butzelaar v Butzelaar*, [1998] SJ No 741 (QB); see also *MacNutt v MacNutt*, [2008] BCJ No 1831 (SC) (stepfather ordered to pay interim child support on short-term basis pending determination of biological father's child support obligation).

494 *SS v PS*, 2012 ABCA 163; *H(UV) v H(MW)*, 2008 BCCA 177; *Peacock v Peacock*, [1999] NBJ No 313 (QB); *Dovicin v Dovicin*, [2002] OJ No 5339 (SCJ); *Boyko v Boyko*, 2010 SKQB 247; but compare *RLS v MNR*, [2005] BCJ No 52 (SC); *Cook v Kilduff*, [2000] SJ No 482 (QB).

495 *SM v RP*, [1998] QJ No 4119 (CS); compare *Stevenson v Perry*, [2005] BCJ No 1664 (SC); *Cook v Kilduff*, [2000] SJ No 482 (QB).

496 *TDO v RGO*, [2000] BCJ No 524 (SC).

497 *Janes v Janes*, [1999] AJ No 610 (QB); *Squires v Severs*, [2000] BCJ No 1083 (SC); *SM v RP*, [1998] QJ No 4119 (CS).

498 *Howlett v Howlett*, [2004] OJ No 3566 (SCJ).

499 *Stere v Stere; Herron, Third Party* (1980), 19 RFL (2d) 434 (Ont HCJ). And see *Spring v Spring* (1987), 61 OR (2d) 743 (UFC), wherein Mendes da Costa UFCJ suggested a time limitation for support orders linked to the duration of the *de facto* parent/child relationship.

500 *Aamodt v Aamodt*, [2000] BCJ No 1912 (SC); *RAV v SMIV*, [2007] BCJ No 2808 (SC).

be ordered to contribute towards designated expenses that fall within section 7 of the Guidelines in addition to providing medical and dental insurance coverage for the children through his employer.[501] There is nothing in the wording of section 5 of the *Federal Child Support Guidelines* that precludes its application in section 7 cases. In some circumstances, it may be appropriate to order that a step-parent pay more than a biological parent, having regard to the child's needs and the relative means of the step-parents and the biological parents.

Courts in some provinces traditionally imposed the primary responsibility for child support on the natural parent. For example, courts in British Columbia,[503] New Brunswick,[504] and Saskatchewan[505] have in the past resolved that where a child's natural father has been providing ongoing child support and continues to do so, the applicant must prove (1) that the support is inadequate, and (2) that nothing further can be expected from the natural father before the court will order support against the non-biological parent. These criteria pre-date the *Federal Child Support Guidelines* and require review in light of *Chartier v Chartier*,[506] although it is noteworthy that the judgment of the Supreme Court of Canada does not purport to address the implications of section 5 of the *Federal Child Support Guidelines*, which expressly confers a broad discretion on the court to order child support against a spouse or former spouse who stands in the place of a parent in such amount as the court considers appropriate, having regard to the Guidelines and any other parent's legal duty to support the child.[507] Insofar as there is no comparable provision whereby a court can take account of "any other parent's legal duty to support the child" when determining the amount of child support to be paid by a biological or adoptive parent, section 5 of the *Federal Child Support Guidelines* impliedly endorses the principle of primary and secondary obligations of child support as between biological or adoptive parents and step-parents or persons who stand in the place of parents to other people's children.[508] Given that *Chartier v Chartier* does not address the implications of section 5 of the Guidelines, there is nothing in the judgment of the Supreme Court of Canada that precludes a court from reducing the amount of prospective or retroactive[509] child support payable by a step-parent, even to zero, if that is found to be appropriate.[510]

---

501 *Ibid.*

502 *Azougarh v Maliakkal*, 2010 ONCJ 610.

503 *Delargy v Ciolfi*, [1999] BCJ No 1335 (SC); *Quinn v Quinn*, [1999] BCJ No 2099 (SC) (dismissal of application for interim support); but see *contra Reich v Sager*, [1997] BCJ No 2850 (CA), rev'g [1995] BCJ No 225 (SC).

504 *Williamson v Williamson* (1991), 31 RFL (3d) 378 (NBQB).

505 *Forbes v Forbes* (1994), 2 RFL (4th) 121 (Sask QB); compare *Kotylak v Kotylak*, [1999] SJ No 430 (QB).

506 [1999] 1 SCR 242; and see *Kotylak v Kotylak*, [1999] SJ No 430 (QB).

507 *Dutrisac v Ulm*, [2000] BCJ No 1078 (CA); *H(UV) v H(MW)*, 2008 BCCA 177; *Boivin v Smith*, 2013 ONCJ 426; *Woodrow v Lepoudre*, 2022 SKQB 143.

508 *Collins v Collins*, 2008 NLUFC 31; *WJA v STS*, [2001] NSJ No 151 (CA); *MacArthur v Demers*, [1998] OJ No 5868 (Gen Div). Compare *Symons v Taylor*, [2000] OJ No 2703 (SCJ). For express recognition in Manitoba of the primary obligation of biological or adoptive parents and the secondary obligation of persons who stand in the place of those parents, see the *Family Maintenance Act*, RSM 1987, c F20, s 36, as amended by SM 1997, c 56, s 4; *The Manitoba Child Support Guidelines*, s 5.

509 *NP v IV*, 2013 BCSC 1323. See also *SLL v DBL*, 2022 SKKB 277.

510 *Dutrisac v Ulm*, [2000] BCJ No 1078 (CA); *Sandhals v Lorette*, [2001] BCJ No 34 (SC) (divorced husband ordered to pay all tuition costs for biological and non-biological children but only required to pay table amount of child support for his own biological children); *H(UV) v H(MW)*, 2008 BCCA 177; *NP v IV*, 2013 BCSC 1323; *MML v PMF*, [2005] SJ No 514 (QB).

Section 5 of the *Federal Child Support Guidelines*, which permits a court to deviate from the applicable table amount of child support having regard to another parent's obligation to support the child, cannot be invoked by a biological or adoptive parent.[511] In determining the respective child support obligations of the natural father and the stepfather in *H(UV) v H(MW)*,[512] the judgment of the British Columbia Court of Appeal endorsed the following principles:

1) A natural parent cannot invoke section 5 of the Guidelines even though a step-parent is concurrently liable to pay child support. There can be no "balancing" or "apportionment" of the table amount of child support payable by the natural parent by reason of the step-parent's concurrent liability. The obligation of the natural parent to pay the applicable table amount of child support pursuant to section 3(1) of the Guidelines can only be modified or affected by the obligation of the step-parent in those discretionary situations specified by the Guidelines, namely, in circumstances involving children over the provincial age of majority (section 3(2)(b)), incomes over $150,000 (section 4), special or extraordinary expenses (section 7), shared parenting time (section 9), or undue hardship (section 10).[513]
2) A natural parent is not released from his obligation to pay the applicable table amount of child support by a prior consensual undertaking on the part of the step-parent to shoulder primary responsibility for supporting the natural parent's children.
3) The natural parent's legal obligation to pay the applicable table amount of child support is not discharged by voluntary payments of his own choosing made for the benefit of the children.
4) As was stated by the British Columbia Court of Appeal in *Dutrisac v Ulm*,[514] in the context of the provincial *Child Support Guidelines*, the judgment of the Supreme Court of Canada in *Chartier v Chartier*[515] does not preclude a court from concluding that a step-parent should pay a reduced amount or no amount of child support, if that is deemed appropriate in the exercise of the judicial discretion conferred by section 5 of the Guidelines.
5) Where it is practicable to do so, the amount of child support payable by the natural parent must be determined in order to determine the appropriate amount of child support to be paid by the step-parent. Once the former amount has been ascertained, the

---

511 *H(UV) v H(MW)*, 2008 BCCA 177; see also *Reis v Thompson*, 2009 ABQB 156; *MS v CS*, 2009 NBCA 66; *KK v AK*, 2012 NBQB 276; *Boivin v Smith*, 2013 ONCJ 426; *Wright v Zaver*, [2002] OJ No 1098 (CA); *Dolsen v Lariviere*, 2015 SKQB 127. Compare *Reis v Thompson*, 2009 ABQB 156 and *Thierman v Tymchuk*, 2021 ABQB 902, applying section 51(5) of the Alberta *Family Law Act*.

512 2008 BCCA 177. See also *DMD v RLD*, 2015 BCSC 2332 at para 215; *Sullivan v Struck*, 2018 BCCA 256; *MS v CS*, 2009 NBCA 66; *LMA v PH*, 2014 ONSC 1707; *Lamb v Copeland*, 2015 ONSC 3547 (application under *Family Law Act*, RSO 1990, c F-3); *Spry v Shetler*, 2021 ONSC 603 (application under *Family Law Act*, RSO 1990, c F-3); *Currie-Johnson v Johnson*, 2015 SKQB 315. And see the nine principles formulated by SS Bondy J in *Boivin v Smith*, 2013 ONCJ 426 at para 102. As to the apportionment of section 7 expenses, see *Guinn v Descoteau*, 2013 BCSC 1408; *Woodrow v Lepoudre*, 2022 SKQB 143.

513 See *PRR v JCG*, 2013 NBQB 405; *Wright v Zaver*, [2002] OJ No 1098 (CA) at para 30; *Sutherland v Schlamp*, 2014 SKQB 34.

514 2000 BCCA 334.

515 [1998] 1 SCR 242.

step-parent's obligation should be determined in light of that amount and the notional amount of child support payable by the primary caregiving parent, having regard to the objectives specified in section 1 of the Guidelines.

In the words of Newbury JA:

> Thus a "fair standard of support," objectivity of calculation, and reduction of conflict between parents are relevant to the determination of "appropriate" support by the stepparent. On the other hand, s. 5 does not, in my view, confer a discretion that is so broad as to encompass "*all*" the circumstances of a case . . . or "fairness" to the father arising from a kind of promissory estoppel against the stepparent (as was suggested by the chambers judge in this case).
>
> Given the "children-first" perspective of the Guidelines . . . , primacy should be given to the children's standard of living.[516] Where for example the stepparent provided a standard to the children during the period of cohabitation that was materially higher than that which the natural parents can provide by means of their Guidelines amounts, a court might find it appropriate to make an order against the stepparent that is designed to provide the higher standard, or something approximating it, "on top of" the other parents' support. However, where the "piling" of Guidelines amounts would result in a standard beyond one that is reasonable in the context of the standard the children have previously enjoyed, such a "windfall" or "wealth transfer" . . . is unlikely to be "appropriate."[517] At the other end of the spectrum, where the three (or more) parents' Guidelines "contributions" together are needed to provide the children with a reasonable standard of living, then both the stepparent and the parent(s) may well be required to pay full Guidelines amounts. Or, where one of the natural or adoptive parents is not present or is unable to pay any support, the stepparent may well have to pay his or her full table amount. The Legislature has left it to the judgment of trial and chambers judges in the first instance to fashion orders that are "appropriate" under s. 5. At the same time, the Guidelines system is not thereby jettisoned in favour of a "wide open" discretion. The inquiry must, like the Guidelines themselves, focus on the children and their needs.[518]

A similar approach was endorsed in the following conclusions of Aston J, of the Ontario Superior Court of Justice, in *MacArthur v Demers*:

> [para 28] Section 5 of the guidelines only applies if the respondent is not the child's biological parent. The following step-by-step approach offers one way of structuring the exercise of judicial discretion under section 5:
>
> 1. Determine the guideline amount payable by the respondent. This will involve consideration of the table amount, any section 7 add-ons and any undue hardship adjustment.
> 2. Determine the "legal duty" of any other . . . parent to contribute to the support of the child. As noted above, this will be established by a pre-existing order or agreement or by a guideline calculation. The words in section 5 "any other parent's legal duty to support the child" would include the [primary caregiving] parent, but the guideline scheme

516 See *LMA v PH*, 2014 ONSC 1707.

517 See *SLA v BAA*, 2013 NBQB 372.

518 *Ibid* at paras 40–41. See also *Shen v Tong*, 2013 BCCA 519; *Shaw v Arndt*, 2016 BCCA 78; *Spry v Shetler* 2021 ONSC 603 (application under *Family Law Act*, RSO 1990, c F-3).

assumes the [primary caregiving] parent meets this duty by sharing his or her household standard of living with the child.[519]

3. In considering whether it is "appropriate" to reduce the respondent's obligation under the guidelines, once [it has been established] that another . . . parent (or parents) has (have) a legal duty to support the child, the onus ought to shift to the [primary caregiving] parent to demonstrate why the respondent's obligation should not be reduced by that of other . . . parent(s).

[para 29] The [primary caregiving] parent might satisfy that onus, in whole or in part, by demonstrating that

(a) the "legal duty" of the other . . . parent(s) is (are) unenforceable, or
(b) such a reduction is inconsistent with the stated objectives in section 1 of the guidelines.[520]

In proceedings instituted under the British Columbia *Family Law Act*, an additional factor to consider in determining a step-parent's child support obligation is the length of time the child lived with the step-parent.[521]

Although a biological father cannot invoke section 5 of the *Federal Child Support Guidelines* to reduce the applicable table amount of child support payable by him, his court-ordered contribution to the child's section 7 expenses may be determined so as to reflect the mother's option to proceed for a contribution towards the same expenses by her divorced husband who stood in the place of a parent to the child prior to their divorce and has ongoing parenting time with the child.[522]

The child support obligation of a husband, who has demonstrated a settled intention to treat his wife's child from a previous relationship as a child of his family within the meaning of section 1(1) of the Ontario *Family Law Act*, is not negated by the mother's right to claim child support against the estate of the deceased father, but the amount of child support may be adjusted to take account of the child's receipt of a state-subsidized "orphan's benefit" in consequence of the biological father's death.[523] In contrast, a biological father's obligation to pay the applicable table amount of child support to his child's aunt, who has demonstrated a settled intention to treat the child as a member of her family, is unaffected by the child's entitlement to the orphan's benefit in consequence of his mother's death.[524]

From time to time, courts have provided an alternative means of limiting the extent of a step-parent's child support obligation by imposing a time limit on the duration of the order[525] or by ordering lump sum support.[526] It is open to a court to impose restrictions on the

---

519 See *Mayer v Mayer*, 2013 ONSC 7099.

520 [1998] OJ No 5868 (Gen Div); see also *RAV v SMIV*, [2007] BCJ No 2808 (SC); *Hiscock v Hiscock*, 2014 NLTD(F) 14; *GNP v LAG*, 2001 NSSC 165; *Hari v Hari*, 2013 ONSC 5562; *Nicholauson v Nicholauson*, 2019 SKQB 287.

521 *Henderson v Bal*, 2014 BCSC 1347 (stepfather for ten years required to pay the full table amount of child support where the child's father had died); *Bouzane v Martin*, 2014 BCSC 1690 (fixed-term support).

522 *Woolsey v Redman*, [2003] SJ No 823 (QB).

523 *Cassar-Fleming v Fleming* (1996), 20 RFL (4th) 201 (Ont Ct Gen Div).

524 *Perovic v Nagtzaam*, [2001] OJ No 3462 (Ct J).

525 *RAV v SMIV*, [2007] BCJ No 2808 (SC); *O'Hara v O'Hara*, [1995] NBJ No 291 (review order); *Collins v Collins*, 2008 NLUFC 31; *Millward v Millward*, [2003] OJ No 1517 (SCJ). Compare *Pittillo v Pittillo*, 2012 ABQB 109.

526 *Hall v Becker*, 2009 BCSC 1607.

duration of child support obligations pursuant to the express provisions of sections 15.1(4) and 17(3) of the *Divorce Act,* which regulate original and variation child support applica tions respectively. There is no obvious rationale, however, for a court to impose time con straints on an order for the support of a dependent child under the age of majority, merely because the obligor is not the biological parent of the child, except in circumstances where the step-parental order is intended to serve as a stopgap until steps can be taken to obtain a child support order against the biological parent.[527]

The *Federal Child Support Guidelines* specifically direct the court to have regard only to two considerations — namely, the Guidelines amount and any other parent's legal duty to support the child. The *Alberta Child Support Guidelines* go further and direct the court to have regard to the factors set out in section 51(5) of the *Family Law Act,*[528] which reads as follows:

> (5) Notwithstanding subsection (1), the obligation of a mother or father to provide child support outweighs the obligation of a person standing in the place of a parent to provide child support and in determining the amount and duration of child support a person standing in the place of a parent must pay, the court shall consider the following:
> (a) the amount determined in accordance with the prescribed guidelines;
> (b) the amount of child support that is being paid or should be paid by the father or mother, or both, of the child;
> (c) the duration of the relationship between the person standing in the place of a parent and the child for whose benefit the order is sought;
> (d) any other factor that the court considers relevant.

It has been concluded that cases interpreting the *Federal Child Support Guidelines* may be useful in the interpretation of the *Alberta Child Support Guidelines.*[529]

There is no single answer to the question whether there is any obligation to bring other parents before the court on any section 5, or similar, application. Although formulas have a surface attraction, they cannot respond to the many variables of multiple parenthood.[530] court should not reduce the amount of support that a child is potentially entitled to receive from a step-parent on the basis that the biological parent has a child support obligation, if there is actually no prospect of support from that source.[531] The court's obligation to ensure procedural fairness requires a biological parent to be given notice of proceedings involving a step-parent, if there is any possibility that the biological parent will be called upon to resume or increase his or her child support obligation. The *Divorce Act* and the *Federal Child Support Guidelines* are silent on the question of who has the responsibility for bringing the additional parent before the court. There may be situations where this responsibility should fall on the primary caregiving parent, for example, where the other biological parent is still

527 *Millward v Millward,* [2003] OJ No 1517 (SCJ); see also *Vongrad v Vongrad,* [2005] AJ No 632 (QB); *RAV v SMIV,* [2007] BCJ No 2808 (SC).

528 SA 2003, c F-4.5.

529 *Reis v Thompson,* 2009 ABQB 156.

530 *Janes v Janes,* [1999] AJ No 610 (QB); *Squires v Severs,* [2000] BCJ No 1083 (SC).

531 *Thierman v Tymchuk,* 2021 ABQB 902; *LMA v PH,* 2014 ONSC 1707; *Spry v Shetler,* 2021 ONSC 603 (application under *Family Law Act,* RSO 1990, c F-3).

involved with the child or has an apparent ability to pay child support. In other situations, the responsibility for bringing the biological parent before the court should fall on the person who stands in the place of a parent to the child and against whom a child support order is sought. Neither the *Divorce Act* nor the *Federal Child Support Guidelines* provides a procedure whereby multiple parents can be brought before the court so as to provide the court with an opportunity to allocate any financial responsibility between them, but the decision of the Supreme Court of Canada in *Chartier v Chartier*[532] supports the notion of joint and several liability and provincial Rules of Court usually provide for the adding of parties to a proceeding.[533] The exact procedural mechanism for adding parents to a child support proceeding has not been fully developed by the courts,[534] but the use of Zoom or similar technology might well provide a partial solution.

Section 5 of the *Federal Child Support Guidelines* should not be interpreted so as to permit a parent to unilaterally transfer the full obligation of child support to the step-parent or person who stood in the place of a parent to the child by refusing to identify or proceed against the other biological parent.[535]

When ordering the applicable table amount of support to be paid by a spouse who stands in the place of a parent to one of the children, the court may direct the recipient to pursue the natural parent and advise the payor whether the pursuit is successful, so as to enable the payor to bring an application to reduce the amount previously ordered.[536]

A step-parent or spouse who stands in the place of a parent may be entitled to add the natural father as a party to a child support proceeding.[537] Where it is just and convenient to do so, the judicial discretion to add a party defendant should be exercised generously so as to facilitate an equitable apportionment of the child support obligation.[538] In ideal circumstances, all persons who are under an obligation to support a child will be before the court so that their respective obligations can be determined.[539] However, there are often practical obstacles to giving effect to the obligation of multiple parents to support their child when one of them, usually the father, may have long ago disappeared from the scene. Provincial rules of court that provide for the adding of parties may alleviate the problem by allowing a parent to seek child support concurrently from the step-parent and the natural parent where the

---

532 [1999] 1 SCR 242.

533 *Janes v Janes*, [1999] AJ No 610 (QB) (application by step-parent to reduce child support denied, but leave granted to bring biological non-custodial parent before the court to determine their respective liabilities to contribute to the child's support); see also *GC v CH*, [2008] BCJ No 2371 (SC); *Rowsell v Rowsell*, [2000] NJ No 254 (SC); *Weinert v Weinert*, [2005] OJ No 584 (SCJ); *Cook v Kilduff*, [2000] SJ No 482 (QB).

534 See *MHR v JM*, 2011 BCSC 1622 at para 9, Loo J, citing Marie Gordon, "Third-Party Child Support: A Post-*Chartier* Review" (2001) 18 *Canadian Journal of Family Law* 327 at paras 71–74.

535 *Cook v Kilduff*, [2000] SJ No 482 (QB); *SMC v DLH*, [2008] PEIJ No 34 (SC). See also *Woodrow v Lepoudre*, 2022 SKQB 143.

536 *Lucier v Lucier*, [1999] BCJ No 402 (SC); see also *Thierman v Tymchuk*, 2021 ABQB 902.

537 *Snow v Snow*, 2013 ABQB 146; *Pye v Pye*, [1995] BCJ No 1315 (SC); *Ross v Ross*, [2001] MJ No 317 (QB); *McBride v McBride*, [2001] NWTJ No 69 (SC); *Walker-Bodnarek v Bodnarek*, [2005] SJ No 658 (QB). Compare *Baskin v Rogers*, 2010 NWTSC 73.

538 *Pye v Pye*, [1995] BCJ No 1315.

539 *Dusseault v Dolfo and McGarry*, [1998] BCJ No 1209 (Prov Ct); *Thorvaldson v Vanin* (1996), 25 RFL (4th) 273 (Sask QB) (application under *The Family Maintenance Act, 1997*, SS 1990–91, c F-6.1); *Cook v Kilduff*, [2000] SJ No 482 (QB). Compare *Nelson v Nelson*, [1999] AJ No 242 (QB).

latter parent lives within the same province as the divorcing or divorced spouses,[540] but the possibility of third-party applications for contribution or indemnity tend to ignore practicalities, not least of which are the absence of statutory authority,[541] the potential difficulty in tracing a missing parent, the prohibitive cost of litigation, and the perennial problem of the enforcement of orders that are obtained.

The right to pursue a claim for support against the father does not rest solely with the mother but can be exercised by the stepfather against whom child support is being sought. Adding the father as a party is usually the most just and convenient way of permitting all issues to be determined at the same time, if there is not already an existing order against the natural father. Pleadings respecting a claim for child support by a mother under the *Divorce Act* may be amended to permit the stepfather to present his claim against the father under the British Columbia *Family Law Act*. The court has jurisdiction under section 5 of the *Federal Child Support Guidelines* to vary the amount of support to be paid by the stepfather, having regard to the father's legal duty to support the child, but such a reduction should not be ordered until the court is satisfied as to the father's obligation to support the child. The court may accordingly conclude that the stepfather should be denied relief in the absence of an order for child support against the natural father.[542] Under the current provisions of the *Family Law Act*, and in contrast with the former *Family Relations Act*, a child support order is no longer available against a step-parent who is still resident with the child's parent. Section 149(3)(b) of the *Family Law Act* provides that a child support order "may only be made against a stepparent if the stepparent and the child's parent are separated."[543]

Although a court may refuse to add the natural parent of a child as a party to a divorce proceeding in which child support is sought against a spouse who stands in the place of a parent to the child, the natural parent may be ordered to provide complete and updated financial and property statements, to submit to examination for discovery, and to attend the trial for the purposes of giving evidence and producing any requested documents.[544]

Judicial opinion has been divided on the question whether a current spouse who stands in the place of a parent to a child can or should be joined in a proceeding wherein the payor or recipient of child support seeks to vary an existing order. Subrule 7(5) of the *Family Law Rules* provides that a court may order that any person who should be a party shall be added as a party.[545] In *Johnson v Johnson*,[546] on a procedural motion to amend the statement of claim, an Ontario court permitted the applicant to join the other parent's new spouse as a party to the claim for child support but the court expressly refrained from addressing the merits of the claim. In *Nelson v Nelson*,[547] PLG Smith J of the Alberta Court of Queen's Bench expressly declined to follow *Johnson v Johnson* and concluded that the term "spouse" in section 5 of

---

540 *Pye v Pye* (1995), 15 RFL (4th) 76 (BCSC); *Thorvaldson v Vanin* (1996), 25 RFL (4th) 273 (Sask QB).

541 *Stere v Stere; Herron, Third Party* (1980), 19 RFL (2d) 434 (Ont HCJ) (spouse standing in place of parent is unable to invoke natural parent's obligation in third-party proceedings); see also *Robinson v Domin* [1998] BCJ No 1145 (SC).

542 *Clarke v Clarke*, [1998] BCJ No 2370 (SC).

543 *KHM v JMF*, 2014 BCPC 246 at para 67, Harrison J.

544 *Singh v Singh*, [1997] BCJ No 1550 (SC), Master Powers.

545 *Azougarh v Maliakkal*, 2010 ONCJ 610.

546 (1998), 38 RFL (4th) 279 (Ont Ct Gen Div); see also *Azougarh v Maliakkal*, 2010 ONCJ 610.

547 [1999] AJ No 242 (QB); see also *Woodrow v Lepoudre*, 2022 SKQB 143.

the *Federal Child Support Guidelines* refers to a spouse who is or was a party to the divorce action and does not extend to persons who subsequently marry the original parties to the divorce proceedings. She further concluded that the phrase "any other parent's legal duty to support the child" in section 5 of the *Federal Child Support Guidelines* is sufficiently broad to include the legal support obligation of the biological parent of a child, of a former spouse who stood in the place of a parent to the child, and of a current spouse who stands in the place of a parent to the child.[548] Justice PLG Smith also concluded that, if the *Divorce Act* or provincial statutes or rules of court permitted joinder, it was unnecessary for the effective and complete determination of the matter before the court to add the new spouse as a party to the action to vary the amount of child support because the powerful tool of an adverse inference would be available against a party whose new spouse declined to co-operate. As she cogently observed:

> [para 51] In my view, if there is a legal remedy which would require the new spouses to disclose, (which I find there is not by virtue of s. 17(1) of the *Divorce Act*, but leave open the possibility under some provinces' Provincial Legislation) it would be similar to the application at bar, but would be framed under R. 38 as the new spouse being a necessary party by virtue of their "legal duty" to support the child under s. 5. While this approach was not argued before me, it is my view that the vast majority of cases can be fairly and justly determined without recourse to adding a party. The adverse inference is a powerful tool, and not a difficult one to raise from an evidentiary point of view in family law context, against the party whose new spouse declines to cooperate. Further, there are good policy reasons to avoid litigation inside intact marriages. It is not hard to see that the legal interests of co-plaintiffs or of plaintiffs and third parties are not the same. There is also the concern that allowing the addition of new spouses as parties in child support matters will create a flood of litigation.
>
> [para 52] However, I do not mean to preclude, by these comments, the possibility that a new spouse's legal duty to support the parties' children may precipitate a successful application to join that new spouse as a defendant or third party on the right facts and law. In my view, the facts required to be successful in such an application would have to demonstrate that while the adverse inference may lead to the complete determination of the matter, the inference would not lead to an effectual determination, and the lack of effect touches upon the children's best interests. Alberta law, as it now stands, does not permit action against *a loco parentis* parent still married and living with the biological parent. The Alberta law differs from Ontario and Manitoba law (see Reasons of Nation J. in *K.(M.J.) v. M. (J.D.)* (1998), 167 D.L.R. (4th) 334).

The problem of dividing the child support obligation between sequential parents and step-parents has evoked the following observations from Southin JA of the British Columbia Court of Appeal:

> The question of the extent to which someone who is not a parent either by blood or adoption should continue to be held responsible, perhaps for years, for children who may have no interest in him or her at all and whose natural parent may have acquired a new spouse, is a troubling one which appears to be arising more frequently and is deserving of more than cursory attention. It is not a question to be answered by the "blunt instrument" approach.

548 Compare *Mayer v Mayer*, 2013 ONSC 7099 at paras 93–94. See also *KHM v JMF*, 2014 BCPC 246.

The problem was addressed by Mr. Justice Thackray in *Sharratt v. Green* (1995), 11 R.F.L. (4th) 386. His approach seems to me to have much to recommend it. He commented, at p. 392:

> The case at bar illustrates the potential for a large number of people to attain the role of "parent." At some point in this progression the obligation of one or other of the "parents" must surely be subject to variation or even cancellation, depending on the circumstances of the case . . . .

In the case at bar four persons may have a duty to support the children: the mother, their natural father, the appellant, and Mr. More. It does not seem to me to be right in principle that the necessary support should be apportioned on the footing that as the appellant had the broadest back he must bear the broadest burden. I think it at least doubtful that the first family obligation concept to which the learned judge refers has any place when the children are not the natural or adopted children of the person from whom support is sought.[549]

In Alberta, section 51(5) of the *Family Law Act* provides that the obligation of a mother or father to provide child support outweighs the obligation of a person standing in the place of a parent to provide child support and in determining the amount and duration of child support a person standing in the place of a parent must pay, the court shall consider the following:

(a) the amount determined in accordance with the prescribed guidelines;
(b) the amount of child support that is being paid or should be paid by the father or mother, or both, of the child;
(c) the duration of the relationship between the person standing in the place of a parent and the child for whose benefit the order is sought;
(d) any other factor that the court considers relevant.[550]

In a decision of the Manitoba Court of Appeal that pre-dated the implementation of child support guidelines, it was held that the primary obligation of the parents to support their child under section 36 of *The Family Maintenance Act* (Manitoba) is not lessened by their youthful age or by the willingness of a grandparent to stand *in loco parentis* to the child, but it is limited by their own abilities to pay.[551]

Several provincial statutes have in the past expressly stipulated that the support obligation of a birth or adoptive parent outweighs the obligation of a person who stands in the place of that parent.[552] In Ontario, this statutory provision was repealed when provincial child support guidelines were implemented. There is something to be said in favour of endorsing the principle that the primary obligation to support children should fall on their natural parents and that only a secondary obligation should fall on step-parents or persons who

549 *Beatty v Beatty*, [1997] BCJ No 995 (CA); see also *CMC v GWC*, [1998] BCJ No 2344 (SC); *Adler v Jonas* [1998] BCJ No 2062 (SC).

550 *Reis v Thompson*, 2009 ABQB 156; *Thierman v Tymchuk*, 2021 ABQB 902.

551 *W(EG) v P(ME)* (1996), 25 RFL (4th) 270 at 271–72 (Man CA) (applying s 36(4) of *The Family Maintenance Act* whereby the support obligation of a person standing *in loco parentis* to a child is secondary to that of the parents).

552 See *W(EG) v P(ME), ibid*; *A(DR) v M(RM)* (1997), 30 RFL (4th) 269 (Ont Ct Gen Div) (applying s 33(7) of the *Family Law Act*, RSO 1990, c F3 as it then was); *M(DE) v S(HJ)* (1996), 25 RFL (4th) 264 (Sask QB) (applying s 3(2) of *The Family Maintenance Act, 1997*, SS 1991, c F-6.1).

stand in the place of parents. If step-parents or persons who stand in the place of parents to children cannot unilaterally terminate the parent/child relationship and thereby avoid child support obligations,[553] the same is particularly true of natural or adoptive parents.[554] It is well established that parenting time and child support are not dependent on each other. Consequently, a natural or adoptive parent should be unable to avoid liability for child support by dropping out of a child's life. The practicalities of the particular case may, of course, result in an accessible step-parent or person who stands in the place of the parent assuming the primary obligation for child support, but this should not become the norm where the natural or adoptive parent can readily be called to account. This principle should not prevent a step-parent or person who stands in the place of a parent from being required to pay supplementary child support where his or her income exceeds that of the natural or adoptive parent. Such an approach is quite consistent with the wide discretion conferred on the courts by section 5 of the federal and provincial child support guidelines. In the absence of any formula under the *Divorce Act* or the *Federal Child Support Guidelines*, the court has a discretion under section 5 of the Guidelines to apply what it perceives as an eminently fair and reasonable approach.[555]

In Nova Scotia, once a judge has decided that a "possible father" shall pay child support pursuant to section 11 of the *Parenting and Support Act*, the judicial discretion to deviate from the table amount specified in the *Child Support Guidelines* is limited to circumstances where the father can demonstrate undue hardship within the meaning of section 10 of the Guidelines. Where the "possible father" does not dispute that he is the child's biological father, the fact that other persons stood *in loco parentis* to the child does not reduce his obligation to pay the applicable table amount of child support under the Guidelines.[556] The mother's delay in seeking support for the child is not a barrier to an order for support because child support is the child's right and the child is not accountable for a parent's delay. Any reduction in the father's income after the trial judge's disposition should be addressed by way of a variation proceeding. A father is not entitled to complain of inadequate assistance from counsel whom he consulted before proceeding to act on his own behalf at the trial.[557]

Section 33(7)(b) of the Ontario *Family Law Act* contemplates that the duty to support a child should be apportioned between the child's parents, but a biological parent cannot invoke section 5 of the *Ontario Child Support Guidelines* against a step-parent and thereby avoid paying the full table amount of child support. The discretionary jurisdiction under section 5 of the provincial guidelines only applies if the parent against whom a child support order is sought stands in the place of a parent to the child or is not a natural or adoptive parent. Issues of fairness are not a relevant consideration in this context.[558]

A former "common law" husband against whom child support is sought pursuant to the Ontario *Family Law Act* is entitled to add the biological father to the child support proceeding, notwithstanding that the mother did not pursue any such claim. Furthermore,

553 *Chartier v Chartier*, [1999] 1 SCR 242.

554 *Ibid.*

555 *Boyle v Boyle*, [1998] OJ No 3783 (Gen Div).

556 *WJA v STS*, [2001] NSJ No 151 (CA).

557 *Ibid.*

558 *Budden v Briggs*, [2003] OJ No 5528 (SCJ); see also *Reiss v Reiss*, [2001] SJ No 37 (QB) (judicial refusal to add biological father to child support proceedings involving adoptive parents).

an agreement to waive the biological father's child support obligation as a trade-off against possible parenting rights constitutes no bar to a court-ordered reduction in the full table amount of child support payable by the "common law husband" in light of the biological father's concurrent legal obligation to support the children.[559]

A step-parent who has been granted primary care of a child may seek a child support order from the child's biological father under the Ontario *Family Law Act*, notwithstanding the existence of a child support order made under the *Divorce Act* whereby the mother is liable to pay child support to the step-parent.[560]

A court may reduce the amount of support payable by a step-parent with respect to his stepchildren because of their receipt of death benefits and pension benefits as a result of their biological father's death.[561]

4) Independent Actions between Sequential Parents

In *Chartier v Chartier*,[562] Bastarache J observed that the obligations of the biological parent and the step-parent "are all joint and several" and "the issue of contribution is one between all of the parents who have obligations towards the child, whether they are biological parents or step-parents; it should not affect the child."[563] In reaching this conclusion, reliance was placed on the decision of the Alberta Court of Appeal in *Theriault v Theriault*, wherein Kerans JA stated:

> [para 21] In my view, the obligation of parents, whether they be two or twenty, towards a child are all joint and several . . . If the parent before us seeks contribution, he should sue for it. Meanwhile, he must support the child. I would reject this ground of appeal.
>
> [para 22] I do not agree with the somewhat contrary reasoning in *Lewis v. Lewis* (1987), 11 R.F.L. (3d) 402 (Alta. Q.B.), and *Williamson v. Williamson* (1991), 31 R.F.L. (3d) 378 (N.B.Q.B.). In these cases, the judges stated that the primary obligation for support of a child rests with the natural father. In both cases, the judge made support against the step-parent conditional on pursuit of the natural parent. The judge in *Lewis* offered no support for his statement, and the judge in *Williamson* cited *Lewis*.
>
> [para 23] It may well be that the obligation of the natural father has primacy, but that is not a universal proposition. It would very much depend on the circumstances of the case, including the actual roles performed by the two fathers in the course of the upbringing of the child. In any event, that is best decided in a proceeding for contribution among the parents, not a proceeding for support by or for the child.
>
> [para 24] It is not in the best interests of the child for a judge to deny support from one parent for lack of pursuit of another. I agree with the approach taken by Miller A.C.Q.B., as he then was, in *Johnson v. Johnson*, 23 R.F.L. 293, [1975] W.W.D. 167 (Alta. T.D.). He made an order for support against a step-parent despite the existence of an order against the natural

559 *Kaszas v Guinta*, [2001] OJ No 2572 (SCJ).
560 *Couture v Ferguson*, [2003] OJ No 942 (SCJ).
561 *Bagu v Bagu*, [2004] SJ No 279 (QB).
562 [1999] SCJ No 79 at para 42.
563 *Azougarh v Maliakkal*, 2010 ONCJ 610.

parent. On the other hand, I have no quarrel with an admonition, almost always in the best interests of the child, that a further source of support be pursued on behalf of the child.[564]

Joint and several liability in tort law has been described as "obscure and under-theorized."[565] In the context of family law, a theoretical or conceptual framework for joint and several liability and the right of a step-parent to seek contribution from the biological parent is non-existent. The obligations of step-parents and biological parents are not assimilated or interchangeable under section 5 of the *Federal Child Support Guidelines*. Clearly, the table amounts of child support may vary because the annual incomes of a step-parent and biological parent are different or they may vary because the stepchild is one of several children in the parent's household. Even more significant is the fact that section 5 of the *Federal Child Support Guidelines* and its provincial/territorial counterparts can only be invoked where an order for child support is being sought against a step-parent or person standing in the place of a parent. In these circumstances, a court may find it appropriate to reduce the amount of child support payable by the step-parent in light of the biological parent's concurrent legal obligation to support the child. However, a biological parent cannot invoke section 5 or any other section of the Guidelines and thereby avoid paying the full table amount of child support solely on the ground that a concurrent legal obligation is owed by a step-parent or other person who stood or stands in the place of a parent to the child. The discretionary jurisdiction under section 5 of the provincial guidelines only applies if the parent against whom a child support order is sought stands in the place of a parent to the child and is not a biological or adoptive parent.[566] Issues of fairness are not a relevant judicial consideration in this context; "the Guidelines trump fairness."[567]

It has been suggested that the joint and several liability of multiple parents and the right to sue for a contribution would best be decided in a proceeding for contribution among the parents, not a proceeding for support by or for the child.[568] As was pointed out by Krever J in *Stere v Stere, Herron, Third Party*,[569] however, a biological parent's obligation to support a child is simply a factor that may result in the reduction of the amount payable by a step-parent; there is no right vested in the step-parent to institute independent or third-party proceedings asserting a right to an indemnity or contribution in his or her own right. Although the judgment of the Supreme Court of Canada in *Chartier v Chartier* implies that all parents can be brought before the same court in order to settle the issues of "joint and several liability" and acknowledges the responsibility of the step-parent to make the case for a "contribution" being made by the biological parent, it does not provide any legal foundation for independent

---

564 [1994] AJ No 187 (CA).

565 Hazel Carty, "Joint Tortfeasance and Assistance Liability" (1999) 19 LS 489, citing P Birks "Civil Wrongs: A New World" in *Butterworths Lectures 1990–91* (London: Butterworths, 1992) 100. As Hazel Carty further observes: "The leading text is still G. Williams, *Joint Torts and Contributory Negligence* (London: Stevens, 1951)."

566 *H(UV) v H(MW)*, 2008 BCCA 177; *KF v TB*, 2012 NBQB 144; *Wright v Zaver*, [2002] OJ No 1098 (CA). See also *Reis v Thompson*, 2009 ABQB 156; *Robinson v Domin*, [1998] BCJ No 1145 (SC); *MacArthur v Demers*, [1998] OJ No 5868 (Gen Div).

567 *KF v TB*, 2012 NBQB 144; *Mohr v Baxter*, [1999] OJ No 1541 (Prov Div).

568 *Theriault v Theriault*, [1984] AJ No 187 (CA); *Johb v Johb*, [1998] SJ No 603 (CA).

569 (1980), 30 OR (2d) 200 (HCJ); compare *Clarke v Clarke*, [1998] BCJ No 2370 at paras 41–42 (SC); see also *Robinson v Domin*, [1998] BCJ No 1145 (SC).

claims for a contribution as between step-parents and biological parents, nor would any such claim be apparent under the doctrine of unjust enrichment. In an annotation to *Primeau v Primeau,*[570] which has since been judicially endorsed,[571] Professor McLeod observed:

> In *Stere v. Stere*, 30 O.R. (2d) 200, 19 R.F.L (2d) 434, 19 C.P.C. 188, 116 D.L.R. (3d) 703 (H.C.), the court refused to explore the multiple parent dilemma. If, as *Primeau* suggests, a psychological parent is to be forever liable for support, the same should be required of the natural parent. If a mother refuses to pursue rights against the natural father, then the psychological father should have that right. The *Family Law Act* grants such a right. It is within judicial authority to grant a corresponding right under legislation which does not expressly so provide.
>
> Pursuant to the doctrine of contribution, where one co-obligor pays more than his share of a common responsibility, he is entitled to recover from the other. Where a demand is made, at law, on one, he is entitled to join the other and have the matter dealt with at one time to prevent multiplicity of litigation.[572]

Whatever the validity of Professor McLeod's observations may be under the former discre tionary child support regime, they appear to be impractical in the context of fixed amounts of child support under the provincial/territorial tables found in the *Federal Child Support Guidelines*, because there is no direct correlation between the amounts payable by the co-obligors, which depend solely on the obligor's income and the number of children of the marriage that the obligor is required to support. In the words of Gray J in *Varga v Varga*, "parents and step-parents are not entitled to seek indemnity against each other. The obliga tion of another parent is merely a factor that could result in the diminution of the amount a parent might be called on to pay. The other parent should either be before the court, or other evidence of that parent's status should be adduced."

K. CONDUCT

A parent's substantial delay[574] in seeking child support does not bar an appropriate order where there is a current need. The fact that a parent has not been pressed for support in the past must not be allowed to operate to the prejudice of the child.[575] In a proceeding for child support the prejudicial effect of a delay in filing an application must be subordinated to the best interests of the child. A biological father may be ordered to pay the applicable table amount of child support, notwithstanding the mother's waiver of periodic child support some fifteen years previously and notwithstanding the stepfather's current obligation to pay substantial child support.[576]

---

570 (1986), 2 RFL (3d) 113 (Ont HCJ).

571 *Kolada v Kolada*, [1999] AJ No 376 (QB).

572 GHL Fridman & JG McLeod, *Restitution* (Toronto: Carswell, 1982) at 365–80; see also *ibid* at 402–10.

573 [2009] BCJ No 626 (SC), citing *H(UV) v H(MW)*, 2008 BCCA 177, [2008] BCJ No 717 at para 38.

574 See Phillip M Epstein & Ilana I Zylberman, "Support for Adult Children in Cases of Estrangement: The Parent as Wallet" in The Law Society of Upper Canada, *Special Lectures 2006: Family Law* (Toronto: Irwin Law, 2007) 233.

575 *G(G) v H(J)* (1996), 22 RFL (4th) 69 (NWTSC) (application under *Domestic Relations Act*); *WJA v STS*, [2001] NSJ No 151 (CA) (application under *Family Maintenance Act*); *DAW v WMZ*, [2000] SCJ No 2391 (SCJ).

576 *DAW v WMZ*, *ibid.*

It has been asserted that fault has no place in the determination of child support rights and obligations.[577] The obligation of a parent to support a child in accordance with the Guidelines is not abrogated by the conduct of the other parent, however morally reprehensible that conduct might be.[578] Child support is a right of the child and should not be eroded by parental misconduct, such as the denial of parenting privileges to the support obligor.[579] Before the implementation of the *Federal Child Support Guidelines* on 1 May 1997, a court could reduce,[580] suspend, or terminate the payment of child support as a result of the deliberate actions of the primary caregiving parent in frustrating court-ordered parenting time granted to the support payor,[581] although it would decline to do so when it could harm the child.[582] It is not clear whether this judicial discretion to terminate or suspend child support payments continues to be exercisable under section 15.1(4) of the *Divorce Act* or whether it has been abrogated by section 3 of the *Federal Child Support Guidelines*.[583] A child's conduct or attitude towards a parent or step-parent has sometimes been considered in determining the right to and amount[584] of child support, particularly where the cost of post-secondary education for a mature child is involved.[585] It may still be relevant under section 3(2)(b) or section 7(1)(e) of the Guidelines in circumstances involving a child of or over the age of provincial majority who is pursuing post-secondary education.[586] Where a child and a parent no longer communicate with each other, the court is left to determine whether the relationship was terminated unilaterally by the child, in which case support may not be payable, or whether the payor parent has been significantly involved in the relationship's deterioration. There must be clear and unequivocal actions taken by the child to exclude the parent from his or her life. As well, the termination must not have been justified by the actions of the parent.[587] The onus rests with the parent to prove that the child has unilaterally terminated the relationship,

---

577 *Caterini v Zaccaria*, 2010 ONSC 6473; see also *O'Donnell v O'Donnell*, 2011 NBQB 56; *LTG v WH and MH* (1989), 89 NSR (2d) 67 (Fam Ct), Levy J, disapproving *Welner v Welner* (1984), 64 NSR (2d) 72 (Fam Ct), Niedermayer J.

578 *JAA v SRA*, [1999] BCJ No 634 (CA); see also *Bjornson v Bjornson* (1970), 2 RFL 414 (BCCA); *McLaughlin v McLaughlin*, [2004] SJ No 716 (QB) (stepfather); compare *Hamel-Smith v Gonsalves*, [2000] AJ No 430 (QB); *Wilbur v MacMurray* (1991), 38 RFL (3d) 74 (NBQB); *Dyck v Dyck* (1979), 1 Sask R 43 (QB).

579 *Lee v Lee* (1990), 29 RFL (3d) 417 (BCCA); *McGregor v McGregor* (1994), 148 NBR (2d) 176 (CA); *Martin v Martin*, [1998] NJ No 323 (CA); *Twaddle v Twaddle* (1995), 46 RFL (2d) 337 (NSCA); *Newman v Bogan*, 2010 NWTSC 69; *Carwick v Carwick* (1972), 6 RFL 286 (Ont CA); *Sveinbjornson v Deurbrouck*, [1998] SJ No 853 (QB) (application for remission of arrears). Compare *Turecki v Turecki* (1989), 19 RFL (3d) 127 (BCCA); *Hughes v Hughes*, 2014 BCCA 196; *Hamel-Smith v Gonsalves*, [2000] AJ No 430 (QB).

580 For a post-Guidelines reduction, see *Kuffner v Kuffner*, 2012 SKQB 427.

581 *Welstead v Bainbridge* (1994), 2 RFL (4th) 419 (Ont Prov Ct).

582 *McGregor v McGregor* (1994), 148 NBR (2d) 176 at 185–86 (CA); *Welstead v Bainbridge* (1994), 2 RFL (4th) 419 (Ont Prov Ct).

583 See *Johb v Johb*, [1998] SJ No 603 (CA) but compare *Chartier v Chartier*, [1999] 1 SCR 242.

584 See *Menegaldo v Menegaldo*, 2012 ONSC 2915 at paras 148–56.

585 *Farden v Farden* (1993), 48 RFL (3d) 60 (BCSC); *LG v RG*, 2013 BCSC 983; *Broaders v Broaders*, 2014 NLTD(F) 13; *Law v Law* (1986), 2 RFL (3d) 458 (Ont HCJ); *Friesen v Braun*, 2020 SKQB 253. See also *Fincham v Fincham*, 2017 ONSC 4279.

586 *Marsland v Gibb*, 2000 BCSC 471; *KKS v JSS*, 2019 BCSC 136; *Hrechka v Andries*, [2003] MJ No 114 (QB); *Szitas v Szitas*, 2012 ONSC 1548; *Fernquist v Garland*, [2005] SJ No 747 (QB); compare *Michaud v Michaud*, [2005] AJ No 1095 (QB); *Dykman v Dykman*, 2011 BCSC 883.

587 *Szitas v Szitas*, 2012 ONSC 1548; *Warsh v Warsh*, 2012 ONSC 6903; *Foster v Amos*, 2010 SKQB 409; see also *CLC v BTC*, 2012 BCSC 736 (mentally disabled adult child).

notwithstanding the parent's meaningful efforts to maintain a positive relationship with the adult child.[588] As the Manitoba Court of Appeal observed in *Rebenchuk v Rebenchuk*, parent/child estrangement is a particularly difficult issue. "[S]elfish or ungrateful children who reject [a] parent without justification should not expect to be supported through their years of higher education. But this factor rarely stands alone as the sole ground for denying support unless the situation is 'extremely grave' (*Pepin v Jung*, [2003] OJ No 1779 (SCJ))),"[589] and the threshold for such a finding is high.[590] In a paper entitled "Child Support for Estranged Adult Children," presented in November 2010 at a Superior Court of Justice Judge's Conference in Toronto, David L Corbett J thoroughly reviewed the legislation and judicial authorities. He provided the following summary:

(a) Contrary to certain recent literature, there has not been "growing judicial recognition" that the quality of the relationship should have a bearing on child support.
(b) Courts have been willing to impose a few specific responsibilities on adult support recipients, and may properly do so, but not conditions that include maintaining a social relationship with a parent.
(c) The statutory basis for taking the quality of the child-parent relationship into account is dubious.
(d) There is appellate authority permitting the court to place some weight on the parent-child relationship, but that authority is more ambiguous than trial and motions court decisions suggest.
(e) On the current state of the law, there seems to be a discretion to take this factor into account, though few courts do, and fewer have found it a significant factor in a support decision.
(f) The better view is that if conduct is ever relevant, it should only be in truly egregious cases of misconduct by a child against a parent.[591]

Although a court may find it inappropriate to deny child support because of an estranged parent/child relationship where the evidence is not indicative of culpability or unilateral rejection of the paying parent by the adult child,[592] it may conclude that it is reasonable to impose a condition on the right to continuing support that the child provide the paying

588 *Fiorino v Fiorino*, 2013 ONSC 2445.

589 2007 MBCA 22 at para 56; see also; *KNH v JPB*, 2019 ABQB 511; *VMH v JH*, 2020 ABQB 156; *Sharma v Sharma*, 2022 MBQB 27; *Swerid v Swerid*, 2022 MBQB 94; *CC v MR*, 2013 NBQB 330; *LeBlanc v LeBlanc* 2015 NBQB 164; *Nafar-Ross v Raahemi*, 2018 ONSC 3054; *Droit de la famille—121520*, 2012 QCCA 1143; *BM v PM*, 2019 SKQB 36; *Stephens v Stephens*, 2019 SKQB 114. And see *Urquhart v Loane*, 2016 PECA 15. Compare *Oleksiewicz v Oleksiewicz*, 2017 BCSC 228.

590 *Olszewski (Willick) v Willick*, 2009 SKCA 133 at para 34; *Tagseth v Tagseth*, 2016 SKQB 66; see also *Beach v Tolstoy*, 2015 ONSC 7248; *LAU v LLL*, 2016 PESC 3; *Magotiaux v Magotiaux*, 2016 SKQB 406.

591 Cited with approval in *Shaw v Arndt*, 2016 BCCA 78; *CMR v LFR*, 2019 BCCA 371; *Janmohamed v Janmohamed*, 2020 BCSC 432; *Sidhu v Chima*, 2020 BCSC 768; *MB v FA*, 2011 MBQB 7; *Caterini v Zaccaria*, 2010 ONSC 6473; and *AVR v MJA*, 2016 SKQB 272. See also *Marthinsen v Marthinsen*, 2020 BCSC 619; *Stenhouse v Stenhouse*, 2011 ABQB 530 at para 34; *Wawzonek v Page*, 2015 ONSC 4374; *Vantomme v Vantomme*, 2014 SKQB 227.

592 *McCargar v McCargar*, [1997] AJ No 678 (QB); *Alonzo v Alonzo*, [2000] BCJ No 2389 (SC); *Hrechka v Andries*, [2003] MJ No 114 (QB); *MV v DV*, [2005] NBJ No 505 (QB); *Green v Green*, [2005] NJ No 165 (CA); *Anthony v Anthony*, 2009 NSSC 343; *Pohlod v Bielajew*, [1998] OJ No 1770 (Gen Div) (child under age of majority); *Cennon v Cennon*, [1999] SJ No 504 (QB).

parent with copies of all academic reports, keep him or her informed of the costs associated with attending university and of other sources of income such as scholarships or employment, and discuss with him or her in a meaningful way educational plans before the beginning of any semester.[593] It has also been asserted that, while an estranged relationship between an adult child and the paying parent may not justify the immediate denial or reduction of child support, the child may ultimately be called upon to bear the consequence of persisting in the estrangement and that consequence may be cessation of child support.[594] This approach has been judicially questioned in circumstances of long-term estrangement on the basis that it is unfair to place such a burden on the child, when the responsibility for cementing a meaningful relationship with the child lay with both parents.[595] It is apparent from the caselaw that the quality of the parent/child relationship is rarely determinative in the absence of other factors negating the child support obligation,[596] unless the circumstances are extremely grave and exceptional as, for example, where the parent was the victim of abuse and the child had other resources to fall back on.[597] In *Fernquist v Garland*,[598] the mother's long history of parental alienation and the adult children's present refusal to pursue even a modest relationship with their father or at least participate in counselling for the purpose of resolving real or perceived issues was a significant factor that was taken into account in determining that the adult children did not satisfy the definition of "children of the marriage" within the meaning of section 2(1) of the *Divorce Act*. This judgment can be compared with the more recent judgment of the Saskatchewan Court of Appeal in *Olszewski (Willick) v Willick*[599] wherein support was sought for two adult children while they continued their post-secondary education. Applying the factors set out in *Bradley v Zab*[600] and *Farden v Farden*[601] as relevant to determining whether the two daughters were eligible for support as "children of the marriage" within the meaning of section 2(1) of the *Divorce Act*, the trial judge made the following findings: (1) an inter-spousal agreement indicated that both parents intended their daughters to pursue post-secondary education; (2) neither of the daughters carried a full credit load in any semester; (3) one daughter never applied for a student loan or other financial assistance and the same was probably true of the other daughter; (4) one daughter switched programs without advising her father; (5) the other daughter did not inform her father of her educational plans and her attendance at university in the fall of 2006, and her academic performance was poor. The trial judge also found that both daughters earned substantial income from part-time employment and he was not satisfied that they lacked the ability to contribute to their

593 *Lewis v Correia*, 2014 ABQB 314; *Ciardullo v Ciardullo* (1995), 15 RFL (4th) 121 (BCSC); *Hradowy v Hradowy*, 2011 MBQB 64; *MV v DV*, [2005] NBJ No 505 (QB); *CC v MR*, 2013 NBQB 330; *Rosenberg v Rosenberg*, [2003] OJ No 2962 (SCJ).

594 *Wahl v Wahl*, [2000] AJ No 29 (QB); *McLean v McLean*, 2013 ABQB 700; *Dalke v Dalke*, 2012 BCSC 173; *Khoee-Solomonescu v Solomonescu*, [1997] OJ No 4876 (Gen Div); *Fraser v Jones* (1995), 17 RFL (4th) 218 (Sask QB). See also *DDG v GNG*, 2019 MBQB 98 at para 111.

595 *JK v SD*, [1999] QJ No 4155 (CS) but see *Marsland v Gibb*, [2000] BCJ No 558 (SC).

596 *Wahl v Wahl*, [2000] AJ No 29 (QB).

597 *Dalep v Dalep* (1987), 11 RFL (3d) 359 (BCSC).

598 [2005] SJ No 747 (QB); see also *Moore-Orlowski v Johnston*, [2006] SJ No 389 (QB); *Ollinger v Ollinger*, 2006 SKQB 433.

599 2009 SKCA 133; see also *Billett v Billett*, 2013 SKQB 269.

600 [1996] SJ No 5 (Sask CA).

601 [1993] BCJ No 1315 (BCSC).

own support. The trial judge undertook a detailed analysis of the eighth factor in *Farden v Farden*, namely, whether the adult children had unilaterally terminated their relationship with their father. He determined that the father wished to maintain a relationship with his two daughters but there was no reciprocity on their part, the only relationship that they sought with their father being a financial one. He held that the daughters were not entitled to treat him in a disdainful manner and yet continue to reach into his wallet. In the opinion of the Saskatchewan Court of Appeal, it was clear that the trial judge had concluded that the daughters had unilaterally withdrawn from the relationship with their father and this was the determining factor that led the trial judge to hold that the daughters were no longer entitled to support as "children of the marriage." Citing relevant caselaw, including *Hamel v Hamel*,[602] *Saunders v Saunders*,[603] and *Rebenchuk v Rebenchuk*,[604] the Saskatchewan Court of Appeal asserted that "unilateral withdrawal rarely stands alone as a factor disentitling an adult child to maintenance and that the threshold for such a finding is high." Reviewing the evidence in light of this precept, it concluded that the trial judge erred by placing too much emphasis on the daughters' poor treatment and disdain of the father. In the opinion of the Saskatchewan Court of Appeal, it was clear from the evidence that the lack of communication after September 2006 between father and daughters was mutual, with each stonewalling the other except for a few abortive attempts by one of the daughters to reconnect with her father. The proper conclusion to be drawn from all of the evidence of the father/daughter relationship before September 2006 and the relative silence thereafter was that the father and daughters were fighting, and this mutual fight was prolonged and sustained by the litigation and the intervention of the mother. Furthermore, even if the circumstances as a whole were construed as a unilateral withdrawal by the daughters, the high threshold for a finding that it disentitled the daughters to maintenance had not been met. In the appellate court's opinion, application of the *Farden* and *Zaba* factors as a whole did not warrant the trial judge's finding that the daughters were no longer "children of the marriage" within the meaning of section 2(1) of the *Divorce Act*. It was clear that the daughters were not able to withdraw from their father's charge while pursuing their post-secondary education after all of those factors were considered and balanced. The matter was, therefore, remitted to the trial judge for a determination of the extent of the father's child support obligations, either by way of the table amount of child support plus section 7 expenses or, if that approach were deemed inappropriate, then by a determination of an appropriate amount under section 3(2)(b) of the *Federal Child Support Guidelines*, having regard to the condition, means, needs, and other circumstances of the daughters and the financial ability of each of the parents to contribute to the support of their daughters. The Saskatchewan Court of Appeal observed that many of the same factors canvassed by the trial judge as relevant to the issue of whether the daughters were "children of the marriage" would again come into play respecting his determination under section 3(2) of the Guidelines of what is appropriate. Without limiting the scope of the trial judge's inquiry, the Saskatchewan Court of Appeal stated that examples of such factors could include the unjustifiable failure of the daughters to keep their father informed of their educational situation for the 2006 fall semester and how that affects the father's obligations

602 2001 SKCA 115.

603 (1988), 14 RFL (3d) 225 (Sask CA).

604 2007 MBCA 22; see also *Winstanley v Winstanley*, 2016 MBCA 17; *Swerid v Swerid*, 2022 MBQB 94.

for that semester as well as the ability of the daughters and their mother to contribute towards the costs of the post-secondary education.[605]

A court may grant time-limited support or a review order with respect to an adult child pursuing post-secondary education in order to allow the child to re-establish contact with the obligor from whom the child is estranged.[606] In recognition of the fact that a reconciliation will need the intervention of a skilled counsel, the court may order the estranged parent to pay the costs of counselling.[607]

In *Chartier v Chartier*,[608] the Supreme Court of Canada specifically ruled that a person who stands in the place of a parent to a child during matrimonial cohabitation cannot unilaterally terminate the parent/child status on spousal separation and thereby evade the child support obligation. Although the Supreme Court of Canada did not specifically address the situation where the adult child is responsible for severance of the parent/child relationship, the language of Bastarache J's judgment in *Chartier v Chartier* is sufficiently wide to warrant the conclusion that such severance by the child does not terminate the parent/child status for the purpose of determining the right, if any, to child support.[609]

Variation of a child support order requires proof of a change of circumstances since the order was granted. If a father's application to vary is founded on the sole basis that the child has unilaterally terminated her relationship with him but the parent/child estrangement had existed for more than three years prior to the granting of the child support order, the required change of circumstances will not be established. In dismissing the father's appeal on this issue in *Vezina v Vezina*,[610] the Saskatchewan Court of Appeal observed that the father could reapply for variation to address the adult child's eligibility for ongoing child support while pursuing post-secondary education.

Parenting time with the child is not conditional in any way upon the payment of child support.[611] A parental agreement that the father shall neither exercise parenting time with the children nor pay child support constitutes no basis for denying a child's application for support under the Ontario *Family Law Act* when the child attains the age of majority but is pursuing full-time post-secondary education or training.[612]

A child under the provincial age of majority who is still attending school should not be denied support because he or she is not maintaining contact with the parent called upon to pay child support. This is the case whether or not the primary caregiving parent has contributed to the child's attitude and behaviour.[613]

605 As to the rehearing, see *Olszewski v Willick*, 2010 SKQB 289.

606 *Bennett v Bennett* (1997), 34 RFL (4th) 290 (Ont Ct Gen Div).

607 *Ibid.*

608 [1999] 1 SCR 242.

609 *Cox v Cox*, [1999] NJ No 242 (UFC). See also Section J(2), above in this chapter.

610 [2006] SJ No 105 (CA).

611 *Loughran v Loughran*, [2000] NSJ No 41 (SC).

612 *Hyde v Lang* (1996), 22 RFL (4th) 317 (Ont Ct Gen Div). See also *Black v Black* (1995), 19 RFL (4th) 442 (BCCA).

613 *Pohlod v Bielajew*, [1998] OJ No 1770 (Gen Div).

Determination of Income; Disclosure of Income

A. WHOSE INCOME?

The obligor's income is the foundation on which the provincial and territorial tables fix the monthly amount of child support. The income of the other spouse may also be relevant in cases involving a child over the age of majority or obligors who earn more than $150,000 per year. In addition, the income of the other spouse and possibly that of his or her household members will be relevant to claims for special or extraordinary expenses under section 7 of the *Federal Child Support Guidelines*, to situations involving split or shared parenting time under sections 8 and 9 of the Guidelines and to claims of undue hardship under section 10 of the Guidelines.

B. WRITTEN AGREEMENT AS TO ANNUAL INCOME

Where both spouses agree in writing on the annual income of a spouse, the court may consider that amount to be the spouse's income for the purpose of the *Federal Child Support Guidelines* if the court thinks that the amount is reasonable having regard to the income information provided under section 21 of the Guidelines.[2] Speaking to section 15(2) of the *Federal Child Support Guidelines in Boutin v Boutin*, Barrington-Foote JA, of the Saskatchewan Court of Appeal, stated:

> [62] … The fact that s. 15(2) requires that the judge have regard to income information provided under s. 21 does not mean that they can consider *only* that information. In particular, it does not mean that a judge can only find the agreement to be reasonable if they are satisfied that the payor will be obliged to pay essentially the same amount of child support as if no agreement had been made.… Nor need they turn a blind eye to everything but strictly financial

1 *Auer v Auer*, 2015 ABQB 67.

2 SOR/97-175, as amended, s 15(2); *Hayden v Hayden*, 2011 ABQB 731; *PHH v NRY*, 2015 BCSC 320; *Wood ford v Horne*, 2015 NSSC 208; *Richard v Holmes*, 2020 ONSC 6485; *Boutin v Boutin*, 2023 SKCA 41. See also *Liggett v Doucet*, 2021 ONSC 3886.

considerations. The question of whether an agreement is reasonable permits a more nuanced enquiry than that, in a manner that also takes proper account of factors such as threats and foot dragging to avoid rewarding such unacceptable behaviour.[3]

Where a father derives his income from his private corporation and the parents have negotiated a separation agreement with competent independent legal advice that provides a mechanism for ongoing financial disclosure and a determination of the father's annual income having regard to the fact that the father's tax year end does not coincide with that of his corporation, the court may uphold the agreement pursuant to section 15(2) of the *Federal Child Support Guidelines* even though the difference in the fiscal year of the parent and his corporation results in a one-year delay in the parent's reporting of the receipt of dividends from the corporation.[4]

The court has a duty to ensure that a child support order reflects the parent's true income. Spousal acknowledgement of a specified income in minutes of settlement does not estop a party from subsequently asserting hidden income and may warrant an order for further financial disclosure, but a court should not sanction a "fishing expedition" and may impose the penalty of costs if the allegation of a higher income is not substantiated.[5]

C. DETERMINATION OF ANNUAL INCOME; USE OF CRA T1 GENERAL FORM; STATUTORY ADJUSTMENTS

1) General Observations

Subject to section 15(2) of the *Federal Child Support Guidelines*, which deals with written agreements,[6] sections 16 to 20 of the Guidelines define how income is to be determined by the court in order to apply the Guidelines.[7] For the purpose of those sections and also section 21,[8] words and expressions used therein, which are not otherwise defined in section 2 of the Guidelines, have the meanings assigned to them under the *Income Tax Act*.[9]

The objective of sections 16 to 20 of the *Federal Child Support Guidelines* is to establish an amount that fully and fairly reflects the income available for child support purposes.[10]

An examination of sections 16 to 20 and Schedule III of the *Federal Child Support Guidelines* makes it abundantly clear that the calculation of income for the purpose of applying the Guidelines can be extremely complex. The degree of complexity will vary according to the source of income and the particular circumstances of the case. Relevant factors include whether the spouse or former spouse is self-employed or earns commission income, investment income, or dividend income and whether he or she has received capital gains. The

---

3 *Boutin v Boutin*, 2023 SKCA 41 at para 62.

4 *Miner v Miner*, [2004] OJ No 3303 (CA).

5 *Guarino v Guarino*, [1999] OJ No 4836 (SCJ).

6 See *Miller v White*, 2022 PESC 4. And see Section B, above in this chapter.

7 *Snow v Wilcox*, [1999] NSJ No 453 (CA).

8 Section 21 of the *Federal Child Support Guidelines* defines the financial disclosure obligations of a spouse who is applying for a child support order and whose income information is necessary to determine the amount of the order.

9 *Federal Child Support Guidelines*, SOR/97-175, s 2(2); *Bhandari v Bhandari*, [2002] OJ No 658 (SCJ).

10 *WLG v ACG*, 2021 SKCA 112.

difficulties will be compounded when the spouse or former spouse has voluntarily relin quished employment or is underemployed, or failed to realize the income earning potential of property. The time has come when lawyers and judges must use computer software pro grams in order to determine the appropriate amount of child support. Gone are the days of freewheeling negotiations and submissions premised on supposed going rates. Now, the arithmetical calculations must be precisely applied and access to a reliable computer data base or an accountant is essential if errors are to be avoided in the more complex cases.[11]

Fluctuations in income during the year are only relevant to the determination of the obligor's annual income; they do not permit parties or the courts to reassess the monthly amount of child support on a regular ongoing basis during the year.[12]

Section 16 of the *Federal Child Support Guidelines* calls for a flexible approach that is based on fairness to both parties. Accounting procedures applicable for the purpose of the *Income Tax Act* are not necessarily the same for the Guidelines.[13]

Where the obligor's income tax liabilities play a significant role in the determination of his or her income, the court may grant an order for child support on the assumption that the obligor's claim to a high deduction for taxes is legitimate, while reserving jurisdiction to adjust the order in light of any new information that may be received.[14]

A determination of income should be based on demonstrated earning capacity and not on self-serving speculation.[15] The fact that the obligor's income is derived from intensive and physically demanding labour does not warrant any adjustment to that income under the Guidelines. Although such income may not be sustainable over the long term, children are entitled to a level of support that reflects the obligor's actual income, regardless of the ease or difficulty in earning it.[16]

Remuneration from public service or from secondary employment is not excluded from an obligor's income in assessing the amount of child support that is payable.[17]

2) Basic Steps for Determining Income

In *Chan-Henry v Liu*,[18] Kent J of the British Columbia Supreme Court set out the following three-step process for determining a parent's income for child support purposes:

> [164] First, reference is made to the spouse's "total income" as set out in line 150 (now line 15000) of a standard form Income Tax Return ("ITR"). That ITR requires the spouse to itemize income from a wide variety of sources including:
>
> - employment income;
> - pensions;

11 *Meuser v Meuser*, [1998] BCJ No 2808 (CA).

12 *Lachapelle v Vezina*, [2000] OJ No 3171 (SCJ).

13 *Griffin v Griffin*, [1999] BCJ No 397 (SC); *GRR v JES*, 2020 NBQB 154 at para 72.

14 *Kaderly v Kaderly*, [1997] PEIJ No 74 (TD).

15 *Asadoorian v Asadoorian*, [1997] OJ No 3115 (Gen Div).

16 *Yagelniski v Yagelniski*, [1999] SJ No 35 (QB).

17 *Young v Young*, [1998] BCJ No 453 (SC).

18 2018 BCSC 2140 at paras 164–66; see also *Mach v Mach*, 2021 BCSC 1655 at para 176, citing *Sullivan v Struck*, 2015 BCCA 521; *KAB v PDM*, 2023 BCSC 1156.

- disability benefits;
- (un)employment insurance benefits;
- dividends from corporations;
- interest and other investment income;
- rental income;[19]
- taxable capital gains;
- income received from RRSPs;
- social assistance payments;[20] and
- any "other income."

[165] The second step is to adjust the line 150 (now line 15000) total income of a spouse in accordance with Schedule III of the Guidelines. Among other things, adjustments are made respecting:

- certain employment expenses;
- social assistance;
- dividends from taxable Canadian corporations;
- capital gains and capital losses;
- business investment losses;
- employee stock options;
- net self-employment income;
- partnership or sole proprietorship income;
- capital cost allowance for property.

[166] The third step is to make any applicable adjustments/determinations under ss. 17–19 of the *Guidelines*, which address fluctuating patterns of income, consideration of pre-tax corporate income where the spouse is a shareholder, director or officer of the corporation, and imputing income to a spouse in a wide variety of circumstances including such things as intentional under/unemployment, failing to use property to generate income, unreasonable deduction of expenses from income, and deriving income from dividends, capital gains or other sources taxed at a lower rate or not at all.

Judicial determination of a parent's income under the *Federal Child Support Guidelines* requires a court to examine both income and earning capacity. In *Murphy v Murphy*, Martinson J of the British Columbia Supreme Court[21] formulated the following step-by-step approach: Part I — Determine what a parent actually earns, and Part II — Determine whether additional income should be attributed to supplement the actual earnings. Each part has the following four steps.

Part I — Actual Earnings

- Step One — Gather mandatory information pursuant to financial disclosure requirements.

19 See *Evans v Evans*, 2023 ONSC 3919 at para 78.

20 Compare *Bradford v Bradford*, 2022 BCSC 595 (funds received for the care of a developmentally disabled adult).

21 [2000] BCJ No 1253 (SC); see also *DNL v CNS*, 2013 BCSC 858 at paras 30–32, Pearlman J.

- Step Two — Examine separately each source of income identified in the Canada Revenue Agency's T1 General form and use the most current information available to predict the parent's prospective annual earnings from each source.
- Step Three — Review historical patterns of income over the last three taxation years to determine whether the predicted income under Step Two is the fairest determination of annual income from each source. If it is not, the historical pattern of earnings can be used to predict the parent's prospective annual income from each source.
- Step Four — Total the predicted income from each source.

Part II — Imputing Income

- Step Five — Assess the parent's earning capacity in light of whether a parent is underemployed, unreasonably deducts expenses from income, is not using property to generate income, or is hiding income behind a corporate veil.
- Step Six — Determine whether the parent receives any income tax benefits or concessions or benefits under a trust.[22]
- Step Seven — Decide whether a parent is seeking to avoid the payment of child support by diverting income or not making full financial disclosure.
- Step Eight — Decide whether any other supplemental income should reasonably be attributed to the parent.

And in *Olchowecki v Olchowecki*,[23] Wilkinson J of the Saskatchewan Court of Queen's Bench stated:

> The basic approach in the determination of income is therefore:
>
> (1) to employ s. 16 to determine annual income for the year in which the application is heard, using the most current source(s) of income information available;
>
> (2) the combined effect of ss. 16 and 17 dictates that if there is a material difference between the historical pattern of income and the determination under s. 16, the latter should be questioned for fairness;
>
> (3) mere fact of difference does not make the s. 16 determination unfair. The degree of permanence associated with the difference, the quality of the change in income from historical levels, and the reasons giving rise to the change must all be considered: See: *Fuzi v. Fuzi*, [1999] B.C.J. No. 2263 (B.C.S.C.);
>
> (4) there is an additional test of fairness applied to a s. 16 determination of income if s. 18 is implicated. If the income earner is a shareholder, director or officer of a corporation, the determination of income may include:
>
> (a) all or part of the pre-tax income of the corporation or any related corporation for the most recent taxation year; or,
>
> (b) an amount not exceeding that pre-tax income which is commensurate with the services provided to the corporation.

---

22 See *Bledin v Bledin*, 2021 ONSC 3815; *Veskovic v Nielsen*, 2022 SKCA 134.

23 2005 SKQB 144 at para 10; see also *MH v AB*, 2019 SKCA 135, leave to appeal to SCC denied 2020 CanLII 36067 (SCC); *ACG v WLG*, 2020 SKQB 43; *Merrifield v Merrifield*, 2021 SKCA 85; *MacLennan v MacLennan*, 2021 SKCA 132, *Goertzen v Goertzen*, 2024 SKCA 45 at para 99.

Added to the pre-tax income are any amounts paid to or on behalf of persons who are not at "arm's length" unless the payments are proved to be reasonable;

(5) fairness in the application of s. 18 will depend on the nature of the relationship between the income earner and the corporation, the nature of the corporation's business, the legitimate calls on the corporate income, and the corporation's capitalization requirements, with the court having the ability to consider the historical income pattern of the spouse and non-recurring gains or losses: See: *Kowalewich v. Kowalewich*, [2001] B.C.J. No. 1406, 2001 BCCA 450, (2001), 19 R.F.L. (5th) 330 (B.C.C.A.) and *Boser v. Boser*, [2003] S.J. No. 714, 2003 SKQB 477, 240 Sask. R. 55 (Q.B.);

(6) lastly, s. 19 operates to impute additional income in appropriate circumstances, including, but not limited to, the enumerated situations in subparagraphs (a) through (i). Furthermore, imputed income can be used for the purpose of determining a pattern of income over three years pursuant to s. 17 as well as current income: See: *Schnell v. Schnell*, [2001] S.J. No. 704, 2001 SKCA 123, 213 Sask. R. 174 (C.A.).

3) Section 16 and Schedule III Adjustments

Section 16 of the *Federal Child Support Guidelines* provides that, subject to sections 17 to 20, the annual income of a spouse is determined using the sources of income set out under the heading "Total income" in the T1 General form that is issued by the Canada Revenue Agency and adjusted in accordance with Schedule III.[24] While using the previous year's line 150 (now line 15000) income as the basis for the next year's payment obligations will often be a fair, inexpensive way of determining child support obligations,[25] it will be grossly unfair if a dramatic change has occurred that deprives the support creditor of substantial child support for a year or cripples the support debtor by imposing a level of payments that cannot be afforded.[26] The T1 General form identifies the sources that make up total income as: employment income; commissions; old age security pension; Canada or Quebec Pension Plan benefits; disability benefits;[27] other pensions or superannuation; unemployment insurance benefits; dividends; interest and other investment income; partnership income; rental income;[28] capital gains;[29] registered retirement savings plan income; other income; business income; professional income; commission income; farming income; fishing income; workers' compensation payments; social assistance payments;[30] and net federal supplements.[31] Capital gains and registered retirement savings plan income are sources of income that are subject

24 *Darlington v Moore*, 2013 NSSC 103; *Szitas v Szitas*, 2012 ONSC 1548; *Morrissey v Morrissey*, 2015 PECA 16; *Pearson v Pearson*, 2004 SKQB 348 (union dues and automobile expenses must be deducted under Sch III).

25 *Farnsworth v Chang*, 2014 ONSC 1871, citing *Bak v Dobell*, 2007 ONCA 304 at para 30.

26 *Gibson v Gibson*, 2011 ABQB 564. See also *Walls v Walls*, 2014 BCSC 586.

27 See *Mullins v Mullins*, 2016 ABQB 226; *SMS v SMU*, 2021 BCSC 933 (non-taxable disability pension grossed up); *Myles v Armstrong*, 2011 NBQB 61; *Taylor v Sherlow*, 2014 ONSC 6614. See also *Crossley v Vorell*, 2021 BCSC 2484.

28 See *Appu v Appu*, 2014 ONSC 19; *Evans v Evans*, 2023 ONSC 3919 at para 78.

29 *Qaraan v Qaraan*, 2014 ONCA 401; *Wetsch v Kuski*, 2017 SKCA 77.

30 See *Mullins v Mullins*, 2016 ABQB 226. See also *Crossley v Vorell*, 2021 BCSC 2484.

31 *Darlington v Moore*, 2013 NSSC 103.

to adjustment as described in Schedule III and they may in fact be excluded if their inclusion will not lead to a fair determination of the spouse's income.

The basis for the exclusion of an income or part of an income is outlined in sections 17 to 20 of the Guidelines.[32] In determining income, a court must consider taxable benefits even though the parent does not receive them in cash because they are "income sources" set out under the heading of Total Income in the T-1 General form.[33]

In assessing or imputing income, the court must take into account income from all sources, including retroactive income from an arbitral award[34] or pay equity settlement, rental income, interest payments, and disability payments.[36] Section 16 of the Guidelines does not permit or require a court to use gross business income to derive income for child support purposes. The court should look to net business income, which is part of the total of income under line 150 (now line 15000) of the T1 income tax return, but the court can impute income under section 19(1)(g) of the Guidelines if the obligor unreasonably deducts expenses from income.[37]

Section 16 and Schedule III of the Guidelines provide the starting point for determining parental income. Section 17 of the Guidelines, which empowers a court to take account of a parent's fluctuating annual income over the last three years, and section 19 of the Guidelines, which empowers a court to impute income to a parent, are only triggered when section 16 and Schedule III of the Guidelines would fail to provide the fairest determination of the par ent's current and anticipated annual income.[38] Specified adjustments to the spouse's income provided under Schedule III of the Guidelines include the following:

a) the spouse's employment expenses that would be deductible under sections 8(1)(d) to (j) and (n) to (q) of the *Income Tax Act* are deducted;[39]
b) CPP contributions and Employment Insurance premiums under section 8(1)(l.1) of the *Income Tax Act* are deducted if paid in respect of another employee who has acted as an assistant or substitute for the spouse;[40]
c) child support that is included to determine total income in the T1 General form issued by the Canada Revenue Agency is to be deducted;

---

32 *Ibid.*

33 *Chin v Chow*, [1998] BCJ No 1278 (SC); *Froese v Froese*, 2010 MBQB 156; *Boissy v Boissy*, [2004] OJ No 3400 (SCJ).

34 *Levesque v Meade*, 2010 NBQB 270.

35 *Gagnier v Gagnier*, [2002] OJ No 2183 (SCJ).

36 *Brosteneants v Brosteneants*, [1999] OJ No 819 (Gen Div); see *Boissy v Boissy*, [2004] OJ No 3400 (SCJ) (taxable benefits to be included).

37 *MT v JS*, 2023 BCCA 64; *Appu v Appu*, 2014 ONSC 19.

38 *Luckett v Luckett*, [2002] SJ No 232 (QB). See also *Warren v Warren*, 2021 ABQB 213 (restricted share units; subsequent loss in value).

39 *Jarbeau v Pelletier*, [1998] OJ No 3029 (Prov Div) (meals and lodgings of railway employee held deductible under *Income Tax Act*, s 8(1)(e); union dues deductible under s 8(1)(i); motor vehicle expenses deductible under s 8(1)(j)); *Haimanot v Haimanot*, [2002] SJ No 12 (CA) (union dues); *Larocque v Larocque*, 2011 SKQB 140 (subsistence and clothing allowances); *Sobczak v Evraire*, 2013 ONSC 1249 (automobile expenses); *Smith v Smith*, 2013 ONCJ 657 (motor vehicle expenses). See also *ADJ v FJ*, 2022 BCSC 600; *Haras v Camp*, 2018 ONSC 3456; *BM v PM*, 2019 SKQB 36.

40 *Guidelines to Amend the Federal Child Support Guidelines*, SOR/97-563, s 12, amending SOR/97-175, s 1(i) of Sch III. As to health care premiums, see *Neilly v Neilly*, 2019 ABCA 504 at paras 14–18.

d) spousal support received from the other spouse is deducted in calculating income for the purpose of determining the amount of child support under the applicable provincial or territorial table;[41]
e) spousal support paid to the other spouse is deducted in calculating income for the purpose of determining an amount respecting special or extraordinary expenses under section 7 of the Guidelines;[42]
f) social assistance income is adjusted to only include the amount determined to be attributable to the spouse;[43]
g) the taxable amount of dividends from Canadian corporations received by the spouse is replaced by the actual amount of those dividends received by the spouse;[44]
h) the taxable capital gains realized in a year by the spouse are replaced by the actual amount of capital gains realized by the spouse in excess of actual capital losses suffered by the spouse in that year;[45]
i) the actual amount of business investment losses suffered by a spouse during the year are deducted;[46]
j) the spouse's carrying charges and interest expenses that are paid by the spouse and that would be deductible under the *Income Tax Act* are deducted;[47]
k) where the net self-employment income of the spouse is determined by deducting an amount in respect of salaries, wages or management fees, or other payments, paid to or on behalf of persons with whom the spouse does not deal at arm's length, that amount shall be added, unless the spouse establishes that the payments were necessary to earn the self-employment income and were reasonable in the circumstances;[48]

---

41 *Saunders v Saunders*, 2020 ABCA 226; *Bowes v Bowes*, 2021 NLCA 10; *Mudronja v Mudronja*, 2020 ONCA 569; see also *O'Brien v O'Brien*, 2011 NBQB 179 (adjustment for lump sum spousal support).

42 *Russell v Russell*, [2002] BCJ No 1983 (SC); *O'Brien v O'Brien*, 2011 NBQB 179; *Magee v Magee*, [1997] SJ No 468 (QB).

43 *Mullins v Mullins*, 2016 ABQB 226; *Martel v Martel*, [2001] OJ No 759 (Ct J).

44 *Plett v Plett*, 2009 BCSC 227; *NP v MCP*, 2012 BCSC 1843; *Dickson v Dickson*, 2009 MBQB 274; *Hanrahan-Cox v Cox*, 2011 NSSC 182; *Plese v Herjavec*, 2018 ONSC 7749; *Stephen v Stephen*, [1999] SJ No 479 (QB). See also *MC v JO*, 2017 NBCA 15; *CRP v NDP*, 2023 NBKB 197. Compare *Brown v Brown*, 2014 BCCA 152. And see *AMW v BW*, 2018 ABQB 518 at paras 14–17.

45 *Plett v Plett*, 2009 BCSC 227; *Dickson v Dickson*, 2009 MBQB 274; *C v S*, 2010 NBQB 252; *Kendry v Cathcart*, [2001] OJ No 277 (SCJ); compare *Andersen v Andersen*, [1997] BCJ No 2496 (SC).

46 *McCaffrey v Dalla Longa*, 2008 ABQB 183; *Kohlman v Bergeron*, 2015 ABCA 410; *Warren v Warren*, 2021 ABQB 213.

47 *McCaffrey v Dalla Longa*, 2008 ABQB 183; *MHG v DJG*, [2006] BCJ No 275 (SC); *TC v AJ*, 2021 BCSC 1696 (deduction of legal fees incurred to obtain a child support order); *Andres v Andres*, [1999] MJ No 103 (*sub nom Cornelius v Andres*) (1999), 170 DLR (4th) 254 (Man CA) (mortgage payments respecting rental property; principal not deductible under s 18(1)(b) of *Income Tax Act*; interest deductible under s 20(1)(c) of *Income Tax Act*); *Dickson v Dickson*, 2009 MBQB 274 (deduction of carrying charges paid); *C v S*, 2010 NBQB 252; *McBennett v Danis*, 2021 ONSC 3610 at paras 297–99 (legal fees to pursue support); *Haimanot v Haimanot*, [2002] SJ No 12 (CA); *Boutin v Boutin*, 2023 SKCA 41. See also *McKenzie v McKenzie*, 2014 BCCA 381; *SLD v WAD*, 2020 BCSC 690; *Forester v Odjick*, 2021 BCSC 789; *ARJ v ZSH*, 2021 BCSC 274.

48 *Holtby v Holtby*, [1997] OJ No 2237 (Gen Div); *Stewart v Stewart*, [2000] SJ No 149 (QB). See also *Dickson v Dickson*, 2009 MBQB 274.

l) where the spouse reports income from self-employment that includes income for the reporting year plus a further amount earned in the prior year, the spouse may deduct the amount earned in the prior period, net of reserves;
m) spousal income includes any deduction for an allowable capital cost allowance with respect to real property;[49]
n) where the spouse earns income from a partnership or sole proprietorship, any amount included in income that is properly required by the partnership or sole proprietorship for purposes of capitalization shall be deducted from the spouse's income;[50]
o) where the spouse has received, as an employee benefit, stock options to purchase shares of a Canadian-controlled private corporation, or a publicly traded corporation that is subject to the same tax treatment as a Canadian-controlled private corporation, and has exercised the options during the year, the difference between the value of the shares at the time the options are exercised and the amount paid for the shares and any amount paid to acquire the options is added to the spouse's income for the year in which the options are exercised;[51] and if the spouse has disposed of the shares during a year, deduct from the income for that year the difference determined under section 13(1).[52]
p) if a spouse is deemed to have received a split-pension amount under paragraph 60.03(2)(b) of the *Income Tax Act* that is included in that spouse's total income in the T1 General form issued by the Canada Revenue Agency, deduct that amount.[53]

Premiums paid on a parent's behalf by an employer for life insurance are not deductible under Schedule III of the *Child Support Guidelines*.[54]

Where a mother receives an annual income from her current husband pursuant to an income splitting arrangement to secure income tax advantages, it may be fair and reasonable to accept this income, which is reported on her CRA T1 General form, as her income under the *Federal Child Support Guidelines* for the purpose of apportioning section 7 expenses between the two parents.[55]

The payment of church tithes is a discretionary expense that cannot take priority over child support obligations. Such payments made through the obligor's professional corporation may be considered as part of his or her personal income for the purposes of calculating her child support obligation in light of sections 16 and 18 of the *Federal Child Support Guidelines*.

---

49 *McCaffrey v Dalla Longa*, [2008] AJ No 335 (QB); *Ghosn v Ghosn*, [2006] NSJ No 33 (SC); *Roberts v Roberts*, 2011 ONSC 7130; *Monkman v Monkman*, 2013 SKQB 80.

50 *TLB v RB*, 2010 BCSC 710; *Evanow v Lannon*, 2018 BCCA 208; *Ghosn v Ghosn*, [2006] NSJ No 33 (SC) *Abelman v Abelman*, 2017 ONSC 1810 at paras 65–68; see also *Dickson v Dickson*, 2009 MBQB 274.

51 Schedule III, s 13(1). See *Gibson v Gibson*, 2011 ONSC 4406 (shares not included in income until they vest). Compare *Sarro v Sarro*, 2011 BCSC 1010, applying s 17 of the *Federal Child Support Guidelines*; *Walker v Walker*, 2024 ONSC 198. And see below, (j) "Stock Options."

52 Schedule III, s 13(2); see also *Walker v Walker*, 2024 ONSC 198; Aaron Franks, "Deferred Compensation Versus Current Support Obligations" in Law Society of Upper Canada, *Special Lectures 2006: Family Law* (Toronto: Irwin Law, 2007) 273.

53 *Guidelines Amending the Federal Child Support Guidelines*, SOR/2009-181 11 June 2009.

54 *PJC v PLC*, 2024 NBKB 42 at para 89, citing *Chippett v Fudge*, 2019 NLSC 29.

55 *Ohlmann v Ohlmann*, [2005] AJ No 140 (QB).

56 *Zubek v Nizol*, 2011 BCSC 776.

a) Federal and Provincial Government Benefits; Canada Child Benefit and GST Credits

Child-related government benefits and refundable credits such as the Canada Child Benefit, the National Child Benefit Supplement, the GST credit (including any portion for the children), the refundable medical expense credit, the Child Disability Benefit, and the various provincial benefit and credit schemes, are included in a spouse's income for the purpose of applying the With Child Support formula under the *Spousal Support Advisory Guidelines*, but these benefits and credits are not treated as income for table amount purposes under the *Federal Child Support Guidelines*.[57]

Child tax credits and GST/HST rebates are not included in the recipient spouse's income.[58] They do not constitute a source of income under the T1 General form,[59] although they may be taken into account in determining a spouse's "means" for the purpose of applying section 9(c) of the *Federal Child Support Guidelines* in cases involving shared parenting arrangements.[60] Similarly, GST credits and child tax credits should not be considered as income for the purpose of allocating section 7 expenses under the *Federal Child Support Guidelines*,[61] but they may be included in the "means" of the recipient parent pursuant to section 7(1) of the Guidelines.[62]

b) Employment Expenses

Where the requirements of section 6(6) of the *Income Tax Act* are satisfied, an obligor who is an employee can exclude a living allowance from his or her income under the Guidelines. The requirements are (1) that the allowance does not exceed a reasonable amount; (2) the employee must work at special work site, a location where the duties performed are of a temporary nature; (3) the employee must maintain a self-contained principal residence at another location that is available for occupancy but to which he or she cannot be reasonably expected to return from the special work site on a daily basis; and (4) the employee's duties must require him or her to be away from the principal residence at least thirty-six hours, including travel time.[63] If an allowance is specifically excluded from income under the *Income*

---

57 See the *Federal Child Support Guidelines*, Sch I, notes 5 and 6; *Murray v Murray*, 2021 ABQB 539 at paras 44–45, Mandziuk J; *Miller v White*, 2022 PESC 4 at para 89.

58 *EMO v WRO*, 2003 BCCA 191 at para 37; *Pitcher v Pitcher*, [2002] NJ No 358 (UFC); *Migwans v Lovelace*, 2011 NWTSC 54; *Scott v Chenier*, 2015 ONSC 7866; *Pelletier v Kakakaway*, 2002 SKCA 94; compare *Gillie v Ritchie*, [2001] NSJ No 440 (SC).

59 *EMO v WRO*, 2003 BCCA 191; *Stokes v Stokes*, [2002] NJ No 249 (SC); *Moulson v Graves*, [2002] OJ No 2582 (SCJ); *Ironstand v Ironstand* (1999), 45 RFL (4th) 159 (Sask QB); see *contra Wedsworth v Wedsworth*, [2000] NSJ No 209 (SC).

60 *Reber v Reber*, [2002] BCJ No 1281 (SC), disapproving *O'Regan v O'Regan* (2001), 194 NSR (2d) 257 (SC); *Luedke v Luedke*, [2004] BCJ No 1157 (CA); *Gannon v Gannon*, 2014 NSSC 113. And see text in Chapter 6. As to apportionment of the parental entitlement to the Canada Child Benefit in shared parenting situations, see *Friesen v The Queen*, 2022 TCC 53, which is reviewed in detail in Chapter 6, B(10) "Canada Child Benefit; Eligible Dependant Tax Credit."

61 *Stewart v Stewart*, 2009 BCSC 917; *Marcella v Marcella*, 2016 SKQB 407; compare *Mullins v Mullins*, 2016 ABQB 226.

62 *MJB v WPB*, [2004] MJ No 123 (QB); *Francis v Filion*, [2003] OJ No 1138 (SCJ); compare *King v King*, [2004] SJ No 527 (QB). See also *SS v JG*, 2021 NSSC 228 at paras 121–22 (Canada Child Benefit and GST credit).

63 *Hickey v Gaulton*, 2013 NLTD(G) 156.

Tax Act, as opposed to being an expense that is deductible from income pursuant to section 1 of Schedule III of the Guidelines, then it does not enter the picture at all and section 19(1)(g) of the Guidelines cannot be invoked to attribute any portion of the allowance as additional income to the obligor because such an allowance is unrelated to deductible expenses.[64]

Expenses received for travel, meals, and accommodation should not be included in an employed spouse's income where these funds were actually used for the purposes intended. A tax-free living allowance for a member of the provincial or territorial legislature should not be treated as income for the purpose of applying the *Federal Child Support Guidelines* Such an allowance is essentially reimbursement for expenses incurred to earn an income. A deduction from income of meal expenses by a long distance truck driver should reflect the amount allowed by the *Income Tax Act*; a court is not entitled to deduct any higher amount to reflect the actual expenses and the US/Canadian dollar exchange rates.[67] A housing allow ance, which constitutes a taxable benefit, should be included in determining the obligor's income under the *Federal Child Support Guidelines*.[68] A monthly allowance may be treated as income where more than half of it represented an expatriation allowance and a child allowance.[69] A *per diem* allowance for employment expenses may be attributed to a parent as income insofar as it exceeds the expenses incurred.[70]

A motor vehicle allowance may be included in a parent's income for Guidelines pur poses but travel expenses will be allowed when they fall within section 8(1)(h) of the *Income Tax Act*.[71] An automobile allowance and related payments received from an employee have, nevertheless, been excluded from a parent's income when they were revenue neutral in terms of the benefits received and the expenditures incurred.[72] Although automobile expenses may be deductible from the parent's income pursuant to Schedule III, sections 1(f.1) and (h) of the Guidelines, the tax savings, which are consequential to this allowed deduction, may be added back into the Guidelines income of the parent.[73] The deduction for motor vehicle travel expenses will arise where the employee: (1) is ordinarily required to work away from his employer's place of business[74] or in different places; (2) is required by his employer to pay his own travelling expenses; and (3) does not receive an allowance for travelling expenses from

---

64 *Kyle v Kyle*, [1998] SJ No 55 (QB); *AMT v RDC*, 2012 SKQB 85; compare *Wright v Wright*, [1998] AJ No 1167 (QB) (taxable allowances for field duty, clothing, and accumulated leave included in obligor's income).

65 *Whittleton v Whittleton*, 2003 ABQB 513; *Calver v Calver*, 2014 ABCA 63; *Smith v Hookey*, [1999] NJ No 243 (UFC).

66 *O'Brien v O'Brien*, [1999] NWTJ No 56 (SC); see also *McCaffrey v Dalla Longa*, 2008 ABQB 183.

67 *DAT v SLP*, 2018 NBQB 135; *O'Dell v Kraugh*, [1999] SJ No 51 (QB). Compare *Sampson v Sampson*, [1999] NSJ No 104 (TD) (meal and travel expenses; partial deduction from obligor's income).

68 *Esligar v Esligar*, [1999] NBJ No 150 (CA); *VSJ v LJG*, [2004] OJ No 2238 (SCJ) (non-taxable portion of free rental accommodation grossed up before being added back into parent's Guidelines income); *LSP v JRP*, [2002] SJ No 35 (QB).

69 *Horton v Horton*, [1999] OJ No 4855 (SCJ).

70 *Ralph v Ralph*, [2001] NJ No 238 (SC) (full *per diem* allowance included in parent's income but not grossed up as a tax-free allowance where some expenses were incurred).

71 *Myers v Myers*, [2000] NSJ No 367 (SC); *Simpson v Simpson*, [2004] OJ No 2564 (SCJ); *Santos v Potter* 2010 SKQB 115.

72 *Ralph v Ralph*, [2001] NJ No 238 (SC); *VSG v LJG*, [2004] OJ No 2238 (SCJ). See also *KM v SW*, 2014 BCSC 2240.

73 *Shaw v Shaw*, [2002] OJ No 2782 (SCJ).

74 *Gartman v Hancheroff*, 2015 BCSC 160.

his employer that is tax-exempt. The cost of commuting to and from one's home to place of work is not tax-deductible. The taxable travel allowance received by the employee will have been included in income. The taxable allowance or benefit itself is not deducted. It is only the actual expenses that the employee is entitled to claim under the applicable provisions of the *Income Tax Act* that will be deducted. These employment expenses will be reported on a Canada Revenue Agency Form T777.[75] If a parent seeks to claim that certain employment expenses should be deducted from his or her income pursuant to Schedule III of the *Federal Child Support Guidelines*, the onus falls on the parent to provide the necessary evidence to establish that should occur.[76] Taxable benefits relating to a parent's use of a company vehicle are part of the parent's income for the purposes of the *Income Tax Act* and section 16 of the *Federal Child Support Guidelines*. There is nothing in Schedule III of the Guidelines dealing with adjustments to income that call for taxable benefits to be deducted in determining a parent's Guidelines income. Only motor vehicle travel expenses actually incurred and deductible in accordance with section 8(1) of the *Income Tax Act* are deductible from the parent's Guidelines income pursuant to section 1 of Schedule III of the Guidelines.[77]

In *Calver v Calver*, the Alberta Court of Appeal stated (at para 16):

> Several cases have declined to impute income based on job-related payments for travel and living expenses, see e.g., *McCaffrey v. Dalla Longa*, [2008] A.J. No. 335 (Q.B.); *Jordan v. Jordan*, 2005 SKQB 129; *Dartige v. Dartige*, 1997 CanLII 1100 (Sask QB); *O'Brien v. O'Brien*, 1999 CanLII 6800 (NWT SC). Various rationales exist: it would be unjust to attribute income that is meant to reimburse a party for costs incurred in the course of employment; the *Income Tax Act*, RSC 1985, c 1 (5th Supp) excludes from income certain benefits relating to special work sites or remote work locations; living allowances are not income under the *Federal Child Support Guidelines*, SOR/97-175; it would be inconsistent with the *Guidelines* to add a travel allowance to income when the *Guidelines* specifically authorize the deduction from income of travel expenses paid directly by an employee (Schedule III, section 16(1)); and these amounts can be speculative since they may depend on the number of days away from home. The fact that an employee need not account for such an allowance has been considered irrelevant to the allowance's treatment: *O'Brien* at para 6.[78]

And in *Webster v Webster*,[79] wherein one-half of the father's living expenses were reasonably imputed to him as Guidelines income, Pearlman J of the British Columbia Supreme Court extracted the following principles from relevant caselaw:

> (a) generally, a living-out allowance paid for the recovery of work-related travel and living expenses will not be treated as income under the *Guidelines*;
>
> (b) living-out allowances are intended to compensate the recipient spouse for the extra costs associated with working away from home;

75 *Chopek v McKenzie*, 2015 MBQB 207; *BNM v PJM*, 2017 SKQB 331.

76 *ADJ v FJ*, 2022 BCSC 600; *Chopek v McKenzie*, 2015 MBQB 207; *Boutin v Boutin*, 2023 SKCA 41 at para 90.

77 *BNM v PJM*, 2017 SKQB 331; *Boutin v Boutin*, 2023 SKCA 41 at para 90.

78 *Calver v Calver*, 2014 ABCA 63 at para 16.

79 2014 BCSC 730 at para 37; see also *Stromquist v Stromquist*, 2020 BCSC 1556.

(c) in all the cases where courts have excluded living-out allowances from the recipient spouse's *Guideline* income, there has been some evidence that the recipient actually incurred extra costs associated with working away from home, although the recipient was not required to account for the whole amount of the allowance; and
(d) under s. 19(1) of the *Guidelines*, the court has a broad discretion to impute such amount of income to a spouse as it considers appropriate in the circumstances.

c) Social Assistance Benefits

Social assistance benefits constitute income under the *Federal Child Support Guidelines* but must be adjusted under section 4 of Schedule III to include only the amount attributable to the recipient spouse, although the full amount may be attributed where there is no evidence of any proportionate breakdown.[80]

d) Dividend Income

In determining a parent's income under the *Federal Child Support Guidelines*, section 5 of Schedule III requires the court to replace the taxable amount of dividends received from taxable Canadian corporations with the actual amount of the dividends received.[81]

In *Austin v Austin*,[82] Smith J of the Ontario Superior Court of Justice held that section 5 of Schedule III of the Guidelines applies where dividends are received from a Canadian corporation that is not owned or controlled by either spouse;[83] it does not preclude a court from imputing additional income to a spouse who is the sole shareholder of a company and who elects to receive dividends from the company in lieu of salary. Justice Smith observed that section 19(1)(h) of the *Federal Child Support Guidelines* expressly empowers a court to impute income to a spouse who "derives a significant portion of income from dividends, capital gains or other sources that are taxed at a lower rate than employment or business income."[84] Furthermore, section 18(1) of the Guidelines empowers a court to impute cor porate income to a spouse who is a shareholder, director, or officer of a corporation, if the spouse's annual income as determined by section 16 of the Guidelines does not fairly reflect all the money available for the payment of child support. In *Riel v Holland*,[85] the Ontario Court of Appeal affirmed that where a parent arranges his or her business affairs so as to pay substantially less income tax, sections 18 and 19 of the Guidelines may be applied to gross up the income received so as to promote fairness and consistency in quantifying the amount

---

80 *Perron v Hlushko*, 2015 ABQB 595; *Chambers v Chambers*, [1998] NWTJ No 54 (SC); *SA v EA*, 2010 NBQB 61; *Kelly v Kelly*, 2013 ONSC 6733; *Helle-Wort v Brisson*, [2001] YJ No 113 (SC); compare *JET v CDT*, [2001] AJ No 1054 (QB); *Hamilton v Hamilton*, 2010 NSSC 198. And see *Bradford v Bradford*, 2022 BCSC 595 (funds received for the care of a developmentally disabled adult).

81 *Bohn v Bohn*, 2016 ABCA 406 at para 28; *Ramachala (Holland) v Holland*, 2020 ABQB 432.

82 [2007] OJ No 4283 (SCJ); see also *Campbell v Campbell*, 2016 MBQB 57; *DE v LE*, 2014 NBCA 67; *Hamilton v Hamilton*, 2010 NSSC 198; *Taillefer v Taillefer*, 2013 ONSC 6105; *Rawluk-Harness v Harness*, 2014 ONSC 2531; *Howe v Howe*, 2013 SKQB 74. Compare *Leis v Leis*, 2014 ABCA 36; *Lightle v Kotar*, 2014 BCCA 69.

83 See also *Perdue v Perdue*, 2014 NBQB 262 at para 40; *Tucker v Tucker*, 2019 SKQB 317; and see *MH v AB*, 2019 SKCA 135, leave to appeal to SCC denied 2020 CanLII 36067 (SCC), discussed below.

84 See also *Shaw v Przybylski*, 2014 ABQB 667 at paras 35–45; *MC v JO*, 2017 NBCA 15; compare *Brown v Brown*, 2014 BCCA 152.

85 (2003), 42 RFL (5th) 120 (Ont CA).

of child support payable by salaried parents and those who receive monetary benefits in another form that attracts less tax. In *Austin v Austin*, Smith J observed that the husband did not actually reduce the overall amount of the taxes paid when his corporate and personal taxes were combined. However, as stated by Lane J in *Manis v Manis*,[86] "[t]he fundamental principle is that the Court must estimate the actual means which the paying parent has available for child support." Applying this principle in *Austin v Austin*, Smith J found it appropriate to impute additional income to the husband pursuant to section 19(1)(h) of the Guidelines, or to use section 18(1) of the Guidelines based on the amount available for distribution by the corporation by way of salary, after a reasonable amount was allowed for retained earnings, thus producing a result that ensured consistency between a parent earning a salaried income and the parent who received dividends from his private corporation in lieu of salary. And see *Dand v Ady* wherein McIntyre J of the Saskatchewan Court of Queen's Bench (Family Law Division) stated:

> Section 5 of Schedule III to the *Federal Child Support Guidelines* (SOR/97-175) ("*Guidelines*") speaks to replacing the taxable amount of dividends from taxable Canadian corporations received by a spouse by the actual amount of dividends received for the purposes of determining income pursuant to s. 16 of the *Guidelines*. This is appropriate in circumstances such as where the spouse is receiving investment income by way of dividends. However, where the spouse is a shareholder of a company and receives dividends from the company in lieu of salary, it is more appropriate for the spouse's income to be determined by using the taxable amount of the dividend. See, for example, *Gursky v. Gursky*.[87] This approach puts the spouse who receives a dividend in lieu of salary in the same position as a spouse who receives the same amount simply as salary.[88]

Speaking to this issue at length in *MH v AB*,[89] after reviewing relevant caselaw, Kalmakoff JA, of the Saskatchewan Court of Appeal, concluded:

> [71] It is apparent . . . that the trial judge calculated the appellant's income for 2015 and 2016 using the following formula:
>
> line 150 income [now line 15000] + pre-tax income of corporation – actual dividend paid to the appellant
>
> [72] Included in the appellant's line 150 income for each of those years was the dividend paid to him by the professional corporation, grossed up to reflect its taxable value. . . .
>
> . . .
>
> [102] In *Howe v Howe*, 2013 SKQB 74 (CanLII) [*Howe*], Barrington-Foote J. (as he then was) cited *Austin* as a helpful analysis but determined that in the particular factual circumstances before him, where the mother earned the bulk of her income in the form of dividends

86 [2000] OJ No 4539 (SCJ).

87 2008 SKQB 253; see also *Tucker v Tucker*, 2019 SKQB 317; *MH v AB*, 2019 SKCA 135, leave to appeal to SCC denied 2020 CanLII 36067 (SCC).

88 2014 SKQB 101 at para 6. For additional caselaw, see *AMW v BW*, 2018 ABQB 518; *Babich v Babich*, 2015 SKQB 22 at para 69; *Podruchny v Evans*, 2018 SKQB 262. See also *Campbell v Campbell*, 2016 MBQB 57; *MC v JO*, 2017 NBCA 15; *Tucker v Tucker*, 2019 SKQB 317.

89 2019 SKCA 135 at paras 64–110.

from her own company and the father was a teacher who received all of his income as salary, it was not to appropriate to use the grossed-up value of the dividends when calculating the mother's income for child support purposes. This was because Barrington-Foote J. attributed the pre-tax income from the mother's company to her under s. 18(1) of the *Guidelines* and, in light of that, the consistency of treatment required by the *Guidelines* was achieved by using the actual amount of the dividend paid, rather than imputing the grossed-up amount under s. 19(1)(h).

[103] In *Howe*, Barrington-Foote J. recognized, correctly in my view, that attribution of pre-tax income from the corporation alone will often achieve the goal of consistency in the treatment of income for child support purposes. This is entirely consistent with the thread running through the jurisprudence, namely that the discretion provided in s. 19(1)(h) must be exercised in tandem with s. 18(1) to ensure that the income of the party receiving dividends from a corporation properly reflects all the money available for child support purposes, and achieves the consistency of treatment required by the *Guidelines.*

[104] In some cases where a party receives dividend income from a closely-held corporation, achieving those goals will require the court to attribute corporate pre-tax income under s. 18(1) of the *Guidelines.* In others, it will be appropriate to impute the grossed-up value of dividends received from the corporation under s. 19(1)(h) to achieve those goals. There may also be instances in which it is appropriate to do both, and yet others in which it is appropriate to do neither. It all depends on the particular circumstances of the case.

[105] It is also trite to say that the decision to attribute corporate income under s. 18(1), or to impute the grossed-up value of a dividend under s. 19(1)(h) instead of using the actual amount of the dividend cannot be arbitrary. It must be based on evidence which supports the conclusion that doing so is appropriate and necessary to reflect the amount of money truly available for child support purposes, and to achieve the consistency of approach required by the *Guidelines.*

[106] In this case, the trial judge did both; that is, he attributed the pre-tax income of the corporation to the appellant under s. 18(1) of the *Guidelines*, and he imputed the grossed-up value of the dividends under s. 19(1)(h). While he gave detailed reasons as to why attributing corporate income under s. 18(1) was appropriate and necessary, the judge failed to conduct any analysis of the evidence with respect to imputation under s. 19(1)(h). He simply cited *Dand* and concluded that because the appellant received a substantial amount of his income in the form of dividends from his own corporation in 2015 and 2016, imputation of the grossed-up value of the dividends should occur. He did not analyse whether the way in which the appellant structured his income actually resulted in tax benefits that made imputation of the grossed-up value of the dividends necessary to achieve consistency of treatment. Nor did he consider whether the requisite consistency had already been achieved through attributing pre-tax corporate income under s. 18(1). The failure to conduct such an analysis was, in my view, an error in principle.

[107] The trial judge also erred in principle, in my view, by finding that it was appropriate to impute the grossed-up value of the dividends as income under s. 19(1)(h) rather than substituting the actual amount under s. 16 via Schedule III, s. 5 in the absence of evidence supporting such a finding. In this case, there was simply no evidence from which to conclude that, by paying dividends to himself from the corporation in the amounts that he

did, the appellant had received a tax advantage of such a nature as to make imputation of the grossed-up amount of the dividends under s. 19(1)(h) of the *Guidelines*, in addition to attributing the pre-tax value of corporate income under s. 18(1), appropriate.

[108] It falls, then, to this Court to intervene. Based on the evidence that was before the trial judge, and considering the decision to attribute the full amount of the appellant's pre-tax corporate income to him for the purpose of calculating child support, I see no basis upon which to impute the grossed-up value of the appellant's dividend income rather than using the actual amount paid. The appellant had already paid tax — at the corporate level — on the corporate income, before paying himself the dividend, and again — at the personal level — on the taxable amount of the dividend. Applying the reasoning set out in paragraph 15 of *Howe*, I see no basis in the evidence to conclude that any measure other than the attribution of pre-tax corporate income was necessary to reflect the full amount of income available to the appellant for child support purposes or achieve consistency of approach under the *Guidelines*.

Different considerations may apply where non-recurring dividend income is paid to a child support obligor but the attendant circumstances signify that the obligor's lifestyle and capacity to pay child support are not thereby enhanced. In *Brown v Brown*,[90] in ordering a father to pay retroactive child support for the years 2008 and 2009, a chambers judge excluded from the father's Guidelines income substantial dividends paid to him by his corporate employer under "a form of retirement package" for senior management employees. The essential characteristic of the package was that the employees acquired shares in the company, which they were required to pay for out of future dividends paid on the shares. The employees were to benefit from the shares only upon the sale or liquidation of the company "in the distant future" and they could not sell the shares or use them to raise funds. Addressing the dividend income paid to Mr Brown, which went to pay down the purchase price of the shares and to pay the taxes resulting from the dividend income, the chambers judge accepted the submission that while the dividends were classified as income for tax purposes, they had no impact on Mr Brown's ability to pay child support and it would be unfair to take them into account in determining his income under the *Federal Child Support Guidelines* for the purpose of quantifying a retroactive child support award. In upholding this decision, the British Columbia Court of Appeal concluded that the dividends received in 2008 and 2009 were of a non-recurring nature that fell within section 17(1) of the *Federal Child Support Guidelines* because they were paid on a one-off basis at the discretion of the principal of the company and they did not form part of Mr Brown's regular income stream. And in the appellate court's opinion, whether the dividends should be included or excluded from the father's Guidelines income depended on the court's assessment of the "fairest determination of [the father's] income." But the fairness referred to in section 17(1) of the *Federal Child Support Guidelines* is not subjective or elusive. It must be determined in light of the objectives set out in section 1 of the Guidelines. In particular, a court should bear in mind the objective that children should continue to benefit from the financial means of their parents

90 2014 BCCA 152; compare *Perdue v Perdue*, 2014 NBQB 262. See also *Foster v Sauvé*, 2019 BCSC 1656; *Block v Block*, 2020 BCSC 1694; *Lussier v Ritchie*, 2023 BCSC 1817; compare *Loehr v Loehr*, 2023 BCSC 2229. And see *Howard v Howard*, 2020 ABQB 292 (liquidated pension payment viewed as non-recurring gain).

after separation: (Guidelines, section 1(a)) and also the objective that parents and children should receive consistent treatment in similar circumstances (Guidelines, section 1(d)). Citing *Marinangeli v Marinangeli*,[91] the British Columbia Court of Appeal stated that in many cases, the objective that the parents' financial means be available for child support will be of overriding importance. But unlike its previous judgment in *Vincent v Vincent*,[92] wherein dividend income was included in the father's Guidelines income because it represented an income resource that could readily have been diverted for child support purposes instead of being re-invested in another business, Mr Brown's dividend income did not provide an income resource that could be used for child support purposes. Consequently, the objective set out in section 1(a) of the *Federal Child Support Guidelines* could not be seen as supporting the inclusion of the dividends in Mr Brown's Guidelines income. Turning next to the objective of promoting consistency and predictability in accordance with section 1(d) of the Guidelines, the British Columbia Court of Appeal observed that "[i]n order to achieve this goal, courts have, in determining whether non-recurrent dividend income should be excluded under section 17(1), attempted to characterize the nature of the income and to analogize it to other forms of income that are clearly included or excluded in calculating Guideline[s] income": (per Groberman JA at paragraph 34). Concluding that the dividends received by Mr Brown were not ordinary income that would be included in his Guidelines income, and that they were not analogous to a return of capital that would be excluded from a parent's Guidelines income, the British Columbia Court of Appeal drew an analogy between Mr Brown's "share purchase agreement scheme" and a registered company pension plan. Applying this analogy, the appellate court opined that "[t]he characterization of the dividends as analogous to employer contributions to a pension plan recognizes the fact that the dividends are not part of Mr Brown's ordinary remuneration" and also the fact that "[b]ut for the existence of the share purchase scheme, Mr Brown would receive no dividends." Thus, "[t]he dividends were more closely analogous to employer contributions to a pension plan than to employee contributions" (para 38). And given the Guidelines objective that "spouses and children who are in similar circumstances" should be treated consistently, it was appropriate to treat Mr Brown's dividend income in the same way as employer contributions to pension plans and to exclude the dividends from his Guidelines income. The appellate court made it clear, however, that the exclusion did not extend to Mr Brown's prior contribution of $10,000 to the share purchase scheme nor to any future profit-sharing entitlements that Mr Brown might be required to pay into, because these payments come out of ordinary income and are analogous to employee contributions to pension plans that are included in the employee contributor's Guidelines income.

e) Capital Gains

In determining income, section 6 of Schedule III of the *Federal Child Support Guidelines* stipulates that taxable capital gains[93] must be converted to the actual amount of capital gains

91 (2003), 66 OR (3d) 40 at para 30 (CA).

92 2012 BCCA 186.

93 See Julien D Payne, "Some Notable Family Law Decisions from 2012 to 2014" (2015) 43 *Advocates' Quarterly* 131 at 153.

realized in excess of actual capital losses.[94] Regular capital gains are included in income pursuant to section 6 of Schedule III of the Guidelines where they are annual recurring amounts.[95] A non-recurring capital gain may be excluded from an obligor's annual income pursuant to section 17(1) of the Guidelines,[96] or may be included where the simple use of employment income would be unfair in light of the attendant circumstances.[97] There are numerous factors that should be taken into account in assessing whether the inclusion of a non-recurring capital gain should be included as a fair determination of income.[98] Capital gains attributable to a parent's rollover of his investment portfolio to a holding company may be excluded from the parent's income when they may never be realized in actuality.[99] Where a spouse or former spouse has investments in the stock market so arranged as to attract capital gains tax only at some future time, the court may conclude that the prospect of future gain is counterbalanced by the prospect of future loss so as to render it artificial to ascribe the character of income to the possibility of a future capital gain.[100]

Because income tax is payable on only one half of any capital gains and child support under the Guidelines is based upon pre-tax income, section 19(1)(h) of the Guidelines permits the court to gross up the amounts to reflect the equivalent income taxed at the normal rate.[101]

f) Non-Arm's-Length Payments

Pursuant to section 9 of Schedule III of the *Federal Child Support Guidelines*, third-party non-arm's-length salaries, benefits, wages, management fees, or other payments are included in a self-employed spouse's income, unless they were necessary to earn that income and they were reasonable in the circumstances.[102] Once such non-arm's-length payments are established, the onus falls on the spouse who seeks to deduct them to provide evidence of their necessity and reasonableness.[103]

---

94 *Plett v Plett*, 2009 BCSC 227; *Coghill v Coghill*, [2006] OJ No 2602 (SCJ); *Wilson v Wilson*, [1998] SJ No 236 (QB); *Wetsch v Kuski*, 2017 SKCA 77; *Matechuk v Kopp (Yaworenko)*, 2020 SKQB 196. Compare *Vincent v Vincent*, 2012 BCCA 186 (profit from sale of principal residence).

95 *Mascarenhas v Mascarenhas*, [1999] OJ No 37 (Gen Div). For a review of cases for and against the inclusion of capital gains in the obligor's Guidelines income, see *Maurier v Maurier*, 2022 ABKB 856.

96 *Bell v Bell*, 2011 BCSC 212; *McNeil v McNeil*, 2013 NBCA 65; *Leet v Beach*, 2010 NSSC 433; *Arnold v Washburn*, [2001] OJ No 4996 (CA); *Loran v Loran*, 2009 SKQB 514; compare *Schick v Schick*, 2008 ABCA 196, citing *Marinangeli v Marinangeli*, [2003] OJ No 2819 (CA).

97 *MAW v PCW*, 2014 ABQB 703; *Schick v Schick*, 2008 ABCA 196, citing *Marinangeli v Marinangeli*, [2003] OJ No 2819 (CA); *Vincent v Vincent*, 2012 BCCA 186; *Kendry v Cathcart*, [2001] OJ No 277 (SCJ) (capital gain spread over three years in determining obligor's income); *More v Shurygalo*, 2010 SKQB 203 (partial inclusion).

98 *MAM v DLL*, 2018 BCSC 2114; *Murphy v Howes*, 2021 NSSC 354 at para 32.

99 *DMCT v LKS*, 2008 NSCA 61.

100 *Pitt v Pitt*, [1997] BCJ No 1528 (SC).

101 *Gagnon v Petke*, [2008] BCJ No 879 (SC); *Wetsch v Kuski*, 2017 SKCA 77. Compare to *Vincent v Vincent*, 2012 BCCA 186.

102 *Clark v Clark*, 2012 BCCA 297; *Leger v Leger*, [2000] NBJ No 52 (QB); *Nichol v Johnson*, [2003] SJ No 736 (QB).

103 *Snow v Wilcox*, [1999] NSJ No 453 (CA); *Fidyk v Hutchison*, 2013 SKQB 27.

g) Fiscal Year-End Adjustments

In *Tweel v Tweel*,[104] Jenkins J of the Prince Edward Island Supreme Court excluded from the obligor's income under the *Federal Child Support Guidelines* business income reported from previous taxation years in consequence of the 1995 amendments to the *Income Tax Act* which required unincorporated taxpayers to adopt a fiscal year end based on the calendar year. Such exclusion would appear to follow directly from the application of section 10 of Schedule III of the Guidelines.[105] Two Ontario courts have, nevertheless, concluded that a court has no jurisdiction under section 10 of Schedule III of the *Federal Child Support Guidelines* to adjust the annual income of a spouse so as to deduct any additional tax burden arising from the year-end amendments to the *Income Tax Act*.[106]

h) Capital Cost Allowances on Real Property

Any capital cost allowance permitted to a spouse under the *Income Tax Act* with respect to real property, as distinct from personal property, must be added back into the spouse's income under section 11 of Schedule III of the Guidelines.[107] Section 11 of Schedule III to the Guidelines refers not to a corporation's deductions but to a spouse's deductions for an allow able capital cost allowance with respect to real property.[108] Section 11 of Schedule III of the Guidelines should not be read into the analysis of available corporate income under section 18 of the Guidelines. However, a payee spouse will not be disadvantaged by the omission of an equivalent provision in section 18, because if there is a finding that the spouse's annual income does not reflect what is actually available to him for child support, a court can consider (1) the pre-tax income of the corporation, or (2) the value of the spouse's services to the company. And the former measure will necessarily add back all tax deductions subsequently utilized by the corporation, including amortization.[109] After reviewing the above text and relevant Canadian caselaw respecting the jurisdiction to adjust for capital cost allowances claimed by companies, Forgeron J, of the Supreme Court of Nova Scotia, in *Wolfson v Wolfson* concluded:

> Given the remedial nature of the *Guidelines*, their stated objectives, and the case authorities, I find that I have the jurisdiction to adjust for the CCA claimed by Mr. Wolfson's companies either pursuant to ss. 18 or 19 of the *CSG* or through s. 11 of Schedule III. My preference is for such a calculation to occur under s. 18 or s. 11 because s. 19 would place the evidentiary burden on the spouse who lacks control of the asset and the associated evidence. In this case the burden is of no consequence, because even if it rests on Ms. Wolfson, she has overwhelmingly satisfied it.[110]

---

104 [2000] PEIJ No 9 (SC).

105 See, to like effect, *Garrett-Rempel v Garrett-Rempel*, [2000] BCJ No 1771 (SC).

106 *Merritt v Merritt*, [1999] OJ No 1732 (SCJ); *Lepage v Lepage*, [1999] SJ No 174 (QB).

107 *de Goede v de Goede*, [1999] BCJ No 330 (SC); *Shaw v Shaw*, [1997] MJ No 400 (QB); *Fidyk v Hutchison* 2013 SKQB 27.

108 *PMR v MHR*, 2011 BCSC 1621.

109 *O'Kane v Lillqvist-O'Kane*, 2022 ABKB 661 at para 180; *Boykiw v Boykiw*, 2013 BCSC 1107 at paras 33–36, Schulters J; see also *Wolfson v Wolfson*, 2021 NSSC 260; *Krammer (Ackerman) v Ackerman*, 2020 SKQB 280 at paras 80–88, Megaw J.

110 *Wolfson v Wolfson*, 2021 NSSC 260 at para 362; see also *Ward v Murphy*, 2023 NSSC 370.

i) Partnership Income

Section 12 of Schedule III to the *Federal Child Support Guidelines* provides that where a parent earns income through a partnership or sole proprietorship, the parent can deduct any amount included in income that is properly required for the partnership or sole proprietorship for the purposes of capitalization. Section 12 of Schedule III of the Guidelines, which relates to partnership income and the deduction of any amount required for purposes of capitalization, has been applied to mortgage payments on rental properties owned jointly by the spouses.[111] Capitalization refers to the cash needed to operate on a day-to-day basis to cover expenses such as staff, office rental, leases or purchases of furniture or equipment,[112] but section 12 does not permit deductions from income for the acquisition of an asset, such as an interest in a partnership or the shares of a corporation, even though that interest may generate future income.[113] Capitalization is, in effect, the cash needed for the partnership to operate. It is needed in order to generate income. It is well settled that where an increase in a capital account is properly required to operate a business or partnership, that increase will result in a decrease in available Guidelines income for support purposes.[114] In the final analysis, section 12 of Schedule III of the Guidelines should be interpreted in a way that confers sufficient discretion to ensure that the outcome is fair and the parent does not build up capital assets at the expense of his or her children's right to support.[115]

j) Stock Options

Section 13(1) of Schedule III of the Guidelines provides for profit generated by the exercise of stock options[116] to be added to the obligor's income for the year in which the options are exercised,[117] but section 17 of the Guidelines confers a discretion on the court to take account of the non-recurring nature of such profits and to allocate such portion of them to the obligor's current annual income as the court considers appropriate.[118] In an explanatory note of section 13 of Schedule III of the Guidelines, which was amended as of 1 August 2001, the Department of Justice, Canada makes the following observations:

---

111 *de Goede v de Goede*, [1999] BCJ No 330 (SC); see also *Evanow v Lannon*, 2018 BCCA 208.

112 *Ghosn v Ghosn*, [2006] NSJ No 33 (SC); *McLellan v McLellan*, 2020 NSSC 161.

113 *Boniface v Boniface*, [2007] BCJ No 2303 (SC); *MGH v KLDH*, 2020 NBCA 46; *McLellan v McLellan*, 2020 NSSC 161. But compare *Foster v Sauvé*, 2019 BCSC 1656. And see *SME v JAE*, 2020 BCSC 332.

114 *SME v JAE*, 2020 BCSC 332 at paras 38–42, Weatherill J, citing *Richardson v Richardson*, 2013 BCCA 378 and *Boniface v Boniface*, [2007] BCJ No 2303 (SC).

115 *Grant v Grant*, [2001] NSJ No 100 (SC). See also *CRE v KLE*, 2011 BCSC 291 at paras 9–22, wherein the relevant caselaw is reviewed.

116 See Aaron Franks, "Deferred Compensation Versus Current Support Obligations" in The Law Society of Upper Canada, *Special Lectures 2006: Family Law* (Toronto: Irwin Law, 2007) at 273–89.

117 *JDG v JJV*, 2016 BCSC 2389; see also *Crossley v Vorell*, 2021 BCSC 2484.

118 *Sarro v Sarro*, 2011 BCSC 1010 (Guidelines, s 17 applied); compare *Bell v Glynn*, [2000] BCJ No 1505 (SC) (stock options exercised but excluded from obligor's income because they were non-recurring amounts and had already been included in the family assets pool). See also *Arnold v Washburn*, [2001] OJ No 4996 (CA); *Coghill v Coghill*, [2006] OJ No 2602 (SCJ) (no justification for exercising discretion under s 17 of Guidelines); *Pomozova v Mann*, 2010 ONCA 212; *Walker v Walker*, 2024 ONSC 198 at paras 39–79. As to an income tax gross up being applied to earnings from the exercise of stock options, see *Kowalski v Kowalski*, [2008] AJ No 257 (QB).

A minor amendment was made to the *Federal Child Support Guidelines* effective August 1, 2001. The changes to Schedule III, section 13, reflect changes announced in the federal government's February 2000 Budget.

The words "publicly traded corporation that is subject to the same tax treatment with reference to stock options as a Canadian-controlled private corporation," were added to section 13 to reflect announced changes to the *Income Tax Act*.

Before Budget 2000, stock options were sometimes treated differently depending on where the employee worked. The stock options of employees working for Canadian controlled private corporations (CCPC) and stock options of employees of non-CCPCs received different tax treatments. The income benefit of a stock option of a company that is not a CCPC was included in income for tax purposes at the time the option was *exercised*. The income benefit of a CCPC stock option was included in income for tax purposes when the option shares were *sold*.

Section 13 of the Guidelines now makes the income treatment for options issued by CCPCs the same as for non-CCPCs. It ensures that the income benefit of CCPC stock options is included in income for guideline purposes in the year in which the option is *exercised* even though the amount will not necessarily be taxed in that year. A deduction under subsection 13(2) is permitted in the year the option shares are sold to prevent double counting.

The budget proposed that the taxation of gains on certain employee stock options in public company shares be postponed to when the shares are sold (instead of when the option is exercised). To ensure consistent income treatment of all stock options under the Guidelines, section 13 required an amendment to include both CCPC options and non-CCPC options.

Pursuant to section 16 of the *Federal Child Support Guidelines* and section 13 of Sched ule III of the Guidelines, profits generated by the exercise of stock options constitute "income" for the year in which the options are exercised.[119] It does not follow, however, that all or any of this income will be included in a parent's income for the purpose of determining the amount of child support to be paid. Where income from the exercise of stock options does not form part of a recurring stream of income and skews a parent's annual income in assessing child support, the court may exclude the stock option profits from the parent's income in assessing child support. Such discretionary jurisdiction arises pursuant to section 17 of the *Federal Child Support Guidelines* where the court is of the opinion that the fairest determination of a parent's annual income is thereby achieved. Whether a court should include or exclude all or some of the profits realized by a parent's exercise of stock options in a particular year from the Guidelines income to be attributed to that parent for that year will depend upon the attendant circumstances. Relevant factors for consideration might include: (1) the non-recurring nature of that particular source of income; (2) the existence of a substantial annual income from other sources; and (3) inclusion in the parent's Guidelines income of the income yield from the parent's investment portfolio that arose from the exercise of the stock options. While affirming the above principles in *Arnold v Washburn*,[120] the Ontario Court of Appeal further concluded that, although stock option profits may be excluded from a parent's

119 *Gagnon v Petke*, [2008] BCJ No 879 (SC); *JDG v JJV*, 2016 BCSC 2389.

120 [2001] OJ No 4996 (CA). For an insightful critique, see James G McLeod, "Annotation" (2002) 20 RFL (5th) 236 at 237–42. See also *Bell v Bell*, 2011 BCSC 212; *McNeil v McNeil*, 2013 NBCA 65.

"income" for the purpose of determining the applicable table amount of child support under section 3(1) of the *Federal Child Support Guidelines*, such profits may be relevant under section 3(2)(b) of the Guidelines to a parent's "financial capacity" to contribute to the support of an adult child who is pursuing post-secondary education. Where stock options represent an accepted regular means of compensation, income may be imputed to their owner pursuant to section 19(1)(h) of the Guidelines when the options are exercised, if at that time they amount to a significant portion of the obligor's income.[121] In *Walker v Walker*, Audet J, of the Ontario Superior Court of Justice, provided the following detailed analysis of the treatment of stock options as income under the Federal Child Support Guidelines:

> [45] Stock options offered to employees are an accepted means of compensation and for the purpose of assessing support and they are to be treated as income subject to the Court's discretion to exclude them under s. 17 of the *Federal Child Support Guidelines*, SOR/97-175 (hereinafter referred to as "the Guidelines"). This is clearly set out in Schedule III, s. 13 . . . .
>
> [46] As set out in in this provision, there are two income components to share purchase options (stock options). Firstly, there is the monetary value received by the employee resulting from the ability to purchase shares from the employer company at a price that is lower than market value. This is often referred to as the "cash value". Pursuant to Schedule III, s. 13(1) of the Guidelines, that value is added to the payor's income in the year that the shares are purchased (when the option to purchase shares is exercised) even though for income tax purposes the income may only need to be reported when the underlying shares are later sold.
>
> [47] Secondly, there is the financial benefit, in the form of a capital gains, which is realized at the time the underlying shares are disposed of. The capital gains form part of the payor's income during the year the shares are sold. To avoid double-dipping, the cash value added to the payor's income in the year of purchase is deducted from the gains realized during the year of their sale. This is set out in Schedule III, s. 13(2) of the Guidelines.
>
> [48] The treatment of stock options under the Guidelines (as opposed to their treatment under the *Income Tax Act*, R.S.C. 1985, c. 1 (5th Supp.)), was summarized by the Ontario Court of Appeal in *Marinangeli v. Marinangeli* (2003), 2003 CanLII 27673 (ON CA) . . . as follows:
>
>> . . . Options granted as an employee benefit are to be valued and added to a spouse's income for the year in which the options are exercised under Schedule III and s. 13(1) of the Guidelines. Once the value of the option has been determined the court has a discretion to exercise under s. 17. If, as a result of the exercise of the options, the court is of the opinion that the spouse's income results in an amount that is not fair to the paying spouse, for example, because this is a one-time payment, the court can look at the spouse's income over the last three years and determine an amount that is fair and reasonable in light of the receipt of a non-recurring amount during those years.
>
> [49] It is undisputable in this case that the father's ability to purchase shares from his employer provides him with significant financial benefits, in the form of the cash value received at the time he exercises his stock options, in the form of dividends payable on Paid

121 *Marinangeli v Marinangeli*, [2003] OJ No 2819 (CA). See also *Schick v Schick*, 2008 ABCA 196.

Shares, and in the form of capital gains he realizes when he sells the underlying shares in the manner permitted by the Plan. . . .

[50] While the timing for the inclusion of stock option income (cash value or capital gains) in a payor's yearly income for support purposes is made clear in Schedule III, what is not clear is whether the payor should be left with complete discretion as to the *timing* for the exercise of available stock options or the sale of the underlying shares. This issue arises because an employee can choose whether and when to exercise stock options and delay the sale of the underlying shares (once vested) to defer compensation for many years and "shield income" beyond the time when support terminates.

[51] This was one of the issues that arose in the case of *Patterson v. Patterson* (2006), 2006 CanLII 53701 (ON SC), 36 R.F.L. (6th) 268 (Ont. S.C.). . . .

. . .

[55] The court in *Patterson* not only concluded that the *timing* of a payor's exercise of share options was one that ought to be considered as part of the analysis under s. 19 of the Guidelines, but that the *timing* of the sale of the underlying shares could also be considered under s. 19. The court stated the following at para. 116:

> The husband takes the position that the *Marinangeli* case is stating that options are included in income, but only in the year they are exercised. I do not agree that the court is dealing with the timing of the exercise of the option. The court ruled that options are included in income. They have not addressed the issue of whether they should be considered as income once vested and available to the payor under section 19 of the guidelines.

[56] The relevant parts of s. 19 of the Guidelines read as follow:

> **Imputing income**
> **19** (1) The court may impute such amount of income to a spouse as it considers appropriate in the circumstances, which circumstances include the following:
> [...]
> (d) it appears that income has been diverted which would affect the level of child support to be determined under these Guidelines; [and]
> (e) the spouse's property is not reasonably utilized to generate income.

[57] The court [in *Patterson*] concluded, at paras. 122, 128, that stock options available to the husband should form part of his income for support purposes during the year they vested regardless of whether he chose to exercise them (sell them) or not:

> Section 13 of Schedule III is clearly subject to section 17-20. I believe that section 19 of the guidelines should be utilized when it comes to stock options in this case. Options of some type have been available for the past ten years on an annual basis. If I only accept them as income once exercised, there could be easily over a million dollars in income that is unavailable for purposes of child support once the various termination periods arise. Under paragraph 19(1)(*e*), this would, in my view, be a case of the spouse's property not being reasonably utilized to generate income.
>
> [...]

The principle of imputing income for unexercised stock options, in my view, is not very different from imputing income for retained earnings, or pre-tax corporate income. In each case, there is an order that property must be better utilized to generate income. It is as though income has been diverted. Both paragraphs 19(1)(*d*) and 19(1)(*e*) are relevant.

[58] The same conclusion was reached by the court in the case of *De Zen v. De Zen* (2001), 2001 CanLII 28139 (ON SC), 20 R.F.L. (5th) 326 (Ont. S.C.), at para. 42.

[59] The above is relevant because the mother in this case is seeking to impute to the father dividend income which he would have received had he elected to purchase all the shares made available to him by Ledcor every year since the parties separated. The mother also takes the position that the father should be deemed to have sold the underlying shares (those he elected to purchase) in the year they became vested, regardless of whether he chose to sell them at that time, and imputed an income commensurate to the gains he would have realized from their sale.

[60] There are very few cases dealing with the specific issue of *timing* in relation to stock options in Ontario or elsewhere in the country since *Patterson* was released. A key finding in both the *Patterson* and *De Zen* cases was that the payor was intentionally deferring significant income which would have unquestionably been available to him had he exercised his options when vested. Further, the evidence supported the clear conclusion that the payor would have gained a substantial financial benefit if he had sold them at that time.

[61] In my view, the decision to impute income to a payor for unexercised stock options (failure to purchase shares offered) or unrealized vested stock options (failure to sell the underlying shares when they vest) should not be automatic in every case and requires a careful analysis of many factors. While it would be clearly unfair to allow a payor to defer compensation available to him or her for the purpose of minimizing a support obligation, it would also be unfair to impute additional income on a payor in circumstances where there are valid reasons for the deferral of income. In my view, the following non-exhaustive factors are relevant to this analysis;

- In relation to the exercise of stock options (buying the shares offered by the company at a discounted rate):
  a. What are the terms pursuant to which stock options can be exercised?
  b. Is the employee required to finance the purchase?
  c. If so, what are the financing terms?
  d. Is there a requirement for the employee to pay a portion of the purchase price up front (in which case the employee must have immediate access to cash)?
  e. Must the financed portion be paid back with the use of the employee's future earnings (thus diminishing the employee's available income in future years)? Or is the company essentially "gifting" the shares to the employee?
  f. Would a reasonable person in the same circumstances exercise the stock options?
  g. What was the employee/payor's practice in relation to the exercise of stock options during the marriage? Has his/her practice changed post-separation? Is there a valid justification for such change? What would have likely happened if the family had remained intact?

- In relation to the sale of the underlying shares (disposing of the shares previously acquired at a discounted rate):
  h. What are the terms upon which vested shares can be realized?
  i. What are the restrictions, if any, associated with their sale?
  j. How long can an employee defer their sale?
  k. Does the employee have any control over the deferral?
  l. What are the reasons/justifications for the deferral? For instance, if the company is not performing well and the shares would be sold at a low profit, a deferral might be reasonably justified;
  m. Is the deferral (of part or all available compensation) reasonable from a tax, retirement, or estate planning perspective?
  n. What is the purpose of the stock option package? Is it to help executive employees build a retirement fund or is it meant to supplement the employee's income while serving other corporate interests (such as attracting and retaining executive talent while tying executive employees' compensation to their and the company's overall performance and success)?
  o. Would a reasonable person sell in the same circumstances?
  p. What was the employee/payor's practice in relation to vested shares and the deferral of compensation during the marriage? Has his/her practice changed post-separation? Is there a valid justification for such change? What would have likely happened if the family had remained intact?

[62] When it comes to the exercise of stock options, the primary consideration appears to be whether it is financially feasible for the employee to exercise his or her option and if so, whether it makes clear financial sense to do so at any given point in time. When it comes to the sale of the underlying vested shares, the primary consideration would seem to be whether there are any valid reasons for the employee's deferral of available compensation, or whether the employee is simply (and intentionally) deferring same for the main purpose of minimizing existing or future support obligations.

[63] In either case, the nature of a payor's support obligation may be an important factor. Both parents have a positive obligation to maximize their income to support their children to the best of their ability. The deferral of compensation which [is] readily available to a payor, to the detriment of children's current needs and well-being, should not be permitted unless there are valid reasons. Similarly, when a recipient's entitlement to spousal support is strongly compensatory, there will be a heightened expectation that he/she will be able to continue to share in the future wealth available to the payor as a result of the recipient's significant contributions during the relationship. In that case, there may be a stronger expectation on the payor to maximize his/her income each year, including by exercising stock options available to him/her (if financially able to do so), and to elect to immediately receive compensation (for instance realizing on vested shares) as soon as it becomes available, unless market conditions or other valid justifications militate in favour of a deferral.

[64] In the case at hand, the financial benefits available to the father through his employer's Share Purchase Plan is an integral part of his compensation package as an executive employee of Ledcor....

[65] Nonetheless, I am not prepared to impute to the father the additional income (of any kind) that he would have earned if he had exercised all the share purchase options offered to him by his employer in any given year. There are many reasons why the father has, over the past three years, declined to exercise all (or any) of the share options offered to him. These are the same reasons why he may not fully exercise these options in the future.

[67] Similarly, I am not prepared to impute to the father an income commensurate with the capital gains he would have realized had he elected to sell the shares he owned immediately upon vesting. There are many reasons why I decline doing so in this case. . . .

[73] For all those reasons, I am not prepared to impute income to the father on account of unexercised share purchase options or on account of unrealized vested shares for the years 2020 to present. Evidence may demonstrate that it would be reasonable to do so in the future, but based on the evidence before me, I find that it would not be appropriate to do so for the past three years.

[74] However, the cash value of the stock options he did exercise during those three years (he only did so in 2022) should be included in his income during the year of their purchase. Also, any capital gains flowing from the future sale of any underlying shares will be part of his income for support purposes during the year they are sold (as adjusted in accordance with Schedule III, s. 13 of the Guidelines).[122]

k) Union Dues

Union dues are deductible as of right from a parent's gross income for the purpose of determining the parent's Guidelines income. Section 1(g) of Schedule III to the *Federal Child Support Guidelines* requires the deduction to be made; no residual discretion is vested in the court.[123] However, a careful reading of section 8 of the *Income Tax Act* makes it clear that Canada Pension Plan contributions and *Employment Insurance Act* premiums are only deductible if they are paid on behalf of another individual employed or acting as "an assistant or substitute to perform the duties of the taxpayer's [spouse's or former spouse's] office or employment."[124]

l) Spousal Support Payments

Spousal support paid to the other spouse or former spouse is not deductible from the obligor's income in determining the applicable provincial or territorial table amount of child support.[125] Spousal support received from the other spouse is deducted from the overall income of the recipient spouse for the purpose of determining the applicable table amount of child support.[126] To calculate the income of each spouse or former spouse for the purposes of any order

122 *Walker v Walker*, 2024 ONSC 198 at paras 45–74.

123 *Stewart v Stewart*, [2004] AJ No 362 (QB); *Llewellyn v Llewellyn*, [2002] BCJ No 542 (CA); *LPH v JMR*, 2021 BCSC 1282; *Budyk v Sol*, [1998] MJ No 252 (CA); *PJC v PLC*, 2024 NBKB 42; *Stratton v Smith*, [2005] NJ No 101 (UFC); *Staples v Callender*, 2010 NSCA 49; *White v White*, 2015 NSCA 52; *Tucesku v Tucesku*, 2015 NSSC 281 (compulsory mess dues); *Walker v Rutledge*, [2002] OJ No 4521 (SCJ); *REG v TWJG*, 2011 SKQB 269.

124 *Guidelines to Amend the Federal Child Support Guidelines*, SOR/97-563, s 12; see also *Phillips v Phillips*, [1997] BCJ No 2376; *Munn v Munn*, [1999] OJ No 738 (CA); *Krislock v Krislock*, [1997] SJ No 698 (QB).

125 *Mabbett v Mabbett*, [1999] NSJ No 125 (SC); *Westcott v Westcott*, [1997] OJ No 3060 (Gen Div).

126 *Federal Child Support Guidelines*, SOR/97-175, Sch III, s 3(a); *Saunders v Saunders*, 2020 ABCA 226; *Hanrahan-Cox v Cox*, 2011 NSSC 256; *Boissy v Boissy*, [2004] OJ No 3400 (SCJ); *Mudronja v Mudronja*, 2020 ONCA 569.

for special or extraordinary expenses under section 7 of the *Federal Child Support Guidelines* spousal support payments must be deducted from the payor's income and included in the recipient's income.[127] Sections 3 and 3.1 of Schedule III of the *Federal Child Support Guidelines,* which expressly deal with the payment and receipt of spousal support with respect to the applicable table amount of child support and special or extraordinary expenses sought under section 7 of the Guidelines, have generated some uncertainty as to their potential effect. In *Sherlow v Zubko,*[128] the court refused to attribute income to a spouse on the basis of spousal support received from a prior spouse, notwithstanding that such spousal support constitutes taxable income that might properly fall within the ambit of section 16 of the *Federal Child Support Guidelines.* In the context of an application for child support under the *Ontario Child Support Guidelines,* which are substantively identical to the federal Guidelines, Lack J of the Ontario Superior Court has offered the following criticism: Where an order for spousal support is appropriate, the calculation of income for the purposes of the Guidelines is circuitous and tedious, if claims are made for special or extraordinary expenses under section 7 of the Guidelines or if undue hardship within the meaning of section 10 of the Guidelines is pleaded. This ensues from the fact that, whereas spousal support paid or received is ignored in calculating the income of the parties for the purpose of determining the amount of child support under the applicable provincial table, the receipt of spousal support is included in a spouse's income and is excluded from the income of the payor spouse for the purposes of determining a claim for section 7 expenses. A conundrum thus results from section 38.1(1) of the Ontario *Family Law Act* which, like section 15.3 of the *Divorce Act,* provides that child support takes precedence over spousal support. While such priority is to be accorded to child support, the calculation of section 7 expenses cannot be undertaken until spousal support is assessed. A similar conundrum arises under the undue hardship provisions of section 10 of the *Federal Child Support Guidelines* because the court must deny such a claim, if the potential obligor's household standard of living is higher than that of the recipient household, but any such comparison necessitates a prior determination of the amount, if any, of spousal support to be ordered. The problems of the court are compounded where no information has been provided dealing with the net impact of potential orders.[129]

m) Child Support Payments

From time to time, courts have been faced with the question whether the base amount of child support payable pursuant to the applicable provincial table (or in substitution therefor in cases where the court has a discretion to deviate from the table amount) is relevant to the determination of either spouse's income when the court apportions the respective spousal

---

127 *Federal Child Support Guidelines,* SOR/97-175, Sch III, s 3.1 (deduction only referred to); *Jang v Jang,* [2001] AJ No 563 (QB); *SJB v RDBB,* 2019 ABQB 624; *Werenka v Werenka,* 2021 ABQB 789; *Galloway v Galloway,* [2008] BCJ No 94 (CA); *Marquez v Zapiola,* 2013 BCCA 433; *O'Brien v O'Brien,* 2011 NBQB 179 (lump sum spousal support); *MacDiarmid v MacDiarmid,* 2014 NBQB 12; *Walsh v Walsh,* [2006] NJ No 33 (UFC); *Jahn-Cartwright v Cartwright,* 2010 ONSC 923; *Ludmer v Ludmer,* 2014 ONCA 827 (deduction from payor's income); *LAU v LLL,* 2016 PECA 15; *Mehlsen v Mehlsen,* 2012 SKCA 55; *Leland v Klette,* 2013 SKQB 277. See also *Ostapchuk v Ostapchuk,* [2003] OJ No 1733 (CA). And see Chapter 5, Section C.

128 [1999] AJ No 644 (QB).

129 *Schmid v Smith,* [1999] OJ No 3062 (SCJ).

contributions to a child's special or extraordinary expenses that are allowed pursuant to section 7 of the Guidelines. Given that periodic child support payments made pursuant to a pre-Guidelines agreement or order are deductible from the payor's taxable income and are taxable in the recipient spouse's income, such payments constitute a "source of income" to the payee within the meaning of section 16 of the Guidelines. Consequently, in order to exclude such payments, which are intended to address the child's basic needs, from being taken into account in the proportionate parental sharing of a child's special or extraordinary expenses, section 2 of Schedule III of the *Federal Child Support Guidelines* expressly provides that the court shall "deduct" from the payee's Guidelines income "any child support received that is included to determine total income in the T1 General form issued by the Canada Revenue Agency."[130] In *Ostapchuk v Ostapchuk*,[131] counsel were in agreement that the basic amount of child support that is payable according to the applicable provincial table or in substitution therefor is not deductible from the payor's income nor added to the payee's income for the purpose of apportioning section 7 expenses under the Guidelines in accordance with the respective parental incomes. Because of conflicting judicial rulings on this issue in the past,[132] the Ontario Court of Appeal in *Ostapchuk v Ostapchuk* decided to resolve the issue for itself. In doing so, it made no mention of section 16 of the *Federal Child Support Guidelines* nor of section 2 of Schedule III of the Guidelines. Instead, it drew inferences from the Guidelines' treatment of spousal support payments and in particular from section 3(2) of Schedule III of the Guidelines, which stipulates that "to calculate income for the purpose of determining an amount under section 7 of these Guidelines, deduct the spousal support paid to the other spouse." The first inference drawn by the Ontario Court of Appeal was that by directing that spousal support be deducted from the payor's income, such support would "by implication correspondingly, be included in the payee's income in calculating income for determining section 7 payments." Such an inference is consistent with section 16 of the Guidelines because spousal support payments clearly constitute a "source of income" under the heading "Total income" in the CRA T1 General form. The second inference drawn from section 3(2) of Schedule III by the Ontario Court of Appeal was that "the express mention of spousal support in calculating section 7 expenses necessarily implies that child support be excluded from the determination of income for this purpose." As the Ontario Court of Appeal observed, this is a logical distinction because spousal support goes to a parent's ability to contribute towards section 7 expenses whereas basic child support payments do not. From the payor's perspective, the Ontario Court of Appeal observed that the child support obligation not only extends to the applicable table amount of child support; it also includes allowable section 7 expenses. This is in accord with the presumptive rule established by section 3(1) of the *Federal Child Support Guidelines*. Consequently, the Ontario Court of Appeal concluded that there is no reason to separate the base amount of child support from section 7 expenses in the context of determining the payor's income under the Guidelines for the purpose of apportioning any

130 *Magee v Magee*, [1997] SJ No 468 (QB).

131 [2003] OJ No 1733 (CA). See also *Ross v Dunphy*, 2009 NBQB 281 (deduction of child care expenses for obligor's second family denied); *Walsh v Walsh*, [2006] NJ No 33 (UFC); *Marcella v Marcella*, 2016 SKQB 407.

132 See, for example, *Peltz v Peltz*, [2000] OJ No 3778 (SCJ); *Whittle v Clements*, [1998] NJ No 140 (UFC); *Prince Edward Island (Director of Maintenance Enforcement) v Skinner*, [2000] PEIJ No 29 (TD).

allowed special or extraordinary expenses between the parents. From the payee's perspective, the Ontario Court of Appeal observed that the base amount of child support is intended to accommodate the child's average day-to-day needs and cannot, therefore, be indicative of the ability of the recipient parent to contribute to the child's special or extraordinary expenses under section 7 of the Guidelines. By way of concluding its analysis, the Ontario Court of Appeal observed that "if Parliament had intended child support payments to be a separate consideration in calculating income for section 7 expenses, it would have expressly provided for this as it did in the case of spousal support payments."

4) Personal and Business Expenses and Losses

It has long been recognized that, for income tax purposes, some legitimately deducted expenses have a personal component because the *Income Tax Act* does not impose the requirement that an expense must be wholly or exclusively incurred for the purpose of trade in order to be deductible.[133] Legitimate business expenses may be deducted from the obligor's gross income for the purpose of applying the *Federal Child Support Guidelines*[134] but the court must take care to avoid the deduction of personal benefits that have been provided by the business.[135] An obligor who seeks to substantially reduce his or her income on account of business losses must provide full financial disclosure and explanation of the losses. Expenses unrelated to earning an income cannot generally be used to reduce income.[136] The onus of proving that business expenses are reasonable falls on the support obligor.[137] In *Cunningham v Seveny*,[138] the Alberta Court of Appeal confirmed that:

- When a self-employed parent argues that his or her gross income should be reduced by business expenses for purposes of calculating income for child support, the onus of proving that the expenses are reasonable is clearly on that parent.
- A parent claiming a deduction for business-related expenses must present evidence to justify the expenses.
- If the claimed expenses also resulted in a personal benefit to the parent claiming the deduction, "an explanation is required for why those expense deductions (or a part of them) should not be attributed to the parent's income for child support purposes."

---

133 *Williams v Williams*, [1997] NWTJ No 49 (SC).

134 *Beaudry v Beaudry*, 2010 ABQB 119; *Shaw v Shaw*, [1997] MJ No 400 (QB); *Brown v Brown*, [1997] NBJ No 287 (QB); *Wedge v McKenna*, [1997] PEIJ No 75 (TD); *Droit de la famille—152697*, 2015 QCCA 1738.

135 *Bohn v Bohn*, 2016 ABCA 406 at para 25; *MT v JS*, 2023 BCCA 64; *Zadera v Zadera*, 2023 BCSC 1880; *MWDP v MAG*, 2019 NBQB 62; *Snow v Wilcox*, [1999] NSJ No 453 (CA); *Sarafinchin v Sarafinchin*, [2000] OJ No 2855 (SCJ); *Tice v Tice*, [1998] SJ No 742 (QB).

136 *Bohn v Bohn*, 2016 ABCA 406; *Kuntz v Kuntz*, [1998] SJ No 743 (QB); see also *Henderson-Jorgensen v Henderson-Jorgensen*, 2013 ABQB 213; *Desrosiers v Pastuck*, 2016 NSSC 308.

137 *Henderson-Jorgensen v Henderson-Jorgensen*, 2013 ABCA 328, citing *Snow v Wilcox*, 1999 NSCA 163; *Bohn v Bohn*, 2016 ABCA 406; *ACS v CJS*, 2021 BCSC 1193; *Zadera v Zadera*, 2023 BCSC 1880. See also *Delichte v Rogers*, 2018 MBQB 75 at paras 136–37, Little J; *Yovcheva v Hristov*, 2019 ONSC 1007.

138 2017 ABCA 4; see also *Ruffell v Ruffell*, 2021 ABCA 39; *Murray v Murray*, 2021 ABQB 539; *ACS v CJS*, 2021 BCSC 1193.

- Even if expenses have been approved for income tax purposes by the Canada Revenue Agency, this does not mean that the test for deducting expenses from income for child support purposes has been met.
- "Child support is the right of the child. A parent's legal obligation to pay child support that fairly reflects the parent's income in accordance with child support guidelines is not to be constrained or limited by income tax statutes that may confer entitlements in relation to deductibility of business expenses."[139]

In the words of Schutz JA of the Alberta Court of appeal in *Cunningham v Seveny*, "[t]he evidential and persuasive onus under sections 18-21 of either the federal or provincial *Guidelines* as to the reasonableness of expenses, rests with the self-employed or corporate parent throughout, and is the most effective means by which to serve the best interests of the child."[140]

A parent is not entitled to claim an income deduction for *ex gratia* payments made to a third party as an expression of his gratitude for their support of his business.[141]

Business expenses can be addressed under either section 18(2) or section 19(1)(g) of the Federal Child Support Guidelines where a corporation is involved but section 19 will be the only option available where a sole proprietorship or partnership is in issue[142] Section 7 of Schedule III of the *Federal Child Support Guidelines* entitles a spouse to deduct from his or her income the actual amount of business investment losses sustained by the spouse during the year. The right to deduct a non-recurring business investment loss under this section only arises after the loss has actually been incurred. A prospective future loss, such as might arise from a potential lawsuit, does not fall within the ambit of the section.[143]

5) Commission Income; Bonuses; Stock Options; Severance Packages

A parent who asserts that his or her line 150 (now line 15000) income on the income tax return is not the fairest way of determining annual income pursuant to sections 16 and 17 of the Guidelines, has the onus of rebutting the presumption in favour of the "total income" line. "Fairness" and "reasonableness" within the meaning of section 17 of the Guidelines must be considered in relation to both of the spouses and to the children. A signing bonus, even though spread over more than one year, may constitute a non-recurring amount within the meaning of section 17 of the Guidelines but the court has a discretion to determine what, if any, amount of signing bonus should fairly be included in the parent's income.[144] The court may conclude that it is not "fair and reasonable" within the meaning of section 17 of the Guidelines to include that portion of the parent's signing bonus that was used to extinguish pressing debts.[145]

---

139 Quoted by Williams J in *Sawma v Zeidan*, 2018 ONSC 4319 at para 29. See also *MT v JS*, 2023 BCCA 64.

140 *Cunningham v Seveny*, 2017 ABCA 4 at para 28; see also *Zdyb v Zdyb*, 2017 ABQB 44; *Vavrek v Vavrek*, 2019 ABCA 235; *Destine v Cloutier*, 2022 ABCA 331; *JC v AAG*, 2020 BCSC 1485.

141 *Scott v Scott*, [2004] NBJ No 468 (CA); see also *Delichte v Rogers*, 2018 MBQB 75.

142 *MT v JS*, 2023 BCCA 64 at paras 9–10; see also *Code v McLeod*, 2023 BCSC 1686.

143 *Omah-Maharajh v Howard*, [1998] AJ No 173 (QB).

144 As to the deferral of management bonuses, see *Korkola v Korkola*, [2009] OJ No 343 (SCJ).

145 *Shaw v Shaw*, [2002] OJ No 2782 (SCJ).

Where a work performance bonus has been paid for several years, but its contingent nature, which is premised on certain levels of cost savings being achieved, renders it unfair to impute an average or fixed amount for the current year, the bonus may be taken into account, if and when paid, by adding it to the parent's base annual income and having the parent pay a lump sum adjustment payment representing the difference between the child support paid and the child support payable in light of the bonus added to the parent's base income.[146] An order for the payment of the applicable table amount of child support may be made subject to quarterly adjustment to reflect the payor's commission income over and above his base salary.[147] Recurring bonuses may be included in an obligor's income under the *Federal Child Support Guidelines*, subject to an adjustment if future bonuses do not materialize.[148] Where the division of matrimonial property is not in issue, bonuses and benefits associated with the exercise and disposition of stock options that are historically part of an obligor's compensation package may constitute income for the purposes of assessing support under the *Federal Child Support Guidelines.* In cases where bonuses are received at the end of a pay period, any support payments for the period in which the bonuses were earned are subject to a possible readjustment and a lump sum may be ordered to take into account that the bonuses are available at infrequent times. A severance package also constitutes income for the purposes of the Guidelines where it represents an acceleration of income that would normally be earned by the recipient over a specified period. The fact that the obligor receives the severance package as a lump sum or receives preferential tax treatment by transferring all or part of it to an RRSP does not change its characterization as income. The disposition of stock options that results in a taxable capital gain may also be considered income. If the aforementioned benefits are included in a division of matrimonial property, the amount of income to be attributed to the obligor may require reassessment.[149] Bonuses that are unlikely to continue may be disregarded in determining the obligor's income, even though section 17(1) of the Guidelines confers a discretion on the court to take into account such portion of a non-recurring amount as the court considers appropriate.[150]

Income for the purpose of applying the Guidelines includes severance pay, which represents an acceleration of income, in addition to whatever other earnings the obligor may have.[151] Determination of the obligor's income in light of a severance package is unaffected by his or her election to tax shelter part of the payments, but a *pro rata* adjustment is

146 *Goodwin v Goodwin*, [2002] SJ No 45 (QB). Compare *Gibson v Gibson*, 2011 ONSC 4406. See also *Forester v Odjick*, 2021 BCSC 789; *Easton v Coxhead*, 2018 ONSC 4784.

147 *Bhoi v Bhoi*, [2001] OJ No 4864 (SCJ).

148 *Sutcliffe v Sutcliffe*, [2001] AJ No 629 (Alta QB); *Oswald v Oswald*, [2001] MJ No 73 (QB).

149 *MacDonald v MacDonald*, [1997] AJ No 1262 (CA); *Vitagliano v Di Stavalo*, [2001] OJ No 1138 (SCJ). See also *DeWolfe v McMillan*, 2011 NSSC 301 (severance pay).

150 *Spanier v Spanier*, [1998] BCJ No 452 (SC).

151 *LR v DT*, [1998] SJ No 733 (QB), citing *MacDonald v MacDonald* (1997), 209 AR 178 (CA); see also *Steeves v English*, [2004] AJ No 632 (CA); *McKenzie v Perestrelo*, 2014 BCCA 161; *KJP v BSJG*, 2024 BCSC 167; *Levesque v Meade*, 2010 NBQB 270; *Burgess v Burgess*, 2016 NLCA 11; *MF v MW*, 2011 NSFC 2; *Williams v Steinwand*, 2017 NWTSC 50; *Andrews v Andrews*, [1999] OJ No 3578 (CA); *Beach v Tolstoy*, 2015 ONSC 7248; *Scory v Scory*, [1999] SJ No 644 (CA); *Holtzman v Holtzman*, 2012 SKQB 74; compare *Thompson v Scullion*, [2000] NBJ No 209 (QB). And see *Lafontaine v Lafontaine*, 2011 ONSC 1833 (settlement of claim for damages for wrongful dismissal included in recipient's income and excluded from property equalization); *Lisitza v Herle (Lisitza)*, 2022 SKQB 71.

appropriate in calculating the obligor's annual income, where the severance pay represented more than one year's income.[152] Lump sum severance and vacation payments may be taken into account for the purpose of attributing an annual income to a spouse. The investment of part of the severance package in stock options does not reduce the child support obligations applicable during the period to which the severance package relates.[153] Severance pay and termination allowances may be taken into account in calculating the obligor's income,[154] even though they are already spent.[155] In determining the prospective income of a parent who receives a very substantial severance package on the involuntary termination of her employment and thereafter acquires new employment that yields a much lower income, the court may use a "forward averaging" approach that spreads the severance income over subsequent years, thereby recognizing that a severance package is intended to provide a monetary amount that can be used to soften the blow of changing circumstances through a reasonable period of transition.[156]

In *Murdoch-Woods v Zywina*,[157] a father as a result of severance became eligible for Employment Insurance retraining benefits, which provided no living allowance and were payable directly to college. Characterizing the retraining benefits as being in the nature of a capital expenditure that would provide the father with a capital asset, namely retraining to facilitate his employment and increase his income earning capacity, the retraining benefits were excluded from the father's Guidelines income.

6) Problems with Self-Employed Parents

Judicial determination of the income of wage earners is relatively easy because their tax returns generally provide a true reflection of their income. Where obligors are self-employed and operate a business, the net income reported on their personal income tax return is not necessarily a true reflection of their personal income for the purpose of determining their child support obligations.[158] When faced by such parties, the court must meticulously examine the financial records placed before the court.[159]

Several difficulties previously encountered when dealing with self-employed persons have been summarized in the following observations of Gunn J of the Saskatchewan Court of Queen's Bench in *Gorgichuk v Gordichuk*:[160]

---

152 *AJL v JTB*, 2020 ABQB 649; *McKenzie v Perestrelo*, 2014 BCCA 161; *Campbell v Campbell*, 2012 NSCA 86; *Gervasio v Gervasio*, [1999] OJ No 1366 (Gen Div); see also *McIntyre v Veinot*, 2016 NSSC 8 at paras 425–31.

153 *Crawford v Crawford*, [1998] OJ No 885 (Gen Div).

154 *MacDonald v MacDonald* (1997), 57 Alta LR (3d) 195 (CA); *Wallace v Wallace*, [1998] BCJ No 2086 (SC); *PDR v JER*, [2005] NBJ No 51 (QB); *Rondeau v Kirby*, [2003] NSJ No 436 (SC), aff'd [2004] NSJ No 143 (CA); *Walliser v Pouliot*, [2005] SJ No 580 (QB); *Lisitza v Herle (Lisitza)*, 2022 SKQB 71. Compare *Pomozova v Mann*, 2010 ONCA 212.

155 *Vincent v Tremblett*, [1998] NJ No 292 (SC).

156 *CAB v MSCS*, 2006 BCSC 1393.

157 2011 ONSC 705.

158 *Omah-Maharajh v Howard*, [1998] AJ No 173 (QB); *Snow v Wilcox*, [1999] NSJ No 453 (CA); *Babich v Babich*, 2015 SKQB 22.

159 *Williams v Williams*, [1997] NWTJ No 49 (SC).

160 *Gorgichuk v Gorgichuk*, [1997] SJ No 211 at paras 65–68 (QB); see also *Wasuita v Wasuita*, [1998] AJ No 695 (QB); *Woodward v Woodward*, 2016 SKQB 301; *Birnie v Birnie*, 2019 SKQB 303.

In *Pyper v. Neville* (1995), 132 Sask. R. 300 at 303 (Q.B.), Halvorson J. commented on the utility of the support Guidelines recommended in the "Federal/Provincial/Territorial Family Law Committee's Report and Recommendations on Child Support":

> A third observation is the difficulty inherent in referring to the support tables where the payor is a farmer or other self-employed person. Gross income is meaningless as a measure of ability to pay. Reasonable expenses in earning that income must be deducted. This leaves net income as the figure against which the tables should be applied. That can be unfair too, as it understates real cash available. This can be remedied to a degree by adding depreciation back in before implementing the tables.

This issue has also been canvassed by the Alberta Court of Appeal in *Levesque v. Levesque* (1994), 4 R.F.L. (4th) 375 at p. 388 (*per curiam*):

> The calculation of gross income does not, of course, work as simply for the self-employed as for those who are employed for wages. They have business expenses that must be put against gross income. For them, the judge must do a calculation of what, as near as can be, would be the gross income were the party employed for wages. While we cannot offer detailed assistance, we warn judges not necessarily to use the tests employed by the *Income Tax Act* for the calculation of expenses. Some of these, as, for example, capital cost allowance, reflect tax policy not related to the issue before us.

In *Jones v. Jones* (1994), 4 R.F.L. (4th) 293 at 317 (Sask. Q.B.) Gerein J. made the following comments in considering capital cost allowance as it related to a farm business:

> It is readily apparent from the foregoing that the respondent's disposable income was considerably more than his taxable income. At the same time, it would be unfair to simply treat all of the capital cost allowance as income available for normal living expenses. This approach would ignore the reality that there are capital costs involved in operating a farm and that money should be set aside for the purpose of replacing equipment as it wears out. Accordingly, this must be taken into account in determining the respondent's ability to provide financial support.

The approach in *Jones* was adopted by McLellan J in *Keenleyside v Keenleyside.*[161]

Although the above observations pre-dated the implementation of the *Federal Child Support Guidelines*, they remain applicable to a determination of income under the Guidelines.[162] As Wilkinson J of the Saskatchewan Court of Queen's Bench observed in *Poff v Fenell*

> Because of the latitude farmers have to "manage" their income under the cash method of accounting and through the use of deferred crop payments, prepaid expenses, inventory adjustments, capital cost allowance, the treatment of operating expenses and incentive programs, the court would be greatly assisted in the discharge of their function if an accounting

161 (1996), 140 Sask R 31 (QB).

162 *Andres v Andres*, [1999] MJ No 103 (CA).

of farm production and expenses was presented on an accrual basis. This would provide a more realistic picture of true farm income.[163]

However, as Danyliuk J of the Saskatchewan Court of Queen's Bench pointed out in *Heidel v Heidel*, "[t]he accrual method of income calculation is not a panacea. It may work in some cases for the determination of a farmer's income, but not in others. . . . [T]he accrual method is not one of universal application. Determination of a farmer's income is a question of fact. As such, resolution of that issue depends heavily on the evidence before the Court."[164]

Some of the issues relating to the income of farmers and the self-employed are addressed in Schedule III of the *Federal Child Support Guidelines*, although significant problems remain. As Turcotte J of the Saskatchewan Court of Queen's Bench observed in *LJL v LRS*:

> To arrive at a determination of a farmer's income for child support purposes, our courts have adopted a flexible approach, having regard for the provisions of ss. 15 to 20 of the *Guidelines*. This flexible approach allows for consideration of the reasonableness of farming expenses claimed by a farmer for income tax purposes in determining the income for child support purposes. Expenses which may be subject to adjustment include inventory adjustments, capital cost allowance claims and assessing the extent to which farming expenses claimed for tax purposes include a personal component that benefits the farmer. The flexible approach to determination of a farmer's income for child support purposes also allows for the use of statistical information for comparative purposes; using an average of farming income over a three year period; and at times imputing income based on a farmer's ability to maintain off-farm employment in addition to earning income as a farmer.[165]

7) Student Loans

A student loan cannot be viewed as income in the hands of the recipient but a student bursary is equivalent to a grant and is income in the year it is actually received under the *Income Tax Act* and for the purposes of the federal or provincial Guidelines.[166] Although student loans are not income under section 16 of the *Federal Child Support Guidelines*, benefits received by the father under the *Employment Insurance Act* to help further his education are income under section 16 for the purpose of determining the amount of child support to be paid.[167]

8) Future Commissions

A monthly advance against future commissions does not constitute income for the purpose of assessing the appropriate amount of child support or for determining the amount of arrears at the date of trial.[168]

---

163 [1998] SJ No 608 at para 10 (QB).
164 2013 SKQB 8 at para 19; see also *Labrecque v Labrecque*, 2014 SKCA 59.
165 2013 SKQB 168 at para 58; see also *Woodward v Woodward*, 2016 SKQB 301; *MacLachlan v MacLachlan*, 2020 SKQB 117 at para 20.
166 *Fraser v Gallant*, [2004] PEIJ No 5 (SC); *Marquis v Marquis*, 2013 SKQB 76.
167 *Giao v McCready*, [2005] NSJ No 50 (SC).
168 *Edwards v Edwards* (1997), 31 RFL (4th) 320 (Alta CA) (issues remitted to trial judge).

9) Exclusions from Income

Workplace Safety and Insurance Board payments and Canada Pension Plan disability payments constitute "income" under section 16 of the *Federal Child Support Guidelines* but the Child Tax Credit,[169] GST rebate, and any child care subsidy do not constitute income under that section. Workplace Safety and Insurance Board payments should be grossed up to take account of their tax-free status.[170] An income tax refund is not income for the purpose of the Guidelines.[171] Settlement proceeds arising from wrongful dismissal are included in a spouse's income under the Guidelines, after deductions have been made for legal fees and disbursements and for reimbursement of Employment Insurance benefits.[172]

Income signifies money or benefit received by way of entitlement; gratuitous benefits received from a church or family member should not be treated as income.[173] A government benefit for the respite care of a mentally challenged child is excluded from a parent's income where the benefit is directly payable to the respite worker.[174]

A lump sum received for pain and suffering, as distinct from income replacement, under a personal injuries settlement does not constitute income for the purpose of the *Federal Child Support Guidelines*, although the interest earned thereon does.[175]

Repayment of a shareholder loan is not income under the *Federal Child Support Guidelines*,[176] but such repayment of capital may result in the judicial imputation of income on the basis that the capital asset is not being reasonably utilized to generate income within the meaning of section 19(1)(e) of the Guidelines.[177]

Dividend income that is received by a spouse on a periodic basis by way of property entitlement has been excluded from the calculation of the recipient's income under the *Federal Child Support Guidelines*, notwithstanding that it constitutes income for taxation purposes.[178]

---

169 Compare *Mullins v Mullins*, 2016 ABQB 226 at para 9, Jeffrey J.

170 *DAT v SLP*, 2018 NBQB 135. See also *Dahlgren v Hodgson*, [1998] AJ No 1501 (CA); *Mullins v Mullins*, 2016 ABQB 226; *Dedoscenco v Beauchamp*, [2005] BCJ No 1053 (SC) (CPP and WCB disability pensions grossed up; WCB personal care allowance not grossed up); *MS v EJS*, 2017 BCSC 564; *Prince v Soenen*, 2015 MBQB 31; *Callahan v Brett*, [2000] NJ No 354 (SC) (workers' compensation benefits and private disability pension); *Coadic v Coadic*, [2005] NSJ No 415 (SC); *Peterson v Horan*, [2006] SJ No 333 (CA); *SMM v DPG*, [2003] YJ No 98 (SC). Re gross up of workers' compensation, compare *Landry v Landry*, 2012 ONSC 7187 at para 5; see also *Storey v Simmons*, 2013 ABQB 168 and compare *Starling v Starling*, 2016 SKQB 112 (spousal support).

171 *Rapoport v Rapoport*, 2011 ONSC 4456; see also *Dahlgren v Hodgson*, [1998] AJ No 1501 (CA); *Flanagan v Heal*, [1998] SJ No 805 (QB) (child tax credit).

172 *Griffin v Griffin*, [1999] BCJ No 397 (SC).

173 *Booth v Booth*, [2000] BCJ No 2544 (SC).

174 *Moulson v Graves*, [2002] OJ No 2582 (SCJ).

175 *Tibbo v Bush*, [2000] NSJ No 352 (Fam Ct) (issue left unresolved as to whether the capital settlement constituted "means" that might justify an order under s 7 of the Guidelines in the absence of any order for the table amount of child support).

176 *Rudachyk v Rudachyk*, [1999] SJ No 312 (CA). For a nuanced review of relevant caselaw, see *CRP v NDP* 2023 NBKB 197 at paras 247–66, Colford J.

177 *Waese v Bojman*, [2001] OJ No 2009 (SCJ); see also *JR v NR*, 2017 BCSC 455; *CRP v NDP*, 2023 NBKB 197.

178 *Dunham v Dunham*, [1998] OJ No 4758 (Gen Div).

10) RRSPs; Pensions

A parent has a legal obligation to earn as much as he or she is reasonably capable of earning to meet the obligations to support the children. Where a parent has a pension plan from which he or she can immediately receive benefits, he or she cannot avoid paying child support because he does not wish to take his pension at a reduced rate.[179]

Compulsory contributions to RRSPs are not deductible from the obligor's income for the purpose of applying the *Federal Child Support Guidelines*.[180] An employer's contribution to a spouse's pension plan does not constitute "income" within the meaning of section 16 of the *Federal Child Support Guidelines*.[181] The Alberta Court of Appeal has, nevertheless, concluded that the court retains a discretion to include such contributions in the employed spouse's income for the purpose of the *Federal Child Support Guidelines*, although it should decline to do so in the absence of good reason for such inclusion.[182] Given the definition of "income" under the Guidelines, it is difficult to conceive how such contributions can be properly categorized as income under the Guidelines, even though courts retain a discretion to impute income in circumstances other than those listed in section 19(1) of the Guidelines.

Pension payments constitute income, not property instalment payments, under section 16 of the *Federal Child Support Guidelines*.[183] Withdrawals from RRSPs constitute income under section 16 of the Guidelines.[184] As RRSP withdrawals are included in line 15000 income on a tax return and there is no exemption set out in the *Federal Child Support Guidelines*, there is a presumption they are included as income for child support purposes and the spouse making the RRSP withdrawals bears the burden of demonstrating that treating them as income would not lead to the fairest determination of income.[185] Such withdrawals cannot be said to involve "double dipping" on the basis that the RRSPs have already been taken into account under a spousal claim for the equalization of the net family properties, because the notion of double dipping is by its nature inapplicable to child support, which reflects the right of the child, rather than the right of the primary caregiving parent.[186] However, RRSPs are not always included as income because the cashing in of such investments may represent

---

179 *Lenko v Lenko*, 2011 BCSC 28.

180 *Lepage v Lepage*, [1999] SJ No 174 (QB). Compare *Lussier v Ritchie*, 2023 BCSC 1817 and see *Loehr v Loehr*, 2023 BCSC 2229.

181 *Ennis v Ennis*, [2000] AJ No 75 (CA); *Redlick v Redlick*, 2013 BCSC 1155; *Purdue v Purdue*, 2014 NBQB 262; *Chippett v Fudge*, 2019 NLSC 29, compare *PJC v PLC*, 2024 NBKB 42.

182 *Ennis v Ennis*, [2000] AJ No 75 (CA).

183 *Harris v Harris*, [1999] AJ No 484 (QB).

184 *FDM v EGM*, 2023 ABCA 100; *Lemire v Lemire*, 2016 BCSC 2340; *Dickson v Dickson*, 2009 MBQB 274; *MR v JR*, 2018 NBCA 12; *PJC v PLC*, 2024 NBKB 42; *Pitt v Tee*, 2016 NWTSC 40; *Fraser v Fraser*, 2013 ONCA 715; *Ludmer v Ludmer*, 2014 ONCA 827; *Richard v Holmes*, 2020 ONSC 6485; *Holtzman v Holtzman*, 2013 SKQB 408. See also *LDW v KDM*, 2011 ABQB 384 (redemption of RRSPs excluded on basis of double dipping but included in matrimonial property division); *Warren v Warren*, 2021 ABQB 213; *Brown v Brown*, 2012 NBCA 11; compare *Belot v Connelly*, 2013 MBQB 98, citing TW Hainsworth, *Child Support Guidelines Service* (Aurora, ON: Canada Law Book, 1998) at 5–14 to 5–15. *Kelland v Stanley*, 2013 NLTD(F) 40; *Osman v ElKadi*, 2015 ONSC 1124; *Lisko v Lisko*, 2016 SKQB 38.

185 *Boon v Boon*, 2022 BCSC 1444 at para 5, Edelmann J; see also *FDM v EGM*, 2023 ABCA 100.

186 *Stevens v Boulerice*, [1999] OJ No 1568 (SCJ); *Mylrea v Benoit*, [2003] OJ No 2921 (SCJ); see also *Steeves v English*, [2004] AJ No 632 (CA); *Brown v Brown*, 2012 NBCA 11; *Perrier v Daigle*, 2012 NSSC 54; *Francis v Filion*, [2003] OJ No 1138 (SCJ). Compare *Boon v Boon*, 2022 BCSC 1444; *Belot v Connelly*, 2013 MBQB 98; *Owen v Owen*, 2015 ONSC 4002, citing *Difede v Difede*, [2007] OJ No 622 (SCJ).

non-recurring income that falls within section 17(1) of the Guidelines.[187] The propriety of including an RRSP withdrawal as income for child support purposes is fact dependent.[188] *Dillon v Dillon*,[189] the trial judge was found to have erred in adding cashed-out RRSP con tributions to the father's employment income that already included new contributions in a similar amount. To include both the contributions and the withdrawal as income amounted to a double counting and a material overstatement of the parent's income, which constituted a palpable and overriding error of fact. Pursuant to SOR/2009-181, 11 June 2009,[190] Sched ule III of the *Federal Child Support Guidelines* has been amended to include the following provision:

> **Split-pension amount**
>
> 14 If a spouse is deemed to have received a split-pension amount under paragraph 60.03(2)(*b*) of the *Income Tax Act* that is included in that spouse's total income in the T1 General form issued by the Canada Revenue Agency, deduct that amount.

In a regulatory impact statement included with the amendment but not constituting part of the Guidelines, the following observations have been made:

> The Pension Income Splitting program was implemented under the *Income Tax Act*, in 2007, to allow Canadian residents to allocate up to one-half of their eligible pension income to their spouse or common-law partner for tax purposes. This has the effect of lowering a couple's household tax liability. It also has the effect of artificially increasing the gross income of the recipient, even though there is no actual transfer of funds to him or her. As such, because the calculation of child support is based on a parent's total income, if a recipient is also a child support payor, his or her child support obligation is increased as a direct result of his or her artificially increased total income. This is an unintended impact of pension income splitting on child support calculations. Since there is no transfer of funds, this impact is contrary to the Federal Guidelines' fundamental principle that child support should be based on a parent's ability to pay. Furthermore, the Federal Guidelines do not currently include a relief mechanism permitting the allocated pension amount to be deducted from the recipient's total income for the purpose of calculating child support.
>
> An amendment to Schedule III of the Federal Guidelines is necessary to address the impact of pension income splitting on the calculation of child support.
>
> This amendment ensures that the amount of pension income received by a person, in accordance with the Pension Income Splitting program, does not have an impact on the

---

187 *Haig v Whitmore*, 2015 ABQB 267; *McKenzie v Perestrelo*, 2014 BCCA 161 at paras 82–83; *CAM v TCH* 2016 BCSC 1756; *Belot v Connelly*, 2013 MBQB 98 at paras 68–70; *Kelland v Stanley*, 2013 NLTD(F) 40; *Leet v Beach*, 2010 NSSC 433; *Mitchell v Mitchell*, [2002] OJ No 2504 (SCJ) (cashing in of RRSP viewed as liquidation of capital); *Mask v Mask*, [2008] OJ No 423 (SCJ); compare *Lemire v Lemire*, 2016 BCSC 2340; *Pitt v Tee*, 2016 NWTSC 40; *Fraser v Fraser*, 2013 ONCA 715; *Ludmer v Ludmer*, 2014 ONCA 827; *Horowitz v Nightingale*, 2015 ONSC 190.

188 *DYP v NPT*, 2015 NBQB 67; *Kelland v Stanley*, 2013 NLTD(F) 40. See also *Richard v Holmes*, 2020 ONSC 6485 at para 34.

189 [2005] NSJ No 548 (CA); see also *JK v DK*, 2010 NBQB 23; *PJC v PLC*, 2024 NBKB 42; *Croft v Foote*, 2023 NLCA 36; *Campbell v Campbell*, 2012 NSCA 86.

190 See *Canada Gazette*, Vol 143, No 13, 24 June 2009.

calculation of child support where that person is also a parent paying child support. The objectives of this amendment are

- to maintain the principle on which the Federal Guidelines are based, i.e. that parents have a joint financial obligation to maintain the children of the marriage in accordance with their ability to contribute;
- to ensure that income used under the Federal Guidelines continues to reflect a person's actual ability to pay; and
- to uphold the fairness, predictability and consistency of the determination of child support under the Federal Guidelines.

Description and rationale

The amendment to Schedule III of the Federal Guidelines permits the deduction of the allocated pension splitting amount from the recipient's income used for child support purposes. The amendment is intended to neutralize the impact of pension income splitting on the application of the Federal Guidelines by ensuring that the parent's income used for the purposes of applying the Federal Guidelines reflects their actual ability to pay child support.

It is worth noting that the amendment only allows the deduction from the recipient's income, not the transferor's. This is because pension income splitting does not affect a transferor's total income. In addition, the court retains its discretion to impute any income to spouses, under section 19 of the Federal Guidelines.

This amendment does not affect the rules established under the *Income Tax Act* regarding the Pension Income Splitting program.

Although split-pension amounts received under paragraph 60.03(2)(b) of the *Income Tax Act* can be deducted from a parent's income pursuant to section 14 of Schedule III,[191] a payout of accumulated sick leave credits does not trigger any corresponding deduction.[192]

11) Work Done but Unbilled

In determining an obligor's income, the inclusion of work done, but not billed, may produce an unrealistically high figure for income, which does not reflect cash on hand out of which support must be paid. In that event, the court may apply the "matching principle" to work in progress, which is sanctioned for income tax purposes by the Canadian Institute of Chartered Accountants. This principle signifies that the income for any given year should most accurately reflect the balance between the revenues for that year and the expense and effort that have produced those revenues.[193]

191 *LeBlanc v LeBlanc*, 2015 NBQB 164.

192 *Blumer v Dancey*, 2010 ONSC 5707.

193 *Augaitis v Augaitis*, [1998] OJ No 1795, 40 RFL (4th) 341 at 343–46 (Gen Div) (money received from former firm on winding up included in income in lieu of what would normally have been work in progress).

12) Trust Funds

Section 19(1)(i) of the *Federal Child Support Guidelines* confers discretionary jurisdiction on a court to impute income to a spouse who receives "income or other benefits" from a trust. Doing so does not require mathematical precision, and the court does the best that it can in the circumstances.[195] This broad language suggests that distributions from a trust, whether from the income or the capital of the trust, constitute part of the "means" of a payor spouse and may be taken into account in calculating a spouse's income for support purposes and tax-free capital distributions from the trust may be grossed up.[196]

13) Seasonal Employment

Courts should fix child support on the basis of an obligor's annualized income where the obligor is engaged in seasonal employment and receives employment insurance benefits when unemployed.[197] Monthly child support is ordered on the basis of the obligor's annual income. It is the obligor's responsibility to budget so as to accommodate seasonal unemployment.

14) Damages; Structured Settlements

An award of damages or a structured settlement providing for non-pecuniary loss and the cost of future care does not constitute "income" within the meaning of section 16 of the *Federal Child Support Guidelines*. The receipt of such payments does not fall within section 19(1)(b) of the Guidelines, which empowers a court to impute income to a parent whose "income" is exempt from federal and provincial income tax, nor do such payments fall within section 19(1)(h) of the Guidelines, which empowers a court to impute income where funds are acquired through dividends, capital gains, or other sources of income that are taxed at a lower rate than employment or business income or that are exempt from tax. Insofar as an award of damages or structured settlement and a CPP disability benefit provide an award for loss of earning capacity, such payments constitute "income" within the meaning of the Guidelines, but a court may decline to gross up the payments received under the structured settlement when they were calculated on the basis of the disabled parent's gross income loss. Lump sum payments under the annuity that are specifically earmarked for the disabled parent's children from his first marriage are not "income" under the Guidelines.[199]

---

194 See *Elhert v Sailer*, 2023 ABCA 371 (order for financial disclosure by family trust).

195 *SAM v JAB*, 2023 BCSC 2110 at para 29, Stephens J.

196 *Bledin v Bledin*, 2021 ONSC 3815; see also *Veskovic v Nielsen*, 2022 SKCA 134.

197 *SGS v CLS*, [2004] OJ No 2177 (SCJ).

198 *Peters v Evenson*, [2003] BCJ No 948 (SC).

199 *MK v RAS*, [2004] BCJ No 2930 (SC); *Mason v Mason*, 2013 ONSC 5974. See also *Buckingham v Buckingham*, 2013 ABQB 155; *Storey v Simmons*, 2013 ABQB 168 at para 2; *Stasiewski v Stasiewski*, 2007 BCCA 205; *Fraser v Fraser*, 2013 ONCA 715 at paras 108–11; *Tookenay v Laframboise*, 2015 ONSC 2898; *AVR v MJA*, 2016 SKQB 272. Compare *CAL v DEL*, 2019 BCSC 1483; *Doucet v Doucet*, 2020 BCSC 1218 (spousal support); *Starling v Starling*, 2016 SKQB 112 (spousal support).

The fact that the proceeds of a disability settlement have the character of capital and are not income for tax purposes does not necessarily determine whether the settlement proceeds can form the basis of imputation of income under section 19 of the *Federal Child Support Guidelines*.[200] A capital amount paid in a personal injuries settlement for future income loss may be taken into account in fixing a parent's annual income under the *Federal Child Support Guidelines*,[201] even if the money has already been spent.[202]

Settlement funds paid to a parent on account of the copyright infringement of his musical compositions constitute income for child support purposes pursuant to section 15 of the *Federal Child Support Guidelines*, subject to the deduction of necessary legal and accounting fees incurred in negotiating the settlement. And if the funds are tax-free, they may be grossed up pursuant to section 19(1)(h) of the *Federal Child Support Guidelines*.[203] This conclusion is sound whether or not the settlement funds constitute a source of income within the meaning of section 16 of the Guidelines because the jurisdiction of the court to impute income pursuant to section 19(1) of the Guidelines is not confined to the circumstances listed under that section 19(1)(b)[204] and the settlement funds represent a loss of income by way of royalties.

15) Foster Parent's Allowance

It may be appropriate to include a portion of a foster parent's allowance as income for the purpose of calculating child support.[205]

D. MOST CURRENT INFORMATION TO BE USED

Where, for the purpose of the *Federal Child Support Guidelines*, including any determination of income, any amount is determined on the basis of specified information, the most current information must be used.[206] Implicit in that requirement, however, is that it be the most reliable and accurate "current information" available.[207] A child is entitled to be supported according to the payor's current income, if ascertainable, and if not, by a reasonably accurate estimate of the payor's current income with an adjustment at year's end once the actual

200 *Myles v Armstrong*, 2011 NBQB 61. See also *Laurain v Clarke*, 2011 ONSC 7195.

201 *SP v BM*, 2013 BCSC 1825, citing *MK v RAS*, 2004 BCSC 1798 and *KLK v EJGK*, 2010 BCSC 1437.

202 *Meggerson v Geisbrect*, [2006] SJ No 79 (QB) (calculation of annual investment yield of capital amount added to the parent's current employment income).

203 *Mobin v Stephens*, 2013 ONCJ 53.

204 See *Bak v Dobell*, 2007 ONCA 304.

205 *Lonergan v Lonergan*, 2011 ONSC 1410. See also *JJR v JFM*, 2013 NBQB 253.

206 *Federal Child Support Guidelines*, SOR/97-175, s 2(3); *Ramachala (Holland) v Holland*, 2020 ABQB 432; *Piper v Piper*, 2010 BCSC 1718; *Trevors v Jenkins*, 2011 NBCA 61; *Stanford v Cole*, [1998] NJ No 300 (SC); *Koester v Koester*, 2014 NSSC 367; *MacNeil v MacNeil*, [2000] NWTJ No 4 (SC); *White v White*, 2015 NSCA 52; *Andrews v Andrews*, [1999] OJ No 3578 (CA); *Moreton v Inthavixay*, 2020 ONSC 4881; *Brown v Pierce*, 2018 PECA 23; *Miller v White*, 2022 PESC 4; *Keogan v Weekes*, [2004] SJ No 583 (CA); *Ritchie v Solonick*, [1999] YJ No 66 (SC). See also *VC v PR*, 2016 NBQB 90 at paras 128–29; *SEB v JTM*, 2019 NBQB 76 at para 64.

207 See *Ryder v Kent*, 2016 NLTD(F) 1 at para 15, Sheahan J; see also *GF v JACF*, 2016 NBCA 21.

income is known.[208] The obligor's income for the calendar year in which the application is heard is the income to be considered for the purpose of applying the *Federal Child Support Guidelines.*[209] Reliable current information should be used as opposed to historical informa tion.[210] In determining the amount of child support payable under the applicable provincial or territorial tables, the projected annual income, not historical income, is the income figure to be used.[211] Although past income may provide an obviously important basis upon which to predict future income, support is payable from what the obligor will earn, not what he or she has earned.[212] Where the evidence establishes on the balance of probabilities that the obligor's present and future income will be substantially different from historical income, a court cannot base the calculation of child support on the no longer representative past income levels.[213] If changes have occurred, the court will expect to receive evidence of the actual earnings for the current year.[214]

In *Gagnon v Gagnon*,[215] MacDonald J of the Nova Scotia Supreme Court states:

> A review of court decisions about the calculation of income provides the following guidance:
>
> - A court should determine a parent's Guideline income for the upcoming 12 months after the decision to pay is to be made.
> - A court may assume that a parent will earn the same or a similar amount in a upcoming year as he or she did in the previous year unless there is clear evidence to the contrary.
> - A court may extrapolate upcoming yearly income from a payor's year to date income when there is clear evidence that the prior year's income is not an indication of what upcoming income will be.

The previous year's income cannot be used when the obligor's current income is known, absent a circumstance where it is necessary to average the previous three years of earnings as provided by section 17 of the Guidelines or where the court imputes income under sec tion 19 of the Guidelines.[216] In determining income, the objective is to find the most reliable or fairest indicators as to what the individual's current income is.[217] But this does not mean that a current financial statement is conclusive, especially when it is inconsistent with the last income tax return. Section 2(3) of the Guidelines read in context with sections 16 to 20 of the Guidelines illustrates two principles. The first is that the obligor's annual income, not sim

---

208 *ZAM v AVT*, 2018 ABQB 319, citing *Lavergne v Lavergne*, 2007 ABCA 169 at para 17; *EL v ML*, 2021 BCSC 835.

209 *de Goede v de Goede*, [2000] BCJ No 5 (SC); *Coghill v Coghill*, [2006] OJ No 2602 (SCJ); *Morrissey v Morrissey*, 2015 PECA 16.

210 *Lee v Lee*, [1998] NJ No 247 (CA); *White v White*, 2015 NSCA 52; *Scott v Chenier*, 2015 ONSC 7866; *JLP v TRP*, 2019 SKQB 293.

211 *KB v MA*, 2019 NBQB 90 at para 63; *Matechuk v Kopp (Yaworenko)*, 2020 SKQB 196.

212 *MTP v TP*, 2019 NBQB 80; *Lee v Lee*, [1998] NJ No 247 (CA); *Holtby v Holtby*, [1997] OJ No 2237 (Gen Div); *Tweel v Tweel*, [2000] PEIJ No 9 (SC); *Matechuk v Kopp (Yaworenko)*, 2020 SKQB 196.

213 *Lee v Lee*, [1998] NJ No 247 (CA); see also *JM v KB*, 2012 NBQB 243; *Tauber v Tauber*, [2001] OJ No 3259 (SCJ); *Livingston v Trainor*, [2002] PEIJ No 46 (SC); *Matechuk v Kopp (Yaworenko)*, 2020 SKQB 196; *Ritchie v Solonick*, [1999] YJ No 66 (SC).

214 *Stupak v Stupak*, [1997] SJ No 302 (QB); *Fawcett-Kennett v Kennett*, 2016 SKQB 111.

215 2011 NSSC 486 at para 28; see also *FA v NA*, 2018 NBQB 215.

216 *MKR v JAR*, 2015 NBCA 73 at para 27, Baird JA; *Matechuk v Kopp (Yaworenko)*, 2020 SKQB 196.

217 *ML v LAL*, 2015 NBQB 150; *Ryder v Kent*, 2016 NLTD(F) 1; *Babich v Babich*, 2015 SKQB 22.

ply his or her monthly income, must be determined. The second is that the current annual income so determined should be a reliable and equitable measure of what the obligor will continue to receive annually, for it is this amount that determines the level of child support to be paid pursuant to the Guidelines.[218] The most reliable current information in some cases may be historical data and in other fact situations it may be gleaned from the evidence.[219] "Most current information" in section 2(3) of the Guidelines is not limited to information for a time period that has yet to expire. The court may look at the pattern of income over preceding tax years in addressing an anticipated loss in the current year.[220] Where the court considers it appropriate, the annual income of a spouse may be determined by reference to the obligor's last income tax return[221] or by extrapolation from the year-to-date earnings[222] or pay stubs.[223] In many cases, the previous year's income tax return for an individual with the same employment and relatively stable income provides a proxy for the payor's current income.[224] Where the spouse's prior year's income is not predictive of what the spouse is likely to earn in the upcoming year, the court generally determines the spouse's income for the upcoming twelve months from when child support will be paid.[225] This is especially appropriate where there has been a significant recent decrease in the spouse's income,[226] but a court should decline to determine a parent's prospective annual income from year-to-date earnings where the types of income typically lack consistency throughout the year.[227] A court may endorse the use of a parent's previous year's income to determine child support payable in the following year where greater certainty and security will be thereby promoted and the court will avoid the deficiencies inherent in attempting to address ongoing payments on the basis of the current year.[228] Where the parties have for several years functioned well under a system that required the exchange of the previous year's tax returns, and where to attempt to impose a process of exchanging current income information subject to *ex post facto* review and audit would likely create the opportunity for conflict, then the previous system of determining income meets the test of fairness under the Guidelines and is in the best interests of the child.[229]

---

218 *ML v LAL*, 2015 NBQB 150; *Coghill v Coghill*, [2006] OJ No 2602 (SCJ); *Hansvall v Hansvall*, [1997] SJ No 782 (QB).

219 *MTP v TP*, 2019 NBQB 80.

220 *Giene v Giene*, [1998] AJ No 1305 (QB); *Picco v Picco*, [2000] NJ No 64 (UFC).

221 *Bland v Bland*, [1999] AJ No 344 (QB) (income imputed on basis of previous year's earnings where minimal earnings recorded for first two months of current year, during which time the parties were engaged in hotly contested litigation). See also *BDD v GTS*, 2021 BCSC 1010 at para 29.

222 *Francis v Francis*, [1999] AJ No 1190 (QB) (current annual income determined by projections based on current hourly rate); *SMM v KCM*, [2005] BCJ No 1197 (SC); *Branch v Branch*, [2003] NBJ No 50 (QB); *Green v Green*, [2005] NJ No 165 (CA); *Iselmoe v Iselmoe*, [2003] OJ No 4076 (SCJ); *Morrissey v Morrissey*, 2015 PECA 16; *Walliser v Pouliot*, [2005] SJ No 580 (QB).

223 *Willis v Willis*, 2010 ABQB 534; *Oswald v Oswald*, [2001] MJ No 73 (QB); *Beck v Weisgerber*, [1999] SJ No 560 (QB) (matter to be revisited in event of layoff).

224 *Wilk v Martin-Wilk*, 2023 SKCA 64 at para 47, Tholl JA.

225 *Scott v Chenier*, 2015 ONSC 7866.

226 *Chambers v Chambers*, [1998] NWTJ No 54 (SC); *Coghill v Coghill*, [2006] OJ No 2602 (SCJ).

227 *MHG v DJG*, [2006] BCJ No 275 (SC).

228 *LAK v AAW*, [2005] AJ No 1140 (QB); *TM v DM*, 2014 NBQB 132 at para 18; *Koester v Koester*, [2003] OJ No 5406 (SCJ).

229 *Hodge v Jones*, 2011 ONSC 2363. See also *KAMR v WHG*, 2014 BCSC 103.

Projecting an annual income from a very limited pay period may be somewhat speculative, in which event the court may choose to exercise some discretion in determining a spouse's probable annual income.[230] Projected earnings for the current year may be a more reliable indicator of the obligor's income than historical information that includes non-recurring amounts, but historical information may be relied upon to assess the obligor's probable overtime pay.[231] A court should always be vigilant when facing an assertion that runs contrary to the historical pattern of conduct,[232] but judicial recourse to the historical pattern of income does not justify an imputation of additional income where there has been a genuine reduction of income that reflects market conditions.[233] Judicial recourse to the parent's pre-separation pattern of considerable overtime income may not constitute a reliable basis for imputing prospective overtime income to the parent after the spousal separation.[234]

Section 16 of the *Federal Child Support Guidelines* stipulates that income is determined using the sources of income set out under the heading Total Income in the T1 General form issued by the Canada Revenue Agency. This section does not direct the court to determine income on the basis of the amount set out in the preceding year's tax return. Rather, it requires the determination of income to be made by reference to the "sources of income" set out in the T1 General tax form.[235] It is the sources of income — not their historical amounts — that must be considered pursuant to section 16 of the Guidelines.[236] The basic responsibility of the court is to determine a fair figure for the current income from which support is to be paid. Quantifying child support by reference to the current year's income can create practical difficulties, particularly where the payor's income fluctuates or is uncertain. In addition, where yearly updates are necessary it is often more practical to order that the parties rely on the previous year's income. As a result courts often rely on the previous year's income as the best indicator of current income.[238] In some cases, a court will look to the income disclosed by line 150 (now line 15000) of the parties' tax return from the last calendar year. In other cases, that amount is not a reliable and equitable measure of current income. Although courts often use the previous year's income tax return to determine Guidelines income for the current year, the question of whether that is the correct approach turns on whether it is the best evidence of current income. If, for example, an obligor's income has permanently increased due to

---

230 *MTP v TP*, 2019 NBQB 80; *Ritchie v Solonick*, [1999] YJ No 66 (SC).

231 *CAG v DJG*, [1998] SJ No 796 (QB).

232 *MTP v TP*, 2019 NBQB 80; *Ward v Ward*, [1999] OJ No 458 (Gen Div) (judicial refusal to assume future reduction in obligor's overtime pay). See also *Dornick v Dornick*, [1999] BCJ No 2498 (CA) (issue remitted to trial court where respondent's sworn statement of anticipated income did not reflect fluctuations in three preceding years).

233 *MLR v SLR*, 2020 ABQB 444; *ML v LAL*, 2015 NBQB 150; *Alexander v Alexander*, [1999] OJ No 3694 (SCJ).

234 *RS v TS*, [2005] NBJ No 448 (SC).

235 *Lavergne v Lavergne*, 2007 ABCA 169; *CLE v BMR*, 2010 ABCA 187; *DS v JSR*, 2014 NBQB 111; *Dillon v Dillon*, [2005] NSJ No 548 (CA); *Scott v Chenier*, 2015 ONSC 7866; *Morrissey v Morrissey*, 2015 PECA 16; *Rasmussen v MacDonald*, [1997] SJ No 667 (QB) at paras 13–14.

236 *Lee v Lee*, [1998] NJ No 247 (CA); *Lavergne v Lavergne*, 2007 ABCA 169; *Tauber v Tauber*, [2001] OJ No 3259 (SCJ).

237 *HT v SS*, 2010 NBQB 312; *Hawco v Myers*, [2005] NJ No 378 (CA); *RS v TS*, [2005] NBJ No 448 (SC); *Coghill v Coghill*, [2006] OJ No 2602 (SCJ).

238 *KAMR v WHG*, 2014 BCSC 103; *Peterson v Peterson*, 2019 SKCA 76 at paras 70–71. See also *Wehrhahn v Murphy*, 2014 ABCA 194.

a change in employment, child support should be calculated on the basis of the increased income. The same is true if the payor's income has permanently decreased, assuming it is not appropriate to impute income pursuant to section 19 of the Guidelines, or to take account of the last three years' income due to patterns, fluctuations, or non-recurring amounts.[239]

If the historical record does not provide a reliable foundation for assessing income, the court may impute income on the basis of the anticipated future income earning capacity according to the best evidence available.[240] In the case of an employed spouse or former spouse who is obliged to disclose income information, section 21(1)(c) of the Guidelines requires disclosure of a recent statement of earnings setting forth the total earnings paid in the year to date. This is intended to allow the court to calculate what the spouse's current annual earnings are for the purposes of applying section 16 of the Guidelines.[241] Although the production of the three most recent tax returns and notices of assessment or reassessment may assist the court in a number of ways, the objective of the court is to find the most reliable indicator of the individual's current annual income. In pursuing this objective, the court should have regard to all of the information before it, including the three most recent tax returns, the year to date income of an employee spouse, and any other evidence that is placed before the court that might assist in determining the individual's present annual income. An individual who asserts that his or her current annual income is going to be less than that of previous years has the onus of providing substantive verification or explanation of the anticipated change. The nature of the verification or explanation will depend on the circumstances of the case but the bald assertion that a reduced income is anticipated will not suffice.[242] Judicial determination of the obligor's income by reference to his or her income tax return for the preceding year,[243] or by averaging the income over those years,[244] may be inappropriate where there is credible evidence that overtime income is likely to decrease.

In assessing the amount of child support under the Guidelines, a court should have regard to current income, rather than speculate about future income.[245] However, a court may assess child support in light of an anticipated increase in the obligor's income where the future increase is not speculative.[246] Although a court should determine the amount of child support on the facts existing at the time of the order, including facts that do not then exist but will likely exist in the immediate future on the balance of probabilities, a court should not engage in crystal ball gazing by addressing more remote future contingencies. If and when those contingencies arise, they can be addressed by a further application to the court. Where the obligor's historical income may not be consistent with his or her future earning potential, the court may reserve the right for counsel to re-address the issue of child support on the basis of a more realistic appreciation of the obligor's income.[247] Alternatively,

239 *Lutz v Lutz*, 2014 SKQB 146 at para 10, Barrington-Foote J.
240 *Herbert v Herbert*, [1999] AJ No 1241 (QB); *HT v SS*, 2010 NBQB 312; *RS v TS*, [2005] NBJ No 448 (SC).
241 *JM v KB*, 2012 NBQB 243; *Rasmussen v MacDonald*, [1997] SJ No 667 (QB).
242 *Ibid*.
243 *Hunter v Hunter*, [1998] OJ No 1527 (Gen Div).
244 *Reynolds v Reynolds*, [1999] SJ No 7 (QB).
245 *Tremaine v Tremaine*, [1997] AJ No 379 (QB).
246 *Fibiger v Fibiger*, [1998] BCJ No 187 (SC); *Gray v Gray*, [1998] OJ No 2175 (Gen Div).
247 *Close v Close*, [1997] OJ No 3288 (Gen Div).

a court may order a monthly advance based on the preceding year's income that is subject to adjustment when income for the current year is known. The court also has the discretion to order payments in anticipation of an increased income that is subject to adjustment when the income for the current year is known.[248]

A parent who asserts that his or her annual income will be less in the current year than it was in the past assumes the onus of verifying that assertion by providing evidence to support it.[249]

Employment insurance benefits may be judicially perceived as the best indicator of a parent's current annual income where the parent's employment and income status are in a state of flux and are unpredictable.[250]

For the purpose of making the fairest determination of a parent's current annual income, section 16 of the *Federal Child Support Guidelines* permits a court to average the pattern of income over the preceding three years pursuant to section 17 of the Guidelines and to impute income to a parent pursuant to section 19 of the Guidelines. While permitting recourse to sections 17 and 19 of the Guidelines, section 16 does not provide that they are mutually exclusive.[251]

In determining a parent's current income, the court may take account of the declining economy in the community in which the parent is employed.[252]

Section 17 of the *Manitoba Child Support Guidelines* mandates that the starting point for determining a parent's income is to look at the "Total income" heading (line 15000) on the parent's income tax return. The court must then be satisfied that the parent will likely receive that amount during the current year. If the court is satisfied that current income will not provide the fairest determination of annual income, the court may have regard to the parent's income over the last three years and determine a fair and reasonable amount in light of any pattern over those three years. Historical averaging over three years is inappropriate where the parent's income as an investment broker has undergone a significant decline because of a sustained bear stock market and earnings for the current year are no better than the previous year. Child support is payable from future income but a court cannot predict the future of the stock market. Consequentially, annualization of the parent's earnings for the current year may provide the best yardstick for determining the parent's Guidelines income for the purpose of determining child support.[253] Additional income may be imputed to the parent pursuant to section 18(1)(e) of the *Manitoba Child Support Guidelines* on the basis that his property was not reasonably used to generate income in that he received no interest on a corporate debenture that he held, and pursuant to section 18(1)(g) of the Guidelines because of the commingling of business perks and personal expenses.[254]

---

248 *JM v KB*, 2012 NBQB 243; *McDonald v Gross*, [1998] SJ No 301 (QB). See also *DYP v NPT*, 2015 NBQB 67; *Fawcett-Kennett v Kennett*, 2016 SKQB 111; *HMS v MH*, 2019 SKQB 311 at paras 28–29.

249 *Bishop v Bishop*, [2001] SJ No 47 (QB).

250 *Hannam v Boone*, [2000] NJ No 319 (Prov Ct).

251 *Schnell v Schnell*, [2001] SJ No 704 (CA); see also *Hackett v Hackett*, [2001] NJ No 317 (SC); *Stein v Stein*, [2001] NSJ No 550 (SC).

252 *MLR v SLR*, 2020 ABQB 444; *Garrett-Rempel v Garrett-Rempel*, [2000] BCJ No 1771 (SC).

253 *Spiring v Spiring*, [2002] MJ No 424 (QB).

254 *Ibid.*

E. PATTERN OF INCOME

Section 17(1) of the *Federal Child Support Guidelines* enables courts to deal with erratic or fluctuating incomes[255] by providing that if the court is of the opinion that the determination of a spouse's annual income from a source of income under section 16 would not be the fairest determination of that income, the court may have regard to the spouse's income over the last three years and determine an amount that is fair and reasonable in light of any pattern of income, fluctuation in income or receipt of a non-recurring amount during those years.[256] Section 17 of the *Federal Child Support Guidelines*[257] provides the court with a broad discretion to consider a three-year time frame where it would more fairly determine income;[258] it no longer speaks directly to "averaging" a parent's income over the preceding three years but it may still be appropriate to do that to arrive at a fair and reasonable determination of a parent's prospective income.[259] As is pointed out by the British Columbia Court of Appeal in *Reid v Reid*, however, while section 17 of the Guidelines provides the court with a broad discretion to average income over a period of years and to exclude certain income, the discretion is not to be exercised arbitrarily.[260] Section 17 of the Guidelines relies on the more recent past to predict the near future and does not adopt averaging as a default methodology.[261] As affirmed by the British Columbia Court of Appeal in *Harras v Lhotka*,[262]

> the averaging approach to income determination under s 17 is very fact specific. Generally speaking, averaging will be applied where income fluctuates, or where the payor has not demonstrated a lasting decline in earnings. Ultimately, it depends on fairly calculating the amount of income reasonably available to pay child support. Depending on the reasons for a pattern of fluctuating income (or . . . declining income[263]), averaging may be more or less appropriate.

In *Phillips v Saunders*, Willcock JA, of the British Columbia Court of Appeal, stated that

> [t]he discussion that follows in *Harras* supports the view that s. 17 averaging is appropriate where there are large annual fluctuations in income *(Dornik v. Dornik*, 1999 BCCA 627; *Cornelissen v. Cornelissen*, 2003 BCCA 666) and inappropriate where there is evidence

---

255 See Chapter 9, Section C.

256 *Federal Child Support Guidelines*, s 17(1), as amended by SOR/2000-337, s 4; *Steeves v English*, [2004] AJ No 632 (CA); *Harras v Lhotka*, 2016 BCCA 246; *Reid v Reid*, 2017 BCCA 73; *Stewart v Stewart*, [2004] MJ No 272 (QB); *Trevors v Jenkins*, 2011 NBCA 61 (averaging income over four years); *Sobczak v Evraire*, 2013 ONSC 1249; *Stelter v Stelter*, 2012 SKCA 117; *Potzus v Potzus*, 2017 SKCA 15.

257 SOR/97-237, s 17, as amended by SOR/2000-337, s 4; *Reid v Reid*, 2017 BCCA 73.

258 *More v Shurygalo*, 2010 SKQB 203. See also *SAN v JMS*, 2011 BCSC 963 (refusal to look back over six years).

259 *Elfar v Elfar*, 2012 ABCA 375; *Tataryn v Kriese*, 2024 BCSC 75 at paras 51–52; *Delaney v Delaney*, 2014 NLTD(F) 28; *Raymond-Theoret v Smith*, 2011 ONSC 7215; *Quiquero v Quiquero*, 2016 ONSC 6696; *Fidyk v Hutchison*, 2013 SKQB 27. For guidance as to when income averaging is appropriate, see *Harras v Lhotka*, 2016 BCCA 246 at paras 26–36. And see *AJB v JM*, 2020 BCSC 242.

260 *Reid v Reid*, 2017 BCCA 73 at para 122, cited in *Zilic v Zilic*, 2019 BCSC 1482 at para 187.

261 *Akkawi v Habli*, 2017 ONSC 6124, citing *Mason v Mason*, 2016 ONCA 725 at para 138: *Yovcheva v Hristov*, 2019 ONSC 1007; *Lesko v Lesko*, 2021 ONCA 369.

262 2016 BCCA 246 at para 35; see also *Espersen v Espersen*, 2017 BCSC 1206.

263 See *MT v JS*, 2020 BCSC 203, var'd 2023 BCCA 64.

of consistently declining or consistently increasing income (*de Bruijn v. de Bruijn*, 2011 BCSC 1546; *Jakob v. Jakob*, 2010 BCCA 136).[264]

But there does not appear to be any single principle that can be drawn from the cases. Where the spouses have established a mechanism for determining Guidelines income over several years, a court may find it appropriate not to alter their method of calculating income changes.[266]

While a three-year average is commonly used, there is precedent for using a longer time period.[267] "Fairness" and "reasonableness" within the meaning of section 17 of the Guidelines must be considered in relation to both spouses and the children. If a choice needs to be made as to the priority between children on the one hand and spouses on the other, that choice must be made in favour of the children. A court ought not to isolate one idiosyncratic year and may seek to determine a pattern of income over the preceding three years. Section 17(1) of the *Federal Child Support Guidelines* is only applicable if the court is of the opinion that a determination of income under section 16 of the Guidelines will not provide the fairest determination.[268] Where the obligor's income has progressively increased[269] or decreased in each of the three most recent taxation years, section 17(1) of the *Federal Child Support Guidelines* empowers the court to determine the obligor's income on the basis of his or her most recent taxation year. Fluctuations in annual income lend themselves to averaging over the preceding three taxation years under the authority of section 17(1) of the *Federal Child Support Guidelines*[271] or the court may adopt the mean income[272] or determine such other amount as it deems appropriate.[273] The court should establish an obligor's current annual income according to the best evidence available. This may sometimes require averaging, sometimes not.[274] Current earnings, rather than averaging, may be a far better indicator of the obligor's probable annual income, particularly in an economy where employment is sometimes scarce and where there can be wide fluctuations.[275] Under sections 2(1) and 16 of

264 *Phillips v Saunders*, 2020 BCCA 265 at para 24 (spousal support).

265 *MWDP v MAG*, 2019 NBQB 62.

266 *Aquilina v Winn*, 2016 ONSC 4530 at para 44, Timms J.

267 *PKC v JRR*, 2014 BCSC 932 at para 143, Wong J; see also *Harras v Lhotka*, 2016 BCCA 246, citing *Ouellette v Ouellette*, 2012 BCCA 145 (imputing income based on averaging over five years); *Hemsworth v Hemsworth*, 2002 BCSC 648 (four-year average was used); *Quiquero v Quiquero*, 2016 ONSC 6696; *Burke v Poitras*, 2020 ONSC 3162 (five-year average used). See also *WLG v ACG*, 2021 SKCA 112.

268 *LFG v KG*, [2004] AJ No 493 (QB); *Grossi v Grossi*, [2005] BCJ No 125 (CA); *Decaen v Decaen*, 2013 ONCA 218; *Holtzman v Holtzman*, 2013 SKQB 408.

269 *Jakob v Jakob*, 2010 BCCA 136; *Stevens v Stevens*, 2012 BCSC 1698; *Roberts v Roberts*, [2000] OJ No 3234 (SCJ); *James v Belosowsky*, 2012 SKQB 316.

270 *Ostlund v Ostlund*, [2000] BCJ No 1158 (SC); *MT v JS*, 2020 BCSC 203, var'd 2023 BCCA 64.

271 *Grossi v Grossi*, [2005] BCJ No 125 (CA); *MM v AM*, 2008 NBQB 305; *Carew v Ricketts*, [2003] NJ No 52 (SC); *Allaire v Allaire*, [2003] OJ No 1069 (CA); *MacIntyre v MacIntyre*, [2001] PEIJ No 39 (SC); *Nichol v Johnson*, [2003] SJ No 736 (QB).

272 *Lavoie v Wills*, [2000] AJ No 1359 (QB).

273 *Cornborough v Cornborough*, [1997] BCJ No 1981 (SC); see also *Shipka v Shipka*, [2001] AJ No 213 (QB) (annual income reported over four taxation years; current annual income assessed on basis of average over last two years); *Michaud v Michaud*, [2005] AJ No 1095 (QB) (average of income over three middle years of last five years to avoid anomalies).

274 *Herbert v Herbert*, [1999] AJ No 1241 (QB).

275 *Bell v Bell*, [1999] BCJ No 1999 (CA); see also *Pallot v Pallot*, 2010 BCSC 1146.

the *Federal Child Support Guidelines*, a court is required to make a determination of annual income for the year in which the application for child support is heard, based on the most current information available in respect of each source of income identified in the T1 General form issued by the Canada Revenue Agency. Although section 17 of the Guidelines permits departure from a determination made under section 16 of the Guidelines, having regard to a pattern of income over the three most recent tax years, where the application of section 16 would not provide the fairest determination of annual income, a difference in the amounts under sections 16 and 17 of the Guidelines does not itself justify a finding of unfairness. The degree of permanence associated with the difference is a material consideration,[276] as is the size of the difference, the reason for it, and the use to which the extra income was put.[277] The current provisions in the Guidelines respecting the determination of annual income have been judicially perceived as remarkable for their uncertainty, given the specific objectives defined in section 1 of the Guidelines to promote fair standards, reduce conflict, improve efficiency in the legal process, and ensure consistent treatment of spouses and children in similar circumstances.[278] Using a three-year average may be appropriate where there are fluctuations due to discretionary bonuses[279] or overtime hours[280] and the obligor's testimony concerning an anticipated reduction in overtime pay for the current year is unsupported by any other evidence.[281] Averaging an obligor's income over three years pursuant to section 17(1) of the Guidelines may be deemed inappropriate because of aberrations or huge fluctuations in the pattern of income[282] or because there is no current expectation of unusual future fluctuations.[283] Averaging the obligor's annual income over the preceding three income taxation years is inappropriate where there has been a fundamental change that affects the income that is likely to continue into the future.[284] A court may refuse to rely on the previous pattern of income from employment where the obligor has been laid off for an indefinite period by his or her employer, but in reducing the amount of child support on an application to vary, the court may direct the obligor to immediately inform the payee of any future resumption of employment so that the payments can be adjusted.[285]

It is inappropriate to rely on the averaging provisions of section 17(1) of the *Federal Child Support Guidelines* to reduce the obligor's income where his or her current income is known and will not decrease in future years.[286] In addition to averaging corporate earnings

---

276 *Fuzi v Fuzi*, [1999] BCJ No 2263 (SC) (determination of interim child support; obligor's annual income fixed pursuant to s 17(1)(b) of Guidelines at the mid-point between the average employment income for each of the last three taxation years and the amount determined under s 16 of the Guidelines); *TM v DM*, 2014 NBQB 132; see also *Steward v Ferguson*, 2012 BCSC 279.

277 *Belot v Connelly*, 2013 MBQB 98 at para 60.

278 *Fuzi v Fuzi*, [1999] BCJ No 2263 (SC).

279 *James v James*, [1998] OJ No 1301 (Gen Div).

280 *Francis v Francis*, [1999] AJ No 1190 (QB); *James v James*, [1998] OJ No 1301 (Gen Div); *Baerg v Baerg*, [1997] SJ No 808 (QB).

281 *McAfee v McAfee*, [1998] BCJ No 413 (SC).

282 *Frerichs v Frerichs*, [1998] AJ No 388 (QB); *Bell v Bell*, 1999 BCCA 497; *Hendrickson v Hendrickson*, [2005] NSJ No 395 (SC); *Waese v Bojman*, [2001] OJ No 2009 (SCJ).

283 *Frerichs v Frerichs*, [1998] AJ No 338 (QB).

284 *TM v DM*, 2014 NBQB 132 at para 16; *Augaitis v Augaitis*, [1998] OJ No 1795 (Gen Div).

285 *TM v DM*, 2014 NBQB 132; *Cavanaugh v Cavanaugh*, [2001] NSJ No 312 (SC).

286 *Johnson v Checkowy*, [1997] SJ No 451 (QB).

over several years to take account of a recent loss of substantial contracts, a court may direct a further review after a few months to provide a safeguard against an unreliable attribution of income.[287]

Section 17(1) of the Guidelines confers a broad discretion on the court where a spouse has received a non-recurring amount of income in any of the three most recent tax years. Resorting to three-year averaging under section 17 may be appropriate in the case of a large, one-time capital gain from the sale of a business where there is no suggestion that the proceeds of the sale were re-invested in an equivalent business.[289] A "windfall" or one-time success fee relating to a specific transaction may be excluded from the determination of an obligor's income under the *Federal Child Support Guidelines*. A share option may be similarly excluded where there is no current value attached and it is too far from fruition to be properly considered as income.[290] A non-recurring withdrawal from an RRSP or the liquidation of a pension may be excluded from income,[291] but a severance package will not be treated in the same way insofar as it represents replacement of income lost until new employment can be found.[292] A pay equity settlement may be excluded from the current annual income of the recipient spouse as being paid on account of income received in previous years,[293] although it has been asserted that a heavy onus falls on the recipient to establish such an exclusion.

A court may take account of non-recurring capital gains arising from the sale of a parent's business in determining the income of that parent.[295] Exclusion of a capital gain from a parent's annual income as a non-recurring amount is an option, but not a requirement under section 17 of the *Federal Child Support Guidelines*.[296] As Harris J of the British Columbia Supreme Court observed in *JMD v RMJD*,[297] each case is fact specific and given the nature of the capital gain, the court has in some cases determined that a non-recurring gain should not be included in income for Guideline purposes.[298] In other cases, a non-recurring gain has been brought into income for Guideline purposes because the capital gain is properly seen in substance as income that enhances the financial means of the obligor.[299]

A parent who wishes to exclude a "non-recurring amount" from his or her annual income pursuant to section 17 of the *Federal Child Support Guidelines* has the burden of persuading

---

287 *Hill v Monkhouse*, [1998] SJ No 278 (QB).

288 *Stevens v Stevens*, [1999] AJ No 1550 (QB) (RRSPs); *LLL v BAL*, 2010 BCSC 301; *Rondeau v Kirby*, [2003] NSJ No 436 (SC), aff'd [2004] NSJ No 143 (CA); *Tait v Barker*, 2016 MBQB 148 at para 105; *Pollitt v Pollitt*, 2010 ONSC 1617; *More v Shurygalo*, 2010 SKQB 203.

289 *Fraser v Fraser*, 2011 BCSC 1852.

290 *Horning v Horning*, [2000] BCJ No 189 (SC). See also *Brown v Brown*, 2014 BCCA 152 (non-recurring dividend income tied to employee retirement package).

291 *Lavoie v Wills*, [2000] AJ No 1359 (QB); *McKenzie v Perestrelo*, 2014 BCCA 161; *Ludmer v Ludmer*, 2014 ONCA 827; *Wotton v Banks*, [2001] PEIJ No 22 (SC); see also *Lemire v Lemire*, 2016 BCSC 2340; *Brown v Brown*, 2012 NBCA 11; *LaPalme v Hedden*, 2012 ONSC 6758.

292 *Lavoie v Wills*, [2000] AJ No 1359 (QB).

293 *Young v Rodgers*, [2000] OJ No 4564 (SCJ).

294 *Gagnier v Gagnier*, [2002] OJ No 2183 (SCJ).

295 *Shields v Shields*, [2006] AJ No 569 (QB); *Tamke v Tamke*, [2001] SJ No 791 (QB).

296 *Phillips v Delaney*, [2001] PEIJ No 86 (SC).

297 2011 BCSC 1295 at para 24.

298 See, for example, *Krupa v Krupa*, 2010 BCSC 1400; *JMD v RMJD*, 2011 BCSC 1295; see also *Tait v Barker*, 2016 MBQB 148 at para 105.

299 See, for example, *Shields v Shields*, 2006 ABQB 368; *Schick v Schick*, 2008 ABCA 196.

the court to do so.[300] A capital gain realized from the sale of a business may be spread over three years or even over five years where the parent entered into a non-competition covenant for the period of time.[301]

In *Ewing v Ewing*,[302] the Alberta Court of Appeal held that the principle of fairness, which guides the court in determining a parent's income for the purpose of fixing child support, applies with equal force to both prospective and retroactive orders and there is nothing in the *Federal Child Support Guidelines* that limits the application of section 17 to prospective support orders.[303] Courts must be alert to the nature of any non-recurring gain and whether it was derived from a disposition of capital. This is particularly true when non-recurring gains result from the sale of assets, such as a business interest, from which the parent's income was previously derived and the proceeds need to be invested to provide future income. In making money available for child support, courts must guard against "killing the goose that laid the golden egg." In these circumstances, the fairest method of determining the parent's income may be to exclude the non-recurring gain. On the other hand, where the non-recurring gain is in the nature of an employment bonus, as might arise upon the exercise of stock options, its inclusion in calculating the parent's income in accordance with section 16 of the Guidelines may not be unfair. In addition to considering the nature of the non-recurring gain, a court may also need to consider whether that gain would have resulted in a change in the lifestyle of the family, had it remained intact. If the family's lifestyle would have been unaffected by the non-recurring gain, a section 16 calculation that includes the gain may not be the fairest method of calculating the parent's income for child support purposes. By way of further guidance, the Alberta Court of Appeal in *Ewing v Ewing*[304] sets out the following non-exhaustive list of matters for a court to consider in determining whether a section 16 calculation is fair in light of non-recurring gains or major fluctuations in the pattern of the payor's income:

- Is the non-recurring gain a sale of assets that formed the basis of the payor's income?
- Will the capital generated from a sale provide a source of income for the future?
- Are the non-recurring gains received at an age when they constitute the payor's retirement fund, or partial retirement fund, such that it may not be fair to consider the whole amount, or any of it, as income for child support purposes?[305]

---

300 *Usova v Harrison*, 2010 BCSC 723.

301 *Blais v Blais*, [2001] SJ No 468 (QB).

302 2009 ABCA 227; see also *Emslie v Emslie*, 2015 ABQB 581; *JMD v RMJD*, 2011 BCSC 1295; *Dunnett v Dunnett*, 2018 BCCA 262; *Shock v Shock*, 2019 BCSC 2179; *Block v Block*, 2020 BCSC 1694; *Belot v Connelly*, 2013 MBQB 98; *McNeil v McNeil*, 2013 NBCA 65; *Boylan v MacLean*, 2018 NSSC 15; *Favero v Favero*, 2013 ONSC 4216. Compare *Merritt v Merritt*, 2010 ONSC 4959. See also *DeWolfe v McMillan*, 2011 NSSC 301 (severance pay).

303 See also *Brown v Brown*, 2014 BCCA 152, in Section C(3)(d), above in this chapter.

304 *Ewing v Ewing*, 2009 ABCA 227 at para 35. And see *Emslie v Emslie*, 2015 ABQB 581; *Howard v Howard*, 2020 ABQB 292 (liquidated pension payment viewed as non-recurring gain under s 17); *Felts v Silvestre*, 2021 BCSC 523; *SLD v WAD*, 2021 BCSC 942; *Chan-Henry v Liu*, 2021 BCCA 318; *Tait v Barker*, 2016 MBQB 148; *PJC v PLC*, 2024 NBKB 42; *Murphy v Howes*, 2021 NSSC 354; *Fournier v Labranche*, 2019 ONSC 4651; *Van Boekel v Van Boekel*, 2020 ONSC 5265; *Wetsch v Kuski*, 2017 SKCA 77; *Matechuk v Kopp (Yaworenko)*, 2020 SKQB 196. And see *Howard v Howard*, 2020 ABQB 292 (liquidated pension payment viewed as non-recurring gain under s 17(1) of the Guidelines). See also *Warren v Warren*, 2021 ABQB 213 (restricted share units; subsequent loss in value).

305 See *Warren v Baird*, 2015 ABQB 479.

- Is the payor in the business of buying and selling capital assets year after year such that those amounts, while the sale of capital, are in actuality more in the nature of income?
- Is inclusion of the amount necessary to provide proper child support in all the circumstances?
- Is the increase in income due to the sale of assets that have already been divided between the spouses, so that including them as income might be akin to redistributing what has already been shared?
- Did the non-recurring gain even generate cash, or was it merely the result of a restructuring of capital for tax or other legitimate business reasons?[306]
- Does the inclusion of the amount result in wealth distribution as opposed to proper support for the children?

Finding that the chambers judge had carefully considered the nature of the non-recurring gains that were substantially out of line with the historical pattern of the father's income, and perceiving a risk of "killing the goose that lays the golden egg," the Alberta Court of Appeal saw no reason to interfere with the chambers judge's conclusion that a section 16 calculation of the father's income would be unfair and that section 17 of the Guidelines justified averaging the father's income on a three-year rotational basis. The Alberta Court of Appeal noted, however, that section 17 of the *Federal Child Support Guidelines*, as amended in 2000, does not require that fair income be established by averaging the obligor's income over three years. The court may use an averaging formula, or it may remove all or part of the non-recurring gains from its calculation of the obligor's income, or it may take whatever steps it deems appropriate to arrive at an income that is fair for child support purposes.

A parent who wishes to use a three-year average or to exclude a "non-recurring amount" from income under section 17 of the Guidelines has the burden of proving that "the determination of the parent's annual income under section 16 of the Guidelines would not be the fairest determination."[307] Capital gains arising from a sale of shares are included in a parent's annual income for the year in which they were received. A parent is not entitled to exclude capital gains from income for the purpose of a judicial determination of the respective contributions to be made by each parent towards their children's section 7 expenses under the *Federal Child Support Guidelines*. Where the focus of the inquiry is to determine the fairest annual income of a parent for one particular year, as opposed to predicting an income for a future year, the onus to be met to exclude a non-recurring amount pursuant to section 17 of the Guidelines is high and the judicial discretion should be exercised in the context of the objectives set out in section 1 of the Guidelines.[308]

Where a parent's income in the last taxation year is grossly distorted by a lump sum disability payment, the court may apportion that payment over a specified number of years and caution future courts to recognize that the income disclosed in future tax returns will understate the parent's income for the purpose of applying the *Federal Child Support Guidelines*.

306 See *Van Boekel v Van Boekel*, 2020 ONSC 5265. And see *Block v Block*, 2020 BCSC 1694.

307 *Shields v Shields*, 2006 ABQB 368; *Bouzane v Martin*, 2014 BCSC 1690; *Levesque v Meade*, 2010 NBQB 270; *Fung v Lin*, [2001] OJ No 456 (SCJ); *Krzak v Erixon*, 2008 SKQB 468.

308 *Gibson v Gibson*, [2002] OJ No 1784 (SCJ); *Howe v Tremblay*, [2007] OJ No 4043 (SCJ).

309 *Feucht-Fender v Hepworth*, [2000] SJ No 620 (QB).

When averaging a parent's income over three years for the purpose of determining his or her current annual income under the *Federal Child Support Guidelines*, section 16 of the Guidelines does not compel the court to rely on the pattern of income revealed in the obligor's income tax returns. Additional income may be imputed to the parent pursuant to section 19 of the Guidelines before the averaging process is undertaken. Section 16 of the Guidelines permits recourse to both sections 17 and 19 of the Guidelines, but does not provide that they are mutually exclusive. A parent who fails to make full and complete financial disclosure should not expect any indulgence from the court.[310]

There is no provision in the *Federal Child Support Guidelines*, other than the court's right to impute income, to determine income on anything other than an annual basis. If it were otherwise, unnecessary litigation could be triggered by obligors with seasonal incomes or monthly income fluctuations. Unless exceptional circumstances exist, support should be based on annual income where it is available, not on monthly variations.[311] Where a parent's monthly income fluctuates, that parent should budget accordingly so as to provide regular monthly table amounts of child support based on the parent's annual income.[312]

Where there has been a recent reduction in business income due to the loss of a primary customer, a parent's currently reduced monthly draw from the business may provide an inadequate basis for determining his annual income where it was not clear that business profits will be affected over the longer term. Fluctuating business income is addressed in sections 17 and 18 of the *Federal Child Support Guidelines*. Two basic principles can be discerned, namely, (1) the support payor makes payments on the basis of currently available income, although adjustments can subsequently be made if the amount chosen as the current standard proves too high or too low; (2) where there is fluctuating income, the assessment of income may have to be dealt with over a relatively lengthy period of time. Monthly adjustments are not envisaged. Annual adjustments based on a court order for the production of ongoing financial information are appropriate in light of section 25 of the Guidelines. Indeed, it is difficult to understand why an annual written request for financial information is not sought as a matter of course in all child support disputes, without recourse to the court. Such a request is expressly authorized by section 25 of the Guidelines. Given the filing of annual personal income tax returns on or before 30 April, relevant financial information should be available by 15 May of each year. Section 25 of the Guidelines not only envisages the production of personal income tax returns in accordance with section 21(1) of the Guidelines; section 25 also encompasses corporate tax returns in accordance with section 21(1)(f) of the Guidelines.[313]

Section 17(2) of the *Federal Child Support Guidelines* deals with non-recurring losses by providing that, where a spouse has incurred a non-recurring capital or business investment loss, the court may, if it is of the opinion that the determination of the spouse's annual income under section 16 would not provide the fairest determination of the annual income, choose not to apply sections 6 and 7 of Schedule III, and adjust the amount of the loss, including related expenses and carrying charges and interest expenses, to arrive at such amount as the

310 *Schnell v Schnell*, [2001] SJ No 704 (CA); see also *Hackett v Hackett*, [2001] NJ No 317 (SC); *Stein v Stein*, [2001] NSJ No 550 (SC).

311 *Albinet v Albinet*, [2003] MJ No 44 (CA).

312 *Creaser v Creaser*, [2002] NSJ No 542 (SC).

313 *Yeoman v Luhtala*, [2002] AJ No 1504 (QB).

court considers appropriate.[314] Speaking to this issue in *Kohlman v Bergeron*, which involved the conjoint operation of section 17(2) of the *Alberta Child Support Guidelines* and section 8 of Schedule III, which corresponds to section 7 of Schedule III of the *Federal Child Support Guidelines*, the Alberta Court of Appeal, stated:

> **17** The chambers judge erred in her interpretation of s. 17(2) by finding, in effect that the child's best interest always trumped allowing business losses as a deduction from the payor's income in the journey to setting child support. This interpretation would result in s. 8 of Schedule III never operating, as the mere fact that a child needs to be supported would mean a payor could never deduct business losses as expressly permitted by that section. That is not what s. 17(2) provides. Rather, business losses permitted to be claimed for income tax purposes may be claimed in establishing child support obligations unless a judge concludes that doing so "would not provide the fairest determination of annual income."
>
> **18** The relevant inquiry includes, but is not confined, to the following questions:
>
> a) Was the investment made in good faith in the expectation of profit?
>
> b) Was there a reasonable likelihood of profit being made from the business in which the loss was incurred at the time the investment was made?
>
> c) Documentary proof of the portion of the loan advanced by a family member, the interest rate paid on the loan and proof of actual repayment.
>
> d) Whether the entire loan had been repaid during the years over which retroactive child support is claimed and if not, what portion was repaid in each relevant year.
>
> e) Whether any portion of the loan remains unpaid and, if so, when it is required to be paid by the underlying loan documentation.
>
> f) The size of the loan in comparison to the payor's income from all other sources.
>
> **19** Evidence addressing each of these considerations will allow the judge to determine whether it would be fair to allow any or all of the payor's business losses by way of assessing the actual quantum of these loses and the degree of risk undertaken by the payor and his wife at the time of investing in [the business]. Allowing the deduction of some or all of the business loss in setting guideline income is premised on the proposition that had the business made income, that income would have been added to the payor's employment income for the purposes of setting child support.[315]

A parent who contends that non-recurring losses should be set off against business income for the purpose of determining child support must provide comprehensive records of income and expenses in support of the contention.[316] A non-recurring business loss that has already been incurred and written off cannot be notionally spread out over future years so as to reduce the obligor's income pursuant to section 17(2) of the Guidelines. To allow any deduction for such a loss would generate a distorted picture of the obligor's real income available for the payment of child support.[317]

---

314 See *Kohlman v Bergeron*, 2015 ABCA 410; *TC v AJ*, 2021 BCSC 1696; *Bhandari v Bhandari*, [2002] OJ No 658 (SCJ).

315 2015 ABCA 410.

316 *Pakka v Nygard*, [2002] OJ No 3858 (SCJ).

317 *Merritt v Merritt*, [1999] OJ No 1732 (SCJ).

F. INCOME OF SHAREHOLDER, DIRECTOR, OR OFFICER OF CORPORATION; ADJUSTMENT OF CORPORATION'S PRE-TAX INCOME

Where a spouse is a shareholder, director, or officer of a corporation and the court is of the opinion that the amount of the spouse's annual income as determined under section 16 does not fairly reflect all the money available to the spouse for the payment of child support, the court may consider the situations described in section 17 of the Guidelines and determine the spouse's annual income to include (a) all or part of the pre-tax income of the corporation, and of any corporation that is related to that corporation, for its most recent taxation year; or (b) an amount commensurate with the services that the spouse provides to the corporation, provided that the amount does not exceed the pre-tax income of the corporation.[318] In determining the pre-tax income of a corporation for this purpose, all amounts paid by the corporation as salaries, wages or management fees, or other payments, to or on behalf of persons with whom the corporation does not deal at arm's length must be added, unless the shareholding spouse establishes that the payments were reasonable in the circumstances.[319] Section 18 of the Guidelines provides authority for the court to impute corporate income to a party on an interim basis if the court does not accept that the income calculated pursuant to section 16 of the Guidelines accurately reflects the amount available for child support.[320] But a judge hearing an interim application must apply the relevant principles concerning the burden of proof in a cautious and conservative manner to reflect the reality that the respondent will often be unable and could not reasonably be expected to provide full disclosure and a detailed explanation of financial and other matters relevant to the application.[321] If the child support obligor, though not the sole shareholder of the corporation, is in a position to influence how pre-tax income is used then, depending on all of the circumstances, it may be appropriate to attribute pre-tax corporate income to him or her.[322]

---

318 *Federal Child Support Guidelines*, s 18(1); see *Ewing v Ewing*, [2007] AJ No 217 (CA); *Miller v Joynt*, 2007 ABCA 214; *Kowalewich v Kowalewich*, [2001] BCJ No 1406 (CA); *Vincent v Vincent*, 2012 BCCA 186; *Kopp v Kopp*, 2012 BCCA 140; *Evanow v Lannon*, 2018 BCCA 208; *Nesbitt v Nesbitt*, [2001] MJ No 291 (CA); *Verwey v Verwey*, 2007 MBCA 102; *Dyck v Dyck*, 2008 MBCA 135; *Scott v Scott*, [2004] NBJ No 468 (CA); *Gosse v Sorensen-Gosse*, 2011 NLCA 58; *Hann v Elms*, 2016 NLTD(F) 15; *Keown v Procee*, 2014 ONSC 7314; *Stelter v Stelter*, 2012 SKCA 117; *Thompson v Bear*, 2014 SKCA 111; *Potzus v Potzus*, 2017 SKCA 15, subsequent proceedings, *Potzus v Potzus*, 2018 SKQB 55 (joint and several personal and corporate liability); *EAG v DLG*, 2010 YKSC 23. See also *Kosior v Kosior*, 2013 SKQB 42, citing Dinyar Marzban & Jamie R Wood, "Lifting the Corporate Veil: Income Determinations for Shareholders, Directors and Officers Under Section 18 of the *Federal Child Support Guidelines*" (2012) 31 *Canadian Family Law Quarterly* 1.

319 *Federal Child Support Guidelines*, s 18(2); *Kinasewich v Kinasewich*, [2001] AJ No 1185 (QB); *BMD v CND*, 2010 BCSC 1785; *MDA v MS*, [2008] NBJ No 498 (QB); *Gosse v Sorensen-Gosse*, 2011 NLCA 58; *Hendrickson v Hendrickson*, [2005] NSJ No 395 (SC); *Bedi v Bedi*, [2004] OJ No 2207 (SCJ); *Shepherdson v Shepherdson*, [2008] OJ No 4703 (SCJ); *Hesson v Hesson*, [2000] SJ No 257 (QB); *Walker v Walker*, 2019 SKCA 96.

320 *MacLachlan v MacLachlan*, 2020 SKQB 117 at para 20; see also *Krammer (Ackerman) v Ackerman*, 2020 SKQB 280.

321 *Merrifield v Merrifield*, 2021 SKCA 85 at para 37, Barrington-Foote JA; see also *Rolinger v Rolinger*, 2021 ABQB 474.

322 *Guenther v Guenther*, 2016 SKQB 322 at para 20.

Two appellate judgments from British Columbia and from Newfoundland and Labrador offer significant guidance as to the interpretation to be accorded to section 18 of the Guidelines. The first is *Kowalewich v Kowalewich*,[323] wherein the British Columbia Court of Appeal formulated the following principles:

- A court need not look for signs of bad faith or undeclared personal benefits before imputing income to a parent pursuant to sections 17 or 18 of the Guidelines.[324] Nor should a court look only to section 18(1)(b) of the Guidelines to determine the value of the parent's services to a company that the parent owns or controls.
- The attribution of pre-tax corporate income to a parent pursuant to section 18(1)(a) of the Guidelines does not strip that parent or his or her corporation of the income attributed. It is simply used as a measuring rod for the purpose of fixing the parent's annual income on the basis of which the amount of child support will be determined.
- The purpose of section 18 of the Guidelines is to allow the court to lift the corporate veil to ensure that money received as income by the paying parent fairly reflects all of the income reasonably available for the purpose of assessing child support. A court's effort to ensure fairness does not require a court to second-guess business decisions. What it does require is that a parent's allocation of pre-tax corporate income between business and family purposes be assessed for fairness by an impartial tribunal when parents cannot reach agreement on priorities as they would in an intact family. To determine whether "Total income" in the T1 General form issued by the Canada Revenue Agency fairly reflects a parent's income in the context of child support, a court might ask what a reasonable and well-informed parent would make available for child support in the circumstances of the particular business over which the parent exercises control, having regard to the objectives under section 1 of the Guidelines, the underlying parental obligation to support children in accordance with parental means under section 26(2) of the *Divorce Act*, and any applicable situation arising from income fluctuations or non-recurring gains or losses under section 17 of the Guidelines. The question of whether some or all of the pre-tax income of a corporation should be attributed to a payor to achieve that purpose depends on the facts.[326]
- No explicit guidance is provided as to how a parent or a court might go about choosing whether to use the corporate income method of attribution under section 18(1)(a) of the Guidelines or the personal services attribution method under section 18(1)(b) of the Guidelines. Section 18 suggests, however, two considerations in the pre-conditions for its application: (1) which method produces an annual income that more fairly reflects all the income available for the assessment of child support? and (2) which method does the nature of the parent's relationship with the corporation support?

---

323 [2001] BCJ No 1406 (CA). See also *KAW v MEW*, 2020 ABCA 277; *Quinton v Kehler*, 2020 BCCA 254 at para 85; *Wolfson v Wolfson*, 2021 NSSC 260; *Krammer (Ackerman) v Ackerman*, 2020 SKQB 280; *King v King*, 2021 SKQB 201. And see *AB v MH*, 2018 SKQB 317, citing Dinyar Marzban & Jamie R Wood, "Lifting the Corporate Veil: Income Determinations for Shareholders, Directors and Officers Under Section 18 of the *Federal Child Support Guidelines*" (2013) 31 *Canadian Family Law Quarterly* 1.

324 See also *Potzus v Potzus*, 2017 SKCA 15.

325 *KAW v MEW*, 2020 ABCA 277 at para 19; *Ward v Murphy*, 2023 NSSC 370; *Potzus v Potzus*, 2017 SKCA 15.

326 *Merrifield v Merrifield*, 2021 SKCA 85 at para 47, Barrington-Foote JA.

Section 18 also permits reference to the "situations described in section 17" and thus to the parent's income pattern over the preceding three years. The nature of the parent's relationship with the corporation may sometimes be decisive. Section 18 of the Guidelines applies not only to a parent who wholly controls a corporation;[327] it also applies to a parent who shares corporate ownership and control with others. Where a parent wholly owns a corporation, the attribution of corporate income under section 18(1)(a) of the Guidelines is likely to be the fairer method of determining parental income, because it allows a court to include not only reasonable payment for personal services rendered to the corporation but also a reasonable return on the parent's entrepreneurial capacity and investment. These are sources of income that an intact family would utilize. Moreover, it not only permits but requires the inclusion of the income of companies related within the meaning of the *Income Tax Act* and of non-arm's-length payments made without value to the company.

- There may be factors in particular cases that will recommend to the court the personal services method of attributing income under section 18(1)(b) of the Guidelines, as for example, where the corporation's only business is the provision of the personal services of its owner. There may also be cases where stability of income will persuade a trial judge to use the personal services method, having regard to situations under section 17 of the Guidelines.
- Section 18(1)(a) of the Guidelines allows a court to include all the pre-tax income of a corporation for the most recent taxation year in a parent's annual income for Guidelines purposes, but this is not required and courts should not make the inclusion of pre-tax corporate income the default position.
- The only explicit guidance provided as to how much of a corporation's pre-tax income should be included in the parent's annual income is found in the words "the court may consider the situations described in section 17." That section refers to the historical income pattern of a spouse and to non-recurring gains and losses. Regard should also be paid to the nature of the corporation's business and any evidence of legitimate calls on its corporate income for the purposes of that business. Money needed to maintain the value of the business as a viable going concern will not be available for support purposes and should not be included in determining a parent's annual income.
- Although an appellate court should not tinker with a trial judge's exercise of discretion, it may reduce the amount of corporate income attributed to a parent where the trial judge has paid insufficient regard to the evidence of legitimate business needs in determining what portion of pre-tax corporate income to include in the parent's annual income.

Speaking to the relationship between sections 16 and 18 of the *Federal Child Support Guidelines* in Willcock JA, of the British Columbia Court of Appeal, in *Quinton v Kehler* stated:

> [85] . . . First, the *Guidelines* should be interpreted in light of their stated objectives, including the ability to calculate child support in an objective manner that ensures consistent treatment

327 See *KAW v MEW*, 2020 ABCA 277 at para 15 (control without shareholder status).

of spouses and children who are in similar circumstances. Second, under a s. 18 approach, the corporate income method is likely to be the fairer method of determining income of an individual who wholly controls a corporation. This method allows a court to include all income available for child support an intact family would utilize. Third, where that approach is appropriate, pretax corporate earnings, not retained earnings or earnings after payment of taxes, are the starting point for an assessment of *Guidelines* income. Fourth, where a company is wholly owned by the payor, the onus is on the payor to provide evidence that his pretax corporate earnings are not available to him....

> [90] ... The choice between s.16 and s.18 analyses is a choice of measuring rods where the objective is to select the most accurate measure of the payor's pretax income. It is not a search for available cash. To again use the words of Huddart J.A., the result of the exercise is not to "strip a spouse of their available money" (at para. 41).
>
> [91] If pretax corporate earnings are not considered to be available for the payment of child support, because corporate taxes are exigible, the *Guidelines* income of unincorporated partners and the *Guidelines* income of incorporated partners will be set at different levels, which might be appropriate for tax purposes (in part because the tax system is designed to equalize the taxes paid by each), but cannot have been the intention of the drafters of the *Guidelines* for whom consistent treatment of spouses in similar circumstances was an objective.[328]

Building on the principles set out in the leading decision of the British Columbia Court of Appeal in *Kowalewich v Kowalewich* and having regard to the onus of proof under section 18 of the Guidelines, as defined in *Miller v Joynt*[329] and *Hausmann v Klukas*,[330] the Newfoundland and Labrador Court of Appeal in *Gosse v Sorensen-Gosse*[331] expressed the following opinion on the interpretation and application of section 18(1)(a) of the *Federal Child Support Guidelines*:

- Section 18(1)(a) of the Guidelines provides that where a spouse is a shareholder, director, or officer of a corporation and the court is satisfied that the spouse's T1 Income Tax Form does not fairly reflect all the money available to the spouse for the payment of child support, the court may include all or part of the pre-tax income of the corporation for the most recent taxation year to the spouse's annual income for the purpose of determining the appropriate amount of child support to be paid.
- The pre-tax income of the corporation will be adjusted pursuant to section 18(2) of the Guidelines to add non-arm's-length payments and benefits, unless they were reasonable under the circumstances.
- The pre-tax income of the corporation may be adjusted having regard to capital cost allowances claimed by the corporation.[332]

---

328 *Quinton v Kehler*, 2020 BCCA 254 at paras 85 and 90.

329 2007 ABCA 214.

330 2009 BCCA 32 and 2009 BCCA 320; see also *Sweeney v Sweeney*, 2016 ABQB 131; *ANH v LDG*, 2018 BCSC 2012, citing *Hausmann v Klukas*, 2009 BCCA 32; *Reid v Faubert*, 2019 NSCA 42; *McLellan v McLellan*, 2020 NSSC 161; *Potzus v Potzus*, 2017 SKCA 15.

331 2011 NLCA 58; see also *Reid v Reid*, 2018 NLSC 33.

332 See also *Gossen v Gossen*, [2003] NSJ No 113 at para 83 (SC).

- Determining the annual income for child support purposes of a spouse who is a shareholder has nothing to do with the retained earnings of the corporation. Such a determination does not require paying out retained earnings. Whether or not the corporation has a pot of money, and whether the child of the parties was deprived of anything, is totally irrelevant to determining the income available to a spouse for child care.
- Section 18(1)(a) of the Guidelines does not make clear whether the discretion to impute "all" or "part" of the pre-tax corporate income is a general discretion, applicable to any corporation in which the spouse is a shareholder, or whether the discretion to impute all of the income only arises where the spouse is the sole shareholder, and a part of the income, proportionate to the shareholding, where the spouse owns only part of the shares. It is reasonable to conclude that the latter is the correct interpretation.[333]
- Many professionals manage their practices through corporations, either as sole shareholders or one of several shareholders.[334] The necessity of imputing Guidelines income on the basis of shareholdings in these circumstances is obvious. It is equally obvious that the fact that a doctor or lawyer or engineer chooses to record his or her professional income through a wholly owned corporation does not justify reducing the pre-tax corporate income by factors that would not warrant reducing an unincorporated professional's income.[335]
- The attribution of pre-tax corporate income to a spouse pursuant to section 18(1)(a) of the Guidelines does not strip that spouse or his or her corporation of the income attributed. It is simply used as a measuring rod for the purpose of fixing the spouse's annual income on the basis of which the amount of child support will be determined. Neither imputing pre-tax corporate income to a shareholder, nor adjusting the amount shown as pre-tax corporate income to offset non-cash expensing in the course of establishing the basis for calculating child support obligations under the Guidelines, requires the corporation to alter its financial records or its business decisions in any manner. It does not require the actual transfer of any of its financial resources to the sole shareholder. That remains a decision of the corporation, as guided and directed by the sole shareholder. The corporation is not a party to the action and no order is directed at the corporation. In the case of a sole shareholder, the effect is, essentially, to ignore the corporate structure, for Guidelines income assessment purposes only, and treat the shareholding spouse in the same manner as that spouse would be treated if the business were carried on in the name of that spouse personally.
- A court need not look for signs of bad faith or undeclared personal benefits before imputing income to a spouse pursuant to sections 18(1)(a) of the Guidelines.
- The purpose of section 18 of the Guidelines is to allow the court to lift the corporate veil to ensure that money received as income by the paying spouse fairly reflects all of the income reasonably available for the purpose of assessing child support. A court's effort to ensure fairness does not require a court to second-guess business decisions

333 See to like effect, *Chapman v Summer*, 2010 BCCA 237; *REG v TWJG*, 2011 SKQB 269. And see *Merrifield v Merrifield*, 2021 SKCA 85.

334 See *Guenther v Guenther*, 2016 SKQB 322 at para 20, discussed in the text above.

335 See *Quinton v Kehler*, 2020 BCCA 254.

nor "place the largest available shovel in the company store." What it does require is that a spouse's allocation of pre-tax corporate income between business and family purposes be assessed for fairness by an impartial tribunal when the spouses cannot reach agreement on priorities as they would in an intact family.

- To determine whether "Total income" in the T1 General form issued by the Canada Revenue Agency fairly reflects a spouse's income in the context of child support, a court might ask what a reasonable and well-informed parent would make available for child support in the circumstances of the particular business over which the spouse exercises control, having regard to the objectives under section 1 of the Guidelines, the underlying obligation to support children in accordance with one's means under section 26(2) of the *Divorce Act*, and any applicable situation arising from income fluctuations or non-recurring gains or losses under section 17 of the Guidelines.
- The corporation's pre-tax income will be assumed to be available to the shareholding spouse for the payment of child support, unless there is clear evidence led by that spouse to support the conclusion that re-investment is necessary to sustain the company as a viable enterprise. It is not open to a judge to speculate about the needs of the corporation in absence of any supporting evidence.
- Where the spouse is a shareholder of a corporation, the test is whether or not the income, calculated in accordance with the Canada Revenue Agency T1 General form, "clearly reflect[s] all the money available to the spouse for the payment of child support." Section 18(1)(a) of the Guidelines provides that "the court may consider the situations described in section 17," namely, a fluctuating income pattern and non-recurring gains and losses. Pursuant to the options available under section 17, this could result in adding, solely for purposes of calculating child support obligations, to the corporation's stated income, any capital losses used to set off capital gains during that year, or even the ignoring of business investment losses (see Guidelines, section 17 and Schedule III, paragraphs 6 and 7). It does not and cannot alter the corporation's stated income or affect any decision relevant to the determination of its income.
- Subject to the exclusion of amounts necessary to meet legitimate business calls substantiated by the evidence, the Guidelines are clearly intended to include as income available for child support, all income over which the spouse has discretionary control, whether that income is recorded as being received personally or by a corporation. Where the corporation is wholly owned by the spouse, that can only mean 100% of the pre-tax income that is not subject to a retention requirement to meet existing legitimate obligations of the corporation.

While some common themes emerge from the foregoing cases, each case must be decided on its own facts.[336]

Speaking to factors relevant to determining whether corporation pre-tax income should be attributed to a parent under section 18 of the *Federal Child Support Guidelines*, Chappel J of the Ontario Superior Court of Justice in *Thompson v Thompson*:

---

336 *Chekowski v Howland*, 2013 ABCA 299.

92 A review of the case-law relating to section 18 indicates that courts have considered the following factors in determining whether all or a portion of a corporation's pre-tax income should be included in a party's income:

a) The historical pattern of the corporation for retained earnings.
b) The restrictions on the corporation's business, including the amount and cost of capital equipment that the company requires.
c) The type of industry the corporation is involved in, and the environment in which it operates.
d) The potential for business growth or contraction.
e) Whether the company is still in its early development stage and needs to establish a capital structure to survive and [grow].
f) Whether there are plans for expansion and growth, and whether the company has in the past funded such expansion by means of retained earnings or through financing.
g) The level of the company's debt.
h) How the company obtains it financing and whether there are banking or financing restrictions.
i) The degree of control exercised by the party over the corporation, and the extent if any to which the availability of access to pre-tax corporate income is restricted by the ownership structure.
j) Whether the company's pre-tax corporate income and retained earnings levels are a reflection of the fact that it is sustained primarily by contributions from another related company.
k) Whether the amounts taken out of the company by way of salary or otherwise are commensurate with industry standards.
l) Whether there are legitimate business reasons for retaining earnings in the company. Monies which are required to maintain the value of the business as a going concern will not be considered available for support purposes. Examples of business reasons which the courts have accepted as legitimate include the following:
   (i) The need to acquire or replace inventory;
   (ii) Debt-financing requirements;
   (iii) Carrying accounts receivable for a significant period of time;
   (iv) Cyclical peaks or valleys in cash flow;
   (v) Allowances for bad debts;
   (vi) Allowances for anticipated business losses or extraordinary expenditures; and
   (vii) Capital acquisitions.[337]

In *Ward v Murphy*, Van den Eynden JA of the Nova Scotia Court of Appeal observed:

> Here are some general, non-exhaustive, considerations that may assist in deciding whether income should be attributed under s. 18:
>
> - Attribution of pre-tax corporate income to a payor pursuant to s. 18(1)(a) is a factual exercise, undertaken by a judge on a case-by-case basis.

---

337 2013 ONSC 5500 at para 92; see also *Duffus v Frempong-Manso*, 2015 ONSC 7051; *Wade v Wade*, 2016 ONSC 1056.

- A judge is not required to add any pre-tax corporate income to a payor's income. The *Guidelines* merely allow for a judge to do so.
- The reasonableness of a deduction is a discretionary determination; however, the objective is to ensure the allocation of pre-tax corporate income between business and family purposes is fair. At the end of the day, one should not interfere with reasonable economic decisions needed to meet corporate sustainability.
- The onus rests on the shareholder parent to establish that pre-tax income of the corporation is not available for support purposes. This means the parent, who is typically the payor, must lead evidence that the pre-tax corporate income is not available for support purposes because it will jeopardize the capacity of the corporation to meet its financial obligations.
- When deciding the amount of pre-tax corporate income to attribute to the payor, consideration should be given to:
  » What is the nature of the business?
  » Is there a business reason for retaining earnings?
  » What is the historical practice for retaining earnings?
  » What degree of corporate control does the payor exercise?
  » Is there only one principal shareholder or other *bona fide* arm'slength shareholders involved?
  » Depreciation;
  » Possible economic downturns;
  » Return on invested capital; and
  » If the corporation, after adding back expenses to the pre-tax corporate income, has an overall negative pre-tax income (also known as a loss), no amount of pre-tax corporate income can be attributed to the payor's income.[338]

And in the words of McIntyre J of the Saskatchewan Court of Queen's Bench in *Dand v Ady*

> 14 If the court is to apply s. 18, it is pre-tax net corporate earnings and not retained earnings that are to be used (*Nykiforuk v. Richmond*, 2007 SKQB 433). In considering s. 18, it is helpful if the court can consider the business practices of the company, both before and after the separation, taking into account any pattern that may be evident. The court will look at factors such as pre-tax income of the corporation; the nature of the business and whether there is a reasonable need to retain earnings; the corporate share structure and any shareholders' agreements; the company's operational requirements and, if the court is to consider attributing pre-tax income to a spouse, is there in fact money available to the spouse through the corporation.[339]

While it is important to be cautious respecting the use of retained earnings in the assessment of resources available for support, it is important not to overlook them when claims are being advanced that a business, whether it be a farm, a ranch, or otherwise, needs to minimize the potential use of corporate income for support in order to create a reserve

338 *Ward v Murphy*, 2022 NSCA 20 at para 153. See also *MT v JS*, 2023 BCCA 64.
339 2014 SKQB 101 at para 14.

for future expenses.[340] Non-arm's-length benefits and payments to a "common law spouse" may be added to a parent's income under section 18(2) of the Guidelines, except insofar as such payments reflected necessary and reasonable recompense for services when measured against industry standards applicable to similar work rendered in similar circumstances.[341] Remuneration paid by the obligor's company to his children or to his "common law spouse" and her child who are discharging the normal duties of employees and being paid normal rates are treated as arm's-length transactions and give rise to no attribution of income to the obligor under the Guidelines.[342] The following criteria set out by the Canada Revenue Agency in IT-419R2 apply in determining whether parties are dealing at arm's length:

a) Is there a common mind which directs the bargaining for both parties to a transaction?
b) Are the parties acting in concert?
c) Is there "de facto" control?

The IT-419R2 definition of non-arm's length also refers to parties "acting in a highly interdependent manner," and an "element of common interest."[343]

Section 18 of the *Federal Child Support Guidelines* is designed to address the unfairness that would result if a parent were to manipulate his or her income through a corporate structure and thereby avoid child support obligations. Corporations and businesses must operate in the real world, however, and there may be legitimate reasons for maintaining retained earnings in a corporation and not making them available to shareholder owners by way of salary or dividend. As Yungwirth J of the Alberta Court of Queen's Bench observed in *Sweezey v Sweezey*:

> Factors which courts have considered in determining whether all or part of a corporation's pre-tax income should be included in a shareholder's income for child support purposes include:
>
> a. the nature of the corporation's business;
> b. the historical spending patterns of the corporation;
> c. the role the shareholder spouse plays in the corporation;
> d. whether the shareholder spouse is the sole shareholder;
> e. the degree of control exercised by the shareholder spouse;
> f. the benefits received by non-arm's length persons as a result of payment of corporate expenses; . . .
> h. whether the company's pre-tax income is required to manage the business and ensure its ongoing financial viability.[344]

340 *MacLachlan v MacLachlan*, 2020 SKQB 117 at para 28, Brown J.

341 *Kinasewich v Kinasewich*, [2001] AJ No 1185 (QB); *Miner v Miner*, [2004] OJ No 3303 (CA); *REG v TWJG*, 2011 SKQB 269; compare *Boser v Boser*, [2003] SJ No 714 (QB) (payments made prior to cohabitational relationship deemed at arm's length).

342 *Miner v Miner*, [2004] OJ No 3303 (CA); *Hesson v Hesson*, [2000] SJ No 257 (QB).

343 *BMD v CND*, 2010 BCSC 1785.

344 *Sweezey v Sweezey*, 2016 ABQB 131 at para 56; see also *Kondics v Kondics*, 2017 ABQB 493; *VOE v LLE*, 2018 ABQB 940.

In *Bembridge v Bembridge*,[345] MacDonald J of the Supreme Court of Nova Scotia added:

> [36] Other courts examining this issue have commented that decisions made pursuant to section 18 [of the Guidelines] require a court to understand (for example):
>
> - the historical practice of the corporation for retaining earnings;
> - the restrictions on the corporation's business including the amount and cost of capital equipment required;
> - the type of industry is involved and the environment in which it operates;
> - the potential for business growth or contraction;
> - the level of debt;
> - how the corporation obtains its financing and whether there are banking or financing restrictions;
> - the control exercised by the parent over the corporation.
>
> [37] This list is not exhaustive. Failure to understand exactly where the additional money can be found to increase the parent's income can lead to an incorrect result and ultimately, if the parent cannot find the expected additional money, may undermine the operation of the corporation and eventually "kill the goose that lays the golden egg."

And in *Brophy v Brophy*,[346] Linhares de Sousa J of the Ontario Superior Court of Justice listed the following questions and considerations in light of relevant caselaw:

> 1. Because of the separate legal entity of the corporation, should there be a general reluctance by the court to automatically attribute corporate income to the shareholder?
> 2. Is there a business reason for retaining earnings in the company?
> 3. Is there one principal shareholder or are there other *bona fide* arm's length shareholders involved?
> 4. What is the historical practice of the corporation for retaining earnings?
> 5. What degree of control is exercised by the spouse over the corporation?

In *Koester v Koester*,[347] Staychyn J of the Ontario Superior Court of Justice observed that the principles summarized in *Brophy v Brophy*, above, are consistent with the following factors outlined in periodical literature:

> (a) To what extent is the availability of access to pre-tax corporate income restricted by the ownership structure?
>
> (b) What restrictions on availability are imposed by nature of the corporation's business including the amount of capital equipment required, the nature of the industry in which the company operates, the outlook in terms of expansion or contraction, the level of debt as well as any banking or financing restrictions?
>
> (c) Historical trends and practices of the corporation.

---

345 2009 NSSC 158 at paras 35–36; see also *Croissant v Croissant*, 2022 SKCA 5.

346 [2002] OJ No 3658 at para 36 (SCJ). See also *C v S*, 2010 NBQB 252; *Reid v Reid*, 2018 NLSC 33; *Hendrickson v Hendrickson*, [2005] NSJ No 395 (SC); *Tremblay v Tremblay*, 2016 ONSC 588.

347 [2003] OJ No 5406 at para 34 (SCJ), citing Vivian Alterman, "Looking Through the Corporate Veil — Attributing Corporate Income for Federal Guidelines Purposes" (December 1999) 14 *Money & Family Law* 89–92. See also *Ramsay v Mackintosh*, 2013 ABQB 80; *Pallot v Pallot*, 2010 BCSC 1146; *MDA v MS* [2008] NBJ No 498 (QB); *Thompson v Thompson*, 2013 ONSC 5500; *ACG v WLG*, 2020 SKQB 43.

Applying these criteria, Staychyn J refused to impute additional income to a father who had a 50 percent interest in a private company, where the drawing down of its retained earnings would threaten the growth and survival of the company and was strongly opposed by the co-owner of the company who was at arm's length from the father.

It is pre-tax net corporate earnings and not retained earnings that should be used in applying section 18 of the Guidelines.[348] While it is important to be cautious respecting the use of retained earnings in the assessment of resources available for support, it is important not to overlook them when claims are being advanced that a business needs to minimize the potential use of corporate income for support in order to create a reserve for future expenses.[349] In *Nykiforuk v Richmond*,[350] Ryan-Froslie J (as she then was) of the Saskatchewan Court of Queen's Bench (Family Division) observed that, in determining whether to exercise its discretion pursuant to section 18 of the Guidelines, the court must be satisfied that additional money is actually available and that it can be paid to the shareholder without endangering the financial viability of the company. Merely looking at the retained earnings of the corporation is of limited assistance. Retained earnings are a shareholder's equity in the corporation (its assets less its liabilities). They do not represent cash available for distribution, nor do they reflect the pre-tax income of the corporation. In making a determination pursuant to section 18 of the Guidelines, a wide range of factors must be considered, including:

1) The pre-tax income of the corporation;
2) The nature of the business involved (Is it capital intensive or service-oriented? Is it subject to seasonal fluctuations or economic cycles?);
3) The corporate share structure, including any obligation imposed by shareholders' agreements;
4) The financial position and general operations of the company (What are the company's operating requirements, its inventory, accounts receivable and accounts payable? Are there bank covenants which may affect payment out of funds? Is there a necessity to upgrade equipment, etc.?); and
5) Is the company a well-established one or merely in its start-up phase?

Fairness in the application of section 18 will depend on the nature of the relationship between the obligor and the corporation, the nature of the corporation's business, the legitimate calls on the corporate income, and the corporation's capitalization requirements, with the court having the ability to consider the historical income pattern of the spouse and non-recurring gains or losses.[351] In *Beeching v Beeching*,[352] Wilkinson J of the Saskatchewan Court of Queen's Bench summarized relevant judicial decisions as follows:

> In the case law, legitimate business reasons for retaining earnings in a corporation have included: (1) the need to acquire or replace inventory; (2) debt-financing requirements;

---

348 *Miller v Joynt*, 2007 ABCA 214; *Johnson v Barker*, 2017 NSCA 53; *Reid v Faubert*, 2019 NSCA 42; *McLellan v McLellan*, 2020 NSSC 161; *Wolfson v Wolfson*, 2021 NSSC 260; *Mayer v Mayer*, 2013 ONSC 7099.

349 *Birnie v Birnie*, 2018 SKQB 87 at para 34, Brown J.

350 2007 SKQB 433; see also *Johnson v Barker*, 2017 NSCA 53; *Reid v Faubert*, 2019 NSCA 42; *Wolfson v Wolfson*, 2021 NSSC 260.

351 *More v Shurygalo*, 2010 SKQB 203.

352 (1998), 169 Sask R 18 at para 27 (QB); see also *Guenther v Guenther*, 2016 SKQB 322.

(3) carrying accounts receivable for a significant period of time; (4) cyclical peaks or valleys in cash flow; (5) allowances for bad debts; (6) allowances for anticipated business losses or extraordinary expenditures; and (7) capital acquisitions.

An appellate court will not interfere with the refusal of a trial judge to impute income to a shareholding parent on the basis of the retained earnings of a private corporation, where there is evidence upon which the trial judge can properly conclude that the retention of earnings represents a prudent business measure.[353] Although a portion of significant retained earnings of a company in which the obligor is the sole shareholder and driving force may be judicially attributed to the obligor under the Guidelines,[354] a court may decline to make such attribution on the basis of a company's retained earnings where they reflect the busi ness pattern in place before the spousal separation.[355] Courts are disinclined to interfere with business decisions where such interference could undermine the viability of a business. Consequently, a court may refuse to impute income to a shareholding spouse in excess of his or her annual corporate salary where the retained earnings of the corporation are being used to build up necessary inventory at an early stage of business development; different considerations might be applicable once the business is firmly established.[356] A court may refuse to impute income to a parent on the basis of retained earnings in the parent's private corporation where the business is highly volatile and it is prudent to set aside funds for future use as an income source. However, where the parent faces the prospect of paying child sup port for his second family, it may be appropriate to revisit the issue and incorporate some portion of retained earnings into the respondent's annual income, particularly if he seeks to invoke the undue hardship provisions of section 10 of the *Federal Child Support Guidelines*

The ability of a sole shareholder of a company to control the income received is open to abuse and requires careful judicial scrutiny under the *Federal Child Support Guidelines* Additional income may be imputed to the obligor under sections 19(1)(a) and (d) of the Guidelines, if the income received is unrealistic and the availability of money in the company is evidenced by circumstances, such as the repayment of a shareholder loan. Some eviden tial basis must exist to justify such an imputation. The court may also impute income to the obligor under section 19(1)(e) of the Guidelines where property is not reasonably used to generate income.[358] This section empowers the court to impute additional income where the obligor's income is needlessly low.[359] However, a court should decline to impute income pursuant to section 19(1)(e) of the Guidelines where it is unrealistic to expect a parent to liquidate his or her capital holdings and invest the proceeds.[360]

353 *Hollenbach v Hollenbach*, [2000] BCJ No 2316 (CA).

354 *Brokop v Stepenoff*, [1999] SJ No 574 (QB) (application under *Saskatchewan Child Support Guidelines* and *The Family Maintenance Act, 1997*, SS 1997, c F-6.2).

355 *Bakken v Bakken*, [1999] SJ No 559 (QB).

356 *Hesson v Hesson*, [2000] SJ No 257 (QB); see also *JT v KC*, 2011 BCSC 1723; *Denbok v Thuet*, [2000] OJ No 4671 (SCJ).

357 *Denbok v Thuet, ibid.*

358 See *YL v GL*, 2020 BCSC 808 at para 365 (annual rate of return of 3 percent is used when imputing income pursuant to s 19(1)(e) of the Guidelines in the absence of evidence that establishes a higher rate).

359 *Rudachyk v Rudachyk*, [1999] SJ No 312 (CA).

360 *Bucholtz v Smith*, [2001] BCJ No 1872 (SC); *Livingston v King*, 2022 BCSC 1906.

Where the lifestyle of the obligor is inconsistent with his or her stipulated income, the court may attribute income to the obligor based on the pre-tax income of a family company and the obligor's ability to draw significant amounts from the company for household living expenses.[361] Income may be readily imputed to an obligor with a history of minimizing his or her salary and utilizing his or her companies for the payment of personal expenses.[362] An obligor cannot treat personal and business expenditures as interchangeable and thereby reduce his or her income for the purpose of applying the *Federal Child Support Guidelines*.[363] Income may be imputed to a self-employed parent who uses business expenses for personal purposes and any such expenses may be grossed up before being attributed as income of the parent under the Guidelines.[364] Income may be imputed to an obligor whose income is artificially low because of low draws from a personal corporation.[365] However, a court should be cautious before attributing income to an obligor that reflects previous high draws from his or her business. Draws from a business may be no more than a measure of a person's cash flow needs and they may have to be repaid if the income to support them is not forthcoming. Draws may fail to provide a true picture of the actual income from a sole proprietorship, partnership, or corporation. Where practicable, a court should carefully evaluate the statements of income and expenditures of the business and, in doing so, is not bound to accept the statements at face value.[366]

An obligor's income may be assessed at less than draws from the company over the preceding fiscal year where management compensation over many years generated a lesser amount.[367] Allegations respecting personal expenses and retention of cash from corporate sales may be rejected by the court when they are not substantiated by evidence and the claimant could have had the corporate records audited but declined to do so.[368]

Income may be imputed to an obligor on the basis of the payment of personal expenses by his or her company and the availability of additional income in light of the company's pre-tax earnings that the obligor has the authority to withdraw, but the court may refuse to treat all of the company's pre-tax earnings as realistically available to pay child support.[369]

A spouse who asserts that all or part of the pre-tax income of a corporation should be included in the income of the other spouse must demonstrate some basis upon which section 18 of the *Federal Child Support Guidelines* should apply. Once the court is satisfied that it is appropriate to impute income, the onus shifts to the spouse who utilizes the corporation to build up retained earnings or to incur expenses to establish that they are reasonable having regard to the business. The rationale for this shift in onus is that the shareholder knows much more about the business than the recipient spouse and is therefore in the best position to explain why some or all of the company's pre-tax income is not available for support or can

361 *Shelleby v Shelleby*, [1997] OJ No 2608 (Gen Div).

362 *Hauger v Hauger*, [2000] AJ No 753 (QB); *Estrela v Estrela*, [1997] OJ No 2916 (Gen Div).

363 *Adams v Adams*, [2000] AJ No 247 (QB); *Bucholtz v Smith*, [2001] BCJ No 1872 (SC).

364 *Riel v Holland*, [2003] OJ No 3901 (CA); see *contra Kinasewich v Kinasewich*, [2001] AJ No 1185 (QB).

365 *Bhopal v Bhopal*, [1997] BCJ No 1746 (SC); *Forward v Martin*, [1999] NBJ No 433 (QB); *Yeo v Yeo*, [1998] PEIJ No 100 (SCTD).

366 *Westcott v Westcott*, [1997] OJ No 3060 (Gen Div).

367 *Stanbridge v Stanbridge*, [1998] BCJ No 193 (SC).

368 *Ibid.*

369 *Moss v Moss*, [1997] NJ No 299 (SC).

identify individuals who could be called as witnesses to address the issue.[370] The onus of proof is on the payor spouse to provide clear evidence that a corporation's pre-tax income is not available for support, and the court should not have to ferret out the necessary information from inadequate or incomplete financial disclosure.[371] There are some corporations or enterprises that by their nature require significant injections of capital from time to time to operate. A personal services corporation, generally speaking, is not such a corporation. In the absence of legitimate calls on the pre-tax corporate income of a company, children and a spouse are entitled to support based on the full income available to the payor spouse.[372]

There are several reasons the entirety of pre-tax corporate income might not be attributed to an individual, including, *inter alia*, absence of control, operational and capital requirements, debt servicing, and banking covenants. The attribution of income must not result in a situation that puts the corporation at risk, encroaches on its capital, or interferes with the rights of third parties. The reasons the payor resists the attribution of the totality of corporate pre-tax income must be carefully examined.[373]

In *Thompson v Bear*,[374] Klebuc JA of the Saskatchewan Court of Appeal observed that there are conflicting decisions on the interpretation to be accorded to section 18(1)(a) of the *Federal Child Support Guidelines* in circumstances where section 17(1) of the Guidelines is applied. One line of cases interprets the conjoint operation of sections 18(1)(a) and 17(1) of the Guidelines as entitling the court to attribute to the shareholding parent an annual sum equal to the average of the pre-tax income of a corporation during the preceding three years, even if that sum exceeds the corporation's pre-tax income for its most recent tax year. The second line of cases interprets the conjoint operation of sections 18(1)(a) and 17(1) of the *Federal Child Support Guidelines* in a manner that limits the authority of the court to attribute to the parent no more than the pre-tax income of a corporation for its most recent taxation year. Klebuc JA's closely reasoned analysis of the conflicting judicial decisions and his endorsement of the second line of cases is highly persuasive; it provides that a court should consider section 17 as part of the process of assessing whether "all or part of the pre-tax income of the corporation . for the most recent taxation year" should be attributed to the parent. While the attribution of corporate income is limited to the amount of the most current year's pre-tax corporate income, a court is fully entitled to scrutinize a corporation's historical earnings and other financial information to determine what portion of the current year's income should be attributed.

---

370 *Mayer v Mayer*, 2013 ONSC 7099 at paras 57–58, citing *Goett v Goett*, 2013 ABCA 216. See also *Sydor v Keough*, 2019 MBCA 119 at para 25.

371 *SLD v WAD*, 2020 BCSC 690 at para 39; *de la Fuente v Breen*, 2021 BCSC 2000.

372 *Teja v Dhanda*, 2009 BCCA 198 (entire pre-tax income of personal services corporation imputed to parent where the corporation was used to build up substantial savings); see also *VC v PR*, 2016 NBQB 90; *Kosior v Kosior*, 2013 SKQB 42.

373 See *Birnie v Birnie*, 2018 SKQB 87 at paras 23–24, citing *Potzus v Potzus*, 2017 SKCA 15 at para 14.

374 2014 SKCA 111; see also *Potzus v Potzus*, 2017 SKCA 15; *Aalbers v Aalbers*, 2017 SKCA 43; *Croissant v Croissant*, 2022 SKCA 5. And see *ANH v LDG*, 2018 BCSC 2012, citing *Hausmann v Klukas*, 2009 BCCA 32; *AB v MH*, 2018 SKQB 317. Compare *Mason v Mason*, 2016 ONCA 725 (spousal support). Compare also *Wolfson v Wolfson*, 2021 NSSC 260; *Walker v Walker*, 2019 SKCA 96. And see *MT v JS*, 2023 BCCA 64, discussed in discussed in Franks & Zalev, "This Week in Family Law," 7 August 2023 (Thomson Reuters).

375 *Dungey v Dungey*, 2020 SKCA 138, cited in *Merrifield v Merrifield*, 2021 SKCA 85; see also *WLG v ACG* 2021 SKCA 112.

In *O'Neill v O'Neill*,[376] Harvison Young J, in endorsing the first line of cases stated that "[a] literal and restrictive interpretation of section 18(1)(a) would create an incentive for litigants seeking to avoid or minimize support obligations to manipulate the success or lack thereof of the corporation for the year preceding the trial." Any such manipulation, however, could be addressed by applying section 19 of the *Federal Child Support Guidelines*.[377] Although section 18 of the Guidelines allows the court to attribute corporate income to a parent only for the immediate preceding year, it may be possible to apply section 19(1)(d) or (e) of the Guidelines as an additional potential source to impute retained corporate earnings to a parent.[378] The accumulation of retained earnings in a corporation may result in an imputation of income pursuant to section 19 of the Guidelines where an obligor is not properly utilizing his or her property to generate income by, for example, failing to declare dividends when it is appropriate to do so.[379] Relevant caselaw in Alberta,[380] British Columbia,[381] Manitoba,[382] Newfoundland and Labrador,[383] and Saskatchewan[384] asserts that in circumstances where a payor spouse has retained earnings in his company, the onus is on that spouse to convince the court that there are valid business reasons for doing so. Where the parent is the sole shareholder, director, and officer of the corporation, the onus will be a heavy one.[385] Where a parent is financially responsible and frugal, he has not taken out a salary commensurate with his efforts, there is no evidence that he used the business to deduct personal expenses, the wife will profit from his financial prudence, there is no indication that he had any intention of avoiding his child support obligation, and he might need to refinance the company to meet significant debts following the court-ordered distribution of matrimonial property, the court may conclude that section 18(1)(b) is the more appropriate option in imputing additional income to the parent.[386] It has been asserted that pre-tax income of a parent's corporation is likely to be attributed to the parent, if it can be taken without seriously undermining the finances of the corporation

---

376 (2007), 39 RFL (6th) 72 (Ont SCJ). But see *contra*: *Thompson v Thompson*, 2013 ONSC 5500 at para 65, Chappel J. And see *Wolfson v Wolfson*, 2021 NSSC 260.

377 Compare, for example, *Goett v Goett*, 2013 ABCA 216, wherein the pre-tax income of a corporation was imputed to a parent for child support purposes under the conjoint operation of ss 18 and 19 of the *Federal Child Support Guidelines* when the parent was not a shareholder, director, or officer of the corporation but was the controlling mind and *de facto* owner of the corporation. See also *MT v JS*, 2023 BCCA 64; *Code v McLeod*, 2023 BCSC 1686; *MC v JO*, 2017 NBCA 15; *Henderson v Henderson*, 2021 NBQB 88; *Walker v Walker*, 2019 SKCA 96. And see *Ward v Murphy*, 2022 NSCA 20, wherein the lack of clarity around the intersection/application of ss 18 and 19 of the Guidelines is reviewed.

378 *Nesbitt v Nesbitt*, [2001] MJ No 291 (CA); *Verwey v Verwey*, 2007 MBCA 102; *Dyck v Dyck*, 2008 MBCA 135; *Cook v McManus*, [2006] NBJ No 334 (QB); see also *Giene v Giene* (1998), 234 AR 355 (QB); *Hodgkinson v Hodgkinson*, 2011 BCSC 634 at paras 38–42; *O'Neill v O'Neill*, [2007] OJ No 1706 (SCJ); *Hann v Elms*, 2016 NLTD(F) 15; compare *C v S*, 2010 NBQB 252; *Thompson v Bear*, 2014 SKCA 111; *Potzus v Potzus*, 2017 SKCA 15; *Walker v Walker*, 2019 SKCA 96.

379 *Trueman v Trueman*, [2000] AJ No 1301 (QB); *Morley v Morley*, [1999] SJ No 31 (QB).

380 *Miller v Joynt*, 2007 ABCA 214.

381 *Hausmann v Klukas*, 2009 BCCA 32; *KW v LH*, 2018 BCCA 204.

382 *Dyck v Dyck*, 2008 MBCA 135.

383 *Gosse v Sorensen-Gosse*, 2011 NLCA 58.

384 *Labrecque v Labrecque*, 2014 SKCA 59.

385 *Ibid.*

386 *MJW v BJW*, [2006] AJ No 7 (QB); *Cook v McManus*, [2006] NBJ No 334 (QB); see also *Potzus v Potzus*, 2017 SKCA 15.

and if it is available to the parent or could be made available.[387] The key word under section 18 is the word "available." There is a substantial difference between the company that is wholly owned and directed by the payor parent and one in which he is not the controlling mind. Likewise there is also a difference between a company that generates its income solely from the work of the payor, for example, a medical doctor or a dentist, and a company that operates retail stores.[389] To find *de facto* control a person must have the clear right and ability to effect a significant change in the directorship of the company or to influence in a very direct way the shareholders who would otherwise have the ability to elect the board of directors. In determining who has control of a corporation, a court may consider the following factors: (1) who decides when dividends are declared and when the corporate funds are dispensed? (2) how has control been exercised in the past in the real sense? (3) who exercises complete control of finances, policies, and business practices of the corporation? (4) who is the *de facto* shareholder and controlling mind of the business? (5) who can influence in a very direct way the shareholders who would otherwise have the ability to elect the board of directors?, and (6) who is in a position to influence the amounts paid out by the corporation and to influence how the pre-tax income is used?[391] Corporate income attribution may be appropriate, however, even where a parent does not control the corporation, where, for example, control is held by a cooperative relative, and there is a past practice of the parent receiving compensation.[392]

Although it can be useful to call experts to testify as to the financial needs of the business and the purpose and legitimacy of any expenses, the court has a discretion, in assessing income, to employ common sense when it analyzes financial information.[393] Where an existing court order restricts the amount of compensation to be paid to a parent shareholder in order to prevent a dissipation of assets pending a distribution of property pursuant to provincial statute, the freedom to attribute additional income to a parent pursuant to section 18 of the *Federal Child Support Guidelines* is circumscribed.[394]

The ability to impute income pursuant to section 18 of the Guidelines is discretionary, not mandatory, but the discretion must be exercised judicially.[395] The fact that a spouse draws no income from the corporation or draws less than could possibly be taken is not itself sufficient to warrant an imputation of income under section 18 of the Guidelines. What the court must consider is whether it is reasonable for a corporation to retain part of its earnings rather than paying them out to the spouse. In determining what is reasonable, the court should review the tax returns of the spouse as well as the financial statements and tax returns of the companies involved. It may be significant if the parent took income or benefits from the company in the past but ceased to do so after the spousal separation. Such conduct may lead to the inference that money is being left in the company in order to reduce the parent's liability for child

---

387 *Cook v McManus*, [2006] NBJ No 334 (QB); *Kendry v Cathcart*, [2001] OJ No 277 (SCJ).

388 *Kowalewich v Kowalewich*, 2001 BCCA 450; *Pallot v Pallot*, 2010 BCSC 1146.

389 *Pallot v Pallot, ibid.*

390 *Potzus v Potzus*, 2017 SKCA 15 at para 49.

391 *LFR(H) v RBH*, 2021 NBQB 50 at paras 25–26, d'Entremont J, citing *Potzus v Potzus*, 2017 SKCA 15 at paras 45–51.

392 See *Leitch v Novac*, 2020 ONCA 257 at para 36 (availability of the tort of conspiracy examined).

393 *Ursel v Ursel*, 2014 BCSC 1219.

394 *Ibid.*

395 *Adams v Adams*, 2011 ABQB 576, citing *Miller v Joynt*, 2007 ABCA 214.

support. Intentional under-drawing of income is not the only matter that the court should consider. A spouse may have no intention of evading his or her child support obligations but may, nevertheless, have unreasonably left income in the company that should be considered when assessing child support. In determining whether this is so, the court must consider the pre-tax income of the corporation and whether the services rendered to the corporation by the shareholding spouse are adequately compensated for, as well as the capital that is reasonably required for it to function, grow, and become more competitive in the marketplace. The court should seek to balance the objective of providing reasonable child support and promoting the company's reasonable objectives. Where the court is satisfied that a corporation can reasonably pay out additional income to its shareholding spouse without undermining the financial health of the corporation, the court may include in the spouse's income under the Guidelines all or part of the pre-taxation income of the corporation. Section 11 of Schedule III of the *Federal Child Support Guidelines* directs the court to adjust a spouse's annual income by including "the spouse's deduction for an allowable capital cost allowance with respect to real property." This provision does not entitle a court to directly add back a corporate capital cost allowance on real property into the spousal shareholder's Guidelines income. The only way in which a court may take account of the corporate capital cost allowance lies in its ability to include in the spouse's income all or part of the pre-tax income of the corporation in accordance with section 18(1)(a) of the Guidelines. A spouse's practice of not drawing income from either of two companies in which he is the sole shareholder may be found to be reasonable, if he has an income from full-time employment that will itself generate reasonable child support, and the companies in which he has a controlling interest have very modest liquid assets because their holdings are made up of buildings, land, and appliances, all of which are essential for the corporate business activities. Courts rarely require a spouse to borrow money or sell property in order to provide child support, particularly when the spouse has other means of providing reasonable child support. Many spouses upon divorce have equity in various assets, such as real property or RRSPs and there is no reason why a spouse should not retain the equity that he holds as a corporate shareholder without having additional income imputed to him on this basis for the purpose of increasing the reasonable amount of child support paid out of his full-time employment income.[396]

In determining whether all or part of the pre-tax income of a company should be attributed to a spouse under section 18(1)(a) of the *Federal Child Support Guidelines*, a court will not normally interfere with the internal management of a company, particularly where arm's-length shareholders are involved and there is no evidence that the management decisions were unreasonable, or made in bad faith, or contrary to the interests of the company.[397] Evidence of the applicant's chartered accountant that is based solely on financial statements of the company may be rejected by the court, where no consideration was given to the long-range plans or philosophy of the primary shareholders of the company or their business practices.[398] Cases in which courts have included corporate income in the obligor's income under section 18 of the Guidelines usually involve circumstances where the spouse is the

396 *Cook v McManus*, [2006] NBJ No 334 (QB); *Gossen v Gossen*, [2003] NSJ No 113 (SC).

397 *Rudulier v Rudulier*, [1999] SJ No 366 (QB).

398 *Ibid.*

sole shareholder,[399] but this is not a precondition to the application of section 18 of the *Federal Child Support Guidelines.*[400] While the ability to lift the corporate veil is particularly important in the case of a sole shareholder who has the ability to control the income of the corporation, it is not restricted to wholly-owned private companies.[401]

A shareholder's loan that is repaid is not income under the *Income Tax Act* nor under the *Federal Child Support Guidelines.* The only specific adjustment the court is directed to make to a corporation's pre-tax income is for amounts paid to persons not at arm's length under section 18(2) of the Guidelines. Any adjustment to the corporation's pre-tax income for capital cost allowance must be derived from the court's entitlement to include all or part of the pre-tax income of the corporation under section 18(1)(a) of the Guidelines. The courts have sometimes required a full exploration of the attendant circumstances before adding back capital cost allowance on property other than real property, but in other situations, including interim child support applications, the courts have been willing to add back a fixed percentage. Each case must be decided on its own merits and a resolution may be deferred until evidence is available that would assist the court in reaching a determination.[402] In the final analysis, the treatment of capital cost allowance on personal property for the purpose of ascertaining the obligor's income is to be determined according to the merits of the particular case and no consistent pattern can be expected.[403]

In applying section 18 of the *Federal Child Support Guidelines,* the historical earnings of a private corporation may be relied upon to estimate the future income available to a parent in light of the existing retained earnings of the corporation.[404]

In considering an adjustment of income under section 18 of the Guidelines, the court must strike a balance between maintaining the ongoing operations of the company and determining an amount of income that fairly reflects the money available to a parent for the payment of child support.[405]

Periodic payments made for the purpose of redeeming a spouse's shares in a company should not be deducted from the company's revenues, when determining the other spouse's imputed income under sections 18(1)(a) and 19(1) and (2) of the *Federal Child Support Guidelines.*[406] A court may decline to impute income to an obligor who is the sole shareholder in a company established for charitable purposes, where no income is taken from the company, even though the obligor may receive some benefit when entertaining persons who contribute to the charitable work.[407]

A search for the fairest determination of parental income must take into account a parent's control of private companies and the intertwining of personal affairs. A parent is not

---

399 *Bowen v Bowen,* [2001] OJ No 480 (SCJ); *Beeching v Beeching,* [1998] SJ No 355 (QB); *Stephen v Stephen* [1999] SJ No 479 (QB).

400 *Jensen v Jensen,* 2018 BCSC 283; see also *Guenther v Guenther,* 2016 SKQB 322 at para 20.

401 *Kowalewich v Kowalewich,* 2001 BCCA 450; *Chapman v Summer,* 2010 BCCA 237; *Gosse v Sorensen-Gosse,* 2011 NLCA 58; *REG v TWJG,* 2011 SKQB 269.

402 *Beeching v Beeching,* [1998] SJ No 355 (QB).

403 *Ruecker v Ruecker,* [1998] SJ No 408 (QB).

404 *Peterson v Peterson,* [2001] AJ No 1044 (QB).

405 *Chapman v Summer,* 2010 BCCA 237; *Kopp v Kopp,* 2012 BCCA 140; *Desrosiers v Pastuck,* 2016 NSSC 308; *Tauber v Tauber,* [2001] OJ No 3259 (SCJ); *Dobson v Dobson,* [2005] SJ No 686 (QB).

406 *Dunham v Dunham,* [1998] OJ No 4758 (Gen Div).

407 *Covington v Covington,* [1999] AJ No 5 (QB).

entitled to divest the assets of a business corporation of which he is the sole shareholder by means of charitable donations, nor can a parent artificially reduce his income by drawing on a shareholder loan to subsidize his living expenses instead of withdrawing income from the companies under his control. If this occurs, corporate income may be imputed to that parent pursuant to section 18 of the *Federal Child Support Guidelines.* An alternative basis for imputing income to the sole shareholding parent may be found under section 19 of the Guidelines where it appears that income has been diverted (s 19(1)(d)), where the parent's property is not reasonably used to generate income (s 19(1)(e)), where expenses have been unreasonably deducted from income to fund charitable donations (s 19(1)(g)), or where there has been a failure to provide income information that is legally required (s 19(1)(f)).[408]

Although a court may add the after-tax income of the obligor's holding company to his professional income, it may refuse to attribute the pre-tax income of the company to the obligor under section 18(1)(b) of the *Federal Child Support Guidelines,* having regard to the historical pattern of dealings with the company.[409]

The provisions of sections 18(1) and 18(2) of the Guidelines speak only to the most recent taxation year.[410] Pre-tax income and retained earnings are not the same and must not be confused in an application under section 18 of the Guidelines. As the British Columbia Court of Appeal stated in *Hausmann v Klukas,*[411] retained earnings in a company's financial statement represent equity, not cash. Only the pre-tax income of a corporation for the most recent taxation year may be included in a spouse's annual income under section 18(1)(a) of the Guidelines. Section 18 is not directed at retained corporate earnings over several years but such retained earnings may result in the imputation of income to a spouse under section 19 of the Guidelines.[412] Section 18(3) of the *Manitoba Child Support Guidelines* empowers a court to impute income to a parent who is the sole shareholder of a private corporation by including "all or part of the pre-tax income of the corporation . . . for the most recent taxation year." The reference to "the most recent taxation year" means the most recent year for which financial statements are available.[413] Section 19(1)(e) of the *Manitoba Child Support Guidelines* does not apply to retained earnings of a corporation, unless it can be shown that the obligor has control of the corporation and has caused the corporation to unduly retain its earnings.[414]

408 *Volken v Volken,* [2001] BCJ No 1344 (SC). See also *CRP v NDP,* 2023 NBKB 197.

409 *Merritt v Merritt,* [1999] OJ No 1732 (SCJ).

410 *Lahanky v Lahanky,* 2011 NBQB 84.

411 2009 BCCA 32. See also *Stockall v Stockall,* 2020 ABQB 229 at para 33; *Vincent v Vincent,* 2012 BCCA 186 at para 55; *Gosse v Sorensen-Gosse,* 2011 NLCA 58; *Johnson v Barker,* 2017 NSCA 53; *Reid v Faubert,* 2019 NSCA 42; *Potzus v Potzus,* 2017 SKCA 15. As to the significance of retained corporate earnings under sections 18 and 19 of the *Child Support Guidelines* and improper intermingling of the steps undertaken in determining a parent's income under sections 16 to 19 of the Guidelines, see *Bembridge v Bembridge,* 2009 NSSC 158; *Thompson v Thompson,* 2013 ONSC 5500.

412 *Tucker v Tucker,* 2019 SKQB 317 at para 35; see also *Grossi v Grossi,* [2005] BCJ No 125 (CA); *Cook v McManus,* [2006] NBJ No 334 (QB); compare *Boser v Boser,* [2001] SJ No 347 (QB); *Hodgkinson v Hodgkinson,* 2011 BCSC 634. See also *Boser v Boser,* [2003] SJ No 714 (QB); *Rudachyk v Rudachyk,* [1999] SJ No 312 (CA); *Jarvis v Parker,* [2008] SJ No 47 (QB).

413 *Blanchard v Kemp,* [2000] MJ No 506 (CA).

414 *Blaine v Sanders,* [2000] MJ No 149 (QB) (retention of earnings by corporation found insufficient to warrant imputation of income under s 19(1)(e) of the Guidelines on the basis that "the spouse's property is not reasonably utilized to generate income").

Where an obligor's income is channelled through a corporation in which he and his current wife each have a 50 percent interest, the obligor cannot shield himself against a judicial attribution of income under section 11 of Schedule III of the *Federal Child Support Guidelines* on the basis that capital cost allowances were not personal, but corporate. Section 18 of the Guidelines empowers the court to take account of the pre-tax income of a company where the obligor is a shareholder, director, or officer of the company.[415]

Section 18 of the *Federal Child Support Guidelines* does not justify a court incorporating a legitimate corporate expense in the shareholding parent's Guidelines income.[416]

In the absence of evidence that a parent is unreasonably building up retained corporate earnings rather than taking out the money as personal income, a court will not impute additional income to that parent simply because there is a time lag in the reporting of income because of the fact that his personal tax year end and his corporation's tax year end do not coincide.[417]

A corporation and the person who controls it are "related persons" and are deemed not to deal with each other at arm's length under sections 251(1)(a) and 251(2)(b) of the *Income Tax Act*. A parent who runs a personal service private corporation has the onus of establishing that the salary received from the corporation is reasonable compensation for the services rendered. Absent relevant evidence and in light of previously demonstrated earning capacity, a court may attribute all of a recently established corporation's pre-tax income to the controlling parent for the purpose of determining the amount of interim child support to be paid. If the subsequent first annual statement of the corporation and required supplemental evidence subsequently point to a contrary disposition, an application to vary the interim order may be entertained.[418]

On an application to vary an interim child support order, there may be insufficient information available to warrant the judicial imputation of additional income to a parent based on retained earnings of his private corporation, but additional income may be imputed where he had previously engaged in income splitting with the applicant but discontinued this practice after the spousal separation.[419]

There is ample jurisprudence for the discretionary inclusion of a portion of a corporation's retained earnings or the pre-tax income of the corporation in the controlling shareholder's income for child support purposes. There is no reason why a non-operating corporate status should be considered an exception under section 18 of the *Federal Child Support Guidelines* Cases under section 18 provide little guidance on the appropriate amount or percentage of the corporation's retained earnings or pre-tax income that should be imputed to a parent; this is because corporations have differing objectives, revenues, and expense patterns. When future increases to the retained earnings are not likely because of the non-operating status of the corporation and where the use of the retained earnings is purely discretionary and unrelated to any essential business efficacy, the court may conclude that it would be

415 *Jaasma v Jaasma*, [1999] AJ No 1186 (QB).

416 *Barker v Barker*, [2002] BCJ No 1193 (CA).

417 *Miner v Miner*, [2004] OJ No 3303 (CA).

418 *Olchowecki v Olchowecki*, [2005] SJ No 192 (QB); see also *Potzus v Potzus*, 2017 SKCA 15.

419 *Biddle v Biddle*, [2005] OJ No 737 (SCJ).

inappropriate to add the entire retained earnings in one lump sum, having regard to the personal income tax implications of imputing a single lump sum to the shareholding parent.[420]

Since the purpose of the *Federal Child Support Guidelines* is to arrive at an annual income for the parent that is fair and accurate in all the circumstances, section 18 of the Guidelines may be invoked not only to increase the income revealed in line 150 (now line 15000) of the obligor's income tax return but also to reduce it. If the amount of income declared in the parent's income tax return is based on corporate and personal tax planning that does not reflect the actual income available to the parent, the court may adjust the amount identified in line 150 (now line 15000) of the parent's income tax return so as to establish a fair and realistic income for the purpose of determining the amount of child support to be paid pursuant to the *Federal Child Support Guidelines*.[421]

In granting an order for corporate financial disclosure pursuant to section 18(1)(a) of the Guidelines, the court may direct that the financial information shall be provided in a form that lends itself to analysis by counsel for the other parent.[422]

Income from a family trust may be considered along similar lines to the examples used in section 18 of the Guidelines for the purpose of determining an appropriate attribution of income.[423]

The British Columbia Rules of Court require the disclosure of the financial statements of companies controlled by parties to family litigation and makes provision whereby a failure to comply entitles the court to draw an adverse inference against the party or attribute income to that party in an amount the court considers appropriate.[424]

The pre-tax income of a corporation can be imputed to a parent for child support purposes under the conjoint operation of sections 18 and 19 of the *Federal Child Support Guidelines* when the parent is not a shareholder, director, or officer of the corporation but is the controlling mind and *de facto* owner of the corporation.[425]

G. IMPUTING INCOME

1) Listed Circumstances under Section 19 of Guidelines

In determining the annual income of a spouse or former spouse, section 19 of the *Federal Child Support Guidelines* provides that the court may impute such amount of income as it considers appropriate in the circumstances, which include the following nine circumstances:

420 *Vance v Kovacs*, [2005] NBJ No 540 (QB) (20 percent attribution of corporate retained earnings to father deemed appropriate in the present case pursuant to ss 18(1) and 19(1)(e) of the *Federal Child Support Guidelines;* judicial refusal to impute additional earnings on the basis of intentional underemployment within the meaning of s 19(1)(a) of Guidelines in light of the judicial adding of corporate retained earnings to the parent's income).

421 *Bartkowski v Bartkowski*, [2003] BCJ No 720 (SCJ); *TLB v RB*, 2010 BCSC 710.

422 *Stang v Stang*, [2002] AJ No 106 (QB).

423 *Penner v Penner*, [1998] MJ No 353 (QB) (application under *Manitoba Child Support Guidelines*); see also *Veskovic v Nielsen*, 2022 SKCA 134.

424 *Wang v Wang*, [2003] BCJ No 2211 (SC) (annual income of $100,000 imputed to father who failed to provide financial statements of Taiwan company in which he owned a 78 percent interest).

425 *Goett v Goett*, 2013 ABCA 216; see also *Sweeney v Sweeney*, 2016 ABQB 131.

1) the spouse or former spouse is intentionally underemployed or unemployed, other than where the underemployment or unemployment is required by the needs of a child of the marriage or any child under the age of majority or by reasonable educational or health needs of the spouse or former spouse;
2) the spouse or former spouse is exempt from paying federal or provincial income tax;
3) the spouse or former spouse lives in a country that has effective rates of income tax that are significantly lower than those in Canada;[426]
4) it appears that income has been diverted that would affect the level of child support to be determined under the Guidelines;
5) the property of the spouse or former spouse is not reasonably utilized to generate income;[427]
6) the spouse or former spouse has failed to provide income information when under a legal obligation to do so;[428]
7) the spouse or former spouse unreasonably deducts expenses from income;
8) the spouse or former spouse derives a significant portion of income from dividends, capital gains, or other sources that are taxed at a lower rate than employment or business income;[429] and
9) the spouse or former spouse is a beneficiary under a trust and has been or may be in receipt of income or other benefits from the trust.[430]

2) Non-Exhaustive List under Section 19 of Guidelines

The list of circumstances under section 19 of the *Federal Child Support Guidelines* that entitles a court to impute income to a spouse or former spouse does not purport to be com prehensive and does not interfere with the power of the court to impute income in other circumstances.[431] As part of its general discretionary authority under section 19 (1) of the *Federal Child Support Guidelines,* a court may impute income to a party if there is evidence showing that the party's position respecting their income is not credible for any reason. The nine circumstances set out in section 19(1) of the Guidelines all involve situations where the income is understated or does not adequately reflect the obligor's real ability to contribute to the support of a child. There is nothing in section 19(1) to suggest that other appropri ate circumstances must be analogous to those listed.[433] However, any new category should be

426 See *Pousette v Janssen,* 2023 BCCA 176, supp reasons 2023 BCCA 272.

427 See *YL v GL,* 2020 BCSC 808 at para 365 (annual rate of return of 3 percent is used when imputing income pursuant to s 19(1)(e) of the Guidelines in the absence of evidence that establishes a higher rate). See also *WLG v ACG,* 2021 SKCA 112.

428 *Heuft v Bramwell,* 2021 ABQB 642; *VKG v IG,* 2023 ONSC 6329.

429 See *Healey v Healey,* 2024 BCCA 68.

430 See *Healey v Healey,* 2024 BCCA 68; *Veskovic v Nielsen,* 2022 SKCA 134.

431 *Simpson v Bettenson,* 2014 ABCA 21; *TAL v SDB,* 2018 ABQB 589; *Ouellette v Ouellette,* 2012 BCCA 145; *Rhys-Williams v Rhys-Williams,* 2023 BCSC 164; *Healey v Healey,* 2024 BCCA 68; *Chiasson v Doucet,* 2014 NBCA 49 at para 9; *CRP v NDP,* 2023 NBKB 197; *Ward v Murphy,* 2022 NSCA 20; *Bak v Dobell,* 2007 ONCA 304; *Korman v Korman,* 2015 ONCA 578; *Le v Nguyen,* 2022 ONSC 6265; *Madi v King,* 2023 ONCA 443; *Walker v Walker,* 2019 SKCA 96; *Goertzen v Goertzen,* 2024 SKCA 45 at para 90.

432 *VKG v IG,* 2023 ONSC 6329 at para 259, Chappel J.

433 *CMMR v RWAR,* 2011 NBQB 159; *Favero v Favero,* 2013 ONSC 4216; *Korman v Korman,* 2015 ONCA 578.

consistent with the rationale underlying section 19(1) and the objectives set out in section 1 of the Guidelines.[434] It has been judicially asserted that in order to expand the circumstances in which income may be imputed to an obligor, the circumstances should bear some similarity to the enumerated circumstances in section 19 of the Guidelines. These circumstances fall into two categories: (1) those related to external factors such as income tax laws and (2) those related to the conduct of the obligor, such as underemployment, failure to provide income information, or the unreasonable deduction of expenses from income.[435] In *C v S*, Tuck J of the New Brunswick Court of Queen's Bench stated:

> 57 There are other circumstances other than those enumerated in the *Guidelines* which may give rise to an imputation of income. I believe how closely said circumstances relate to or are similar to the enumerated circumstances in Section 19 is certainly a factor to consider. However I believe more germane to whether a particular set of circumstances may lead to an imputation of income would be an examination of said circumstances in their entirety and in their context to see if they appropriately support an inference that would lead to an appropriate imputation of income. In short, common sense should be the viewfinder through which such decisions are formulated. A holistic approach should be adopted.
>
> 58 For example, besides the circumstances enumerated in Section 19 there may be appropriately an imputation of income when one receives a benefit. Considerations as to whether such a benefit should result in an imputation of income may include considerations such as:
>
> - By receiving the benefit, does it replace items that would have in probability been purchased anyways?
> - Is the benefit a luxury item that would not have been acquired by the payor with their income if it had not been conferred on or given to them?
> - In short, does the receipt of the benefit free up income for child support purposes? Does the receipt of any benefit lead to the provision of a pool of funds appropriately accessible for income that would be income for child support purposes?[436]

Losses from risky stock investments, though deductible from a parent's taxable income, may be added back into the parent's income under the Guidelines by way of a judicial imputation of income to the parent.[437] It may, in a particular fact situation, be appropriate to attribute income to a spouse or former spouse on the basis of significant capital assets,[438] although it is important to recognize that any substantial diminution of the capital assets may in the long term reduce the income generated by them. Accordingly, any imputation of income

---

434 *Lobo v Lobo*, [1999] AJ No 113 (QB); *Charles v Charles*, [1999] BCJ No 395 (SC); *Fong v Fong*, 2010 MBQB 5; *DLM v JAM*, 2008 NBCA 2; *Slater v Slater*, 2010 NSSC 353; *Beilstein v Beilstein*, [1999] NWTJ No 34 (SC); *Bak v Dobell*, 2007 ONCA 304; *Trang v Trang*, 2013 ONSC 1980; *Chace v Chace*, [1998] PEIJ No 64 (TD); *McGowan v McGowan*, [2003] SJ No 515 (QB); see also *MWM v HLM*, 2010 NBCA 86; *AVR v MJA*, 2016 SKQB 272.

435 *SAC v SEC*, 2015 MBQB 61 (criminal conduct); *Bowes v Bowes*, 2021 NLCA 10 at para 36; *Risen v Risen*, [1998] OJ No 3184 (Gen Div); *Bak v Dobell*, 2007 ONCA 304 (family gifts excluded from parent's income); *MAK v KAB*, [2000] PEIJ No 8 (SC); *McGowan v McGowan*, [2003] SJ No 515 (QB).

436 2010 NBQB 252; see also *VC v PR*, 2016 NBQB 90 at para 143.

437 *McGowan v McGowan*, [2003] SJ No 515 (QB).

438 *Bushell v Bushell*, [2000] AJ No 1499 (QB) (income imputed to parent on sale of business by grossing up non-taxable non-competition lump sum payment after spreading it over a three-year period).

from this source must attempt to take account of the financial needs of the children while minimally impairing the continued ability of the supporting parent to generate long-term income from the assets.[439] An adverse inference may arise from non-disclosure of income quite apart from any express provision found in the *Federal Child Support Guidelines*.[440]

Future earning potential may result in the imputation of income.[441] An order may be graduated to reflect imputed future income based on a perceived earning potential and the court may reserve the right to make a retroactive adjustment if the obligor finds more remunerative employment than anticipated.[442] A student loan does not resemble any of the circumstances that may warrant an imputation of income under sections 19(1)(a) to (i) of the Guidelines and the obligation to repay the loan may be properly regarded as of fundamental importance in determining that it does not constitute income for the purpose of applying section 7 of the Guidelines.[443] Income may be judicially imputed to a parent whose employer provides subsidized accommodation.[444]

3) Evidence

Section 19 of the Guidelines does not require a court to impute income; it confers a discretion on the court to do so in circumstances where the court finds it appropriate.[445] The onus is on the person requesting an imputation of income to establish an evidentiary basis for such a finding[446] but this does not relieve the parent against whom the imputation of income is sought from making full and complete financial disclosure so as to ensure that the information required to make a decision on the issue is before the court.[447] Once a party seeking the imputation of income presents the evidentiary basis suggesting a *prima facie* case for imputation of income, the onus shifts to the individual seeking to defend the income position he is taking.[448] Imputation of income must be based on evidence and not speculation.[449] A court cannot arbitrarily select an amount as imputed income.[450] Income should not be imputed on the basis of suspicion where relevant evidence is lacking.[451] The court cannot assume facts;

---

439 *Hryhoriw v D'Lugos*, [1997] SJ No 636 (QB).

440 *Ninham v Ninham*, [1997] OJ No 2667 (Gen Div).

441 *Andersen v Andersen*, [1997] BCJ No 2496 (SC); *Ninham v Ninham*, [1997] OJ No 2667 (Gen Div).

442 *Quintal v Quintal*, [1997] OJ No 3444 (Gen Div).

443 *Maynard v Maynard*, [1999] BCJ No 325 (SC).

444 *DMES v WLS*, [2003] MJ No 185 (QB).

445 *Primrose v Hanlon*, [2000] BCJ No 82 (SC); *Monahan-Joudrey v Joudrey*, 2012 ONSC 5984.

446 *Tarapaski v Tarapaski*, 2009 ABCA 365; *DNL v CNS*, 2013 BCSC 858; *Russell v Russell*, 2011 MBQB 274; *MacDonald v MacDonald*, 2016 NSSC 290; *Homsi v Zaya*, 2009 ONCA 322; *Studzinski v Studzinski*, 2020 ONSC 2540; *Morrissey v Morrissey*, 2015 PECA 16; *BNM v PJM*, 2017 SKQB 331.

447 *Mansoor v Mansoor*, 2012 BCSC 602; *Szitas v Szitas*, 2012 ONSC 1548; *Beaudoin v Stevens*, 2023 ONSC 4401; see also *Kaushal v Kaushal*, 2023 ABCA 155 at para 5.

448 *Peters v Atchooay*, 2022 ABCA 347; *Horbas v Horbas*, 2020 MBCA 34 at para 34; *KW v GW*, 2022 NBKB 236; *AD v ME*, 2022 NBKB 249; *SM v JA*, 2023 NLCA 1; *Lo v Lo*, 2011 ONSC 7663; *McKenna v McKenna*, 2015 ONSC 3309; *BNM v PJM*, 2017 SKQB 331.

449 *Heuft v Bramwell*, 2021 ABQB 642; *Piper v Piper*, 2010 BCSC 1718; *Bowes v Bowes*, 2021 NLCA 10.

450 *Horbas v Horbas*, 2020 MBCA 34 at para 39; *McKenna v McKenna*, 2015 ONSC 3309 at para 41, Skarica J; *Yeung v Bui-Yeung*, 2024 SKCA 35 at para 47.

451 *Laflamme v Laflamme*, [1998] AJ No 292 (QB); *JK v DK*, 2010 NBQB 23; *Poff v Fenel*, [1998] SJ No 608 (QB); see also *GF v JACF*, 2016 NBCA 21; *BNM v PJM*, 2017 SKQB 331.

facts must be proven.[452] Courts should take a cautious approach to imputing income on an interim motion.[453] Although a court is not entitled to impute an arbitrary amount of income to the father pursuant to section 19(1) of the *Federal Child Support Guidelines*, the right to child support should not undermine a parent's failure to comply with financial disclosure obligations and unwillingness to engage in court proceedings. In such circumstances, a court may find that a fair and reasonable approach would be to impute the parent's income to be consistent with the increase in the cost of living according to the Bank of Canada Inflation Calculator since the parent's income was last known.[454] A failure to produce documentation or to answer questions respecting corporate benefits received with respect to such things as mortgage payments and automobile expenses may justify an imputation of income.[455] A general authority to impute income to a spouse in certain circumstances is not sufficient to warrant doing so in every case. There must be a rational and solid evidentiary basis that justifies such an imputation,[456] although the burden of adducing evidence about the reasonableness of the income level of a self-employed professional must fall at least in part on the professional who is the only one with the requisite knowledge.[457] An adverse inference may be drawn against a spouse who elects not to rebut presumptive evidence of additional sources of income.[458] Where a litigant is stonewalling or being evasive, a court may impute income based on speculation, but in the absence of such conduct, a court normally requires some evidentiary foundation before income is to be attributed to a spouse. Although a court may take judicial notice of the legal aspects of filing private and corporate income tax returns, the scope of judicial notice does not signify that judges can analyze the finer points of corporate income tax returns without expert assistance. Judges are not entitled to take judicial notice of matters of fact unless they are notorious and the implications of retained corporate earnings fall outside the scope of being notorious facts. Some sort of evidentiary foundation is required before an attribution of income is made in these circumstances.[459] Although a court should refuse to act on unsubstantiated allegations of hidden income in an affidavit filed in support of an interim application for child support, the issue may be further explored at the pre-trial settlement conference or later in the litigation process.[460]

In the absence of adequate financial and business records, the court may take account of circumstantial evidence, such as the parent's lifestyle during matrimonial cohabitation,[461]

---

452 *Anderson v Anderson*, 2010 ABQB 763; *AD v ME*, 2022 NBKB 249.

453 *Moreton v Inthavixay*, 2020 ONSC 4881; *Merrifield v Merrifield*, 2021 SKCA 85.

454 *El Himili v Benmoussa*, 2022 ONSC 5311 at paras 28–29, Somji J; see also *Beaudoin v Stevens*, 2023 ONSC 4401.

455 *Koenen v Koenen*, [2001] AJ No 223 (CA).

456 *Kalchuk v Kalchuk*, [2000] AJ No 813 (QB); *Lafrentz v Palmer*, 2021 BCSC 1332; *Bishop v Bishop*, 2017 MBQB 97; *DLM v JAM*, 2008 NBCA 2; *White v White*, 2015 NSCA 52; *Yhard v Mulvihill*, 2017 NSSC 101; *Scholes v Scholes*, [2003] OJ No 3432 (SCJ) (Ontario Wage Survey relied upon); *Burisch v Gosal*, 2007 ONCA 569; *Cheng v Sze*, 2020 ONSC 937 at para 64; *Farooq v Farooq*, 2023 ONSC 3679; *de Pimentel v Rodriguez*, 2024 ONSC 2844; *Morrissey v Morrissey*, 2015 PECA 16; *Yeung v Bui-Yeung*, 2024 SKCA 35 at para 47.

457 *Gordon v Norris*, 2018 BCSC 188; *West v West*, [2001] OJ No 2149 (SCJ).

458 *Mansoor v Mansoor*, 2012 BCSC 602.

459 *Watkin v Hall*, [1998] MJ No 310 (QB). As to the application of judicial notice of provincial economic conditions as they impact job prospects in the context of a child support claim involving imputed income, see *Locke v Bramwell*, 2016 NSSC 300 at paras 8–18.

460 *Segall v Fellinger*, [1998] SJ No 253 (QB).

461 *Mansoor v Mansoor*, 2012 BCSC 602; *Bishop v Bishop*, 2017 MBQB 97.

credit card charges and bank statements, income disclosure on a mortgage application, and the amount of damages sought for lost wages in an action against the parent's former employer.[462] Statements made in a loan application can be evidence for imputation of income. Imputation of income is a judicial exercise that requires a rational basis. Courts cannot impute income arbitrarily.[464] A failure to provide financial information is inconvenient and aggravating, but section 19 of the Guidelines is not an invitation to judges to pull out of the air any income attribution figure they might fancy. Rule 19.02(1) of the Ontario *Rules of Civil Procedure* provides that a defendant noted in default is deemed to admit all allegations of fact in the statement of claim. Although no similar provision is found in the Rules of the Provincial Division for Family Law Proceedings, failure to defend is a fact that may be considered in determining the respondent's ability to pay child support. Where the applicant acknowledges that the respondent is unemployed, the court may refuse to attribute income to the respondent on the ground that there is no evidence on which income can be imputed.[465] Simply providing a court with statistical information on average earnings from the jurisdiction where the parent resides does not meet the onus to establish the appropriateness or reasonableness of an order imputing income to a parent who fails to appear or file a response.[466]

The evidence of a professional recruiter may be judicially relied upon for the purpose of imputing income to a parent on the basis of intentional unemployment or underemployment under section 19(1) of the *Federal Child Support Guidelines*.[467] An unemployed parent must actively seek out employment. The failure of a husband to provide timely disclosure of efforts to find employment entitles the court to rely on expert testimony called by the wife as to the husband's earning potential.[468] Speaking to the issue of expert evidence as to a parent's income in *Ramlochan v Ramlochan*,[469] Corbett J of the Ontario Superior Court of Justice has stated:

> A court will not accept an expert's opinion solely on the basis of the expert's "authoritative claim." That is, it is not sufficient for an expert to show that (a) she is an expert; (b) she has looked into a matter; (c) she has reached a conclusion; and (d) therefore the court should accept her conclusion. Rather, the expert should explain her assumptions, describe the material evidence and observations upon which the expert relies, describe the analysis and reasoning the expert has used to reach her conclusion, set out her conclusion, including any limitations or qualifications to that conclusion. The opinion is not just the "bottom-line" conclusion, but the entire intellectual exercise of assumptions, evidence, analysis, reasoning, conclusions and limitations and qualifications of that conclusion. It is then possible for the

---

462 *AG v BR*, [2005] BCJ No 127 (SC).

463 *McKenna v McKenna*, 2015 ONSC 3309 at para 146, citing *Lo v Lo*, 2011 ONSC 7663.

464 *Chiasson v Doucet*, 2014 NBCA 49; *Stafford c Stafford*, 2023 NBCA 39; *Johnson v Barker*, 2017 NSCA 53; *Drygala v Pauli* (2002), 29 RFL (5th) 293 (Ont CA). As to the cautious judicial approach to the use of governmental income surveys, see *Jahan v Chowdhury*, 2016 ONCJ 503, citing *Caine v Ferguson*, 2012 ONCJ 139 at para 32.

465 *Fawcett v Hurd*, [1998] OJ No 4345 (Gen Div).

466 *JAL v AAJ*, 2020 YKSC 7 at para 17, Veale J.

467 *Dalgleish v Dalgleish*, [2003] OJ No 2918 (SCJ); see also *TBT v LCG*, [2004] AJ No 289 (QB) (reliance on government website); *JC v BW*, 2024 NSSC 95.

468 *Swanson v Swanson*, [2004] OJ No 5266 (SCJ) (vocational assessment).

469 2010 ONSC 4323.

court to understand and apply the expert's opinion on the basis of the facts, as found by the court, and to weigh competing opinions on contested issues.

4) Earning Capacity; Intentional Underemployment or Unemployment

Section 19(1)(a) of the *Federal Child Support Guidelines* confers a discretion[470] on the court to impute such income as it deems appropriate to a spouse who "is intentionally under-employed or unemployed, other than where the underemployment or unemployment is required by the needs of a child of the marriage or any child under the age of majority or by reasonable educational or health needs of the spouse."[471] Appellate courts in British Columbia,[472] Manitoba,[473] New Brunswick,[474] Newfoundland and Labrador,[475] Nova Scotia,[476] Ontario,[477] Quebec,[478] and Saskatchewan[479] have long concluded that section 19(1)(a) of the Guidelines is not confined to circumstances where a parent deliberately seeks to evade his or her child support obligations or recklessly disregards his or her children's financial needs while pursuing his or her personal choice of employment or lifestyle. Although such deliberate or reckless conduct, where it exists, weighs heavily in the exercise of the court's discretion to impute income

---

470 *SDM v KFM*, [2004] BCJ No 67 (SC); *Kochar v Kochar*, 2014 ONSC 3220; *Algner v Algner*, [2008] SJ No 182 (QB).

471 See Rollie Thompson, "Slackers, Shirkers, and Career-Changers: Imputing Income for Under-Employment and Unemployment" in The Law Society of Upper Canada, *Special Lectures 2006: Family Law* (Toronto: Irwin Law, 2007) 153–82, (2007) 26 *Family Law Quarterly* 135; Lorne MacLean, Fraser MacLean, Kaye Booth & Oliver Spinks, "COVID-19 and Canadian Spousal and Child Support: There Is a Light at the End of the Tunnel but How Long Is the Tunnel?" County of Carleton Law Association, Annual Institute of Family Law 2021, 23 March 2021, Ottawa. As to the imputation of income to a parent on the basis of intentional underemployment or unemployment pursuant to s 19(1)(a) of the *Federal Child Support Guidelines* in the post-COVID pandemic era, see the judgment of Dewolfe Fam Ct J in *RC v AL*, 2021 NSFC 01. And see *Bowes v Bowes*, 2021 NLCA 10 at para 77, Butler JA. As to the impact of COVID-19 on averaging annual income over three years under s 17 of the *Federal Child Support Guidelines*, see *ARJ v ZSH*, 2021 BCSC 274; *Church v Church*, 2021 MBQB 20 at paras 20–21. See also *McClelland v Harrison*, 2021 ABCA 89. As to imputing income on the basis of a parent's refusal to be vaccinated against COVID-19, see *Lyons v Lyons*, 2022 SKQB 70 (interim spousal support order); see also *Almon v Hill*, 2022 NSSC 310. For an excellent summary of principles relating to the judicial imputation of income on the basis of intentional unemployment or underemployment, see the judgment of Pazaratz J in *Abumatar v Hamda*, 2021 ONSC 2165 at para 28; see also *Lavoie v Lavoie*, 2024 ABCA 85 (shared parenting); *Evans v Evans*, 2023 ONSC 3919 at para 77.

472 *Van Gool v Van Gool*, [1998] BCJ No 2513 (CA); *TK v RJHA*, 2015 BCCA 8; *Beissner v Matheusik*, 2015 BCCA 308.

473 *Donovan v Donovan*, [2000] MJ No 407 (CA); *Schindle v Schindle*, [2001] MJ No 564 (CA); *Steele v Koppanyi*, [2002] MJ No 201 (CA).

474 *DLM v JAM*, 2008 NBCA 2; *JF v GF*, 2016 NBQB 46.

475 *Duffy v Duffy*, 2009 NLCA 48. See also *DB v HMB*, 2019 NLSC 105.

476 *Montgomery v Montgomery*, [2000] NSJ No 1 (CA); see also *Smith v Helppi*, 2011 NSCA 65.

477 *Drygala v Pauli* (2002), 29 RFL (5th) 293 (CA); *Riel v Holland*, [2003] OJ No 3901 (CA); *Akkawi v Habli*, 2017 ONSC 6124; *Lavie v Lavie*, 2018 ONCA 10. For an excellent summary of relevant principles and Ontario caselaw, see *Tillmanns v Tillmanns*, 2014 ONSC 6773 at paras 48–81; *Verhey v Verhey*, 2017 ONSC 2216; *Templeton v Nuttall*, 2018 ONSC 815; *McBennett v Danis*, 2021 ONSC 3610. And see *Yeung v Silva*, 2016 BCSC 1682 at paras 43–52, Dardi J.

478 *Droit de la famille — 1275*, 2012 QCCA 87; *Droit de la famille — 133554*, 2013 QCCA 2176.

479 *Pontius v Murray*, 2011 SKCA 121; *Pellegrini v Tkach*, 2023 SKCA 85, leave to appeal denied 2024 CanLII 25741 (SCC).

to a parent, the proper test for the judicial imputation of income to a parent pursuant to section 19(1)(a) of the Guidelines is perceived in the aforementioned appellate judgments as being a test of reasonableness. According to this criterion, the court must have regard to the parent's capacity to earn in light of such factors as employment history, age, education, skills, health, available employment opportunities, and the standard of living enjoyed during the marriage.[480] In *Peters v Atchooay*,[481] a five-member panel of the Alberta Court of Appeal, revisited *Hunt v Smolis-Hunt*,[482] wherein the Alberta Court of Appeal, by a majority of 2:1, had concluded that the judicial imputation of income under section 19(1)(a) of the *Federal Child Support Guidelines* is confined to circumstances where a parent deliberately seeks to evade child support obligations through their choice of employment or lifestyle. After a detailed review of *Smolis-Hunt* and relevant caselaw across Canada, the Alberta Court of Appeal in *Peters v Atchooay* rejected the deliberate evasion test and endorsed the reasonableness as exemplified by the following summary of section 19(1)(a) principles:

> [92] The following is a non-exhaustive list of principles to guide the determination of whether to impute income under s 19(1)(a):
>
> 1. *General Duty to Work*. There is a duty to seek employment where a parent is healthy and can work. A parent's limited work experience or job skills do not justify a failure to pursue lower skilled employment or employment in which the necessary skills can be learned on the job. While this may mean a job at the lower end of the wage scale, parents cannot refuse to take reasonable steps to support their children simply because they cannot obtain interesting or highly paid employment. Nor can a high-earning or highly skilled parent refuse employment indefinitely by holding out for employment commensurate with their skills and previous level of earning, job title or seniority.
> 2. *Earning Capacity Used to Assess Reasonableness*. When determining whether to impute income on the basis of under-employment or unemployment, a court must consider what is reasonable in the circumstances. The starting point is the payor's earning capacity, which is the objective measure by which the reasonableness of the parent's decision or conduct is assessed. Earning capacity is determined based on factors like age, education, experience, skills, and health of the payor, along with availability of work, the freedom to relocate, and other obligations.
> 3. *Discretion*. Income will not be imputed where a parent's decision to earn less than the maximum they are capable of making is found to be reasonable. Nor is there a presumption that a career choice resulting in a reduction in income is unreasonable.
> 4. *Obligation to Support Children is the Overarching Goal*. The reasons for under-employment or unemployment must be objectively scrutinized. A parent is required to act in a manner reflective of his or her obligations and cannot be excused from support obligations in furtherance of unrealistic, unproductive or non-remunerative career aspirations. Persistence in unremunerative employment or repeated education initiatives may also entitle the court to impute income. Parental self-fulfillment is a consideration but does not trump child support requirements.

480 For an excellent summary of the principles applicable under s 19(1)(a) of the *Federal Child Support Guidelines*, see *Algner v Algner*, [2008] SJ No 182 (QB), cited with approval in *Pellegrini v Tkach*, 2023 SKCA 85, leave to appeal denied 2024 CanLII 25741 (SCC).

481 2022 ABCA 347; see also *Khan v Khan*, 2022 ABCA 370; *Kaser v Kaser*, 2023 ABKB 6.

482 2001 ABCA 229.

5. *Agreements Contextualize Reasonableness.* The parties' pre-separation agreements or social contracts have some weight in determining *Guidelines* income, but they are not determinative. The parenting arrangement, and the payor's involvement or lack of involvement with the children, the length or time the arrangement has been in place, and the ages of the children may be considered in assessing the reasonableness of the payor's under-employment or unemployment.
6. *Reasonableness Is Not Fixed in Time.* The payor's history of paying child support and providing financial disclosure are objective measures by which to assess the reasonableness of the payor's employment decision or conduct. What is reasonable (or unreasonable) is determined at one point in time and will not necessarily remain static for the entire time the children are owed support.
7. *The Ultimate Onus Rests on the Party Opposing Imputation.* Assuming the financial disclosure requirements have been met, the onus is on the party opposing imputation to prove on a balance of probabilities: 1) that the under-employment or unemployment was not voluntary, that is, not due to their own decision or conduct; or, 2) that the under-employment or unemployment is as a result of one of the listed exceptions in s 19(1)(a). If neither circumstance applies, that party must establish on a balance of probabilities that their under-employment or unemployment is reasonable, having regard to all the existing circumstances. However, where it is an initial application, the person seeking an imputation of income under s 19(1)(a) has a preliminary onus to establish some basis for the imputation sought. Either way, each stage of the analysis requires evidence that is as objective as possible. Bare assertions will not suffice.

[93] On the issue of amount, a court cannot choose an arbitrary number; "there must be a rational basis underlying the selection of any such figure ... grounded in the evidence".... However, if a reasonable figure can be determined in between earning capacity and actual earnings that is grounded in the evidence, it may be the more appropriate amount to impute in circumstances where the payor's actual income is unreasonable.[483]

Once unemployment or underemployment is established against a parent, the onus shifts to that parent to prove one of the exceptions under section 19(1)(a) of the Guidelines.[484] In determining whether unemployment or underemployment is required by virtue of a parent's reasonable education needs, the following questions should be considered:

(a) How many courses must be taken and when?
(b) How much time must be devoted in and out of the classroom to ensure continuation in the program?
(c) Are the academic demands such that the spouse is excused from pursuing part-time work? Could the program be completed over a longer period with the spouse taking fewer courses so that the spouse could obtain part-time employment?

483 *Peters v Atchooay*, 2022 ABCA 347 at paras 92–93; see also *Lavoie v Lavoie*, 2024 ABCA 85 (shared parenting); *Shumate v Patrick*, 2023 ABKB 98; *Ma v Xu*, 2023 ABKB 346; *Mohamud v Abdullahi*, 2023 ABKB 371; *Yu v Zhu*, 2024 ABKB 154; *CP v AP*, 2024 ABKB 334; *LKB v JG*, 2023 NBQB 90.

484 *Cowan v Cowan*, 2018 ONSC 2495 at para 25, citing *Ffrench v Williams*, 2016 ONCJ 105.

(d) If the rigours of the program preclude part-time employment during the regular academic school year, is summer employment reasonably expected?
(e) Can the spouse take cooperative courses as part of the program and earn some income in that way?[485]

In *Donovan v Donovan*,[486] Steel JA of the Manitoba Court of Appeal endorsed the fol lowing six principles as relevant when determining whether income should be imputed to a parent pursuant to section 19(1)(a) of the *Federal Child Support Guidelines*:

1. There is a duty to seek employment in a case where a parent is healthy and there is no reason why the parent cannot work. It is "no answer for a person liable to support a child to say he is unemployed and does not intend to seek work or that his potential to earn income is an irrelevant factor" (*Van Gool v. Van Gool*[487]).
2. When imputing income on the basis of intentional under-employment, a court must consider what is reasonable under the circumstances. The age, education, experience, skills and health of the parent are factors to be considered in addition to such matters as availability of work, freedom to relocate and other obligations.
3. A parent's limited work experience and job skills do not justify a failure to pursue employment that does not require significant skills, or employment in which the necessary skills can be learned on the job. While this may mean that job availability will be at the lower end of the wage scale, courts have never sanctioned the refusal of a parent to take reasonable steps to support his or her children simply because the parent cannot obtain interesting or highly paid employment.[488]
4. Persistence in unremunerative employment may entitle the court to impute income.
5. A parent cannot be excused from his or her child support obligations in furtherance of unrealistic or unproductive career aspirations.
6. As a general rule, a parent cannot avoid child support obligations by a self-induced reduction of income.

And as Steel JA of the Manitoba Court of Appeal further observed in *Donovan v Don ovan*, "the concept of reasonableness must be assessed in light of the joint ongoing legal obligations of the parents to maintain their children."[489]

---

485 See *Sweeney v Sweeney*, 2018 ONSC 6499 at para 15.

486 (2000), 150 Man R (2d) 116 at para 21 (CA). See also *Hanson v Hanson*, [1999] BCJ No 2532 (SC); *Watts v Willie*, [2004] BCJ No 2482 (CA); *Beissner v Matheusik*, 2015 BCCA 308; *SGW v JDF*, 2023 BCSC 1851; *Rana v Rana*, 2024 BCSC 49; *Campbell v Campbell*, 2014 MBCA 104; *Horbas v Horbas*, 2020 MBCA 34; *Blanchard v Maxwell*, 2022 MBQB 113; *DLM v JAM*, 2008 NBCA 2; *MM v MS*, 2021 NBQB 183; *Moody v Holden*, 2015 NLTD(F) 45; *Smith v Helppi*, 2011 NSCA 65; *SM-M v SM*, 2022 NSSC 256; *IC v MC*, 2023 NSSC 170; *Hawkins v Hawkins*, 2019 ONSC 7149; *DBB v DMB*, 2017 SKCA 59; *Pellegrini v Tkach*, 2023 SKCA 85, leave to appeal denied 2024 CanLII 25741 (SCC). For a more detailed summary of the principles applicable under s 19(1)(a) of the *Federal Child Support Guidelines*, see *Algner v Algner*, [2008] SJ No 182 (QB); see also *Daniel-DeFreitas v Francis*, 2012 ONSC 515 at paras 57–58.

487 (1998), 113 BCAC 200 (CA).

488 See *KAL v KJL*, 2017 BCSC 651.

489 2000 MBCA 80 at para 20, cited with approval in *Gallant v Houde*, 2017 BCCA 391. See also *Horbas v Horbas*, 2020 MBCA 34 at para 25.

Delivering the opinion of the Newfoundland and Labrador Court of Appeal in *Duffy v Duffy*,[490] Welsh JA elicited the following principles from relevant caselaw dealing with the judicial imputation of income to a parent under the *Federal Child Support Guidelines*:

1. The fundamental obligation of a parent to support his or her children takes precedence over the parent's own interests and choices.
2. A parent will not be permitted to knowingly avoid or diminish, and may not choose to ignore, his or her obligation to support his or her children.
3. A parent is required to act responsibly when making financial decisions that may affect the level of child support available from that parent.
4. Imputing income to a parent on the basis that the parent is "intentionally under-employed or unemployed" does not incorporate a requirement for proof of bad faith. "Intentionally" in this context clarifies that the provision does not apply to situations beyond the parent's control.
5. The determination to impute income is discretionary, as the court considers appropriate in the circumstances.
6. Where a parent is intentionally under-employed or unemployed, the court may exercise its discretion not to impute income where that parent establishes the reasonableness of his or her decision.[491]
7. A parent will not be excused from his or her child support obligations in furtherance of unrealistic or unproductive career aspirations or interests. Nor will it be acceptable for a parent to choose to work for future rewards to the detriment of the present needs of his or her children, unless the parent establishes the reasonableness of his or her course of action.
8. A parent must provide proper and full disclosure of financial information. Failure to do so may result in the court drawing an adverse inference and imputing income.

Justice of Appeal Welsh further stated that the amount of imputed income must be supported by the evidence, although some degree of imprecision may be inevitable.

And in *Pretty v Pretty*,[492] Forgeron J of the Nova Scotia Supreme Court distilled the following principles from the caselaw:

a. The discretionary authority found in s. 19 must be exercised judicially, and in accordance with rules of reasons and justice — not arbitrarily. A rational and solid evidentiary foundation, grounded in fairness and reasonableness, must be shown before a court can impute income: *Coadic v. Coadic*.[493]

490 2009 NLCA 48 at para 35; see also *Drover v Drover*, 2020 NLCA 9; *Bowes v Bowes*, 2021 NLCA 10; *Fincham v Fincham*, 2017 ONSC 4279; *Cowan v Cowan*, 2018 ONSC 2495.

491 See also *Horbas v Horbas*, 2020 MBCA 34 at para 28.

492 2011 NSSC 296 at para 72; see also *Campbell v Campbell*, 2016 MBQB 57, citing *MacDonald v Pink*, 2011 NSSC 421 at para 24; *Ducharme v Ducharme*, 2019 MBQB 72; *Abbott v Abbott*, 2014 NLTD(F) 2; *McIntyre v Veinot*, 2016 NSSC 8; *JC v BW*, 2024 NSSC 95 at para 77.

493 2005 NSSC 291; see also *White v White*, 2015 NSCA 52; *CAV v LCM*, 2020 NSSC 168; *NK v RE*, 2021 NSSC 13.

b. The goal of imputation is to arrive at a fair estimate of income, not to arbitrarily punish the payor: *Staples v. Callender*.[494]

c. The burden of establishing that income should be imputed rests upon the party making the claim, however, the evidentiary burden shifts if the payor asserts that his/her income is less than in prior years, or if ill health, or the needs of a child are advanced to justify the unemployment or under-employment: *MacDonald v. MacDonald*;[495] *MacGillivary v. Ross*.[496]

d. The court is not restricted to actual income earned, but rather, may look to income earning capacity, having regard to subjective factors such as the payor's age, health, education, skills, employment history, and other relevant factors. The court should look to what is reasonable and fair in the circumstances: *Van Gool v. Van Gool*;[497] *Hanson v. Hanson*;[498] *Saunders-Roberts v. Roberts*;[499] and *Duffy v. Duffy*.[500]

e. A party's decision to remain in an unremunerative employment situation, may entitle a court to impute income where the party has a greater income earning capacity. A party cannot avoid support obligations by a self-induced reduction in income. A party cannot be relieved of support obligations to further an unrealistic or unproductive career: *Marshall v. Marshall*;[501] and *Duffy v. Duffy*.[502]

A three-step analysis of section 19(1)(a) of the *Federal Child Support Guidelines* has been judicially endorsed. First, the court must determine whether the parent is intentionally underemployed or unemployed. Bad faith or an improper purpose is not necessary to estab lish that the respondent's unemployment is intentional. Second, if the parent is intentionally underemployed or unemployed, the court must determine whether that is justified by the needs of a child of the marriage, by the needs of any child under the age of majority, or by the reasonable educational or health needs of the parent. Third, if none of these exceptions apply, then the court must decide whether to exercise its discretion and impute income to the parent.[503] While a parent may be justified in taking early retirement due to the cumulative effect of physical ailments and stress associated with his former employment, income may be imputed to that parent where he can be reasonably expected to pursue some form of less stressful employment.[504] A parent who decides to change his or her career and thereby suffers a substantial drop in income must be able to explain why the decision was reasonable under

---

494 2010 NSCA 49.

495 2010 NSCA 34.

496 2008 NSSC 339; see also *O'Connor v Merlo*, 2020 ONSC 2531 at paras 60–61.

497 (1998), 113 BCAC 200.

498 [1999] BCJ No 2532 (SC); see also *Gordon v Norris*, 2018 BCSC 188; *Yhard v Mulvihill*, 2017 NSSC 101.

499 2002 NWTSC 11.

500 2009 NLCA 48.

501 2008 NSSC 11.

502 2009 NLCA 48.

503 *Drygala v Pauli* (2002), 29 RFL (5th) 293 (Ont CA); see also *Lavoie v Lavoie*, 2024 ABCA 85 (shared parenting); *RTC v NMC*, 2021 BCSC 2273; *Kopp v Burke*, 2014 MBQB 247; *BC v MC*, 2011 NBQB 285; *Bowes v Bowes*, 2021 NLCA 10; *Dalton v Clements*, 2016 NSSC 38; *Terracol v Terracol*, 2012 ONSC 2801; *O'Connor v Merlo*, 2020 ONSC 2531 at paras 60–61; *Beisel v Henderson*, [2004] SJ No 413 (QB); *Rafan v Rauf*, 2020 SKQB 107; *MAB v HIL*, 2010 YKSC 8.

504 *Kopp v Burke*, 2014 MBQB 247; *BC v MC*, 2011 NBQB 285; *Beisel v Henderson*, [2004] SJ No 413 (QB).

the circumstances; absent such an explanation, income may be imputed to that parent.[505] A court may also impute income to a parent whose change of career was triggered by dismissal from previous employment because of professional misconduct.[506] An obligor will not be permitted to voluntarily earn less income in order to pay less support, and if income is lacking, may be required to make up the deficiency out of means other than income.[507] Income may be imputed to a parent who refuses to pay court ordered child support and uses his very substantial capital in lieu of income to live on.[508] It is not for a court to dictate a person's future employment but the earning capacity of a spouse should be measured against what is reasonable in light of his or her background, education, training, and work experience.[509] The decision-making freedom of a separated or divorced spouse should not be held to a higher standard than that of a spouse in an intact marriage. However, the fact that an ex-spouse is unlikely to have any significant input in the decision places the burden squarely on a support paying separated or divorced spouse to make a decision to accept financial change that can be justified as being reasonable in light of his responsibilities to his dependants.[510] Where there is no available market for a parent's specialized accreditation, that parent must look at other viable options and take reasonable steps to secure employment commensurate with his or her age, health, education, skills, and work history.[511] A court should not impute additional income to a parent who changes his or her employment for legitimate reasons. In addressing the issue of alleged intentional underemployment, the court should take into consideration: (1) the capacity of the parent to work or to be trained for work; (2) the steps the parent has already taken to obtain employment commensurate with such factors as age, state of health, education, skills, and work history; (3) the litigation history itself; and (4) the relationship between the parties.[512] If underemployment is established, the onus is on the underemployed spouse to establish that his or her "educational plan is a reasonable one."[513]

A court should refuse to impute income to a parent whose earning capacity is impaired by a disability.[514] Income may be judicially imputed to a disabled parent whose personal injury settlement partially reflects lost earning capacity, where the applicant for child support has no entitlement to share in the settlement by way of a court-ordered property distribution.[515] A court may refuse to impute income where the obligor took advantage of new "temporary absence" provisions of employment because of family-related stress.[516] A parent, who claims

505 *Williams v Williams*, [2007] NJ No 257 (UFC); *Everill v Everill*, [2005] NSJ No 37 (SC); *Cole v Cole*, [2005] OJ No 5191 (SCJ); *Algner v Algner*, [2008] SJ No 182 (QB).

506 *Stadnyk v Stadnyk*, [2004] SJ No 355 (QB).

507 *Baker v Baker* (1990), 27 RFL (3d) 76 (BCCA); *Sarchfield v Sarchfield* (1990), 103 NBR (2d) 81 (QB), rev'd (1990), 109 NBR (2d) 335 (CA).

508 *Fraser v Fraser*, 2012 ONSC 685.

509 *IG v LG*, [2000] AJ No 113 (QB); *Desrochers v Desrochers*, [2004] BCJ No 1465 (SC); *B-JG v BD*, 2023 NBKB 30; *Yar v Yar*, 2015 ONSC 151; *Hein v Hein*, 2009 SKQB 23.

510 *Rondeau v Kirby*, [2003] NSJ No 436 (SC), aff'd [2004] NSJ No 143 (CA); see also *Taylor v Taylor*, [2009] AJ No 22 (QB).

511 *Kolada v Kolada*, [1999] AJ No 609 (QB); *MacLean v MacLean*, [2003] PEIJ No 16 (TD).

512 *Cherry v Cherry*, [2004] OJ No 2881 (SCJ).

513 *Galpin v Galpin*, 2018 BCSC 1572.

514 *Tapper v Connolly*, [2002] NJ No 83 (SC). Compare *Hutchison v Gretzinger*, [2007] OJ No 5058 (SCJ) (drug addiction). See also *Dunbar v Saunders*, 2021 BCSC 193.

515 *Neufeld v Neufeld*, [2001] BCJ No 1682 (SC); see also *Parkes v Mones*, [2001] SJ No 777 (QB).

516 *Peters v Peters*, [1999] SJ No 392 (QB).

that his or her earning potential is impaired by ill health, has the burden of establishing a meaningful link between his or her health and the underemployment or unemployment. A parent who asserts a continued inability or reduced ability to earn income because of an ongoing medical condition has the burden of proving that on the balance of probabilities. In most cases, that will require opinion evidence from a properly qualified medical expert. In the words of London-Weinstein J, of the Ontario Superior Court of Justice, in *Mansour v Hassan*:

> The following considerations must be considered where the purported reason for the under employment or unemployment is based on a health concern:
>
> - There is a duty to seek employment in a case where a person is healthy, *Drygala, supra.*
> - A health limitation may constitute a reasonable explanation for unemployment or under employment. The onus rests on the party advancing this explanation to provide evidence both as to the nature and magnitude of the health problem; and also the connection between the health issue and the person's capacity to earn any income. *Cogent medical evidence in the form of a detailed medical opinion should be provided by the payor in order to satisfy the court that the reasonable health needs justify a decision not to work. Stoangi v. Petersen,* 2006 CanLII 24124 (SCJ).
> - The payor must establish that any medical excuse for being underemployed is reasonable. *Rilli v. Rilli,* 2006 CanLII 34451 (SCJ).
> - Support pay[o]rs must make reasonable efforts to address whatever medical limitations they may have to earn income. This means following up on medical recommendations to address those limitations. C.V. *v* S.G., 2019 ONCJ 159 (OCJ).
> - In considering the amount of income to be imputed, the court should consider the payor's capacity to earn an income when taking into consideration their age, education, health, work history and availability of work that is within the scope of their capabilities. *Crowe v. McIntyre,* 2014 ONSC 7106 at para 29.
> - In assessing the imputation of income, the evidentiary basis for that assessment may be less than complete, as long as it is enough to permit the court to exercise its discretion in rendering a decision. *Balanco v. Grummett,* 2022 SCC 37 at paras 96, 99 and 121.[519]

Problems of proof may arise when an alleged lack of earning capacity is attributed to ill health. Even if medical opinion is submitted in support of the allegation, a judge may be uncertain of the merits of the allegation. In some cases, doubt can be resolved by an order for the production of past and present medical records that may contain information to sub stantiate or refute the allegation.[520] In other cases, this is not feasible. In that event, a judge may order a stay of proceedings until such time as an applicant undergoes a physical and/ or mental examination before a non-partisan qualified medical practitioner or specialist. A similar approach may be adopted when a defaulting spouse seeks to explain the non

---

517 *Mitansky v Mitansky,* [2000] AJ No 179 (QB); *MacGillivary v Ross,* 2008 NSSC 339; *Fisher v Rogers,* 2012 ONSC 669.

518 *Marino v Marino,* 2008 BCSC 1402; *Klein v Klein,* 2019 SKQB 268.

519 *Mansour v Hassan,* 2023 ONSC 2054 at para 15 (emphasis added).

520 *Hallworth v Hallworth* (1987), 14 BCLR (2d) 209 (SC); *Latimer v Latimer* (1979), 24 OR (2d) 134 (Ont HCJ).

521 *Proctor v Proctor* (1979), 26 OR 394 (Div Ct), aff'd (1980), 28 OR (2d) 776n (CA).

payment of support by reason of alleged ill health affecting the financial ability to pay. The failure to undergo an examination would warrant an adverse inference being drawn against the defaulter.[522] A parent's imprisonment due to his abuse of one of his children impacts his current capacity to pay child support but not his obligation to the children who would be financially penalized, but enforcement of his child support obligations may be suspended during his incarceration and for a designated period thereafter. Such wilful misconduct is no different than a parent's misuse of alcohol or drugs that other courts have equated to intentional underemployment.[523]

Income may be judicially imputed to a parent on the basis of intentional underemployment within the meaning of section 19(1)(a) of the *Federal Child Support Guidelines* where he retrained for employment following an injury sustained in the workplace but failed to provide evidence of any attempt to find higher income employment that reflected his new qualifications.[524]

Imputing income under section 19(1)(a) of the *Federal Child Support Guidelines* provides a means whereby a court requires parents to realize their full earning capacity so as to discharge their joint and ongoing obligation to support their child pursuant to section 26.1(2) of the *Divorce Act*. Section 19(1)(a) of the *Federal Child Support Guidelines* authorizes a court to impute income only when the parent is intentionally underemployed or intentionally unemployed. A parent is intentionally underemployed when that parent chooses to earn less than he or she is capable of earning. A parent is intentionally unemployed when he or she chooses not to work, when capable of doing so. Income should not be imputed when a change of employment was reasonable. Reasonableness is to be assessed in light of the joint parental obligation to support the children and the legal duty of a parent to realize his or her full earning capacity. There are two aspects of earning capacity. The first relates to the parent's qualifications, including such factors as age, education, experience, skills, and health. The second relates to such matters as the availability of work, freedom to relocate, and other obligations.[525] Not every voluntary change of employment that results in a reduced income is unreasonable

---

522 Compare *McIntosh v McIntosh* (1985), 46 RFL (2d) 249 at 260 (BCSC), citing *Levesque v Comeau*, [1970] SCR 1010.

523 *Billingsley v Billingsley*, 2010 ONSC 3381; see also *DCC v DWC*, 2022 CarswellNB 645 (KB), discussed in Franks & Zalev, "This Week in Family Law," 10 April 2023 (Thomson Reuters); and see *CP v AP*, 2024 ABKB 334; *NDS v JAS*, 2020 BCSC 1034; *Rideout v Woodman*, 2016 NSSC 205; *Saunders-Roberts v Roberts*, 2002 NWTSC 11; *Haggis v Sokolski*, 2023 ONSC 469; and compare *Sheridan v Cupido*, 2018 ONSC 5817 at paras 13–16 (imprisonment; refusal to impute income on interim application); *Cote v Taylor*, 2013 ONSC 5428 (imprisonment; refusal to impute income). And see *Henderson-Jorgensen v Henderson-Jorgensen*, 2013 ABQB 213 (alcohol addiction); *MSB v LMB*, 2012 BCPC 520 (cocaine addiction); *Wong v Wong*, 2012 NSSC 430; *Walpole v Walpole*, 2012 ONSC 2731 (spousal support). As to whether addiction should be considered a disability or a matter of choice with respect to the imputation of income on the basis of intentional unemployment or underemployment within the meaning of s 19(1)(a) of the *Child Support Guidelines*, see the comprehensive review of relevant caselaw in the judgment of Malfair J in *SMR v ELM*, 2019 BCPC 236.

524 *Lowe v Lowe*, [2006] OJ No 128 (SCJ).

525 *Hanson v Hanson*, [1999] BCJ No 2532 (SC); *Barker v Barker*, 2005 BCCA 177; *QP v QN*, 2017 BCSC 400; *Houghton v Houghton*, [2000] MJ No 298 (QB); *MAA v JMA*, 2011 NBQB 298; *Hackett v Hackett*, [2001] NJ No 317 (SC); *Smith v Helppi*, 2011 NSCA 65; *Tybring v Tybring*, [2003] NWTJ No 81 (SC); *Daniel-DeFreitas v Francis*, 2012 ONSC 515 at para 58; *Grenier v Imbeault*, 2018 ONSC 6467; *Molnar v Bruton*, 2013 SKQB 301.

and thus "intentional" for the purpose of section 19(1)(a) of the Guidelines. Section 19(1) of the Guidelines, when read in conjunction with section 26.1(2) of the *Divorce Act*, confers a broad discretion on the court to determine the appropriate circumstances in which to impute income; such a determination is made on a case-by-case basis.[526] Where insufficient time has passed to permit a determination to be made whether there has been a significant and long lasting change of income and the parent has failed to provide full financial disclosure, a court may decline to order an income-based reduction in the amount of child support by way of a variation order, although a reduction may be warranted where one of the children of the marriage has taken up residence with the payor for a specified period.[527]

It is not a function of the court to mandate a business plan but the court may impute additional income to a parent whose business plan generates unnecessarily high expenses and also reduces the parent's earning capacity below its reasonable potential.[528] A parent is not entitled to persist in relatively unremunerative business activities and then seek variation of an existing child support order on the basis of his significantly reduced income earning capacity after an involuntary termination of previous employment, where that parent can reasonably be expected to upgrade his skills to find suitable employment albeit at a some what lower wage than that previously earned.[529]

A court may impute income to the recipient on the basis that he is "intentionally under-employed or unemployed" within the meaning of section 19(1)(a) of the Guidelines where he chooses to live frugally by depleting his capital rather than seeking out employment for which he is qualified.[530]

A parent is not required to work more than full time to fulfill the duty to support his children[531] but a parent who chooses to work less than a regular work week must justify that choice by the needs of the children or suffer the loss personally.[532]

A parent's unexplained early retirement from employment may warrant the judicial imputation of income to that parent on the basis of his intentional underemployment or unemployment within the meaning of section 19(1)(a) of the *Federal Child Support Guidelines*.[533]

Criminal conduct that prevents the earning of income may constitute intentional under employment or unemployment.[534]

When imputing income, the court may stagger amounts over a period of time to allow the obligor to fully realize his or her earning potential, or defer the operation of the child

526 *Peters v Atchooay*, 2022 ABCA 347; *MAA v JMA*, 2011 NBQB 298.

527 *Tynan v Moses*, [2002] BCJ No 197 (SC); see also *Bowes v Bowes*, 2021 NLCA 10 at para 68.

528 *Guy v Tulloch*, [2004] OJ No 2197 (SCJ) (husband allowed time to restructure chiropractic practice).

529 *BJM v KFB*, [2003] BCJ No 581 (SC) (income imputed to parent but in lower amount than that earned from previous employment; child support order varied accordingly).

530 *Paniccia v Butcher*, [2003] OJ No 1880 (SCJ).

531 *Fong v Fong*, 2011 BCSC 42.

532 *Barker v Barker*, 2005 BCCA 177; *Shock v Shock*, 2019 BCSC 2179.

533 *Natywary v Natywary*, [2003] OJ No 5628 (Div Ct).

534 *SAC v SEC*, 2015 MBQB 61; *Courchesne v Courchesne*, [2007] OJ No 442 at para 13 (SCJ); *Hutchison v Gretzinger*, [2007] OJ No 5058 at paras 23–24 (SCJ). See also *DCC v DWC*, 2022 CarswellNB 645 (KB) discussed in Franks & Zalev, "This Week in Family Law," 10 April 2023 (Thomson Reuters).

support order for a brief period of time to enable the obligor to put his or her affairs in order before paying the monthly child support and expenses.[535]

A court may refuse to impute additional income to a parent on the basis of underemployment, where the parent has accepted a lower paying job, but one that provides a more reliable income.[536] For most parents with child support obligations, there is likely a range of reasonable career options and a parent is not always compelled to choose the one that provides the greatest income. Some leeway must be given to a parent to organize his working life in a way that promotes his own self-actualization. On the other hand, a parent must weigh in the balance his or her obligations to support a child and cannot unfairly disregard the needs of a child. While this approach may create an element of uncertainty in the determination of a parent's income under the Guidelines, this is balanced by a fairer outcome for the child.[537]

Section 19(1)(a) does not apply to situations where, through no fault of their own, spouses are laid off, terminated, or given reduced hours of work.[538] A court may refuse to impute income to a parent whose earning ability is limited by his health to sedentary types of employment, where that parent has been pursuing an education to increase his earning potential, but the court may impose a time zone within which the parent is expected to find employment, failing which the matter may be brought back for judicial review.[539]

Where a parent is entitled to bank overtime hours and vacation pay towards pre-retirement leave pursuant to his or her union's collective agreement, the court may refuse to impute income to the parent on that basis, if the scheme represents a genuine policy of pre-retirement leave and there is no evidence that the parent was seeking to artificially reduce the level of income upon which child support would be assessed.[540]

A court may refuse to impute additional income to a parent whose current employment status is the product of a prior joint spousal retirement plan and the economic circumstances in the local area.[541]

A parent who seeks to justify underemployment or unemployment by virtue of the pursuit of educational upgrading or a university education must satisfy the court of the reasonableness of the program. Information should be provided to the court concerning such matters as the nature of the program and alternatives available for its completion that may enable the parent to earn some income.[542] Where income is imputed on the basis that the parent can earn some part-time income while pursuing university studies, the amount fixed under section 19(1)(a) of the Guidelines should not be arbitrarily selected; the exercise of the court's discretion must reflect the evidence. Relevant factors to consider include the age, education, experience, skills and health of the parent, the availability of job opportunities, the number of hours that can reasonably be spent in employment in light of the parent's overall obligations including educational demands, and the hourly rate that the parent can

535 *Visnjic v Visnjic*, [2000] OJ No 1018 (SCJ).

536 *Levesque v Levesque*, [2001] MJ No 43 (QB); *Ffrench v Ffrench*, [2001] NSJ No 82 (CA).

537 *Peters v Atchooay*, 2022 ABCA 347; *MAA v JMA*, 2011 NBQB 298; *Leveille v Lemieux*, [2002] OJ No 3422 (SCJ).

538 *Fincham v Fincham*, 2017 ONSC 4279 at para 17, Audet J.

539 *Beisel v Henderson*, [2004] SJ No 413 (QB).

540 *Dorman v Dorman*, [2001] BCJ No 1635 (SC).

541 *Beaudry-Fortin v Fortin*, [2001] BCJ No 1880 (SC).

542 *Ropchan v Moen*, 2022 ABKB 811; *Baberakubona v Kanso*, 2014 ONSC 697; *MAB v HIL*, 2010 YKSC 8.

reasonably be expected to earn. Absent evidence on these matters, the court may impute a percentage of the income previously earned by the parent.[543]

A court should refuse to impute income to a spouse on the basis of intentional under employment, where supplementary education or training would be required before returning to employment in a field in which the spouse graduated before marriage.[544] Income may be imputed to a full-time university student who has the capacity to earn a substantial income during the summer[545] or from lucrative part-time employment.[546] Student loans are not "sources of revenue" in the Canada Revenue Agency's T1 General form and are not included in a spouse's annual income under section 16 of the *Federal Child Support Guidelines*. Stu dent loans and grants may, nevertheless, permit a court to impute income to a spouse pursu ant to section 19(1) of the Guidelines,[547] even though part of them are repayable and not all of them will be available for living expenses because of the cost of tuition, books, and materials.

Trial judges should be cautious of bald assertions made by a spouse that he or she is unable to work for health-related reasons.[548] As is pointed out by Goebel J of the Saskatchewan Court of Queen's Bench in *Giesbrecht v Storos*,[549] referring to the remarks of Ryan-Froslie JA in *Kosolofski v Kosolofski*,[550] "it is too broad to say that 'independent evidence must be presented in every case but, if available, it should be produced — or an explanation provided as to why it was not.'" Income may be imputed to a spouse who alleges ill health as an explanation for not seeking employment, where there is no sufficient medical evidence to substantiate the allegation[551] and the obligor's conduct is indicative of efforts to evade his or her child support obligation,[552] or where the spouse, though partially disabled, is capable of undertaking light sedentary work.[553] Income has been imputed under the *Manitoba Child Support Guidelines* to an obligor who elected to take early retirement allegedly by reason of "burn out," where there was no indication that the obligor could not pursue alternative employment.[554]

An obligor is not permitted to assume an obligation to support aging parents in pref erence to discharging the legal obligation to support his children. Income may be imputed to an obligor whose lengthy unpaid work history for his parents demonstrates an earning capacity.[555]

---

543 *AMD v AJP*, [2002] OJ No 3731 (CA).

544 *Schmid v Smith*, [1999] OJ No 3062 (SCJ).

545 *Fibke v Fibke*, [1999] AJ No 172 (QB); *Sookorukoff v Sookorukoff*, [1998] BCJ No 2892 (SC); *Carson v Buziak*, [1998] SJ No 229 (QB).

546 *Pauli v Pauli*, [2001] OJ No 150 (SCJ).

547 *Razavi v Aavani*, [1998] BCJ No 1885 (SC); *Coppens v Cal*, [1998] SJ No 871 (QB).

548 *Irvine v Beausoleil*, 2020 SKQB 281.

549 2017 SKQB 40 at para 7.

550 2016 SKCA 106 at para 61.

551 *Allen v Allen*, [2002] AJ No 133 (QB); *Millar v Millar*, [1998] BCJ No 2489 (SC); *Wolbaum v Royal*, [1998] SJ No 235 (QB). Compare *Fraser v Fraser*, 2013 ONCA 715; *Irvine v Beausoleil*, 2020 SKQB 281.

552 *Wolbaum v Royal*, [1998] SJ No 235 (QB).

553 *British Columbia (Director of Maintenance Enforcement) v CJH*, [2002] BCJ No 1373 (Prov Ct) (personal injuries settlement also considered); *AMP v RP*, [1998] OJ No 2540 (Gen Div). See also *Fraser v Fraser*, 2013 ONCA 715.

554 *Donovan v Donovan*, [2000] MJ No 407 (CA) (obligor deemed capable of matching former income by a combination of existing pension income plus earned income from alternative employment).

555 *Bloomfield v Bloomfield*, [2000] SJ No 655 (QB).

Persistence in unremunerative employment or unrealistic or unproductive career aspirations or interests may entitle the court to impute income.[556] A parent is not entitled to invest in a speculative business venture at the expense of his children's right to receive support in accordance with a pre-existing court order. Should a parent do so, a court is entitled to impute income to that parent based on his or her historical earning capacity and future earning potential.[557] High risk income generating endeavours, whether gambling, day trading, or speculating, can generate losses or very low income as well as substantial gains. However, while the downside of the risk may be acceptable to the parent, it is not reasonable or fair that child support should be based on negative incomes or income levels close to the poverty line. Where a professional gambler's income has widely fluctuated and it has suffered a severe downturn that generates no child support or minimal child support, a court may find it inappropriate to apply either section 16 or 17 of the *Ontario Child Support Guidelines* and, exercising its discretion under section 19 of the Guidelines, it may impute an annual income to the parent based on his pre-gambling income from regular employment.[558]

Courts will not sanction the refusal of a parent to support his or her children simply because he or she cannot find satisfying employment, provided that there is employment available that reflects the capacity and qualifications of that parent.[559] An obligor is not entitled to decline menial employment where no other employment opportunities are available.[560] The court may impute income based on the minimum wage rate where there is a paucity of evidence but the parent is apparently in good health and has, at least, limited skills for which there is a job market.[561] A court may impute income to a parent who voluntarily takes up residence in a foreign jurisdiction where employment is unavailable.[562] A failure to make reasonable efforts to acquire part-time or seasonal employment may justify a judicial imputation of income based on unrealized earning capacity.[563] His or her normal annual salary may be attributed to a teacher who has a reduced structured salary level over four years to provide for a self-financed sabbatical in the fifth year, where the teacher is not currently engaged in other employment but has a demonstrated ability to earn supplementary income.[564] Where a spouse threatened by loss of employment elects to defer part of his or her salary to provide for retraining, a court may refuse to attribute the deferred income to that spouse during the current year.[565] A judicial determination as to whether a spouse is intentionally underemployed becomes increasingly difficult when disclosure requests for

---

556 *Elliott v Elliott*, 2010 ABQB 789; *Watts v Willie*, 2004 BCCA 600; *Donovan v Donovan*, [2000] MJ No 407 (CA); *MAA v JMA*, 2011 NBQB 298; *Duffy v Duffy*, 2009 NLCA 48; *Beilstein v Beilstein*, [1999] NWTJ No 34 (SC); *Drygala v Pauli* (2002), 29 RFL (5th) 293 (Ont CA); *MAK v KAB*, [2000] PEIJ No 8 (SC); *Yeung v Bui-Yeung*, 2024 SKCA 35 at para 37.

557 *MAA v JMA*, 2011 NBQB 298; *White v White*, [2001] NSJ No 558 (SC), aff'd [2002] NSJ No 248 (CA); *Blais v Blais*, [2001] SJ No 468 (QB).

558 *Quesnel v Erickson*, 2012 ONSC 4335.

559 *Van Gool v Van Gool*, [1998] BCJ No 2513 (CA).

560 *Schick v Schick*, [2000] NWTJ No 12 (SC).

561 *Allen v Allen*, [2002] AJ No 133 (QB); *CYJ v RJ*, 2022 BCSC 1901; *Schick v Schick*, [2000] NWTJ No 12 (SC); *Raymond-Theoret v Smith*, 2011 ONSC 7215. Compare *de Pimentel v Rodriguez*, 2024 ONSC 2844.

562 *Legere v Legere*, [2001] NSJ No 173 (SC).

563 *Ibid.*

564 *Kennedy v Sinclair*, [2001] OJ No 1837 (SCJ).

565 *Abear v Abear*, [1998] BCJ No 2894 (SC).

relevant information are refused. In these circumstances, a judge or Master of the Supreme Court of British Columbia may refer an application respecting child support for a hearing before the Registrar, to be followed by a report and recommendation to the court.[566]

Income may be imputed under section 19 of the *Federal Child Support Guidelines* to an obligor who voluntarily reduces his or her income during a planned career change. Section 19(1)(a) of the Guidelines, which empowers a court to impute income on the basis of "intentional" underemployment, is not confined to circumstances where an obligor seeks to evade child support obligations or recklessly disregards the children's needs in the pursuit of his/her career aspirations. The issue is one of reasonableness, in the resolution of which the court should not be confined to an examination of the obligor's circumstances; the court should look at all the circumstances, including the financial circumstances of the children, in order to ensure the payment of a fair standard of support in accordance with the objectives defined in section 1 of the *Federal Child Support Guidelines*.[567] A court may impute income to a parent on the basis of "intentional unemployment" within the meaning of section 19(1)(a) of the *Federal Child Support Guidelines*, where the parent chooses to attend college in pursuit of a new career and this decision was not reasonable in light of the attendant circumstances.

A court may impute income to a father who is currently unemployed and close to retirement age, where the court is satisfied that he is intentionally unemployed within the meaning of section 19(1)(a) of the *Federal Child Support Guidelines*. The amount of income to be prospectively imputed may have regard to his high skill level and financial success as a salesman in the field of telecommunications in the past, but should also reflect that future opportunities are likely to be less lucrative than those in the past due to his age and reduced opportunities in the field of telecommunications.[569]

A court may refuse to impute additional income to a parent where a change of employment and reduced income arose from a legitimate desire to spend more time with his children. A parent's *bona fide* career change made in order to establish a more satisfactory and secure future that could benefit his children when they are older may justify a judicial refusal to impute additional income to a parent who is pursuing a doctorate in order to advance his future career development.[570]

Income may be imputed to a spouse under the *Federal Child Support Guidelines* where it would be reasonable for that spouse to assume full-time, rather than part-time employment.[571] After imputing income on the basis of intentional underemployment or unemployment, a court may order disclosure of any change in the obligor's employment status and annual disclosure of his or her income tax return.[572]

Income may be imputed on the basis of "intentional unemployment" within the meaning of section 19(1)(a) of the *Federal Child Support Guidelines* to a child support obligor who has a child from his or her current marriage and remains at home with that child instead of

566 *Le Bourdais v Le Bourdais*, [1998] BCJ No 2488 (SC).

567 *Peters v Atchooay*, 2022 ABCA 347; *DL v ML*, 2012 NBQB 382; *Montgomery v Montgomery*, [2000] NSJ No 1 (CA); *West v West*, [2001] OJ No 2149 (SCJ); compare *Goudie v Buchanan*, [2001] NJ No 187 (UFC).

568 *Stoate v Stoate*, [2005] OJ No 1655 (SCJ); compare *Hogan v Matthew*, [2005] SJ No 684 (QB).

569 *Trick v Trick*, [2003] OJ No 1263 (SCJ).

570 *Goudie v Buchanan*, [2001] NJ No 187 (UFC).

571 *Patrick v Patrick*, [1999] BCJ No 1245 (SC).

572 *LCB v RJS*, [1999] BCJ No 1427 (SC).

seeking out employment after a reasonable time has elapsed from the child's birth.[573] A parent who chooses to work less than a regular work week must justify that choice by the needs of the children or suffer the loss personally. He or she cannot effectively transfer part of the cost of that choice to her children.[574] In *McCaffrey v Paleolog*,[575] Chiasson JA of the British Columbia Court of Appeal stated that it is recognized that generally a newborn child or a very young aged child needs care at home, but childbirth does not provide automatic relief from a parent's child support obligations. The circumstances of each situation must be evaluated and any period of non-support must be reasonable in the circumstances. The financial condition of the obligor's present family should be considered. The financial circumstances of the first family may also be relevant, for example, where the second family is affluent and the first family is destitute. The circumstances may compel an almost immediate return to work or may provide for full or part-time in-home assistance. Assisted child care may be unavailable or only available on a limited basis. In considering the applicability of section 19(1)(a) of the Guidelines, the court should be given every assistance by the parties so as to take into account all relevant factors that bear upon the reasonableness of a period of relief from child support, always recognizing that the burden is on the parent who seeks a hiatus from the obligation to provide child support to prove that a period of underemployment or unemployment is required by the needs of a child.

Courts generally appear more indulgent towards mothers who seek to reduce their first-family child support obligations because of second-family responsibilities, but courts must avoid creating a double standard for stay-at-home fathers. A parent's obligation to support the children of a dissolved marriage is not avoidable by a wish to remain at home with a child born of a subsequent relationship until that child attains school age.[576] And a parent's desire to be available for his or her child before and after school is insufficient reason to justify underemployment in the absence of evidence of the child's special need and income may be judicially imputed to that parent pursuant to section 19(1)(a) of the *Federal Child Support Guidelines*.[577]

A spouse's limited work experience and job skills do not justify a failure to pursue employment that does not require significant skills or employment in which the necessary skills can be learned on the job. While this may mean that job availability will be at the lower end of the wage scale, courts have never sanctioned the refusal of a parent to take reasonable steps to support his or her children simply because they cannot obtain interesting or highly paid employment. Courts have made it abundantly clear that a parent is expected to take

---

573 *McCaffrey v Paleolog*, 2011 BCCA 378. See also *Koch v Koch*, 2012 BCCA 378; *Loscerbo v Loscerbo*, [2008] MJ No 246 (QB) (reduced hours of employment); *Terracol v Terracol*, 2010 ONSC 6442; *Zieglgansberger v Venyige*, [2003] SJ No 791 (QB). As to the relevance of child care expenses and the loss of a child care subsidy on remarriage, see *Hamelin v Bratlien*, 2011 BCSC 708.

574 *Mahannah v Mahannah*, 2012 BCSC 403.

575 2011 BCCA 378 at paras 58–59. See also *CCR v TAR*, 2016 BCSC 519; *Arnett v Arnett*, 2018 BCSC 1982; *Ghent v Busse*, 2016 ONSC 5282. And see *Demers v Moar*, 2004 ABCA 380; *Spring v Spring*, 2022 ABCA 19.

576 *Tatlock v Lays*, [2001] AJ No 962 (QB); compare *Fauth v Fauth*, [2002] AJ No 580 (QB); *Sevier v Sevier*, [2003] BCJ No 1540 (SC). See also *Lamontagne v Culham*, 2013 SKQB 96, aff'd 2013 SKCA 100.

577 *Llewellyn v Llewellyn*, [2002] BCJ No 542 (CA), citing *Van Gool v Van Gool* (1999), 44 RFL (4th) 331 (BCCA); *Donovan v Lee*, [2002] MJ No 226 (QB).

reasonable steps to obtain employment commensurate with their age, health, education, skills, and work history.[578] A parent may have to consider relocating in order to find employment.[579] An obligor may be found to be intentionally underemployed within the meaning of section 19 of the *Federal Child Support Guidelines* in light of his or her previous actions and attitudes.[580]

Income may be attributed to a spouse or former spouse whose evidence as to income is inconsistent with his or her past record of achievement. Alleged business reversals that are coincidental with the institution of support proceedings may lead a court to conclude that the respondent's evidence lacks credibility.[581]

A court may attribute income to spouses or former spouses who have the skills to supplement their income or whose income is greater or could be greater than that declared[582] but, if income is to be imputed in this manner, there should be sufficient evidence to substantiate the imputation.[583] The circumstances upon the basis of which a court is called upon to impute income under section 19 of the *Federal Child Support Guidelines* should be proved by affidavit or oral evidence.[584] A court should not attribute income to an obligor based on former employment that is no longer available, practicable, or reasonable.[585] Although income may be attributed to a spouse or former spouse based on employment skills,[586] a court should refuse to impute historical earnings where similar employment is no longer available and the withdrawal from previous employment was justified.[587] An obligor's decision to take other less remunerative employment, rather than await termination of his employment, may not be so imprudent as to justify imputing his former level of income to him for the purpose of assessing child support.[588] A conservative estimate of prospective income may be called for having regard to the unpredictability of the market.[589] A spouse or former spouse who has deliberately limited his employment opportunities in order to avoid child support obligations may be expected to obtain secondary employment that will facilitate the discharge of those obligations.[590] A court should err on the side of conservatism in imputing income to

---

578 *Van Gool v Van Gool*, [1998] BCJ No 2513 (CA); *Campbell v Campbell*, 2014 MBCA 104.

579 *Goulet v Racher*, [2002] BCJ No 2430 (SC); *Durant v Durant*, [2001] NSJ No 10 (SC); *MacLean v MacLean* [2003] PEIJ No 16 (TD); see also *Hackett v Hackett*, [2001] NJ No 317 (SC).

580 *Ibid.*

581 *Schom-Moffatt v Moffatt*, [1997] BCJ No 2055 (SC); see also *Depace v Michienzi*, [2000] OJ No 453 (SCJ).

582 *Channer v Hoffman-Turner*, [1997] AJ No 1002 (QB); *Bablitz v Bablitz* (1994), 10 RFL (4th) 84 (BCCA); *Sheppard v Sheppard* (1992), 44 RFL (3d) 1 (Nfld CA); *Bekeros v Bekeros* (1989), 19 RFL (3d) 432 (Ont UFC); *Daku v Daku*, [1999] SJ No 330 (QB).

583 *McNulty v McNulty*, [1998] MJ No 518 (QB); *Leet v Leet* (1994), 131 NSR (2d) 19 (TD); *Wong v Wong* (1990), 27 RFL (3d) 215 (Ont CA); *Quintal v Quintal*, [1997] OJ No 3444 (Gen Div).

584 *Vivier v Vivier*, [1997] MJ No 414 (QB).

585 *Phillips v Phillips* (1995), 14 RFL (4th) 113 (Alta CA); *Bayliss v Bayliss*, [2000] MJ No 52 (QB); *Farnell v Farnell*, [2002] NSJ No 491 (SC); *Hearn v Bacque*, [2006] OJ No 2385 (SCJ); *Lotten v Lotten*, [2003] SJ No 831 (QB).

586 *Smith v Smith*, [1997] AJ No 1265 (QB).

587 *Gran v Gran*, [1997] SJ No 330 (QB); see also *Stiver v Mercer*, [2000] OJ No 568 (SCJ) (income imputed discounted by 25 percent to account for transition in light of unavailability of return to same employment).

588 *Rains v Rains*, [1997] OJ No 2516 (Gen Div); see also *Canuel v Canuel*, [1997] BCJ No 1654 (CA).

589 *Perry v Perry*, [1997] BCJ No 1567 (SC).

590 *D(GA) v D(G)* (1995), 11 RFL (4th) 270 (Alta QB).

a parent who voluntarily takes up a second job to supplement his or her basic income.[591] A parent is not required to maintain two jobs that will force her to work seven days a week.[592]

As a general rule, a spouse or former spouse cannot avoid child support obligations by a self-induced reduction of income.[593] Children should not bear the responsibility of a parent's foolish, if not deliberate, lack of judgment in relinquishing employment, where that parent can make use of a substantial asset base, including severance and pension benefits, if difficulty is encountered in paying court-ordered child support in addition to personal living expenses.[594] Only in exceptional circumstances will a spouse or former spouse be entitled to make a change of employment with a consequential reduction in the ability to pay child support.[595] Such an exception may arise where an obligor chooses a career path with short-term pain for long-term gain. In such a case, the child should benefit as the obligor's income eventually increases.[596] A parent cannot elect to pursue less remunerative employment because of the freedom that self-employment provides.[597] Child support obligations cannot be evaded by either parent ceasing employment in order to pursue further education.[598] An unemployed spouse or former spouse has a duty to seek employment so that he or she can earn the income necessary to pay child support, unless earning an income is precluded by reason of mental or physical disability.[599] A court may refuse to impute income on the basis of a spouse's early retirement where no further evidence is before the court.[600] A court may also refuse to impute income for the time being to an obligor who has worked in his family's previously successful business and who seeks to revive it rather than seek alternative employment. In these circumstances, however, the court may stipulate that the obligor seek alternative employment, if the effort to revive the family business is not successful by a designated date, and may further stipulate that the failure to do so will justify an imputation of income in line with the obligor's qualifications for employment.[601] Income may be imputed to a spouse whose employment is terminated for cause and who makes no effort to seek alternative employment or retrain.[602] Long-term retirement planning, by way of a reduced work load and the maximization of RRSP contributions, may be a laudable

---

591 *Wedsworth v Wedsworth*, [2000] NSJ No 209 (SC); see also *Ollivier v Zarins*, [2003] BCJ No 298 (SC) (judicial refusal to impute income to parent who withdrew from second position on weekends).

592 *Mitchell v Hill*, [2000] MJ No 228 (QB); *Hamilton v Hamilton*, [1999] NBJ No 297 (QB); *White v White*, 2015 NSCA 52.

593 *LHG v CBG*, [1998] AJ No 542 (QB); *Garcia v Rodriguez* (1997), 29 RFL (4th) 329 (BCCA); *Peach v Peach*, [2003] NSJ No 41 (Fam Ct); *Maceus-Agyckum v Agyckum*, [2005] OJ No 1306 (SCJ); *Weibe v Oviatt*, [1998] SJ No 303 (QB).

594 *BDW v HGW*, [1999] AJ No 997 (QB).

595 *Babyak v Antosh* (1990), 26 RFL (3d) 280 (Sask QB).

596 *Williams v Williams*, [1997] NWTJ No 49 (SC); compare *Motyka v Motyka*, [2001] BCJ No 52 (CA); *Shock v Shock*, 2019 BCSC 2179.

597 *Lobo v Lobo*, [1999] AJ No 113 (QB).

598 *Hurst v Hurst*, [1999] AJ No 165 (QB); *Stiver v Mercer*, [2000] OJ No 568 (SCJ); *Anwender-Rempel v Rempel*, [2004] SJ No 646 (QB).

599 *Sigurdson v Sigurdson* (1980), 7 Sask R 422 (UFC).

600 *Barnsley v Barnsley*, [1998] OJ No 5332 (Gen Div); see also *Stevens v Boulerice*, [1999] OJ No 1568 (Gen Div) (retiree in mid-fifties not obliged to take on further work at low rate of pay).

601 *Pela v Pela*, [1998] SJ No 804 (QB).

602 *Baldini v Baldini*, [1999] BCJ No 1426 (SC); *Hall v Hall*, [1999] OJ No 453 (Gen Div); *McGowan v McGowan*, [1998] SJ No 662 (QB).

objective, but should not be permitted at the expense of the children whom the obligor can well afford to support.[603]

Income may be imputed to a parent on the basis of judicial notice being taken of excel lent employment opportunities available and the parent's recent earnings over a period of three months.[604]

Although an adverse inference may be drawn from non-disclosure of income, this requires factual underpinning.[605]

Income may be imputed to a parent with a comfortable lifestyle in northern Ontario who failed to take advantage of greater employment opportunities in the south.[606]

Income may be imputed to a father with a demonstrated earning capacity in Canada prior to his leaving his wife and children and taking up residence abroad.[607]

Any imputation of income by a chambers judge on the basis of intentional underemploy ment or unemployment under section 19(1)(a) of the Guidelines requires a solid grounding in evidence.[608] Findings of fact that turn on the credibility of one of the parties or witnesses cannot be resolved by reviewing conflicting affidavits. A *viva voce* trial of the underlying issue may be required to allow a judge the opportunity to observe the parties and receive evidence from other important sources.[609]

Income may be judicially imputed to a parent on a stepped-up basis over several years where the court is not satisfied that parent has made reasonable efforts to realize her income earning capacity.[610]

Income may be imputed to a spouse with questionable employment potential but very substantial assets.

5) Unreported Income; Underground Economy

A court may impute income under the *Federal Child Support Guidelines* where the obligor does not report cash receipts on his or her income tax return.[611]

A bare assertion of "under the table" income, unsupported by any evidence, will not justify any imputation of income over and above that specified in the parent's income tax returns.[612] Where additional income is imputed to a parent who engages in the so-called "underground economy," the undeclared taxable income may be grossed up to take account

603 *Pietrus v Preston*, [1999] SJ No 34 (QB).
604 *Roszko v Roszko*, [2000] AJ No 920 (QB).
605 *KJP v BSJG*, 2024 BCSC 167; *Ninham v Ninham*, [1997] OJ No 2667 (Gen Div).
606 *Midena v Collette*, [2000] OJ No 4429 (Ct J).
607 *Hitchens v Hitchens*, [2004] OJ No 2019 (SCJ).
608 *Walker v Walker*, [2001] AJ No 553 (CA); *Rozen v Rozen*, [2001] BCJ No 1633 (SC).
609 *Walker v Walker*, [2001] AJ No 553 (CA); see also *LRS v SSD*, 2020 ABCA 206.
610 *Cipriano v Hampton*, 2015 ONSC 349 at para 15.
611 *Sorya v Parmar*, 2012 BCSC 129 (unreported taxi fares grossed up for income tax); *Xu v Chu*, 2019 BCCA 414 (hidden cash sales grossed up for income tax); *Parsons v Clarke*, [2002] NJ No 162 (SC); *Zeggelaar v Zeggelaar*, 2024 NSSC 34; *Kereluk v Kereluk*, [2004] OJ No 4337 (SCJ) (tips, including income tax gross up); but see *contra BM v ALG*, 2014 NSSC 443 at paras 22–23 (refusal to gross up unreported income).
612 *Kalchuk v Kalchuk*, [2000] AJ No 813 (QB); *X(RL) v X(JF)*, [2002] BCJ No 1889 (SC).

of its tax-free nature, notwithstanding the parent's liability to be reassessed by the Canada Revenue Agency.[613]

6) Vocational Assessment

The court may grant an order for a vocational and aptitude assessment of a spouse in order to determine the income earning potential of that spouse. Although the granting of an order for a vocational and aptitude assessment by a registered psychologist is discretionary, the choice of the assessor is determined by the party moving for the assessment.[614]

7) Forgivable Loans; Family Gifts

As the Alberta Court of Appeal stated in *CRC v DAJC*:

> [20] As a general rule, gifts are not included in the payor parent's guideline income but courts retain discretion to impute them in appropriate circumstances. Gifts to payor parents have been attributed as income when they are regular, long standing, materially affect the payor parent's standard of living and are likely to continue: *Hartley v Del Pero*, 2017 ABQB 1 at para 128; *Bak* at para 76. In this context, gifts are not limited to transfers of property ownership to the payor spouse. Regular payments of a payor parent's everyday living expenses and his or her luxury expenditures may be imputed as income in appropriate circumstances: *Del Pero* at paras 144, 154, 156; *AEA v HE*, 2016 ABPC 84 at paras 66, 94; *Korman v Korman*, 2015 ONCA 578 at para 55, 65 & 67.[615]

In *Bak v Dobell*,[616] Lang JA of the Ontario Court of Appeal identified several factors that a court will consider in determining whether it is appropriate to include a receipt of gifts in a parent's income. They "include the regularity of the gifts; the duration of their receipt; whether the gifts were part of the family's income during cohabitation that entrenched a particular lifestyle; the circumstances of the gifts that earmark them as exceptional; whether the gifts do more than provide a basic standard of living; the income generated by the gifts in proportion to the payor's entire income; whether they are paid to support an adult child through a crisis or period of disability; whether the gifts are likely to continue; and the true purpose and nature of the gifts." And in *Whelan v O'Connor*,[617] Mackinnon J of the Ontario Superior Court of Justice endorsed the following principles:

---

613 *Dowe v Dowe*, [2001] NSJ No 313 (SC); *Ali v Williams-Cespedes*, 2015 ONSC 3560.

614 *Minthorn v Minthorn*, [1992] OJ No 1233 (Gen Div).

615 *CRC v DAJC*, 2020 ABCA 143 at para 20; *Russell v Ullett Russell*, 2021 ABQB 769; *Zheng v Yang*, 2020 MBQB 146. For a detailed review of caselaw on treating gifts as a support-tappable resource, see *Godin v Stone*, 2022 ABQB 86 at paras 122–34.

616 2007 ONCA 304; see also *Mortson v Kminkova*, 2021 ABQB 476; *Andreassen v Andreassen*, 2016 BCSC 1196; *KAL v KJL*, 2017 BCSC 651; *Russell v Russell*, 2011 MBQB 274; *Zheng v Yang*, 2020 MBQB 146; *Korman v Korman*, 2015 ONCA 578 (income imputed where settled pattern of parental monetary gifts); *Salehi v Tawoosi*, 2016 ONSC 540 at paras 82–83; *Teitler v Dale*, 2017 ONSC 248; *MB v SBB*, 2018 ONSC 4893. Compare *AL v JN*, 2017 NBCA 25; *Droit de la famille—1991*, 2019 QCCA 137.

617 (2006), 28 RFL (6th) 433 at para 21 (Ont SCJ); see also *Russell v Ullett Russell*, 2021 ABQB 769 at para 65; *SR v BE*, 2011 BCSC 1586; *Seaton v Zheng*, 2013 ONSC 4469.

1. The court should be cautious in imputing income on the basis of gifts when so doing would have the effect of transferring a child support obligation to someone who, legally, does not have that obligation.
2. Income is generally imputed where a parent is not properly utilizing earning capacity or other resources to support his or her children.
3. Factors supporting income imputation on the basis of gifts include:
   a. the gifts represent a significant portion of the recipient's overall income;
   b. the gifts are part of a planned or intentional diversion of income or substitution for income previously earned from this source; and,
   c. there is reliance upon the regular and ongoing nature of the gifts as an income source in lieu of pursuing other remunerative employment commensurate with the abilities of the respondent.
4. Failure to make full disclosure is a frequent factor in cases where income is imputed.

A court may impute income to a parent who is the beneficiary of a forgivable loan from his or her employer.[618]

8) Income Tax Concessions

The *Federal Child Support Guidelines* base support payments on the payor's gross taxable income. One of the objectives of the Guidelines is to ensure "consistent treatment" of those who are in "similar circumstances." Thus, there are provisions to impute income where a parent is exempt from paying tax, lives in a lower taxed jurisdiction, or derives income from sources that are taxed at a lower rate. Where a parent pays substantially less tax or no tax on income received, the income must be grossed up for the purpose of determining the amount of child support to be paid. This is the only way to ensure the consistency mandated by the legislation.[619] Pursuant to section 19(1)(b) of the *Federal Child Support Guidelines* income may be imputed where a parent is exempt from paying federal or provincial income tax.[620] Examples include: workers' compensation benefits;[621] disability pension or insurance

618 *BLS v JMS*, 2010 BCSC 1319; *Myers v Myers*, [2000] NSJ No 367 (SC) (loan apportioned over two taxation years); compare *CLY v DGY*, 2013 ONSC 6550.

619 *Hall v Hall*, [2006] AJ No 563 (QB); *Peters v Atchooay*, 2022 ABCA 347 at para 104; *Kuznecov v Kuznecov*, [2006] BCJ No 1155 (SC); *Church v Church*, 2021 MBQB 20; *Ward v Murphy*, 2023 NSSC 370; *Orser v Grant*, [2000] OJ No 1429 (SCJ); *Caterini v Zaccaria*, 2010 ONSC 6473; *Pollitt v Pollitt*, 2010 ONSC 1617; *MH v AB*, 2019 SKCA 135 at para 89, leave to appeal to SCC denied 2020 CanLII 36067 (SCC). Compare *Vincent v Vincent*, 2012 BCCA 186.

620 *Mullins v Mullins*, 2016 ABQB 226.

621 *Dahlgren v Hodgson*, [1998] AJ No 1501 (CA); *Mullins v Mullins*, 2016 ABQB 226; *Dedoscenco v Beauchamp*, [2005] BCJ No 1053 (SC) (CPP and WCB disability pensions grossed up; WCB personal care allowance not grossed up); *MS v EJS*, 2017 BCSC 564; *Prince v Soenen*, 2015 MBQB 31; *Callahan v Brett* [2000] NJ No 354 (SC) (workers' compensation benefits and private disability pension); *DAT v SLP*, 2018 NBQB 135; *Coadic v Coadic*, [2005] NSJ No 415 (SC); *Peterson v Horan*, [2006] SJ No 333 (CA); *SMM v DPG*, [2003] YJ No 98 (SC). Re gross up of workers' compensation, compare *Landry v Landry* 2012 ONSC 7187 at para 5; see also *Storey v Simmons*, 2013 ABQB 168 and compare *Starling v Starling* 2016 SKQB 112 (spousal support).

benefits;[622] foreign resident income;[623] income earned by Indigenous person living and working on a First Nations reserve;[624] receipt of cash/in kind payments;[625] Canadian Armed Forces foreign service allowance;[626] foster care payments;[627] curling revenue;[628] and gambling winnings.[629]

An obligor's income may be grossed up to reflect tax benefits resulting from donations of cultural property, such as rare books, maps, or art.[630]

Income may be imputed to a parent on the basis of his exemption from income tax while working abroad and on the basis of free accommodation and free use of an automobile being provided to him.[631]

If a parent's foreign income is subject to significantly lower rates of income tax than those applicable in Canada, the court has the discretionary jurisdiction under section 19(1)(c) of *Federal Child Support Guidelines* to impute such income as it considers appropriate under those circumstances. Before exercising that discretion, a court may require reliable evidence of the foreign tax rate and may also find it necessary to address other economic factors, such as increased health care costs in the foreign jurisdiction.[632] In the words of Neilson JA of the British Columbia Court of Appeal in *Gonabady-Namadon v Mohammadzadeh*:[633]

---

622 *Rooker v Rooker*, 2017 ABCA 87, leave to appeal to SCC denied on 26 October 2017, 2017 CanLII 71233; *Walgren v Walgren*, [2002] BCJ No 881 (SC); *DS v EPS*, 2011 BCSC 1102 (wage replacement portion of the respondent's ICBC benefits grossed up); *McKenzie v Perestrelo*, 2014 BCCA 161 (disability pension grossed up); *Mathusz v Carew*, 2011 NLTD(F) 28; *Vaughan v Vaughan*, 2014 NBCA 6; *Darlington v Moore*, 2013 NSSC 103; *Tobin v Tobin*, 2019 NSSC 314; *Davis v Davis*, 2022 NSSC 212 (tax-free disability pension grossed up); *Hewitt v Rogers*, 2018 ONSC 1384 (assessment of child support in light of tax-free lump sum disability payments); *Dyck v Highton*, [2003] SJ No 600 (QB) (disability pension not grossed up); *GL v KH*, 2020 SKQB 167 (housekeeping and house maintenance benefits included as income for child support purposes, but no gross up for income tax purposes). But see *LF v CGC*, 2014 BCSC 1069, citing *Storey v Simmons*, 2013 ABQB 168 in concluding that a veterans' disability pensions are not income for Guidelines purposes; see also *Frigon v Blanchard*, 2014 MBQB 212. Compare *Lozinski v Lozinski*, 2017 BCCA 280 (shared parenting); *Starling v Starling*, 2016 SKQB 112 (spousal support). See also *Blaskavitch v Smith*, 2023 ONSC 2133.

623 *Johnston v Johnston*, [2004] AJ No 333 (QB); *Morgan v Morgan*, [2000] BCJ No 431 (SCJ); *Paul v Dennis*, 2012 NSSC 366; *McLean v Vassel*, [2004] OJ No 3036 (SCJ).

624 *Peters v Atchooay*, 2022 ABCA 347 at para 104; *Alexander v Alexander*, 2010 BCSC 1674; *Young v Marshall*, 2018 NSSC 211; *Roote v Thompson*, [2005] OJ No 5590 (SCJ); *Kaiswatum-Thomson v Thomson*, [2004] SJ No 406 (CA).

625 *MacNeil v Garney-MacNeil*, 2012 ONSC 3332; *Myers v Myers*, 2013 ONSC 170 (cash payments grossed up by 35 percent, representing nonpayment of income tax); compare *BM v ALG*, 2014 NSSC 443.

626 *Hiscock v Hiscock*, 2014 NLTD(F) 14; *Dunleavy v Comeau*, 2019 ONSC 4535; *Reynolds v Andrew*, [2008] SJ No 532 (QB).

627 *Kovich v Kreut*, [1998] BCJ No 2586 (SC); *Minski v Minski*, [2002] SJ No 773 (QB).

628 *Smith v Smith*, [1999] MJ No 74 (QB).

629 *Kuznecov v Kuznecov*, [2006] BCJ No 1155 (SC).

630 *SP v RP*, [2010] OJ No 1642 (SCJ).

631 *Morgan v Morgan*, [2000] BCJ No 431 (SC) (certain business expenses allowed with respect to maintenance of lease on former office in Canada; storage charges for furniture disallowed where not an arm's-length transaction); see also *Stevens v Stevens*, 2012 BCSC 1698.

632 *Chalifoux v Chalifoux*, 2008 ABCA 70; *Ward v Ward*, [2001] BCJ No 1206 (SC); *Anderson v Anderson*, [2005] MJ No 243 (QB); *Anthony v Anthony*, 2009 NSSC 343; *Pomozova v Mann*, 2010 ONCA 212; compare *ADB v SAM*, [2006] NSJ No 252 (SC) (cost of living to be disregarded).

633 2009 BCCA 448. See also *Pousette v Janssen*, 2023 BCCA 176, supp reasons 2023 BCCA 272; *Almeida v Malek-Gilani*, 2018 ONSC 5699.

When a non-resident payor's tax rate is significantly different than Canadian tax rates, the usual practice under ss. 19(1)(c) and 20 of the *Guidelines* is to convert his or her gross foreign income to Canadian dollars at a fair exchange rate, then look to the evidence of the applicable foreign tax rate to calculate his net income, and then determine what gross income would be required to yield the same net income at Canadian tax rates. Finally, it may be necessary to examine the "bundle of services" that both governments provide in exchange for the tax dollars paid. These matters are often the subject of expert evidence: *Patrick v. Patrick*, [1999] B.C.J. No. 1245 (S.C.) at paras. 12–19, *Ward v. Ward*, 2001 BCSC 847, 19 R.F.L. (5th) 232 at paras. 34–40, *Watson v. Watson*, 2006 BCSC 256, [2006] B.C.J. No. 329 at paras. 22–29.

Income may be grossed up for spouses who are exempt from paying Canadian income-taxes. Grossing up the tax free income earned by an Indian on a reserve for the purpose of applying the *Federal Child Support Guidelines* does not constitute a breach of Treaty rights. Income may be imputed to an obligor whose foreign income generates lower tax liabilities than would be applicable in Canada, where no evidence is adduced to show that the benefits of lower foreign taxation are offset by higher costs of living.[635] In such a case, the foreign income will be converted into the equivalent amount of Canadian dollars for the purpose of applying the Guidelines.[636]

Income may be imputed to an obligor who receives essentially tax-free income from a family trust, but the gross up should reflect that the funds must be dedicated to the use of the children and for no other purpose.[637]

A court may impute income to a farmer in an attempt to equate his or her income to that of a wage earner who does not have deductions of the magnitude available to the self-employed.[638] Income may be imputed to a self-employed spouse with substantial tax write-offs.[639] Personal benefits accruing from business expenses may result in the imputation of income[640] and they may be grossed up to reflect their tax-free status to the parent.[641]

An income tax refund from a previous year is not included in an obligor's income under section 16 of the *Federal Child Support Guidelines*.[642]

9) Failure to Make Financial Disclosure

Where a parent has failed to provide up-to-date financial disclosure, the court may draw an adverse inference and impute appropriate income to that parent.[643] However, there must

634 *Merasty v Merasty* (2000), 194 Sask R 91 (QB); see also *Solomon v Solomon*, [2001] OJ No 2996 (SCJ).
635 *Nkwazi v Nkwazi*, [1998] SJ No 571 (QB).
636 *Ibid.*
637 *Penner v Penner*, [1998] MJ No 353 (QB) (application under *Manitoba Child Support Guidelines*).
638 *Wasuita v Wasuita*, [1998] AJ No 695 (QB).
639 *Cabernel v Cabernel*, [1997] MJ No 375 (QB); *Naidoo v Naidoo*, [2004] OJ No 1458 (SCJ).
640 *Ennis v Ennis*, [1999] AJ No 352 (QB); *Crawford v Crawford*, [1999] SJ No 238 (QB).
641 *Orser v Grant*, [2000] OJ No 1429 (SCJ); *Sarafinchin v Sarafinchin*, [2000] OJ No 2855 (SCJ); *Riel v Holland*, [2003] OJ No 3901 (CA); *Van Vroenhoven v Van Vroenhoven*, [2009] OJ No 995 (SCJ); see contra *Johnson v Johnson*, [2000] BCJ No 2065 (SC).
642 *Levasseur v Ellis*, [2004] NSJ No 248 (SC).
643 *Kretschmer v Terrigno*, 2012 ABCA 345; *Bodine-Shah v Shah*, 2014 BCCA 191; *Verwey v Verwey*, [2007] MJ No 309 (CA); *SAD v MA*, 2019 NBQB 85; *Dewan v Dewan*, 2012 ONSC 503; *Burke v Poitras*, 2020 ONSC 3162; *Studzinski v Studzinski*, 2020 ONSC 2540; *VKG v IG*, 2023 ONSC 6329.

be an evidentiary basis for attributing additional income to a parent.[644] A figure cannot be simply plucked from the air but a suspicion of undisclosed income may be substantiated by the parent's prior tax returns, property holdings, or by the parent's lifestyle and annual expenditures that are unaffordable on the income reported by the parent.[645] It may not be ideal to make such important decisions by inference from records, but a party who is not forthcoming with direct information takes the risk that circumstantial evidence will be invoked against that party.[646]

The failure of an obligor to furnish relevant financial information by filing a BC Form 89 financial statement entitles the court to impute income to the obligor pursuant to section 19(1)(f) of the *Federal Child Support Guidelines* and to draw an adverse inference against him under section 23 of the Guidelines. Evidence of historical earnings and deferred earnings may be taken into account in fixing the annual income to be imputed to the obligor. Additional income may be imputed where the obligor resides in a foreign jurisdiction that has a lower tax base than Canada. Income in foreign currency must be converted into Canadian dollars. In terms of the appropriate foreign exchange rate, the court may average the Bank of Canada rate over the preceding twelve months to arrive at the parent's Canadian income for the purpose of applying the *Federal Child Support Guidelines*.[647]

In addition to the express powers to impute income under section 19 of the *Federal Child Support Guidelines*, a failure to file income tax returns and other financial data, as required by section 21(1) of the *Federal Child Support Guidelines*, entitles the other spouse to have an application for child support set down for a hearing in accordance with section 22(1)(a) of the Guidelines and, at such a hearing, the court may, pursuant to section 23 of the Guidelines, impute income to the offending spouse in such amount as is considered appropriate.[648] Judicial imputation of income may be justified by the obligor's failure to provide relevant financial information coupled with the inadequacy of the evidence produced to support his assertion of inability to work due to depression and stress.[649]

10) Lifestyle

In *Bak v Dobell*,[650] Lang JA of the Ontario Court of Appeal observed that "lifestyle is not income, but rather evidence from which an inference may be drawn that the payor has undisclosed income that may be imputed for the purpose of determining child support."[651] This observa-

644 *ML v BH*, 2012 NBQB 233; *Studzinski v Studzinski*, 2020 ONSC 2540.

645 *Parham v Jiang*, 2013 ONSC 6003 at para 43; *Arlt v Arlt*, [2003] SJ No 713 (QB).

646 *Li v Wong*, 2010 ABCA 296; *Poursadeghian v Hashemi-Dahaj*, 2010 BCCA 453; *Zeggelaar v Zeggelaar*, 2024 NSSC 34; *Crosbie v Crosbie*, 2012 ONCA 516.

647 *KV v TE*, [2004] BCJ No 792 (SC); *Pousette v Janssen*, 2023 BCCA 176, supp reasons 2023 BCCA 272. See also *Mastin v Mastin*, 2019 NSSC 248; *Beaudoin v Stevens*, 2023 ONSC 4401.

648 *Janmohamed v Janmohamed*, 2020 BCSC 432; *Cole v Cole*, [2000] NSJ No 74 (SC); *Alexander v Alexander*, [1999] OJ No 3694 (SCJ).

649 *Pamma v Pamma*, [1999] BCJ No 2252 (SC).

650 2007 ONCA 304; see also *Hartley v Del Pero*, 2010 ABCA 182; *Simpson v Bettenson*, 2014 ABCA 21; *Burke v Poitras*, 2020 ONSC 3162.

651 2007 ONCA 304 at para 43; see also *Kretschmer v Terrigno*, 2012 ABCA 345; *Simpson v Bettenson*, 2014 ABCA 21; *CRC v DAJC*, 2020 ABCA 143 at para 19; *Sullivan v Struck*, 2015 BCCA 521; *Bishop v Bishop*, 2017 MBQB 97; *C v S*, 2010 NBQB 252 at para 206; *CMM v DGC*, 2015 ONSC 1815 (application by

tion reflects pre-existing caselaw, including *Davids v Davids*[652] and *Biamonte v Biamonte,* which demonstrates that a parent's lifestyle can inform the question of whether that parent has diverted income or under-reported income so as to justify the judicial imputation of income for the purpose of calculating child support. The inadequacy of the income information provided by the obligor may entitle the court to impute an income based on all of the evidence presented. The court may take cognizance that the lifestyle of the obligor indicates a higher income than that indicated.[654] Income may be imputed to a spouse whose lifestyle or household budget is inconsistent with his or her tax returns and whose personal expenses are channelled through his or her private business. In these circumstances, it is incumbent on the court to impute a fair annual income for the purpose of establishing the child support obligation and not to allow "creative accounting" to be used to evade that obligation.[655] Where the credibility of a self-employed husband respecting his annual income from driving a taxi was deemed inconsistent with his lifestyle, evidence from an independent taxi driver who knew neither party was admitted respecting the earning potential of drivers in the City of Toronto and income was imputed to the husband on the basis of this evidence.[656] A court should decline to attribute income to an obligor on the basis of his or her lifestyle, insofar as that lifestyle is enhanced by the independent income of the obligor's spouse.[657] Income may be imputed to a parent who has benefitted over the years and continues to benefit from his family's generosity.[658]

11) Investments; Financial Management

Investment income may be attributed to an obligor on the basis of capital investments,[659] substantial lottery win,[660] or an interest-free loan of money to a friend.[661] Business income may be imputed to an obligor based on a projected percentage return on his or her investment.[662] Investment income, which is earned on a regular basis and likely to continue in the future,[663] should be taken into consideration.[664] The deployment of income for investment

child under *Family Law Act,* RSO 1990, c F3); *McKenna v McKenna,* 2015 ONSC 3309; *Sich v Sich,* 2014 SKQB 174 at paras 43–47.

652 [1998] OJ No 2859 (Gen Div).

653 (1998), 36 RFL (4th) 349 (Ont Ct Gen Div).

654 *Motyka v Motyka,* [2001] BCJ No 52 (CA); *DNL v CNS,* 2013 BCSC 858; *Ghosn v Ghosn,* [2006] NSJ No 33 (SC); *Heard v Heard,* 2014 ONCA 196; *Richardson v Richardson,* 2016 SKQB 356; *Kelly v Lyle,* [2001] YJ No 90 (SC). Compare *Fleury v Fleury,* 2009 ABCA 43.

655 *Stamp v McIntosh,* [1998] AJ No 429 (QB); see also *Lavoie v Wills,* [2000] AJ No 1359 (QB) (income tax gross up of household expenses to determine parental income after allowance made for current spouse's contribution); *Dunham v Dunham,* [1998] OJ No 4758 (Gen Div); *Bagu v Bagu,* [2004] SJ No 279 (QB).

656 *Chen v Chen,* [2000] OJ No 1176 (SCJ).

657 *Tapper v Connolly,* [2002] NJ No 83 (SC); *Lacroix v D'Aoust,* 2011 ONSC 5586.

658 *Haq v Haq,* [2003] OJ No 4687 (SCJ); compare *Bak v Dobell,* discussed in Section G(7), above in this chapter; see also *Fleury v Fleury,* 2009 ABCA 43.

659 *Parks v Parks,* [2000] OJ No 2863 (SCJ) (judicial adoption of conservative interest rate of 5 percent per year).

660 *DLA v JTA,* [1999] AJ No 312 (QB); *Bartole v Parker,* [2006] SJ No 349 (QB).

661 *Fuller v Fuller,* [2000] OJ No 4726 (Ct J).

662 *TAL v SDB,* 2018 ABQB 589; *Fleury v Fleury,* 2009 ABCA 43; *Kawalewich v Kawalewich,* [1997] BCJ No 1419 (SC).

663 *Johnson v Checkowy,* [1997] SJ No 451 (QB).

664 *Wishart v Wishart* (1990), 29 RFL (3d) 68 (BCSC); *Syvitski v Syvitski* (1988), 86 NSR (2d) 248 (Fam Ct); *Sloggett v Sloggett* (1989), 19 RFL (3d) 148 (Ont HCJ); *Bell v Griffin,* [1997] PEIJ No 86 (TD).

cannot take priority over the reasonable support expectations of family dependants, even if this requires the disposal of the investments.[665] The imprudent management of financial affairs should not operate to the economic prejudice of the children,[666] nor should an intentional depletion of a parent's business assets.[667] A parent, who is obligated to pay child support, must protect that obligation from risky ventures and cannot seek to reduce the amount of child support to help recover from business misadventures.[668] A parent cannot seek to reduce his or her child support obligation by acting recklessly or irresponsibly nor rely upon an inability to pay that has been self-induced, as, for example, by a depression of income, a reduction of assets, lassitude in maximizing earning potential, or increasing the debt load.[669]

Statements made by a party as to their income as disclosed in loan applications can be evidence that warrants judicial imputation of income. The way business was conducted may also be compelling. Was business conducted in a transparent manner, or were there attempts to hide income from the taxation authorities? Was income split between the parties, thereby reducing the income of the respondent? All of these are factors that may go to a finding of imputation of income in the hands of one party or another.[670]

12) Bank Records

Income may be imputed to a parent where banking records are indicative of a higher income than that asserted.[671]

13) Income Splitting

Where each spouse received income from a corporation or family business before separation to provide a mechanism for income splitting for tax purposes and this practice terminated after spousal separation, income may be attributed to the obligor that is equivalent to the pre-separation joint income of the spouses.[672]

Income splitting by an obligor and his or her new spouse, which is unsupported by evidence that the new spouse is employed by the obligor's company, may warrant an imputation of income to the obligor.[673] A parent is not entitled to shield income by establishing a corporate structure for conducting business under which his new wife earns the lion's share of their household income. In these circumstances, a judicial inference may be drawn that the parent enjoyed the same earning capacity before and after the incorporation of the

665 *Grant v Wolansky* (1994), 4 RFL (4th) 365 (Alta QB); *Johnson v Johnson* (1982), 27 RFL (2d) 10 (BCSC).
666 *Monette v Jordan*, [1997] NSJ No 337 (TD).
667 *Bhullar v Bhullar*, [2001] OJ No 3034 (SCJ).
668 *Kidson v Techentin* (1994), 129 NSR (2d) 228 (Fam Ct); see also *Bakken v Bakken* (1995), 11 RFL (4th) 246 (Sask QB).
669 *Wundele v Wundele* (1994), 8 RFL (4th) 325 (BCCA).
670 *Lo v Lo*, 2011 ONSC 7663 at para 60, McDermot J.
671 *Schluessel v Schluessel*, [1999] AJ No 1555 (QB); *Van Deventer v Van Deventer*, [2000] BCJ No 37 (CA).
672 *Kowalewich v Kowalewich*, [1999] BCJ No 1715 (SC); *McLellan v McLellan*, [1999] NBJ No 348 (QB); *Brokop v Stepenoff*, [1999] SJ No 574 (QB).
673 *Butler v Butler*, [1999] OJ No 940 (Gen Div). See also *REG v TWJG*, 2011 SKQB 269 (common law partner); *Schaefer v Schaefer*, 2014 SKQB 8.

business.[674] Salaries or benefits paid to a self-employed obligor's children or other relatives may result in an attribution of income to the obligor in the absence of information that the amounts were paid under arm's-length conditions or were necessary expenses incurred in earning the obligor's income.[675] A court should refuse to impute income to an obligor on the basis of alleged income splitting with his new spouse, where that spouse works in the business and receives her entitlement to reasonable remuneration.[676]

14) Capital Assets

Income may be imputed to a parent on the basis of the ownership of considerable assets, with the amount of child support to be open to review when those assets fall subject to the other parent's property equalization claim.[677] A spouse's ownership and occupation of a mortgage-free home does not justify the attribution of additional monthly income to that spouse.

15) Diversion of Income

A court has the discretion to impute income to a parent for child support purposes where it appears that income has been diverted, which would affect the level of child support to be determined.[679] A court should refuse to impute income pursuant to section 19(1)(d) of the *Federal Child Support Guidelines* on the basis of an alleged diversion of income, where the wife's allegation that the husband had the ability to manipulate the time when earned commissions would be paid to him is found to be without substance in light of the evidence of the husband's employer and a long-standing policy whereby commissions were paid in the quarter following that in which they were earned.[680]

16) Unreasonable Expenses; Capital Cost Allowances; Optional Inventory Adjustments

Section 19(2) of the *Federal Child Support Guidelines* expressly provides that, for the purpose of determining whether a spouse or former spouse has unreasonably deducted expenses from income under section 19(1)(g) of the Guidelines, the reasonableness of an expense deduction is not solely governed by whether the deduction is permitted under the *Income Tax Act*.[681] Section 19(1)(g) of the Guidelines applies to sole proprietorships and can also apply

674 *Potter v Graham*, [2004] AJ No 1133 (QB); *McLeod v McLeod*, [2002] BCJ No 1817 (SC).

675 *Sarafinchin v Sarafinchin*, [2000] OJ No 2855 (SCJ); *Auckland v McKnight*, [1999] SJ No 652 (QB).

676 *Cary v Cary*, [1999] SJ No 569 (QB); see also *Blaine v Sanders*, [2000] MJ No 149 (QB) (obligor and new wife joint shareholders in company); *Lyttle v Bourget*, [1999] NSJ No 298 (SC) (parties dating but not cohabiting).

677 *Ostrovskaia v Ostrovsky*, [2001] OJ No 640 (SCJ).

678 *Spezowska v Reed*, [1998] AJ No 730 (QB).

679 *Federal Child Support Guidelines*, s 19(1)(d); *Elhert v Sailer*, 2023 ABCA 371 (order for financial disclosure by family trust).

680 *R v R*, [2000] OJ No 2830 (SCJ), var'd [2002] OJ No 1095, 24 RFL (5th) 96 (CA).

681 *Stockall v Stockall*, 2020 ABQB 229; *Dornick v Dornick*, [1999] BCJ No 2498 (CA); *Friesen v Friesen*, 2021 BCSC 2447 at para 42; *Shaw v Shaw*, [1997] MJ No 400 (QB); *MGH v KLDH*, 2020 NBCA 46; *Snow v Wilcox*, [1999] NSJ No 453 (CA); *Riel v Holland*, [2003] OJ No 3901 (CA); *Ludmer v Ludmer*, 2014 ONCA

where there is an incorporated business.[682] The fact that the *Income Tax Act* allows certain deductions for the calculation of income does not make such deductions reasonable for the purpose of applying the *Federal Child Support Guidelines* and the court may impute income where expenses have been unreasonably deducted.[683] A parent who controls a corporation is obligated to provide a breakdown of any personal benefits received from the corporation, and the failure to do so can result in the court presuming that certain payments made by the corporation have a personal component.[684]

Caution should be used when exercising judicial discretion to impute income under section 19(1)(g) of the Guidelines.[685] In *Osmar v Osmar*, Aston J stated:

> There is a substantial body of case-law under s. 19(1)(g) of the Guidelines, not all of it consistent. It is fair to conclude that judicial discretion in this area makes the determination of income more of an art than a science. In my view, the Guidelines require the court to examine expenses from the perspective of balancing the business necessity against the alternative of using those funds for child support. The court should respect the right of self-employed persons to run their business as they see fit, but may, nevertheless, question whether particular expenditures ought to be indirectly subsidized by lower child support.[686]

In order to impute claimed business expenses back into a parent's income pursuant to section 19(1)(g) of the Guidelines, it is not necessary to establish that the party who has claimed the deductions has acted improperly or outside the norm for claiming expenses in the income tax context. Rather, the issue is whether the full deduction of the expense results in a fair representation of the actual disposable income that is available to the party for personal expenses. In determining whether business expenses claimed by a party are unreasonable, the court must balance the business necessity of the expense against the alternative of using those monies for the purposes of child support. A party who seeks to deduct business expenses from their income for child support purposes has an obligation to explain the reasons for the expenses and how they were calculated and must provide documentary proof of the expenses in an organized manner so that the court can make a proper determination as to the reasonableness of the expense from the standpoint of the child support calculation.[687] The onus rests upon the parent seeking to deduct expenses from income to

---

827; *Van Boekel v Van Boekel*, 2020 ONSC 5265; *Haggerty v Haggerty*, 2023 ONSC 377; *Goertzen v Goertzen*, 2024 SKCA 45 at para 90. As to the burden of proof, see *Roseberry v Roseberry*, 2015 ABQB 75.

682 *Friesen v Friesen*, 2021 BCSC 2447 at para 39; *MT v JS*, 2023 BCCA 64.

683 *Scott v Scott*, [2006] AJ No 1740 (CA); *PCJR v DCR*, [2003] BCJ No 792 (CA); *Barry v Davis*, 2021 BCSC 546; *Shaw v Shaw*, [1997] MJ No 400 (QB); *Cook v McManus*, [2006] NBJ No 334 (QB); *Hollett v Vessey*, [2005] NSJ No 538 (SC); *Riel v Holland*, [2003] OJ No 3901 (CA); *Hill v Hill*, [1999] SJ No 145 (QB) (home-office expenses).

684 See *Claughton v Bokenfohr*, 2018 ABQB 1053, citing *Sweezey v Sweezey*, 2016 ABQB 131.

685 *Taylor v Hitchman*, 2013 ONCJ 655 at para 34, Parent J.

686 (2000), 8 RFL (5th) 368 at para 5 (Ont SCJ); see also *LMK v JMK*, 2015 MBQB 1; *Kerr v Erland*, 2014 ONSC 3555.

687 *Monahan-Joudrey v Joudrey*, 2012 ONSC 5984 at paras 33–34, Chappel J; see also *Zdyb v Zdyb*, 2017 ABQB 44, citing *Cunningham v Seveny*, 2017 ABCA 4; *JC v AAG*, 2020 BCSC 1485.

provide meaningful supporting documentation in respect to those deductions, failing which an adverse inference may be drawn.[688]

Although there may be good reason to look behind the income tax return of a self-employed spouse to determine whether business expenses should be allowed in the context of the Guidelines, a court is fully entitled to find that the expenses are reasonable and should not be added back into the spouse's income for the purpose of determining the child support to be paid.[689] The adoption of the "reasonableness" criterion in section 19 of the Guidelines underlines the fact that the provisions of the *Income Tax Act* are designed for different purposes than the *Federal Child Support Guidelines*.[690] The *Income Tax Act* is concerned with raising revenue or providing incentives for certain types of investments, and a strict application of its provisions may fail to provide a realistic picture of how much income is, or should be, available for the assessment of child support.[691] A court should not rely on "paper losses" allowed for income tax purposes that do not affect the income flowing through the parent's hands on a regular basis.[692] Reductions in rental income for "hard costs" relating to rental income are appropriate for the purpose of calculating child support but not all deductions are necessarily allowable.[693] A parent may be entitled to deduct reasonable expenses against rental income,[694] but the amount may be reduced for Guidelines purposes below the amount permitted under the *Income Tax Act* where the parent fails to discharge the onus of proving that the tax deducted expenses were incurred with respect to the repair or maintenance of the rental suite as distinct from the entire residence, which comprised a personal section as well as the rental accommodation.[695] Although section 19(1)(g) of the Guidelines refers to the unreasonable deduction of expenses from income, it does not necessarily require proof that the spouse has acted improperly or outside the norm in deducting the expenses from his or her taxable income.[696] An important consideration is whether there is a personal benefit derived from the business expenses that employed people would have to pay for from their income.[697] Even though the court is not bound by fixed rules, certain types of expenses should not be permitted to reduce the payor's income in determining his or her child support obligation. Some prohibited expenses have been expressly legislated in this context. For example, capital cost allowances with respect to real property must be included in a spouse's

---

688 *Murphy v Howes*, 2021 NSSC 354 at para 27; *Zeggelaar v Zeggelaar*, 2024 NSSC 34; *Wilson v Wilson*, 2011 ONCJ 103; *Mildren v Mildren*, 2013 ONSC 1435.

689 *Luedke v Luedke*, [2004] BCJ No 1157 (CA); *C v S*, 2010 NBQB 252; *Gossen v Gossen*, [2003] NSJ No 113 (SC).

690 *Murphy v Howes*, 2021 NSSC 354 at para 28.

691 *Cook v McManus*, [2006] NBJ No 334 (QB); *DYP v NPT*, 2015 NBQB 67; *Beilstein v Beilstein*, [1999] NWTJ No 34 (SC); *DL v GSL*, [2001] OJ No 2824 (SCJ); *Roy v Roy*, [1999] SJ No 680 (QB).

692 *Cook v McManus*, [2006] NBJ No 334 (QB); *Ralph v Ralph*, [2001] NJ No 238 (SC).

693 *DYP v NPT*, 2015 NBQB 67; *Bennett v Bonatsos*, 2014 ONSC 1048; see also *Dorion v Merkley*, 2014 ONSC 1777.

694 *Tse v Fiddis*, 2009 BCSC 1579; *Graves v Eager* (2002), 29 RFL (5th) 313 (Ont CA); *Appu v Appu*, 2014 ONSC 19; see also *Evans v Evans*, 2023 ONSC 3919 at para 78.

695 *Dorman v Dorman*, [2001] BCJ No 1635 (SC).

696 *Cook v McManus*, [2006] NBJ No 334 (QB); *Smith v Smith*, 2014 NSSC 15; *Szitas v Szitas*, 2012 ONSC 1548; *Wilson v Wilson*, [1998] SJ No 236 (QB); compare *Koren v Blum*, [2000] PEIJ No 121 at para 25 (CA) ("the authorities are not consistent" on whether s 19(1)(g) of the Guidelines "should be applied in the absence of some hint of bad faith or unreasonable conduct").

697 *Szitas v Szitas*, 2012 ONSC 1548; see also *MT v JS*, 2023 BCCA 64.

income under section 11 of Schedule III of the *Federal Child Support Guidelines*,[698] because real property does not decline in value and wear out over time to the point that it has to be replaced.[699] If the legislature had intended capital cost allowance on personal property to be automatically added back into income, it would have said so. Its failure to do so reinforces the conclusion that a reasonable capital cost allowance, or depreciation, for equipment necessary for the transaction of business is an appropriate deduction from the obligor's income under the Guidelines. Depreciation is a real expense, not merely a "paper" write-off. A court should ask itself in each case whether the rate of depreciation or capital cost allowance being used fairly reflects the useful working life of the asset in question and whether it is reasonable to expect that the equipment will be replaced when it wears out.[700] Although section 19(2) of the Guidelines stipulates that the reasonableness of an expense is not "solely" governed by whether it is permissible under the *Income Tax Act*, the use of the word "solely" suggests that deductibility under the *Income Tax Act* should be given considerable weight in determining what is reasonable. The judicial discretion should be exercised in a reasoned and consistent manner, having regard to the *Income Tax Act* and recognized accounting principles that have been uniformly applied by the spouse over a period of years.[701] It does not follow that a portion of capital cost allowance claimed on non-real property cannot be added back into income. Full deduction of such an allowance may be unreasonable. In some instances, a full exploration of income and expenses, capital acquisitions, and the state of depreciable property may be necessary before a decision can be taken whether to add back capital cost allowance on non-real property, but a comprehensive review is not always necessary.[702] Capital cost allowances respecting personal property will not be added to the obligor's income, unless the evidence indicates that the obligor is deducting capital cost allowances unreasonably in calculating his or her income for tax purposes. There should be no arbitrary reduction in the capital cost allowance under the Guidelines but there is nothing in the Guidelines to prevent an examination of individual items to avoid a deduction based on an unwarranted claim. A challenge does not necessitate an expensive appraisal of equipment for which capital allowance is claimed. It involves a determination of the likelihood of the equipment being replaced, the cost of any replacement, and perhaps the continued need of such equipment for the production of income. The object of the inquiry is to ascertain whether the capital cost allowance is real and required or whether it is more in the nature of a book entry with a consequent artificial reduction in income.[703] Because capital cost allowances under the *Income Tax Act* are based on a prescribed rate of depreciation, which may differ significantly from actual depreciation that reflects the cost of equipment spread over its estimated lifespan, evidence of the useful life of a piece of equipment may be admitted, as

---

698 *Trueman v Trueman*, [2000] AJ No 1301 (QB); *BAC v DLC*, [2003] BCJ No 1303 (SC); *Roberts v Roberts*, 2011 ONSC 7130; *Koren v Blum*, [2000] PEIJ No 121 (CA); *Rudachyk v Rudachyk*, [1999] SJ No 312 (CA); *King v King*, 2021 SKQB 201.

699 *Tidball v Tidball*, [1999] OJ No 904 (Gen Div); *More v Shurygalo*, 2010 SKQB 203.

700 *Trueman v Trueman*, [2000] AJ No 1301 (QB); *Tidball v Tidball*, [1999] OJ No 904 (Gen Div); *More v Shurygalo*, 2010 SKQB 203.

701 *Balaski v Balaski*, [1999] SJ No 259 (QB).

702 *Wilson v Wilson*, [1998] SJ No 236 (QB); *Dean v Friesen*, [1999] SJ No 424 (QB).

703 *Trueman v Trueman*, [2000] AJ No 1301 (QB); *Rudachyk v Rudachyk*, [1999] SJ No 312 (CA); *Dean v Friesen*, [1999] SJ No 424 (QB).

in other areas of civil litigation, from manufacturers, equipment dealers, auctioneers, appraisers, insurance adjusters, commercial renters, and the like. The courts should apply generally accepted accounting principles. Once the useful working life of the equipment is known, some basic analysis can be attempted, although different circumstances may neces sitate different methods of analysis.[704] The annual hours of use of the equipment, if known, should be relied upon rather than average use, and a formula that allows for salvage value at the end of the equipment's working life is appropriate.[705] The incremental effect of optional inventory adjustments, in that they are added to income in one year and are deducted as an expense in the next, may also need to be reviewed by an appropriate analysis of expenses, such as fertilizer, pesticide, or gasoline, with evidence being adduced as to the normal and reasonable expenditures for a farming operation of the size and nature before the court. Unless and until the court is presented with farming statements calculated by the accrual method, whereby it can relate specific expenses to specific crop production, any appropriate analysis of the expenses is precluded. Absent such evidence, the court cannot conclude that the expenses are unreasonably deducted from income.[706] The court may, nevertheless, find it appropriate to impute income pursuant to section 19(1)(d) or (e) of the *Federal Child Sup port Guidelines* on the basis that income has been diverted that would affect the amount of child support under the Guidelines or on the basis that the obligor's property is not reason ably used to generate income.[707] On interim applications, courts rarely have more than income tax returns and contradictory affidavits of the parties. The facts of the particular case must determine what portion of capital cost allowance, if any, should be added back to the obligor's income for the purpose of assessing child support under the Guidelines. Where dire need exists, courts are inclined to consider capital cost allowance as an unreasonable expense under the Guidelines.[708] Income attributed to obligors with respect to the capital cost claimed on account of equipment has ranged from 0 to 100 percent.[709] Even if the claimed capital cost allowance is not an actual out-of-pocket expense, there must be reason able provision for equipment depreciation and eventual replacement, where that equipment provides the means whereby the claimant earns his or her income. In the absence of evidence respecting a reasonable depreciation rate or any evidence that the deduction is unreasonable, the court may accept the capital cost allowance available under the *Income Tax Act* and refuse to attribute this amount as additional income.[710] The following factors have been identified by the Manitoba Court of Appeal as relevant for consideration in deciding whether or not capital cost allowances should be imputed back into income:

1. Was the CCA deduction an actual expense in the year?
2. Was the CCA deduction greater than or less than the cost of acquisitions during the same time period?

---

704 *Huber v Yaroshko*, [2000] SJ No 201 (QB); *Schwark v Schwark*, [2000] SJ No 489 (QB) (reliance placed on Saskatchewan Agriculture and Food, "Farm Machinery Custom and Rental Rate Guide, 2000").

705 *Schwark v Schwark*, [2000] SJ No 489 (QB).

706 *Ibid.*

707 *Ibid.*

708 *Poff v Fenel*, [1998] SJ No 608 (QB); see also *Trueman v Trueman*, [2000] AJ No 1301 (QB).

709 *Hauger v Hauger*, [2000] AJ No 753 (QB); *Simpson v Palma*, [1998] SJ No 581 (QB).

710 *Desrochers v Desrochers*, [1998] MJ No 379 (QB).

3. Was the CCA deduction greater than or less than the repayments of principal with respect to chattels in question?
4. Was the CCA deduction the maximum allowable CCA deduction?
5. Was it necessary to take the CCA deduction in that year?
6. How much of a loss in a business year resulted in that year?
7. Are the chattels for which the CCA was claimed truly needed for business purposes?
8. [Have] the chattels for which the CCA was claimed truly depreciated?
9. Is it foreseeable that future chattel purchases will not be required?
10. Is there a pattern of spending which establishes a greater real income than income tax returns indicate?
11. If the children were living with the spouse, would they benefit from the actual income earned by the spouse?
12. Is there a dire need for child support?

After enumerating these factors, the judgment affirmed that no general rule can be readily established as to when capital cost allowances should be imputed as income under section 19 of the Guidelines. Each case must be decided on its own merits, after scrutinizing the business in respect of which the capital cost allowance is being claimed, the equipment on which the deduction is being claimed, and the capital cost allowances claimed in past years, as well as the justification advanced by the party making the claim.[711] Although the Manitoba Court of Appeal listed twelve factors as relevant for consideration, it may not be necessary to address each factor in every case. In *Szitas v Szitas*,[712] Chappel J of the Ontario Superior Court of Justice identified the following additional factors as relevant:

1. Whether the capital cost allowance deduction claimed in the year in question corresponds generally with the actual depreciation of the property for which it was claimed.
2. Is there an intention to replace the chattel(s) in relation to which the deduction is claimed? If there is an intention to replace it, what is the cost of replacement and when will it need to be replaced?
3. Does the chattel continue to serve a useful function for the business?
4. Did the party claiming the capital cost allowance deduction set aside funds during the years in which the deduction is claimed for the purchase of new equipment?
5. Is the capital cost allowance deduction a real expense or a book entry to simply reduce income? Is it reasonable and necessary?
6. What capital acquisitions are needed in the foreseeable future to sustain or expand the business?

When the capital cost allowance on personal property is challenged under the Guidelines, the court will focus on the likelihood of the particular asset being replaced, the cost of replacement, and the question whether the asset will continue to be needed for the production of

711 *Andres v Andres*, [1999] MJ No 103 (*sub nom Cornelius v Andres*) (1999), 170 DLR (4th) 254 (Man CA); see also *CGL v DKL*, 2016 ABQB 71; *Luedke v Luedke*, [2004] BCJ No 1157 (CA); *Karisik v Chow*, 2010 BCCA 548; *AA v CA*, 2012 BCSC 1419; *LMK v JMK*, 2015 MBQB 1; *Wyndels v Minuk*, 2019 MBQB 96; *JR v CR*, [2005] NSJ No 502 (SC); *Szitas v Szitas*, 2012 ONSC 1548; *Koren v Blum*, [2000] PEIJ No 121 (CA); *Petterson v Petterson*, 2010 SKQB 418.

712 2012 ONSC 1548 at para 64.

income. The primary object of the analysis is to determine whether the deduction claimed is real or more in the nature of a book entry.[713] A bare submission, without evidence, is an insufficient basis for concluding that the capital cost allowance on personal property is properly excluded from Guidelines income, but if there is some evidence supporting the reasonableness of the expense beyond the fact that it is allowable under the *Income Tax Act*, the court is unlikely to deny the deduction in calculating the parent's Guidelines income. Similarly, the court will not second-guess the rates permitted under the *Income Tax Act* and *Regulations* unless the allowable rate seems unusual or based on a specific tax policy rather than on the likely economic life of the asset in question.[714] It is always a matter of assessing the reasonableness of a capital cost allowance for personal property and other expense deductions for Guidelines' income purposes. When a parent is engaged in a business where technology is a salient factor, assets required for the business will often depreciate as they become outmoded and need to be replaced on a regular basis; consequently, a capital cost allowance is a realistic factor to consider in such a business.[715] Where capital cost allowance deductions are made through a private corporation in which the parent is the sole shareholder, the court may pierce the corporate veil in the interests of achieving justice under the Guidelines and add back the deductions into the parent's personal income for the purpose of applying the Guidelines. Before a court can impute income to a parent by adding back CCA claimed on corporate assets, it must follow a two-step process under section 18 of the Guidelines: first, it must adjust the corporate pre-tax earnings by adding back some or all of the CCA; and, second, it must then impute some or all of the adjusted pre-tax earnings to the spouse.[717]

The court may disallow an inventory election that results in an artificial reduction of the obligor's income in a particular year.[718] Neither Schedule III nor section 19 of the Guidelines specifically authorizes a court to adjust a spouse's farm income by ignoring the deemed income arising by way of an inventory adjustment, but a court may ignore or adjust any expense lawfully claimed, if it distorts the spouse's true income. The exercise of the right to ignore or adjust inventory adjustment income and expenses requires the court to redo the spouse's income and cash flow calculation over a period of years. Such unwinding often results in a lower average income and cash flow being assigned over the immediately preceding years and an increase in income for the current year. A court may decline to attribute additional current income to the obligor based on an inventory adjustment, where the adjustment has been made consistently over several years preceding the breakup of the family, no evidence or submissions have been advanced to suggest that the expenses claimed are unreasonable within the meaning of section 19(1) of the Guidelines, and an unstructured judicial adjustment of expenses taken in accordance with recognized accounting and income

---

713 *Beaudry v Beaudry*, 2010 ABQB 119; *Rudachyk v Rudachyk*, [1999] SJ No 312 (Sask CA).

714 *Egan v Egan*, [2002] BCJ No 896 (SC).

715 *Luedke v Luedke*, [2004] BCJ No 1157 (CA).

716 *Trueman v Trueman*, [2000] AJ No 1301 (QB); *Gosse v Sorensen-Gosse*, 2011 NLCA 58; *Rudachyk v Rudachyk*, [1999] SJ No 312 (CA). Compare *Richardson v Richardson*, 2013 BCCA 378; *Gossen v Gossen* [2003] NSJ No 113 at para 83 (SC).

717 *More v Shurygalo*, 2010 SKQB 203. Compare *Gossen v Gossen*, [2003] NSJ No 113 at para 83 (SC). See also *Richardson v Richardson*, 2013 BCCA 378.

718 *Desrochers v Desrochers*, [1998] MJ No 379 (QB); *Voth v Voth*, [2004] MJ No 137 (QB); *Daku v Daku*, [1999] SJ No 330 (QB); *Tamke v Tamke*, [2001] SJ No 791 (QB).

tax reporting methods could cause irretrievable damage to one or all parties.[719] When there is a marked departure from accounting practices utilized in previous years, an onus rests on the party asserting that departure to provide a credible explanation for so doing.[720] Given that optional inventory adjustment rules are an artificial device for averaging income for income tax purposes, if they are used in determining income under the *Federal Child Support Guidelines*, they must be consistently applied in that additions and deductions must be taken into account.[721] Inventory adjustments and capital cost allowances that reduce a farmer's income on his income tax returns to a negligible amount are not necessarily added back into his income for the purpose of determining the amount of support payable under the *Federal Child Support Guidelines*, but if marginal farming circumstances condemn him to a perennial annual income of virtually zero, the court may impute income to him on the basis of his duty to seek out alternative employment to meet his child support obligation.[722] Optional inventory adjustments employed by farmers in the cash method of accounting, though appropriate as a means of averaging income for tax purposes, should be excluded in calculating a farmer's income under the Guidelines.[723] Where the determination of a parent's income under the *Prince Edward Island Child Support Guidelines* involves capital cost allowances or optional inventory adjustments, it is not sufficient for that parent to simply provide copies of relevant income tax returns as required by section 21 of the Guidelines. This will not enable the trial judge to conduct the necessary analysis and make an appropriate determination of parental income under the Guidelines. The parent asserting the deducted expenses must justify the reasonableness of the deductions.[724]

A court may decline to take the forgiveness of loans into account in assessing a farmer's income.[725]

While offsetting farm losses may lower the obligor's income tax payable on off-farm income, it does not follow that such losses will be allowed to reduce the obligor's income for the purposes of the *Federal Child Support Guidelines*.[726] Some courts have allowed such losses, at least in part;[727] others have asserted that such losses should not normally be allowed.[728] In the final analysis, the issue would appear to be one of reasonableness.[729] Consequently a court may refuse to allow a parent to deduct farming losses from his or her other income where there is a consistent pattern of farm losses that make it difficult to conclude that the property

---

719 *Balaski v Balaski*, [1999] SJ No 259 (QB); *Dean v Friesen*, [1999] SJ No 424 (QB).

720 *Homenuk v Homenuk*, [1999] SJ No 263 (QB).

721 *DN v CR*, [1999] SJ No 403 (QB).

722 *Hudson v Markwart*, [2003] SJ No 264 (QB); compare *JDK v CEM*, 2009 MBQB 175.

723 *Poff v Fenel*, [1998] SJ No 608 (QB); *Krzak v Erixon*, 2008 SKQB 468.

724 *Koren v Blum*, [2000] PEIJ No 121 (CA); compare *Egan v Egan*, [2002] BCJ No 896 (CA), Newbury JA, dissenting; *Rush v Rush*, [2002] PEIJ No 29 (SC).

725 *DN v CR*, [1999] SJ No 403 (QB).

726 *Nicholauson v Nicholauson*, 2019 SKQB 287.

727 *Gibb v Gibb*, [2005] BCJ No 2730 (interim proceeding); *Cole v McNeil*, [2001] NBJ No 37 (QB); *Dreger v Dreger*, [2000] SJ No 11 (QB); compare *Johnson v Johnson*, 2012 SKCA 87.

728 *TLK v DNK*, [1999] SJ No 401 (QB); see also *Botha v Botha*, [2000] AJ No 1533 (QB); *McMahon v Hodgson*, [2002] OJ No 555 (SCJ); *Van Boekel v Van Boekel*, 2020 ONSC 5265 (cutting horse activity was a hobby not a business); *Nichol v Johnson*, [2003] SJ No 736 (QB).

729 *Putnam v Putnam*, 2010 NSSC 115; *Swan v Swan*, 2024 SKCA 2; see also *Thomas v Thomas*, 2019 NLCA 32. And see *Swan v Swan*, 2024 SKCA 2 at paras 42–46.

is being reasonably utilized to generate income.[730] A parent is not entitled to set off farm losses against employment income for the purpose of determining the amount of support payable under the *Federal Child Support Guidelines*, where the history of annual losses is likely to continue unless the parent reorganizes his affairs. A parent who chooses to operate a farm at a loss cannot expect his former wife, his children, or the public to subsidize the operation when there are reasonable alternatives open, such as renting the farm property.[731]

Special care must be taken when scrutinizing the expenses of self-employed spouses. The court should focus on expenses that were necessarily incurred to earn income. Discretionary expenses, such as entertainment or promotional expenses, even if deductible from taxable income, may be more readily reduced or disallowed, as may also capital cost depreciation for use of an office in the home or automobile expenses.[732] Previous judicial decisions do not provide a magic formula for reviewing or discounting business expenses but may offer some indication of when a court might refuse to recognize a deduction or, at least, scrutinize it very carefully. To this extent, they may be useful in determining whether particular expenses are reasonable or whether income should be attributed pursuant to section 19(1)(g) of the *Federal Child Support Guidelines* on the basis that the spouse has unreasonably deducted expenses from his or her income. The court must also have regard to Schedule III of the Guidelines for regulated specific adjustments, which are themselves subject to the operation of sections 17 through 20 of the Guidelines.[733]

Repeated annual losses from a supplementary part-time business may be allowed by the Canada Revenue Agency for income tax purposes, but may not be deductible from the obligor's income in calculating support under the *Federal Child Support Guidelines*.[734] Where an obligor seeks to deduct secondary business or farming losses from his or her income, the court may look to the criteria applied by the Canada Revenue Agency in determining whether the business is being operated with a reasonable expectation of profit. Where the operation is too small to give any hope of profit, where the owner devotes little time to operation and has not employed other persons, where there is little ongoing capital investment, and where the operation reports little or no gross income for several years, the court may conclude that the operation does not constitute a business with any reasonable expectation of profit and the losses or expenses should not be deducted from the obligor's income. But the start-up and ongoing expenses of a business in the early stages of its development are often more substantial than the income generated. Consequently, a court may conclude that any assumption that the business has no reasonable expectation of profit would be premature, in which event the court should refuse to impute additional income to the obligor pursuant to sections 19(1) and (2) of the *Federal Child Support Guidelines*.[735] Income may be imputed to an obligor because of benefits received from a business corporation, such as

---

730 *Smith v Smith*, [2001] AJ No 1420 (CA); *Roberts v Roberts*, 2011 ONSC 7130; *Koronkiewicz v Gottselig*, [2006] SJ No 339 (QB); *Johnson v Johnson*, 2012 SKCA 87.

731 *Myketiak v Myketiak*, [2001] SJ No 85 (CA); *Johnson v Johnson*, 2012 SKCA 87.

732 *CMP v PEP*, [1999] AJ No 1478 (QB); *Murphy v Howes*, 2021 NSSC 354; *Szitas v Szitas*, 2012 ONSC 1548; *Crawford v Crawford*, [1998] SJ No 322 (QB).

733 *Omah-Maharajh v Howard*, [1998] AJ No 173 (QB); *Snow v Wilcox*, [1999] NSJ No 453 (CA).

734 *LAK v AAW*, [2005] AJ No 1140 (QB); *Kyung v Bowman*, [1999] BCJ No 1305 (SC); *Hradowy v Hradowy* 2011 MBQB 64; *Proulx v Proulx*, [2009] OJ No 1680 (SCJ); *Bowering v Bowering*, [2001] SJ No 657 (QB).

735 *Sackney v Ficko*, [1999] SJ No 27 (QB) (application for interim child support).

expenses associated with the personal use of a vehicle, travel, and entertainment expenses.[736] Where taxable benefits, such as the use of a company vehicle, have not been reported to the Canada Revenue Agency, the court may impute income to the recipient for the purpose of determining his or her income under the *Federal Child Support Guidelines*.[737]

Where business expenses are added back into a parent's income under the *Federal Child Support Guidelines*, they should be grossed up to reflect their tax-free status to the parent.[738]

17) Barter Arrangements

Barter arrangements involving the obligor may also justify an attribution of income under the Guidelines.[739]

18) Casual Earnings

Income may be imputed to a spouse on the basis of casual earnings unconnected with employment.[740] Non-taxable income from curling activities may be grossed up for income tax under the *Manitoba Child Support Guidelines*, after deductions are allowed for legitimate expenses for out-of-town travel, accommodation, and needs. Given the nature of these earnings, the court may grant an order for ongoing annual disclosure of the obligor's curling revenue and expenses.[741]

19) Underutilized Assets

Where the earned income of spouses is insignificant, the court may impute income to them based on their respective capital assets that are capable of generating income, even though the assets are tax sheltered.[742] The *Federal Child Support Guidelines* emphasize income as the fundamental criterion for determining child support and provide little guidance where a parent is asset rich but income poor. Courts are now beginning to address this issue and have imputed income on the basis that assets may be sold or rearranged in order to generate income for support payments.[743] Section 19(1)(e) of the Guidelines expressly empowers a court to attribute income if a spouse's property is not reasonably used to generate income. Imputing income on the basis of underutilized capital assets is not subject to readily identifiable rules, but section 19(1)(e) of the Guidelines does not require that the obligor deliberately pursue a

736 *Penney v Boland*, [1999] NJ No 71 (UFC).

737 *See v See*, [1999] OJ No 698 (Gen Div).

738 *Hall v Hall*, [2006] AJ No 563 (QB); *Kuznecov v Kuznecov*, [2006] BCJ No 1155 (SC); *Voth v Voth*, [2004] MJ No 137 (QB); *Riel v Holland*, [2003] OJ No 3901 (CA); see also *Sarafinchin v Sarafinchin*, [2000] OJ No 2855 (SCJ); *Dias v Dias*, 2015 ONSC 7512; *Ouellette v Uddin*, 2018 ONSC 4520; compare *Johnson v Johnson*, [2000] BCJ No 2065 (SC). See also *Bordin v Bordin*, 2015 ONSC 3730 at paras 89–92 (gross up to be made at marginal, not average, tax rate).

739 *SAD v MA*, 2019 NBQB 85; *See v See*, [1999] OJ No 698 (Gen Div).

740 *Re Gill*, [1999] BCJ No 820 (Prov Ct).

741 *Smith v Smith*, [1999] MJ No 74 (QB).

742 *Caccamo v Kenny*, [1998] OJ No 4123 (Gen Div).

743 *Beilstein v Beilstein*, [1999] NWTJ No 34 (SC), citing *Pentland v Pentland*, [1998] OJ No 2678 (Gen Div) and *BLMG v DJEG*, [1998] MJ No 278 (QB). See also *MacDougall v MacDougall*, [2005] NSJ No 129 (SC).

policy of evading his or her child support obligations.[744] A judicial review to ascertain whether assets are underutilized as income producers is appropriate to prevent a wealthy spouse from avoiding child support obligations solely because his or her income is negligible. Income may be imputed by reason of the underutilization of assets within the meaning of section 19(1)(e) of the Guidelines where there is vacant property that could be rented, where money is loaned without interest or at a very low rate of interest, or where there are unproductive assets available for disposal or reinvestment. Section 19(1)(e) of the Guidelines is intended to authorize an imputation of income where the actual income is needlessly low. To some degree, it will generate an arbitrary figure, but the use of section 19(1)(e) of the Guidelines does provide some opportunity for the exercise of judicial discretion to assure the payment of reasonable and fair child support.[745] Where the obligor has received substantial gifts from his or her parents, a reasonable income yield of a portion of the gift may be attributed to the obligor in assessing child support, even though a substantial portion of the gifts has already been spent. To ignore the income potential of such a substantial windfall would be inconsistent with the stated objective in section 1 of the Guidelines, which seeks to ensure that children continue to benefit from the financial means of both parents after separation.[746] Income may be imputed under section 19(1)(e) of the Guidelines where the obligor will have a substantial capital sum available for investment after the equalization of the spousal net family property has been effectuated.[747] A court may decline to impute income under section 19(1)(e) of the Guidelines on the basis of the unreasonable non-utilization of assets to generate income where the asset in question was the matrimonial home occupied by the mother and daughter.[748]

20) Cohabitant's or Spouse's Income

Income has been attributed to a spouse whose household expenses are shared by an unmarried cohabitant,[749] but widespread adoption of this practice would undermine the predictability and certainty sought to be achieved by the provincial and territorial tables under the *Federal Child Support Guidelines.* Different considerations apply, however, in those situations where the Guidelines expressly confer a judicial discretion in the exercise of which the court is required to take into account the means or ability to pay of the parties. The income of a spouse cannot be attributed to a parent against whom child support is claimed[750] and an application should, therefore, be dismissed where the parent has no independent source of income and is not intentionally unemployed or underemployed.[751] Any contrary interpretation of "income" would fly in the face of section 16 of the *Federal Child Support Guidelines* and would undermine the consistency that was sought to be achieved in the establishment of provincial and territorial tables that fix a specific amount of child support that is based on the obligor's income and the number of "children of the marriage" who are entitled to support.

744 See *Schoff v Schoff*, 2020 SKQB 290 (spousal support).
745 *Rudachyk v Rudachyk*, [1999] SJ No 312 (CA).
746 *Ellis v Carpenter*, [1999] OJ No 934 (Gen Div).
747 *Kowalski v Kowalski*, [1997] OJ No 4050 (Gen Div); *Schoff v Schoff*, 2020 SKQB 290 (spousal support).
748 *Rattenbury v Rattenbury*, [2000] BCJ No 889 (SC).
749 *Courchesne v Charlebois*, [1998] OJ No 2625 (Prov Ct); *MacNaught v MacNaught*, [1998] PEIJ No 27 (TD).
750 *Kavanagh v Kavanagh*, [1999] NJ No 358 (SC); *Parsons v Clarke*, [2002] NJ No 162 (SC).
751 *Corbett v Lanteigne*, [1998] BCJ No 2207 (SC).

Spousal income might, nevertheless, be relevant in those situations arising under sections 3(2)(b),[752] 4(b)(ii),[753] and 9[754] of the *Federal Child Support Guidelines* wherein the court is granted a discretion that is to be exercised having regard to the "condition[s], means, needs, and other circumstances" of the parties or under section 7(1) of the Guidelines, which refers to the "means of the [parties]."[755] Spousal income may also be relevant to the exercise of judicial discretion under section 5 of the Guidelines where child support is sought against a person who stands in the place of a parent.[756] Spousal income is also relevant in the context of a plea of undue hardship under sections 10(1) and (2) of the Guidelines[757] and in any comparison of the living standards in the respective households under sections 10(3) and (4) of the Guidelines.[758]

21) Shareholder Loans

In *Rudachyk v Rudachyk*,[759] the Saskatchewan Court of Appeal concluded that the repayment of a shareholder's loan is not income for the purpose of applying the *Federal Child Support Guidelines*. However, as Mesbur J of the Ontario Superior Court observed in *Waese v Bojman*,[760] any such repayment of capital may result in the judicial imputation of income on the basis that the capital asset is being underutilized to produce income within the meaning of section 19(1)(e) of the Guidelines. Again, in *Tauber v Tauber*,[761] Mesbur J concluded that income should be imputed to a parent pursuant to section 19(1)(e) of the Guidelines where the company owed a significant amount of money to the shareholding parent and no interest was being paid on the money.

Income may be attributed to a parent pursuant to sections 19(1)(d) and (h) of the *Federal Child Support Guidelines* on the basis that commission payments to that parent became artificially low as a result of funnelling the money through the parent's shareholder's loan account. In imputing income under these circumstances, the court may gross up the payments received to reflect the fact that the shareholder's loan payments are tax-free.[762]

In *Hesse v Hesse*,[763] Veit J of the Alberta Court of Queen's Bench held that legitimate shareholder loan repayments received at an appropriate time will not normally be characterized as income. However, section 18(1) of the *Federal Child Support Guidelines* may be engaged where a child support obligor does not receive income from a company by which he or she is employed and of which he or she is a shareholder, director, or officer, but receives only repayment of a shareholder loan. Where the subsection is engaged, the court must assess the fairness of the income situation. If the corporation had the funds available to repay

752 See Chapter 3, Section J.
753 See Chapter 9, Section B.
754 See Chapter 6.
755 See Chapter 1, Section H and Chapter 5, Section B.
756 See Chapter 3, Section J.
757 See Chapter 7, Section G.
758 See Chapter 7, Section J.
759 [1999] SJ No 312 (CA); see also *Dobson v Dobson*, [2005] SJ No 686 (QB).
760 [2001] OJ No 2009 (SCJ).
761 [2001] OJ No 3259 (SCJ).
762 *Gray v Gray*, [2002] MJ No 274 (QB).
763 2010 ABQB 314. See also *CRP v NDP*, 2023 NBKB 197.

the loan, it had the funds available to pay a draw instead. The child support obligor in this situation bears the onus of establishing the validity of the corporate decision that deprived him or her of income. If no valid corporate objective is proved, then the obligor's child support obligation may be based on pre-tax corporate income available. In *Pallot v Pallot*, Chamberlist J of the British Columbia Supreme Court found that the father's withdrawals from his shareholder's loan account in 2010 represented monies available to him under sec tion 18(2) of the Guidelines.

In a detailed summary of relevant caselaw relating to the question whether a court may impute income to a parent who receives payments by way of shareholder's loans in a private corporation, Colford J of the New Brunswick Court of King's Bench in *CRP v NDP* observed:

> [249] A review of case law across the country confirms the issue is a live one in that there are considerably conflicting decisions on whether a partial or full repayment of a shareholder's loan should be imputed as income. In the end like many legal issues, determinations appear to be fact driven.
>
> [250] Recently the Alberta Court of Queen's Bench has this to say in *Wilson v Holmes*, [2022] AJ No 269, Q.L. at para. 63:
>
>> The orthodox view is that a shareholder's loan balance (money owing to him or her by the corporation) is not income to the shareholder, either as a static number or on full or partial repayment to the shareholder: *Rudachyk v Rudachyk*, 1999 CanLII 12271 (SKCA) (para 11: "There is no question the repayment of a shareholder's loan is not income . . ."); *Merrifield v Merrifield*, 2021 SKCA 85 (para 43); *Dai v Ding*, 2019 ONSC 6118 (Gilmore J.) (para 281); and *Walshe v Walshe*, 2021 MBQB 259 (Menzies J.) (para 41). . . .
>
> [252] Conversely, there [have] also been many cases where courts in other jurisdictions have imputed income on the basis that the shareholder loan was being underutilized to produce income within the meaning of section 19(1)(e) of the *FCSG*, (see *Waese v. Bojman*, 2001 CanLII 28221 (ON SC), [2001] O.J. No. 2009).
>
> [253] Similarly, section 19(1)(e) has also been applied in circumstances where the corporation owed a significant amount of money to the shareholding spouse and interest was not being paid on the funds, (see *Tauber v. Tauber*) 2001 CanLII 28234 (ON SC), [2001] O.J. No. 3259 and *Kerr v. Evland* [2014] O.J. No. 3032).
>
> [254] In *Hogan v Hogan*, 2004 Carswell Ont. 3896 [2004 CanLII 31372 (ONSC)] at para 137, the court was very prepared to impute income to the payor spouse based on repayments to his shareholder loan account. . . .
>
> [255] Similarly, in *Pallot v Pallot*, [2010] B.C.J. No. 1600, the Court found the shareholder loan account represented monies available to Mr. Pallot under s. 18(2) of the *FCSG*. In that case, the court determined that the shareholder loan account was being utilized and treated by the defendant as monies available to him. In the Court's view this was not an uncommon business practice.
>
> [256] Courts have also engaged s.18(1) of the *FCSG* where a support obligor does not receive income from a corporation in which he or she is employed and of which they are

764 2010 BCSC 1146.

a shareholder director or officer, but receive only repayment of a shareholder loan. When considering an adjustment under s.18, the Court must strike a balance between maintaining the ongoing operations of the company and determining an amount of income that fairly reflects the amount of money available for the payment of support. . . .

[258] Our Court of Appeal in *C.(M). v. O.(J)* [2017] N.B.C.A.No.15 addressed facts similar to those before the court in this instance. . . .

[259] The Court had this to say about shareholder's loans and the motion judge's treatment of the account in paragraphs 17-19 of the decision:

> 17. . . . As was found by Marshall J. in *W. (M.J.) v. W. (B.J.)*, 2006 ABQB 19, [2006] A.J. No. 7 (Alta. Q.B.) (QL), a shareholders loan is a "means by which a company has free use of capital" to assist in its operations. For small corporations, these loans may be "an integral part of a successful operation". The maintenance of a shareholder's loan account accords with the "basic approach of drawing as little as possible from the company and returning profits to the company" as a means of supplementing working capital. Marshall J. concluded such a loan is "very similar to an asset such as the shares in a company. It is, in effect, part of the Company structure" (see paras. 26-27). It is not "income" to the shareholder but is considered a return of principal.
>
> 18. In *Vincent v. Vincent*, 2012 BCCA 186, [2012] B.C.J. No. 818 (B.C.C.A.) (QL), the court concluded the following:
>
>> Clearly, both the income and capital dividends were available to the father for personal use and thus for child support. He chose to invest them in Robannah by way of a shareholder's loan in 2007, thereby increasing his equity in that company. In *Hausmann*, Kirkpatrick J.A., writing for this Court, noted at para. 11 that shareholders' loans are properly treated as equity, not debt, just as retained earnings are equity, not cash (at para. 66). [para. 55]
>
> 19. In *Chekowski v. Howland*, 2013 ABCA 299, [2013] A.J. No. 923 (Alta. C.A.) (QL), the court observed "each case must be decided on its own facts" (para. 14). *In the case at bar, Mr. C. bore the onus to establish the shareholders account was in essence a repayment for funds he advanced to sustain the operation of the company and therefore they were not available to him for child support. The motion judge concluded Mr. C. did not discharge that onus. I would not interfere with her decision. . . .*

[264] I agree with Ms. P that there is more money available to Mr. P than what is apparent from his guideline income. Mr. P has not in my view, discharged the onus of establishing the due to shareholder accounts were used solely as a repayment of funds advanced by him to sustain the operation of the company. . . .

[266] Accordingly, for the years 2016 to 2023, Mr. P 's income will be imputed in the amounts set out by Ms. P and summarized previously pursuant to sections 19(1)(a) and (h) of the *FCSG*. The exception being the sum identified for 2017, which properly calculated from the audited financial statement is $55,727.00.[765]

765 *CRP v NDP*, 2023 NBKB 197 at paras 249–66.

22) Personal Injuries Settlement

Income may be imputed to a parent on the basis that a portion of a personal injuries settlement received from third parties constituted income replacement.[766]

23) Overtime

Overtime income is relevant to the amount of child support[767] but the annual income to be attributed to the obligor may be discounted where employment is seasonal and the amount of overtime is variable.[768] A distinction has been drawn between mandatory and discretionary overtime income. Although a spouse may not be obliged to work overtime, income may be attributed to that spouse based on his or her perceived ability to pay child support in light of the historical pattern of his or her overtime income.[769] A judicial imputation of income should not be based on the obligor's assumption of excessively long hours of work, unless the previous pattern of overtime income is unlikely to change.[770] A past history of overtime income does not warrant its inclusion in a parent's projected income for the current year where the opportunity for ongoing overtime income has been eliminated.[771] Judicial decisions on the issue of including or excluding possible overtime income are resolved on the particular facts of the case. While refusing to impute overtime income to the parent, a court may direct the parent to annually provide copies of her income tax return to the recipient parent and to pay an adjusted amount of child support for the preceding year if the income actually received exceeds that previously attributed to the parent.[772] Seeking to provide guidance as to the circumstances that a court should take into account in determining what, if any, income from overtime employment should be imputed to a parent who is already engaged in regular full-time employment, Tuck J, in *RS v TS*,[773] offers the following opinion and non-exhaustive list of relevant factors for consideration:

> [para 44] Each overtime case is of course unique and fact driven. In the result there can not be developed a list of factors or guideposts to be considered in relation to the overtime issue that are exhaustive or weighted. Some obvious factors that may be considered in a principled approach to the issue of assessing reasonableness in this regard I think would have to include some of the following considerations as appropriate.
>
> 1. The necessity of overtime in relation to appropriate support needs. The determination of said necessity to include as appropriate a consideration of the condition, means and

---

766 *MK v RAS*, 2004 BCSC 1798; *Dalton v Craig*, [2002] OJ No 4686 (CA) (trial judgment varied by an order for retroactive child support in the amount of $100,000); *HAP v DBC*, 2015 YKSC 4.

767 *Davie v Davie*, [1998] BCJ No 1691 (SC); *Leet v Leet*, [2002] NBJ No 87 (QB) (periodic adjustment of child support envisaged); *Depace v Michienzi*, [2000] OJ No 453 (SCJ); *Katerynych v Hamel*, [2004] SJ No 329 (QB); see also *Federal Child Support Guidelines*, SOR/97-175, s 21(1)(c).

768 *Delaney v Delaney*, [1997] BCJ No 1675 (SC).

769 *Rainer v Rainer*, [2000] AJ No 918 (QB); *Guignard v Guignard*, [2009] OJ No 2267 (SCJ).

770 *Ames v Ames*, [1999] BCJ No 1816 (SC); *Penney v Penney*, [2001] NJ No 85 (SC); *White v White*, 2015 NSCA 52; see also *Peters v Atchooay*, 2022 ABCA 347 at para 74.

771 See *Ladouceur v Dupuis*, 2020 ONSC 8048 (overtime income no longer available following support obligor's promotion).

772 *Schenkeveld v Schenkeveld*, [2002] MJ No 69 (CA).

773 *RS v TS*, [2005] NBJ No 448 (QB).

needs of the affected parents, and the extent of the effect of removal of the disputed overtime amount from income on the pre-existing standard of living enjoyed by affected parties.

2. The issue of any potential reasonable detrimental reliance created by the past working of the disputed overtime.
3. Are the best interests of any children adversely impacted by working the questioned overtime hours, i.e. does same adversely affect the appropriate care of or the appropriate exercise of access to the children in question.
4. The extent to which the elimination of the questioned overtime is a deliberate attempt to avoid otherwise necessary support obligations.
5. A consideration, in context of the overtime in question, of the age and health of the payor.
6. The training, experience and education of the payor.
7. The nature of the actual overtime work, i.e. quantity, type of work (sedentary or labour intensive), how much notice of the availability or obligation with respect to particular overtime is provided and the effect of same.
8. The amount of overtime with respect to which there is reason to believe there will be some consistency of availability and appropriate ability to work.
9. The purpose of past overtime worked. Was it worked of necessity or for a specific purpose i.e. debt reduction, purchase of luxury item etc. and to what extent said need still exists.
10. Whether the working of the overtime is mandatory or discretionary from the employer's perspective. Is the working of the questioned overtime to some measure expected or advisable in relation to a person's employment, i.e. employer expectation, historical practice, trade practice or otherwise?
11. The potential affect of overtime on lifestyle and life quality issues, recognizing the need for all persons not to be unnecessarily thwarted in their pursuit of [a] rewarding balanced and fulfilled life.
12. Recognition of legitimately arising obligations of others with respect to the support in question.
13. Such other factors and considerations as [are] appropriate in particular circumstances.

[para 45] The considerations noted of course are not necessarily mutually exclusive.

24) Free or Subsidized Accommodation

Courts have treated free or subsidized accommodation as income for the purposes of calculating child support.[774] In *CLE v BMR*,[775] the Alberta Court of Appeal was called upon to determine a parent's income under the *Federal Child Support Guidelines* in circumstances where he received a financial subsidy from his employer to offset the exceedingly high cost of renting accommodation in Fort McMurray, Alberta, to which he had been transferred by the bank that employed him. The employer reported the subsidy as a taxable benefit in the amount of $650 per month on the parent's T4 slip. The question before the appellate

774 *JT v TK*, 2018 NSSC 42 at para 29, Beaton J.
775 2010 ABCA 187.

court was whether that was the appropriate amount to be attributed to the parent for the purpose of determining his income under the *Federal Child Support Guidelines.* Delivering the majority opinion of the Alberta Court of Appeal, Côté JA observed that section 16 of the Guidelines stipulates that, in determining a parent's income, the court must have regard to the sources of income set out under the heading "Total income" in the T1 General form, not simply to the amount reported in line 150 (now line 15000) of the parent's income tax return. Accepting that free or subsidized housing from an employer constitutes income for the purposes of the *Income Tax Act* and the *Federal Child Support Guidelines,* Côté JA concluded that the amount reported by an employer as a taxable benefit in the employee's T4 or T4A slip is not necessarily determinative of the value of the financial benefit received. In the particular circumstances of this case, Côté JA noted that the parent had not sought the transfer to Fort McMurray but accepted it in part because of the housing subsidy. He further noted that, without the subsidy, an employee would experience a significantly lower standard of living than similar employees serving the bank elsewhere in Canada. He, therefore, concluded that the value of the housing subsidy granted to the father should be determined having regard to the average Canadian monthly costs of renting similar accommodation.

In *Nielsen v Nielsen,*[776] the British Columbia Court of Appeal upheld the chambers judge's imputation of an annual income of $200,000 to the divorced husband on the basis of his intentional underemployment within the meaning of section 19(1)(a) of the *Federal Child Support Guidelines,* but allowed the husband's appeal insofar as an additional $42,000 was imputed to him as income in consequence of his enjoyment of free accommodation provided by a friend. In deciding to impute the rental value of the accommodation as income to the husband, the chambers judge had relied on *Morgan v Morgan,*[777] wherein the spouse was provided with free housing as part of his employment abroad. However, as the British Columbia Court of Appeal observed in *Nielsen,* the value of the free accommodation in *Morgan* was essentially part of the employee spouse's remuneration. The British Columbia Court of Appeal stated that there are circumstances where it would be appropriate for a court to exercise its discretion to impute income to a spouse who enjoys free accommodation. Such would be the case, for example, where the spouse would have earned additional income if he had to pay for housing. Imputing additional income would also be appropriate where a spouse is providing a service in exchange for free accommodation, as is often the case with managers of apartment buildings. In *Nielsen,* however, the free housing provided to the husband was unrelated to his employment and it was not payment for any service rendered. Accordingly, the chambers judge erred in imputing to the husband the rental value of his free accommodation as additional income.

Income may be imputed to the parent for allowing a friend to occupy a room in his residence rent free on a long-term basis.[778]

---

776 2007 BCCA 604; see also *Johnson v Johnson,* 2011 BCCA 190; *JCM v MJM,* 2018 NBCA 42.

777 2000 BCSC 371. See also *Nugent v Nugent,* 2011 NLTD(F) 4 (housing benefit grossed up).

778 *Terracol v Terracol,* 2010 ONSC 6442.

25) Income from Illegal Activity

Speaking to imputing income based on illegal activities in *BGMS v JEB*,[779] Fleming J of the British Columbia Supreme Court observed:

> [198] Denying any involvement in drug dealing, the respondent also argued the law does not permit the court to order the payment of child support based on an income that will be earned illegally, relying upon *S.J.S. v. Y.W.P.*, 2017 BCSC 798 (CanLII). In that case, the father was a self-proclaimed gangster. The parties enjoyed an extravagant lifestyle during the relationship funded by his criminal activity. Justice Baird concluded he could not impute an income to the husband that he would resort to crime to earn. The same concern about encouraging or requiring a person to continue criminal activity to comply with a child support order was expressed in *L.A.R. v. E.J.R.*, 2014 BCSC 966 (CanLII). Justice Schultes held it was not feasible as a matter of public policy to impute income to the father based on his illegal earnings from marijuana grow operations.
>
> [199] A different approach has been taken when dealing with past income. In *G.D. v. L.E.*, 2013 BCSC 798 (CanLII), for example, Justice McEwan ordered the husband to pay retroactive child support based on a higher income earned while his illegal "agricultural activities were continuing."
>
> [200] Similarly, *M.L.P. v. M.J.M.*, 2012 BCCA 395 (CanLII), allowed an appeal from a decision that permitted the husband to retroactively vary his child support obligation. After he stopped drug trafficking he was unemployed and spent his savings from illegal income on debt obligations. The Court of Appeal noted he had significantly underpaid his child support in the past having failed to disclose the considerable income he earned through the drug trade....
>
> [202] Clearly it is in BED's best interests for the respondent to cease his involvement in drug trafficking, in addition to making other profound personal changes. This as well as the broader public policy issue lead me to conclude that I cannot properly impute an income to the respondent that will likely require him to continue his illegal and dangerous business activities.

26) Foster Care Allowances

To the extent that a foster care allowance provides some form of compensation to the foster parent over and above expenses, some portion of it should be treated as income for child support purposes.[780] Money paid to a spouse for the foster care of children may be segregated into expenses and a fee for service. A distinction should be drawn between costs directly incurred by the spouse for the children and costs "allocated" to the children by the administrators of the foster care program. Notional rental income should be disallowed where there is no evidence that rental costs would be lower if foster children were not present in the home. After deducting the appropriate expenses and determining the fee for service

779 2018 BCSC 1628. See also *Blumer v Blumer*, 2004 BCSC 314 at paras 30–33.

780 *Cole v Cole*, 2010 BCSC 1330; see also *Bradford v Bradford*, 2022 BCSC 595 (funds received for the care of a developmentally disabled adult).

component of the money received, the consequential income must be grossed up for income tax in order to determine the spouse's total income for the purpose of assessing the amount of child support to be ordered.[781]

27) Legal Fees

Legal fees incurred in litigation involving support claims are not deductible from the payor's Guidelines income.[782]

28) Interim Orders

Evidence on an interim application for child support may well be less precise than what may be established at trial, and it is always open to the trial judge to readjust income findings dependent on the nature of the evidence presented at trial. It is incumbent on a party seeking a judicial imputation of income against a parent to provide the court with sufficient informa tion from which a reasonable inference can be drawn. A court should not engage in crystal ball gazing and should not impute income under section 18 of the *Manitoba Child Support Guidelines* without an evidentiary foundation.[783]

29) Applications to Vary

If support was initially calculated based on the court's acceptance of a payor's "declared" income, then changes in the declared income in subsequent years are indicative of a material change on an application to vary an order for child support. But if the original support order was based upon "imputed" income, a more comprehensive analysis is required on a motion to change. The court must consider: (a) why income was imputed on the original application and whether it is still appropriate to impute income to achieve a fair result; and (b) how the court quantified the imputed income and whether similar calculations are still applicable.[784] A party who ignores a court order requiring income disclosure and/or who fails to attend court when required, absent a reasonable explanation, does so at his or her own peril and an obligor's very tardy disclosure compliance should not ground a successful application to retroactively vary or vacate prior orders for child support on the basis of a material change of circumstances. In the words of Martin J, speaking for the Supreme Court of Canada, in *Colucci v Colucci*:

> Of course, a payor whose income was originally imputed because of an initial lack of disclosure cannot later claim that a change in circumstances occurs when he or she subsequently

781 *Kovich v Kreut*, [1998] BCJ No 2586 (SC).

782 *Sobczak v Evraire*, 2013 ONSC 1249; *Aalbers v Aalbers*, 2017 SKCA 43. But see *McBennett v Danis*, 2021 ONSC 3610 at paras 297–99 (legal fees to pursue support).

783 *Spiring v Spiring*, [2002] MJ No 424 (QB).

784 *Trang v Trang*, 2013 ONSC 1980; see also *Colucci v Colucci*, 2021 SCC 24 at para 63; *Reid v Chambers* 2022 ABKB 634; *Rana v Rana*, 2020 BCSC 1232; *Cross v Thompson*, 2019 MBQB 44; *Currie v Currie*, 2022 NSSC 23; *PW v CM*, 2021 NSSC 127; *Ruffolo v David*, 2016 ONSC 754; *Gray v Rizzi*, 2016 ONCA 152 at para 34; *Van Boekel v Van Boekel*, 2020 ONSC 5265; *Aalbers v Aalbers*, 2017 SKCA 43.

785 *Janiten v Moran*, 2019 ABCA 380; *Michaud v Kasali*, 2021 ONSC 6847.

produces proper documentation showing the imputation was higher than the table amount for their actual income. The payor cannot rely on their own late disclosure as a change in circumstances to ground a variation order (*Gray*, at paras. 33–34). This would "defeat the purpose of imputing income in the first place" and act as "a disincentive for payors to participate in the initial court process" (*Trang v. Trang*, 2013 ONSC 1980, 29 R.F.L. (7th) 364, at para. 53).[786]

30) Appeals

An appellate court should not disturb a trial judge's imputation of income to a parent, unless there is a manifest error or a significant misapprehension of the evidence.[787] In addressing a trial court's determination of a parent's income, including the judicial imputation of income, an appellate court must intervene when there is a material error, a serious misapprehension of the evidence or an error in law, but an appellate court cannot overturn a support order simply because it would have made a different decision or balanced the factors differently.[788] Consequently, an appellate court should refuse to interfere with a trial judge's refusal to impute income to a parent who opted for lesser paid employment so as to spend more time with his children, notwithstanding that the appellate court was "troubled" by this finding of fact by the trial judge.[789]

H. CHILD'S ACCESS TO INCOME

Section 3(1) of the *Federal Child Support Guidelines* establishes a presumptive rule whereby the usual amount of child support to be ordered will be the applicable provincial or territorial table amount. The amount of child support provided by the applicable provincial or territorial table is premised on the obligor's income, without regard to the condition, means, needs or other circumstances of the child.[790] In exceptional circumstances, however, a child's assets or income are relevant in determining the amount of child support to be paid. For example, a court may order a lower amount than the table amount of child support pursuant to section 3(2)(b) of the *Federal Child Support Guidelines* where the child is of the age of majority and is a beneficiary under a trust fund,[791] or has part-time employment that enables the child to contribute to post-secondary education expenses,[792] or where an unemployable adult child is entitled to a provincial disability pension.[793] A child's access to income is also relevant when special or extraordinary expenses are being sought under section 7 of the *Federal Child Support Guidelines* because the guiding principle in such cases is that the spouses or former spouses must share those expenses in proportion to their respective income, but only

786 *Colucci v Colucci*, 2021 SCC 24 at para 63; *Michaud v Kasali*, 2021 ONSC 6847; *Tyndall v Tyndall*, 2022 ONSC 131.

787 *Riad v Riad*, [2002] AJ No 1338 (CA).

788 *Beissner v Matheusik*, 2015 BCCA 308; *Schnell v Schnell*, [2001] SJ No 704 (CA); see also *Brown v Brown*, [2002] OJ No 862 (CA).

789 *Schindle v Schindle*, [2001] MJ No 564 (CA).

790 *Penney v Boland*, [1999] NJ No 71 (UFC); *Stokes v Stokes*, [1999] OJ No 5192 (SCJ).

791 *Merritt v Merritt*, [1999] OJ No 1732 (SCJ).

792 *Pitt v Pitt*, [1997] BCJ No 1528 (SC).

793 *Burhoe v Goff*, [1999] NBJ No 296 (QB); *Turner v Ansell*, 2012 ONSC 2598; *Klette v Leland*, 2014 SKCA 122.

after deducting from the expenses, "the contribution if any, from the child."[794] Furthermore, section 9 of the Guidelines, which regulates cases involving shared parenting time for not less than 40 percent of the year, requires the court to have regard to the "conditions, means, needs and other circumstances of each spouse and of any child for whom support is sought." In addition, section 10(3) and Schedule II of the Guidelines, which provide for comparison of the income of the respective households for the purpose of determining whether a plea of undue hardship can be upheld, envisage that the income of a child in either household will be taken into account.

The amount of support ordered for an adult child pursuing post-secondary education may be relatively small, where the child receives an income and can reasonably be expected to reduce his or her expenses to reflect that income.[796]

I. INCOME OF NON-RESIDENT SPOUSE; CURRENCY EXCHANGE RATE

Section 20(1) of the *Federal Child Support Guidelines* provides that, subject to subsection 2, where a spouse is a non-resident of Canada, his or her annual income is determined as though he or she were a resident of Canada. Where income is earned in a foreign jurisdiction, section 20 of the Guidelines requires its conversion into Canadian dollars in light of the applicable currency exchange rate.[797] Because there can be wide and rapid fluctuations in currency exchange rates, it may be desirable to determine the rate of exchange on the basis of the average or median rate over the preceding year, thereby avoiding unnecessary applications where there are frequent fluctuations in the exchange rate.[798]

Section 19(1)(c) of the Guidelines empowers a court to impute income to a foreign resident whose income tax liability is significantly lower than that applicable to a Canadian resident.[799] Pursuant to section 20(2) of the *Federal Child Support Guidelines*, in the converse situation where a foreign resident parent has effective rates of income tax that are significantly higher than those applicable in the province where the other parent habitually resides, the foreign resident's annual income will be the amount that the court determines

794 *Whitley v Whitley*, [1997] BCJ No 3116 (SC); *Fraser v Fraser*, [2001] OJ No 3765 (SCJ) (children's access to trust funds).

795 Compare *Perron v Hlushko*, 2015 ABQB 595 (disability benefits).

796 *Newman v Thompson* (1997), 30 RFL (4th) 143 (Man CA).

797 *Pousette v Janssen*, 2023 BCCA 176, supp reasons 2023 BCCA 272; *EKR v GAW*, [1997] MJ No 501 (QB); *Hare v Kendall*, [1997] NSJ No 310 (TD); *Mascarenhas v Mascarenhas*, [1999] OJ No 37 (Gen Div), aff'd (2000) 18 RFL (5th) 148 (Ont Div Ct) (caveat added).

798 *Walker v Walker*, 2019 ABQB 385; *Ward v Ward*, [2001] BCJ No 206; *JD v YP*, 2015 BCSC 321; *Saunders v Saunders*, 2011 NSCA 81; *Simpkin v Hasson*, 2016 NSSC 82; *Bennett v Bonatsos*, 2014 ONSC 1048; *LSP v JRP*, [2002] SJ No 35 (QB); compare *Horton v Horton*, [1999] OJ No 4855 (SCJ) (trial judge opted for the average of the over-the-counter rate and the rate reported at the date of the hearing). See also *Kelly v White*, [2002] OJ No 5397 (SCJ); *Pawlus v Pawlus*, [2004] OJ No 5706 (SCJ); *VKG v IG* 2023 ONSC 6329 at paras 249–50. Compare *JF v GF*, 2016 NBQB 46 (monthly chart ordered in light of "convulsive fluctuations" in exchange rate).

799 *Pousette v Janssen*, 2023 BCCA 176, supp reasons 2023 BCCA 272.

to be appropriate taking those rates into consideration.[800] Section 20 of the *Federal Child Support Guidelines* includes no provision for circumstances where the non-resident parent faces a significantly higher cost of living in the foreign jurisdiction that is unrelated to the operative income tax regime.[801]

J. SOCIAL ASSISTANCE

Parents have the same financial responsibility to their children, whether or not their income comes from limited sporadic minimum wage income or from CPP benefits or social assistance.[802] Spouses and parents should not be relieved of their support obligations at the expense of the taxpayer.[803] The reluctance of a parent to engage the legal process until coerced into doing so by a provincial agency does not affect the substantive legal issues to be determined on an application for child support.[804] Deduction of the father's child support payment from the mother's social assistance entitlement provides no basis for reduction or elimination of the father's child support obligation.[805] There is no rule that a welfare recipient should not be required to make support payments.[806] A primary caregiving parent's receipt of social assistance constitutes no reason to reduce the other parent's obligation to pay child support to the amount that the recipient is entitled to retain without reimbursement to the provincial treasury.[807] Deviation from the basic table amount of child support payable under the provincial child support guidelines may be justified, however, where the primary caregiving parent is on social assistance and would receive only $100 of any amount ordered and the other parent, with a modest income, is providing indirect benefits for the children by the purchase of an automobile and payment of expenses related thereto. Such a judicial disposition may be made because a court may order an amount that differs from the Guidelines amount, where special arrangements have been made for the benefit of the children and the application of the provincial guidelines would be inequitable in the circumstances.[808] Economic benefits accruing to the children from a shared parenting arrangement should not be undermined by court-ordered support under section 9 of the *Federal Child Support Guidelines* that would simply reimburse the provincial treasury for income assistance provided to the mother.[809] A court has no jurisdiction to order that special or extraordinary expenses payable pursuant to

800 See *Guidelines Amending the Federal Child Support Guidelines*, SOR/2020-247, 23 November 2020; *Canada Gazette*, Part II, Volume 154, Number 25. And see *LRS v SSD*, 2020 ABCA 206; *VC v JDB*, 2009 NSSC 25.

801 See *JGT v TN*, [2001] AJ No 1426 (QB); *ADB v SAM*, [2006] NSJ No 252 (SC); *Connelly v McGouran*, [2006] OJ No 993 (CA).

802 *Dooley v Dooley*, [2000] NSJ No 252 (SC).

803 *Friesen v Friesen* (1995), 16 RFL (4th) 449 (Man QB) (dismissal of application for remission of child support arrears); compare *Maxwell v Brandel*, [1998] BCJ No 1327 (SC).

804 *Barry v Rogers*, [2001] NJ No 123 (SC).

805 *Barry v Rogers*, *ibid*; *Young v Young*, [1999] NSJ No 63 (SC); compare *Gillie v Ritchie*, [2001] NSJ No 440 (SC) (s 7 expenses under the *Federal Child Support Guidelines*).

806 *MacDuff v MacDuff* (1994), 97 Man R (2d) 188 (CA); compare *Lucas v Evans* (1994), 135 NSR (2d) 367 (Fam Ct).

807 *Selberis v Selberis*, [1994] BCJ No 1336 (SC); *KMB v JY*, [1999] BCJ No 280 (SC).

808 *Griffith v Wolfram*, [1998] BCJ No 2970 (Prov Ct) (order for $200 per month instead of the table amount of $360 granted on assumption that obligor would continue present voluntary contributions).

809 *Kirkpatrick v Bellvau*, [2000] BCJ No 2481 (SC).

section 7 of the *Federal Child Support Guidelines* shall not be deductible from the financial assistance received by the primary caregiving parent from public funds.[810] Financial subsidies received from the provincial government to cover certain costs with respect to a disabled child may not be treated as income of the primary caregiving parent for the purpose of determining child support under section 9 of the *Federal Child Support Guidelines*, but may be taken into account in determining a claim for special or extraordinary expenses under section 7 of the Guidelines with respect to another child of the marriage.[811]

The applicable table amount of child support is calculated by reference only to the oblig or's income. Federal or provincial monthly benefits paid to or for a child of a disabled parent are not deductible from the provincial table amount of monthly child support that is payable under the *Federal Child Support Guidelines*,[812] but a court may refuse to impute additional income to a disabled parent on the basis of a non-taxable annuity payable in consequence of an automobile accident.[813] The conjoint operation of the *Federal Child Support Guidelines* and the Canada Pension Plan, whereby benefits payable to or for the benefit of the children of a disabled contributor to the Canada Pension Plan are excluded from consideration in the assessment of the applicable provincial table amount of support under the Guidelines, does not violate equality rights under section 15(1) of the *Canadian Charter of Rights and Freedoms*.[814] Although a parent's obligation to pay child support is not reduced or satisfied by the payment of CPP disability benefits to the children, such payments may be included in the recipient parent's income in undertaking a comparison of the household incomes for the purpose of determining whether the other parent is eligible to claim undue hardship under section 10 of the *Federal Child Support Guidelines*.[815] And benefits payable to or for the benefit of the children of a disabled contributor to the Canada Pension Plan are taken into account in shared parenting situations under section 9(c) of the Guidelines.[816]

The income of the primary caregiving parent or child is relevant only where there are special or extraordinary expenses within the meaning of section 7 of the Guidelines or where the court has a discretion,[817] such as under section 3(2) of the Guidelines if the child has attained the provincial age of majority,[818] or under section 5 of the Guidelines, which relates to the child support obligation of a spouse who stands in the place of a biological or adoptive parent,[819] or in shared parenting situations falling within section 9 of the Guidelines,[820]

---

810 *Giles v Villeneuve*, [1998] OJ No 4492 (Gen Div).

811 *Dunham v Dunham*, [1998] OJ No 4758 (Gen Div); see also *Mullins v Mullins*, 2016 ABQB 226.

812 *Kaupp v Kaupp*, [2008] AJ No 668 (QB); *McLachlan v McLachlan*, [2002] BCJ No 386 (SC); *MJB v WPB* [2004] MJ No 123 (QB); *Callahan v Brett*, [2000] NJ No 354 (SC); *Mathusz v Carew*, 2011 NLTD(F) 28; *Vickers v Vickers*, [2001] NSJ No 218 (CA); *Hill v Davis*, [2005] NSJ No 274 (CA); *Hunter v Hunter* [2001] NWTJ No 62 (SC); *Sipos v Sipos*, [2007] OJ No 711 (CA); *Turner v Ansell*, 2012 ONSC 2598; *Peterson v Horan*, [2006] SJ No 333 (CA); see *contra Mullen v Mullen*, [1998] NBJ No 338 (QB). See also *Levesque v Levesque*, [2003] SJ No 848 (QB); *Jones v Jones*, [2005] SJ No 284 (QB) (shared parenting under s 9 of *Federal Child Support Guidelines*).

813 *Dyck v Highton*, [2003] SJ No 600 (QB).

814 *Wadden v Wadden*, [2000] BCJ No 1287.

815 *Campbell v Campbell*, 2016 MBQB 57.

816 *ML v SP*, 2015 NBQB 249. See also *Crossley v Vorell*, 2021 BCSC 2484.

817 *Vickers v Vickers*, [2001] NSJ No 218 (CA); see also *Peterson v Horan*, [2006] SJ No 333 (CA).

818 *Burhoe v Goff*, [1999] NBJ No 296 (QB); *Turner v Ansell*, 2012 ONSC 2598.

819 *Fedoruk v Jamieson*, [2002] BCJ No 503 (SC).

820 *Jones v Jones*, [2005] SJ No 284 (CA), citing *Vickers v Vickers*, [2001] NSJ No 218 (CA).

under section 10 of the Guidelines in circumstances of undue hardship.[821] On an application for special or extraordinary expenses under section 7 of the Guidelines, an obligor is not entitled to be credited dollar for dollar with respect to Canada Pension Plan payments made to children in consequence of the obligor's disability, but the amount received by the other parent will be included in that parent's income for the purpose of determining the proportionate parental contributions towards the expenses.[822] An adult child's receipt of personal[823] or parental[824] benefits may be taken into account in fixing the amount of support that is appropriate for an adult child who is pursuing post-secondary education. In Saskatchewan, the payment of benefits under the Canada Pension Plan to the children of a disabled parent has been held not to constitute "special provisions" for the benefit of the children within the meaning of section 3(4)(a) of *The Family Maintenance Act, 1997*[825] and similar reasoning can be applied to sections 15.1(5) and 17(6.2) of the *Divorce Act.*

A retroactive lump sum benefit payable to the child of a disabled contributor under the Canada Pension Plan is not sufficiently direct to qualify as a contribution by the disabled parent to arrears of child support.[826] An adult child who is in receipt of benefits under Alberta's program of Assured Income for the Severely Handicapped is not entitled to support from a parent when no additional financial need has been determined.[827]

Where an adult child has returned to the care of a parent because of illness or disability, state subsidies received for that child under provincial statute have been regarded as a relevant consideration in determining what amount, if any, the other parent should be required to contribute to that child's support. In the absence of a general parental obligation to support adult children, the obligation of the state to support the adult child may be placed ahead of that of the parents, having regard to their financial circumstances.[828] But the fact that the state has agreed to subsidize a special needs child's necessaries of life does not automatically relieve the parents of their support obligations under the *Divorce Act,* if they can reasonably supplement the bare necessities provided for by the state.[829] While an order for the table amount of child support under sections 3(1)(a) and 3(2)(a) of the *Federal Child Support Guidelines* may be inappropriate by reason of the disabled adult child's receipt of government assistance, an order for child support may be appropriate under section 3(2)(b) of the Guidelines, having regard to the "condition, means, needs and other circumstances of the child and the financial ability of each [parent] to contribute to the support of the child."[830]

---

821 *Alfaro v Alfaro,* [1999] AJ No 1062 (QB); *Dixon v Fleming,* [2000] OJ No 1218 (SCJ); compare *Van Harten v Van Harten,* [1998] OJ No 1299 (Gen Div).

822 *MJB v WPB,* [1999] MJ No 314 (QB).

823 *Welsh v Welsh,* [1998] OJ No 4550 (Gen Div), applying *Harrington v Harrington* (1981), 33 OR (2d) 150 (CA).

824 *Bort v Derworiz,* [1998] SJ No 177 (QB).

825 *Malbeuf v Malbeuf,* [1999] SJ No 635 (QB); *Peterson v Horan,* [2006] SJ No 333 (CA); see also *Fedoruk v Jamieson,* [2002] BCJ No 503 (SC) in Chapter 10, Section G. But see *May-Rutter v Crisp,* [2002] OJ No 2689 (Div Ct).

826 *Williams v Williams* (1995), 18 RFL (4th) 129 at 131–32 (Ont Div Ct) (trial court in error in deciding that parent was entitled to deduct lump sum benefit from child support arrears).

827 *Buzon v Buzon,* [1999] AJ No 371 (QB) (applying s 3(2)(b) of the *Federal Child Support Guidelines*).

828 *Harrington v Harrington* (1981), 33 OR (2d) 150 (CA); see also *Ploughman v Ploughman* (1989), 78 Nfld & PEIR 170 (Nfld TD); *Riddell v Blackburn,* [2003] SJ No 53 (QB).

829 *Buckley v Holden* (1991), 32 RFL (3d) 182 (BCSC).

830 *Briard v Briard,* 2010 BCCA 431; see also *SAD v MA,* 2019 NBQB 85.

A mother's receipt of CPP and WCB benefits in a monthly amount on the death of her child's biological father may be taken into account when the step-parent is ordered to pay support pursuant to section 5 of the *Federal Child Support Guidelines.*[831]

K. INCOME INFORMATION

Sections 21 to 26 of the *Federal Child Support Guidelines* provide as follows with respect to the acquisition and disclosure of information concerning income:[832]

> **Obligation of applicant**
>
> **21** (1) A spouse who is applying for a child support order and whose income information is necessary to determine the amount of the order must include the following with the application:
>
> (a) a copy of every personal income tax return filed by the spouse for each of the three most recent taxation years;
>
> (b) a copy of every notice of assessment or re-assessment issued to the spouse for each of the three most recent taxation years;
>
> (c) where the spouse is an employee, the most recent statement of earnings indicating the total earnings paid in the year to date, including overtime or, where such a statement is not provided by the employer, a letter from the spouse's employer setting out that information including the spouse's rate of annual salary and remuneration;
>
> (d) where the spouse is self-employed, the following documents for the three most recent taxation years, namely
>
> (i) the financial statements of the spouse's business or professional practice, other than a partnership, and
>
> (ii) a statement showing a breakdown of all salaries, wages, management fees or other payments or benefits paid to, or on behalf of, persons or corporations with whom the spouse does not deal at arm's length;
>
> (e) where the spouse is a partner in a partnership, confirmation of the spouse's income and draw from, and capital in, the partnership for its three most recent taxation years;[833]
>
> (f) where the spouse controls a corporation, for its three most recent taxation years
>
> (i) the financial statements of the corporation and its subsidiaries, and
>
> (ii) a statement showing a breakdown of all salaries, wages, management fees or other payments or benefits paid to, or on behalf of, persons or corporations with whom the corporation, and every related corporation, does not deal at arm's length; and
>
> (g) where the spouse is a beneficiary under a trust, a copy of the trust settlement agreement and copies of the trust's three most recent financial statements.[834]

831 *Leibel v Davis*, [2001] SJ No 208 (QB).

832 See *KAB v PDM*, 2023 BCSC 1156; *Ali v McCurdy*, 2022 MBQB 36, applying *Manitoba Child Support Guidelines*, s 20(2). See also Thomas Bastedo & Samantha Kennedy, "Child Expense Budgets: Use and Abuse" (May 2001) 16 *Money & Family Law* 35–38.

833 *Snow v Wilcox*, [1999] NSJ No 453 (CA).

834 *Veskovic v Nielsen*, 2022 SKCA 134.

Obligation of respondent

(2) A spouse who is served with an application for a child support order and whose income information is necessary to determine the amount of the order, must, within 30 days after the application is served if the spouse resides in Canada or the United States or within 60 days if the spouse resides elsewhere, or such other time limit as the court specifies, provide the court, as well as the other spouse or the order assignee,[835] as the case may be, with the documents referred to in subsection (1).

Special expenses or undue hardship

(3) Where, in the course of proceedings in respect of an application for a child support order, a spouse requests an amount to cover expenses referred to in subsection 7(1) or pleads undue hardship,[836] the spouse who would be receiving the amount of child support must, within 30 days after the amount is sought or undue hardship is pleaded if the spouse resides in Canada or the United States or within 60 days if the spouse resides elsewhere, or such other time limit as the court specifies, provide the court and the other spouse with the documents referred to in subsection (1).

Income over $150,000

(4) Where, in the course of proceedings in respect of an application for a child support order, it is established that the income of the spouse who would be paying the amount of child support is greater than $150,000, the other spouse must, within 30 days after the income is established to be greater than $150,000, if the other spouse resides in Canada or the United States or within 60 days if the spouse resides elsewhere, or such other time limit as the court specifies, provide the court and the spouse with the documents referred to in subsection (1).

Making of rules not precluded

(5) Nothing in this section precludes the making of rules by a competent authority, within the meaning of section 25 of the Act, respecting the disclosure of income information that is considered necessary for the purposes of the determination of an amount of a child support order.

Failure to comply

22 (1) Where a spouse fails to comply with section 21, the other spouse may apply

(a) to have the application for a child support order set down for a hearing, or move for judgment; or

(b) for an order requiring the spouse who failed to comply to provide the court, as well as the other spouse or order assignee, as the case may be, with the required documents.

Costs of the proceedings

(2) Where a court makes an order under paragraph (1)(a) or (b), the court may award costs in favour of the other spouse up to an amount that fully compensates the other spouse for all costs incurred in the proceedings.

---

835 Section 2(1) of the *Federal Child Support Guidelines*, SOR/97-175, defines "order assignee" as meaning "a minister, member or agency referred to in subsection 20.1(1) of the [*Divorce*] *Act* to whom a child support order is assigned in accordance with that subsection."

836 See *Auer v Auer*, 2015 ABQB 67.

Adverse inference

23 Where the court proceeds to a hearing on the basis of an application under paragraph 22(1)(a), the court may draw an adverse inference against the spouse who failed to comply and impute income to that spouse in such amount as it considers appropriate.[837]

Failure to comply with court order

24 Where a spouse fails to comply with an order issued on the basis of an application under paragraph 22(1)(b), the court may

(a) strike out any of the spouse's pleadings;[838]

(b) make a contempt order against the spouse;[839]

(c) proceed to a hearing, in the course of which it may draw an adverse inference against the spouse and impute income to that spouse in such amount as it considers appropriate;[840] and

(d) award costs in favour of the other spouse up to an amount that fully compensates the other spouse for all costs incurred in the proceedings.

Continuing obligation to provide income information

25 (1) Every spouse against whom a child support order has been made must, on the written request of the other spouse or the order assignee, not more than once a year after the making of the order, and as long as the child is a child within the meaning of these Guidelines, provide that other spouse or the order assignee with

(a) the documents referred to in subsection 21(1) for any of the three most recent taxation years for which the spouse has not previously provided the documents;

(b) as applicable, any current information, in writing, about the status of any expenses included in the order pursuant to subsection 7(1); and

(c) as applicable, any current information, in writing, about the circumstances relied on by the court in a determination of undue hardship.

Below minimum income

(2) Where a court has determined that the spouse against whom a child support order is sought does not have to pay child support because his or her income level is below the minimum amount required for application of the tables, that spouse must, on the written request of the other spouse, not more than once a year after the determination and as long as the child is a child within the meaning of these Guidelines, provide the other spouse with the documents referred to in subsection 21(1) for any of the three most recent taxation years for which the spouse has not previously provided the documents.

Obligation of receiving spouse

(3) Where the income information of the spouse in favour of whom a child support order is made is used to determine the amount of the order, the spouse must, not more than once a year after the making of the order and as long as the child is a child within the meaning

---

837 *Poursadeghian v Hashemi-Dahaj*, 2010 BCCA 453; *Jon v Jon*, 2011 NSSC 419. Compare *Armstrong v Armstrong*, 2012 BCCA 166.

838 *Blackburn v Rose*, [1999] OJ No 4361 (SCJ).

839 *Ibid.*

840 *Le Page v Porter*, [2000] OJ No 2574 (SCJ).

of these Guidelines, on the written request of the other spouse, provide the other spouse with the documents and information referred to in subsection (1).

Information requests

(4) Where a spouse or an order assignee requests information from the other spouse under any of subsections (1) to (3) and the income information of the requesting spouse is used to determine the amount of the child support order, the requesting spouse or order assignee must include the documents and information referred to in subsection (1) with the request.[841]

Time limit

(5) A spouse who receives a request made under any of subsections (1) to (3) must provide the required documents within 30 days after the request's receipt if the spouse resides in Canada or the United States and within 60 days after the request's receipt if the spouse resides elsewhere.

Deemed receipt

(6) A request made under subsections (1) to (3) is deemed to have been received 10 days after it is sent.

Failure to comply

(7) A court may, on application by either spouse or an order assignee, where the other spouse has failed to comply with any of subsections (1) to (3)

(a) consider the other spouse to be in contempt of court and award costs in favour of the applicant up to an amount that fully compensates the applicant for all costs incurred in the proceedings; or

(b) make an order requiring the other spouse to provide the required documents to the court, as well as to the spouse or order assignee, as the case may be.

Unenforceable provision

(8) A provision in a judgment, order or agreement purporting to limit a spouse's obligation to provide documents under this section is unenforceable.

Provincial child support services

26 A spouse or an order assignee may appoint a provincial child support service to act on their behalf for the purposes of requesting and receiving income information under subsections 25(1) to (3), as well as for the purposes of an application under subsection 25(7).

As Gates J of the Alberta Court of Queen's Bench observed in *Auer v Auer*,[842] financial disclosure is essential to determining child support, but given the inherently invasive nature of financial disclosure, the court must be satisfied that the information requested is relevant and reasonably necessary as opposed to a fishing expedition. It is the mandatory disclosure obligations under section 21 of the Guidelines that supply the necessary information that enables a court to determine whether the application of section 16 will provide the fairest

841 *Guidelines Amending the Federal Child Support Guidelines*, SOR/97-563, s 3, amending SOR/97-175, s 25(4).

842 2015 ABQB 67 at paras 12–13.

determination of annual income. Section 21 disclosure is absolutely necessary before a court can commence its analysis under sections 16 to 20. Given the incontestable evidentiary burden imposed by subsection 18(2) of the Guidelines upon the spouse who controls a cor poration, to establish that salaries, wages or management fees, or other payments or benefits, to or on behalf of persons with whom the corporation does not deal at arm's length were reasonable in the circumstances, persons who control corporations who fail to fully and honestly comply with section 21 disclosure obligations do so at their peril.[843] In the words of the Alberta Court of Appeal in *Ripulone v Smith*:

> [9] The *Child Support Guidelines* are to be interpreted purposively and are intended to establish a fair standard of support for children that ensures they will continue to benefit from the financial means of both parents after separation. This Court has previously made clear that disclosure obligations are just that; legal obligations to the children and to the court, and must be treated accordingly. This Court has also made clear, and we reiterate, that the disclosure provisions are to be interpreted broadly and a court cannot make an informed decision unless and until full and complete disclosure is made under s 21(1) or (2) of the Guidelines. A parent challenging the reasonableness of corporate or business expenses is not required to first establish a *prima facie* case that such expenses are unreasonable. Disclosure must be provided in a transparent and understandable format. It is not sufficient for a parent to provide disorganized bundles of receipts, papers, and bank statements, nor is it acceptable to tell the other parent to "talk to my accountant." Rather, the required disclosure must be sufficient to allow meaningful review by the recipient parent and be sufficiently complete and comprehensible that, if called upon, a court can readily discharge its duty. The evidentiary and persuasive onus rests with the self-employed or corporate parent throughout. In other words, the self-employed or corporate parent cannot avoid paying his or her fair share of child support by failing to fully and properly disclose in a timely matter: *Cunningham v Seveny*; *Goett v Goett*. . . .
>
> [11] The *Child Support Guidelines* function when parents appreciate the economic obligations attendant with being parents and provide coherent admissible evidence to support their position as to the income available to fulfill that obligation. Where disclosure is stymied, obfuscated or simply refused, courts must respond and are charged with the task, albeit challenging, of imputing income. This is an imperfect science, but the objective is to find a level of support that is justifiable and reasonable and commensurate with what appears to be the parent's financial ability to pay. It is improper, however, to rely on submissions masquerading as evidence in doing so.[844]

But as Jones J of the Alberta Court of Queen's Bench cautions in *SER v JS*:

> [55] In *Cunningham* [*v Seveny*, 2017 ABCA 4], the Court of Appeal seems to suggest that there may be limits to the reasonableness of efforts to secure pre-trial disclosure. Balance is needed. At paragraph 35 the Court notes:

---

843 *Wildeman v Wildeman*, 2014 ABQB 732 at paras 26 and 37, Schultz J.

844 2018 ABCA 167 at paras 9 and 11. For a detailed review of disclosure in a corporate income context, see *Rolinger v Rolinger*, 2021 ABQB 474.

> Simply put, parties ought not to be put to time-wasting, money-draining line-by-line justifications for every dollar that has been spent. In keeping with the foundational rules, pre-trial disclosure must not become a process that wholly consumes the very parental resources that otherwise would be available for child support. And, parties must bear in mind that supervising courts will continue to take a very dim view of litigation antics or abuses that detract from, or thwart, the overarching objectives of child support legislation, the foundational rules and disclosure obligations.[845]

The obligation of a respondent parent to provide income information is triggered by section 21(2) of the *Federal Child Support Guidelines* at the time when the parent is served with an application for a child support order. This is in contrast to the case where a child support order has already been made, where the obligation arises simply upon a written request being made in accordance with the provisions of section 25 of the Guidelines.[846] In *Rasmussen v MacDonald*,[847] McIntyre J of the Saskatchewan Court of Queen's Bench stated:

> 13 The Guidelines are predicated upon the court making a determination as to what the parties current income is. Section 16 says that income is determined "using the sources of income set out under the heading 'Total income' in the T1 General form issued by Revenue Canada." The court is not directed to determine income on the basis of the preceding year's tax return but rather by reference to sources of income contained in the T1 General. In the case of a party obliged to disclose income information who is an employee, ss. 21(1)(c) requires disclosure of a recent statement of earnings setting forth total earnings paid in the year to date. In my view this is intended to allow the court to calculate what the person's current annual earnings are for the purposes of the sources of income referred to in s. 16. Section 2(3) reinforces my view that the court is to determine, as best it can, what a party's current earnings are.
>
> 14 Production by a party of his or her three most recent tax returns and notices of assessment or re-assessment may assist the court in a number of ways, including:
>
> (1) In the case of an employee on salary, unless the evidence indicates a material change of circumstances in the current year which will affect the party's earnings in the current year, one would expect the year to date earnings, once annualized, should be relatively consistent with the previous year's tax return. If it is not, it may be a circumstance requiring explanation.
>
> (2) Prior years tax returns may indicate reoccurring sources of income such as taxable capital gains or taxable dividends which are not reflected in the year to date statement of earnings but which must be factored in to determine the parties income for the purposes of the Guidelines.
>
> (3) Where prior tax returns indicate an income that fluctuates from year to year, the court may determine income on the basis set forth in either ss. 17(1)(a) or 17(1)(b).

The aforementioned provisions establish a new minimum standard for financial disclosure in child support proceedings. They are complemented by section 10(4) of the *Federal*

845 2020 ABQB 267 at para 55.

846 *RWG v SIG*, [2002] SJ No 231 (QB).

847 (1997), 34 RFL (4th) 451 at paras 13–14; see also *ML v LAL*, 2015 NBQB 150.

Child Support Guidelines, which together with Schedule II imposes additional financial disclosure to enable a comparison of the household living standards to be undertaken by the court in cases where undue hardship is established.[848] Sections 21 and 25 of the *Federal Child Support Guidelines,* and indeed the entire Guidelines themselves, when read as a whole, appear to provide for minimum requirements in relation to documentary disclosure. These starting points are generally sufficient for most support applications.[849] Although the first and primary focus of the *Federal Child Support Guidelines* is on the income of the spouse against whom an order is sought, this focus changes to include the income of the applicant if there is split or shared parenting time[850] or if the standard of living test set out in section 10 of the Guidelines must be applied in the determination of a claim of undue hardship.[851]

The responsibility for providing accurate and full disclosure with respect to financial documentation falls on the spouse or former spouse who possesses the information.[852] Section 21 of the *Federal Child Support Guidelines* imposes specific requirements respecting financial disclosure where child support is in issue. An employee who has the ability to deduct employment and vehicle expenses in a manner similar to a self-employed person has a positive obligation to provide not only adequate, but also comprehensive records of income and expenses. This does not mean audited statements, but it does mean a package from which the recipient spouse can draw conclusions on the basis of which the amount of child support can be established.[853] Where the disclosure is inadequate and inferences are to be drawn, they should be favourable to the spouse who is confronted with the challenge of making sense out of financial disclosure and against the spouse whose records are inadequate or whose response to the obligation to produce is so unhelpful that cumbersome calculations and intensive and costly investigations or examinations are necessary. Given an ongoing failure to pay child support that reflects the parent's income over preceding years, the court may order retroactive child support to be paid to make up the shortfall between the amount actually paid and the amount that should have been paid.[854]

In *Antonio v Shaw,*[855] the appellant wife challenged the direction of a case management judge requiring her to provide disclosure of financial statements of a private company in which she held a 40 percent interest. Prior to their marriage, the parties had executed an agreement that protected certain assets of the wife in the event of a divorce. The respondent husband was impugning the validity of the prenuptial agreement. Issues of spousal and child support were also disputed. The appellant argued that the disclosure order contravened the provisions of section 21(2) of the *Federal Child Support Guidelines,* which requires a spouse who "controls" a private corporation to disclose its financial statements. She also argued that the financial statements were not relevant if the prenuptial agreement was valid. The Alberta Court of Appeal found no reviewable error in the case management judge's decision. It noted that subsection 21(5) of the *Federal Child Support Guidelines* expressly provides

848 *Buhr v Buhr,* [1997] MJ No 565 (QB).
849 *JEH v PLH,* 2014 BCSC 125 at para 24, Abrioux J.
850 *Gore-Hickman v Gore-Hickman,* [1999] SJ No 30 (QB).
851 *Cross v Cross,* [1997] BCJ No 1741 (SC).
852 *Cameron-Masson v Masson,* [1997] NSJ No 207 (Fam Ct).
853 *Mildren v Mildren,* 2013 ONSC 1435.
854 *Meade v Meade,* [2002] OJ No 3155 (SCJ); *Crisp v Crisp,* 2012 ONSC 521.
855 2010 ABCA 141; compare *Pele-Tolaini v Tolaini,* 2010 ABCA 223.

that nothing in that section precludes a court from making rules respecting the disclosure of income information. It then observed that the "Court of Queen's Bench *Family Law Practice Note 2* authorizes the use of a Notice to Disclose to require a party having a one percent interest in a privately held corporation to disclose financial statements" and "[t]his requirement expands the disclosure provisions of the Guidelines, but is not inconsistent with them." While accepting the appellant's submission that the validity of a prenuptial agreement should ordinarily be determined before financial disclosure is ordered, the Alberta Court of Appeal observed that this was not the sole issue that required determination. Spousal support and child support issues also needed to be resolved. Holding that the value of the appellant's interests in the privately held company was relevant to these two issues, the Alberta Court of Appeal upheld the direction of the case management judge and dismissed the wife's appeal.

Section 21 of the *Federal Child Support Guidelines* sets out financial information to be produced, but the British Columbia *Rules of Court* authorize a more detailed disclosure of business documents than those required by section 21 of the Guidelines.[856] While the court may order the production of relevant documents stored in a hard drive, the British Columbia *Supreme Court Family Rules* do not authorize an unrestricted search of a digital storage device.[857] In determining the boundaries of financial disclosure under the Nova Scotia *Civil Procedure Rules* having regard to relevance, sensitivity and proportionality, the following ten non-exhaustive considerations have been judicially endorsed:

1. *Connection*: What is the nature of the claim and how do the issues and circumstances relate to the information sought to be produced?
2. *Proximity*: How close is the connection between the sought-after information, and the matters that are in dispute? Demonstrating that there is a close connection would weigh in favour of its compelled disclosure, whereas a distant connection would weigh against its forced production.
3. *Discoverability*: What are the prospects that the sought-after information will be discoverable in the ordered search? A reasonable prospect or chance that it can be discovered will weigh in favour of its compelled disclosure.
4. *Reliability*: What are the prospects that if the sought-after information is discovered, the data will be reliable (for example, has not been adulterated by other unidentified non-party users)?
5. *Proportionality*: Will the anticipated time and expense required to discover the sought-after information [be] reasonable having regard to the importance of the sought-after information to the issues in dispute?
6. *Alternative measures*: Are there other, less intrusive means available to the applicant, to obtain the sought-after information?
7. *Privacy*: What safeguards have been put in place to ensure that the legitimate privacy interests of anyone affected by the sought-after order will be protected?

---

856 *Charles v Charles*, [2005] BCJ No 117 (SC) (application to reduce child support on the basis of the father's reduced income adjourned for three months to enable the wife's accountant to obtain information and documentation in addition to that previously provided). See also *Kuznecov v Kuznecov*, [2006] BCJ No 1155 (SC); see also *JEH v PLH*, 2014 BCSC 125 applying the *Supreme Court Family Rules*; *KAB v PDM*, 2023 BCSC 1156.

857 *Etemadi v Maali*, 2021 BCSC 1003 at para 13.

8. *Balancing*: What is the result when one weighs the privacy interests of the individual; the public interest in the search for truth; fairness to the litigants who have engaged the court's process; and the court's responsibility to ensure effective management of time and resources?
9. *Objectivity*: Will the proposed analysis of the information be conducted by an independent and duly qualified third-party expert?
10. *Limits*: What terms and conditions ought to be contained in the production order to achieve the object of the **Rules**, which is to ensure the just, speedy and inexpensive determination of every proceeding?[858]

An order may be granted to compel the respondent to produce financial disclosure in accordance with the requirements of section 21(1) of the *Federal Child Support Guidelines* and also Rule 13(12) of the Ontario *Family Law Rules*, which provides for the updating of financial statements.[859]

The court has the discretionary jurisdiction to order financial disclosure on an application respecting child support whenever the best interests of the children warrant such an order, but the court should exercise restraint when the parties have entered into a carefully drafted agreement on disclosure because the father's tax year and his private corporation's tax year do not coincide.[860]

A court may order a spouse or former spouse to disclose any change in his or her employment or earning status to the obligee or to a provincial support enforcement office or to the court on a timely basis and to disclose his or her efforts to find employment.[861] Failure to make income disclosure as directed by the court may justify an order for retroactive child support that reflects increases in the obligor's income over several years since the direction was made.[862]

The expression "controls a corporation" in section 21(1)(f) of the *Federal Child Support Guidelines* may be reasonably interpreted as meaning "has a controlling interest in a corporation"; a spouse who has no ownership interest in the corporation, even though he or she is a director, fails to meet that definition.[863] In *Bezanson v Bezanson*, however, Chiasson J of the Supreme Court of Nova Scotia observed:

> [20] Are the tax returns and financial statements of the companies relevant to either the determination of Peter Bezanson's income or the value of his shareholdings? The requested documentation may be relevant to these issues. The ultimate issue of relevance is left to the trial judge but at the preliminary fact finding stage, the documents are *prima facie* relevant as defined by the pleadings. As noted in *Laushway v. Messervey, supra*, there must be a more liberal interpretation of disclosure at the pre-trial stage than at trial.

---

858 *McDonald v McDonald (Mombourquette)*, 2023 NSSC 153 at para 15, citing *Laushway v Messervey & Sobeys Group Inc*, 2014 NSCA 7 at para 32. See also *PM v BM*, 2024 ONSC 1297 at para 9, Conlan J.

859 *Agresti v Hatcher*, [2004] OJ No 910 (SCJ).

860 *Miner v Miner*, [2004] OJ No 488 (SCJ), aff'd [2004] OJ No 3303 (CA).

861 *PA v FA*, [1997] BCJ No 1566 (SC); *Cornish v Cornish*, [2001] NJ No 116 (SC); *Monette v Jordan*, [1997] NSJ No 337 (TD); *Mattila v Liski*, [1997] SJ No 495 (QB).

862 *Pelletier v Lukasik*, [1999] OJ No 2649 (SCJ).

863 *Goerlitz v Paquette*, [1998] AJ No 491 (QB); compare *Pastway v Pastway*, [1999] OJ No 2525 (SCJ). See also *SER v JS*, 2020 ABQB 267; *Lahanky v Lahanky*, 2011 NBQB 84.

[21] Counsel for Peter Bezanson argued that the corporate disclosure requested was irrelevant to a consideration pursuant to s. 21(1)(f) of the *Federal Child Support Guidelines*. The position of Peter Bezanson is that he is not in control of the companies in question and, as such, the disclosure is irrelevant. This argument does not address the issues of financial disclosure which may arise pursuant to s. 18 of the *Federal Child Support Guidelines*.

[22] Section 21(1)(f) makes the financial disclosure sought mandatory if the party controls a company. Section 18 provides that further disclosure may be warranted, even if the spouse is not in control of a company, if the income noted in the T1 general form "does not fairly reflect all the money available to the spouse for the payment of child support." The issue of additional monies available to Peter Bezanson is at the root of the issues of support.[864]

On an application for the production of corporate documents under section 21 of the *Federal Child Support Guidelines* and Rule 60A(2)(b) of the British Columbia *Rules of Court*, the court may order that minutes of the executive committee relating to a decision to change an obligor's remuneration and benefits are of relevant probative value and ought to be produced. Other documents may be excluded, however, where their probative value is outweighed by the potential of prejudice to the corporation that is not a party to the proceeding.[865]

Section 21 of the *Federal Child Support Guidelines* imposes mandatory financial disclosure requirements on an application for child support but does not preclude a court from imposing additional requirements where it deems it appropriate.[866] Section 21(1)(f) of the *Federal Child Support Guidelines* and Rule 69.24.1 of the Ontario *Rules of Civil Procedure* do not restrict a court's jurisdiction to order disclosure of documents other than those thereby stipulated.[867]

A parent's failure to make the required corporate financial disclosure under section 21(1)(f)(ii) of the *Federal Child Support Guidelines* entitles a court to impute income against that parent pursuant to sections 18 and 19 of the Guidelines. Financial disclosure under section 21(1)(f)(i) of the Guidelines entails locating the requisite documents and is not satisfied by deluging a parent with unsorted documents that reflect a "catch me if you can" approach.[868]

The obligation to make financial disclosure in proceedings for child support may not be ousted by the provisions of a marriage contract.[869] Financial disclosure may be ordered by the court, notwithstanding that the provisions of a separation agreement include a waiver of any future right to financial disclosure and the payor parent acknowledges his ability and willingness to pay whatever amount of child support the court decides to order. Where the financial circumstances are complex, the court may initially limit the amount of disclosure but reserve a right to order further disclosure, should this be subsequently found necessary. The court may order the sealing of sensitive information relating to the payor's investment

---

864 *Bezanson v Bezanson*, 2021 NSSC 126 at paras 20–22.

865 *Greenwood v Greenwood*, [1999] BCJ No 846 (SC).

866 *Dougherty v Jepson*, [2002] OJ No 1349 (SCJ). See also *Sweezey v Sweezey*, 2016 ABQB 131 and Section G(17), above in this chapter.

867 *Fielding v Fielding*, [1999] OJ No 2072 (Gen Div) (dismissal of motion for leave to appeal).

868 *Sarafinchin v Sarafinchin*, [2000] OJ No 2855 (SCJ). For a detailed review of disclosure in a corporate income context, see *Rolinger v Rolinger*, 2021 ABQB 474.

869 *Pastway v Pastway*, [1999] OJ No 2525 (SCJ) (respondent with 25 percent interest ordered to produce income and expense portion of company's annual financial statements for three most recent taxation years); see also *Pastway v Pastway*, [2000] OJ No 3062 at paras 8 and 15 (SCJ).

and trading strategies where public disclosure would be prejudicial to him and contrary to the best interests of the children in terms of his ongoing earning capacity.[870]

Section 21(1) of the *Federal Child Support Guidelines* imposes specific mandatory requirements as to financial disclosure and these requirements extend to partnerships that result in income splitting between the obligor and his new spouse.[871]

In addressing a discretionary family trust in *LFR(H) v RBH*, d'Entremont of the New Brunswick Court of Queen's Bench observed:

> Paragraph 21(1)(g) of the *Federal Child Support Guidelines* indicates that if a spouse is a beneficiary of a trust, then the trust settlement agreement and income tax returns relating to the trust for the three recent years should be disclosed. Ms. R. argues that she is a "discretionary" beneficiary of the trust. The *Guidelines* do not differentiate between a beneficiary who has a faint hope of receiving something some day or a beneficiary possessing a more fixed and predictable expectation as an award. The *Guidelines* simply say that if a spouse is a beneficiary of a trust, then the disclosure requirements of paragraph 21(1)(g) apply.[872]

A foreign resident, who invokes the jurisdiction of an Alberta court to reduce spousal and child support arrears and ongoing monthly support, must comply with the financial disclosure requirements imposed by section 21 of the *Federal Child Support Guidelines.* A parent, as the beneficiary under a foreign trust, may be ordered to disclose the trust settle ment agreement and copies of the trust's three most recent financial statements pursuant to section 21(1)(g) of the *Federal Child Support Guidelines.* Such disclosure must be made, unless the parent called upon to produce the prescribed documents proves that production is impossible.[873]

The disclosure requirements of the *Federal Child Support Guidelines* may be supple mented by different, but not conflicting, provincial rules of practice and procedure. While compliance with the conjoint operation of such disclosure requirements may be onerous, they must be complied with, especially by an applicant who seeks to reduce his or her child support obligations based on a material change of circumstances. The federal and provincial rules should not be used as a shield to avoid the disclosure necessary to make an appropriate order.[874] Full financial disclosure is vital to any determination of the right to, amount, and duration of, support. Where a trial judge has declined to grant a motion for full disclosure and production of relevant documents, the appellate court may order such disclosure and production as an alternative to drawing an adverse inference against the spouse who failed to make full disclosure. Pending compliance with such a ruling, the balance of the appeal may be stayed.[875]

Under the British Columbia *Family Law Act,* there has been a fundamental shift in how financial disclosure is addressed. Previously, under the *Family Relations Act,*[876] disclosure

870 *Quinn v Keiper*, [2005] OJ No 5034 (SCJ).
871 *Snow v Wilcox*, [1999] NSJ No 453 (CA).
872 *LFR(H) v RBH*, 2021 NBQB 50 at para 32; see also *Veskovic v Nielsen*, 2022 SKCA 134.
873 *Darel v Darel*, [2002] AJ No 1200 (QB).
874 *Le Bourdais v Le Bourdais*, [1998] BCJ No 2488 (SC).
875 *Ewing v Ewing* (1987), 7 RFL (3d) 168 (Sask CA). And see *Hauff v Hauff* (1994), 5 RFL (4th) 419 (Man CA); *Edwards v Edwards* (1994), 5 RFL (4th) 321 (NSCA).
876 RSBC 1996, c 128.

was addressed through the process of demands, discoveries, and court orders. Under the *Family Law Act*, there is a statutory duty to disclose from the outset.[877] Family Rule 5-1(28)(f) of the British Columbia *Supreme Court Family Rules* provides that the court may draw an adverse inference against a party when that party fails to comply with disclosure requirements. This is consistent with the general discretion of the court to draw adverse inferences against litigants who fail to meet their documentary disclosure obligations.[878] In proceedings for periodic or lump sum support, the mandatory duty to file a property and financial statement pursuant to the British Columbia *Supreme Court Rules* cannot be circumvented by the respondent's assertion that he has means sufficient to satisfy any support order and the details of his assets and income are, therefore, irrelevant. The requisite filing is designed to provide the court with the information that is needed to determine the needs of the parties, their ability to pay, and the proper amount of support. A support order, particularly a lump sum order, ought not to be made in a vacuum. Furthermore, in light of the difficulty that can arise with respect to the enforcement of support orders, it is relevant to know the nature, extent, and location of assets, income, and expenses, and the form in which they are held, so that the court can tailor its order to properly protect and secure the future of the person receiving support.[879] Furthermore, the future may bring an application to vary by one party or the other and non-disclosure prior to the original order would leave no yardstick against which to measure any alleged change of circumstances.[880]

Section 21(5) of the *Federal Child Support Guidelines* provides a minimum standard of financial disclosure and expressly contemplates additional requirements being imposed under provincial and territorial rules of court.[881] Examples of additional requirements are to be found under Rules 70.05, 70.07, 70.08, and 70.09 of the Manitoba *King's Bench Rules*, which set out the financial information that must be filed with the originating process, the answer, a reply, and in an emergency. While there is no provision in the *Federal Child Support Guidelines* similar to section 20(8) of the *Manitoba Child Support Guidelines*, the court has a residual discretion in either context to order the disclosure of all relevant current financial information that is necessary to determine the appropriate amount of child support to be paid.[882]

On an application to vary a pre-Guidelines child support order where the respondent is habitually resident outside Manitoba, the *Federal Child Support Guidelines* apply, not the *Manitoba Child Support Guidelines*. The disclosure requirement of section 21 of the *Federal Child Support Guidelines* relates to income or revenues derived from trust or commercial vehicles. Section 21(5) of the *Federal Child Support Guidelines* provides that nothing in the section precludes the making of rules by a competent rule making authority. Rule 70.05 of the Manitoba *King's Bench Rules* requires financial disclosure by the filing of Form 70D

877 *MAM v DLL*, 2018 BCSC 2114 at para 93, Ker J.

878 *Armstrong v Armstrong*, 2010 BCSC 1686.

879 *Yi v Yung* (1994), 52 BCAC 1; see also *Trefry v Sweeney* (1995), 15 RFL (4th) 309 (NS Fam Ct), aff'd (1995), 15 RFL (4th) 315 (NSTD) (application for child support order under *Family Maintenance Act*, RSNS 1989, c 160).

880 *Trefry v Sweeney* (1995), 15 RFL (4th) 309 (NS Fam Ct).

881 For a detailed discussion of the several ways existing in Alberta for personal and corporate disclosure to be obtained from the opposing party where prospective or retroactive child support is being sought, see *Roseberry v Roseberry*, 2015 ABQB 75 at paras 65–101. See also *Wiebe v Treissman*, 2017 BCSC 1523.

882 *Nykvist v Nykvist*, [2004] MJ No 411 (CA).

where an issue relating to support or property division is raised in an originating process, but this requirement is inapplicable to a variation proceeding, because such a proceeding is not an originating process. Where no claim is made seeking to impute income pursuant to section 19(1)(e) of the *Federal Child Support Guidelines* on the basis that the spouse's property is not reasonably utilized to generate income, a motion for financial disclosure relating to the respondent's assets and liabilities may be dismissed as being too broadly based.[883]

In the context of an interim application for spousal support and child support under *The Family Maintenance Act* (Manitoba), the implementation of the provincial child support guidelines does not create a regime whereby anything asked for must be disclosed, or matters that are properly the subject of examination, interrogatories, or requests for particulars should henceforth be sought pre-emptively on motion. An expert's affidavit asserting that further financial information is required to assess a party's income must be supported by reasons that satisfy the court that additional disclosure is required. Section 20(8) of the *Manitoba Child Support Guidelines* obliges a parent to provide "all relevant current financial information" at the "hearing." No distinction is made between interim and final hearings. This requirement must be read in light of section 20(1) of the Guidelines and its reference to "income information" and in light of section 8 of *The Family Maintenance Act* (Manitoba), as interpreted in *Silver v Silver*,[884] whereby a spouse, who is entitled to full disclosure of matters germane to a maintenance order, is not entitled to resort to special disclosure provisions of *The Family Maintenance Act* (Manitoba) to obtain financial and accounting information concerning claims under *The Marital Property Act* (Manitoba). A court must be persuaded that the information is current, relevant, and necessary, both in the context of the interim nature of the proceedings and to a determination of income or to a consideration of the "means, needs and circumstances" of the party from whom financial disclosure is sought. Section 18 of the Guidelines (and the factors giving rise to imputation of "income" or adjustments to corporate pre-tax income), issues of "appropriateness" under section 4, and issues of special or extraordinary expenses under section 7 provide touchstones of relevance. Invariably, however, what amounts to "current relevant financial information" depends upon the facts of each case, having regard to the stage and nature of the proceedings and the issues before the court. Submissions on costs may be deferred until the disclosure ordered has taken place, at which time the court will be better placed to assess the reasonableness of the requests, their need on an interim basis in light of the expense and time involved, and the discrepancies, if any, between the initial disclosure and that which was subsequently obtained.[885]

Under the *New Brunswick Rules of Court*, Rule 72.14 requires the filing of a financial statement (Form 72J) when issues of child support are before the court. When the information disclosed and the documentary evidence is insufficient to allow a party to properly address the issues, the court can exercise its discretion and order additional relevant disclosure as well as the production of additional relevant documents.[886] On a motion for additional financial disclosure, the court should consider: (1) past compliance with other

---

883 *Sharpe v Sharpe*, [2001] MJ No 406 (QB) (application to vary child support order in light of respondent's lottery win).

884 (1990), 30 RFL (3d) 211 (Man CA).

885 *Minuk v Minuk*, [1999] MJ No 188 (QB).

886 *Lahanky v Lahanky*, 2011 NBQB 84; see also *PD v CD*, 2011 NBQB 239.

disclosure orders on the part of the responding party, (2) the cost of producing the requested items, (3) whether the outstanding items are essential to the issue of the respondent's income for support purposes, (4) whether the court would be able to fairly and justly adjudicate the support issues absent the requested items, (5) how reasonable the requesting party has/will be on the timeline for providing the requested items, (6) whether the requested items can be fairly characterized as over-reaching, (7) whether the requesting party has been vigilant in repeatedly asking for the items, (8) whether a lesser remedy would suffice, and (9) whether the requesting party has discharged the burden of proof.[887]

Section 21 of the *Federal Child Support Guidelines* set out the minimum financial disclosure that must be provided when a claim for child support or contribution to section 7 expenses is made. Where a party has complied with their minimum financial disclosure obligations set out in the *Family Law Rules* and the *Federal Child Support Guidelines*, a more detailed and in-depth analysis of their financial situation may be required if questions arise whether the income reported is an accurate reflection of their true income. As child support is the right of the child, who is typically not a party in child support proceedings, it is incumbent upon the court to err on the side of more extensive disclosure if this is necessary to ensure that the child receives the full protection of the law and the most fulsome benefit of support from their parents.[888]

The financial disclosure provisions of the *Federal Child Support Guidelines* and the Saskatchewan *King's Bench Rules* requiring the filing of financial statements in child support proceedings are not exhaustive. They merely set out the mandatory obligations for financial disclosure on an application dealing with child support. Saskatchewan *King's Bench Rule* 617 provides for a form of interrogatory whereby, once in a proceeding or more often with leave of court or on consent, a party may require a response to a maximum of fifteen written questions relating to financial or property information. Where there is an objection to answering any of the questions, either party may apply to the court for a determination of the validity of the objection.[889]

The disclosure requirements of the *Federal Child Support Guidelines* are supplemented by further requirements under the Saskatchewan *King's Bench Rules*. In addition, the court has always been able to draw an adverse inference against a party who fails to call a witness or produce relevant documents. If a party stonewalls, is evasive, or makes only partial financial disclosure, the objectives of the *Federal Child Support Guidelines* may be undermined; to prevent this, it is open to the court to impute income to that party.[890] The Saskatchewan *King's Bench Rules* are the servants of justice, not its master, and no conflict exists between those Rules and the *Federal Child Support Guidelines*.[891]

In the absence of proper financial disclosure, the court may look to other evidence, including circumstantial evidence, to impute income.[892] Where an obligor offers no cred-

887 *JG v T-LG*, 2020 ONSC 5217, citing *Pasquali v Cox*, 2017 ONSC 7654 at para 12.

888 See *Spettigue v Varcoe*, 2011 ONSC 6618 wherein diverse sanctions for financial non-disclosure are examined.

889 *Marchand v Boon*, [2004] SJ No 76 (QB).

890 *Friedt v Fraser*, [2002] SJ No 150 (QB).

891 *Kidder v Lackten*, [2003] SJ No 729 (CA).

892 *TMH v PJH*, 2020 BCSC 804 at para 265, citing *Poursadeghian v Hashemi-Dahaj*, 2010 BCCA 453.

ible evidence upon which the court can rationally determine his or her income, the court may inferentially determine an annual income in any one or more of three ways, namely (1) examine the obligor's lifestyle; (2) attribute "going wage rates" for persons with the oblig or's qualifications and training; and (3) examine the obligor's past employment history, if it is practicable and reliable.[893]

The various options available to the court under section 24 of the *Federal Child Support Guidelines* to address the non-disclosure of financial information do not expressly include an adjournment, although the court undoubtedly has the jurisdiction to order an adjournment in the unlikely event that it finds it appropriate to do so.[894] Bureaucratic reasons should not stand in the way of contempt proceedings where the administration of justice is undermined by non-compliance with court orders.[895]

L. ONGOING DISCLOSURE

Pursuant to section 25(1) of the *Federal Child Support Guidelines*, a spouse or former spouse against whom a child support order has been made must provide designated financial infor mation annually on the written request of the other spouse or former spouse.[896] Section 25(1) provides a convenient reference point to ascertain whether a court has previously under valued the obligor's earning capacity.[897] Any agreement that purports to limit the statutory right of a parent to request such annual financial disclosure is unenforceable by virtue of sec tion 25(8) of the *Federal Child Support Guidelines*.[898] Many separation agreements include an express provision for annual financial disclosure and a duty to make such disclosure may be implied under a separation agreement.[899] Absent any statutory or contractual duty or any prior judicial direction for ongoing financial disclosure in the existing child support order, a parent's failure to disclose an increased annual income does not automatically trigger entitlement to a retroactive increase in the child support order.[900]

Section 25(1) of the *Federal Child Support Guidelines* operates independently of the court's discretion to order ongoing financial disclosure and may render exercise of the judi cial discretion unnecessary.[901] Where there is an existing court order providing for the annual exchange of financial information by the parents, it is an abuse of process, in the absence of any exceptional circumstance, for a parent to seek financial disclosure more frequently than once yearly.[902] In granting, refusing, or varying an order for child support, it is not uncom

893 *Depace v Michienzi*, [2000] OJ No 453 (SCJ).

894 *Blackburn v Rose*, [1999] OJ No 4361 (SCJ).

895 *Ibid.*

896 *MKR v JAR*, 2015 NBCA 73.

897 *Williams v Williams*, [1997] NWTJ No 49 (SC); *Rust v Rust*, [2003] SJ No 394 (CA) (court-ordered quarterly financial disclosure deemed inappropriate).

898 *DLB v PJB*, [2005] AJ No 207 (QB); *Manuele v O'Connell*, 2012 NSSC 271. See also *Troisi v Gillen*, 2013 ONCJ 677.

899 *Marinangeli v Marinangeli*, [2003] OJ No 2819 (CA).

900 *Marinangeli v Marinangeli*, *ibid*; *Walsh v Walsh*, [2004] OJ No 254 (CA); *Horner v Horner*, [2004] OJ No 4268 (CA); see also *MDA v MS*, [2008] NBJ No 498 (QB); *Tochor v Kerr*, 2011 SKQB 42. And see Chapter 11, Section K(4).

901 *Hourie v Anderson*, [1998] SJ No 754 (QB).

902 *Rivard v Rivard*, [2004] AJ No 589 (QB).

mon for courts to expressly direct either or both of the spouses to provide copies of their respective income tax returns to the other spouse or former spouse within weeks of having filed their returns.[903] A court order for annual financial disclosure may be appropriate where the obligor's income is based on commissions[904] or is likely to improve.[905] Non-compliance with a court order for the timely production of income tax returns and Canada Revenue Agency assessments and reassessments may be penalized by an order for substantial costs being made against the party in default.[906]

When ordering annual financial disclosure, the court may direct that an obligor's documents shall be notarized because of previous contemptuous conduct in withholding information and providing misleading information.[907]

A court may order the annual disclosure of business or corporate information, such as the income tax returns, balance sheet, and statement of income and retained earnings for the previous year.[908] An order for the annual disclosure of specified corporate documents may be deemed necessary to ensure that child support remains at an appropriate level.[909]

Where child support payments are ordered to be made to the Director of Maintenance Enforcement, the court may order the obligor to supply information concerning his or her income or any change of address to the Director, together with a copy of his or her annual income tax return and notice of assessment.[910]

A failure to make ongoing income disclosure may be remedied by a retroactive child support order.[911] Where minutes of settlement provide for the variation of periodic child and spousal support in the event of a material change of circumstances, a spouse and parent whose financial circumstances thereafter change may have an implied obligation to notify the other spouse of these changes and a failure to do so may justify orders for retroactive child support and retroactive spousal support to a date preceding an application to vary.[912]

Both sections 21 to 25 of the *Federal Child Support Guidelines* and Rule 63A of the *Yukon Supreme Court Rules* require full and timely financial disclosure in cases involving child support. Rule 63A(21) provides that financial information must be kept current. In *BJG v DLG*,[913] Martinson J of the Yukon Territory Supreme Court states:

---

903 *JFW v PCW*, [2001] AJ No 1145 (CA); *Arif v Arif*, [2005] AJ No 1559 (CA); *LHMK v BPK*, 2012 BCSC 435; *Fong v Charbonneau*, [2005] MJ No 124 (QB); *Everill v Everill*, [2005] NSJ No 37 (SC); *Gibson v Gibson*, 2011 ONSC 4406; *Jenkins v Quinn*, [2005] PEIJ No 75 (SC); *Ulsen v Keating*, 2014 SKQB 364.

904 *Vallis v Vallis*, [1998] NSJ No 342 (TD).

905 *Moreau v Moreau*, [2004] AJ No 1296 (QB).

906 *Bray-Long v Long*, [2000] NSJ No 10 (SC); see also *Block v Baltimore*, [2000] MJ No 132 (QB).

907 *Berki v Berki*, [1999] OJ No 843 (Gen Div).

908 *Lavoie v Wills*, [2000] AJ No 1359 (QB); *Soucie v Soucie*, 2010 BCSC 1783. See also *Hokhold v Gerbrandt*, 2012 BCSC 1683 (corporate year-end financial statements of 31 October to be disclosed by 15 November of each year).

909 *Raiku v Kokkinis*, [2000] BCJ No 1703 (SC).

910 *MacKinnon v Marshall*, [1998] NSJ No 537 (Fam Ct); *Pomerleau v Agopsowicz*, [1999] OJ No 1967 (SCJ); *Enman v Enman*, [2000] PEIJ No 48 (SC); see also *Williams v Williams*, [2000] NJ No 317 (UFC) (parent directed to provide copy of pay stubs to Unified Family Court on a weekly basis).

911 *Huggins v Huggins*, [1999] NSJ No 494 (SC).

912 *Marinangeli v Marinangeli*, [2003] OJ No 2819 (CA); *Fisher v Green*, [2003] OJ No 2745 (SCJ).

913 2010 YKSC 33.

> 40 The Yukon Supreme Court has repeatedly emphasized the importance of full and timely disclosure. That point was reinforced by the Yukon Court of Appeal in *Holmes v. Matkovich*.[914] There are many compelling reasons for the disclosure requirements in child support cases.
>
> 41 They are in furtherance of the objective of the *Guidelines* of establishing a fair standard of support for children that ensures that they continue to benefit from the financial means of both parents after separation: s. 1(a).
>
> 42 Early disclosure allows the parents to stabilize their financial situation by putting reasonable and timely interim arrangements in place. It also allows them to move towards an early resolution, either by way of settlement, or a timely trial. Information needs to be kept current so that the parents can continue to work on settlement, prepare for trial, or both.
>
> 43 Non-disclosure has a negative impact on both the settlement process and the trial preparation process. When a parent has to spend time, energy and money to obtain the disclosure to which that parent is entitled, that will usually escalate the dispute rather than create a climate where the focus is on settlement. Conflict of this sort can adversely affect children.
>
> 44 Non-disclosure also adversely affects the trial itself. Time that should be used to focus on the merits of the case ends up being used to resolve disputes over disclosure.
>
> 45 Full disclosure is mandatory before a fair and equitable settlement can be reached, that in fact ensures that the children benefit from the financial means of both parents. If that disclosure is inadequate, the agreement reached based on the inadequate disclosure is vulnerable; more costly, time consuming and draining litigation can result.

Judicial directions may be issued respecting annual income disclosure to a provincial child support recalculation office.[915] In *How v How*,[916] the Manitoba Court of Appeal endorsed the practice of including provisions in court orders for the annual recalculation of the table amount of child support and section 7 expenses through the child support recalculation office.

Some provincial statutes expressly provide for annual financial disclosure and the automatic recalculation of child support by a designated government agency. Pursuant to Division 1.1 of the *Family Law Act*, SA 2003, c F-4.5, if a parent fails to provide the required documentation, the amount of child support under an existing order or binding agreement will be automatically recalculated for the first year as if the payor's income had increased by 10 percent. A further 3 percent will be added for each additional year the order was granted or recalculated. The maximum deemed income increase is 25 percent and is applied to orders where five or more years have passed since the parental income levels were determined. Pursuant to section 55.51(4) of the *Family Law Act* (Alberta), where a payor or a recipient fails to provide the recalculation program with income information in respect of a child support order made under the *Divorce Act* (Canada), the Director of the Child Support Recalculation Program may apply to the court on such notice as the court may direct for an order respecting the determination of the income of the payor or the recipient for the purposes of a recalculation of child support. The Director may also request permission to do future recalculations without the need for repeated attendances at the court.[917] Section 24.1 of the

914 2008 YKCA 10.

915 *DC v PC*, 2017 PESC 26 at para 47.

916 2010 MBCA 11.

917 *Moshuk v Moshuk*, 2010 ABQB 540.

Ontario Child Support Guidelines provides for the annual disclosure of designated financial information but no similar obligation arises under the *Federal Child Support Guidelines.*[918]

Sections 25.01 to 25.1(7) of the *Divorce Act*[919] expressly empower the federal Minister of Justice to enter into an agreement with a province to allow for the administrative calculation and recalculation of child support as prescribed in those sections.

M. NON-DISCLOSURE OF INCOME OR ASSETS OR OF MATERIAL CHANGE OF CIRCUMSTANCES

Courts must take appropriate steps to ensure that a parent does not benefit from failing to provide timely, accurate, and complete financial disclosure.[920] A strong message needs to be sent to those individuals who are non-compliant with financial disclosure, and who, despite being given the opportunity to do so, simply disregard the court process.[921] An adverse inference may be drawn against a spouse or former spouse who fails to make full disclosure of his or her income and expenses and the resulting income or earning capacity attributed to such a spouse or former spouse may be in a higher amount than that acknowledged in the evidence.[922] A failure to produce accurate and complete financial information may entitle the court to draw an adverse inference that the non-disclosing party earns at least as much income as the other spouse or former spouse.[923] The obligor's concealment of income may justify an order for retroactive lump sum child support that reflects the differential between the acknowledged and the true income of the obligor.[924]

An adverse inference does not exist in a vacuum.[925] If a primary caregiving parent refuses to disclose business assets, a court may refuse to grant an order with respect to designated expenses under section 7 of the *Federal Child Support Guidelines* on the ground that it is unable to apportion the expenses.[926]

A parent, who is required to provide support for a child in attendance at a school, college, or university, is entitled to proof of the child's continued enrolment in the educational

918 *Montgomery v Jones*, 2015 ONSC 4540 (SCJ); *Williamson v Williamson*, 2016 ONSC 1180; *MA v NM*, 2021 ONSC 5468.

919 See also s 26(1)(c) of the *Divorce Act* (regulation-making authority of Governor in Council).

920 *Tschudi v Tschudi*, 2010 BCCA 170 (retroactive child support deemed appropriate by appellate court); *Windrem v Beck*, 2024 NSSC 71 at para 33. And see generally, Chapter 11, Section K(4). For an insightful review of the impact of the lack of financial disclosure in proceedings for support and property equalization, see the judgment of Fowler Byrne J of the Ontario Superior Court of Justice in *Studzinski v Studzinski*, 2020 ONSC 2540 at paras 6–12. See also *Kaushal v Kaushal*, 2023 ABCA 155; *Kantor v Kantor*, 2023 ABCA 237, discussed in Franks & Zalev, "This Week in Family Law," 20 November 2023 (Thomson Reuters). As to financial disclosure and the availability of the tort of conspiracy to ensure that third parties, such as relatives and new partners, cannot assist a spouse in hiding income and/or assets in an attempt to defeat the other spouse's legitimate support or property claims, see *Leitch v Novac*, 2020 ONCA 257 at paras 44–47.

921 *GC v DC*, 2010 NBQB 81 at para 49, Baird J (imputation of income and order for costs); *Windrem v Beck*, 2024 NSSC 71.

922 *Windrem v Beck*, 2024 NSSC 71; *Plowman v Plowman* (1995), 16 RFL (4th) 82 (Ont Ct Gen Div); *Udaipaul v Kissoon*, [2005] OJ No 5535 (SCJ).

923 *Almeida v Almeida* (1995), 11 RFL (4th) 131 (Alta QB); *Windrem v Beck*, 2024 NSSC 71.

924 *Carty v Jones* (1995), 15 RFL (4th) 367 (Ont Prov Div); see also *Windrem v Beck*, 2024 NSSC 71.

925 *Holtby v Holtby*, [1997] OJ No 2237 (Gen Div).

926 *Woolgar v Woolgar* (1995), 10 RFL (4th) 309 (Nfld UFC).

institution before the commencement of any new academic year. This does not automatically require the other parent to secure transcripts, certificates, or receipts to prove that the child is still in attendance. It does signify, however, that such proof should be provided in a timely fashion when the production of such proof is sought. If proof is not forthcoming, the supporting parent would be justified in paying the money into court pending receipt of satisfactory proof, although this could present difficulty when the enforcement of support obligations is controlled by the provincial bureaucracy.[927] Where a parent has wilfully failed to disclose a change of circumstances that warrants the termination of child support, the court may order reimbursement of the overpayment and, if such payment is not made, may direct that future support payments for a second child be temporarily suspended until the overpayment has been recovered.[928]

A court may decline to entertain an application to reduce child support where the applicant has failed to provide the financial information required by section 21 of the *Federal Child Support Guidelines*.[929]

In *Berry v Berry*,[930] the British Columbia Court of Appeal observed that the evidence must support the conclusions reached and a failure to comply with the rules with respect to financial disclosure constitutes justification for an appellate court ordering a rehearing before the Supreme Court of British Columbia. In *Berry*, the appellate court also referred to its judgment in *Elensky v Elensky*,[931] which confirms the practice of the British Columbia Court of Appeal not to hear appeals concerning variation orders, where the obligor has unilaterally reduced the amount previously ordered and no convincing explanation has been given of his or her impossibility of compliance with the order.

N. DISCLOSURE BY THIRD PARTIES OR NON-PARTIES

Manitoba courts have asserted that, in the absence of a claim of undue hardship under section 10 of the *Federal Child Support Guidelines*, there is no basis on which a court can consider anything but spousal income and, consequently, financial disclosure by third parties living with a spouse is not compellable.[932] While this is true in circumstances where the application is confined to the table amount of child support, it may be inappropriate in circumstances where the Guidelines confer a discretionary jurisdiction on the court to deviate from the table amount of child support having regard to the financial ability of a parent or his or her condition, means, and other circumstances. For example, where the application involves an adult child who is pursuing post-secondary education away from home, the presumptive rule under sections 3(1)(a) and 3(2)(a) of the Guidelines in favour of the table amount may be inappropriate. Then, section 3(2)(b) of the Guidelines would be triggered with the consequence that the court must determine the appropriate amount

927 *Hansen v Hansen* (1995), 13 RFL (4th) 335 (Ont Ct Gen Div).

928 *Ibid.*

929 *Tougher v Tougher*, [1999] AJ No 848 (QB).

930 2002 BCCA 151 at para 151; see also *LMH v GDH*, 2011 BCCA 443.

931 (1993), 50 RFL (3d) 231 (BCCA); see also *LMH v GDH*, 2011 BCCA 443.

932 *Ireland v McMillan*, [1997] MJ No 496 (QB); see also *Baum v Baum*, [2000] BCJ No 2565 (SC); *Dey v Malhotra*, 2013 ONSC 2469 at para 16. As to financial disclosure by non-parties under the Saskatchewan *Queen's Bench Rules*, see *Krammer v Ackerman*, 2020 SKQB 207.

of child support having regard to "the financial ability of each spouse to contribute to the support of the child." This phrase is broad enough to take account of a common law spouse's contributions to a parent's household or other expenses, even if the common law spouse is under no legal obligation to support the child.[933]

Trial judges should be receptive to making orders for full financial disclosure by parties formerly living in a married or marriage-like arrangement[934] in circumstances where the *Federal Child Support Guidelines* confer a discretion on the court that is conditioned on the means or financial ability of a spouse to contribute towards a child's support. It does not follow that a court has *carte blanche* to order the disclosure of any financial information respecting an individual who is not a party to the proceeding. The party seeking production must show that the proposed intrusion into the third party's affairs is relevant and necessary to enable the court to assess the situation.[935]

A bald statement in an affidavit may not provide a sufficiently compelling case for disclosure.[936] A court should not be asked to compel a party to provide financial information concerning a non-party who has no notice of the proceedings and no opportunity to make his or her own submissions to the court.[937] In *Nelson v Nelson*,[938] Veit J of the Alberta Court of Queen's Bench concluded that the current spouse of a recipient of child support is not under a legal duty to disclose his or her income under the *Federal Child Support Guidelines*, although there is a possibility of an adverse inference being drawn against the recipient spouse where a judicial discretion arises that requires the court to have regard to the "financial ability" or "means" of a spouse, as occurs, for example, under section 3(2)(b) of the Guidelines with respect to children over the age of provincial majority, under section 4(b)(ii) of the Guidelines where the obligor's annual income exceeds $150,000, on a claim for special or extraordinary expenses under section 7 of the Guidelines, in circumstances involving shared parenting time under section 9 of the Guidelines,[939] and in cases of undue hardship falling within section 10 of the Guidelines. In *Hebert v Orsini*,[940] Veit J held that a mere allegation of undue hardship will not suffice to justify an order for financial disclosure by a parent's new spouse. A parent who has a support obligation must establish a *prima facie* case that the stringent criteria of "undue hardship" within the meaning of section 10 of the *Federal Child Support Guidelines* have been met before an order will be granted that requires financial disclosure to be made by a non-party.

The word "means" in section 7(1) of the *Nova Scotia Child Support Guidelines* includes the income and assets of the applicant and of the applicant's spouse.[941] When seeking special or extraordinary expenses thereunder, the applicant must disclose his or her household

---

933 *JO v MMM*, 2010 BCSC 1237.

934 *Hersey v Hersey* (1993), 47 RFL (3d) 117 (NBCA); *Edwards v Edwards* (1994), 5 RFL (4th) 321 at 344 (NSCA); *Orser v Grant*, [2000] OJ No 5493 (SCJ); compare *Kaupp v Kaupp*, [2008] AJ No 668 (QB).

935 *Buhr v Buhr*, [1997] MJ No 565 (QB); see also *Gottinger v Runge*, 2018 SKQB 343.

936 *Bodman v Bodman*, [1998] MJ No 62 (QB).

937 *Ibid.*

938 [1999] AJ No 242 (QB).

939 See *AHB v CLB*, 2019 BCCA 349 at paras 35–37; but compare *HM-T v DRGM*, 2023 NBKB 180.

940 2010 ABQB 309.

941 *HBC v CEM*, [2001] NSJ No 263 (Fam Ct), citing *Nelson v Nelson*, [1999] AJ No 242 (QB); see *contra* *Cochrane v D'Andrea*, [2005] OJ No 1536 (SCJ).

income. A court cannot require a non-party to disclose income information but can order the applicant to disclose "all resources, assets, income from investments, spouse's income and investments."[942]

In *Kent v Kent*,[943] the Newfoundland and Labrador Court of Appeal formulated a nuanced approach to mandatory financial disclosure by persons who are married to or cohabit with support obligors. At paragraphs 93 and 94, the appellate court articulates the following general principles:

> 93 The new spouse or partner of a payor spouse has no obligation to support the payor's former spouse: *Davignon v. Davignon*.[944] Consequently, a court should not simply include the partner's income, in whole or in part, in the payor's income to determine his or her ability to pay spousal support: *Meiklejohn v. Meiklejohn*.[945] However, a payor's new spouse's income and other resources *may* be taken into account in establishing a payor's ability to pay because the new spouse or partner is expected to contribute his or her fair share to their household expenses.
>
> 94 With respect to child support, in the absence of a new spouse or partner having assumed the parent role to the children of the former marriage, she or he has no obligation to support the payor's children from that former marriage. . . . However, as in spousal support, the presence of the new spouse or partner may have an impact on the payor's ability to pay.

Extrapolating from these broad general principles in the light of the cited caselaw, the appellate court endorsed the following legal propositions:

1) The income of a second spouse or partner is not considered to be the income of the support obligor. What needs to be considered is the economic impact of the presence of that person on the support obligor's ability to pay. The impact may be neutral or the support obligor's expenses may have increased or decreased as a result of sharing the household with that person.
2) To reduce the expenses of the obligor by the income of the new spouse or partner would be to do indirectly what you cannot do directly—add the income of the new spouse to that of the obligor. However, it would be equally wrong for the obligor to increase his or her household expenses by assuming all the responsibility for a new family, where the other adult in the household is in a position to contribute.
3) Where the law permits reference to the means or financial capacity of the support obligor, it does not follow that the income and other financial information of his or her new spouse or partner, including information regarding companies owned solely by that spouse or partner, must, *ipso facto*, be made available to the court. Such a result could unnecessarily interfere with the privacy rights of a non-party who has no obligation to the spouse or children of the support obligor.

---

942 *HBC v CEM*, [2001] NSJ No 263 (Fam Ct).

943 2010 NLCA 53 [emphasis in original]. See also *Politis v Politis*, 2018 ONSC 323 (spousal support).

944 (2001), 5 RFL (5th) 37 (Ont CA).

945 (2001), 19 RFL (5th) 167 (Ont CA).

4) As the Saskatchewan Court of Appeal pointed out in *Wright v Wright*,[946] wherein the support recipient had repartnered, "[n]o precise or rigid formula can be applied, but rather the approach must remain flexible to deal with the circumstances of each particular case." That approach balances the privacy interest of a third party against the interests of the parties to the action.
5) In the absence of an absolute legal requirement that a third party provide financial information, the party seeking access to such information must demonstrate that the interference with the privacy of the third party is necessary in the particular circumstances and the extent to which it is necessary.
6) Even where a court determines that certain financial information must be provided it does not follow that all financial information, no matter what its precise nature and no matter the degree of its specificity, must be provided.
7) It is not always necessary to know the actual amount of the third party's income. Sometimes the appropriate contribution of the new spouse or partner to household expenses can be determined on a percentage basis and as long as that person is assuming that amount or more, there is no necessity of quantifying the third party's income, let alone the financial circumstances of the third party's company. In some circumstances the contribution makes no difference to the obligor's obligation.

The Newfoundland and Labrador Court of Appeal provided a non-exhaustive list of examples relating to the balancing of interests to illustrate the importance of examining the circumstances of each case in order to determine whether, and to what degree, the financial information is necessary to resolve the issues in the particular case. It observed that the most obvious situation where financial information from the new spouse or partner can properly be ordered is where the support obligor, with the assistance of his new spouse or partner, may have divested or hidden personal or corporate income through their business dealings. It further observed that if a support obligor claims that his or her ability to pay is lessened because the new spouse or partner cannot contribute his or her fair share to the cost of the household, the obligor often voluntarily presents evidence of the third party's earnings to demonstrate an increased demand on the obligor spouse by the second family and a corresponding reduction in ability to pay support to the first family. Failure to provide such supporting information may result in the court assuming a division of responsibility within the household to the detriment of the obligor's position. Of course, second families often comprise more than two people. Thus, the obligation of the support obligor and his or her new spouse or partner within that unit will be influenced by whether there are children of either in the household, the roles of each *vis-à-vis* the children, and whether the support of those children is being contributed to by others. Another factor is that the addition of the new partner may result in a need for larger accommodation. Even where a court is persuaded that access to financial information regarding a third party is required, it does not follow that all such information must be provided. As Steel JA observed in *Bates v Welcher*,[947] the applicant must satisfy the court that the information requested is relevant and reasonably necessary as opposed to a fishing expedition.

946 (1996), 141 Sask R 44 at para 27.

947 2001 MBCA 33; see also *Friedman v Friedman*, 2018 MBQB 91.

In summation, the Newfoundland and Labrador Court of Appeal concluded:

> 112 It follows from this analysis that one cannot say that just because the quantum of spousal support or section 7 expenses is in play it necessarily follows that the specific income level and other financial information of a new partner of the payor spouse is automatically relevant and can be required to be produced by subpoena directed to that non-party partner. The analysis must be more nuanced than that. The Court must consider how and to what extent any of that information may be necessary to resolve the specific support issues as they present themselves in the context of the specific case. Because of the potential impact on the partner's privacy interests, if that information should be provided, the timing becomes a relevant consideration, as well as whether the information could be obtained in a less intrusive way from another source.
>
> 113 Accordingly, we conclude that when the trial judge ruled that because, in the abstract, the income of a payor spouse's new partner *might* in a given case be relevant to (or to use his terminology, "relate to") the issues of spousal support and section 7 expenses in the sense that the presence of the partner in the new relationship has to be factored, in a general manner, into the equation, it necessarily follows that detailed financial information about income levels must always be relevant and produced, he erred.

The appeal was, therefore, allowed and the relevance of the documentation sought was remitted to the trial judge for determination on the basis of the principles defined by the appellate court.

A parent can be ordered to produce documents received from his employer corporation and to answer questions concerning benefits, such as mortgage payments or automobile expenses, received from the company. A failure to produce requested documents or to answer questions may justify an inference being drawn as to the receipt of benefits. The com pany itself cannot be ordered to produce documents without proper notice being served.

The *Federal Child Support Guidelines* set out specific requirements respecting financial disclosure and their ambit should not be enlarged unnecessarily when privacy interests are properly claimed; privacy rights in relation to third parties must be given the protection that is required. The fact that a parent has served as a director of corporate entities at various times does not necessarily establish a right to broad corporate financial disclosure under sec tion 18 of the Guidelines, although limited disclosure may be warranted, if the information provided to the court points to possible avoidance of appropriate child support payments.

The *Federal Child Support Guidelines* do not impose any obligation on third parties, such as corporations, to produce financial documents.

In *Elhert v Sailer*,[950] wherein a family trust was ordered to provide financial statements, the Alberta Court of Appeal observed that in family law matters, certain subject-specific disclosure obligations, or methods of disclosure, arise under legislation and regulation. But these specific provisions do not supplant the basic disclosure obligation in Part 5 of the Alberta *Rules of Court*, which provides mechanisms for obtaining disclosure of relevant and material records and information. Rule 5.13 of the Rules provides a mechanism for obtaining

948 *Koenen v Koenen*, [2001] AJ No 223 (CA); see also *Bates v Welcher*, [2001] MJ No 93 (CA).
949 *Stang v Stang*, [2002] AJ No 106 (QB).
950 2023 ABCA 371 at paras 20–27.

production of relevant and material records from non-parties by stating that a court may order a person who is not a party to produce a record at a specified date, time, and place, if the record is under the control of that person, there is reason to believe that the record is relevant and material, and the person who has control of the record might be required to produce it at trial. To obtain an order for production from a non-party, notice of the application must be served on the party affected by it, and the applicant must generally show that: the records exist; they are under the control of the non-party; they are relevant and material; they cannot be obtained from a party; and it is appropriate to order the non-party to produce the records. For the purposes of disclosure under the Rules, a party has control over a record where it has a legal right to access the record. And the court has the discretion to impute income to a parent for child support purposes where it considers that appropriate in the circumstances, including where it appears that income has been diverted, which would affect the level of child support to be determined or where the parent is a beneficiary under a trust and is or will be in receipt of income or other benefits from the trust.

The British Columbia *Rules of Court* provide for the production of documents by non-parties, but only when there is a substantive issue to which documents relate. There must be more than a simple inquiry as a prelude to a possible application to vary an existing order for child support. Even when there is a matter in issue that justifies an order for non-parties to produce financial documents, the court may impose restrictions on the use to which the material can be put so as to limit as much as possible infringement on the rights of non-parties.[951]

Section 20(2)(g) of the *Manitoba Child Support Guidelines* provides for the disclosure of a corporation's financial statements over its three most recent taxation years where a parent whose income is in dispute "controls" the corporation. The meaning assigned to words used in the *Income Tax Act* applies to the *Manitoba Child Support Guidelines* pursuant to section 2(2) of the Manitoba Guidelines. The word "control" in section 20(2) of the Manitoba Guidelines should, therefore, be interpreted to signify legal control, rather than *de facto* control that focuses on the potential influence that a person may have over the affairs of a corporation. The word "control" under the *Income Tax Act* and the Manitoba Guidelines contemplates the right of control that rests in the ownership of such a number of shares as carries with it the right to a majority of the votes in the election of the Board of Directors. Since section 20(2)(g) of the Manitoba Guidelines corresponds exactly to section 21(f) of the *Federal Child Support Guidelines*, cases from other provinces are relevant. The drafters of the Manitoba Guidelines must be taken to have adopted the concept of "*de jure* control" that applies under the *Income Tax Act*. It must be remembered that sections 20(1) and (2) of the Manitoba Guidelines only set out the minimal mandatory financial disclosure requirements. They were intended to apply to the majority of applications. Where a parent has majority voting control over a corporation, he or she can provide the requisite disclosure without difficulty. Where the parent does not have majority voting control, the situation becomes more complex because the ability to comply is compromised, as are the privacy concerns of the corporation and its other directors and shareholders. That is not to say that there is no

951 *Chapman v Chapman*, [1998] BCJ No 2401 (SC); see also *Stang v Stang*, [2002] AJ No 106 (QB); *Kuznecov v Kuznecov*, [2006] BCJ No 1155 (SC).

ability to order financial disclosure in appropriate situations but it does not exist as of right under section 20(2)(g) of the Manitoba Guidelines. The requirements for financial disclosure in section 20 of the Manitoba Guidelines operate as a pyramid. First, in section 20(1), a party, whose income information is necessary to determine the amount of child support, must file with the court at the same time that the application is begun very minimal information, which will be sufficient for the most common type of application. Section 20(2) is designed to deal with the next most common situation. It details a number of other pieces of financial information, which must be disclosed after receiving a written request from the other parent. The court does not need to become involved at this point in ordering financial disclosure. The parent is entitled as of right to this type of disclosure upon written request. Section 20(2) takes care of many common situations where the payor is self-employed, or in a partnership or receiving other types of income, including where the payor parent is in control of a cor poration. However, the court does have the discretion to order further and better disclosure of financial information if it is necessary and relevant in that particular application. Where, for example, the financial information requested and filed under section 20(2) is insufficient, the court may order more information to be disclosed (section 20(7)). Moreover, the court retains a residual discretion to order even further financial information that it considers relevant to the application. Section 20(8) provides that "nothing in these Guidelines shall be construed as limiting the obligation of a parent whose financial information is necessary to determine the amount of the order to provide all relevant current financial information to the other parent and the court at the time of the hearing of the application." This provision would seem to be a catch-all. There may be information that is relevant to the application, but is not specified in section 20(2). By virtue of section 20(8), the court can order its produc tion so long as it is the financial information of the payor parent. What amounts to "current relevant financial information" will depend on the facts of each case, having regard to the stage and nature of the proceeding and the issues before the court. In addition to invoking the financial disclosure provisions of section 20 of the *Manitoba Child Support Guidelines* party to an application for child support may invoke the Manitoba *King's Bench Rules*. Section 25(1) of the *Federal Child Support Guidelines* expressly provides that the financial disclosure provisions thereunder do not exclude the operation of provincial rules of court. No corres ponding section exists under the *Manitoba Child Support Guidelines*, but the absence of any such express provision does not preclude the conjoint operation of disclosure requirements under the *Manitoba Child Support Guidelines* and the Manitoba *King's Bench Rules*. Section 18(3) of the Manitoba Guidelines empowers a court to impute income to a parent who is a shareholder, director, or officer of a corporation, even in circumstances where the parent does not control the corporation. In order to fulfill its obligation under this subsection, the court must be able to compel disclosure of corporate financial statements pursuant to the Manitoba *King's Bench Rules* relating to financial disclosure by a non-party. The financial disclosure provisions of the *Manitoba Child Support Guidelines* are not exhaustive. They define a minimum standard for financial disclosure with residual discretion in the court to order further and better disclosure of relevant information as set out in section 20(8) of the Guidelines. Where a gap exists, recourse may be had to the Manitoba *King's Bench Rules* In both contexts, however, there is no *carte blanche*; relevance is the touchstone; what may not be relevant at an early stage of the litigation may become relevant after discovery, in which event further motions for financial disclosure may be warranted. For the avoidance of multiple motions, a broad definition of relevance should be adopted, but relevance, not speculation, must still be proven before disclosure can be ordered. Manitoba *King's Bench Rule* 30.02(4) empowers a court to order financial disclosure by a corporation "controlled directly or indirectly" by a party to litigation. The existence of a family relationship is not determinative of influence resulting in control.[952]

In *Colizza v Arnot*,[953] the Manitoba Court of Appeal held that while, clearly, there are circumstances where the court may pierce the corporate veil for the purpose of attempting to obtain financial disclosure, or where it may order the examination of a non-party as part of such a purpose, such orders must be founded upon evidence and not simply suspicion. The evidence revealed that the father was employed by Stanford, a company owned by his wife, but he was not a shareholder, director, or officer of Stanford. The father's evidence that his employment income of $88,000 per annum exceeded the normal range for a person with similar qualifications was uncontradicted and there was no evidence that income to which he was entitled was being diverted by Stanford or otherwise. Reviewing the evidence before the motions judge together with the legal requirements respecting financial disclosure by non-parties, whether under the *Federal Child Support Guidelines* or Rule 30 of the Manitoba *King's Bench Rules*, the Manitoba Court of Appeal held that the respondent mother had failed to discharge the onus of establishing that an order for the disclosure of financial information by Stanford or an order for the examination of Ms Colizza ought to be made. The order of the motions judge was accordingly vacated.

Although a court may lack the jurisdiction to order financial disclosure by an adult child who receives child support while pursuing post-secondary education, the obligor may be declared entitled to apply for variation of the child support order, if he or she is not provided with relevant information.[954] A court may grant an order for the disclosure of income tax returns and notices of assessment and reassessment relating to children under the age of majority, notwithstanding the primary caregiving parent's withdrawal of an application for expenses under section 7 of the *Federal Child Support Guidelines*. The primary caregiving parent may also be required to disclose trust documents and corporate tax returns and notices of assessment and reassessment.[955]

In *Pastway v Pastway*,[956] Reilly J of the Ontario Superior Court of Justice formulated the following principles respecting the production of documents and discovery of non-parties under Rule 30.10 (production of documents) and Rule 31.10 (examination for discovery) of

952 *Bates v Welcher*, [2001] MJ No 93 (CA) (evidence in this case rendered it unnecessary for the Manitoba Court of Appeal to address whether the meaning of "controlled directly or indirectly" as used in Rule 30.02(4) of the Manitoba *King's Bench Rules* refers to "*de facto*" control in light of s 256(5.1) of the *Income Tax Act*). See also *AL v JT*, 2010 NBQB 419; *LFR(H) v RBH*, 2021 NBQB 50 at paras 26–27; *SAC v MAB*, [2002] NSJ No 128 (Fam Ct) (applicant not entitled to introduce evidence in support of allegation that the respondent, a minority shareholder, had *de facto* control of the company in which his mother was the majority shareholder). And see, generally, *Leinburd v Leinburd*, [2003] MJ No 456 (QB). Compare *MC v JO*, 2017 NBCA 15; *Henderson v Henderson*, 2021 NBQB 88 at para 73.

953 [2007] MJ No 499 (CA).

954 *Clark v Clark*, [1998] BCJ No 1934 (SC).

955 *Orser v Grant*, [2000] OJ No 5493 (SCJ); see also *Veskovic v Nielsen*, 2022 SKCA 134.

956 [2000] OJ No 3062 (SCJ).

the Ontario *Rules of Civil Procedure*. Rule 30.10 does not apply to applications or motions; the words "action" and "trial" in paragraphs (a) and (b) of Rule 30.10 are essential words that define the scope of that Rule. Any inherent jurisdiction to order production of documents by a non-party should only be exercised in the clearest of circumstances where an injustice would otherwise ensue. The same philosophy underlies Rule 30.10 and Rule 31.10, namely, a party seeking disclosure and production of documents must attempt to do so from the other party before resorting to these Rules to compel disclosure and production from non-parties. Rule 31 of the Ontario *Rules of Civil Procedure* provides a comprehensive scheme for exam ination for discovery but Rule 31.10 curtails the right to examine non-parties. Leave will be granted to allow the discovery of non-parties only when the moving party has been unable to obtain the information sought from other parties to the litigation and when there has been a refusal, actual or constructive, on the part of the person sought to be examined to provide the information voluntarily. Rule 39.03 of the Ontario *Rules of Civil Procedure* provides a fairly broad right to examine any person before or at a motion hearing but this Rule cannot be invoked simply as a subterfuge to obtain discovery of a non-party that would not be allowed under Rule 31.10. In *Bailey v Bailey*[957] the court set out the following six criteria that must be satisfied to justify the court's exercise of its discretion to order production and disclosure from a non-party pursuant to Rule 19(11) of the Ontario *Family Law Rules*:

(a) The documents are in a non-party's control;
(b) The documents are available only to the non-party;
(c) The documents are not protected by legal privilege;
(d) It would be unfair for the party seeking the disclosure to proceed without the information sought;
(e) The documents sought are relevant and necessary; and
(f) Notice is provided to the non-party.

Subrule 19(11) allows more fulsome disclosure where the six-part test is satisfied and the applicant establishes that unfairness would result without the requested disclosure.[958] And Rule 20(5) of the Ontario *Family Law Rules* provides that the court may, on motion, order that a person (whether a party or not) be questioned by a party or disclose information by an affidavit or other method about any issue in the case, if the following conditions are met:

1. It would be unfair to the party who wants the questioning or disclosure to carry on the case without it;
2. The information is not easily available by another method;
3. The questioning or disclosure will not cause unacceptable delay or undue expense.

Speaking to this Rule in *Weber v Merritt*,[959] Madsen J of the Ontario Superior Court of Justice stated:

> [29] The onus on a motion for non-party disclosure and/or questioning is on the moving party. *Re the Estate of Harold Edwin Ballard*, 1995 CarswellOnt 1332 at 16.

957 2012 ONSC 2486. Compare to *Duleba v Sorge*, 2018 ONSC 6022.
958 *Jordan v Stewart*, 2014 ONSC 5797 at paras 29–32, Mitchell J.
959 2018 ONSC 3086; see also *Hohl v Hohl*, 2021 ONSC 2182.

[30] The starting point is to consider the context, and the purpose for which the Rule is invoked. *Ireland v. Ireland*, 2011 ONCA 623 (Can LII) at 28.

[31] The Court has held that the test under Rule 19(11) is an objective test which requires an analysis outside the litigant's belief system: "suspicion and conjecture will not suffice." See *Santilli v. Piselli*, 2010 CarswellOnt 3317 at paragraph 12. There is no reason that the test would not be the same under Rule 20(5).

[32] In *Re the Estate of Harold Edwin Ballard, supra* at 15, in the context of the *Rules of Civil Procedure*, the Ontario Court of Appeal set out six factors to be considered by the Motions judge when faced with a motion for non-party disclosure:

a. The importance of the documents in the litigation;
b. Whether production at the discovery stage of the process as opposed to production at Trial is necessary to avoid unfairness to the Applicant;
c. Whether the discovery of the defendants with respect to the issues to which the documents are relevant is adequate and if not, whether the responsibility for that inadequacy rests with the defendants;
d. The position of the non-parties with respect to production;
e. The availability of the documents or their informational equivalent from some other source which is available to the moving party;
f. The relationship of the non-parties from whom production is sought, to the litigation and the parties to the litigation. Non-parties who have an interest in the subject matter of the litigation and whose interests are allied with the party opposing production should be more susceptible to a production order than a true "stranger" to the litigation.

[33] Rule 20(5) has been held to be more permissive than the comparable Rule in the *Rules of Civil Procedure*, and to give judges more liberal and generous discretion. As noted by Justice Turnbull in *Hagey-Holmes v. Hagey*, 2005 CarswellOnt 2840 at 32:

> That makes eminent sense when one considers that in matrimonial litigation, spouses and family members may be "used" to shield income or other assets that might be relevant in the assessment of spousal support, child support, or net family equalization issues.

[34] So too in *Loeb v. Loeb*, 2013 CarswellOnt 3247 at 42, the Court noted that it is not uncommon in the family law context for family members and their businesses to align themselves to support and protect a family member defending a property or support claim.

[35] At the same time, as set out in *Boyd v. Fields*, 2006 CarswellOnt 8675 at 12, as with all disclosure requests in the family law context, whether from parties or non-parties, while full and frank disclosure is a fundamental tenet of the *Family Law Rules*, "there is also an element of proportionality, common sense, and fairness built into these rules." Disclosure obligations must be assessed in light of Rule 2(3).

[36] As stressed by Justice Kristjanson in *Politis v. Politis*, 2018 ONSC 323 (Can LII), in the family law context, the test for compelling third party disclosure set out in *Re Ballard, supra*, "must be supplemented to take into account two critical values, privacy and

proportionality." She notes, in the context of new partners, that privacy interests of third parties must be carefully balanced against the interests of the parties in the proceeding.

[37] Non-parties are generally protected from potentially intrusive, costly, and time-consuming processes of discovery *except in circumstances specifically addressed* by the *Rules*. See *Santilli v. Piselli, supra*. As Justice McGee noted therein at paragraph 13: "The discovery process must be kept within reasonable bounds."

[38] There must be an evidentiary basis to show that the documents sought or the questioning requested is relevant. The request for disclosure from a non-party and the request for questioning should not amount to a fishing expedition. *Campbell v. Wentzell*, 2015 CarswellOnt 15086 at 47. Disclosure is not a weapon and is not intended to overreach. *Saunders v. Saunders* 2015 CarswellOnt 2209 at para. 13.

O. SANCTIONS FOR NON-DISCLOSURE

A correct determination of income is vital to the proper assessment of child support under the *Federal Child Support Guidelines*. If a spouse or former spouse fails to comply with the disclosure requirements, a variety of options are available to the court pursuant to the express provisions of the Guidelines. Where a spouse or former spouse fails to provide the income information set out in section 21 of the *Federal Child Support Guidelines*, section 22(1) of the Guidelines entitles the other spouse (a) to seek to have the application for child support set down for a hearing or to move for judgment; or (b) to apply for an order requiring compliance with section 21. After granting an order in either of these circumstances, the court may order costs in favour of the other spouse up to an amount that fully compensates the other spouse for all costs incurred in the proceedings.[960] Where the court proceeds to a hearing, an adverse inference may be drawn against the spouse or former spouse who failed to make disclosure and the court may impute such income to that spouse or former spouse as may be deemed appropriate.[961] Where the spouse or former spouse fails to comply with a court order under section 22(1)(a) of the *Federal Child Support Guidelines*, the court may

1) strike out any of that spouse's pleadings;
2) make a contempt order against that spouse;
3) proceed to a hearing in which it may draw an adverse inference against the spouse or former spouse and impute income to that spouse in such amount as it considers appropriate; and
4) order costs in favour of the other spouse that fully compensates the other spouse for all costs incurred in the proceedings.[962]

960 *Federal Child Support Guidelines*, SOR/97-175, s 22(2); *Cole v Cole*, [2000] NSJ No 74 (SC); *Vollmer v Vollmer*, [1998] OJ No 5389 (Gen Div).

961 *Federal Child Support Guidelines*, s 23; *Motyka v Motyka*, 2001 BCCA 18; *Mansoor v Mansoor*, 2012 BCSC 602; *Vollmer v Vollmer*, [1998] OJ No 5389 (Gen Div); *Seidlikoski v Hall* (1998), 40 RFL (4th) 427 (Sask QB).

962 *Federal Child Support Guidelines*, s 24; see *MR v JR*, 2018 NBCA 12; *Vollmer v Vollmer*, [1998] OJ No 5389 (Gen Div).

The availability of an indemnity for costs in relation to the respondent's non-disclosure of financial information presupposes that the applicant has also made full financial disclosure. Where an indemnity for costs is available, the amount payable will be set by a taxing officer in the absence of agreement between the parties.[963] If the court is asked to fix the costs, the claimant should provide the court with an outline of the costs requested.[964] Section 213(2)(d)(ii) of the British Columbia *Family Law Act*[965] empowers the court to order the payment of an amount not exceeding $5,000 to or for the benefit of a party, or a spouse or child whose interests were affected by the non-disclosure of information or the incomplete, false, or misleading disclosure but the court may decline to impose this sanction where it has not been impeded from arriving at the obligor's income for the purpose of determining the child support obligation.[966]

Failure to comply with an order for financial disclosure can not only result in the judicial imputation of income; it can also result in a penalty up to $5,000 under section 36.1(2) of *The Family Maintenance Act*.[967] This remedy is separate and apart from any other sanctions the court might impose as a consequence of a contempt finding.[968]

Both the Ontario *Family Law Rules* and the *Federal Child Support Guidelines* emphasize the importance placed on full and timely disclosure. In order to promote early resolution or timely litigation, the Ontario *Family Law Rules* have created a process heavily reliant on full disclosure at the earliest possible opportunity. Numerous Rules deal with the issue of disclosure and provide clear sanctions for a failure to disclose.[969] Rules 19 and 20 set up the process. Severe sanctions for failure to comply with a disclosure order are found in Rules 1(8), 13(7), 14(23), and 19(10). A litigant may find his or her pleadings struck and the case proceeding without his or her participation. Although it is an expense to litigants to take out an order, when one seeks to rely on a disclosure endorsement, it should be taken out as an order and served on the party who is to provide the disclosure. This is especially important if the disclosing party is unrepresented because then there can be no doubt about the importance of disclosure. Before imposing sanctions for non-disclosure, the court should consider the clarity of the disclosure request, the continued relevance of the requested disclosure, and the probative value of the missing disclosure weighed against the difficulty of obtaining the disclosure.[970]

A failure to disclose income may justify both a retroactive and a prospective increase in the amount of a child support order in respect of which variation is sought.[971]

---

963 *Zeeper v Zeeper*, [2000] AJ No 309 (QB).

964 *Ibid.*

965 SBC 2011, c 25.

966 See *Burke v Burke*, [2003] BCJ No 2324 (SC) (application under s 92(1) of the *Family Relations Act*, RSBC 1996, c 128); *Watson v Watson*, [2006] BCJ No 329 (SC) (fine deemed inappropriate where no wanton disregard of prior court order for financial disclosure). The *Family Relations Act* has now been superseded by the *Family Law Act*, SBC 2011, c 25.

967 CCSM c F20.

968 *Hradowy v Hradowy*, 2011 MBQB 64.

969 *Biddle v Biddle*, [2005] OJ No 737 (SCJ), Blishen J. For a detailed review of the Ontario disclosure rules, see *Shamli v Shamli*, [2004] OJ No 4999 (SCJ), Rogers J.

970 *Chernyakhovsky v Chernyakhovsky*, [2005] OJ No 944 (SCJ).

971 *Allen v Allen* (1994), 9 RFL (4th) 48 (BCSC).

Insufficient information available to the court respecting the respondent's income may result in a stay of divorce judgment under section 11(1)(b) of the *Divorce Act*. A judicial direction may be issued for financial disclosure in accordance with the requirements of section 21 of the *Federal Child Support Guidelines* to enable the court to order child support and grant the divorce judgment. A failure to comply with the judicial direction may result in an order for costs on a solicitor and client basis pursuant to section 22(2) of the Guidelines. A failure to provide required financial information may also justify a judicial imputation of income under section 19(1)(f) of the Guidelines or it may warrant the court entertaining a motion by counsel for the petitioner to take evidence and receive documents as to the respondent's income, by deposition or otherwise, from persons employed by the respondent's employer. In a proceeding for child support, section 23 of the *Ontario Child Support Guidelines* empowers a court to draw an adverse inference against a parent who fails to provide proper financial disclosure and the court may impute income to that parent in such amount as it considers appropriate. Parents who are self-employed have a positive obligation to put forward not only adequate but also comprehensive records of income and expenses.[973]

An application for variation of a child support order should be dismissed where the applicant fails to provide court-ordered annual disclosure of his income and the disclosure requirements of section 21 of the *Federal Child Support Guidelines* have not been complied with.[974] Only in rare instances should a party applying to reduce his or her child support obligation be heard where that party has failed to make full disclosure.[975]

Wilful failure to comply with a court order for financial disclosure may trigger a finding of contempt. Section 49 of the *Family Law Act* empowers the Ontario Court of Justice to punish contempt with a maximum fine of $5,000 or imprisonment for a period not exceeding ninety days, or both. Additional sanctions for contempt are found under Rule 31(5) of the Ontario *Family Law Rules*. Clause 31(5)(c) permits the court to order the party in contempt to pay an amount to the other party. The purpose of a finding of contempt and the imposition of an appropriate sanction is twofold: (1) to provide an incentive for the contemnor to purge the contempt and bring himself into compliance with the pre-existing court order; and (2) to operate as a general deterrent by sending a message to support payors that they cannot frustrate the intent of the law by failing to support their children adequately as a result of non-compliance with court orders for financial disclosure.[976] In *Sharpley v Sharpley*,[977] the Ontario Court of Justice, having found beyond a reasonable doubt that the father had wilfully failed to provide financial disclosure as required by a prior court order, held that he should pay to the mother the sum of $6,024, which represented the difference between the amount of child support paid and the amount that should have been paid, failing which the father was to be imprisoned for six days. In addition, the father was prohibited from filing any motion to vary or any document in response to a motion to vary until he had purged his contempt.

---

972 *Cole v Cole*, [2000] NSJ No 74 (SC); see also *Bakshi v Bakshi*, 2011 ONSC 3557.

973 *Paul v Dennis*, 2012 NSSC 366; *Reyes v Rollo*, [2001] OJ No 5110 (SCJ); *Bakshi v Bakshi*, 2011 ONSC 3557. See also *Beaudoin v Stevens*, 2023 ONSC 4401.

974 *Rivard v Rivard*, [2004] AJ No 589 (QB).

975 *Terry v Francis*, [2004] NSJ No 366 (CA).

976 *Sharpley v Sharpley*, [2005] OJ No 5697 (Ct J).

977 *Ibid*.

P. FINANCIAL STATEMENTS AND BUDGETS

The former practice of filing detailed financial statements, which included a children's budget,[978] has been substantially affected by the *Federal Child Support Guidelines* in cases where the amount of child support is exclusively determined by reference to the applicable provincial or territorial table. Given the focus of the tables on the obligor's income in determining the amount of child support payable, it is no longer appropriate or necessary for the parties to file detailed financial statements that purport to define their personal expenses and those of the children. The provincial and territorial child support tables are based exclusively on the obligor's income and the number of children and are not budget driven.[979] A case-by-case analysis of children's budgets does not produce predictable results and makes settlements problematic.[980] However, relevant financial data must be provided in situations falling outside the provincial or territorial tables.[981] There is no universal requirement, however, that primary caregiving parents prepare child expense budgets in all cases wherein judicial discretion exists.[982]

The income of an applicant is only necessary to determine the amount of child support in limited circumstances, namely, where

1) the child has attained the age of majority;
2) the annual income of the obligor spouse exceeds $150,000;
3) the spouse against whom an order is sought stands in the place of the natural parent;
4) a claim is made for special or extraordinary expenses under section 7 of the *Federal Child Support Guidelines*;
5) each spouse has more than 60 percent of parenting time with one or more children of the marriage;[983]
6) each spouse has shared parenting time for not less than 40 percent of the year; and
7) either spouse seeks to invoke the undue hardship provisions of section 10 of the *Federal Child Support Guidelines*.

In any of these circumstances, the information and documentation specified in section 21 of the *Federal Child Support Guidelines* is mandatory.[984] Where the claim for child support is confined to the amount payable under the applicable provincial table, an order dispensing with the applicant's filing of a financial statement pursuant to Rule 48(3) or 74 of the Ontario *Rules of Civil Procedure* may be granted. Although there is no specific rule that allows the court to relieve the applicant from the mandatory delivery of a financial statement and the authority for such dispensation can only flow from Rule 6(1), this Rule should be construed

---

978 See Thomas Bastedo & Samantha Kennedy, "Child Expense Budgets: Use and Abuse" (May 2001) 16 *Money & Family Law* 35–38.

979 *Plester v Plester*, [1997] BCJ No 1862 (SC); see also *Gray v Gray*, [1997] OJ No 4652 (Gen Div).

980 *Middleton v MacPherson*, [1997] AJ No 614 (QB), citing *Levesque v Levesque* (1994), 4 RFL (4th) 375 (Alta CA).

981 *Simon v Simon*, [1997] OJ No 4145 (Gen Div), rev'd on other grounds [1999] OJ No 4492 (CA).

982 *Francis v Baker*, [1999] SCR 52; Chapter 9, Section B.

983 See *Federal Child Support Guidelines*, s 2(1) (definition of "majority of parenting time") and s 8 ("split parenting time"), as amended by SOR/2020-247.

984 *Gray v Gray*, [1997] OJ No 4652 (Gen Div).

so as to avoid the need for a party to complete and deliver a form that is irrelevant to the issue before the court.[985]

On an application to vary a child support order pursuant to the *Federal Child Support Guidelines*, assets and debts may be relevant, in which event a short-term financial statement must be completed in accordance with the Ontario *Rules of Civil Procedure*.[986]

Section 21 of the *Federal Child Support Guidelines* specifically provides that a spouse who controls a corporation must produce for the court the financial statements of the corporation and its subsidiaries for the three most recent taxation years and a statement showing a breakdown of all salaries, wages, management fees, or other payments or benefits paid in respect of non-arm's-length transactions.[987] Section 21 of the Guidelines is silent on production of corporate income tax returns.[988] There is no definition of a "financial statement" in the *Federal Child Support Guidelines*. Consequently, the term must be considered as having an ordinary meaning. A corporate financial statement is a financial statement prepared by an accountant that shows the complete corporate financial picture, including notes as to how the statement was prepared. A financial statement usually comprises a statement of corporate assets and liabilities, revenues from all sources, expenses, and a statement of retained earnings.[989] An obligor cannot avoid full financial disclosure by undertaking to pay all of the children's expenses. The Guidelines impose a mandatory directive for disclosure of the required financial records.[990] Non-disclosure triggers the remedies set out in sections 22, 23, and 24 of the Guidelines.[991]

Use of a sealing order to prevent public access to the family's financial information may be appropriate but only in the clearest of cases. Compliance with a sealing order relating to financial information may require counsel to segregate financial and other data.[992] Counsel may be granted the opportunity to apply for an order whereby the parties would be identified by their initials rather than by their names before the reasons for judgment are circulated to publishers. Where no such request is made by the specified date, the reasons may be released with the full names of the parties.[993]

985 *Ibid.*

986 *Stevens v Boulerice*, [1999] OJ No 1568 (SCJ).

987 *MC v JO*, 2017 NBCA 15; *Delaney v Delaney*, 2014 NLTD(F) 28; *Wildeman v Wildeman*, 2014 ABQB 732.

988 *AEF v LAF*, 2011 PESC 23.

989 *Vollmer v Vollmer*, [1998] OJ No 5389 (Gen Div).

990 *Ibid.*

991 See Section O, above in this chapter.

992 *Pakka v Nygard*, [2002] OJ No 3858 (SCJ).

993 *Ibid.*

Special or Extraordinary Expenses

A. DISTINCTIONS BETWEEN ORDINARY AND EXTRAORDINARY EXPENSES; DEFINITION OF EXTRAORDINARY EXPENSES

The court may, on the request of either spouse or former spouse,[1] provide in a child support order for the payment of any of the following expenses, or any portion of those expenses, taking into account the necessity of the expense in relation to the child's best interests and the reasonableness of the expense, having regard to the means of the spouses or former spouses and those of the child and to the family's spending pattern prior to the separation:

1) child care expenses incurred as a result of the employment, illness, disability, or education or training for employment of the spouse who exercises the majority of parenting time;
2) that portion of the medical and dental insurance premiums attributable to the child;
3) health-related expenses that exceed insurance reimbursement by at least $100 annually per illness or event, including orthodontic treatment, professional counselling provided by a psychologist, social worker, psychiatrist or any other person, physiotherapy, occupational therapy, speech therapy, prescription drugs, hearing aids, glasses, and contact lenses;
4) extraordinary expenses for primary or secondary school education or for any educational programs that meet the child's particular needs;
5) expenses for post-secondary education; and
6) extraordinary expenses for extracurricular activities.[2]

A reference to "special or extraordinary expenses" appears in the marginal note to section 7 of the *Federal Child Support Guidelines* but the term "special expenses" does not appear in the body of section 7. Section 7 of the *Federal Child Support Guidelines* gives the court the discretion to order payment of an amount over and above the regular table amount. However,

1 *Middleton v MacPherson*, [1997] AJ No 614 (QB).

2 *Federal Child Support Guidelines*, SOR/97-175, s 7(1). For a useful discussion of s 7 expenses, see *Clarke v Clarke*, 2014 BCSC 824 at paras 48–54, cited in *Sea v He*, 2022 BCSC 2169; *Cervi v McDonald*, 2021 ONSC 1843.

in order to qualify for a section 7 order, the expenses must be proven to be "special" or "extra ordinary" in some way. This is because the basic table amounts of child support are designed to cover all the "ordinary" costs of raising a child. Food, shelter, clothing, and other neces sities are all ordinary, as are many educational, extracurricular, and recreational expenses. Recreational sports and other similar extracurricular activities such as dance lessons, com munity sports leagues, ski trips, etc., will not generally qualify as special or extraordinary expenses unless the child's participation goes beyond that of an ordinary child.[4] Special," as distinct from "extraordinary," expenses are generally added more or less as a routine matter, provided that they are not unreasonably high,[6] but controversy can arise with respect to the "necessity" for a child to be engaged in extracurricular activities.[7]

Section 7 of the Guidelines is not presumptive; it indicates that a court may on either spouse's request[8] provide for an amount to cover all or any portion of the expenses enumer ated, which expenses may be estimated taking into account the necessity of the expenses in relation to the child's best interests and the reasonableness of the expenses in relation to means of the spouses and those of the child and to the family's spending pattern prior to separation. The onus is on the parent seeking a contribution to plead and prove the expense. Although expenses may be estimated, there must be some cogent evidence of a particular expense. Failing to consult is generally treated as a relevant — sometimes decisive — factor in gauging a parent's exposure to section 7 expenses.[11]

An order for special or extraordinary expenses under section 7 of the *Federal Child Sup port Guidelines* is not premised on a prior or concurrent order for the payment of the basic table amount of child support.[12] A non-primary residential parent may seek contribution to a child's extraordinary expenses for extracurricular activities and the amount ordered may be set-off against the table amount of child support payable by the non-primary residential parent.[13] While ordering a *pro rata* sharing of all of the allowable expenses under section 7 of the Guidelines, a court may order that the mother shall assume the primary responsibility for dealing with certain designated expenditures while the father shall assume the primary responsibility for the others.[14]

---

3 *Clarke v Clarke*, 2014 BCSC 824 at paras 48–49, Baird J; *TMR v SMS*, 2019 NBQB 40 at para 16; *MSD obo NC v AL*, 2022 NBQB 21.

4 *Santelli v Trinetti*, 2019 BCCA 319 at para 152, citing *Dorey v Havens*, 2019 BCCA 47 at para 44; *Bernardin v Bernardin*, 2020 BCSC 807.

5 *MSD obo NC v AL*, 2022 NBQB 21; *Slade v Slade*, [2001] NJ No 5 (CA); *VC v JDB*, 2009 NSSC 25. Compare *Olaitan v MacDougall*, 2014 PECA 5.

6 *Sharf v Sharf*, [2000] OJ No 4052 (SCJ).

7 *MD v PD*, 2023 NBKB 202; *Russell v Russell*, 2012 NSSC 258.

8 See *H v J*, 2017 NBQB 69 (application by uncle and grandmother).

9 *Carruthers v Carruthers*, 2015 BCSC 104; *Cook v Cook*, 2016 NBQB 55 citing *H v C*, 2010 NBQB 120; *Bradley v Brooks*, 2015 NLTD(F) 34; *Vantomme v Vantomme*, 2014 SKQB 227.

10 *Howe v Lorette*, 2017 NBQB 119 at para 253, Wooder J; see also *MR v JR*, 2018 NBCA 12; *MD v PD*, 2023 NBKB 202.

11 *Joe-Joe v Joe-Joe*, 2023 ABKB 551 at para 21, Lema J; see also *Meier v Sirman*, 2023 ABKB 704 at para 71, citing *AE v AE*, 2021 ONSC 8189.

12 *Whitley v Whitley*, [1997] BCJ No 3116 (SC); *Davis v Davis*, [1999] BCJ No 1832 (SC); but see *contra Hannigan v Hannigan*, [1998] BCJ No 3177 (SC).

13 *Van Bilsen v Van Bilsen*, [2003] OJ No 4657 (SCJ).

14 *Fisher v Fisher*, [2001] OJ No 5477 (SCJ).

Although child care expenses, medical and dental insurance, health-related expenses, and post-secondary educational expenses need not be extraordinary under sections 7(1)(a), (b), (c), and (e) of the *Federal Child Support Guidelines* in order to warrant a judicial allocation, expenses for primary or secondary school education or for any educational programs that meet a child's particular needs under section 7(1)(d) of the Guidelines and expenses for extracurricular activities under section 7(1)(f) of the Guidelines must be extraordinary in order to be allowable.[15] All expenses, however, must meet the tests of necessity and reasonableness set out in section 7(1) of the Guidelines.[16] The onus falls on the applicant who seeks special or extraordinary expenses under section 7 of the *Federal Child Support Guidelines* to prove that the expenses are necessary in relation to the child's best interests and reasonable having regard to the parental financial circumstances.[17]

Effective 1 May 2006, section 7 of the *Federal Child Support Guidelines* was amended to promote clarity and consistency in the definition of "extraordinary expenses" under sections 7(1)(d) and 7(1)(f) of the Guidelines.[18] Pursuant to section 7(1.1)(a) of the amended Guidelines, expenses are extraordinary if they exceed an amount that the requesting parent can reasonably cover. In determining whether the expenses are reasonably affordable, the court must consider the income of the requesting spouse and any child support received. Where section 7(1.1)(a) is inapplicable in that the expenses do not exceed an amount that the requesting spouse can reasonably cover, the court will determine whether the expenses are extraordinary by taking into account the following five factors:

- the amount of the expense in relation to the income of the spouse requesting the amount, including the amount of child support received;
- the nature and number of the educational programs and extracurricular activities;
- any special needs and talents of the child or children;
- the overall cost of the programs and activities; and
- any other similar factor that the court considers relevant.[19]

These factors indicate the significant discretion reposed in the court of first instance to determine what is or is not an extraordinary expense based on the evidence before the court.

---

15 *Bodine-Shah v Shah*, 2014 BCCA 191; *KKS v JSS*, 2019 BCSC 136; *WL v RW*, [2005] NBJ No 470 (QB); *Hiscock v Hiscock*, 2014 NLTD(F) 14; *Bocaneala v Bocaneala*, 2014 NSSC 450; *Hoover v Hoover*, [1997] NWTJ No 43 (SC); *MacKinnon v MacKinnon*, [2005] OJ No 1552 (CA); *Titova v Titov*, 2012 ONCA 864; *Beisel v Henderson*, [2004] SJ No 413 (QB); *MDL v CR*, 2020 SKCA 44.

16 *MA v FHA*, 2011 BCSC 1047; *KKS v JSS*, 2019 BCSC 136; *NSC v DC*, 2011 NBQB 229; *Bocaneala v Bocaneala*, 2014 NSSC 450; *Williams v Steinwand*, 2014 NWTSC 74; *Titova v Titov*, 2012 ONCA 864; *Zigiris v Foustanellas*, 2016 ONSC 7528; *Beisel v Henderson*, [2004] SJ No 413 (QB); *JC v SAW*, 2008 YKSC 95.

17 *Hamilton v Hamilton*, 2010 BCSC 844; *MD v PD*, 2023 NBKB 202; *Abbott v Crane*, [2004] NJ No 292 (UFC); *Mastin v Mastin*, 2019 NSSC 248; *Clark v Clark*, 2012 ONSC 1026; *Olaitan v MacDougall*, 2014 PECA 5; *Carmichael v Douglas*, [2008] SJ No 474 (QB); *MDL v CR*, 2020 SKCA 44.

18 SOR/2005-400, s 1 (28 November 2005), *Canada Gazette*, Vol 139, No 25 (14 December 2005). And see *FJN v JK*, 2019 ABCA 305 at para 72, leave to appeal to SCC denied 2020 CanLII 8218 (SCC); *AM v GM*, 2018 BCSC 942; *LKS v DMCT*, 2008 NSCA 61. As to ongoing judicial uncertainty and lack of consistency, see *Simpson v Trowsdale*, 2007 PESCTD 3, MacDonald J.

19 *CJT v GAT*, 2012 ABQB 193; *LAM v SCM*, 2020 BCSC 67; *Beruschi v Muller*, 2021 BCSC 78; *LKS v DMCT*, 2008 NSCA 61; *Hardayal v Asrula*, 2018 ONSC 6948; *MDL v CR*, 2020 SKCA 44; *JC v SAW*, 2008 YKSC 95.

An important consideration is the total income of the spouse in receipt of child support but there is no formula and the court must have regard to the evidence before it concludes whether all, some, or none of the expenses in sections 7(1)(d) and/or (f) are extraordinary. In *LKS v DMCT*, it was stated that it is "preferable to deal first with subsection 7(1) [of the Guidelines] to determine whether the expenses are necessary in relation to the child's best interests and reasonable in relation to the means of the parents before dealing with the definition of extraordinary expenses in subsection 7(1A)."[21]

To qualify as a section 7 expense, the applicant must meet the thresholds stated in sections 7(1) and 7(1A) of the *Federal Child Support Guidelines*. In *MacDonald v Pink*,[22] Forgeron J of the Nova Scotia Supreme Court distilled the following principles from relevant Nova Scotia caselaw:

a. Section 7 of the *Guidelines* provides the court with the jurisdiction to grant a discretionary award.
b. The starting point is the assumption that the table amount will ordinarily be sufficient to provide for the needs of the child.[23] The burden therefore rests on the party asserting the claim. Proof is on a balance of probabilities and based upon clear, cogent, and convincing evidence.
c. The sec. 7 analysis is fact specific — one that must be determined on a case by case basis taking into consideration the necessity and reasonableness of the expense, and the [parental] obligation . . . to contribute to the expense.
d. Section 7 cases determined prior to the 2006 amendment may not be applicable.
e. It is preferable to first determine whether expenses are necessary in relation to the child's best interests, and reasonable in relation to the means of the parents under sec. 7(1) before determining the applicability of sec. 7(1A) of the *Guidelines*.[24]
f. If the court decides that the expenses meet the requirements of sec. 7(1), then activity expenses must be further scrutinized pursuant to sec. 7(1A).
g. Section 7(1A) calls for a two part test. First, the court is to determine whether or not the claimed expenses exceed those which the [primary caregiving] parent could reasonably cover given her total income, and the amount of child support being received.
h. If the first test is not applicable, then the court must have recourse to sec. 7(1A)(b). This second test requires the court to review a number of factors, including a proportionality inquiry, and an inquiry into the nature and number of activities, any special needs or talent of the child, the overall cost of the activities, and any other similar and relevant factors.
i. The [primary caregiving] parent does not need to prove that a child is at an elite level in order to have an extracurricular activity included as a sec. 7 expense.

---

20 *Gaspers v Gaspers*, 2008 SKCA 94.

21 2008 NSCA 61 at para 27; *Boylan v MacLean*, 2018 NSSC 15; *Krammer (Ackerman) v Ackerman*, 2020 SKQB 280. Compare *LAM v SCM*, 2020 BCSC 67; *D (DE) v J (QR)*, 2019 PESC 39 at para 13.

22 2011 NSSC 421 at para 55; *Fedortchouk v Boubnoy*, 2018 NSSC 66; *Krammer (Ackerman) v Ackerman*, 2020 SKQB 280.

23 *Carroll v Richardson*, 2014 NSSC 293.

24 *LKS v DMCT*, 2008 NSCA 61.

In *Delichte v Rogers*,[25] Steel JA, who delivered the judgment of the Manitoba Court of Appeal, provided an excellent summary of many of the principles that govern applications for extraordinary expenses for schooling and for extracurricular activities under section 7 of the *Federal Child Support Guidelines*. The following eighteen considerations have been extracted, often verbatim, from her reasons for judgment:

1) The table amount of child support covers all ordinary expenses of child-rearing. Any special or extraordinary expenses are governed by section 7 of the *Federal Child Support Guidelines*. Section 7 of the Guidelines provides some flexibility because not all family needs are the same.[26]
2) Although child care expenses, medical and dental insurance, health-related expenses, and post-secondary educational expenses need not be extraordinary under section 7(1)(a), (b), (c), and (e) of the *Federal Child Support Guidelines* in order to warrant a judicial order, expenses for primary or secondary school education or for any educational programs that meet a child's particular needs under section 7(1)(d) of the Guidelines and expenses for extracurricular activities under section 7(1)(f) of the Guidelines must be extraordinary in order to be allowable.[27]
3) Pursuant to section 7(1.1)(a) of the Guidelines, expenses are extraordinary if they exceed an amount that the requesting parent can reasonably cover, taking into account the income of the requesting spouse and any child support received. Thus, the term "extraordinary expense" must be understood within the particular family's means and circumstances.[28] If the expenses do not exceed an amount the requesting spouse can reasonably cover, then the court will consider the five factors listed in section 7(1.1)(b) to determine whether the expenses can still be classified as extraordinary in the circumstances. The five factors to consider under section 7(1.1)(b) are: (1) the amount of the expense in relation to the income of the spouse requesting the amount, including the amount of child support received, (2) the nature and number of the educational programs and extracurricular activities, (3) any special needs and talents of the child or children, (4) the overall cost of the programs and activities, and (5) any other similar factor that the court considers relevant.
4) On an initial application, the onus is upon the applicant to prove that the claimed expenses fall within one of the categories listed under section 7(1) since the categories listed are exhaustive.[29]
5) Extracurricular activities have been broadly held to include any activity outside the regular school curriculum, although not activities such as family vacations.[30] Everyday

---

25 2013 MBCA 106; see also *FJN v JK*, 2019 ABCA 305, leave to appeal to SCC denied 2020 CanLII 8218 (SCC); *BNM v PJM*, 2017 SKQB 331 (cellphone expenses are not s 7 expenses).

26 See *Andries v Andries* (1998), 159 DLR (4th) 665 at para 11, Twaddle JA.

27 See also *Bodine-Shah v Shah*, 2014 BCCA 191; *JAM v JPM*, 2019 BCSC 654.

28 See *Correia v Correia*, 2002 MBQB 172 at paras 7 and 10; and *Holeman v Holeman*, 2006 MBQB 278 at para 42.

29 *Graham v Graham*, 2008 MBQB 25 at para 62; *Howe v Lorette*, 2017 NBQB 119 at para 251.

30 *Raftus v Raftus* (1998), 166 NSR (2d) 179 at para 22 (CA).

clothing does not fall within section 7 expenses, although the costs of equipment and uniforms that related to an extracurricular activity may qualify.[31]

6) When the actual amount of the expense is difficult to ascertain, the expenses may be estimated; however, there must be some evidence to support the estimation of the expenses, otherwise the court cannot determine whether the requesting spouse is able to reasonably cover a totally unknown expense.[32]
7) Where a court determines that an amount to cover extraordinary expenses should be awarded, the contribution generally will be in proportion with the spouses' respective incomes (section 7(2)), but not always. The court may order a different contribution, depending on the specific circumstances of the case.[33] For example, the courts have occasionally departed from the general rule of contribution in accordance with the parties' respective incomes in situations where the payor's [exercise of parenting time] costs are unusually high.[34] Or a court may depart from the general principle of an income-based *pro rata* sharing of the child's expenses where the parents have agreed to equally share the expenses, or where there is a substantial disparity between the parental incomes, as for example, where one parent's income is barely sufficient to provide for his or her own needs and the other parent has ample ability to shoulder the expense.
8) Even if the expenses fall within one of the categories listed in section 7(1), the court must still be satisfied that the expenses are reasonable and necessary before ordering the sharing of the expenses.[35]
9) In determining whether the two-part test of necessity and reasonableness outlined in section 7(1) has been satisfied, the court is to take the following factors into account: (1) the necessity of the expense in relation to the child's best interests; and (2) the reasonableness of the expense in relation to the means of the spouses and those of the child; and (3) the family's spending pattern prior to the separation.
10) Courts have generally considered that the test of necessity does not connote only the necessities of life, but, rather, may include things that are "suitable to or proper for his station in life bearing in mind his requirements at the time."[36] Courts have looked to activities that have aided the child's development and health. So, for example, participation in sports activities has been held to be necessary in relation to the child's best interests.[37]
11) With regard to private schooling, the British Columbia Court of Appeal has held that a trial judge correctly considered private schooling to be necessary where both parties affirmed the importance of private Catholic school for their daughters and had serious reservations about public school. This agreement was determined to be "strong evidence

31 *Walsh v Walsh*, 2006 NLUFC 7 at paras 62–64.

32 See *Ferguson v Thorne*, 2007 NBQB 66 at paras 63–65; see also *MR v JR*, 2018 NBCA 12.

33 See *EKR v GAW* (1997), 122 Man R (2d) 120 at paras 15–17 (QB); see also *Delichte v Rogers*, 2018 MBQB 75 at para 188; *Soleimani v Melendez*, 2019 ONSC 36; *Droit de la famille — 191160*, 2019 QCCA 1098.

34 *Carmichael v Douglas*, 2008 SKQB 320 at paras 31–32; *Brown v Hudon*, 2004 SKQB 294 at para 24. See also *MDL v CR*, 2020 SKCA 44 (capping of tutoring expenses and extraordinary expenses for extracurricular expenses).

35 *Ibid*.

36 See *Hiemstra v Hiemstra*, 2005 ABQB 192 at paras 52–53.

37 See *Fong v Charbonneau*, 2005 MBQB 92; and *Correia v Correia*, 2002 MBQB 172; *Richer v Freeland*, 2019 ONSC 6840.

to support a finding of necessity in relation to the children's best interests."[38] In other cases, the court has been stricter about proving necessity, in particular with regard to tuition for private school. For example, in *Steele v Koppanyi*,[39] Helper JA determined that "[t]here is no evidence to support a finding that [the child's] best interests necessitate his attending a private school" (at para 46), despite the fact that the child had attended private school for several years.

12) In many cases, the issue of necessity is not really discussed. The lack of discussion about "necessity" was commented upon by MacDonald J in *TLS v DJM*, as follows:

> The requirement for evidence from which a conclusion of "necessity" can be made is generally overlooked and this may occur because many parents agree, after separation, to share these expenses proportionally. This prior agreement may remove the prerequisite that the court determine whether a particular expense is "necessary."[40]

13) Furthermore, in many cases, it quickly becomes apparent that the "real" issue is whether the expense is reasonable in relation to the means of the spouses, and whether the expense is reasonable in light of the parties' spending pattern pre-separation. In that regard, it is necessary to focus on the *means* of the parties, not just their incomes. Caselaw indicates that the means of the parties should be interpreted broadly to include a consideration of all financial resources, including capital assets, income distribution, debt load, third-party resources that impact upon the parties' means, [exercise of parenting time] costs, obligations to pay spousal or other child support orders, spousal support received, and any other relevant factors.[41]

14) The courts have indicated that the following matters can be considered when assessing the reasonableness of the expense in relation to the means of the spouses:
    - the combined income of the parties
    - the fact that two households must be maintained
    - the extent of the expense in relation to the parties' combined level of income;
    - the debt of the parties
    - any prospect for a decline or increase in the parties' means in the near future
    - whether the [other] parent was consulted regarding the expense prior to the expense being incurred[42]

15) The reasonableness of the expense in relation to the family's spending pattern prior to the separation is also a factor that the court is required to take into account (section 7(1)). In *Correia v Correia*, Allen J indicated that "[a]n examination of this factor helps to see if the activity was one which would have been likely to be supported by the parents when together and thus considered by both to be in the child's best interests." In fact, the pre-separation pattern of spending may assist the court on the issue of reasonableness and necessity even where the expense seems relatively excessive.[43] The court

---

38 *McDonald v McDonald*, 2001 BCCA 702 at para 27; see also *KKS v JJS*, 2019 BCSC 136.

39 2002 MBCA 60.

40 2009 NSSC 79 at para 48.

41 See *Leskun v Leskun*, 2006 SCC 25 at para 29.

42 See *Soleimani v Melendez*, 2019 ONSC 36.

43 See, for example, *Winseck v Winseck* (2008), 235 OAC 38 at paras 30–31 (SCJ).

should, therefore, consider the family's lifestyle and activities prior to the separation, although the weight given to this factor may have to be re-evaluated in light of the dissolution of the marriage, the fact that there will now be two households to support, and the decreased means of the parties.[44] Obviously, where the means of the parties have dropped substantially after separation, judicial reliance on the family's pre-separation spending pattern will be less appropriate.

16) Where there has been a history of spending for an extraordinary expense, but that expense has increased to what could be considered an unreasonable level, the court may order the payor to contribute to a portion of the expense in recognition of the prior history of spending.[45] Also see *Iddon v Iddon*,[46] wherein Corbett J set a cap of $7,000 annually on the amount of the private school expense prior to ordering its apportionment between the parties, and *BBW-B v DMB*,[47] wherein Smith J set a cap of $75 per month on the amount the payor had to contribute to extracurricular activities.
17) While it is clear that a lack of consultation with the other spouse does not automatically preclude the proper apportionment of an extraordinary expense, it is a factor the judge can take into account when exercising his or her discretion. In some cases, the courts have reduced the payor's contribution due to the lack of consultation.[48]
18) Ultimately, the decision as to whether a particular expense will be considered necessary and reasonable depends on the facts of the particular case and the hearing judge's discretion.

Four separate but related issues arise under section 7 of the *Federal Child Support Guidelines*, namely,

1) the expenses must fall within one of the categories specified;
2) they must be a necessity in relation to the child's best interests;
3) they must be reasonable, having regard to the means of the spouses and child and the spending pattern before separation; and
4) the court must determine whether the expenses claimed are adequately provided for by the applicable provincial table under the Guidelines.[49]

The test for awarding section 7 expenses was described by the Ontario Court of Appeal in *Titova v Titov* as follows:

> In awarding s. 7 special and extraordinary expenses, the trial judge calculates each party's income for child support purposes, determines whether the claimed expenses fall within

---

44 *NMM v NSM*, 2004 BCSC 346 at paras 111–13.

45 *Doherty v Doherty* (2001), 19 RFL (5th) 46 (Ont SCJ); *Abelson v Mitra*, 2008 BCSC 1197 at para 95; and *Magee v Faveri*, [2007] OJ No 4826 at para 42 (SCJ).

46 [2006] OJ No 237 at paras 72–80 (SCJ).

47 2005 SKQB 462 at paras 35–38.

48 See *Pepin v Jung*, [1997] OJ No 4604 (Gen Div). See also *Meier v Sirman*, 2023 ABKB 704 at para 71, citing *AE v AE*, 2021 ONSC 8189; *Glenn v Glenn*, 2018 BCSC 2.

49 *Trueman v Trueman*, [2000] AJ No 1301 (QB); *Yensen v Yensen*, [2003] BCJ No 2086 (SC); *Budden v Combden*, [1999] NJ No 199 (SC); *Russell v Russell*, 2012 NSSC 258; *Park v Thompson*, [2005] OJ No 1695 (CA); *Titova v Titov*, 2012 ONCA 864 at para 23; *Rush v Rush*, [2002] PEIJ No 29 (SC). See also *Smith v Smith*, 2016 ONSC 4622 citing *Kloc v Wozniak*, 2013 ONCJ 363 at paras 28–37.

one of the enumerated categories of s. 7 of the Guidelines, determines whether the claimed expenses are necessary "in relation to the child's best interests" and are reasonable "in relation to the means of the spouses and those of the child and to the family's spending pattern prior to the separation." If the expenses fall under s. 7(1)(d) or (f) of the Guidelines, the trial judge determines whether the expenses are "extraordinary." Finally, the court considers what amount, if any, the child should reasonably contribute to the payment of these expenses and then applies any tax deductions or credits.[50]

Section 7 expenses cannot be determined in a vacuum. A court cannot determine whether any individual expenses may be necessary and reasonable without knowing the totality of the expenses.[51]

The test of necessity under section 7(1) of the Guidelines is not synonymous with the bare necessities of life; it refers to things suitable to or proper for the child's station in life bearing in mind his or her requirements at the time.[52] The reasonableness of the expenditure under section 7(1) of the Guidelines is more difficult to determine because it brings into play economic realities.[53] Whereas a parent is presumed capable of paying the applicable table amount of child support established by the Guidelines, it cannot be assumed that the parents can afford to contribute to section 7 expenses under the Guidelines. However, the fact that parents may have to scrimp somewhat in their discretionary spending is not a particularly persuasive argument against finding a particular expense to be eligible.[54] Section 7(1) of the Guidelines requires the court to look to the means of the parents. The income of the parties is only one of the factors to consider in assessing the "reasonableness" of an expense. Additional factors to be considered include "capital, income distribution, debt load, third party resources which impact upon a parent's ability to pay, [exercise of parenting] costs, obligations to pay spousal or other child support orders, spousal support received and any other relevant factors."[55] Other relevant factors include the fact that two households must be maintained, the extent of the expense in relation to parental income, any prospects for a financial decline or increase in the near future, and whether the other parent was consulted regarding the expense prior to its being incurred.[56] In the words of MacDonald J of the Nova Scotia Supreme Court in *Russell v Russell*:

> Not only must an expense be necessary, it must be reasonable in relation to the means of the spouses and those of the child and the family's spending pattern prior to the separation. To determine a parent's "means" one must examine not only annual income but also the

---

50 2012 ONCA 864 at para 23; see also *FJN v JK*, 2019 ABCA 305, leave to appeal to SCC denied 2020 CanLII 8218 (SCC); *Homann v Briscoe*, 2020 NSSC 52; *Williams v Steinwand*, 2014 NWTSC 74; *Craig v Niro*, 2022 ONSC 5178; *El Ouazzani v Chabini*, 2022 ONSC 5773; *D(DE) v J(QR)*, 2019 PESC 39.

51 *Melnyk v Glynn*, 2012 BCSC 219.

52 *TLS v DJM*, 2009 NSSC 79; *MacDonald v Pink*, 2011 NSSC 421; *Bruno v Keinick*, 2012 NSSC 336.

53 *Trueman v Trueman*, [2000] AJ No 1301 (QB), *TLS v DJM*, 2009 NSSC 79.

54 *Hiemstra v Hiemstra*, [2005] AJ No 287 (QB).

55 *Piwek v Jagiello*, 2011 ABCA 303, citing *Raftus v Raftus* (1998), 159 DLR (4th) 264 at 275; *Hawkins v Hawkins*, 2019 ONSC 7149.

56 *Bland v Bland*, [1999] AJ No 344 (QB); *Piwek v Jagiello*, 2011 ABCA 303; *Damphouse v Damphouse*, 2020 ABQB 101; *Correia v Correia*, [2002] MJ No 248 (QB); *Clink v Leydier*, [2007] MJ No 482 (QB); *Marunic v Liberty*, 2014 ONSC 957; *Hawkins v Hawkins*, 2019 ONSC 7149; *Meszen v Meszen*, 2021 ONSC 224; *JC v SAW*, 2008 YKSC 95.

> mandatory and voluntary deductions from that income, the resulting net disposable income, the child tax benefits and credits available to the parent, the GST credit available and the cost of living for each parent. A parent must be able to cover his or her reasonable cost of living. Each must be able to pay for a residence, food, clothing, transportation and all of the incidentals required to maintain a household for themselves and the children when the children are in his or her care. To focus only on income in a section 7 analysis would be inequitable and may prevent a parent from having a meaningful relationship with a child because he or she, for justifiable reasons, has insufficient net income to maintain a suitable residence and provide for the child when in his or her care. Some section 7 expenses result from voluntary parental decisions, recreational costs for example. Courts should not necessarily require a parent to contribute to those costs when the parent's means indicate his or her ability to pay will only be achieved if that parent alters what a court has considered to be reasonable living expenses. Courts inclined to do so should be satisfied the parent can in fact "live on less money" before ordering a contribution to a section 7 expense.[57]

In determining the reasonableness of the expenses, the young age of the child at the time of separation may render the pre-separation pattern of spending of little assistance, but the court may have regard to a post-separation pattern of voluntary payment over a period of years as indicative of an ongoing ability to pay. The court may also take account of the fact that future expenses will be payable over an abbreviated period of time.[58] Child care expenses, medical and dental insurance premiums, health care expenses, and post-secondary education expenses are all covered by section 7 and should be proportionately shared, if the spouses are able to pay. Orders for medical and dental insurance coverage should be utilized pursuant to section 6 of the Guidelines before the court has resort to the health-related expenses provisions of section 7 of the Guidelines.[59] Expenses relating to primary or secondary school education or the special educational needs of a child as well as expenses for extracurricular activities will only be allowed if they are "extraordinary" within the meaning of section 7(1.1) of the *Federal Child Support Guidelines*.[60]

An order for a contribution to special or extraordinary expenses under section 7 of the *Federal Child Support Guidelines* is discretionary both as to entitlement and the amount. The child support amounts fixed by the provincial or territorial tables reflect average expenditures on children; section 7 expenses do not lend themselves to average. Section 7 of the Guidelines provides flexibility because not all family needs are the same.[62] The reasonableness and necessity of child care expenses, health-related expenses, and extraordinary expenses for extracurricular activities may need to be assessed in light of the fact that they are sought for special needs children.[63]

---

57 2012 NSSC 258 at para 28.

58 *Trueman v Trueman*, [2000] AJ No 1301 (QB); *Schwark v Schwark*, [2000] SJ No 489 (QB).

59 *Budden v Combden*, [1999] NJ No 199 (SC).

60 SOR/2005-400.

61 Section 7(2). See also *Soleimani v Melendez*, 2019 ONSC 36; *Buckley v Blackwood*, 2019 ONSC 6918; *Smith v Smith*, 2016 ONSC 4622, citing *Kloc v Wozniak*, 2013 ONCJ 363 at paras 28–37; *El Ouazzani v Chabini*, 2022 ONSC 5773.

62 *Young v Young*, [2000] NBJ No 93 (CA); *Carmichael v Douglas*, [2008] SJ No 474 (QB).

63 *ALY v LMY*, [2001] AJ No 506 (QB); *Kirk v Kirk*, [2001] BCJ No 773 (SC); *Csecs v Csecs*, [2001] OJ No 1424 (SCJ).

Some judges have asserted that section 7 add-ons are the exception, not the rule,[64] at least insofar as extraordinary expenses under sections 7(1)(d) and 7(1)(f) are concerned.[65] Even if an expense is "extraordinary," it must also be necessary and reasonable within the meaning of section 7(1) of the Guidelines.[66] A parent does not have *carte blanche* to enrol a child in any number of extracurricular activities and then look to the other parent to share all of the costs.[67]

Orders for expenses under section 7 of the *Federal Child Support Guidelines*, other than post-secondary education expenses, are typically found in cases involving children under the age of majority. Although orders for parental contributions towards health-related expenses for disabled adult children and towards post-secondary education expenses for adult children are unexceptional, it is relatively rare for parents to be ordered to contribute towards extraordinary expenses for the extracurricular activities of adult children. In principle, however, provided the definition of "extraordinary" is satisfied and the expenses are reasonable and necessary within the meaning of section 7 of the *Federal Child Support Guidelines*, there is no legal obstacle to orders being granted relating to the extracurricular activities of adult children, although the children themselves may be expected to make a financial contribution towards the expenses where this is feasible or to curtail their extracurricular activities to some degree.[68]

Current involvement in post-secondary education and extracurricular activities does not constitute a prerequisite to a claim for special and extraordinary expenses under section 7 of the *Federal Child Support Guidelines*.[69] Judicial rules may be laid down with respect to future expenses falling within section 7 of the *Federal Child Support Guidelines*.[70]

The onus falls on the parent seeking section 7 proportionate sharing to prove that expenses are or will be incurred and that they fall within the scope of section 7(1), which is exhaustive.[71] Claims for expenses under section 7 of the Guidelines must be supported by relevant evidence. Absent such evidence, the court may find it too speculative to make an order.[72] The applicant must furnish evidence of the costs involved under the listed categories of allowable expenses under section 7 of the Guidelines, but the court may take judicial notice of the difference between the single and family rates under Alberta Health Care coverage.[73]

In determining the amount of a child's expenses to be paid pursuant to section 7 of the *Federal Child Support Guidelines*, the court has a discretion to estimate the amount so long as the estimate is based on an evidentiary foundation. Section 7 of the *Federal Child Support Guidelines* addresses expenses actually incurred or about to be incurred. It does

64 *Johnston v Johnston*, [2004] AJ No 333 (QB); *Casey v Casey*, [2000] NBJ No 102 (QB); *Budden v Combden*, [1999] NJ No 199 (SC); *Sanders v Sliede*, [2009] OJ No 1657 (SCJ); *Engebretson v Pellettieri*, [1998] SJ No 411 (QB).

65 *WL v RW*, [2005] NBJ No 470 (QB).

66 *Sanders v Sliede*, [2009] OJ No 1657 (SCJ).

67 *Bradley v Brooks*, 2015 NLTD(F) 34; *Smola v Roger*, [2002] OJ No 1254 (SCJ).

68 *Beninger v Beninger*, 2007 BCSC 1306.

69 *Re Gill*, [1999] BCJ No 820 (Prov Ct).

70 *Lavoie v Wills*, [2000] AJ No 1359 (QB).

71 *Lundrigan v Lundrigan*, 2009 NLUFC 28.

72 *MHG v DJG*, [2006] BCJ No 275 (SC) (leave to re-apply upon necessary evidence being provided); *Corkum v Clarke*, [2000] NSJ No 285 (Fam Ct).

73 *Edwards v Edwards*, [2002] AJ No 24 (QB).

not accommodate a parental "wish list"; there must be a reasonable expectation that the expense will soon be incurred. "If and when" orders should be avoided but "here and now" or "here and almost now" orders are appropriate. Wherever possible, the court should be asked to deal with known amounts, but the fact that the amount is unknown is not by itself a bar to ordering section 7 expenses.[74] Section 7(1) of the *Federal Child Support Guidelines* as amended effective 1 November 2000, makes it clear that a court may accept an estimate of anticipated expenses. Reliance on an estimate may be deemed appropriate in order to facilitate an expedited process and avoid further legal costs.[75] In *Griffeth v Griffeth*,[76] Dickson J of the Saskatchewan Court of Queen's Bench observed that there are alternatives available to a court when an application for special or extraordinary expenses under section 7 of the *Federal Child Support Guidelines* is based on an estimate of future expenses. The court may determine the kind of expense to be shared and order reimbursement of the appropriate amount upon production of receipts. This approach is fraught with difficulty. First, the order may be unenforceable by the Maintenance Enforcement Office. Second, before an expense can be judicially determined to be reasonable, necessary, or extraordinary within the meaning of section 7(1) of the Guidelines, the amount must be known. Third, requiring one parent to pay the entire expense and then seek reimbursement may place an unbearable strain on that parent's budget. In the opinion of Dickson J, a preferable approach to determining a parent's monthly contribution to future section 7 expenses would be to require the applicant to present an estimate, thereby enabling the court to determine necessity, reasonableness, and, where appropriate, whether the expenses are extraordinary. Compliance with section 7 could then be achieved by ordering the appropriate contribution to be paid, subject to a subsequent accounting and adjustment between the parents after the actual expense is incurred. This would ensure that a contribution will be made only for expenses actually incurred.

A court may cap the allowable children's expenses under section 7 of the *Federal Child Support Guidelines* to reflect a parent's limited ability to pay.[77]

An interspousal contract for the payment of child-related expenses is enforceable according to its terms even though the expenses fall outside the ambit of special or extraordinary expenses within the meaning of section 7 of the *Federal Child Support Guidelines*.[78]

A spouse who is called upon to contribute to expenses under section 7 of the *Federal Child Support Guidelines* is entitled to disclosure respecting any such expenses. The purpose of disclosure is to ensure that the other party has an adequate opportunity to assess the information provided and govern themselves accordingly.[79]

Section 7 of the *Federal Child Support Guidelines* should not become an indirect vehicle for spousal support. The applicant has the burden of proving the reasonableness of any expenses sought and the costs associated with a proposed expenditure and a claim for expenses may be rejected on the basis that the evidentiary burden has not been discharged.

---

74 *Myke v Myke*, [2000] OJ No 2056 (SCJ); *JB v DM*, 2014 ONSC 7410.

75 *Trueman v Trueman*, [2000] AJ No 1301 (QB); *Reeder v Leach*, [2001] SJ No 757 (QB).

76 [2001] SJ No 742 (QB).

77 *PML v BGL*, [2003] AJ No 1401 (QB); *MDL v CR*, 2020 SKCA 44 at para 97; *Mardanisamani v Farshad* 2022 SKQB 160.

78 *Champagne v Champagne*, [2001] SJ No 290 (QB).

79 *Burt v Burt*, [1998] AJ No 1228 (QB).

80 *Ennis v Ennis*, [1999] AJ No 352 (QB); *Casey v Casey*, [2000] NBJ No 102 (QB).

Given hostility between the parents, the court may devise a protocol to ensure a parent's timely court-ordered contribution to section 7 expenses under the *Federal Child Support Guidelines*.[81]

All the children should be treated fairly in determining the parental contributions to special or extraordinary expenses under section 7 of the *Federal Child Support Guidelines*.[82]

An application for special and extraordinary expenses under section 7 of the *Federal Child Support Guidelines* may be dismissed because the parent's obligation to support a second family renders him incapable of making any contribution to these expenses, except by undertaking to include the child under his health insurance plan.[83] A court-ordered contribution to the children's extraordinary expenses relating to their schooling and their extracurricular activities cannot be ordered against a parent who lacks the financial ability to make a contribution and a court-ordered contribution should not be made at the sacrifice of the extremely limited funds that are available for parenting visits.[84]

Notwithstanding the restrictive definition of "total income" under section 16 of the *Federal Child Support Guidelines*, all income of both spouses, including resources such as child tax benefits, should be included in assessing the apportionment of expenses under section 7(2) of the Guidelines.[85] Variation of an order respecting special or extraordinary expenses under section 7 of the Guidelines requires consideration of any change in the income of either spouse in order for the court to make the appropriate *pro rata* adjustment in light of section 7(2) of the Guidelines.[86]

B. EXHAUSTIVE LIST OF DESIGNATED EXPENSES; DEFINITION OF "MEANS"

The list of special and extraordinary expenses under sections 7(1)(a) to (f) of the *Federal Child Support Guidelines* is exhaustive; if a claim does not fall within any of the listed categories, it must be dismissed.[87] Any affidavit submitted on behalf of the party making the request must detail the claims under the various headings of section 7(1) of the Guidelines.[88] Capital expenses for a home and contents do not fall within the ambit of the exhaustive list of expenses under section 7 of the Guidelines.[89] Expenses incurred for respite care of a severely disabled adult child have been found to fall outside the ambit of section 7 of the corresponding *British Columbia Child Support Guidelines*,[90] but it is appropriate for a court to address the cost of respite care through spousal support under section 15.2(6)(b)

---

81 *Crowdis v Crowdis*, [2003] SJ No 371 (QB).

82 *Wilson v Wilson*, [1999] BCJ No 2458 (SC).

83 *Gillespie v Gormley*, [2002] NBJ No 344 (QB).

84 *Ollivier v Zarins*, [2003] BCJ No 298 (SC).

85 *MJB v WPB*, [2004] MJ No 123 (QB); compare *Gold v Romhanyi*, 2006 BCSC 443.

86 *Khoee-Solomonescu v Solomonescu*, [2000] OJ No 743 (Div Ct).

87 *Clarke v Clarke*, 2014 BCSC 824; *Corey v Corey*, 2010 NBQB 112; *Walsh v Walsh*, [2006] NJ No 33 (UFC) (clothing expenses are not allowable under section 7); *Corkum v Clarke*, [2000] NSJ No 285 (Fam Ct); *Hoover v Hoover*, [1997] NWTJ No 43 (SC); *Vidal v Dunn*, 2018 ONSC 2801 (criminal defence expenses ineligible); *Morley v Morley*, [1999] SJ No 31 (QB).

88 *Middleton v MacPherson*, [1997] AJ No 614 (QB).

89 *Kendry v Cathcart*, [2001] OJ No 277 (SCJ).

90 *Stanton v Solby*, [1999] BCJ No 1348 (SC).

of the *Divorce Act*.[91] Expenses such as entertainment, pets, vacations, school fees, school supplies, children's allowances, meals outside the home, personal grooming, and clothing do not constitute expenses contemplated by section 7 of the *Federal Child Support Guidelines* Expenses associated with driving an automobile or recreational vehicle[93] may fall outside the parameters of section 7 of the Guidelines but a court-ordered contribution under section 7 is sometimes granted for driving lessons.[94] Section 7 of the Guidelines is not intended to offer a full indemnification of all of a parent's out-of-pocket monthly expenses for a child.

Successful claims for additional support by way of special or extraordinary expenses under section 7 of the Guidelines must be supported by sufficient evidence and documentation to enable the court to determine both the necessity and reasonableness of the expenses within the parameters of section 7(1) of the Guidelines.[96] A parent who seeks expenses under section 7 of the Guidelines has the onus of providing details concerning the actual or anticipated expenses and furnishing evidence on the basis of which the court can determine the necessity of the expense in relation to the child's best interests and the reasonableness of the expenses having regard to the financial circumstances of the parents and child and the family's pre-separation spending pattern.[97] An application for special or extraordinary expenses may be dismissed for lack of relevant evidence, without prejudice to a re-application on more comprehensive material.[98] An obligation of financial disclosure falls on both parties under section 21 of the Guidelines where an application is made for expenses under section 7 of the Guidelines.[99] Judicial discretion to provide for the child-related expenses was deemed necessary because the child support amounts fixed by the provincial or territorial tables reflect average expenditures on children and the aforementioned expenses do not lend themselves to averages.[100] Section 7, therefore, provides some degree of flexibility because not all family needs are the same. However, the court should maintain the applicable table amounts except in cases where to do so would clearly provide too much or too little money to meet the child's reasonable needs.[101] Although some observers regard the basic provincial table amounts of child support as too low, they have been legislated and it is improper for a

---

91 *ALY v LMY*, [2001] AJ No 506 (QB).

92 *MSD obo NC v AL*, 2022 NBQB 21; *CSW v TDS*, 2023 SKKB 182.

93 *Moss v Moss*, [1997] NJ No 299 (SC).

94 *Savage v Savage*, [1997] AJ No 1244 (QB); *McLean v McLean*, 2013 ABQB 700 (driving lessons); *McLaren v McLaren*, [1998] BCJ No 2485 (SC) (learning to drive); *Beninger v Beninger*, [2005] BCJ No 1781 (SC); *LHMK v BPK*, 2012 BCSC 435 (driving lessons); *Newman v Tibbetts*, [2004] NBJ No 72 (QB); *Moss v Moss*, [1997] NJ No 299 (SC); *Turple v Turple*, 2011 NSSC 150 (driving lessons); *Kilrea v Kilrea* [1998] OJ No 3677 (Gen Div) (increased insurance premiums); *Taylor v Sherlow*, 2014 ONSC 6614 (driving lessons). Compare *LL v GB*, 2008 ABQB 536; *Earles v Earles*, 2006 BCSC 221; *MMA v SAT*, 2016 NBQB 109 (driving lessons); *Myers v Myers*, [2010] NJ No 329 (UFC) (driving lessons). Compare also *LF v RB*, 2021 BCSC 464 (automobile insurance; fuel costs).

95 *Thomson v Howard*, [1997] OJ No 4431 (Gen Div).

96 *Olaitan v MacDougall*, 2014 PECA 5; *Engebretson v Pellettieri*, [1998] SJ No 411 (QB).

97 *Olaitan v MacDougall*, 2014 PECA 5; *Hinkson v Hinkson*, [1998] SJ No 568 (QB).

98 *Shentow v Bewsh*, [1998] OJ No 3142 (Gen Div) (uncontested application); *Meakin v Meakin*, [1999] SJ No 649 (QB).

99 *Engebretson v Pellettieri*, [1998] SJ No 411 (QB). See also *Olaitan v MacDougall*, 2014 PECA 5.

100 See Regulatory Impact Analysis Statement, which accompanies but is not part of the *Federal Child Support Guidelines*, published in the *Canada Gazette*, Part II, Vol 131, 16 April 1997 at 1121.

101 *Miller v McClement*, [1997] SJ No 761 (QB).

court to readjust the support by adding extra support under section 7 of the *Federal Child Support Guidelines* in circumstances not contemplated by that section.[102]

Section 7 of the *Federal Child Support Guidelines* vests a broad discretion in the court to determine both the right to expenses and the amount to be paid.[103] The court may allow all, any, or none of the expenses claimed.[104] In exercising its discretion, the court takes into account the necessity of the expense in relation to the child's best interests and the reasonableness of the expense, having regard to the means of the spouses or former spouses, the means of the child, and the family's spending pattern prior to separation.[105]

The reference to "the family's spending pattern before separation" in section 7 of the Guidelines does not signify that the expenses in question must have been of a type that were incurred before separation but it is easier to find reasonableness if the expenses were of a kind that the family had incurred before separation.[106] The stringent requirements imposed by the undue hardship provisions of section 10 of the Guidelines have no application to a claim for special or extraordinary expenses under section 7 of the Guidelines. Whether such expenses are "reasonable" is to be determined within the discretionary parameters specifically set out in section 7 of the Guidelines.[107] Three questions should be asked with respect to whether a parent should be ordered to contribute towards expenses under section 7 of the Guidelines, namely:

1) Is the expense necessary in light of the child's best interests?
2) What is the family's spending pattern during cohabitation?
3) Is there an ability to pay a *pro rata* share of the expense?

The application for expenses under section 7 of the Guidelines should be dismissed if the answer is no to any of the above questions.[108] A line-by-line review of a spouse's budget to determine his or her disposable income is not required. The function of the court is to look at the "means" of the parents along with the other criteria under section 7(1) of the Guidelines in a general way in order to determine each spouse's share of the expenses incurred.[109] Court-ordered provision for special or extraordinary expenses in addition to the basic table amount of child support is not automatic. The onus falls on the person seeking such expenses to prove why they should be allowed.[110] The ability to pay or contribute towards special or extraordinary expenses is a critical factor[111] that may render it necessary for the court to accord priority to certain types of expenses over others, for example,

102 *Smith v Smith*, [1997] OJ No 4833 (Gen Div).
103 *MacNeil v MacNeil*, 2013 ONSC 7012.
104 *Calcada v Ferreira*, [2002] BCJ No 1802 (SC); *Bergman-Illnik v Illnik*, [1997] NWTJ No 93 (SC); *Giles v Villeneuve*, [1998] OJ No 4492 (Gen Div); *Carmichael v Douglas*, [2008] SJ No 474 (QB).
105 *Myke v Myke*, [2000] OJ No 2056 (SCJ); *Olaitan v MacDougall*, 2014 PECA 5; *Krislock v Krislock*, [1997] SJ No 698 (QB).
106 *Myke v Myke*, [2000] OJ No 2056 (SCJ).
107 *JL v AA*, 2013 NBQB 121; *Ward v Ward*, [1999] OJ No 458 (Gen Div).
108 *Ward v Ward*, *ibid*.
109 *PMJ v ADJ*, [2003] BCJ No 1144 (CA); *Giles v Villeneuve*, [1998] OJ No 4492 (Gen Div).
110 *Fisher v Heron*, [1997] PEIJ No 77 (TD); *Hansvall v Hansvall*, [1997] SJ No 782 (QB).
111 *Ibid*.

special medical expenses over extraordinary expenses for extracurricular activities.[112] It is counter-productive to order expenses that are beyond the means of the spouses even though they may reflect their previous lifestyle.[113] A claim for special or extraordinary expenses will be denied where there has been no pre-separation pattern of such expenses and the expenses are neither necessary nor reasonable in light of the extremely limited income of the spouses.[114] An obligor may be ordered to pay all of the allowable special or extraordinary expenses where the recipient spouse or former spouse has insufficient means to contribute to those expenses.[115] The "family's spending pattern prior to the separation" may need to be reassessed as a consequence of the separation. For example, expenses that might have been regarded as normally within the household budget before separation may be regarded as no longer reasonable when the overall family income has to be shared between two households on divorce.[116] Conversely, necessary additional expenses of child care may be triggered by the separation.[117] Judicial reliance on the family's pre-separation spending pattern may be rendered inappropriate where the payor's income, through no fault of his own, has substan tially dropped after the spousal separation.[118]

The financial resources available for each spouse or former spouse to meet his or her own basic needs must be considered in assessing their respective abilities to contribute towards both the special and extraordinary expenses listed under section 7 of the *Federal Child Support Guidelines*.[119] A court may conclude that extraordinary expenses for extracurricu lar activities are beyond the means of the family because of a paramount need for spousal support.[120] Although section 15.3 of the *Divorce Act* requires a court to give priority to child support over spousal support, this does not signify that an order for much needed spousal sup port should yield to an order for extraordinary expenses for extracurricular activities that are optional and non-essential in character.[121] A continuation or increase of extraordinary expenses for extracurricular activities may be dependent on the primary caregiving parent's acquisition of full-time employment.[122] "Means" under section 7(1) of the Guidelines denotes the potential capacity of a person to provide support and not merely the actual resources at one's disposal.[123] The means of the parties may exceed their income[124] because "means"

112 *Fisher v Heron*, [1997] PEIJ No 77 (TD).
113 *Blumes v Blumes*, [1998] AJ No 346 (QB).
114 *Dixon v Dixon*, [1997] AJ No 692 (QB).
115 *Cabernel v Cabernel*, [1997] MJ No 375 (QB).
116 *Krawczyk v Krawczyk*, [1998] OJ No 2526 (Gen Div).
117 Compare *Bially v Bially*, [1997] SJ No 352 (QB) (interim order for child care expenses based on pre-separation cost).
118 *Robski v Robski*, [2001] NSJ No 454 (SC).
119 *Fisher v Heron*, [1997] PEIJ No 77 (TD).
120 *Miller v Miller*, [1997] BCJ No 1322 (SC).
121 See *Federal Child Support Guidelines*, SOR/97-175, Sch III, s 3(2); see also *Lyttle v Bourget*, [1999] NSJ No 298 (SC).
122 *Young v Vincent*, [1997] NSJ No 163 (Fam Ct).
123 *Levesque v Levesque* (1994), 4 RFL (4th) 375 (Alta CA); *Vey v Vey* (1979), 11 BCLR 193 (CA); *Marchak v Fleury* (1995), 15 RFL (4th) 458 (Man QB); *Plowman v Plowman* (1995), 16 RFL (4th) 82 (Ont Ct Gen Div).
124 *Bland v Bland*, 1999 ABQB 236; *Piwek v Jagiello*, 2011 ABCA 303; *Ebrahim v Ebrahim*, [1997] BCJ No 2039 (SC); *CL v SF*, 2009 NBQB 129.

comprise money resources and wealth.[125] The "means" of the spouses or former spouses and of the child includes all pecuniary resources, capital assets, income from capital assets or from employment, earning capacity, and any other source from which gains or benefits are received, together with, in certain circumstances, money that a person does not have in possession but that is available to such persons.[126] In reviewing the "means" of the parties under section 7(1) of the Guidelines, the court may address ways in which funds can be made available to satisfy a contribution to special or extraordinary expenses. The reduction or elimination of unreasonable or unnecessary personal expenses constitutes one possible avenue to achieve that end.[127] The "means" of a spouse under section 7 of the *Federal Child Support Guidelines* includes child support payments received from a *de facto* step-parent.[128] The exercise of parenting time costs may be considered when assessing the means of a parent for the purpose of determining whether expenses under section 7 of the *Federal Child Support Guidelines* are reasonable.[129] In considering the means of the spouses under section 7 of the Guidelines, the Canada Child Benefit is a factor that can be taken into account.[130]

A claim for a contribution to expenses under section 7 of the *Federal Child Support Guidelines* is predicated upon the premise that the party is seeking a contribution to actual expenses incurred. Section 7 is not a basis for submitting a shopping list of estimated expenses for a variety of activities for the purposes of simply increasing the monthly child support payable. The party seeking contribution for section 7 expenses should provide sufficient details to satisfy the court the expense is being incurred, or will be incurred, and particulars of the actual expense involved. The party seeking such contribution also has the burden of ensuring that the evidence or material submitted establishes that the expense meets the qualifying criteria applicable to the specific category of expense claimed as well as the qualifying criteria found in the opening words of section 7(1).[131]

Where the evidence of special or extraordinary expenses is insufficient to satisfy the court that an order should be made pursuant to section 7 of the *Federal Child Support Guidelines*, the court may grant leave to the applicant to return to court with further and better particulars.[132]

A court cannot delegate its jurisdiction to determine proper special or extraordinary expenses under section 7 of the Guidelines by ordering a lump sum payment coupled with an absolute discretion in the recipient parent to spend the amount as he or she thinks fit.[133]

Judicial calculations respecting special or extraordinary expenses under section 7 of the *Federal Child Support Guidelines* may be declared subject to review by counsel who may also be instructed to determine the mechanism by which the payments shall be made.[134]

---

125 *RL v BI*, [1997] QJ No 4450 (CS).
126 *Strang v Strang*, [1992] 2 SCR 112; *Leskun v Leskun*, [2006] 1 SCR 920.
127 *BRAA v RVA*, [1998] NSJ No 579 (Fam Ct).
128 *Harder v Harder*, [2000] BCJ No 467 (SC).
129 *Howlett v Rach*, [2000] SJ No 752 (QB).
130 *LAW v MRE*, 2009 BCSC 490.
131 *Krislock v Krislock*, [1997] SJ No 698 (QB).
132 *Ennis v Ennis*, [2000] AJ No 75 (CA); *Andries v Andries*, [1997] MJ No 301 (QB), var'd [1998] MJ No 196 (CA).
133 *Wanstall v Walker*, [1998] BCJ No 1808 (SC).
134 *Savage v Savage*, [1997] AJ No 1244 (QB).

C. SHARING OF EXPENSES AS GUIDING PRINCIPLE; EFFECT OF SPOUSAL SUPPORT

In determining the amount of an expense or the contribution thereto under section 7 of the *Federal Child Support Guidelines*, the guiding principle is that the spouses or former spouses should share the expense in proportion to their respective incomes after deducting any contribution from the child or other liable parent.[135] When a person who stands in the place of a parent is ordered to pay support, any orders with respect to section 7 expenses are discretionary and the court may deviate from the standard proportional distribution.[136] the opinion of the British Columbia Court of Appeal, a parent may earn insufficient income to pay the table amount of child support under the *Federal Child Support Guidelines* but it does not necessarily follow that a person earning an income below the minimum Guidelines amount would not be required to contribute to section 7 expenses.[137] Having regard to their age and financial ability, a court may require children to make a financial contribution to expenses relating to their extracurricular activities, but not to their health-related expenses where their father has health insurance coverage.[138] To respond thoroughly to a request for a contribution to special or extraordinary expenses, the court and the responding spouse requires information about the circumstances of the child. In the event that the children do not cooperate in providing the information,[139] they are at risk of not having their eligibility for section 7 expenses established. The disclosure of a child's Income Tax Return and Notice of Assessment is within the range of documents that should be available to the court and the parties.[140]

Section 7(2) of the Guidelines establishes a guiding principle, rather than a fixed rule or requirement, with respect to the sharing of special or extraordinary expenses that fall within the ambit of section 7(1) of the Guidelines.[141] There is, therefore, some judicial flexibility and

---

135 *Federal Child Support Guidelines*, SOR/97-175, s 7(2); *Milanovich v Joldzic-Milanovich*, [1997] AJ No 754 (QB); *LHMK v BPK*, 2012 BCSC 435; *TAF v MWB*, 2013 MBQB 213; *GF v JACF*, 2016 NBCA 21; *Budden v Combden*, [1999] NJ No 199 (SC); *Ruck v Ruck*, 2016 NSSC 45; *Natywary v Natywary*, [2003] OJ No 5628 (CA); *Knight v Frobel*, 2018 ONSC 3651; *D (DE) v J (QR)*, 2019 PESC 39; *HAK v TJW*, 2011 SKQB 68. See also *Harder v Harder*, [2000] BCJ No 467 (SC) (proportionate sharing of s 7 expenses between biological parents, after due account taken of child support payments of *de facto* step-parent). Compare *Burley v Burley*, 2009 ONCA 2.

136 *Woodrow v Lepoudre*, 2022 SKQB 143 at para 32, Haaf J.

137 *House v Pritchard*, 2021 BCCA 122 at para 31.

138 *Goodwin v Goodwin*, [2002] SJ No 45 (QB).

139 See *CJT v GAT*, 2019 ABQB 851.

140 *Provost v Marsden*, 2010 NSSC 162, citing section 25 of the *Federal Child Support Guidelines*.

141 *Delichte v Rogers*, 2013 MBCA 106; *MDL v CR*, 2020 SKCA 44 at para 94; see also *PJD v WKW*, 2019 BCSC 1188; *Delichte v Rogers*, 2018 MBQB 75; *Smith v Smith*, 2014 NSSC 15; *Staples v Callender*, 2020 NSSC 365; *Ludmer v Ludmer*, 2014 ONCA 827; *Rayes v Dominguez-Cortes*, 2015 ONSC 3693; *Zhao v Xiao*, 2023 ONCA 453, leave to appeal to SCC denied 2023 CanLII 115636 (SCC); *Droit de la famille—101016*, 2010 QCCA 926; *Mardanisamani v Farshad*, 2022 SKQB 160.

discretion in the allocation of such expenses,[142] or in their denial.[143] The court may depart from the general principle of an income-based *pro rata* sharing of a child's expenses where the parents have agreed to equally share the expenses[144] or where there is a substantial disparity between the parental incomes,[145] as for example, where one parent's income is barely sufficient to provide for his or her own needs and the other parent has ample ability to shoulder the expense.[146] Past and present family support obligations may preclude a parent from making a proportionate, or any, contribution to otherwise reasonable expenses falling within the meaning of section 7 of the Guidelines.[147] Courts may deviate from a proportionate sharing of special or extraordinary expenses under section 7(2) of the Guidelines in cases of unequal time-sharing that satisfy the 60:40 percent rule under section 9 of the Guidelines[148] or where one parent assumes the responsibility for transportation costs associated with the exercise of parenting time.[149]

Section 7(2) of the Guidelines does not mandate a rigid formula that automatically relieves separated and divorced parents from contributing to the cost of their children's post-secondary education when the children are able to obtain student loans. Each case must be considered in the context of the financial circumstances of all three potential contributors (the two parents and the child), having regard to the factors in section 7(1) of the Guidelines, and in the context of the objectives of the Guidelines.[150]

Several options are available to the court in light of the phrase "the contribution, if any, of the child" in section 7(2) of the Guidelines. If the child has no actual or potential sources of income, no deduction will be made before apportioning the allowed section 7 expenses between the parents. If the child has income, the court may decline to order the child to make a contribution to the expenses or may treat only part of the income as a contribution to be made by the child.[151] Income may be imputed to an adult child on the basis of a presumed earning capacity during the summer months for the purpose of determining the child's proper contribution towards his post-secondary education expenses. However, a court should not deviate from the guiding principle of apportioning such expenses according to the respective parental incomes after due account is taken of the child's contribution merely because of an

---

142 *KA v TD*, [2008] AJ No 600 (QB) (mother solely responsible for children's special needs); *Bowers v Bowers*, [2000] BCJ No 1108 (SC) (parental agreement); *GRR v JES*, 2020 NBQB 154 at para 78 (financial pressure); *Pitcher v Pitcher*, [2002] NJ No 358 (UFC); *Bell-Angus v Angus*, [2000] OJ No 2074 (SCJ) (parental agreement); *CR v IA*, [2001] OJ No 1053 (SCJ) (substantial disparity between parental resources); *Cudmore v Cudmore*, [2000] PEIJ No 39 (SC); *MDL v CR*, 2020 SKCA 44; see also *Wilson v Wilson*, [1999] BCJ No 2458 (SC) (retroactive order).

143 *DLP v SJ*, 2010 NSSC 107; *Simmons v Wilcox*, [2001] OJ No 2923 (SCJ).

144 *Tapper v Connolly*, [2002] NJ No 83 (SC); compare *Ennis v Ennis*, [2000] AJ No 75 (CA).

145 *Plett v Plett*, 2010 BCSC 758; *Hatfield v Hatfield*, [2000] NSJ No 211 (SC); *Richter v Vahamaki* (2000), 8 RFL (5th) 194 (Ont SCJ).

146 *EKR v GAW*, [1997] MJ No 501, 32 RFL (4th) 202 (QB); *Murphy v Murphy*, [1998] NJ No 304 (SC); *Rayes v Dominguez-Cortes*, 2015 ONSC 3693.

147 *Tack v Fournier*, [1998] MJ No 596 (QB) (order granted under s 7 with stipulations as to priority of pre-existing order).

148 *McCurdy v Morisette*, [1999] BCJ No 2292 (SC).

149 *Zho v Chen*, [2000] OJ No 4520 (SCJ).

150 *Menegaldo v Menegaldo*, 2012 ONSC 2915.

151 *Reyes v Rollo*, [2001] OJ No 5110 (SCJ) (adult child's scholarships excluded from apportionment of post-secondary expenses).

estranged relationship between the child and one of the parents.[152] A student loan may constitute a "contribution . . . from the child" to post-secondary education expenses within the meaning of section 7(2) of the *Federal Child Support Guidelines* and thereby exclude the need for any parental contribution.[153] It would be a mistake, however, to assume that a student loan will always be taken into account to reduce or eliminate the liability that would otherwise be imposed on the parents under section 7 of the Guidelines. The issue really turns on the reasonableness of taking account of any such loans in light of the case. Grants, scholarships, and bursaries are treated on a different footing insofar as they involve a net transfer of resources to the child without any obligation of repayment. It has thus been held that a student loan is not a "benefit" within the meaning of section 7(3) of the *Federal Child Support Guidelines* that must be automatically taken into account in determining the amount to be ordered in respect of expenses sought under section 7 of the Guidelines.[154]

It is uncertain why the guiding principle in section 7(2) of the Guidelines refers specifically to the respective "incomes" of the spouses or former spouses whereas section 7(1) uses the broader term "means."[155] In *Mills v Mills*,[156] Master Powers, of the British Columbia Supreme Court, had regard to the respective means of the former spouses and not simply their respective incomes in concluding that the obligor's contributions to after-tax daycare expenses should be reduced because of his obligation to support his child from a new relationship. And in *Baum v Baum*,[157] Martinson J of the British Columbia Supreme Court concluded that, in assessing the respective parental contributions to child care expenses, the court should take account of the "means," not just the income, of each parent pursuant to section 7(1) of the *Federal Child Support Guidelines*. The guiding principle of *pro rata* sharing of expenses in light of the respective "incomes" of the parents, which is established by section 7(2) of the Guidelines, was stated to be subject to the overriding mandatory provisions that regulate the exercise of judicial discretion under section 7(1) of the Guidelines. Consequently, a judicial discretion was deemed to vest in the court that enables it to have regard to the economic well-being of the spouses and their overall household income in light of newly formed spousal partnerships. In *Speakman v Willis*,[158] however, McEwan J of the British Columbia Supreme Court declined to endorse the reasoning of Martinson J in *Baum v Baum*, above, because section 7(1) of the Guidelines addresses the reasonableness of the expense, whereas section 7(2) addresses the relative apportionment of allowable expenses as between the parents. Justice McEwan consequently concluded that the court was not compelled to take account of the income of a parent's current spouse in apportioning allowable section 7 expenses between the

---

152 *Phillips v Phillips*, [2002] OJ No 717 (SCJ).

153 *Mascarenhas v Mascarenhas*, [1999] OJ No 37 (Gen Div).

154 *Maynard v Maynard*, [1999] BCJ No 325 (SC); *Lee-Broomes v Broomes*, 2012 ONSC 2195, citing *Roth v Roth*, 2010 ONSC 2532 at para 168. See also *Winstanley v Winstanley*, 2016 MBCA 17.

155 *Ollivier v Zarins*, [2003] BCJ No 298 (SC); *Simpson v Palma*, [1998] SJ No 581 (QB); see also *Piwek v Jagiello*, 2011 ABCA 303; *Reyes v Rollo*, [2001] OJ No 5110 (SCJ); *Divorce Act*, s 26.1(2). For a definition of "income," see the *Federal Child Support Guidelines*, SOR/97-175, ss 2 and 15–20.

156 [1997] BCJ No 2258 (SC).

157 [2000] BCJ No 2565 (SC); see also *Mullins v Mullins*, 2016 ABQB 226; *LAF v CPM*, 2015 BCSC 281; *Klimm v Klimm*, 2018 BCSC 5; *Tack v Fournier*, [1998] MJ No 596 (QB); *Kent v Kent*, 2010 NLUFC 5; *Olaveson v Olaveson*, [2007] OJ No 2431 (SCJ); *Bear v Thomson*, 2013 SKQB 270.

158 [2003] BCJ No 1465 (SC); see also *LHMK v BPK*, 2012 BCSC 435 at paras 97–98; *JC v SAW*, 2008 YKSC 95 at para 15.

parents. In *HBC v CEM*,[159] Comeau CJ of the Nova Scotia Family Court held that the definition of "means" in section 7(1) of the *Nova Scotia Child Support Guidelines* includes the income of a parent's spouse. A contrary opinion was expressed by Mazza J of the Ontario Superior Court of Justice in *Cochrane v D'Andrea*, who concluded that the income of a new spouse of either parent should not be taken into account in apportioning allowable expenses under section 7 of the *Federal Child Support Guidelines* where that spouse does not stand in the place of a parent to the child.[160] The question arises whether any reconciliation of the above opinions can be achieved on the basis that section 7(2) of the Guidelines establishes a "guiding principle," not a fixed or absolute rule, for the sharing of expenses in proportion to the respective incomes of the parents, thereby leaving a residual discretion in the court to take account of the income or assets of an obligor's new partner where the attendant circumstances of the case render this appropriate. Even if the income of a parent's new spouse is not ordinarily relevant to the issue of section 7 expenses under the *Federal Child Support Guidelines*, it may be deemed relevant to a primary caregiving parent's claim for child care expenses where a full-time nanny also takes care of that parent's stepchildren.[161]

Some section 7 expenses may be paid by one spouse and some by the other spouse. The key is that the expense is to be shared in proportion to the respective spousal incomes, regardless of who pays.[162] If each spouse or former spouse assumes the responsibility for some expenses but not others, an apportionment must be carried out for each expense individually, and the responsibility for payment must be spelled out in the order. A simple solution in some cases is for the court to add together all the expenses, apportion the total amount payable by each spouse or former spouse according to their respective incomes, and designate the party who shall pay.[163]

Although section 7(2) of the Guidelines provides that the guiding principle in determining the amount to cover special or extraordinary expenses is that it be shared between the spouses or former spouses proportionately to their incomes after deducting any contribution by the child, the court is not confined to these factors in exercising its discretion. Other relevant factors may include the inadequacy of the petitioner's income information, the nature of her employment, and the availability of a financial contribution from the petitioner's family.[164] A court may also take account of the value of volunteer services rendered by the applicant in "working off" her share of a child's section 7 expenses.[165] Where the original order for child support provided that the parents would share the costs of the child's enrolment in private school and the father argued that he ought not to have to pay his share of the child's private school tuition because the mother worked off a significant portion of the fees, the Alberta Court of Appeal agreed with the chambers judge's ruling that the mother's volunteering of her time had value and the proportionate sharing of expenses under section 7 of the *Federal Child Support Guidelines* needed to be calculated in the face of that reality.[166]

---

159 [2001] NSJ No 263 (Fam Ct). Compare *NSC v DC*, 2011 NBQB 229.

160 [2005] OJ No 1536 (SCJ).

161 *Hudson v Klassen*, [2005] SJ No 167 (QB).

162 *Kofoed v Fichter*, [1997] SJ No 558 (QB), aff'd [1998] SJ No 338 (CA).

163 *Middleton v MacPherson*, [1997] AJ No 614 (QB).

164 *LHMK v BPK*, 2012 BCSC 435; *Yunger v Zolty*, 2011 ONSC 5943.

165 *Steeves v English*, [2004] AJ No 632 (CA).

166 *Schick v Schick*, 2008 ABCA 196.

A proportionate sharing of section 7 expenses may be assessed in light of income imputed to a parent[167] or in light of the respective assets of wealthy parents whose incomes are not readily ascertainable.[168]

Neither spouse nor former spouse has the right to make unilateral decisions with respect to discretionary exceptional expenses for the children.[169]

Where the expenses are uncertain or are expected to fluctuate, the court may designate the percentage that the obligor shall pay, having regard to the income of each spouse or former spouse[170] and may direct the recipient spouse or former spouse to provide future authenticated statements or receipts[171] and to disclose any change.[172] An order for special or extraordinary expenses made in percentage terms rather than a fixed amount can promote accuracy and avoid future recourse to the court.[173]

The court may direct that the obligor's contribution to special or extraordinary expenses shall be paid in designated instalments.[174]

Where there is a claim for special or extraordinary expenses under section 7 of the *Federal Child Support Guidelines*, spousal support paid to the other spouse is to be deducted from the obligor's income for the purpose of determining the amount to be paid under section 7 of the Guidelines.[175] Spousal support received by the other spouse is included in that spouse's income but child support is excluded by section 2 of Schedule III of the *Federal Child Support Guidelines*.[176] Consequently, spousal support will have to be determined before an allocation can be made for the purpose of section 7 expenses.[177] It is a reasonable interpretation of the Guidelines and Schedule III to consider a lump sum payment of spousal support as though it was amortized over the years it was meant to address when determining the parties' incomes for purposes of calculating their proportionate share of section 7 expenses.[178]

Section 7(2) of the *Manitoba Child Support Guidelines* states that "[t]he guiding principle" is that the costs of extraordinary expenses are to be "shared by the parents in proportion to their respective incomes above the threshold level of income below which no amount of child support is payable." It also takes account of any contribution from the child.[179]

---

167 *Lobo v Lobo*, [1999] AJ No 113 (QB); *LHMK v BPK*, 2012 BCSC 435.

168 *SHA v WDA*, [2002] BCJ No 1007 (SC).

169 *Sperker v Sperker* (1994), 2 RFL (4th) 243 (NSCA); see also *Pearse v Pearse*, 2010 BCSC 117.

170 *Tallman v Tomke*, [1997] AJ No 682 (QB); *Hunt v Quinn*, [1998] BCJ No 2234 (SC); *Cameron-Masson v Masson*, [1997] NSJ No 207 (Fam Ct); *McCoy v Hucker*, [1998] OJ No 2831 (Gen Div); *Kapell v Richter*, [1997] SJ No 796 (QB).

171 *Tallman v Tomke*, [1997] AJ No 682 (QB); *Van Wynsberghe v Van Wynsberghe*, [1997] OJ No 2566 (Gen Div); *Kapell v Richter*, [1997] SJ No 796 (QB).

172 *Van Wynsberghe v Van Wynsberghe*, [1997] OJ No 2566 (Gen Div).

173 *McCoy v Hucker*, [1998] OJ No 2831 (Gen Div).

174 *Cameron-Masson v Masson*, [1997] NSJ No 207 (Fam Ct); *MacLellan v MacLellan*, [1998] NSJ No 349 (TD).

175 *Federal Child Support Guidelines*, SOR/97-175, Sch III, s 3.1; *Anderson v Anderson*, [2005] MJ No 243 (QB); see also *Cameron-Masson v Masson*, [1997] NSJ No 207 (Fam Ct); *Schmid v Smith*, [1999] OJ No 3062 (SCJ); *Mudronja v Mudronja*, 2020 ONCA 569; *L'Heureux v L'Heureux*, [1999] SJ No 437 (QB).

176 *Sherlow v Zubko*, [1999] AJ No 644 (QB); *Zilic v Zilic*, 2021 BCCA 107; *Anderson v Anderson*, [2005] MJ No 243 (QB); *Schmid v Smith*, [1999] OJ No 3062 (SCJ); *L'Heureux v L'Heureux*, [1999] SJ No 437 (QB)

177 *Galliford v Galliford*, [1998] BCJ No 268 (SC); *Zilic v Zilic*, 2021 BCCA 107; *L'Heureux v L'Heureux*, [1999] SJ No 437 (QB).

178 *SKS v AAS*, 2023 BCSC 1777 at para 105, citing *Zilic v Zilic*, 2021 BCCA 107 at para 116.

179 *Nguetsop v Nguetsop*, 2014 MBQB 131.

D. SUBSIDIES; TAX DEDUCTIONS OR CREDITS

Subject to an exception with respect to the Universal Child Care Benefit under section 7(4) of the Guidelines,[180] in determining the amount of an expense under section 7(1) of the *Federal Child Support Guidelines*, the court must take into account any subsidies, benefits, or income tax deductions or credits[181] relating to the expense and any eligibility to claim a subsidy, benefit, or income tax deduction or credit relating to the expense.[182] If through no fault of the parent, the availability of a subsidy is unknown, the court may decline to deduct the value of the available subsidy.[183]

Sections 118.5 and 118.6 of the *Income Tax Act* provide for tuition, education, and textbook tax credits. Pursuant to section 7(3) of the Guidelines, these tax credits must be taken into account by the court when it grants an order for the payment of section 7 expenses under the *Federal Child Support Guidelines*.[184] Section 118.9 of the *Income Tax Act* allows a student to transfer an unused tuition tax credit to a parent, but the credit cannot be split between

---

180 For the specific language of the amendments and an excellent "Regulatory Impact Analysis Statement," see SOR/2007-59 (*Guidelines Amending the Federal Child Support Guidelines*), *Canada Gazette*, II, 328 (Vol 141, No 7 (4 April 2007)). The Canada Child Benefit program replaced the Canada Child Tax Benefit, National Child Benefit, and Universal Child Care Benefit. Whereas the Universal Child Care Benefit was taxable, the Canada Child Benefit is tax-free. Although the Universal Child Care Benefit has now been superseded, a taxpayer can still apply for a retroactive payment for months prior to July 2016 but there is a 10-year limitation period for applications made after June 2016. Insofar as retroactive child support payments may also be ordered for a period dating back beyond July 2016, if the criteria spelled out in *DBS v SRG; LJW v TAR; Henry v Henry; Hiemstra v Hiemstra*, [2006] 2 SCR 231 are satisfied, s 7(4) of the *Federal Child Support Guidelines* is still required at the present time.

181 As to the potential risk of losing the "equivalent to spouse" credit under the *Income Tax Act* where an agreement or order provides for each spouse to pay a contribution towards a child's special or extraordinary expenses under s 7 of the *Federal Child Support Guidelines*, see the Department of Justice Canada, *The Child Support Newsletter*, Vol 10 (Winter 2000) at 2, ch 1, s B; see also *Shewchuk v Canada*, [2000] TCJ No 398.

182 *Federal Child Support Guidelines*, SOR/97-175, s 7(3); see *Mullins v Mullins*, 2016 ABQB 226 (grossed up Canada Child Tax Benefit and National Child Tax Benefit Supplement to be included in mother's income in calculating section 7 expenses; Child Disability Benefit also relevant to disability driven expenses); *Andries v Andries*, [1997] MJ No 301 (QB), var'd [1998] MJ No 196 (CA) (eligibility for pharmacare); *Canada v Canada-Somers*, 2008 MBCA 59 (tuition tax credit); *FM v TH*, 2016 NBCA 29 at para 36; *TMD v JPG*, 2018 NBCA 15; *JCM v MJM*, 2018 NBCA 42; *Walsh v Walsh*, [2006] NJ No 33 (UFC) (parties free to provide s 7(3) information to secure adjustment of court-ordered apportionment of s 7 expenses); *Bocaneala v Bocaneala*, 2014 NSSC 450 (fitness tax credit); *Ruck v Ruck*, 2016 NSSC 45 (tuition tax credit; education and textbook tax credit); *SS v JG*, 2021 NSSC 228 at paras 121–22 (Canada Child Tax Benefit and GST credit); *Daniel-DeFreitas v Francis*, 2012 ONSC 515 (fitness tax credit); *Menegaldo v Menegaldo*, 2012 ONSC 2915 at para 181 (tuition, education, and textbook tax credits); *Bennett v Bonatsos*, 2014 ONSC 1048 (child care tax deduction); *Rush v Rush*, [2002] PEIJ No 29 (SC) (tax implications of child care); *Olaitan v MacDougall*, 2014 PECA 5 (entitlement to child care subsidy); *LAU v LLL*, 2016 PECA 15 (university fees); *Bennett v Bennett*, [1999] SJ No 728 (QB) (state-subsidized child care); *Lenz v Lenz*, [2008] SJ No 130 (QB) (reimbursement of overpayment); *Brooke v Hertz*, 2008 SKQB 461 (tuition tax credit); compare *MDL v CR*, [2004] SJ No 326 (QB) (child care subsidy); *Mundle v Mundle*, [2001] NSJ No 111 (SC). See also *Baum v Baum*, [2000] BCJ No 2565 (SC) (overriding judicial discretion exists under section 7(1) of Guidelines).

183 *Schill v Schill*, 2012 ONSC 3503.

184 *Knowles v Green*, 2014 NSSC 290; *Foster v Amos*, 2010 SKQB 409. Compare *Koback v Koback*, 2013 SKCA 91 at paras 16–24.

the parents. However, the court can factor in a transfer to one of the parents by realigning the child support to reflect the overall financial realities.[185]

Insofar as a student loan presupposes repayment, it does not constitute a benefit to be automatically taken into account under section 7(3) of the Guidelines.[186] Before apportioning special or extraordinary expenses between the parties under section 7 of the Guidelines, the court should deduct any contribution that has been made to those expenses by family relatives or community groups.[187]

An order for a contribution to the expenses of a special needs child may be granted under section 7 of the *Ontario Child Support Guidelines* where provincial financial aid is insufficient to cover all reasonable needs of the child.[188]

Section 7(3) of the Guidelines is expressed in mandatory language that requires the court to take relevant tax considerations into account in determining the amount of an expense under section 7(1) of the Guidelines.[189] Eligibility for income tax relief must be considered for the purpose of assessing expenses under section 7 of the *Federal Child Support Guidelines* even if such relief is not actually sought by the recipient spouse.[190] Judicial notice has been taken of a spouse's entitlement to income tax relief with respect to child care expenses. Although the court must take into account the tax consequences associated with the expense, it may be impossible to determine their implications until the end of the taxation year. In that event, the court can at best only estimate the tax impact of the expenses and calculate the proportionate share of each spouse on the basis of the estimated net cost of the expense. One way of ensuring a fair proportionate sharing of the expenses is to direct each parent to pay his or her proportionate share of the expenses when they fall due and to later share in the tax benefit on the same proportionate basis, when it is ascertained.[193] In order to accommodate this result, the court may direct the parties to exchange their income tax returns within a specified time after filing, with leave being granted to return to the court, if agreement cannot be reached after the exchange of the income tax information.[194] A court may refuse to allow income tax calculations respecting child care expenses to be deferred

---

185 *Rebenchuk v Rebenchuk*, 2007 MBCA 22.

186 *Maynard v Maynard*, [1999] BCJ No 325 (SC).

187 *Giles v Villeneuve*, [1998] OJ No 4492 (Gen Div).

188 *de Oliviera v Kohlfurst*, [1999] OJ No 3504 (Ct J).

189 *SER v JS*, 2020 ABQB 267; *McLaughlin v McLaughlin*, [1998] BCJ No 2514 (CA) (issue remitted to Registrar or Master of the Supreme Court of British Columbia for calculation); *Chen v Ma*, 2022 MBQB 114 (day care expenses); *Bennett v Bonatsos*, 2014 ONSC 1048; *LAU v LLL*, 2016 PECA 15.

190 *Laskosky v Laskosky*, [1999] AJ No 131 (QB); *Zehr v MacConnell*, 2012 NWTSC 80; *Skiba v Skiba*, [2000] OJ No 76 (SCJ); *Leibel v Davis*, [2001] SJ No 208 (QB); compare *Petipas v Petipas*, [2000] NSJ No 133 (SC); *Mundle v Mundle*, [2001] NSJ No 111 (SC).

191 *Schmid v Smith*, [1999] OJ No 3062 (SCJ).

192 *Middleton v MacPherson*, [1997] AJ No 614 (QB).

193 *Potter v Graham*, [2004] AJ No 1133 (QB); *Shambrook v Shambrook*, [2003] BCJ No 548 (SC); *Murphy v Murphy*, [1998] NJ No 304 (SC); *Provost v Marsden*, 2010 NSSC 162; *Kusnir v Kusnir*, [2001] OJ No 3491 (Ct J); *Paton (Bushko) v Bushko*, [1999] SJ No 49 (QB); compare *Johnson v Punga*, [1998] SJ No 633 (QB) (order for adjustment of payments either by additional disbursement or rebate after requisite tax calculations); *Crowdis v Crowdis*, [2003] SJ No 371 (QB).

194 *NS v RC*, 2009 BCSC 1676; *Murphy v Murphy*, [1998] NJ No 304 (SC); *Paton (Bushko) v Bushko*, [1999] SJ No 49 (QB); *Crowdis v Crowdis*, [2003] SJ No 371 (QB).

until the end of the taxation year because of the difficult or highly conflictual relationship between the spouses.[195]

The failure of a parent to obtain receipts for child care expenses does not preclude a claim for a contribution to these expenses under section 7 of the *Federal Child Support Guidelines*, nor does the absence of receipts signify that no allowance will be made under section 7(3) of the Guidelines for any income tax saving that might have accrued to the primary caregiving parent if properly claimed. A court is entitled to accept a stipulated amount as an estimate that is permitted under the *Federal Child Support Guidelines*.[196]

The net after-tax cost of child care expenses under section 7(1) of the *Federal Child Support Guidelines* must be calculated on the basis that any tax deductions or credits available to the recipient spouse independently of the children for whom support is being sought should be disregarded in making the calculation; the payor is not entitled to benefit from any of the payee's deductions or credits that do not relate to the children's expenses.[197]

A parent may be disentitled to deduct child care expenses from her taxable income where her "common-law spouse" earned no income from a fledgling business. Section 63(2) of the *Income Tax Act* entitles only the spouse with the lower positive income to claim the child care expense deduction and a "common-law spouse's" negative income is properly characterized as a positive income of zero under section 3(f) of the *Income Tax Act*. Notwithstanding any unfairness, the fact that some working parents derive a greater benefit from sections 3(f) and 63(2) of the *Income Tax Act* than others does not contravene the equality rights that are guaranteed by section 15(1) of the *Canadian Charter of Rights and Freedoms*.[198]

Where the court is required to consider factors such as subsidies, benefits, or income tax deductions or credits as set out in section 7 of the *Federal Child Support Guidelines*, the party seeking the section 7 expenses is expected to provide the court with any appropriate adjustment on account of these factors.[199]

A primary caregiving parent may decline to apply for subsidized daycare for a child, but eligibility for such a subsidy must be factored in and deducted from the child's daycare expenses when a contribution to the expenses is sought from the other parent pursuant to section 7 of the *Federal Child Support Guidelines*.[200]

A court may refuse to grant an order to preclude the father from paying his share of daycare costs directly to the service provider and claiming a deduction from his taxable income, where the dispute had never been referred to the Canada Revenue Agency for resolution and the wife has not made out a convincing case for any such order.[201]

A court may order a lump sum payment of private school fees or periodic payments to establish a post-secondary education fund to be made directly to the appropriate third

---

195 *Torti v Torti*, [2001] OJ No 1827 (SCJ); *Gibson v Gibson*, [2008] SJ No 373 (QB).

196 *Nixon v Nixon*, 2014 SKQB 264.

197 *Kelly v Kelly*, [1998] AJ No 228 (QB), supplementary reasons [1998] AJ No 423 (QB).

198 *Whalen v Canada*, [2001] TCJ No 81.

199 *Calogheros v Calogheros*, [2001] BCJ No 2391 (SC); *Myke v Myke*, [2000] OJ No 2056 (SCJ); *Krislock v Krislock*, [1997] SJ No 698 (QB); compare *Gillie v Ritchie*, [2001] NSJ No 440 (SC).

200 *Leung v Lee*, 2004 BCSC 234; *MDL v CR*, [2004] SJ No 326 (QB); compare *Lecompte v Jensen*, 2011 ONSC 3223.

201 *McKenzie v Petrie*, [2003] BCJ No 808 (SC).

party to enable the payor to take advantage of any income tax benefits that might thereby be available as a result of such direct payments.[202]

A father is not entitled to a non-refundable tax credit in relation to a child's medical expenses pursuant to section 118.2 of the *Income Tax Act* where his claim relates to fees paid to a registered psychologist who undertook a parenting plan assessment. Although payments to a psychologist may, in certain circumstances, be deductible pursuant to section 118(2)(l) of the *Income Tax Act*, it must be clearly established that any such payment was made for qualifying "medical expenses." A parenting assessment sought to determine the best inter ests of the children and recommend a parenting plan is not undertaken to obtain a medical diagnosis, effect a treatment, or prevent any disease or illness in relation to the children.[203] father's payment of his child's tuition fees does not trigger a deduction under the *Income Tax Act* for child care expenses where the mother reimburses the father for the tuition fees paid by him.[204] The costs of a child's skiing lessons are not deductible as child care expenses under the *Income Tax Act* where they resulted from recreational activities and were unrelated to the father's discharge of employment duties.[205]

E. PARTICULARS OF EXPENSE TO BE SPECIFIED IN ORDER

Where a court provides for the payment of any of the above expenses, the court must specify in the child support order, though not necessarily in the reasons for judgment, the particu lars of any expense described in section 7(1), the child to whom the expense relates, and the amount of the expense or, where that amount cannot be determined, the proportion to be paid in relation to the expense.[206]

F. ADD-ONS OR SET-OFFS

The expenses under section 7 of the *Federal Child Support Guidelines* have been loosely called "add-ons." This terminology is misleading because an order under section 7 of the Guidelines does not presuppose a prior or concurrent order for a basic or table amount of child support.[207] Furthermore, with the exception of child care expenses under section 7(1)(a) of the Guidelines, a court order respecting the sharing of designated special or extraordin ary expenses may be made in favour of a spouse or former spouse who has been ordered to assume the primary responsibility for the child's support.

202 *Greenwood v Greenwood*, [1998] BCJ No 729 (SC).

203 *Yaskiel v Canada*, [2005] TCJ No 600.

204 *Ibid.*

205 *Ibid.*

206 *MacKinnon v MacKinnon*, 2015 NBQB 1324; *Jackman v Tarrant*, [2000] NJ No 250 (Prov Ct); and see Chapter 11, Section F.

207 *Johnson v Johnson*, [1998] BCJ No 1080 (SC).

G. DIRECT AND HIDDEN COSTS OF PRIMARY CAREGIVING PARENT

The designated expenses under section 7 of the *Federal Child Support Guidelines* refer only to third-party expenses directly incurred by the claimant and not to any hidden costs incurred by a primary caregiving parent,[208] although personal and hidden costs incurred by such a parent may ground a claim for spousal support.[209]

H. PERIODIC OR LUMP SUM PAYMENTS

An order respecting expenses under section 7 of the *Federal Child Support Guidelines* need not specify periodic payments. Unlike ongoing weekly, fortnightly, or monthly basic child support payments, expenses under section 7 may be isolated, sporadic, or recurring at irregular intervals. The court may decline to fix a specific amount of money to meet designated expenses; it may simply order that all or a fixed percentage of past, present, or future expenses shall be paid after a proper account has been submitted to the obligor,[210] although such an order may present some difficulty in circumstances wherein automatic enforcement processes are invoked to ensure due compliance with the order. Pursuant to section 11 of the *Federal Child Support Guidelines*, the court may require expenses to be discharged by periodic payments or by a lump sum or by a combination of both.

I. CHILD CARE EXPENSES

Section 7 of the *Federal Child Support Guidelines* confers a discretion on the court to order the payment of all or part of child care expenses incurred as a result of the employment, illness, disability, or education or training for employment of the spouse who exercises the majority of parenting time.[211] Pursuant to section 2(1) of the *Federal Child Support Guidelines*, "majority of parenting time" means a period of time that is more than 60 percent of parenting time over the course of a year.[212] No discretion is conferred on the court where child care expenses are incurred for the above reasons by the other spouse. Even if reciprocal orders are not permissible, however, the same result may be achieved indirectly, because any child care expenses incurred by the other spouse may be considered in determining his or her contribution to the primary caregiving parent's child care expenses.[213] This flows from the fact that the discretion conferred by section 7(1) of the Guidelines specifically requires the court to have regard to the "means" of the spouses and section 7(2) provides a guiding principle, not an absolute requirement, that expenses be shared in proportion to the respective

208 See s 7(2) of the *Federal Child Support Guidelines*, which applies the respective incomes of the spouses as the guiding principle, not the value of their contributions. Compare *Willick v Willick*, [1994] 3 SCR 670, 6 RFL (4th) 161 at 204.

209 *Moge v Moge*, [1992] 3 SCR 813.

210 *Sikler v Snow*, [2000] SJ No 271 (QB); see also *Abulnaga v Jamshidian*, [2002] BCJ No 535 (SC).

211 *Vollmershausen v Vollmershausen*, 2013 ONSC 4273; see also *Hsieh v Lui*, 2017 BCCA 51.

212 See *Guidelines Amending the Federal Child Support Guidelines*, SOR/2020-247, 23 November 2020; *Canada Gazette*, Part II, Volume 154, Number 25.

213 See *Rockwell v Rockwell*, [1998] BCJ No 3240 (SC).

parental incomes. Unlike section 7(a) of the Guidelines, sections 7(b) to (f) empower either parent to seek a contribution to other special or extraordinary expenses.

Child care expenses do not need to be "extraordinary" under section 7 of the *Federal Child Support Guidelines*, but they must satisfy the dual tests of reasonableness and necessity set out in section 7(1) of the Guidelines.[214]

Child care expenses may be denied under section 7 of the *Federal Child Support Guide lines* where an obligor's family is able to provide child care,[215] although a court may refuse to disturb existing daycare arrangements that have worked well for a substantial period of time.[216]

A court may exercise its discretion by refusing to order any contribution to child care expenses, having regard to substantial government subsidies received by the primary care giving parent, coupled with the other parent's exercise of parenting time for almost 40 per cent of the year.[217] A contribution to child care expenses may be reduced to take account of child-connected expenses incurred by the contributing spouse.[218]

The existence of child care expenses does not give the employed primary caregiving parent an automatic right to receive a contribution to these expenses from the other parent. Where the other parent has high extra-provincial parenting expenses to which the primary caregiving parent makes no contribution, the court may exercise its discretion by declining to grant an order for section 7 expenses.[219]

Child care expenses must be actually incurred; no claim is available for prior unpaid child care under section 7 of *Federal Child Support Guidelines*[220] or for free transportation provided by a spouse's employer.[221]

An unemployed parent is not entitled to claim contribution to a child's preschool expenses under section 7 of the Guidelines.[222] An order for a contribution to child care expenses may be made pursuant to section 7 of Guidelines, however, where the applicant becomes unemployed and is seeking new employment; section 7 is to be interpreted liberally where child care expenses are required to enable the applicant to research the market and find a new job.[223] Where a parent is upgrading his or her skills for entry into the labour force, the other parent may be ordered to pay all child care expenses up to a designated monthly maximum.[224] An order apportioning child care expenses may be expressly declared to be

---

214 *Tang v Tang*, [1998] BCJ No 2890 (SC); *Fowler v Fowler*, 2014 NLTD(F) 25; *Raftus v Raftus* (1998), 166 NSR (2d) 179 (CA); *Park v Thompson*, [2005] OJ No 1695 (CA); *Vollmershausen v Vollmershausen*, 2013 ONSC 4273; *Olaitan v MacDougall*, 2014 PECA 5.

215 *Shipka v Shipka*, [2001] AJ No 213 (QB); *C(NS) v C(D)*, 2011 NBQB 229 (father's new stay-at-home wife); compare *ECH v WEH*, [2003] BCJ No 715 (SC). As to whether family members are entitled to be remunerated for child care services, see *Sage v Sage*, 2014 ONSC 1330.

216 *Erickson v Erickson*, [2001] BCJ No 71 (SC); *MJM v CM*, 2013 NBQB 228.

217 *Mavridis v Mavridis*, [1999] BCJ No 1935 (SC).

218 *Enman v Enman*, [2000] PEIJ No 48 (SC).

219 *Brown v Hudon*, [2004] SJ No 437 (QB); compare *Boyko v Boyko*, 2010 SKQB 247.

220 *L'Heureux v L'Heureux*, [1999] SJ No 437 (QB).

221 *Budden v Combden*, [1999] NJ No 199 (SC); see also *JM v GKM*, [2001] NBJ No 227 (QB) (transportation expenses to daycare denied).

222 *Badley v Badley*, [2000] NSJ No 443 (SC); *JR v CR*, [2005] NSJ No 502 (SC).

223 *SM v RP*, [1998] QJ No 4119 (CS).

224 *Bakken v Bakken*, [1999] SJ No 559 (QB).

conditional on the applicant's actual pursuit of a contemplated educational course with its resulting additional child care expense.[225]

In situations where resources are available, the court will allow child care costs for an employed parent as a legitimate expense.[226] Even though child care may be a necessity, the amount of the obligor's contribution may be limited by the ability to contribute.[227] A court should refuse to order a contribution towards child care expenses where a parent lacks the financial ability to meet this additional obligation.[228] A primary caregiving parent's application for a contribution to child care costs may also be denied because of the other parent's exercise of parenting time costs.[229] Where child care costs are found excessive, the court may reduce the amount before calculating the respective contributions of each spouse or former spouse to these costs.[230] The availability of an older sibling to undertake babysitting responsibilities does not necessarily preclude an order for the sharing of child care expenses under section 7 of the Guidelines.[231] Babysitting expenses paid to an older stepsibling may be the subject of an order for a parental contribution under section 7 of the *Federal Child Support Guidelines*.[232]

A claim for child care expenses may be denied where the child is twelve years of age and, therefore, old enough to care for herself,[233] but a twelve-year-old child should not be expected to regularly babysit a younger sibling in order to reduce child care expenses.[234] The provision of consistent and reliable child care on a regular basis may be inconsistent with the delegation of this responsibility to older siblings and may render a financial contribution from the other parent reasonable and necessary within the meaning of section 7 of the *Federal Child Support Guidelines*.[235]

Child care costs can vary substantially according to the age of the child, the type of care, whether the care is full-time or part-time, and the ability to pay, but they must be reasonable and necessary. Section 7(1) of the *Federal Child Support Guidelines* specifically limits the judicial discretion to provide for the payment of all or any expenses by requiring the court to take into account the necessity of the expense in relation to the child's best interests and the reasonableness of the expense, having regard to the means of the spouses and those of the child and to the family's spending pattern before the separation.[236] Notwithstanding the last

---

225 *Segall v Fellinger*, [1998] SJ No 253 (QB).

226 *Murray v Murray* (1991), 35 RFL (3d) 449 (Alta QB).

227 *Zsiak v Bell*, [1998] BCJ No 2233 (SC); *Wedsworth v Wedsworth*, 2000 NSCA 108.

228 *Kennedy v Kennedy*, [1997] NSJ No 450 (Fam Ct).

229 *Chaput v Chaput*, [1997] OJ No 4924 (Gen Div).

230 *Tallman v Tomke*, [1997] AJ No 682 (QB); *Kramer v Kramer*, [1999] MJ No 338 (QB); *Hendrickson v Hendrickson*, [2005] NSJ No 395 (SC) (changing needs over time may justify variation order).

231 *Laskosky v Laskosky*, [1999] AJ No 131 (QB); *Nakazawa v Klassen*, [2005] BCJ No 1847 (SC); *Chernyakhovsky v Chernyakhovsky*, [2005] OJ No 944 (SCJ).

232 *Gero v Joseph*, [1999] AJ No 1658 (QB).

233 *Acorn v DeRoche*, [1997] PEIJ No 82 (TD); compare *Gormley v Gormley*, [1999] PEIJ No 83 (SC) (contribution to child care expenses for eleven-year-old child deemed appropriate). See also *Abelson v Mitra*, [2008] BCJ No 1672 (SC) (overnight absences of primary caregiving parent).

234 *Levesque v Levesque*, [1999] OJ No 3056 (SCJ); *Bear v Thomson*, 2013 SKQB 270.

235 *McLaughlin v McLaughlin*, [1998] BCJ No 2514 (CA); *Levesque v Meade*, 2010 NBQB 270.

236 *Wait v Wait*, [2000] BCJ No 1282 (CA) (primary caregiving parent entitled to contribution towards child's daycare expenses but not entitled to incur higher expenses by enrolling child in Montessori school); *Kramer v Kramer*, [1999] MJ No 338 (QB).

mentioned consideration, courts will, no doubt, take account of reasonable and necessary child care expenses triggered by the fact of separation.

In order to qualify for a court-ordered contribution under section 7(1)(a) of the *Federal Child Support Guidelines*, the applicant must adduce evidence to show that the child care expenses were incurred as a result of the employment, illness, disability, or education or training for employment of the spouse who has more than 60 percent of parenting time over the course of a year.[237] A parent who has part-time employment is not entitled to call on the other parent for a *pro rata* contribution towards full-time child care.[238] A contribution to the cost of a full-time nanny will be denied where the parent chooses not to be employed and does not suffer from any disability that warrants the employment of a nanny.[239] Babysitting expenses that are incidental to a parent's recreational or other activities fail to qualify under section 7(1)(a) of the Guidelines,[240] necessary though they may be to the welfare of an employed parent. Section 7(1)(a) is addressed to third-party expenses, although a parent's personal assumption of the responsibility for child care may be considered in determining the right to, amount, and duration of spousal support.[241]

The court may order a parent to contribute towards the cost of a nanny where this is deemed preferable to lower cost daycare.[242] Various factors may justify the choice of a nanny over other forms of child care and the fact that the nanny discharges housecleaning and other responsibilities does not necessarily justify any reduction in the allocation of child care expenses under section 7 of the Guidelines,[243] although it may justify a discounting of the nanny's expenses.[244] The costs of a full-time nanny may be nominally adjusted to reflect the fact that the nanny also performs some household services for the primary caregiving parent's new family in addition to caring for a child of the marriage.[245] On an application for expenses under section 7(1)(a) of the *Federal Child Support Guidelines* to meet the costs of a live-in nanny, it is appropriate for the court to consider whether some less costly child care arrangements would be appropriate.[246] Where an application for spousal support is joined with the claim for such expenses, the court should look at the overall situation in determining the type and amount of expenses that require a contribution under section 7(1)(a) of the Guidelines.[247] An order for a contribution to child care expenses under section 7 of the Guidelines may be higher during the summer months when a live-in nanny would be

---

237 See *Federal Child Support Guidelines*, s 7(1)(a), SOR/2020-247, 23 November 2020. See also *Odermatt v Odermatt*, [1998] BCJ No 55 (SC); *Jeans v Jeans*, [2000] NJ No 42 (UFC) (transportation costs included where parent disabled); *Keller v Black*, [2000] OJ No 79 (SCJ); compare *Wright v Wright*, [1998] AJ No 1167 (QB); *Clink v Leydier*, [2007] MJ No 482 (QB).

238 *Kramer v Kramer*, [1999] MJ No 338 (QB).

239 *Forzley v Forzley*, [1997] BCJ No 2881 (SC).

240 *Forrester v Forrester*, [1997] OJ No 3437 (Gen Div).

241 *Brockie v Brockie* (1987), 5 RFL (3d) 440 at 447–48 (Man QB), Bowman J, aff'd (1987), 8 RFL (3d) 302 (Man CA), cited with approval by L'Heureux-Dubé J in *Moge v Moge*, [1992] 3 SCR 813, 43 RFL (3d) 345.

242 *Loewen v Traill*, [1998] BCJ No 466 (SC); *Takach v Rose*, [2001] BCJ No 865 (SC) (finder's fee excluded; cost of nanny based on forty-eight weeks per year).

243 *Low v Robinson*, [2000] AJ No 96 (QB); *Kneller v Kneller*, [2004] BCJ No 2439 (SC).

244 *Robski v Robski*, [2001] NSJ No 454 (SC).

245 *Diehl v Diehl*, [1998] AJ No 1303 (QB); *Zehr v MacConnell*, 2012 NWTSC 80.

246 *AJK v SLM*, [2003] OJ No 2180 (SCJ); *Richardson v Richardson*, 2016 SKQB 356.

247 *Nataros v Nataros*, [1998] BCJ No 1417 (SC).

appropriate and lower during the school year when the child care needs and costs relating thereto will be substantially reduced.[248] The age of the children is a very significant factor when considering whether the expense of a nanny is necessary and reasonable in relation to the means of the spouses.[249] An order whereby the parents are required to share the costs of a full-time nanny in proportion to their respective incomes may be time limited until the child enters Grade 9.[250] The need for child care changes drastically as children reach their teens but some assistance in their care may be justified where the primary caregiving parent works extremely long hours in a demanding career.[251]

Necessary taxi fares in transporting children to and from daycare may be included when the court orders a parent to contribute to "child care expenses" pursuant to section 7(1)(a) of the *Federal Child Support Guidelines*.[252]

Private school fees may fall within the ambit of "child care expenses" under section 7(1)(a) of the *Federal Child Support Guidelines*, if they are reasonable in light of the cost of child care generally.[253]

Child care expenses are to be shared by the spouses or former spouses in proportion to their respective incomes after deducting from the expense the contribution, if any, from the child and after account is taken of any subsidies, benefits, or income tax deductions or credits relating to the expense or any eligibility therefor.[254] The child tax credit represents an additional financial capacity that should be taken into account in ordering a *pro rata* contribution to daycare expenses under section 7 of the *Federal Child Support Guidelines*.[255] Although child care expenses will be ordered in proportion to the respective incomes of the spouses or former spouses,[256] it is the net after-tax cost that should be so apportioned.[257] The entire cost will be apportioned in accordance with the respective spousal incomes where no tax benefits are available to the recipient spouse because his or her low income is insufficient to attract tax.[258]

Where child care expenses are incurred but the amount is uncertain because of fluctuating hours of employment, the court may grant an order for a proportionate sharing of the expenses in accordance with the respective spousal incomes, with a quarterly accounting to be made with respect to the costs involved net of tax and other subsidies.[259] It may be wiser,

248 *Gibillini v Gibillini*, [1998] OJ No 2860 (Gen Div); compare *Wanstall v Walker*, [1998] BCJ No 1808 (SC).
249 *LAW v MRE*, 2009 BCSC 490.
250 *Wanstall v Walker*, [1998] BCJ No 1808 (SC).
251 *Barker v Barker*, [2005] BCJ No 687 (CA); compare *Loran v Loran*, [2007] SJ No 371 (QB).
252 *Pitcher v Pitcher*, [2002] NJ No 358 (UFC).
253 *Wait v Wait*, [2000] BCJ No 1282 (CA).
254 *Federal Child Support Guidelines*, SOR/97-175, ss 7(2) & 7(3); *Coppens v Cal*, [1998] SJ No 871 (QB).
255 *Loughran v Loughran*, [2000] NSJ No 41 (SC).
256 *Estrela v Estrela*, [1997] OJ No 2916 (Gen Div); *Bially v Bially*, [1997] SJ No 352 (QB).
257 *Keller v MacDonald*, [1998] AJ No 1294 (QB); *SER v JS*, 2020 ABQB 267 at para 94; *Johnson v Punga*, [1998] SJ No 633 (QB). And see David Kitai, "A Game Changer for Family Law" *Law Times* (28 February 2020), which briefly reviews the impact of Ontario's Childcare Access and Relief from Expenses (CARE) tax credit on child support and spousal support.
258 *Baerg v Baerg*, [1997] SJ No 808 (QB).
259 *Hart v Hart*, [1997] SJ No 692 (QB).

however, for courts to order that any net after-tax adjustment be made after the filing of the annual tax return. This has been done in several cases.[260]

A parent who is seeking a contribution towards child care expenses pursuant to section 7 of the *Federal Child Support Guidelines* must prove that expenses have been incurred. Evidence of "estimated costs" for the room and board of a live-in grandparent does not suffice. Absent cogent evidence to the contrary, child care provided by a live-in family member is deemed to be "free" child care and is not subject to payment from the separated parent.[261]

A mother's application for the sharing of costs of after school care under section 7 of the Guidelines may be dismissed where the children can go to their father's home after school until their mother picks them up after work.[262] A contribution to child care expenses should not be reduced, however, where it would be unreasonable to impose additional parenting time on the obligor's new family until the child has adjusted to the divorce.[263]

In granting an order for the proportionate sharing of reasonable daycare costs based on the respective parental incomes, the court may conclude that the best interests of the child will be served by balancing the importance of the child's contact with his paternal grandfather with the need for the child to have social interaction with other children at a daycare facility.

On an application to vary a consent order for child support, a claim for child care expenses may be dismissed when it is triggered by the mother's arbitrary decision to remove the child from the care of the paternal grandmother and hire a babysitter while the mother is at work.[265]

The availability of an older sibling to undertake babysitting responsibilities does not necessarily preclude an order for the sharing of child care expenses under section 7 of the Guidelines.[266] Babysitting expenses paid to an older stepsibling may be the subject of an order for a parental contribution under section 7 of the *Federal Child Support Guidelines.*

Fluctuating child care expenses may be addressed by an order for a basic monthly payment, coupled with periodic adjustments to reflect the actual costs incurred by the primary caregiving parent.[268] Monthly contributions to child care expenses may be eliminated during the summer when the child will be in the care of one of the parents.[269] Child care expenses may be amortized over twelve months even though they are only incurred during the school year.[270] A parent's contribution to child care expenses may be reduced in consequence of his or her personal assumption of additional child care responsibilities.[271]

---

260 See Section D, above in this chapter.

261 *Aukstuolyte v Balchun*, [2005] OJ No 3363 (SCJ). Compare *Suchanek v Suchanek*, 2010 BCSC 1271.

262 *Spanier v Spanier*, [1998] BCJ No 452 (SC); *Woode v Woode*, [2002] SJ No 55 (QB).

263 *McCrea v McCrea*, [1999] BCJ No 1514 (SC).

264 *Willford v Schaffer*, [2003] SJ No 840 (QB).

265 *CJB v ECB*, [2003] NSJ No 362 (Fam Ct).

266 *Laskosky v Laskosky*, [1999] AJ No 131 (QB); *Nakazawa v Klassen*, [2005] BCJ No 1847 (SC); *Chernyakhovsky v Chernyakhovsky*, [2005] OJ No 944 (SCJ).

267 *Gero v Joseph*, [1999] AJ No 1658 (QB). See also *Sage v Sage*, 2014 ONSC 1330 (grandparent's right to remuneration).

268 *Scott v Scott*, [2002] OJ No 1418 (SCJ).

269 *Greenwood v Greenwood*, [1998] BCJ No 729 (SC).

270 *MacKenzie v MacKenzie*, [1998] BCJ No 2416 (SC); *Tang v Tang*, [1998] BCJ No 2890 (SC).

271 *Carter v Sprague*, [1999] NSJ No 2 (Fam Ct).

A claim for child care expenses may be inferentially included where the applicant is seeking "such other and further relief" as "the court may deem just and expedient," if the applicant's financial statement clearly indicates the monthly expenses for child care.[272]

Child care expenses may be denied where the applicant claims a global amount without differentiating between expenses relating to children of the marriage and expenses relating to a child from a subsequent marriage.[273]

In dismissing an application for child care expenses under section 7 of the Guidelines for lack of information respecting the after-tax cost and the applicant's income and consequential *pro rata* share of these expenses, the court may grant leave to renew the application when sufficient information is available.[274]

A claim for child care expenses may be significantly reduced by the court where a substantial amount of the expenses were incurred as a consequence of the applicant's business undertakings outside of regular employment that generated losses rather than profits.[275] The amount of the claim may also be reduced because the applicant was a teacher whose hours away from home during her regular employment largely coincided with those of the children, thereby reducing the need for child care during the week and also the summer months.[276] A parent may be called upon to meet any child care costs attributable to the extra supervision of children arising from his or her conduct.[277]

Where the costs of child care will vary every month according to the parenting time arrangements negotiated by the parties, the court may direct that receipts shall be provided on the fifteenth day of each month following such payments. The court may further direct that the obligor shall have the opportunity to provide child care services rather than incur the expense.[278]

A primary caregiving mother is entitled to claim a proportionate share of prenatal and childbearing costs pursuant to section 9(1)(f)(i) of *The Family Maintenance Act, 1997* (Saskatchewan).[279] Such costs constitute "child care" expenses and include maternity clothing and baby furnishings. The fact that the mother received government assistance does not exempt the father from his responsibility under the Act and his proportionate contribution to these expenses should not be reduced because the items in question may have some future resale value. Where insufficient information is available to accurately determine the proportionate share of each parent based on their respective incomes, an equal sharing of the expenses may be found to be fair.[280] An order for a contribution towards a child's daycare expenses may be granted on specified conditions relating to proof of the hours and cost of attendance, the provision of receipts, and the payor's right to claim daycare expenses for tax purposes.[281]

---

272 *Crawley v Tobin*, [1998] NJ No 293 (SC).

273 *Omah-Maharajh v Howard*, [1998] AJ No 173 (QB); see also *Merasty v Merasty*, [2000] SJ No 341 (QB) (right to re-apply with better material).

274 *Osiowy v Osiowy*, [1998] SJ No 573 (QB).

275 *MacLellan v MacLellan*, [1998] NSJ No 349 (TD).

276 *Ibid.*

277 *Ibid.*

278 *Wilson v Wilson*, [1999] BCJ No 2458 (SC).

279 SS 1997, c F-6.2.

280 *MDL v CR*, [2004] SJ No 326 (QB).

281 *Greenslade v Porter*, [2004] NJ No 184 (UFC).

J. MEDICAL AND DENTAL INSURANCE; MEDICAL, DENTAL, OR HEALTH-RELATED EXPENSES

Section 6 of the *Federal Child Support Guidelines* provides that, in making a child support order, where medical or dental insurance coverage is available to either or both[282] of the spouses or former spouses through his or her employer or otherwise at a reasonable rate, the court may order that coverage be acquired or continued.[283] Child support orders normally include provision whereby health insurance coverage will be maintained for eligible dependants. Where this is placed at risk by an obligor's threat to quit employment, the court may order an additional amount of support to replace the health insurance coverage.[284] An order for medical and dental insurance coverage may be struck out on appeal where there is no evidence of such coverage being available through employment nor is there any evidence of the cost of such coverage through a private provider.[285] Where there is existing medical and dental insurance coverage through employment, its continuance should be virtually automatic.[286] The court may grant an order under section 6 of the *Federal Child Support Guidelines* for the reinstatement of cancelled medical and dental insurance available to a spouse through employment.[287] An order for dental and medical insurance under section 6 of the Guidelines is supplementary to the amount of child support payable under the applicable provincial or territorial table and should not be deducted from the amount payable pursuant to the applicable table.[288] Judicial directions may be issued respecting the processing of medical and dental claims through the obligor's insurance plan where difficulties have been encountered in the past[289] and a recalcitrant party can thereafter expect an order for substantial costs against him or her.[290] The court may direct the insured spouse to authorize the insurer to deal directly with his or her spouse in the reimbursement of medical or dental claims with respect to a child of the marriage. In the event this is unacceptable to the insurer, the court may direct the insured spouse to immediately reimburse the other spouse in the same percentage as the plan pays to the insured spouse. If rejected in whole or in part, the court may further direct the spouses to share the expense.[291]

Section 6 is complemented by sections 7(1)(b) and (c) of the *Federal Child Support Guidelines*, which provides that in a child support order the court may, on either spouse's or former spouse's request, provide for the payment of the following expenses, or any portion of those expenses, taking into account the necessity of the expense in relation to the child's best interests and the reasonableness of the expense, having regard to the means of the spouses

282 *Young v Vincent*, [1997] NSJ No 163 (TD).

283 *Colbourne v Colbourne*, 2014 ABQB 547; *KLW v LPW*, 2012 NBQB 91; *Morgan v Morgan*, [2006] NJ No 9 (SC); *Lockerby v Lockerby*, 2010 NSSC 282; *Kingston v Kelly*, [1999] PEIJ No 52 (SC) (order under *PEI Child Support Guidelines*); *Martel v Martel*, [2000] SJ No 322 (QB); compare *MDL v CR*, [2004] SJ No 326 (QB).

284 *Dickinson v Dickinson*, [1998] OJ No 4815 (Gen Div).

285 *Tkachuk v Bigras*, [1997] OJ No 5453 (Gen Div).

286 *Robski v Robski*, [1997] NSJ No 444 (TD).

287 *Jackson v Holloway*, [1997] SJ No 691 (QB).

288 *Bowers v Bowers*, [2000] BCJ No 1108 (SC).

289 *Friesen v Lague*, [2001] SJ No 125 (QB).

290 *Ibid.*

291 *Scharf v Scharf*, [1998] OJ No 199 (Gen Div).

and those of the child and to the family's spending pattern prior to the separation: section 7(1)(b) provides for that portion of the medical and dental insurance premiums attributable to the child;[292] and section 7(1)(c) provides for health-related expenses that exceed insurance reimbursement by at least $100 annually,[293] including orthodontic treatment,[294] professional counselling provided by a psychologist, social worker, psychiatrist, or any other person,[295] physiotherapy, occupational therapy, speech therapy,[296] prescription drugs, hearing aids, glasses, and contact lenses. The $100.00 threshold in section 7(1)(c) of the *Federal Child Support Guidelines* is not a deductible but a threshold. Once the threshold is exceeded, the entire amount of the section 7 expense is chargeable but any payments made by a medical insurer are deductible.[297]

Section 6 of the *Federal Child Support Guidelines* should be utilized whenever possible before resorting to section 7 of the Guidelines, because section 6 provides a significant benefit to children at little or no expense to the parents in that the insurance premiums, if any, will normally be significantly less than the amount of the expenses that would otherwise be incurred if no insurance coverage were available.[298] Any expenses in excess of those reimbursed through a medical or dental insurance plan may be ordered to be shared proportionately in accordance with the respective spousal incomes.[299] Reciprocal obligations may be imposed on the parents to maintain coverage for the children under their employment health and dental plans, with any expenses not covered being shared proportionately in accordance with the respective parental incomes.[300]

Medical expenses may be viewed as a whole, rather than individually, in determining whether they are reasonable and necessary within the meaning of section 7(1) of the *Federal Child Support Guidelines*.[301]

With respect to necessary health-related expenses, ability to pay is the deciding factor.[302] Expenses for private nursing care will be denied where there is no money available to meet such expenses.[303] A child in receipt of a disability pension may be required to contribute towards his or her medical expenses.[304]

---

292 *Wall v Eeles*, [2006] BCJ No 142 (SC); *Walsh v Walsh*, [2006] NJ No 33 (UFC); *Rudulier v Rudulier*, [1999] SJ No 366 (QB).

293 *Federal Child Support Guidelines*, s 7(1)(c), as amended by SOR/2000-337, s 1; *Ryan v Ryan*, 2010 ABQB 672; *Finch v Finch*, 2014 BCSC 2144 at paras 15–16; *Corkum v Clarke*, [2000] NSJ No 285 (Fam Ct); *Baram v Bakshy*, [2000] OJ No 2349 (SCJ); *Woode v Woode*, [2002] SJ No 55 (QB).

294 *Moss v Moss*, [1997] NJ No 299 (SC); *Croft v Foote*, 2023 NLCA 36; *O'Brien v O'Brien*, [1999] NWTJ No 56 (SC); *Bell v Griffin*, [1997] PEIJ No 86 (TD).

295 *Ohlmann v Ohlmann*, [2005] AJ No 140 (QB) (counsellor to provide court with full report outlining progress made and how additional counselling would benefit the children); *Moss v Moss*, [1997] NJ No 299 (SC) (need for counselling not established); *Sharf v Sharf*, [2000] OJ No 4052 (SCJ) (counselling expenses deemed excessive).

296 *Tubbs v Phillips*, [2000] SJ No 282 (QB).

297 *Colbourne v Colbourne*, 2014 ABQB 547; *Speirs v Speirs*, 2011 ONSC 3712.

298 *Hansvall v Hansvall*, [1997] SJ No 782 (QB); see also *Budden v Combden*, [1999] NJ No 199 (SC).

299 *MacLellan v MacLellan*, [1998] NSJ No 349 (TD); *Hansvall v Hansvall*, [1997] SJ No 782 (QB).

300 *Bellman v Bellman*, [1999] BCJ No 1196 (SC).

301 *Giles v Villeneuve*, [1998] OJ No 4492 (Gen Div).

302 *Bell v Griffin*, [1997] PEIJ No 86 (TD); *Sharf v Sharf*, [2000] OJ No 4052 (SCJ).

303 *Van Harten v Van Harten*, [1998] OJ No 1299 (Gen Div).

304 *Ibid*.

Although medical and dental premiums attributable to the child are allowable expenses under section 7(1)(b) of the *Federal Child Support Guidelines*, life insurance premiums are excluded.[305]

A court should refuse to apportion medical and dental insurance premiums under section 7(1)(b) of the *Federal Child Support Guidelines* where the obligor incurs no additional expense by including children of the marriage under his or her employer's insurance plan.

Where there is no evidence as to the portion of the medical and dental premiums attributable to the children, such as the difference between the rate for a single person as against the rate for family coverage, or such coverage as would include the children, the court should not guess the cost that may be attributable to the children.[307]

Where health insurance coverage is lost because a parent moves to another country, that parent may be ordered to pay a proportion of the cost of replacement coverage taken out by the primary caregiving parent, with the proportionate amount reflecting the respective spousal incomes.[308]

Section 7(1)(c) of the *Federal Child Support Guidelines* does not provide a comprehensive list of health-related expenses. Health-related expenses include necessary and reasonable expenses incurred for medical treatment, dental and orthodontal services,[309] chiropractic services,[310] psychological or counselling services,[311] and optical services,[312] but may not include personal expenses incurred by a spouse or former spouse who stays with a child undergoing treatment out of town.[313] The use of the word "including" within section 7(1)(c) of the Guidelines makes it clear that the various treatments and medical items are merely examples of health-related expenses that are encompassed within that subsection. The generality of the phrase "health-related expenses" is not restricted to only the therapies and medical items that are listed within the subsection.[314] A court may grant an order for a contribution to a parent's and child's transportation expenses associated with the child's ill health or disability.[315] The cost of a private or semi-private room in a hospital or other treatment centre or the reasonable costs for supplementary employee insurance to provide these benefits might also constitute a reasonable and necessary expense in the circumstances of a particular case. Food and footwear may constitute health-related expenses within the meaning of section 7(1)(c) of the *Federal Child Support Guidelines* where they are rendered necessary by

---

305 *Moss v Moss*, [1997] NJ No 299 (SC).

306 *Middleton v MacPherson*, [1997] AJ No 614 (QB).

307 *Krislock v Krislock*, [1997] SJ No 698 (QB).

308 *Rains v Rains*, [1997] OJ No 2516 (Gen Div); see also *St Arnaud v St Arnaud*, [1998] BCJ No 3155 (SC).

309 *Kennedy-Dalton v Dalton*, [2000] NJ No 41 (UFC) (orthodontal expenses); *Rosenberg v Rosenberg* (1987), 11 RFL (3d) 126 (Ont SC) (orthodontal expenses).

310 *Hellinckx v Large*, [1998] BCJ No 1462 (SC); *Welsh v Welsh*, [1998] OJ No 4550 (Gen Div); see *contra Michaud v Michaud*, [2003] AJ No 1601 (QB).

311 *Wilde v Wilde*, [1998] AJ No 430 (QB); *Wallace v Wallace*, [2002] BCJ No 1558 (SC); *GMS v DBS*, [1999] NJ No 278 (UFC); *CJI v VMW*, [2000] OJ No 4292 (SCJ).

312 *Sosnowski v Sosnowski*, [2000] BCJ No 1883 (SC).

313 *Tallman v Tomke*, [1997] AJ No 682 (QB). For a contrary stance, see *Kenney v Kenney*, [2000] AJ No 333 (QB).

314 *Marcella v Marcella*, 2016 SKQB 407 at para 20, Zuk J (father to pay his proportionate share of the costs of purchasing a specially equipped van to safely transport disabled child in wheelchair); see also *LRS v SSD*, 2020 ABCA 206.

315 *TAF v JSM*, [1999] BCJ No 1576 (SC); *Welsh v Welsh*, [1998] OJ No 4550 (Gen Div).

the child's medical condition. Costs will be assessed on the basis of expenses over and above those that would have been incurred for a child without the condition.[316] Diaper expenses for a child with developmental delays may fall within section 7(1)(c) of the Guidelines.[317] The Guidelines refer to "health-related expenses," not "medically necessary" expenses. Where appropriate, therefore, a court may order a parent to contribute to some of the expenses relating to homeopathic and naturopathic remedies used in treating a child, even though the parent had objected to such remedies during the marriage.[318] Over-the-counter medications and supplies that most families encounter over a period of time may be excluded in view of the specific identification of "prescription drugs" under section 7(1)(c) of the *Federal Child Support Guidelines*.[319] Non-prescription medications are allowable expenses under section 7 of the Guidelines only in unusual circumstances where relatively high costs are involved.[320]

Health-related expenses within the meaning of section 7(1)(c) of the Guidelines include the expenses of professional service providers and products. The capital cost of a wheelchair ramp may fall within section 7(1)(c) of the Guidelines but the court may permit the capital cost to be amortized, without interest, over five years.[321] Expenses for travel associated with a child's illness are a legitimate, albeit unusual, section 7 expense.[322] As was observed by Johnstone J of the Alberta Court of Queen's Bench in *ALY v LMY*,[323] Canadian judgments are divided on the question whether respite care provided for the benefit of the parent of a special needs child can constitute a child care-related expense or health-related expense under section 7(1)(a) and (c) respectively of the *Federal Child Support Guidelines*. While disallowing the expense under either of these two headings, Johnstone J concluded that it would be appropriate for the court to address the issue of respite care through a spousal support order premised on section 15(2)(6)(b) of the *Divorce Act*.

Spouses or former spouses who claim all or part of health-related expenses should, where practicable, alert the other spouse or former spouse before the expenses are incurred.[324] Notification may not be possible in cases involving emergency treatment.

A court may refuse to grant an order for medical and optical expenses under section 7(1)(c) of the *Federal Child Support Guidelines* where those expenses are substantially covered by the obligor's group insurance policy with an employer but, in that event, the court may direct the obligor to advise the obligee of the rules applicable to the policy and to process any claim by the obligee in a timely manner.[325]

An appellate court may decline to interfere with the manner in which the chambers judge has ordered medical and dental premiums and expenses to be paid, where the chambers

---

316 *Keller v MacDonald*, [1998] AJ No 1294 (QB); *Noiles v Noiles*, [2007] NBJ No 393 (QB).

317 *Greenslade v Porter*, [2004] NJ No 184 (UFC).

318 *Miceli v Miceli*, [1998] OJ No 5460 (Gen Div); compare *Blaine v Sanders*, [2000] MJ No 149 (QB) (non-prescription herbal remedies excluded, except on consent).

319 *Armaz v Van Erp*, [2000] OJ No 1544 (SCJ); *Wurmlinger v Cyca*, [2003] SJ No 247 (QB).

320 *Michaud v Michaud*, [2003] AJ No 1601 (QB).

321 *Corkum v Clarke*, [2000] NSJ No 285 (Fam Ct).

322 *Schill v Schill*, 2012 ONSC 3503. See also *Cook v Cook*, 2016 NBQB 55 at para 35; *Matechuk v Kopp (Yaworenko)*, 2020 SKQB 196.

323 [2001] AJ No 506 (QB).

324 *Andrews v Andrews*, 531 NE2d 219 (Ind Ct App 1988).

325 *Andries v Andries*, [1997] MJ No 301 (QB), var'd [1998] MJ No 196 (CA).

judge has adopted the most practical approach having regard to continuing acrimony between the parents.[326]

In order to address future eventualities, a court may direct that "the parties shall share the children's exceptional uninsured medical, optical and dental expenses in proportion to their incomes at the time of such expenses, upon the condition that neither party will incur non-emergency medical, optical or dental expenses for the children without prior consulta tion with the other with respect to the necessity, timing and cost of the expense."[327]

A court may order health-related expenses to be paid in designated instalments.[328] Where the parents have a capital sum with which to pay for uninsured orthodontic treatment, it may be preferable to use those funds rather than amortize the costs and pay them monthly.

An order for health-related expenses may be declared retroactive to the date when the insurance coverage terminated.[330]

K. EXTRAORDINARY EDUCATIONAL EXPENSES; PRIVATE SCHOOL

Section 7(1)(d) of the *Federal Child Support Guidelines* confers a discretion on the court to provide for the payment of all or part of extraordinary expenses for primary or secondary school education or for any educational programs that meet the child's particular needs. Pursuant to section 7(1.1) of the *Federal Child Support Guidelines*,[332] which amendment became effective on 1 May 2006, the definition of "extraordinary" expenses has been clarified. The amendment provides a two-part definition. First, in accordance with section 7(1.1)(a), expenses are extraordinary if they "exceed those that the spouse requesting an amount for the extraordinary expenses can reasonably cover." This is determined having regard to the income of the requesting spouse as well as any child support received. This element of the definition relates to the requesting spouse's ability to pay for the expenses. If the expenses exceed those that the requesting spouse can reasonably cover, they are extraordinary. Where section 7(1.1)(a) does not apply because the expense does not exceed the amount that the requesting spouse can reasonably cover, the second part of the definition, set out in section 7(1.1)(b), applies. Section 7(1.1)(b) directs courts to determine whether the expenses are extraordinary, having regard to five factors, namely,

1) the amount of the expenses in relation to the income of the spouse requesting the amount (including the child support amount);
2) the nature and number of the education programs and extracurricular activities;
3) any special needs and talents of the child or children;

---

326 *CRHE v FGE*, [2004] BCJ No 1057 (CA).
327 *Raynor v Raynor*, [1997] NSJ No 411 (TD), Davidson J.
328 *Seiferling v Langmaier*, [1998] SJ No 84 (QB).
329 *Jensen v Siagris*, [1998] BCJ No 743 (SC).
330 *McCoy v Hucker*, [1998] OJ No 2831 (Gen Div).
331 See Section A, above in this chapter.
332 SOR/2005-400, s 1, 28 November 2005, *Canada Gazette*, Vol 139, No 25, 14 December 2005.
333 *Orring v Orring*, [2006] BCJ No 1520 (SC) (learning centre expenses of $5,000 not "extraordinary" for father with after-tax income of $110,000); *NZ v OZ*, 2015 BCSC 2130; *Kramchynsky v Kramchynsky*, 2013 MBQB 56; *Gordinier-Regan v Regan*, 2011 NSSC 297; *Homier v Paquette*, 2011 ONSC 3319; *MDL v CR*, 2020 SKCA 44.

4) the overall costs of the programs and activities; and
5) any other similar factors that the court considers relevant.[334]

The opening words of section 7(1) require the court to take into account the necessity of the expense in relation to the child's best interests and the reasonableness of the expense, having regard to the means of the spouses and those of the child and to the family's spending pattern prior to the separation,[335] and the guiding principle under section 7(2) calls for a sharing of the expenses in proportion to the respective spousal incomes in the absence of any contribution from the child.[336] Private school fees are generally considered extraordinary educational expenses under section 7(1)(d) of the Guidelines but they must also be reasonable and necessary.[337] It is not enough to show that the child will find the school experience delightful and instructive.[338] A court may be unable to make a finding as to the necessity of the expense in relation to the child's best interests and may be unable to apply the guiding principle of proportionate sharing where the applicant fails to make full disclosure as to his or her income.[339] In determining the father's obligation to contribute to the children's private school expenses, judicial account may be taken of the importance of the children's emotional well-being and the necessity that their mother not be too stressed by her parenting role after discharging heavy professional obligations during the day.[340]

High school graduation costs do not constitute extraordinary expenses for secondary school education within the meaning of section 7(1)(d) of the *Federal Child Support Guidelines*.[341]

The purchase of a computer may not fall within sections 7(1)(d) or (f) of the Guidelines, if households having the income of the spouses would normally have a computer available for the use of their children,[342] or if no evidence has been adduced to establish that a computer was a necessary purchase.[343] The purchase of a computer to assist a special needs student[344]

334 *CLE v BMR*, 2010 ABCA 187; *LHMK v BPK*, 2012 BCSC 435; *Beruschi v Muller*, 2021 BCSC 78; *KEK v LEL*, 2010 MBQB 266; *LKS v DMCT*, 2008 NSCA 61; *Ward v Ward*, 2015 ONSC 6221; *Gaspers v Gaspers*, 2008 SKCA 94; see also *Hosseini v Kazemi*, 2010 BCSC 666 (donations to RESP taken into account).

335 *CLE v BMR*, 2010 ABCA 187; *Calcada v Ferreira*, [2002] BCJ No 1802 (SC); *Croll v Croll*, [2003] BCJ No 2937 (SC) (tutoring expenses disallowed); *KEK v LEL*, 2010 MBQB 266; *LJM v GSM*, [2006] NBJ No 202 (QB); *Gordinier-Regan v Regan*, 2011 NSSC 297; *Hoover v Hoover*, [1997] NWTJ No 43 (SC); *Andrews v Andrews*, [1999] OJ No 3578 (CA); *Beach v Tolstoy*, 2015 ONSC 7248; *Fitzgerald v Gerlich*, [2003] OJ No 1946 (SCJ) (Catholic school fees); *RL v BI*, [1997] QJ No 4450 (CS); *Beisel v Henderson*, [2004] SJ No 413 (QB); *MDL v CR*, 2020 SKCA 44.

336 *Calcada v Ferreira*, [2002] BCJ No 1802 (SC); *LJM v GSM*, [2006] NBJ No 202 (QB); *Khoee-Solomonescu v Solomonescu*, [1997] OJ No 4876 (Gen Div); *Tubbs v Phillips*, [2000] SJ No 282 (QB).

337 *DJE v PAE*, 2014 ABCA 403 (private school expenses); *NZ v OZ*, 2015 BCSC 2130; *Korman v Korman*, 2015 ONCA 578; *Chong v Donnelly*, 2021 ONSC 5263.

338 *Fisher v Pade*, [2001] BCJ No 1469 (SC); *NMM v NSM*, [2004] BCJ No 642 (SC) (fees to be paid until end of current school year); *DI v SI*, 2011 BCSC 1788; *LHMK v BPK*, 2012 BCSC 435; *LJM v GSM*, [2006] NBJ No 202 (QB); *Gordinier-Regan v Regan*, 2011 NSSC 297.

339 *Cross v Cross*, [1997] BCJ No 1741 (SC).

340 *SM v PEN*, [2003] QJ No 14125 (CS); compare *Holeman v Holeman*, [2006] MJ No 456 (QB).

341 *Covin v Covin*, 2021 NBQB 228; *Morley v Morley*, [1999] SJ No 31 (QB); see *contra Beninger v Beninger*, [2005] BCJ No 1781 (SC).

342 *Wanstall v Walker*, [1998] BCJ No 1808 (SC).

343 *Kingston v Kelly*, [1999] PEIJ No 52 (SC).

344 *Rumpel v Wills*, 2010 SKQB 397.

or an accomplished student[345] in fulfilling her school assignments has, nevertheless, been found to be a reasonable and necessary extraordinary expense within the meaning of section 7(1)(d) of the Guidelines where it was readily affordable in light of the parental incomes.

An order for a contribution to the cost of a scholastic assessment to determine whether a child is gifted falls within the ambit of section 7(1)(d) of the *Federal Child Support Guidelines*.[346]

Tuition fees to upgrade high school marks may be characterized as an extraordinary expense for secondary school education under section 7(1)(d) of the Guidelines, but an order for a contribution to this expense may be refused where the course was not completed. A court may order a contribution to be made towards the costs of a tutor for a child who is encountering academic problems, but proper receipts must be provided.[348] An order for contribution to the costs of a tutor may be conditioned on full consultation between the parents prior to arrangements for a tutor being made.[349] The cost of tutoring has been found to qualify as an eligible extraordinary expense where a child is experiencing academic difficulties but courts have also found tutoring costs to qualify as a section 7(d) expense when a child is not struggling academically but wants to enhance his or her academic potential. Even where the evidence shows the child would benefit from tutoring, however, courts retain the discretion to decline to make an order for cost sharing if the payor has insufficient means to contribute to that expense or it may impose a cap on the allowable expenses to reflect a parent's limited ability to pay.[350] Extraordinary education expenses are those that extend beyond the basic school program.[351] Routine school fees, general school supplies, field trips, normal transportation, and school lunches are regarded as "usual expenses" rather than "extraordinary expenses" within the meaning of section 7 of the *Federal Child Support Guidelines* The basic amounts of child support provided by the applicable provincial or territorial table under the *Federal Child Support Guidelines* reflect an average of what parents at various income levels spend on their children, but the tables provide no clear indication as to what is an extraordinary educational expense.[353] In the absence of clarification, no hard and fast rules can or should apply to the determination of whether particular expenses constitute extraordinary expenses within the meaning of section 7(1)(d) of the Guidelines, although it may be helpful to the court if evidence is adduced of the expenses normally associated with

345 *Wurmlinger v Cyca*, [2003] SJ No 247 (QB).

346 *Nataros v Nataros*, [1998] BCJ No 1417 (SC).

347 *Newman v Tibbetts*, [2004] NBJ No 72 (QB).

348 *Massler v Massler*, [1999] AJ No 206 (QB); *LHMK v BPK*, 2012 BCSC 435; *Newman v Tibbetts*, [2004] NBJ No 72 (QB); *Lyttle v Bourget*, [1999] NSJ No 298 (SC); *Schwark v Schwark*, [2000] SJ No 489 (QB). See also *AJL v JTB*, 2020 ABQB 649 at para 83 (extraordinary expenses for extracurricular expenses).

349 *Bennett v Bennett*, [1999] SJ No 728 (QB).

350 *MDL v CR*, 2020 SKCA 44 at paras 88, 90, and 97, Schwann JA.

351 *Middleton v MacPherson*, [1997] AJ No 614 (QB); *Ebrahim v Ebrahim*, [1997] BCJ No 2039 (SC); *Covin v Covin*, 2021 NBQB 228.

352 *CLE v BMR*, 2010 ABCA 187; *NZ v OZ*, 2015 BCSC 2130; *MSD obo NC v AL*, 2022 NBQB 21; *Walsh v Walsh*, [2006] NJ No 33 (UFC) (books for school); *Raymond-Theoret v Smith*, 2011 ONSC 7215; *McEachern v McEachern*, [1998] SJ No 507 (QB).

353 See *MSD obo NC v AL*, 2022 NBQB 21; *Sagl v Sagl*, [1997] OJ No 2837 (Gen Div), wherein the court concluded that the applicable table amount of child support, namely $1,725, was sufficient to cover any private school fees that might be incurred.

enrolment in a local public school.[354] School expenses cannot be categorized as extraordinary simply on account of the number of children to whom they relate, because the basic table amount of support increases with the number of children,[355] although it must be borne in mind that the table amounts reflect economies of scale according to the number of children, whereas school expenses are not discounted having regard to the number of children in respect of whom they are payable.

Extraordinary expenses associated with home schooling must reflect the special needs of the child.[356]

An order for the proportionate sharing of private school fees may be granted pursuant to section 7 of the *Federal Child Support Guidelines* where a child has experienced difficulties in public school and would be more likely to attain reasonable educational goals by a transfer to a private school that the parents can afford.[357] An order for a contribution to private school expenses may be denied where there is no evidence to show that the public system of education would not be equally effective in meeting the child's needs.[358] The mere fact that the child has been attending private school does not signify that the expense is necessary and must continue.[359] Academic or social needs might make it a necessity in the child's best interest to attend private school.[360] Where a parent has acted reasonably in enrolling a child in private school, child support may be provided to reflect the costs of the child's education.[361] A parent who unilaterally registers a child in private school may be denied a contribution to the child's expenses.[362] An order for a contribution to the expenses of a private school may be granted, even though the expenses were not part of the family's spending pattern before the spousal separation.[363] The pattern of expenses before the separation may not be particularly relevant where the child was not attending school when the parents separated.[364] Laura W Morgan, an American commentator,[365] has identified the following factors as relevant to the provision of expenses for private schooling:

---

354 *Middleton v MacPherson,* [1997] AJ No 614 (QB).

355 *Moss v Moss,* [1997] NJ No 299 (SC).

356 *Andrews v Andrews,* [1999] OJ No 3578 (CA).

357 *Greenwood v Greenwood,* [1999] BCJ No 2093 (SC) (judicial refusal to vary consent order); *Pohlod v Bielajew,* [1998] OJ No 3345 (Gen Div). See also *DI v SI,* 2011 BCSC 1788.

358 *Potter v Graham,* [2004] AJ No 1133 (QB); *NZ v OZ,* 2015 BCSC 2130; *Hanrahan-Cox v Cox,* 2011 NSSC 256; *Bhupal v Bhupal,* 2013 ONSC 60; see also *Steiger v Steiger,* [1999] AJ No 129 (QB). Compare *Casals v Casals,* [2006] OJ No 5602 (SCJ); *Seltsas v Seltsas,* [2008] OJ No 4948 (SCJ).

359 *Bhupal v Bhupal,* 2013 ONSC 60.

360 *Gordinier-Regan v Regan,* 2011 NSSC 297; *Banfield v Banfield,* 2012 NSSC 68.

361 *Lennox v Frender* (1990), 27 RFL (3d) 181 (BCCA); *Robinson v Robinson* (1989), 22 RFL (3d) 10 (Ont HCJ); compare *Vandervort v Brettler* (1989), 22 RFL (3d) 160 (Ont HCJ).

362 *Potter v Graham,* [2004] AJ No 1133 (QB); *Cornelissen v Cornelissen,* [2002] BCJ No 1459 (SC); *Colizza v Arnot,* [2000] MJ No 176 (CA); *Maginley v Maginley,* [2003] NSJ No 35 (SC); *Banfield v Banfield,* 2012 NSSC 68 (retroactive support reduced); *L'Heureux v L'Heureux,* [1999] SJ No 437 (QB).

363 *Krislock v Krislock,* [1997] SJ No 698 (QB).

364 *Pohlod v Bielajew,* [1998] OJ No 1770 (Gen Div).

365 Laura W Morgan, *Child Support Guidelines: Interpretation and Application,* loose-leaf (New York: Aspen Law and Business, 1996–2010) §4.05[b]; see also *LHMK v BPK,* 2012 BCSC 435; *Andrews v Andrews,* [1999] OJ No 3578 (CA).

> whether one or both parents attended private school; whether the child has been enrolled in a private school prior to the divorce;[366] whether there has been an expectation that the child would have a private education, by express agreement or otherwise; whether the parents can afford a private education;[367] and whether the child has a special need for private school that public schools cannot provide,[368] making private education in the best interests of the child.

She further asserts that "[these] considerations would also justify . . . [expenses] for music lessons or other cultural activities" and that "[when] private education costs are awarded, the court should award such expenses only to the extent that they are actually incurred and not paid from other sources."[369] The fact that the children did not attend private school in the past is not conclusive and an appellate court may direct a rehearing where the trial judge paid insufficient attention to such factors as the educational history of the parents that included extensive private schooling, the children's private preschooling, the talent that the children developed over a long period of separation, and the ability to pay of a parent.[370] Affordability does not, of itself, justify the enrolment of children in private school where there is no family history or pre-separation intention to enroll the children in private school.[371]

Once it is established that a private school education is in a child's best interests and is reasonable having regard to the means of the spouses and the family's pre-separation pattern of spending, incidental expenses that flow naturally from enrolment in the school, such as transportation and uniform costs, will ordinarily be included in the after-tax expenses to be shared by the parents in accordance with their respective incomes.[372]

Where a child with behavioural problems has been placed in a private school, each parent may be ordered to contribute to the expenses as being reasonable and in the child's best interests, even though the cost is a burden on both parents.[373]

In determining the extent, if any, to which a parent should contribute to private school expenses of children of the marriage, the court may assess each child independently and thereby reach differing outcomes.[374] However, a court should not lightly deny one child the same benefits of private school as those enjoyed by another sibling, where there are no financial obstacles to the payment of the requisite costs.[375]

---

366 *Van Deventer v Van Deventer*, [2000] BCJ No 37 (CA); *Rivett v Bylund*, [1998] OJ No 325 (Gen Div); *Korman v Korman*, 2015 ONCA 578; compare *BAC v DLC*, [2003] BCJ No 1303 (SC).

367 *Stelter v Klingspohn*, [1999] BCJ No 2926 (SC); *Steele v Koppanyi*, [2002] MJ No 201 (CA); *TLS v DJM* 2009 NSSC 79; *Maloney v Maloney*, [2004] OJ No 5828 (Div Ct); *Korman v Korman*, 2015 ONCA 578.

368 *TAP v JTP*, 2009 BCSC 970; *TLS v DJM*, 2009 NSSC 79; *Shankman v Shankman*, [2001] OJ No 3798 (SCJ); *Williamson v Rezonja*, 2014 ONCJ 72 at para 52.

369 Laura Morgan, *Child Support Guidelines: Interpretation and Application*, loose-leaf (New York: Aspen Law and Business, 1996–2010) §4.05[b]; see also *Andrews v Andrews*, [1999] OJ No 3578 (CA); *Hall v Galbraith*, 2023 ONSC 2161 at para 31.

370 *Cochrane v Zarins*, [1998] BCJ No 756 (SC).

371 *Potter v Graham*, [2004] AJ No 1133 (QB).

372 *Wanstall v Walker*, [1998] BCJ No 1808 (SC).

373 *Comeau v Comeau*, [1997] NSJ No 409 (TD).

374 *Burton v Burton*, [1997] NSJ No 560 (TD); see also *Ostlund v Ostlund*, [2000] BCJ No 1158 (SC).

375 *Bell-Angus v Angus*, [2000] OJ No 2074 (SCJ); *Korman v Korman*, 2015 ONCA 578.

Where the total cost of private school education is not reasonably within the means of the parents but alternative sources are available, the court may cap the maximum total cost for section 7 expenses proportionate to the incomes imputed to the parents.[376]

A court may order a lump sum payment of private school fees to be made directly to the school so as to entitle the payor to obtain the tax benefits of such a payment.[377]

Expenses for private school will be denied where they are unreasonable, given the parents' incomes and the expenses of the two households.[378]

Private school expenses, though reasonable for a short period of transition, may become unreasonable in the long term,[379] especially where a change in circumstances reduces the parental income.[380] An application for the payment of private school tuition fees will be dismissed, notwithstanding that the children are flourishing under that system, where the obligor's debt load renders such expense a luxury that the parents cannot afford.[381] It may be delightful and instructive for a preschool child to attend a Montessori school, but the criteria to be applied under section 7(1) of the Guidelines are premised on "need" and "means."[382] In the absence of persuasive evidence that a child has any needs different from those of other normal children, private school fees are not an extraordinary expense that should be imposed on an unwilling parent.[383]

A claim for extraordinary secondary school educational expenses under section 7(1)(d) of the *Federal Child Support Guidelines* may be dismissed for lack of relevant evidence without prejudice to the right to re-apply with appropriate supporting materials.[384]

L. EXPENSES FOR POST-SECONDARY EDUCATION

Section 7(1)(e) of the *Federal Child Support Guidelines* empowers a court to provide for the payment of some or all of post-secondary education expenses.[385] To qualify as post-secondary education expenses, the expense must be sufficiently connected to the program of study and that can only be true where the expense in question is not one that would otherwise have been incurred.[386]

An application for expenses for post-secondary education under section 7(1)(e) of the *Federal Child Support Guidelines* may be deemed premature, where the child has a history

---

376 *Iddon v Iddon*, [2006] OJ No 237 (SCJ).

377 *Greenwood v Greenwood*, [1998] BCJ No 729 (SC).

378 *Kramchynsky v Kramchynsky*, 2013 MBQB 56; *RPS v KJS*, 2014 ONSC 1385.

379 *Pilotte v Pilotte*, 2013 NSSC 24.

380 *McDonald v McDonald*, [2001] BCJ No 2570 (CA).

381 *Lyttle v Bourget*, [1999] NSJ No 298 (SC). See also *Hall v Hall*, [2006] AJ No 563 (QB).

382 *Wait v Wait*, [2000] BCJ No 1282 (CA) (primary caregiving parent entitled to contribution towards less expensive child care costs); compare *JMG v FG*, [2001] OJ No 3010 (SCJ) (retroactive order for *pro rata* sharing of after-tax Montessori preschool expenses).

383 *Wait v Wait*, [2000] BCJ No 1282 (CA), cited in *Wells v Watson*, [2000] BCJ No 1638 (SC) (application successful); *JLT v JDNT*, 2011 BCSC 855; *RPS v KJS*, 2014 ONSC 1385. Compare *Dostie v Poapst*, 2014 ONSC 6959.

384 *Fisher v Gerrard*, [1998] SJ No 688 (QB).

385 See Chapter 3, Section E.

386 *Craig v Niro*, 2022 ONSC 5178 at paras 24–25 (purchase of furniture and appliances, food, and toiletries characterized as post-secondary education expenses).

of changing his or her plans and has not been accepted for admission to university or community college.[387]

Although section 7(1)(e) of the *Federal Child Support Guidelines* and of the *Ontario Child Support Guidelines* may provide an advantage with respect to the post-secondary education of children of divorced or separated parents, which is not shared by children of an intact marriage, there is no contravention of sections 7 and 15 of the *Canadian Charter of Rights and Freedoms.*[388]

Post-secondary education expenses do not have to be "extraordinary" in order to satisfy section 7(1)(e) of the *Federal Child Support Guidelines,* but they must satisfy the tests of necessity and reasonableness defined in section 7(1).[389] The costs of post-secondary education or training are placed fairly high on the scale of necessity in relation to the child's best interests. Whether the expenses are also reasonable must be assessed having regard to the means of the parties and of the child and to the family's pre-separation spending pattern.

Expenses for post-secondary education may include tuition, books and other supplies, and necessary transportation costs.[391] Where the table amount of basic child support is deemed inappropriate because the adult child is living away from home while attending university, the post-secondary education expenses under section 7 of the Guidelines will include tuition and institutional expenses, room and board or equivalent expenses, and books, travel, and miscellaneous expenses reasonably attributable to the pursuit of that education.[392] The court must avoid the double counting of such costs as accommodation and food when an order for the table amount of child support is coupled with an order for a contribution to the child's expenses while attending an out-of-town university.[393]

Expenses for post-secondary education under section 7(1)(e) of the *Federal Child Support Guidelines* are not confined to children over the provincial age of majority in respect of whom section 3(2)(b) of the Guidelines might be invoked.[394] However, section 7(1)(e) may be invoked with respect to children over the age of majority for whom child support has been fixed in accordance with the applicable provincial or territorial table pursuant to section 3(2)(a) of the *Federal Child Support Guidelines.*

There are a number of things that the court is required to consider in relation to post-secondary education expenses. The court must determine whether the expenses are reasonable having regard to the means of the spouses and child and the family's spending pattern before separation. It is also necessary to determine whether an expense has arisen solely as a result of post-secondary education or whether some portion is already factored into the basic amount provided by the applicable provincial or territorial table. Contributions of the child made possible from his or her earnings are to be deducted from the expenses. The

387 *Cowan v Cowan,* [2001] AJ No 669 (QB).

388 *Souliere v Leclair,* [1998] OJ No 1393 (Gen Div).

389 *Odermatt v Odermatt,* [1998] BCJ No 55 (SC); *Kavanagh v Kavanagh,* [1999] NJ No 358 (SC).

390 *Kusnir v Kusnir,* [2001] OJ No 3491 (Ct J).

391 *MV v DV,* [2005] NBJ No 505 (QB); *St Amour v St Amour,* [1997] NSJ No 363 (TD); *Cervi v McDonald,* 2021 ONSC 1843; compare *Newman v Newman,* [1998] NJ No 269 (UFC) (automobile insurance deducted).

392 *LHMK v BPK,* 2012 BCSC 435; *Cervi v McDonald,* 2021 ONSC 1843.

393 *Pollock v Rioux,* [2004] NBJ No 467 (CA); *MacPherson v MacPherson,* [2005] OJ No 3448 (SCJ); see also *CRC v DAJC,* 2020 ABCA 143.

394 See *Nadeau v Mitchell,* [1997] OJ No 2833 (Gen Div); see Chapter 3, Section J.

court must also take into account subsidies, benefits, and income tax deductions or credits relating to the expenses. Where the only evidence is the applicant's notional estimate of what it may cost for tuition, books, and living expenses, the court may conclude that there is insufficient information available to enable the court to fashion an order in the absence of further evidence.[395] A claim for post-secondary education expenses may be adjourned or dismissed without prejudice to the right to re-apply where insufficient evidence is provided of the child's ability or inability to contribute to the expenses.[396] An adult child is expected to contribute to his or her college expenses to the extent that is reasonable. The applicant or the adult child must furnish accurate and meaningful information so that the court can assess what the child's contribution should be. A failure to provide such information entitles the court to draw an adverse inference for the purpose of determining the child's contribution.[397] An assessment may be declined as premature until the child is accepted at university[398] or until such time as post-secondary education costs have been incurred.[399]

In calculating the amount of child support to be paid to enable a child to pursue university studies, the court should take account of the child's capacity to contribute to the cost out of his or her own income, and bursaries, scholarships, or student loans.[400] An adult child is expected to contribute towards the cost of post-secondary education or training by maximizing his or her income, whether by scholarships, bursaries, loans, or summer employment,[401] but his or her availability for part-time employment while at college is to be determined in light of the academic demands for successful completion of the program.[402] The opportunity to pursue post-secondary education is a privilege, not a right, and an adult child may be required to take advantage of student loans. The appropriate level of the child's loan obligation should be determined by reference to the child's means and capabilities, the financial capacity of the parents and a fair balance between the child and the parents.[403] There is no hard-and-fast rule that student loans ought to be required only when the means of the child combined with those of the parents leaves a shortfall.[404] An adult child who is pursuing university studies should not be expected to incur substantial debt, if the child is contributing to his or her subsistence in a significant way and the parent against whom the relief is claimed is capable of providing the necessary child support. Under these circumstances, the amount

---

395 *LJM v GSM*, [2006] NBJ No 202 (QB); *Magnes v Magnes*, [1997] SJ No 407 (QB).

396 *Louisseize v Louisseize*, [1999] OJ No 5000 (SCJ); *Nkwazi v Nkwazi*, [1998] SJ No 571 (QB).

397 *LJM v GSM*, [2006] NBJ No 202 (QB); *Gibson v Gibson*, [2002] OJ No 1784 (SCJ); compare *Morgan v Morgan*, [2006] BCJ No 1795 (SC). See also *CJT v GAT*, 2019 ABQB 851.

398 *Kennedy-Dalton v Dalton*, [2000] NJ No 41 (UFC); *SDB v PW*, [1998] NSJ No 565 (Fam Ct).

399 *Wilk v Re*, [1997] AJ No 732 (QB); *LJM v GSM*, [2006] NBJ No 202 (QB).

400 *Tobias v Tobias*, [2000] AJ No 346 (QB); *WPN v BJN*, [2005] BCJ No 12 (CA); *Hughes v Hughes*, [1997] NBJ No 261 (QB); *Selig v Smith*, 2008 NSCA 54; *Cervi v McDonald*, 2021 ONSC 1843; *Minish v Timmons*, 2021 ONSC 7622; *Simard v Simard*, [2000] SJ No 539 (CA).

401 *Wahl v Wahl*, [2000] AJ No 29 (QB); *WPN v BJN*, [2005] BCJ No 12 (CA); *Bradley v Zaba* (1996), 22 RFL (4th) 52 (Sask QB); see also *Liscio v Avram*, [2009] OJ No 3406 (SCJ); compare *Reyes v Rollo*, [2001] OJ No 5110 (SCJ) (adult child's scholarship excluded from apportionment of expenses).

402 *Wahl v Wahl*, [2000] AJ No 29 (QB); *WPN v BJN*, [2005] BCJ No 12 (CA); *Liscio v Liscio*, [2009] OJ No 3406 (SCJ); *Bradley v Zaba* (1996), 22 RFL (4th) 52 (Sask QB).

403 *Johnson v Johnson*, [1998] BCJ No 1080 (SC); *Ross v Dunphy*, 2009 NBQB 281; *Selig v Smith*, 2008 NSCA 54; *Neufeld v Neufeld*, [2003] OJ No 5382 (Div Ct); *Cervi v McDonald*, 2021 ONSC 1843; *Nygren v Johnson*, 2011 SKQB 12.

404 *Selig v Smith*, 2008 NSCA 54; compare *Rebenchuk v Rebenchuk*, 2007 MBCA 22.

of child support may be fixed so as to enable the child to live on a zero-deficit basis.[405] Courts have a very broad discretion in determining how to balance the many competing considerations relevant to determining the respective responsibilities of the parents and the child to cover the post-secondary education costs of an adult child still considered to be a child of the marriage for the purpose of the *Federal Child Support Guidelines*. Relevant cases indicate that there is a growing trend to impose one-third to one-half of the responsibility on the adult child, to be met by part-time employment, scholarships, or student loans, depending on the talents and choices of the child, and the balance on the parents, proportional to their respective incomes. However, this is far from invariable; it depends on the incomes and circumstances of the parties.[406]

Expenses under section 7(1)(e) of the Guidelines may be denied where a child who attends university can totally finance his or her own studies through savings, student loans, or employment income,[407] or where an adult child is living in her own apartment with her mother's consent and the father is making voluntary payments to cover the child's post-secondary education and living expenses.[408] The fact that grandparents help pay the expenses of their grandchildren does not in the ordinary course absolve a parent from financial responsibility.[409] Gifts received by the child may also be taken into account, although it does not follow that the child should exhaust his or her savings before seeking support from a parent. In *Dunn v Dunn*,[411] Fry J of the Newfoundland and Labrador Supreme Court, Family Division, stated that "[t]he case law suggests that a student who seeks parental support for his post-secondary education should contribute an appropriate amount, which has been suggested as anywhere between 25–40 percent. There is no hard and fast rule." The applicant or the adult child must furnish accurate and meaningful information so that the court can assess the parents' and the child's appropriate contribution. A failure to provide such information entitles the court to draw an adverse inference for the purpose of determining the child's contribution.[412] In *Roth v Roth*,[413] Ricchetti J of the Ontario Superior Court of Justice provided the following useful summary of principles governing an adult child's obligation to contribute towards his or her post-secondary expenses pursuant to section 7 of the *Federal Child Support Guidelines*:

---

405 *SB v RB*, [2000] QJ No 3298 (CS); see also *MacDonald v MacDonald*, [2001] NSJ No 498 (SC).

406 *Dunn v Dunn*, 2013 NLTD(F) 7 at para 41; *Fleming v Boyachek*, 2011 SKCA 11; *Firkola v Firkola*, 2017 SKQB 31; *Youle v Galloway*, 2018 SKQB 211; compare *Semancik v Saunders*, 2011 BCCA 264; see also *Werenka v Werenka*, 2021 ABQB 1023; *Wiewiora v Wiewiora*, 2014 MBQB 218; *Corby v Corby*, 2015 ONSC 2700.

407 *Herriot v Herriot*, [2003] BCJ No 1274 (SC); *Evans v Evans*, [1998] SJ No 91 (QB).

408 *Krill v Krill*, [2000] AJ No 163 (QB).

409 *Mistry v Mistry*, 2019 ONSC 193, citing *Squires v Crouch*, 2016 ONCA 774, at para 12.

410 *Davis v Davis*, [1999] BCJ No 1832 (SC) (scholarship fund set up by maternal grandparents); *Finn v Levine*, [1997] OJ No 2201 (Gen Div); see also *Lewi v Lewi*, [2006] OJ No 1847 (CA) (trust funds); *Fearon v Tzeng Fearon*, 2021 ONSC 7545 .

411 2013 NLTD(F) 7 at para 41, citing James G McLeod & Alfred A Mamo, *Annual Review of Family Law, 2011* (Toronto: Carswell, 2012) at 269–99; see also *Vardy v Vardy*, 2015 NLTD(F) 36; *Bauer v Noonan*, 2005 SKQB 427; compare *Foster v Amos*, 2010 SKQB 409 at paras 57–60 (no fixed allocation; amount is discretionary being based on the particular circumstances).

412 *RPS v KJS*, 2014 ONSC 1385 at para 106, Stevenson J; *Fearon v Tzeng Fearon*, 2021 ONSC 7545.

413 2010 ONSC 2532 at para 16; see also *Cervi v McDonald*, 2021 ONSC 1843 at paras 53–62.

a) Generally, post secondary education is considered a necessary expense in the best interests of the children. . . .
b) The reasonableness of the expense considers the means of the spouses or former spouses *and* the means of the child.
c) Children have an obligation to make a *reasonable contribution* to their own post-secondary education or training. This does not mean that all of a child's income should necessarily be applied to the costs of the child's further education. The court should consider whether the child should be entitled to some personal benefit from the fruits of his or her labours.[414]
d) Grants, scholarships and bursaries are generally treated as a reduction of the education expense as they involve a net transfer of resources to the child without any obligation of repayment.
e) A student loan is not a "benefit," within the meaning of section 7(3) of the Guidelines that must be automatically taken into account in determining the amount to be ordered in respect of s. 7 expenses. A student loan *may constitute*, in whole or in part, a "contribution. from the child" to post-secondary education expenses within the meaning of section 7(2) of the Guidelines and thereby exclude or reduce the need for any parental contribution. This turns on the reasonableness of taking account of any such loans in the circumstances of the case.
f) In determining the amount of an expense or the contribution thereto under section 7 of the *Federal Child Support Guidelines*, the guiding principle is that, once the court has determined the appropriate amount of contribution by the spouses or former spouses, the spouses or former spouses should share the expense in proportion to their respective incomes after deducting any contribution from the child, or other liable parent.

A diploma program at a private college may be equated with a university degree program for the purpose of determining the father's obligation to contribute to his daughter's expenses for post-secondary education under section 7 of the *Federal Child Support Guidelines*. An adult child is not disentitled to section 7 expenses simply because her choice of post-secondary education did not reflect her father's expectations. An adult child is entitled to make her own choice provided that it is reasonable and there is a reasonable expectation of success. In ordering the father to contribute towards the adult child's post-secondary education expenses in addition to paying the applicable table amount of child support, the court must avoid duplicating the provision for food and shelter that is included in the applicable table amount of child support. Although the father's obligation to pay section 7 expenses terminates on the adult child's graduation from college, the court may direct the applicable table amount of child support to be paid for three months after graduation to allow time for the adult child to find employment.[415]

Although an adult child may be enrolled in an extra-provincial post-secondary institution, a parent's contribution towards the child's expenses may be judicially limited to the cost of attending the hometown university[416] or to an amount that falls in between the costs

414 See *TMR v SMS*, 2019 NBQB 40; see also *O'Connor v O'Connor*, 2022 ONSC 3482.
415 *Jordan v Bolt*, [2004] NJ No 417 (SC).
416 *Oates v Oates*, [2004] OJ No 2984 (SCJ); *Lidstone v Lidstone*, [2001] PEIJ No 118 (SC).

of a hometown and an out-of-province education.[417] An adult child's choice of an Ivy League institution, such as Princeton, for his or her college education may be justified, however, by the child's receipt of a full athletic scholarship.[418]

Costs associated with the use of an automobile may be allowed where there is no public transportation available.[419] Extra accommodation expenses that are based solely on the child's personal lifestyle choice may be excluded from allowable expenses under section 7 of the *Federal Child Support Guidelines*, where other appropriate accommodation is available at a significantly lower cost.[420]

Section 7 of the *Federal Child Support Guidelines* confers a discretion on the court to order the payment of a contribution to a child's post-secondary education expenses. The court is under no compulsion to make such an order and may conclude that any contribution would be inappropriate, having regard to the potential obligor's inability to pay.[421]

Full financial information is required for a court to determine parental contributions to the post-secondary education expenses of an adult child under section 7(1)(e) of the *Federal Child Support Guidelines*.[422]

Middle-class parents are expected to make some sacrifice to ensure that their children achieve their full academic potential, whereas parents of modest means may be unable to contribute towards their child's post-secondary education.[423]

A court may conclude that it is premature to embark upon speculation whether children in their pre-teen or early teenage years will be pursuing post-secondary education and decline to make an order in that regard.[424] An order compelling a parent to contribute to a RESP, or to establish a separate fund for a child's future post-secondary education,[426] may be deemed inappropriate where any post-secondary education lies several years in the future. Some courts have ordered spouses to set money aside for their children's future post-secondary education,[427] but it is questionable how far courts are entitled to deal with future contingencies when applying the *Divorce Act* and the *Federal Child Support Guidelines*. An application for release of money held in an education fund because the oldest child has plans to attend university may be dismissed as premature where the child's plans have not been finalized and an immediate release would trigger income tax consequences.[429]

A court may declare that either parent is at liberty to apply to vary the amount payable by way of section 7 expenses, if there is a material change in the child's expenses, or in the

417 *Dunn v Dunn*, 2013 NLTD(F) 7.
418 *Lavdovsky v Lavdovsky*, [1998] BCJ No 1952 (SC).
419 *Pope v Janes*, 2014 NLTD(F) 27; compare *Foster v Amos*, 2010 SKQB 409 at paras 52–56.
420 *Moss v Moss*, [1997] NJ No 299 (SC).
421 *Alonzo v Alonzo*, [2000] BCJ No 2389 (SC); *Barnett v Barnett*, [2001] PEIJ No 71 (SC).
422 *Tweel v Tweel*, [2000] PEIJ No 9 (SC).
423 *AWH v CGS*, [2007] NSJ No 262 (SC); *Brosteneants v Brosteneants*, [1999] OJ No 819 (Gen Div).
424 *Cavanaugh v Glass*, [2001] OJ No 457 (SCJ) (children aged fourteen and sixteen).
425 *Luedke v Luedke*, [2004] BCJ No 1157 (CA); *Larosa v Larosa*, [2003] MJ No 203 (QB); *JB v DM*, 2014 ONSC 7410.
426 *Dalgleish v Dalgleish*, [2003] OJ No 2918 (SCJ).
427 *McCrea v McCrea*, [1999] BCJ No 1514 (SC); *Thompson v Thompson*, [1999] SJ No 317 (QB).
428 *LFF v KG*, [2004] AJ No 493 (QB). See Chapter 11, Section I.
429 *Giammarco v Moccia*, [2005] OJ No 5506 (SCJ).

sources of funds available to partially satisfy the cost of education, or in the income of the parents.[430] Such a direction is not required, however, in order for variation to be sought.

Recent decisions dealing with the treatment of RESPs for child support purposes have held that where one parent has made post-separation contributions to the plan, it will not be included in child support calculations. Rather, it is viewed as a pre-payment of future obligations by the parent establishing the plan. To determine otherwise would eliminate any incentive for such plans to be established.[431]

A parent may be ordered to reimburse a child whose RESP or trust fund for post-secondary education has been misused or mismanaged by the parent[432] and pre-judgment interest may be ordered on the amount due.[433]

M. EXTRAORDINARY EXPENSES FOR EXTRACURRICULAR ACTIVITIES

Section 7(1)(f) of the *Federal Child Support Guidelines* confers a discretion on the court to provide for the payment of all or part of any extraordinary expenses for extracurricular activities.[434] In *Russell v Russell*, MacDonald J of the Nova Scotia Supreme Court states:

> I will comment upon the definition of the word extracurricular first. Dictionary definitions of this word refer to activities performed by students that fall outside the realm of the school curriculum but are supported by or are under the auspices of the school attended by the student. The dictionary meaning of this word does not include what I will refer to as recreational activities although many extracurricular activities are also recreational. This difference has not been noted as far as I have been able to determine by courts rendering decisions under section 7. Courts have interpreted the words "extracurricular activities" to include any type of recreational activity in which a child may be engaged whether it is under the auspices of their school or not. I have used this latter interpretation although I am not at all satisfied that those who passed or approved of the child support guidelines ignored the distinction between the word extracurricular and the word recreational.[435]

The fact that an expense relates to an extracurricular activity does not automatically bring the entire amount within section 7 because the basic child support under the applicable table is presumed to include an allowance for some extracurricular activities.[436] Where the parents'

---

430 *Davis v Davis*, [1999] BCJ No 1832 (SC).

431 *Foster v Amos*, 2010 SKQB 409. See also *Nykolyshyn v Dalton*, 2022 ABKB 860; *Pereverzoff v Pereverzoff*, 2017 BCSC 687. And see Chapter 11, Section I(3).

432 *Stones v Stones*, [2002] BCJ No 2521 (SC); *Regaudie v Thomas*, [2002] OJ No 2231 (SCJ).

433 *Regaudie v Thomas*, *ibid*. For excellent commentary on whether RESPs constitute property for the purpose of inter-spousal property division under provincial legislation, see Philip Epstein, "Epstein's This Week in Family Law," 6 September 2018 (Thomson Reuters), which examines *Elias v Elias*, 2018 CarswellOnt 10816, citing *McConnell v McConnell*, 2015 ONSC 2243 in light of *M(CS) v L(WS)*, 2015 CarswellBC 2674; *Barnes v Bates*, 2014 CarswellBC 1410 (BCSC); and *Sodhi v Sodhi*, 2014 BCSC 1622; see also *Labatte v Labatte*, 2022 ONSC 4787, discussed *sub nom L v L* in Franks & Zalev, "This Week in Family Law," 12 September 2022 (Thomson Reuters).

434 See Section A, above in this chapter.

435 2012 NSSC 258 at para 26.

436 *Laurie v Laurie*, 2002 BCCA 317 at para 5; *Lee v Chung*, 2011 BCSC 404; *MSD obo NC v AL*, 2022 NBQB 21.

income is relatively high, some extracurricular activities, even if they are expensive, may not qualify as extraordinary expenses. The same may not necessarily be true if the parents' income is at the lower end of the scale, because in those cases, the table amount of child support payable may only be sufficient to cover basic expenses.[437] A primary caregiving parent has an obligation to give notice to the other parent of extraordinary expenses expected to be incurred. If, having done so, the other parent unreasonably refuses to agree to share in the expenses, then the primary caregiving parent is quite justified in pursuing the other parent for contribution.[438]

Prior to an amendment of section 7 of the *Federal Child Support Guidelines*, which became effective on 1 May 2006, judicial opinions differed on the meaning to be assigned to the phrase "extraordinary expenses for extracurricular activities." Some courts asserted that the term "extraordinary" was to be construed objectively without regard to spousal incomes. On this interpretation, the words "extraordinary expenses for extracurricular activities" was given the plain meaning of "unusual" or "exceptional" expenses and a determination was made, not in light of parental income, but having regard to the nature of the activities and the nature or extent of the expenses. The respective spousal incomes only became relevant under this interpretation if the court found that the expenses were unusual and also necessary in the child's best interests, in which event the spousal incomes would be considered by the court in determining whether an amount, and what amount, should be ordered to be paid. Other courts adopted a subjective approach by concluding that the particular expenses must be unusual in their nature or amount when compared to those ordinarily incurred by a family of similar means in similar circumstances and the court had to consider the means of both of the parents and the children in making its determination. As was pointed out by the British Columbia Court of Appeal in *McLaughlin v McLaughlin*,[439] judicial controversy on the meaning of the phrase "extraordinary expenses for extracurricular activities" in section 7 of the *Federal Child Support Guidelines* was fuelled by the lack of direction in the Guidelines themselves. After an exhaustive review of conflicting appellate rulings, the British Columbia Court of Appeal favoured the subjective interpretation of section 7(1)(f) of the Guidelines by concluding that the court, in determining whether expenses fall within that section, should take into consideration such factors as the combined income of the parties, the nature and amount of individual expenses, the nature and number of activities, any special needs or talents of the children, and the overall cost of the activities.

In consequence of the lack of judicial consistency in defining "extraordinary expenses" under both section 7(1)(d) (extraordinary education expenses) and section 7(1)(f) (extraordinary expenses for extracurricular activities) of the *Federal Child Support Guidelines*, section 7 has been amended as of 1 May 2006 to include section 7(1.1), which sets out a specific definition of "extraordinary expenses."[440] The amendment mirrors the definition adopted in 2001 under the *Manitoba Child Support Guidelines*,[441] except with respect to who can

437 *Williams v Steinwand*, 2014 NWTSC 74 at para 82, Charbonneau J.

438 *ZDD v RCG*, 2004 BCSC 1239 at para 31; *Lee v Chung*, 2011 BCSC 404.

439 [1998] BCJ No 2514 (CA).

440 SOR/2005-400, s 1, 28 November 2005, *Canada Gazette*, Vol 139, No 25, 14 December 2005.

441 See *Correia v Correia*, [2002] MJ No 248 (QB); *Laurie v Laurie*, [2004] MJ No 87 (QB); *KEK v LEL*, 2010 MBQB 266; *Gard v Gard*, 2013 MBQB 128; *Bishop v Bishop*, 2017 MBQB 97.

apply for relief. While under the *Federal Child Support Guidelines* either spouse can seek an amount for special or extraordinary expenses, under the *Manitoba Child Support Guidelines* only the parent with final decision-making authority respecting the child's education and activities can do so.[442] Both the federal and the Manitoba Guidelines provide a two-part definition. First, pursuant to section 7(1.1)(a), expenses are extraordinary if they "exceed those that the spouse requesting an amount for the extraordinary expenses can reasonably cover." This is determined having regard to the income of the requesting spouse as well as any child support received. This element of the definition relates to the requesting spouse's ability to pay for the expenses. If the expenses exceed those that the requesting spouse can reasonably cover, they are extraordinary. The tests of necessity and reasonableness set out in section 7(1) of the Guidelines continue to apply to extraordinary expenses under sections 7(1)(d) and 7(1)(f). Where section 7(1.1)(a) does not apply (because the expense does not exceed the amount that the requesting spouse can reasonably cover), the second part of the definition, set out in section 7(1.1)(b), applies. Section 7(1.1)(b) directs the court to determine whether the expenses are extraordinary having regard to the following five factors:

1) the amount of the expense in relation to the income of the spouse requesting the amount (including the child support amount)
2) the nature and number of the educational programs and extracurricular activities
3) any special needs and talents of the child or children
4) the overall costs of the programs and activities
5) any other similar factor that the court considers relevant[443]

These factors largely correspond to those in *McLaughlin v McLaughlin*.[444] Only if the court concludes that an expense is extraordinary will the court turn its attention to the additional requirements of necessity and reasonableness within the meaning of section 7(1) of the *Federal Child Support Guidelines*.[445]

In *Staples v Callender*,[446] the Nova Scotia Court of Appeal rejected the trial judge's suggestion that extracurricular sports activities must be at an "almost elite level" in order to warrant consideration as section 7 expenses. It concluded that this was not consistent with the requirements of section 7(1)(f) and section 7(1A)(a) of the Guidelines. Each case requires a fact specific analysis.

It is impossible to list specific categories of expenses as falling within the ambit of section 7(1)(f) of the Guidelines. An assessment of the particular facts by the trial judge is of primary importance and an appellate court should not substitute its own discretion for that of the trial judge where there is no demonstrated error of law.[447]

---

442 *JSG v MFG*, 2011 MBQB 177.

443 See *CLE v BMR*, 2010 ABCA 187; *LAM v SCM*, 2020 BCSC 67; *Bishop v Bishop*, 2017 MBQB 97; *LM v TM*, 2012 NBQB 238; *Hiscock v Hiscock*, 2014 NLTD(F) 14; *LKS v DMCT*, 2008 NSCA 61; *Muise v Fox*, 2013 NSSC 349; *Ward v Ward*, 2015 ONSC 6221; *JC v CS*, 2009 PESC 8; *Gaspers v Gaspers*, 2008 SKCA 94; *Hennenfent v Loftsgard*, 2015 SKQB 289. And see Professor Rollie Thompson, "The Chemistry of Support: The Interaction of Child and Spousal Support" (2006) 25 *Canadian Family Law Quarterly* 251.

444 [1998] BCJ No 2514 (CA). See also *SJP v CAP*, 2010 BCSC 1426; *LAM v SCM*, 2020 BCSC 67.

445 *AM v GM*, 2018 BCSC 942; *Chambers v Chambers*, 2004 MBQB 239; *Gard v Gard*, 2013 MBQB 128.

446 2010 NSCA 49.

447 *Barker v Barker*, [2005] BCJ No 687 (CA); *Kofoed v Fichter*, [1998] SJ No 338 (CA).

Although the table amounts of child support under the *Federal Child Support Guidelines* apparently include some allowance for expenditures incurred for the extracurricular activities of children, there is no readily available information to indicate what portion of the applicable table amount is allocated to meet these expenses. Accordingly, courts lack any clear guidance as to when expenses for extracurricular activities are ordinary and when they are extraordinary. As Veit J of the Alberta Court of Queen's Bench observed in *MacIntosh v MacIntosh*, "it would be helpful if some guideline, based perhaps on a percentage of the total income of the parents, could help identify which extracurricular activities belong in the 'extraordinary' category."[448] Given the absence of any such guidance, there is a substantial lack of consistency in the judicial disposition of applications for extraordinary expenses for extracurricular activities under section 7(1)(f) of the *Federal Child Support Guidelines*, but modest expenses arising from a child's participation in extracurricular activities are covered by basic child support.[449]

Section 7 of the Guidelines places an onus on a parent who seeks expenses for the children's extracurricular activities to establish why those expenses should be allowed. Such expenses should not be added as a matter of course.[450]

Section 7(1)(f) of the *Federal Child Support Guidelines* applies only to extracurricular activities; a family vacation is not an extracurricular activity[451] but a summer camp for the children may qualify.[452]

Not all expenses for extracurricular activities will qualify for sharing between the spouses or former spouses. Such expenses must be "extraordinary" in order to qualify under section 7 of the *Federal Child Support Guidelines.*[453] Basic expenses, such as the costs of registration in a community sports league, or normal costs commonly associated with sport, such as the purchase of ordinary equipment and minimal travel costs are not extraordinary expenses and should be discounted from any exceptional expenses.[454] A sports expense becomes "extraordinary" and is therefore capable of requiring a section 7 analysis if it is an expense that goes beyond what could reasonably be expected to be covered within the confines of the normal table amount of child support.[455] A child's pursuit of a sporting career may be an important consideration where extra expenses are thereby generated.[456] In determining whether a child support order should provide for an amount to cover all or some extraordinary expenses for extracurricular activities, the court takes into account the necessity of the expense in relation to the child's best interests and the reasonableness of the expense, having regard to the current means of the spouses and those of the child and to the family's spending pattern

448 [2003] AJ No 728 at para 42 (QB). Compare *Simpson v Trowsdale*, [2007] PEIJ No 7 (TD); *DA(R)A v DJR* [2008] PEIJ No 20 (TD), wherein a formula was judicially proposed and implemented.

449 *Craig v Niro*, 2022 ONSC 5178 at para 45.

450 *LM v TM*, 2012 NBQB 238; *Aucoin v Aucoin*, [2002] PEIJ No 13 (SC).

451 *Arnold v Washburn*, [2001] OJ No 4996 (CA).

452 *Levesque v Meade*, 2010 NBQB 270.

453 *CLE v BMR*, 2010 ABCA 187; *EDM v JCDM*, [2007] BCJ No 2644 (SC); *MSD obo NC v AL*, 2022 NBQB 21; *Pitcher v Pitcher*, [2002] NJ No 358 (UFC); *Park v Thompson*, [2005] OJ No 1695 (CA); *Kofoed v Fichter*, [1998] SJ No 338 (CA).

454 *WL v RW*, [2005] NBJ No 470 (QB); *LM v TM*, 2012 NBQB 238; *MSD obo NC v AL*, 2022 NBQB 21; *Olaveson v Olaveson*, [2007] OJ No 2431 (SCJ); *Bear v Thomson*, 2013 SKQB 270.

455 *Richer v Freeland*, 2019 ONSC 6840 at para 27, Kurke J.

456 *WL v RW*, [2005] NBJ No 470 (QB).

prior to the separation.[457] When expenses are anticipated but not incurred, the claim for such expenses may be dismissed as premature, although a court may accept a reliable estimate of anticipated expenses to expedite the process and avoid further legal costs.[458]

A court should not apply its personal values in determining whether an expense is extraordinary. The standard of living during cohabitation should be considered in addition to the other considerations defined by section 7 of the *Federal Child Support Guidelines*.[459]

The cumulative total of expenses incurred for the children's extracurricular activities may render the expenses extraordinary; even though the expenses relating to any single activity would not be regarded as extraordinary.[460] Some expenses for extracurricular activities may be extraordinary; others may not.[461] Having regard to the fact that the table amount of child support builds in a certain amount for extracurricular expenses,[462] the norm for what are ordinary expenses increases as the family income increases;[463] ordinary expenses for a family income of $30,000 are less than what is normal for a family income of $60,000.[464] It may be difficult to determine where ordinary expenses for extracurricular activities end and extraordinary expenses begin, but the court must make that determination based on the facts of each particular case.[465] To the extent that extracurricular expenses are found to be extraordinary the court still retains a discretion whether to order any contribution to be paid, having regard to the necessity of the expenses and their reasonableness as defined in section 7 of the *Federal Child Support Guidelines*.[466] In most middle income families, standard expenses for extracurricular activities are ordinary and covered by the applicable table amount. The same expenses for a low income family would be extraordinary because the applicable table amount of child support would be required to meet basic needs.[467] In *Nixon v Nixon*, Wilkinson J of the Saskatchewan Court of Queen's Bench opined that Statistics Canada data on average recreational expenditures by household by province may serve as a barometer of what might be considered reasonable spending on extracurricular activities.[468]

If expenses are found to be extraordinary, the court must then determine whether they are necessary and reasonable under section 7(1) of the *Federal Child Support Guidelines*. In addressing the reasonableness of extraordinary expenses, the court has regard to the means

---

457 *Trueman v Trueman*, [2000] AJ No 1301 (QB); *EDM v JCDM*, [2007] BCJ No 2644 (SC); *WL v RW*, [2005] NBJ No 470 (QB); *Myers v Myers*, [2000] NSJ No 367 (SC); *Hulley v Carroll*, [2007] OJ No 4820 (SCJ); *Bear v Thomson*, 2013 SKQB 270.

458 *Trueman v Trueman*, [2000] AJ No 1301 (QB); *MSD obo NC v AL*, 2022 NBQB 21.

459 *Gray v Gray*, [1998] OJ No 2291 (Gen Div).

460 *MacLellan v MacLellan*, [1998] NSJ No 349 (TD); *Bear v Thomson*, 2013 SKQB 270; compare *MacEachern v MacEachern*, [1999] NSJ No 62 (TD); *Anger v Anger*, [2004] OJ No 3422 (UFC). See also s 7(1.1)(b) of the *Federal Child Support Guidelines*, SOR/2005-400, 28 November 2005, s 1.

461 *Barker v Barker*, [2005] BCJ No 687 (CA); *Olaveson v Olaveson*, [2007] OJ No 2431 (SCJ); *Reynolds v Reynolds*, [1999] SJ No 7 (QB).

462 *Nataros v Nataros*, [1998] BCJ No 1417 (SC).

463 *Clegg v Downing*, [2004] AJ No 1511 (QB); *Nataros v Nataros*, [1998] BCJ No 1417 (SC); *Yeo v Yeo*, [1998] PEIJ No 100 (SCTD).

464 *Campbell v Martijn*, [1998] PEIJ No 33 (SC).

465 *Nataros v Nataros*, [1998] BCJ No 1417 (SC).

466 *Nataros v Nataros, ibid; JC v MC*, 2014 NBQB 161.

467 *Trueman v Trueman*, [2000] AJ No 1301 (QB); *DiPasquale v DiPasquale*, [1998] NWTJ No 58 (SC); *Nitkin v Nitkin*, [2006] OJ No 2769 (SCJ).

468 2014 SKQB 264 at para 44, citing "Spending Patterns in Canada, Table 2," online: www.statcan.gc.ca.

of the parents and the child. This is a financial question and fairness does not enter into the analysis until the court has determined that the extraordinary expenses are reasonable. Given such a finding, the court will then determine whether it is fair to order payment of all or some portion of the expenses. In this context, it is appropriate for the court to consider whether the activity was encouraged by both parents and whether there was consultation between the parents before the expenses were incurred. Where a sperm donor father has had no relationship with his fifteen-year-old daughter since her birth, a court may find it unfair to require him to contribute retroactively to expenses incurred by the mother in promoting the child's wish to become a champion skater but a contribution to future expenses may be deemed fair after the mother's claim for such expenses has been brought to the father's attention. In assessing the expenses connected with out-of-town competitions, the court may take account of travelling expenses incurred by the mother where it would be inappropriate for the child to travel and stay alone.[469]

Extraordinary expenses for extracurricular activities include expenses for recreational activities as well as expenses related to a child's special talents.[470] Evidence of a special talent in a sport can be established through the evidence of a parent.[471] Even if a child is extremely talented, an order for a contribution to the extraordinary expenses of that activity will be denied where the cost is not reasonable in light of the modest means of the parents.[472]

"Extracurricular" activities are those activities that fall outside the scope of the child's program of education.[473] Extracurricular activities encompass activities that lie outside regular school and are not confined to education in a narrow sense.[474] They may be defined as activities that fall outside the regular or normal school curriculum or that fall outside one's regular duties or routines.[475] The determination of whether a particular extracurricular activity falls within section 7(1)(f) of the *Federal Child Support Guidelines* depends on the circumstances of each case.[476] Extraordinary expenses for extracurricular activities involve expenditures above and beyond those connected with average day-to-day activities.[477]

The test of necessity relates to the best interests of the child and is not one of strict necessity;[478] money spent on a child will usually benefit that child and thereby satisfy the necessity criterion imposed by section 7(1) of the Guidelines.[479] A child does not require any special talent for an activity's expenses to qualify as necessary.[480] Expenses may be deemed neces

---

469 *Clegg v Downing*, [2004] AJ No 1511 (QB).

470 *Middleton v MacPherson*, [1997] AJ No 614 (QB); *Ebrahim v Ebrahim*, [1997] BCJ No 2039 (SC); *Cox v Cox*, [1999] NJ No 242 (UFC); *Racette v Gamauf*, [1997] PEIJ No 123 (TD).

471 *KAMR v WHG*, 2014 BCSC 103 at para 50, Punnett J.

472 *Bland v Bland*, [1999] AJ No 344 (QB); *LM v TM*, 2012 NBQB 238. Compare *Strickland v Strickland*, [1998] OJ No 5869 (Gen Div) (interim order for contribution to extremely high costs of teenage Olympic hopeful; fixed-term order; payment conditioned upon other parent's undertaking to reimburse payor for one-half of mortgage payments and municipal taxes on matrimonial home).

473 *Ibid.*

474 *Ibid.*

475 *Omah-Maharajh v Howard*, [1998] AJ No 173 (QB); *LM v TM*, 2012 NBQB 238.

476 *Ibid.*

477 *MSD obo NC v AL*, 2022 NBQB 21; *Bergman-Illnik v Illnik*, [1997] NWTJ No 93 (SC).

478 *Omah-Maharajh v Howard*, [1998] AJ No 173 (QB); as to relevant considerations, see *Russell v Russell* 2012 NSSC 258 at para 27; *MacNeil v MacNeil*, 2013 ONSC 7012.

479 *Trueman v Trueman*, [2000] AJ No 1301 (QB).

480 *Omah-Maharajh v Howard*, [1998] AJ No 173 (QB); *Raftus v Raftus*, [1998] NSJ No 119 (CA).

sary when they relate to activities, such as sports, that aid in the development of a child's character and health to their full potential.[481] As MacDonald J of the Nova Scotia Supreme Court observed in *Pilotte v Pilotte*:

> As is the case with all "best interest" decisions, everything will be determined based upon the information provided about the child, his or her character, interests, strengths, weaknesses, challenges, and previous and present involvement in extracurricular activities; and about the family, how decisions about these activities were made in the past and presently, the support each parent provided and will provide to permit and encourage the child's participation, and whether the activities may impede a child's opportunity to develop a relationship with a parent.[482]

The issue of whether expenses are reasonable, given the means of the spouses and those of the child and the family's established spending pattern before separation, will depend on the circumstances of the particular case.[483] New post-separation activities are not precluded,[484] although they should be carefully scrutinized in the court's determination whether the expenses are reasonable in the absence of similar expenses prior to the spousal separation.[485] New activities often arise as a matter of course as children grow older[486] or where the children were very young when their parents separated.[487] Care must be exercised to ensure that expenses for extracurricular activities do not become automatic "add-ons" to the basic provincial table amount of child support.[488] Having regard to the means of the parents, a court may conclude that it should disallow the expenses sought because it would be more reasonable for the parents to find less costly extracurricular activities for their children.[489] It is not open to a parent to select any activity, regardless of cost, and then demand that the other parent contribute to the cost.[490] Neither parent has a *carte blanche* to enrol a child in an activity and then demand an automatic contribution to the cost from the other parent.[491] Neither parent has the right to impose excessive demands on the other parent respecting extraordinary expenses for extracurricular activities; such expenses must satisfy the threshold tests of necessity and reasonableness.[492] A court may allow some but not all of the extraordinary expenses claimed for extracurricular activities, having regard to their reasonableness in

481 *DiPasquale v DiPasquale*, [1998] NWTJ No 58 (SC); *MacNeil v MacNeil*, 2013 ONSC 7012; *Yeo v Yeo*, [1998] PEIJ No 100 (SCTD).

482 2013 NSSC 24 at para 50.

483 *Omah-Maharajh v Howard*, [1998] AJ No 173 (QB); *Morrissette v Ball*, [2000] BCJ No 73 (SC); *DiPasquale v DiPasquale*, [1998] NWTJ No 58 (SC).

484 *Campbell v Martijn*, [1998] PEIJ No 33 (TD) (spousal separation fifteen years previously).

485 *Omah-Maharajh v Howard*, [1998] AJ No 173 (QB).

486 *Omah-Maharajh v Howard, ibid*; *Doherty v Doherty*, [2001] OJ No 2400 (SCJ).

487 *Trueman v Trueman*, [2000] AJ No 1301 (QB).

488 *Hedderson v Kearsey*, [1998] NJ No 62 (SC).

489 *Miller v Hayduk*, [1998] SJ No 465 (QB); *Guillet v Guillet*, [1999] SJ No 266 (QB) (extracurricular expenses denied because of "meagre financial resources").

490 *Trueman v Trueman*, [2000] AJ No 1301 (QB); *Piller v Piller*, [1998] NJ No 179 (SC); *Waller v Waller*, [1998] OJ No 5387 (Gen Div).

491 *DiPasquale v DiPasquale*, [1998] NWTJ No 58 (SC).

492 *Ackland v Brooks*, [2001] BCJ No 1733 (SC); *Thomson v Howard*, [1997] OJ No 4431 (Gen Div); *MDL v CR*, 2020 SKCA 44.

light of the means of the spouses or former spouses,[493] or it may deny all of them.[494] Each case must be decided on its own merits. For example, there may be a greater need for extracurricular activities in a relatively small urban environment or in a remote environment where there are limited resources available to children.[495]

The wishes of the children will not justify an order under section 7 of the *Federal Child Support Guidelines* where no corresponding family spending pattern existed before the spousal separation.[496] The family's pre-separation spending pattern may have little or no evidential value, however, where the separation occurred several years before the application for such expenses was brought, or where the children's interests and talents change as they grow older,[497] or there may be the present means to provide for extraordinary expenses that would not have been consistent with the family's pre-separation spending pattern.[498] court should treat all children of the marriage fairly in allocating extraordinary expenses for extracurricular activities, although it may take account of their differing needs.[499] A court is not required to apportion parental expenses equally between the children. Their respective situations may require the court to independently assess the needs of each child, as for example, where one of the children has special talents or special needs.[500]

A court may seek to encourage extracurricular activities for children who are traumatized by divorce where the expenses associated with the activities are legitimate and affordable.

Where the parties cannot agree on the extent to which they should support a child's extracurricular activities, the court may cap the obligor's maximum contribution at a designated amount.[502]

A court may grant an interim order for the payment of extraordinary expenses for extracurricular activities, notwithstanding that the spouses will need to address the question of whether or not they can continue to offer these extracurricular activities to their children.

A claim for extraordinary expenses for extracurricular activities may be denied where no evidence has been adduced as to the costs involved.[504] Where future costs are uncertain but will be incurred, the court may grant an order for reimbursement of all or part of those costs upon the production of an invoice or receipt.[505]

---

493 *Kinasewich v Kinasewich*, [1997] AJ No 1220 (QB); *GR v TR*, [2005] BCJ No 1496 (SC); *Addison v Schneider*, [1999] MJ No 300 (QB); *MacLellan v MacLellan*, [1998] NSJ No 349 (TD); *Bergman-Illnik v Illnik*, [1997] NWTJ No 93 (SC); *Pepin v Jung*, [1997] OJ No 4604 (Gen Div); *El Ouazzani v Chabini*, 2022 ONSC 5773; *Walker-Bodnarek v Bodnarek*, [2005] SJ No 658 (QB) (financial cap imposed).

494 *Dennison v Kubic*, [2003] BCJ No 461 (SC); *Bowering v Bowering*, [1998] NJ No 305 (SC); *Strickland v Strickland*, [1999] OJ No 2293 (SCJ) (priority accorded to costs of post-secondary education over high costs of competitive skating at elite level).

495 *Bergman-Illnik v Illnik*, [1997] NWTJ No 93 (SC).

496 *Vecchioli v Vecchioli*, [1999] AJ No 799 (QB).

497 *Salo v Boguist*, [1998] OJ No 5786 (Gen Div); *Racette v Gamauf*, [1997] PEIJ No 123 (TD).

498 *Meuser v Meuser*, [1998] BCJ No 1614 (SC), var'd [1998] BCJ No 2808 (CA).

499 *Massler v Massler*, [1999] AJ No 206 (QB).

500 *Fransoo v Fransoo*, [2001] SJ No 121 (QB).

501 *Godfrey-Smith v Godfrey-Smith*, [1997] NSJ No 544 (TD); see also *MDL v CR*, 2020 SKCA 44.

502 *DJE v PAE*, 2014 ABCA 403; *Carrothers v Carrothers*, [1997] BCJ No 1535 (SC); *LM v TM*, 2012 NBQB 238; *Magee v Faveri*, [2007] OJ No 4826 (SCJ).

503 *Bially v Bially*, [1997] SJ No 352 (QB).

504 *Acorn v DeRoche*, [1997] PEIJ No 82 (TD).

505 *Racette v Gamauf*, [1997] PEIJ No 123 (TD); *Krislock v Krislock*, [1997] SJ No 698 (QB).

A court may estimate special or extraordinary expenses likely to be incurred but an evidentiary foundation must be laid in order for the court to do so.[506] As Kirchner J of the Supreme Court of British Columbia noted in *Galloway v Galloway*, "[c]ourts have shown a certain amount of flexibility in the level of detail needed for such estimates" and "have generally been prepared to work with rough budget amounts, or budgets lacking significant detail, so long as they are able to determine the reasonable costs of the child."[507]

A primary caregiving parent should not be disproportionately compensated with respect to extraordinary expenses for extracurricular activities arising from the other parent's non-exercise of parenting time where the primary caregiving parent contributed to this state of affairs.[508]

High costs relating to country club membership and activities may constitute extraordinary expenses for extracurricular activities within the meaning of section 7 of the *Federal Child Support Guidelines*, having regard to the pre-separation family lifestyle and the current incomes and assets of the spouses.[509]

A court may find that a parent is unable to afford any contribution towards the children's expenses relating to their extracurricular activities, having regard to his or her obligation to pay the applicable table amount of child support and the priority that must be accorded to his or her obligation to contribute towards necessary child care, special needs educational expenses, and the children's health and dental expenses.[510] A parent is not entitled to run up high expenses for the children's extracurricular activities and then plead an inability to contribute to more critical basic expenses that fall within the ambit of section 7 of the *Federal Child Support Guidelines*.[511] Expenses for recreational activities should take a back seat to counselling costs associated with re-establishing parenting time with an alienated child with the aid of a highly qualified therapist.[512]

In order to avoid repeated applications, a court may devise a formula that the spouse may use as the basis for determining future child support payments in light of mandated disclosure relating to the previous year's expenses respecting extracurricular activities.[513]

Where parents agree to share extraordinary expenses for their child's extracurricular activities but disagree on the method of payment, the court may order each parent to make direct payment to the service provider in a timely way.[514]

---

506 *Price v Holman-Price*, 2014 NLTD(F) 30; *Lewis v Carlson-Lewis*, [2001] SJ No 117 (QB).
507 *Galloway v Galloway*, 2022 BCSC 10 at para 26
508 *Stanbridge v Stanbridge*, [1998] BCJ No 193 (SC).
509 *Greenwood v Greenwood*, [1998] BCJ No 729 (SC).
510 *Hudson v Klassen*, [2005] SJ No 167 (QB); see also *Stuart v Multan*, 2006 MBQB 238.
511 *Lavoie v Wills*, [2000] AJ No 1359 (QB).
512 *Lewis v Lewis*, [2000] AJ No 556 (QB).
513 *Young v Young*, [1998] BCJ No 1120 (SC).
514 *Peters v Peters*, [1999] SJ No 392 (QB).

CHAPTER 6

Split and Shared Parenting Time Arrangements[1]

A. SECTION 8 OF THE GUIDELINES: SPLIT PARENTING TIME DUE TO SEPARATION OF SIBLINGS

Section 8 of the *Federal Child Support Guidelines* provides that if there are two or more children and each spouse has the majority of parenting time with one or more of those children,[2] the amount of a child support order is the difference between the amount that each would otherwise pay if a child support order were sought against each of the spouses.[3] Pursuant to section 2(1) of the *Federal Child Support Guidelines*, "majority of parenting time" means a period of time that is more than 60 percent of parenting time over the course of a year.[4] Given possible future changes in the parental incomes, parents may be judicially directed to exchange complete copies of their income tax returns by 15 May of each year.[5] Where the parents earn the same income and each is responsible for the support of a child of the marriage, the court may decline to make any order for child support[6] and the section 7 expenses may be ordered to be shared equally.[7] The language of section 8 of the Guidelines suggests that a parent who intends

1 See *Guidelines Amending the Federal Child Support Guidelines*, SOR/2020-247, 23 November 2020; *Canada Gazette*, Part II, Volume 154, Number 25.

2 See, generally, Carol Rogerson, "Child Support Under the Guidelines in Cases of Split and Shared Custody" (1998) 15 *Canadian Journal of Family Law* 11; see also Kim Hart Wensley, "Shared Custody — Section 9 of the *Federal Child Support Guidelines*: Formulaic? Pure Discretion? Structured Discretion?" (2004) 23 *Canadian Journal of Family Law* 63.

3 *LDW v KDM*, 2011 ABQB 384 (conjoint operation of ss 8 and 9 of *Federal Child Support Guidelines*); *SEH v SRM*, [1999] BCJ No 1458 (SC) (split time-sharing involving biological child and stepchild; set-off under s 8 of *Federal Child Support Guidelines*); *Pozzolo v Pozzolo*, 2020 BCCA 281; *TM v DM*, 2014 NBQB 132; *Fitzpatrick v Fitzpatrick*, [2000] NJ No 62 (UFC); *Tran v Tran*, 2013 NSSC 280; *Bergman-Illnik v Illnik*, [1997] NWTJ No 93 (SC); *Monahan-Joudrey v Joudrey*, 2012 ONSC 5984; *MacLean v MacLean*, [2003] PEIJ No 16 (TD); *Agioritis v Agioritis*, 2011 SKQB 257. Compare *Dudka v Dudka*, [1997] NSJ No 526 (TD).

4 See *Guidelines Amending the Federal Child Support Guidelines*, SOR/2020-247, 23 November 2020; *Canada Gazette*, Part II, Volume 154, Number 25.

5 *Hladun v Hladun*, [2002] SJ No 476 (QB).

6 *Cram v Cram*, [1999] BCJ No 2518 (SC).

7 *Pretty v Pretty*, 2011 NSSC 296.

to invoke the section should be seeking support for the child in his or her care from the other parent.[8] Bilateral orders may be granted for child support where each parent has primary care of one or more children of the marriage.[9] Section 8 of the *Federal Child Support Guidelines,* unlike section 9, provides no judicial discretion in the assessment of child support.[10]

Section 8 of the Guidelines cannot be invoked by a respondent with respect to children of a previous marriage, where insufficient evidence is adduced to establish a *prima facie* case that the applicant stood in the place of a parent to those children.[11]

Section 8 of the *Federal Child Support Guidelines* may be applied where each of the parents provides a home for one or more of their dependent children, even though one of the children is an adult attending university.[12] Section 8 of the Guidelines will not be satisfied, however, where the evidence is insufficient to establish that the adult child is a "child of the marriage" within the meaning of the *Divorce Act.*[13] Pursuant to section 3(2)(b) of the *Federal Child Support Guidelines,* a trial judge may be justified in deviating from the applicable table amount because one of the children is over the age of provincial majority and is not totally dependent on either parent.[14] Pursuant to section 17(6.2) of the *Divorce Act,* a court may order the differential between the two table amounts to be paid for only ten months of the year, so as to maintain conformity with the ten months' pattern established by the divorce judgment.[15]

There have been cases wherein a court has increased the normally applicable amount payable in cases of split primary care of the children under section 8 of the *Federal Child Support Guidelines* because a child would be required to live frugally in one parental household, while enjoying a luxurious lifestyle in the other parental household.[16] Deviation from the amount normally payable under section 8 is usually encountered in extraordinary cases, where there are grossly disparate lifestyles.[17] In the absence of a finding of undue hardship, however, section 8 of the Guidelines provides no residual discretion to the court to deviate from the differential between the two table amounts, as articulated in that section.[18] A significant disparity in the lifestyles in the two households may be addressed, however, by an order for spousal support or a variation order for increased spousal support.[19] Although there may be little difference from an economic standpoint between split parenting time arrangements under section 8 of the Guidelines and shared parenting time arrangements under section 9

8 *Tanner v Simpson,* [1999] NWTJ No 71 (SC).

9 *Holman v Bignell,* [2000] OJ No 3405 (SCJ).

10 *Wright v Wright,* [2002] BCJ No 458 (SC); *Kavanagh v Kavanagh,* [1999] NJ No 358 (SC). And see *Pozzolo v Pozzolo,* 2020 BCCA 281.

11 *Auckland v McKnight,* [1999] SJ No 652 (QB).

12 *Khoee-Solomonescu v Solomonescu,* [1997] OJ No 4876 (Gen Div); see also *Sutcliffe v Sutcliffe,* [2001] AJ No 629 (QB); *Davis v Davis,* [1999] BCJ No 1832 (SC); *Kavanagh v Kavanagh,* [1999] NJ No 358 (SC); *Bauer v Noonan,* [2005] SJ No 616 (QB).

13 *Tanner v Simpson,* [1999] NWTJ No 71 (SC).

14 *Richardson v Richardson,* [1997] OJ No 2795 (Gen Div); see also *Alexander v Alexander,* [1999] OJ No 3694 (SCJ).

15 *Waller v Waller,* [1998] OJ No 5387 (Gen Div); compare *Ellis v Ellis,* [1997] PEIJ No 119 (TD); Section B, below in this chapter.

16 *Scharf v Scharf,* [1998] OJ No 199 (Gen Div); see also *Snyder v Snyder,* [1999] NBJ No 32 (QB); *Farmer v Conway,* [1998] NSJ No 536 (TD).

17 *Plante v Plante,* [1998] AJ No 1206 (QB); *Inglis v Birkbeck,* [2000] SJ No 227 (QB).

18 *Horner v Horner,* [2004] OJ No 4268 (CA); *KO v CO,* [1999] SJ No 29 (QB).

19 *Aschenbrenner v Aschenbrenner,* [2000] BCJ No 1950 (SC).

of the Guidelines, the broad discretion conferred on the court by section 9 is not mirrored in the provisions of section 8, in the absence of an intermingling of split and shared parenting time arrangements involving the same family.

The application of section 8 of the Guidelines may result in an order that falls short of equalizing the children's lifestyles.[20]

A court may refuse to interfere with a spousal agreement that pre-dated implementation of the *Federal Child Support Guidelines*, where the children are living under a split parenting time arrangement and the application of the Guidelines would leave the mother in desperate financial straits.[21] A court may also take account of a post-Guidelines agreement in calculating the appropriate set-off to be made, where one of the children goes to live with the payor after the execution of the agreement that provided for higher amounts of child support than would have been payable under the Guidelines.[22]

The undue hardship provisions of section 10 of the *Federal Child Support Guidelines* apply to split parenting time arrangements falling within section 8 of the Guidelines.[23] Section 8 of the *Federal Child Support Guidelines* may generate an unfair advantage for the higher income earning spouse insofar as the differential in the table amounts that is payable to the lower income spouse may be less than the support that the lower income earning spouse is required to contribute for the child in the higher income home. Given these circumstances, a court may conclude that a finding of undue hardship is warranted under section 10 of the Guidelines.[24] Section 10(2)(d) of the Guidelines has no application to a case of split parenting time arrangements, if the child in question is a "child of the marriage" within the meaning of section 2 of the *Divorce Act*.[25]

Where each parent has the majority of parenting time with one or more of the children but the income of one of the parents falls short of the minimum threshold under the applicable provincial table, the other parent will be required to pay the full table amount of support for the child in the primary care of the low- or no-income parent.[26]

In addition to ordering payment of the differential between the two table amounts pursuant to section 8 of the *Federal Child Support Guidelines*, a court may order a sharing of special or extraordinary expenses under section 7 of the Guidelines in proportion to the respective parental incomes,[27] or in such other proportion as the court deems reasonable.[28]

A court may refuse to apply section 8 of the *Federal Child Support Guidelines* so as to reduce the amount of support payable where no satisfactory evidence is adduced concerning the respondent's income.[29]

---

20 *Kendry v Cathcart*, [2001] OJ No 277 (SCJ).

21 *Barker v Barker*, [1999] BCJ No 2020 (SC).

22 *Stevens v Stevens*, [1999] AJ No 1550 (QB); compare *Park v Park*, [1999] OJ No 5078 (SCJ).

23 *Schaan v Schaan*, [2000] BCJ No 61 (SC).

24 *MacLeod v Druhan*, [1997] NSJ No 573 (Fam Ct).

25 *Schmid v Smith*, [1999] OJ No 3062 (SCJ).

26 *Estey v Estey*, [1999] NSJ No 226 (SC); *Fraser v Gallant*, [2004] PEIJ No 5 (SC); *Hamonic v Gronvold*, [1999] SJ No 32 (QB). Compare *KO v CO*, [1999] SJ No 29 (QB).

27 *LDW v KDM*, 2011 ABQB 384; *Patrick v Patrick*, [1999] BCJ No 1245 (SC); *Tran v Tran*, 2013 NSSC 280; *Sayong v Aindow*, [1999] NWTJ No 63 (SC); *Fraser v Fraser*, [2001] OJ No 3765 (SCJ); *Fransoo v Fransoo*, [2001] SJ No 121 (QB).

28 Compare *Tooth v Knott*, [1998] AJ No 1395 (QB); see Section B(2), below in this chapter.

29 *Pitura v Pitura*, [1999] NWTJ No 70 (SC).

B. SECTION 9 OF THE GUIDELINES: SHARED PARENTING TIME; 40 PERCENT RULE

1) Basic Provisions of Section 9 of the Guidelines

Section 9 of the *Federal Child Support Guidelines* provides that if each spouse exercises not less than 40 percent of parenting time with a child over the course of a year, the amount of the child support order must be determined by taking into account

a) the amounts set out in the applicable tables for each of the spouses or former spouses;
b) the increased costs of shared parenting time arrangements; and
c) the conditions, means, needs, and other circumstances of each spouse or former spouse and of any child for whom support is sought.[30]

The language of section 9 is imperative in that its provisions are to be applied if the 40 percent criterion is satisfied. A court has no discretion to depart from the 40 percent minimum threshold, although a discretion exists with respect to the quantification of child support under sections 9(a), (b), and (c) of the Guidelines. These criteria are conjunctive; they must all be considered if the 40 percent test has been satisfied.[31]

Although there are factors other than the parental incomes to be considered under section 9 of the *Federal Child Support Guidelines*, a court is not entitled to disregard the income that should be imputed to a parent.[32] It is also relevant to consider the assets and liabilities of each parent under section 9(c).[33]

It is important to lead evidence relating to sections 9(b) and 9(c) of the Guidelines.[34]

2) The 40 Percent Rule

The spouse who invokes section 9 of the Guidelines has the onus of proving that he or she cares for the child at least 40 percent of the time over the course of a year,[35] which is the equivalent of 146 days[36] or 3504 hours[37] of the year or an average of 67.2 hours per week.[38]

30 See *Guidelines Amending the Federal Child Support Guidelines*, SOR/2020-247, 23 November 2020; *Canada Gazette*, Part II, Volume 154, Number 25.

31 *Lee v Taggart*, 2015 BCSC 1959 (interim order); *Atte v Atte*, 2021 BCSC 133; *SAH v KAH*, 2022 NBCA 17; *HS v PW*, 2016 NLCA 67; *Costa v Petipas*, [2006] PEIJ No 39 (SC); *JAF v PU*, 2019 YKSC 68.

32 *Klassen v Morrow*, [2002] AJ No 909 (CA).

33 *Vlek v Graff*, 2013 BCSC 1906.

34 *Green v Green*, [2000] BCJ No 1001 (CA); *Vlek v Graff*, 2013 BCSC 1906; *Cabot v Mikkelson*, [2004] MJ No 240 (CA); *Slade v Slade*, [2001] NJ No 5 (CA); *Contino v Leonelli-Contino*, [2005] 3 SCR 217.

35 *Tooth v Knott*, [1998] AJ No 1395 (QB); *EG v DG*, 2022 ABCA 129 at para 8; *Caldwell v Caldwell*, 2011 BCSC 1019; *McGrath v McGrath*, [2006] NJ No 201 (UFC); *Gardiner v Gardiner*, [2007] NSJ No 367 (SC); *Gauthier v Hart*, 2011 ONSC 815; *LL v MC*, 2013 ONSC 1801; *MacNaught v MacNaught*, [1998] PEIJ No 27 (TD); *Holtzman v Holtzman*, 2011 SKQB 10.

36 *Handy v Handy*, [1999] BCJ No 6 (SC); *Hamm v Hamm*, [1998] NSJ No 139 (TD); *Gardiner v Gardiner*, [2007] NSJ No 367 (SC); *Yovcheva v Hristov*, 2022 ONSC 5284, citing *LL v MC*, 2013 ONSC 1801 at para 37.

37 *Ramachala (Holland) v Holland*, 2020 ABQB 432 at para 44; *Claxton v Jones*, [1999] BCJ No 3086 (Prov Ct); *Yovcheva v Hristov*, 2022 ONSC 5284; *Taccone v Taccone*, 2023 ONSC 1646.

38 *JF v GF*, 2016 NBQB 46.

In determining whether a parent has "not less than 40 percent of parenting time with a child over the course of a year" within the meaning of section 9 of the *Federal Child Support Guidelines*, some cases support an interpretation requiring twelve consecutive months and if they are not a calendar year, that they are at least neither random nor specifically selected in order to reach the threshold. Other cases show a willingness to consider any consecutive twelve-month period, past or future, providing there is logic to the period chosen.[39] In *Gosse v Sorensen-Gosse*,[40] Wells JA of the Newfoundland and Labrador Court of Appeal ventured the following opinion:

> There is nothing in the *Guidelines* to require application of the formula to a calendar year, or to a year determined on any other specific basis. I would conclude that the basis for determination of the time frame against which to measure the required percentage of [parenting time] would depend on the circumstances in each case, considered in the context of any compelling practicalities. One cannot imagine that the phrase "over the course of a year" was ever intended to have indeterminate beginning and ending times, depending on what one spouse or the other may wish to assert in the circumstances. Such an interpretation would invite confusion and abuse. As well, a calendar year is the normal basis for calculating the income of a spouse in order to determine the level of financial responsibility for child support. In the ordinary course, the phrase, "over the course of a year" should, absent compelling reason to do otherwise, be taken to mean over the course of a calendar year. In the case of shared [parenting time] beginning at some point during the year, that point must be the beginning point. Then, common sense and practicality would dictate that the initial period would end at the end of that calendar year and calendar years used thereafter, unless there was some compelling reason to use a year determined on a basis other than a calendar year.

It has been held that shared parenting need not have already existed for one year in order for section 9 of the Guidelines to be triggered.[41] All that is required is that the parenting arrangement has been in place for a sufficiently substantial period of time to enable the court to infer that it is expected to continue during the course of the year.[42] Although there may be times when the child is in a parent's primary care for more than 40 percent of the time over a specific period, section 9 of the Guidelines only applies where the threshold is or will be met "over the course of a year."[43] Section 9 applies to interim orders as well as permanent orders,[44] although an express reservation of the right of a trial judge to make an adjustment may be deemed appropriate. Shared parenting time may be minimal in some months while considerable in others, but it must average 40 percent of the time over the course of a year. The requirements of section 9 are not satisfied merely because a parent exceeds the 40 percent criterion over several months during a twelve-month period. Section 9 of the Guidelines does not entitle a parent to claim a rebate in payments of child support where

39 *Gauthier v Hart*, 2011 ONSC 815, MacKinnon J; *Ramachala (Holland) v Holland*, 2020 ABQB 432 at paras 39–41.

40 2011 NLCA 58 at para 126; see also *Morrissey v Morrissey*, 2015 PECA 16.

41 *Chickee v Chickee*, [2000] OJ No 2769 (SCJ); compare *Walsh v Walsh*, [2006] NJ No 33 (UFC).

42 *Gardiner v Gardiner*, [2007] NSJ No 367 (SC); *Haney v Haney*, [2005] OJ No 2329 (SCJ).

43 *ADJ v TDP*, 2017 BCSC 2360 at para 23.

44 *Chickee v Chickee*, [2000] OJ No 2769 (SCJ).

special circumstances involve a temporary increase in the time the children spend with that parent.[45] Where there is no formal written agreement or order in place, a court should exercise caution before applying section 9 of the Guidelines to what may be short-term parenting arrangements. An application may be deemed premature where no track record has been established.[46] Where a new parenting time schedule has been devised to reduce the stressful environment in which the children have been living, a court may adjourn an application to vary child support until the parenting regime has been in force for a minimum of six months, so that there will be a reliable record on which the court can determine the amount of time spent by the children with each parent and the application of section 9 of the Guidelines to that situation.[47]

There is no universally accepted method for determining whether a parent spent not less than 40 percent of parenting time with a child over the course of a year for the purpose of section 9 of the *Federal Child Support Guidelines*.[48] In *Froom v Froom*,[49] the trial judge found the 40 percent threshold met by counting days, not hours. Counsel for the father conceded that the 40 percent test would not have been met if hours, not days, had been counted. The majority judgment of the Ontario Court of Appeal refused to find any error on the part of the trial judge, having regard to the absence of any universally accepted method for determining the 40 percent threshold. The minority judgment would have allowed the appeal because the hours calculation was perceived as producing a more accurate figure in the circumstances of this particular case.[50]

The critical issue facing the Manitoba Court of Appeal in *Mehling v Mehling*[51] was the method for determining whether the 40 percent threshold under section 9 of the *Manitoba Child Support Guidelines* had been satisfied. Having acknowledged that courts have no discretionary authority to disregard the 40 percent threshold, Hamilton JA observed that judicial opinions have differed on how to determine whether that threshold has been met. Some courts have favoured a strictly mathematical approach that may even involve hourly calculations.[52] Other courts have placed emphasis on the functioning of the particular shared parenting time regime.[53] These differences of approach arise from the fact that the relevant criterion under section 9 of the Guidelines is the amount of time that the children are in the care and control of a parent, not the amount of time that the parent is physically

45 *B-JG v BD*, 2023 NBKB 30 at para 92; *Lussier v Lussier*, [2001] OJ No 169 (Ct J).

46 *Ibid.*

47 *Murphy v Murphy*, [1999] BCJ No 318 (SC).

48 *Ramachala (Holland) v Holland*, 2020 ABQB 432; *Maultsaid v Blair*, 2009 BCCA 102; *Lekakis v Lekakis*, 2023 BCSC 376; *Mehling v Mehling*, 2008 MBCA 66; *FM v TH*, 2016 NBCA 29 at para 20; *AA v JA*, 2023 NBKB 210; *Ransom v Coulter*, 2014 NWTSC 55; *Kerr v Pickering*, 2013 ONSC 317 at para 34, citing *Froom v Froom*, [2005] OJ No 507 (CA); *Clarke v Dowe*, 2016 ONSC 4773; *Nderitu v Kamoji*, 2017 ONSC 2617; *B (LD) v S (RN)*, 2019 PESC 44.

49 [2005] OJ No 507 (CA); see also *Quercia v Francioni*, 2011 ONSC 6844; compare *Paddon v Paddon*, [2006] NBJ No 1 at paras 37–42 (QB); *Taccone v Taccone*, 2023 ONSC 1646 at paras 37–38.

50 See also *Desjardins v Bouey*, 2013 ABQB 714; *Brougham v Brougham*, 2009 BCSC 897; *B(LD) v S (RN)*, 2019 PESC 44.

51 2008 MBCA 66, [2008] MJ No 172. See also *Yakimitz v Chorkwa*, 2013 ABQB 443; *Maultsaid v Blair*, 2009 BCCA 102; *Abbott v Meadus*, 2014 NBQB 18; *DA v SA*, 2017 SKQB 108.

52 *Jebb-Waples v Waples*, 2014 ABQB 26 (hourly calculation); *ADJ v TDP*, 2017 BCSC 2360; *Arlt v Arlt*, 2014 ONSC 2173.

53 *Ramachala (Holland) v Holland*, 2020 ABQB 432 at para 44.

present with the children.[54] After reviewing relevant appellate decisions from across Canada, the Manitoba Court of Appeal in *Mehling* favoured a functional approach, but concluded that a decision as to the proper approach falls within the discretion of the presiding judge. A non-exhaustive list of relevant factors to be considered in applying a functional approach is set out in the judgment. They include:

- the desirability of flexible parenting time schedules
- the stated desire of the children to spend additional time with the parent seeking to meet the 40 percent threshold
- who is responsible for the children while they are at school or in daycare
- who is responsible for meal preparation, including school lunches
- summer vacation and holiday arrangements
- whether parenting time has in fact been exercised in accordance with the governing agreement or court order

Speaking to this issue in *Ransom v Coulter*,[55] Vertes J of the Northwest Territories Supreme Court has stated:

> 14 It is I think an understatement to say that the imposition of the 40% threshold has been a contentious issue that has resulted in a proliferation of litigation over how to count that 40%. The predominant debate in the jurisprudence is whether the 40% should be considered in a holistic fashion, or if the courts should engage in a detailed time accounting exercise. And the jurisprudence offers little to no consensus. There is certainly no guidance from the Supreme Court of Canada on the issue.
>
> 15 In *Mehling v. Mehling*, [2008] M.J. No. 172 (C.A.), the Manitoba Court of Appeal reviewed reported decisions from across Canada and came to the conclusion that a flexible and holistic approach should be taken to calculating the 40% requirement. . . .
>
> 16 Similarly, appellate courts in British Columbia and Ontario have held that there is no universally accepted method for determining 40% but that it is necessary to avoid rigid calculations and consider whether parenting is truly shared: *Maultsaid v. Blaid* (2009), 78 R.F.L. (6th) 45 (B.C.C.A.); *Froom v. Froom* (2005), 11 R.F.L. (6th) 254 (Ont. C.A.).
>
> 17 However, many other cases have emphasized the unassailable fact that a calculation must still be done since the legislature has decreed that, before the shared parenting calculation can be applied, the court must be satisfied that a child spends not less than 40% of his or her time with the payor parent. So, even though many cases accept that a flexible and holistic approach should be taken, they still undertake a precise mathematical calculation of not just days but the hours that the payor parent has the child in his or her care. This has resulted in situations where a parent was found to have [parenting time with] the child for 39.6% or 39.3% of the time over the course of a year and therefore failing to meet the threshold: see, for example, *Gauthier v Hart* (2011), 100 R.F.L. (6th) 178 (Ont. S.C.J.); *Petterson v. Petterson* (2010), 92 R.F.L. (6th) 241 (Sask. Q.B.).
>
> 18 The Alberta Court of Appeal has made clear that, however the time is calculated, there must still be a calculation: *L.C. v. R.O.C.*, 2007 ABCA 158. "Deeming" that the 40

54 See *BNM v PJM*, 2017 SKQB 331; see also *Irvine v Beausoleil*, 2020 SKQB 281.

55 2014 NWTSC 55.

> percent threshold is met is not acceptable practice. As stated in that case (at para. 11): "For the purposes of calculating child support, the percentage allocation of [parenting] time must conform to the actual evidence on this point." …
>
> 26 … I agree with the cases that say that a court may assess child-parent time as meeting the 40% criterion without a tight accounting of hours and days. But there must be evidence whereby a court can reasonably conclude that the child spends such a sizeable percentage of time with the paying parent that the 40% level is achieved.[56]

Courts have encountered difficulty in determining whether the 40 percent criterion is satisfied.[57] The calculations may be undertaken on an hourly, daily, weekly, or monthly basis, or any combination of these, depending on the circumstances of the case.[58] However, as Hoegg JA of the Newfoundland and Labrador Court of Appeal observed in *HS v PW*, "[w]hile there may be some variation in how a court determines the 40 percent threshold, there must be a valid determination that the 40 percent threshold is met before a Judge has the discretion to depart from ordering the table amount of child support on this basis. This is not a debatable point in this jurisdiction or elsewhere in Canada."[59]

If the parent/child contact is less that 40 percent over the course of a year, the court is not burdened by the discretion arising under section 9 of the Guidelines[60] and a court may conclude that a short-term state of affairs that prevailed in the artificial climate developing during the spousal dispute cannot constitute the basis for a long-term decision.[61]

Some courts apply a presumption that the primary caregiving parent starts with 100 percent of the time, thus requiring the other parent to prove that he or she has had parenting time with the child for not less than 40 percent of the year.[62] But it is not the amount of time actually spent with that parent relative to the amount of time actually spent with the other parent that is relevant.[63] Time that a child spends sleeping or at school or daycare[64] or with a nanny or babysitter[65] is not to be ignored in determining whether a parent satisfies the requirements of section 9 of the Guidelines. Section 9 of the Guidelines may require the

---

56 See also *Hall v Zaidel*, 2017 BCSC 2045.

57 *Green v Green*, [2000] BCJ No 1001 (CA).

58 *LC v ROC*, 2007 ABCA 158; *Jebb-Waples v Waples*, 2014 ABQB 26 (hourly calculation); *ADP v TDP*, 2017 BCSC 2360 (hourly calculation); *Maultsaid v Blair*, 2009 BCCA 102; *Taccone v Taccone*, 2023 ONSC 1646 (hourly calculation); *B (LD) v S (RN)*, 2019 PESC 44 (hourly calculation); *Jarocki v Rice*, [2003] SJ No 178 (QB); compare *Anderson v Anderson*, [2000] BCJ No 522 (SC).

59 2016 NLCA 67 at para 15, Hoegg JA. See also *Meier v Sirman*, 2023 ABKB 704; *Foster v Sauvé*, 2019 BCSC 1656 at para 27; *AA v JA*, 2023 NBKB 210; *CRB v KJM*, 2023 NBKB 224 at para 262.

60 *LC v ROC*, [2007] AJ No 513 (CA); *Sonne v Wurzer*, 2011 BCSC 609; *Flasch v Flasch*, [2007] SJ No 653 (QB).

61 *MacNeil v MacNeil*, [2000] NWTJ No 4 (SC); *Brodland v Brodland*, [1997] SJ No 688 (QB).

62 *Desjardins v Bouey*, 2013 ABQB 714; *Georgelin v Bingham*, 2011 BCSC 47; *Walsh v Walsh*, [2006] NJ No 33 (UFC); *Meloche v Kales*, [1997] OJ No 6335 (Gen Div); *Sarkozi v Pereira*, 2012 ONSC 4011; *Ferguson v Ferguson*, [2005] PEIJ No 22 (SC).

63 *Giene v Giene*, [1998] AJ No 1305 (QB); *Evans v Evans*, [2004] BCJ No 986 (SC).

64 *Kolt v Kolt*, 2009 ABQB 305; *Hall v Hall*, [1997] BCJ No 1191 (SC); *Penner v Penner*, [1998] MJ No 353 (QB) (application under *Manitoba Child Support Guidelines*); *Walsh v Walsh*, [2006] NJ No 33 (UFC); *Sirdevan v Sirdevan*, [2009] OJ No 3796 (SCJ); *MacNaught v MacNaught*, [1998] PEIJ No 27 (TD); *Lepage v Lepage*, [1999] SJ No 174 (QB). Compare *Barnes v Carmount*, 2011 ONSC 3925.

65 *Dennett v Dennett*, [1998] AJ No 440 (QB); *Mosher v Martin*, [1997] NJ No 180 (SC); compare *Willford v Schaffer*, [2003] SJ No 840 (QB) (time spent with paternal grandfather excluded in calculating child's time with father).

court to count the hours for which each parent has responsibility for the child but the court is not required to inquire into the sleeping patterns of the children,[66] although hours spent sleeping should be credited to the parent in whose home they were sleeping.[67] To exclude time spent by a child in school from calculation of the time a child is the responsibility of a parent ignores the reality of child rearing.[68] Time spent in school or daycare should be included in the calculation as time with the parent having care and control of the child.[69] This accords with the definition of "parenting time" in section 2(1) of the *Divorce Act* whereby parenting time means the time that a child of the marriage spends in the care of a person, whether or not the child is physically with that person during that entire time. The relevant criterion is the amount of time that the children are in the care and control of the parent, not the amount of time that the parent is physically present with the children.[70] Parents who spend time with a child for part of a day, such as mid-week evenings, should not be credited for a full day in undertaking the calculation under section 9 of the Guidelines, if the primary caregiving parent would have been called upon if anything had happened while the child was at school.[71] If only part of a day is spent with a parent, it is simpler, clearer, and fairer to account for the time on the basis of the number of hours spent with that parent or during which that parent assumes responsibility for the child.[72] Where an agreement is specific as to when parenting time starts and ends, an hourly accounting is preferable.[73] The primary caregiving parent will be credited with time that a child spends sleeping or at school, except for those hours when the other parent is actually exercising parenting time or the child is sleeping in that parent's home.[74] The existence of an order or agreement for joint guardianship or for shared parental decision-making authority is not a criterion for the application of section 9 of the Guidelines. Although an existing order or agreement may be relevant, the court must consider the actual parenting arrangements.[75]

---

66 *Vargas v Berryman*, 2010 BCSC 542; *Pearson v Pearson*, [2002] SJ No 10 (QB), affirmed on appeal except for modification of parenting time provisions, Sask CA, 17 December 2002, leave to appeal to SCC refused, [2003] SCCA No 75.

67 *Vargas v Berryman*, 2010 BCSC 542; *Torrone v Torrone*, 2010 ONSC 661.

68 *Crofton v Sturko*, [1998] BCJ No 38 (SC); *Evans v Gravely*, [2000] OJ No 4748 (SCJ); compare *Barnes v Carmount*, 2011 ONSC 3925.

69 *Giene v Giene*, [1998] AJ No 1305 (QB); *Maultsaid v Blair*, 2009 BCCA 102; *Arlt v Arlt*, 2014 ONSC 2173; *Fidyk v Hutchison*, 2013 SKQB 27. As to the impact of a shared parenting time arrangement, see *Bexon v McCorriston*, 2019 ONSC 6060.

70 *Bolton v Bolton*, 2022 ABQB 277; *Crofton v Sturko*, [1998] BCJ No 38 (SC); *Hamm v Hamm*, [1998] NSJ No 139 (TD); *Arlt v Arlt*, 2014 ONSC 2173; *Nderitu v Kamoji*, 2017 ONSC 2617; *Ferguson v Ferguson*, [2005] PEIJ No 22 (SC); *DA v SA*, 2017 SKQB 108; *BNM v PJM*, 2017 SKQB 331.

71 *Lepage v Lepage*, [1999] SJ No 174 (QB).

72 *Kolada v Kolada*, [1999] AJ No 609 (QB); *Bolton v Bolton*, 2022 ABQB 277; *Knudsen v Knudsen*, 2012 BCSC 1315; *McGrath v McGrath*, [2006] NJ No 201 (UFC); *D'Urzo v D'Urzo*, [2002] OJ No 2415 (SCJ); *LL v MC*, 2013 ONSC 1801; *Kelly v Wright*, 2014 ONSC 6285; *Jarocki v Rice*, [2003] SJ No 178 (QB); compare *Gass v Garland*, [2003] PEIJ No 126 (SC).

73 *Kelly v Wright*, 2014 ONSC 6285.

74 *Cusick v Squire*, [1999] NJ No 206 (SC); *LL v MC*, 2013 ONSC 1801; *DA v SA*, 2017 SKQB 108.

75 *CRB v KJM*, 2023 NBKB 224 at para 264; *Ransom v Coulter*, 2014 NWTSC 55, citing *Fidyk v Hutchison*, 2013 SKQB 27.

Where there is shared parenting time, the court should review the attendant circumstances to determine which parent assumed the responsibility for dealing with the school[76] and, particularly, which parent would first be contacted in the event of an emergency.[77] However, a court may refuse to credit a "stay-at-home parent" with all the hours that the children spend in school, where the other parent provides the children with lunches and supplies and other services on their overnight stays.[78] The allocation of school time to only one of the parents may not be reflective of the spirit or reality of the shared parenting time arrangement, where both parents have significant involvement in their children's lives and schooling.[79] For example, both parents may actively participate at the same time in school or extracurricular activities involving their children. The court must consider the existing *de facto* arrangements, as distinct from the *de jure* parenting regime under any pre-existing order or agreement.[80] In cases involving adult children attending university, section 9 may be invoked even though neither parent can be said to have the child in his or her primary care. No court order is necessary in order for "shared parenting time" to arise within the meaning of section 9 of the *Federal Child Support Guidelines*. Conversely, the existence of a court order is no guarantee that the 40 percent criterion under section 9 of the Guidelines has been satisfied.[81] The breakdown of time-sharing must be such as to fall within the 40 percent rule.[82] If it is 40 percent or more, the exercise becomes more intricate, requiring a consideration of the applicable table amount of child support, the increased costs of shared parenting time arrangements, and the conditions, means, needs, and other circumstances of each spouse and of any child for whom support is sought.[83]

One parent cannot unilaterally insist upon keeping the children for extra time in order to satisfy section 9 of the Guidelines.[84] A spouse whose conduct has resulted in a unilateral change in pre-existing shared parenting time arrangements should not expect to be rewarded in consequence of that change.[85] Where court-ordered parenting time is wrongfully frustrated by the other parent, the benefit of any doubt in determining whether the the 40 percent criterion has been met under section 9 of the Guidelines should be given to the parent whose parenting time has been improperly curtailed.[86] A child's refusal to visit a parent may preclude the application of section 9 of the Guidelines.[87]

---

76 See *Ferguson v Ferguson*, 2005 PESCTD 16 at para 37, for a list of relevant considerations; see also *ALM v NJO*, 2015 BCSC 70; *Barnes v Carmount*, 2011 ONSC 3925.

77 *Mavridis v Mavridis*, [1999] BCJ No 1935 (SC); compare *Gass v Garland*, [2003] PEIJ No 126 (SC).

78 *Carver v Carver*, [2001] PEIJ No 130 (SC). Compare *B (LD) v S (RN)*, 2019 PESC 44.

79 *Penner v Penner*, [1999] MJ No 88 (QB) (application under *Manitoba Child Support Guidelines*); see also *Barnes v Carmount*, 2011 ONSC 3925; *Tweel v Tweel*, [2000] PEIJ No 9 (SC).

80 *PT v IT*, [2004] NJ No 98 (SC); *Tweel v Tweel*, [2000] PEIJ No 9 (SC).

81 *Crofton v Sturko*, [1998] BCJ No 38 (SC); *Maultsaid v Blair*, 2009 BCCA 102; *Ball v Ball*, [1998] SJ No 572 (QB).

82 *Mol v Mol*, [1997] OJ No 4060 (Gen Div); see also *SC v SH*, 2016 NLCA 43.

83 *Crick v Crick*, [1997] BCJ No 2222 (SC); *Cabot v Mikkelson*, [2004] MJ No 240 (CA).

84 *Ness v Ness*, [1999] BCJ No 262 (CA).

85 *Billark v Billark* (1996), 36 RFL (4th) 361 (Ont Ct Gen Div).

86 *Sorensen v Kelly*, [2003] BCJ No 950 (SC).

87 *Metzner v Metzner*, [1997] BCJ No 2903 (SC), rev'd on other grounds [1999] BCJ No 1607 (CA).

The 40 percent requirement under section 9 of the Guidelines must be met, regardless of the spirit of the parenting arrangement.[88] No residual judicial discretion exists to deviate from the applicable provincial table amount of basic child support in cases that fall just short of reaching the 40 percent plateau.[89] There is no discretionary jurisdiction in the court to address the unfairness of a situation where the parenting time falls just short of the 40 percent mark, nor to make allowances for additional costs in the absence of "undue hardship" within the meaning of section 10 of the *Federal Child Support Guidelines*.[90] Section 9 of the Guidelines is only met when the 40 percent mark is reached. If the mark can only be reached in a speculative fashion by reference to possible time when parenting time may be exercised, section 9 of the Guidelines cannot be invoked.[91]

Section 9 of the *Federal Child Support Guidelines* is inapplicable unless the time-sharing arrangements place the burden of daily care and responsibility in the hands of the spouse invoking the section for not less than 40 percent of the time "over the course of a year."[92] There can be no section 9 adjustment of the amount payable under the Guidelines, unless parenting time is in fact exercised for the stipulated period.[93] The calculation is to be made on the basis of actual parenting time rather than by reference to the terms of any pre-existing court order.[94] Any notion that each week or month should have a unique amount of support to reflect its time-sharing arrangements is inconsistent with the language and objective of section 9 of the Guidelines. Consequently, an obligor is not entitled to a set-off or to court-ordered support for the summer months when the child is residing with the obligor.[95] It has, nevertheless, been held that the normal proportionate sharing of child care costs under section 7 of the Guidelines may be adjusted to reflect the time and energy spent on the children by the parent who fails to satisfy the 40 percent criterion established by section 9 of the Guidelines.[96]

It has been suggested that it might be possible to avoid complicated arithmetical calculations that will vary from year to year by counting the child's arrival day at one parent's home as that parent's day and the child's departure day as the other parent's day.[97] However,

---

88 *Dennett v Dennett*, [1998] AJ No 440 (QB); *CRB v KJM*, 2023 NBKB 224; *Ransom v Coulter*, 2014 NWTSC 55; *LL v MC*, 2013 ONSC 1801; *Fidyk v Hutchison*, 2013 SKQB 27; see also *Tweel v Tweel*, [2000] PEIJ No 9 (SC).

89 *SR v BE*, 2011 BCSC 1586; *McGrath v McGrath*, [2006] NJ No 201 (UFC); *Gauthier v Hart*, 2011 ONSC 815.

90 *de Goede v de Goede*, [1999] BCJ No 330 (SC).

91 *Martinez v Olson*, [1998] AJ No 1137 (QB); *CRB v KJM*, 2023 NBKB 224 at para 269.

92 *Brubaker v Brubaker*, [1999] AJ No 879 (QB); *NMPH v LLH*, [2006] BCJ No 67 (SC); *Ellis v Ellis*, [1997] PEIJ No 119 (TD); *Gore-Hickman v Gore-Hickman*, [1999] SJ No 503 (QB).

93 *Bradshaw v Davidson*, [1999] OJ No 1391 (Gen Div) (alleged interference with right to 40 percent parenting time found insufficient to trigger s 9 of Guidelines).

94 *Borutski v Jabbour*, [2000] OJ No 5173 (SCJ).

95 *Ellis v Ellis*, [1997] PEIJ No 119 (TD); compare *Waller v Waller*, [1998] OJ No 5387 (Gen Div); see Section A, above in this chapter.

96 *Tooth v Knott*, [1998] AJ No 1395 (QB).

97 *Middleton v MacPherson*, [1997] AJ No 614 (QB). But see *contra Cross v Cross*, [1997] BCJ No 1741 (SC), wherein it was opined that the costs associated with exercising overnight parenting time generally include costs of grooming, providing a school lunch, paying transportation expenses, and occasionally paying for school supplies or other charges, so that it would seem reasonable to add the school attendance hours following overnight parenting time into the computation of time; see also *Whalen v Whalen*, 2010 NSSC 432.

an apportionment of days might have to be undertaken when, for example, a parent exercises non-overnight mid-week parenting time or when the child's arrival and departure occur at different times of the day.[98]

In determining whether the 40 percent criterion under section 9 of the *Federal Child Support Guidelines* has been met, a detailed time accounting that is broken down into hours, part days, days, and weeks is often impractical, undesirable, and unnecessary. Faced with conflicting evidence and the difficulty of measuring time with scientific precision, the issue becomes a matter of judgment not amenable to a fixed time accounting exercise. The question to be determined is whether the paying parent spends such a sizable percentage of time with the child or children that, on any reasonable view of the evidence and considering the advantage that may accrue to a child in spending the occasional additional day, part day, or hour with a parent, the court can reasonably say that the 40 percent criterion has been achieved. Even if it has been achieved, it does not compel an automatic reduction in the amount of child support to be paid. A father's application to reduce the amount of child support because the children are now spending more time with him may be rejected after due consideration of the relevant factors specified in sections 9(a), (b), and (c) of the *Federal Child Support Guidelines*, given the mother's unemployment while she pursues education to enhance her earning capacity and the fact that the father's fixed expenses, such as housing arising from the shared parenting arrangement have not appreciably increased and the variable expenses for food, clothing, and the like do not place him under any undue financial pressure.[99]

Where a court is satisfied that the minimum 40 percent criterion has been met, it is not compelled to make a formal finding of the precise percentage of time that each parent is responsible for the child. There is nothing in section 9 of the Guidelines to suggest that the amount of child support must invariably reflect the percentages of shared parenting time. A contextual approach is required that does not place undue reliance upon percentages or formulae. Shared parenting time is usually expensive for both parents and it cannot be assumed that once the 40 percent threshold is met, the parent who spends more time with the child will have higher costs than the parent who spends less time with the child. Even if a finding is made with respect to the percentage of the year that each parent is responsible for the child, this neither avoids nor assists in the financial analysis that must be undertaken pursuant to sections 9(b) and 9(c) of the Guidelines, which respectively require the court to have regard to any proven increased costs of the shared parenting time regime and to the relative standards of living available in the two households and the ability of each parent to absorb the costs required to maintain an appropriate standard of living.[100]

---

98 *Middleton v MacPherson*, [1997] AJ No 614 (QB); *Billark v Billark* (1996), 36 RFL (4th) 361 (Ont Ct Gen Div); see also *Kolada v Kolada*, [1999] AJ No 609 (QB); *Gore-Hickman v Gore-Hickman*, [1999] SJ No 503 (QB).

99 *Cooke v Cooke*, 2011 BCCA 44; *DLC v FMC*, 2011 BCCA 444; *Cabot v Mikkelson*, [2004] MJ No 240 (CA); *Froom v Froom*, [2005] OJ No 507 (CA).

100 *Stewart v Stewart*, 2007 MBCA 66; *Wolfson v Wolfson*, 2021 NSSC 260; *Hamam v Mantello*, 2020 ONSC 4948; *MA v NM*, 2021 ONSC 5468.

3) Shared Parenting Time under Section 9 of the *Federal Child Support Guidelines* — SCC Definitive Ruling on Relevant Criteria

The amount of child support to be paid pursuant to section 9 of the *Federal Child Support Guidelines* when the minimum 40 percent parenting time criterion has been satisfied must be determined by taking into account (a) the amounts set out in the applicable tables for each spouse; (b) the increased costs of shared parenting time arrangements; and (c) the conditions, means, needs, and other circumstances of each spouse and of any child for whom support is sought.[101] In *Contino v Leonelli-Contino*,[102] the Supreme Court of Canada held that section 9 of the Guidelines establishes a distinct and separate regime in cases of shared parenting time[103] that promotes flexibility and fairness by ensuring that the economic reality and particular circumstances of each family are accounted for.[104] The listed three factors in section 9 of the Guidelines all structure the exercise of judicial discretion and no single factor prevails.[105] The weight given to each of the three factors will vary according to the particular circumstances of each case.[106] Because section 9 of the Guidelines sets out the specific criteria to be applied in shared parenting time arrangements involving a minimum 60:40 time-sharing over the year, there is no presumption in favour of ordering the full table amount of child support plus allowable section 7 expenses as prescribed by section 3(1) of the Guidelines. Nor is there any presumption in favour of reducing a parent's child support obligation below that amount because, after an analysis of all three factors in section 9, a court may conclude that the normal Guidelines amount should be paid in full under the circumstances of a particular shared parenting time arrangement, having regard to the attendant financial circumstances.[107] A simple set-off between the table amounts payable by each parent is an appropriate starting point under section 9(a) of the Guidelines,[108] but it must be followed by an examination of the factors specified in sections 9(b) and (c) of the

101 *GF v JACF*, 2016 NBCA 21; *ASL v LSL*, 2020 NBCA 15. As to a nesting arrangement whereby each of the parents is allotted specific blocks of time with the children in the family home and its impact on the determination of child support, see *MacLennan v MacLennan*, 2021 SKCA 132.

102 [2005] 3 SCR 217 (majority judgment, 8:1, Fish J dissenting). And see DA Rollie Thompson, "Annotation, *Contino v Leonelli-Contino*" (2006) 19 RFL (6th) 239, cited with approval in *GJL v MJL*, 2017 BCSC 688. For an excellent detailed summary of the criteria defined in *Contino v Leonelli-Contino*, [2005] 3 SCR 217, see *Khairzad v McFarlane*, 2015 ONSC 7148 at paras 65–69; *Boyko v Fitzgerald*, 2022 BCSC 614; *Cherewyk v Cherewyk*, 2018 MBCA 13, citing *Kolisnyk v Loscerbo*, 2010 MBCA 1; *Beaudoin v Stevens*, 2023 ONSC 4401. And see *JCM v MJM*, 2018 NBCA 42, citing Professor Rollie Thompson, "Case Comment: *Contino v Leonelli-Contino*" (2004), 42 RFL (5th) 326; see also *MacDonald v Brodoff*, 2020 ABCA 246; *Peters v Atchooay*, 2022 ABCA 347. As to the application of section 9 of the Guidelines in light of section 4 of the Guidelines where the obligor's annual income exceeds $150,000, see *BPE v AE*, 2016 BCCA 335; see also *KMR v IWR*, 2020 ABQB 77; *Russell v Ullett Russell*, 2021 ABQB 769 at paras 17–25; *SRM v NGTM*, 2020 BCSC 468; *KAC v JDEC*, 2020 BCSC 1373; *Prime v Prime*, 2021 SKQB 130.

103 *BPE v AE*, 2016 BCCA 335.

104 See *Gottinger v Runge*, 2018 SKQB 343 at para 20.

105 *Adams v Adams*, 2011 ABQB 576; *Steward v Ferguson*, 2012 BCSC 279; *Smederovac v Eichkorn*, 2020 MBCA 57; *Ludlow v Harkins*, 2014 NLTD(G) 23; *Martin v Martin*, [2007] MJ No 449 (QB); *GF v JACF*, 2016 NBCA 21; *Bolleter v Livingstone*, 2015 NWTSC 47; *Costa v Petipas*, [2006] PEIJ No 39 (SC); *Heigh v Rubidge*, 2010 SKCA 80.

106 *Bleoo v Bleoo*, 2011 ABQB 16; *Vlek v Graff*, 2013 BCSC 1906; *Ratajczak v Ratajczak*, 2010 ONSC 4286.

107 *Schick v Schick*, 2008 ABCA 196.

108 See *Royer v Peters*, 2021 ONSC 1637.

Guidelines and the continuing ability of the recipient parent to meet the financial needs of the child, especially in light of the fact that many costs are fixed.[109] All of the costs associated with the children should be considered under section 9(b) of the Guidelines.[110] Expenses that may be properly considered "avoidable" will not necessarily always be considered by the court.[111] Simply assuming that the costs would be reduced in the recipient parent's household and increased in the payor parent's household as a result of the child's presence constitutes an error.[112] When both parents are making effective contributions, it is necessary to verify how each parent's actual contribution compares to the table amount that is prescribed for each of them. Such a review will provide the judge with better insight in deciding whether adjustments should be made to the set-off amount based on the actual sharing of child-related expenses. The court retains the discretion to modify the set-off amount where, considering the financial situation of the parents, it would lead to a significant variation in the standard of living experienced by the children as they move between the respective households.[113] Section 9(b) of the Guidelines recognizes that the total cost of raising children may be greater in shared parenting time situations.[114] The court will examine the budgets and actual expenditures of both parents in addressing the needs of the children and determine whether shared parenting time has resulted in increased costs globally. These expenses will be apportioned between the parents in accordance with their respective incomes.[115] Section 9(c) of the Guidelines vests the court with a broad discretion to analyze the resources and needs of both the parents and the children. A broad and flexible interpretation has been accorded to the phrase "conditions, means, needs and other circumstances" in section 9(c) of the *Federal Child Support Guidelines.*[116] In *Ortynski v Ortynski,*[117] for example, it was held that section 9(c) captured wealthy paternal grandparents' contributions,[118] and in *Reber v Reber,*[119] child tax benefits and a daycare subsidy were considered on the same basis. In *SAH v KAH*, Baird JA, of the New Brunswick Court of Appeal, stated:

> [I]t is also incumbent upon a spouse to reveal, as part of their budgetary disclosure, any financial assistance they receive from third parties. This would apply to common-law partners,

---

109 *Conway v Conway*, 2011 ABCA 137; *Destine v Cloutier*, 2022 ABCA 331, citing *MacDonald v Brodoff*, 2020 ABCA 246 at para 12; *Peters v Atchooay*, 2022 ABCA 347; *Stockall v Stockall*, 2020 ABQB 229; *BPE v AE*, 2016 BCCA 335; *Robertson v Vega Soto*, 2019 BCSC 1140; *Graham v Graham*, 2013 MBCA 66; *Smederovac v Eichkorn*, 2020 MBCA 57; *MGH v KLDH*, 2020 NBCA 46; *SAH v KAH*, 2022 NBCA 17; *Moody v Holden*, 2015 NLTD(F) 45; *MWDP v MAG*, 2019 NBQB 62; *ASL v LSL*, 2020 NBCA 15; *Boudreau v Marchand*, 2012 NSCA 79; *Hemond v Galano*, 2013 ONSC 6929; *Moreton v Inthavixay*, 2020 ONSC 4881; *Costa v Petipas*, [2006] PEIJ No 39 (SC); *MacLennan v MacLennan*, 2021 SKCA 132. Compare *Briggs v Kasdorf*, 2020 BCSC 1702; *GRR v JES*, 2020 NBQB 154 at paras 98–101.

110 *Adams v Adams*, 2011 ABQB 576; *REQ v GJK*, 2019 BCSC 1116; *Ludlow v Harkins*, 2014 NLTD(G) 23.

111 *Ferris v Longhurst*, 2014 SKQB 294 at para 31, Megaw J.

112 *Adams v Adams*, 2011 ABQB 576 at para 18.

113 *Walling v Holosney*, 2011 BCSC 104; *Carnegie v Carnegie*, 2008 MBQB 249; *LP v SP*, 2022 NSSC 197; *Hussain v Saunders*, 2021 NSSC 166; *MA v NM*, 2021 ONSC 5468; *Wetsch v Kuski*, 2017 SKCA 77.

114 *Wetsch v Kuski*, 2017 SKCA 77 at para 137.

115 *Scott v Scott*, [2006] BCJ No 1701 (SC); *Stewart v Stewart*, [2006] MJ No 190 (QB); *MA v NM*, 2021 ONSC 5468; *Costa v Petipas*, [2006] PEIJ No 39 (SC).

116 *Lozinski v Lozinski*, 2017 BCCA 280 at para 45, Dickson JA; see also *Gottinger v Runge*, 2018 SKQB 343.

117 2014 BCSC 73 at para 45.

118 See also *Wetsch v Kuski*, 2017 SKCA 77.

119 2002 BCSC 884 at para 76.

roommates and family members who live with a parent and who contribute towards household expenses, and would include the receipt of non-taxable subsidies, benefits, grants, and cash as examples.[120]

It is important to keep in mind the objectives of the Guidelines that require a fair standard of support for children and fair contributions from both parents. The court will look at the standard of living of the child in each household and the ability of each parent to absorb the costs required in order to maintain the appropriate standard of living in the circumstances.[121] In the words of Steel JA, of the Manitoba Court of Appeal, in *Smederovac v Eichkorn*:

> The purpose of section 9 is not to equalize household incomes, but rather to make adjustments for any significant and appreciable variations in household standards of living and the financial realities of the parties, including the ability to absorb costs related to maintaining a similar standard of living (see *Wetsch v Kuski*, 2017 SKCA 77 at paras 138-39).[122]

Up-to-date financial statements and/or child expense budgets are necessary for a proper evaluation of section 9(b) and (c) of the Guidelines.[123] Many courts have extracted expenses directly relating to the children as well as a portion of the expenses for the benefit of the children from each parent's statement of expenses.[124] There is no need to resort to section 7 or section 10 of the Guidelines either to increase or to reduce support, since the court has full discretion under section 9(c) to consider "other circumstances" and order the payment of any amount above or below the table amounts.[125] It may be that the undue hardship provisions of section 10 would apply in an extraordinary situation. It is important that the parents lead evidence relating to sections 9(b) and 9(c) of the Guidelines and courts should demand information from them when the evidence is deficient. A court should neither make "common sense" assumptions about costs incurred by the payor parent, nor apply a multiplier to account for the fixed costs of the recipient parent, such as has been done by some courts in the past.[126]

The judgment in *Contino* denounces a strict formulaic approach to the determination of child support in shared parenting time situations and emphasizes the need for relevant financial evidence to be adduced so that the court can address the factors specified in sections 9(b) and (c) of the Guidelines in addition to taking account of the table amount payable by each parent, as required by section 9(a).[127] Given the Supreme Court of Canada's assertion that a

---

120 2022 NBCA 17 at para 31; see also *HM-T v DRGM*, 2023 NBKB 180.

121 *Vlek v Graff*, 2013 BCSC 1906; see also *Rolls v Whittaker-Rolls*, 2010 MBQB 12; *NW v MV*, 2023 NBKB 160; *Muise v Fox*, 2011 NSSC 258; *Wolfson v Wolfson*, 2021 NSSC 260; *Amos v Fischer*, 2013 SKQB 49.

122 2020 MBCA 57 at para 35.

123 *Vlek v Graff*, 2013 BCSC 1906; *ASL v LSL*, 2020 NBCA 15; *Woodford v MacDonald*, 2014 NSCA 31; *Mayer v Mayer*, 2013 ONSC 7099; compare *Moniz v Deschamps*, 2010 ONSC 598. Compare *GRR v JES*, 2020 NBQB 154 at paras 98–101, citing *MacDonald v Brodoff*, 2020 ABCA 246 at para 59.

124 *Abbott v Abbott*, 2014 NLTD(F) 2 at para 135, McGrath J.

125 *Stockall v Stockall*, 2020 ABQB 229 at para 70; *Johnson v Johnson*, 2011 BCCA 190; *MM v AM*, 2008 NBQB 305; *Smith v Smith*, 2011 NSSC 269; *MA v NM*, 2021 ONSC 5468; *Costa v Petipas*, [2006] PEIJ No 39 (SC); *Wetsch v Kuski*, 2017 SKCA 77.

126 *Moreau v Fliesen*, [2008] BCJ No 1925 (SC); *Plourde v Morin*, [2005] NSJ No 505 (SC); *Hilliard v Johnston*, 2010 ONSC 5819; compare *Martin v Martin*, [2007] MJ No 449 (QB).

127 *Smederovac v Eichkorn*, 2020 MBCA 57; *SAH v KAH*, 2022 NBCA 17; *Torrone v Torrone*, 2010 ONSC 661: *Wetsch v Kuski*, 2017 SKCA 77. Compare *Krammer (Ackerman) v Ackerman*, 2020 SKQB 280.

child should not suffer a noticeable decline in his or her standard of living from any change in the parenting regime, a distinction may need to be drawn between original applications for child support and variation applications that can trigger the so-called cliff effect, in that a modest increase in the time spent with the child could result in an unjustifiable reduction in the amount of child support payable if a strict formulaic approach were applied.[128] The "cliff effect" can only be resolved by the court paying due regard to the criteria specified in sections 9(b) and (c) of the Guidelines. If evidence relating to these criteria is not initially adduced, the court may grant an adjournment to permit the necessary evidence to be provided. It is not open to the court to make unsubstantiated assumptions as to the increased costs of a shared parenting time arrangement or to apply any arbitrary multiplier to the set-off amount instead of requiring relevant evidence to be adduced. While mandatory financial statements and child-related budgets may be fraught with difficulties, as parents confuse necessary expenditures with their preferred wish lists, trial judges are well placed to resolve any such conflict.[129]

The judgment in *Contino* states that the broad discretion conferred by section 9(c) of the Guidelines empowers the court to order an overall amount of child support that includes special or exceptional expenses that would otherwise fall within section 7 of the Guidelines.[130] As was observed in *Slade v Slade*,[131] special or extraordinary expenses may be ordered in shared parenting time situations pursuant to section 7 of the Guidelines or they may be considered under the broad provisions of section 9(c) of the Guidelines. Neither option is foreclosed by the judgment in *Contino* and a severance of the basic amount of child support from allowable section 7 expenses may be advantageous in facilitating future variations.

The judgment of the Supreme Court of Canada in *Contino* represents a balanced approach to reconciling the inherent flexibility of the judicial discretion conferred by section 9 of the *Federal Child Support Guidelines* with the objective of providing some measure of consistency and predictability. The judgment in *Contino* does not rule out the fixing of child support on the basis of a simple set-off of the respective table amounts, provided that, in so doing, the additional factors in sections 9(b) and (c) of the *Federal Child Support Guidelines* are considered.[132] It is common on interim applications for the parties to use a simple set-off of their respective child support obligations to arrive at a net payable amount, rather than assembling the evidence that would be required to consider all of the factors that potentially inform a full analysis under section 9 of the Guidelines.[133] In order to determine the correct table amounts under section 9(a), a court must first determine each party's annual income

---

128 *Martin v Martin*, 2007 MBQB 296; *Foss v Foss*, 2011 NSSC 115; *Miller v Volk*, [2009] OJ No 3297 (SCJ); *Costa v Petipas*, [2006] PEIJ No 39 (SC).

129 *JC v MC*, 2014 NBQB 161.

130 *Stewart v Stewart*, [2006] MJ No 190 (QB).

131 [2001] NJ No 5 (CA); see also *ML v SP*, 2015 NBQB 249.

132 *Waugh v Waugh*, 2010 BCSC 110; *MGH v KLDH*, 2020 NBCA 46; *Dillon v Dillon*, [2005] NSJ No 548 (CA); *Beggair v Nixon*, [2006] NWTJ No 26 (SC); *Amos v Fischer*, [2006] SJ No 72 (QB). See also *Conway v Conway*, 2011 ABCA 137; *Woodford v MacDonald*, 2014 NSCA 31; *Dyck v Bell*, 2015 BCCA 520; *GF v JACF*, 2016 NBCA 21; *Kuski v Wetsch*, 2017 SKCA 77. Compare *Krammer (Ackerman) v Ackerman*, 2020 SKQB 280. As to the prevalent default to the set off approach under s 9(a) of the Guidelines, see *MacDonald v Brodoff*, 2020 ABCA 246.

133 *Renshi v Renshi*, 2022 BCSC 1942 at para 46, Elwood J.

in accordance with sections 15 to 20 of the Guidelines, which includes imputation of income under section 19.[134] If there is limited information available to the court and the incomes of the parents are not widely divergent, a simple set-off between the table amounts of child support may be deemed appropriate.[135] Where there is a substantial disparity between the parental incomes and the child's standard of living would be significantly reduced by a simple set-off approach, it behooves the court to adjourn the proceeding so that requisite evidence can be provided that will enable the court to apply the criteria defined in sections 9(b) and (c) of the Guidelines.[136] In circumstances where the primary residence parent is also the primary income earner, it is particularly important to consider sections 9(b) and 9(c) of the Guidelines to ensure that a proper amount of child support is paid. The overall objective is to provide an appropriate standard of living in both households.[137] The determination of an equitable division of the costs of support for children in shared parenting time situations is not amenable to simple solutions. Any attempt to apply strict formulae fails to recognize the diversity of families. A contextual approach that takes into account all three factors enunciated in section 9 of the Guidelines must be applied.[138]

Citing *Contino v Leonelli-Contino*,[139] Armstrong J of the British Columbia Supreme Court, in *Flick v Flick*,[140] identified the following factors for consideration in determining the amount of support to be paid in a shared parenting time situation under section 9 of the *Federal Child Support Guidelines*:

- the language of s. 9 warrants emphasis on flexibility and fairness (para 39)
- it requires acknowledgement of the overall situation of the parents and the needs of the child (para 39)
- the weight of each factor under s. 9 will vary with the particulars of the case (para 39)
- take into account the financial situations of both parents (para 40)
- calculating the set-off amount is the starting point, not the end of the enquiry (para 49)
- the set-off amount does not take into account actual spending patterns as they relate to variable costs [or] the fact that fixed costs of the recipient parent are not reduced by the increased spending of the payor (para 48)
- the court retains the discretion to modify the set-off amount where, considering the financial realities of the parents, it would lead to a significant variation in the standard of living experienced by the child as they move from one household to the other (para 51)
- one of the overall objectives of the Guidelines is, to the extent possible, to avoid great disparities between households (para 51)

---

134 *MacDonald v Brodoff*, 2020 ABCA 246 at para 46; *Peters v Atchooay*, 2022 ABCA 347 at paras 87–91; *Ramachala (Holland) v Holland*, 2020 ABQB 432.

135 *JC v MC*, 2014 NBQB 161; see also *Burgess v Burgess*, 2016 NLCA 11.

136 *Ramachala (Holland) v Holland*, 2020 ABQB 432; *LDF v SJF*, 2010 BCSC 1055; see also *Jellis v Jellis*, 2016 BCSC 2270.

137 *Vargas v Berryman*, 2010 BCSC 542; *Wetsch v Kuski*, 2017 SKCA 77.

138 *Miller v Volk*, [2009] OJ No 3297 (SCJ); *Sirdevan v Sirdevan*, [2009] OJ No 3796 (SCJ).

139 2005 SCC 63.

140 2011 BCSC 264 at para 64; see also *Garm v Straker*, 2011 BCSC 1104; *DI v SI*, 2011 BCSC 1788; *Gottinger v Runge*, 2018 SKQB 343; *Prime v Prime*, 2021 SKQB 130. And see the judgment of Chappel J of the Ontario Superior Court of Justice in *Kerr v Pickering*, 2013 ONSC 317 at para 32; *Ortynski v Ortynski*, 2014 BCSC 73.

- the court must examine the budgets and actual expenses of both parents in addressing the needs of the child and to determine if shared [parenting time] has in effect resulted in increased costs globally (para 52)
- increased costs would normally result from a duplication and the child effectively being given two homes (para 52)
- the expenses will be apportioned between the parents in accordance with their incomes (para 53)
- the analysis should be contextual and remain focused on the particular facts of each case
- the court has full discretion under s. 9(c) to consider "other circumstances" (para 72)
- courts should demand information relating to s. 9(b) and (c) when the evidence filed is deficient (para 57)

In *Sydor v Sydor*,[141] Midwinter J of the Manitoba Court of Queen's Bench listed the following considerations:

1) There is no presumption of a table amount.
2) No automatic reduction for shared [parenting time].
3) No formula is mandated.
4) No use of prorated set off.[142]
5) No multipliers.
6) No need to separate out section seven expenses.
7) No need to use section 10 as the Court has discretion under section 9(c) to do the appropriate thing to avoid undue hardships in the exercise of its discretion apart from an extraordinary situation.

While *Contino* cautions against being formulaic, certainty, predictability, and a minimization of opportunities for conflict between the parties may be overriding considerations in considering go-forward calculations. Once the appropriate support obligation has been determined, the parties may need a simple calculation that they can use each year to calculate the support amount after exchanging their income tax returns and notices of assessment for the previous year. In *Hodge v Jones*,[143] to achieve the measure of certainty that the parties had enjoyed in the past and would require for the future, the court ordered that their future support obligations for child support would be varied after an exchange of the previous year's tax returns and notices of assessment by calculating the set off under section 9(a) of the Guidelines and adding one third the difference between the set off and the full table amount.

In a summary of their review of post-*Contino* cases published in June 2006, Jennifer Blishen J and Michèle Labrosse, a family law practitioner, express the following conclusion:

> Given the Supreme Court of Canada's emphasis on a discretionary rather than a "formulaic" or "mathematical" approach to calculating child support under s 9 of the *Child Support Guidelines*, it is not surprising that recent cases have widely differing results depending on their circumstances. The results range from a determination that no child support was

141 2011 MBQB 38 at para 25.

142 See *Royer v Peters*, 2021 ONSC 1637.

143 2011 ONSC 2363.

payable (see *Lowe v. Lowe*, [2006] O.J. No. 128 (S.C.J.)), to the use of a straight set-off (see *Dillon v. Dillon*, [2005] N.S.J. No. 548 (C.A.)), to orders for the full Table amount or close to it in situations where there is a significant disparity in the incomes, assets and/or expenses of the parties (see *Kennedy v. Kennedy*, [2006] B.C.J. No. 509 (S.C.), *Elliott v. MacAskill*, [2005] N.S.J. No. 479 (Fam. Ct.), *Mendler v. Mendler*, [2006] O.J. No. 878 (S.C.J.) and *Easton v. McAvoy*, [2005] O.J. No. 5479 (Ct. J.)).[144]

In *Dagg v Chenier*,[145] Cornell J of the Ontario Superior Court of Justice refers to a later study undertaken by Professor Rollie Thompson wherein the following findings and conclusions were expressed:

> 24 In an article entitled "The TLC of Shared Parenting: Time, Language and Cash," presented at the Law Society of Upper Canada's *7th Annual Family Law Summit 2013*, Professor Thompson undertook a review of the 2012 cases which considered *Contino*. He found that of the thirty-two reported decisions, twenty ended up at the straight set-off amount, five were above the set-off and five were below the set-off amount. He summarizes his findings at p. 21 as follows:
>
> > What this brief survey reveals is that the straight or simple set-off has become the default solution in many s. 9 cases, despite the wide discretion espoused by *Contino*. Child expense budgets are avoided. Section 7 expenses are dealt with separately. Courts make adjustments up or down from the set-off based upon some sense of "fairness." Only rarely do courts appear to consider net disposable income or other measures of household standard of living, despite the Supreme Court's emphasis upon that concern. We do not see the emergence of any formulaic solution in the cases to date, hardly surprising given the holdings in *Contino*.[146]

And in *Martin v Martin*,[147] Little J, of the Manitoba Court of Queen's Bench, observed:

> [86] At some point, one must wonder whether it is appropriate to consider amendments to the shared [parenting time] provisions of Section 9 if only to create a presumption — if not one in favour of the table or the set-off amount, then one in favour of the mid-point. If the range of support between the table and set-off amounts is broad enough so that a mid-point is not a sensible compromise in a particular case, that party can then bear the onus to establish a different result is appropriate.
>
> [87] Until such time as something is done, I can only wonder how many parents may mortgage their own and their children's lives.

144 Justice Jennifer Blishen & Michèle Labrosse, "Shared Custody and Child Support after *Contino*" (Paper presented to the County of Carleton Law Association, 15th Annual Institute of Family Law, 2 June 2006) at tab 1cii.

145 2014 ONSC 336; see also *TH v JH*, 2016 NBQB 6; *Prime v Prime*, 2021 SKQB 130.

146 And see *MacDonald v Brodoff*, 2020 ABCA 246; *Peters v Atchooay*, 2022 ABCA 347. See also Beth Ambury, "The Cost of Shared Parenting: An Analysis of Section 9 from 2016 to 2017" (2020) 39 CFLQ 1.

147 2007 MBQB 296 at paras 86–87.

4) Increased Costs: Section 9(b) of the Guidelines

Section 9(b) of the *Federal Child Support Guidelines* takes account of any increased costs of time-sharing arrangements associated with maintaining two households, a consideration that may not be adequately addressed by reference only to the difference in table amounts payable by each spouse.[148] Section 9(b) does not refer merely to the expenses assumed by the payor parent as a result of the increase in parenting time from less than 40 percent to more than 40 percent. Rather, it recognizes that the total cost of raising children may be greater in shared parenting time situations and that these expenses will be apportioned between the parents in accordance with their respective incomes.[149] The judgment of the Supreme Court of Canada in *Contino* underscores the need for evidence of the actual spending patterns of the parents with the onus on the payor parent to demonstrate that his or her increase in the actual time spent with the child directly results in additional costs for him or her.[150] It has been suggested that the reference in section 9(b) to the increased costs of time-sharing arrangements refers to the need to reduce the amount payable by the higher income spouse in order to reflect that spouse's increased costs from having the children, but this suggestion imposes an unduly restrictive interpretation on the provisions that is not explicitly required by section 9(b) and pays insufficient attention to ongoing infrastructure costs that exist, regardless of any shared parenting time arrangement.

Unequal time-sharing coupled with one spouse's assumption of significant monthly expenses for the children may justify an order for child support in an amount substantially exceeding a simple set-off of the applicable table amounts, even though the incomes judicially imputed to the spouses are comparable in amount.[151] Increased costs may be associated with parenting arrangements on an equal time-sharing basis in consequence of a parent's need for a two-bedroom apartment to accommodate a teenage child. Judicial deviation from an arithmetical application of the table amounts is warranted where higher child support is justified to reflect increased costs of reasonable rental accommodation.[152]

The onus of proving increased costs of shared parenting time falls on the parent who seeks to reduce the amount of child support to be paid.[153] Increased costs of shared parenting time arrangements under section 9(b) of the Guidelines will only be considered where evidence of those costs has been adduced.[154] Increased costs to the spouse who invokes section 9 of the *Federal Child Support Guidelines* would include increased food and travel costs. An analysis of increased costs has been said to involve some kind of "before and after" comparison that should be addressed by counsel or the parties,[155] but any such comparison may be impractical if the shared parenting time arrangements follow immediately upon

148 *Dennett v Dennett*, [1998] AJ No 440 (QB); *ALM v NJO*, 2015 BCSC 70; *Ludlow v Harkins*, 2014 NLTD(G) 23; *Fisher v Fisher*, [2001] OJ No 5477 (SCJ).

149 *Jellis v Jellis*, 2016 BCSC 2270 at para 20, Hinkson CJ; *Wolfson v Wolfson*, 2021 NSSC 260; *Moreton v Inthavixay*, 2020 ONSC 4881.

150 *CLB v AHB*, 2013 BCCA 472.

151 *Hughes v Alfano*, [2006] BCJ No 133 (SC).

152 *Veugelers v Yeoh*, [1999] OJ No 3962 (SCJ).

153 *Adams v Adams*, 2011 ABQB 576; *Lane v Hustings-Lane*, [2005] NJ No 379 (SC).

154 *Schick v Schick*, 2008 ABCA 196; *Hubic v Hubic*, [1997] SJ No 491 (QB). Compare *Martin v Martin*, [2007] MJ No 449 (QB).

155 *MacNaught v MacNaught*, [1998] PEIJ No 27 (TD).

spousal separation. It should also be borne in mind that increased expenses incurred by one parent are not necessarily offset by reduced expenses being incurred by the other parent. Furthermore, housing, food, clothing, and other expenses incurred by the respective parents are not necessarily correlated to the time spent with each parent and such expenses are often difficult to calculate for the purpose of invoking section 9(b) of the Guidelines.[156] Although a standardized affidavit might help to alleviate this problem to some degree, difficulties would continue to exist.[157]

A mother's assumption of extra responsibility for providing meals to the children during the week may be insufficient to warrant judicial deviation from a straight set-off of the applicable table amounts of child support where the court is not satisfied that the increased costs of the shared parenting arrangement thereby fall more on the mother than on the father.[158]

a) Judicial Discretion to Deviate from Set-Off under Section 9(c) of Guidelines

Section 9(c) requires the court to take into account the conditions, means, needs, and other circumstances of each spouse and any child[159] for whom an order is sought. Among the factors the court may consider under section 9(c) are the actual spending patterns of the parents, the ability of each parent to bear the increased costs of shared parenting time and the standard of living in each household.[160] Of particular importance under this subsection is the standard of living for the children in each household: to the extent that it is practicable, children should not suffer a noticeable decline in their standard of living.[161] The court will be especially concerned here with the ability of each parent to absorb the costs required to maintain the appropriate standard of living in the circumstances.[162]

The criteria defined in section 9(c) of the Guidelines confer a substantial discretion on the court in its assessment of the appropriate amount of child support.[163] The discretion should be exercised in a principled manner. There are various factors that may be considered, including the following:

1) the exercise of the discretion must respond to the needs of the particular family; there is no single formula that can be applied to all families;
2) child care budgets may be informative, but they are not determinative of the appropriate amount of child support to be ordered;

---

156 *Adams v Adams*, 2011 ABQB 576.

157 *Green v Green*, [2000] BCJ No 1001 (CA); *Martin v Martin*, [2007] MJ No 449 (QB). See also *Jellis v Jellis*, 2016 BCSC 2270.

158 *Reber v Reber*, [2002] BCJ No 1281 (SC).

159 *ML v SP*, 2016 NBQB 249.

160 *ALM v NJO*, 2015 BCSC 70 at para 106, Greyell J; *Hamam v Mantello*, 2020 ONSC 4948; *MA v NM*, 2021 ONSC 5468.

161 *Perron v Hlushko*, 2015 ABQB 595; *LAB v MLB*, 2012 BCSC 1066; *ML v SP*, 2016 NBQB 249; *Ludlow v Harkins*, 2014 NLTD(G) 23; *Hussain v Saunders*, 2021 NSSC 166; *Dagg v Chenier*, 2014 ONSC 336; *HAK v TJW*, 2013 SKQB 70; *Prime v Prime*, 2021 SKQB 130.

162 *CLB v AHB*, 2013 BCCA 472; *Wolfson v Wolfson*, 2021 NSSC 260; *Prime v Prime*, 2021 SKQB 130.

163 *Perron v Hlushko*, 2015 ABQB 595; *Green v Green*, [2000] BCJ No 1001 (CA); *Smederovac v Eichkorn*, 2020 MBCA 57; *Neil v Neil*, [2003] NJ No 146 (SC); *Haney v Haney*, [2005] OJ No 2329 (SCJ); compare *Harrison v Harrison*, [2001] OJ No 470 (SCJ); *McLaughlin v McLaughlin*, [2004] SJ No 716 (QB).

3) a distinction may be drawn between cases where both parents play an equal role in the lives of their children and those cases where one parent assumes the primary responsibility notwithstanding that the other parent satisfies the 40 percent criterion which triggers section 9 of the Guidelines; and
4) a substantial disparity between the parental incomes is significant where a reduction of the applicable table amount payable by the higher income parent will operate to the detriment of the children's standard of living in the lower income parent's household.[164]

The significance of section 9(a) of the Guidelines may vary from case to case, depending on the differences in parental incomes and assets, the amount of time the children spend with each parent, and the manner in which the children's expenses are incurred and paid for.[165] Notwithstanding that courts may favour a straight set-off of the table amounts under section 9(a) of the Guidelines where there is no convincing evidence of increased costs of shared parenting time arrangements nor of the conditions, means, needs, and other circumstances of either spouse or of the children that warrant a different amount from the set-off amount,[166] there will be cases where a straight set-off would be unfair as, for example, where that amount of support would generate a much lower standard of living in one household than in the other. Although section 9 should not be perceived as spousal support nor as a means of equalizing the respective household incomes, the court must ensure that there is an adequate amount of resources to meet the children's needs in both households. The interests of the children will not be served if the amount of child support is barely enough to meet their basic needs in the lower income home, while they enjoy a luxurious lifestyle in the other home.[167] In these circumstances, sections 9(b) and (c) of the Guidelines take on a special importance, because the application of section 9(a) alone would fly in the face of the *Divorce Act*, which postulates the determinative criterion of the best interests of the children in parenting dispositions and the importance of maintaining maximum contact between the children and both of their parents on or after divorce.[168] Whatever may result from the application of sections 9(a) and (b) of the Guidelines, the comparative means and needs of the parties and their children may compel another result. Having regard to the language of section 9(c) of the Guidelines, the court has, in the final analysis, the discretion to do what seems appropriate in all the circumstances.[169] A shared parenting time arrangement that falls within section 9 of the Guidelines does not inevitably lead to any adjustment or reduction in the table amount of support payable by the higher income parent.[170] A court may decline

164 *Shaw v Shaw*, [2002] OJ No 2782 (SCJ); *Prime v Prime*, 2021 SKQB 130.
165 *Fisher v Fisher*, [2001] OJ No 5477 (SCJ); *DI v SD*, [2003] YJ No 74 (SC).
166 *TVC v MLH*, 2015 ABQB 668; *SR v BE*, 2011 BCSC 1586; *Abbott v Abbott*, 2014 NLTD(F) 2.
167 *Ames v Ames*, [1999] BCJ No 1816 (SC) (mother with modest income entitled to full table amount of child support); *Schellenberg v Schellenberg*, [2001] MJ No 233 (QB); *Fox v Fox*, 2007 NBQB 243; *Smith v Smith*, 2011 NSSC 269 at para 71; *Magee v Faveri*, [2007] OJ No 4826 (SCJ); *Carver v Carver*, [2001] PEIJ No 130 (SC); *Orth v Orth*, [1999] SJ No 886 (QB) (full table amount reduced by 30 percent).
168 *Giene v Giene*, [1998] AJ No 1305 (QB).
169 *Spiess v Spiess*, 2021 ABQB 961 at para 9; compare *Armstrong v Armstrong*, 2010 BCSC 1686 (increased spousal support to reflect differential lifestyles in the two homes).
170 *Schick v Schick*, 2008 ABCA 196; *ALM v NJO*, 2015 BCSC 70; *JSG v MFG*, 2011 MBQB 177; *Lickfold v Robichaud*, [2008] OJ No 4117 (SCJ); *Costa v Petipas*, [2006] PEIJ No 39 (SC); *Deagnon v Folk*, 2009 SKQB 499.

to order a set-off between the two table amounts of child support where the differential is counterbalanced by the assumption of increased costs by one parent associated with the shared parenting time arrangement,[171] or where the costs of the parenting arrangement do not increase the costs of a parent beyond what they would be if the child were with that parent less than 40 percent of the time.[172] Where parenting arrangements exist on a 60:40 time-sharing basis, a court may order the applicable table amount to be paid without any adjustment for time-sharing but may relieve the payor of making any contribution to the other parent's child care expenses.[173] Alternatively, an order for the payment of the differential between the two table amounts under section 9 of the Guidelines may be supplemented by an order for the payment of child care expenses under section 7 of the Guidelines.[174]

Net worth is a valid consideration under a section 9(c) analysis, and capital assets and business operations, such as rental properties, are a legitimate consideration.[175] The fact that a spouse is sharing household expenses with a new partner may be a relevant factor to consider under section 9(c) of the Guidelines,[176] but the bare assertion that a spouse is living with someone else is not enough.[177]

Section 9(c) invites consideration of any number of relevant factors, including but not limited to special or extraordinary expenses that fall within section 7 of the *Federal Child Support Guidelines*.[178] Inheritances and monetary gifts received from family members do not constitute "income" under section 16 of the *Federal Child Support Guidelines* but should be considered, as should the value of a parent's residence, as part of the full net worth of the recipient parent that is to be taken into account in shared parenting time situations in which the court is required to have regard to the "conditions, means, needs and other circumstances" of each parent pursuant to section 9(c) of the Guidelines.[179] CPP benefits paid for the children of disabled contributors should also be taken into account.[180]

In exercising its discretion under section 9 of the Guidelines, the court should have regard to section 26.1(2) of the *Divorce Act*, which imposes a joint financial obligation on the spouses or former spouses to support the children of the marriage in accordance with

---

171 *Leavitt v Leavitt*, [1999] BCJ No 648 (SC); see also *Claxton v Jones*, [1999] BCJ No 3086 (Prov Ct).

172 *Evans v Gravely*, [2000] OJ No 4748 (SCJ); *Buhler v Buhler*, 2012 SKQB 366; see also *Lavoie v Wills*, [2000] AJ No 1359 (QB) (food costs factored into adjustment of full table amount of child support).

173 *McCurdy v Morisette*, [1999] BCJ No 2292 (SC).

174 *Johnson v Bradford*, [1999] AJ No 678 (QB).

175 *Woodford v MacDonald*, 2014 NSCA 31.

176 *GJL v MJL*, 2017 BCSC 688; *Rolls v Whittaker-Rolls*, 2010 MBQB 12; *HM-T v DRGM*, 2023 NBKB 180; *LP v SP*, 2022 NSSC 197; *Schick v Schick*, [2000] NWTJ No 12 (SC); *Ratajczak v Ratajczak*, 2010 ONSC 4286; *Kuski v Wetsch*, 2013 SKQB 70. Compare *Johnson v Johnson*, 2011 BCCA 190; *BPE v AE*, 2016 BCCA 335; *AHB v CLB*, 2019 BCCA 349 at paras 35–37; *Bernardin v Bernardin*, 2020 BCSC 807. For an excellent review of the impact of repartnering under section 9 of the *Federal Child Support Guidelines*, see *Spiess v Spiess*, 2021 ABQB 961, which is reviewed in Franks & Zalev, "This Week in Family Law," 2 May 2022 (Thomson Reuters); *Gottinger v Runge*, 2018 SKQB 343; see also Elliott S Birnboim & Daniella Murynka, "Section 9 and Second Families" (2015) 93:1 *Canadian Bar Review* 39, 2015 CanLIIDocs 138; *NW v MV*, 2023 NBKB 160.

177 *Soderberg v Soderberg*, [1998] NWTJ No 128 (SC). See also *Atte v Atte*, 2021 BCSC 133 at para 33.

178 *Penner v Penner*, [1999] MJ No 88 (QB) (application under *Manitoba Child Support Guidelines*); *Rolls v Whittaker-Rolls*, 2010 MBQB 12.

179 *CRHE v FGE*, [2004] BCJ No 1057 (CA). See also *HAK v TJW*, 2013 SKQB 70 (spouse's income).

180 *ML v SP*, 2016 NBQB 249.

their relative abilities to contribute to the performance of that obligation.[181] Income may be imputed to a parent for the purpose of applying sections 9(a) and (c) of the Guidelines.[182] A parent's receipt of the Canada Child Benefit and of a daycare subsidy does not constitute "income" under section 16 of the *Federal Child Support Guidelines* for the purpose of applying section 9(a) of the Guidelines. However, the benefit and subsidy are relevant to that parent's "means" under section 9(c) of the Guidelines in that they may reduce the disparity that would otherwise have been substantial between the standards of living in the respective households and may consequently justify a straight set-off between the table amounts of child support under section 9(a) of the Guidelines.[183]

If one spouse spends more time with the children and incurs substantially more of their everyday necessary expenses than the other spouse, the court may conclude that it is improper to only order a top-up amount that reflects the differential between their respective table amounts.[184]

A set-off of the respective table amounts may be deemed inappropriate where one parent bears the lion's share of the children's expenses. In these circumstances, the court may order the full table amount of child support to be paid by the parent who incurs few, if any, of the expenses,[185] or such lesser amount as has been determined under a prior consent order.[186]

A court may conclude that the economic realities are such as call for no abatement of the full table amount and no set-off, where any disposition would generate wide disparities in the child's amenities in the respective households.[187]

A court may refuse to order a parent to pay support for children living under a shared parenting time arrangement where any court-ordered payment would simply reimburse the provincial treasury for income assistance paid to the mother at the expense of the economic well-being of the children.[188]

A court may deviate from the set-off amount for a limited time to enable the parents to adjust to the shared parenting regime.[189]

5) Reasons for Decision

A court is not required to record the reasons for its decision provided the factors under sections 9(a), (b), and (c) of the Guidelines are taken into account, although for the sake of clarity it would be advisable to do so.[190]

---

181 *Hubic v Hubic*, [1997] SJ No 491 (QB).

182 *RJO v ACO*, [2000] BCJ No 2562 (SC); *Loscerbo v Loscerbo*, [2008] MJ No 246 (QB).

183 *Reber v Reber*, [2002] BCJ No 1281 (SC); *Luedke v Luedke*, [2004] BCJ No 1157 (CA); see also *Foss v Foss*, 2011 NSSC 115. Compare *Johnson v Johnson*, 2011 BCCA 190.

184 *Georgelin v Bingham*, 2011 BCSC 47; *Rosati v Dellapenta*, [1997] OJ No 5047 (Gen Div).

185 *Richards v Richards*, [1998] BCJ No 2657 (SC); *Johnstone v Johnstone*, [1998] OJ No 5337 (Gen Div).

186 *Richards v Richards*, [1998] BCJ No 2657 (SC).

187 *Coles v Coles*, [2002] BCJ No 1142 (SC); *Graham v Graham*, 2013 MBCA 66; *Weismiller v Jolkowski*, [2000] OJ No 1775 (SCJ); *Weir v Landry*, [2003] PEIJ No 116 (SC); see also *NP v MCP*, 2012 BCSC 1843.

188 *Kirkpatrick v Bellvau*, [2000] BCJ No 2481 (SC).

189 *Belot v Connelly*, 2013 MBQB 98.

190 *Middleton v MacPherson*, [1997] AJ No 614 (QB).

6) Mixed Parenting Time Arrangements and Blended Families

There has been judicial divergence across Canada on the application of section 9 of the *Federal Child Support Guidelines* where there is a hybrid of parenting arrangements in that different time-sharing regimes apply to different children in the family.[191] In *Wouters v Wouters*,[192] M-E Wright J of the Saskatchewan Court of Queen's Bench concluded that a two-stage analysis should occur when there is a hybrid of parenting arrangements. The starting point should deal with those children whose parenting is not shared. They are not part of the shared parenting time arrangements encompassed by section 9 and the presumptive rule arising under section 3 of the Guidelines applies to these children. It is only after the support obligation arising under section 3 has been addressed that the court should turn its attention to the support of those children whose parenting is shared. The two-stage analysis has been consistently applied in Saskatchewan.[193] A similar approach was endorsed by Vertes J of the Northwest Territories Supreme Court in *McBride v McBride*,[194] wherein the following conclusions were expressed. If there is a hybrid of parenting arrangements whereby one child is living in a shared parenting time arrangement but a second child is not, the court must segregate the determination of support for each child. A hybrid of parenting arrangements calls for the application of different formulas under the *Federal Child Support Guidelines*. The court cannot simply mix different arrangements into a melange *and* then apply one formula. Where section 9 of the Guidelines is triggered with respect to one child and section 5 of the Guidelines applies to the other child, the court cannot simply pull a number out of the air that appears to be fair. Although both sections 9 and 5 of the Guidelines confer a discretion on the court, different factors must be taken into account under each section.[195] Although the support rights of different categories of children have to be examined sequentially in the context of the diverse applicable sections under the Guidelines, rigid compartmentalism cannot usually be maintained because the applicable table amounts of child support are based on the obligor's income and the number of children for whom support is sought and the table amounts reflect economies of scale where children are residing under the same roof. In *Hofsteede v Hofsteede*,[196] Marshman J of the Ontario Superior Court of Justice conceded that the wording of the Guidelines might, at first blush, dictate that the approach in *Wouters v Wouters* is the proper one. However, Marshman J accepted the reasoning of Vogelsang J in

---

191 See, for example, *Blair v Callow* (1998), 41 RFL (4th) 44 (BCSC); *Ferster v Ferster*, [2002] BCJ No 172 (SC) (formula devised for melange of split and shared parenting time arrangements); *EGP v SLP*, 2009 BCSC 1221; *JRB v SCB*, 2011 BCSC 1683; *JC v MC*, 2014 NBQB 161; *Delaney v Delaney*, 2014 NLTD(F) 28; *SM-M v SM*, 2022 NSSC 256; *Seguin v Masterson*, [2004] OJ No 2176 (SCJ) (judicial review of several possible options); *Dagg v Chenier*, 2014 ONSC 336; *Costa v Petipas*, [2006] PEIJ No 39 (SC); *Wouters v Wouters*, [2001] SJ No 232 (QB).

192 [2001] SJ No 232 (QB), see also *Burgess v Burgess*, 2016 NLCA 11; *Kaul v Hart*, 2012 ONSC 7186; *Shoukri v Mishriki*, 2012 ONSC 7336; *King v McSymytz*, 2015 SKQB 224; *Basso v Reesor*, 2015 SKQB 329; *BNM v PJM*, 2017 SKQB 331; *Prime v Prime*, 2021 SKQB 130; *CSW v TDS*, 2023 SKKB 182.

193 *Keast v Keast*, 2016 SKQB 124 at para 15.

194 [2001] NWTJ No 69 (SC); see also *MPT v RWT*, 2008 YKSC 94.

195 *McBride v McBride*, [2001] NWTJ No 69 (SC); see also *TLR v RWR*, [2006] BCJ No 409 (SC).

196 [2006] OJ No 304 (SCJ); see also *Dyck v Bell*, 2015 BCCA 520; *JC v MC*, 2014 NBQB 161; *Thompson v Thompson*, 2013 ONSC 5500; *NH v JH*, 2017 ONSC 6607.

Burns v Burns,[197] who observed that the table amounts prescribed by the *Federal Child Support Guidelines* recognize the principle of economies of scale when children are residing under the same roof. Thus, the table amount for three children is less than the table amount for one child plus the table amount for two children, before any *Contino* adjustment is made by virtue of a set-off or the application of sections 9(b) and (c) of the Guidelines. Applying the reasoning in *Burns* to the facts in *Hofsteede v Hofsteede*, wherein the older of two children resided primarily with the mother and the younger child spent equal time with both parents, Marshman J found it more appropriate to apply section 8 (split parenting time) and section 9 (shared parenting time) to the situation rather than sections 3 and 9. Consequently, in calculating the child support to be paid, Marshman J first determined the father's table amount of support for the two children and the wife's table amount of support for one child and effectuated a set-off between these two amounts. Marshman J then reviewed the children's budgets prepared by both parents and increased the set-off amount to reflect the increased costs of the shared parenting time arrangement with respect to the younger child and the mother's assumption of a disproportionate share of the overall child-related expenses. In *Thompson v Thompson*,[198] Chappel J of the Ontario Superior Court of Justice stated:

> Turning to the principles that apply in hybrid child care arrangements, a review of the current case-law reveals broad support for the approach which Zisman J. adopted in the case of *Sadkowski v. Harrison-Sadkowski*.[199] In that case, the court described two possible approaches to hybrid claims, namely the "two-step" analysis and the "economies of scale" analysis. The former approach involves first calculating the child support owing relating to the children whose [parenting] is not shared, based on section 3 of the *Guidelines*, then separately calculating the support owed for the child in a shared [parenting] arrangement using a straight set-off amount, and adding the two sums. The latter "economies of scale" involves calculating the full *Table* amount owed by the parent with shared care of children for the total number of children in the care of the parent who has both primary and shared care of children, and setting that amount off by the full *Table* amount payable by the parent with both primary and shared care for the total number of children with the parent who has shared care. Zisman J. held that the set-off calculation using the "economies of scale" approach is the proper starting point for the analysis of hybrid claims. She concluded that this set-off calculation serves only as a starting point for the child support analysis, and is not presumptive. The second step in determining hybrid claims is to carry out a *Contino* inquiry to determine whether adjustments are necessary in order to achieve the goal of establishing fair levels of support for the children from both parents. This step involves the court examining the budgets and actual expenditures of each parent to determine whether adjustments are necessary in order to ensure that the children enjoy relatively comparable standards of living in each household. The approach which Zisman J. described in this case has since been followed in subsequent

---

197 (1998), 40 RFL (4th) 32 (Ont Ct Gen Div); see also *Poohkay v Thomlison*, 2022 ABQB 282; *Murphy v Murphy*, 2012 ONSC 1627; *Granter v Tricco*, 2018 ONSC 6906.

198 2013 ONSC 5500 at para 42; see also *Clark v Leska*, 2014 ONSC 268. And see *Dyck v Bell*, 2015 BCCA 520; *JC v MC*, 2014 NBQB 161; *Delaney v Delaney*, 2014 NLTD(F) 28: *Fedortchouk v Boubnoy*, 2018 NSSC 66 at paras 143–46, O'Neil, ACJ; *Basso v Reesor*, 2015 SKQB 329.

199 2008 ONCJ 115; see also *Dagg v Chenier*, 2014 ONSC 336; *Dyck v Bell*, 2015 BCCA 520.

> cases, including *Murphy v. Murphy*[200] and *Lalonde v. Potier.*[201] I conclude that this approach is the appropriate one to follow, as it recognizes the economies involved when fixed costs are shared between more than one child, and accords with the general principles which the Supreme Court of Canada adopted in *Contino* in the case of shared [parenting] arrangements.

In *Doyle v Doyle,*[202] the British Columbia Court of Appeal found that the chambers judge had erred by failing to apply the *Federal Child Support Guidelines* on a variation application after finding that a change of circumstances had occurred in consequence of the older of two children taking up residence with the father and thereby changing the equal time-sharing regime that had previously been implemented with respect to both of the children. After reviewing the submissions of both parties with respect to the potential application of sections 8 and 9 of the Guidelines, the British Columbia Court of Appeal concluded that additional evidence was required and the application to vary should be remitted to the British Columbia Supreme Court for a new hearing to enable both parents to provide the necessary evidence and to permit a proper determination to be made as to whether the parenting time arrangements fell within section 8 or 9 of the Guidelines, or some combination thereof and, if within section 9, to consider and weigh each of the factors listed in subsections (a), (b), and (c). And in *Dyck v Bell,*[203] the British Columbia Court of Appeal held that a chambers judge had erred in applying the two-stage approach to a hybrid parenting situation in which one of the two children lived primarily with the mother and the other child spent equal time with each of the parents under an alternating weekly parenting arrangement. Speaking for the court, Harris JA stated:

> 27 The error arose because the trial judge should have adopted what is referred to as the "economies of scale" approach: see *E.G.P. v. S.L.P.*, 2009 BCSC 1221 at paras. 18–23, and *R.B. v. L.M.L.*, 2014 BCSC 134 at paras. 44–47. On that approach, the starting point of the analysis would be a payment based on the table amount of Mr. Bell for two children, less the table amount of Ms. Dyck for one child. This would amount to $976 per month based on the *Guideline* incomes used by the chambers judge. The court would then be required to consider the application of s. 9 of the *Guidelines* in accordance with the principles set out in *Contino.*

According to Jollimore J of the Nova Scotia Supreme Court, who endorsed the economies of scale approach:

> In New Brunswick, Newfoundland and Labrador, Ontario, and British Columbia, the economies of scale approach is used. In Saskatchewan, Yukon, and Northwest Territories the two-stage approach is used.[204]

---

200 2012 ONSC 1627.

201 2013 ONSC 1513.

202 [2006] BCJ No 523 (CA). See also *Johal v Johal*, 2013 BCSC 1592; *Migwans v Lovelace*, 2011 NWTSC 54.

203 2015 BCCA 520; see also *BSW v WFW*, 2023 BCSC 1925.

204 *Harrison v Falkenham*, 2017 NSSC 139 at para 30; see also *Miller v Miller*, 2021 NSSC 152; *SM-M v SM*, 2022 NSSC 256. And see *Poohkay v Thomlison*, 2022 ABQB 282; *CAM v JC*, 2021 PESC 41 (economies of scale approach adopted).

7) Section 7 and Other Expenses

Section 9(c) of the Guidelines confers a broad discretion on the court, which envisages a consideration of many factors, including but not limited to special or extraordinary expenses falling within section 7 of the Guidelines.[205] The court need not follow a strict application of the table amount and an apportionment of section 7 expenses; instead, it can fix an amount by considering these matters together.[206] Special and extraordinary expenses may be granted in shared parenting time situations pursuant to section 7 of the Guidelines[207] or they may be considered under the broader provisions of section 9(c) of the Guidelines.[208]

An order for the proportionate sharing of clothing and other expenses may be granted under section 9 of the *Federal Child Support Guidelines*,[209] even though an order for a contribution to these expenses would not be justified under section 7 of the Guidelines.[210]

8) Evidence

Where there is a serious dispute as to the amount of time-sharing on an application to reduce the amount of child support pursuant to section 9 of the Guidelines, a court may be disinclined to resolve the dispute on a summary basis without prior cross-examination of the parties.[211] The diversity of factors that have been considered by the courts in determining whether the 40 percent criterion of section 9 of the *Federal Child Support Guidelines* has been satisfied, demonstrate the vital importance of detailed evidence being adduced with respect to the parenting arrangements, including the times when each parent is responsible for and cares for the children.[212] Where there is an order for child support in a shared parenting time situation, the court may issue a direction for the exchange of information whenever any change occurs in the financial circumstances of either parent.[213]

A court cannot weigh the credibility of conflicting affidavits respecting an alleged denial of parenting time on an interim application to vary child support and may decline to take account of an artificial situation that has only briefly existed.[214]

---

205 *Contino v Leonelli-Contino*, [2005] 3 SCR 217; *AEC v GBH*, [1998] NSJ No 580 (Fam Ct); see also *McCurdy v Morisette*, [1999] BCJ No 2292 (SC); *Klein v Martin*, 2010 MBQB 159; *Smith v Smith*, 2011 NSSC 269.

206 *Contino v Leonelli-Contino*, [2005] 3 SCR 217; *Scott v Scott*, [2006] BCJ No 1701 (SC); *Kimber v Nikkari*, [2000] SJ No 326 (QB).

207 *Cahill v Weaver*, [2005] AJ No 1121 (QB); *Waugh v Waugh*, 2010 BCSC 110; *Slade v Slade*, [2001] NJ No 5 (CA); *Mason v Mason*, [2006] NSJ No 227 (SC); *Wolfson v Wolfson*, 2021 NSSC 260; *Dowling v Dowling*, [2005] OJ No 2682 (Div Ct); *Harvey v Armbruster*, 2014 SKQB 363.

208 *Contino v Leonelli-Contino*, [2005] 3 SCR 217; *CLB v AHB*, 2013 BCCA 472; *Slade v Slade*, [2001] NJ No 5 (CA); *Wolfson v Wolfson*, 2021 NSSC 260.

209 *Frost v Frost*, [2000] OJ No 1600 (SCJ); compare *Luedke v Luedke*, [2004] BCJ No 1157 (CA).

210 *Mertler v Kardynal*, [1997] SJ No 720 (QB).

211 *Solonenko v Stice*, [1998] SJ No 291 (QB).

212 *Tweel v Tweel*, [2000] PEIJ No 9 (SC).

213 *Abear v Abear*, [1998] BCJ No 2894 (SC).

214 *Propp v Dobson*, [1998] SJ No 703 (QB).

9) Negative Aspects of Section 9 of the Guidelines

One unfortunate aspect of section 9 of the Guidelines is that it leads to a situation where spouses may argue about parenting time in an attempt to avoid or take advantage of section 9[215] either at the time of the original application for child support or thereafter. Several courts have expressed concern about the arbitrariness and possible unfair operation of the 40 percent threshold and its potential detrimental impact on parenting arrangements.[216] For example, the parent with primary responsibility for the care and upbringing of the children may be reluctant to agree to an order for liberal and generous parenting time for the other parent unless the order makes it clear that the generosity does not exceed 40 percent of the child's time with the other parent.[217] There is a real concern that section 9 of the Guidelines may induce a primary caregiving parent to discourage maximum contact between the child and the other parent because of the economic consequences that may ensue under section 9 of the Guidelines.[218] Conversely, the other parent may seek shared parenting for 40 percent of the child's time for the sole purpose of reducing the amount of child support that would otherwise be payable.[219] The 40 percent criterion under section 9 of the federal and provincial child support guidelines also has serious limitations in that it excludes the quality of time spent with the children and may result in a "default assignment" of school hours to the parent who has primary care of the children when they are out of school.[220] Where parenting times are in issue as well as child support, the 40 percent criterion under section 9 of the Guidelines should be viewed in light of the provisions of the *Divorce Act* that endorse the best interests of the child as the determinative consideration in parenting and in light of its endorsement of maximum contact between the child and each parent insofar as it is consistent with the child's best interests.[221] Where appropriate, potential detrimental effects of section 9 of the Guidelines may be averted by the court's endorsement of pre-existing shared parenting time arrangements that have prevailed over a significant period of time.[222]

An order that provides for substantial time-sharing by the parents should not be adapted to accommodate the financial interest of the payor of child support. A parent who will spend between 37.2 and 38.1 percent of the time with his children under a proposed parenting arrangement endorsed by the Office of the Children's Lawyer should not be granted an order that brings the time-sharing up to 40 percent so as to reduce child support pursuant to section 9 of the *Federal Child Support Guidelines*. The proper approach to determining a parenting regime for children is based on their best interests, not on the financial implications of that regime.[223]

---

215 *Lopatynski v Lopatynski*, [1998] AJ No 1312 (QB); *McKerracher v McKerracher*, [1997] BCJ No 2257 (SC); *Green v Green*, [2000] BCJ No 1001 (CA); *Simpson v Simpson*, [1999] PEIJ No 73 (SC); *Propp v Dobson*, [1998] SJ No 703 (QB).

216 *Dennett v Dennett*, [1998] AJ No 440 (QB); *Hall v Hall*, [1997] BCJ No 1191 (SC); *Rosati v Dellapenta*, [1997] OJ No 5047 (Gen Div); *MacNaught v MacNaught*, [1998] PEIJ No 27 (TD).

217 *Hall v Hall*, [1997] BCJ No 1191 (SC).

218 *Hall v Hall*, *ibid*; *Propp v Dobson*, [1998] SJ No 703 (QB).

219 *Lavoie v Wills*, [2000] AJ No 1359 (QB); *Ball v Ball*, [1998] SJ No 572 (QB).

220 *Penner v Penner*, [1998] MJ No 353 (QB) (application under *Manitoba Child Support Guidelines*).

221 *Ibid.*

222 *MAF v WAF*, [1998] SJ No 224 (QB).

223 *Taillon v Taillon*, [2005] OJ No 1116 (SCJ).

10) Canada Child Benefit; Eligible Dependant Tax Credit[224]

The Canada Child Benefit program replaces the Canada Child Tax Benefit, National Child Benefit, and Universal Child Care Benefit. Although the Canada Child Benefit does not form part of the recipient's income, it is a relevant consideration under section 9 of the Guidelines.[225] Eligibility to receive the Canada Child Benefit and to claim tax credits or deductions is governed by the *Income Tax Act* and a court exercising its family law jurisdiction cannot override the eligibility requirements set out in that Act. If there are disputes over eligibility, the Tax Court of Canada has exclusive jurisdiction to resolve the issue.[226] Pursuant to current legislation, the Canada Child Benefit and the child component of the GST/HST credit is payable to the parent who fulfills the primary responsibility for the care and upbringing of the children. To address situations where the children spend time with each parent on an approximately equal basis or for not less than 40 percent during the month, eligibility for the CCB and the GST/HST credit is extended to each parent, with the amounts being determined by reference to each parent's adjusted family net income. In *Friesen v The Queen*, Graham J of the Tax Court of Canada stated:

> [8] The definition of "shared-custody parent" was amended in 2021 in response to the Federal Court of Appeal decisions in *Lavrinenko v. The Queen* (2019 FCA 151) and *Morrissey v. The* Queen (2019 FCA 56). The amendments were retroactive to 2011.
>
> [9] Parents are now considered shared-custody parents if they meet three tests: they must not be cohabitating spouses or common-law partners; they must reside with the child either at least 40 percent of the time in the month or on an approximately equal basis; finally, they must each primarily fulfil the responsibility for the care and upbringing of the child when the child resides with them. . . .
>
> [35] Based on the clear language of the provision and the statements made in the explanatory notes that accompanied the new legislation, I conclude that the new definition contemplates a situation where a parent normally meets the 40 percent threshold but temporarily slips below it in a given month because, for example, of illness, vacations, or something similar.
>
> [36] In my view, the new provision is a very practical solution to the fact that, while parenting occurs on an ongoing basis, entitlement to the Canada Child Benefit is determined on a monthly basis. The amendment provides a level of consistency for parents in the often unpredictable world of raising children.
>
> [37] The addition of the approximately equal basis test appears to have been designed to recognize that irregularities in a given month may upset an otherwise established schedule but that, over time, these irregularities will balance out.
>
> [38] I can think of a number of possible examples where the provision could apply. One parent may take the children for a week's vacation over spring break and the other parent may later take them on a similar vacation in July. One parent may have to leave town one weekend to attend a friend's wedding and the other parent may take the children for the

224 See also Chapter 1, Section B.

225 *LRC v JMC*, 2008 BCSC 408; *JC v MC*, 2014 NBQB 161; *Gannon v Gannon*, 2014 NSSC 113.

226 *Gannon v Gannon*, 2014 NSSC 113; *Cook v Ballantyne*, 2022 SKQB 172; see also *Furlan v The Queen*, 2018 TCC 25 (shared parenting time).

> weekend. Finally, a child could be sick and the parents might decide not to move the child from his or her current location with one parent in order to keep him or her comfortable. In each of these examples, I am picturing either a month where parenting time is unequal but will be roughly balanced out over the course of time or a month in which an unusual event or occurrence has interfered with the parents' established schedules.[227]

Shared parenting arrangements may affect the right to claim the eligible dependant tax credit (formerly known as the "equivalent to spouse" tax credit) under the *Income Tax Act*. Section 118(5) of the *Income Tax Act* precludes a co-parent who is paying child support from obtaining the tax credit.[228] The different statutory treatment of co-parents who are not required to pay child support and co-parents who are required to pay child support does not violate equality rights guaranteed by section 15 of the *Canadian Charter of Rights and Freedoms*.[229] A payor who is precluded from claiming the credit in respect of a particular child because he or she is paying child support for that child still may be able to claim a credit in respect of another child for which no child support is being paid.[230]

Section 118(5.1) of the *Income Tax Act* currently provides as follows:

> Where, if this Act were read without reference to this subsection, solely because of the application of subsection (5), no individual is entitled to a deduction under paragraph (*b*) or (*b*.1) of the description of B in subsection (1) for a taxation year in respect of a child, subsection (5) shall not apply in respect of that child for that taxation year.

As Woods J observed in *Perrin v Canada*,[231] "[t]his provision is intended to avoid the harsh application of s 118(5) where both spouses pay child support for the same child in the relevant year. It is designed to enable one of the spouses to claim the tax credit under paragraph 118(1)(b) in these circumstances." Consistent with these observations, the Canada Revenue Agency has published the following policy statement:

> If you *and* another person were required to make support payments for the child . . . and as a result, *no one* would be entitled to claim the amount for an eligible dependant for the child, you can still claim this amount providing that you and the other person(s) paying support agree that you will be the one to make the claim. If you do not agree on who will claim this amount for the child, no one will be allowed to claim them.[232]

Commenting on the above issues in *Cleasby v Cleasby*, McIntyre J of the Saskatchewan Court of Queen's Bench has stated:

---

227 *Friesen v The Queen*, 2022 TCC 53 at paras 8–9 and 35–38; see also *Scott v The King*, 2022 TCC 131.

228 *Haynes v Canada*, 2013 TCC 84, citing *Verones v Canada*, 2013 FCA 69; *Cleasby v Cleasby*, 2013 SKQB 67; *Ochitwa v Canada*, 2014 TCC 263; *Stevenson v The Queen*, 2018 TCC 176; *Bayrack v The Queen*, 2019 TCC 53. Compare *Ruel v The Queen*, 2017 TCC 93; *Brown v Brown*, 2020 BCCA 53 at para 81. And see Steven Benmore, "Separated Parents Don't Always Share the Tax Credit" *The Lawyers Weekly* 33:38 (21 February 2014).

229 *Donovan v Canada*, 2005 TCC 667; *Calogeracos v Canada*, 2008 TCC 389.

230 PricewaterhouseCoopers, *One Step at a Time: Tax Rules for Family Law Practitioners 2011* (PricewaterhouseCoopers, 2011) at 14–15. See also *Shewchuk v Canada*, [2000] TCJ No 398, applying s 118(5) of the *Income Tax Act*.

231 2010 TCC 331; see also *Verones v Canada*, 2012 TCC 291; *Haynes v Canada*, 2013 TCC 84.

232 General Income Tax and Benefit Package for 2008—Guide, Returns, Schedules. Modified 6 January 2009.

> The Canada Child Benefits Booklet T4114 published by the Canada Revenue Agency provides that in a case of shared [parenting], each parent will receive 50% of the child tax benefit that he or she would have received if the child had lived with that parent all of the time. The Canada Revenue Agency General Income Tax and Benefit Package indicates that if a parent does not have a spouse or common law partner and is supporting a dependant, a parent may claim an amount for an eligible dependant (AED) as a tax credit. This used to be referred to the equivalent to spouse tax credit. However a parent may not claim the AED for a child for whom the parent is required to make child support payments. While the wording of an agreement or order can be an important factor in the case of a shared parenting arrangement, if both parents are required to pay child support resulting in a set-off, Canada Revenue Agency appears to take the position that no one is entitled to claim the AED or the federal child amount tax credit for such a child unless the parents agree on who will be making the claim. Canada Revenue Agency takes the position that if the parents cannot agree, then neither of them may claim the AED or the federal child amount tax credit (FCTC).[233]

11) Variation Orders

A child support order based on the shared parenting time of children may be varied to reflect a change in the income level of one of the parents[234] or the assumption of new family relationships and obligations.[235] On an application to vary an order of child support granted pursuant to section 9 of the *Federal Child Support Guidelines*, the applicant must prove a change of circumstances within the meaning of section 17(4) of the *Divorce Act* and section 14(b) of the *Federal Child Support Guidelines*. The change must be material, substantive, unforeseen, and of a continuing nature. Where a parent has been ordered to pay the full table amount of child support, notwithstanding that the shared parenting time arrangements fall within section 9 of the *Federal Child Support Guidelines*, minor changes in the parenting regime to accommodate the child's entering kindergarten do not justify a variation order.[236] In *Clarke v Babensee*,[237] the British Columbia Court of Appeal found that the appellant father had failed to demonstrate a reviewable error. While acknowledging that on an absolute scale there had been a change in the parental incomes, the mother's having increased while the father's decreased, the British Columbia Court of Appeal stated that "the income of a spouse is but one consideration in the support regime established by section 9 of the Guidelines and as *Contino* holds, no one factor in that analysis should prevail. More to the point, it is but one consideration in the constellation of factors set out in section 14(b) of the Guidelines," which explicitly refers to "any change in the condition, means, needs or other circumstances of either spouse or of any child who is entitled to support."

233 2013 SKQB 67 at para 16. See also *Nixon v Nixon*, 2014 SKQB 264; *CPB v Canada*, 2013 TCC 118; *Letoria v Canada*, 2015 TCC 221; *Belway v Canada*, 2015 TCC 249; *LLH v CCH*, 2019 BCSC 1346 at para 267. As to the spousal equivalent and child deduction in a split parenting time case, see *Harder v Canada*, 2016 CarswellNat 4358 (TCC [Informal Procedure]), discussed in FAMLNWS 2016-50 (19 December 2016). See also *Brown v Brown*, 2020 BCCA 53 at paras 72–83.

234 *Wouters v Wouters*, [2002] SJ No 520 (QB), var'd [2005] SJ No 340 (CA).

235 *Plourde v Morin*, [2005] NSJ No 505 (SC).

236 *Heigh v Rubidge*, 2010 SKCA 80.

237 2009 BCCA 122 at para 23.

Where a shared parenting time agreement provided for a designated monthly amount for child support and the agreement was incorporated in an order for corollary financial relief granted at the time of divorce, a modest increase in the amount of time spent with the children by the paying parent may be insufficient to warrant any variation of the existing order, if the few extra days have no real financial impact on the parents.[238] The provisions of section 9 of the *Nova Scotia Child Support Guidelines* mirror section 9 of the *Federal Child Support Guidelines*; consequently, the principles defined by the Supreme Court of Canada in *Contino v Leonelli-Contino*[239] apply to a shared parenting time arrangement that falls within section 9 of the provincial guidelines. An application to vary a consent order for shared parenting time may be denied where (1) it is apparent that the modest increase in the amount of time the children spend with their father has not significantly increased his parenting expenses or reduced those of the mother and no useful purpose would be served by adjourning the variation application to permit the self-represented litigants to provide detailed financial disclosure and child-related budgets; and (2) termination of child support would compromise the economic well-being of the children and the standard of living provided by the mother.[240]

Where parenting arrangements have materially changed so as to trigger the application of section 9 of the *Federal Child Support Guidelines*, there are four factors in the background that are relevant concerns. The first factor to consider is the purpose behind section 9 of the Guidelines. The assumption under section 9 is that a shared parenting time situation will increase the overall costs for both parents as a result of duplication, with the result that payment of the basic Guidelines amount would be unfair. The second factor is the "cliff effect," which results from the sudden drop in the support payable to a parent when the other parent crosses the threshold between 39 percent and 40 percent of the child's time. Third, there is the view that variation is more readily justified if a parent has less means than the primary caregiving parent and would have difficulty in meeting increased expenses. Fourth, the court must not give undue weight to section 9(a) of the Guidelines, which refers to the table amounts payable by each parent. The court must also consider section 9(b), which addresses the increased costs of shared parenting time, and section 9(c), which requires the court to have regard to the conditions, means, needs, and other circumstances of each parent and of any child for whom support is sought.[241] The importance of applying sections 9(b) and (c) of the Guidelines to counteract the "cliff effect" of a simple set-off of the respective table amounts of child support under section 9(a) is underlined in the judgment of the Supreme Court of Canada in *Contino v Leonelli-Contino*.[242] Recipient parents may have validly incurred expenses based on legitimate expectations of how much child support would be received. The court must, therefore, consider the actual spending patterns of the parents, the ability of each to bear the increased costs of shared parenting time arrangements (which

238 *Fletcher v Keilty*, [2003] NBJ No 10 (QB), aff'd [2004] NBJ No 152 (CA).

239 [2005] 3 SCR 217.

240 *Elliott v MacAskill*, [2005] NSJ No 479 (Fam Ct).

241 *CRHE v FGE*, [2003] BCJ No 2129 (SC), aff'd [2004] BCJ No 1057 (CA).

242 [2005] 3 SCR 217; see Section B(3), above in this chapter. See also *Kolisnyk v Loscerbo*, 2010 MBCA 1; *Church v Chafe*, 2010 NLTD(F) 31.

entails considerations of assets, liabilities, income levels, and disparities) and the standard of living for the child in each household.[243]

While section 9 of the Guidelines gives the court flexibility, it does not give the paying spouse an automatic right to a reduction in the support payable because a shared parenting time arrangement has come to exist.[244] Although a change in parenting arrangements that results in alternating weekly parenting may trigger the application of section 9 of the *Federal Child Support Guidelines*, the court may conclude that the higher income parent shall continue to pay the full applicable table amount of child support where the other parent's ability to financially provide for the children while in her care is a matter of serious concern. The recipient parent may be ordered to notify the payor of any future employment and the rate of pay.[245]

A court may refuse to interfere with the provisions of a comprehensive settlement by increasing the amount of child support to be paid, where reasonable provision is being made for the children by way of an agreed amount of periodic child support under a consensual shared parenting time situation and the wife's application for an increased amount of child support is simply an indirect attempt to obtain spousal support under the guise of child support, the wife having lost her previous entitlement to spousal support by entering into a "common law" relationship.[246] Similarly, a father's increased time with children under a parenting regime that already falls subject to section 9 of the *Federal Child Support Guidelines* does not warrant variation of the amount of child support payable with respect to those children under a prior consent order, where such increased time was contemplated by the consent order and there is no evidence of any increased costs.[247]

12) Provincial Guidelines

Section 9 of the *Manitoba Child Support Guidelines* calls for a three-stage analysis that starts with a consideration of whether or not the applicable table amount payable under the Guidelines by each parent is to be altered and then, and only then, does the court proceed to steps two and three, which call for a review, based on the evidence, of the increased costs associated with the shared parenting time arrangements, and then finally, the conditions, means, needs, and other circumstances of each parent and child. Parents cannot simply claim that they have additional costs because of a shared parenting time arrangement. They must prove what those costs are. If the motions judge did not have the factual foundation on which to arrive at a reasoned analysis, an appellate court may remit the matter back to the motions court so that the requisite evidence can be provided.[248]

The *Ontario Child Support Guidelines* are not concerned with standing or with jurisdiction; they are concerned only with the amount of child support, if any, that should be ordered. Section 9 of the *Ontario Child Support Guidelines* may be invoked by a parent who

---

243 *Martin v Martin*, 2007 MBQB 296; *Kolisnyk v Loscerbo*, 2010 MBCA 1; *Foss v Foss*, 2011 NSSC 115.

244 *Contino v Leonelli-Contino*, [2005] 3 SCR 217; *Kielesinski v Kielesinski*, 2011 BCSC 538.

245 *Park v Walsh*, [2003] NJ No 63 (SC).

246 *Roth v Gallagher*, [2003] BCJ No 260 (SC).

247 *Lake v Lake*, [2004] NBJ No 61 (QB).

248 *Cabot v Mikkelson*, [2004] MJ No 240 (CA).

spends less time with the children but satisfies the 40 percent time-sharing criterion set out therein. In calculating whether a parent exercises not less than 40 percent of parenting time with a child over the course of a year, section 9 of the Guidelines confers no discretion on the court. Section 9 calls for the court to apply simple arithmetic in determining whether the 40 percent plateau has been reached. If the 40 percent criterion is satisfied, there is no clearly defined approach as to how a court should balance the factors specified in sections 9(a), (b), and (c) of the Guidelines. Several different formulae have been used but there are also cases that eschew any formula in favour of a broader approach that emphasizes means and needs. Unlike section 3(2) and section 4 of the Guidelines, section 9 of the Guidelines creates no presumption in favour of the payment of the applicable table amount of child support but, at the same time, there is nothing to prevent the court from balancing the stipulated criteria and exercising its discretion by ordering the obligor to pay the full table amount of child support so that the child may, so far as is practicable, enjoy the same standard of economic well-being as was enjoyed prior to the parental separation.[249]

13) Conclusion

The variety of different approaches adopted by the courts in exercising their discretion under section 9 of the federal and provincial child support guidelines renders the law totally unpredictable and thereby fosters litigation. It would be appropriate, therefore, for the Minister of Justice to re-examine the operation and application of section 9 of the Guidelines with a view to providing clarification and a higher degree of predictability than currently exists.

249 *Robblee v Reid*, [2003] OJ No 429 (SCJ).

CHAPTER 7

Undue Hardship

A. GENERAL OBSERVATIONS

Section 10(1) of the *Federal Child Support Guidelines* provides that a court may, on the appli cation of either spouse or former spouse,[1] make a child support order in an amount that is different from one that would have been determined in accordance with sections 3 to 5, 8, or 9 of the Guidelines if the court finds that the spouse or former spouse making the application, or a child in respect of whom the application is made, would suffer undue hardship as a result of an order in an amount determined under those sections. Undue hardship may, therefore, be invoked as a justification for deviating from the amount of child support prescribed by the applicable provincial or territorial table, or in cases involving children over the age of major ity under section 3(2)(b) of the Guidelines, or for the purpose of qualifying the application of section 4 of the Guidelines involving obligors with income over $150,000, or under section 5 of the Guidelines whereby the support obligation owed to a child of the marriage by a spouse or former spouse who stands in the place of a parent may be affected by a natural or adoptive parent's child support obligation,[2] or to qualify the application of section 8 of the Guidelines where each spouse has the primary care of at least one child of the marriage,[3] or in cases of shared parenting time under section 9 of the Guidelines.[4] In deviating from the Guidelines that would be applicable but for undue hardship, the court may, on the application of either spouse or former spouse, set child support at a higher or lower level than would otherwise be payable. The same high threshold test of "undue hardship" applies whether the payor or the payee invokes section 10 of the Guidelines[5] but successful applications by payees are rare.

1 *Middleton v MacPherson*, [1997] AJ No 614 (QB); *Lavoie v Lavoie (Lillos)*, 2011 ABQB 781; *MS v JC*, 2010 PESC 50 (application by obligor).

2 *Locke v Goulding*, 2012 NLCA 8.

3 *Scharf v Scharf*, [1998] OJ No 199 (Gen Div).

4 *Kerr v Kerr*, [2002] BCJ No 1468 (SC) (stringent test of undue hardship not satisfied); *Locke v Goulding*, 2012 NLCA 8; compare *Contino v Leonelli-Contino*, [2005] 3 SCR 217; see Chapter 6, Section B(3).

5 *Suian v Suian*, [2002] BCJ No 1328 (SC).

6 *Saby v MacIntosh*, [2002] BCJ No 1813 (SC); *Eckert v Eckert*, 2018 MBQB 117.

Courts should be cautious when a finding of undue hardship is being sought by the recipient spouse because of the potential for abuse and should not permit section 10 to be invoked by the payee as an indirect vehicle for the payment of spousal support or for imposing a child support obligation on other members of the obligor's household.[7] Economic hardship faced by the payee should be addressed by means of an application for spousal support.[8] Three potential issues arise pursuant to section 10 of the *Federal Child Support Guidelines* when undue hardship is pleaded, namely

(a) whether undue hardship exists;
(b) whether a comparison of the standard of living in each household precludes the exercise of judicial discretion; and
(c) how the court should exercise its discretion.[9]

A claim of undue hardship under section 10 of the *Federal Child Support Guidelines* should be included in the pleadings or they should be amended to include such a claim before the court makes any such finding.[10] A judicial determination under section 10 of the *Federal Child Support Guidelines* presupposes a series of steps being undertaken, including a consideration of all relevant evidence, findings of fact being made, and the application of the criteria set out in that section. These are functions of a trial judge, not of an appellate court; in their absence, an appellate court should remit the matter for reconsideration by the trial court.[11]

It is not possible to determine whether undue hardship will exist if the child support order is limited to the amount fixed by the Guidelines, without first knowing the amount of spousal support, if any, to be ordered. While section 15.3(1) of the *Divorce Act* requires the court to give priority to child support where there are concurrent applications for spousal and child support, consideration of an application for increased child support based on undue hardship within the meaning of section 10 of the *Federal Child Support Guidelines* must be deferred until the matter of spousal support has been determined.[12] The amount of spousal support to be paid and received must then be taken into account in comparing the standard of living of the respective households under Schedule II of the *Federal Child Support Guidelines* for the purpose of determining whether the requirements of section 10(3) of the Guidelines have been satisfied.[13]

The undue hardship provisions of section 10 of the *Federal Child Support Guidelines* create a fairly narrow judicial discretion to deviate from the Guidelines. Undue hardship

---

7 *Middleton v MacPherson*, [1997] AJ No 614 (QB); *Saby v MacIntosh*, 2002 BCSC 1144; *Jeans v Jeans*, [2000] NJ No 42 (UFC); *Williams v Williams*, [1997] NWTJ No 49 (SC); *Racette v Gamauf*, [1997] PEIJ No 123 (TD); *O'Hara v O'Hara*, [1997] SJ No 482 (QB). See also *MS v JC*, 2010 PESC 50 at para 22.

8 *Kehler v Kehler*, [2001] AJ No 1048 (QB).

9 *Smith v Smith*, [1999] AJ No 1180 (QB); *Blanchard v Blanchard*, 2019 ABCA 53; *Swain v Montanaro*, 2016 ONSC 4295 at para 10, Smith J; *Reid v Faubert*, 2019 NSCA 42; *Guenette v Morrisey*, 2019 ONSC 4326.

10 *Branch v Branch*, [2003] NBJ No 50 (QB); *Locke v Goulding*, 2012 NLCA 8. See also *Henderson v Micetich*, 2021 ABCA 103 at para 78.

11 *Brandt v Brandt*, [2003] NJ No 168 (CA) (trial judge in error in failing to consider faxed affidavit of parent resident abroad; support order set aside by appellate court, rehearing ordered).

12 *Galliford v Galliford*, [1998] BCJ No 268 (SC); *Schmid v Smith*, [1999] OJ No 3062 (SCJ) (application under Ontario *Family Law Act* and *Ontario Child Support Guidelines*).

13 *Ibid.*

is a tough threshold to meet.[14] The test for undue hardship requires that the hardship be severe and unreasonable.[15] Furthermore, the use of the word "may" in section 10(1) of the Guidelines clearly demonstrates that any deviation from the Guidelines amount is discretionary, even if the court finds undue hardship and a lower standard of living in the obligor's household.[16] Although there is little judicial guidance on when this residual discretion will be exercised, it is inappropriate to exercise it where the parent alleging undue hardship has wilfully refused to pay child support.[17] The presumptive rule under section 3 of the *Federal Child Support Guidelines* should not be displaced in the absence of specific and cogent evidence why the applicable table amount would cause an "undue hardship."[18] Section 10 of the Guidelines is only available where excessively hard living conditions or severe financial consequences would result from the payment of the Guidelines amount.[19] A court should refuse to find undue hardship where a parent can reasonably reduce his or her expenses and thereby alleviate hardship.[20] In the absence of the circumstances that constitute "undue hardship" under section 10 of the *Federal Child Support Guidelines*, a court has no residual discretion to lower the applicable table amount of child support under the Guidelines. If a parent has difficulty paying the table amount of child support because of other financial commitments that fall short of constituting "undue hardship" within the meaning of section 10 of the Guidelines, that parent must rearrange his or her financial commitments; the child support obligation takes priority.[21] In most cases wherein the undue hardship provisions of the Guidelines are met by the obligor, there is only a reduction in the amount of support; the child support obligation is rarely extinguished, although circumstances may arise where this is the appropriate disposition.[22] One way to rationalize the amount of child support to be paid when a paying parent demonstrates undue hardship is by reference to how much that parent would be required to pay for one family consisting of the total number of children for which he or she is legally responsible. Upon being satisfied that undue hardship is made out, the court considers what the basic obligation would be if the children were all in one family

14 *Hanmore v Hanmore*, [2000] AJ No 171 (CA); *Kimmerly v Henschel*, 2016 ABQB 540; *Van Gool v Van Gool*, [1998] BCJ No 2513 (CA); *LCT v RK*, 2017 BCCA 64; *Bassett v Magee*, 2020 BCSC 1994; *Campbell v Campbell*, 2016 MBQB 57; *Turner v Yerxa*, [2002] NBJ No 199 (QB); *Locke v Goulding*, 2012 NLCA 8; *Pretty v Pretty*, 2011 NSSC 296; *Locke v Bramwell*, 2016 NSSC 300; *Corbett v McEachren*, 2017 NSSC 108; *Cole v Jerome*, 2017 NWTSC 28; *Praetzel v Porter*, 2022 NWTSC 19; *Harvey v Sturk*, 2016 ONSC 4669; *Racette v Gamauf*, [1997] PEIJ No 123 (TD); *Barber v Barber*, 2011 SKQB 131.

15 *Corbett v McEachren*, 2017 NSSC 108, citing *LCT v RK*, 2017 BCCA 64 at para 83; *Callwood v Purdy*, 2021 ONSC 5815; see also *Hull v Kornilov*, 2024 BCSC 82; *Reid v Faubert*, 2019 NSCA 42; *Vardy v Vardy*, 2019 NSSC 285.

16 *CWT v KAT*, 2013 ABQB 678; *X(RL) v X(JF)*, [2002] BCJ No 1889 (SC); *LCT v RK*, 2017 BCCA 64; *Skorulski v Zupan*, 2012 MBQB 98; *Locke v Goulding*, 2012 NLCA 8; *Murphy v Bert*, 2007 NSSC 376; *Praetzel v Porter*, 2022 NWTSC 19; *Swain v Montanaro*, 2016 ONSC 4295; *Callwood v Purdy*, 2021 ONSC 5815; *Barber v Barber*, 2011 SKQB 131.

17 *RDO v CJO*, [2003] BCJ No 1179 (SC).

18 *Hanmore v Hanmore*, [2000] AJ No 171 (CA); *Scott v Scott*, [2000] BCJ No 1147 (SC); *Locke v Goulding*, 2012 NLCA 8; *Tutty v Tutty*, [2005] NSJ No 514 (SC).

19 *Ellis v Ellis*, [1999] NSJ No 78 (CA).

20 *Badry v Badry*, [2004] BCJ No 2432 (SC); *Locke v Goulding*, 2012 NLCA 8; *SM v RP*, [1998] QJ No 4119 (CS).

21 *MacEachern v Hardy*, 2010 NSSC 246; *Ritchie v Solonick*, [1999] YJ No 66 (SC).

22 *Alfaro v Alfaro*, [1999] AJ No 1062 (QB); *Tutty v Tutty*, [2005] NSJ No 514 (SC); *Larkin v Jamieson*, [2000] PEIJ No 65 (SC).

and then apportions that amount amongst each of the children. But to be fair to everyone, additional factors, such as differences in the cost of living and the receiving parent's actual costs of living, may need to be taken into account.[23]

Where the obligor has a low income, a court may order a modest amount of child support as a "symbolic" gesture to reinforce the parental role,[24] but such an order may be deemed unnecessary in light of the attendant circumstances of the particular case.[25]

In its final report on child support guidelines, the Federal/Provincial/Territorial Family Law Committee suggested that a court would only make a finding of undue hardship in lower income families because parents with higher incomes would rarely find difficulty in paying the required amount of child support.[26] It should be borne in mind, however, that it is not only an obligor who can invoke undue hardship for the purpose of reducing child support; the recipient may also invoke undue hardship under section 10 of the *Federal Child Support Guidelines* for the purpose of increasing the amount of child support. Such latter claims are likely to be rare because of the potential applicability of section 7 being invoked to deal with special or extraordinary expenses incurred with respect to the child.

Undue hardship is objectively ascertained. A bald assertion that the obligor cannot afford to pay does not satisfy the requirements of section 10 of the *Federal Child Support Guidelines* and the motives of the applicant who is seeking child support are generally irrelevant.[27] A court may decline to find undue hardship where it is not satisfied as to the *bona fides* of a recent arrangement to pay monthly support for a child from the obligor's previous relationship.[28]

The *Federal Child Support Guidelines* were designed to provide certainty with respect to the amount of child support to be paid to the parent who is primarily responsible for the care of the children. They are based on prescribed formulae and are not intended to provide much discretion for a trial judge. Parliament has severely circumscribed the judicial discretion in determining child support in order to promote consistency, certainty, and an overall increase in the amount of child support. The presumptive rule whereby a primary caregiving parent receives the applicable provincial table amount of child support is not displaced by economic hardship on the part of the payor spouse, unless that hardship satisfies the stringent requirements imposed by the "undue hardship" provisions of section 10 of the *Federal Child Support Guidelines*.[29] Pursuant to section 10 of the *Federal Child Support Guidelines*, the court must first be satisfied that circumstances exist that would cause the applicant or a child to suffer undue hardship. Section 10(2) of the Guidelines sets out a non-exhaustive list of factors that may cause undue hardship. Second, even if a finding of undue hardship is made, the court must still refuse to deviate from the Guidelines amount, where the court is of the opinion

---

23 *Cole v Jerome*, 2017 NWTSC 28 at paras 56–58, Shaner J, citing *Bumpus v Benoit*, 2004 PESCTD 60.

24 *Dixon v Fleming*, [2000] OJ No 1218 (SCJ).

25 *Larkin v Jamieson*, [2000] PEIJ No 65 (SC).

26 Federal/Provincial/Territorial Family Law Committee (Canada), *Report and Recommendations on Child Support* (Ottawa: Department of Justice, 1995) at 29, para 5.2.3; see also *Cahill v Weaver*, [2005] AJ No 1121 (QB); *Raynor v Raynor*, [1997] NSJ No 411 (TD); *Douglas v Faucher*, 2014 ONSC 4045.

27 *Sampson v Sampson*, [1998] AJ No 1214 (QB); *Bosgra v Squires*, [2001] NWTJ No 78 (SC).

28 *White v White*, [2000] BCJ No 516 (SC).

29 *Anderson-Devine v Anderson*, [2002] MJ No 46 (QB); *KB v MA*, 2019 NBQB 90; *Locke v Goulding*, 2012 NLCA 8.

that the household of the party asserting undue hardship would have a higher standard of living than the recipient household even after allocating the applicable Guidelines amount.[30] It is clear from the opening words of section 10(3) of the *Federal Child Support Guidelines* that a comparison of the standard of living of the two households will only be undertaken after there has been a prior determination of undue hardship.[31] Consequently, an obligor is not entitled to financial disclosure respecting third parties who live in the same household as the primary caregiving parent until circumstances constituting undue hardship have been established by the obligor.[32] On a practical level, however, it is for the court to ensure that neither party engages in an abuse of process and both counsel are expected to exercise common sense and act in the best interests of their clients. On the one hand, simply advancing a claim of undue hardship, whether the claim has merit or not, does not trigger an automatic right to income information concerning all members of each household. On the other hand, information should not be withheld solely for tactical reasons in cases where there is potential merit to the claim and non-disclosure will serve only to delay proceedings and increase the costs of the parties.[33]

The existence of a lower standard of living in the obligor's household does not of itself justify a finding of undue hardship.[34] A parent who earns an annual income of $25,000 will not, therefore, be absolved of financial obligations towards his or her child simply because the primary caregiving parent's household has two income earners and a combined annual income in excess of $150,000.[35]

The onus of proving that the requirements of section 10 of the *Federal Child Support Guidelines* have been satisfied falls upon the party who invokes the plea of undue hardship.[36] Such a finding cannot be made in the absence of full disclosure of his or her household income and expenses.[37] However, it has been asserted that once the obligor has established a *prima facie* case of undue hardship, the onus shifts to the recipient household to prove that the party claiming undue hardship would have a higher household standard of living

---

30 *Hanmore v Hanmore*, [2000] AJ No 171 (CA); *Van Gool v Van Gool*, [1998] BCJ No 2513 (CA); *Kelly v Kelly*, 2011 BCCA 173; *Hull v Kornilov*, 2024 BCSC 82; *MN v CGF*, 2019 BCSC 1406; *Eckert v Eckert*, 2018 MBQB 117; *WL v NDH*, 2014 NBQB 214; *Locke v Goulding*, 2012 NLCA 8; *Gaetz v Gaetz*, [2001] NSJ No 131 (CA); *Reid v Faubert*, 2019 NSCA 42; *Newman v Bogan*, 2010 NWTSC 69; *Camirand v Beaulne*, [1998] OJ No 2163 (Gen Div); *Belliveau v Arsenault-Dawson*, [2001] PEIJ No 114 (SC); *Varga v Varga*, 2013 SKQB 22; *LARA v DSB*, 2009 YKSC 74.

31 *Kelly v Kelly*, 2011 BCCA 173; *Kaur v Khurana*, 2022 BCSC 1613; *Russell v Doucet*, [2012] NBJ No 114 (QB); *Green v Green*, [2005] NJ No 165 (CA); *Locke v Goulding*, 2012 NLCA 8; *Gaetz v Gaetz*, [2001] NSJ No 131 (CA); *Costa v Perkins*, 2012 ONSC 3165; *Hourie v Anderson*, [1998] SJ No 754 (QB).

32 *Nishnik v Smith*, [1997] SJ No 812 (QB).

33 *Russell v Russell*, [1998] OJ No 2234 (Gen Div); *Jackson v Holloway*, [1997] SJ No 691 (QB).

34 *Kimmerly v Henschel*, 2016 ABQB 540; *Gaetz v Gaetz*, [2001] NSJ No 131 (CA); *Ross v Ross*, [2001] NSJ No 184 (CA); *Phelan v Verni*, 2013 ONSC 2893; *Callwood v Purdy*, 2021 ONSC 5815; *Dougan v Clark*, [2003] PEIJ No 87 (SC); *Jackson v Holloway*, [1997] SJ No 691 (QB); see also *DLD v RAG*, 2010 BCSC 1080.

35 *AA v JA*, 2023 NBKB 210 at para 125; *Birss v Birss*, [2000] OJ No 3692 (Div Ct).

36 *Van Gool v Van Gool*, [1998] BCJ No 2513 (CA); *JJ v AM*, 2011 NBQB 368; *Locke v Goulding*, 2012 NLCA 8; *Ellis v Ellis*, [1999] NSJ No 78 (CA); *Williams v Steinwand*, 2014 NWTSC 74; *Russell v Russell*, [1998] OJ No 2234 (Gen Div); *Kelly v Kingston*, [2000] PEIJ No 22 (SC); *Uhrich-Cormier v Cormier*, [2000] SJ No 595 (QB).

37 *Cross v Cross*, [1997] BCJ No 1741 (SC); see also *Tack v Fournier*, [1998] MJ No 596 (QB) (application under *Manitoba Child Support Guidelines*); *Locke v Goulding*, 2012 NLCA 8.

than that enjoyed by the recipient household if the court elected not to deviate from the amount otherwise payable under the Guidelines.[38] An advisory test is provided in Schedule II to assist in the calculation of the household standard of living. Section 10(4) of the *Federal Child Support Guidelines* does not require the court to use the test set out in Schedule II of the Guidelines.[39]

The obligor's failure to file a sworn financial statement as required by section 20 of the *Federal Child Support Guidelines* may preclude a finding of undue hardship under section 10 of the Guidelines.[40]

The absence of requisite information may compel dismissal of a claim of undue hardship without prejudice to the claimant's right to renew the claim at a later date.[41]

There is no legal basis for restricting the application of the undue hardship provisions of section 10 of the *Federal Child Support Guidelines* to interim proceedings for child sup port, but their application may require greater caution because of the limitations of affidavit evidence.[42]

Where the obligor's sole source of income is social assistance, the court must apply some measure of common sense and reason in applying the undue hardship provisions of the Guidelines.[43]

Given a finding of undue hardship, the court may conclude that a parent should be relieved from paying any child support either prospectively or retroactively.[44]

A plea of undue hardship under section 10 of the Guidelines may be adjourned to allow additional information to be provided concerning the obligor's eligibility, if any, for dis ability benefits.[45] Exercise of the judicial discretion under the undue hardship provisions of section 10 of the *Federal Child Support Guidelines* may result in an order for no support or for reduced support.[47]

The undue hardship provisions of the Guidelines may be applied to reduce the amount of lump sum retroactive child support as well as the prospective periodic child support payments that would otherwise have been ordered.[48] A parent is not entitled to assert undue hardship where the inability to pay child support was self-induced after the order had been granted.

Income may be imputed to a parent and his spouse for the purpose of determining whether the "undue hardship" provisions of section 10 of the *Federal Child Support Guide lines* have been met. On a variation application arising from a parenting change, the level of income previously imputed to a parent is not conclusive as to current income, given that a material change in circumstances may have occurred since the original order. A mother

---

38 *Nishnik v Smith*, [1997] SJ No 812 (QB); compare *Kelly v Kingston*, [2000] PEIJ No 22 (SC).

39 *Hull v Kornilov*, 2024 BCSC 82; *Tack v Fournier*, [1998] MJ No 596 (QB); *Johnson v Downey*, 2021 NSSC 2; *Camirand v Beaulne*, [1998] OJ No 2163 (Gen Div); *Nishnik v Smith*, [1997] SJ No 812 (QB).

40 *Kramer v Kramer*, [1999] MJ No 338 (QB).

41 *Nagy v Tittemore*, [1997] SJ 810 (QB).

42 *Boppart v Boppart*, [1999] BCJ No 555 (SC).

43 *Peck v Peck*, [1998] NSJ No 286 (TD).

44 *Kennedy-Dowell v Dowell*, [2002] NSJ No 123 (SC).

45 *Griffiths v Griffiths*, [1999] AJ No 283 (QB).

46 *White v Rushton*, [1998] BCJ No 1227 (SC).

47 *Ostafie v Ostafie*, [2001] SJ No 149 (QB).

48 *Miller v Ufoegbune*, [2000] OJ No 3979 (SCJ).

49 *Sporer v Sporer*, [2000] OJ No 2413 (SCJ).

may be entitled to question the father's new spouse directly for the purpose of ascertaining whether additional income might be imputed to the father's household that could affect how the court would deal with the effect of proven undue hardship.[50]

The judgment of the Newfoundland and Labrador Court of Appeal in *Locke v Goulding*[51] provides an excellent review of the judicial discretion to deviate from the presumptive rule under section 3(1) of the *Federal Child Support Guidelines* in favour of the applicable table amount of child support on the basis of a finding of undue hardship within the meaning of section 10 of the Guidelines in circumstances where the support obligor is required to support children from successive marriages. The following principles have been distilled from the judgment:

1) Section 3(1)(a) of the Guidelines prescribes a presumptive rule in favour of the applicable table amount of child support.
2) A court may deviate from the table amount of child support on the basis of undue hardship if the requirements of section 10 of the Guidelines are satisfied.
3) In the absence of a finding of undue hardship under section 10 of the Guidelines, a court has no jurisdiction to reduce the applicable provincial table amount of support payable to children of the parent's first marriage by taking account of his or her legal obligation to support children born of a second marriage. Before a court can find undue hardship under section 10(2)(d) of the Guidelines on the basis that a parent must also support the children of a second marriage, there must be cogent and persuasive evidence that undue hardship would result from an order for the table amount of child support to be paid for the children of the first marriage. If a parent remarries and has more children when he or she already has a responsibility to support the children from a previous marriage, that parent is ordinarily expected to organize his or her affairs so as to honour the pre-existing obligation.
4) A claim of undue hardship under section 10 of the Guidelines should be included in the pleadings and supported by full financial disclosure.
5) The onus of proving undue hardship falls upon the party who invokes section 10 of the Guidelines.
6) A judicial determination under section 10 of the Guidelines presupposes a consideration of all relevant evidence, findings of fact being made, and the application of the criteria set out in that section.
7) An undue hardship analysis involves several steps. The table amount of child support payable under section 3(1) of the Guidelines must first be determined. Then, the evidence in support of the claim for undue hardship must be evaluated in relation to the circumstances listed under section 10(2) of the Guidelines or any other circumstances (as the list is not exhaustive) that reasonably invite consideration of undue hardship. This evaluation must recognize that undue hardship is a high threshold to meet. It goes beyond difficulty or inconvenience; the hardship must be "excessive, extreme, improper,

50 *Ben-Ami v Ben-Ami*, [2001] OJ No 5109 (SCJ) (father's new spouse ordered to answer questions directed towards her income since this procedure would be more likely to achieve accuracy and timeliness than if the father were to endeavour to provide the information).

51 2012 NLCA 8; see also *Davis v Davis*, 2016 NLTD(F) 2; *DB v HMB*, 2019 NLSC 105.

unreasonable, [or] unjustified." Section 10(2) of the Guidelines sets out circumstances that *may* constitute undue hardship within the meaning of section 10(1) of the Guidelines. Merely showing that one of the circumstances listed in section 10(2) exists is not sufficient to meet the requirement of establishing undue hardship. The applicant must show that the circumstances relied upon *will* create undue hardship if the table amount of child support is ordered. The claimant must prove that his or her obligations and expenses cannot be reasonably managed so as to enable him or her to pay the table amount of child support and how and why it is that he or she will suffer undue hardship if ordered to pay the table amount of child support. If the claimant is unable to prove this, his or her claim of undue hardship must fail at this stage. A general reference to the overall expense of a new household will not suffice to support a claim of undue hardship; there must be full disclosure of the support obligor's household income and expenses.

8) If the evidence supports a finding of undue hardship under section 10(2) of the Guidelines, the court *must* undertake a standards-of-living comparison under section 10(3) of the Guidelines. A comparison of the standard of living of the two households will be undertaken pursuant to section 10(3) of the Guidelines only when there has been a prior determination of undue hardship.
9) An optional test for conducting a standards-of-living comparison is found in Schedule II of the Guidelines. Without attempting to catalogue the factors that compose a standards-of-living comparison, it involves more than a straightforward comparison of household incomes. Even Schedule II contemplates imputing income to any member of the household, which includes the spouse of a payor parent. But Schedule II does not account for all factors relevant to one's standard of living. The value of a two-parent household as opposed to a single-parent household, high medical costs, or a multitude of other circumstances could well inform a standards-of-living comparison.
10) If the court determines that, after paying the table amount of child support, the standard of living of the support obligor's household would remain higher than (or perhaps equal to) that of the recipient household, the claim must be denied. Furthermore, the use of the word "may" in section 10(1) of the Guidelines clearly demonstrates that any deviation from the table amount of child support is discretionary, even if the court finds undue hardship and a lower standard of living in the obligor's household.
11) If a court ultimately exercises its discretion and grants the claim for undue hardship, section 10(6) of the Guidelines requires the court to record its reasons for doing so.

B. STRINGENT CRITERION OF UNDUE HARDSHIP

"Undue hardship" implies that section 10 of the *Federal Child Support Guidelines* imposes substantial limitations on the court's jurisdiction to deviate from the amount of child support that would otherwise be granted pursuant to the Guidelines. The Guidelines must be applied and the court is given no discretion to "fudge" them if there is no finding of undue hardship.[52] Parents are expected to exhaust all efforts to increase their incomes and decrease discretionary expenses before consideration can be given to reduce a child support

52 *Tallman v Tomke*, [1997] AJ No 682 (QB).

obligation.[53] Section 10 of the *Federal Child Support Guidelines* must be interpreted in light of the objectives defined in section 1 of the Guidelines. The objectives of predictability and consistency cannot be achieved if courts frequently deviate from the applicable provincial or territorial table as a result of section 10 applications.[54] The objectives of the *Federal Child Support Guidelines*, which are set out in section 1 of the Guidelines, would be defeated if courts adopted a broad definition of "undue hardship" or if applications under section 10 of the Guidelines became the norm, rather than the exception.[55] Judicial interpretation of the Guidelines cannot depend on what the court regards as appropriate policy or what is fair.[56] The requirement that the hardship be "undue" signifies that a stringent criterion will be applied. Some degree of economic hardship may be the inevitable consequence of separation and divorce. In order to meet the requirements of section 10(1), the hardship must be more than awkward or inconvenient; it must be severe, exceptional, excessive, disproportionate, unwarranted, or out of the ordinary, rather than the inevitable consequence of dividing limited resources between two households. The use of the term "undue" implies something more than the hardship that ensues from a lower standard of living after divorce.[57]

A court will decline to find undue hardship where a parent can reorganize his financial affairs and thereby alleviate the hardship.[58] The judicial discretion is severely limited, therefore, in average situations.[59] The obligor's spending habits are irrelevant to the issue of undue hardship but the income earned or the earning capacity of the obligor's current spouse is relevant to the issue of undue hardship. While the obligor's current spouse has no obligation to support the obligor's child from a previous relationship, that spouse must contribute towards the support of her own children and to that extent increases the obligor's capacity to discharge his support obligation to the child of his previous relationship.[60] Undue hardship will not be found in a variation proceeding where the reduction of support results from the direct application of the *Federal Child Support Guidelines*.[61]

53 *Pretty v Pretty*, 2011 NSSC 296, citing *McPhee v Thomas*, 2010 NSSC 367.

54 *Kelly v Kelly*, 2011 BCCA 173; *Philibert v Webber*, 2011 BCSC 623; *Locke v Goulding*, 2012 NLCA 8; *Camirand v Beaulne*, [1998] OJ No 2163 (Gen Div).

55 *Hanmore v Hanmore*, [2000] AJ No 171 (CA); *LCT v RK*, 2017 BCCA 64; *Beisel v Henderson*, [2004] SJ No 413 (QB).

56 *Osmar v Osmar*, [2000] OJ No 2060 (SCJ); *Bates v Bates*, [2000] OJ No 2269 (CA); *Birss v Birss*, [2000] OJ No 3692 (Div Ct). Compare *Forrest v Forrest*, [2006] NSJ No 136 (SC).

57 *Hanmore v Hanmore*, [2000] AJ No 171 (CA); *CLE v BMR*, 2010 ABCA 187; *Van Gool v Van Gool*, [1998] BCJ No 2513 (CA); *Kelly v Kelly*, 2011 BCCA 173; *Hull v Kornilov*, 2024 BCSC 82; *Schenkeveld v Schenkeveld*, [2002] MJ No 69 (CA); *Canada v Canada-Somers*, 2008 MBCA 59; *Gillespie v Gormley*, [2003] NBJ No 369 (CA); *Comeau v Newman*, 2021 NBQB 197; *MSD obo NC v AL*, 2022 NBQB 21; *AA v JA*, 2023 NBKB 210; *Locke v Goulding*, 2012 NLCA 8; *Reid v Faubert*, 2019 NSCA 42; *Newman v Bogan*, 2010 NWTSC 69; *Costa v Perkins*, 2012 ONSC 3165; *Smith v Reynolds*, 2020 ONSC 4459; *JABD v RAB*, 2012 PESC 6; *Beisel v Henderson*, [2004] SJ No 413 (QB).

58 *Gillespie v Gormley*, [2003] NBJ No 369 (CA).

59 *Hanmore v Hanmore*, [2000] AJ No 171 (CA); *Schenkeveld v Schenkeveld*, [2002] MJ No 69 (CA); *Jeans v Jeans*, [2000] NJ No 42 (UFC); *Hoover v Hoover*, [1997] NWTJ No 43 (SC); *Charlton v Dodman*, [2000] SJ No 821 (QB).

60 *Charlton v Dodman*, *ibid*.

61 *Ibid*.

C. CIRCUMSTANCES THAT MAY CAUSE UNDUE HARDSHIP

Section 10(2) of the *Federal Child Support Guidelines* set outs the following non-exhaustive list of circumstances that may constitute "undue hardship" within the meaning of section 10(1) of the Guidelines:

(a) the spouse has responsibility for an unusually high level of debts reasonably incurred to support the spouses and their children prior to the separation or to earn a living;[62]

(b) the spouse has unusually high expenses in relation to exercising parenting time with a child;[63]

(c) the spouse has a legal duty under a judgment, order or written separation agreement to support any person;

(d) the spouse has a legal duty to support any child, other than a child of the marriage, who is

  (i) under the age of majority, or

  (ii) the age of majority or over but is unable, by reason of illness, disability or other cause to obtain the necessaries of life; and

(e) the spouse has a legal duty to support any person who is unable to obtain the necessaries of life due to an illness or disability.

Circumstances that may lead to a finding of undue hardship are not limited to those listed in section 10(2).[64] Undue hardship may arise from a combination of the circumstances listed under sections 10(2)(a) to (e) of the *Federal Child Support Guidelines*,[65] or from a combination of circumstances, some of which fall within the categories listed while others fall outside.[66] All five grounds in the list of circumstances under section 10(2) of the Guidelines relate in one way or another to the financial costs associated with past or present obligations to children or other persons to whom a spouse has an obligation to support.[67] The circumstances listed in section 10(2) of the Guidelines are not exhaustive nor do their existence mandate a conclusion that undue hardship exists.[68] Merely showing that one or more of the circumstances enunci ated in section 10 exists is not sufficient to meet the requirement of establishing undue hard ship. The applicant must go on to show that given those circumstances they will suffer undue hardship if they are required to pay child support in accordance with the table.[69] The proper course is to determine whether the factors in section 10(2) of the Guidelines exist or there are other factors that, in the circumstances of the particular case, create undue hardship in that

---

62 See *Bassett v Magee*, 2020 BCSC 1994.

63 See *Guidelines Amending the Federal Child Support Guidelines*, SOR/2020-247, 23 November 2020; *Canada Gazette*, Part II, Volume 154, Number 25.

64 *Campbell v Campbell*, 2016 MBQB 57 (father's health costs); *Eckert v Eckert*, 2018 MBQB 117; *Swain v Montanaro*, 2016 ONSC 4295.

65 *MacFarlane v MacFarlane*, [1999] BCJ No 3008 (SC); *Dorge v Dorge*, 2012 MBQB 97; *Santos v Potter*, 2010 SKQB 115.

66 *Goudie v Buchanan*, [2001] NJ No 187 (UFC) (application under *Newfoundland Child Support Guidelines* *Wainman v Clairmont*, [2004] NSJ No 69 (SC).

67 *Jeans v Jeans*, [2000] NJ No 42 (UFC); *Bergman-Illnik v Illnik*, [1997] NWTJ No 93 (SC); *Jackson v Holloway*, [1997] SJ No 691 (QB).

68 *Locke v Goulding*, 2012 NLCA 8; *Min v Soe*, [2008] OJ No 927 (SCJ).

69 *Locke v Goulding*, 2012 NLCA 8; *Barber v Barber*, 2011 SKQB 131.

they cause excessive suffering.[70] The examples in section 10(2) of the Guidelines, although not an exhaustive list of circumstances that constitute undue hardship,[71] support the conclusion that Parliament intended to provide sufficient flexibility to deal with special circumstances in an equitable way, without opening the floodgates to applications alleging undue hardship under section 10 of the Guidelines. The examples, while not exhaustive, do provide guidance as to the nature of the circumstances that Parliament intended the courts to consider in dealing with a plea of undue hardship.[72] If the courts are not strict in limiting any expansion to circumstances that are as serious, exceptional, or excessive as those listed, the purpose of the Guidelines would be defeated.[73] Although section 10 of the *Federal Child Support Guidelines* sets out a non-exhaustive list of situations that may give rise to a finding of undue hardship, the boundaries of undue hardship are financial, and the emotional health and well-being of family members cannot trigger a finding of undue hardship.[74]

Some courts have expressly endorsed the application of the *ejusdem generis* rule in the context of section 10 of the Guidelines.[75] Other courts have asserted that courts are permitted to consider anything that might have an impact upon a determination of undue hardship.[76] In *Larkin v Jamieson*,[77] for example, personal medical expenses, an ability to have a place to receive the visiting children, and the cost of furthering one's education for the purpose of finding suitable employment were all taken into account to justify a finding of undue hardship. There is nothing in the language of section 10 of the Guidelines to support a rigid application of the *ejusdem generis* rule.[78] Undue hardship within the meaning of section 10 of the *Federal Child Support Guidelines* requires a judicial determination on a case-by-case basis.[79] Undue hardship may properly include such considerations as living at or below the poverty line and cost-of-living indexes.[80] Personal care expenses arising out of the disability of a parent may warrant a finding of undue hardship.[81] An assertion of higher taxes and a higher cost of living in the foreign country where the obligor resides is of little assistance to a court, where there is no expert assessment of raw data furnished to the court and the obligor fails to identify and quantify how he or she would be affected.[82] The existence of one of the listed categories of undue hardship under section 10(2) of the *Federal Child Support Guidelines* does not itself presuppose that the court must make a finding of undue hardship.[83]

70 *McArthur v McArthur*, [1999] BCJ No 1239 (SC); *Smith v Hookey*, [1999] NJ No 243 (UFC).

71 *Reiter v Reiter*, [1997] BCJ No 2835 (SC); *JJ v AM*, 2011 NBQB 368; *Jeans v Jeans*, [2000] NJ No 42 (UFC); *Kennedy-Dowell v Dowell*, [2002] NSJ No 123 (SC); *Hoover v Hoover*, [1997] NWTJ No 43 (SC); *Schmid v Smith*, [1999] OJ No 3062 (SCJ); *Larkin v Jamieson*, [2000] PEIJ No 65 (SC); *Jackson v Holloway*, [1997] SJ No 691 (QB).

72 *Camirand v Beaulne*, [1998] OJ No 2163 (Gen Div); see also *MacDonald v Seguin*, 2011 NSSC 337.

73 *Adams v Loov*, [1998] AJ No 666 (QB); *CA v SF*, [1997] QJ No 3989 (CS).

74 *Gillespie v Gormley*, [2003] NBJ No 369 (CA).

75 See, for example, *Russell v Russell*, [1998] OJ No 2234 (Gen Div).

76 *Loosdrecht v Loosdrecht*, [1998] BCJ No 1629 (SC); see also *Kennedy-Dowell v Dowell*, [2002] NSJ No 123 (SC).

77 [2000] PEIJ No 65 (SC).

78 *Scharf v Scharf*, [1998] OJ No 199 (Gen Div).

79 *Kennedy v Kennedy*, [1997] NSJ No 450 (Fam Ct); *Larkin v Jamieson*, [2000] PEIJ No 65 (SC).

80 *Ibid.*

81 *Dyck v Highton*, [2003] SJ No 600 (QB).

82 *Schmid v Smith*, [1999] OJ No 3062 (SCJ).

83 *Mayo v O'Connell*, [1998] NJ No 239 (SC); *Hansvall v Hansvall*, [1997] SJ No 782 (QB).

Such a finding involves a degree of subjective judicial discretion in light of the attendant circumstances, but undue hardship cases constitute the exception rather than the rule. Although the aforementioned list focuses on undue hardship being sustained by either or both of the spouses or former spouses, it is important to appreciate that undue hardship within the meaning of section 10 of the *Federal Child Support Guidelines* includes undue hardship to a child of the marriage in respect of whom the application is made. Indeed, the child is the one who is the focus of the inquiry into hardship and no penalty should attach to the child for any alleged fault of the primary caregiving parent.[85]

Undue hardship may be found where the obligor's after-tax and after-support income would be so low that he or she would be left unable to support himself or herself.[86] Undue hardship may be reasonably assumed where the payor of child support receives social assistance benefits.[87]

An obligor is not entitled to assert undue hardship within the meaning of section 10 of the Guidelines where any hardship arises from personal choice.[88] Section 10 of the Guidelines presupposes that some financial obligation exists. A desire to salvage the family business, however honourable, will not trigger a finding of undue hardship even though the list under section 10(2) of the Guidelines is not exhaustive.[89]

Past history respecting parenting and the absence of child support payments has been deemed irrelevant to a claim of undue hardship under section 10 of the *Federal Child Support Guidelines*.[90]

In exceptional circumstances arising under the former judicial discretionary child support regime, a court could deviate from the norm of cash payments. In the words of Carr J of the Manitoba Court of Queen's Bench:

> Normally, one expects a cash contribution from a . . . parent who clearly has the wherewithal to so provide. The mere purchase of items is not normally sufficient or appropriate. Here, however, the parties have an arrangement that has been satisfactory to both for eight years, and nothing has changed to make the arrangement any less appropriate now than it was when the parties agreed to it. Most of the items that she purchases are, for this child at least, necessaries in that if she did not buy them, the father would do so.[91]

In Nova Scotia, one spouse was ordered to provide meat, eggs, milk, and vegetables in addition to periodic financial support,[92] and another spouse was ordered to pay child support in the form of a tax-free housing allowance.[93] In Ontario, a father was ordered to purchase clothing for his daughter up to a designated annual value.[94] Such orders might be possible

84 *Hansvall v Hansvall, ibid.*
85 *Scharf v Scharf*, [1998] OJ No 1996 (Gen Div).
86 *Bell v Griffin*, [1997] PEIJ No 86 (TD).
87 *Kelly v Kingston*, [2000] PEIJ No 22 (TD).
88 *Pela v Pela*, [1998] SJ No 804 (QB).
89 *Ibid.*
90 *Harder v Harder*, [2000] BCJ No 467 (SC).
91 *Picken v Picken* (1991), 37 RFL (3d) 250 at 252 (Man QB).
92 *Matthews v Matthews* (1990), 96 NSR (2d) 376 (TD), var'd (1991), 34 RFL 201 (NSCA).
93 *Dunn v Dunn* (1995), 14 RFL (4th) 50 (NSTD).
94 *Booth v Vucetic* (1989), 19 RFL (3d) 240 (Ont Fam Ct).

under the *Federal Child Support Guidelines*, if the requirements of undue hardship under section 10 of the Guidelines were satisfied.

D. FAMILY DEBTS OR EMPLOYMENT EXPENSES

It is a well-established principle that the payment of child support takes priority over the payment of debts. It is presumably for this reason that debts as a basis for deviating from the Guidelines have been circumscribed by the express provisions of section 10(2)(a) of the *Federal Child Support Guidelines*. In order to satisfy section 10(2)(a) of the Guidelines, the debts must satisfy each of the following three conditions:

1) they must be of an unusually high level;
2) they must have been reasonably incurred; and
3) they must have been incurred in order to support the spouses and their children prior to the separation or to earn a living.[95]

Having determined that undue hardship exists and that the standard of living in the debtor father's household is lower than that in the mother's household, the court must still determine whether any reduction in the applicable table amount of child support is warranted and, if so, in what amount and for how long. In dealing with this last issue, the court may have regard not only to the financial circumstances of the father, but also to the amount of child support previously agreed between the parents. The existence of an unusually high level of debts does not entitle the father to pay reduced child support forever. The court may order the father to pay less than the table amount of child support for a specified time, after which the then applicable table amount of child support will become payable, with leave being granted to the mother to apply for a variation order if circumstances change, including any change arising from the father's earning a substantially increased annual income or the alleviation of his debt problems by resorting to bankruptcy.[96]

An unusually high level of family debt, which exceeds the value of the family assets, may warrant an interim child support order in a lower amount of child support than the applicable table amount, subject to a reassessment of the issue of undue hardship after the family assets have been sold.[97]

A court should not deviate from the applicable table amount of child support on the basis of alleged undue hardship within the meaning of section 10 of the *Federal Child Support Guidelines* in the absence of specific and cogent evidence as to why the circumstances constitute undue hardship. It is not enough to assert an unusually high level of debt; the debts must have been incurred to support the family prior to separation or to earn a living.

95 *Jackson v Holloway*, [1997] SJ No 691 (QB); see also *Polack v Sterling*, 2010 ABQB 122; *Philibert v Webber*, 2011 BCSC 623; *Elliott v Melnyk*, 2014 NSSC 446; *Tanner v Simpson*, [1999] NWTJ No 71 (SC); *Wislesky v Wislesky*, [1999] OJ No 1220 (Gen Div); *MLS v BJM*, 2011 SKQB 163. Compare *JDF v GEW*, [2007] NSJ No 116 (Fam Ct).

96 *Semeschuk v Biletski*, [2004] SJ No 200 (QB).

97 *Hebert v Klebeck*, [2005] SJ No 775 (QB).

Particulars relating to the debts must be provided, which might well include the annual costs of servicing the debt.[98]

A failure to alleviate debt problems, when able to do so, is an important factor for consideration.[99] Debts reasonably incurred to earn a living may fall short of being unusually high, having regard to the income of the debtor and his or her current spouse.[100] Whether outstanding family debts create undue hardship so as to satisfy the requirements of section 10 of the *Federal Child Support Guidelines* largely depends on the debtor's level of income.[101] The assumption of a substantial family debt load by one spouse may be of little or no consequence where there is a vast difference between spousal incomes on marriage breakdown, especially if the debt resulted from conscious and deliberate choice on the part of that spouse.[102] Debts incurred with respect to a prior[103] or subsequent[104] family do not satisfy the criteria set out in section 10(2)(a) of the Guidelines. Child support clearly takes priority over the discharge of commercial debts. If this were not the case, taxpayers who ultimately bear the burden of public assistance for family dependants could be indirectly subsidizing the discharge of commercial debts to general creditors in circumstances where bankruptcy is a viable option. The preservation of a reasonable standard of living for dependent children on family breakdown or divorce would also be threatened if commercial debts took precedence. It is for these reasons that debt as a basis for deviating from the Guidelines amount of child support has been circumscribed by the prerequisites of section 10(2)(a). Its operation is restricted to circumstances in which the family unit, having enjoyed a benefit in the past as a result of debt incurred, may have to share in the present burden of that debt.[106] Alternatively, the debt must enable the obligor to earn a living from which child support can be paid.[107] The words "reasonably incurred to support the spouses and their children prior to the separation or to earn a living," which expressly appear in section 10(2)(a) of the *Federal Child Support Guidelines*, must be given some meaning and the only apparent meaning is that they are words of limitation, that circumscribe the types of debt that can amount to undue hardship to those therein described.[108] A plea of undue hardship under section 10 of the *Federal Child Support Guidelines* may be dismissed where the financial circumstances in the obligor's household reflect lifestyle decisions that negatively affect his household income, namely the decision to have children with his new spouse, the fact that she was not working outside the home,

98 *Uhrich-Cormier v Cormier*, [2000] SJ No 595 (QB); see also *Redlick v Redlick*, 2013 BCSC 1155.

99 *Dick v Knoblauch*, [1998] SJ No 631 (QB).

100 *Hedderson v Kearsey*, [1998] NJ No 62 (SC).

101 *NMPH v LLH*, [2006] BCJ No 67 (SC); *MacNeil v MacNeil*, [2000] NWTJ No 4 (SC) (access to overtime income).

102 *Pearce v Pearce*, [1999] BCJ No 2278 (SC), citing *Turcotte v Turcotte* (1996), 22 RFL (4th) 364 (Ont Ct Gen Div).

103 *Tack v Fournier*, [1998] MJ No 596 (QB) (application under *Manitoba Child Support Guidelines*).

104 *Russell v Russell*, [1998] OJ No 2234 (Gen Div); *Jackson v Holloway*, [1997] SJ No 691 (QB); *Flanagan v Heal*, [1998] SJ No 805 (QB); compare *Stevenson v Stevenson*, [1999] BCJ No 324 (SC); *Hollett-Collins v Hollett*, [2002] NJ No 292 (SC).

105 *Diminie v Diminie*, [1995] OJ No 59 (Gen Div); compare *Bedard v Bedard*, [2003] OJ No 862 (SCJ) (pre-existing wage assignment to commercial creditors).

106 *Russell v Russell*, [1998] OJ No 2234 (Gen Div); *Jackson v Holloway*, [1997] SJ No 691 (QB); compare *Dick v Knoblauch*, [1998] SJ No 631 (QB).

107 *Russell v Russell*, [1998] OJ No 2234 (Gen Div).

108 *Adams v Loov*, [1998] AJ No 666 (QB).

and his decision to take parental leave.[109] Debts for housing and transportation that reflect a lifestyle choice, rather than necessary expenses to earn a living, will not ground a plea of undue hardship under section 10(2)(a) of the Guidelines.[110]

Pursuant to section 10(5) of the Guidelines, where the court orders a different amount of child support under section 10(1) of the Guidelines because of a high level of debts, it may establish a reasonable time for the repayment of the debts and specify in the child support order the amount of child support payable at the end of that time. The amount of table support payable may be phased in over several months to reflect future reductions in the monthly amounts required by the obligor to discharge outstanding debts.[111]

An inability to acquire assets and savings does not warrant an extension of the non-exhaustive list of circumstances of undue hardship under section 10 of the Guidelines.[112]

An unusually high level of family debts within the meaning of section 10(1)(a) of the Guidelines does not warrant deviation from the normal Guidelines amount of child support, where the standard of living in the obligor's household remains higher than that of the recipient spouse's household after payment of the normal amount.[113] A point may be reached at which it becomes impossible to discharge family debts to third parties and child support obligations. At that point, bankruptcy may be the only available option in order for priority to be accorded to the child support payments.

E. UNUSUALLY HIGH EXPENSES IN RELATION TO EXERCISING PARENTING TIME WITH A CHILD;[114] PAYMENT OF CHILD SUPPORT TO NON-PRIMARY CAREGIVING PARENT

There are three major aspects of section 10 of the *Federal Child Support Guidelines* concerning expenses in relation to exercising parenting time with a child.[115] First, the court has a discretion to order an amount of child support that differs from the Guidelines figure, but does not have to do so. Second, the expenses must be "unusually high" in order to support a plea of undue hardship.[116] Typically, such expenses occur in situations where the non-primary caregiving parent either spends an unusual amount of time with his children or there is an unusual distance to be travelled between his residence and that of the primary care parent.[117]

---

109 *Hollett v Vessey*, [2005] NSJ No 538 (SC).

110 *Tutty v Tutty*, [2005] NSJ No 514 (SC).

111 *Aulatjut v Aulatjut*, [1997] NWTJ 125 (SC).

112 *Veltkamp v Veltkamp*, [1998] SJ No 34 (QB).

113 *Lebrun v Lebrun*, [1999] OJ No 3393 (SCJ).

114 See *Guidelines Amending the Federal Child Support Guidelines*, SOR/2020-247, 23 November 2020; *Canada Gazette*, Part II, Volume 154, Number 25. For useful guidance on undue hardship arising from unusually high expenses in relation to exercising parenting time with a child, see the judgment of Lema J of the Alberta Court of Queen's Bench in *SDH v ARH*, 2019 ABQB 212 at para 70.

115 *Paradon v Ratzlaff*, 2019 SKQB 86.

116 *Ewaniw v Ewaniw*, [1998] AJ No 704 (QB); *Kelly v Kelly*, 2011 BCCA 173; *Bouzane v Martin*, 2014 BCSC 1690 (legal expenses excluded); *Pollock v Rioux*, [2004] NBJ No 467 (CA); *Pretty v Pretty*, 2011 NSSC 296; *MacNeil v MacNeil*, [2000] NWTJ No 4 (SC); *Praetzel v Porter*, 2022 NWTSC 19; *Pace v Barry*, 2019 ONSC 1739; *Roemer v Roemer*, [2003] SJ No 499 (QB) (suspension of child support for one year). For a review of relevant cases, see *Deveau v Groskopf*, [2000] SJ No 281 (QB).

117 *Zivot v Tobey*, 2009 MBQB 269.

Third, even where there are unusually high expenses in relation to exercising parenting time with a child, the court may order a different amount of child support only upon finding that the obligor would otherwise suffer undue hardship.[118] Whether expenses in relation to exercising parenting time with a child are unusually high is relative to a parent's financial means and should be determined in light of the obligor's disposable income.[120] A claim that undue hardship arises from unusually high expenses in relation to exercising parenting time with a child must be dismissed, if the obligor's household would enjoy a higher standard of living than the recipient's household after payment of the applicable Guidelines amount,[121] but they may be taken into account in quantifying spousal support.[122] The determination of undue hardship must be made in light of present circumstances, not what has occurred in the past.

Expenses incurred to travel a long distance can constitute undue hardship but section 10(2)(b) of the Guidelines is not restricted to parenting time costs for long distance parents nor is it limited to travel costs.[124] A finding that parenting time expenses are "unusually high" within the meaning of section 10(2)(b) of the *Federal Child Support Guidelines* is fact specific. Some expenses for transportation and food are to be expected; only amounts in excess of basic expenditures can be classified as "unusually high." Courts have considered whether the mode of transportation is reasonable in light of available alternatives, the distance travelled, the frequency of contact, the linkage to vacation time for the parent, the overall annual cost of exercising parenting time with a child and its relationship to the parent's annual income. An undue hardship claim may succeed by the conjoint operation of sections 10(2)(b) and 10(2)(c) of the Guidelines where high parenting time costs exist in addition to the obligation to support a second family. Given findings of undue hardship and of a lower standard of living in the obligor's household, the court should not permit the standard of living of the children in each family to diverge too widely. Accommodation may be achieved by disallowing section 7 expenses or by a set-off of parenting time costs against these expenses.

---

118 *Omah-Maharajh v Howard*, [1998] AJ No 173 (QB); *Hull v Kornilov*, 2024 BCSC 82; *Williams v Williams*, [1997] NWTJ No 49 (SC); *Praetzel v Porter*, 2022 NWTSC 19 at para 9; *Scammell v Davies*, [1999] SJ No 298 (QB).

119 *McDermott v McDermott*, [2006] BCJ No 1380 (SC); *SS v DS*, 2013 NSSC 384; *Williams v Steinwand*, 2014 NWTSC 74.

120 *Dixon v Fleming*, [2000] OJ No 1218 (SCJ); see also *Walker v Walker*, [1999] AJ No 828 (QB) (annual costs of $3,537 not unusually high for parent with attributed income of $62,000); *Kempkes v Kempkes*, [2000] BCJ No 1018 (SC) (annual parenting costs of $4,000 not unusually high for parent with annual income of $48,145); *Casey v Casey*, [2004] NBJ No 434 (QB) (expenses of $200 per month not unusually high for parent earning $53,200 per year); *Kennedy-Dowell v Dowell*, [2002] NSJ No 123 (SC) (parent relieved from paying any child support); *Tanner v Simpson*, [1999] NWTJ No 71 (SC) (annual costs of $2,000 not unusually high for parent earning $80,000 per year); *Champion v Champion*, [2001] PEIJ No 129 (SC); *Santos v Potter*, 2010 SKQB 115; *Paradon v Ratzlaff*, 2019 SKQB 86. Compare *Schmid v Smith*, [1999] OJ No 3062 (SCJ).

121 *Omah-Maharajh v Howard*, [1998] AJ No 173 (QB); *CLE v BMR*, 2010 ABCA 187; *Eadie v Eadie*, [1998] NBJ No 352 (QB); *Brink v Young*, 2011 ONSC 4955.

122 *Brink v Young, ibid.*

123 *Byrne v Byrne*, [1999] BCJ No 1087 (SC); *GL v KH*, 2020 SKQB 167.

124 *CWT v KAT*, 2013 ABQB 678.

125 *Deveau v Groskopf*, [2000] SJ No 281 (QB).

Where the best interests of the children so require, a parent may be required to sacrifice some extra-provincial visits so that the appropriate amount of child support can be provided.[126]

The usual expenses incurred by a non-primary caregiving parent in relation to exercising parenting time with a child cannot be relied upon for the purpose of establishing a claim of undue hardship within the meaning of section 10(1) of the *Federal Child Support Guidelines*.[127] However, the costs of exercising parenting time with a child may be unusually high; for example, where there are very heavy travel costs attributable to the distances between the parental residences[128] or where cheap public transportation is unavailable or inappropriate. In such cases, a parent who incurs such unusually high expenses may be entitled to claim undue hardship for the purpose of reducing the amount of child support or expenses that would otherwise be paid to the primary caregiving parent.[129] Onerous transportation costs that will be incurred in the exercise of parenting time may clearly warrant an adjustment of the amount of child support where parenting time would otherwise be impossible.[130] Travel, food, and other expenses that increase the costs of parenting time with the child must be assessed in light of the reasonableness of the parent's decision as to the manner in which parenting time is to be exercised.[131] Although a court may accept that the cost of parenting time and related travel is substantial, it may not be satisfied on a balance of probabilities that these costs could not be rearranged or reduced to enable the parent to better meet his child support obligations.[132] Additional costs associated with exercising parenting time with a disabled child may also be considered in the assessment of child support.[133] Instead of modifying the monthly amount of support payable under the *Federal Child Support Guidelines* to take account of unusually high parenting time expenses, a court may order that the designated amount of child support shall not be payable for any month in which the obligor has parenting time for four consecutive weeks.[134] In determining whether parenting time expenses should be factored into the assessment of child support, caution must be exercised so that generous parenting time privileges do not render it impossible for the primary caregiving parent to provide adequately for the children.[135] The needs of the children do not diminish because one of the parents incurs unusually high expenses in relation to exercising parenting time with the children.[136]

---

126 *Hahn v Hahn*, [2001] AJ No 571 (QB).

127 *Ewaniw v Ewaniw*, [1998] AJ No 704 (QB); *MJM v ADEM*, 2012 NBQB 71; *Bosgra v Squires*, [2001] NWTJ No 78 (SC); *Fontaine v Andall*, [1998] SJ No 510 (QB).

128 *Smith v Smith*, [1999] AJ No 1180 (QB) (parent obliged to seek employment in foreign jurisdiction); *BAC v DLC*, [2003] BCJ No 1303 (SC); *Edwards v Edwards*, [2001] PEIJ No 51 (SC) (confirmation hearing with respect to extra-provincial provisional order); *Fontaine v Andall*, [1998] SJ No 510 (QB).

129 *Federal Child Support Guidelines*, SOR/97-175, s 10(2)(b); see also *Sutherland v Sutherland*, [1998] BCJ No 342 (SC); *Boucher v Boucher*, [1997] NBJ No 43 (QB); *Taylor v Taylor*, [1999] SJ No 541 (QB); compare *Williams v Williams*, [1997] NWTJ No 49 (SC).

130 *Pyper v Neville* (1995), 14 RFL (4th) 262 (Sask QB).

131 *Scammell v Davies*, [1999] SJ No 298 (QB).

132 *Hart v Talbot*, 2010 NSSC 311.

133 *Green v Green* (1995), 11 RFL (4th) 207 (Alta QB).

134 *Tanner v Simpson*, [1997] NWTJ No 22 (SC); see also *Lang v Racine*, [1998] NSJ No 584 (SC) (table amount payable for ten months of each year).

135 *Gunn v Gunn* (1994), 10 RFL (4th) 197 at 200 (Man CA); see also *KHP v RP*, [1997] BCJ No 1166 (SC).

136 *NCL v AJL*, [2001] NWTJ No 102 (SC). As to counterbalancing increased costs to both parents arising from occasional visits, see *Walker v Rutledge*, [2002] OJ No 4521 (SCJ).

A judge may refuse to find that expenses in relation to exercising parenting time with the children are unusually high after taking into account the distances between communities within the province[137] and the opportunity to share travel costs,[138] or the exceptionally high income of the parent.[139] A court may find that the costs of extra-provincial travel are not "unusually high" within the meaning of section 10 of the *Federal Child Support Guidelines* when compared to typical costs of intra-provincial travel. In these circumstances, the court must refuse to order any adjustment of the applicable table amount of child support, but it may reduce the contribution towards special or extraordinary expenses falling within section 7 of the Guidelines.[140]

A spouse or former spouse who voluntarily changes his or her provincial residence may not be entitled to relief from consequentially high expenses in relation to exercising parenting time with the children that were clearly foreseeable,[141] but a primary caregiving parent who changes his or her residence may be granted less child support than that provided under the applicable provincial table, where increased expenses in relation to exercising parenting time with the children create undue hardship for the other parent within the meaning of section 10 of the *Federal Child Support Guidelines*.[142]

It is doubtful whether a primary caregiving parent can invoke section 10(2)(b) of the Guidelines in circumstances where his or her expenses are increased because of the other parent's repeated non-compliance with court ordered or consensual parenting time arrangements, although such a claim might be made pursuant to section 10(1) and independently of section 10(2)(b) if the primary caregiving parent or the child thereby suffers undue economic hardship.[143] It remains to be seen whether undue hardship to the primary caregiving parent can arise from a legitimate denial of parenting time to the other parent or whether either spouse or former spouse can successfully claim undue hardship where unusually high expenses are incurred as a result of supervised parenting time. The requirements of section 10 of the *Federal Child Support Guidelines* will not be satisfied where parenting time has rarely, if ever, been exercised,[144] but the claimant may be entitled to reopen the issue upon a resumption of the exercise of parenting time.[145]

In the context of section 10(2)(b) of the *Federal Child Support Guidelines*, it seems reasonable to assume that undue hardship refers to undue financial hardship as distinct from the psychological harm that might result from a parent's failure to accept his or her responsibilities to preserve meaningful contact with a child of the marriage, unless such harm generates health-related expenses such as fall within the meaning of section 7(1)(c) of the Guidelines.

137 *Fontaine v Andall*, [1998] SJ No 510 (QB).
138 *Beeler v Beeler*, [1997] SJ No 612 (QB).
139 *Salvadori v Kebede*, [1998] BCJ No 1819 (SC).
140 *Button v Button*, [1999] NJ No 130 (UFC).
141 *Williams v Williams*, [1997] NWTJ No 49 (SC).
142 *Adams v Loov*, [1998] AJ No 666, 40 RFL (4th) 222 (QB); *Vinderskov v Vinderskov*, [2002] BCJ No 2428 (CA).
143 *Hill v Ilnicki*, [2000] AJ No 1219 (QB).
144 *Herbert v Herbert*, [1999] AJ No 1241 (QB); *Sutton v Sutton*, [1999] BCJ No 1933 (SC); *GMS v DBS*, [1999] NJ No 278 (UFC) (order allowed no physical time sharing; amount also questionable in light of "seat sales" and visits to province on business).
145 *Mayo v O'Connell*, [1998] NJ No 239 (SC).

A court cannot assume that undue hardship exists because of allegedly unusually high expenses in relation to exercising parenting time with a child where the claimant fails to file relevant financial information.[146]

A court may determine whether unusually high expenses in relation to exercising parenting time with a child have been reasonably incurred without scrutinizing every penny spent, particularly if the costs are not incurred in the city where the parent resides.[147]

High expenses in relation to exercising parenting time with the children may be found insufficient to trigger a finding of "undue hardship" within the meaning of section 10 of the *Federal Child Support Guidelines*, but sufficient to warrant lowering the monthly instalments payable by the obligor against fixed arrears of child support.[148]

Expenses in relation to exercising parenting time that arise with respect to a child, other than a child of the marriage, do not fall within the express provisions of section 10(2)(b) of the *Federal Child Support Guidelines* because the definition of "child" under section 2 of the Guidelines is expressly confined to a child of the marriage. Given that section 10(2) of the Guidelines does not provide an exhaustive list of factors that may warrant a finding of undue hardship, it remains to be seen whether the courts will interpret section 10(2)(b) so as to exclude a plea of undue hardship arising with respect to the exercise of parenting time with respect to a child, other than a child of the marriage, thereby reversing the position that existed before the implementation of the *Federal Child Support Guidelines* on 1 May 1997.[149]

Unusually high expenses in relation to exercising parenting time with a child that are insufficient to warrant deviation from the applicable provincial or territorial table amount of child support because the obligor's household enjoys a higher standard of living than the recipient household are relevant to the obligor's means and ability to contribute towards the cost of post-secondary education for the child and to pay spousal support.[150]

Ordinarily, it is the primary caregiving parent who is entitled to receive child support. However, this is not inevitably the case. The spouses or former spouses have a joint financial obligation to maintain the children of the marriage in accordance with their relative abilities to contribute to the performance of that obligation.[151] Consequently, there may be circumstances wherein the primary caregiving parent may be required to pay support to the other parent to assist that parent to support the children during the exercise of parenting time.[152]

A claim for a reduction of the applicable table amount of child support is only permissible in the context of the undue hardship provisions of section 10 of the *Federal Child Support Guidelines*.[153] Although the expenses incurred in the exercise of parenting time may be unusually high, the court may conclude that they fall short of establishing undue hardship,

---

146 *Hare v Kendall*, [1997] NSJ No 310 (TD); *Lutz v Sequeira*, [2000] SJ No 460 (QB).

147 *Aker v Howard*, [1999] OJ No 651 (Gen Div).

148 *Llewellyn v Llewellyn*, [2002] BCJ No 542 (CA).

149 See *Deane v Deane* (1995), 14 RFL (4th) 55 (Ont Ct Gen Div).

150 *Kaderly v Kaderly*, [1997] PEIJ No 74 (TD); see also *Wislesky v Wislesky*, [1999] OJ No 1220 (Gen Div) (high parenting time costs deemed relevant to "add-ons" under s 7 of Guidelines).

151 *Divorce Act*, RSC 1985 (2d Supp), c 3, as amended by SC 1997, c 1, s 26.1(2).

152 *Jaques v Marlin* (1995), 11 RFL (4th) 224 (Ont UFC); *Walsh v Walsh*, [1996] OJ No 3970 (Gen Div); *Jackson v Jackson*, 2023 SKCA 70; see also *Levesque v Levesque* (1994), 4 RFL (4th) 375 at 386–87 (Alta CA); *RLS v DCM*, [2003] BCJ No 1030 at paras 30–31 (SC); *Droit de la famille — 1118*, [1988] RDF 308 (Que CS).

153 *Epp v Robertson*, [1998] SJ No 684 (QB).

which must be "exceptional, excessive or disproportionate" to meet the requirements of section 10 of the *Federal Child Support Guidelines*.[154] While maximum contact between children and both of their parents is ordinarily in the children's best interests, it must be balanced against the obligation of a parent to satisfy the children's basic needs by the payment of child support.[155] Nothing in the Guidelines authorizes a court to order a primary caregiving parent to make a financial contribution towards the other parent's expenses in exercising parenting time with a child.[156] Prior to the implementation of the *Federal Child Support Guidelines* on 1 May 1997, however, a court could make such an order pursuant to either section 15(4) or section 16(6) of the *Divorce Act*.[157] And it is doubtful whether section 10 of the *Federal Child Support Guidelines* limits this jurisdiction, given that the provisions of section 15(4) are currently mirrored in section 15.1(4) of the *Divorce Act*, as amended by the SC 1997, c 1, and section 16(6) of the *Divorce Act* is unaffected by the 1997 amendments.[158] This issue was not specifically addressed in *Cutmiski v Aubert*,[159] wherein the primary caregiving parent was ordered to pay the transportation expenses of the children to enable them to visit the other parent, but the court refused to set off these expenses against the court-ordered child support payments. In *Holtskog v Holtskog*,[160] the Saskatchewan Court of Appeal concluded that the trial judge erred in ordering the primary caregiving parent to contribute one-half of the monthly airfare arising from extra-provincial visits after rejecting the plea that unusually high expenses were incurred in relation to exercising parenting time that would justify a finding of undue hardship within the meaning of section 10 of the Guidelines. Where a parent has failed to satisfy the specific requirements of the undue hardship provisions in section 10 of the *Federal Child Support Guidelines*, however, the court may take expenses incurred in relation to exercising parenting time into consideration in determining the amount of "add on" support to be paid by that parent pursuant to section 7 of the Guidelines.[161] In *RBN v MJN*,[162] Campbell J of the Nova Scotia Supreme Court questioned whether *Holtskog v Holtskog* precluded an order for the payment or sharing of expenses in relation to exercising parenting time with a child in the absence of a finding of undue hardship. In ordering the primary caregiving parent to pay all of the extra-provincial transportation costs resulting from her relocation of the children, Campbell J stated that the authority to order a contribution to such costs comes from the *Divorce Act* itself, both under section 15.1(4), which permits the court to impose terms, conditions, or restrictions in connection with a support order and

---

154 *MEL v BGL*, 2012 BCSC 1841; *LWH v SC*, 2012 NBQB 2.

155 *MEL v BGL*, 2012 BCSC 1841.

156 *South v South*, [1998] BCJ No 962 (SC).

157 RSC 1985 (2d Supp), c 3.

158 See *Ruel v Ruel*, 2006 ABCA 170; *Peregrym v Peregrym*, 2011 ABQB 558; *Ellis v Ellis*, 1999 CanLII 4274 (NSCA); *McMahon v Sharaput*, 2011 ONSC 3399; *Lebouthillier v Manning*, 2014 ONSC 4081; *MacPhail v MacPhail*, [2000] PEIJ No 41 (SC). Compare *Greene v Greene*, 2010 BCCA 595; *Gray v Metcalf*, 2011 ABQB 773.

159 [1998] SJ No 825 (QB). Compare *Fenster v Fenster*, 2011 ONSC 3852 (court order for consensual set-off of parenting time costs against child support).

160 [1999] SJ No 304 (CA). See also *Domzalska v Desjardins*, 2017 ABQB 177; *Greene v Greene*, 2010 BCCA 595; *RF v JM*, 2017 SKQB 51.

161 *Uhrich-Cormier v Cormier*, [2000] SJ No 595 (QB); see also *Koval v Brinton*, 2010 NSCA 78.

162 [2002] NSJ No 530 (SC); see also *RJM v EM*, 2015 BCSC 414 at para 89; *Tucesku v Tucesku*, 2015 NSSC 281; *Lebouthillier v Manning*, 2014 ONSC 4081; *Thompson v Gordon*, 2009 SKQB 323; *RF v JM*, 2017 SKQB 51.

under section 16(6) of the *Divorce Act*, which provides a similar jurisdiction with respect to a parenting order. As Campbell J observes, "there is no logical reason to deny a claim for a contribution or full payment of [parenting time] costs by the [primary caregiving] parent merely because the undue hardship claim failed." The judicial controversy is resolved to some extent by section 16.95 of the *Divorce Act* as amended by SC 2019, c 16, which expressly provides that if a court authorizes the relocation of a child of the marriage, it may provide for the apportionment of costs relating to the exercise of parenting time by a person who is not relocating between that person and the person who is relocating the child.[163]

In *Ritchie v Solonick*,[164] Vertes J of the Yukon Territory Supreme Court was unable to make a finding of undue hardship but, nevertheless, relieved the obligor from paying the monthly amount of child support during the one month of the year when the children were in his exclusive care. It is doubtful, however, whether a court can deviate from the applicable table amount by ordering that it shall not be paid during the month when the children are residing with the obligor. The tables appear to be formulated on the basis that the obligor's annual income must yield the designated amount for every month of the year. Unusually high expenses in relation to exercising parenting time with a child may fall within the ambit of the undue hardship provisions of section 10 of the *Federal Child Support Guidelines* or could trigger section 9 of the Guidelines if the parenting time represents not less than 40 percent of the time that the child spends with that parent over the course of the year, but absent either of these two situations, it is difficult to perceive on what basis a court can deviate from the applicable table amount of monthly child support by relieving the obligor from one or more monthly payments.

F. DUTY UNDER COURT ORDER OR SEPARATION AGREEMENT TO SUPPORT ANY PERSON

A spouse or former spouse may seek to establish undue hardship on the ground that he or she has a legal duty to support any person pursuant to a court order or written separation agreement.[165] An order must have been granted by a court of competent jurisdiction, although there is no requirement that it be a Canadian court. The order or agreement may relate to a duty of support owed to any person, including a spouse, former spouse, child, or a parent. Where the support obligation is consensual, it must arise under a written separation agreement. Support obligations arising under a marriage contract do not satisfy the requirements of section 10(2)(c) of the *Federal Child Support Guidelines*.

163 See Andrea Himel & Debra Paulseth, "1-800-ZOOM-ME: A Divorce Act Update on Post-Relocation Parenting Time, Travel Costs and Child Support" (2022) 41 CFLQ 195.

164 [1999] YJ No 66 (SC).

165 *Federal Child Support Guidelines*, SOR/97-175, s 10(2)(d).

G. LEGAL DUTY TO SUPPORT ANY CHILD OTHER THAN A CHILD OF THE MARRIAGE; SEQUENTIAL FAMILIES

Undue hardship may arise pursuant to section 10(2)(d) of the *Federal Child Support Guidelines* where a spouse or former spouse has a legal,[166] as distinct from a moral,[167] duty to support a child, other than a child of the marriage, who is under the age of provincial majority, or who is the age of majority or over but unable, by reason of illness, disability, or other cause, to obtain the necessaries of life.[168] A legal duty to support a child of the marriage falls outside the ambit of section 10(2)(d) of the Guidelines and precludes a finding of undue hardship thereunder.[169] Section 10(2)(d), unlike section 10(2)(c), does not require that the legal duty of support arise pursuant to a court order or written separation agreement. It may arise pursuant to provincial statute even in the absence of any court order or agreement as, for example, where the obligor has formed a new relationship and owes a duty of support to children born of that relationship or to whom the obligor stands in the place of a parent as a consequence of his or her marital or cohabitational relationship.[170]

A support obligation owed to a child other than a "child of the marriage" within the meaning of the *Divorce Act* may be pertinent to the obligor's invoking the "undue hardship" provisions of section 10 of the *Federal Child Support Guidelines* but, in that event, the fact that the father shares the cost of raising that child with another adult person must also be considered.

The court should not deviate from the applicable provincial or territorial table amount under the *Federal Child Support Guidelines* where the obligor has a demonstrable ability to pay that amount, notwithstanding his or her obligation to support another child.[172] An obligor may be called upon to more effectively manage his or her financial affairs so as to accord precedence to an order for child support over debts and non-necessities.[173]

In determining whether a legal obligation to support a child generates undue hardship where the child is an adult pursuing post-secondary education, relevant considerations include:

1) the obligor's substantial income;
2) the availability of other financial assistance for the child;
3) the adult child's ability to contribute to his or her own support through part-time employment; and
4) the lack of objective evidence of any financial hardship.[174]

---

166 *Andrada v Garcia*, [1998] BCJ No 2980 (Prov Ct); *Bosgra v Squires*, [2001] NWTJ No 78 (SC); *Bedard v Bedard*, [2003] OJ No 862 (SCJ); *MS v JC*, 2010 PESC 50.

167 *Parker v Parker*, [2003] NSJ No 139 (SC).

168 *JJ v AM*, 2011 NBQB 368; *Smith v Hookey*, [1999] NJ No 243 (UFC); *Brouse v Brouse*, [1999] OJ No 1834 (Gen Div) (child support reduced to nominal amount of $1 per month); *Kelly v Kingston*, [2000] PEIJ No 22 (SC); *Pelletier v Kakakaway*, [2002] SJ No 448 (CA).

169 *Schmid v Smith*, [1999] OJ No 3062 (SCJ).

170 See, for example, *Family Law Act*, RSO 1990, c F3, s 31. And see *MS v JC*, 2010 PESC 50.

171 *Tremaine v Tremaine*, [1997] AJ No 379 (QB); compare *Jacques v Jacques*, [1997] SJ No 265 (QB).

172 *Tanner v Simpson*, [1997] NWTJ No 22 (SC); *Hansvall v Hansvall*, [1997] SJ No 782 (QB); see also *Mayo v O'Connell*, [1998] NJ No 239 (SC).

173 *Tanner v Simpson*, [1997] NWTJ No 22 (SC); see also *MacEachern v Hardy*, 2010 NSSC 246.

174 *Tanner v Simpson*, [1999] NWTJ No 71 (SC).

A court should be cautious in accepting differentials between the cost of living in different communities as a factor that might cause undue hardship because any cost-of-living adjustment could undermine the objectives set out in section 1 of the *Federal Child Support Guidelines* or render the Guidelines almost meaningless in such jurisdictions as the Northwest Territories.[175]

Sequential families and the associated legal duty to support the children of such families are not uncommon. The assumption of second family obligations may inevitably create a certain degree of economic hardship but that hardship is not necessarily "undue."[176] The payment of child support is often perceived as a financial hardship by the payor and the new family, but their subjective perceptions do not satisfy the test of undue hardship. Awkwardness or inconvenience or the need to interfere with the existing financial planning strategy in the new payor household will not suffice. Undue hardship is not to be equated with financial difficulty, budgetary cutbacks, restraints, or financial re-evaluations. Undue hardship signifies that there is hardship that is excessive, extreme, disproportionate, improper, unreasonable, or unjustified.[177] A parent who pleads undue hardship on the basis of a co-existing obligation to support the child of a second family must prove that the hardship is different from that normally experienced by parents of second families.[178] In the case of a second family, the obligor should provide clear and cogent evidence, not conjecture or speculation, from which an inference can reasonably be drawn that the children in the second family would suffer significant deprivation if the table amount was ordered for the children of the first relationship. "Deprivation" means with respect to food, clothing, shelter, or some medical or other health need.[179] The fact that the obligor's household standard of living is lower than that of the spouse or former spouse, due in part to his or her legal duty to support another child, does not automatically create circumstances of undue hardship.[180] Courts are not required, therefore, to equalize the rights of half-siblings from sequential families. Absent undue hardship as defined above, the "first in time prevails" as between the children of sequential families.[181] The above stringent criteria were applied by the Nova Scotia Court of Appeal in *Gaetz v Gaetz*.[182]

---

175 *Ibid.*

176 *Schenkeveld v Schenkeveld*, [2002] MJ No 69 (CA); *Locke v Goulding*, 2012 NLCA 8; *Phillips v Bourque*, [2000] NBJ No 13 (SC); *Camirand v Beaulne* (1998), 160 DLR (4th) 749 (Ont Ct Gen Div); *Varga v Varga*, 2013 SKQB 22. See also *Soleimani v Melendez*, 2019 ONSC 36.

177 *Hanmore v Hanmore*, [2000] AJ No 171 (CA); *Van Gool v Van Gool*, [1998] BCJ No 3513 (CA); *Kelly v Kelly*, 2011 BCCA 173; *MN v CGF*, 2019 BCSC 1406; *Toews v Toews*, [1998] MJ No 346 (QB); *Gillespie v Gormley*, 2003 NBCA 72; *Moores v McLellan*, 2018 CarswellNB 48, 2018 CarswellNB 49, annotated in FAMLNWS 2018-16 (16 April 2018); *Locke v Goulding*, 2012 NLCA 8; *Johnson v Downey*, 2021 NSSC 2; *Laraque v Allooloo*, [1999] NWTJ No 49 (SC) (application under *NWT Child Support Guidelines*); *Pace v Barry*, 2019 ONSC 1739; *Jackson v Jackson*, 2023 SKCA 70; *BJG v DLG*, 2010 YKSC 33.

178 *Steele v Koppanyi*, [2002] MJ No 201 (CA); *Moores v McLellan*, 2018 CarswellNB 48, 2018 CarswellNB 49.

179 *Reid v Nelson* (2002), 30 RFL (5th) 153 (Ont Ct J); *Harvey v Sturk*, 2016 ONSC 4669; see also *Newman v Bogan*, 2010 NWTSC 69.

180 *Jones v Chappell*, 2009 ABQB 728; *Van Gool v Van Gool*, [1998] BCJ No 2513 (CA); *CGR v JLR*, 2020 BCSC 842; *Schenkeveld v Schenkeveld*, [2002] MJ No 69 (CA); *Smith v Hookey*, [1999] NJ No 243 (UFC); *Camirand v Beaulne*, [1998] OJ No 2163 (Gen Div); *Waite v Clements*, [2002] PEIJ No 8 (SC); *Messier v Baines*, [1997] SJ No 627 (QB).

181 See *Soleimani v Melendez*, 2019 ONSC 36.

182 [2001] NSJ No 131 (CA); see also *Ross v Ross*, [2001] NSJ No 184 (CA). And see *Locke v Goulding*, 2012 NLCA 8; *Birss v Birss*, [2000] OJ No 3692 (CA).

In a commentary on that judgment, Professor DA Rollie Thompson concludes that "some appeal courts have seriously overshot the mark in establishing a 'tough' test for undue hard ship, to the point of causing serious individual injustice by their adherence to the Table amounts."[183] Professor Thompson contends that his review of some 260 reported undue hardship cases since March 1997 provides little or no indication that a more flexible judi cial approach to undue hardship would open the floodgates to doubtful claims.[184] However, the low incidence of undue hardship cases is, no doubt, attributable at least in part to the stringent criteria imposed in early appellate decisions under the Guidelines.[185] Whether a more flexible approach in these cases would have opened the floodgates to "undue hardship" claims is a matter for speculation. Be that as it may, Professor Thompson is undoubtedly correct in asserting that *Gaetz v Gaetz* is questionable insofar as it interprets section 10(2) of the Guidelines as providing an exhaustive list of circumstances that constitute "undue hardship," despite the "open-ended language" of that section. A close examination of the trial and appellate judgments in *Gaetz v Gaetz* emphasizes that legal practitioners and judges would do well to bear in mind that a parent who has been ordered to pay child support is not thereby disqualified from obtaining an order for periodic spousal support.[186]

A claim of undue hardship arising out of the cost of a second family is not necessarily restricted to the circumstances identified in section 10(2)(d) of the *Federal Child Support Guidelines*, but a general reference to the overall expense of a new household will not suffice to support a claim of undue hardship in the absence of special or unique circumstances. Evidence of undue hardship might arise from having to change accommodation, giving up a needed vehicle, or operating on a restricted diet.[188] An obligor's responsibility for a second family will not warrant a finding of undue hardship where the expenses relating thereto were voluntarily assumed and within the obligor's control.[189] A separated or divorced parent is expected to organize his or her affairs with due regard to any pre-existing child support obligation.[190] An applicant who seeks to reduce child support on the ground of undue hard ship generated by obligations to a second family may have to explain why his or her common law spouse is not employed or likely to be employed in the near future.[191] A lifestyle decision of the obligor and his common law spouse that she will stay at home and look after their child is a relevant circumstance to be considered, where the obligor asserts that the child of his common law relationship will suffer undue hardship from the loss of extracurricular activities, if the obligor is compelled to pay the table amount of support for the children

183 DA Rollie Thompson, "Case Comment: *Gaetz v Gaetz*" (2000) 15 RFL (5th) 82 at 86.

184 *Ibid.*

185 See *Hanmore v Hanmore*, [2000] AJ No 171 (CA); *Van Gool v Van Gool*, [1998] BCJ No 2513 (CA).

186 *Varcoe v Varcoe*, [2000] OJ No 229 (SCJ) (interim orders); *Richter v Vahamaki* (2000), 8 RFL (5th) 194 (Ont SCJ).

187 *Locke v Goulding*, 2012 NLCA 8; *Camirand v Beaulne*, [1998] OJ No 2163 (Gen Div); *Jackson v Holloway* [1997] SJ No 691 (QB).

188 *Sutton v Sutton*, [1999] BCJ No 1933 (SC). For other relevant considerations, see *Belansky v Belansky*, [2009] OJ No 5480 at para 26 (SCJ).

189 *Camirand v Beaulne*, [1998] OJ No 2163 (Gen Div).

190 *Russell v Russell*, [1998] OJ No 2234 (Gen Div); *MS v JC*, 2010 PESC 50.

191 *Schluessel v Schluessel*, [1999] AJ No 1555 (QB); *Hansen v Hansen*, [1998] OJ No 4982 (Gen Div); *MS v JC*, 2010 PESC 50.

of his previous marriage.[192] There is no automatic relief from the child support obligations merely because the obligor's household lives below the poverty line. When such an obligor has established undue hardship and a household standard of living lower than that of the recipient household, the court must look at all the circumstances of each of the parties before determining the amount of child support to be paid. Relevant factors to be considered are the long lasting failure of the obligor to provide financial assistance, the primary caregiving parent's consequential assumption of an unfair share of the burden of raising the child, and the presence of another adult in the obligor's household who is not currently employed and whom the obligor supports.[193] An obligor cannot escape liability for child support on the basis that payments will provide no direct benefit to the children but will simply reimburse the province for social assistance paid to the primary caregiving parent.[194]

Where section 10 of the *Federal Child Support Guidelines* is deemed applicable by reason of the undue hardship generated by the obligations owed to a second family, the court may conclude that variation of an existing child support order is justified, but that a reduction, rather than the elimination, of the child support obligation owed to the children of a previous marriage is more appropriate.[195]

Where the requirements of section 10 of the Guidelines have been met, the court may deduct from the obligor's annual income the amount of support that would be payable under the Guidelines for the child[ren] in the obligor's home and fix the amount of support for the children of the obligor's first family having regard to the revised income amount.[196] In the absence of a finding of undue hardship under section 10 of the *Federal Child Support Guidelines*, a court has no jurisdiction to reduce the applicable provincial table amount of support payable in respect of children of the marriage by taking account of the obligor's legal duty to support other children.[197]

The fact that the payor and his second family are living at a lower standard of living than that of his first family is not necessarily sufficient to justify a finding of undue hardship. Although it may appear unfair and discriminatory that the second family may have to endure a lower standard of living than the children of the first family, the government has set forth that policy in the Guidelines.[198] Even with a finding of undue hardship, the obligor's legally enforceable new-family obligations cannot reduce the standard of living of a "child of the marriage" below that enjoyed in the obligor's current household.[199] Where undue hardship is established in consequence of the obligation to support the children of two families, the court may deviate from the applicable table amount of basic child support and may also decline to order any contribution to be made to necessary child care expenses under section 7 of the *Federal Child Support Guidelines*. In exercising its discretion to this effect, the

---

192 *McPhee v McPhee*, [1999] BCJ No 337 (SC).

193 *Sampson v Sampson*, [1998] AJ No 1214 (QB).

194 *Lucas v Gallant*, [2000] AJ No 457 (QB).

195 *Wlodarczyk v Wlodarczyk*, [2002] BCJ No 1940 (SC).

196 *Hookey v Smith*, [1998] NJ No 238 (SC).

197 *Coe v Coe*, [1999] BCJ No 1373 (SC); *Locke v Goulding*, 2012 NLCA 8; *McLean v Rice*, [2005] OJ No 576 (SCJ).

198 *Waite v Clements*, [2002] PEIJ No 8 (SC); compare *Gillespie v Gormley*, [2002] NBJ No 344 (QB). See also *Zubek v Nizol*, 2011 BCSC 776.

199 *Van Gool v Van Gool*, [1998] BCJ No 2513 (CA); *Russell v Russell*, [1998] OJ No 2234 (Gen Div); *Dean v Friesen*, [1999] SJ No 424 (QB).

court must interpret the Guidelines in a way that best serves the interests of all the children involved, even though only one child is the subject of the litigation.[200] Such exercise of judicial discretion enables the court to ensure, to the extent possible, that the children of both families are treated equitably;[201] their respective standards of living should not diverge too widely.[202] The court must consider the welfare of all of the obligor's children and ensure that they receive consistent treatment and opportunities.[203] The amount ordered may need to be revisited in the event of an older child pursuing post-secondary education.[204]

Where undue hardship is found within the meaning of the Guidelines and the affected parent's household income is significantly less than the low income measures amount in Schedule II of the Guidelines, the court may conclude that no order for child support should be granted.[205]

H. LEGAL DUTY TO SUPPORT A SICK OR DISABLED PERSON

Undue hardship under section 10(1) of the *Federal Child Support Guidelines* may be found because a spouse or former spouse has a legal duty to support any person who is unable to obtain the necessaries of life due to an illness or disability.[206]

Voluntary support of a sick sibling constitutes no basis for a finding of undue hardship under the *British Columbia Child Support Guidelines*.[207]

I. REASONABLE TIME TO OVERCOME HARDSHIP

Pursuant to section 10(5) of the *Federal Child Support Guidelines*, where the court orders a different amount of child support after making a finding of undue hardship under section 10(1) of the Guidelines, it may specify, in the child support order, a reasonable time for the satisfaction of any obligation arising from the circumstances that cause undue hardship and the amount payable at the end of that time. This provision is likely to be most frequently invoked in situations where unusually high family debts are the cause of the hardship,[208] but it is by no means expressly confined to those situations. In *Bourque v Phillips*,[209] undue hardship was found under section 10(2)(c) of the *Nova Scotia Child Support Guidelines*, where the father was obliged to pay fixed-term spousal support under a separation agreement, but the court concluded that the undue hardship would cease to exist once the time-limited spousal support obligation terminated.

---

200 *Hughes v Bourdon*, [1997] OJ No 4263 (Gen Div).

201 *Messier v Baines*, [1997] SJ No 627 (QB); see also *Tuesday v Daniels*, [2002] MJ No 316 (QB); *Gillespie v Gormley*, [2002] NBJ No 344 (QB); *Douglas v Ward*, [2006] SJ No 57 (QB).

202 *Deveau v Groskopf* (2000), 192 Sask R 227 (QB).

203 *Louisseize v Louisseize*, [1999] OJ No 5000 (SCJ); see also *KWF v EW*, [2000] OJ No 147 (SCJ).

204 *Louisseize v Louisseize*, [1999] OJ No 5000 (SCJ).

205 *Bahnman v Bahnman*, [1999] SJ No 888 (QB). For judicial criticism of the inflexibility of the low income measure, see *JABD v RAB*, 2012 PESC 6 at para 15.

206 *Federal Child Support Guidelines*, SOR 97-175, s 10(2)(e); see *Maloney-Chumney v Maloney-Chumney* [1999] NBJ No 108 (QB).

207 *Chatwin v Falbo*, [1998] BCJ No 2862 (Prov Ct).

208 *Aker v Howard*, [1998] OJ No 5562 (Gen Div).

209 [2000] NSJ No 13 (SC).

An application for increased child support may be granted by virtue of a change of circumstances within the meaning of section 14 of the *Federal Child Support Guidelines* when the respondent's annual income has increased and a previous finding of undue hardship is no longer tenable because the respondent is no longer liable to pay court-ordered support for two children of a prior marriage.[210]

J. JUDICIAL DISCRETION IN CASES OF UNDUE HARDSHIP CIRCUMSCRIBED BY COMPARISON OF STANDARD OF LIVING IN RESPECTIVE HOUSEHOLDS

A finding of undue hardship within the meaning of section 10 of the *Federal Child Support Guidelines* does not require the court to deviate from the amount of child support that would be ordered in the absence of undue hardship. A finding of undue hardship simply provides the court with the discretionary power to deviate from the norm.[211] There will be cases where the court will be faced by circumstances in which both households are facing undue hardship. In these circumstances, the court might decide in favour of one of the affected parties, for example, the child, or it might seek to balance the competing interests of the respective households. However, it is not possible for the court to deviate from the norm under sections 3 to 5 or 8 or 9 of the *Federal Child Support Guidelines*, if the household of the spouse pleading undue hardship would, after payment of the normal amount under the Guidelines, have a higher standard of living than the household of the other spouse[212] or spouses.[213] Such a case would fall subject to section 10(3) of the Guidelines, which specifically provides as follows:

> **Standards of living must be considered**
> 10 (3) Despite a determination of undue hardship under subsection (1), an application under that subsection must be denied by the court if it is of the opinion that the household of the spouse who claims undue hardship would, after determining the amount of child support under any of sections 3 to 5, 8 or 9, have a higher standard of living than the household of the other spouse.

There is nothing in section 10(3) of the Guidelines to prevent a court from taking account of the relative cost of living in two countries but relevant evidence must first be available to enable the court to undertake the comparison.[214]

Pursuant to section 10(4) of the *Federal Child Support Guidelines*, in comparing standards of living for the purpose of section 10(3), the court typically uses the comparison of

---

210 *Casey v Casey*, [2004] NBJ No 434 (QB).

211 *Locke v Goulding*, 2012 NLCA 8; *Tutty v Tutty*, 2005 NSSC 338; *Williams v Williams*, [1997] NWTJ No 49 (SC).

212 *Dean v Barrett*, [2004] AJ No 183 (CA); *JAA v SRA*, [1999] BCJ No 634 (CA); *Noel v Noel*, [2001] MJ No 441 (CA) (Addendum); *Skorulski v Zupan*, 2012 MBQB 98; *MJM v ADEM*, 2012 NBQB 71; *Locke v Goulding*, 2012 NLCA 8; *Tutty v Tutty*, [2005] NSJ No 514 (SC); *Williams v Williams*, [1997] NWTJ No 49 (SC); *Russell v Russell*, [1998] OJ No 2234 (Gen Div); *Hardy-Generoux v Generoux*, [2001] PEIJ No 52 (TD); *Dyck v Highton*, [2003] SJ No 600 (QB).

213 *O'Connor v O'Connor*, [1999] OJ No 362 (Gen Div) (three prior relationships; onus on obligor under provincial child support guidelines not discharged).

214 *Lafleur v Donoghue*, [2005] OJ No 5416 (SCJ).

household standards of living test set out in Schedule II of the Guidelines.[215] Schedule II provides as follows:

SCHEDULE II

(Subsection 10(4))

COMPARISON OF HOUSEHOLD STANDARDS OF LIVING TEST

Definitions

1 The definitions in this section apply in this Schedule.

average tax rate [Repealed, SOR/2000-337, s. 7].

child means a child of the marriage or a child who:

(a) is under the age of majority; or

(b) is the age of majority or over but is unable, by reason of illness, disability or other cause to obtain the necessaries of life.

household means a spouse and any of the following persons residing with the spouse:

(a) any person who has a legal duty to support the spouse or whom the spouse has a legal duty to support;

(b) any person who shares living expenses with the spouse or from whom the spouse otherwise receives an economic benefit as a result of living with that person, if the court considers it reasonable for that person to be considered part of the household; and

(c) any child whom the spouse or the person described in paragraph (a) or (b) has a legal duty to support.[216]

taxable income means the annual taxable income determined using the calculations required to determine "Taxable Income" in the T1 General form issued by The Canada Revenue Agency.

Test

2 The comparison of household standards of living test is as follows:

STEP 1

Establish the annual income of each person in each household by applying the formula:

$$A - B - C$$

where:

A is the person's income determined under sections 15 to 20 of these Guidelines, and

B is the federal and provincial taxes payable on the person's taxable income. Where the information on which to base the income determination is not provided, the court may impute income in the amount it considers appropriate.

215 *Reiter v Reiter*, [1997] BCJ No 2835 (SC); *WJA v STS*, [2001] NSJ No 151 (CA); *Reid v Faubert*, 2019 NSCA 42; *Larkin v Jamieson*, [2000] PEIJ No 65 (SC); *Fontaine v Andall*, [1998] SJ No 510 (QB).

216 *Guidelines Amending the Federal Child Support Guidelines*, SOR/97-563, s 10, amending SOR/97-175, s 1 (definition of "household").

C is the person's source deductions for premiums paid under the *Employment Insurance Act* and contributions made to the *Canada Pension Plan* and the *Quebec Pension Plan.*

Where the information on which to base the income determination is not provided, the court may impute income in the amount it considers appropriate.[217]

STEP 2

Adjust the annual income of each person in each household by:

(a) deducting the following amounts, calculated on an annual basis:

  (i) any amount relied on by the court as a factor that resulted in a determination of undue hardship,[218] except any amount attributable to the support of a member of the household that is not incurred due to a disability or serious illness of that member;

  (ii) the amount that would otherwise be payable by that person in respect of a child to whom the order relates, if the pleading of undue hardship was not made;

    (A) under the applicable table, or

    (B) as is considered by the court to be appropriate, where the court considers the table amount to be inappropriate;

  (iii) any amount of support that is paid by the person under a judgment, order or written separation agreement, except:

    (A) an amount already deducted under subparagraph (i), and

    (B) an amount paid by the person in respect of a child to whom the order referred to in subparagraph (ii) relates; and

(b) adding the following amounts, calculated on an annual basis:

  (i) any amount that would otherwise be receivable by the person in respect of a child to whom the order relates, if the pleading of undue hardship was not made;

    (A) under the applicable table, or

    (B) as is considered by the court to be appropriate, where the court considers the table amount to be inappropriate;

  (ii) any amount of child support that the person has received for any child under a judgment, order or written separation agreement.[219]

STEP 3

Add the amounts of adjusted annual income for all the persons in each household to determine the total household income for each household.

STEP 4

Determine the applicable low-income measures amount for each household based on the following:

---

217 *Guidelines Amending the Federal Child Support Guidelines*, SOR/2005-400, s 6.

218 *SEM v JJR*, 2013 ONSC 86.

219 *Guidelines Amending the Federal Child Support Guidelines*, SOR/97-563, s 11, amending SOR/97-175, Sch II, ss 2(a) & (b); see *Fontaine v Andall*, [1998] SJ No 510 (QB), wherein Gerein J concluded that the amendment constitutes a movement from the general to the specific and demonstrates an intention that only the basic table support be taken into account. See also *MacKinnon v Marshall*, [1998] NSJ No 537 (Fam Ct) (application under *Nova Scotia Child Support Guidelines*).

Low-income Measures

Household Size	*Low-income Measures Amount*
One Person	
1 adult	$10,382
Two persons	
2 adults	$14,535
1 adult and 1 child	$14,535
Three persons	
3 adults	$18,688
2 adults and 1 child	$17,649
1 adult and 2 children	$17,649
Four persons	
4 adults	$22,840
3 adults and 1 child	$21,802
2 adults and 2 children	$20,764
1 adult and 3 children	$20,764
Five Persons	
5 adults	$26,993
4 adults and 1 child	$25,955
3 adults and 2 children	$24,917
2 adults and 3 children	$23,879
1 adult and 4 children	$23,879
Six Persons	
6 adults	$31,145
5 adults and 1 child	$30,108
4 adults and 2 children	$29,070
3 adults and 3 children	$28,031
2 adults and 4 children	$26,993
1 adult and 5 children	$26,993
Seven Persons	
7 adults	$34,261
6 adults and 1 child	$33,222
5 adults and 2 children	$32,184
4 adults and 3 children	$31,146
3 adults and 4 children	$30,108
2 adults and 5 children	$29,070
1 adult and 6 children	$29,070

Household Size	Low-income Measures Amount
Eight Persons	
8 adults	$38,413
7 adults and 1 child	$37,375
6 adults and 2 children	$36,337
5 adults and 3 children	$35,299
4 adults and 4 children	$34,261
3 adults and 5 children	$33,222
2 adults and 6 children	$32,184
1 adult and 7 children	$32,184

STEP 5

Divide the household income amount (Step 3) by the low-income measures amount (Step 4) to get the household income ratio for each household.

STEP 6

Compare the household income ratios. The household that has the higher ratio has the higher standard of living.

For the purpose of the comparison of the household standards of living test under Schedule II of the *Ontario Child Support Guidelines,* the portion of social assistance received on behalf of the children by the primary caregiving parent is not to be included in the recipient's adjusted annual income under Schedule III of the Guidelines.[220]

Use of Schedule II of the *Federal Child Support Guidelines* is not mandatory when a court undertakes the required comparison of the respective household living standards in light of a finding of undue hardship. Judicial refusal to apply Schedule II of the Guidelines may be justified where the income ratio under that Schedule is not reflective of the funds available to the primary caregiving parent by way of child support, child tax benefits, social assistance, and provincial family bonuses.[221]

The onus falls on the party who invokes the undue hardship provisions of section 10 of the Guidelines to undertake the required comparison of household living standards under Schedule II of the Guidelines. It is the responsibility of counsel to demonstrate the impact of Schedule II and this responsibility is not discharged by simply presenting raw data and leaving it to the court to struggle with the calculation.[222]

An onus falls on the respondent to make full disclosure of household income when seeking to rely on a plea of "undue hardship" under section 10 of the *Federal Child Support Guidelines.* It is no answer to assert that the applicant seeking child support has also failed to make full disclosure of household income.[223]

The comparison of household incomes test under section 10(4) of the *Federal Child Support Guidelines* and of the *Ontario Child Support Guidelines* does not contravene section 7

220 *Martel v Martel,* [2001] OJ No 759 (Ct J).

221 *Williams v Smith,* [2001] AJ No 248 (QB) (downward adjustment of table amount deemed appropriate); *Ash v Summat,* [2003] BCJ No 2027 (SC).

222 *McDonald v McDonald,* [1998] BCJ No 3150 (SC).

223 *Bosgra v Squires,* [2001] NWTJ No 78 (SC).

of the *Canadian Charter of Rights and Freedoms*; a child's right to support is paramount to an individual's right to privacy.[224]

Paragraph (a) of Step 2 in section 2 of Schedule II, as amended effective 9 December 1997, signifies that when the household standard of living is calculated, no allowance is deducted from the obligor's income for the costs of raising the children of the second marriage, unless the expenses relate to illness or disability.[225] Only the applicable table amount of child support or its equivalent is deductible under Step 2 in section 2 of Schedule II; extraordinary expenses are not deductible.[226]

The comparable standard of living test in section 10(3) of the *Federal Child Support Guidelines* compares households, not just the spouses or former spouses themselves, and a claim of undue hardship will be dismissed unless the claimant provides sufficient evidence to enable the court to compare the standard of living in each household.[227] The use of the word "household" in sections 10(3) and (4) and Schedule II of the Guidelines signifies that a "common law spouse's" actual or imputed income should be taken into account in undertaking the comparison of household living standards,[228] but income received for the direct support of foster children has been excluded from the application of Schedule II of the Guidelines. In comparing the incomes of each household under Schedule II of the *Federal Child Support Guidelines*, the obligation of a common law partner of the spouse or former spouse to pay tax deductible spousal support and non-tax deductible child support should be taken into account, even though that partner cannot personally invoke the undue hardship provisions of section 10 of the Guidelines.[230]

Where undue hardship is pleaded within the meaning of section 10 of the *Federal Child Support Guidelines*, the court has no jurisdiction to order the "common law partner" of either parent to disclose financial information, but the court may draw an adverse inference and impute an income pursuant to section 23 of the Guidelines. A "common law partner" may be presumed to contribute financially to the household for the purpose of a judicial comparison of the respective household incomes under section 10(3) and (4) of the Guidelines.[231]

The obligation of a parent asserting undue hardship to provide financial information relating to a cohabitant's income cannot be avoided by reliance on the terms of a cohabitation agreement that purports to preclude such disclosure.[232]

A child of the marriage who is living in a shared parenting time arrangement should be considered as part of the household of each spouse or former spouse in applying Schedule II of the *Federal Child Support Guidelines*.[233] Although the definition of "household" under Schedule II does not include the children of a common law partner living with the spouse or

224 *Souliere v Leclair*, [1998] OJ No 1393 (Gen Div).

225 *Swift v Swift*, [1998] OJ No 501 (Gen Div); *Duffee v Scott*, [2003] SJ No 212 (QB).

226 *Matthews v Hancock*, [1998] SJ No 617 (QB).

227 *Locke v Goulding*, 2012 NLCA 8; *Holtby v Holtby*, [1997] OJ No 2237 (Gen Div).

228 *Zorn v Zorn*, [1998] BCJ No 3014 (SC); *LLF v JD*, [2004] NSJ No 466 (Fam Ct); compare *Kaupp v Kaupp*, [2008] AJ No 668 (QB).

229 *Zorn v Zorn*, [1998] BCJ No 3014 (SC).

230 *Middleton v MacPherson*, [1997] AJ No 614 (QB).

231 *Cecotka v Cecotka*, [2000] AJ No 7 (QB); compare *Ben-Ami v Ben-Ami*, [2001] OJ No 5109 (SCJ).

232 *Fleury v Fleury*, [2000] OJ No 3021 (Ct J).

233 *Ibid.*

former spouse, section 10(2)(d) of the Guidelines may apply with respect to such children so as to trigger a plea of undue hardship by the spouse or former spouse and warrant a deduction from his or her income under Step 2(a)(i) of Schedule II.[234]

In determining whether a party who asserts undue hardship under section 10 of the *Federal Child Support Guidelines* will be disentitled to relief on the ground that his or her household standard of living is higher than that of the recipient's household, the court may impute income to that party on the basis of intentional underemployment or unemployment within the meaning of section 19 of the Guidelines.[235]

Some difficulty may be experienced in determining the income of all persons in each household, even in cases where the composition of each household is beyond dispute and not in a transitional stage. Although sections 21 to 25 of the *Federal Child Support Guidelines* impose mandatory disclosure requirements on one or both of the spouses or former spouses, as the case may be, together with sanctions for non-compliance, these provisions do not extend to other members of either household, such as children, new partners, or parents. However, section 21(5) of the *Federal Child Support Guidelines* specifically empowers the competent rule making authorities in any province or territory to make additional rules respecting the disclosure of information for the purpose of determining the amount of a child support order.

Although the *Federal Child Support Guidelines* do not provide a mechanism for the court to order the production of income information by a non-party,[236] Step 1 of Schedule II of the Guidelines does stipulate that where the information on which to base the income determination is not provided, the court may impute income in the amount it considers appropriate. Accordingly, if there is another individual in the household whose income information should be considered and there is no disclosure of that information, it would be advisable for the spouse or former spouse to provide such information as he or she may be aware of so that the court may determine whether or not to impute income.[237] Income may be imputed to a "common law spouse" who has demonstrated an earning capacity but deliberately chosen not to seek employment.[238]

Where an obligor seeks a reduction in the amount of child support due to undue hardship, the recipient parent is not relieved of the duty of financial disclosure under section 21 of the *Federal Child Support Guidelines* by conceding a higher household standard of living than that enjoyed in the obligor's household. In order to reach a decision on whether there should or should not be any deviation from the amount otherwise payable under the Guidelines, the court must know the precise financial picture of the recipient household. Although such a concession eliminates the need for the court to undertake a comparison of the respective households pursuant to section 10(3) of the Guidelines, it does nothing to assist the court in determining what reduction, if any, should be ordered.[239]

234 *Ibid.*
235 *Warren v Warren*, [1998] NBJ No 315 (QB).
236 But see *Tanner v Simpson*, [1999] NWTJ No 71 at para 57 (SC).
237 *Tanner v Simpson*, *ibid*; *St Mars v St Mars*, [1997] SJ No 700 (QB).
238 *Toews v Toews*, [1998] MJ No 346 (QB); see also *Zorn v Zorn*, [1998] BCJ No 3014 (SC).
239 *Cuddie v Cuddie*, [1998] BCJ No 159 (SC).

Although GST and Child Tax Credits do not constitute "income" within the meaning of section 16 of the Guidelines, it is essential to take them into account in undertaking a comparison of the household living standards under section 10(3) of the Guidelines.[240]

In undertaking a comparison of the standards of living in the respective households, the court is not obliged to use the model set out in Schedule II of the *Federal Child Support Guidelines*,[241] although a comparative analysis necessarily includes some aspects of Schedule II.[242] The object of Schedule II is to provide a mechanism that results in a fair determination.[243] Schedule II has potential limitations when applied without regard for individual circumstances. There may be other criteria the court will prefer to apply in determining which household has the higher standard of living.[244] For example, costs of living can vary considerably depending on urban or rural locations and employment and lifestyle imperatives.[245] undertaking a comparison of the household living standards, the court may "gross up" support payments that fall subject to the former deduction/inclusion income tax regime.[246] Foreign health care costs may also be relevant to such a comparison.[247] A court could admit expert evidence on the issue of standards of living, although that might prove to be prohibitively costly and unduly speculative in many cases. The court could use some comparison model of its own creation or it could apply a variation of the model set out in Schedule II. Even the definition of "household," which is set out in section 1 of Schedule II, could be judicially redefined for the purpose of applying a different model under section 10(3) of the Guidelines, although courts would be wise to avoid adding to the confusion. Professor Bala has observed:

> Since s. [10](4) is permissive, one can argue that other factors might be considered, such as cost-of-living differences between two locations. It might be possible to make individualized economic arguments for those expenses analogous to those in s. [10](2)(a), (b) and (c) that, for instance, a spouse's unavoidable medical expenses, necessitated by a disability, affect "standard of living."[248]

While it is not mandatory for the court to apply Schedule II of the Guidelines in comparing the household standards of living, the court will expect counsel to undertake and submit an appropriate calculation to the court.[249] Although section 10(3) of the *Federal Child Support Guidelines* specifically requires a court to deny an application based on undue hardship where the household of the spouse or former spouse claiming undue hardship would have a higher standard of living than the prospective recipient household, it provides no guidance as to what the court should do where it finds that the spouse or former spouse claiming

---

240 *Ash v Summat*, [2003] BCJ No 2027 (SC); *Pelletier v Kakakaway*, [2002] SJ No 448 (CA).

241 *Omah-Maharajh v Howard*, [1998] AJ No 173 (QB); *Loosdrecht v Loosdrecht*, [1998] BCJ No 1629 (SC); *Tack v Fournier*, [1998] MJ No 596 (QB) (application under *Manitoba Child Support Guidelines*); *Camirand v Beaulne*, [1998] OJ No 2163 (Gen Div); *Ironstand v Ironstand*, [1999] SJ No 250 (QB).

242 *Loosdrecht v Loosdrecht*, [1998] BCJ No 1629 (SC).

243 *Ibid*.

244 *Toews v Toews*, [1998] MJ No 346 (QB), citing *Woolhouse v Jarosz*, [1998] SJ No 62 (QB).

245 *Woolhouse v Jarosz*, *ibid*, citing *Hansvall v Hansvall*, [1997] SJ No 782 (QB).

246 *Tack v Fournier*, [1998] MJ No 596 (QB).

247 *Ibid*.

248 Nicholas Bala, "Ottawa's New Child Support Regime: A Guide to the Guidelines" (1996) 21 RFL (4th) 301 at 326.

249 *Jackson v Holloway*, [1997] SJ No 691 (QB); see also *Reid v Faubert*, 2019 NSCA 42.

undue hardship has a lower household standard of living than that of the other spouse. In the absence of any guidance, a court may conclude that the amount of child support to be ordered should substantially equate the two household income ratios.[250] There is no exact mathematical formula to determine the adjustment to be made to the applicable table amount of child support where the undue hardship provisions of section 10 of the Guidelines have been met. Judicial decisions provide no hard and fast rules as to how the court should exercise its discretion. Equalization of the household income ratio in the order for child support may be appropriate in some cases, but not in others.[251] A valid separation agreement, though not an absolute bar to an application for child support some years later, may be a relevant consideration in dealing with the undue hardship provisions of the Guidelines, where one of the parties assumed new family obligations after execution of the agreement.[252]

K. REASONS FOR DEVIATION FROM NORM TO BE JUDICIALLY RECORDED

Where a court decides to deviate from the amount of child support that would be granted under sections 3 to 5 or 8 or 9 of the *Federal Child Support Guidelines* on the ground of undue hardship, section 10(6) of the Guidelines requires the court to record its reasons for doing so.[253] A written endorsement, unlike a recorded tape of a judicial proceeding, will provide a necessary permanent record of the purpose of section 10(6) of the Guidelines.

L. SECTION 7 EXPENSES

The undue hardship provisions of section 10 of the *Federal Child Support Guidelines* would appear to be inapplicable to claims for special or extraordinary expenses under section 7 of the Guidelines. Although section 10 of the *Federal Child Support Guidelines* empowers a court to deviate from the amount of child support determined under any of sections 3 to 5, 8, or 9 of the Guidelines on the basis of undue hardship, and section 3(1)(b) of the Guidelines specifically incorporates a reference to section 7 of the Guidelines, it would be illogical to apply section 10 of the Guidelines to applications for special or extraordinary expenses, given that section 7(1) of the Guidelines requires the court to have regard to the "reasonableness of the expenses in relation to the means of the spouses" in determining what, if any, parental contribution to such expenses should be ordered. The test of "reasonableness" under section 7 of the Guidelines is not nearly as stringent as the requirements respecting undue hardship that are imposed by section 10 of the Guidelines. Consequently, a failure to establish undue hardship in a claim for the applicable table amount of child support does not preclude the

---

250 *Reiter v Reiter*, [1997] BCJ No 2835 (SC); *Dean v Friesen*, [1999] SJ No 15 (QB).

251 *DL v ML*, 2012 NBQB 382.

252 *Aker v Howard*, [1999] OJ No 651 (Gen Div).

253 *Middleton v MacPherson*, [1997] AJ No 614 (QB); *CAE v MD*, 2011 NBCA 17; *Locke v Goulding*, 2012 NLCA 8.

court from denying a correlative claim for special or extraordinary expenses under section 7 of the Guidelines where hardship, whether undue or not, would otherwise ensue.[254]

M. SHARED PARENTING TIME

Subject to a possible extraordinary situation, there is no need to resort to the undue hardship provisions of section 10 of the *Federal Child Support Guidelines* in shared parenting time situations falling within section 9 of the Guidelines because the court has full discretion under section 9(c) to consider "other circumstances" in fixing the amount of child support.

254 *WM v DO*, [1999] AJ No 1338 (QB); *ANH v MKC*, 2010 NBQB 120; *Pitcher v Pitcher*, [2002] NJ No 358 (UFC); *WL v NDH*, 2014 NBQB 214; *Koval v Brinton*, 2010 NSCA 78; *Staples v Callender*, 2020 NSSC 365; *Camirand v Beaulne*, [1998] OJ No 2163 (Gen Div); *Olaitan v MacDougall*, 2014 PECA 5; *Nishnik v Smith*, [1997] SJ No 812 (QB). Compare *Kaupp v Kaupp*, [2008] AJ No 668 (QB); *Lidstone v Lidstone*, [2003] PEIJ No 77 (SC); *Dougan v Clark*, [2003] PEIJ No 87 (SC).

255 See *Contino v Leonelli-Contino*, [2005] 3 SCR 217; see Chapter 6, Section B(3). See also *Wetsch v Kuski* 2017 SKCA 77; *Hinds v Jacobs*, 2018 SKQB 51 (retroactive child support).

CHAPTER 8

Impact of Child Support on Spousal Support

A. PRIORITY OF CHILD SUPPORT OVER SPOUSAL SUPPORT; EFFECT OF CHILD SUPPORT ORDER ON ASSESSMENT OF SPOUSAL SUPPORT

Section 15.3 of the *Divorce Act* provides as follows:

> **Priority to child support**
>
> 15.3 (1) Where a court is considering an application for a child support order and an application for a spousal support order, the court shall give priority to child support in determining the applications.
>
> **Reasons**
>
> (2) Where, as a result of giving priority to child support, the court is unable to make a spousal support order or the court makes a spousal support order in an amount that is less than it otherwise would have been, the court shall record its reasons for having done so.
>
> **Consequences of reduction or termination of child support order**
>
> (3) Where, as a result of giving priority to child support, a spousal support order was not made, or the amount of a spousal support order is less than it otherwise would have been, any subsequent reduction or termination of that child support constitutes a change of circumstances for the purposes of applying for a spousal support order, or a variation order in respect of the spousal support order, as the case may be.[1]

The priority accorded to child support under section 15.3 also applies to variation pro ceedings.[2] If spousal support is less than it would otherwise had been as a result of the child

1 *Maka v Maka*, 2015 ONSC 3480.

2 See *Divorce Act*, RSC 1985 (2d Supp), c 3, s 17(6.6).

support, then when the child support terminates, it is a change of circumstances that allows for a variation in the spousal support order.[3]

Section 15.3 and section 17(6.6) of the *Divorce Act* address the situation where the application for child support and the application for spousal support involve members of the same family. They do not establish priorities as between sequential families.[4] For example, a former divorced wife's order for spousal support will not be subject to a statutory priority in favour of the obligor's children from a second subsequently dissolved marriage. The difficulties that have plagued the courts respecting the competing claims of sequential families remain unresolved.

Where a needs-based spousal support order is precluded by the husband's inability to pay after judicial regard is paid to the statutory priority that applies to child support orders, the husband may be directed to provide the wife with a copy of his income tax return on an annual basis so that she may revisit the issue of spousal support when appropriate.[5]

In granting an order for periodic spousal support, a court may declare the amount to be less than would have been ordered but for the priority to be accorded to the needs of the children under section 15.3 of the *Divorce Act*.[6] In ordering the termination of a spousal support obligation having regard to the statutory priority to be accorded to the child support obligation, the court may acknowledge that economic self-sufficiency is an attainable goal for the former recipient of spousal support and declare that this factor will be closely scrutinized if section 15.3(3) of the *Divorce Act* is subsequently invoked in an attempt to reinstate a spousal support obligation.[7]

Although section 15.3(1) of the *Divorce Act* requires the court to give priority to child support over spousal support, this does not signify that special or exceptional expenses should be ordered under section 7 of the *Federal Child Support Guidelines* to supplement the basic amount of child support payable under the applicable provincial or territorial table, where such a supplementary allocation would render a spouse destitute.[8] The priority of child support, including section 7 expenses,[9] over spousal support that is mandated by section 15(3)(1) of the *Divorce Act* does not preclude the court from giving consideration to spousal support and looking at the overall picture in determining the appropriate contribution, if any, to be made to special or extraordinary child-related expenses.[10] An order for interim spousal support may be subject to reduction in the event of a subsequent successful claim for special or extraordinary expenses under section 7 of the Guidelines.[11]

---

3 *Willms v Willms*, 2020 BCCA 51 at para 22, citing *McIntosh v McIntosh*, 2007 BCSC 1331; *Harrison v Harrison*, 2020 BCSC 1203. See also *MLO v DGO*, 2023 MBKB 171 at paras 89–94.

4 *Hilborn v Hilborn*, [2007] OJ No 3068 (SCJ).

5 *Rausch v Rausch*, [2004] SJ No 171 (QB).

6 *Peters v Peters*, [2002] NSJ No 413 (SC); *Beatty v Beatty*, [2000] OJ No 1755 (SCJ).

7 *Kozub v Kozub*, [2002] SJ No 407 (QB).

8 *Lyttle v Bourget*, [1999] NSJ No 298 (SC); *Kaderly v Kaderly*, [1997] PEIJ No 74 (TD); see also *Cameron-Masson v Masson*, [1997] NSJ No 207 (Fam Ct).

9 *Andrews v Andrews*, [1999] OJ No 3578 (CA) (priority over spousal support given to extraordinary expenses for children's schooling pursuant to s 38.1(i) of Ontario *Family Law Act*).

10 *Nataros v Nataros*, [1998] BCJ No 1417 (SC); see also *Wilson v Wilson*, [2004] BCJ No 116 (SC).

11 *Shentow v Bewsh*, [1998] OJ No 3142 (Gen Div).

A parent who is ordered to pay periodic child support is not thereby disqualified from obtaining an order for periodic spousal support.[12] Child support and spousal support, though sometimes intertwined, are based on distinct principles. The fact that the receipt of one may offset the payment of the other does not preclude an order for both kinds of relief in appropriate circumstances.[13] But given the different income tax treatment accorded to periodic child support and periodic spousal support, a court should not order a direct set-off of child support payable to the primary caregiving parent and spousal support payable by that parent.[14]

A primary caregiving parent's obligation to provide financially for a child of the marriage takes priority over the obligation to pay spousal support to the other parent and may result in a reduction of the amount of spousal support that would otherwise be ordered[15] or the denial of any order for spousal support.[16] A primary caregiving parent cannot avoid the obligation to pay a reasonable amount of spousal support on the dissolution of a long marriage by calling upon the other parent to live at or below the poverty level in order for the primary caregiving parent to provide a child of the marriage with luxuries.[17]

Where a child has special needs due to a chronic illness, this may be taken into account in determining the ability of the payor spouse to pay spousal support when that individual is already committing significant resources to the child.[18]

Where the spousal incomes are approximately equal after the payment of child support, a court may refuse to order spousal support until the child support obligation is eliminated.[19]

The cessation of child support payments does not inevitably justify an increase in the amount of spousal support payments.[20]

In consequence of giving priority to child support, a court may be unable to grant a spousal support order because the obligor has no ability to pay any amount to satisfy the demonstrated need of the other spouse.[21] Although periodic spousal support may be reduced or denied where child support obligations impair the obligor's ability to pay,[22] a lump sum spousal support payment may be practical.[23] In granting a lump sum order for spousal support, the court may expressly acknowledge a potential future right to periodic spousal support under section 15.3(3) of the *Divorce Act*.[24] Where spousal support has been denied or reduced

12 *Varcoe v Varcoe*, [2000] OJ No 229 (SCJ) (interim orders).

13 *Richter v Vahamaki* (2000), 8 RFL (5th) 194 (Ont SCJ).

14 *Noble v Boone*, 2010 NLTD 65; *Stokes v Stokes*, [1999] OJ No 5192 (SCJ). Compare *Edgar v Edgar*, 2012 ONCA 646.

15 *Schick v Schick*, [1997] SJ No 447 (QB).

16 *Trehearne v Trehearne*, [2000] AJ No 1632 (QB).

17 *Reyher v Reyher* (1993), 48 RFL (3d) 111 (Man QB).

18 *Broder v Broder* (1994), 93 Man R(2d) 259 (QB).

19 *Rupert v Rupert*, [1999] NBJ No 5 (QB).

20 *Davis v Davis*, [2000] NSJ No 86 (SC).

21 *Bell v Bell*, [1997] BCJ No 2826 (SC); *Falbo v Falbo*, [1998] BCJ No 1497 (SC) (application for interim spousal support adjourned indefinitely); *CJD v CED*, 2020 PESC 21; *Cooper v Cooper*, [2002] SJ No 226 (QB).

22 *D'Entremont v D'Entremont*, [2001] NSJ No 586 (SC); *Norlander v Norlander* (1989), 21 RFL (3d) 317 (Sask QB); see also *Hunt v Smolis-Hunt*, [2001] AJ No 1170 (CA) (spousal support to be revisited by trial court in light of appellate court's disposition of appeal respecting child support); *Kenning v Kenning* (1995), 11 RFL (4th) 216 (BCSC).

23 *Kapogianes v Kapogianes*, [2000] OJ No 2572 (SCJ); *Lepage v Lepage*, [1999] SJ No 174 (QB); compare *Whalen v Whalen*, [2000] OJ No 2658 (SCJ).

24 *Lepage v Lepage*, [1999] SJ No 174 (QB).

to accommodate child support payments, spousal support may be awarded or increased when the child support obligations cease.[25] A court may direct that an order for periodic spousal support shall be increased by the amount by which child support is reduced when each of the children ceases to be entitled to support.[26] Before making any order, it is important to keep in mind that periodic payments for child support that are ordered after 1 May 1997 are tax-free, whereas periodic spousal support payments are deductible from the payor's taxable income and are taxable in the hands of the recipient spouse.[27] Courts must not overlook this difference when ordering, what is in effect, the conversion of child support payments into spousal support payments at some future date. An order whereby spousal support will be increased to a designated monthly amount on termination of the obligor's duty to pay court ordered child support may be expressly declared to be subject to further variation by reason of a material change of circumstances,[28] although such a declaration is presumably unnecessary.

Although section 15.3(1) of the *Divorce Act* gives priority to child support over spousal support where applications for both are brought in the same proceeding, the spousal support claim must be dealt with first if the applicant seeks increased child support on the ground of undue hardship under section 10 of the Guidelines.[29]

A nominal amount of spousal support of $1 per year may be ordered having regard to the priority to be placed on child support obligations.[30] It has been asserted, however, that "in case" nominal orders serve no useful purpose because the parties are free to re-apply in the event of a change of circumstances.[31]

Where periodic child support has been ordered, the amount should be grossed up for income tax for the purpose of determining the obligor's capacity to pay periodic spousal support[32] or the obligor's entitlement to receive spousal support from a primary caregiving parent.[33]

Where the combined income of the two spousal households has been substantially diminished in consequence of the application of the *Federal Child Support Guidelines* and accompanying amendments of the *Income Tax Act*, which took effect on 1 May 1997, a court may conclude that this constitutes a change of circumstances that warrants a reduction of the amount of spousal support under a pre-existing order so that the overall reduction in total income may be shared on some equitable basis by the former spouses.[34] On an applica tion to vary the spousal support order on this basis, the court must be provided with accurate information concerning the after-tax income of the spouses before and after 1 May 1997.[35]

---

25 *Sneddon v Sneddon* (1993), 46 RFL (3d) 373 (Alta QB); *Peters v Peters*, [2002] NSJ No 413 (SC); *MacArthur v MacArthur*, [2004] NSJ No 209 (SC); *Gray v Gray*, 2014 ONCA 659; *CJD v CED*, 2020 PESC 21.

26 *McLean v McLean*, [1997] OJ No 5315 (Gen Div); see also *Smith v Smith* (1998), 36 RFL (4th) 419 at 425 (Ont Ct Gen Div); *Gritti v Gritti*, [2001] OJ No 1363 (SCJ); *Cusack v Cusack*, [1999] PEIJ No 90 (SC).

27 See *Rondeau v Kirby*, [2003] NSJ No 436 (SC), aff'd [2004] NSJ No 143 (CA).

28 *Lackie v Lackie*, [1998] OJ No 888 (Gen Div).

29 *Galliford v Galliford*, [1998] BCJ No 268 (SC).

30 *Young v Young*, [1999] NSJ No 63 (SC).

31 *Frydrysek v Frydrysek*, [1998] BCJ No 394 (SC).

32 *Hama v Werbes*, [1998] BCJ No 2682 (SC).

33 *Stokes v Stokes*, [1999] OJ No 5192 (SCJ).

34 *Desjardins v Desjardins*, [1999] MJ No 70 (CA) (minority opinion of Huband J). The majority opinion of Scott CJM, with Monnin JA concurring, expressly declined to speculate on this issue.

35 *Ibid.*

the absence of such information, an appellate court may conclude that a trial judge's order for a substantial reduction in the amount of court-ordered spousal support cannot be sustained, having regard to the financial disparity and apparent inconsistency between the old and new orders for spousal and child support, and may direct a new hearing on the issue of the amount of spousal support.[36]

In assessing the amount of spousal support to be paid by a high income spouse, the court may take into consideration the indirect benefits conferred on the applicant by a concurrent periodic child support order in an exceptionally high amount.[37]

Section 15.3(2) of the *Divorce Act* provides that where a court is unable to make a spousal support order or makes an order in a reduced amount because of the priority accorded to child support, the court "shall record its reasons for having done so."[38] Thomas Bastedo, a senior family law practitioner from Toronto, has concluded that "it is difficult to accept that the court will insist on section 15.3(2) as a precondition for its exercise of jurisdiction under subsection (3)."[39] But, as B Lynn Reierson, a Halifax family law practitioner, has shrewdly observed:

> Although s. 15.3(3) of the *Divorce Act* establishes an automatic variation threshold, where the child support order relates to young children the opportunity to apply s. 15.3(3) to a spousal support variation application may not arise for many years. Entitlement on a compensatory basis, where need is not acute, may be very difficult to revisit at that future time.[40]

The impact of the *Federal Child Support Guidelines* on spousal support is not confined to their substantive significance in light of section 15.3 of the *Divorce Act*. The effect of specific disclosure requirements under sections 21 to 26 of the *Federal Child Support Guidelines* has spread over into the context of spousal support.[41]

Child support takes priority over spousal support under section 38.1 of the Ontario *Family Law Act* where the obligor is faced with their competing demands on his income.[42]

B. IMPLICATIONS OF CHILD CARE DURING MARRIAGE AND AFTER DIVORCE ON SPOUSAL SUPPORT ENTITLEMENT

Sections 15.2(6)(b) and 17(7)(b) of the *Divorce Act* empower a court to equitably apportion the indirect financial consequences of child rearing between divorcing or divorced spouses by means of spousal support. Professor Ellen Zweibel has identified four distinct indirect and direct costs of child rearing, namely:

---

36 *SAJM v DDM*, [1999] MJ No 118 (CA).

37 *Davis v Davis*, 2013 NBQB 115; *R v R*, [2000] OJ No 2830 (SCJ), var'd [2002] OJ No 1095, 24 RFL (5th) 96 (CA); *Ghremida v Elgahwas*, 2023 SKCA 23 at para 43.

38 *Lepp v Lepp*, 2008 BCSC 448.

39 Thomas Bastedo, "Impact of Child Support Guidelines on Spousal Support" (November 1999) 11:3 *Matrimonial Affairs*, CBAO Family Law Section Newsletter 1 at 27.

40 B Lynn Reierson, "The Impact of Child Support Guidelines on Spousal Support Law and Practice" (Paper presented to Federation of Law Societies and Canadian Bar Association, The 2000 National Family Law Program, St John's, Newfoundland, 10–13 July 2000) ch 23-1 at 1.

41 *Ibid* at 10–11.

42 *Schmid v Smith*, [1999] OJ No 3062 (SCJ); see also *Andrews v Andrews*, [1999] OJ No 3578 (CA).

(i) the indirect costs of the increased responsibility of child care falling on a single parent and the cost of time spent on household, child rearing and nurturing tasks;
(ii) the increased direct costs of services purchased to meet the needs of the child, such as work related child care, babysitters, assistance with household tasks;
(iii) the hidden increased costs associated with shopping and housing functions; and
(iv) lost employment opportunity costs.[43]

As L'Heureux-Dubé J observed in *Moge v Moge*,[44] a woman's ability to support herself after divorce is often significantly affected by her role as primary caregiver to the children both during the marriage and after the divorce. Her sacrifices include loss of training, work place security and seniority, absence of pension and insurance plans, and decreased salary levels. These losses may arise from the woman's role as primary caregiver, regardless of whether or not she was employed outside the home. Bearing these considerations in mind, lawyers and courts should reject the notion that short-term marriages with children warrant only short-term spousal support and that any such support should be reduced or terminated when the youngest child is old enough to attend school.

On marriage breakdown and divorce, poverty is essentially a parenting problem. It is not single women with employment potential who suffer most. It is single mothers who must shoulder both economic and parenting burdens. This must be borne in mind under sections 15.2(6)(a), (b), and (c) and 17(7)(a), (b), and (c) of the *Divorce Act*. As L'Heureux-Dubé J has stated extra-judicially: "Through judicial discretion, these objectives must be interpreted and applied in a way that does not perpetuate the feminization of poverty and further diminish the economic condition of women after divorce."[45]

---

43 Ellen B Zweibel, "Valuing the Custodial Parents' Contribution: Dealing with Increased Monetary and Non-monetary Costs Absorbed by the Custodial Parent" in Canadian Advisory Council on the Status of Women, *Summary Notes* (Critical Review of Child Support Guidelines Workshop, Ottawa, 22–24 May 1992), cited by L'Heureux-Dubé J in *Willick v Willick*, [1994] 3 SCR 670, 6 RFL (4th) 161 at 202–3.

44 [1992] 3 SCR 813.

45 Justice Claire L'Heureux-Dubé, "Economic Consequences of Divorce: A View from Canada" (1994) 31 *Houston Law Review* 451 at 489.

CHAPTER 9

Low- and High-Income Earners; Annual Income over $150,000

A. LOW-INCOME EARNERS

The provincial or territorial tables under the *Federal Child Support Guidelines* have a minimum annual income or poverty threshold below which no fixed amount of basic child support is payable[1] and any existing order should be terminated.[2] In these circumstances, however, a court may direct the obligor to provide the primary caregiving parent[3] or the provincial maintenance enforcement office[4] with financial statements at designated intervals.

Where a parent is relieved of the legal obligation to pay the basic amount of table support because his or her income falls below the minimum threshold, a court may also reject any claim to expenses under section 7 of the *Federal Child Support Guidelines* even though "means" under section 7(1) of the Guidelines is a broader concept than income earning capacity in that "means" includes all of a person's pecuniary resources, capital assets, income from employment or earning capacity, and any other source from which a person receives gains or benefits, together with, in certain circumstances, money that the person does not have in possession but which is available to that person. The fact that the Guidelines do not prescribe a basic child support payment for parents with income below the minimum threshold reflects the reality that everyone requires a certain amount of money simply to survive. It would appear to be

---

1 *Sampson v Sampson*, [1998] AJ No 1214 (QB); *Adamson v Adamson*, [1998] BCJ No 2697 (CA); *Smith v Smith*, [2005] BCJ No 480 (SC) (a court is not entitled to take the parent's new spouse's income into account); *Mabbett v Mabbett*, [1999] NSJ No 125 (SC); *Larkin v Jamieson*, [2000] PEIJ No 65 (SC); *RBK v AMK*, [1997] SJ No 599 (QB); compare *Uto v Szemok*, [2005] BCJ No 1417 (SC).

2 *Oliver v Oliver*, [1998] AJ No 340 (QB); *Thistle v Thompson*, [2000] NJ No 57 (SC) (prospective and retroactive variation with partial remission of arrears); *PM v DJT*, [1999] OJ No 4955 (SCJ); *Gershon v Shulson*, [1998] SJ No 811 (QB).

3 *Oliver v Oliver*, [1998] AJ No 340 (QB); *PM v DJT*, [1999] OJ No 4955 (SCJ); *Gershon v Shulson*, [1998] SJ No 811 (QB).

4 *Dietz v Dietz*, [1998] SJ No 197 (QB).

irrational if a parent who is unable to pay the base level of child support can be compelled to contribute to special or extraordinary expenses under section 7 of the Guidelines.[5]

If a parent's annual income falls below the minimum threshold under the provincial table, a court should not seek to circumvent the consequential exemption from liability by ordering a reapportionment of that parent's RRSP so as to indirectly accomplish what cannot be directly achieved, where the economic welfare of the children would be better advanced by that parent having the means to restore himself or herself to a financially independent state as quickly as possible so that a fair contribution can then be made to the support of the children.[6]

Absent undue hardship, a low-income disabled parent is obligated to pay the applicable table amount of child support.[7] Subject to the overriding jurisdiction of the court to deviate from the Guidelines amount of child support in cases of undue hardship, as defined in section 10 of the Guidelines, a parent whose income exceeds the minimum threshold under the applicable provincial table should be ordered to pay the designated amount of child support, regardless of the fact that the children's needs are more than amply met by their primary caregiving parent. Child support is a right of the child and reflects part of the role that each parent should play. The payment of child support reinforces the parental role and input and thereby reflects the best interests of the children, provided that the contributing parent's income is also sufficient to meet the direct and indirect expenses incurred by that parent on behalf of the children.[8]

B. ANNUAL INCOME OVER $150,000

Section 4 of the *Federal Child Support Guidelines* provides two approaches to the assessment of child support where the annual income of the spouse against whom a child support order is sought exceeds $150,000. Pursuant to section 4(a) of the Guidelines, the amount of child support is determinable in accordance with section 3 of the Guidelines, whereby the amount will be ordinarily established by reference to the applicable provincial or territorial table, together with any additional amount that may be payable for special or extraordinary expenses falling within section 7 of the Guidelines.[9] The provincial and territorial tables establish a fixed monetary amount of support to be paid by an obligor whose annual income is $150,000. Insofar as the obligor's income exceeds $150,000, the monthly table amount of child support is increased above that payable at the $150,000 level by a designated percentage of the obligor's income over $150,000. Pursuant to section 4(b) of the *Federal Child Support Guidelines*, if the court considers the amount payable under section 3 of the Guidelines to be inappropriate, the amount of child support will be assessed as follows:

---

5 *Cornelius v Andres*, [1998] MJ No 86 (QB).

6 *Frydrysek v Frydrysek*, [1998] BCJ No 394 (SC).

7 *Hunter v Hunter*, [2001] NWTJ No 62 (SC).

8 *Petrocco v Von Michalofski*, [1998] OJ No 200 (Gen Div); see also *Nolte v Nolte*, [2001] SJ No 362 (QB).

9 See *Francis v Baker*, [1999] 3 SCR 250; *Omah-Maharajh v Howard*, [1998] AJ No 173 (QB); *Braich v Braich*, [1997] BCJ No 1764 (SC); *Leger v Leger*, [2000] NBJ No 52 (QB); *Davids v Davids*, [1998] OJ No 2859 (Gen Div); *Bachorick v Verdego*, [1999] SJ No 450 (CA); *Ghremida v Elgahwas*, 2023 SKCA 23. See also *Klette v Leland*, 2014 SKCA 122. Compare *Cross v Batters*, 2016 SKCA 71.

1) in respect of the first $150,000 of the spouse's income, the amount set out in the applicable table for the number of children under the age of majority to whom the order relates;
2) in respect of the balance of the spouse's income, the amount that the court considers appropriate, having regard to the condition, means, needs, and other circumstances of the children who are entitled to support and the financial ability of each spouse to contribute to the support of the children; and
3) the amount, if any, determined under section 7 with respect to special or extraordinary expenses.[10]

The court may build section 7 expenses into the monthly support amount without expressly setting them out as a separate line item.[11]

The court has no discretion under either section 4(a) or 4(b) of the Guidelines to interfere with the table amount payable in respect of the first $150,000 of the obligor's annual income. The discretion conferred on the court by section 4(b) of the Guidelines applies only to the obligor's annual income in excess of $150,000.[12] A court will be disinclined to deviate from the applicable provincial table amount of child support where the obligor's annual income does not vastly exceed $150,000[13] or where the recipient spouse is unable to contribute towards the support of the children.[14]

Deviation from the applicable provincial table amount of basic child support in cases where the obligor's annual income exceeds $150,000 is only appropriate under section 4 of the *Federal Child Support Guidelines* if there is clear and compelling evidence to warrant doing so.[15] Although an obligor is not required to call evidence to rebut the presumption in favour of the table amount of child support, such a parent clearly takes the risk that a motions judge will see nothing in the evidence before him to call into question the appropriateness of the table amount.[16] The table amount must be ordered, unless it is found inappropriate. What is inappropriate must be determined on the facts of the particular case.[17] A father's obligation to support additional children born of his current marriage does not warrant deviation from the applicable table amount payable to the children of his previous marriage, where

10 *Moors v Moors*, 2013 ABQB 740; *Braich v Braich*, [1997] BCJ No 1764 (SC); *Rémillard v Rémillard*, 2014 MBCA 101 at paras 64–68; *Ghosn v Ghosn*, [2006] NSJ No 33 (SC); *Cross v Batters*, 2016 SKCA 71.

11 *Cross v Batters*, *ibid* at para 34, Richards CJS.

12 *Salvadori v Kebede*, [1998] BCJ No 1819 (SC); *Rémillard v Rémillard*, 2014 MBCA 101. As to the possible application of section 3(2)(b)of the Guidelines, see *Klette v Leland*, 2014 SKCA 122 (adult child with disability awarded significantly less than the overall table amount of child support).

13 *McIver v McIver*, [1998] AJ No 1012 (QB); *Sarro v Sarro*, 2011 BCSC 1010; *Dickinson v Dickinson*, [1998] OJ No 4815 (Gen Div); *Rémillard v Rémillard*, 2014 MBCA 101.

14 *Chrintz v Chrintz*, [1998] OJ No 3289 (Gen Div).

15 *Francis v Baker*, [1999] 3 SCR 250; *KLH v SH*, 2018 ABQB 41; *Metzner v Metzner*, [2000] BCJ No 1693 (CA); *Hollenbach v Hollenbach*, [2000] BCJ No 2316 (CA); *MacDonald v MacDonald*, [2002] BCJ No 121 (CA); *Vincent v Vincent*, 2012 BCCA 186; *MLG v KGG*, 2021 BCSC 682; *Davis v Davis*, 2013 NBQB 115 (interim proceeding); *Dickson v Dickson*, 2009 MBQB 274; *Lahanky v Lahanky*, 2011 NBQB 220; *Virc v Blair*, 2016 ONSC 49; *Cherneski v Rathwell*, 2013 SKCA 133; *Klette v Leland*, 2014 SKCA 122; *Jones v Jones*, 2017 SKCA 46.

16 *Sharpe v Sharpe*, [2004] MJ No 56 (CA) (variation order for payment of applicable table amount of support upheld by majority of 2:1).

17 *Plester v Plester*, [1998] BCJ No 2438 (SC); *Turk v Turk*, [2008] OJ No 397 (SCJ); *Lepage v Lepage*, [1999] SJ No 174 (QB).

the lifestyle in his current household is higher than that in his previous wife's household. Furthermore, the fact that the children of his former marriage did not enjoy a pre-separation lifestyle equivalent to that which will be achieved by an order for the payment of the applicable table amount of child support does not render the table amount inappropriate where the father's income has substantially increased over the years following the divorce. A finding under section 4(b)(ii) of the Guidelines that the amount determined under section 3 is "inappropriate" should not be made lightly. The objectives of the Guidelines as defined in section 1 of the *Federal Child Support Guidelines* will not be promoted if determination of child support in accordance with section 3 is too readily departed from without clear and compelling evidence to warrant doing so.[18] A spouse cannot avail himself or herself of section 4(b) of the Guidelines in the absence of material that satisfies the court that the table amount would be inappropriate. Section 4 of the Guidelines sets out a two-step process to be followed when dealing with an obligor whose annual income exceeds $150,000. First, the court must satisfy itself that the table amount of support respecting the income in excess of $150,000 may be deemed inappropriate. This is a threshold determination and a reason must be articulated why the strict table amount is inappropriate. Only if it is deemed inappropriate will the court assess support on the income exceeding $150,000, having regard to the condition, means, needs, and other circumstances of the children and the financial ability of each spouse to contribute to that support. There is nothing in section 4(a), however, that precludes a court from considering the factors listed in section 4(b)(ii) of the Guidelines in determining whether the table amount is inappropriate. There is consequently some overlap of consideration in sections 4(a) and (b) of the Guidelines.[19]

In *Francis v Baker*,[20] the Supreme Court of Canada held that the meaning of the word "inappropriate" in section 4(b) of the *Federal Child Support Guidelines* is its ordinary dictionary meaning of "unsuitable" or inadvisable. Courts, therefore, have the discretion to either increase or reduce the amount of child support prescribed by a strict application of the provincial or territorial table insofar as the obligor's annual income exceeds $150,000. Children must always receive at a minimum the table amount of child support payable on the first $150,000 of their parent's annual income. They can further expect that a fair additional amount will be ordered with respect to that portion of the parent's annual income that exceeds $150,000. The closer the paying parent's income is to $150,000, the more likely it is that the table amount will be ordered.[21] Child support undeniably involves some form of wealth transfer to the children and will often produce an indirect benefit to the primary caregiving parent, but the objectives specified for the *Federal Child Support Guidelines* do not displace the *Divorce Act*, which dictates that the maintenance of children, rather than household equalization or spousal support, is the purpose of child support.[22] This is explicitly articulated in section 26.1(2) of the *Divorce Act*. Although relevant caselaw indicates that an order for child support under section 4 of the *Federal Child Support Guidelines* has as its objective the maintenance of the child(ren) rather than household income equalization or spousal support, there is nothing wrong with

---

18 *Davis v Davis*, 2013 NBQB 115.

19 *Plester v Plester*, [1998] BCJ No 2438 (SC); *CLL v SWJ*, 2013 BCSC 917.

20 [1999] 3 SCR 250.

21 *Rémillard v Rémillard*, 2014 MBCA 101; *Jones v Jones*, 2012 SKQB 59.

22 *Cross v Batters*, 2016 SKCA 71. See also *Potzus v Potzus*, 2017 SKCA 15; *ACG v WLG*, 2020 SKQB 43.

a recipient parent reallocating her money freed up by increased child support to build up assets, such as an RRSP.[23] Courts should not be too quick to find that the table amount of child support is excessive or that it constitutes an unwarranted wealth transfer or spousal support. Need is only one of the factors for the court to consider in determining whether the table amount is inappropriate. There may come a point, however, where the table amount is so much in excess of the children's reasonable needs that it no longer qualifies as support.[24] The greater the excess of the obligor's income over the discretionary threshold of $150,000, the greater the need for a careful analysis of the actual means, needs, and circumstances of the parties and the children to arrive at a fair award.[25]

The *Federal Child Support Guidelines* are predicated on a cost estimation of child rearing, rather than on an attempt to equalize familial resources and living standards as between the parents. The party who seeks deviation from the table amount has the onus of rebutting the presumption that the table amount is appropriate.[26] This does not compel that party to testify or call evidence and no unfavourable conclusions should be drawn from a failure to do so. A party seeking deviation from the table amount may simply choose to question the evidence of the opposing party. Whatever tactics are adopted, the evidence as a whole must be sufficiently clear and compelling to warrant departure from the table amount. There must be an articulable reason for deviating from the table amount, but the relevant factors will inevitably differ from case to case. The condition, means, needs, and other circumstances of the children and the financial abilities of both spouses are designated factors to be taken into account under section 4(b) of the *Federal Child Support Guidelines.*[27] These factors are relevant both to the initial determination whether the table amount is inappropriate and to the quantification of the appropriate amount of support that should be paid in respect of the obligor's income in excess of $150,000. Only after examining all the circumstances of the case, including the above designated factors, should a court find the table amount to be inappropriate. The court must be provided with all the necessary information and this will often require child expense budgets that provide some evidence, albeit imperfect, of the child's needs. This is consistent with section 21(4) of the *Federal Child Support Guidelines,* which requires the primary caregiving parent to provide certain financial information within thirty days after learning that the obligor's annual income exceeds $150,000. There is no universal requirement, however, that primary caregiving parents prepare child expense budgets in all cases in which section 4 is invoked,[28] although the more a parent's income exceeds $150,000, the more likely it is that budgets will be required.[29] It is a matter that should be left for trial

23 *Cherneski v Rathwell*, 2013 SKCA 133; *MacLennan v MacLennan*, 2021 SKCA 132.

24 *LLL v BAL*, 2010 BCSC 301; *Davis v Davis*, 2013 NBQB 115; *MacLennan v MacLennan*, 2021 SKCA 132.

25 *SRM v NGTM*, 2014 BCSC 442, citing *SG v KG*, 2012 BCSC 1937 at para 121, Sewell J.

26 *JGT v TN*, [2001] AJ No 1426 (QB); *Steward v Ferguson*, 2012 BCSC 279; *ADJ v FJ*, 2022 BCSC 600; *Davis v Davis*, 2013 NBQB 115; *Lamb v Hoffman*, [2000] NSJ No 156 (SC); *Simon v Simon*, [1999] OJ No 4492 (CA); *Droit de la famille—3148*, [2000] RJQ 2339 (CS); *Jones v Jones*, 2012 SKQB 59 (*prima facie* case must be established on interim application); *Cherneski v Rathwell*, 2013 SKCA 133; compare *Canada v Canada-Somers*, 2008 MBCA 59; *MDA v MS*, [2008] NBJ No 498 (QB).

27 *SRM v NGTM*, 2014 BCSC 442.

28 See Thomas Bastedo & Samantha Kennedy, "Child Expense Budgets: Use and Abuse" (May 2001) 16 *Money & Family Law* 35.

29 *Sarafinchin v Sarafinchin*, [2000] OJ No 2855 (SCJ).

judges to determine on a case-by-case basis. It is appropriate to provide a budget to assist the court in assessing need by including possible future expenditures if increased child support is awarded.[30] Where a parent's annual income exceeds $1 million, a court may conclude that it is unable to assess the appropriate amount of child support according to the criteria defined by the Supreme Court of Canada in *Francis v Baker* until a child expense budget is filed.[31] Where the obligor's annual income does not greatly exceed $150,000, a trial judge may conclude that the added cost and delay of requiring a budget cannot be justified. Trial judges are not required to adjust child support orders to be in line with submitted budgets. Unfortunately, many child expense budgets have been notoriously unreliable and largely discredited as wish lists artificially tailored to the preconceived end of showing that monthly expenses substantially exceed monthly income. Preparation of a child expense budget is not an exact science and may result in overestimating or underestimating the amounts involved. This does not render it objectionable for trial judges to exercise their discretion by ordering child expense budgets to be prepared. Under the Guidelines, however, primary caregiving parents are entitled to the applicable table amount, unless it is shown to be inappropriate. It follows that primary caregiving parents are not required to justify each and every budget expense.[32]

Courts should be wary of quickly discarding the figures set out in child expense budgets, unless there is some obvious duplication or other readily apparent anomaly. The proper balance will be struck by requiring the obligor to demonstrate that budgeted child expenses are so high as to "exceed the generous ambit within which reasonable disagreement is possible." The sheer size of the overall table amount cannot give rise to a presumption that the amount is inappropriate. The burden of proof remains with the party seeking to pay a reduced amount. There is no predetermined cap or limit on child support.[33]

The unique economic situation of high-income earners must be acknowledged and the level of expenses that would support the table amount must be unarguably excessive in order for a court to deviate from the table amount. The question of appropriateness is not to be determined from the perspective of the children's lifestyle in previous years when the parents cohabited, if the table amount is not out of line with the standard of living enjoyed by children of similarly wealthy parents. The fact that the children have never enjoyed the lifestyle usually associated with the kind of wealth possessed by their father is no reason for doubting the appropriateness of the overall table amount of child support. Children should not be penalized by the prior frugality of a parent, nor by the failure of the applicant parent to provide a budget itemizing expenses that meet the table amount. It is not reasonable to hold the children to the stringent pre-separation lifestyle imposed by their father nor by their mother's budget, which is based on the amount being paid by the father, when the post-separation income and lifestyle of the father have improved dramatically. While a budget may be helpful in dealing with the issue of whether the table amount is appropriate, it is not determinative of that issue. On the threshold question of appropriateness, it is not for the applicant to justify the table amount by the presentation of a persuasive budget; rather, the onus falls on the obligor to demonstrate by clear and compelling evidence that the table amount is

30 *Cherneski v Rathwell*, 2013 SKCA 133.
31 *Njegovan v Melnuk*, [2000] MJ No 409 (QB).
32 *Sarafinchin v Sarafinchin*, [2000] OJ No 2855 (SCJ).
33 *El Gahwas v Ghremida*, 2020 SKQB 311, citing *Francis v Baker*, [1999] 3 SCR 250.

inappropriate. The British Columbia Court of Appeal has stated that a wealthy parent faces a formidable onus at the threshold stage; if this is thought to create a hardship or unfairness, the remedy lies with Parliament.[34] It does not follow that the lifestyle of the parties before separation is an irrelevant consideration in determining whether the overall table amount of child support is appropriate where the obligor earns more than $150,000 per year, nor that the receiving parent's budget should be ignored, nor that children are automatically entitled to a lifestyle commensurate with the payor's income, nor that the appropriateness of the applicable table amount should be determined by reference to the spending habits of other wealthy families, rather than the situation of the children in question. In deciding whether the obligor has rebutted the presumption in favour of the table amount by presenting clear and convincing evidence that it is not appropriate, it will be relevant to consider the parties' lifestyle before and after separation, the budget or plan the receiving parent has for the children along with the values and aspirations of the family when it was a unit. These are only some of the factors that have to be weighed and, like all relevant factors, their weight is a matter of judgment in each case. There may be a difference in outcome as between interim and permanent orders because findings that can only be made at trial may have an influence on what is appropriate. Whether a family's practice of accumulating savings is a factor that relates to capital rather than income is a matter that is more properly addressed at trial when all the financial aspects of the dispute between the parties are before the court.[35] A luxurious child-related budget does not necessarily constitute a functional wealth transfer to the child or *de facto* spousal support, although it may do so where the budget constitutes an overt attempt to bring proposed expenditures in line with the overall table amount of child support but the expenditures are totally out of line with the child's needs as reflected by the family's spending pattern prior to separation.[36] The reasonable needs of children of wealthy parents include not only expenses for basic needs but also a large element of discretionary spending.[37] In determining what are reasonable discretionary expenses for the children over and above their basic monthly expenses, the court may not only have regard to the pre-separation lifestyle of the family but also to the substantial means of both parents.[38] A child's entitlement is not conditioned, however, on whether the parents cohabited and established a standard of living together before or after the child's birth.[39] The needs of the child as reflected in the child care budget are only one of the factors to be considered in determining whether the applicable table amount of support is inappropriate under section 4(b)(ii) of the Guidelines. Another factor for consideration is the circumstance that the child is the child of a wealthy parent and ought not to be required to live at a standard of living far lower than the ability of the parent to provide. The standard of living of the parent is not mentioned as a factor under section 4(b)(ii) of the Guidelines, but it may enable the court to put into some context

---

34 *Hollenbach v Hollenbach*, [2000] BCJ No 2316 (CA); *Hathaway v Hathaway*, 2014 BCCA 310; *PKM v JDM*, 2019 BCSC 625; *R v R*, [2002] OJ No 1095 (CA); *Potzus v Potzus*, 2017 SKCA 15. Compare *Ewing v Ewing*, 2009 ABCA 227.

35 *MacDonald v MacDonald*, [2002] BCJ No 121 (CA); see also *R v R*, [2002] OJ No 1095 (CA).

36 *Tauber v Tauber*, [2001] OJ No 3259 (SCJ).

37 *R v R*, [2002] OJ No 1095 (CA); *Merrifield v Merrifield*, 2021 SKCA 85 at para 39.

38 *MacDonald v MacDonald*, [2002] BCJ No 2320 (SC).

39 *Pakka v Nygard*, [2002] OJ No 3858 (SCJ).

the parent's complaint that the standard of living provided by the table amount (or the budget amount, if it is higher) is inappropriate. An order for the payment of the applicable table amount of child support, in the monthly sum of $15,091.54, does not exceed the legitimate boundaries of reasonableness where it represents less than 12 percent of the parent's expenses or 8 percent of his income.[40]

An unusual dramatic increase in annual income does not, of itself, render the table amount of child support unfair or inappropriate.[41]

In *Metzner v Metzner*,[42] Finch JA of the British Columbia Court of Appeal formulated the following nine principles as flowing from the judgment of the Supreme Court of Canada in *Francis v Baker*:

(1) Parliament created a presumption in favour of the overall table amount in all cases.

(2) The table amount applicable to the obligor's income insofar as it exceeds $150,000 may be increased or decreased by the court, but the party seeking such deviation must rebut the presumption in favour of the table amount.

(3) Clear and compelling evidence is required for a court to deviate from the table amount.

(4) Parliament has expressly listed in section 4(b)(ii) of the *Federal Child Support Guidelines* the factors relevant to determining the appropriateness or inappropriateness of applying the overall table amount or any deviation from the table amount ordinarily applicable to the obligor's annual income in excess of $150,000.

(5) Courts should determine whether the table amount is inappropriate only after examining all circumstances, including the factors expressly set out in section 4(b)(ii) of the Guidelines.

(6) Section 4(b)(ii) of the Guidelines emphasizes the "centrality" of the actual situation of the children;[43] the actual circumstances of the children are at least as important as any single element of the legislative purpose underlying that section. A proper construction of section 4 of the Guidelines requires that the objectives of predictability, consistency and efficiency on the one hand, which are defined in section 1 of the Guidelines, be balanced with those of fairness, flexibility and recognition of the actual "condition, means, needs and other circumstances of the children" on the other.

(7) While child support payments unquestionably result in some kind of wealth transfer to the children which results in an indirect benefit to the non-paying parent, the objectives of child support payments must be borne in mind. The *Federal Child Support Guidelines* have not displaced the *Divorce Act* which has as its objective the maintenance of children, rather than household income equalization or spousal support.

(8) The court must have all necessary information before it in order to determine whether the table amount applicable to the obligor's annual income in excess of $150,000 is

---

40 *Ibid.*

41 *Fung v Lin*, [2001] OJ No 456 (SCJ).

42 [2000] BCJ No 1693 (CA); see also *Hathaway v Hathaway*, 2014 BCCA 310; *Reid v Reid*, 2017 BCCA 73; *Briggs v Kasdorf*, 2020 BCSC 1702; *MLG v KGG*, 2021 BCSC 682; *Rémillard v Rémillard*, 2014 MBCA 101; *MDA v MS*, [2008] NBJ No 498 (QB); *Mercer v Rosenau*, 2013 NLCA 64; *REG v TJG*, 2011 SKQB 269, especially para 204; *Potzus v Potzus*, 2017 SKCA 15; *BJL v DBL*, 2018 SKQB 213, citing *IE v SG*, 2017 SKQB 257.

43 *RWG v SIG*, [2002] SJ No 231 (QB) (table amount of support deemed inappropriate for adult child addict).

inappropriate. If the evidence provided is a child expense budget, "the unique economic situation of high income earners" must be considered.

(9) A parent who seeks to impugn the reasonableness of a child's expenses must demonstrate that the budgeted expense is so high "as to exceed the generous ambit within which reasonable disagreement is possible."[44]

In *Sirdevan v Sirdevan*,[45] Graham J of the Ontario Superior Court of Justice endorsed the following principles:

(1) High income earners are in a unique economic situation in that expenses which may in other situations be considered unreasonable, may, in a high income situation be reasonable. Therefore, in order to challenge budgets, payors in high income situations must demonstrate that budgeted expenses are so high as to exceed the generous ambit within which reasonable disagreement is possible.

(2) In situations where the table amount is so excessive in comparison to the reasonable needs of the children that support under the table is no longer just child support but a *de facto* wealth transfer or spousal support, the table amount should be reduced. This is in keeping with s. 26.1(2) of the *Divorce Act* which dictates that maintenance of children, rather than household equalization or spousal support, is the object of support payments.

(3) Child support payments will often produce an indirect benefit to the [primary caregiving] parent and the court should not be too quick to find that Guideline figures enter the realm of wealth transfer or spousal support.

(4) An award of discretionary expenses is not unreasonable and may be high in high income situations.

(5) In high income cases, reasonableness of discretionary expenses replaces the concept of need.

(6) While budgets are not exact, [primary caregiving] parents need not justify every expense and courts should be wary about discarding the figures in such budgets too quickly. Courts should bear in mind that where one figure is over-estimated, another figure may be under-estimated.

(7) Ordinarily when the parties have established a family lifestyle and pattern of expenditure, these will be relevant considerations to determining what amount of child support is appropriate having regard to the children's condition and needs. The weight of such evidence will vary depending upon all the relevant circumstances but where a payor parent's income has risen substantially after separation, the children are entitled to benefit from that increase.

(8) Comparison with the budgets of other wealthy families is not required.

And in *Ewing v Ewing*,[46] the Alberta Court of Appeal extracted the following principles from the judgment of the Supreme Court of Canada in *Francis v Baker*:

44 *Ibid*.

45 [2009] OJ No 3796 (SCJ).

46 2009 ABCA 227; see also *Moors v Moors*, 2013 ABQB 740; *AJL v JTB*, 2020 ABQB 649; *Rémillard v Rémillard*, 2014 MBCA 101; *Gould v Gould*, 2013 SKCA 34; *Klette v Leland*, 2014 SKCA 122; *Potzus v Potzus*, 2017 SKCA 15.

i. There is a presumption that the Table applies to all incomes, including incomes over $150,000. A party seeking to deviate from the Table has the onus of rebutting the presumption. (paras. 41, 43)

ii. Children can expect the Table amount on the first $150,000 and a fair additional amount for that portion that exceeds $150,000. The closer the amount is to $150,000, the more likely it is that the Table amount will be awarded. (para. 41)

iii. Where the presumption is rebutted, the *Guideline* figures can be increased or reduced under section 4. (para. 42)

iv. The test for deviation from the Table amount is that the evidence in its entirety must be sufficient to raise a concern that the Table amount is inappropriate.[47] The evidence for departure from the *Guidelines* must be clear and compelling. A party seeking deviation is not required to testify or adduce evidence and no unfavourable conclusion should be drawn from a failure to do so. It is recognized that a party may not possess the required relevant evidence. (para. 43)

v. The actual situation of the children is central, and the condition, means, needs and other circumstances of the children must be considered in the assessment of the initial determination of inappropriateness and the determination of appropriate support. (para. 44) No single element of legislative purpose is to be given more weight than the actual circumstances of the children (para. 39). A proper construction of section 4 requires that the objectives of predictability, consistency and efficiency on the one hand, be balanced with those of fairness, flexibility and recognition of the actual "condition, means, needs and other circumstances of the children" on the other. (para. 40)

vi. To determine appropriateness the court must be armed with sufficient information, and trial judges have discretion to determine on a case-by-case basis whether a child expense budget is required to provide that information and they have the power to order it. (para. 45) [Primary caregiving] parents are not required to produce child expense budgets in all cases under section 4.

vii. Although frequently child support results in a benefit to the wife, the legislative objective is maintenance for the children rather than household income equalization or spousal support. (para. 41)

viii. While standard of living can be considered in assessing need, at some point support payments will meet even a wealthy child's reasonable needs. When the Table amount is so in excess of the child's reasonable needs it must be considered a functional wealth transfer to a parent, or *de facto* spousal support. (para. 41)

ix. The test for whether expenses are reasonable will be met by the paying parent if the budgeted expenses are so high as to "excee[d] the generous ambit within which reasonable disagreement is possible": *Bellenden v. Satterthwaite*, [1948] 1 All E.R. 343 at 345. (para. 49)

Applying these principles in *Ewing v Ewing*, the Alberta Court of Appeal held that the chambers judge had committed four errors. First, he imposed too strict a burden on the father to rebut the presumption in favour of the overall table amount. While "clear and

47 *Merritt v Merritt*, 2010 ONSC 4959; *Olszewski v Willick*, 2010 SKQB 289.

compelling evidence" is required, the chambers judge erred in describing the onus of "formidable."[48] All that is required according to *Francis v Baker* is that the entirety of the evidence is sufficient to "raise a concern" about whether the overall table amount is inappropriate. Once that threshold is met, the payee's failure to adduce evidence on the matter, as a matter of common sense, rather than an evidentiary burden, might well result in an unfavourable finding. Second, the chambers judge erred by failing to examine "the condition, means, needs and other circumstances of the children." Consideration of these factors is not to be displaced by an assumption that children are automatically entitled to share in the entirety of their parent's wealth. Third, the chambers judge did not engage in any analysis of the father's evidence, which raised a concern that the overall table amount of child support was inappropriate. Fourth, the chambers judge mistakenly concluded that the mother had not been receiving child support in the amount of $13,776, as ordered in 2007. Consequently, to the extent that he considered the circumstances and lifestyles of the children, he did so in an erroneous factual context by ignoring the mother's receipt of $13,776 per month for approximately twenty-three months. Regarding the issue of whether the father's evidence was sufficiently compelling to raise a concern about the propriety of ordering the table amount, the Alberta Court of Appeal observed that the monthly amount of child support had substantially increased over the years since the parents separated. Furthermore, despite the increase in the amount of child support from $6,000 to $13,776 per month in 2007, a review of the available evidence revealed no change in the condition, means, needs, and other circumstances of the children, other than the purchase of a vehicle for one of the children. In the opinion of the Alberta Court of Appeal, the evidence suggested that the level of support received since 2007 met, and indeed, may well have exceeded the reasonable needs of the children. Consequently, the Alberta Court of Appeal concluded that the father had satisfied the burden of proving that the table amount of child support would be inappropriate. With respect to what amount of child support would be appropriate, the Alberta Court of Appeal observed that this issue would ordinarily be remitted to the Court of Queen's Bench for an assessment based on such further budgetary information as a judge directs. In this appeal, however, since the holding of the Alberta Court of Appeal was based, in part, on the fact that the monthly payment of $13,776 had not resulted in any increased benefit to the children, it would be difficult to order anything beyond that amount, notwithstanding any increase in the father's income. In the result, the husband's cross-appeal was allowed and child support was left at $13,776, the amount ordered in 2007. Thus, the mother's application to vary child support retroactively for the years 2005 and 2006 was denied.

The judgment in *Ewing* introduces welcome checks and balances in the context of orders for child support granted pursuant to section 4 of the *Federal Child Support Guidelines*. If followed in other Canadian jurisdictions, it is likely to result in a more conservative approach towards "discretionary expenses" under section 4 of the *Federal Child Support Guidelines*.

In *REG v TWJG*,[49] Ryan-Froslie J (as she then was) of the Saskatchewan Court of Queen's Bench distilled the following principles from *Francis v Baker*:

48 Compare *Hollenbach v Hollenbach*, [2000] BCJ No 2316 (CA); *Hathaway v Hathaway*, 2014 BCCA 310; *R v R*, [2002] OJ No 1095 (CA).

49 2011 SKQB 269; see also *Cherneski v Rathwell*, 2014 SKQB 399; *Merrifield v Merrifield*, 2021 SKCA 85.

(i) In enacting s. 3 of the *Guidelines*, Parliament intended that there would be a presumption in favour of the Table amount of child support. (See: *Francis v. Baker, supra*, at para. 42);

(ii) Table support will apply on the first $150,000 of income. (See: *Francis v. Baker, supra*, at para. 41);

(iii) The Table amount of child support over and above $150,000 can be increased or decreased under s. 4 of the *Guidelines* if the party seeking such a deviation rebuts the presumption that the Table amount is "appropriate." (See: *Francis v Baker, supra*, at para. 42);

(iv) "Inappropriate" in the context of s. 4 of the *Guidelines* means "unsuitable." (See: *Francis v. Baker, supra*, at para. 40);

(v) There must be clear and convincing evidence for departing from the Table amount. (See: *Francis v. Baker, supra*, at para. 43);

(vi) The relevant factors with respect to determining the appropriate Table support are specified in s. 4(b)(ii), i.e. the condition, needs, means and other circumstances of the children and the financial abilities of both spouses to contribute to the support of the children. (See: *Francis v. Baker, supra*, at para. 44);

(vii) While child support payments may result in a transfer of "wealth" to the children which indirectly benefits a non-paying parent, the objectives of child support must be kept in mind. The *Guidelines* have not displaced the *Divorce Act* which has as its objective the maintenance of children rather than the equalization of household incomes or spousal support. (See: *Francis v. Baker, supra*, at para. 41);

(viii) A proper construction of s. 4 of the *Guidelines* requires that the objectives of predictability, consistency and efficiency on the one hand be balanced with those of fairness, flexibility and recognition of the actual condition, needs, means and other circumstance of the children on the other hand. (See: *Francis v. Baker, supra*, at para. 40); and

(ix) The closer the paying parent's income is to the $150,000 threshold, the more likely it is that the Table amount of child support will be awarded. (See: *Francis v. Baker, supra*, at para. 41).

C. HIGH-INCOME SPOUSE OR FORMER SPOUSE WITH SHORT CAREER

Professional entertainers and athletes have attracted special problems where their income peaks at a very high level but is expected to decrease dramatically with the passage of time. Several American courts have produced a creative solution to this problem by establishing a trust to deal with future child support payments when the income declines.[50] Although the flexibility exhibited by the American courts might be impossible to achieve in Canada under section 4(a) of the *Federal Child Support Guidelines*,[51] a similar constraint may not

50 See, for example, *In re JT (KD)*, 16 Fam L Rep (BNA) 1046 (NY Fam Ct 1989); *In re Paternity of Tukker MO*, 544 NW2d 417 (1996). See also *In re Marriage of Stamberg*, 218 Ill App 3d 333, 578 NE2d 261 (1991) (foreseeable loss of income due to pending criminal prosecution). And see, generally, Laura W Morgan, *Child Support Guidelines: Interpretation and Application*, loose-leaf (New York: Aspen Law & Business, 1996–) §4.07(b)[4], "The High-Income Parent with the Short Career."

51 See *Bachorick v Verdejo*, [1999] SJ No 450 (CA); compare *Simon v Simon*, [1999] OJ No 4492 (CA).

apply to the combined application of section 4(b) of the *Federal Child Support Guidelines* and section 15.1(4) of the *Divorce Act,* which empowers a court to make child support orders for a definite or indefinite period or until a specified event occurs and to impose such terms, conditions, and restrictions on the order as the court thinks fit and just.[52]

52 *OM v AK,* [2000] QJ No 3224 (CS).

CHAPTER 10

Effect of Order or Agreement or Other Arrangement That Benefits Child; Consent Orders

A. ADVANTAGES AND LIMITATIONS OF PARENTAL SETTLEMENTS

Negotiated settlements are much better than court imposed orders for dealing with the eco nomic consequences of divorce. The parties themselves know best how to optimize and apply their limited resources. The flexibility available to them in negotiations far exceeds the lati tude of the court in interpreting and applying the legal principles and rules to the facts of the particular case, especially with the advent of the *Federal Child Support Guidelines*. Neither the parties nor the court can foresee all contingencies but, unlike the parties, the court will not be involved in the ongoing administration of the result. A court cannot possibly address all potential scenarios that may befall the family members and where future events do occur that cause a material change of circumstances, the court is an awkward forum for the reso lution of those matters.[1] The law recognizes that giving deference to previously agreed-to provisions of child support encourages spouses to resolve their own affairs.[2] As Dorgan J of the British Columbia Supreme Court stated in *Haber v Nicolle*,[3] "the equilibrium achieved by a fairly negotiated agreement is subject to upset when only one piece of a complex puzzle is substantially altered." However, subject to the statutory qualifications hereafter considered, child support is the right of the child and the jurisdiction of the court to order interim or permanent child support pursuant to the *Divorce Act* cannot be ousted by the terms of a spousal or parental agreement or by minutes of settlement.[4] Contractual covenants do not suffice to negate child support obligations that would otherwise ensue from the parent/child

1 *Kaderly v Kaderly*, [1997] PEIJ No 74 (TD).

2 *Goulding v Keck*, 2014 ABCA 138; *HB v JB*, 2019 ABQB 321; *Bradshaw v Bradshaw*, 2011 BCSC 1103; see also *DBS v SRG; LJW v TAR; Henry v Henry; Hiemstra v Hiemstra*, [2006] 2 SCR 231 at para 78; *Chutter v Chutter*, 2016 BCSC 2407; *MGH v KLDH*, 2020 NBCA 46.

3 2011 BCSC 210 at para 45.

4 *Richardson v Richardson*, [1987] 1 SCR 857; *Willick v Willick*, [1994] 3 SCR 670; *Wildeman v Wildeman*, 2014 ABQB 732; *Reid v Reid*, 2017 BCCA 73; *Aquilini v Aquilini*, 2019 BCSC 1146; *Sidhu v Chima*, 2020 BCSC 768; *ADJ v FJ*, 2022 BCSC 600; *Renshi v Renshi*, 2022 BCSC 1942; *Horbas v Horbas*, 2020 MBCA 34 at para 37; *MGH v KLDH*, 2020 NBCA 46; *Picco v Picco*, [2000] NJ No 64 (UFC); *Kroupa v Stoneham*

relationship.[5] An agreement that a parent will not seek to vary a child support order even in the event of a material change will not be given effect by a court.[6] Where a separation agreement purports to fix the amount of child support payable, a material change, since the execution of the agreement is not required before a judicial review of child support, can be undertaken in accordance with the *Federal Child Support Guidelines*.[7] An agreement purporting to cap periodic child support payments constitutes no bar to an order for the payment of the applicable table amount under the *Federal Child Support Guidelines*, where there are no special provisions in the agreement that directly or indirectly benefit the children so as to render the table amount inequitable.[8] Agreed payments into an investment trust fund for a child's future education do not constitute "special provisions" under section 17(6.2) of the *Divorce Act* that entitle the payor to divert his child support payments in excess of a specified monthly amount into the trust fund. Child support is intended to meet the current needs of the child, and a parent's diversion of payments into an investment fund for the child's future education does not reduce the obligation to pay the appropriate amount of current support.[9] Parents cannot bargain away their children's right to support. A proposed consent order that waives child support entitlement is not justified by psychological benefits ensuing from the avoidance of litigation. A chambers judge should not rubber stamp a proposed consent order without addressing relevant factors pertaining to child support. A consent order that provides that the primary caregiving parent's application shall be dismissed "as though there had been a trial on the merits" is not a "child support order" within the meaning of the *Divorce Act* and the *Federal Child Support Guidelines*, and any subsequent application for support should be brought under section 15.1 of the *Divorce Act*, not by way of a variation proceeding under section 17 of the *Divorce Act*. Consequently, there is no need to prove that a material change of circumstances has occurred since the consent order was granted.[10]

Child support and the exercise of parenting time are not interdependent and parents cannot barter away these rights without regard to the child's best interests and cannot consensually oust the jurisdiction of the courts to determine the appropriate level of child support at any time.[11]

2011 ONSC 5824; *Franke v Franke*, 2012 SKQB 204; *Daniel v Daniel*, 2022 SKKB 279; compare *Quercia v Francioni*, 2011 ONSC 6844. See also *GG v JTG*, 2013 ABQB 726; *MKR v JAR*, 2015 NBCA 73.

5 See *Chartier v Chartier*, [1999] SCJ No 79; *Richardson v Richardson*, [1987] 1 SCR 857; *Doe v Alberta*, 2007 ABCA 50; *Johannson v Haaranen*, 2018 ABQB 554; *Kopp v Kopp*, 2012 BCCA 140; *Goundrey-Beskau v Beskau*, 2015 BCSC 168; *Powell v Powell*, 2019 BCSC 303; *MEL v PRH*, 2018 NBQB 224; *CMM v DGC*, 2015 ONSC 1815 (application by child under *Family Law Act*, RSO 1990, c F3); *Skotnicki v Cayen*, 2019 ONSC 4831; *Kozak v Moore*, 2020 SKQB 22.

6 *LW v FW*, 2022 BCSC 642 at para 27, Veenstra J.

7 *Kopp v Kopp*, 2012 BCCA 140; *MEL v PRH*, 2018 NBQB 224 (consent order). *See also Sidhu v Chima*, 2020 BCSC 768 (application under BC *Family Law Act*).

8 *Jeannotte v Jeannotte*, [2004] SJ No 445 (QB); see also *Goundrey-Beskau v Beskau*, 2015 BCSC 168. Compare *DSS v NMG*, 2012 PESC 12.

9 *Cherneski v Rathwell*, 2013 SKCA 133.

10 *Lambright v Brown*, [2003] BCJ No 2612 (CA).

11 *DAW v WMZ*, [2000] SCJ No 2391 (SCJ), citing *Richardson v Richardson*, [1987] 1 SCR 857, wherein it was pointed out that child support, like the exercise of parenting time, is the right of the child.

An interim child support order in accordance with the *Federal Child Support Guidelines* is not precluded by a spousal agreement negotiated without legal advice. Incidental matters relating to life insurance and income tax refunds may also be addressed.[12]

A retroactive increase in child and spousal support payable under a separation agreement may be justified by the obligor's failure to disclose a severance package from a former employer.[13]

The Court of Queen's Bench of Alberta has held that it should not lightly disturb a mediated comprehensive settlement achieved through the alternative judicial resolution facilities except insofar as there is evidence of a material change of circumstances after the settlement was reached. If parties can simply float a trial balloon in the mediation process, its value will be significantly diminished and the more cumbersome and expensive litigation process will resurface to the detriment of constructive attempts to resolve family disputes away from the adversarial atmosphere of the courtroom.[14] However, a parental waiver of support is not binding on the child or the courts where inadequate provision has been made for the child. The test of inadequacy must be measured against the federal or provincial child support guidelines and the provisions of sections 15.1(5) to (8) and 17(6.2) to (6.5) of the *Divorce Act* Parents cannot trade off child support against the exercise of parenting time.[16]

An application to vary child support is not precluded by the terms of a separation agreement that provides that no such application shall be brought for a specified number of years.

Spouses or former spouses may agree that the amount of child support shall exceed that available under the *Federal Child Support Guidelines*,[18] but the amount and duration of agreed child support payments remain governed by the *Divorce Act* and the *Federal Child Support Guidelines*, not by the agreement.[19] Courts are reluctant to interfere with agreements entered into freely by competent adults that benefit the children to a greater extent than the amount payable under the Guidelines.[20] Receiving less money as a result of the application of the provincial child support guidelines does not necessarily mean that the result would be inequitable, but a court should not lightly disregard a comprehensive settlement that intermingles spousal and child support in providing higher child support than would ordinarily be ordered.[21] Parents are required to contribute to their child's support pursuant to the *Divorce Act* and the *Federal Child Support Guidelines*, but nothing prevents them from being indulgent and contributing more than would otherwise be available under

12 *Ferguson v Ferguson*, [1999] AJ No 1107 (QB).

13 *Simons v Simons*, [1999] SCJ No 1437 (SCJ) (order for child support and spousal support granted pursuant to s 56(4)(a) of the Ontario *Family Law Act*).

14 *Varga v Varga*, [1998] AJ No 646 (QB).

15 *Bosse v Bosse* (1996), 19 RFL (4th) 54 (NBQB); *W(CSJ) v W(BH)* (1996), 24 RFL (4th) 432 (NSCA); *G(G) v H(J)* (1996), 22 RFL (4th) 69 (NWTSC); *Seeley v McKay*, [1998] SCJ No 2857 (Gen Div).

16 *Black v Black* (1995), 19 RFL (4th) 442 (BCCA); *DAW v WMZ*, [2000] SCJ No 2391 (SCJ).

17 *King v King*, [1998] NJ No 283 (SC).

18 *Wilson v Daffern*, [1998] BCJ No 2899 (SC); *Dicks v Dicks*, [2000] OJ No 3964 (SCJ).

19 *Wilson v Daffern*, [1998] BCJ No 2899 (SC). See also *Sutherland v Sutherland*, 2023 ABCA 121.

20 *Barker v Barker*, [1999] BCJ No 2020 (SC); *Balcom v Balcom*, [1999] NSJ No 458 (QB); *Adams v Mustard* [2002] SCJ No 3363 (SCJ); *Jay v Jay*, [2003] PEIJ No 1 (TC); *BLGR v LMR*, [1998] SJ No 583 (QB); compare *Garrett-Rempel v Garrett-Rempel*, [2000] BCJ No 1771 (SC); *Brown v Brown*, [2003] SCJ No 4988 (SCJ). See also *Pederson v Pederson*, [2001] BCJ No 2252 (SC).

21 *Babcock v Babcock*, [1999] SCJ No 391 (Prov Div) (application under *Ontario Child Support Guidelines*

the Guidelines.[22] Where the contract provides for payment to be made to the mother, the court should not order payment to be made directly to the child, simply because the father prefers such an arrangement.[23] A court has no jurisdiction to order support to be payable when a child ceases to be a "child of the marriage" as defined in section 2(1) of the *Divorce Act*, regardless of the terms of an inter-spousal contract.[24]

A court is entitled to vary a spousal agreement entered into for the purpose of conforming to the *Federal Child Support Guidelines* where the parties made errors in calculating the obligor's income.[25]

Where both spouses agree in writing on the annual income of a spouse, the court may treat that amount as the spouse's income for the purpose of applying the *Federal Child Support Guidelines*, if the court considers that the amount is reasonable having regard to the income information provided under section 21 of the Guidelines.[26]

B. RELEVANT STATUTORY PROVISIONS

Far-reaching provisions concerning the effect of a spousal agreement are found in sections 15.1(5), 15.1(7), and 15.1(8) of the *Divorce Act*, SC 1997, c 1, which provide as follows:

> **Court may take agreement into account**
>
> 15.1 (5) Notwithstanding subsection (3), a court may award an amount that is different from the amount that would be determined in accordance with the applicable guidelines if the court is satisfied
>
> (a) that special provisions in an order, a judgment or a written agreement respecting the financial obligations of the spouses,[27] or the division or transfer of their property, directly or indirectly benefit a child, or that special provisions have otherwise been made for the benefit of a child; and
>
> (b) that the application of the applicable guidelines would result in an amount of child support that is inequitable given those special provisions.
>
> **Consent orders**
>
> (7) Notwithstanding subsection (3), a court may award an amount that is different from the amount that would be determined in accordance with the applicable guidelines on the consent of both spouses if it is satisfied that reasonable arrangements have been made for the support of the child to whom the order relates.
>
> **Reasonable arrangements**
>
> (8) For the purpose of subsection (7), in determining whether reasonable arrangements have been made for the support of a child, the court shall have regard to the applicable guidelines. However, the court shall not consider the arrangements to be unreasonable solely because the amount of support agreed to is not the same as the amount that would otherwise

22 *Kuling v Kuling*, [2004] SJ No 520 (QB); *Cook v Cook*, [2007] SJ No 332 (QB).

23 *Kuling v Kuling*, [2004] SJ No 520 (QB).

24 *Ibid*. Compare to *LL v GRB*, 2009 ABCA 356.

25 *Roshau v Roshau*, [1997] BCJ No 2589 (SC).

26 *Federal Child Support Guidelines*, SOR/97-175, s 15(2).

27 *McGrath v McGrath*, [2001] BCJ No 1555 (SC); *Miller v White*, 2018 PECA 11.

have been determined in accordance with the applicable guidelines. Corresponding provisions to those in sections 15.1(5), (7) and (8) of the *Divorce Act* apply to variation orders for child support under sections 17(6.2), (6.4) and (6.5) of the *Divorce Act*.[28]

In *Gobeil v Gobeil*,[29] the Manitoba Court of Appeal held that the trial judge had erred in upholding the child support provisions of the separation agreement on the basis of a *Miglin*[30] analysis instead of determining the applicable amount of child support under the *Federal Child Support Guidelines*, as required by section 15.1(3) of the *Divorce Act*. Only two exceptions are admitted to this requirement. Pursuant to section 15.1(5) of the *Divorce Act*, the court may deviate from the Guidelines amount of child support where a separation agreement includes "special provisions" that provide direct or indirect benefits for the child that render the Guidelines amount of child support inequitable. The second exception arises pursuant to section 15.1(7) of the *Divorce Act* whereby a court may grant a consent order that deviates from the Guidelines amount of child support if the court is satisfied that reason able arrangements have been made for the support of the child to whom the order relates. Neither of these exceptions was argued, nor were they applicable in *Gobeil*, according to the Manitoba Court of Appeal. Consequently, the trial judge was found to have erred in failing to determine the husband's income pursuant to the Guidelines to establish the amount of child support payable and this matter was remitted to the Court of Queen's Bench (Family Division) for determination.

Sections 15.1(5) and 17(6.2) of the *Divorce Act* create a tripartite test. The court must find (1) special provisions, (2) that benefit the child in a specified way either directly or indirectly, and (3) that would render the normal amount payable under the *Federal Child Support Guidelines* inequitable by reason of the special provisions.[32] While an application for spousal support may trigger a finding of "double dipping" as between the spouses in light of a prior division of matrimonial property,[33] the concept of "double dipping" is inapplicable in a child support proceeding wherein the division of matrimonial property is not linked to child support in any way.[34]

C. MEANING OF "SPECIAL PROVISIONS" AND "INEQUITABLE" UNDER SECTIONS 15.1(5) AND 17(6.2) OF *DIVORCE ACT*

It is not clear whether the term "special provisions" in sections 15(1)(5)(a) and 17(6.2)(a) of the *Divorce Act* means "particular" or "out of the ordinary or unusual."[35] It has been asserted that a "special provision" within the meaning of section 15.1(5) of the *Divorce Act* must be

28 As to the effect of the child support obligor's death on the enforcement of a consent order to pay lump sum child support in instalments, see *McLeod v McLeod*, 2013 BCCA 552.

29 [2008] MJ No 19 (CA); *Bradshaw v Bradshaw*, 2011 BCSC 1103; *Reid v Reid*, 2017 BCCA 73.

30 See *Miglin v Miglin*, [2003] 1 SCR 303.

31 See *Nicholl v Nicholl*, 2020 BCCA 173; see also *MLG v KGG*, 2021 BCSC 682.

32 *Shields v Shields*, [2006] AJ No 569 (QB); *Anderson-Devine v Anderson*, 2002 MBCA 166 at para 16; *Riddell v Riddell*, 2013 MBQB 4.

33 See *Boston v Boston*, [2001] 2 SCR 413.

34 *Alpugan v Baykan*, 2014 ABCA 152; *HB v AB*, 2010 ABCA 279.

35 *Wang v Wang*, [1997] BCJ No 1678 (SC), aff'd [1998] BCJ No 1966 (CA); compare *Wright v Zaver*, [2002] SCJ No 1098 (CA). See also *Brost v Brost*, [2004] YJ No 104 (SC).

one that, in whole or in part, replaces the need for ongoing support of the children.[36] In *Bromm v Bromm*,[37] Ryan-Froslie J (as she then was) of the Saskatchewan Court of Queen's Bench stated:

> 74 The law with respect to s. 15.1(5) is far from settled. Courts of Appeal across this country faced with interpreting this subsection have adopted different approaches as to what constitutes a "special provision."
>
> 75 In *Danchuk v. Danchuk*, 2001 BCCA 291, 15 R.F.L. (5th) 328, the British Columbia Court of Appeal, at para 27, held that a "special provision" must at a minimum "... either encompass some pre-payment of child support or reflect a financial or property obligation beyond that which the law would normally impose."
>
> 76 In *Wright v. Zaver* (2002), 24 R.F.L. (5th) 207 (Ont. C.A.), the Ontario Court of Appeal split with respect to what constitutes a "special provision" under the Ontario provincial legislation. The majority of the Court held that a "special provision" must be out of the ordinary or "unusual," a position also adopted by the Nova Scotia Court of Appeal in *MacKay v. Bucher*, 2001 NSCA 120, (2001), 196 N.S.R. (2d) 293. A minority of the Ontario Court of Appeal in *Wright v. Zaver*, at para 90, found that to qualify as a special provision, there was no requirement that the provision be out of the ordinary or unusual so long as the provision replaced "... in whole or in part, the need for support..."
>
> 77 The leading case in this province is the Saskatchewan Court of Appeal decision in *Peterson v. Horan, supra*. While that case involved provincial legislation, the provision in issue is identical to s. 15.1(5) of the *Divorce Act*. Accordingly the principles set out in *Peterson v. Horan* are applicable to this case.
>
> 78 *Peterson v. Horan, supra* dealt with the issue of whether a payment made by the Canada Pension Plan to the child of a disabled contributor constitute "special provisions otherwise made" for the benefit of the child. While the Court of Appeal was split in its determination of that issue, Cameron J.A. did provide guidance as to the meaning of the term "special provisions." At paras 35 and 36 he stated:
>
>> [35] Now, the term "special provisions" is employed in the context of creating an exception to the general requirement that the amount accord with that called for by the *Guidelines*. This suggests that what the Legislature had in mind were provisions that are out of the ordinary in the sense they do not ordinarily feature in the determination of the amount of money prescribed by the *Guidelines*. Take, for example, a father who agrees on separation that mother and child should continue to reside in the family residence and that he will continue to pay the rent or make the mortgage payments. These provisions are of benefit to the child but are ordinarily of no account under the *Guidelines*, for ordinarily they do not fall within any of the exceptions furnished by the *Guidelines*.
>>
>> [36] This is but a simple example of what the Legislature seems to have had in mind in enacting the statutory exception contained in subsection 3(4), but it serves

36 *Manuele v O'Connell*, 2012 NSSC 271; *Wright v Zaver*, [2002] SCJ No 1098 (CA). And see *Miller v White*, 2018 PECA 11 (interim order for third-party payments in lieu of interim child support payments).

37 2010 SKQB 85; see also *Hanson v Hanson*, 2019 SKCA 102; *Matechuk v Kopp (Yaworenko)*, 2020 SKQB 196; *Granquist v Lemond*, 2022 SKCA 90; *Daniel v Daniel*, 2022 SKKB 279.

to identify the import of the subsection and the attributes of "special provisions" that "benefit a child" or that "have . . . been made for the benefit of a child." As the example suggests, such provisions will usually possess the following attributes:

- they are unusual or out of the ordinary in the sense they do not feature in determining the amount of maintenance in accordance with the *Guidelines*;
- they serve to contribute to the maintenance of the child; and
- they serve in effect to partially discharge the parent's obligation to provide for the maintenance of the child and tend, therefore, to reduce the need, at least in part, for the amount of maintenance called for by the *Guidelines*.

Consequently, medical and dental insurance and life insurance benefits that are conferred on children do not satisfy the requirements of section 15.1(5) of the *Divorce Act*.[38] There is discretion under section 15.1(5) of the *Divorce Act* to take payments under the BC Adoption Assistance Program into account when determining a parent's section 3 obligations.[39]

Courts will be called upon to examine a wide variety of agreements to determine whether they contain "special provisions" within the meaning of sections 15.1(5) and 17(6.2) of the *Divorce Act*. Some agreements will have been prepared by legal counsel; others will not. Some will have been entered before, and others after, the Guidelines were implemented. Some will expressly purport to set out "special provisions"; others will not. Some agreements will provide more, others will provide less, than the amounts payable under the Guidelines. The particular circumstances facing each family and their children will obviously differ from case to case. Consequently, the determination of whether an agreement contains "special provisions" will depend on the unique circumstances of the individual case.[40] An agreement made with knowledge of the Guidelines that provides for child support in an amount greater than that payable under the Guidelines may, in itself, be a "special provision."[41] In *MacKay v Boucher*,[42] the Nova Scotia Court of Appeal observed that there is no inconsistency in a court refusing to vary an agreement providing for support exceeding the Guidelines amount, yet increasing a lower award to the Guidelines level, because a higher support award is always in the child's best interests, unless it reaches a level where it is no longer child support but becomes a transfer of wealth. The term "inequitable" in sections 15(1)(5)(b) and 17(6.2)(b) of the *Divorce Act* is capable of several meanings depending on the subject of comparison. It could refer to inequity as between the parties, or as between a child and parent, or as between these parties and others in the community to whom the Guidelines apply. The last construction is raised by section 1(d) of the Guidelines, which defines one of their objectives as being "to ensure consistent treatment of spouses and children who are in similar circumstances." Notwithstanding this declared objective, the term "inequitable" relates to the parties and requires consideration of both the circumstances giving rise to the written agreement or order and their circumstances at the time of the application. This interpretation recognizes the give and take of settlement negotiations and the interrelationship of the

38 *Hall v Hall*, [1997] BCJ No 1191 (SC); *Bellingham v Bellingham*, [2003] MJ No 348 (QB); *Burns v Burns* [1998] SCJ No 2602 (Gen Div).

39 *CSH v EMH*, 2013 ABQB 660, but compare *KLS v JES*, 2010 ABQB 410.

40 *Finney v Finney*, [1998] BCJ No 1848 (SC).

41 *Finney v Finney, ibid*; *Schryver v Schryver*, 2013 ONSC 3082; compare *Biggar v Biggar*, [1998] SJ No 570 (QB).

42 2001 NSCA 120 at para 50.

terms reflected in an agreement or order.[43] In the absence of evidence of undue hardship within the meaning of section 10 of the *Federal Child Support Guidelines*, a pre-existing spousal agreement with special provisions that benefit the children constitutes no bar to the application of the Guidelines where the needs and circumstances of the children have changed since the agreement and where no inequitable consequences would ensue from the application of the Guidelines in these circumstances.[44]

D. AMBIT OF JUDICIAL DISCRETION

Section 15.1(5) of the *Divorce Act* is inapplicable to an oral agreement, but sections 15.1(7) and (8) are not similarly circumscribed.[45]

Consensual arrangements for child support may be varied by an order granted pursuant to the Guidelines without proof of a material change of circumstances.[46] The words "special provisions" within the meaning of section 15.1(5)(a) of the *Divorce Act* signify unique provisions, other than periodic payments for the support of a child. Spousal reapportionment of property,[47] transfers of property in trust for the benefit of the children, or substantial lump sum amounts in satisfaction of debts or future child support obligations might constitute examples of unique or special provisions.[48] But as Barrington-Foote JA of the Saskatchewan Court of Appeal pointed out in *Hanson v Hanson*:[49]

> An unequal division of family assets or liabilities does not necessarily engage the exception created by s. 15.1(5) of the *Divorce Act*: *de Rooy v Bergstrom*, 2010 BCCA 5 (CanLII) at paras 56-61, 282 BCAC 26; *Epp v Robertson* (1998), 1998 CanLII 13515 (SKQB), 171 Sask R 315 (QB) at para 13 [*Epp*]. A party seeking the benefit of s. 15.1(5) must meet a two-part test. First, they have the onus to satisfy the court that the provisions at issue directly or indirectly benefit the child, or that special provisions have otherwise been made for the benefit of the child. Second, if they do, they must also satisfy the court it would be inequitable to apply the *Guidelines*: *Epp* at paras 11–13; *Lutz v Sequeira*, 2000 SKQB 319 (CanLII), 195 Sask R 87. Justice Wilkinson addressed the second element of this test in *Epp*: [20] Once a finding has been made that special provisions exist, it must be determined whether, given those provisions, the amount of child support determined under the Guidelines would be inequitable. As stated in *Wang v. Wang* (1997), 1997 CanLII 1299 (BC SC), B.C.J. No. 1678 (QL) (B.C. S.C. [In Chambers]) and

43 *Wang v Wang*, [1997] BCJ No 1678 (SC); *MGH v KLDH*, 2020 NBCA 46; *Epp v Robertson*, [1998] SJ No 684 (QB).

44 *Fisher v Heron*, [1997] PEIJ No 77 (TD).

45 *McIllwraith v McIllwraith*, [1999] NBJ No 129 (QB).

46 *Erickson v Erickson*, [2001] BCJ No 71 (SC); see also *Garrett-Rempel v Garrett-Rempel*, [2000] BCJ No 1771 (SC) (application under *Family Relations Act*).

47 *Duncan v Duncan*, [1999] BCJ No 2201 (CA). See also *Zhao v Xiao*, 2023 ONCA 453, leave to appeal to SCC denied 2023 CanLII 115636 (SCC).

48 *Fonseca v Fonseca*, [1998] BCJ No 2772 (SC); see also *CTG v RRG*, 2016 SKQB 387; *Hanson v Hanson*, 2019 SKCA 102; *Granquist v Lemond*, 2022 SKCA 90.

49 2019 SKCA 102 at para 20; see also *Granquist v Lemond*, 2022 SKCA 90; *Daniel v Daniel*, 2022 SKKB 279. And see para 22 wherein Barrington-Foote JA observed: "As noted in *Bromm v Bromm*, 2010 SKQB 85 (CanLII), 353 Sask R 198, there have been some differences in the approach taken to the meaning of 'special provision' between provinces."

> *Eilers v. Eilers*, [1998] B.C.J. No. 1021 (QL) (B.C.S.C.), the term "inequitable" relates to the parties and requires a consideration of both the circumstances of the parties giving rise to the order or agreement and their circumstances at the time of the application. Such an interpretation recognizes the give and take of settlement discussions and the interrelationship of terms which will be reflected in a settlement agreement or order.

As stated in *Peterson v Horan*,[50] special provisions that benefit a child or that have been made for the benefit of a child will usually possess the following attributes:

- they are unusual or out of the ordinary in the sense they do not feature in determining the amount of maintenance in accordance with the *Guidelines*;
- they serve to contribute to the maintenance of the child; and
- they serve in effect to partially discharge the parent's obligation to provide for the maintenance of the child and tend, therefore, to reduce the need, at least in part, for the amount of maintenance called for by the *Guidelines*.

Shared parenting arrangements that fall short of meeting section 9 of the *Federal Child Support Guidelines* do not constitute "special provisions" for the benefit of the children under section 15.1(5)(a) of the *Divorce Act*.[51]

There is no requirement that a separation agreement must be filed with the court so that it can be treated as a court order for the purpose of an application to vary its terms under section 17 of the *Divorce Act* and section 14 of the *Federal Child Support Guidelines*. An original application for child support may be brought pursuant to section 15.1 of the *Divorce Act*, and upon such an application, it is unnecessary to prove any change of circumstances, since the execution of the agreement before an order can be made in accordance with the *Federal Child Support Guidelines*.[52] Section 15.1(5) of the *Divorce Act* confers a discretion on the court to order an amount different from the Guidelines, if special provisions of the agreement benefit a child and the Guidelines amount would be inequitable in light of the special provisions. The same criteria apply whether the benefits provided by the agreement are higher or lower than the Guidelines amount.[53] The Guidelines are presumptively applicable and the onus of proof falls on the spouse who requests the court to deviate from the Guidelines pursuant to section 15.1(5) of the *Divorce Act*.[54] A reduction in the obligor's income that reflects an isolated event may not warrant a reduction in an agreed amount of child support pursuant to the application of the Guidelines, where the recipient spouse received less than an equal share of the matrimonial property in return for a higher amount of child support than would have been otherwise payable.[55] The terms of a separation agreement should not be characterized as "special provisions" where the Guidelines are capable of achieving the same objectives as those sought to be achieved by the agreement. The Guidelines should be

---

50 2006 SKCA 61 at para 36; *Granquist v Lemond*, 2022 SKCA 90.

51 *Handy v Handy*, [1999] BCJ No 6 (SC).

52 *Davie v Davie*, [1998] BCJ No 1691 (SC).

53 *Garard v Garard*, [1998] BCJ No 2076 (CA) (application to vary under s 17 of *Divorce Act*); *Cane v Newman*, [1998] OJ No 1776 (Gen Div); *BLGR v LMR*, [1998] SJ No 583 (QB).

54 *Johnston v Johnston*, [1998] NSJ No 177 (TD); *Cane v Newman*, [1998] OJ No 1776 (Gen Div); *Hanson v Hanson*, 2019 SKCA 102.

55 *Epp v Robertson*, [1998] SJ No 684 (QB).

applied where they provide a better and fairer method of calculating support and they are in the best interests of the child.[56]

Where a court finds that special provisions of a separation agreement indirectly benefit the children so as to render immediate application of the Guidelines inequitable, section 15.1(4) of the *Divorce Act* may be invoked to enable the court to give deference to the separation agreement, while at the same time taking into account present and future changes by ordering that the applicable table amount of child support shall be payable at a designated future date. Given that the basic table amount of child support is readily ascertainable by reference to the obligor's income, such an order does not constitute crystal ball gazing.[57]

A transfer of the equity in the matrimonial home to the primary caregiving parent coupled with a trade-off of higher spousal support against lower child support may constitute "special provisions" within the meaning of section 15.1(5) of the *Divorce Act* that render an order for the applicable table amount of child support inequitable. Given such circumstances, the court may decline to bring the child support provisions of the separation agreement in line with the normal Guidelines amount of child support, but may conclude that the agreed amount of periodic support for the children shall be modestly increased to reflect the children's current needs.[58]

An unequal division of assets or liabilities between the spouses does not in itself confer benefit on the child nor does it signify that the origin of any indirect benefit to the child was by a special provision that renders the application of the Guidelines inequitable within the meaning of section 15.1(5) of the *Divorce Act*.[59] An unequal reapportionment of the matrimonial home under minutes of settlement does not constitute a "special provision" that warrants judicial deviation from the normal Guidelines amount of child support under section 15.1(5) of the *Divorce Act*, where such reapportionment is explicable by the wife's sacrifice of her career development during a long marriage.[60] A separation agreement or court order that provides for long-term exclusive possession of the former matrimonial home by the primary caregiving parent and the children of the marriage may not suffice to trigger the application of section 15.1(5) of the *Divorce Act*.[61] Although such an agreement or order may provide stability for the children, section 15.1(5) of the *Divorce Act* is directed towards financial, not psychological, benefits.[62]

Conflicting evidence of the parties as to their unexpressed intent is unhelpful and the court should not speculate whether the obligor gave up some entitlement on the basis of some notion of pre-paying child support.[63] Courts should refrain from speculating and making assumptions about an agreement in the absence of persuasive evidence that a division

---

56 *Cane v Newman*, [1998] OJ No 1776 (Gen Div).

57 *Webb v Webb*, [1999] OJ No 507 (Gen Div) (seven-year deferral); see also *Martin v Martin*, [1999] OJ No 813 (Gen Div) (no date fixed for future payments).

58 *Bellingham v Bellingham*, [2003] MJ No 348 (QB).

59 *de Rooy v Bergstrom*, 2010 BCCA 5; *Stokes v Stokes*, [2002] NJ No 249 (SC); *Epp v Robertson*, [1998] SJ No 684 (QB); compare *Duncan v Duncan*, [1999] BCJ No 2201 (CA); *Corder v Corder*, 2009 BCSC 915; *Darbyson v Darbyson*, [1998] SCJ No 2173 (Gen Div).

60 *Rozen v Rozen*, [2002] BCJ No 2192 (SC).

61 *Monney v Monney*, [1999] MJ No 17 (QB).

62 *Ibid.*

63 *Wallace v Wallace*, [1998] BCJ No 203 (SC).

of assets created a direct or indirect benefit for the child that warrants deviation from the Guidelines.[64]

Where a purportedly final separation agreement includes no special provisions within the meaning of section 15.1(5) of the *Divorce Act* that replace the need for ongoing child support, the court should apply the Guidelines if their application provides a higher amount of child support than that provided by the agreement. An obligor's claim that it would be unfair or inequitable to apply the Guidelines in light of the purportedly final agreement does not satisfy the requirements of section 15.1(5) of the *Divorce Act* where there are no special provisions in the agreement that benefit the child. The fact that the obligor has complied with the separation agreement does not signify that he or she is suffering an injustice simply because the legislation has determined that a person of his or her means should pay more, nor can the obligor complain that the basic amount of child support payable under the provincial and territorial tables in the Guidelines is based solely on the obligor's income. The tables reflect the amount that a parent with a particular level of income is expected to contribute towards the costs of child rearing; in this way, the children share in increases or decreases in the other parent's income just as they would if the family still lived together.[65]

Sections 15.1(5) and 17(6.2) of the *Divorce Act* are confined to situations where a financial benefit is conferred on children. While the exercise of parenting time provisions of a spousal agreement do not entitle a court to deviate from the Guidelines pursuant to section 15.1(5) of the *Divorce Act*, section 10 of the *Federal Child Support Guidelines* may warrant consideration if expenses relating to the exercise of parenting time are unusually high and the payor's household standard of living is lower than that of the recipient spouse's household.[66]

In an application under section 15.1 of the *Divorce Act* where there is a pre-existing separation agreement, the court must first decide whether it should exercise its discretion not to apply the *Federal Child Support Guidelines*. If it concludes that the Guidelines should be applied, the court must then decide whether an amount less than that required by the Guidelines should be ordered on the basis that the separation agreement contains special provisions that directly or indirectly benefit the child so as to render application of the Guidelines inequitable within the meaning of section 15.1(5) of the *Divorce Act*. A six-step procedure has been formulated by Martinson J of the British Columbia Supreme Court to address these two issues:

1) Identify the child support provisions in the agreement.
2) Identify any special provisions in the agreement as defined in section 15.1(5) of the *Divorce Act*.
3) Determine the Guidelines amount as though there were no separation agreement.
4) Compare the Guidelines amount to the provisions of the separation agreement to see whether reasonable arrangements have been made in light of the Guidelines standard.
5) If reasonable arrangements have been made, the court will decline to make an order under the Guidelines and the terms of the separation agreement will prevail; if reasonable arrangements have not been made, the Guidelines should be addressed.

---

64 *Young v Young*, [1998] BCJ No 453 (SC).

65 *Duffield v Duffield*, [1998] BCJ No 184 (SC).

66 *Demonte v Demonte*, [1998] BCJ No 1041 (SC); *Greene v Greene*, 2010 BCCA 595.

6) In addressing the Guidelines, compare the Guidelines amount to the special provisions and child support provisions to see if an order different from the Guidelines amount should be ordered; if it should be, decide what amount is appropriate; if it should not be, apply the Guidelines amount determined in the third step.[67]

A separation agreement may be upheld pursuant to section 15.1(5) of the *Divorce Act* where higher spousal support is provided to offset the less than Guidelines amount of child support and the overall effect is beneficial to all family members because of the differential treatment of periodic spousal support payments and periodic child support payments under the *Income Tax Act*.[68]

Where parents have negotiated a comprehensive agreement that subsumes child support under spousal support and the recipient spouse's circumstances warrant increased spousal support, the court may order increased spousal support without interfering with child support on the basis that the income tax consequences of the agreement operate to the advantage of both spouses and benefit their children under the existing shared parenting arrangement.[69]

The primary caregiving parent's receipt of social assistance does not constitute a "special provision" within the meaning of section 15.1(5) of the *Divorce Act*.[70]

Although section 17(6.1) of the *Divorce Act* states that the court making a variation order in respect of child support shall do so in accordance with the applicable Guidelines, section 17(6.2) stipulates an overriding provision whereby the court may order an amount that deviates from the Guidelines if the court is satisfied: (a) that special provisions in an order or written agreement respecting the financial obligations of the spouses, or the division or transfer of property, directly or indirectly benefit a child, or that special provisions have otherwise been made for the benefit of a child; and (b) that the application of the Guidelines would result in an amount of child support that is inequitable given those special provisions.[71] Both of these prerequisites may exist so as to justify dismissal of an application to vary child support where the parties have addressed their financial obligations, including child support, in the context of a comprehensive settlement that provides, *inter alia*, that one parent shall maintain the former matrimonial home for occupation by the children when in his or her care.[72] An unequal division of matrimonial property or of the matrimonial home will be insufficient to warrant deviation from the *Federal Child Support Guidelines*, unless it constitutes a "special

---

67 *Baum v Baum*, [1999] BCJ No 3025 (SC) (transfer of family home to wife who gave up her interest in the husband's company did not amount to "special provisions" under section 15.1(5) of *Divorce Act*; court was not satisfied that reasonable arrangements had been made for the child where the agreement provided a taxable monthly amount of $500 for child support and the Guidelines would generate a non-taxable monthly sum of $468; Guidelines applied); see also *Rozen v Rozen*, [2001] BCJ No 1633 (SC), applying the *Baum v Baum* six-step approach to a post-Guidelines spousal agreement. And see *Hammond v Maloney*, 2008 NLUFC 37.

68 *Da Silva v Da Silva*, [2004] SCJ No 1976 (SCJ). Compare *Grzelak v Grzelak*, [1997] SCJ No 4838 (Gen Div).

69 *McGrath v McGrath*, [2001] BCJ No 1555 (SC).

70 *TDO v RGO*, [2000] BCJ No 524 (SC).

71 *Hutchings v Hutchings*, [1999] BCJ No 2897 (CA) (application of s 8 of *Federal Child Support Guidelines* excluded by prior lump sum payment in full satisfaction of future child support obligations); *Danchuk v Danchuk*, [2001] BCJ No 755 (CA); *Tutty v Tutty*, [2005] NSJ No 514 (SC); *Koot v McLaren*, [2003] SJ No 214 (QB).

72 *Wedge v McKenna*, [1997] PEIJ No 75 (TD).

provision" that replaces or reduces the need for ongoing support for the children.[73] The onus of proving that an unequal division of matrimonial property on the marriage breakdown renders it inequitable to order the applicable Guidelines amount of child support falls on the spouse who invokes section 15.1(5) of the *Divorce Act*. The onus will not be discharged where it is not clear that the unequal division will benefit the children and the financial circumstances of the parents have undergone material changes since their separation.[74] Section 17(6.2) of the *Divorce Act* cannot be invoked to justify deviation from the *Federal Child Support Guidelines* where any special benefit to children resulting from consensual arrangements was not so great as to render the application of Guidelines inequitable.[75] An argument of detrimental reliance cannot be invoked by an obligor who remarries and has more children on the assumption that the consensual arrangements were final, unless the circumstances are such as to trigger a finding of undue hardship within the meaning of section 10 of the Guidelines.[76] An unequal property division in return for a waiver of spousal and child support does not preclude a subsequent order for support of the children who are undertaking post-secondary education where this was not within the contemplation of the spouses when they negotiated their settle ment several years previously.[77]

A primary caregiving parent's willingness to take less than the applicable Guidelines amount of child support does not justify a court deviating from the Guidelines.

The phrase "or that special provisions have otherwise been made for the benefit of the child" in sections 15.1(5)(a) and 17(6.2)(a) of the *Divorce Act* does not specifically require that special provisions be made by the divorcing or divorced spouses. A family trust established by a parent[78] or grandparent may fall within the ambit of either section.[79] Where a parent has settled trust funds for the benefit of children of the marriage, a court should not interfere with the administration of the trust. The court may, nevertheless, conclude that it would be inequitable for the primary caregiving parent to receive the applicable amount payable under the Guidelines in addition to funds provided by the trust for the maintenance, education, or advancement of the children. In that event, the court may direct that the other parent's obligation to pay the Guidelines amount shall be reduced proportionately to any payments made from the trust for the support of the children. The fact that funds have not previously been withdrawn from the trust fund for the benefit of the children does not preclude such a court-ordered set-off.[80]

Living arrangements whereby divorced parents maintain separate lives in a single home are insufficient to warrant a finding of "special provisions" for the benefit of the children within the meaning of section 17(6.2) of the *Divorce Act*. The payment of a higher net amount of child support under the new child support and income tax regimes is not considered as

---

73 *Omah-Maharajh v Howard*, [1998] AJ No 173 (QB); *Garard v Garard*, [1998] BCJ No 2076 (CA); *Danchuk v Danchuk*, [2001] BCJ No 755 (CA); *Picco v Picco*, [2000] NJ No 64 (UFC); *Lutz v Sequeira*, [2000] SJ No 460 (QB).

74 *Lutz v Sequeira*, *ibid*.

75 *Aker v Howard*, [1998] SCJ No 5562 (Gen Div); *Morrison v Morrison*, [2001] YJ No 521 (SC).

76 *Aker v Howard*, *ibid*.

77 *MacDonald v Simpson*, [1998] SCJ No 1045 (Gen Div).

78 *Davidson v Davidson*, [1998] AJ No 1040 (QB).

79 See *Tauber v Tauber*, [1999] OJ No 359 (Gen Div).

80 *Davidson v Davidson*, [1998] AJ No 1040 (QB).

rendering the application of the *Federal Child Support Guidelines* inequitable under section 17(6.2) of the *Divorce Act*. An obligor is expected to restructure his or her financial affairs so as to accord priority to child support over the personal acquisition of a capital asset by way of equity in a home.[81]

In granting a variation order with respect to child support, section 17(6.2) of the *Divorce Act* empowers a court to reduce the normal Guidelines amount of child support that would be payable in light of the obligor's increased annual income, if prior minutes of settlement at the time of the existing order included special provisions benefitting the children by relieving their primary caregiving parent of the obligation to share the responsibility for family debts incurred prior to the marriage breakdown.[82]

When the criteria set out in section 17(6.2) of the *Divorce Act* are satisfied, the judicial discretion enables the court not only to deviate from the amount that would be payable under the Guidelines; it also enables the court to refuse to vary the existing order in any way.[83] Where the obligor's financial circumstances have deteriorated since the agreement and order, the court may regard the reduced amount of child support payable under the applicable provincial table as appropriate, while leaving unchanged the agreed division of special and extraordinary expenses in proportion to the respective parental incomes.[84]

A court may retroactively incorporate the terms of a separation agreement in a divorce judgment and order the sharing of extraordinary expenses for extracurricular activities of the children that were incurred by the primary caregiving parent over several years following divorce.[85]

There is nothing in section 15.1(5) or section 17(6.2) of the *Divorce Act* that prevents a court from dealing with child-related expenses in a similar manner to the basic amount of child support where the best interests of the children are served by judicial endorsement of a parental agreement. In determining whether extracurricular and educational expenses are "extraordinary" within the meaning of section 7 of the *Federal Child Support Guidelines*, the court has regard to the combined annual income of the parents. Expenses totalling approximately $4,700 per year are not extraordinary expenses for parents with a combined annual income of almost $115,000. The court may, nevertheless, refuse to interfere with a parental agreement for the payment of such expenses and may decline to disturb their undertakings that the expenses will be paid on a 50/50 basis rather than a *pro rata* basis.[86]

---

81 *Chan v Chan*, [1999] BCJ No 1155 (SC) (order pre-dating implementation of Guidelines on 1 May 1997 varied to accord with basic table amount and appropriate s 7 expenses under the *Federal Child Support Guidelines*).

82 *Anderson-Devine v Anderson*, [2002] MJ No 484 (CA).

83 *Gore-Hickman v Gore-Hickman*, [1999] SJ No 503 (QB), citing *Kuntz v Chow*, [1998] SJ No 23 (QB); see also *Morrison v Morrison*, [2001] YJ No 521 (SC).

84 *Shepherd v Shepherd*, [1998] BCJ No 2159 (SC).

85 *Wilson v Wilson*, [1999] BCJ No 2458 (SC).

86 *Pederson v Pederson*, [2001] BCJ No 2252 (SC).

E. COURT RECORDS

Where a court deviates from the applicable Guidelines pursuant to section 15.1(5) or section 17(6.2) of the *Divorce Act*, the court must record its reasons for doing so.[87]

F. CONSENT ORDERS

A consent order for child support may be granted in an amount that exceeds the requirements of the *Federal Child Support Guidelines*.[88] It has also been suggested that a court should be loath to change negotiated child support arrangements to which the parents wish to adhere, even though they provide an amount of support modestly lower than the applicable table amount under the *Federal Child Support Guidelines*.[89] It is submitted, however, that courts should be cautious about allowing parents the freedom to pay or receive lower periodic child support payments than those required by the applicable table, unless there are circumstances other than the agreement itself that warrant deviation from the applicable table amount and any additional special or extraordinary expenses to which the children may be entitled under section 7 of the Guidelines.[90]

With respect to consent orders, a finding under section 15.1(7) of the *Divorce Act* that reasonable arrangements have been made for the support of a child to whom the order relates, presupposes that adequate information has been provided to the court about the economic and other circumstances of the spouses and the children, including any special or extraordinary expenses likely to be incurred on behalf of the children. Sufficient evidence must be presented to the court to enable it to make an informed judgment. A bald assertion that reasonable arrangements have been made for the support of a child does not warrant a consent order that deviates from the Guidelines. Such a bald assertion is not evidence but a conclusion to be determined by the court after an evaluation of any supporting evidence.

A court may refuse to endorse a shared parenting agreement for the nonpayment of child support where a substantial disparity exists between the respective parental incomes and their expenses,[92] but where there will be no imbalance between the standards of living that the children will enjoy in the two households, the court may apply section 15.1(7) of the *Divorce Act* by giving effect to a parental agreement providing for alternating weekly parenting time with neither parent being required to pay child support.[93]

A consent order for child support may be varied where there has been a material change by virtue of a sudden and significant increase in post-secondary education costs.[94]

---

87 *Divorce Act*, ss 15.1(6) and 17(6.3); see *Middleton v MacPherson*, [1997] AJ No 614 (QB); *Fournier v Phelan*, [2000] SCJ No 2638 (Div Ct); And see *Miller v White*, 2018 PECA 11 (interim order for third-party payments in lieu of interim child support payments).

88 *O'Sanlou v O'Sanlou*, [1998] BCJ No 684 (SC).

89 *McIllwraith v McIllwraith*, [1999] NBJ No 129 (QB).

90 See *Gale v Dawson*, 2015 BCSC 1795 applying section 150(2) of *Family Law Act*, SBC 2011, c 25 (special residential and travel arrangements made to promote parent/child relationship).

91 Compare *Dumas v Dumas* (1992), 43 RFL (3d) 260 (Alta QB), applying *Divorce Act*, s 11(1)(b). See, generally, Julien D Payne, *Payne on Divorce*, 4th ed (Scarborough, ON: Carswell, 1996) at 86–90.

92 *Connors v Connors*, [1999] BCJ No 2793 (SC).

93 *Warren v Warren*, [2001] NJ No 262 (SC).

94 *Otto v Between*, [1996] OJ No 4786 (Gen Div).

A court may grant a consent order for an amount greater than that required by the *Federal Child Support Guidelines*[95] and may ratify an agreed amount of expenses for extracurricular activities even though they do not satisfy the test of being "extraordinary" within the meaning of section 7 of the Guidelines.[96]

G. PROVINCIAL LEGISLATION AND GUIDELINES

Section 150(4) of the *Family Law Act* (BC) empowers a court to deviate from the normal amount payable under the *Federal Child Support Guidelines* if the provisions in an order or written agreement respecting the financial obligations of the parties, or the division or transfer of their property, directly or indirectly benefit the child, or special provisions have otherwise been made for the benefit of the child, and the application of the Guidelines would be inequitable in light of those provisions. A father's transfer of his interest in the former matrimonial home to the mother will not be regarded as providing an indirect benefit to his biological child and stepchild so as to justify an order for reduced child support if no significant equity is involved that could provide an ongoing benefit to the children. Furthermore, Canada Pension Plan payments to the children of a disabled father are not to be credited to the father's child support obligation as "special provisions" directly benefitting the children. Section 150(4) of the *Family Law Act* (BC) envisages some financial arrangement made by one or both of the parents for the continuing support of the children. Section 150(4) might also include provision for a child's financial security made by a grandparent or other relative, or even by a "new" parent, but Canada Pension Plan benefits are paid automatically, by operation of statute, and not because of any specific action on the part of the disabled parent or any third party. Insofar as such payments are made to a stepchild, however, a court may conclude that they should be taken into account pursuant to section 5 of the *Federal Child Support Guidelines* in determining the stepfather's obligation to support that child. In exercising its discretion under section 5 of the Guidelines, a court is not confined to the circumstances specified in section 5 of the Guidelines and section 150(4) of the *Family Law Act* (BC).[97]

A lump sum payment, which purports to constitute a final and binding resolution of child support rights and obligations, does not preclude a subsequent application for periodic support under the *Federal Child Support Guidelines*.[98] The attendant circumstances may, nevertheless, entitle the court to deviate from the normal table amount of child support by ordering a lower amount on the basis that the lump sum settlement falls within section 150(4) of the *Family Law Act* (BC) in that the lump sum constitutes a "special provision" for the benefit of the child that renders future payment of the full table amount inequitable. The court may also refuse to order retroactive child support except for a few months prior to its prospective order.[99]

---

95 *Simpson v Simpson*, [1997] BCJ No 2885 (SC); *Blair v Blair*, [1997] SCJ No 4949 (Gen Div).

96 *Blair v Blair*, *ibid*.

97 *Fedoruk v Jamieson*, [2002] BCJ No 503 (SC).

98 *MacKay v Bucher*, 2001 NSCA 120; see also Chapter 13, Section M; see also *Wright v Zaver*, [2002] SCJ No 1098 (CA).

99 *MT v BC*, [2001] BCJ No 2791 (Prov Ct).

A purportedly final consent order for lump sum support of an extramarital child made at the time of the child's birth may be varied pursuant to section 37 of the *Family Maintenance Act* (NS)[100] so as to provide future payment of the applicable table amount of child support under the provincial guidelines in addition to any allowed special or extraordinary expenses under section 7 of the Guidelines. Such variation requires proof of a change of circumstances since the granting of the order but this requirement is satisfied in the case of a pre-Guide lines order by the implementation of the provincial guidelines. It is not necessary to prove a "material change of circumstances" that satisfies the criteria defined in *Willick v Willick* whereby the change had to be such that, if known at the time, would likely have resulted in different terms. For a court to uphold a pre-Guidelines agreement or order that does not conform to the Guidelines, the requirements of section 10(3) of the *Family Maintenance Act* (NS) must be satisfied. Section 10(3) provides that a judge may order maintenance that differs from the Guidelines amount where (1) the order contains a special provision that directly or indirectly benefits the child and (2) the application of Guidelines would result in an amount of child maintenance that is inequitable. A lump sum order for child support may be perceived as making special provision that directly or indirectly benefits the child insofar as it replaces the need for ongoing child support, and inequity may ensue within the meaning of section 10(3) of the *Family Maintenance Act* (NS) if an order granted in the Guidelines amount would result in exposing the payor to duplicate amounts of child support. The special provision that has been made by way of the pre-Guidelines lump sum order must be judged in comparison with the amount that would be payable as a result of applying the Guidelines. In assessing inequity, it is the payor's current financial situation that is relevant, not the circumstances existing when the special provision was made. There may be occasions, however, when the payor's former circumstances will be taken into account, for example, where the parent can demonstrate that his or her current financial obligations directly relate to the payment of purportedly final lump sum child support. There is no inconsistency in a court refusing to vary an agreement or consent order providing for support exceeding the Guidelines amount, yet increasing a lower amount to the Guidelines level; both courses of action will typically reflect the best interests of the child.[102]

In *Wright v Zaver*,[103] which arose in the context of the Ontario *Family Law Act* and the *Ontario Child Support Guidelines*, minutes of settlement had been executed by the parents of a child in 1985 and were incorporated in a court order. The father agreed to pay a lump sum of $4,000 as child support and waived exercising parenting time with his child to permit the mother to get on with her life. The mother formed another spousal relationship some five years later but this marriage, which also resulted in the birth of a child, broke down after nine years. The mother's husband undertook to pay and was paying the applicable table amount of support for the two children—his own biological child and his stepchild. The mother, nevertheless, sought support from the father of her first child who was ordered to pay the applicable table amount of child support. Section 37(2.3) of the Ontario *Family Law Act* empowers a court to deviate from the *Ontario Child Support Guidelines*, if special provisions have otherwise been

100 See now *Parenting and Support Act*, RSNS 1989, c 160, as amended.

101 [1994] 3 SCR 670.

102 *MacKay v Bucher*, 2001 NSCA 120.

103 [2002] SCJ No 1098 (CA); see also *Deiter v Sampson*, [2004] SCJ No 904 (CA).

made for the benefit of a child that render the application of the Guidelines inequitable. All five judges of the appellate panel agreed that it would not be inequitable to order the father to pay the full table amount of child support, notwithstanding the mother's receipt of ongoing periodic child support from her husband. Justice of Appeal Simmons, with whom Feldman JA concurred, was of the opinion that the 1985 child support arrangements coupled with the stepfather's assumption of child support obligations both before and after the marriage breakdown constituted "special provisions" under section 37(2.3) of the Ontario *Family Law Act*, although they did not render inequitable a prospective order for the father to pay the applicable table amount of child support. Justice of Appeal Simmons asserted that "special provisions" within the meaning of section 37(2.3) of the Ontario *Family Law Act* must replace, in whole or in part, the need for ongoing child support but concluded that there is no additional requirement that the "special provisions" be unusual or out of the ordinary. Justice of Appeal Sharpe, with whom Carthy and Charron JJA concurred, agreed that "special provisions" must replace, in whole or in part, the need for ongoing child support, but was of the opinion that they must be out of the ordinary or unusual in order to satisfy the requirements of section 37(2.3) of the Ontario *Family Law Act*. Justice of Appeal Sharpe declined to definitively determine whether the stepfather's ongoing child support payments constituted "special provisions" under section 37(2.3) of the Act. It was unnecessary to make a definitive ruling in this context because Sharpe JA found that the stepfather's ongoing child support payments did not render the father's obligation to pay the table amount of child support inequitable under section 37(2.3) of the Ontario *Family Law Act*. Two reasons were given by Sharpe JA. First, there was the fact that the stepfather was, in any event, liable to pay the applicable table amount of support for his own biological child of the marriage and the difference between this amount and the amount that he was currently paying for the two children, his biological child and his stepchild, was insufficient to produce any significant increase in the mother's personal standard of living. Second, any incidental increase in her personal standard of living was legally irrelevant because child support is a right of the child, not a right of the primary caregiving parent. In the minority judgment of Simmons JA, paramount weight on the issue of inequity had been placed on the mother's inability to meet her first child's needs, even with the benefit of the additional resources provided by the stepfather. Justice of Appeal Simmons concluded that the first child's needs should not be assessed on a minimalist basis and that an order for the father to pay the applicable table amount of child support would not be an undue financial burden for him, nor was it likely to provide a surplus that would unfairly increase the mother's standard of living.

A disproportionate property division in favour of the mother, coupled with the father's waiver of spousal support, may be insufficient to satisfy section 33(12) of the Ontario *Family Law Act*, which entitles the court to deviate from ordering the applicable Guidelines amount of child support, where special provisions in a separation agreement directly or indirectly benefit the children so as to render an order for the Guidelines amount of support inequitable because of those special provisions. The majority judgment of the Ontario Court of Appeal in *Wright v Zaver*, discussed above, applies an objective test to determine whether there are unusual or out-of-the-ordinary provisions that replace or reduce the children's ongoing need for support. The question is not whether the parents subjectively intended to benefit the children, but whether the provisions actually benefit the children when viewed objectively. This test has a child-centred focus and the children's entitlement to support should not be compromised by a parent's mismanagement of property received under an unequal division of the spousal net family properties. Even if "special provisions" are found, the court cannot deviate from the Guidelines amount, unless the court concludes that it would be inequitable to apply the Guidelines in light of those special provisions.[104]

A separation agreement, which is filed with a court under section 35 of the Ontario *Family Law Act*, may be varied in light of a material change of circumstances or if evidence unavailable at the previous hearing subsequently becomes available. The Supreme Court of Canada in *Willick v Willick*[105] defined a material change as one that, if known at the time of the order, would likely have resulted in different terms. Section 37(2.2) of the Ontario *Family Law Act* and section 17(6.1) of the *Divorce Act* require the court to apply the *Federal Child Support Guidelines* on an application to vary a child support order. There is little or no discretion available to the court to deviate from the Guidelines. The only exceptions are found in sections 37(2.3) and 37(2.5) of the Ontario *Family Law Act* and sections 17(6.2) and 17(6.4) of the *Divorce Act*. Unless one of the aforementioned provisions applies, if one family member benefits from conversion to the Guidelines amount, there is no judicial discretion to deviate from the Guidelines. If, however, the after-tax cost to the payor is higher under the Guidelines and the after-tax benefit to the payee is less, the court should not make an order in accordance with the Guidelines. A payor may invoke the Guidelines to reduce the level of child support even where the payor's financial circumstances have improved or remained the same and those of the recipient spouse and children have not improved. "Special provisions" in a separation agreement for the benefit of the children may justify a reduction in the amount of table support payable under the Guidelines, but only where the court finds that the application of the Guidelines would be "inequitable" in light of the "special provision" benefitting the children.[106] A court may refuse to interfere with a consent order whereby the father agreed to pay higher child support than the Guidelines amount because of the mother's medical condition, the special needs of the children, and the father's inability to exercise parenting time and provide respite to the mother. Whilst upholding the consent order on the basis that it would be inequitable to reduce the amount of child support to that prescribed by the Guidelines, partial remission of accrued child support arrears may be ordered because of a temporary reduction in the father's income.[107]

In the context of an application for child support under section 33 of the Ontario *Family Law Act*, section 56(1.1) of the Act provides that, in determining child support, the court may disregard any pertinent provision of a domestic contract, where the court considers the provision unreasonable, having regard to the *Federal Child Support Guidelines* as well as to any other provision in the agreement relating to the support of the child. The applicant has the burden of proving that the terms of the domestic contract should be disregarded. A court cannot conclude that a contractual provision is inadequate on its face on no other basis than the existence of the Guidelines. There must be judicial consideration of whether the support provision meets or fails to meet the needs of the child, having regard to any other relevant

---

104 *Deiter v Sampson*, [2002] SCJ No 4160 (SCJ), aff'd [2004] SCJ No 904 (CA).

105 [1994] 3 SCR 670.

106 *Osmar v Osmar*, [2000] SCJ No 2060 (SCJ) (amount of child support payable under duly filed separation agreement reduced to reflect the table amount payable under the Guidelines).

107 *Morrison v Morrison*, [2001] YJ No 521 (SC).

provisions in the domestic contract. Where the contract makes provision for a transfer of property or some other financial benefit that purports to meet the needs of the child, in whole or in part, that provision must be considered and assessed as well as the Guidelines. The support provisions of section 33 of the Act come into play only after a determination is made under section 56(1.1) that the contractual provision falls short of meeting the needs of the child. At that point, the *onus* shifts to the respondent.[108]

In *Blagaich v Blagaich*,[109] pursuant to the terms of a settlement executed at the time of their divorce in Maryland, the father agreed to pay child support in accordance with the *Maryland Child Support Guidelines* until each child reached the age of eighteen or graduated from high school. The settlement further provided that any future dispute would be governed by Maryland law and would be submitted to a Maryland court. The mother relocated with the three children to Ontario shortly after the execution of the settlement. In response to the mother's motion for retroactive and prospective child support payments in accordance with the *Ontario Child Support Guidelines*, the father brought a cross-motion seeking a finding that jurisdiction vested in the Maryland Circuit Court and that support be paid in accordance with its prior order. Holding that the father had attorned to the jurisdiction of the Ontario Superior Court by attending to argue before it, Wood J observed that section 58 of the *Family Law Act* (Ontario) requires a foreign domestic contract to comply with the law of Ontario and, in particular, sections 33(4) and 56 of the *Family Law Act* in order to be enforceable. Pursuant to section 56(1.1) of the *Family Law Act*, a court may disregard any provision of a domestic contract that is unreasonable in light of the *Ontario Child Support Guidelines*, unless there is a counterbalancing benefit conferred on the children. In Ontario, the *Family Law Act* and the *Ontario Child Support Guidelines* impose an obligation on parents to support their adult children who are engaged in full-time post-secondary education. This contrasts with Maryland law, which provides that support ceases when a child attains the age of eighteen. Given the respondent's residence with the children in Ontario, she was entitled to apply to an Ontario court for child support in accordance with the law of Ontario and section 33(11) of the *Family Law Act* prescribes the application of the *Ontario Child Support Guidelines*. Accordingly, the provision in the settlement requiring that child support be determined in accordance with the *Maryland Child Support Guidelines* was rendered unenforceable by operation of section 58 of the *Family Law Act* and could not constitute a bar to the mother's application for child support.

Parties are encouraged to consensually resolve child support rights and obligations by section 35 of the Ontario *Family Law Act*, but if their wish is to embody agreed child support provisions in an order, the court must, before granting an order, be provided with and have regard to the relevant financial information required by section 21 of the *Ontario Child Support Guidelines*. A sworn financial statement in accordance with Rule 44(3) of the *Ontario Court (Provincial Division) Family Rules*[110] must also be filed. The court must have regard to "all the circumstances of the parties," including very specific financial and non-financial considerations set out in section 33(9) of the Ontario *Family Law Act*. The additional work

---

108 *Spencer v Irvine*, [1999] SCJ No 1493 (SCJ).

109 [2007] SCJ No 3399 (SCJ).

110 RRO 1990, Reg 199.

and expense involved in meeting the above requirements may appear to be unfair but are deemed necessary by the legislature in order to protect the interests of children. Whether they will ultimately result in a benefit that exceeds their cost is an open question. Clients are free to resolve the issue of child support free from judicial intervention but, if they wish an agreement to take on the force of a court order, they have no choice but to fulfil the above requirements.[111]

The payment of benefits under the Canada Pension Plan to the children of a disabled parent does not constitute "special provisions" for the benefit of the children within the meaning of section 3(4)(a) of *The Family Maintenance Act, 1997* (Saskatchewan).[112] The Saskatchewan Court of King's Bench has no general jurisdiction to vary the child support provisions of an interspousal contract but has the discretion to deal with such an application as an original application for a child support order under *The Family Maintenance Act, 1997*. In that event, it will be necessary for the court to determine whether the interspousal contract directly or indirectly benefits the children so as to render inequitable an order for support in accordance with the *Federal Child Support Guidelines*.[113]

H. ARTIFICIAL INSEMINATION

Sections 48, 53, 85, and 86 of the Alberta *Family Law Act*[114] provide qualified recognition to parental agreements but such agreements cannot oust the supervisory jurisdiction of the court to grant child support orders, guardianship orders, and parenting orders to protect the needs and best interests of children. The rights to liberty and security that are guaranteed by section 7 of the *Canadian Charter of Rights and Freedoms* have received a large and liberal interpretation, but they do not extend to guarantee freedom of contract. Furthermore, section 7 can only be triggered where there is a breach of principles for fundamental justice. Accordingly, sections 53, 85, and 86 of the *Family Law Act* are not constitutionally deficient because they do not guarantee private ordering, even on matters as potentially personal as parenting. In applying these principles to the facts in *Doe v Alberta*, Martin J concluded that the applicants could not enter into a binding and determinative agreement whereby the male partner would have no parental rights or responsibilities and no child support obligation towards his unmarried cohabitant's child born as a result of her artificial insemination by an unknown donor.[115]

---

111 *D(J) v J(J)* (1998), 42 RFL (4th) 335 (Ont Prov Div).

112 SS 1997, c F-6.2; *Malbeuf v Malbeuf*, [1999] SJ No 635 (QB), citing *Blain-Hughes v Blain* (1998), 39 RFL (4th) 327 (Ont Ct Gen Div) (application to vary child support order under ss 37(2.3)(a) and (b) of Ontario *Family Law Act*); *Peterson v Horan*, [2006] SJ No 333 (CA); compare *MJB v WPB*, [2004] MJ No 123 (QB).

113 *Nicolson v Prekaski*, [2004] SJ No 714 (QB).

114 SA 2003, c F-4.5.

115 [2005] AJ No 1719 (QB).

Form and Types of Order

A. DIVERSE TYPES OF ORDER

The diverse types of support order that may be granted pursuant to sections 11 and 12 of the Guidelines are as follows:

1) An order to pay a lump sum;
2) An order to secure a lump sum;
3) An order to pay and secure a lump sum;
4) An order to pay periodic sums;
5) An order to secure periodic sums;
6) An order to pay and secure periodic sums.

The court is not restricted to making only one type of order. A combination of the various types of order may be accommodated.

When child support is granted, it is usually ordered to be paid on a periodic basis — weekly, fortnightly, or monthly. A court has no jurisdiction under section 12 of the Guidelines to order an obligor to transfer property in satisfaction of his child support obligation.[1] Indeed, even the mutual consent of the spouses would appear insufficient to confer jurisdiction on the courts to order a transfer of property in the exercise of jurisdiction under section 12 of the Guidelines, although an out-of-court-settlement could be negotiated by the spouses or an order to pay might be enforced by way of execution against the land or other assets of the obligor.

In *Giao v McCready*,[2] a father on social assistance was ordered to pay nominal child support of $1 per month and directed to keep the mother and the Director of Maintenance Enforcement informed of any income changes as soon as they occurred. The father was also required to provide his income tax returns and notices of assessment on an annual basis to the mother and the Director of Maintenance Enforcement.

1 See *McConnell v McConnell* (1975), 11 NBR (2d) 19 (CA).

2 [2005] NSJ No 50 (SC).

B. INTERIM ORDERS

A court may grant an interim order for child support pending the determination of an application for a permanent order.[3] Interim and permanent orders fall subject to the same criteria in that both types of order must ordinarily be made in accordance with the applicable guidelines.[4] An interim order, like a permanent order, may be made for a definite[5] or indefinite period or until a specified event occurs and the court may impose such terms, conditions, or restrictions in connection with the interim order as it thinks fit and just.[6]

An interim order for child support may be unnecessary where the parents continue to reside under the same roof.[7]

Interim proceedings are not geared for the final determination of issues. The evidence is entirely by affidavit and the court lacks the benefit of seeing the parties and their witnesses testify in open court and having their evidence tested under cross-examination. Interim proceedings are summary in nature and provide a rough justice at best. The merits of the case are not thrashed out in interim proceedings.[8] Interim relief is not generally available to resolve contested issues. A trial or pre-trial allows for a more thorough and judicious resolution of the issues. Generally, most issues should not be resolved in chambers upon conflicting affidavit evidence.[9]

1) Types of Interim Order

Section 11 of the *Federal Child Support Guidelines* expressly empowers the court to order interim support by way of such lump sum and/or periodic sums as the court deems reasonable. On an application for interim child support and for the proportionate sharing of extraordinary expenses relating to extracurricular activities, a lump sum may be granted respecting actual expenses being incurred, pending resolution of diverse issues at trial. Section 12 of the *Federal Child Support Guidelines* expressly confers jurisdiction on the court to make orders to pay or secure, or to pay and secure, interim support.

2) Effect of Reconciliation on Interim Order

If an interim support order is terminated by an unsuccessful spousal reconciliation, a new order can be obtained simply by bringing back the original motion and filing a supplementary affidavit to establish the new facts.[11]

---

3 *Divorce Act*, RSC 1985 (2d Supp), c 3, s 15.1(2).

4 *Ibid*, s 15.1(3). Compare to *Miller v White*, 2018 PECA 11 (interim order).

5 *Gordinier-Regan v Regan*, 2011 NSSC 297.

6 *Divorce Act*, RSC 1985 (2d Supp), c 3, s 15.1(4).

7 *Moore v Fernandes*, [2001] OJ No 5192 (SCJ); compare *VLN v SRN*, 2019 ABQB 849.

8 *Sochowski v Sochowski*, 2020 ABCA 59 at para 11; *Gibb v Gibb*, [2005] BCJ No 2730 (SC); *ZAS v TS*, 2022 BCSC 435; *McConkey v McConkey*, 2022 ONSC 4600; *Miller v White*, 2018 PECA 11 (interim order); *CTG v RRG*, 2016 SKQB 387.

9 *Lafrentz v Palmer*, 2021 BCSC 1332; *Jacobson v Jacobson*, 2011 SKQB 402; *Poultney v Poultney*, 2011 SKQB 420. See also *Long v Sun*, 2019 BCSC 2129.

10 *Fuzi v Fuzi*, [1999] BCJ No 2263 (SC).

11 *Grail v Grail* (1990), 27 RFL (3d) 317 (Ont Master), aff'd (1990), 30 RFL (3d) 454 (Ont Ct Gen Div).

3) Effect of Divorce on Interim Order

An interim order for support may be granted pursuant to the *Divorce Act* once a petition for divorce has been filed.[12] An interim order is not automatically terminated by the pronouncement of a divorce. Section 15.1(2) of the *Divorce Act* permits an interim order to continue until a permanent order is granted.[13] An interim order may post-date a divorce judgment and may be the result of undertakings made by a party at the divorce hearing.[14]

4) Relationship Between Federal Divorce Legislation and Provincial/Territorial Legislation

The institution of divorce proceedings in one province does not stop the applicant from seeking interim child support in another province under provincial legislation.[15] Where a support order under provincial legislation is outstanding, a subsequent order for interim relief in a divorce proceeding may supplement[16] or incorporate[17] the former order where the means and needs of the respective spouses warrant. An order for support made pursuant to provincial legislation, even if intended to be final, does not bar a subsequent application for interim support by way of corollary relief in divorce proceedings.[18] Any such application deals with the matter *de novo* and does not require proof of a change of circumstances.[19] However, an application in a divorce proceeding for interim support in the same amount as that awarded under provincial legislation has been dismissed on a preliminary objection because it is improper to embark on an identical application as one already determined.[20]

5) Relevance of Ultimate Entitlement; Definition of "Child of the Marriage"

A court cannot undertake an intensive investigation of the facts on a motion for interim child support. Where the court is satisfied on the available material that there is a likelihood that permanent support will be ordered, an interim child support order is appropriate.[21]

Where an issue is raised on an application for interim child support as to whether the respondent stood in the place of a parent to the child, the court must be satisfied that a *prima facie* case has been established before granting an order.[22] To establish a *prima facie*

---

12 *Mitchell v Mitchell* (1993), 129 NSR (2d) 351 (TD); *Sauve v Watson*, 2021 ONSC 4188; compare *Zemliak v Zemliak* (1992), 40 RFL (3d) 181 (Man CA).

13 *Boznick v Boznick* (1993), 45 RFL (3d) 354 (BCSC).

14 *Wedgwood v Wedgwood* (1988), 69 Nfld & PEIR 134 (Nfld UFC).

15 *Purse v Purse* (1987), 50 Man R (2d) 9 (QB).

16 *Gobeille v Savard*, [1975] CA 94 (Que CA).

17 *Asselstine v Asselstine*, unreported, 14 February 1972 (Ont CA).

18 *Jochimski v Jochimski* (1994), 2 BCLR (3d) 191 (SC); *Goodfellow v Goodfellow* (1982), 38 OR (2d) 54 (HCJ).

19 *B(R) v B(M)* (1989), 19 RFL (3d) 92 (Ont HCJ).

20 *Mudrinic v Mudrinic* (1978), 6 RFL (2d) 326 at 328 (Ont HCJ).

21 *Richardson v Richardson*, [2002] OJ No 2463 (SCJ).

22 *TIM v TLM*, [2003] BCJ No 2902 (SC); *Bell v Bell*, [2006] OJ No 2843 (SCJ); *Wojcichowsky v Wojcichowsky*, 2009 SKQB 89.

case, there must be evidence before the court as to the nature and quality of the respondent's relationship with the children.[23]

Interim child support may be ordered on the basis of *prima facie* evidence that one spouse stood in the place of a parent to the other spouse's child from a prior relationship, without prejudice to a trial judge's right to revisit the issue.[25] An order should be denied where there is insufficient material before the court to warrant such a finding.[26] The applicant assumes the onus of establishing a *prima facie* case that her spouse stood in the place of a parent to the applicant's child.[27]

A court will not order a step-parent to pay interim child support where the affidavit evidence is contradictory and the court is unable to determine whether or not the step-parent stood in the place of a parent to his wife's children from her previous marriage. Where there is a genuine triable issue or a *prima facie* case has not been made, the matter should be resolved by a trial judge who can order retroactive child support if a parent/child relationship is established on the evidence.[28]

On an interim application, an applicant must establish a *prima facie* case of entitlement and, if there is a significant conflict on the evidence, the matter should be determined at pre-trial or trial.[29] Faced with conflicting affidavits on an application for interim child support, a chambers judge may conclude that a *prima facie* case has not been established that the respondent stood in the place of a parent to the child and that it will take a trial to sort the matter out. An appellate court should not disturb that conclusion unless the chambers judge has abused his or her discretion by acting on some wrong principle, by disregarding some material fact, or by failing to act judicially.[30]

6) Application of *Federal Child Support Guidelines*

Interim support should cover those needs that will arise from the time of the application until the litigation is completed.[31] Because the interim process and the volume of motions prevent the kind of decisive and informed findings possible only after a trial, it is the task on an interim motion to consider the situations of the parties as they appear at the time of the interim order and foreseeable future.[32] Extended delays in trials and supervening material changes accompanying those delays may be dealt with by motions to vary when necessary.

---

23 *Sankey v Aydt*, [2004] SJ No 673 (QB).

24 *MacDonald v Moutter*, [2000] BCJ No 2114 (SC); *MacArthur v Demers*, [1998] OJ No 5868 (Gen Div); *Sullivan v Sullivan*, [1999] OJ No 3973 (CA) (application under *Family Law Act*); *Widdis v Widdis*, [2000] SJ No 614 (QB).

25 *Benoit v Benoit*, [2000] OJ No 1019 (SCJ).

26 *Hanson v Hanson*, [1999] BCJ No 2532 (SC), citing *Newson v Newson* (1998), 115 BCAC 151; *Tamke v Tamke*, [2001] SJ No 791 (QB).

27 *McNaughton v Murray*, [2002] SJ No 223 (QB) (onus not discharged in the light of conflicting affidavits).

28 *Bourgon v Paquette*, [2004] OJ No 3236 (SCJ).

29 *Lygouriatis v Gohm*, 2006 SKQB 448.

30 *Miller v Pchajek*, [2005] SJ No 29 (CA) (leave to appeal denied).

31 *Titchener v Titchener* (1991), 31 RFL (3d) 173 (BCSC) (interim spousal support).

32 *Schultz v Schultz* (1994), 3 RFL (4th) 422 (Ont Ct Gen Div); see also *Resch v Resch* (1995), 12 RFL (4th) 410 (Man CA); *Mullins v Mullins* (1995), 12 RFL (4th) 461 (Nfld UFC).

33 *Schultz v Schultz* (1994), 3 RFL (4th) 422 (Ont Ct Gen Div).

Thereafter, it remains for the trial judge, in her unfettered discretion, to make or deny a permanent order based on the evidence adduced at trial, unless the parties resolve matters earlier by mutual agreement.[34]

Section 15.1(3) of the *Divorce Act* expressly provides that the court making an order for interim child support under section 15.1(2) of the *Divorce Act* shall do so in accordance with the applicable provisions of the *Federal Child Support Guidelines* or their federally designated provincial counterpart.

7) Interim-Interim Orders; Adjournments

If an applicant for interim support can show a *prima facie* entitlement to child support under the *Federal Child Support Guidelines* and an adjournment is sought by the respondent to permit cross-examination on the applicant's affidavit or the filing of documents in opposition to the application and such an adjournment would result in a delay of several weeks or months, it may be reasonable to require the respondent to make some financial provision to the applicant on granting the adjournment. An order to this effect is frequently referred to as an interim-interim order and can be properly characterized as an order for interim support.[35] In order to determine the applicable table amount of support under the *Federal Child Support Guidelines* and the right, if any, to special or extraordinary expenses under section 7 of the Guidelines, it is necessary to determine the income of the parties. A court may experience some difficulty in determining the appropriate interim-interim disposition, because of contradictory affidavits that have not been scrutinized by way of cross-examination. Except in rare circumstances, however, the court must grant an interim-interim order to ensure reasonable provision for the children until an interim order can be granted on the return of the motion. In endeavouring to grant an appropriate interim-interim order, the court must make findings based on a reasonable interpretation of the facts as presented by the parties. On a return of the motion after cross-examinations have been conducted, the amounts provided by the original order can be retroactively adjusted.[36]

Interim-interim orders are "band-aid" orders intended to be of short duration until the parties have furnished complete financial information to the court. When this is done, the court may order interim support in an amount less than that provided by the interim-interim order. Cases that preclude respondents from seeking a downward variation of permanent support orders until they have been put in good standing have no direct application to interim-interim orders.[37]

Ordinarily, there should only be one interim-interim order in support applications before cross-examinations are conducted and one interim order after cross-examination. Thereafter, the parties should get on to trial or settle a final order.[38]

---

34 *Ibid.*

35 *Sugar v Sugar* (1976), 23 RFL 248 (Ont CA).

36 *Lopez v Lopez*, [1998] OJ No 5370 (SC); see also *BJG v KRG*, [2001] AJ No 1310 (QB).

37 *Harris v Harris* (1982), 37 OR (2d) 552 (UFC).

38 *McEachern v McEachern* (1994), 5 RFL (4th) 115 (Ont Ct Gen Div).

8) Effect of Delay

Delay in bringing an application for interim support may negate need insofar as support for the applicant spouse is concerned, but should not operate to the prejudice of a child in respect of whom interim financial relief is sought.[39] A parent's delay in bringing a motion has no bearing on the obligation to pay interim child support, because support is the right of the child who should not be penalized by the failure of the parent to seek prompt relief.

An interim motion for child support may be allowed to proceed without a prior case conference, notwithstanding the absence of any emergency, where the interests of justice would not be served if the interim motion were not considered immediately.[41]

9) Voluntary Payments

Voluntary payments do not create a legal obligation to continue such payments; if it were otherwise, spouses would be reluctant to make temporary payments on a voluntary basis.

10) Graduated Payments

In determining the amount of interim child support having regard to the obligor's actual and anticipated income, the court may order a designated sum for the immediate future and a lesser sum after expiry of a fixed period.[43]

11) Fixed-Term Orders

Short-term interim orders, with leave to re-apply, may provide an appropriate foundation for negotiations between the parents.[44]

A fixed-term interim support order may be appropriate to encourage a party to bring the matter to trial as expeditiously as possible,[45] but a child of the marriage should not be penalized by such an order.

A fixed-term order for child support may be appropriate to provide some degree of certainty for the primary caregiving parent and child, although such an order may be varied if future adjustments prove to be necessary.[46]

---

39 *Ohayon v Ohayon*, [1969] OJ No 381 (Ont HCJ).
40 *MacArthur v Demers*, [1998] OJ No 5868 (Gen Div).
41 *Pakka v Nygard*, [2002] OJ No 3858 (SCJ).
42 *Fisher v Fisher* (1990), 28 RFL (3d) 324 (Ont HCJ).
43 Compare *Leask v Leask* (1975), 24 RFL 275 (BCSC).
44 *Ollinger v Ollinger*, [1999] SJ No 218 (QB).
45 *Cafik v Cafik* (1993), 46 RFL (3d) 321 (Ont Ct Gen Div).
46 *Melik v Ducholke*, [2004] AJ No 1190 (QB); *Wallace v Wallace*, [1998] BCJ No 2086 (SC); *Pawlus v Pawlus*, [2004] OJ No 5706 (SCJ).

12) Interim Spousal Support; Interim Child Support

Interim child support may be granted even when interim spousal support is denied to the applicant.[47] The converse is also true.[48]

13) Retroactive Interim Orders

Although the court has the discretion to order interim support payable as of the date considered appropriate, interim orders are usually made effective as of the date of service of the notice of motion, which is the formal demand for payment.[49] While there may be reasons why an order should not be so backdated, these should be stated; otherwise, an appellate tribunal may conclude that the discretion was not exercised judicially in departing from the date of service of the notice of motion.[50] A court may make a provisional determination of a parent's annual income for the purpose of granting an interim order for prospective and retroactive child support pending further financial disclosure, where the child support being paid is clearly far too low in light of the *Federal Child Support Guidelines*. The calculation of retroactive child support under these circumstances may be declared subject to review and recalculation after financial disclosure has been provided.[51] In granting an interim child support order with retroactive effect to the month in which the motion was brought, the motion judge may expressly preserve the applicant's right to seek further retroactivity at trial.[52]

Where retroactivity will be of relatively short duration and encompasses a period during which the parties were negotiating, there is no reason why the issue of retroactivity cannot be dealt with on an interim motion, because the trial judge will be no better placed to determine the issue than the motion judge.[53] In *Steinhuebl v Steinhuebl*,[54] where the applicant unequivocally asserted an intention to seek support but the launching of proceedings was delayed while *bona fide* negotiations between the solicitors were carried on promptly and expeditiously, it was held that interim support might be ordered effective from the date when the demand for support had been made. The court considered that to insist in all cases that interim support could not be obtained until after an application therefore had been brought might precipitate the early launching of motions, which would seriously interfere with the possibilities of consensual resolution.

If there are substantial issues to be argued and retroactivity is sought from a date preceding the application for interim child support, the issue of retroactivity should be left to the trial judge.[55] For example, the issue of retroactive child support may be left for the trial judge to determine because it would require a pre-determination of one of the issues set

---

47 *Hryhoriw v Hryhoriw* (1973), 9 RFL 287 (Sask QB); see also *Horne v Horne* (1989), 19 RFL (3d) 399 (BCSC).

48 *Lopez v Lopez* (1993), 48 RFL (3d) 298 (Ont Ct Gen. Div).

49 *Woroniuk v Woroniuk*, 2011 MBQB 268.

50 *Butilkin v Butilkin*, [1972] OJ No 280 (CA); see also *Smith v Smith*, [1999] BCJ No 1399 (SC); *AL v OG*, [2000] QJ No 912 (CS); compare *Staples v Callender*, 2010 NSCA 49.

51 *MacIntosh v MacIntosh*, [2003] AJ No 728 (QB).

52 *Torti v Torti*, [2001] OJ No 1827 (SCJ).

53 *Gregorash v Comuzzi*, [1999] OJ No 1856 (SCJ).

54 (1970), 2 RFL 317 (Ont CA).

55 *ALY v LMY*, [2001] AJ No 506 (QB); *Villeneuve v Lafferty*, [1999] NWTJ No 128 (SC); *Gregorash v Comuzzi*, [1999] OJ No 1856 (SCJ). Compare *McConkey v McConkey*, 2022 ONSC 4600.

for trial, namely, whether director fees payable to the petitioner as a result of the sale of certain shares constitute income for the purpose of the *Federal Child Support Guidelines* matrimonial property that is subject to statutory division between the parties.[56] It has been judicially asserted that there is no mechanism in an interlocutory proceeding to make a final determination as to the right to retroactive child support. Consequently, a retroactive order, whereby child support becomes payable from a date preceding the application, such as the date of spousal separation, should not be granted in a proceeding for interim child support; any such retroactive order should be made after trial.[57] However, retroactive child support may be ordered on an application for interim child support when the facts and law are clear and there is no triable issue.[58] Such an award remains an interim order and, in principle, subject to variation, but once the issue of retroactive support is concluded in chambers in a clear case, the parties may find it unnecessary to further address the issue by way of a pre-trial conference or a trial.[59] When the facts and the law are in dispute and the situation is unclear, the issue of retroactive support should be left to the trial judge, failing settlement by means of a pre-trial conference.[60] Motions for temporary orders are not well-suited to dealing with retroactive claims where there is a lack of clarity on factual and financial issues due to competing affidavits. These issues are better determined by the give and take of the negotiation process or, if necessary, by trial with oral testimony and cross-examination.[61]

14) Subsequent Adjustment of Interim Order

An interim order for child support does not preclude a final order for retroactive child sup port that pre-dates the interim order.[62] Where the amount of child support was originally fixed by a parental agreement and the amount was reasonable, that amount may be used, rather than the Guidelines amount, in quantifying the arrears of child support to be paid.

Where the annual income of the obligor is unpredictable, a court may fix the monthly amount of interim child support on the basis of the average of the obligor's annual income over the preceding three years, but may direct a future accounting when the actual income becomes known in the following year, at which time any income in excess of that imputed will require an upward adjustment and the payment of those arrears and, if the actual income is lower than that imputed, a downwards adjustment of the monthly payments will be cred ited against the subsequent years' support.[64] An interim order may be retroactively adjusted upwards at trial if the obligor's income was in fact higher than anticipated; it can also be

56 *Wouters v Wouters*, 2001 SKQB 142.

57 *Mills v Mills*, [1999] SJ No 177 (QB).

58 *Graham v Tomlinson*, 2010 SKCA 101; see also *Hennenfent v Loftsgard*, 2015 SKQB 289; *Grose v Grose* 2016 SKQB 339; *CTG v RRG*, 2016 SKQB 387; *Podruchny v Evans*, 2018 SKQB 262.

59 *Graham v Tomlinson*, 2010 SKCA 101.

60 *Mayson-Blacklaws v Blacklaws*, 2011 SKQB 334; *Kozak v Moore*, 2020 SKQB 22; see also *Denis v Denis* 2012 SKQB 49 (variation of separation agreement). As to variation applications based on affidavit evidence, see *Lamontagne v Culham*, 2013 SKQB 96, citing *Malinowski v Malinowski*, 2010 SKQB 27.

61 *Douglas v Faucher*, 2014 ONSC 4045 at para 11, James J. See also *Miller v White*, 2018 PECA 11.

62 *Thomas v Thomas*, 2014 ABQB 481 at para 48; see also *CTG v RRG*, 2016 SKQB 387.

63 *Collinge v Collinge*, [2004] BCJ No 1707 (SC).

64 *Gregorash v Comuzzi*, [1999] OJ No 1856 (SCJ).

retroactively adjusted downwards if the obligor's income subsequently turns out to be lower than expected.[65]

The fact that the permanent order for child support differs from the interim order is not self-sufficient to justify a retroactive adjustment of the interim order.[66] A trial judge may grant a retroactive order for the applicable table amount of child support and for "add-ons" with respect to child care expenses falling within section 7 of the *Federal Child Support Guidelines*, where inequities would otherwise result under a pre-existing interim order. In fixing the amount payable under the court-ordered retroactive adjustment, the court will determine what amount should have been payable under the Guidelines in light of the parental income and deduct the amount already paid.[67]

A court may grant an interim order for retroactive child support where the obligor has been paying less than the applicable table amount of child support, without prejudice to the right of a trial judge to increase the period of retroactivity or the amount payable after the obligor's income has been determined on more substantial evidence.[68]

An order for retroactive child support may be deemed appropriate where better information is available to the trial judge than was available to the chambers judge on the motion for interim support. The responsibility of a trial judge to ensure that a reasonable amount of support has been paid when the interim order was in effect is more obvious when the chambers judge expressly indicated that the amount stipulated in the interim order was without prejudice to the right to seek a retroactive adjustment at trial.[69] The doctrine of *res judicata* does not prevent retroactive adjustment of an interim order by the trial judge.[70] Lump sum retroactive support or permanent support orders that are intended to compensate for inadequate interim orders are the exception rather than the rule.[71]

Retroactive variation of a consent order for interim child support may be ordered by the trial judge where the obligor's income fell short of that previously imputed to him.[72]

A court may refuse to retroactively reduce interim support orders for spousal and child support because of the attendant circumstances, including the modest amounts involved, the payor's delay in returning to court, and his prior default in making support payments. Prospective payments may be adjusted, however, to reflect the income judicially attributed to the parent after consideration of the evidence and the *Federal Child Support Guidelines*.[73]

15) Interim and Permanent Orders; Effect of Delay Before Trial

Interim applications usually fall short of providing the full information and particulars necessary for a long-term disposition. An interim support order is temporary and is intended to

65 *NMM v NSM*, [2004] BCJ No 642 (SC). See also *JSG v MFG*, 2011 MBQB 177.
66 *Dyck v Highton*, [2003] SJ No 600 (QB).
67 *Leis v Leis*, [2002] OJ No 4306 (SCJ). See also *Woroniuk v Woroniuk*, 2011 MBQB 268.
68 *VAW v RL*, [2004] OJ No 3418 (SCJ).
69 *Vitagliano v Di Stavolo*, [2001] OJ No 1138 (SCJ).
70 *DL v GSL*, [2001] OJ No 2824 (SCJ).
71 *Zdan v Zdan*, [2001] MJ No 444 (QB).
72 *Plett v Plett*, [2002] BCJ No 2078 (SC); *Cooper v Cooper*, [2004] OJ No 5096 (SCJ) (overpayments set off against property division entitlements).
73 *LSP v JRP*, [2002] SJ No 35 (QB).

tide the parties over until the matter can be resolved on a permanent basis. An interim order is not binding on a trial judge who will be called upon to render a decision after hearing all the evidence.[74] The judicial substitution of a permanent order for child support in place of an interim order does not require a material change of circumstances.[75] A trial judge making a final support order is entitled to review an existing interim order to determine if any adjustments in the financial relationship between the parties are required. Such a review may provide for a retroactive increase or decrease in the amount of support payable.[76] An order for permanent child support may be more substantial in amount than a pre-existing interim order, but the decision in favour of an increased amount after appropriate evidence has been adduced does not necessarily render the interim order inappropriate and, therefore, in need of a retroactive lump sum adjustment.[77] A trial judge is not compelled to top up an interim support order by a lump sum or supplementary periodic payments in light of a subsequent attribution of income.[78]

16) Right to Be Heard; Adjournments

In order for a court to determine disputed issues in interim proceedings, both parties must have a real opportunity to place evidence before the court. In granting an adjournment to enable a spouse to present relevant evidence, conditions may be imposed to ensure that the necessary evidence is brought before the court in a timely manner.[79]

In *Guptill v Guptill*,[80] it was held that a judge's failure to afford the respondent's solicitor an opportunity to cross-examine the applicant and his failure to rule on the request for an adjournment effectively precluded the respondent from having his day in court. Counsel for the parties must always be permitted to test their opponent's affidavit evidence.[81] A court should not grant interim relief based merely on an applicant's untested evidence.[82] Where there has been an unreasonable delay in bringing the application for interim support, it would be a proper exercise of judicial discretion to grant the respondent's request for an adjournment without imposing any immediate obligation to pay interim support.[83]

17) Variation of Interim Orders

Although sections 15.1(2) and 17 of the *Divorce Act* and section 14 of the *Federal Child Support Guidelines* include no express provision for the variation, rescission, or suspension of

74 *Smith v Smith*, [2001] AJ No 1420 (CA); *FJN v JK*, 2019 ABCA 305 at para 55; *Sutherland v Sutherland*, 2023 ABCA 121; *Doerksen v Houlahan*, 2012 MBQB 110; *DAT v SLP*, 2018 NBQB 135; *BM v KR*, 2022 NBCA 50 at para 61; *Crook v Crook* (1992), 42 RFL (3d) 297 (NSTD); *Wharry v Wharry*, 2016 ONCA 930.

75 *Allen v Allen*, [2000] BCJ No 2474 (SC).

76 *Durocher v Klementovich*, 2013 ABCA 115; *Cherewyk v Cherewyk*, 2018 MBCA 13; *Cisecki v Cisecki*, 2011 ONSC 1343; *ACG v WLG*, 2020 SKQB 43.

77 *Stephen v Stephen*, [1999] SJ No 479 (QB).

78 *L'Heureux v L'Heureux*, [1999] SJ No 437 (QB).

79 *Martindale v Martindale* (1990), 30 RFL (3d) 229 (Man CA) (interim parenting orders).

80 (1987), 11 RFL (3d) 278 (NSCA).

81 *Magionas v Magionas* (1988), 12 RFL (3d) 194 (NSCA).

82 *Gibb v Gibb*, [1987] OJ No 982 (HCJ).

83 *Sugar v Sugar* (1976), 23 RFL 248 (Ont CA); compare *Leigh v Leigh* (1976), 26 RFL 282 (Ont HCJ).

interim child support orders, courts have the inherent jurisdiction to vary an interim support order under the *Divorce Act* when the assumptions on which the order was made later prove to have been clearly understated or where material changes have occurred on an interim basis.[84] The jurisdiction to vary, rescind, or suspend interim child support orders survives under section 15.1(2) of the *Divorce Act*, notwithstanding that section 17(1)(a) of the Act expressly provides only for applications to vary, rescind, or suspend "a support order" being made by "either or both *former* spouses."[85] Section 17(1)(a) is clearly directed at permanent, not interim, orders. Any contrary interpretation of section 17(1)(a)[86] is inconsistent with the definitions of "support order," "child support order," and "spousal support order" in section 2(1) of the *Divorce Act*, which refer only to permanent child support orders and spousal support orders granted pursuant to sections 15.1(1) and 15.2(1) respectively, and thereby exclude interim orders granted pursuant to sections 15.1(2) and 15.2(2). Section 17(1)(a) of the *Divorce Act* cannot be construed, therefore, as precluding an application to vary, rescind, or suspend an interim order during the subsistence of the marriage, where circumstances would justify a change in that order. Justice Vertes of the Northwest Territories Supreme Court has suggested that section 14 of the *Federal Child Support Guidelines* directly applies to both interim and permanent orders for child support[87] but this interpretation overlooks the opening words of section 14 of the Guidelines, whereby it purports to apply "[for] the purposes of section 17(4) of the [*Divorce*] *Act*." There is no doubt, however, that courts continue to have an inherent jurisdiction to vary interim orders under section 15.1(2) of the *Divorce Act* and, in so doing, they are required to apply the *Federal Child Support Guidelines* in accordance with the express provisions of section 15.1(3) of the *Divorce Act*.[88]

Proof of a material change since previous interim-interim orders were made is not necessary where the court is currently in a position to make a finding with respect to the husband's income and make an appropriate interim order based on that finding.[89]

An application to vary an interim order need not be heard by the same judge who made the original order. It has been asserted that when a court has jurisdiction over the parties, it may vary an interim order made under the *Divorce Act* by a superior court in another province.[90]

Although the *Federal Child Support Guidelines* apply to interim orders granted pursuant to the *Divorce Act*, there is still merit in the long-standing approach that applications to vary interim orders should not be encouraged and that a heavy onus falls on a party who seeks to

---

84 *Jaggs v Jaggs*, 2018 BCSC 1578; *Lahanky v Lahanky*, 2011 NBQB 220 (withholding of full and accurate financial disclosure); *Janmohamed v Janmohamed*, 2014 BCSC 107; *BDD v GTS*, 2021 BCSC 1010; *Wakeman v Wakeman*, 2021 BCSC 1095; *Gilkinson v Nichols*, 2023 ONSC 1504; *CTG v RRG*, 2016 SKQB 387, citing *Prescesky v Prescesky*, 2015 SKCA 111 wherein the term "inherent" is questioned; *WLG v ACG*, 2021 SKCA 112.

85 *Hama v Werbes*, [1999] BCJ No 2558 (SC); see also *Stannard v Stannard* (1991), 34 RFL (3d) 249 (Alta QB); *McLeod v McLeod* (1993), 45 RFL (3d) 181 (NS Fam Ct); *Monkhouse v Monkhouse* (1987), 10 RFL (3d) 445 (Sask QB).

86 See *Heschel v Heschel* (1991), 119 AR 35 (QB); *Dupont v Dupont* (1993), 47 RFL (3d) 273 (BCSC); *Validen v Validen* (1990), 30 RFL (3d) 163 (Man QB); *Biddle v Biddle*, [2005] OJ No 737 (SCJ); *Wolkowski v Doroshenko*, [2002] SJ No 170 (QB).

87 *Beilstein v Beilstein*, [1999] NWTJ No 34 (SC).

88 *Janmohamed v Janmohamed*, 2014 BCSC 107.

89 *Haq v Haq*, [2003] OJ No 4687 (SCJ).

90 *Scott v Scott*, [1999] SJ No 659 (QB).

vary an interim order. If a party is unhappy with an interim arrangement, the action should be brought to trial where all relevant facts can be adequately analyzed. A court may refuse to vary an interim order for child support where the obligor's earning capacity is in dispute and would be better left for the trial judge who could order a retroactive decrease, if appropriate, and adjust the future child support payments accordingly.[91] Orders to vary interim support should not be granted lightly, particularly where an appropriate adjustment can be made at the trial. There is a heavy onus on a person who moves to vary an interim order instead of proceeding to trial.[93] The applicant must meet the burden of establishing a material change in circum stances, having regard to the obligor's income with respect to the basic table amount and the condition, means, needs, and other circumstances of the parties and of the child where the amount of child support falls subject to the exercise of judicial discretion under sections 3 to 5, 7, and 9 of the *Federal Child Support Guidelines*. Applications to vary orders for interim relief are rare and are not to be encouraged[94] in the absence of a supervening inability to pay. Where there has been a substantial reduction in the payor's income, a downward variation may be appropriate,[96] but a parent who invokes poverty or an inability to pay as a reason to vary an interim child support order must be prepared to make the fullest financial disclosure.

The following policy reasons have been judicially identified to explain why courts should not vary orders for interim support in the absence of a compelling change of circumstances that would result in serious prejudice to either or both parties if the order were left untouched:

1) Interim orders are often based on conflicting affidavit evidence without the benefit of examinations for discovery and complete financial disclosure;
2) The parental obligation to support a child is based on earning capacity, not simply on the income earned;
3) Children should not bear the brunt of temporary changes in their parents' financial circumstances;
4) The best interests of children are served by an expeditious order for permanent child support; and
5) Adjustments can usually be made for any prior inequities by the trial judge who has the benefit of full financial disclosure and can review all relevant evidence.[98]

---

91 *Anderson v Anderson*, [2000] AJ No 752 (QB); *McInnes v Young*, [1998] NWTJ No 91 (SC).

92 See *Leontowicz v Leontowicz*, 2020 ABCA 324 at para 9; *Rolinger v Rolinger*, 2021 ABQB 474; *Sutherland v Sutherland*, 2023 ABCA 121; *Drozdzik v Drozdzik* (1992), 39 RFL (3d) 138 (BCCA); *Cherewyk v Cherewyk* 2018 MBCA 13; *Dumont v Dumont* (1987), 86 NBR (2d) 183 (QB); *Miller v Miller* (1994), 4 RFL (4th) 33 (NSCA); *Nova Scotia (Community Services) v EL*, 2020 NSSC 193; *Connell v Connell*, [2006] PEIJ No 12 (SCTD); *Merrifield v Merrifield*, 2021 SKCA 85. Compare *Werden v Werden*, [2005] OJ No 5257 (Sup Ct).

93 *Stannard v Stannard* (1991), 34 RFL (3d) 249 (Alta QB); *Jaggs v Jaggs*, 2018 BCSC 1578; *Coley v Coley* (1981), 20 RFL (2d) 327 (Man CA).

94 *Cherewyk v Cherewyk*, 2018 MBCA 13; *Carvell v Carvell*, [1969] 2 OR 513 (CA); *Biddle v Biddle*, [2005] OJ No 737 (SCJ).

95 *Witt v Johnson*, 2022 ABQB 105; *Nein v Nein* (1991), 36 RFL (3d) 417 (Sask QB).

96 *Hama v Werbes*, [2000] BCJ No 1556 (SC) (substantial reduction in obligor's income coupled with significant delay in getting to trial); see also *Hunt v Hunt* (1994), 94 Man R (2d) 81 (QB) (application under *The Family Maintenance Act*, RSM 1987, c F-20); *Renpenning v Renpenning* (1992), 103 Sask R 23 (QB).

97 *Beilstein v Beilstein*, [1999] NWTJ No 34 (SC).

98 *Hama v Werbes*, [1999] BCJ No 2558 (SC), Martinson J; *Lussier v Lussier*, 2012 MBQB 274.

On an application to vary an order for interim support, the court may order a retroactive variation of the order by reason of the obligor's reduced capacity to pay arising from temporary unemployment.[99] The power to vary the order retroactively may be exercised even though the notice of motion does not specifically seek retroactive variation,[100] but the party should be given an adequate opportunity to respond to any belated application. Given the nature of the respective proceedings, a court is more likely to remit arrears of child support that have accrued under an interim order than under a permanent order.[101]

Continuing negotiations constitute no bar to variation of an interim order for child support.[102]

Arrears of child support and spousal support that have accrued under interim orders are not discharged by a subsequent discontinuance of the action but judicial remission of part of the arrears may be justified by the obligor's severe decline in income after the interim orders were granted.[103]

The Supreme Court of British Columbia lacks jurisdiction to vary an interim child support order of the Provincial Court.[104]

18) Appeals of Interim Orders[105]

In British Columbia, an appeal from an order for interim support from a Master lies to the Supreme Court rather than the Court of Appeal.[106]

Appellate courts have endorsed a general policy of not disturbing interim orders and are very reluctant to interfere with interim support orders, unless there is an obvious error or patent injustice that must be immediately corrected.[107] Appeals respecting interim support orders are generally discouraged and will usually be dismissed, unless the trial date is so far in advance that the matter must be reviewed.[108] This is so because an appeal of an interim order can become an excuse to delay the trial.[109] The appellate court will intervene in interim support matters if it is clearly of the opinion that the amount awarded is inordinately high or if an

99 See *Fedorovich v Fedorovich* (1974), 15 RFL 386 (Alta TD), applying *McIndoe v McIndoe* (1966), 57 WWR 577 (Sask QB) and *Belof v Belof* (1972), 9 RFL 60 (Sask QB); *Guy v Guy* (1975), 22 RFL 82 (Ont HCJ).

100 *Fedorovich v Fedorovich* (1974), 15 RFL 386 (Alta TD).

101 *Mickey v Mickey*, [1998] BCJ No 1805 (SC).

102 *Smith v Smith*, [1999] BCJ No 1399 (SC).

103 *Greco v Greco*, [2000] OJ No 3594 (SCJ) (reduced arrears to be paid by monthly instalments without interest; monthly instalments to increase when child no longer eligible for ongoing periodic support; reduced arrears to be paid in entirety upon obligor's receipt of inheritance).

104 *Schlichting v Gauld*, [1999] BCJ No 928 (SC).

105 As to whether leave to appeal is necessary, see Chapter 15, Section D.

106 *De Grandis v De Grandis* (1990), 28 RFL (3d) 45 (BCSC).

107 *Rogers v Lowe*, [2001] BCJ No 2329 (SC); *Cherewyk v Cherewyk*, 2018 MBCA 13; *SS v DS*, 2010 NSCA 74; *Miller v White*, 2018 PECA 11; *Droit de la famille — 142281*, 2014 QCCA 1692 (interim spousal support); *Potzus v Potzus*, 2017 SKCA 15.

108 *Leontowicz v Leontowicz*, 2020 ABCA 324 at para 9; *Graveline v Graveline*, 2024 ABCA 31 at para 13; *Phillips v Phillips* (1985), 43 RFL (2d) 462 at 463 (BCCA); *Loesch v Walji*, 2008 BCCA 214; *Benoit v Benoit*, 2019 MBCA 106; *Hickey v Hickey* (1994), 2 RFL (4th) 65 (NSCA); *Foss v Foss* (1991), 31 RFL (3d) 367 (Sask CA); *Merrifield v Merrifield*, 2021 SKCA 85.

109 *Langevin v Langevin* (1955), 10 RFL (4th) 229 (Alta CA).

error in law has been demonstrated.[110] An appellate court should not interfere with an interim order unless it is clearly wrong and exceeds the wide ambit of reasonable solutions that are available in summary interim proceedings,[111] although trial judges must adhere to the applicable provincial or territorial tables in determining the amount of child support except insofar as the *Federal Child Support Guidelines* or section 15.1 of the *Divorce Act* provide otherwise.

An appeal from an interim order does not operate to stay the execution of the order unless so ordered by a judge or by the officer whose decision is complained of.[112]

There is no statutory or inherent authority in any Ontario court to grant or reaffirm an order for interim corollary relief pending an appeal from the judgment in the trial proceeding.

C. PERIODIC AND LUMP SUM PAYMENTS

1) Section 11 of Guidelines

Section 11 of the *Federal Child Support Guidelines* provides that the court making a child support order may require the spouse against whom the order is made to pay the amount in periodic payments, in a lump sum, or in a lump sum and periodic payments. No criteria are defined to indicate when a lump sum might be appropriate,[114] but they are relatively rare and are only made in special circumstances.[115]

2) Limits on Judicial Discretion

Although lump sum child support and orders to secure child support are now regulated by sections 11 and 12 of the *Federal Child Support Guidelines*, instead of by the provisions of the *Divorce Act*, it has been judicially asserted that no policy change has thereby ensued. This may be true in the sense that lump sum orders for prospective child support are still exceptional[117] and caselaw suggests that a specific or immediate need for a lump sum must be shown, or there must be a history of default,[118] or a record of poor money management, or an inclination to risk the family's economic security.[119] In the words of Smith J of the British Columbia Supreme Court in *Santelli v Trinetti*:

> Such orders are exceptional and restricted to cases where there are special circumstances such as animosity between the parties, the paying party's inability to make periodic payments,

---

110 *Loesch v Walji*, 2008 BCCA 214; *Bacon v Bacon* (1991), 33 RFL (3d) 170 (Sask CA); compare *Webster v Lusty* (1992), 44 RFL (3d) 56 (Man CA).

111 *Haigh v Haigh* (1987), 9 RFL (3d) 301 (BCCA); *Webster v Lusty* (1992), 44 RFL (3d) 56 (Man CA); *Wellman v Gilcash*, [2003] NBJ No 214 (CA); *Sypher v Sypher* (1986), 2 RFL (3d) 413 at 413–14 (Ont CA).

112 *Parkinson v Parkinson* (1974), 16 RFL 135 (Ont HCJ).

113 *Siemieniuk v Siemieniuk* (1976), 7 RFL (2d) 90 (Ont CA).

114 *Tauber v Tauber*, [2001] OJ No 3259 (SCJ).

115 *Santelli v Trinetti*, 2019 BCCA 319; *Shock v Shock*, 2019 BCSC 2179; *SLH v AWH*, 2020 YKSC 12.

116 *Strand v Strand*, [1999] AJ No 545 (QB).

117 See *Santelli v Trinetti*, 2019 BCCA 319; *PMZ v DJT*, 2023 BCSC 1444 at paras 242–45.

118 *Strand v Strand*, [1999] AJ No 545 (QB); *Hunt v Smolis-Hunt*, [2001] AJ No 1170 (CA); *SJB v RDBB*, 2019 ABQB 624; *Mansoor v Mansoor*, 2012 BCSC 602; *Tauber v Tauber*, [2001] OJ No 3259 (SCJ).

119 *Wilson v Eronchi*, [2000] NWTJ No 3 (SC) (application under *Children's Law Act*); *AL v OG*, [2000] QJ No. 912 (CS).

difficulties enforcing orders for support, and the risk that the available monies will be otherwise squandered or dissipated. They are more common where children are only two or three years away from being self-supporting: *Komori v. Malins*, 1996 CanLII 470 (BC CA), 24 R.F.L. (4th) 1, at paras. 71 and 72.[120]

Given that the *Federal Child Support Guidelines* normally determine a monthly amount of table support on the basis of the obligor's income and the number of children entitled to support, there are limitations on the right of a court to order prospective lump sum child support pursuant to section 11 of the Guidelines.[121] Absent a finding of undue hardship within the meaning of section 10 of the Guidelines,[122] lump sum orders may be available by way of retroactive child support, section 7 expenses, or pursuant to section 3(2)(b) of the Guidelines for the support of a child over the age of majority,[123] but a court has no general discretionary jurisdiction under section 11 of the *Federal Child Support Guidelines* to order lump sum child support. If the attendant circumstances, such as a history of default or the likelihood of future default, render a lump sum order necessary to protect the financial interests of the child, the periodic amount of child support must first be determined and then converted into a lump sum payment, preferably with the aid of actuarial evidence.[124] Some of the limitations relating to lump sum child support orders may be addressed by an order to secure periodic child support payments that is available under section 12 of the *Federal Child Support Guidelines*.[125]

The ensuing analysis, which incorporates cases decided under the pre-Guidelines child support regime, must be understood as falling subject to the aforementioned inherent limitations concerning the jurisdiction of the court to order lump sum support under section 11 of the Guidelines.

3) Consent Orders for Lump Sum in Lieu of Periodic Child Support

Section 15.1(7) of the *Divorce Act* empowers a court to order an amount of child support that is different from the amount that would be determined under the *Federal Child Support Guidelines* if both spouses consent and the court is satisfied that reasonable arrangements have been made for the support of the children. A court may consequently grant a consent order that provides lump sum support to meet the post-secondary education costs of adult children.[126] Similarly, a court may conclude that reasonable arrangements for the support

---

120 *Santelli v Trinetti*, 2018 BCSC 300 at para 192. As to discounting a lump sum order for child support to reflect present value and future contingencies, see *PMZ v DJT*, 2023 BCSC 1444.

121 *Ibid*; see also *Erikson v Cabeza*, [2002] BCJ No 286 (SCJ); compare *Hunt v Smolis-Hunt*, [2001] AJ No 1170 (CA). And see *Purtzki v Saunders*, 2016 BCCA 344. Compare *Hewett v Hewett*, 2016 BCSC 2429 at para 39.

122 See Section C(5), below in this chapter.

123 *Finlay v Finlay*, [2004] NBJ No 448 (QB).

124 *Scorgie v Scorgie*, [2006] OJ No 225 (SCJ); *Chamanlall v Chamanlall*, [2006] OJ No 251 (SCJ). See also *MEC v DEJ*, [2009] BCJ No 766 (SC) (lump sum for two years; periodic support thereafter); *KAL v KJL*, 2017 BCSC 651; *GKD v CSD*, 2021 BCSC 367; *Segat v Segat*, 2015 ONCA 16; *Studzinski v Studzinski*, 2020 ONSC 2540.

125 *Finlay v Finlay*, 2004 NBQB 138.

126 *Alexander v Alexander*, [1999] OJ No 3694 (SCJ).

of the children have been achieved by minutes of settlement that provide for the transfer of the obligor's equity in the matrimonial home to the parent with whom the children will be living while attending university, such transfer, in effect, constituting a lump sum payment in lieu of periodic support under the Guidelines.[127]

4) Lump Sums in Addition to Periodic Sums to Reflect Bonuses

A court may order a lump sum in addition to periodic child support to reflect actual and projected bonuses that the obligor has received or will receive as a supplement to his annual income,[128] but an application by the obligor to delay payment of a portion of the applicable table amount of child support until the annual bonus is received may be dismissed where the obligor has been making insufficient contributions to the support of the children.[129]

5) Undue Hardship May Trigger Lump Sum

A court may order lump sum child support in addition to[130] or in lieu of[131] periodic child sup port where undue hardship would be suffered by the children, if there were strict adherence to an income based assessment under the *Federal Child Support Guidelines.*

6) Lump Sum by Instalments

Lump sum child support may be ordered to be paid in two[132] or more instalments.

7) Lump Sum Interim Orders

In the absence of a failure to recognize an obvious obligation or an attempt to avoid it, a parent should not ordinarily be ordered to pay a lump sum for child support on an interim basis. The purpose of an interim order is to make temporary provision for children pending trial. An order for lump sum child support should not ordinarily be made until the spousal property division has been finalized and all material facts are known.[133]

8) Lump Sum Capitalization of Periodic Support

In granting a lump sum order for child support instead of an order for periodic payments, it is customary for the courts to capitalize the periodic payments that would otherwise have

---

127 *Khullar v Khullar*, [1999] AJ No 1260 (QB) (mother entitled to renew application for support in the event of a material change of circumstances).

128 *Jackson v Holloway*, [1997] SJ No 691 (QB).

129 *Schmid v Smith*, [1999] OJ No 3062 (SCJ).

130 *Gibney v Gibney*, [1998] BCJ No 632 (SC).

131 *Trebilcock v Trebilcock*, 2012 ONCA 452.

132 *Ibid.*

133 *Dram v Foster*, 2009 MBCA 125. Compare *Chiaramonte v Chiaramonte*, 2012 ONSC 6886 at para 22 (interim spousal support).

been ordered.[134] Thus, lump sum child support may be ordered on the basis of actuarial evidence respecting capitalization of the periodic support payable pursuant to the applicable provincial table under the *Federal Child Support Guidelines* where there is a real possibility that the obligor would not comply with an order for periodic support.[135]

9) Periodic Support as the Norm

Although the amount of child support under the applicable provincial table is calculated on a monthly basis, the court may order proportionate payments to be made on a weekly[136] or fortnightly basis.[137] Lump sum orders have generally been restricted to cases involving special circumstances and seem to be more commonly ordered when the children are within two or three years of becoming self-supporting.[138] Lump sum child support has been awarded where the obligor's unemployment is intentional.[139]

Section 11 of the *Federal Child Support Guidelines* empowers the court to order a lump sum in place of periodic support for the children but the lump sum must reflect the support otherwise due under the Guidelines.[140] There are exceptional situations where the courts have found lump sum orders to be appropriate, for example, where a parent has failed to discharge financial responsibilities in the past or is likely to do so in the future,[141] where no voluntary payments were made during the period of separation,[142] or where the obligor has a history of irresponsible money management.[143] Lump sum child support is rarely appropriate, unless there is no reasonable alternative. A lump sum that seeks to capitalize the amount of child support that would otherwise be payable under a periodic order cannot reflect the annual adjustments envisaged for periodic child support orders under the Guidelines. A lump sum based on present earnings denies the opportunity for adjustment to reflect a rise or fall in the payor's income and the ability of children to benefit from annual increases in remuneration.[144] Actuarial calculations may be judicially endorsed, however, that take account of such prospective increases in the capitalization of the lump sum to be paid in

134 *BAS v GDS*, [2000] AJ No 192 (QB); *Venco v Lie*, 2009 BCSC 831 (lump sum pre-payment of table amount of child support for three years.); *MacDonald v MacDonald*, [1997] OJ No 4250 (CA); *Jones v Jones*, [2001] SJ No 199 (QB).

135 *KV v TE*, [2004] BCJ No 792 (SC); *GKD v CSD*, 2021 BCSC 367; *Swanson v Swanson*, [2004] OJ No 5266 (SCJ).

136 *Smith v Smith*, [2001] NSJ No 8 (SC); *Duffy v Duffy*, [1999] OJ No 3663 (Gen Div) (weekly payments judicially perceived as more likely to be paid).

137 *McLaughlin v McLaughlin*, [1999] BCJ No 485 (CA).

138 *Komori v Malins* (1996), 24 RFL (4th) 1 (BCCA); see also *BAS v GDS*, [2000] AJ No 192 (QB); *Ahenkora v Ahenkora*, [1999] BCJ No 1770 (SC).

139 *Swanson v Swanson*, [2004] OJ No 5266 (SCJ); compare *Burry v Burry*, 2011 NLTD(F) 49.

140 *Erikson v Cabeza*, [2002] BCJ No 286 (SCJ).

141 *Deans v Deans*, 2010 ABQB 17; *Purewal v Purewal*, 2011 BCSC 169; *GKD v CSD*, 2021 BCSC 367; *Keogh v Keogh*, [2008] NJ No 228 (SC); *Wilson v Eronchi*, [2000] NWTJ No 3 (SC); *Alford v Che-Alford*, [1999] OJ No 4206 (SCJ) (retroactive and prospective child support obligations to be satisfied by lump sum payment to be paid out of obligor's property entitlement); *Jones v Jones*, [2001] SJ No 199 (QB); compare *Erikson v Cabeza*, [2002] BCJ No 286 (SCJ).

142 *Shinkarik v Shinkarik* (1993), 87 Man R (2d) 39 (QB).

143 *Lobo v Lobo*, [1999] AJ No 113 (QB); *Wilson v Eronchi*, [2000] NWTJ No 3 (SC).

144 *Conron v Conron*, [1999] OJ No 38 (Gen Div).

lieu of periodic child support.[145] Where a parent has alcohol or drug abuse problems that may result in a squandering of income, a court may conclude that it is appropriate to order lump sum child support based on a capitalization of the periodic amounts payable under the federal and provincial child support guidelines until the child attains the age of majority. The lump sum may be ordered to be paid out of the proceeds of sale realized from a spousal property division and the court may direct that the lump sum be used to purchase an annuity that will yield the requisite monthly payments.[146] A lump sum may not be granted where, although justified, there are no liquid assets from which to extract the sum.[147] Lump sum child support may be deemed inappropriate because of an inability to pay.[148] A lump sum is not appropriate simply because the obligor has been a low income earner and will receive a capital sum on the resolution of the spousal property division.

10) Lump Sum Contribution to Section 7 Expenses

There is ample authority asserting that a contribution to special or extraordinary expenses under section 7 of the *Federal Child Support Guidelines* may be made by way of a lump sum. Where a spouse is called upon to contribute to special or extraordinary expenses within the ambit of section 7 of the *Federal Child Support Guidelines*, it may be impractical for the court to order regular periodic payments to meet those expenses. In that event, the court may order a fixed percentage of the expenses to be paid as and when they are incurred and a proper account thereof has been provided to the obligor.[150] A lump sum has been ordered to enable the primary caregiving parent to meet necessary orthodontal expenses for a child. The court's jurisdiction to order a lump sum payment must be made within the context of a child support order granted under the authority of the *Federal Child Support Guidelines* While lump sum orders have only been granted in special circumstances according to cases that pre-date the implementation of the *Federal Child Support Guidelines* on 1 May 1997, a combined reading of sections 7 and 11 of the Guidelines clearly favours the conclusion that lump sum payments are permissible in dealing with special or extraordinary expenses under section 7 of the Guidelines. Indeed, expenses for such matters as orthodontic treatment, professional counselling, prescription drugs, hearing aids, spectacles and contact lenses, primary or secondary education, post-secondary education, and extracurricular activities may involve non-recurring costs that should be discharged by a lump sum payment that avoids the fiction of amortizing those expenses in order to establish monthly payment equivalents.

Where a lump sum is sought for post-secondary education under section 7 of the *Federal Child Support Guidelines*, the court should address the likelihood of the child continuing his

145 *Sleiman v Sleiman*, [2003] OJ No 588 (SCJ).

146 *McIntosh v McIntosh* (1996), 19 RFL (4th) 46 (Man QB); compare *Wilson v Eronchi*, [2000] NWTJ No 3 (SC). See also *GKD v CSD*, 2021 BCSC 367.

147 *Cunha v Cunha* (1994), 99 BCLR 93 (SC).

148 *Richardson v Richardson*, [1997] OJ No 2795 (Gen Div); *Gee v Ng*, [1997] SJ No 350 (QB).

149 See, for example, *Carr v Wilson*, [2005] BCJ No 2353 (SC); *GKD v CSD*, 2021 BCSC 367 at para 79; *Burnett v Burnett*, [1999] OJ No 3063 (SCJ); *Willie v Willie*, [2000] SJ No 750 (QB).

150 *Kapell v Richter*, [1997] SJ No 796 (QB).

151 *Mattes v Mattes*, [1997] NSJ No 191 (TD); *Rosenberg v Rosenberg* (1987), 11 RFL (3d) 126 (Ont HCJ).

152 *Greenwood v Greenwood*, [1998] BCJ No 729 (SC).

or her education.[153] On granting a lump sum as a contribution towards the costs of an adult child's pursuit of post-secondary education, the court may direct that the lump sum shall be refundable, in whole or in part, if the child does not undertake or complete such education.[154]

11) Lump Sum Settlements

A lump sum settlement for child support is enforceable as a contract and may be judicially enforced, notwithstanding a subsequent change of circumstances.[155] However, the best interests of the child must always be considered by the court before any lump sum settlement is implemented.[156] Payment of lump sum child support in the expectation that the ex-wife and her second husband would adopt the children does not preclude an order for ongoing periodic support when the adoption does not proceed by reason of the breakdown of the second marriage. Child support is a right of the child that cannot be bargained away in a spousal settlement. The focus of the court must be on the best interests of the children, which override any understandable feeling of grievance on the part of the obligor. Some relief may be offered the obligor, however, by way of the suspension of the periodic support obligation for a specified period.[157]

12) Reimbursement of Lump Sum

If a parent has paid lump sum support for children who soon thereafter establish their residence with him or her, the payor may be entitled to be compensated and, if this is not possible because the money has already been invested in a home, the court may grant the payor a lien against that home and designate the terms upon which enforcement may ensue.[158]

13) Lump Sum Retroactive Child Support

A court may grant an order for lump sum retroactive child support.[159]

14) Lump Sum on Death of Parent

Where a parent dies after the institution of a child support proceeding, an interim or permanent order for lump sum support to enable adult children to pursue post-secondary education may be granted pursuant to sections 3(2)(b) and 11 of the *Federal Child Support Guidelines*. In assessing the amount of the lump sum to be paid out of the deceased's estate, priority must be accorded to the federal Crown with respect to the deceased's income tax

153 *Deans v Deans*, 2010 ABQB 17.
154 *Coady v Coady*, [1999] OJ No 2305 (SCJ); compare *Hutchings v Hutchings*, [1999] BCJ No 2897 (CA) (application of s 8 of *Federal Child Support Guidelines* excluded by prior lump sum payment).
155 *Bezanson v Falle*, [1998] OJ No 5392 (CA).
156 *Ibid.*
157 *Campbell v Campbell*, [1997] BCJ No 2 (SC).
158 *Vlasveld v Vlasveld*, [1999] BCJ No 1084 (SC).
159 *Taillon v Taillon*, [2005] OJ No 1116 (SCJ). And see Section K(7), below in this chapter. See also *Gray v Ransom*, 2011 SKQB 139.

liabilities, but the child support obligation takes priority of the deceased's ordinary creditors and the declared beneficiaries of the deceased's estate.[160]

15) Variation of Lump Sum Orders

Child support should normally be paid through periodic payments established pursuant to the applicable *Federal Child Support Guidelines*. However, parents are not prevented from negotiating an agreement whereby a lump sum will be provided instead of periodic payments. Such an arrangement may be judicially endorsed pursuant to sections 15.1(5) to (8) of the *Divorce Act*. Article 589 of the *Civil Code of Quebec* also permits child support, as well as spousal support, to be provided in exceptional circumstances by way of a lump sum payment in cash or by instalments. Where parents have executed a well-structured agreement that includes a provision for a lump sum to be paid for the support of their two children on the assumption that the children will complete CEGEP and attend university, such an agreement may be judicially sanctioned by means of a consent order that satisfies the requirements of sections 15.1(7) and (8) of the *Divorce Act*. If one of the two children thereafter decides to leave school rather than pursue a post-secondary education, the court may entertain an application to vary the consent order because that child is no longer a "child of the marriage" within the meaning of section 2(1) of the *Divorce Act* and the assumptions underlying the spousal settlement and consent order have thus been undermined. In addressing the variation application in light of the change of circumstances, section 17(6.2) of the *Divorce Act* empowers the court to reduce the previously agreed lump sum payment to a lower amount based on the remaining child's anticipated completion of university studies.[161]

D. ORDERS TO PAY AND SECURE SUPPORT

1) Section 12 of Guidelines

Pursuant to section 15.1(4) of the *Divorce Act* and section 12 of the *Federal Child Support Guidelines*, there is a broad discretion accorded to trial judges to impose charging orders in appropriate cases.[162] Section 12 of the *Federal Child Support Guidelines* expressly provides that the court may require the amount payable under a child support order to be paid or secured in the manner specified in the order.[163]

2) Orders to Pay and/or Secure Support

An order to secure support, of itself, is not an order to make payments and secure those payments. It is an order to secure and no more. The sole obligation arising under such an order is

---

160 *Hillock v Hillock*, [2001] OJ No 3837 (SCJ). As to the effect of the child support obligor's death on the enforcement of a consent order to pay lump sum child support in instalments, see *McLeod v McLeod*, 2013 BCCA 552.

161 *JC v KS*, [2003] QJ No 4113 (CA).

162 *McMaster-Pereira v Pereira*, 2021 ONCA 547 at para 30, citing *Katz v Katz*, 2014 ONCA 606 at para 71.

163 *Lessard v Lessard*, [1999] AJ No 525 (QB); *JDG v JJV*, 2016 BCSC 2389; *KAL v KJL*, 2017 BCSC 651; *Dool v Dool*, [1997] OJ No 1256 (Gen Div).

to provide the security; having done that, there is no further liability. The parent who is only ordered to secure support does not assume a personal obligation to pay and never becomes a debtor in respect of payments in default. A parent in whose favour an order to secure support is made takes the benefit of the security and must look to it alone; if it ceases to yield the expected income, that parent cannot call upon the other to make good the deficiency.[164] The mutual exclusivity of orders to pay and orders to secure support, which was endorsed by the majority judgment of the Supreme Court of Canada in *Nash v Nash*,[165] no longer prevails under section 12 of the *Federal Child Support Guidelines*. Pursuant to that section, the court may require that the amount payable under a child support order "be paid or secured, or paid and secured" in the manner specified in the order.[166] In view of the aforementioned inherent limitations of an order to secure *simpliciter*, courts are well advised to grant a combined order to pay and secure support where the obligor has income but some additional security is appropriate to ensure due discharge of the court-ordered obligations. Where such an order is granted, realization of the security would not preclude further recourse on the personal obligation to meet any deficiency or ongoing liability. An order to secure may be appropriate when the obligor may be unable to make periodic payments, when the obligor may leave the country with the assets or waste or conceal them, or when the obligee requires some assurance that there will be funds available.[167]

3) Diverse Types of Security

A periodic or lump sum child support order may be secured against real or personal property,[168] including the matrimonial home,[169] or the proceeds of sale thereof,[170] the obligor's statutory property entitlement,[171] or against an obligor's mutual funds,[172] personal injuries monetary settlement or a portion thereof,[173] Canada Savings Bonds,[174] corporate shareholdings,[175] RRSPs,[176] or retirement pension.[177] An important distinction is to be drawn between an order for lump sum child support and an order requiring that a lump sum be set aside

---

164 *Nash v Nash*, [1975] 2 SCR 507; *Cotton v Cotton* (1966), 60 DLR (2d) 117 (BCCA).

165 [1975] 2 SCR 507.

166 *Price v Price* (1994), 5 RFL (4th) 383 (BCSC).

167 See *Bhatthal v Bhatthal* (1990), 28 RFL (3d) 152 (Alta QB); *Ormerod v Ormerod* (1990), 27 RFL (3d) 225 (Ont UFC); *Droit de la famille—1231*, [1989] RDF 189 (Que CS).

168 *Strand v Strand*, [1999] AJ No 545 (QB); *Hama v Werbes*, [2000] BCJ No 1556 (SC) (delivery up of certificate title to foreign immovables as security for spousal and child support obligations); *Shelly v Shelly*, [2004] OJ No 743 (SCJ).

169 *Nand v Nand*, 2011 ABQB 324; *Davari v Namazi*, [1999] BCJ No 116 (SC); *Riel v Holland*, [2003] OJ No 3901 (CA); *Parsalidis v Parsalidis*, 2012 ONSC 2963.

170 *MEL v BGL*, 2012 BCSC 1841; *Dalgleish v Dalgleish*, [2003] OJ No 2918 (SCJ).

171 *JDG v JJV*, 2016 BCSC 2389; *Alford v Che-Alford*, [1999] OJ No 4206 (SCJ); *Campbell v Campbell*, [1998] SJ No 180 (QB).

172 *Baldini v Baldini*, [1999] BCJ No 1426 (SC).

173 *Hernon v Renaud*, [1999] BCJ No 2509 (SC); see also *O'Riordon v O'Riordon* (1987), 11 RFL (3d) 52 (BCCA).

174 *Elgaard v Elgaard* (1986), 1 RFL (3d) 256 (BCSC).

175 *Whittall v Whittall* (1987), 19 BCLR (2d) 202 (SC).

176 *BC v MC*, 2011 NBQB 285; *Wislesky v Wislesky*, [1999] OJ No 1220 (Gen Div).

177 *Deale v Deale* (1995), 15 RFL (4th) 95 (BCSC); *Francis v Filion*, [2003] OJ No 1138 (SCJ); compare *Roby v Roby*, [2003] OJ No 4408 (SCJ).

as security for the payment of child support.[178] An order to secure periodic child support payments may be deemed appropriate where the obligor has a history of dissipating assets; where the obligor is likely to leave the jurisdiction and become an absconding debtor; where the obligor has previously refused to honour a support obligation; or where the obligor has a poor employment history or threatens to leave his employment.[179] An order for periodic child support may be secured against the obligor's entitlement to the remainder of his share of matrimonial property, if the obligor is intentionally underemployed. Where such an order is made, the obligor may be relieved from making periodic child support payments based on his imputed annual income until the lump sum property entitlement has been exhausted. An application for lump sum support to be secured against the obligor's interest in the matrimonial home should be denied where there is no evidentiary basis pointing to prospective default in the payment of periodic child support.[181] A court may conclude that it is in the best interests of the children that the obligor provide security for the child support obligation in the form of a postponement of the sale of the matrimonial home, which may be achieved by an exclusive possession order in favour of the primary caregiving for a fixed period of time, at the end of which the home will be sold and the obligor's share of the proceeds of sale will first be applied to any arrears of child support then outstanding.[182] A certificate of pending litigation is not available to secure a claim for retroactive child support.[183] A conditional prohibition has been imposed on an obligor's employer to preclude the pay out of a lump sum pension entitlement, unless the obligor secures gainful employment and can thus discharge the monthly child support obligation.[184] It is submitted, however, that a court has no jurisdiction to impose legal obligations on a non-party to the litigation. In order to ensure timely payment of child support, the court may order the obligor to provide a designated lump sum in liquid security[185] or in an interest-bearing trust account[186] from which periodic child support payments shall be made. Money previously paid into court may be retained as security, pending resolution of the issue of child support.[187] The power to make or refuse an order to secure support is within the discretion of the court.[188] In exercising its discretion, the court must have due regard to the capital and secured income of the spouse against whom the order to secure is sought.[189] Although the courts may decline to grant an order to secure against property that has no income yielding capacity, an obligor may be ordered to execute a mortgage against the matrimonial home in favour of the obligee.[190] Security for future payments may also be provided by a judicial direction that the obligor execute an appropriate

178 *Chou v Chao* (1996), 21 RFL (4th) 45 (BCSC).
179 *Reid v Catalano*, [2008] OJ No 912 (SCJ).
180 *White v White*, [2002] AJ No 1049 (QB).
181 *Graham v Graham*, [1998] BCJ No 185 (SC).
182 *Lonergan v Lonergan*, [1998] BCJ No 150 (SC).
183 *Lipskaya v Guo*, 2020 BCSC 209, citing *VB v KB*, 2013 SKQB 412 at para 72.
184 *AMP v RP*, [1998] OJ No 2540 (Gen Div).
185 *Braich v Braich*, [1997] BCJ No 1764 (SC).
186 *Hosseini v Assadbeigi*, [1998] BCJ No 1642 (SC).
187 *Scory v Scory*, [1999] SJ No 644 (CA).
188 *Cox v Cox*, [1998] AJ No 1282 (QB); *Parniak v Parniak*, [1999] MJ No 37 (QB).
189 *Barker v Barker*, [1952] P 184 (Eng CA).
190 See, for example, *Van Zyderveld v Van Zyderveld*, [1977] 1 SCR 714; compare *Von Hessert v Von Hessert* (1986), 3 RFL (3d) 27 at 29 (Sask CA).

irrevocable declaration under a life insurance policy. An obligor may be ordered to provide security for periodic support payments by irrevocably designating the obligee as the beneficiary under a life insurance policy or supplementary death benefit plan,[191] but such an order may be inappropriate when the obligee's economic circumstances are not extreme and the obligor has a relatively modest estate and other family dependants to support.[192] A court may direct that the child support order shall constitute a first charge on the obligor's estate.[193] Judicial opinion has not yet finally resolved whether a court has jurisdiction to order an obligor to purchase a life insurance policy to secure child support payments where no policy existed at the date when relief was sought.[194] A mother who seeks to obtain insurance on the father's life to secure the payment of child support arrears and the costs relating thereto may obtain a court order to compel the father to complete a questionnaire and undergo whatever medical testing is required.[195] Where an obligor is ordered to make an irrevocable designation under a life insurance policy in order to secure child support payments, the court may require the obligor to direct her insurer to provide the designated party with annual proof of coverage and notice of any change in or cancellation of the policy immediately upon its occurrence.[196] Where both periodic child support and periodic spousal support are to be secured against an obligor's life insurance, the amounts involved may need to be segregated to reflect differences existing between the amount and duration of the orders.[197] The life insurance provisions of an existing order may be varied as an incident of child support if there is a change in circumstances within the meaning of the *Child Support Guidelines*.[198]

Periodic child support payments may be ordered to be secured by insurance to cover the eventuality of a termination or change in the obligor's employment.[199]

It has been concluded that the meaning of the word "secure" is sufficiently broad to permit a court to order that support be deducted directly from the obligor's wages.[200]

A court may order that all child support arrears and interest payable thereon shall be secured against the defaulter's retirement account and may issue an order restraining the

191 *Inglis v Inglis*, [2001] BCJ No 411 (SC) (designation under obligor's life insurance policy for benefit of children from two relationships); *KAP v KAMP*, 2012 BCSC 811; *KLW v LPW*, 2012 NBQB 91; *Rossiter-Forrest v Forrest* (1994), 129 NSR (2d) 130 (TD); *Van Dusen v Van Dusen*, 2010 ONSC 220; compare *Barry (Wilson) v Wilson* (1990), 29 RFL (3d) 42 at 47 (NBQB). See also *Day v Day* (1994), 129 NSR (2d) 169 (TD); *Cavanagh v Cassidy*, [2000] OJ No 1658 (SCJ) (group life insurance for child of obligor's first marriage reduced to allow provision for child of second marriage); *Leland v Klette*, 2013 SKQB 277. And see *Family Law Act*, SBC 2011, c 25, sections 170–171; *Joffres v Joffres*, 2014 BCSC 1778; *RM v NM*, 2014 BCSC 1755; *MPM v ACM*, 2022 BCSC 122; *Family Law Act*, RSO 1990, c F3, s 34(4); *Katz v Katz*, 2014 ONCA 606. Compare *Malboeuf v Hanna*, 2018 ONSC 6562 and see FAMLNWS 2018-50 (10 December 2018).

192 *Ripley v Ripley* (1991), 30 RFL (3d) 41 (BCCA); see also *Quinton v Kehler*, 2020 BCCA 254.

193 *Miceli v Miceli*, [1998] OJ No 5460 (Gen Div).

194 Compare *Laczko v Laczko*, [1999] OJ No 2577 (SCJ) and *Feinstat v Feinstat*, 2012 ONSC 5339; see also *Berki v Berki*, [1999] OJ No 843 (Gen Div) (direction for purchase of life insurance policy to become moot, if obligor uninsurable); *Rush v Rush*, [2002] PEIJ No 29 (SC). See also *REQ v GJK*, 2019 BCSC 1116 at paras 137–39.

195 *Beattie v Ladouceur*, [2002] OJ No 5501 (SCJ).

196 *Laczko v Laczko*, [1999] OJ No 2577 (SCJ).

197 *F v V*, [2002] OJ No 3900 (SCJ).

198 *Malboeuf v Belter*, 2018 ONSC 6516.

199 *Coathup v Coathup*, [2000] OJ No 289 (SCJ).

200 *Long v Long* (1993), 1 RFL (4th) 110 (Alta QB).

obligor from disposing of or encumbrancing the account until the debt is fully discharged. The court may further suggest that the Family Responsibility Office seize the retirement account in addition to garnishing the defaulter's pay, having regard to the principle that child support obligations take priority over saving for retirement.[201] A court may decline to order security for child support where prior arrears accrued during bankruptcy and there is no apparent need to secure the obligation.[202]

Where arrears of support have accrued notwithstanding the filing of the child support order in the Ontario Family Responsibility Office, because statutory provisions impose a maximum on the amount deductible by the income source, an order to secure child support payments against the obligor's interest in the matrimonial home may be deemed appropriate, and where special needs children are involved, the court may further direct both parents to maintain their existing life insurance policies for the benefit of the children.[203]

An order for periodic child support payments may be secured against the obligor's personal and corporate property interests pursuant to section 12 of the *Federal Child Support Guidelines*.[204] If an order to secure support has been made and the property constituting the security has been determined, the order does not create a floating charge over all the assets of the party who is ordered to give security, but only charges the assets so determined.[205] An order charging all assets is objectionable in form and substance and should not be made.[206] Where an order to secure support is made against a spouse who dies before the property constituting the security has been determined, the order may be enforced against the deceased's estate.[207]

An order to secure should not be made conditional on future considerations that are merely a matter for conjecture, but a token order may be made in contemplation of future contingencies, which would be variable in the event of a material change in the condition, means, needs, or other circumstances of the parties.[208] The power of the court to order security does not extend to confer jurisdiction upon the court to deprive a spouse of his property by ordering its transfer to the other spouse.[209] The jurisdiction to order security for child support under section 12 of the *Federal Child Support Guidelines* does not include any power to order the sale of assets. The terms of an order for realizing on security for support are a very different matter. Past and future support may be secured by a lump sum charge against the former matrimonial home and on the obligor's RRSPs. The court may set out specific terms respecting the charging order and realization of the security in the event of default.

---

201 *Wasney v Wasney*, [1999] OJ No 3389 (SCJ) (balance of arrears to be paid at Guideline rate of $507 per month but Family Responsibility Office free to garnish more).

202 *Cohen v Cohen* (1995), 11 RFL (4th) 1 (BCCA).

203 *Csecs v Csecs*, [2001] OJ No 1424 (SCJ).

204 *Rykert v Rykert*, [2000] OJ No 4453 (SCJ). As to piercing the corporate veil, see further *Wildman v Wildman*, [2006] OJ No 3966 (CA); *Lynch v Segal*, [2006] OJ No 5014 (CA); *O'Neill v O'Neill*, [2007] OJ No 1706 (SCJ); *Potzus v Potzus*, 2018 SKQB 55.

205 *Hyde v Hyde*, [1948] P 198.

206 *Barker v Barker*, [1952] P 184 (Eng CA).

207 *Maclurcan v Maclurcan* (1897), 77 LT 474 (Eng CA); *Mosey v Mosey*, [1956] P 26; *Richardson's Will Trusts v Llewellyn-Evans' Trustees*, [1958] Ch 504.

208 *F v F*, [1967] 2 All ER 660.

209 *Switzer v Switzer* (1969), 1 RFL 262 (Alta CA); *McConnell v McConnell* (1975), 11 NBR (2d) 19 (CA).

210 *Dickinson v Dickinson*, [1998] OJ No 4815 (Gen Div).

4) Justification for Orders to Secure Support Payments

An order to secure child support is usually ordered only when the obligor has wilfully disobeyed previous orders or is likely to ignore future orders.[211] Courts will only grant an order for child support to be secured where there is some reason to suspect that the obligor will not discharge her child support obligations.[212] An order for security may be granted at the conclusion of a trial where the obligor has threatened to quit employment rather than pay child support.[213] The following situations may warrant security being ordered:

1) where the obligor has a history of dissipating assets;
2) where the obligor is likely to leave the jurisdiction and become an absconding debtor;
3) where the obligor has refused to honour a court-ordered or consensual support obligation or has refused to provide support at all;
4) where the obligor has a poor employment history or threatens to leave his employment;
5) where the obligor has no income, savings, or prospect of employment;
6) where the obligor has an extravagant lifestyle and was uncooperative with the payee in the past;
7) where the obligor is outside the jurisdiction at the time of the hearing but has assets within the jurisdiction that are capable of forming a basis for security; and
8) where the obligor has declared that he or she will refuse to pay any eventual support order.[214]

The New Brunswick Court of Appeal in *Milton v Milton*[215] cautioned trial judges from making arbitrary orders securing support payments in the absence of some evidence establishing the amount of security necessary.

5) Variation of Security

An order to secure child support may be varied pursuant to section 17 of the *Divorce Act* by an order reducing the amount of the security.[216]

Under appropriate conditions, an application may be brought for the discharge of a lien registered against the applicant's property to secure payment of child support ordered under the *Divorce Act*.[217] Such an application may be granted without prejudice to the future right to file a further lien to secure any new child support order, where the sole reason for the registrant's refusal to discharge the lien was to impose leverage in order to extract additional support.[218]

---

211 *Oshanek v Oshanek*, [1999] AJ No 680 (QB); *Cohen v Cohen* (1995), 11 RFL (4th) 1 (BCCA); *Koyama v Leigh*, [1998] BCJ No 279 (CA); *RRH v BK*, 2011 BCSC 948.

212 *Kolada v Kolada*, [1999] AJ No 376 (QB); *Armstrong v Armstrong*, [1999] OJ No 2614 (SCJ).

213 *Dickinson v Dickinson*, [1998] OJ No 4815 (Gen Div).

214 See *Edden v Foley*, 2024 ABKB 48; *Davids v Davids*, [1998] OJ No 2859 (Gen Div); *Yenovkian v Gulian*, 2019 ONSC 7279 at para 133.

215 2008 NBCA 87; see also *Calvy v Calvy*, 2012 NBCA 47; *GF v JACF*, 2016 NBCA 21.

216 *Koyama v Leigh*, [1998] BCJ No 2127 (SC).

217 *Johnson v Johnson*, [1999] BCJ No 1064 (SC).

218 *Langstaff v Langstaff*, [1999] BCJ No 327 (SC).

The court may grant an order for the preservation of the obligor's assets so as to ensure an ability to pay child support,[219] but may vary such an order to permit the sale of specific assets where the proceeds of sale are to be used to satisfy arrears of support.[220] The court may direct that any residue shall be held by the obligor's solicitor in trust for the payment of future support.[221]

Where a child maintenance order has been registered against the obligor's real property, an application under section 26(10) of the *Family Maintenance Enforcement Act* (BC) to vacate the registration should be brought by the registered owner, not by prospective purchasers of the property. An appeal may, nevertheless, be allowed to proceed where the chambers judge had not insisted on compliance with this statutory requirement and the interests of all concerned would be best served by resolution of the substantive issue relating to the provision of alternative security. While upholding the chambers judge's decision to reduce the amount of security, the appellate court may find that the chambers judge was in error in granting leave to the obligor to make a further application if his relationship with the child improved. Alternative security is not ordered in every case but may be appropriate in light of a prior default in the payment of child maintenance or where a future default is likely. The obligor has the onus of proving that alternative security is no longer necessary to protect the child's maintenance entitlement. Child maintenance and security relating thereto should not be linked to parenting issues or the degree of bonding between the obligor and the child.

6) Remission to Trial Division by Appellate Court

Where an appellate court concludes that an order for child support should be secured and the parties cannot agree on the security, the matter may be referred back to the trial judge.

7) Order to Restrain Disposition of Assets; Mareva Injunction

An order for security under section 12 of the *Federal Child Support Guidelines* presupposes the existence of a child support order. The court has no statutory jurisdiction to issue a preservation order with respect to a parent's prospective child support obligation. The only means available to prevent a parent from disposing of or dealing with his assets is a *Mareva* injunction, but this requires the applicant to show irreparable harm if the injunction is denied.[224]

An order that child support be paid in a lump sum or that it be secured is an unusual step, even though such orders are envisaged by sections 60(1)(b) and (j) of the *Children's Law Act*.[225] Such orders may be justified where the obligor has a poor past record with respect to child support, or a record of poor money management or an inclination to risk the family's economic security. They may be warranted where there is a risk that support will not be

---

219 *Tkachuk v Bigras*, [1997] OJ No 5453 (Gen Div).

220 *Hama v Werbes*, [1998] BCJ No 2682 (SC).

221 *Ibid.*

222 *BD v LDB*, [2003] BCJ No 648 (CA).

223 *Dyczek v Dyczek*, [1986] OJ No 1085 (CA).

224 *Quinn v Keiper*, [2005] OJ No 5034 (SCJ).

225 SNWT 1997, c 14.

paid or where the obligor has abandoned the family without trace but has left assets behind. Even if the court concludes that a lump sum child support order is unjustified, it may still decide that caution is appropriate in light of the possible mismanagement of substantial lottery winnings. In these circumstances, the court may grant an interim order restraining the disposition of a portion of the winnings until further order of the court, but without prejudice to the obligor's right to apply for a disposition of these funds after presenting an investment plan to the court.[226]

E. DIVISION OF PROPERTY; POSSESSION OF MATRIMONIAL HOME

The *Divorce Act* confers no jurisdiction on a court to order the transfer of a parent's interest in the matrimonial home in satisfaction of lump sum orders for retroactive and prospective child support, but the court may direct the orders to be secured against the obligor's interest in the matrimonial home for so long as the payee parent retains exclusive possession of the home.[227]

Partition and sale of a matrimonial home held by spouses under joint tenancy may be denied where a spouse cannot or will not pay child support.[228]

Where a parent is unable to provide reasonable support for the children, it may be appropriate for a court to grant long-term possession of the former matrimonial home to the primary caregiving parent.[229]

An unequal division of matrimonial property by way of a postponed sale of the matrimonial home may be justified under section 13(h) of the Nova Scotia *Matrimonial Property Act* on the basis of the needs of a child under the age of majority. It is not necessary in every case for the primary caregiving parent to present evidence that harm would be suffered by the child as a result of a move or to demonstrate that there is no adequate alternative shelter.[230] Where a court-ordered matrimonial property division is coupled with an order for child support based on the husband's imputed income, the court may order the husband to transfer his interest in the matrimonial home to his wife and direct her to mortgage back to her husband the amount owing, without interest, until the child attains the age of majority or the home is sold or the mortgage is paid in full, whichever is earlier. This may serve to provide security for child support payments, with any outstanding arrears being deductible from the mortgage payout.[231]

An unequal division of matrimonial property may be ordered pursuant to *The Matrimonial Property Act, 1997* (Saskatchewan) where there is no possibility of obtaining child support, but that should only be done as a last resort.[232] A parent's failure to pay child support does not disentitle him or her to share in an increase in the value of the family home between the date of the application and the date of adjudication where the increase arises from market

226 *Wilson v Eronchi*, [2000] NWTJ No 3 (SC).

227 *Duhnych v Duhnych*, [2004] OJ No 2655 (SCJ).

228 *Hoyer v Hoyer* (1982), 30 RFL (2d) 261 (BCCA); *Wundele v Wundele* (1994), 99 BCLR (2d) 1 (BCCA).

229 *Hoyer v Hoyer* (1982), 30 RFL (2d) 261 (BCCA); *Turner v Turner*, [1998] BCJ No 2615 (CA); *Binczak v Binczak* (1992), 44 RFL (3d) 122 (Ont Ct Gen Div).

230 *Sampson v Sampson*, [1999] NSJ No 379 (CA). Compare *Mayer v Mayer*, [2001] NSJ No 404 (SC).

231 *Durant v Durant*, [2001] NSJ No 10 (SC).

232 *Anderson v Anderson*, [1993] SJ No 342 (QB).

forces and is far in excess of the outstanding child support. It is always possible to quantify the amount of child support outstanding and set-off the respective amounts owed.[233]

Arrears of child support may be ordered to be deducted from the obligor's matrimonial property entitlement.[234]

F. INFORMATION TO BE SPECIFIED IN ORDER

It is imperative that all orders for child support include a recital so that staff, lawyers, and the court can readily determine the financial basis on which an order was made.[235]

Generally, the parties, their attendances, and the documents relied upon should be included in the preamble to an order of the Alberta Court of King's Bench. The purpose of a preamble is to provide a setting for what follows. It should provide context but should not include facts, terms of the order, or reasons for the order. A slightly different approach to the norm exists when dealing with divorce and corollary relief orders. This arises because Rules 561.1 to 579.3 and particularly Rule 575.1 of the *Alberta Rules of Court* prescribe the form of order to follow. The Forms are set out in Schedule B to the Rules. In Forms 17 through 19, over and above the usual context, the order provides for a recitation of the Guidelines income of the respective parties and the names and birth dates of each child. While section 13 of the *Federal Child Support Guidelines* specifies what must be included in a child support order, it does not specify what should be in the preamble. Consequently, the preamble is governed by the Alberta Rules and prescribed Forms, while the body of the order formalizes the court's direction on the various issues raised.[236]

A child support order or variation order made in accordance with the *Federal Child Support Guidelines* must be segregated from spousal support and the child support order must include the following information:

1) the name and birth date of each child to whom the order relates;
2) the income of any spouse whose income is used to determine the amount of the child support order;[237]
3) the amount set out in the applicable provincial or territorial table for the number of children to whom the order relates;
4) the amount determined under paragraph 3(2)(b) for a child the age of majority or over;
5) the particulars of any expense described in section 7(1), the child to whom the expense relates, and the amount of the expense or, where that amount cannot be determined, the proportion to be paid in relation to the expense;[238] and
6) the date on which the first payment is payable and the day of the month on which all subsequent payments are to be made.[239]

---

233 *Williams v Williams*, 2011 SKCA 84.

234 *Alma v Zachary*, [2005] AJ No 772 (QB); *Maskell v Maskell*, [1999] NSJ No 424 (SC).

235 *Young v Vincent*, [1997] NSJ No 163 (TD).

236 *Geherman v Geherman*, [2004] AJ No 1254 (QB).

237 *Mosher v Mosher*, [1999] NSJ No 202 (SC).

238 *TMD v JPG*, 2018 NBCA 15 at para 24.

239 *Federal Child Support Guidelines*, SOR/97-175, s 13; see *Pitt v Pitt*, [1997] BCJ No 1528 (SC); *Rains v Rains*, [1997] OJ No 2516 (Gen Div); *Anderson v Wilkins*, [2002] OJ No 2724 (child care expenses);

The inclusion of the above information is mandatory. It is required for the purposes of facilitating both the enforcement and variation of support orders. It is an error in law for the information required under section 13 of the *Federal Child Support Guidelines* not to be provided in a court order.[240] However, an order for child support is not void simply because the form of the order does not comply with section 13 of the Guidelines. Where an error or slip is made in drawing up a formal order, the trial judge retains jurisdiction to rectify the order and this jurisdiction may also be exercised, in appropriate cases, on appeal.[241]

G. AVOIDANCE OF COMBINED ORDERS FOR CHILD SUPPORT AND SPOUSAL SUPPORT

Periodic child support payments made pursuant to an agreement or order made after 1 May 1997 are no longer deductible from the taxable income of the payor nor are they taxable as income in the hands of the recipient spouse or former spouse. The income tax deduction/inclusion rule still prevails, however, with respect to periodic spousal support. Consequently, it is now imperative to avoid agreements or orders for combined child and spousal support, even when lawyers or the courts are only dealing with interim arrangements.[242] Given that the new tax treatment for periodic child support orders does not apply to periodic spousal support orders, any agreement or court order must state separately the amount of support to be provided to each of them. If this is not done, the global amount of spousal and child support will be treated as child support and will be transferred on a tax-free basis.[243] Quite apart from the different tax consequences applicable to child support and spousal support, it should be borne in mind that global orders for spousal and child support have generated variation problems in the past[244] and that a child support order has priority over a spousal support order.[245]

Spousal support and child support must be segregated into separate orders where an application is brought to vary a combined order for spousal and child support that pre-dated the amendments to the *Divorce Act* and the *Federal Child Support Guidelines*, which came into force on 1 May 1997.[246]

Beckman v Hanna, 2017 SKQB 80.

240 *Tkachuk v Bigras*, [1997] OJ No 5453 (Gen Div); but see *Cross v Batters*, 2016 SKCA 71.

241 *Lee v Lee*, [1998] NJ No 247 (CA); *Fedortchouk v Boubnoy*, 2018 NSSC 66 at para 84; *MDL v CR*, 2020 SKCA 44 at paras 35–38; see also *FM v TH*, 2016 NBCA 29.

242 Compare *Hall v Hall*, [1999] OJ No 453 (Gen Div) (global amount of interim spousal and child support ordered without specific determination concerning imputed income where parties had orally agreed on payment of $1,200 per month prior to obligor's loss of employment; interim order granted without prejudice to right to seek retroactive support when obligor's income finally determined); compare also *BFC v DGW*, [2001] BCJ No 1509 (SC); *Berg v Berg*, [2000] SJ No 118 (QB).

243 *Mercer v Canada*, [2007] TCJ No 13.

244 See Julien D Payne, *Payne on Divorce*, 4th ed (Scarborough, ON: Carswell, 1996) at 247–48.

245 *EW v MMP*, [1997] QJ No 3474 (CS).

246 *Rondeau v Kirby*, [2003] NSJ No 436 (SC), aff'd [2004] NSJ No 143 (CA); *Inns v Inns*, [1999] OJ No 4209 (SCJ).

H. COMMENCEMENT AND DURATION OF ORDERS; EFFECT OF RECONCILIATION

1) Normal Commencement Date

In the absence of any evidence that the payor needs time to organize his affairs, a child support order should ordinarily come into effect not later than the first day of the month immediately following the judicial decision.[247]

2) Fixed-Term and Review Orders

Section 15.1(4) of the *Divorce Act* specifically empowers the court to make an interim or permanent child support order for a definite or indefinite period or until the happening of a specified event. The court may also impose such terms, conditions, or restrictions in connection with the interim or permanent order as it thinks fit and just. Where the financial circumstances or prospects are uncertain, the court may direct that the issues relating to child support be reviewed after a designated period of time.[248] Subject to any judicial directions to the contrary,[249] a child support order declared subject to review after a designated period of time does not require proof of a change of circumstances in order for the review to be undertaken and the situation reassessed.[250] The fact that an order is declared reviewable after a specific period of time does not preclude an earlier application to vary that order pursuant to section 17 of the *Divorce Act* and section 14 of the *Federal Child Support Guidelines*.[251] review order is inappropriate to deal with a child's anticipated graduation from high school. The proper procedure in such a case is to bring an application to vary if a material change in the child's circumstances can be demonstrated after graduation.[252]

3) Duration of Order

Subsection 3(2) of the *Federal Child Support Guidelines* empowers a court to override a provision in a separation agreement that stipulates termination of child support at the age of twenty-one.[253]

Child support may be ordered to be paid until a specified date, unless the child finds full-time employment before that date, in which event the child support payments shall terminate on the last day of the month in which the child commences full-time employment.

---

247 *Reardon v Smith*, [1999] NSJ No 403 (CA) (delay of additional month found to constitute reversible error on appeal); see also *Evans v Evans*, [1999] BCJ No 2919 (SC).

248 *McCargar v McCargar*, [1997] AJ No 678 (QB); *Simms v Simms*, [1997] BCJ No 1553 (SC). See also *DBB v DMB*, 2017 SKCA 59; *LCR v IJER* 2019 SKQB 229.

249 *Loewen v Traill*, [1998] BCJ No 466 (SC).

250 *TM v DM*, 2014 NBQB 132; *Schick v Schick*, [2000] NWTJ No 12 (SC); see, generally, Julien D Payne, *Payne on Divorce*, 4th ed (Scarborough, ON: Carswell, 1996) at 243.

251 *SSG v SKG*, 2022 ABCA 379. See also Payne, *ibid*, citing *Lidstone v Lidstone* (1993), 46 RFL (3d) 203 (NSCA).

252 *Peterson v Peterson*, 2011 SKQB 365, citing *Leskun v Leskun*, 2006 SCC 25.

253 *Kilrea v Kilrea*, [1998] OJ No 3677 (Gen Div).

254 *Olsen v Olsen*, [1997] SJ No 476 (QB).

An order for child support made pursuant to the *Divorce Act* does not automatically terminate upon the child's reaching the age of majority, unless the order expressly so provides. The order will remain in effect until it is varied.[255] The *Divorce Act* offers little guidance concerning the duration of orders, but judicial decisions demonstrate that child support rights and obligations may extend beyond the age of majority.[256] The court may designate a specific period during which support shall be payable.[257] For example, a court may direct that support shall be paid as long as the child attends school, college, or university,[258] or until the child reaches a specific age,[259] which may be variable according to whether the child pursues post-secondary education or training,[260] or marries, or until the child has obtained employment and is self-supporting, whichever event shall occur *first*.[261] In an Alberta case, where a child had emotional problems and required special care, payments were ordered for his support until he attained the age of eighteen years or became self-supporting, whichever shall *last* occur.[262] A court may order that support shall terminate after a child's completion of four years of university education, but may further direct that either parent shall be at liberty to apply for a review of the child's status, if postgraduate studies are thereafter envisaged.[263]

Support payments have also been limited to the period during which the child attends school and continues to reside with the primary caregiving parent.[264] An arbitrary limitation to this effect on the right to child support is unwarranted.[265] Orders may be and have been granted by the courts that provide for child support, notwithstanding that the child does not reside with the primary caregiving parent.[266]

An order that requires a parent to pay monthly support for an "infant child" terminates once the child attains the provincial age of majority. Arrears do not accrue under such an order after the child attains the age of majority. Any extension of the child support obligation requires an application to the court and the onus falls on the applicant to satisfy the court that the adult child remains unable to withdraw from her economic dependence on the

---

255 *Johnson v Johnson*, [1999] BCJ No 1064 (SC).

256 See Chapter 3, Section C.

257 *CGG v CHG*, [2001] AJ No 1410 (QB) (order for fixed period of two years); *Wood v Boere*, 2012 BCSC 252; *Kerr v Kerr* (1975), 20 RFL 312 (Man QB); compare *Corkum v Corkum* (1988), 14 RFL (3d) 275 (Ont HCJ), wherein Misener LJSC rejected a specific age limitation in favour of a general direction that support be payable for as long as the child remained a "child of the marriage"; compare also *Kelly v Lyle*, [2002] YJ No 116 (SC) (application for "sunset clause" denied).

258 *Duncan v Duncan* (1992), 40 RFL (3d) 358 (Alta QB); *Mullin v Mullin* (1989), 24 RFL (3d) 1 (PEI CA); compare *Taplin v Laurie* (1992), 41 RFL (3d) 197 at 199–200 (Man CA).

259 *Yurchuk v Yurchuk* (1976), 2 AR 277 (CA) (eighteen years of age); *Joyce v Joyce* (1987), 8 RFL (3d) 164 (NBQB) (twenty-one years of age); *Stein v Stein* (1975), 10 Nfld & PEIR 358 (Nfld TD) (sixteen years of age); *Wrightsell v Wrightsell* (1973), 11 RFL 271 (Ont SC) (twenty-one years of age); *Ward v Ward* (1988), 13 RFL (3d) 259 (Ont HCJ), rev'd in part (1990), 26 RFL (3d) 149 (Ont CA) (not to extend beyond twenty-four years of age).

260 *Ewaniw v Ewaniw*, [1998] AJ No 704 (QB); see also *Messier v Robillard*, [1999] NJ No 368 (SC).

261 *Wrightsell v Wrightsell* (1973), 11 RFL 271 (Ont SC).

262 *Fuhrman v Fuhrman* (1980), 19 RFL (2d) 404 (Alta QB), var'd (1981), 32 RFL (2d) 129 (Alta CA).

263 *Davis v Davis*, [1999] BCJ No 1832 (BCSC); see also *Cove v Cove*, 2010 NSSC 407.

264 *Clark v Clark* (1971), 4 RFL 27 (Ont SC); *Pongor v Pongor* (1976), 27 RFL 109 (Ont CA); see also *Landry v Landry* (1980), 31 NBR (2d) 16 at 22 (QB); *Cove v Cove*, 2010 NSSC 407.

265 *Harrington v Harrington* (1981), 22 RFL (2d) 40 at 51 (Ont CA).

266 *Barry v Wilson* (1990), 29 RFL (3d) 42 (NBQB); *Clark v Clark* (1971), 4 RFL 27 (Ont SC); see also *Wood v Wood* (1971), 5 RFL 82 (Ont SC); *Sweet v Sweet* (1971), 4 RFL 254 (Ont SC).

parents. The Director of Maintenance Enforcement has no authority to extend the order; that authority rests with the court.[267]

The duration of a child support order may be extended if the child decides to undertake post-secondary studies,[268] but a court may decline to order support where the application is not brought until several years after the completion of post-secondary studies.[269]

4) Stay of Order

A court may stay an order for child support during weeks when the obligor receives no income or benefits and may direct the obligor to immediately notify the Director of Support Enforcement of any changes in the obligor's employment status.[270]

5) Future Child Support

In appropriate circumstances, in the past, courts have fixed child support to be paid in the future, thereby creating an accumulating debt obligation.[271] It is open to question whether such orders are consistent with the *Federal Child Support Guidelines*.[272]

If the cost of day to day support for the children comes to less than the amount of child support paid, the surplus should be diverted to a trust for the children and should not be intermingled with investments in the name of the payee spouse and her new partner.[273]

6) Effect of Spousal Reconciliation

Judicial decisions are not consistent with respect to the effect of spousal reconciliation on pre-existing spousal and child support obligations. In Ontario and Saskatchewan, a resumption of cohabitation in an ultimately unsuccessful attempt at reconciliation has been held to terminate rights and obligations under a pre-existing support order.[274] In British Columbia

---

267 *Goudriaan v Plourde*, [2002] AJ No 272 (QB).

268 *Swannie v Swannie* (1989), 75 Nfld & PEIR 284 (Nfld TD).

269 *Pearson v Pearson* (1995), 16 RFL (4th) 75 (Man QB).

270 *Martin v Martin*, [1997] NJ No 61 (TD).

271 See *Ross v Ross*, [1997] NSJ No 444 (TD); compare *Grey v McNeil*, [1997] NSJ No 87 (TD); see, generally, Julien D Payne, *Payne on Divorce*, 4th ed (Scarborough, ON: Carswell, 1996) at 184 and 263, subheadings "Future Contingencies."

272 In *Robski v Robski*, [1997] NSJ No 444 (TD), Tidman J raised but did not resolve the question whether contingent orders would continue to be possible after implementation of the *Federal Child Support Guidelines* on 1 May 1997.

273 *Reid-Floyd v Kelly*, [1998] NBJ No 19 (QB).

274 *Re Wiley and Wiley* (1919), 49 DLR 643 (Ont HC); *Snyder v Snyder* (1973), 12 RFL 335 (Ont Fam Ct); *Mongrain v Mongrain* (1986), 1 RFL (3d) 330 (Ont HCJ); *Smith v Smith* (1989), 22 RFL (3d) 173 (Ont HCJ), additional reasons at (1989), 22 RFL (3d) 393 (Ont HCJ); *Grail v Grail* (1990), 30 RFL (3d) 454 (Ont Ct Gen Div) (interim support); *Michalchuk v Michalchuk*, 2013 ONSC 5978; *Re Hughes* (1959), 28 WWR 170 (Sask Dist Ct); *Stecyk v Stecyk* (1980), 16 RFL (2d) 255 (Sask Dist Ct), aff'd (1980), 23 RFL (2d) 53 (Sask QB). Compare *Rodbard v Rodbard* (1993), 45 RFL (3d) 451 (Ont Ct Gen Div). As to the termination of parenting orders by spousal reconciliation, see *MacDonald v Keddy-Smith* (1990), 30 RFL (3d) 461 (NS Fam Ct); compare *Clarke v Gale*, 2009 NSSC 170; *Wilson v Wilson*, 1983 CanLII 1165 (Ont Ct J). As to the effect of a resumption of cohabitation on a separation agreement, see *Baron v Baron* (1990), 29 RFL

and Manitoba, on the other hand, it has been held that a valid support order cannot be nullified by anything other than a further order of a court of competent jurisdiction[275] but as a general rule courts will suspend the obligation to pay during the period of cohabitation.[276]

7) Effect of Obligor's Death

Child support obligations have sometimes been declared binding on the obligor's estate, thereby extending the duration of child support beyond the obligor's death.[277] In the absence of any specific direction that the order shall survive the death of the payor, a child support order terminates on the death of the payor[278] except insofar as there may be a statutory provision to the contrary.[279] In the absence of any express declaration that a pre-existing child support order is binding on the deceased obligor's estate, an application under section 17(1) of the *Divorce Act* to retroactively change child support cannot be brought after the death of the payor because the *Divorce Act* does not contain a provision similar to section 34(4) of the Ontario *Family Law Act*,[280] which stipulates that an order for support binds the estate of the person having the support obligation.[281] Where a payor who has a duty to pay support under an agreement or order dies, and the agreement or order is silent about whether that duty continues after the payor's death and is a debt of his or her estate, section 171(3) of the British Columbia *Family Law Act* allows the recipient of that support to apply for an order that the duty to pay support continues despite the death of the payor and is a debt of the estate, based on the factors in section 171(1) of the Act.[282] Where a payee spouse sought to vary a subsisting order for the support of her disabled child but died prior to the hearing, the executors of her estate were held entitled to proceed with the application because the periodic payments were not conditioned on the survival of the payee spouse, being subject only to the condition that the child remain a "[child] of the marriage" within the meaning of section 2 of the *Divorce*

(3d) 37 (Man QB); *Evans v Evans* (1992), 41 RFL (3d) 400 (Nfld TD) (matrimonial property); *Bebenek v Bebenek* (1979), 11 RFL (2d) 137 (Ont CA); *Bailey v Bailey* (1982), 26 RFL (2d) 209 (Ont CA); *Livermore v Livermore* (1992), 43 RFL (3d) 163 (Ont Ct Gen Div); *Hill v Hill* (1990), 29 RFL (3d) 386 (Sask QB).

275 *Wolf v Wolf* (1992), 41 RFL (3d) 391 (BCSC); *Barnesky v Barnesky* (1988), 16 RFL (3d) 450 (Man QB); *Clarke v Gale*, 2009 NSSC 170.

276 *Fitzell v Weisbrod* (2005), 11 RFL (6th) 239 (Ont SCJ); *Ivan v Leblanc*, 2012 ONSC 4445.

277 *Chalmers Estate v Chalmers* (1990), 29 RFL (3d) 54 at 58–59 (Alta QB); *Usova v Harrison*, 2010 BCSC 723; *Wagener v Wagener* (1988), 17 RFL (3d) 308 (Man QB) (order to bind estate for three years after death); *Reddin v Reddin* (1990), 80 Nfld & PEIR 181 (PEITD), aff'd (1992), 94 Nfld & PEIR 328 (PEICA); *Will v Thauberger Estate* (1991), 34 RFL (3d) 432 (Sask QB), var'd (1991), 38 RFL (3d) 68 (Sask CA); see *contra Carmichael v Carmichael* (1992), 43 RFL (3d) 145 (NSCA). See also *Sinclair v McAuley*, 2012 MBCA 86.

278 *Despot v Despot Estate* (1992), 42 RFL (3d) 218 (BCSC); *Terry v Terry Estate* (1994), 1 BCLR (3d) 299 (SC) (specific direction found in this case); *Finnie v Rae* (1977), 16 OR (2d) 54 (HCJ); *Katz v Katz*, 2014 ONCA 606; see *contra Chalmers Estate v Chalmers* (1990), 27 RFL (3d) 54 at 58–59 (Alta QB) (child support); *Johnson v MacLellan Estate*, [2007] AJ No 117 (QB); see also *Droit de la famille—324*, [1987] RJQ 149 (CS).

279 See *Family Law Act*, SA 2003, c F-4.5, s 80; *Family Law Act*, SBC 2011, c 25, sections 170–171; *Joffres v Joffres*, 2014 BCSC 1778; *Bouchard v Bouchard*, 2018 BCSC 1728; *RM v NM*, 2014 BCSC 1755; *Family Law Act*, RSO 1990, c F3, s 34(4); *Katz v Katz*, 2014 ONCA 606.

280 RSO 1990, c F.3.

281 *Blacklock v Tkacz*, 2021 ONCA 630 at paras 6–7.

282 *Bouchard v Bouchard*, 2018 BCSC 1728 at para 34, Donegan J.

Act, 1968.[283] It remains to be seen whether orders binding the obligor's estate will continue to be feasible in light of the implementation of the *Federal Child Support Guidelines* as of 1 May 1997, which establish fixed periodic child support payments that are premised on the obligor's income. Child support obligations arising pursuant to a separation agreement may bind a deceased obligor's estate; whether such obligations do bind the estate turns upon the construction of the agreement.[284]

In determining an adult child's entitlement to support out of the estate of his deceased father while the child is pursuing post-secondary education, section 8(1) of *The Dependants Relief Act* (Manitoba) requires the court to determine the child's financial needs and fix an amount and duration that are reasonable having regard to all the circumstances of the case, including the eleven factors specifically listed. In the absence of exceptional circumstances, the court may place a cap on the child's entitlement at his first degree or four years. The court may apportion the child's educational expenses between both the parents in proportion to their respective means, after due account is taken of the child's responsibility to make a reasonable contribution to his own expenses either by way of part-time employment or student loans. The fact that the child has not been in contact with the obligor for many years prior to the obligor's death may be treated as a neutral factor where the child was not responsible for the breakdown in the parent/child relationship.[285]

Adult children, one of whom is completing post-secondary education and the second of whom is disabled, may be entitled to lump sum support out of their deceased father's estate pursuant to Part V of the Ontario *Succession Law Reform Act.* Section 58(1) of the Act empowers a court to make an order when the deceased has not made "adequate provision for the proper support" of a dependant and the court may make an order it considers adequate for "proper support." What constitutes proper maintenance and support must be determined in light of a variety of circumstances; it cannot be limited to the bare necessities of life. In determining whether a deceased person has made adequate provision for the proper support of particular dependants, the court must examine the claims of all dependants, whether based on need or on legal or moral and ethical obligations and regardless whether they are pursuing a claim in their own right under the Ontario *Succession Law Reform Act.* Although the court might well be justified in ordering that the deceased's entire testamentary estate and notional estate under section 72 of the Act be transferred to the disabled adult child on a strictly needs-based approach, such a disposition may be deemed inappropriate in light of the moral claims that the deceased's widow is entitled to assert notwithstanding her economic self-sufficiency.[287]

Child support arrears owing to a parent at the time of the obligor's death are a first charge against the obligor's estate and can be recovered if the estate has enough funds. RSPs, such

283 SC 1967–68, c 24; *Lesser v Lesser* (1985), 44 RFL (2d) 255 (Ont HCJ), aff'd (1985), 51 OR (2d) 100 (CA); see also *Will v Thauberger Estate* (1991), 34 RFL (3d) 432 (Sask QB), var'd (1991), 38 RFL (3d) 68 (Sask CA).

284 *Wilson v Wilson Estate*, [1998] BCJ No 2516 (SC). As to the impact of proceedings for child support brought against the obligor's estate pursuant to the Ontario *Succession Law Reform Act*, see *Cummings v Cummings*, [2004] OJ No 90 (CA).

285 *CERB v L Estate*, [2004] MJ No 83 (QB) (child entitled to lump sum of $16,500 out of deceased's estate of $96,500).

286 *Cummings v Cummings*, [2004] OJ No 90 (CA).

287 *Ibid.*

as a LIRA, are not part of the deceased's estate and child support arrears cannot be pursued, therefore, when the proceeds of the LIRA are already in the hands of the designated beneficiaries. The child, as an adult full-time student, may, nevertheless, be entitled to pursue an application for support as a "dependant" within the meaning of the Ontario *Succession Law Reform Act* where the deceased did not make adequate provision for the child in her will and, on such application, the court may order "such provision as it considers adequate" pursuant to section 58(1) of the Act. In that event, the requisite amount may be ordered to be paid out of the LIRA, even though its proceeds have already been paid to the designated beneficiaries. The calculation of "adequate" provision under the Ontario *Succession Law Reform Act* is not an exact science. There are no monetary guidelines and the amount is largely a matter of judicial discretion, although the court must have regard to "all the circumstances" of the application pursuant to section 62(1) of the Act. In fixing the amount payable, the child support arrears may be taken into account as a "moral obligation" of the deceased parent, as may also the adult child's own reasonable contribution to her post-secondary and living expenses through summer employment and available student loans and an appropriate contribution of the surviving parent. After reviewing the financial considerations in *Juffs v Investors Group Financial Services Inc*,[288] Belobaba J included one-half of the child support arrears in his calculations, which produced an overall amount of $22,442.80 to be paid out of the LIRA, which had a value of $32,127.81, thus leaving a portion of the LIRA to be shared by the designated beneficiaries, subject to their payment of costs on a partial indemnity basis in this action against them. Without resolving the issue of whether and under what circumstances a financial institution has a duty of care to estate creditors or SLRA claimants when paying out the proceeds of an RSP or LIRA to designated beneficiaries, Belobaba J dismissed a concurrent action in negligence against Investors Group Financial Services Inc on the ground that, given the information it was provided, there was no negligence on the facts of this case.

I. TERMS AND CONDITIONS

1) Section 15.1(4) of *Divorce Act*

Diverse terms, conditions, and restrictions may be imposed on child support orders pursuant to section 15.1(4) of the *Divorce Act*.[289]

2) Speculative and Anticipated Future Contingencies

A court will not determine the amount of child support on the basis of changes that are merely speculative.[290] The court may, nevertheless, anticipate future events that are expected to occur. For example, the court may order that the amount of child support shall decrease in accordance with the applicable provincial table after the division of the obligor's income

---

288 [2005] OJ No 3872 (SCJ).

289 *Muslake v Muslake* (1987), 6 RFL (3d) 280 (Ont UFC).

290 *Walkeden v Zemlak*, [1997] SJ No 601 (QB); see also *White v White*, [1998] BCJ No 2635 (SC); *Aker v Howard*, [1998] OJ No 5562 (Gen Div); *Walker v Gardner*, [2000] PEIJ No 99 (SC).

bearing assets results in a decreased income.[291] A court may temporarily reduce the monthly amount of child support payable under the applicable provincial table of the Guidelines, where the obligor will sustain a loss of employment income and be compelled to rely on employment insurance after necessary medical or surgical treatment.[292] To possibly avert the need and expense of further litigation, an order may be granted to provide for future child support payments while the children complete their post-secondary education.[293] The amount of child support may reflect alternative plans relating to the post-secondary educa tional programs of the respective children.[294]

A court may refuse to make a prospective order based on future contingencies, while advising the parties to consider the possibility of being penalized in costs for ignoring the lessons learned from the current proceeding.[295]

A child support order may be tiered to cover future events.[296] Where the obligor is currently underemployed or unemployed but is likely to achieve better employment in the future, the court may order child support on a graduated basis that is conditional on the obligor's income.[297] A court may order that a certain level of child support be paid while the obligor is unemployed and a higher level of support be paid when the obligor is employed or receiving unemployment insurance benefits.[298]

In *Crick v Crick*,[299] Warren J of the British Columbia Supreme Court concluded that there is no legislative authority whereby the court can set aside a portion of the amount of periodic child support to be paid into a trust account to meet the child's future educational and other needs. A contrary conclusion was reached in *Greenwood v Greenwood*,[300] wherein Burnyeat J of the British Columbia Supreme Court granted an order for the establishment of a post-secondary education fund and further directed that the payor should be entitled to pay the amount directly into the fund and thereby be eligible for any income tax benefits consequently available. Given the disinclination of the courts to grant child support orders that address future contingencies[301] and the well-established principle that support orders should be based on the facts existing at the time of the order or on facts that are foreseen as likely to occur,[302] the conclusion of Warren J in *Crick v Crick* appears to be sound, notwith

291 *RSW v ATW*, [1997] BCJ No 3065 (SC).

292 *Ward v Ward*, [1998] AJ No 63 (QB).

293 *MacDonald v Rasmussen*, [2000] SJ No 660 (QB).

294 *Penney v Boland*, [1999] NJ No 71 (UFC).

295 *Cram v Cram*, [1999] BCJ No 2518 (SC).

296 *McGrath v McGrath* (1998), 86 NSR (2d) 35 (TD).

297 *Agnew v Agnew* (1994), 93 Man R (2d) 243 (QB); *Swerid v Swerid* (1994), 94 Man R (2d) 86 (QB).

298 *Best v Combden*, [1998] NJ No 74 (SC); *Currie v Currie*, [1999] OJ No 2170 (SCJ); *Champion v Champion* (1994), 115 Nfld & PEIR 175 (PEITD); *Atkinson v Atkinson* (1994), 124 Nfld & PEIR 271 (PEITD).

299 [1997] BCJ No 2222 (SC); see also *Livingstone v Livingstone*, [1999] BCJ No 996 (CA) (order for establishment of trust fund set aside on appeal as unnecessary and a potential source of future conflict, but the jurisdictional right, if any, to make such an order was left unresolved).

300 [1998] BCJ No 729 (SC); and see *Greenwood v Greenwood*, [1999] BCJ No 2093 (SC) (judicial dismissal of variation application). See also *Thompson v Thompson*, [1999] SJ No 317 (QB) (parents ordered to contribute on *pro rata* basis to Canadian Scholarship Trust Fund).

301 As to the position under the discretionary child support regime that existed prior to 1 May 1997, when the *Federal Child Support Guidelines* were implemented, see Julien D Payne, *Payne on Divorce*, 4th ed (Scarborough, ON: Carswell, 1996) at 184–85.

302 *Omah-Maharajh v Howard*, [1998] AJ No 173 (QB).

standing that section 15.1(4) of the *Divorce Act* confers a discretion on the court to "impose terms, conditions or restrictions in connection with the order or interim order as it thinks fit and just." The implementation of the *Federal Child Support Guidelines* on 1 May 1997, whereby the basic table amount of child support is based on the obligor's current annual income, militates against the exercise of an overriding judicial discretion to address future contingencies, at least in those cases where the amount of child support is based solely on the applicable provincial table. This analysis accords with the decision of the Saskatchewan Court of Appeal in *Bachorick v Verdejo*,[303] which has been endorsed by the Ontario Court of Appeal in *Simon v Simon*,[304] wherein it was concluded that a court has no jurisdiction under the *Divorce Act* or the *Federal Child Support Guidelines* to build a fund for a child's future education out of the monthly table amount of child support. Any judicial direction to this effect would negate the underlying premise of the *Federal Child Support Guidelines* that the amount of child support reflects the current needs of the children. It would also constitute an unwarranted intrusion on the spending priorities of the primary caregiving parent. The implementation of the Guidelines has not changed the basic principle that a court will not ordinarily compel a primary caregiving parent to account for how child support payments are spent.[305] The role of the court in ordering child support is to establish the appropriate amount of child support, based on the circumstances at the time when the application is heard. It is not a responsibility of the court to guarantee that the standard of living of children will be assured for the future. If that were the case, a court would be required to set aside funds for such possibilities as illness or loss of employment in every case. The *Federal Child Support Guidelines* do not change the role of the court from that which pre-dated their implementation. While the reasoning in *Bachorick v Verdejo* is compelling in the context of the specific order made in that case, a distinction might possibly be made between child support orders in the applicable provincial or territorial table amount and orders granted for the payment of special or extraordinary expenses under section 7 of the *Federal Child Support Guidelines*, although the dangers of crystal ball gazing should not be overlooked. In *OM v AK*,[306] the court ordered less than the applicable table amount of child support pursuant to section 4(b) of the *Federal Child Support Guidelines* on the basis that the applicable table amount was inappropriate, being far in excess of the children's reasonable entitlement. However, because the obligor's high income was likely to be short-lived, the court concluded that the actual needs of the children included their future education and other benefits ordinarily available to high income families. Accordingly, in addition to ordering periodic child support, the court ordered a designated monthly amount to be paid into a trust to meet such future eventualities.

---

303 [1999] SJ No 450 (CA); *Ghremida v Elgahwas*, 2023 SKCA 23. See also Section I(3), below in this chapter.

304 [1999] OJ No 4492 (CA); see also *JS v AB*, 2010 NBQB 429; *Mylrea v Benoit*, [2003] OJ No 2921 (SCJ); compare *Provost v Marsden*, 2009 NSSC 365.

305 See also *KAW v MEW*, 2020 ABCA 277 (structured payments respecting retroactive child support reversed on appeal).

306 [2000] QJ No 3224 (CS).

3) Registered Education Savings Plan

Registered Education Savings Plans are not section 7 expenses, nor are they part of the table amount of child support.[307] Child support is intended to provide for the current needs of the children. A child support order should not address anticipated needs in the distant future. A court may refuse to order a parent to make future payments into a scholarship savings plan or a Registered Education Savings Plan (RESP) to meet future educational needs of the children.[308] Whether assets in an RESP are the property of the subscriber or are held in trust for a beneficiary has not been consistently answered in the caselaw.[309]

4) Retroactive Adjustment of Child Support Based on Subsequent Income Tax Returns; Ongoing Financial Disclosure

In *Sullivan v Struck*,[310] Harris JA of the British Columbia Court of Appeal stated:

> I accept that in calculating a retrospective support order, the correct approach is to use the payor's actual income for the relevant period, if it is readily ascertainable: *Cornelissen v. Cornelissen*, 2003 BCCA 666 at paras. 39-41. This approach is consistent with what the Supreme Court of Canada had to say in *D.B.S. v. S.R.G.*, 2006 SCC 37.

A court may direct either or both of the spouses to annually provide the other spouse with a copy of his duly filed Income Tax Return and Notice of Assessment or Reassessment for the preceding taxation year.[311] If the actual income varies from that utilized for the previous year's calculation of child support, the court may further direct that there shall be a retro active change effective 1 January of the previous year and the deficiency or excess, as the case may be, shall be paid or repaid in a lump sum to the appropriate party.[312] Although an express judicial direction respecting the payment of any such deficiency or excess can clearly be added to an order for child support pursuant to section 15.1(4) of the *Divorce Act*, which expressly empowers a court, in the exercise of its discretion, to impose terms, conditions, or restrictions in connection with the order, the question arises whether retroactive variation is available as of right in the absence of any judicial direction to that effect. In the opinion

---

307 *Smith v Smith*, 2011 NSSC 269 at para 80, Jollimore J; see also *Boylan v MacLean*, 2018 NSSC 15; *Pereverzoff v Pereverzoff*, 2017 BCSC 687.

308 *RY v CSY*, [2001] BCJ No 1570 (SC); *Pereverzoff v Pereverzoff*, 2017 BCSC 687; *JS v AB*, 2010 NBQB 429; *Rhynold v Van der Linden*, 2007 NSCA 72; *Boylan v MacLean*, 2018 NSSC 15; *CM v PM*, 2019 NSSC 250; *Wotton v Banks*, [2001] PEIJ No 22 (SC); *Crosby v Crosby*, [2002] SJ No 164 (QB).

309 See *Labatte v Labatte*, 2022 ONSC 4787 at para 34, Faieta J, citing Kira Domratchev, "Is an RESP a Trust? . . . And So What If It Is?" (May 2021) 40 Est Tr & Pensions J 257; Charles Wagner & Mari Maimets, "Litigation and RESPs," 20th Annual Estates and Trusts Summit, 16 October 2017. See also Chapter 5, Section L: "Expenses for Post-Secondary Education."

310 2015 BCCA 521 at para 78. See also *McCarty v McCarty*, 2016 ABQB 91 (application based on s 18 of Guidelines).

311 *JFW v PCW*, [2001] AJ No 1145 (CA); *Bucholtz v Smith*, [2001] BCJ No 1872 (SC); *Albinet v Albinet*, [2003] MJ No 44 (CA); *Robski v Robski*, [1997] NSJ No 444 (TD); *Currie v Currie*, [1999] OJ No 2170 (SCJ).

312 *Michalezski v Michalezski*, [2002] AJ No 501 (QB); see also *MJB v WPB*, [1999] MJ No 314 (QB) (calculation of child support to be revisited in the event of the obligor's disability claim against a third party being reinstated); *HK v SK*, [2002] NSJ No 475 (SC); *Harris v Mayo*, [2001] OJ No 4751 (SCJ); *Thackeray v Sellstead*, [2001] SJ No 248 (QB).

of McIntyre J of the Saskatchewan Court of Queen's Bench in *Martin v Schaeffer*,[313] where a court determines a parent's current annual income for the purpose of determining the amount of child support to be paid, it does so on the basis of the best information available to the court. The judicial prognosis as to a parent's future income may not be entirely accurate but this does not normally justify any retroactive adjustment of child support once a parent's actual income becomes known. To encourage such applications would result in endless litigation. In *Lavergne v Lavergne*,[314] however, the Alberta Court of Appeal favoured such retroactive adjustment, stating that "[t]he child is entitled to be supported according to the payor's current income, if ascertainable, and if not, by a reasonably accurate estimate of the payor's current income with an adjustment at year's end once the actual income is known." While this approach may be readily applicable to adjust the table amount of child support, difficulties may arise when the original order deviated from the table amount pursuant to the *Federal Child Support Guidelines*.

Where the obligor derives a significant portion of her income from a pension, the court may direct the obligor to keep the primary caregiving parent informed about the status of the pension and any plans to change that status.[315]

A court may direct spouses to keep each other informed of any change in their employment status.[316]

5) Control over Child Support Payments

In the absence of any judicial direction to the contrary, the payor cannot control how the basic table amount of child support is spent by the recipient parent.[317]

Where there is evidence that an adult child will not take court-ordered support from the recipient parent, the court may order the appointment of an independent trustee to administer the funds.[318]

6) Parenting

Child support and parenting are rights of the child. A primary caregiving parent's interference with the exercise of parenting time by the other should be addressed by an application to vary the parenting arrangements. It should not be addressed by judicial endorsement of a parent's request that the payment of court-ordered child support should be linked to or conditioned upon the enjoyment of a positive relationship with the children.[319]

---

313 [2001] SJ No 210 (QB). See also *Clark v Clark*, [2006] OJ No 233 (SCJ).

314 2007 ABCA 169 at para 22 (quantification of retroactive child support); see also *Chalifoux v Chalifoux*, 2008 ABCA 70; *Willis v Willis*, 2010 ABQB 534; *Heppner v Jylli*, 2010 BCSC 1020; *DMA v MS*, [2008] NBJ No 498 (QB); *Kelland v Stanley*, 2013 NLTD(F) 40; *Emmerson v Emmerson*, 2017 ONCA 917. Compare *KAMR v WHG*, 2014 BCSC 103.

315 *Laraque v Allooloo*, [1999] NWTJ No 49 (SC) (application under *NWT Child Support Guidelines*).

316 *Currie v Currie*, [1999] OJ No 2170 (SCJ).

317 *Dahlgren v Hodgson*, [1998] AJ No 1501 (CA) (*Charter* challenge dismissed on its merits in addition to being procedurally defective); *Simon v Simon* (2000), 1 RFL (5th) 119 (Ont CA).

318 *Alexander v Alexander*, [1999] OJ No 3694 (SCJ).

319 *Hillier v Hillier*, [2003] PEIJ No 58 (SC).

7) "Step Down" Provisions

A "step down" provision in a formal order that provides for a reduction in the amount of child support as each child ceases to be eligible for support is unobjectionable, if the respective amounts payable reflect the amounts set out in the *Federal Child Support Guidelines* for that number of children. Such an order filed with the Director of Maintenance Enforcement does not purport to empower the Director to make determinations concerning who is a "child of the marriage." Because a "step down" provision may provide additional clarity to the parties, there is no objection to the inclusion of such a provision in an order, but if the support order is contested, this is an issue that should be addressed at the hearing.[320]

J. COST OF LIVING INDEXATION

Under the former judicial discretionary regime of child support, a court had the statutory jurisdiction to index a periodic child support order against inflation in order to provide for a child's needs. It is questionable how far the judicial discretion to include an annual cost-of-living adjustment in a child support order has survived the implementation of federal and provincial guidelines, whereby a court must presumptively apply the provincial or territorial table in order to quantify periodic child support, because these tables are not conditioned on the cost of living but on the obligor's income. As that income changes, so too does the amount of child support prescribed by the applicable table. The *Federal Child Support Guidelines* are, therefore, self-sufficient and do not require the judicial imposition of a cost-of-living index. Indeed, as one judge has pointed out, any such addition could result in double recovery. Nevertheless, some courts have used cost-of-living indexation, perhaps to offset the possibility that former spouses will not avail themselves of the right to annual disclosure under section 25(1) of the *Federal Child Support Guidelines* or any provincial equivalent.[323]

Different considerations may apply to consensual arrangements that provide for child support payments. In such cases, cost-of-living indexation clauses may be attractive to the spouses or former spouses, although they may become less common except in cases where the child support arrangements were negotiated under the former tax deduction/inclusion regime.

A cost-of-living indexation clause in a separation agreement does not prevent the finding of a material change of circumstances sufficient to warrant an order for the basic amount of child support under the provincial child support guidelines in addition to designated special or extraordinary expenses.[324]

In *Sleiman v Sleiman*,[325] wherein lump sum child support was ordered, full cost-of-living indexation of the annual income attributed to the obligor was incorporated in actuarial

---

320 *Stebner v Stebner*, [2005] AJ No 1556 (QB).

321 *Fein v Fein*, [2001] OJ No 4554 (SCJ); *WG v SG*, 2014 ONSC 3258; *Ouellette v Uddin*, 2018 ONSC 4520.

322 *Whitehead v Whitehead*, [1999] BCJ No 1783 (SC).

323 See, for example, *Rooney v Rooney*, [2003] NJ No 227 (SC); *Davids v Davids*, [1998] OJ No 2859 (Gen Div); *Mayer v Mayer*, [1999] OJ No 5286 (SCJ); *Cavanaugh v Glass*, [2001] OJ No 457 (SCJ); *Laughlin v Cormier*, [1997] PEIJ No 80 (SC).

324 *Denesi v Neves*, [1998] OJ No 736 (Prov Div).

325 [2003] OJ No 588 (SCJ).

calculations and was judicially endorsed because of the impossibility of determining anticipated increases in the obligor's annual income.

K. RETROACTIVE PERMANENT AND VARIATION ORDERS; APPEALS

1) Retroactivity under Sections 15.1 and 17 of *Divorce Act*

While section 15.1 of the *Divorce Act* is silent on the question whether courts may order child support to be paid for a period of time that preceded the commencement of divorce proceedings, the Supreme Court of Canada in *DBS v SRG; LJW v TAR; Henry v Henry; Hiemstra v Hiemstra*[326] accepted the reasoning of the majority judgment in the Alberta Court of Appeal in *Hunt v Smolis-Hunt*[327] that "[a]n order for retroactive child support pre-dating the issuance [of] a petition for divorce is, we suggest, a necessary incident to the dissolution of a marriage" and falls within the legislative authority of the Parliament of Canada.[328] Section 17(1) of the *Divorce Act* expressly empowers a court to retroactively vary child support orders. The exercise of this discretion may result in either reducing the amount of child support or in increasing the amount payable, so as to conform in both instances with the stipulation in section 26(2) of the *Divorce Act* that child support should reflect the joint obligation of the spouses to maintain their children in accordance with their retroactive abilities.[329]

2) Interim Orders

On an application for interim child support[330] or for variation of a permanent order for child support under the *Divorce Act*, it is a common practice for the court to make its order effective as of the date when the proceeding was launched,[331] although a court may find this inappropriate in the circumstances of the particular case.[332] Courts are reluctant to backdate interim child support to a date prior to the filing of the motion because of the limited evidence available at the interim stage of a proceeding.[333]

---

326 [2006] SCJ No 37.

327 [2001] AJ No 1170 at para 32 (CA). See also *Johannson v Haaranen*, 2018 ABQB 554; *S v S*, [2007] NBJ No 422 (QB). And see *JTD v JPD*, 2012 BCSC 343 (retroactive child support denied prior to parental separation).

328 For a review of prior conflicting provincial appellate judgments, see *Mellway v Mellway*, [2004] MJ No 300 (CA).

329 *Dahl v Dahl* (1995), 178 AR 119 (CA); *Chester v Chester*, [2001] AJ No 1475 (QB); *Stebner v Stebner*, [2005] AJ No 392 (QB).

330 See Section B(13), above in this chapter.

331 *Razutis v Garrett*, [1999] BCJ No 1505 (CA); *Worrall v Worrall* (1991), 38 RFL (3d) 435 (Ont Ct Gen Div), applying *Englar v Englar* (1978), 2 RFL (2d) 237 (Ont CA); *Reeves v Reeves*, [2003] PEIJ No 50 (SC); see also *Thomson v Howard*, [1997] OJ No 4431 (Gen Div); *BC v DU*, [1997] BCJ No 2431 (SC) (confirmation order).

332 *Cane v Newman*, [1998] OJ No 2116 (Gen Div).

333 *Reeves v Reeves*, [2003] PEIJ No 50 (SC); *Skormorowski v Bernier*, 2009 SKQB 55. See Section B(13), above in this chapter.

3) Diversity of Judicial Approaches

There is no precise yardstick as to when retroactive child support should be ordered; claims for such relief should be considered on a case-by-case basis.[334] Neither the *Divorce Act* nor the *Federal Child Support Guidelines* imposes any direction or time limitation respecting retroactive support orders. In *MacKinnon v MacKinnon*,[335] the Ontario Court of Appeal concluded that retroactive support relates to claims for support for the period pre-dating the commencement date of the proceeding in which support is claimed; a claim for support after the proceeding has been commenced is characterized as prospective support.[336]

The jurisdiction of the court to order that retroactive child support be paid for a period preceding the date of the application to vary implies a right to order financial disclosure further back in time than the three years that customarily applies to variation applications under section 21 of the *Federal Child Support Guidelines*, although the court may impose temporal limits respecting the additionally required disclosure as a preliminary step to ascertaining whether even more financial disclosure will be required.[337]

An applicant parent's lack of due diligence cannot stop a proper claim for retroactive child support,[338] although a finding of actual acquiescence may go to the question of fairness.[339] Laches, being an equitable remedy, constitutes no defence to a statutory claim for a retroactive increase in child support.[340] If a child's needs can only be met by a retroactive support order, the court should exercise its discretion accordingly but in doing so the court should ensure that the children benefit first and foremost and not the payee parent.[341] However, the fact that the primary caregiving parent will likely be the primary benefactor is no bar to retroactive child support where that parent has borne an unduly onerous financial responsibility for the upbringing of a child in the past,[342] even though the child may soon cease to be a "child of the marriage" within the meaning of section 2(1) of the *Divorce Act*.

It is open to question whether a retroactive order for support should be granted when an application for interim support has been dismissed,[344] but in a proper case a court may grant retroactive support, regardless of whether there has been a prior order for interim support. Failure to bring an interim application for child support constitutes no bar to a retroactive

---

334 *DBS v SRG; LJW v TAR; Henry v Henry; Hiemstra v Hiemstra*, 2006 SCC 37; *Kerr v Baranow* and *Vanasse v Seguin*, [2011] 1 SCR 269 (spousal support); *Brett v Brett*, [1999] OJ No 1384 (CA); *Cennon v Cennon*, [1999] SJ No 504 (QB).

335 (2005), 75 OR (3d) 175 at para 19 (CA).

336 See *Hemond v Galano*, 2013 ONSC 6929 at para 38; *JMG v LDG*, 2016 ONSC 3042. And see *Henderson v Micetich*, 2021 ABCA 103 at para 35; *Boylan v MacLean*, 2018 NSSC 15 at paras 112–13.

337 *Boyda v Boyda*, [1998] AJ No 279 (QB).

338 *Allen v Allen* (1994), 9 RFL (4th) 48 (BCSC).

339 *Keighley v Keighley*, [1998] BCJ No 2845 (SC).

340 *Denesi v Neves*, [1998] OJ No 736 (Prov Div).

341 *MacBeth v MacBeth*, [1998] AJ No 195 (QB); *Lobo v Lobo*, [1999] AJ No 113 (QB).

342 *Collins v Collins*, [1998] AJ No 417 (QB); *Cavanaugh v Ziegler*, [1998] AJ No 1423 (CA); *Barnsley v Barnsley*, [1998] OJ No 5332 (Gen Div).

343 *Collins v Collins*, [1998] AJ No 417 (QB); see also *DBS v SRG; LJW v TAR; Henry v Henry; Hiemstra v Hiemstra*, 2006 SCC 37 at paras 89 and 150.

344 *Burgess v Burgess* (1995), 16 RFL (4th) 388 (Ont CA).

345 *Kerr v Kerr*, [1997] MJ No 6 (QB), considering *Kawaluk v Kawaluk* (1995), 17 RFL (4th) 185 (Man CA). See also *Dahl v Dahl* (1995), 18 RFL (4th) 122 (Alta CA); *Zdan v Zdan*, [2001] MJ No 444 (QB).

order being granted by the trial judge where the obligor was aware of the claim from the onset of court action,[346] but the amount of retroactive support may be reduced where it would cause hardship to the payor and the children in his care.[347] A trial judge may revisit an order for interim child support where the actual financial circumstances of the obligor only became known at the trial and, in such circumstances, an order for lump sum retroactive child support may be deemed appropriate.[348] When a trial judge is asked to deal with a claim for retroactive support that embraces the pre-trial period, the first issue to consider is what child support was properly payable during that period. Such an analysis must be undertaken to determine what adjustment, if any, should be made to a pre-existing interim child support order. The adjustment may operate in either of two ways; it may favour the payor parent or it may favour the recipient parent.[349] If an adjustment is deemed appropriate, the court must determine whether the accrued obligation should be discharged by a lump sum or by periodic payments or by a combination of both.[350]

In granting an order for retroactive child support, the court may order that interest shall be payable on the arrears thereby created.[351]

A retroactive order creating instant child support arrears may be deemed inappropriate where a disabled parent has no present or future capacity to discharge such arrears.[352] An order for retroactive application of the *Ontario Child Support Guidelines* will only be granted where circumstances render it expedient, practical, and fair.[353] While retroactive support may be denied where there is no need demonstrated during the period, there was no debt incurred, and payment ordered may represent a capital windfall,[354] these considerations may not apply when government seeks contribution or recovery of past social assistance payments, and there has been bad faith demonstrated by payor and recipient in arranging a collateral benefit outside the continued payment of public funds.[355]

Retroactive child support may be denied where such an order would amend a comprehensive spousal settlement reached after protracted negotiations at which both spouses were legally represented.[356] Where the obligor paid periodic child support for many years pursuant to a purportedly final settlement, without any expectation that it might subsequently be judicially reviewed, the court may conclude that retroactive child support should not be ordered

---

346 See *Kerr v Baranow* and *Vanasse v Seguin*, [2011] 1 SCR 269 (spousal support).

347 *Fransoo v Fransoo*, [2001] SJ No 121 (QB).

348 *MacMinn v MacMinn* (1995), 17 RFL (4th) 88 (Alta CA); compare *Pearce v Pearce*, [1999] BCJ No 2278 (SC) (judicial refusal to revisit interim order where income imputed fell short of actual income earned); *Enman v Enman*, [2000] PEIJ No 48 (SC).

349 *MacMinn v MacMinn* (1995), 17 RFL (4th) 88 (Alta CA). See also *Doerksen v Houlahan*, 2012 MBQB 110.

350 *Enman v Enman*, [2000] PEIJ No 48 (SC); see also *Tobias v Tobias*, [2000] AJ No 346 (QB) ("instant arrears" arising from retroactive child support order to be paid in designated lump sum instalments over six months).

351 *Hrabluik v Hrabluik*, [1999] MJ No 472 (QB); compare *Campbell v McRudden*, [2001] BCJ No 676 (SC) (interest on retroactive child support deemed inappropriate, even if permissible because it would constitute a windfall); see also *Speirs v Speirs*, 2011 ONSC 3712.

352 *Larosa v Larosa*, [2003] MJ No 203 (QB).

353 *Surette v Surette*, [2000] OJ No 675 (SCJ).

354 *Brett v Brett* (1999), 44 OR (3d) 61 (CA).

355 *Ogonowski v Ogonowska*, [2001] OJ No 335 (SCJ).

356 *Dean v Dean*, [1997] OJ No 3224 (Gen Div).

with respect to the period of time that elapsed before commencement of the application. Similarly, an order for retroactive child support may be deemed inappropriate where an interim-interim order for child support has remained unchanged for several years.[358]

A court may refuse to order retroactive child support either by way of a lump sum order or by way of future additional periodic child support payments where the obligor's ability to pay ongoing prospective periodic child support would be impaired by any additional obligation.[359]

Prospective orders for child support should be based on the obligor's current income, whereas retroactive orders should reflect the obligor's actual or imputed income at the material time.[360]

A court should not grant a retroactive order for reduced child support where this would deprive the children of support for a period of time because of the primary caregiving parent's inability to reimburse the "overpayment."[361]

4) Enumerated Factors Relating to Retroactivity

The judgments of the Supreme Court of Canada in three cases establish the framework for dealing with applications for retroactive child support: (1) *DBS v SRG; LJW v TAR; Henry v Henry; Hiemstra v Hiemstra;*[362] (2) *Michel v Graydon;*[363] and (3) *Colucci v Colucci.*[364] Prior to the judgments of the Supreme Court of Canada in *DBS v SRG; LJW v TAR; Henry v Henry; Hiemstra v Hiemstra,*[365] provincial appellate courts in Canada were divided as to the criteria to be applied in determining whether retroactive child support should be ordered in the diverse situations where such jurisdiction is possessed by the court.[366] In *DBS v SRG; LJW v TAR; Henry v Henry; Hiemstra v Hiemstra,* the seven-person court was divided four to three. Subject to a potential finding of "undue hardship" within the meaning of section 10 of the *Federal Child Support Guidelines,* the minority judgment was disposed to holding parents fully accountable for any failure to pay increased child support in accordance with the Guide

---

357 *Proulx v Zigart,* [1998] AJ No 545 (QB) (application under *Parentage and Maintenance Act,* SA 1990, c P-0.7).

358 *Miceli v Miceli,* [1998] OJ No 5460 (Gen Div).

359 *Ribeiro v Li* (1996), 22 RFL (4th) 459 at 463 (Ont Ct Gen Div).

360 *Porter v Porter,* [1998] NSJ No 426 (SC).

361 *Garrett-Rempel v Garrett-Rempel,* [2000] BCJ No 1771 (SC) (application under *Family Relations Act*).

362 2006 SCC 37.

363 2020 SCC 24. For an insightful review explaining how the Supreme Court of Canada judgment in *Michel v Graydon* modifies the principles relating to retroactive child support orders that were set out in the previous judgment of the Supreme Court of Canada in *DBS v SRG,* see *Henderson v Micetich,* 2021 ABCA 103. See also *Abumatar v Hamda,* 2021 ONSC 2165 at paras 52–60, Pazaratz J; *LB v PE,* 2021 ONCJ 114, Sherr J. And see Rollie Thompson, "The Supreme Court Begins to Rewrite *D.B.S.* in *Michel v. Graydon*" (2020) 39 CFLQ 309; Rollie Thompson, "Retroactive Support After Colucci", County of Carleton Law Association, Ottawa, 30th Annual Institute of Family Law: Day 1, Fall Virtual Program, 14 September 2021; *AF v RR,* 2021 NBCA 37.

364 2021 SCC 24.

365 2006 SCC 37.

366 See, for example, *LS v EP,* [1999] BCJ No 1451 (CA); *Cabot v Mikkelson,* [2004] MJ No 240 (CA); *Lu v Sun,* [2005] NSJ No 314 (CA); *Marinangeli v Marinangeli,* [2003] OJ No 2819 (CA); compare the Alberta Court of Appeal judgments in *DBS v SRG,* [2005] AJ No 2 (CA); *LJW v TAR,* [2005] AJ No 3 (CA); *Henry v Henry,* [2005] AJ No 4 (CA); *Hiemstra v Hiemstra,* [2005] AJ No 27 (CA).

lines as and when their incomes materially increased. The majority judgment adopted a somewhat more conservative approach in endorsing the following conclusions as modified by the subsequent judgments of the Supreme Court of Canada in *Michel v Graydon* and in *Colucci v Colucci*:

1) So-called retroactive orders for child support are not truly retroactive. They simply enforce the pre-existing legal obligation of parents to pay an amount of child support commensurate with their income.[367]
2) When an application for retroactive child support is brought, it is incumbent on the court to analyze the federal or provincial statutory scheme under which the application is brought. Different policy choices by the federal and provincial governments must be judicially respected.[368]
3) The propriety of a retroactive award can only be evaluated after a detailed examination of the facts of the particular case.[369]
4) Retroactive orders should not be regarded as exceptional orders to be granted only in exceptional circumstances. Although the propriety of a retroactive order should not be presumed, it is not confined to rare cases.[370]
5) Child support is a right of the child that cannot be bargained away by the parents.[371] Sections 15.1(5) to (8) and 17(6.2) to (6.5) of the *Divorce Act* control the extent to which parents can consensually determine their child obligations and the criteria defined therein take account of the standards prescribed by the *Federal Child Support Guidelines*. Corresponding legislation is to be found under provincial child support regimes. Courts may order retroactive child support where circumstances have changed or were not as they appeared when a prior agreement was reached or court order was made.[372]
6) The underlying premise of both federal and provincial guidelines is that the amount of child support should reflect the obligor's income.[373]
7) Quite independently of any court order or any steps taken by the prospective recipient, there is a free-standing obligation on parents to support their children commensurate with their income. A parent who fails to do so will have failed to fulfil her child support obligation.[374]
8) Although the Guidelines do not impose a direct obligation on an obligor to automatically disclose income increases and adjust child support payments accordingly, this does not mean that a parent will satisfy the child support obligation by doing nothing. If the income increases without an appropriate increase in the amount of child support paid, there exists an unfulfilled legal obligation that may subsequently merit enforcement by means of a retroactive child support award.[375]

---

367 *DBS v SRG; LJW v TAR; Henry v Henry; Hiemstra v Hiemstra*, 2006 SCC 37 at para 2.

368 *Ibid* at para 54; see also *Michel v Graydon*, 2020 SCC 24.

369 *DBS v SRG; LJW v TAR; Henry v Henry; Hiemstra v Hiemstra*, 2006 SCC 37 at para 6.

370 *Ibid* at para 5; *LPH v JMR*, 2021 BCSC 1282.

371 *DBS v SRG; LJW v TAR; Henry v Henry; Hiemstra v Hiemstra*, 2006 SCC 37 at paras 104 and 172.

372 *Hinz v Davey*, 2022 BCCA 232 (retroactive variation of child support agreement under British Columbia *Family Law Act*).

373 *Ibid* at paras 45, 54, and 166; see also *Colucci v Colucci*, 2021 SCC 24.

374 *DBS v SRG; LJW v TAR; Henry v Henry; Hiemstra v Hiemstra*, 2006 SCC 37 at para 48.

375 *Ibid* at para 59. And see *Colucci v Colucci*, 2021 SCC 24 at para 36.

9) Where retroactive child support is sought pursuant to section 15.1 of the *Divorce Act*, the obligor's interest in certainty must be balanced with the need for fairness and flexibility. Relevant factors for consideration in determining whether a retroactive child support award is justified include whether there is a reasonable excuse why support was not sought earlier by the payee; the conduct, blameworthy or otherwise, of the obligor; the circumstances of the child;[376] and any hardship that would be occasioned by a retroactive award. There is no priority to these factors and none is decisive; the court must take an holistic approach, which requires that account be taken of the interconnected nature of issues of child support, child poverty, and the consequent feminization of poverty. Relevant evidence concerning the aforementioned factors is a prerequisite to an order for retroactive child support; historic income disclosure is insufficient in itself.[378] In the opinion of the Alberta Court of Appeal in *Henderson v Micetich*, the Supreme Court of Canada in *Michel v Graydon* "recast the *DBS* factors, placing the consideration of a recipient parent's reasons for delay in a broader social context and taking an expansive view of blameworthy conduct."[379]

10) An unreasonable delay in seeking support militates against a retroactive child support award but the court must bear in mind that child support is the right of the child and cannot be waived by parental agreement. Courts should not hesitate to find a reason able excuse for the delay where the applicant harbours fears about a vindictive response from the obligor or lacks the financial or emotional means to bring an application or was given inadequate legal advice.[380] In *Michel v Graydon*, the Supreme Court of Canada concluded that with respect to the issue of delay in making an application, "the focus should be on whether the reason provided is understandable" rather than whether the support recipient had a "reasonable excuse" for the delay."[381] As stated by the Alberta Court of Appeal in *Henderson v Micetiich*:

> [41] . . . Most recently, in *Michel*, the Supreme Court recognized there are many reasons for a delay on the part of the recipient parent for bringing an application for increased child support. These may include lack of information regarding the payor's income, particularly lack of knowledge that the income has increased. Delay may also be the result of a lack of access to justice because of a lack of financial resources, or potential intimidation or misleading behavior on the part of the payor. In her concurring judgment in *Michel*, Martin J spoke of delay in this broader social context, considering issues such as intimate partner violence and access to justice. She noted that delay is not itself "inherently unreasonable".

---

376 *Woodland v Kirkham*, 2021 ONSC 8194 at paras 98–102 (order for $564,684.12 retroactive child support from 1 October 2009 to 1 October 2021).

377 *Michel v Graydon*, 2020 SCC 24 at para 100, Martin J, cited in *JM v LC*, 2022 PESC 35.

378 *DBS v SRG; LJW v TAR; Henry v Henry; Hiemstra v Hiemstra*, 2006 SCC 37 at paras 94–116; *LPH v JMR*, 2021 BCSC 1282.

379 *Henderson v Micetich*, 2021 ABCA 103 at para 33. See also *Arnault v Arnault*, 2022 ABQB 176; *Auer v Auer*, 2022 ABCA 376; *Hovey v Hanson*, 2021 NSSC 89 at para 70, Cormier J.

380 *DBS v SRG; LJW v TAR; Henry v Henry; Hiemstra v Hiemstra*, 2006 SCC 37 at para 101.

381 *Perez v Chiris*, 2021 ONSC 101 at para 24, Engelking J; *Laprise v Laprise*, 2023 ONSC 6195.

[42] We agree. In the absence of a clear agreement or court order that waives disclosure requirements or provides for another mechanism to calculate child support, delay will rarely substantially prejudice a payor parent. . . .

[44] Put simply, delay has a very limited role to play in determining the availability and extent of a retroactive child support order. Any delay on the part of a recipient parent must be viewed in light of available information, resources, and social context, including gender, social and economic inequities. Given the structure of the *Guidelines* and the well understood, and now widely accepted, philosophy that child support is an obligation on the part of both parents, the amount of which depends on the payor's income, there will be few cases where delay can be truly seen as unreasonable or a factor that should preclude the award of previously-owed support to children.[382]

Similarly, in *Best v MacKay*, Forgeron J, of the Supreme Court of Nova Scotia, observed:

> There are many reasons why a parent might delay in making an application, including fear of reprisal/violence, fear of litigation and litigation costs, lack of information or misinformation about the payor's income, inability to contact the payor, illness of the child or the parent, lack of emotional means, concerns about the child's relationship with the payor, attempts at reconciliation, mediation, or settlement, or the payor's deliberate delay: para 85. When focusing on the reason for the delay, the court must take into account "a generous appreciation of the social context in which the claimant's decision was made": para 113.[383]

11) Blameworthy conduct, though not a prerequisite to retroactivity,[384] is an important factor to consider in determining the propriety of a retroactive child support award. Blameworthy conduct is accorded an expansive definition and arises whenever a parent knowingly chooses to ignore or evade his child support obligations.[385] Blameworthy conduct has been described as "anything that privileges the payor parent's own interests over their children's right to an appropriate amount of support"[386] and a payor parent has a duty to make full and honest income disclosure.[387] Speaking for the majority in *Michel v Graydon*, Brown J explained the critical importance of full disclosure of income by the payor parent in the *Guidelines* system in the following words:

382 2021 ABCA 103 at paras 41, 42, and 44; see also *Mortson v Kminkova*, 2021 ABQB 476; *Destine v Cloutier*, 2022 ABCA 331; *Fleming v Spence*, 2023 ABCA 315. For a comprehensive summary on reasonable and unreasonable excuses for delay, see *SMF v BWF*, 2019 ABQB 806; see also *Nyereyogona v Schofield*, 2021 ABQB 662.

383 *Best v MacKay*, 2021 NSSC 124 at para 22.

384 *Goulding v Keck*, 2014 ABCA 138; *Howard v Cox*, 2017 ABCA 111; *Tedham v Tedham*, [2003] BCJ No 2554 (CA). As to the relevance of blameworthy conduct by the applicant in failing to disclose the receipt of disability benefits for a child, see *Felts v Silvestre*, 2021 BCSC 523.

385 *Goulding v Keck*, 2014 ABCA 138; *Hartshorne v Hartshorne*, 2010 BCCA 327; *Fallis v Garcia*, [2008] OJ No 2099 (SCJ); *Woodland v Kirkham*, 2021 ONSC 8194.

386 *DBS v SRG; LJW v TAR; Henry v Henry; Hiemstra v Hiemstra*, 2006 SCC 37 at para 106; *Henderson v Micetich*, 2021 ABCA 103; *Best v MacKay*, 2021 NSSC 124 at para 22.

387 As to the significant obligation on payor parents to provide full, honest, and timely income disclosure, see *CC v RT*, 2021 PESC 2, citing *Michel v Graydon*, 2020 SCC 24. And see *Colucci v Colucci*, 2021 SCC 24 wherein the prerequisite of timely financial disclosure is emphasized throughout the unanimous judgment of the Supreme Court of Canada. See also *Woodland v Kirkham*, 2021 ONSC 8194.

> Failure to disclose material information is the cancer of family law litigation (*Cunha v. Cunha* (1994), 1994 CanLII 3195 (BC SC), 99 B.C.L.R. (2d) 93 (S.C.), at para. 9, quoted in *Leskun v. Leskun*, 2006 SCC 25, [2006] 1 S.C.R. 920, at para. 34). And yet, payor parents are typically well aware of their obligation as a parent to support their children, and are subject to a duty of full and honest disclosure — a duty comparable to that arising in matrimonial negotiations (*Brandsema*, at paras. 4749). The payor parent's obligation to disclose changes in income protects the integrity and certainty afforded by an existing order or agreement respecting child support. Absent full and honest disclosure, the recipient parent — and the child — are vulnerable to the payor parent's nondisclosure.[388]

An application for a retroactive decrease in the amount of child support must be paired with full and frank financial disclosure.[389]

In *Henderson v Micetich*, the Alberta Court of Appeal ventured the following opinion:

> Blameworthy conduct in its expansive form is anything that favors the payor to the detriment of the children. It is generally used to overcome the judicially imposed three-year rule put forward in *DBS*. However, as a concept it has limited utility. A retroactive award ought not to be punitive, but rather restorative, providing benefit to the recipient parent and the children. Thus, while blameworthy conduct can militate in favor of an award beyond three years, its absence should not be found to militate against the making of any retroactive order at all.[390]

12) In assessing the obligor's conduct, the court is not confined to looking at blameworthy conduct. Sometimes, an obligor's positive conduct will militate against a retroactive child support award. For example, an order for the payment of retroactive child support may be negated by the obligor's voluntary assumption of substantial child-related expenses.[391] Informal payments made by an obligor should be considered as part of the payor-parent's conduct in crafting a retroactive child support award,[392] but it must be borne in mind that an obligor is not free to decide how the child support obligation shall be discharged.[393]
13) In determining whether a retroactive child support award is justified, the court should have regard to the circumstances of the child as they exist at the time of the application as well as the circumstances of the child as they existed at the time when the support

---

388 *Michel v Graydon*, 2020 SCC 24 at para 33, Brown J. See also *Heuft v Bramwell*, 2021 ABQB 642; *SKR v KSD*, 2021 BCSC 1250 at paras 45–46; *Hovey v Hanson*, 2021 NSSC 89 at para 70; *Tyndall v Tyndall* 2022 ONSC 131. And see *Colucci v Colucci*, 2021 SCC 24 at paras 32 and 48–54, wherein financial disclosure is characterized as "the linch pin holding the child support regime together."

389 *Zuniga v Zuniga*, 2021 BCSC 1625 at para 29.

390 *Henderson v Micetich*, 2021 ABCA 103 at para 57; see also *Mortson v Kminkova*, 2021 ABQB 476.

391 See *DBS v SRG*; *LJW v TAR*; *Henry v Henry*; *Hiemstra v Hiemstra*, 2006 SCC 37 at para 109; *Henderson v Micetich*, 2021 ABCA 103 (mortgage payments on matrimonial home); *AD v AD*, 2018 NBCA 83 at paras 51–52; *Lafrance v Latimer*, 2010 ONSC 1117.

392 *Shears v Gould*, 2014 NLCA 2. See also *DR v EPR*, 2014 BCSC 1912.

393 *Haisman v Haisman* (1994), 22 Alta LR (3d) 56 at paras 79–80 (CA); *UVH v MWH*, 2008 BCCA 177 at para 34; *Tobias v Meadley*, 2011 BCCA 472; *GFW v JLR*, 2012 BCCA 245 (support arrears not discharged by direct payments to adult child); *LBL v SB*, 2010 NBQB 339; *Sanderson v Pennycook*, 2013 NWTSC 48.

should have been paid.[394] It is important to realize, however, that "there is no requirement to prove any need on the part of the children for them to receive as retroactive support amounts that have not been paid as required, and a payor parent cannot avoid a retroactive award by arguing that the recipient parent was able to sufficiently care for the child on his or her own."[395]

14) Hardship to the obligor and his new family dependants is a relevant factor to be considered in determining whether a retroactive child support award is justified.[396] But hardship to the obligor "can only be assessed after taking into account the hardship which would be caused to the child and recipient parent from not ordering the payment of sums owing but unpaid."[397] The minority judgment in *DBS v SRG; LJW v TAR; Henry v Henry; Hiemstra v Hiemstra* clearly spells out that the hardship must be "undue hardship" that satisfies the requirements of section 10 of the *Federal Child Support Guidelines*. While the majority judgment accepts the premise that the Guidelines govern both retroactive and prospective child support orders, Bastarache J's analysis with respect to the impact of hardship is not so clearly defined as to expressly confine its application to circumstances in which the very stringent requirements of section 10 of the Guidelines are satisfied.[398] He does volunteer the statement that "[w]hile hardship for the payor parent is much less of a concern where it is the product of his/her blameworthy conduct, it remains a strong one where this is not the case."[399] He also acknowledges that courts should craft their retroactive awards so as to minimize hardship, for example, by ordering periodic payments over a period of time to discharge the overall amount due. The exercise of this jurisdiction is consistent with section 11 of the *Federal Child Support Guidelines*.[400] Furthermore, if a court wishes to defer the payment of retroactive support or order payment by instalments,[401] it may do so pursuant to section 15.1(4) (original child support orders) or section 17(3) of the *Divorce Act* (variation orders), which empower the court to impose "terms, conditions or restrictions" on its orders. An order

394 *DBS v SRG; LJW v TAR; Henry v Henry; Hiemstra v Hiemstra*, 2006 SCC 37 at paras 110–13. Compare *Hovey v Hanson*, 2021 NSSC 89 at para 70, Cormier J. See also *Best v MacKay*, 2021 NSSC 124 at para 22; *Woodland v Kirkham*, 2021 ONSC 8194.

395 *Henderson v Micetich*, 2021 ABCA 103 at para 60; *Mortson v Kminkova*, 2021 ABQB 476; *Auer v Auer*, 2022 ABCA 376; *AA v JA*, 2023 NBKB 210 at para 91.

396 *DBS v SRG; LJW v TAR; Henry v Henry; Hiemstra v Hiemstra*, 2006 SCC 37 at para 115.

397 *Henderson v Micetich*, 2021 ABCA 103; *Perez v Chiris*, 2021 ONSC 101, citing *Michel v Graydon*, 2020 SCC 24 at para 125; *Mortson v Kminkova*, 2021 ABQB 476; *Best v MacKay*, 2021 NSSC 124 at para 22.

398 *DBS v SRG; LJW v TAR; Henry v Henry; Hiemstra v Hiemstra*, 2006 SCC 37 at paras 114–16; see also *Goulding v Keck*, 2014 ABCA 138; *Smith v Gulka*, 2020 ABQB 32 at paras 82–88; *Henderson v Micetich*, 2021 ABCA 103; *Toronchuk v Wainwright*, 2021 ABQB 862; *MC v JO*, 2017 NBCA 15; *Locke v Goulding*, 2012 NLCA 8; *BW v JG*, 2014 NLCA 5; *Goulding v Goulding*, 2016 NLCA 6; *Fedortchouk v Boubnoy*, 2018 NSSC 66 at paras 219–20; *Costa v Perkins*, 2012 ONSC 3165; *LMA v PH*, 2014 ONSC 1707; *CC v KK*, 2020 PESC 16; *Koback v Koback*, 2013 SKCA 91 at paras 80–87; *Wetsch v Kuski*, 2017 SKCA 77; *Hinds v Jacobs*, 2018 SKQB 51; *DWS v NMJC*, 2017 YKSC 60 at para 116.

399 *DBS v SRG; LJW v TAR; Henry v Henry; Hiemstra v Hiemstra*, 2006 SCC 37 at para 116; see also *Smith v Gulka*, 2020 ABQB 32 at paras 82–88.

400 *DBS v SRG; LJW v TAR; Henry v Henry; Hiemstra v Hiemstra*, 2006 SCC 37 at para 116; *Michaud v Michaud*, [2005] AJ No 1095 (QB); *LMA v PH*, 2014 ONSC 1707.

401 See *DGS v HAS*, 2019 ABQB 887; *LCR v IJER*, 2019 SKQB 229. See also *KAW v MEW*, 2020 ABCA 277 (structured payments reversed on appeal). And see *Colucci v Colucci*, 2021 SCC 24 at para 140.

that establishes how child support arrears are to be paid should not be arbitrary. It must be grounded on the basis of a reasoned and articulated analysis of the financial realities of the parties. A recipient spouse is not a lender or a mortgagee to a payor spouse who owes arrears in support. He or she should not be required to finance the blameworthy conduct of a payor.[402]

15) There are two aspects to the judicial determination of the amount of any retroactive child support award. First, the court must determine the date to which the award should be retroactive. Second, the court must determine the dollar value of its order.[403]

(i) Date of Retroactivity

The majority judgment examines four options as to the appropriate date when retro active child support becomes payable, namely

(a) the date when the application was made to the court;
(b) the date when formal notice was given to the obligor;
(c) the date when effective notice was given to the obligor; and
(d) the date when the amount of child support should have increased.

Given the desirability of parents resolving the issue of child support promptly and without recourse to costly and emotionally draining litigation, the majority judgment favoured the third option. This option does not require the applicant to take any legal action. All that is required is that the topic be broached. After that, the obligor can no longer assume that the *status quo* is fair to the child and his interest in certainty in the management of his affairs is less compelling. While the date of effective notice will usually signal the applicant's attempt to change the child support obligation, an unwarranted prolonged period of inactivity should not be ignored. Consistent with this approach and with section 25(1)(a) of the *Federal Child Support Guidelines*, which limits an applicant's request for financial disclosure by the obligor to the preceding three years, the majority judgment states that "it will usually be inappropriate to make a support award retroactive to a date more than three years before formal notice was given to the obligor." However, the date when increased support should have been paid will sometimes be a more appropriate date from which the retroactive order should start. Such will be the case where the obligor engages in blameworthy conduct, such as intimidation or misrepresentation, and a failure to disclose a material income increase itself constitutes blameworthy conduct. Given such conduct, the presumptive date of retroactivity can be moved back to the time when the obligor's circumstances materially changed. In the final analysis, a retroactive award must fit the circumstances of the case and the date of retroactivity can be adjusted to affect the quantum of the award so as to ensure that the award is appropriate.[404]

---

402 *See TMD v JPG*, 2018 NBCA 15 at para 22, Baird JA.

403 As to delegation of judicial authority with respect to the terms of payment of retroactive child support, see *DAT v SLP*, 2018 NBQB 135 at paras 55–57.

404 See *DBS v SRG; LJW v TAR; Henry v Henry; Hiemstra v Hiemstra*, 2006 SCC 37 at paras 117–25; see also *KD v SD*, 2022 BCSC 1299; *Gauthier v Gauthier*, 2022 BCCA 193; *Livingston v King*, 2022 BCSC 1906; *AM c RB*, 2019 NBBR 170 at para 72, DeWare CJ.

(ii) Amount

Sections 15.1(3) and 17(6.1) of the *Divorce Act* confer a discretion on the courts to determine whether a child support order should be granted but the amount of any order after 1 May 1997 must be "in accordance with the applicable guidelines." However, blind adherence to the table amounts set out in the Guidelines is neither required nor recommended. The first method whereby the court may deviate from the table amount of child support arises where undue hardship is established within the meaning of section 10 of the Guidelines. In addition to cases of undue hardship, courts may exercise their discretion with respect to amount in the diverse circumstances prescribed by sections 3(2) (adult children), 4 (parental annual income in excess of $150,000), and 9 (shared parenting). A second method of adjusting the amount of support payable is exercisable by altering the time period encompassed by the retroactive award. For example, where a court finds that there has been an unreasonable delay after effective notice of the child support claim was first given, the period of excessive delay might be excluded in calculating the retroactive award. Unless the statutory provisions mandate a different outcome, a court should not order retroactive child support in an amount that it considers unfair in light of all the attendant circumstances of the case.[405]

16) In *DBS v SRG; LJW v TAR; Henry v Henry; Hiemstra v Hiemstra*, it was concluded that the use of the phrase "at the material time" in the definition of "child of the marriage" in section 2(1) of the *Divorce Act* refers to the time when the application for retroactive child support was filed and served.[406] Consequently, a child who is over the provincial age of majority and no longer financially dependent on his or her parents at the time of the application is ineligible for a retroactive child support award.[407] It was acknowledged that an exception may arise if a Notice to Disclose/Notice of Motion was filed prior to the application for retroactive support.[408] The jurisdictional limitation discussed in *DBS* does not apply to a parent's alternative claim in contract, and a parent is not precluded from advancing that claim even though it was brought after the children ceased to be children within the meaning of the *Divorce Act*.[409] Furthermore, the fact that an application for the enforcement or variation of child support arrears under an existing order is brought after the children have ceased to be eligible for support does not necessarily preclude the recovery of or the remission of arrears that accrued prior thereto, although it

---

405 See *DBS v SRG; LJW v TAR; Henry v Henry; Hiemstra v Hiemstra*, 2006 SCC 37 at paras 126–30.

406 *Ibid* at paras 88–89; *Smith v Smith*, 2015 SKQB 238 at paras 7–15.

407 *DBS v SRG; LJW v TAR; Henry v Henry; Hiemstra v Hiemstra*, 2006 SCC 37. As to whether the same limitation applies to a variation application under s 17 of the *Divorce Act* or to an original or variation application brought pursuant to provincial legislation, see *Michel v Graydon*, 2020 SCC 24; *Ballanger v Ballanger*, 2020 ONCA 626.

408 *Calver v Calver*, 2014 ABCA 63 at para 28; *VanSickle v VanSickle*, 2012 ONSC 7340, citing *DBS v SRG; LJW v TAR; Henry v Henry; Hiemstra v Hiemstra*, 2006 SCC 37 at para 150. See also *Gordashko v Boston*, [2009] AJ No 404 (QB) (use of CRS process prior to application; blameworthy conduct of obligor); *JP v JAP*, 2010 ABQB 53; *Carmichael v Kiggins*, 2010 ABQB 78; *Elliott v Elliott*, 2010 ABQB 789; *Doherty v Decoff*, [2007] NSJ No 263 (SC); *JDG v JAB*, 2012 NSSC 20. And see *Hnidy v Hnidy*, 2017 SKCA 44.

409 *Hnidy v Hnidy*, 2017 SKCA 44 at para 112, Wilkinson J (*ad hoc*): see also *Galbraith v Galbraith*, 2018 SKQB 157; *McElravey v Healey*, 2019 SKQB 157; *Hanson v Hanson*, 2019 SKCA 102.

may be a relevant consideration.[410] In *Michel v Graydon*,[411] the Supreme Court of Canada concluded that when deciding an application for retroactive child support, a court must analyze the statutory scheme under which the application was brought, and different policy choices made by the federal and provincial governments must be respected. It then determined that section 152 of the *Family Law Act* of British Columbia authorizes a court to retroactively vary a child support order, irrespective of whether the bene ficiary is a "child" at the time of the application, and irrespective of whether the order has expired.[412] In light of *Michel v Graydon*, it remains to be seen whether the Supreme Court of Canada will in future revise the conclusion expressed in *DBS v SRG; LJW v TAR; Henry v Henry; Hiemstra v Hiemstra* that the phrase "at the material time" in the definition of "child of the marriage" in section 2(1) of the *Divorce Act* refers to the time when the application was filed and served. It is quite conceivable that in the context of applications for retroactive child support, as distinct from applications for prospective or ongoing child support, the phrase "at the material time" in the definition of "child of the marriage" in section 2(1) of the *Divorce Act* will in future be interpreted to refer to the time in respect of which retroactive child support is being sought instead of the time when the application was filed and served.

17) In *Colucci v Colucci*,[413] Martin J, writing for a unanimous court, established the following framework for dealing with claims for both retroactive increases and decreases in child support and requests to rescind arrears that the payor properly owes based solely on an alleged inability to pay:

> [113] To summarize, where the payor applies under s. 17 of the *Divorce Act* to retroactively decrease child support, the following analysis applies:

---

410 See *Colucci v Colucci*, 2021 SCC 24. For relevant caselaw before *Colucci v Colucci*, see *Buckingham v Buckingham*, 2013 ABQB 155; *MacCarthy v MacCarthy*, 2015 BCCA 496; *Dring v Ghehle*, 2018 BCCA 435; *SEB v JTM*, 2019 NBQB 76; *McCrate v McCrate*, 2019 NSSC 167 at paras 64–67; *Ross v Welsh*, 2009 SKQB 483; *Kosowan v Vanderstap*, 2016 SKCA 149; compare *McDonald v McDonald*, [2008] BCJ No 1694 (SC); *Suen v Dunn*, 2018 NSSC 17; *Millar v Millar*, 2007 SKQB 25. See also *Lemire v Lemire*, 2016 BCSC 2340; *Lemay c Longpré*, 2014 ONCS 5107.

411 2020 SCC 24. See also *Fleming v Spence*, 2023 ABCA 315; *Brar v Brar*, 2021 BCSC 748 (application for variation order under s 17 of the *Divorce Act*); *Kennedy v Kennedy*, 2022 BCSC 256 (application for varia tion order under s 17 of the Divorce Act); *Pelletier v Richard*, 2021 NBQB 77 at para 61 (application under NB *Family Law Act*, SNB 2020, c 23); *MacKenzie v MacKenzie*, 2022 PESC 20; *JM v LC*, 2022 PESC 35.

412 For a helpful summary of further directions provided by the Supreme Court of Canada in *Michel v Graydon*, 2020 SCC 24, see *Cavanagh v Wagner*, 2020 ONSC 7444 at para 25, McEachern J. Compare *LLM v DRM*, 2022 BSSC 143 at para 66 (Lyster J: "Michel does not overrule the holding in *Dring* [*v Gheyle*, 2018 BCCA 435] that the Court has no jurisdiction to entertain an original application for child support under the FLA where the would-be beneficiary is no longer a 'child.'"); see also *Deng v Zhang* 2022 BCCA 271 at paras 74 and 86.

413 2021 SCC 24. And see Chapter 13, Section S(2). See also *Shumate v Patrick*, 2023 ABKB 98; *AF v RR*, 2021 NBCA 37; *Currie v Currie*, 2022 NSSC 23; *Evans v Evans*, 2023 ONSC 3919; *Folkerts v Folkerts*, 2021 SKQB 290; Rollie Thompson, "Retroactive Support After Colucci," County of Carleton Law Association, Ottawa, 30th Annual Institute of Family Law: Day 1, Fall Virtual Program, 14 September 2021; Jodi Lazare & Kelsey Warr, "A Gender-Based Approach to Historical Child Support: Comment on *Colucci v Colucci*" (2022) 34 CJFL 209, 2022 CanLIIDocs 3244.

(1) The payor must meet the threshold of establishing a past material change in circumstances. The onus is on the payor to show a material decrease in income that has some degree of continuity, and that is real and not one of choice.

(2) Once a material change in circumstances is established, a presumption arises in favour of retroactively decreasing child support to the date the payor gave the recipient effective notice, up to three years before formal notice of the application to vary. In the decrease context, effective notice requires clear communication of the change in circumstances accompanied by the disclosure of any available documentation necessary to substantiate the change and allow the recipient parent to meaningfully assess the situation.

(3) Where no effective notice is given by the payor parent, child support should generally be varied back to the date of formal notice, or a later date where the payor has delayed making complete disclosure in the course of the proceedings.[414]

(4) The court retains discretion to depart from the presumptive date of retroactivity where the result would otherwise be unfair.[415] The *D.B.S.* factors (adapted to the decrease context) guide this exercise of discretion. Those factors are: (i) whether the payor had an understandable reason for the delay in seeking a decrease; (ii) the payor's conduct; (iii) the child's circumstances; and (iv) hardship to the payor if support is not decreased (viewed in context of hardship to the child and recipient if support *is* decreased). The payor's efforts to pay what they can and to communicate and disclose income information on an ongoing basis will often be a key consideration under the factor of payor conduct.

(5) Finally, once the court has determined that support should be retroactively decreased to a particular date, the decrease must be quantified. The proper amount of support for each year since the date of retroactivity must be calculated in accordance with the *Guidelines*.[416]

[114] It is also helpful to summarize the principles which now apply to cases in which the recipient applies under s.17 to retroactively increase child support:

a) The recipient must meet the threshold of establishing a past material change in circumstances. While the onus is on the recipient to show a material increase in income, any failure by the payor to disclose relevant financial information allows the court to impute income, strike pleadings, draw adverse inferences, and award costs. There is no need for the recipient to make multiple court applications for disclosure before a court has these powers.

b) Once a material change in circumstances is established, a presumption arises in favour of retroactively increasing child support to the date the recipient gave the

414 See *Moen v Ropchan*, 2021 ABQB 777; *Reid v Chambers*, 2022 ABKB 634; *Bilodeau v Bilodeau*, 2022 ABKB 799; *Ward v Murphy*, 2023 NSSC 370; *Folkerts v Folkerts*, 2021 SKQB 290.

415 See also *PJM v RMS*, 2021 BCCA 260 at para 42; *Mannell v Mannell*, 2023 ONSC 4209; *Woodrow v Lepoudre*, 2022 SKQB 143.

416 See also *Murray v Murray*, 2021 ABQB 539; *SMP v TMP*, 2022 ABQB 226; *Hinz v Davey*, 2022 BCCA 232 (jurisdiction exists under British Columbia *Family Law Act* to retroactively vary agreement with respect to child support); *CAM v TCH*, 2023 BCSC 1283 at para 79; *DDM v JMM*, 2023 BCSC 1834; *Abdullahi v Warsame*, 2021 ONCJ 449; *Savage v Kaczmarek*, 2022 ONSC 1313.

payor effective notice of the request for an increase, up to three years before formal notice of the application to vary. In the increase context, because of informational asymmetry, effective notice requires only that the recipient broached the subject of an increase with the payor.[417]

c) Where no effective notice is given by the recipient parent, child support should generally be increased back to the date of formal notice.

d) The court retains discretion to depart from the presumptive date of retroactivity where the result would otherwise be unfair. The *D.B.S.* factors continue to guide this exercise of discretion, as described in *Michel*. If the payor has failed to disclose a material increase in income, that failure qualifies as blameworthy conduct and the date of retroactivity will generally be the date of the increase in income.

e) Once the court has determined that support should be retroactively increased to a particular date, the increase must be quantified. The proper amount of support for each year since the date of retroactivity must be calculated in accordance with the *Guidelines*. . . .[418]

[132] I will now consider the scenario in which a payor who has fallen behind on payments seeks full or partial rescission of arrears under s. 17 on the basis of a current and ongoing inability to pay. . . .

[138] . . . [I]n this third category of cases, the payor must overcome a presumption against rescinding any part of the arrears. The presumption will only be rebutted where the payor parent establishes on a balance of probabilities that — even with a flexible payment plan — they cannot and will not ever be able to pay the arrears. . . . Present inability to pay does not, in itself, foreclose the prospect of future ability to pay, although it may justify a temporary suspension of arrears. . . . This presumption ensures rescission is a last resort available only where suspension or other creative payment options are inadequate to address the prejudice to the payor. . . .[419]

[140] The court has a range of available options when faced with proven payor hardship. A court's refusal to rescind arrears does not mean the payor must pay the entire amount immediately. . . . If the court concludes that the payor's financial circumstances will give rise to difficulties paying down arrears, the court ought to first consider whether hardship can be mitigated by ordering a temporary suspension, periodic payments, or other creative payment options. . . .

[141] While the presumption in favour of enforcing arrears may be rebutted in "unusual circumstances," the standard should remain a stringent one. Rescission of arrears based solely on current financial incapacity should not be ordered lightly. It is a last resort in exceptional cases, such as where the payor suffers a "catastrophic injury". . . . The rule should not allow or encourage debtors to wait out their obligations or subvert statutory enforcement regimes that recognize child support arrears as debts to be taken seriously.[420]

---

417 As to the three-year rule, see *Livingston v King*, 2022 BCSC 1906.

418 See also *Vinagreiro v Vinagreiro*, 2022 ABKB 678; *ACS v CJS*, 2021 BCSC 1193; *Caillier v Viray*, 2021 BCSC 2512; *McMaster-Pereira v Pereira*, 2021 ONCA 547 at paras 23–24; *MacNeil v Yeadon*, 2022 NSCA 79; *McCain v McCain*, 2021 ONSC 7744.

419 See also *Moen v Ropchan*, 2021 ABQB 777; *AF v RR*, 2021 NBCA 37.

420 See also *Stark v Tweedale*, 2021 BCSC 1133; *Folkerts v Folkerts*, 2021 SKQB 290.

Although *Colucci v Colucci* dealt with the retroactive variation of an existing child support order, the principles enunciated therein regarding the determination of a presumptive date of retroactivity are equally applicable when making a retroactive award for an initial child support order, with the exception of not having to find a material change in circumstance.[421]

In *Abumatar v Hamda*, Pazaratz J of the Ontario Superior Court of Justice offered the following observations concerning the impact of *Michel v Graydon* on *DBS v SRG; LJW v TAR; Henry v Henry; Hiemstra v Hiemstra*:

> [52] In *D.B.S.* the Supreme Court of Canada outlined several fundamental principles governing orders for child support and requests for retroactive child support. These include:
>
> a. Child support is the right of the child and cannot be bargained away by the parents.
> b. Child support should, as much as possible, provide children with the same standard of living they enjoyed when the parents were together.
> c. Child support is to be calculated based upon the income of the payor parent. The obligation exceeds merely furnishing the "necessities of life."
> d. Retroactive awards are not truly "retroactive". They reflect an obligation which existed at the time, based on ability to pay.
> e. Retroactive awards are not limited to exceptional or rare cases.
>
> [53] In *D.B.S.* the court identified four primary considerations:
>
> 1. Whether the recipient spouse has provided a reasonable excuse for his or her delay in applying for support.
> 2. The conduct of the payor parent.
> 3. The circumstances of the child.
> 4. The hardship that the retroactive award may entail.
>
> [54] None of the above factors are decisive or take priority and all should be considered in a global analysis. In determining whether to make a retroactive award, a court will need to look at all of the relevant circumstances. The payor's interest in certainty must be balanced with the need for fairness and flexibility.
>
> [55] In *Michel v. Graydon* 2020 SCC 24 the Supreme Court recently revisited these principles. The commentary includes the following:
>
> a. Parents know they are liable to pay support in accordance with the Tables, based on their actual income. They know they will be held accountable for underpayment, even if enforcement of their obligations may not always be automatic.
> b. The obligation to support your child exists even if the other parent has not (yet) started a court case.
> c. Retroactive child support is a debt. It represents money that should have been paid. Presumptively, the money is owing and should still be paid, unless there are strong reasons not to do so.
> d. Retroactive child support simply holds payors to their existing (and unfulfilled) support obligations.
> e. The court must be aware of the gender and social dynamics which permeate child support law. When we assess the reasonableness of actions and behaviours by support

421 *Floyd v Rodger*, 2023 MBKB 3 at para 42, Petersen J.

recipients — and the reality is that they are predominantly women — we must take into account all of their experiences, challenges, vulnerabilities, financial limitations, fears, danger, and perceptions as to their actual options.

f. The neglect or refusal to pay child support is strongly linked to child poverty and female poverty.

g. There is nothing exceptional about judicial relief from the miserable consequences that can flow from a payor's indifference to their child support obligations.

Michel v. Graydon refines the approach to be taken on the issue of delay:

a. Rather than ask whether there was a "reasonable excuse" for any delay in bringing an application, the court should examine whether the reason for the delay is "understandable".

b. A delay, in itself, is not inherently unreasonable. The mere fact of a delay does not prejudice an application, as not all factors need to be present for a retroactive award to be granted.

c. Rather, a delay will be prejudicial only if it is deemed to be unreasonable, taking into account a generous appreciation of the social context in which the claimant's decision to seek child support was made.

d. A delay is likely to be more understandable if it is motivated by any one of the following reasons:

    1. Fear of reprisal/violence from the other parent.
    2. Prohibitive costs of litigation or fear of protracted litigation.
    3. Lack of information or misinformation over the payor parent's income.
    4. Fear of counter-application for custody.
    5. The payor leaving the jurisdiction or the recipient unable to contact the payor parent.
    6. Illness/disability of a child or the custodian.
    7. Lack of emotional means.
    8. Wanting the child and the payor to maintain a positive relationship or avoid the child's involvement.
    9. Ongoing discussions in view of reconciliation, settlement negotiations or mediation.
    10. The deliberate delay of the application or the trial by the payor.

e. Delay by a recipient does not constitute a waiver or abandonment of a right to claim the appropriate amount of support which should have been paid.

f. It is generally a good idea to seek child support as soon as practicable. But it is unfair to bar parents from applying for the financial support they are entitled to, simply because they put their safety and that of their children ahead of their financial needs; or because they did not realistically have the ability to access justice earlier.

g. Even if the delay is unreasonable, this does not negate blameworthy conduct by the payor. Indeed, blameworthy conduct may have caused or contributed to the delay.

h. Delay is not determinative. It is one factor and should not be given undue weight.

[56] In *Michel v. Graydon* the Supreme Court provided additional direction on the issue of blameworthy conduct:

a. Courts should apply an expansive definition of blameworthy conduct.

b. While we should take a subjective approach to "reasons for delay", when dealing with blameworthy conduct we should not focus on the payor's intentions. Intention can be a basis on which to *increase* blameworthiness. But the primary focus needs to be on the payor's actions and their consequences.[422]

c. Blameworthy conduct is anything that privileges the payor parent's own interests over his/her children's right to an appropriate amount of support.
d. Blameworthy conduct is not a prerequisite to trigger to the payor's obligation to pay the claimed child support.
e. But where blameworthy conduct is present, it weighs in favour of an award and may also serve to expand the temporal scope of the retroactive award.

[57] With respect to the third *D.B.S.* factor — the circumstances of the child — *Michel v. Graydon* included the following:

a. If a child previously experienced hardship — or if the child needs support at the time of the hearing — this weighs in favour not only of an award, but also of extending the temporal reach of the award.
b. But there need not be any determination of hardship as a pre-requisite to making a retroactive award.
c. A payor's previous support obligation does not disappear when the child no longer requires support. Payors should not perceive an incentive to pay inadequate support, in the hope that retroactivity will hinge on the recipient's ability to prove hardship.
d. Quite commonly the recipient parent caring for the child will personally absorb the hardship created by inadequate support. A primary care parent who prioritizes their child's well-being should not receive less support as a result of choices that protect the child.
e. The fact that the child did not have to suffer hardship because of their custodial parent's sacrifice is not one that weighs against making a retroactive support order. Rather, the recipient parent's hardship, like that of a child, weighs in favour of the retroactive support award and an enlarged temporal scope.
f. The fact that the recipient will indirectly benefit is not a reason to refuse to make the retroactive award of support.

[58] *Michel v. Graydon* stated the following in relation to hardship:

a. While the focus is on hardship to the *payor*, that hardship can only be assessed after taking into account the hardship which would be caused to the *child* and the *recipient parent* from not ordering the payment of sums owing but unpaid.
b. If there is the potential for hardship to the payor, but there is also blameworthy conduct which precipitated or exacerbated the delay, it may be open to the courts to disregard the presence of hardship.
c. The court must remember that the payor had the benefit of the unpaid child support for the full period of time that it was unpaid. Those monies may have funded a preferred lifestyle or the acquisition of property. In contrast, if inappropriate support was being paid, the recipient parent may have been deprived of lifestyle or property opportunities, because they were forced to spend their money (and perhaps incur indebtedness) for the benefit of the child.

422 See also *Gauthier v Gauthier*, 2022 BCCA 193.

d. In all cases, hardship may be addressed by the form of payment.

[59] *D.B.S.* said the following in relation to the start date for support:

a. Where ordered, an award should generally be retroactive to the date when the recipient gave the payor effective notice of his or her intention to seek an increase in support payments. This date represents a fair balance between certainty and flexibility.
b. An earlier date may be appropriate if there is blameworthy conduct by the payor.
c. But generally a retroactive award should not commence earlier than three years before formal notice was given.
d. Effective notice is defined as any indication by the recipient parent that child support should be paid, or that a current amount needs to be renegotiated. All that is required is for the subject to be broached. Once that has been done, the payor can no longer assume that the status quo is fair.
e. But the date of effective notice is not relevant when a payor parent has engaged in blameworthy conduct.

[60] In *Michel* the Supreme Court suggested that rather than ordering retroactive support back to the date of effective notice, it may now be time to simply start ordering payors to pay what they should have paid, as a matter of course.

a. Payors have an absolute — *not a contingent* — obligation to support their children in the amount set out in *Child Support Guidelines*, pursuant to a now long-standing, well-publicized family law regime.
b. By now, every parent should understand that the amount of child support you pay is based on the amount of income you earn. It's a simple, logical concept.
c. If the obligation by the payor and the entitlement by the child are both absolute and unconditional, it makes little sense to invite more complication — and litigation — by adding a condition that "mandatory payments" are only "payable" if the recipient does certain specific things to ask.[423]

In *TM v ZK*, Bokenfohr J of the Alberta Court of Queen's Bench stated that *Colucci v Colucci* provides the following framework for situations wherein the support obligor experienced a material drop in income that affected their ability to make payments as they became due:

- A payor seeking a downward retroactive change must first show a past change in circumstance. This will often be a material change in income. The decrease in income must be "significant and have some degree of continuity, and it must be real and not one of choice" (para 61).
- The payor must disclose sufficient reliable, accurate, and complete evidence for the court to determine when and how far their income fell, and to ascertain whether the change was significant, long lasting, and not one of choice (para 62).
- Once the applicant establishes a change in circumstances a presumption is triggered that support will be varied back to effective notice, up to three years before formal notice (paras 71 and 80).

---

423 *Abumatar v Hamda*, 2021 ONSC 2165 at paras 52–60.

- Effective notice must include sufficient information to allow the recipient to assess the situation, adjust expectations, make necessary changes to lifestyle and expenditures, and make informed decisions (para 88).
- The period of retroactivity is presumed to extend no further than three years before the date of formal notice (para 91). The court retains the discretion, however, to depart from the presumptive date of retroactivity where "the result would otherwise be unfair in the circumstances of a particular case" (para 96).

If a retroactive variation is appropriate, the Guidelines apply in determining the amount of child support (para 109).[424] In *McMaster-Pereira v Pereira*, wherein a recipient of child support applied to retroactively increase child support, Harvison Young JA of the Ontario Court of Appeal observed:

> [23] In summary, the revised approach in *Colucci* requires first that the recipient establish a past material change in circumstances. Once that has been established, a presumption arises in favour of retroactively increasing child support to the date the recipient gave the payor effective notice of the request for an increase, up to three years before formal notice of the application to vary. Effective notice requires only that the recipient broached the subject of a potential increase with the payor. If there was no effective notice, child support should generally be increased back to the date of formal notice. Due to the presumption that is triggered by establishing a past material change in circumstances, the factors in *D.B.S. v. S.R.G.*, 2006 SCC 37, [2006] 2 S.C.R. 231 are no longer necessary in determining whether child support should be retroactively increased. However, they are still relevant in guiding the court's exercise of discretion to depart from the presumptive date of retroactivity where the result would be otherwise unfair. Finally, once the court has determined that support should be retroactively increased to a particular date, the increase must be quantified in accordance with the CSG: *Colucci*, at paras. 6, 71-73 and 114.[[425]]
>
> [24] One of the principles underpinning this approach to the variation of child support is adequate, accurate, and timely financial disclosure: *Colucci*, at paras. 32, 48-54. The child support regime is a system that creates informational asymmetry and is tied to the payor's income, and it would be unfair and contrary to the child's best interests to require the recipient to police the payor's ongoing compliance with their obligations: at para. 49. As the court emphasized, at para. 50:
>
>> This is why frank disclosure of income information by the payor lies at the foundation of the child support regime. In *Roberts v. Roberts*, 2015 ONCA 450, 65 R.F.L. (7th) 6, the Court of Appeal described the duty to disclose financial information as "[t]he most basic obligation in family law". A payor's failure to make timely, proactive and full disclosure undermines the policies underlying the family law regime and "the processes that have been carefully designed to achieve those policy goals". Without proper disclosure, the system simply cannot function and the objective of

---

424 *TM v ZK*, 2021 ABQB 588 at para 30. See also *Hatt v Heather*, 2021 ABQB 878, wherein the court determined that income swings between 1 and 9 percent did not constitute material changes of circumstances on the payor's application for a retroactive reduction of child support. And see *CAM v TCH*, 2023 BCSC 1283 at para 79.

425 See also *Monilaws v Monilaws*, 2022 ABKB 652 at para 36; *McCain v McCain*, 2021 ONSC 7744.

establishing a fair standard of support for children that ensures they benefit from the means of both parents will be out of reach.[426]

Insofar as possible, retroactive support is to be determined based on actual income earned in each year for which it is due.[427] In *Vanos v Vanos*,[428] the Ontario Court of Appeal acknowledged that an obligor's income from the previous year is frequently used as a mat ter of common sense when calculating future child support, because the obligor's actual income for the upcoming year may be incapable of exact determination. However, where the obligor's income is known for the year in respect of which retroactive child support is sought, that is the annual income to be used in determining the amount of retroactive child support to be paid. This conclusion is rooted in common sense and also in section 2(3) of the *Federal Child Support Guidelines*, which stipulates that "[w]here, for the purposes of these Guidelines, any amount is determined on the basis of specified information, the most current information must be used."

In *BM v KR*, French JA of the New Brunswick Court of Appeal observed that

> the adjudication of the child support claim advanced in the application, in relation to the period after the application, is not a retroactive claim regardless of when that claim is determined by the court, at least in the sense of a retroactive claim as contemplated by the Supreme Court in *D.B.S. v. S.R.G.; L.J.W. v. T.A.R.; Henry v. Henry; Hiemstra v. Hiemstra*, 2006 SCC 37, [2006] 2 S.C.R. 231.[429]

Where there is an existing child order requiring annual disclosure of income in the future and automatic adjustment of child support, the aforementioned principles articulated by the Supreme Court of Canada in *DBS v SRG*, *Michel v Graydon*, and *Colucci v Colucci* do not apply.[430]

As a preventative measure that could significantly reduce the number of future claims for retroactive child support, the Alberta Court of Appeal in *DBS v SRG*[431] stated that court orders and negotiated agreements should expressly provide an appropriate mechanism for the future variation of child support obligations to reflect changes in parental income. It is incumbent on courts to ensure the recalculation of child support on a regular basis. At a minimum, orders for child support should routinely include the following provisions unless the attendant circumstances render them inappropriate. First, the payor should be required to annually disclose the financial information, including income tax returns, outlined in

---

426 *McMaster-Pereira v Pereira*, 2021 ONCA 547 at paras 23–24.

427 *Pereverzoff v Pereverzoff*, 2017 BCSC 687, citing *Hsieh v Lui*, 2017 BCCA 51, para 49; *RC v DRC*, 2019 BCSC 1218; *HJ v PJ*, 2020 BCSC 378; *MPM v ACM*, 2022 BCSC 122; *Lewis v Adesanya*, 2014 ONCJ 326 at para 22, Sherr J, citing *Vanos v Vanos*, 2010 ONCA 876; see also *Catizzone v Cowell*, 2016 ONSC 5297; *Emmerson v Emmerson*, 2017 ONCA 917. And see *Colucci v Colucci*, 2021 SCC 24 at paras 113 & 114.

428 2010 ONCA 876; see also *MPM v ACM*, 2022 BCSC 122; *SEB v JTM*, 2019 NBQB 76; *Emmerson v Emmerson*, 2017 ONCA 917.

429 *BM v KR*, 2022 NBCA 50 at para 61; see also *MacKinnon v MacKinnon* (2005), 75 OR (3d) 175 (CA) (retroactive spousal support refers to support sought for any period prior to the initiation of a proceeding).

430 *Dhein v Pratt*, 2016 BCSC 857 at para 44, Hyslop J, citing *MacCarthy v MacCarthy*, 2015 BCCA 496; see also *Chertow v Chertow*, 2005 CanLII 13911 (Ont CA).

431 [2005] AJ No 2 at paras 149–50 (CA).

section 25 of the *Federal Child Support Guidelines*. Second, the court order should specify that the amount is subject to annual recalculation based on the then current income or as agreed upon between the parents. Third, the court order should provide that, if the parents are unable to agree on the amount of child support payable or the date when the adjusted payments will commence, then either parent may apply to the court to resolve the issues and/or make use of available alternative dispute resolution services. The current practice in Alberta requires a mandatory annual disclosure clause in every support order, thereby highlighting the importance of ensuring that financial disclosure is kept up to date.[432]

Since child support is a right of the child, parents cannot negotiate out of their child support obligations and thereby undermine their children's rights. An agreement between the parents that purports to regulate child support on the basis that the parents will share the parenting of the children is of no consequence where the agreement fails to survive because one of the parents is in the military and is posted abroad for several months. The fact that the paying parent voluntarily increased the amount of child support when the shared parenting arrangement was frustrated does not negate the obligation to pay the full amount prescribed by the *Federal Child Support Guidelines*. Applicable legal principles do not permit the children's right to support in accordance with the *Federal Child Support Guidelines* to be varied on the basis of parental good intentions, or parental plans or agreements that are not consistent with the Guidelines, or on the basis of ignorance between the parents when they reach agreements, or on the basis of any other exception, whether morally right or wrong, that does not give the children the rights to which they are legally entitled.[433] However, in *Mann v Mann*,[434] Huddart JA of the British Columbia Court of Appeal observed that "courts may refuse a retroactive order of support where voluntary payments . . . are made and accepted without complaint by a recipient spouse knowledgeable about parental obligations to children and reasonably well-informed about the payor spouse's income and other means, as the trial judge found the appellant was."

Because courts are granting retroactive orders that can be very large in amount they must, of necessity, have the ability to determine whether a child support debtor should be required to pay an order for retroactive child support forthwith or whether an order for a large amount can be paid over a period of time. If a purposive interpretation of section 10(5) of the *Federal Child Support Guidelines* does not allow the court to exercise its discretion in that way, the court can use its inherent jurisdiction to provide a flexible payment regime.[435] Another option is a temporary suspension of the requirement to pay retroactive arrears, subject to a review in the future.[436]

---

432 See *Roseberry v Roseberry*, 2015 ABQB 75 at paras 60–113 wherein the disclosure requirements in Alberta are fully discussed. See also *Damphouse v Damphouse*, 2020 ABQB 101 at para 68. And see *Colucci v Colucci*, 2021 SCC 24 at paras 53 and 112; *LPH v JMR*, 2021 BCSC 1282.

433 *CPZ v TMZ*, [2005] AJ No 1209 (QB); *Doe v Alberta*, 2007 ABCA 50.

434 2009 BCCA 181 at para 21.

435 *Michaud v Michaud*, [2005] AJ No 1093 (QB).

436 See *JL v AA*, 2013 NBQB 121 at para 49; see also *WL v NDH*, 2014 NBQB 214 (court ordered set-off of portion of retroactive child support against obligor's expenses in relation to the exercise of parenting time).

5) Variation Orders

Section 17(1) of the *Divorce Act* expressly empowers a court to vary a pre-existing order for child support either prospectively or retroactively and judicial opinion supports the view that there is discretionary jurisdiction to grant an order for child support that pre-dates the variation judgment and, where appropriate, the court may even order the payment of child support for a period pre-dating the commencement of the variation proceedings.[437] It is not unusual for a court to order any increase to be retroactive to the date of the application, although service of a notice of motion and a notice to disclose does not automatically dictate that an order for increased child support be retroactive to the date of service.[439] Section 17 of the *Divorce Act* empowers a court to retroactively increase the amount of child support pre viously ordered.[440] It also empowers the court to reduce the amount retroactively, in which event all or part of any arrears accruing under the pre-existing order may be cancelled. Most variation applications deal with support reduction, but the court has clear statutory authority to retroactively increase child support. Where support for a child has been over paid in consequence of the primary caregiving parent's deception, the court may conclude that the amount of overpayment should be set off against arrears of support and a retroactive increase of support respecting a second child.[442]

6) Types of Retroactive Order

A court may order that retroactive child support be paid in instalments that are to be added to the prospective child support payments.[443] A retroactive order for child support may be made by way of a lump sum payment[444] and the court may direct a set-off of the lump sum against the obligor's matrimonial property entitlement[445] or against the proceeds of sale of

---

437 See *DBS v SRG; LJW v TAR; Henry v Henry; Hiemstra v Hiemstra*, 2006 SCC 37; see also Section K(4), above in this chapter. And see *MacMinn v MacMinn* (1995), 17 RFL (4th) 88 (Alta CA); *Ennis v Ennis*, [1999] AJ No 352 (QB), var'd (2000), 281 AR 161, [2000] AJ No 75 (CA); *Wishlow v Bingham*, [2000] AJ No 809 (CA); *LS v EP*, [1999] BCJ No 1451 (CA); *Motyka v Motyka*, [2001] BCJ No 52 (CA); *Njegovan v Melnuk*, [2000] MJ No 409 (QB) (negotiation is to be encouraged; retroactive order for increased child support from time when claim first brought to the obligor's notice); *Waterman v Waterman* (1995), 16 RFL (4th) 10 (Nfld CA); *Reardon v Smith*, [1999] NSJ No 403 (CA).

438 *Boyda v Boyda*, [1998] AJ No 279 (QB); *Razutis v Garrett*, [1999] BCJ No 1505 (CA); *Cennon v Cennon* [1999] SJ No 504 (QB).

439 *DLA v JTA*, [1999] AJ No 312 (QB); *Bolingbroke v Bolingbroke*, [2001] AJ No 53 (QB) (defective service no bar to retroactive order where the respondent had adequate notice of the application).

440 *Dahl v Dahl* (1995), 18 RFL (4th) 122 (Alta CA); *Wishlow v Bingham*, [2000] AJ No 809 (CA); *Waller v Waller*, [1998] OJ No 5387 (Gen Div).

441 *Dahl v Dahl* (1995), 18 RFL (4th) 122 (Alta CA); *Simmonds v Turner*, [2005] NSJ No 460 (SC).

442 *Sampson v Sampson*, [1997] OJ No 5356 (Gen Div).

443 *Larson v Boje*, [1999] AJ No 682 (QB); *Budden v Combden*, [1999] NJ No 199 (SC); *Vickers v Vickers*, [2001] NSJ No 218 (CA). See also *KAW v MEW*, 2020 ABCA 277 (structured payments reversed on appeal). And see *Colucci v Colucci*, 2021 SCC 24 at para 140.

444 *MacMinn v MacMinn* (1995), 17 RFL (4th) 88 (Alta CA); *Asadoorian v Asadoorian*, [1997] OJ No 3115 (Gen Div); *Laughlin v Cormier*, [1997] PEIJ No 80 (TD). And see *Colucci v Colucci*, 2021 SCC 24 at para 140.

445 *Lackie v Lackie*, [1998] OJ No 888 (Gen Div).

the former matrimonial home,[446] after adjusting the lump sum to take account of the primary caregiving parent's exclusive possession of the matrimonial home for several years.[447]

7) Effect of Successful Appeal

On a successful appeal respecting the right to and amount of child support, the decision of the appellate court is substituted for the order appealed from. Consequently, the appellate judgment takes effect from the date of the original order. Pursuant to section 21 of the *Divorce Act*, however, the appellate court may direct that its judgment shall take effect only from the date of the decision, although such an exceptional course of action can only be justified where there are circumstances rendering it unjust to do otherwise.[448] Any retroactive decrease in the amount of support resulting from a successful appeal should bear in mind the amount of the overpayment and the ability of the recipient to repay that amount.[449] In granting an appeal for the termination of child support, the appellate court may decline to order the termination of the support payments retroactively to the date of the trial judgment or the date of the variation application, where the money has been already paid and probably spent and the payee has limited resources to repay.[450]

8) Need for Application

Retroactive support must normally be requested in the notice of motion. If requested just before or during the hearing, the obligor must be given a reasonable opportunity to make submissions to the court.[451]

9) Retroactive Orders under Shared Parenting Arrangements

In addressing an application for a retroactive child support order in a shared parenting situation, section 9 of the Guidelines does not mandate a formulaic and non-discretionary approach. The court should be guided in its deliberations by the principle of the fair and equitable sharing of monies actually spent during the period in question based on the respective parental incomes.[452]

A court may refuse to order retroactive child support from the date when a shared parenting regime ended where this would generate substantial "instant arrears" that would

446 *Coady v Coady*, [1999] OJ No 2305 (SCJ).

447 *Ibid.*

448 *Prewada v Prewada* (1993), 48 RFL (3d) 190 (Man CA); see also *H(UV) v H(MW)*, 2008 BCCA 177; *Van Gool v Van Gool*, [1998] BCJ No 2513 (CA); *Birss v Birss*, [2000] OJ No 3692.

449 *Benson v Benson* (1987), 8 RFL (3d) 32 (Nfld CA); see also *Silverman v Silverman* (1987), 10 RFL (3d) 37 (NS Fam Ct); *CG v TL*, 2024 NLCA 1.

450 *Pink v Pink* (1991), 31 RFL (3d) 233 (Man CA); see also *Desjardines v Desjardines* (1991), 31 RFL (3d) 449 (Alta QB); *H(UV) v H(MW)*, 2008 BCCA 177; *LeBlanc v LeBlanc* (1993), 48 RFL (3d) 457 (Man CA).

451 *Esligar v Esligar*, [1999] NBJ No 150 (CA); *MDA v MS*, [2008] NBJ No 498 (QB).

452 *Cuddy v Cuddy*, [1999] OJ No 1399 (SCJ).

be an unreasonable burden, given the father's ongoing child obligation and his financial circumstances.[453]

10) Effect of Bankruptcy

An obligor's bankruptcy does not affect her future child support obligation, but may be relevant where a retroactive child support order is sought after the obligor, her creditors, and trustee in bankruptcy all took positions relying on their understanding of the obligor's financial affairs, which included the fact that child support payments were being made under the former tax deduction/inclusion scheme.[454]

11) Effect of Income Tax Reassessment

A court may refuse to grant a retroactive child support order that would result in the obligor being reassessed for income tax purposes and paying higher taxes, without any substantial tax benefits accruing to the primary caregiving parent and with a windfall accruing to the Canada Revenue Agency. Any marginal losses sustained by the primary caregiving parent as a result of the judicial refusal to order retroactive periodic child support may be addressed by a compensatory lump sum order.[455] A court may refuse to exercise its discretion to grant a variation order for retroactive child support where such retroactivity would result in a windfall to the Canada Revenue Agency at the expense of the family.[456]

12) Significance of Separation Agreement or Minutes of Settlement

After emphasizing that Canadian child support is an application-based system in *DBS v SRG LJW v TAR; Henry v Henry; Hiemstra v Hiemstra*,[457] the Supreme Court of Canada articulated the principle that in most circumstances concerning retroactivity of child support, consider able weight should be given to agreements reached by the parents because these agreements were likely considered holistically by the parents, such that a smaller amount of child support may be explained by a larger amount of spousal support for the primary caregiving parent. Therefore, it is often unwise for courts to disrupt the equilibrium achieved by parents. How ever, as is the case with court orders, where circumstances have changed, or were never as they first appeared, and the actual support obligations of the payor parent have not been met, courts may order a retroactive award so long as the applicable statutory regime permits it.[458] Minutes of settlement that are based on inaccurate information due to the obligor's wilful withholding of financial information may justify a retroactive order for child support in accordance with the *Federal Child Support Guidelines*.[459] A court is not entitled to remit

453 *CYD v JRD*, [2005] BCJ No 2596 (SC).
454 *Olesen v Olesen*, [1999] AJ No 494 (QB).
455 *Addison v Schneider*, [1999] MJ No 300 (QB).
456 *Osmar v Osmar*, [2000] OJ No 2060 (SCJ).
457 2006 SCC 37.
458 *Hargrove v Holliday*, 2010 ABQB 70.
459 *Rozen v Rozen*, [2002] BCJ No 2192 (SC). See also *Goulding v Keck*, 2014 ABCA 138 (father in breach of contractual undertaking to disclose income increases); compare to *McBean v McBean*, 2019 ABCA 1.

child support arrears on the basis of an agreement whereby the primary caregiving parent purported to waive child support if the other parent refrained from exercising parenting time with the children. Parents are not free to barter away the child's right to support.[460]

13) Retroactive Section 7 Expenses

A court may grant a retroactive order for a parent to make a contribution towards special or extraordinary expenses under section 7 of the *Federal Child Support Guidelines*.[461] In exercising its discretion, the court should take account of the attendant circumstances, including any voluntary arrangements between the parents, whether the expenses were known to both parents, the parenting arrangements, and the date of the application for a contribution.[462] Many of the policy issues and factors that are addressed in relation to retroactive basic child support are also applicable to claims for a contribution to section 7 expenses under the *Federal Child Support Guidelines*.[463] However, there is one fundamental difference. Basic child support reflects the right of the child to have his essential needs met. Extraordinary expenses for extracurricular activities are not a basic right of the child and there is no inherent obligation in the parents to pay for such activities.[464] An order for a retroactive contribution to such expenses may be deemed unfair where the father had no knowledge of these expenses and no idea that he might ultimately be called upon to contribute towards them.[465] The court should look to the criteria that govern applications for basic retroactive child support, namely, whether there is a reasonable excuse for why the application was not brought earlier, blameworthy conduct on the part of the obligor or obligee, the present circumstances of the child, and any hardship that would be occasioned by an order for retroactive section 7 expenses.[466] In granting a retroactive order for section 7 expenses, need does not override all other considerations, nor is retroactivity restricted to expenses incurred following an interim application.[467] Limits may be judicially imposed on the retroactivity of an order for a contribution to section 7 expenses so as to promote fairness in light of the attendant circumstances, including the significant delay involved in the claimant's application for a contribution to the expenses.[468] The expectation that the normal period of retroactivity will be restricted to three years before

---

460 *Black v Black* (1995), 19 RFL (4th) 442 (BCCA).

461 *Doucet v Lau*, [2005] AJ No 1809 (QB); *RCT v AKT*, 2023 BCSC 654; *KJP v BSJG*, 2024 BCSC 167 at paras 315–16; *MR v JR*, 2018 NBCA 12; *Maka v Maka*, 2015 ONSC 3480; *Buhler v Buhler*, 2012 SKQB 366; see also *Paynter v Sackville*, 2004 SKQB 258 (retroactive reduction and order for reimbursement of expenses paid after they ceased to be incurred). But see *Selig v Smith*, 2008 NSCA 54; see also Section K(16), below in this chapter.

462 *PCJR v DCR*, [2003] BCJ No 792 (CA). See also *MLR v SLR*, 2020 ABQB 444; *Hatt v Heather*, 2021 ABQB 878; *Pelletier v Richard*, 2021 NBQB 77.

463 *MEKF v FF*, 2015 BCSC 621; *Mastin v Mastin*, 2019 NSSC 248; *Maka v Maka*, 2015 ONSC 3480.

464 *Fedortchouk v Boubnoy*, 2018 NSSC 66 at para 193.

465 *Clegg v Downing*, [2004] AJ No 1511 (QB); *Block v Block*, 2018 BCSC 716, citing *Semancik v Saunders*, 2011 BCCA 264 para 57; *DDR v KTR*, 2019 BCSC 1805.

466 *Semancik v Saunders*, 2011 BCCA 264; *MS v KS*, 2019 BCSC 1458; *Fulcher v Fulcher*, 2012 ONSC 3721; *Chomitzky v Beckstead*, 2012 SKQB 376.

467 *Picco v Picco*, [2000] NJ No 64 (UFC).

468 *CNG v SMR*, [2007] BCJ No 1251 (SC); *Pelletier v Richard*, 2021 NBQB 77; *Sills v Sills*, [2002] OJ No 3679 (SCJ).

formal notice was given to the obligor, in accordance with *DBS v SRG*,[469] applies equally to claims for child support table amounts and for section 7 extraordinary expenses.[470] Retroactivity may be confined to the applicable table amount of child support where the evidence relating to section 7 expenses ranges from vague to non-existent.[471] Where the application for a retroactive order relates to section 7 expenses, it is particularly important that the recipient parent has informed the payor parent in a timely manner of the details of the expenses as they occur.[472]

14) Interest

Pre-judgment and post-judgment interest may be ordered to be paid with respect to a retroactive order for child support.[473]

15) Retroactive Child Support Orders After Adulthood

Child support claims should be brought in a timely fashion. Inchoate support rights cannot be banked and thereafter asserted as relevant to the determination of a spousal property dispute many years later.[474] If retroactive child support, including section 7 expenses, is unavailable after the children have ceased to be eligible for support,[475] its non-availability cannot be circumvented by adult children launching an action for damages based on an alleged breach of fiduciary duty, unjust enrichment or tortious infliction of mental distress or impoverishment upon the children.[476]

16) Jurisdiction of Provincial Court

Although retroactive child support may be ordered pursuant to the *Family Law Act* (Nfld) and retroactivity may be appropriate to cover delay that is attributable to paternity testing, the Provincial Court's jurisdiction to order a lump sum payment is limited by section 40(3)

469 2006 SCC 37.

470 *Martinuk v Graham*, 2015 ONSC 6769 at para 78, Kane J; see also *Small v Small*, 2020 BCSC 707; *Wharry v Wharry*, 2016 ONCA 930.

471 *Guillena v Guillena*, [2003] NSJ No 76 (SC).

472 *Small v Small*, 2020 BCSC 707 at para 245 (reimbursement of retroactive s 7 expenses).

473 *Pope v Janes*, 2014 NLTD(F) 27; *Martin v Sansome*, 2014 ONCA 14 (rate of post-judgment interest reduced on appeal from 10 to 3 percent). See also *NNN v DEB*, 2023 BCSC 1538 (pre-judgment and post-judgment interest on order for reimbursement of overpayments of spousal and child support).

474 *Kazmierczak v Kazmierczak*, [2001] AJ No 955 (QB).

475 See *DBS v SRG; LJW v TAR; Henry v Henry; Hiemstra v Hiemstra*, 2006 SCC 37; see Section K(4), item 16, above in this chapter. See also *Selig v Smith*, 2008 NSCA 54 (s 7 expenses).

476 *Louie v Lastman*, [2001] OJ No 1888 (SCJ), aff'd [2002] OJ No 3521 (CA). For dismissal of the mother's independent action for damages against the father, see *Louie v Lastman*, [2001] OJ No 1889 (SCJ), aff'd [2002] OJ No 3522 (CA). See also *Dopson v Cameron*, [2001] OJ No 3024 (SCJ) (onus of proof not discharged with respect to "historical" claim for support of two adult children who were currently economically self-sufficient).

477 See *Woodland v Kirkham*, 2021 ONSC 8194.

of the Act to circumstances where the dependant "does not have the necessities for life or to prevent the dependant from becoming a public charge."[478]

17) Recalculation of Child Support Where Change in Income During the Year

Retroactive variation of a child support order under section 37 of the Ontario *Family Law Act* may be effectuated by means of an order for the payment of a lump sum that represents the difference between the monthly amounts paid under the order that is sought to be varied and the monthly amounts payable under the variation order. Where the change in income occurs well into the year, the fairest way of achieving the necessary variation may be to recalculate the monthly amount payable under the Guidelines in light of the obligor's overall annual income and subtracting the payments made prior to the variation order; the differential may then be paid in a lump sum.[479]

478 *Ralph v Brockerville,* [2000] NJ No 289 (Prov Ct).

479 *Andrews v Andrews,* [2000] OJ No 4060 (SCJ).

CHAPTER 12

Effect, Registration, and Enforcement of Child Support Orders

A. DEFINITION OF "COURT"

Although corollary orders could be registered and enforced in the Federal Court pursuant to section 15 of the *Divorce Act*, 1968, section 20 of the *Divorce Act* provides only for the registration and enforcement of orders[1] in "any court in a province" and this phrase does not include the Federal Court.[2]

For the purposes of section 20 of the *Divorce Act*, section 20(1) expressly provides that "court" bears the same meaning as that assigned by section 2(1) of the Act. Pursuant to the

---

1 As to interjurisdictional support orders, see ss 18–19 of the *Divorce Act*, RSC 1985 (2d Supp), c 3; see also ss 28–29.5 of the *Divorce Act* whereby the provisions of the *Convention of 23 November 2007 on the International Recovery of Child Support and Other Forms of Family Maintenance* (2007 Hague Child Support Convention) have the force of law in Canada insofar as they relate to subjects that fall within the legislative competence of Parliament. As to the implementation of the *Convention of 19 October 1996 on Jurisdiction, Applicable Law, Recognition, Enforcement and Co-operation in Respect of Parental Responsibility and Measures for the Protection of Children*, see the *Divorce Act*, ss 30–41. And see John-Paul E Boyd, "A Brief Overview of Bill C-78, An Act to Amend the *Divorce Act* and Related Legislation; Part 2: Amendments Relating to Interjurisdictional Agreements and Treaties" (June 2018), online: Canadian Research Institute For Law and the Family https://afccontario.ca/wp-content/uploads/2018/06/Boyd-Overview-of-Bill-C78-Pt-2-June-2018.pdf; Department of Justice, Canada, "The *Divorce Act* Changes Explained: Part II," online: Department of Justice, Canada, www.justice.gc.ca/eng/fl-df/cfl-mdf/dace-clde/index.html. The 2007 Hague Child Support Convention came into force for Canada and applies to the provinces of Manitoba and Ontario on 1 February 2024, and to British Columbia on 1 March 2024. It is expected that the Convention will be progressively implemented in other provinces and territories in Canada: see Department of Justice, Canada, "Enforcement of Child and Spousal Support Payments between Provinces, Territories and Countries," online: www.justice.gc.ca/eng/fl-df/enforce-execution/enforce-execut.html. See also Ontario Family Responsibility Office (FRO) website and the Hague Conference on Private International Law website, subheading "Child Support," online: HCCH.net; and see Andina van Isschot & Annick Boulay, "Strengthening Family Justice Services: Recent Changes to the *Family Orders and Agreements Enforcement Assistance Act* and Canada's Implementation of the 2007 Hague Child Support Convention," County of Carleton Law Association, 33rd Annual Institute of Family Law, 5 April 2024, Montebello, Quebec.

2 *Young v Hubbert* (1987), 8 RFL (3d) 453 (FCTD).

definition of "court" in section 2(1), the Lieutenant Governor in Council of a province may designate a Unified Family Court that is presided over by federally appointed judges as a court of competent jurisdiction for all purposes of the *Divorce Act.* Section 20(1) goes beyond the provisions of section 2(1), however, by also empowering the Lieutenant Governor in Council of a province to designate some other court as a court of competent jurisdiction for the purposes of section 20 of the *Divorce Act.* A Lieutenant Governor in Council may designate a court presided over by provincially appointed judges to exercise enforcement powers in respect of any corollary order registered in that court pursuant to section 20(3)(a) of the *Divorce Act.*[3] The joint operation of sections 20(1) and 20(3) appears to remove any doubt that might otherwise exist concerning the permissibility of extra-provincial enforcement proceedings being brought before provincially appointed judges in respect of support or parenting orders under the *Divorce Act.* It is submitted that the power to enforce corollary orders granted on or after divorce may be exercised by provincially appointed judges and that the exercise of such jurisdiction does not contravene section 96 of the *Constitution Act, 1867.* Indeed, the enforcement of support and parenting orders has increasingly become a function of courts presided over by provincially appointed judges, at least where the order was made in the same province as that in which enforcement is sought. A search for the enforcement practices existing in the provinces and territories prior to 1867 is likely to prove elusive, even in the few provinces that had enacted divorce legislation prior to that date. In Quebec and Newfoundland, judicial divorce was unknown until 1968 and the same appears to be true in Alberta, British Columbia, the Northwest Territories, Ontario, and Yukon, prior to 1867.[4]

B. NATIONAL EFFECT OF COROLLARY ORDERS

Section 20(2) of the *Divorce Act* provides that any corollary order, other than a provisional order under section 18(2), has legal effect throughout Canada. National effect is extended to provincial divorce judgments, as distinct from any corollary orders therein, by the express provisions of section 13 of the *Divorce Act.*[5]

C. ENFORCEMENT AND VARIATION DISTINGUISHED

The powers conferred by section 20(3) of the *Divorce Act* are expressly confined to the enforcement of corollary orders and do not include any jurisdiction to vary, rescind, or suspend such orders.[6] The jurisdiction to vary, rescind, or suspend orders for support or parenting is expressly confined by the provisions of the *Divorce Act* to courts that satisfy the definition of "court" found in section 2(1).[7] Thus, in *Knott v Jacob,*[8] wherein child support had been granted

3 See *Re LeBlanc* (1986), 77 NSR (2d) 49 (TD).

4 See, generally, Christine Davies, *Family Law in Canada* (Toronto: Carswell, 1984) at 325–28.

5 See Julien D Payne, *Payne on Divorce*, 4th ed (Scarborough, ON: Carswell, 1996) ch VI, "Divorce Judgments," Part 3, "National Effect of Divorce and Corollary Orders."

6 See *Ontario (Director of Support & Custody Enforcement) v Sarsfield* (1988), 15 RFL (3d) 192 (Ont Fam Ct); see also *British Columbia (Public Trustee) v Price* (1989), 21 RFL (3d) 51 (BCSC), rev'd (1990), 25 RFL (3d) 113 (BCCA); *Manzoni v Manzoni* (1987), 67 Nfld & PEIR 339 (Nfld TD).

7 See *British Columbia (Director of Maintenance Enforcement) v Fults* (1991), 38 RFL (3d) 80 (BCSC).

8 (1986), 2 RFL (3d) 255 (Ont Fam Ct).

in divorce proceedings in accordance with a pre-existing order of the Provincial Court (Family Division), now the Ontario Court of Justice, James J held that the Supreme Court of Ontario, now the Ontario Superior Court of Justice, has no jurisdiction to direct that any motion to vary the order shall be adjudicated by the Provincial Court (Family Division).[9]

On an application by the Saskatchewan Director of Maintenance Enforcement to enforce a child support order, the presiding judge has no jurisdiction to provide a pragmatic response to practical problems by granting a variation order, where no application for such relief has been brought and the parent in receipt of child support has been denied the opportunity to be heard on the matter.[10] In *Smith v Smith*,[11] the mother had been ordered to pay support for three children pursuant to the *Divorce Act* and the *Federal Child Support Guidelines*. The order provided that the support would continue "for so long as the said children remain children within the meaning of the *Divorce Act* or until further order of this Court." The order was registered under *The Enforcement of Maintenance Orders Act, 1997*.[12] The Director of Maintenance Enforcement instituted default proceedings against the mother seeking arrears that had accrued with respect to the two older children after they attained the provincial age of majority. Within the confines of the maintenance enforcement proceeding, the mother sought a judicial determination that the two older children had ceased to be "children within the meaning of the *Divorce Act*" when they turned eighteen. She argued that her support obligation was extinguished by operation of law when each child attained the provincial age of majority, and that the onus thereafter fell on the father to apply for any continued support with respect to the children's ongoing education. She also challenged the Director's action in taking steps to enforce arrears, stating that he had the power to determine disputes between the parents, the statutory discretion to suspend or refuse to enforce arrears, and the right to apply for a variation of the order on his own initiative. The chambers judge held that he had no jurisdiction to deal with the mother's request for declaratory relief and the remission of arrears in enforcement proceedings in the absence of an agreement between the parents or a variation application brought pursuant to the *Divorce Act*. On the mother's appeal, the Saskatchewan Court of Appeal addressed three specific issues. The first was whether a child support order under the *Divorce Act* terminates by operation of law upon the child's attainment of the provincial age of majority. Looking to the judgments of the Supreme Court of Canada in *Jackson v Jackson*[13] and *Ruttan v Ruttan*,[14] the Saskatchewan Court of Appeal held that a child does not cease to be a "child of the marriage" within the meaning of section 2(1) of the *Divorce Act* only by reason of the fact that he or she has attained the provincial age of majority. Whether a child satisfies the statutory definition is not a question of age but one of continued financial dependence on the parents. Consequently, a child support order does not "self-destruct" when a child attains the provincial age of majority, although a variation

---

9 See also *Lake v Lake* (1988), 11 RFL (3d) 234 (NSCA).

10 *Saskatchewan (Director of Maintenance Enforcement) v Gerbrandt*, [2003] SJ No 569 (CA).

11 2008 SKCA 141.

12 SS 1997, c E-9.21.

13 [1973] SCR 205.

14 [1982] 1 SCR 690. And see Keith B Farquhar, "The Variation, Enforcement and Interpretation of Maintenance Orders in Canada — Some New Aspects of an Old Dilemma" (1982) 60 *Canadian Bar Review* 585; and Keith B Farquhar, "Variation and Enforcement of Maintenance Orders: *Ruttan* Revisited" (1986) 64 *Canadian Bar Review* 534.

application under section 17 of the *Divorce Act* confers jurisdiction on the court to determine the issue.[15] In response to the mother's argument that it was unfair to require payors to shoulder the burden of applying for variation, the Saskatchewan Court of Appeal stated that this was not an onerous exercise because it would often require nothing more than proof that the child's plans after turning eighteen were not made known to the paying parent. Thereafter, the evidentiary burden of establishing the continued dependence of the child would fall on the parent asserting that the child was "unable to withdraw from parental charge" within the meaning of the statutory definition of "child of the marriage" under section 2(1) of the *Divorce Act*. The Saskatchewan Court of Appeal then turned to the second issue, namely, the mother's correlative argument that a court has jurisdiction in enforcement proceedings to review a child's status under the *Divorce Act* and, if appropriate, terminate a support order and rescind arrears. Referring to sections 20(2), (3), and (4) of the *Divorce Act* and to *Ruttan v Ruttan*, discussed above, and its own previous judgment in *Alberding v Alberding*,[16] the Saskatchewan Court of Appeal concluded that, while provincial enforcement mechanisms, such as those contained in *The Enforcement of Maintenance Orders Act, 1997*, can be invoked to enforce support orders granted in divorce proceedings, a judge acting under the authority of provincial legislation cannot entrench on substantive matters governed by the *Divorce Act* that fall within the exclusive authority of Parliament. Furthermore, a judge in enforcement proceedings cannot embark upon an inquiry to determine whether the child is a "child of the marriage" within the meaning of the *Divorce Act*. Such an inquiry must be undertaken in the context of proceedings under the *Divorce Act*, although section 53(7) of *The Enforcement of Maintenance Orders Act, 1997* permits a default hearing and a variation application to be heard together. The third and final issue in this appeal related to the authority of the Director of Maintenance Enforcement. The mother argued that the Director should have refused to enforce the arrears in the face of the parental dispute regarding the eligibility of the two older children for continued support after they attained the provincial age of majority. She further argued that the Director should have applied for variation of the order as he possessed the sole authority to enforce, or refuse to enforce, the registered order. As with the other aspects of the mother's appeal, the Saskatchewan Court of Appeal observed that the mother's argument confused issues of entitlement, which concern the parties, with issues of enforcement, which concern the Director. Reviewing sections 6(1)(c), 8, and 9 of *The Enforcement of Maintenance Orders Act, 1997*, the Saskatchewan Court of Appeal held that the Director did not act improperly in seeking to enforce the arrears. The mother's reliance on *Dueck v Dueck*[17] was misplaced. That case decided that the Director had a discretion with respect to the enforcement of *ongoing* support if there was agreement between the parents that the child had ceased to be dependent. There was no tenable basis, however, for the mother's argument that the Director must possess a similar discretion with respect to *arrears* of support that accrued over a period of time when the parents were in active disagreement as to the children's eligibility for child support. The appeal was, therefore, dismissed.

15 See *Ethier v Skrudland*, 2011 SKCA 17; compare *Haavisto v Haavisto*, 2008 SKQB 446, DEW McIntyre J (variation proceeding).

16 (1989), 74 Sask R 208.

17 2006 SKQB 417.

D. ENFORCEMENT UNDER PROVINCIAL LAWS

Section 20(3)(b) of the *Divorce Act* expressly recognizes alternative means of enforcing corollary orders to those specified in section 20(3)(a) where such means have been provided for by provincial laws. The directors of provincial enforcement plans do not have the authority to vary a court order. Although they may choose the method by which an order is to be enforced, they may not alter the terms or conditions of the order.[18]

E. BURDEN OF PROOF; FAILURE TO ATTEND

The burden of proving inability to pay support or to comply with any other order falls on the party against whom the order was made. The reverse onus whereby the defaulter must prove inability to pay or otherwise face imprisonment is compatible with principles of fundamental justice and does not violate sections 7 or 11 of the *Canadian Charter of Rights and Freedoms*.[19] A respondent who has actual notice of a show cause hearing and who fails to attend cannot complain that his rights under section 7 of the *Canadian Charter of Rights and Freedoms* have been violated, notwithstanding that Rule 7.01 of the Rules and Regulations enacted pursuant to the *Family Court Act*,[20] as amended, has not been duly complied with. Such non-compliance is treated as an irregularity and does not nullify the proceeding where there is no breach of the rules of natural justice.[21]

F. FEDERAL ENFORCEMENT LEGISLATION

Provincial laws respecting the enforcement of support orders have been complemented by federal legislation.[22] The federal legislative framework and limitations regulating the enforcement of support obligations cannot be circumvented or expanded by judicial appointment of a receiver/trustee.[23]

The *Family Orders and Agreements Enforcement Assistance Act*[24] provides for the release of information from designated federal information banks that will assist in locating spouses or parents who act in breach of court orders for support or parenting. This Act also permits the garnishment of federal monies to satisfy support orders or agreements that are in default. An income tax refund constitutes "garnishable money" under section 24 of the *Family Orders and Agreements Enforcement Assistance Act*.[25] The *Family Orders and Agreements Enforcement Assistance Act* was amended by SC 2019, c 16 to allow for the search and release of a

---

18 *McGill v McGill* (1994), 8 RFL (4th) 84 at 86 (Sask QB).

19 *Woloshyn v Woloshyn*, [2000] MJ No 53 (QB); *Mancuso v Mancuso* (1991), 35 RFL (3d) 265 (Ont Prov Div); *Fedorychka v Fedorychka* (1985), 44 RFL (2d) 458 (Sask UFC).

20 RSNS 1967, c 98.

21 *Lecreux v Lecreux*, [1987] NSJ No 293 (Co Ct), citing *Stoddard v Randall* (1985), 72 NSR (2d) 99 (Fam Ct).

22 See the *Garnishment, Attachment and Pension Diversion Act*, RSC 1985, c G-2, as amended by RSC 1985 (2d Supp), c 3, s 29 and by SC 2019, c 16; see also *Weniuk v Weniuk* (1986), 3 RFL (3d) 110 (FCTD).

23 *Beattie v Ladouceur* (1995), 13 RFL (4th) 435 (Ont Ct Gen Div).

24 RSC 1985 (2d Supp), c 4, as amended by SC 1992, c 1.

25 *Marzetti v Marzetti* (1994), 5 RFL (4th) 1 (SCC), wherein the Director of Maintenance Enforcement for Alberta was granted priority over the defaulter's trustee in bankruptcy. See also *Beattie v Ladouceur* (1995), 13 RFL (4th) 435 (Ont Ct Gen Div).

party's income information to courts and provincial services, including provincial enforcement services, for the purposes of establishing, varying, or enforcing support.[26]

G. GARNISHMENT; ATTACHMENT; EXECUTION

The British Columbia Court of Appeal[27] has held that ordinary garnishment law should not be applied to the enforcement of support orders unless it is consistent with the "social purposes" of the British Columbia *Family Maintenance Enforcement Act*. Section 16(4) of the *Family Maintenance Enforcement Act* (BC) sets out only two instances wherein a court may set aside an attachment order: (1) where the attachee is no longer liable; (2) where the Notice of Attachment contains or is based on a material error. Furthermore, the court's power to increase the amount of salary exempt from attachment is also very limited. Section 13.1(3) of the regulation relating to the *Family Maintenance Enforcement Act* (BC) permits a court to increase the normal exemption only if such an increase is necessary to enable the debtor to meet her basic needs for food, shelter, or clothing.[28] Failure to give notice of the filing of a maintenance order or to serve a notice of attachment on a defaulter, coupled with an incorrect statement of the amount of arrears, do not warrant intervention, if the Director of Family Maintenance Enforcement took reasonable steps to serve the respondent and no prejudice was suffered by the respondent as a result of the error in amount.[29]

Where there have been problems with the payment of support on time, with consequential budgeting and planning problems for the payee, and the payor undertakes to make timely payments through the court, an order of the court may direct that if any payment is late, a garnishee notice will be issued without further notice to the parties.[30]

Service of a notice of garnishment by ordinary mail pursuant to Rule 6(2)(a) of the Ontario *Family Law Rules* is *prima facie* evidence that the documents were received by the addressee. If the addressee satisfies the court on the balance of probabilities that the documents were not received, he is not liable to pay the support creditor the amount previously paid to the support debtor in ignorance of the mailed notice of garnishment.[31] The Ontario Court of Justice has no jurisdiction to grant equitable relief nor does it have any jurisdiction to determine the priorities of competing creditors by way of an interpleader motion or declaratory judgment, but a support debtor's interest in a law partnership is garnishable

---

26 See Andina van Isschot, Department of Justice, "FOAEAA Income Disclosure," 29th Annual Family Law Conference, Part 1, County of Carleton Law Association, Ottawa, 1 October 2020. See generally Canada, Department of Justice, *Legislative Background: An act to amend the Divorce Act, the Family Orders and Agreements Enforcement Act and the Garnishment Attachment and Pension Diversion Act and to make consequential amendments to another Act* (Bill C-78, now SC 2019, c 16) (24 January 2019), online: www.justice.gc.ca/eng/rp-pr/fl-lf/famil/c78/03.html. See also *Denial of Licences for Family Orders and Agreements Enforcement Regulations, 2021*, SOR/2020-266. And see *Release of Information for Family Orders and Agreements Enforcement Assistance Regulations*, SOR/2023-125, online: www.canlii.org/en/ca/laws/regu/sor-2023-125/latest/sor-2023-125.html retrieved on 12 March 2024.

27 *British Columbia (Director of Maintenance Enforcement) v IWA Forest Industry Pension Plan (Trustees of)* (1991), 37 RFL (3d) 266 (BCCA).

28 *Vorlicek v Soares*, [1999] BCJ No 3083 (Prov Ct).

29 *Mackechnie v Mackechnie*, [1998] BCJ No 2096 (SC).

30 *MacInnes v MacInnes* (1993), 122 NSR (2d) 329 (Fam Ct).

31 *Ontario (Director, Family Responsibility Office) v Hay*, [2002] OJ No 1335 (Ct J).

under section 43 of the *Partnerships Act*.[32] An employer who fails to comply with an order garnishing a support defaulter's wages is liable to make good the loss.[33] A parent's Canada Pension Plan disability benefits are "garnishable moneys" within the meaning of the *Family Orders and Agreements Enforcement Assistance Act* (Canada) and the *Family Support Orders and Agreements Garnishment Regulations*[34] made thereunder.[35] In *Trick v Trick*,[36] on the termination of his employment in Canada, which triggered payment of a company pension, the husband obtained higher-income employment in Texas but judgment-proofed his US assets. On the wife's motion to enforce her entitlement to $422,192 in arrears of child and spousal support, interest, and costs, the motion judge vested 100 percent of the husband's pension in the wife and ordered the garnishment of 100 percent of the husband's Canada Pension Plan and Old Age Security benefits. On appeal, the motion judge was found to have erred in granting the vesting order with respect to the husband's pension because this order contravened section 66(4) of the *Pension Benefits Act*,[37] which permits execution against a pension benefit but only to a maximum of 50 percent of the benefit. Furthermore, the vest ing order contravened section 65(1) of the *Pension Benefits Act*, which provides that "[e]very transaction that purports to assign, charge, anticipate or give as security money payable under a pension plan is void." Consequently, the vesting order was set aside by the Ontario Court of Appeal and the wife was held entitled only to the garnishment of 50 percent of the husband's company pension. With respect to the motion judge's order for the garnishment of 100 percent of the husband's CPP and OAS benefits, the Ontario Court of Appeal observed that while the Canada Pension Plan[38] and the *Old Age Security Act*[39] prohibit execution of these respective benefits, they are subject to the overriding provisions of sections 24 to 26 of the *Family Orders and Agreements Enforcement Assistance Act*,[40] which render CPP and OAS benefits garnishable in accordance with provincial garnishment law. Given that section 23(1) of the *Family Responsibility and Support Arrears Enforcement Act*[41] caps garnishment of the payor's income source at 50 percent, the Ontario Court of Appeal concluded that the motions judge had erred in garnisheeing 100 percent of the husband's CPP and OAS benefits. Section 65(1) of the *Pension Benefits Act*[42] acts as an absolute bar to charging a pension in respect of child support ordered or accruing in future, but section 66(4) of the Act permits one half of a pension to be seized to satisfy support enforceable in Ontario.[43] Although

---

32 RSO 1990, c P.5. See *Ontario (Director, Family Support Plan) v Freyseng* (1994), 4 RFL (4th) 454 (Ont Prov Div).

33 *Ontario (Director of Support & Custody Enforcement) v Thomas* (1990), 27 RFL (3d) 135 (Ont Dist Ct).

34 SOR/88-181.

35 *MJB v WPB*, [2004] MJ No 123 (QB).

36 [2006] OJ No 2737 (CA); see also *Thompson v Gilchrist*, 2012 ONSC 4137; *Kelly v Kelly*, 2013 ONSC 6733 (LIRA).

37 RSO 1990, c P.8.

38 RSC 1985, c C-8.

39 RSC 1985, c O-9.

40 RSC 1985 (2d Supp), c 4.

41 SO 1996, c 31.

42 RSO 1990, c P.8.

43 *Kelly v Kelly*, 2013 ONSC 6733 at para 38, Pearce J; *Trick v Trick*, 2006 CanLII 22926 (ONCA); *Vetro v Vetro*, 2017 ONSC 7294. See also *Virc v Blair*, 2017 ONCA 849.

garnishment is generally available as a matter of course, it is governed by equitable principles and the court retains discretion as to whether it will permit garnishment proceedings.[44]

The conditions for lifting a continuing garnishment that are imposed by section 28 of *The Enforcement of Maintenance Orders Act, 1997* (Saskatchewan) are not satisfied where there is an ongoing child support obligation.[45] A termination of future obligations under a maintenance order does not prevent enforcement of arrears accrued under that order.[46]

On the application of the support creditor, the court may order the collapse of the defaulter's RRSP.[47]

H. ENFORCEMENT BY PROVINCIAL AGENCIES

One problem that has plagued Canadian law over many years is the degree to which court orders for spousal and child support fall into default. The enforcement of support orders, even those granted in divorce, is primarily regulated by provincial and territorial legislation. Provincial and territorial automatic enforcement processes have been established whereby the enforcement of orders is no longer left to the spouses or parents to whom the money is payable. Orders for support are now registerable with provincial or territorial agencies that monitor the payments and take any necessary steps to enforce orders that have fallen into default.[48] Manitoba, New Brunswick, Newfoundland and Labrador, Nova Scotia, Ontario, and Quebec have adopted an automatic or "opt-out" registration and enforcement system whereby maintenance orders are automatically filed with a maintenance enforcement program at the time of the order. A support recipient may ask to be withdrawn from the program but the payor usually has to agree to the withdrawal and the request can be denied if the recipient is receiving social assistance. Alberta, British Columbia, Prince Edward Island, Saskatchewan, Yukon, the Northwest Territories, and Nunavut have an "opt-in" program, whereby registration is at the option of either the recipient or payor. An exception arises in cases where the recipient is eligible for social assistance, in which event enrolment in the maintenance enforcement program is mandatory.[49]

As an alternative to court applications for variation, several provinces, including Alberta, Manitoba, Newfoundland and Labrador,[50] and Prince Edward Island provide a calculation service that facilitates a regular administrative review, usually annually, of the payor's financial circumstances and possible recalculation of the payment terms in an order, without going to court.[51] Sections 25.01 and 25.1 of the *Divorce Act*[52] empower the federal Minister

44 *Vetro v Vetro*, 2017 ONSC 7294 at para 21, Gray J.

45 *Hamonic v Gronvold*, [2003] SJ No 847 (QB).

46 *Morin v Matheson*, 2018 SKCA 9.

47 *Cail v Cail*, [2003] NBJ No 179 (QB), citing *Prince Edward Island (Director of Maintenance Enforcement) v Campbell*, [1990] PEIJ No 141 (CA).

48 Statistics Canada, *The Daily* (3 March 2008); Statistics Canada, Canadian Centre for Judicial Statistics, *Child and Spousal Support: Maintenance Enforcement Survey Statistics, 2006/2007* (Ottawa: Minister of Industry, 2008).

49 See, generally, Statistics Canada, "A Description of Maintenance Enforcement Services" (17 September 2010).

50 See *Dinn v Dinn*, 2011 NLTD(F) 19.

51 Statistics Canada, "A Description of Maintenance Enforcement Services" (17 September 2010).

52 See also s 26(1)(c) of the *Divorce Act* (regulation-making authority of Governor in Council).

of Justice, on behalf of the Government of Canada, to enter into an agreement with a province authorizing a provincial child support service to calculate or recalculate the amount of child support in accordance with the applicable guidelines where complete and accurate income information is provided by the parents. If either or both spouses do not agree with the amount of the child support calculated or recalculated, they may apply to a court of competent jurisdiction for an order. These statutory provisions allow a recalculation to be performed at the request of either or both former spouses rather than only at "regular intervals" (for example, if there is a job loss during a year); provide for rules allowing for the deeming of income by the calculation services if a spouse refuses to disclose their income information; allow for the recalculation of an interim order; and allow a provincial calculation service to apply the same rules to an order made under the *Divorce Act* as would apply to a support order made under provincial law. Pursuant to sections 20(2) and 20(3) of the *Divorce Act*, a provincial child support service decision that calculates or recalculates the amount of child support under sections 25.01 or 25.1 of the *Divorce Act* has legal effect and is enforceable throughout Canada. In Alberta, pursuant to Division 1.1 of the *Family Law Act* SA 2003, c F-4.5, if a parent fails to provide the required documentation, the amount of child support under an existing order or binding agreement will be automatically recalculated for the first year as if the payor's income had increased by 10 percent. A further 3 percent will be added for each additional year the order was granted or recalculated. The maximum deemed income increase is 25 percent and is applied to orders where five or more years have passed since the parental income levels were determined. Pursuant to section 55.51(4) of the *Family Law Act*, where a payor or a recipient fails to provide the recalculation program with income information in respect of a child support order made under the *Divorce Act* (Canada), the Director of the Child Support Recalculation Program may apply to the court on such notice as the court may direct for an order respecting the determination of the income of the payor or the recipient for the purposes of a recalculation of child support.[53] The Alberta program has no discretion to consider individual circumstances or to conduct an analysis of business expenses that have not been challenged by the Canada Revenue Agency. The Government of Alberta, Child Support Recalculation Program, Information Sheet states:

> Self-employed people can be eligible for certain benefits and income tax deductions that salaried employees are not. Depending on the type and extent of self-employment income, courts may add some of those benefits or deductions back into the calculation when deciding on the self-employed person's income for child support purposes. To make this decision, judges can do a comprehensive review of the self-employed party's finances, examining business and personal financial documents and questioning the party of those documents. Since these reviews involve investigation and discretion, they are not suitable for an administrative recalculation program like RP. Unlike a court, RP cannot use discretion to take into account each person's particular situation. RP has a simple, administrative process that recalculates child support based on Line 150 (now Line 15000) of the parent's filed income tax return as assessed by Revenue Canada. There is a risk that in self-employment situations, tax documents may show less income than is actually available for child support purposes.[54]

---

53 *Moshuk v Moshuk*, 2010 ABQB 540.

54 *Gonek v Gonek*, 2011 ABQB 166 (father judicially precluded from using recalculation program).

In Alberta, child support orders must be paid through the Director of Maintenance Enforcement, unless the recipient withdraws from the program.[55] The practice of the Director of Maintenance Enforcement, whereby a support obligor's compliance with a voluntary payment plan relieves him from the risk of full execution on arrears, has been judicially endorsed in Alberta. However, this concession is only justifiable where the child support obligor makes voluntary payments that do not require the Director to undertake procedures by way of support deduction notices (formerly called garnishees) that would trigger additional administrative costs.[56]

The British Columbia Supreme Court has only limited authority to intervene with respect to procedures invoked by the Director of the Family Maintenance Enforcement Program to enforce a parent's child support obligations by (1) preventing the issue of a driving licence; (2) reporting his indebtedness to the Credit Bureau; (3) registering a lien against his personal property; and (4) filing notices of attachment with the federal government. Judicial intervention is inappropriate where the defaulter's lack of income is due to a refusal to work, rather than an inability to work.[57] Court orders exist and are enforceable until such time as they are varied or terminated by the court. The Family Maintenance Enforcement Program of British Columbia has no authority to give legal advice to people as to the effect of court orders and the obligations thereby imposed. Whether an adult child remains a child of the marriage entitled to support is a matter to be resolved by a court, not by the provincial enforcement agency.[58]

Part VI of *The Family Maintenance Act* (Manitoba), entitled "Enforcement of Maintenance Orders," empowers a designated officer of the Enforcement Branch to initiate various types of proceedings to enforce support obligations that are in default. In *Daniels v Daniels*,[59] Schulman J of the Manitoba Court of Queen's Bench reviewed various statutory provisions and enforcement processes before concluding that monies payable to a support defaulter who is entitled to receive funds under the Indian Residential Schools Settlement may be accessed by the Enforcement Branch pursuant to a court order for the appointment of a receiver. The order for the appointment of the receiver was appealed by Daniels and by the Attorney General of Canada.[60] The Manitoba Court of Appeal held that the receiver order did not offend the terms of the class action settlement and that the supervising judge had "exercised his discretion judicially and for the purpose of securing a just and expeditious resolution of the issues related to the enforcement of Daniels' arrears of child support."[61] Furthermore, Daniels could not successfully challenge the order on the basis of either section 88 or 89 of the *Indian Act*,[62] in circumstances where the payments were pursuant to a settlement agreement rather than federal legislation and both Daniels and his wife were status Indians. With respect to the Attorney General for Canada's arguments that the order for the appointment of a receiver

---

55 *DBC v RMW*, [2004] AJ No 1559 (QB).

56 *Stebner v Stebner*, [2005] AJ No 1556 (QB); see also *Stebner v Stebner*, [2005] AJ No 1625 (QB). And see *Colucci v Colucci*, 2021 SCC 24 at para 140.

57 *KJK v PBK*, [2002] BCJ No 2114 (SC). Compare *Louksr v Assadbeigi*, 2010 BCSC 116.

58 *Collison v Collison*, [2001] BCJ No 2080 (SC).

59 *Daniels v Daniels*, 2010 MBQB 46.

60 *Daniels v Daniels*, 2011 MBCA 94.

61 *Ibid* at para 73.

62 RSC 1985, c I-5.

offended the principle of Crown immunity as well as the principle that the federal Crown can not be bound by provincial legislation, the Manitoba Court of Appeal reviewed the nature of receiver orders and distinguished them from attachment and garnishment orders. It pointed out that "some judges have navigated around Crown immunity by limiting the powers of the receiver to 'receiving.'"[63] This approach has come to be known as a "*Willcock*" order, after *Willcock v Terrell*.[64] The Manitoba Court of Appeal acknowledged that "[t]here is always the practical issue of whether the Crown will cooperate with a *Willcock*-type order" and to facili tate cooperation, close attention must be paid to the wording of the order, which must refrain from purporting to confer powers on the receiver to enforce payment against the Crown. In the words of BM Hamilton JA, who delivered the opinion of the appellate court:

> To summarize, the appointment of the designated officer as receiver of Daniels's DR award under the settlement agreement, in and of itself, does not offend federal Crown immunity. This is so because the law recognizes the possibility of appointing a receiver where such an appointment creates the power to receive and does not constitute an order against the Crown (i.e., it is not coercive).[65]

However, because paragraphs 4 and 8 of the receiver order were coercive against the federal Crown, they offended its Crown immunity. Consequently, the Manitoba Court of Appeal excised these coercive provisions but found it unnecessary to strike the receiver order aside in its entirety, thereby leaving it to the Crown to decide whether it wished to cooperate with the designated officer as a receiver. By following this course of action, the court not only navigated around the issue of Crown immunity; it also navigated around the principle that the federal Crown is not bound by compulsory provincial legislation.

As of 1 March 1992, Ontario implemented a program designed to address the massive delinquency rate of support debtors. Before its implementation, 75 percent of all family support orders were said to be in default and $450 million in support payments was owed. Courts in Ontario now make a support deduction order at the same time as they make an order for spousal or child support. The spouse or parent who is ordered to pay support and who receives regular wages, commissions, pension benefits, annuities, or other income must furnish the name and address of the income source (usually the employer). A support deduction notice is sent to the employer or income source, who is then responsible for deducting the support payments from the payor's income in the same way as income tax, Canada Pension Plan deductions, and unemployment insurance premiums are deducted from income. If the payor changes her address or employment, she must advise the Family Responsibility Office of the change and the name and address of the new employer. Failure to do so can result in a maximum fine of $10,000. When advised of a new employer, the Family Responsibility Office sends a support deduction notice to the new employer without further recourse to the courts.

Wage deductions made by an employer are sent to the office of the Family Responsibility Office, which redirects the payment to the ex-spouse or parent who is entitled to receive

---

63 *Daniels v Daniels*, 2011 MBCA 94 at para 91.

64 [1879] 3 Ex D 323 (CA).

65 *Daniels v Daniels*, 2011 MBCA 94 at para 99.

spousal or child support. If needed, the Family Responsibility Office can use other enforcement procedures, such as garnishment, seizure of property, or show cause hearings. The Family Responsibility Office is a collection agency; it does not underwrite or guarantee the support payment. It merely takes steps to enforce support payments. It is provided free of charge and, with minor exceptions, is not subject to opting out.[66]

Section 23(1) of the Ontario *Family Responsibility and Support Arrears Enforcement Act* stipulates that the total amount deducted by an income source and paid to the Director of the Family Responsibility Office under a support deduction order shall not exceed 50 percent of the net amount owed by the income source to the payor. A court cannot circumvent this section by purporting to exercise its *parens patriae* jurisdiction in ordering the Director to garnish the full amount of child support, although the Director is free to pursue concurrent enforcement remedies, including a move to suspend the obligor's provincial driving privileges.[67]

The duty of public officials to enforce support orders transcends merely private interests. An application to enforce an extra-provincial support order granted in divorce proceedings may, therefore, proceed in the absence of the creditor spouse.[68] Costs may be awarded against enforcement officers who refuse to negotiate or engage in settlement discussions or who fail to deal with issues on a case-by-case basis.[69] A Director of Support and Custody Enforcement should not compel a spouse to seek "interpretation" or clarification of an order as a condition precedent to automatic enforcement. The Director must obtain the best legal opinion and then act upon it.[70] An applicant who is represented by a Family Court officer must furnish the officer with sufficient knowledge and evidence of default, and the reciprocating jurisdiction should be furnished with evidence of when arrears accrued.[71]

Provincial and territorial enforcement programs have encountered difficulty in enforcing support provisions relating to special or extraordinary expenses under section 7 of the *Federal Child Support Guidelines* where the court-ordered contribution is declared to be proportionate to the respective incomes of the spouses but there is no specific amount identified as the appropriate contribution. Income tax deductions or credits, nevertheless, have been ordered to be taken into account by the Maintenance Enforcement Office pursuant to a court-ordered calculation of the respondent's contribution to expenses granted pursuant to section 7 of the *Federal Child Support Guidelines*.[72] The duty and powers of the Director of the Family Responsibility Office under the Ontario *Family Responsibility and Support Arrears Enforcement Act, 1996*[73] centre on the enforcement of support orders and support deduction orders issued by a court. The Family Responsibility Office does not have the

---

66 As to the Director's discretion to refuse to enforce a support order, see *Tsaros v Ontario (Director, Family Responsibility Office)*, 2012 ONSC 2449 (Div Ct).

67 *Gray v Gray*, [1998] OJ No 2291 (Gen Div).

68 *Noel v Earle* (1986), 3 RFL (3d) 387 (Ont Dist Ct), applying *Rae v Rae* (1983), 37 RFL (2d) 16 (Ont HCJ).

69 *Ontario (Director of Support & Custody Enforcement) v Glover* (1987), 11 RFL (3d) 58 (Ont Fam Ct); *Ontario (Director of Support & Custody Enforcement) v McIntyre* (1987), 11 RFL (3d) 89 (Ont Fam Ct); see also *Oldham v King* (1987), 11 RFL (3d) 75 (Man QB).

70 *Rintaluhta v Rintaluhta* (1987), 11 RFL (3d) 397 (Ont Dist Ct). Compare *Caravello v Wickett*, 2011 ONSC 3702.

71 *Kehl v Innes* (1988), 88 NSR (2d) 259 (Fam Ct).

72 *Ridgeway v Ridgeway*, [2000] PEIJ No 4 (SC).

73 SO 1996, c 31.

authority to determine which section 7 expenses are legitimate.[74] Its inability to determine which expenses are legitimate is consistent with its lack of a mandate to interpret court orders where there is disagreement as to their meaning. The inability of the Family Responsibility Office to "approve" special and extraordinary expenses is to be distinguished from a requirement to present receipts to the Family Responsibility Office for a specific category of expense, such as camp expenses or tutoring, in an amount that is not specified by the court. Where the parties disagree about the meaning of an order, the Family Responsibility Office should decline to enforce the order and send the parties back to court to seek clarification.

If the Ontario Family Responsibility Office uses a collection agency to enforce arrears of child support, the fees charged by the agency cannot be set off by the Ontario Family Responsibility Office against the support paid to the primary caregiving parent.[77]

The Minister of Revenue, who is responsible for the collection and disbursement of support payments under the *Act to Facilitate the Payment of Support*,[78] has no authority to vary an order for child support. Such jurisdiction vests in the court and any purported exercise of jurisdiction by the Minister of Revenue is illegal.[79]

The Enforcement of Maintenance Orders Act, 1997 (Saskatchewan) is remedial legislation that should be broadly and liberally interpreted to ensure the attainment of its objectives. While the purpose of the Act is to enforce maintenance orders, such enforcement must be tempered by reasonableness. The language of section 53(1) of the Act, which sets out the types of orders that a court "may" make on a default hearing, is permissive, not mandatory. Although section 53 does not refer directly to the suspension of enforcement, its wording is sufficiently broad to include such orders. The suspension of enforcement does not affect the accrual of arrears. While the Director of the Maintenance Enforcement Office has an obligation to enforce child support orders, that obligation terminates prospectively once the child ceases to be eligible for support under the relevant statutory criteria. The table amounts of support under the *Federal Child Support Guidelines* are based on the obligor's gross annual income and the number of children for whom support is ordered. Section 13 of the Guidelines requires specific information to be included in the formal order so that subsequent adjustments can be easily made. In particular, an order is required to include the name and date of birth of each child to whom the order relates, the income of any parent whose income is used to determine the amount of the child support order, the table amount for the number of children to whom the order relates, the specific amount of support for a child over the provincial age of majority if that amount differs from the table amount, the particulars of any section 7 expenses, including the amount of the expense and the proportion to be paid in relation to the expense, and the date when the order is to commence. In addition, courts usually specify when the order ceases to have effect. Orders granted pursuant to the *Federal Child Support Guidelines* are not global in nature so as to render the number of children covered by the order

---

74 *Caravello v Wickett*, 2011 ONSC 3702.

75 *Ibid*, citing *Graham v Bruto*, [2007] OJ No 656 (SCJ).

76 *Caravello v Wickett*, 2011 ONSC 3702; *Emhecht v Ontario (Family Responsibility Office)*, 2011 ONSC 2644 (SCJ) (order for costs against FRO).

77 *Tu v Tu*, [2000] OJ No 1336 (SCJ).

78 RSQ c P-2.2.

79 *MB v NS*, [2001] QJ No 3039 (SCJ).

irrelevant.[80] Where the order involves a table amount for two or more children and one of them ceases to qualify for support, the tables in the Guidelines dictate the amount to be paid for the remaining children. As Veit J observed in *Stebner v Stebner*,[81] a "step-down" provision in the order, which indicates the amount of support changes with the number of children, is not necessary before an adjustment can be made by a provincial enforcement agency. Once a child ceases to be eligible for support under the court order, the Director of the Maintenance Enforcement Office should adjust the amount to be collected in accordance with the tables. In making that adjustment for the purpose of enforcement, the Director is not "varying the court order" but merely carrying out its terms. Such an adjustment advances the objectives of the *Federal Child Support Guidelines* as well as those of *The Enforcement of Maintenance Orders Act, 1997* (Saskatchewan). The fact that child support orders are not global in nature does not fully answer the question of when the Director should adjust the support payable. There may be a dispute as to when a child ceased to be entitled to support. In that event, Veit J in *Stebner*[82] suggested that in Alberta, the Director pursue the following procedure:

> However, where the support debtor is of the view that a child is no longer a child of the marriage but the support creditor disagrees, the Director may obtain from the debtor evidence in support of the debtor's contention that a child is no longer a child of the marriage. The Director may provisionally accept that evidence and advise the child support creditor, typically the mother, that, as of a certain date, the debtor's support obligation relative to the support of that child has ceased. The child support creditor can either accept the Director's provisional assessment, or bring an application to the court for a determination of the issue. Alternatively, the Director may provisionally reject the evidence tendered by the child support debtor in which case the debtor can either accept the Director's provisional assessment or bring an application to the court for a determination of the issues.

In Saskatchewan, the Director of the Maintenance Enforcement Office has no legislative authority to obtain evidence from the parties or make a provisional determination. He can only adjust the order when the parties agree that a child no longer qualifies for support. In these cases, the Director should adjust ongoing support payments in accordance with the table amount payable for the remaining children. Any arrears should be adjusted to the date agreed upon by the parties or, failing agreement, to the earliest common date not in dispute. If there is disagreement as to this date, an application for variation may be brought. The Director is not required to enforce orders where the amount payable is not readily verifiable. In that event, the Director may withdraw the maintenance order from enforcement pursuant to section 9(1)(d) of *The Enforcement of Maintenance Orders Act, 1997*, leaving it to the parties to seek clarification of the order pursuant to section 9(4) of the Act. Applying the above criteria, Ryan-Froslie J (as she then was) in *Dueck v Dueck*[83] concluded that the Director had erred in treating the child support order as a "global" order by seeking an order that the respondent be imprisoned for the nonpayment of all of the arrears for the three children after

---

80 *Rumpf v Rumpf*, 2000 SKQB 510, Gerein CJQB.

81 2005 ABQB 839.

82 *Ibid* at para 14.

83 [2006] SJ No 578 (QB).

both parents had acknowledged that two of the children had ceased to be eligible for support. She then proceeded to recalculate the arrears in light of the attendant circumstances.

I. SUSPENSION OF DRIVING LICENCE

In Alberta, a person whose driving privileges have been suspended because of support arrears has the option of making arrangements with the Director of Maintenance Enforcement or bringing an application in the Court of King's Bench to forgive the arrears or retroactively reduce support payments. In the absence of any such order or a court-ordered stay of execution, the defaulter must make arrangements that are satisfactory to the Director of Maintenance Enforcement. The court may direct that the defaulter's access to the children shall be terminated if he drives a vehicle with them in it while his licence is suspended. An Alberta court lacks jurisdiction to order the reinstatement of the driving privileges of a support defaulter whose driving licence has been suspended at the request of the Director of Maintenance Enforcement, but a stay of enforcement may be granted for approximately sixty days to permit the defaulter to make suitable arrangements with the Director for an orderly discharge of the arrears.[85]

In British Columbia, a court has only a limited jurisdiction to review the decision of the Director of the Family Maintenance Enforcement Program to issue a direction for the suspension of the driving licence of an obligor who defaults in making support payments. The extent of that authority is found in section 29.2(2) of the *Family Maintenance Enforcement Act* (BC) and in the court's jurisdiction to remit the arrears where it would be grossly unfair not to do so.[86]

An order to restrain the Director of the Ontario Family Responsibility Office from suspending a parent's driving licence may only be made within thirty days after the first notice is served. There is no jurisdiction to extend the thirty-day period. Cogent evidence is required to rebut service that complies with the legislative requirements respecting service by ordinary mail. A support defaulter's bare assertion that no notice was received will not suffice. A court has no jurisdiction to order the reinstatement of a suspended driver's licence where the conditions of section 38(1) of the *Family Responsibility and Support Arrears Enforcement Act* (Ontario) are not satisfied,[87] but the court may urge the Director to exercise his discretion to reinstate the licence where it would be unconscionable not to do so, given the absence of culpable conduct on the part of the support debtor and his inability to earn a reasonable income while unable to drive.[88] The Ontario Court of Justice has no jurisdiction to vary a child support order granted pursuant to the *Divorce Act*. Where a support defaulter in Ontario seeks a refraining order pursuant to section 35 of the *Family Responsibility and Support Arrears Enforcement Act* (Ontario) to prevent the suspension of his driving licence

---

84 *D(GA) v D(G)* (1995), 11 RFL (4th) 270 (Alta QB).

85 *Labine v Fenske*, [2000] AJ No 122 (QB).

86 *KJK v PBK*, [2002] BCJ No 2114 (SC).

87 *Adubofuor v Ontario (Director, Family Responsibility Office)*, [2001] OJ No 708 (CA); see also *McLarty v Ontario (Director, Family Responsibility Office)*, [2001] OJ No 707 (CA); *Harris v Mayo*, [2001] OJ No 4751 (SCJ).

88 *Ontario (Director, Family Responsibility Office) v Pennell*, [2002] OJ No 1816 (Ct J). See also *Alsafouti v Alsafouti*, [2005] OJ No 4079 (SCJ).

because of support arrears that have accrued under an order of the Quebec Superior Court granted pursuant to the *Divorce Act*, the appropriate forum is the Ontario Superior Court of Justice, which is entitled to entertain concurrent motions for an order to refrain and an order to vary the existing child support order.[89]

A court has no jurisdiction under section 43 of *The Enforcement of Maintenance Orders Act, 1997*[90] to order suspension of the cancellation of a defaulter's driving licence where support is more than three months in arrears, but an order of the court suspending the enforcement of child support arrears automatically suspends all provincial enforcement mechanisms.[91] Given that the obligor's poor payment record might tempt him to view an order suspending enforcement as an invitation to ignore his future support obligations, a court may find it preferable to leave it open to the Director of Maintenance Enforcement to cancel the suspension of the obligor's driver's licence but to resume its suspension if the obligor does not comply with his new obligations under a variation order.[92] The suspension of driving privileges is one of many tools the legislature has provided to the Director of Maintenance Enforcement to encourage or compel defaulting payors to pay court-ordered support. The enforcement measures are intended to cause inconvenience, including serious inconvenience, to defaulting payors. Otherwise, they would be ineffective.[93]

J. CROWN'S PRIORITY AS TAX COLLECTOR; OTHER CREDITORS

Where a husband defaults in making support payments, the Crown's assertion of a priority as a tax collector does not constitute a violation of the wife's equality rights under section 15 of the *Canadian Charter of Rights and Freedoms*.[94]

Pursuant to section 4 of the Ontario *Creditor's Relief Act*, lump sum orders for prospective and retroactive child support that are secured by the obligor's interest in the former matrimonial home take priority over other judgment debts, regardless of when an enforcement process is issued or served.[95] Although section 34 of the Ontario *Solicitors Act* confers jurisdiction on a court to protect a solicitor's account by a charging order where the asset

---

89 *Rozzi v Ontario (Director, Family Responsibility Office)*, [2003] OJ No 1723 (Ct J). As to the jurisdiction of a court to grant a refraining order, see generally *Farah v Ontario (Director, Family Responsibility Office)*, 2018 ONCJ 829; and see *Ryckman v Camick*, 2020 ONSC 5429 (denial of passport).

90 SS 1997, c E-9.21.

91 *Scott v Scott*, 1999 SKQB 84 (defaulter's driving licence to be immediately reinstated upon Maintenance Enforcement Office being notified of the court-ordered suspension of enforcement of arrears for designated period of time); see also *NTG v JAMG*, 2022 SKKB 264; compare *Williams v Ontario (Family Responsibility Office, Director)*, [1999] OJ No 5051 (SCJ) (jurisdiction of Ontario Court of Justice to issue refraining order respecting suspension of support defaulter's driving licence by Director of Family Responsibility Office; s 35 of *Family Responsibility and Support Arrears Enforcement Act* applied).

92 *Bindig v Wilchynski*, [2002] SJ No 377 (QB).

93 *DRC v JEM*, 2022 SKQB 26 at para 19, Robertson J.

94 *Wright v Canada (Attorney General)* (1988), 13 RFL (3d) 343 (Ont Div Ct); but see *WB v JV*, [1999] OJ No 3489 at para 15 (SCJ), wherein Kozak J acknowledged that the payment of child support arrears might affect the applicants' ability to pay Revenue Canada but stated that "as between the payment to Revenue Canada and the obligation to pay the child support arrears, it is well settled law that priority is to be given to the payment of child support." Compare *Asre v Asre*, 2011 BCSC 1232.

95 *Duhnych v Duhnych*, [2004] OJ No 2655 (SCJ).

charged is, in truth and substance, the fruit of the action, a charging order cannot be regis tered against property that provides security for child support.[96]

K. COMMITTAL FOR CONTEMPT; RECEIVERSHIP

In *CJD v RIJ*,[97] Graesser J of the Alberta Court of Queen's Bench observed:

> [42] Civil contempt has become a more challenging remedy following *Carey v Laiken*, 2015 SCC 17 (CanLII)....
>
> [43] In that case, the Supreme Court clarified the law regarding civil contempt in a number of aspects:
>
> 1. Civil contempt has three elements which must be established beyond a reasonable doubt (at para 32);
> 2. The first element is that the order alleged to have been breached "must state clearly and unequivocally what should and should not be done" (at para 33);
> 3. A party will not be found in contempt where an order is unclear (at para 33);
> 4. An order may be found to be unclear if, for example, it is missing an essential detail about where, when or to whom it applies; if it incorporates overly broad language; or if external circumstances have obscured its meaning (at para 33);
> 5. The second element is that the party alleged to have breached the order must have had actual knowledge of it (at para 34);
> 6. It may be possible to infer knowledge in the circumstances, or an alleged contemnor may attract liability on the basis of the willful blindness doctrine (at para 34);
> 7. The party allegedly in breach must have intentionally done the act that the order prohibits or intentionally failed to do the act that the order compels (at para 35);
> 8. The contempt power is discretionary (para 36);
> 9. Courts have consistently discouraged its routine use to obtain compliance with court orders (para 36);
> 10. Contempt of court cannot be reduced to a mere means of enforcing judgments; it should be used "cautiously and with great restraint" (para 36);
> 11. It is an enforcement power of last rather than first resort (para 36);
> 12. Where an alleged contemnor acted in good faith in taking reasonable steps to comply with the order, the judge entertaining a contempt motion generally retains some discretion to decline to make a finding of contempt (at para 37); and
> 13. Under Canadian common law that all that is required to establish civil contempt is proof beyond a reasonable doubt of an intentional act or omission that is in fact in breach of a clear order of which the alleged contemnor has notice (at para 38).
>
> [44] The necessity for actual knowledge of the order was reinforced in *Pintea v Johns*, 2017 SCC 23 (Can LII).

The rules and procedures governing contempt applications are complex and counsel must be given a reasonable opportunity to prepare for and respond to a motion involving the

96 *Ibid.*

97 2018 ABQB 287 at paras 42–44.

liberty of the subject.[98] A civil contempt motion is available to enforce compliance with the substance of a court order but is not available as a means of addressing an abuse of the judicial process arising from a material non-disclosure. Where a motions judge has been led to an incorrect conclusion respecting an order for child support because the mother failed to advise the court that the adult child had graduated from university and was, therefore, no longer eligible for child support, the mother cannot be found in contempt of the court order if it included no provision imposing an obligation on her to keep the father or anyone else informed of any change in the child's status. Relief may be available to the father, however, by means of an application for retroactive variation of the child support order to the appropriate date and an order for costs with respect to any such application necessitated by the mother's misconduct.[99]

Where there is more than one avenue open to a party to enforce an order, one of them being committal proceedings for contempt, resort to those other avenues should first be pursued.[100] This does not preclude a court from combining a committal order for default with other remedies available under provincial statute, including the seizure of corporate records and the appointment of the Director of Maintenance Enforcement as receiver and sequestrator of the defaulter's personal and corporate assets.[101]

In *Prescott-Russell Services for Children and Adults v G(N)*,[102] Blair JA of the Ontario Court of Appeal, set out the following three prerequisites for a finding of contempt of court:

1) The order that is breached must state clearly and unequivocally what should or should not be done.
2) The party who disobeys the order must do so deliberately and willfully.
3) The evidence must establish contempt beyond a reasonable doubt.

When the relief sought involves a finding of contempt, the respondent must be put on notice as to the conduct that is alleged to be contemptuous. The better practice is to refer to the alleged misconduct in the notice of motion itself.[103] There is no foundation for contempt proceedings where an order has not been perfected by being drawn and entered and no order was personally served on the party allegedly in contempt. A court should not find a parent

---

98 *Pakka v Nygard*, [2001] OJ No 2934 (SCJ).

99 *Zadegan v Zadegan*, [2003] OJ No 5282 (SCJ).

100 *Sukhram v Sukhram* (1987), 6 RFL (3d) 200 at 202 (Man QB); *Smellie v Smellie* (1987), 8 RFL (3d) 135 at 138–39 (Man QB); *Latreille v Bard*, 2021 ONSC 1290.

101 *Grant v Wolansky* (1994), 4 RFL (4th) 365 (Alta QB). For a useful analysis of relevant caselaw relating to contempt proceedings based on a failure to pay court-ordered support, see *Hokhold v Gerbrandt*, 2018 BCSC 183. As to the scope of an Ontario court's authority to deal with non-compliance with court orders under Rule 1(8) of the Ontario *Family Law Rules*, see *Bouchard v Sgovio*, 2021 ONCA 709, which is reviewed in Franks & Zalev, "This Week in Family Law," 14 February 2022 (Thomson Reuters). And see *Boutin v Boutin*, 2022 ONSC 3239 and 2022 ONSC 4776 (persistent inadequate financial disclosure; contempt; sentencing; investigative receivership), discussed in Franks & Zalev, "This Week in Family Law," 3 October 2022 (Thomson Reuters).

102 (2007), 82 OR (3d) 686 at para 27 (CA); *Hobbs v Hobbs*, 2008 ONCA 598; see also *Heisler v Heisler*, 2012 BCSC 753; *Garnet v Garnet*, 2013 ONSC 6389. For a more detailed analysis of relevant caselaw, including *Carey v Laiken*, 2015 SCC 17, see *Hokhold v Gerbrandt* 2018 BCSC 183; *Lessard v Mahoney*, 2019 BCSC 551.

103 *Sukhram v Sukhram* (1987), 6 RFL (3d) 200 (Man QB).

in contempt of an order that is ambiguous. The proper course is to apply for more specific directions to more precisely define the terms of the order.[104]

An order that fixes the amount of child support arrears but does not order their payment is not enforceable by means of a contempt proceeding.[105]

Default in the payment of court-ordered child support is a serious problem in Canada. There is a need that the sentence imposed for contempt serves as an incentive for the obligor to obey the court order and sends a strong message to other like-minded individuals that disobedience of court orders will not be countenanced.[106] The penalty must reflect the offence and be in proportion to the gravity of the offence and the contemnor's degree of responsibility, recognizing any aggravating and mitigating factors.[107] Relevant caselaw in Ontario points to sentences of incarceration for contempt ranging from a few days to twelve months. In *Beattie v Ladouceur*,[108] the court imposed a sentence of four months' imprisonment having regard to the long history of the case, including the respondent's repeated breaches of numerous court orders, the extent to which his conduct displayed a defiance of court orders, his insincere apology, the fact that the breaches occurred with the respondent's full knowledge and understanding, and the need for specific and general deterrence. Before imposing this sanction, Polowin J referred to *Boucher v Kennedy*,[109] wherein Ferrier J identified eight factors to be considered in addressing the appropriate sanction:

(1) whether the contemnor has admitted the breach;
(2) whether the contemnor had demonstrated a full acceptance of the paramountcy of the rule of law, by tendering a formal apology to the court;
(3) whether the breach was a single act or part of an ongoing pattern of conduct in which there were repeated breaches;
(4) whether the breach occurred with the full knowledge and understanding of the contemnor that it was a breach rather than as a result of a mistake or misunderstanding;
(5) the extent to which the conduct of the contemnor displayed defiance;
(6) whether the order was a private one, affecting only the parties to the suit or whether some public benefit lay at the root of the order;
(7) the need for specific and general deterrence; and
(8) the ability of the contemnor to pay.

Rule 60.11(1) of the Ontario *Rules of Civil Procedure* precludes contempt proceedings being brought to enforce the payment of money, but orders requiring the husband to secure his spousal and child support obligations by an irrevocable letter of credit and to post security for costs with his wife's solicitor are not orders for the payment of money under Rule 60.11(1) of the Ontario *Rules of Civil Procedure*, because neither order constitutes a fixed debt obligation requiring the husband to pay money to his wife.[110] The common practice of denying

104 *Kloczko v Kloczko* (1991), 36 RFL (3d) 424 (Sask QB).
105 *Bloomfield v Bloomfield*, [2000] SJ No 655 (QB).
106 *Moutal v Moutal*, [1997] BCJ No 2463 (SC); *Sharpley v Sharpley*, [2005] OJ No 5697 (Ct J).
107 *Power v Power*, 2020 NSSC 379 at para 19 (Jollimore J) (imprisonment for 4.5 years, subject to purging of contempt).
108 [2002] OJ No 5501 (SCJ).
109 [1998] OJ No 1612 (Gen Div), aff'd [1999] OJ No 3407 (CA).
110 *Dickie v Dickie*, 2007 SCC 8.

an audience to a contemnor pending the purging of the contempt reflects the exercise of judicial discretion which is grounded in the inherent jurisdiction of the court to control its own process and, in Ontario, in section 140(5) of the *Courts of Justice Act,* which empowers the court to stay or dismiss a proceeding as an abuse of process.[111]

Section 2(1) of the Alberta *Maintenance Enforcement Act* empowers a court to imprison a person for a maximum of ninety days for her wilful failure to pay court-ordered support. No particular form of contempt hearing is statutorily prescribed and the usual practice appears to be to proceed by way of affidavit evidence.[112]

In *Trevors v Jenkins,*[113] the New Brunswick Court of Appeal reviewed an order directing the court administrator to prepare the necessary documentation to have the father incarcerated for ten days, if he failed to regularly pay his court-ordered child support. This sanction was directed to take effect on an ongoing basis. Observing that section 35(2)(c) of the New Brunswick *Support Enforcement Act* stipulates that an order for imprisonment shall not be for a period longer than ninety days, notwithstanding that the default has not been remedied, the appellate court was "not convinced that this section permits a continuation of the prospect of incarceration on an indefinite basis without first having a show cause hearing where the payor could explain his or her reason for non-payment." However, since the issue had not been argued and the father's appeal had been allowed with respect to variation of the child support order, the appellate court found it unnecessary to resolve the issue and left it for another day.

A parent with a long history of evading his child support obligation may be required to make some arrangement for the timely discharge of judicially fixed arrears, failing which he may be required to satisfy the court why it should not issue a warrant for his imprisonment, probably for the maximum term of six months pursuant to section 37(3)(j) of the *Maintenance Enforcement Act* (Nova Scotia).[114]

Absent wilful disobedience of a child support order, an obligor should not be committed to prison for nonpayment of court-ordered child support.[115] The Ontario Court of Justice has no inherent jurisdiction to commit a defaulter to jail for contempt. On a motion for committal of a defaulter, the creditor is expected to adduce evidence to show that incarceration is the only coercive measure that would yield results. The debtor may then lead evidence of any unforeseeable event that would make imprisonment unreasonable or oppressive or that would remove the ability to comply with the order.[116]

There is no inherent jurisdiction in the Saskatchewan Court of King's Bench to find a defaulter in contempt of court for nonpayment of child support but *The Enforcement of Maintenance Orders Act, 1997* provides for the enforcement of support orders by way of contempt applications.[117]

A committal order may be made subject to terms and conditions.[118] The purpose of imprisoning those in default of their support obligations is not to punish them but to

---

111 *Ibid.*

112 *Rarick v Rarick,* [2000] AJ No 429 (QB).

113 2011 NBCA 61.

114 *Nova Scotia (Director of Maintenance Enforcement) v Stuckless,* [2003] NSJ No 296 (SC).

115 *Ontario (Director, Family Responsibility Office) v Pennell,* [2002] OJ No 1816 (Ct J).

116 *Lindsay v Lindsay* (1992), 38 RFL (3d) 12 (Ont Prov Div).

117 *Paul v Paul,* [2000] SJ No 780 (QB).

118 See *Thompson v Thompson* (1988), 16 RFL (3d) 415 (Ont HCJ).

persuade them to meet their obligations. It is appropriate, therefore, for a committal order to stipulate that the defaulter can avoid imprisonment altogether or obtain an early release if the arrears of support are fully paid.[119] One of the key features of the *Family Maintenance Enforcement Act* of British Columbia[120] is that the punishment for default is fixed in advance at the default hearing. The committal hearing offers the defaulter a last chance to avoid imprisonment. The presiding judge may vary the order made at the default hearing or decide there should be no imprisonment because of a change of circumstances or because imprisonment would be a grave injustice. Otherwise, the court will order the defaulter to be imprisoned in accordance with the order made at the default hearing.[121] Although the thrust of the *Family Maintenance Enforcement Act* is towards consecutive terms of imprisonment where there have been multiple defaults, this is not an inevitable result. The judge presiding at the committal hearing has a limited area of discretion and may order concurrent terms to be served by the defaulter.[122]

Committal for contempt does not excuse the defaulter from paying court-ordered support during the term of imprisonment. If it were otherwise, the beneficiary of the support would be punished for taking necessary steps to enforce the support order that has fallen into default.[123] Contempt motions must be severely scrutinized and must be properly before the court with direct evidence in support; compliance with the *strictissimi juris* rule is essential; affidavits containing evidence may support an application for prohibition but are insufficient to support a motion for contempt.[124]

Imprisonment for contempt is inappropriate where the default in making support payments continued for many years and the defaulter was lulled into the belief that continued default would not give rise to committal proceedings. Parties are expected to act promptly in instituting court proceedings for contempt and cannot be allowed to appropriate the remedy of committal for themselves to bring forward when it suits their tactical purposes.

Section 30 of *The Family Maintenance Act* (Manitoba), which confers jurisdiction on the Master of the Court of King's Bench to incarcerate a person for non-compliance with a support order, does not violate section 96 of the *Constitution Act, 1867*, nor is it invalid by reason of the prohibitions respecting imprisonment for civil debt and liberty of the subject under paragraph 103(1)(g)(i) of the *King's Bench Act* and *King's Bench Rules* 183(a) and 478. The power under sections 30(3)(a) and 30(6) of *The Family Maintenance Act* to incarcerate a defaulter for a maximum of thirty days following a show cause hearing does not offend sections 7 and 9 of the *Canadian Charter of Rights and Freedoms*, but the sanction of indefinite imprisonment set out under section 30(4)(a) of the Act contravenes both sections 7 and 9 of the *Charter* and is not saved by section 1 of the *Charter*.[126]

---

119 *British Columbia (Director of Maintenance Enforcement) v McLeod* (1994), 88 BCLR (2d) 222 (SC); *Léger v Léger* (1994), 146 NBR (2d) 32 (QB); *Prince Edward Island (Director of Maintenance Enforcement) v Moase*, [2001] PEIJ No 117 (SC).

120 SBC 1988, c 3.

121 *British Columbia (Director of Maintenance Enforcement) v McLeod* (1994), 88 BCLR (2d) 222 (SC).

122 *Ibid.*

123 *L(GM) v L(VA)* (1993), 127 NSR (2d) 66 (Fam Ct).

124 *Dragun v Dragun*, [1984] 6 WWR 171 (Man QB).

125 *Shaw v Van Louie*, [1998] BCJ No 2415 (SC).

126 *Schnell v Schnell*, [1988] 3 WWR 447 (Man QB).

L. ORDER OR AGREEMENT; ELECTION OF REMEDY

The doctrine of election operates to prevent a person from selectively enforcing inconsistent rights.[127] When the relief sought is to either enforce a support order or sue upon a covenant in an agreement, an election must be made. Once the election is made, the support creditor is bound by that election.[128]

M. ENFORCEMENT OF SUPPORT ARREARS AGAINST BANKRUPT DEFAULTER

Any claim for spousal or child support under any court order or agreement made before the bankruptcy of the debtor for amounts accrued in the year before that date, plus any lump sum amount payable under the order or agreement before that date, is provable in proceedings under the *Bankruptcy and Insolvency Act*. Furthermore, priority treatment is accorded to such unpaid support arrears as against all ordinary unsecured creditors of the bankrupt. These rights supplement pre-existing enforcement remedies.[129]

A court-ordered payment relating to the enforcement of child support obligations, including interest and costs, is unaffected by the obligor's assignment in bankruptcy.[130] Bankruptcy does not release a support payor from the obligation to pay child support but a court is able to look at the general circumstances and make retroactive adjustments, with a consequential remission of arrears that have accrued.[131] A costs award with respect to a support order is part of a support award for the purposes of the *Bankruptcy and Insolvency Act* and survives the bankruptcy.[132]

Arrears of child support subrogated to and owing to the Provincial Treasurer of Alberta by virtue of social assistance provided to the family dependants are not extinguished by the discharge of the obligor from bankruptcy. Section 178(1)(c) of the *Bankruptcy and Insolvency Act*[133] does not specify to whom the support debt or liability must be owing and is sufficiently broad to encompass the situation where the provincial government is subrogated to the support rights of the court-ordered recipient by reason of social assistance provided.[134]

N. FRAUDULENT CONVEYANCES AND PREFERENCES

A parent's conveyance of property may be set aside as a fraudulent conveyance under the *Statute of Elizabeth, 1570*, where the parent had thereby intended to evade obligations to his creditors, including the mother of his children to whom child support was payable pursuant to their divorce judgment. The fact that the fraudulent conveyance was primarily directed

---

127 *Francis v McLeod* (1998), 30 BCLR (2d) 163 (SC); *Cameron v Cameron*, [1998] BCJ No 3046 (SC) (claim for child support not precluded by terms of separation agreement).

128 *Despot v Despot Estate* (1992), 42 RFL (3d) 218 (BCSC); *H(CA) v N(BD)* (1987), 10 RFL (3d) 317 (Ont Fam Ct), aff'd (1987), 11 RFL (3d) 429 (Ont Dist Ct); see also *Oxby v Oxby* (1987), 11 RFL (3d) 369 (Sask QB).

129 See Robert A Klotz, "New Enforcement Remedy When Payer Becomes Bankrupt" (1995) 16 RFL (4th) 214. See also *Graves v Graves*, [2003] BCJ No 2240 (SC).

130 *Beattie v Ladouceur*, [2001] OJ No 4852 (SCJ) (judicial review of relevant principles and caselaw).

131 *Dicks v Dicks*, [2000] OJ No 3964 (SCJ).

132 *Lees (Bankruptcy of)*, 2002 BCSC 570; *Manley v Lund*, 2009 BCSC 903.

133 RSC 1985, c B-3.

134 *Russell v Russell*, [2005] SJ No 423 (QB).

at commercial creditors does not preclude the mother from relying on the fraudulent action for the purpose of setting aside the transaction where the mother was clearly a creditor at the time of the transaction, even if the obligor was not then in arrears. No distinction is drawn between past and future support obligations in determining the mother's priority over other creditors under the Alberta *Maintenance Enforcement Act*.[135] An obligor's transfer of property to a close relative may be characterized as fraudulent and declared void under the *Statute of Elizabeth, 1570*, where there is a pre-existing child support order, even though there has been no default in making the periodic payments as of the date of the transfer.[136]

Where a husband transfers his interest in the jointly owned matrimonial home to his wife in consideration for her waiver of spousal and child support under a separation agreement, third-party creditors cannot impugn the conveyance as fraudulent under provincial statute, nor is it void under federal bankruptcy legislation.[137]

O. *LOCUS STANDI* OF CHILD

Although the *Divorce Act* does not give a child of divorcing or divorced parents any standing to apply for a child support order or for the variation of any such order,[138] a child may institute proceedings to enforce an order for his or her support that was granted in prior divorce proceedings.[139] A child who is under a legal disability by virtue of age should commence or defend proceedings by a guardian *ad litem*, but the lack of a guardian *ad litem* is not fatal to proceedings already instituted, being merely an irregularity.[140]

P. CHILD NO LONGER A CHILD OF THE MARRIAGE

An application to enforce a child support order should be dismissed if the child was not a "child of the marriage" within the meaning of section 2(1) of the *Divorce Act* at the relevant period of time when the alleged arrears accrued, but a finding to this effect does not necessarily preclude a finding that thereafter the child was a "child of the marriage" and thereby entitled to support.[141] A court may refuse to reduce arrears of child support even though the defaulter will still be paying them off long after the children have attained the age of majority.

Q. ENFORCEMENT, SUSPENSION, AND REMISSION OF ARREARS

In proceedings to enforce arrears of child support, the defaulter has the onus of showing cause why the order should not be enforced and of satisfying the court that he or she was unable to make the payments as they become due.[144]

---

135 *Proulx v Proulx*, [2002] AJ No 163 (QB).
136 *Fillier v Bubley*, [1997] AJ No 1285 (QB).
137 *Caldwell v Simms* (1995), 11 RFL (4th) 28 (BCSC).
138 *Garbers v Garbers* (1993), 48 RFL (3d) 217 (Ont UFC).
139 *Sloat v Sloat* (1981), 25 RFL (2d) 378 (BCSC).
140 *Ibid*.
141 *Ibid*.
142 *D(GA) v D(G)* (1995), 11 RFL (4th) 270 (Alta QB).
143 See Chapter 13, Section S.
144 *Grant v Wolansky* (1994), 4 RFL (4th) 365 (Alta QB).

Child support obligations take priority over commercial obligations; where there is insufficient money to discharge both, child support must be paid first.[145]

Arrears of child support are not discharged by incidental payments to the children or by the purchase of clothing and other items for the children.[146]

Where the defaulter's income is sufficient only to meet personal minimal and legitimate living expenses, the answer does not lie in an order for payment that is beyond his or her capacity. Such an order would only invite continued default and could lead to emotional stress and the possible loss of any earning capacity.[147]

A defaulting parent's remarriage does not result in the imposition of any obligation on his or her second spouse to make good the default, but that spouse's contribution toward the household expenses may be relevant in determining the defaulter's capacity to pay.[148]

Enforcement of arrears is inappropriate where the obligor is bankrupt or on the verge of bankruptcy.[149]

Although a court may hesitate to order that a defaulter's farm or business be sold to pay arrears of child support if this would have the effect of jeopardizing the defaulter's income and future capacity to pay ongoing child support, a court may properly order that the defaulter convert a portion of existing RRSPs into cash for the purpose of discharging the child support arrears.[150]

Arrears of support do not accrue after a child's adoption, but judicial opinion differs on whether an adoption operates retroactively to eradicate unsecured arrears previously accrued.[151]

Judicial remission of child support arrears is not warranted by a failure of a provincial enforcement agency to discharge its responsibilities. The doctrine of laches cannot be applied against a parent who relies on a government enforcement program.[152]

Where a parent is receiving social assistance, the Minister of Family and Social Services may exercise a right of subrogation, notwithstanding a parental waiver of rights under a child support order, but the right of subrogation does not preclude a court from exercising its statutory discretion to remit arrears of support.[153]

While parents cannot make an enforceable agreement to reduce or ignore child support obligations established by court order, if they have mutually established a reasonable alternative arrangement to the order, the court may consider that arrangement as one factor in deciding whether arrears should be cancelled or reduced. In determining whether the arrangement is a reasonable one, the court must decide if it provides for the child at a

145 *McCallum v McCallum*, [1999] AJ No 1548 (QB).
146 *Davari v Namazi*, [1999] BCJ No 116 (SC); compare *Bale v Bale*, [2001] OJ No 4196 (SCJ).
147 *Rollins v Kutash* (1982), 26 RFL (2d) 444 (Alta Prov Ct).
148 *Rollins v Kutash*, *ibid*; *Mosher v Turner* (1990), 26 RFL (3d) 230 (NSTD).
149 *Saunders v Saunders* (1988), 18 RFL (3d) 298 (NBQB); *Campbell v Campbell* (1989), 79 Nfld & PEIR 179 (PEITD).
150 *Prince Edward Island (Director of Maintenance Enforcement) v Campbell* (1990), 30 RFL (3d) 76 (PEICA). See also *Stefanovic v Stefanovic* (1990), 30 RFL (3d) 201 (BCCA) (enforcement delayed for six months to allow defaulter with real estate to deal with outstanding arrears).
151 See *British Columbia (Director of Maintenance Enforcement) v Lagore*, [1993] BCJ No 899 (Prov Ct); *Nitchie v Nitchie*, [1999] BCJ No 2865 (SC); compare *Fletcher v Bourgeois*, [2004] NSJ No 164 (SC).
152 *Wasney v Wasney*, [1999] OJ No 3389 (SCJ).
153 *Ms M v Mr B*, [2000] AJ No 1497 (QB).

comparable or better level than the child support order and whether it is clearly in the child's best interests. If it does not meet these criteria, it should have no bearing on a determination as to what arrears are owed.[154]

A primary caregiving parent is not entitled to waive child support arrears because such support is an entitlement of the children, but accommodation may be offered to an unemployed defaulter who needs some time to find employment and arrange his affairs so that the arrears may be discharged.[155] Where the obligor has no immediate capacity to pay child support arrears, a court may suspend payment for a specified period of time.[156]

Although a court may decline to remit child support arrears, it may provide some breathing space to the obligor who has engaged in a new business enterprise by ordering the withdrawal of a notice of attachment by the provincial maintenance enforcement authorities and the suspension of prospective periodic payments for several months, during which time the monthly payments will accrue as arrears.[157]

R. ENFORCEMENT BY PROVINCIAL COURT

Where child support has been granted in divorce proceedings, the order may be filed in and enforced by the Provincial Court. Upon such filing, the jurisdiction of the Provincial Court is confined to the enforcement of the order; it does not extend to the variation of the order. Where the defaulting parent is unable to pay the arrears of child support that accrued prior to the enforcement proceedings, the Provincial Court of Alberta may order the payment of a designated amount of monthly support for a fixed period of time pending the hearing of the husband's application to the Court of King's Bench to vary the order for child support. The effect of such an order is neither to vary or cancel the arrears nor to alter the higher amount of periodic payments due under the previous divorce judgment. Such an order may, however, facilitate eventual clarification of the respondent's future obligations.[158]

The *Family Maintenance Act* (BC) anticipates enforcement in the Provincial Court of British Columbia and that is the best court in the province to deal with the enforcement of maintenance orders.[159]

S. ENFORCEMENT OF SEPARATION AGREEMENT

The filing of a divorce petition wherein child support is sought constitutes no basis for applying the doctrine of election so as to deprive the primary caregiving parent of the right to sue for arrears previously accrued under a separation agreement.[160]

Damages may be awarded for breach of a separation agreement that imposes child support obligations and it is open to the parties to include a liquidated damages clause to fix

---

154 *D'Ambrosio v D'Ambrosio*, [2000] BCJ No 1704 (SC).
155 *MJD v JPD*, [2001] BCJ No 107 (SC).
156 *MJD v JPD, ibid*; *White v White*, [2002] NSJ No 248 (CA); *Boudreau v Jarvie*, [2001] OJ No 381 (SCJ).
157 *Feuchter v Feuchter*, [2000] BCJ No 248 (SC).
158 *Rollins v Kutash* (1982), 26 RFL (2d) 444 (Alta Prov Ct).
159 *X(RL) v X(JF)*, [2002] BCJ No 1889 (SC).
160 *Bakes v Kelly* (1995), 15 RFL (4th) 361 at 365–66 (BCCA), Southin JA.

the amount of recovery. Where there are sequential breaches and the separation agreement provides for a specific amount of liquidated damages to be payable for each breach, there is no bar to the court allocating the designated amount of liquidated damages for each breach that has occurred before the date of trial together with pre-judgment and post-judgment interest.[161]

A separation agreement that is duly filed under section 35 of the *Family Law Act* (PEI) may be enforced "as if it were an order of the court." Accordingly, it falls subject to a ten years' limitation period under section 2(1)(f) of the *Limitations Act* (PEI), instead of the six years' limitation period that would have applied under section 2(1)(g) of the *Limitations Act* to the enforcement of the separation agreement prior to its filing with the court.[162]

The Saskatchewan Court of King's Bench has jurisdiction to cancel arrears that have accrued under an agreement for child maintenance that has been filed pursuant to section 11 of *The Family Maintenance Act, 1997*, even though such jurisdiction is not conferred by that particular section.[163]

T. SET-OFF

A court may order child support payments or arrears to be set off against monies due to the obligor by way of a matrimonial property entitlement[164] or pursuant to an order for costs.[165] A set-off of child support against costs will be deemed inappropriate where the financial well-being of a child would be thereby undermined. Faced with that contingency, the court may postpone payment of the court-ordered costs.[166] In *Jamieson v Loureiro*,[167] the British Columbia Court of Appeal upheld a chambers judge's refusal to order an equitable set-off of costs against court-ordered arrears of child and spousal support and future child support payments. Citing *DBS v SRG*[168] in support of the premise that child support is the right of the child, the British Columbia Court of Appeal stated that it was "unable to conceive of a case in which set-off would be allowed against future child support" and "it would be a very

161 *Hall v Cooper*, [1994] OJ No 696, 3 RFL (4th) 29 (Gen Div); see also *McVeetors v McVeetors* (1995), 43 RFL (2d) 113 (Ont CA).

162 *Cameron v Cameron*, [1999] PEIJ No 62 (SC); compare *Surette v Surette*, [2000] OJ No 675 (SCJ).

163 *Frigon v Lepoudre*, [2003] SJ No 575 (QB).

164 *Laskosky v Laskosky*, [1999] AJ No 131 (QB); *Cotey v Cotey*, [2002] BCJ No 2726 (SC); *TDB v LNU*, 2010 NBQB 408; *Etchegary v Etchegary* (1990), 81 Nfld & PEIR 189 (Nfld UFC); *Maskell v Maskell*, [1999] NSJ No 424 (SC); *Robski v Robski*, [2001] NSJ No 454 (SC); *Azimi v Mirzaei*, [2007] OJ No 5007 (CA); *Bolen v Bolen*, 2010 SKQB 202; see also *Risdale v Risdale*, [1999] AJ No 1517 (QB) (order for transfer of matrimonial home and cancellation of maintenance registration on title pursuant to s 183 of Alberta *Land Titles Act*); *Segat v Segat*, 2015 ONCA 16; *Jones v Jones*, [2001] SJ No 199 (QB). Compare *Plimmer v Burke*, 2019 ONSC 1915 and see text to footnotes 168–70, below in this chapter.

165 *Petroczi v Petroczi*, 2011 BCSC 1223; *SC v ASC*, 2011 MBCA 70 at para 57; *TDB v LNU*, 2010 NBQB 408; *MMK v PRM*, [2000] OJ No 2361 (SCJ); *Rego v Santos*, 2015 ONCA 540; see *contra Walsh v Walsh*, [2008] OJ No 98 (SCJ). And see *S v A*, 2023 ONSC 4719.

166 *Bains v Bains*, 2008 ABQB 319.

167 2010 BCCA 52 (CA); see also *DBF v BF*, 2017 ABCA 272; *SAL v BJL*, 2019 ABCA 350 at para 24; *Jamieson v Loureiro*, 2011 BCSC 1251; *Struck v Struck*, 2018 BCSC 44; *LRR v EM*, 2018 NBCA 2; *Izyuk v Bilousov*, 2011 ONSC 7476. Compare *Petroczi v Petroczi*, 2011 BCSC 1223; *Barkhouse v Wile*, 2014 NSCA 11. As to a set-off of unpaid costs against spousal support, see *G(JD) v G(SL)*, 2017 MBCA 117; *Uriu v Rivadeneyra*, 2017 ONSC 7457; *Berta v Berta*, 2019 ONCA 218; see also *Schneider v Owers*, 2022 BCSC 787 (property entitlement and retroactive spousal support).

168 2006 SCC 37 at paras 36 and 38.

rare case in which one would consider set-off against arrears of child support." In its opinion, support to which a child is entitled should not be lost because the person to whom the support is payable may owe, in another capacity, amounts to the payor. There is simply an insufficient connection and an absence of manifest injustice in requiring the payor to pay the full amount of support, even if the costs related to an application to vary child support.

Although some courts have drawn a distinction between a set-off against child support arrears and a set-off against prospective child support payments,[169] the Nova Scotia Court of Appeal in *Barkhouse v Wile*[170] endorsed a more nuanced approach. While it acknowledged that, as stated in *DBS v SRG*, child support is the right of the child, it stated that this does not signify that child support is the "property" of the child in a narrow and technical sense. And a "bright white line analysis,"[171] such as is favoured in *Jamieson v Loureiro*, may not be in the best interests of the child, the parents, or in the public interest. In the words of Bryson JA, of the Nova Scotia Court of Appeal, in *Barkhouse v Wile*:

> 20 Certainly, as a general rule, setting off a spousal debt against child support is undesirable and is to be avoided. However, the circumstances of a particular case may dictate otherwise. Accordingly where:
>
> (a) the debt involved — costs here — was incurred in connection with the support claim;
>
> (b) there is no reasonable prospect that the payor spouse will collect costs from the defaulting payee spouse:
>
> (c) there would be no adverse impact on the children involved;
>
> (d) it would not otherwise be inequitable to order a set-off then it may be appropriate to set-off some or all of child support against costs associated with litigating that issue. However, the burden of establishing no adverse impact on the children should rest with the spouse seeking set-off. In such cases it will be a matter of discretion for the trial judge, considering the foregoing principles, to decide if, and to what extent, set-off should be ordered.

Where an order for child support is granted following a parenting change, the court may direct that arrears outstanding under a previous order shall be set off against the amounts payable under the new order by means of a designated monthly deduction from the currently payable amount under the applicable provincial table set out in the *Federal Child Support Guidelines*.[172]

Given the different income tax treatment accorded to periodic child support and periodic spousal support, a court should not order a direct set-off of child support payable to the primary caregiving parent and spousal support payable by that parent.[173]

---

169 See *Petroczi v Petroczi*, 2011 BCSC 1223; *Pascual v Pascual*, 2018 ONSC 5412 at paras 62–69.

170 2014 NSCA 11 at para 20; see also *Bose v Bose*, 2023 NSSC 269. For an excellent review of Ontario caselaw, see *Starr v Starr*, [2008] OJ No 6042 (SCJ). And see *Rego v Santos*, 2015 ONCA 540; *Pascual v Pascual*, 2018 ONSC 5412.

171 See *Walsh v Walsh*, [2008] OJ No 98 at para 49 (SCJ).

172 *Messier v Robillard*, [1999] NJ No 368 (SC).

173 *Noble v Boone*, 2010 NLTD 65; *Stokes v Stokes*, [1999] OJ No 5192 (SCJ). Compare *Edgar v Edgar*, 2012 ONCA 646.

U. INTEREST

Interest charges may be applied to support arrears.[174] Until such time as the certificate prescribed by section 124(1) of the *Family Services Act* (New Brunswick) issues, a support order is not a "judgment" as defined by Rule 1.04 of the New Brunswick *Rules of Court* and does not attract statutory interest.[175] An order for retroactive child support is not a judgment for debt or damages within the meaning of section 5(1) of *The Pre-judgment Interest Act* (Saskatchewan). Accordingly, a trial judge has no jurisdiction to award pre-judgment interest with respect to such an order.[176] Compare *Tadayon v Mohtashami*[177] wherein the Ontario Court of Appeal held that an application judge erred in failing to award pre-judgment interest on retroactive child support and retroactive spousal support awards because the recipient was *prima facie* entitled to interest on the retroactive support orders pursuant to section 128(1) of the *Courts of Justice Act*.[178]

Interest is not ordered as a penalty; it constitutes compensation for loss of the use of the money. Section 129 of the Ontario *Courts of Justice Act* creates a substantive entitlement to post-judgment interest, whether or not the formal order says so.[179] Interest may, therefore, be granted, even though it was not claimed in the original pleadings, where there is no unfairness thereby caused.[180] In directing the payment of interest, the court may conclude that a previous payment shall be credited against the oldest arrears that were payable.[181] The circumstances may be such that it would be inappropriate to allow interest[182] or a reduction of the previously ordered former interest rate may be justified where that rate has dramatically declined.[183]

In granting an order for prospective or retroactive child support, the court may direct that post-judgment interest shall be payable at a designated rate on all late payments.[184]

A court may order a reduction in the amount of interest to be paid on child support arrears insofar as the amount of the arrears has been judicially reduced. Interest will remain payable on the balance of the arrears where the "gross unfairness" test under section 96(3.1) of the *Family Relations Act* (BC) (now the *Family Law Act*, s 174) has not been satisfied.[185] The court may refuse to cancel or reduce annual default fees where the court is not satisfied

---

174 *Haisman v Haisman* (1994), 7 RFL (4th) 1 (Alta CA); *Cawker v Cawker* (1994), 7 RFL (4th) 282 (BCSC); *Beavis v Beavis*, 2014 BCSC 422; *JCH v SMBH*, 2024 BCSC 54; *Richard v Richard* (1994), 2 RFL (4th) 395 (NBQB); *Allen v Allen* (1991), 32 RFL (3d) 160 (Ont CA); *Mudronja v Mudronja*, 2020 ONCA 569 (enforcement by Family Responsibility Office); *MacGregor v MacGregor*, [1998] PEIJ No 102 (TD).

175 *Bowes v Mattie*, [2003] NBJ No 68 (QB).

176 *Wouters v Wouters*, [2005] SJ No 340 (CA).

177 2015 ONCA 777.

178 RSO 1990, c C.43.

179 *Scaffidi v Scaffidi* (1998), 41 RFL (4th) 166 (Ont Ct Gen Div); see *contra MacKinnon v Duffy*, [2000] OJ No 2948 (SCJ).

180 *Scaffidi v Scaffidi* (1998), 41 RFL (4th) 166 (Ont Ct Gen Div).

181 *Jungaro v Wannamaker* (1990), 26 RFL (3d) 292 (Sask CA).

182 *Pearson v Pearson* (1995), 16 RFL (4th) 75 (Man QB); see also *Welsh v Welsh*, [1998] OJ No 4550 (Gen Div).

183 *Crosbie v Crosbie*, 2012 ONCA 516.

184 *Potter v Graham*, [2004] AJ No 1133 (QB); *McCrea v McCrea*, [1999] BCJ No 1514 (SC); *Dickinson v Dickinson*, [1998] OJ No 4815 (Gen Div).

185 *X(RL) v X(JF)*, [2002] BCJ No 1889 (SC); *Beavis v Beavis*, 2014 BCSC 422.

that "special circumstances" exist within the meaning of section 14.4(6)(c)(ii) of the *Family Maintenance Enforcement Act* (BC).[186]

A court has no jurisdiction to cancel the interest on arrears except where the arrears themselves are cancelled.[187]

V. PIERCING THE CORPORATE VEIL

It is a long-established rule of law that a corporation is a legal entity distinct from its share holders. However, the distinction between a company and its "controlling mind" is not abso lute and, in appropriate circumstances, a court may pierce the corporate veil for the purpose of enforcing third-party rights.[188] In the field of corporate and commercial law, the judicial willingness to look behind a corporation is narrowly circumscribed. There must be suffering caused to a third party that cannot be otherwise remedied. In general, the following circum stances must be present in those fields: (1) the individual must exercise complete control over the finances, policies, and business practices of the company; (2) that control must have been used by the individual to wrongly deprive a third party of his or her rights; and (3) the misconduct must be the reason for the third party's injury or loss. In the area of family law, a somewhat less rigorous approach has been taken by the courts where an individual seeks to shield herself against the legitimate enforcement of support rights and obligations. It is noteworthy that a piercing of the corporate veil is expressly mandated by section 18 of the federal and provincial child support guidelines for the purpose of imputing income to a spouse or parent, although this may simply be the codification of a common practice of the courts across Canada in claims for both spousal and child support. There are important public policy reasons for courts to prevent support obligors from hiding behind the facade of a private company. The nonpayment of support thrusts family dependants onto social assistance and contributes to present levels of child poverty in Canada. If statutory support rights and obligations are not to be frustrated, a court must be free to pierce the corporate veil in appropriate circumstances in order to ensure their enforcement.[189]

For the purpose of enforcing child support, a court may pierce the corporate veil where a defaulter commingles commercial and business expenses, but the piercing of the corporate veil to assist in the resolution of child support issues does not destroy the defaulter's ability to rely on the corporate vehicle for other purposes, including tax and protection from personal liability connected to business operations.[190]

The payor cannot shelter his assets and income behind a corporation and thereby seek to justify a reduction in the amount of support that should be paid.[191]

The obligation to pay child support cannot be avoided by the obligor's assignment of income arising under a consulting contract to a company that is wholly owned by the obligor.

186 *Ibid.*

187 *Armstrong v Armstrong*, [2004] BCJ No 1678 (SC).

188 See *Potzus v Potzus*, 2018 SKQB 55.

189 *Wildman v Wildman*, [2006] OJ No 3966 (CA); *Lynch v Segal*, [2006] OJ No 5014 (CA); see also *Debora v Debora*, [2006] OJ No 4826 (CA) (property equalization); *MLH v DWH*, [2003] AJ No 992 (QB); *Potzus v Potzus*, 2018 SKQB 55.

190 *M(BB) v M(WW)* (1994), 7 RFL (4th) 255 (Alta QB); *MLH v DWH*, [2003] AJ No 992 (QB).

191 *Robinson v Robinson* (1994), 5 RFL (4th) 72 (Ont Ct Gen Div).

Even where the court is unable to conclude that the assignment was made for devious reasons or with fraudulent intent, it may order the obligor as the sole shareholder and controlling force to reassign the income to the obligor personally.[192]

W. DIVISION OF MATRIMONIAL PROPERTY

Arrears of support may be set off against the obligor's equity in the matrimonial home upon the distribution of net proceeds after sale.[193]

Arrears of child support are explicitly recognized in section 21(2)(m) of *The Matrimonial Property Act, 1997* of Saskatchewan as a basis for ordering an unequal distribution of matrimonial property and such an order is appropriate where the court is not confident that the obligor will voluntarily pay the arrears and his status as self-employed creates problems of enforcement.[194]

X. EFFECT OF DEATH

Child support arrears are enforceable against a deceased obligor's estate, subject to the application of the provincial *Limitations Act* and subject also to the court's discretionary jurisdiction to remit all or part of the arrears.[195] Child support arrears also constitute an outstanding debt that is enforceable by the estate of the recipient spouse.[196]

The death of the child in respect of whom support should have been paid does not extinguish child support arrears.[197]

Y. STAY OF ENFORCEMENT

Given that child support obligations should take priority over saving for retirement, an application to stay execution of an order for lump sum child support arrears and to substitute an order for monthly payments against the arrears may be dismissed where the obligor has RRSP savings that can be used to liquidate the arrears.[198]

Enforcement of support arrears may be stayed pending the obligor's receipt of an income tax refund that he or she undertakes to transfer to the debtor spouse, but the court may see fit to direct that the matter shall be brought back within three months if the arrears are not met by transfer of the refund.[199]

---

192 *Blumes v Blumes*, [1998] AJ No 346 (QB).

193 *Swerid v Swerid* (1994), 94 Man R (2d) 86 (QB); *Jukosky v Jukosky* (1990), 31 RFL (3d) 117 (Ont Ct Gen Div).

194 *Burton v Burton*, [1998] SJ No 61 (QB).

195 See *Cooney v Catherwood Estate*, 2016 ONSC 525.

196 *Carpentier v British Columbia (Director of Family Maintenance Enforcement)*, 2017 BCSC 250 (enforcement of child support after mother's death); *Poyntz Estate v Poyntz*, [1998] OJ No 1024 (Gen Div). See also *Bouchard v Bouchard*, 2018 BCSC 1728.

197 *Burbank v Garbutt*, 2012 BCSC 190.

198 *Bland v Bland*, [1999] AJ No 344 (QB).

199 *Blumes v Blumes*, [1998] AJ No 346 (QB).

In *Secours v Secours*,[200] Lee J of the Alberta Court of Queen's Bench concluded that section 25 of the *Maintenance Enforcement Act* (Alberta) does not preclude a court from staying the enforcement of child support arrears for a period exceeding three months where the attendant financial circumstances justify a longer extension. In *Torbey v Torbey*,[201] however, Veit J of the Alberta Court of Queen's Bench concluded that the statutory time limits imposed by sections 25(5) and (6) of the *Maintenance Enforcement Act* (Alberta), which make no provision for any judicial extension, must be applied by the courts. A further stay of child support and spousal support orders in a divorce judgment pending the obligor's pursuit of an application for rescission was found to be not permissible in light of the aforementioned statutory provisions. Even if the statutory time limitations had been found inapplicable, Veit J concluded that the obligor had failed to provide valid reasons for a further stay because he had not proved a justifiable inability to pay the support payments ordered nor had he satisfied the court that the balance of convenience was in his favour.

The Ontario *Rules of Civil Procedure* and the Ontario *Family Law Rules* exempting a support order from the provisions of an automatic stay make sense "because one cannot eat appeal papers during the time it takes these matters to go to appeal."[202]

Z. EFFECT OF RECONCILIATION

Even if a spousal reconciliation does not automatically terminate a court order for child support, a court may be justified in refusing to enforce payments that accrued thereunder during the period of resumed cohabitation.[203]

AA. LACHES; LIMITATION OF ACTIONS

The equitable defence of laches has no direct application to the enforcement of statutory child support obligations[204] but the applicant's unreasonable delay over many years may render the enforcement of arrears inappropriate.[205] The enforcement of child support obligations may be subject to statutory limitation periods.[206] In British Columbia, the right to enforce arrears of child support falls subject to section 3 of the *Limitation Act* of British Columbia, whereby an action on a judgment for the payment of money expires ten years after the date on which the right of enforcement arose. However, the running of the ten-year period is postponed

---

200 [2001] AJ No 956 (QB).

201 [2001] AJ No 1320 (QB).

202 *Fernbach v Fernbach*, [2004] OJ No 1188 at para 28 (SCJ), citing *Brooks-Gualtieri v Gualtieri*, [1998] OJ No 5591 (Gen Div).

203 *Vecchioli v Vecchioli*, [1999] AJ No 799 (QB); *Fitzell v Weisbrod*, [2005] OJ No 791 (SCJ); and see generally Chapter 11, Section H.

204 *Walsh v Walsh*, [1999] NJ No 12 (UFC); *Phiroz v Mottiar* (1995), 16 RFL (4th) 353 (Ont Prov Ct); *JG v MG*, [2008] PEIJ No 33 (SC).

205 *Smith v Smith*, [2001] NSJ No 87 (SC).

206 *Daniels v Lakes* (1987), 11 RFL (3d) 159 (BCCA); *Johnston v Johnston*, [1997] BCJ No 418 (CA); *Cameron v Cameron*, [1999] PEIJ No 62 (SC); *Surette v Surette*, [2000] OJ No 675 (SCJ) (action for enforcement of arrears under separation agreement); *Frigon v Lepoudre*, [2003] SJ No 575 (QB); compare *Pigeon v Pigeon*, [2000] AJ No 1515 (QB). See also *Cooney v Catherwood Estate*, 2016 ONSC 525 (enforcement of child support arrears against obligor's estate).

until such time as the child reaches the age of majority. This extension ensues because the right to support is the right of the child and the law, including section 7 of the *Limitation Act*, recognizes the legal disabilities of children.[207] Corresponding legislation can be found in Prince Edward Island. The right of action on a default accrues as soon as the payment is past due. Consequently, each successive payment that is past due generates a new cause of action. Any payments that have been due more than ten years are unenforceable under section 2(1)(f) of the provincial *Statute of Limitations* and would be cancelled.[208] There is no statutory time limitation period in Manitoba that prevents the recovery of child support arrears, but section 17 of the *Divorce Act* confers a discretion on the court to vary an order retroactively, with a consequential remission of arrears, and the exercise of this discretion may be deemed appropriate where enforcement of the arrears would provide a windfall to the recipient ex-spouse several years after the child attained the age of majority.[209] The filing of a separation agreement containing provisions for child support pursuant to section 35 of the Ontario *Family Law Act* renders the agreement enforceable "as if it were an order of the court." Consequently, the six-year limitation period applicable to contract does not arise; instead, the applicable limitation period is that for judgments of a court, namely, twenty years. Furthermore, child support is the right of the child not the parent and it cannot be waived by a parent's delay or lack of diligence in enforcing the right. The limitation period does not begin to run until the child attains the age of majority.[210] Rule 60.07(2) of the Ontario *Rules of Civil Procedure* provides that, "if six years or more have elapsed since the date of the order, or if its enforcement is subject to a condition, a writ of seizure and sale shall not be issued unless leave of the court is first obtained." Once it is established that the order was obtained within the limitation period, that it is unsatisfied, and that a writ of execution may properly be enforced against the judgment debtor, there is no jurisdiction to refuse an order on equitable grounds. However, a judge does have a discretion not to permit the enforcement of the writ by reason of his or her statutory discretion to remit arrears of support.[211]

The judicial discretion to consider delay in the enforcement of child support arrears is severely restricted. It will be an unusual case where arrears of child support are forgiven or reduced because of a primary caregiving parent's delay in enforcing the order. Delay in enforcing arrears related to a cost-of-living-adjustment (COLA) clause will provide no justification for cancellation or reduction of the arrears where the obligor had the ability to make the payments and has resources currently available to discharge the arrears.[212]

BB. ASSIGNMENT OF ORDERS

Section 20.1 of the *Divorce Act* provides that an order for support may be assigned to a designated federal or provincial Minister of the Crown or to any member of the Council of Yukon

207 *Burbank v Garbutt*, 2012 BCSC 190; see also *Schorath v Schorath*, [2000] AJ No 1050 (QB) (refusal to confirm BC provisional order remitting portion of arrears where adult children were under a permanent disability); *Chatman v Chatman*, 2014 BCSC 430.

208 *Maclean v Jackson* (1996), 24 RFL (4th) 134 (PEITD); *JG v MG*, [2008] PEIJ No 33 (SC).

209 *Watson v Watson*, [1998] MJ No 356 (QB); compare *Wilson v Wilson* (1963), 46 WWR 217 (Man QB).

210 *Young v Rodgers*, [2000] OJ No 4564 (SCJ).

211 *Poyntz Estate v Poyntz*, [1998] OJ No 1024 (Gen Div).

212 *D'Ambrosio v D'Ambrosio*, [2000] BCJ No 1704 (SC).

territory or of the Northwest Territories or of Nunavut. It is uncertain whether section 20.1 vests an exclusive authority in the recipient spouse or parent to assign the support order or whether the court may, of its own initiative, direct an assignment of the order, regardless of the wishes of the recipient spouse or parent.

Section 20.1 is intended to facilitate the enforcement of support orders and provide a means whereby welfare authorities may secure the reimbursement of funds paid out of the public purse to family dependants from the spouse or parent who has wilfully defaulted in making the court-ordered support payments. This section reinforces provincial systems of automatic enforcement that shift the burden of enforcing orders in default from the family dependants themselves to duly appointed enforcement personnel.[213]

Given that a support order may be assigned to a Minister of the Crown or to a provincial agency, the parental obligation to support the children is not automatically terminated by the fact that the children are in foster care. If there has been no assignment, the question to be determined is whether the children have withdrawn from the charge of their parents, in which event the court may order retroactive variation of the order.[214]

CC. FIXING OF ARREARS; PAYMENT BY INSTALMENTS

Arrears of support may be recalculated by applying the Guidelines even though one of the orders in default with respect to the obligor's sequential family relationships pre-dated the implementation of the Guidelines; common sense must prevail where there is no expert accounting and tax evidence to assist the court.[215]

Where a lump sum order for child support arrears would be unrealistic, the court may order the arrears to be paid by designated monthly instalments.[216]

A court may postpone the payment of child support arrears for a reasonable period of time to make reasonable terms for payment, if it seems appropriate, taking into account all the circumstances of a case, including the present financial circumstances of the obligor. Any such accommodation presupposes that there has been complete disclosure of the obligor's financial circumstances.[217]

Arrears of child support may be discharged by part payment under the terms of minutes of settlement that address both past and future child support obligations. Where the parties acknowledge the minutes of settlement to be a binding domestic contract within the meaning of the Ontario *Family Law Act* as well as being capable of incorporation in a court order, the doctrine of substantial performance may be applied to the bilateral contract, where payment of the second of two instalments was late because of the delay of the Canada Revenue Agency in providing a tax refund.[218]

---

213 See *Beauregard v Beauregard* (1991), 38 RFL (3d) 407 (Man QB). For complementary federal legislation aimed at facilitating the enforcement of support and parenting orders across Canada, see the *Family Orders and Agreements Enforcement Assistance Act*, RSC 1985 (2d Supp), c 4, as amended.

214 *Pawliuk v Pawliuk*, [1999] SJ No 268 (QB).

215 *O'Connor v O'Connor*, [1999] OJ No 362 (Gen Div).

216 *Ibid*. And see *Colucci v Colucci*, 2021 SCC 24 at para 140.

217 *Best (Guardian ad litem) v Young*, [1999] BCJ No 280 (SC).

218 *Lariviere v Kelleher*, [1999] OJ No 1824 (SCJ).

DD. SUPPORT DEDUCTION ORDERS

A court may suspend a support deduction order pursuant to section 28 of the Ontario *Family Responsibility and Support Arrears Enforcement Act* only if it finds that it would be unconscionable to require the payor to make support payments in that manner.[219]

EE. PRESERVATION ORDERS

Section 8(1) of *The Family Maintenance Act, 1997* (Saskatchewan) empowers the Saskatchewan Court of King's Bench to grant an interim or final order to restrain the disposition or wasting of assets available to satisfy a claim under the Act. It is not necessary to find an intention on the part of the respondent to waste assets for relief to be granted under section 8. The test is simply whether the disposition or wasting of assets would impair or defeat a claim under the Act. An order under section 8 is not limited to persons against whom a claim is made under the Act, but an order should not be made against a non-party.[220]

FF. REGISTRATION AGAINST LAND

A periodic child maintenance order registered against the obligor's property pursuant to section 23 of the *Maintenance Enforcement Act*[221] does not take priority over a Requirement to Pay of the Canada Revenue Agency served on the support obligor at a time when all the monthly child support payments are current. The use of the word "may" in section 23(5) of the Act makes it clear that an order directing the cancellation of the registration of a maintenance order is in the court's discretion and that such an order may be made on whatever terms the court thinks appropriate. Where the property has been sold and the proceeds of sale have been released to the father by his solicitor after the payment of known debts to the Director of Maintenance Enforcement, the Canada Revenue Agency, and the father's bank, but additional arrears of periodic child support, child-related expenses, and costs have accumulated prior to the current application for discharge of the registration, the court may direct that its cancellation of the registration shall not be registered in the appropriate land registration district until the father has paid the aforementioned amounts. Although the mother's security position with respect to a variation order for lump sum child support may become moot because of a recent additional Requirement to Pay served on the father by the Canada Revenue Agency, the mother may register the substituted order for future lump sum child maintenance under the *Maintenance Enforcement Act* and seek enforcement under all of the provisions of that Act.[222]

---

219 *Fraser v Lewandowski*, [1999] OJ No 1457 (Gen Div).

220 See *VAW v MEH*, 2003 SKQB 255, var'd *VAW v MEH*, 2004 SKCA 104.

221 RSA 2000, c M-1.

222 *Nugent v Nugent*, [2004] AJ No 1161 (QB).

CHAPTER 13

Variation, Rescission, or Suspension of Child Support Orders

A. RELEVANT STATUTORY AND REGULATORY PROVISIONS

Sections 17(4) and (6.1) of the *Divorce Act* provide as follows:

> **Variation, Rescission or Suspension of Orders**[1]
>
> **Order for variation, rescission or suspension**
>
> 17 (1) A court of competent jurisdiction may make an order varying, rescinding or suspending, prospectively or retroactively,
>
> (a) a support order or any provision thereof on application by either or both former spouses. . . .

1 As to interjurisdictional support orders, see ss 18–19 of the *Divorce Act*, RSC 1985 (2d Supp), c 3; see also ss 28–29.5 of the *Divorce Act* whereby the provisions of the *Convention of 23 November 2007 on the International Recovery of Child Support and Other Forms of Family Maintenance* (2007 Hague Child Support Convention) have the force of law in Canada insofar as they relate to subjects that fall within the legislative competence of Parliament. As to the implementation of the *Convention of 19 October 1996 on Jurisdiction, Applicable Law, Recognition, Enforcement and Co-operation in Respect of Parental Responsibility and Measures for the Protection of Children*, see the *Divorce Act*, ss 30–41. And see John-Paul E Boyd, "A Brief Overview of Bill C-78, An Act to Amend the Divorce Act and Related Legislation; Part 2: Amendments Relating to Interjurisdictional Agreements and Treaties" (June 2018), online: Canadian Research Institute For Law and the Family https://afccontario.ca/wp-content/uploads/2018/06/Boyd-Overview-of-Bill-C78-Pt-2-June-2018.pdf; Department of Justice, Canada, "The *Divorce Act* Changes Explained: Part II," online: Department of Justice, Canada www.justice.gc.ca/eng/fl-df/cfl-mdf/dace-clde/index.html. The 2007 Hague *Child Support Convention* came into force for Canada and applies to the provinces of Manitoba and Ontario on 1 February 2024, and to British Columbia on 1 March 2024. It is expected that the Convention will be progressively implemented in other provinces and territories in Canada: see Department of Justice, Canada, "Enforcement of Child and Spousal Support Payments between Provinces, Territories and Countries," online: www.justice.gc.ca/eng/fl-df/enforce-execution/enforce-execut.html. See also Ontario Family Responsibility Office (FRO) website and the Hague Conference on Private International Law website, subheading "Child Support," online: HCCH.net; and see Andina van Isschot & Annick Boulay, "Strengthening Family Justice Services: Recent Changes to the *Family Orders and Agreements Enforcement Assistance Act* and Canada's Implementation of the 2007 Hague Child Support Convention," County of Carleton Law Association, 33rd Annual Institute of Family Law, 5 April 2024, Montebello, Quebec.

Terms and conditions

(3) The court may include in a variation order any provision that under this Act could have been included in the order in respect of which the variation is sought.

Factors for child support order

(4) Before the court makes a variation order in respect of a child support order, the court shall satisfy itself that a change of circumstances as provided for in the applicable guidelines has occurred since the making of the child support order or the last variation order made in respect of that order. . . .

Conduct

(6) In making a variation order, the court shall not take into consideration any conduct that under this Act could not have been considered in making the order in respect of which the variation order is sought.

Guidelines apply

(6.1) A court making a variation order in respect of a child support order shall do so in accordance with the applicable guidelines.

Courts may take agreement, etc., into account

(6.2) Notwithstanding subsection (6.1), in making a variation order in respect of a child support order, a court may award an amount that is different from the amount that would be determined in accordance with the applicable guidelines if the court is satisfied

(a) that special provisions in an order, a judgment or a written agreement respecting the financial obligations of the spouses or the division or transfer of their property, directly or indirectly benefit a child, or that special provisions have otherwise been made for the benefit of a child; and

(b) that the application of the applicable guidelines would result in an amount of child support that is inequitable given those special provisions.

Reasons

(6.3) Where the court awards, pursuant to subsection (6.2), an amount that is different from the amount that would be determined in accordance with the applicable guidelines, the court shall record its reasons for having done so.

Consent orders

(6.4) Notwithstanding subsection (6.1), a court may award an amount that is different from the amount that would be determined in accordance with the applicable guidelines on the consent of both spouses if it is satisfied that reasonable arrangements have been made for the support of the child to whom the order relates.

Reasonable arrangements

(6.5) For the purposes of subsection (6.4), in determining whether reasonable arrangements have been made for the support of a child, the court shall have regard to the applicable guidelines. However, the court shall not consider the arrangement to be unreasonable solely because the amount of support agreed to is not the same as the amount that would otherwise have been determined in accordance with the applicable guidelines. . . .

Copy of order

(11) Where a court makes a variation order in respect of a support order ... made by another court, it shall send a copy of the variation order, certified by a judge or officer of the court, to that other court.

Variation order by affidavit, etc.

17.1 Where both former spouses are habitually resident in different provinces, a court of competent jurisdiction may, in accordance with any applicable rules of the court, make a variation order pursuant to subsection 17(1) on the basis of the submissions of the former spouses, whether presented orally before the court or by means of affidavits or any means of telecommunications, if both former spouses consent thereto.

The provisions of section 17 of the *Divorce Act* are complemented by section 14 of the *Federal Child Support Guidelines,* which provides as follows:

Circumstances for variation

14 For the purposes of subsection 17(4) of the Act, any one[2] of the following constitutes a change of circumstances:

(a) in the case where the amount of child support includes a determination made in accordance with the applicable table, any change in circumstances that would result in a different child support order or any provision thereof;

(b) in the case where the amount of child support does not include a determination made in accordance with a table, any change in the condition, means, needs or other circumstances of either spouse or of any child who is entitled to support;

(c) in the case of an order made before 1 May 1997, the coming into force of section 15.1 of the Act, enacted by section 2 of chapter 1 of the Statutes of Canada, (1997).[3]

Section 17 of the *Divorce Act* and section 14 of the *Federal Child Support Guidelines* codify the circumstances wherein a court may vary a child support order. The role of the court is not that of an appellate tribunal; the validity of the existing order is presumed and the court's role in a variation proceeding is simply to determine whether there has been a change in circumstances since the order was granted that warrants its variation according to the afore mentioned provisions.[4] The judicial assumption that the existing order is correct applies not only to the amount of child support but also to its duration. If the order has expired, an application to continue child support will be treated by analogy to section 17(10) of the *Divorce Act* which deals with the variation of spousal support orders, as an application to vary that falls subject to section 17 of the *Divorce Act* and section 14 of the *Federal Child Support Guidelines* and not as an original application for support under section 15.1 of the *Divorce Act.*[5]

2 *Guidelines Amending the Federal Child Support Guidelines*, SOR/97-563, s 2, amending SOR/97-175, s 14.

3 *Ramachala (Holland) v Holland,* 2020 ABQB 432; *LF v RB,* 2021 BCSC 464; *Van Boekel v Van Boekel* 2020 ONSC 5265. For a useful discussion of general principles relating to the variation of child support orders, see *Weber v Weber,* 2020 ONSC 4098 at paras 63–68.

4 *Zarins v Cochrane,* [1999] BCJ No 2876 (SC). See Lorne MacLean, Fraser MacLean, Kaye Booth & Oliver Spinks, "COVID-19 and Canadian Spousal and Child Support: There Is a Light at the End of the Tunnel but How Long Is the Tunnel?" County of Carleton Law Association, Annual Institute of Family Law 2021, Ottawa, 23 March 2021.

5 *Gervais v Tongue,* [2000] OJ No 529 (SCJ).

B. JURISDICTION

Pursuant to section 5(1) of the current *Divorce Act*, the jurisdiction to vary, rescind, or suspend a permanent order for spousal or child support, or a parenting order vests in the court of the province in which either former spouse is habitually resident, or in a court whose jurisdiction is accepted by the former spouses, provided that the definition of "court" under section 2(1) is satisfied.[6] Pursuant to sections 5(2) and 5(3) of the current *Divorce Act*, where variation proceedings are pending in two courts that would have jurisdiction under section 5(1), the first to be instituted prevails unless it is discontinued,[7] and if the two proceedings are commenced on the same day, the Federal Court has jurisdiction to determine which court retains jurisdiction.[8]

A court has jurisdiction to hear a variation application even when the subject order is under appeal.[9]

C. TRANSFER OF PROCEEDING TO ANOTHER PROVINCE

Section 6(1)of the current *Divorce Act* stipulates that if an application for an order for the exercise of parenting time or parental decision-making responsibility under section 16.1 of the *Divorce Act* is made in a divorce proceeding or corollary relief proceeding to a court in a province and the child of the marriage in respect of whom the order is sought is habitually resident in another province, the court may, on application by a spouse or former spouse or on its own motion, transfer the proceeding to a court in that other province. And section 6(2) provides that if an application for a variation order in respect of a parenting order is made in a variation proceeding to a court in a province and the child of the marriage in respect of whom the variation order is sought is habitually resident in another province, the court may, on application by a former spouse or on its own motion, transfer the variation proceeding to a court in that other province.

D. APPROPRIATE JUDICIAL DISTRICT; CHANGE OF VENUE

Where one of the spouses still resides in the judicial district wherein the divorce was granted, an application to vary support granted by way of corollary relief must be brought in that judicial district,[10] but such jurisdictional rules are not to become an instrument of oppression when one party has ample means and the other has very limited means.[11] It may be possible to change the venue of a motion to a judicial district other than that where the respondent or the respondent's solicitor resides when, for example, financial hardship would result.[12]

6 See *Dixon v Dixon* (1995), 13 RFL (4th) 160 (Alta QB); *Lavoie v Yawrenko* (1992), 44 RFL (3d) 89 (BCCA); *Shipowick v Shipowick*, 2016 MBQB 124; *IJ v TS*, 2015 NBQB 86; *Hiscocks v Marshman* (1991), 34 RFL 12 (Ont Gen Div).

7 See *Winram v Cassidy* (1991), 37 RFL (3d) 230 (Man CA); *Droit de la famille—541*, [1988] RDF 484 (Que CA).

8 As to the criteria to be applied by the Federal Court, see s 5(3) of the *Divorce Act*.

9 *Labrecque v Labrecque*, 2012 SKQB 320.

10 *Droit de la famille—1271*, [1989] RDF 592 (CS).

11 *Martin v Martin* (1988), 14 RFL (3d) 388 (BCCA).

12 *Ridley v Ridley* (1989), 37 CPC (2d) 167 (Ont HCJ).

E. EFFECT OF APPEAL

An application to vary an order for child support may be entertained by reason of changed circumstances, notwithstanding that an appeal is pending against the original order. Although there is jurisdiction to hear an application to vary or rescind a support order that is under appeal,[14] the variation proceeding may be stayed pending the disposition of the appeal in order to avoid multiplicitous proceedings.[15]

F. ENFORCEMENT AND VARIATION DISTINGUISHED UNDER PROVINCIAL LEGISLATION

Orders granted pursuant to the *Divorce Act* have legal effect throughout Canada and may be enforced extra-provincially, but a court may only vary an order in accordance with the *Divorce Act*.[16]

An order for support granted under the *Divorce Act* cannot be varied by an application brought pursuant to provincial statute, nor can any such application seek to remit arrears of support that have accrued under the order.[17]

Although provincial legislation may apply to the enforcement of orders for support granted on or after divorce, such legislation is not a legitimate source of judicial jurisdiction to vary an order for support granted pursuant to the *Divorce Act*.[18] Provincial enforcement legislation cannot be invoked, therefore, as the basis for an order that "arrears under the divorce judgment [will] not continue to accumulate while the respondent [is] unemployed."

G. STATUS OF APPLICANT; EFFECT OF DEFAULT

Section 17(1)(a) of the *Divorce Act* provides that an application to vary, rescind, or suspend a support order or any term thereof may be brought by either or both former spouses. A joint application is permissible under section 17(1)(a). The reference to "former spouse(s)" in section 17(1)(a) presupposes that an application to vary a permanent order for support cannot be instituted before the divorce judgment becomes effective pursuant to section 12 of the *Divorce Act*.[20]

Section 17(1) confers no express authority on third parties to institute proceedings to vary, rescind, or discharge spousal or child support orders, notwithstanding any assignment of such order made pursuant to section 20.1 of the *Divorce Act*.[21] A distinction is to be drawn

---

13 *Preston v Preston* (1981), 22 RFL (2d) 137 (Sask QB).

14 *Gordon v Solmon* (1995), 16 RFL (4th) 403 (Ont CA); *Gresham v Gresham* (1988), 14 RFL (3d) 446 (Sask CA).

15 *Aleixandre v Aleixandre* (1984), 43 RFL (2d) 245 (Ont HCJ).

16 *Divorce Act*, s 20.

17 *Weinstein v Weinstein* (1995), 15 RFL (4th) 353 (BCCA).

18 See *Divorce Act*, s 20(4); *McArthur v Kyle* (1994), 113 DLR (4th) 263 (Ont Ct Gen Div).

19 *Prince Edward Island (Director of Maintenance Enforcement) v Callaghan* (1991), 32 RFL (3d) 117 (PEICA).

20 See Chapter 11, Section B(17).

21 See *Robbins v Robbins* (1986), 43 Man R (2d) 53 (QB); *Pearson v Pearson* (1990), 25 RFL (3d) 79 (NBQB), wherein Logan J held that the Minister of Income Assistance was not entitled to intervene and be added as a party on a divorced husband's application to terminate spousal and child support merely because family members might become a public charge. In *Galan v Galan* (1990), 25 RFL (3d) 225

between proceedings to enforce a support order and proceedings to vary the order.[22] A child, in respect of whom support has been ordered, has no jurisdiction to apply to vary that order under section 17 of the *Divorce Act*, nor has the court any power to exercise a *parens patriae* jurisdiction on behalf of an adult child.[23] It has been held, however, that the words "former spouse" in section 17 of the *Divorce Act* include the personal representative of a deceased former spouse at least with respect to the variation of a child support order.[24]

It is well recognized that a court has a discretion not to entertain an application for variation by a payor spouse who is in continuous default.[25] There is no general principle that a person in arrears of support who has the capacity to pay should in every case be denied a hearing of his or her application to vary the support order.[26]

H. INTERIM VARIATION OF PERMANENT ORDERS

Although interim orders are specifically authorized by sections 15.1(2), 15.2(2), and 16(2) of the *Divorce Act*, no jurisdiction to grant interim orders is explicitly conferred by section 17 of the *Divorce Act*, which empowers a court to make an order varying, rescinding, or suspending, prospectively or retroactively, a final spousal support order, child support order, or parenting order.[27] In British Columbia and Saskatchewan, appellate courts have addressed the issue of whether interim variation orders could be granted under section 11 of the *Divorce Act*, SC 1967–68, c 24 (RSC 1970, c D-4), the predecessor to section 17 of the *Divorce Act*, RSC 1985 (2d Supp), c 3. While acknowledging that there was no jurisdiction to grant interim orders on an application under section 11(2) of the *Divorce Act*, 1968, where variation was sought in respect to an existing order for corollary financial relief, the judgments of *Burton v Burton*[28] and *Frey v Frey*[29] state that an order could be varied pursuant to section 11(2) of the *Divorce Act*, 1968, and then varied again, if injustices might otherwise arise from delay prior to a full review of the attendant circumstances. On the other hand, in *Yeo v Yeo*,[30] the Prince Edward Island Court of Appeal concluded that injustices and hardships that can arise from delay in the full hearing of an application to vary an order under section 17(1) of the *Divorce Act* cannot be addressed by successive orders, the first of which is merely transitional pending a full review of the attendant circumstances. Instead, injustices and hardships must be addressed by expedited hearings and/or by orders for retroactive variation, the latter jurisdiction being expressly recognized by section 17(1) of the current *Divorce Act* but not

(Man CA), however, the Director of Income Security was entitled to be heard on an application to reduce arrears of support where the wife had been largely supported through social assistance.

22 See Section F, above in this chapter.

23 *Garbers v Garbers* (1993), 48 RFL (3d) 217 (Ont UFC).

24 *Chalmers Estate v Chalmers* (1990), 29 RFL (3d) 54 (Alta QB); *Lesser v Lesser* (1985), 44 RFL (2d) 255 (Ont HCJ), aff'd (1985), 51 OR (2d) 100 (CA).

25 *Dickie v Dickie*, [2007] 1 SCR 346; *Burley v Burley*, 2009 ONCA 2.

26 *Pousette v Pousette* (1993), 46 RFL (3d) 152 (BCSC), considering *Parkinson v Parkinson*, [1973] 11 RFL 128 (Ont CA).

27 *Colter v Colter*, 2015 NSSC 2; see also *MR v JR*, 2018 NBCA 12; *Whelan v Whelan*, [2005] NJ No 134 (CA) (spousal support).

28 (1982), 27 RFL (2d) 170 (BCCA); see also *Skemer v Skemer*, 2016 BCSC 1199.

29 [1987] SJ No 322 (CA). See also *Keogan v Weekes*, [2005] SJ No 170 (QB).

30 [1998] PEIJ No 97 (CA).

by section 11(2) of the *Divorce Act*, 1968. The reasoning in *Yeo v Yeo* seems more compelling than the reasoning in *Frey v Frey*. However, the cases have two common features. First, both acknowledge that the relevant statutory provisions confer no jurisdiction on a court to grant an interim order varying an existing final order. Second, both acknowledge the need for the avoidance of injustices or hardships that might arise from delay. Where they differ is in the means whereby such avoidance is secured. Bringing a new perspective to the aforementioned divergence of judicial opinion based on the current approach to statutory interpretation, Jackson JA of the Saskatchewan Court of Appeal in *Prescesky v Prescesky*[31] has ventured the following opinion:

> 41 We have not been asked to overrule *Frey*, nor do I think it is necessary to consider doing so. While I recognize the debate in the jurisprudence as to the proper interpretation of ss. 15.1 [15.2] and 17 of the *Divorce Act*, some observations are in order. First, much of the jurisprudence taking a different approach predates the Supreme Court of Canada's explication of the proper method of statutory interpretation in *Rizzo & Rizzo Shoes Ltd. (Re)*, [1998] 1 SCR 27 at 40–41 [*Rizzo*]. Following the modern approach to statutory interpretation, the words of a provision must be "read in their entire context and in their grammatical and ordinary sense, harmoniously with the scheme of the Act, the object of the Act, and the intention of Parliament" (*Rizzo*, p. 28)....
>
> 42 Second, ss. 15.1 [15.2] and 17 apply to spousal support orders as well as child support. In that regard, it is significant that *Yeo* is a spousal support case. It relies on the "clear" words of the statute and the need for "finality" in spousal support orders. It also leaves open the possibility of a different interpretation for *child support orders*: ...
>
> 44 Third, courts have for some time interpreted s. 15.1 as allowing for successive interim orders.... Again, nothing in the language of s. 15.1 specifically authorizes the making of multiple interim orders, but the application of the principles of statutory interpretation support the conclusion nonetheless. In making this comment, I am addressing the *authority* to make more than one interim order under s. 15.1(2), not the circumstances under which successive orders should be made.
>
> 45 Fourth, *generally speaking*, interim orders are used for "interim" matters....
>
> 46 While that is the general rule, it is also correct that substantive issues are being resolved in Chambers, with the possibility that the decision will be revisited at a later date....
>
> 47 Fifth, the move away from the formalism of another era can be explained in terms of access to justice....
>
> 48 Sixth, section 17 does not use the word "interim" nor does it use the word "final." The word "final" is imported into this area of the law from the practice domain dealing largely with "interlocutory" orders, which can have implications for appellate practice, but have less bearing when determining the rights of children.
>
> 49 Having regard for these considerations, and applying the modern principle of statutory interpretation, and the Supreme Court authority above-mentioned, I conclude that Parliament did not intend to limit the court's authority to vary final orders—in Chambers or otherwise. Section 17(1) specifically confers the authority to vary, rescind or *suspend*,

---

31 2015 SKCA 111 at paras 41–50 [emphasis in original]. See also *Hart v Pownall*, 2020 MBQB 168, citing *Innocente v Innocente*, 2014 ONSC 7082.

prospectively or *retrospectively* any order. The only question is whether it can be done on an interim basis.

50 I see no reason in principle why a court, faced with an application to vary, should not be able to make an interim order pending a final resolution of the matter — in the appropriate case. The affidavit evidence may not rise to the level of certainty needed for a final order, but the judge may nonetheless be satisfied that need, hardship and a change of circumstances dictate that the judge should act immediately rather than waiting to test the evidence and make a final determination. In such circumstances, it would be an exercise in formalism to insist that the matter be set down for a hearing or a trial in order to make a final order — which may exacerbate hardship and surely will increase cost. The better interpretation of ss. 15.1[15.2] and 17 is to permit variation for child and spousal support orders on an interim basis leaving the development of the common law to determine when the discretion to do so should be exercised.

The above reasoning does not draw distinctions between the jurisdiction to vary an interim order for child support and/or spousal support pursuant to sections 15.1 and 15.2 of the *Divorce Act* and the jurisdiction under section 17 of the *Divorce Act* to vary a final order for child support and/or spousal support on an interim basis but it categorically affirms that courts in Saskatchewan have the authority to grant both types of order under the current rules of statutory interpretation.

Applications to vary interim orders should be rare, and there is a heavy onus on the applicant to meet that test, rather than just proceeding to trial and resolving all matters after a full hearing. Furthermore, an appellate court should not interfere with an interim order for support in the absence of a serious error in principle, a substantial misapprehension of the evidence, or if the order is so clearly wrong that it amounts to an injustice. In *Walsh v Walsh*,[32] the Ontario Court of Appeal concluded that in the absence of a finding of a change of circumstances within the meaning of section 17(4) of the *Divorce Act* and section 14 of the *Federal Child Support Guidelines*, a motions judge has no jurisdiction to grant an interim order for the variation of a pre-existing child support order. Furthermore, even when a material change of circumstances is established, a court will only grant a variation order by way of interim relief when the need for an increase is urgent or pressing. In *Innocente v Innocente*, Gautier J of the Ontario Superior Court of Justice stated:

> In those cases where a temporary or interim variation of a final order has been granted, the courts have found what are in my view, exceptional circumstances:
>
> (a) To prevent undue hardship. *Dancsecs v. Dancsecs* (1994), 5 R.F.L. (3d) 64 (Ont. Gen. Div.);
>
> (b) Where the failure to make the interim order would be incongruous or absurd. *Rogers v. Rogers* (1990), 27 R.F.L. (3d) 214 (Ont. H.C.) and *French v. Woods* (1992), 42 R.F.L. (3d) 345 (Ont. Gen. Div.); and
>
> (c) Where there is a pressing and immediate urgency. See *McTaggart v. Hilton*, [1994] O.J. No. 1069.[33]

---

32 [2004] OJ No 254 (CA); see also *Cherewyk v Cherewyk*, 2018 MBCA 13; *A v B*, [2007] OJ No 5555 (SCJ); *Williams v Williams*, 2013 ONSC 220 at para 25.

33 2014 ONSC 7082 at para 45; see also *Lapshinoff v Allen*, 2017 ONSC 1023; *JG v T-LG*, 2020 ONSC 5217; *P v H*, 2022 CarswellOnt 3203 (SCJ).

And the moving party must come to court with "clean hands."[34] An interim order for the variation of a permanent child support order is only warranted where manifest unfairness or injustice would arise if the *status quo* under the existing child support order were maintained until the *viva voce* hearing.[35] Changes in parenting arrangements have been found insufficient to warrant an interim order for reduced child support where the father's income as a farmer could not be resolved by affidavit evidence and required a *viva voce* hearing in which income issues and assertions could be tested by cross-examination.[36]

An application to vary an order for child maintenance pursuant to section 10 of *The Family Maintenance Act, 1997* (Saskatchewan) requires proof of change in circumstances. A chambers judge is not entitled to grant an interim variation order pending trial of an issue as to whether the applicant stood *in loco parentis* to one of the children under the existing order prior to the applicant's recent discovery that he was not the father of the child in question.[37] Where the interests of children are concerned, some courts have purported to exercise their *parens patriae* jurisdiction as a means of securing the interim variation of a permanent order for child support.[38] Many cases across Canada have asserted that child support may be ordered in the exercise of the *parens patriae* jurisdiction.[39] There is, nevertheless, room for some doubt as to whether such jurisdiction can properly be invoked in a proceeding relating to child support, as distinct from a guardianship, parenting, or adoption proceeding. Furthermore, even if such jurisdiction can be invoked to protect the economic interests of a child, there is no reason to assume that it could be invoked to reduce pre-existing child support obligations for the benefit of a parent.

The Ontario Court of Justice has no statutory or *parens patriae* jurisdiction to grant an interim order varying a final order for child support granted pursuant to the Ontario *Family Law Act.* Rule 57.1 of the *Rules of the Ontario Court (Provincial Division) in Family Matters* establishes a new procedure whereby, instead of pleading allegations in a variation application with only a skeletal factual basis outlined, sworn evidence along with documentary support is placed before the court at the outset. This procedure, if properly undertaken,

---

34 *Lapshinoff v Allen*, 2017 ONSC 1023, citing *Clark v Vanderhoeven*, 2011 ONSC 2286.

35 *McRann v McRann*, [2005] SJ No 285 (QB), citing *Keogan v Weekes*, [2005] SJ No 170 (QB); *Lepage v Lepage*, [2006] SJ No 16 (QB).

36 *Keogan v Weekes*, [2005] SJ No 170 (QB).

37 *Hornoi v Cornejo-Bilawchuk*, [2004] SJ No 230 (CA) (existing order for support of both children to remain in effect under appellate court's ruling, but enforcement of arrears suspended and to be dealt with by the trial judge when the *in loco parentis* issue was determined).

38 See *Dahler v Dahler*, [2002] OJ No 2671 (SCJ) (leave granted to appeal an interim-interim variation of a permanent spousal support order). For additional cases adding to the confusion, see Julien D Payne, *Payne on Divorce*, 4th ed (Scarborough, ON: Carswell, 1996) at 314 n27. See also *Wedsworth v Wedsworth*, [2001] NSJ No 239 (CA), wherein jurisdiction to grant an interim order to vary a child support order made under the *Divorce Act* was tacitly assumed.

39 See *Dumas v Dumas* (1992), 41 RFL (3d) 204 (Ont Ct Gen Div) (indexation of child support); *Parr v Lavallee* (1992), 42 RFL (3d) 58 (Ont Ct Gen Div) (jurisdiction to make interim order in variation application); *Hansen v Hansen* (1995), 13 RFL (4th) 335 at 337 (Ont Ct Gen Div) (variation of consent order for child support is not dependent on change of circumstances); *Boyer v Bradley* (1995), 15 RFL (4th) 33 (Ont Ct Gen Div) (interim variation of child support order). See also *Dixon v Dixon* (1995), 13 RFL (4th) 160 (Alta QB); *Hunt v Smolis-Hunt*, [2001] AJ No 1170 (CA); *Re Kuehn* (1976), 2 BCLR 97 (SC); *Baker v Peterson*, [2001] NSJ No 52 (SC); *Reyes v Rollo*, [2001] OJ No 5110 (SCJ).

40 See *Harris v Harris* (1978), 90 DLR (3d) 699 (BCSC) (no inherent equitable jurisdiction over child support).

forecloses any argument made in favour of varying final orders on an interim basis to prevent mischief in clear cases of hardship. Rule 57.1 enables most variation applications to be dealt with expeditiously at first instance, often in chambers, and on a final basis. Rule 57.1(15) permits the court to direct the trial of an issue in stated circumstances. Where it is not possible to make a final variation order at first instance, the court retains the authority to order retroactive variation pursuant to subsection 37(2.1)(a) of the Ontario *Family Law Act*.[41]

I. FUTURE CONTINGENCIES

Courts should make orders based on probabilities, not possibilities.[42] A court will not speculate as to future contingencies and will grant a variation if and when changes occur, not in advance.[43] However, a payor can bring an application to reduce child support based on an anticipated reduction of his or her annual income.[44]

Where spouses are not communicating with each other, it is impractical to make an order that has built into it variations in the amount of support that depend on whether the obligee is employed, drawing unemployment insurance, or has no source of income whatsoever, although such an order may be permitted under section 15(4) of the *Divorce Act*.[45]

J. CHANGE OF CIRCUMSTANCES; ONUS OF PROOF

Absent an appeal or proof of a change of circumstances since the previous order was granted, parties cannot revisit issues already litigated.[46] If support was initially calculated based on the court's acceptance of a payor's "declared" income, then changes in the declared income in subsequent years are indicative of a material change on an application to vary an order for child support. But if the original support order was based upon "imputed" income, a more comprehensive analysis is required on a motion to change. The court must consider: (a) why income was imputed on the original application and whether it is still appropriate to impute income to achieve a fair result; and (b) how the court quantified the imputed income and whether similar calculations are still applicable.[47] If a support order was made in ignorance of material facts and on erroneous assumptions of fact, an application to review that order may be entertained, notwithstanding that there has been little, if any, material change in the condition, means, needs, and other circumstances of either former spouse since the making

41 *Winterburn v Evanchuk*, [1999] OJ No 5968 (SCJ).

42 *MacDonald v Frampton* (1987), 78 NSR. (2d) 258 (Fam Ct); compare *Harris v Gilbert* (1992), 39 RFL (3d) 458 (Ont Ct Gen Div) (nominal order granted in variation proceeding to accommodate any future catastrophe).

43 *Basque v Basque* (1988), 89 NBR (2d) 214 (QB); *Peterson v Peterson*, 2011 SKQB 365. But see Chapter 11, Section I(2).

44 *Kinasewich v Kinasewich*, [2000] AJ No 267 (QB); *Wilson v Wilson*, [1998] 8 WWR 493 (Sask QB).

45 *Droit de la famille—1271*, [1989] RDF 592 (CS).

46 *Rivard v Rivard*, [2004] AJ No 589 (QB); see also *NSC v DC*, 2011 NBQB 229; *Francis v Isadore-Francis*, 2010 NSSC 208.

47 *Trang v Trang*, 2013 ONSC 1980; see also *Jacklin v Daigle*, 2020 NSSC 248; *Ruffolo v David*, 2016 ONSC 754; *Gray v Rizzi*, 2016 ONCA 152 at para 34; *Abdellatif v Abdellatif*, 2015 SKQB 396.

of the order that is sought to be varied.[48] In *Edwards v Edwards*,[49] a support order had been granted in ignorance of the husband's true financial circumstances, such ignorance having been induced by the husband. The court held that on the wife's motion for a new order in substitution for the original order, the court was exercising its inherent jurisdiction as an instrument of justice as distinct from its statutory jurisdiction to vary the order.

On a variation application, the burden falls on the applicant to establish on the balance of probabilities that there has been a material change of circumstances within the meaning of section 17 of the *Divorce Act* and section 14 of the *Federal Child Support Guidelines* Once such a change is established, section 17(6.1) of the *Divorce Act* stipulates that "[a] court making a variation order in respect of a child support order shall do so in accordance with the applicable guidelines."[51] The burden of proof will not be discharged where there is insufficient evidence adduced to establish such a change.[52] Bald assertions made in an affidavit are insufficient to support a finding of a material change of circumstances. Facts in support of the beliefs or conclusions must be sworn to and presented.[53] A parent who seeks to prospectively and retroactively vary an order for child support assumes the onus of prov ing a material change of circumstances since the granting of the order. This onus will not be discharged where the applicant fails to provide reliable business records as to income earned. An adverse inference may be drawn against an applicant who regularly receives cash for jobs undertaken and gives a discount for cash payments without proffering any explanation to the court for such discounts.[54]

When the provisions of the *Divorce Act* and the *Federal Child Support Guidelines* are read as a whole, it is apparent that a consent order summarily dismissing a claim for child support is not a "child support order" and proof of a change of circumstances is not a pre requisite to a subsequent application for child support, which should be brought under section 15.1 of the *Divorce Act* rather than by way of a variation application under section 17 of the *Divorce Act*.[55]

---

48 *Psaila v Psaila* (1987), 6 RFL (3d) 141 (BCCA); *Pelley v Pelley* (1995), 14 RFL (4th) 1 (BCCA); *Hennessey v Hennessey* (1992), 122 NSR (2d) 220 (TD); *Dunsdon v Dunsdon* (1978), 5 RFL (2d) 89 (Ont CA). Compare *Miller v Miller* (1992), 42 RFL (3d) 278 (Sask CA).

49 (1975), 21 RFL 121 (Ont HCJ); see also *Cunningham v Cunningham* (1990), 30 RFL (3d) 159 (BCCA).

50 *Bushell v Bushell*, [2000] AJ No 1499 (QB); *Murphy v Murphy*, 2007 BCCA 500; *Johnson v Johnson*, 2011 BCCA 190; *Donovan v Lee*, [2002] MJ No 226 (QB); *Leger v Allain*, [2002] NBJ No 189 (QB); *Collins v Collins*, [2003] NJ No 278 (SC); *Smith v Smith*, 2011 NSSC 269; *Stanghi v Stanghi*, [2001] OJ No 1892 (CA); *Stevenson v Smit*, 2014 ONCA 521; *Vezina v Vezina*, [2006] SJ No 105 (CA).

51 *CLB v AHB*, 2013 BCCA 472.

52 *Earle v Earle*, [1999] BCJ No 383 (SC); *Duffett v Duffett*, 2010 NLTD(F) 16; *Bakay v Bakay*, [2000] SJ No 781 (QB); *MacAlister v MacAlister*, [1997] YJ No 62 (SC); see also *Tapping v Hetherington*, [1998] BCJ No 2907 (CA) (pre-Guidelines order based on capital holdings); *Snow v Wilcox*, [1999] NSJ No 453 (CA) (filing of income tax returns of self-employed parent does not satisfy the mandatory financial dis closure requirements imposed by s 21(1) of the *Federal Child Support Guidelines*; failure to discharge onus of proving material change on variation application).

53 *MacFarlane v MacFarlane* (1987), 83 NBR (2d) 306 (CA).

54 *OAAF v AAF*, [2001] OJ No 2032 (SCJ).

55 *Lambright v Brown*, [2003] BCJ No 2612 (CA); *MA v FHA*, 2011 BCSC 1047; compare *Danchuk v Danchuk*, 2011 BCCA 291.

A sufficient change of circumstances to justify variation of a child support order may arise from a change in the parenting arrangement[56] or a change in the payor's income[57] or when the child is no longer a "child of the marriage" within the meaning of section 2(1) of the *Divorce Act*.[58]

Amendments to the *Federal Child Support Guidelines* that were implemented on 1 May 2006, on 1 January 2012, and on 22 November 2017 constituted changes of circumstances because they changed the prior table amounts.[59]

Once a change of circumstances has been found to have occurred, the court must rely on the best current information that it has to determine the amount of support payable.[60] Given a change of circumstances since a child support order, a chambers judge has no discretion to deviate from the *Federal Child Support Guidelines*, unless the circumstances fall within sections 17(6.2) to (6.5) of the *Divorce Act* or the circumstances are such as to trigger a finding of undue hardship under section 10 of the Guidelines.[61] Absent undue hardship, an obligor's bankruptcy does not relieve him of his child support obligation.[62]

Nothing in the *Federal Child Support Guidelines* affects the long-standing legal requirement that a material change of circumstances, which is significant and long lasting, must be established as a condition precedent to the variation of a child support order. A parent cannot return to court whenever any change — no matter how insignificant or brief — occurs. To allow this would be contrary to the best interests of the children and contrary to the objectives of the Guidelines. A court may order increased costs when a party has unnecessarily invoked the court's jurisdiction, and where such conduct persists, the court may direct that any future application to vary the existing child support order shall only be brought by leave of court and that any such application should, if possible, be returnable before the same judge.[63]

A trial judge is entitled to reject expert opinions as to the obligor's ability to earn an income from employment if the attendant circumstances negate assumptions made by the experts or there has been a failure to explore the options available for employment.[64]

Children should not bear the brunt of temporary changes in parental financial circumstances; parents with fluctuating incomes should budget accordingly.[65] A parent cannot resume full-time post-secondary education at his or her children's expense, where other alternatives are available to complete the program. A parent who has been ordered to pay support must organize his or her affairs so as to continue to provide the required amount of

---

56 *Burgess v Burgess*, 2013 NLTD(F) 27.

57 *Cherneski v Rathwell*, 2013 SKCA 133.

58 *Barry v Rogers*, [2002] NJ No 115 (SC); *Szitas v Szitas*, 2012 ONSC 1548.

59 *Hodge v Jones*, 2011 ONSC 2363.

60 *Trevors v Jenkins*, 2011 NBCA 61.

61 *Montalbetti v Montalbetti*, [2000] BCJ No 1834 (CA); *Szitas v Szitas*, 2012 ONSC 1548.

62 *Court v McQuaid*, [2005] PEIJ No 24 (SC) (variation application dismissed).

63 *Hamilton v Pearce*, [2001] BCJ No 1546 (SC); see also *Walker v Walker*, 2016 ABQB 181; *Leger v Allain*, [2002] NBJ No 189 (QB); *Szitas v Szitas*, 2012 ONSC 1548; *Harder v Harder*, [2003] SJ No 429 (QB). Compare *ADB v SAM*, [2006] NSJ No 252 (SC).

64 *Stanghi v Stanghi*, [2001] OJ No 1892 (CA).

65 *Kinasewich v Kinasewich*, [2000] AJ No 267 (QB).

child support and income may be imputed to such a parent on an application for variation of the existing child support order.[66]

A change of circumstances within the meaning of section 17(4) of the *Divorce Act* and section 14 of the *Federal Child Support Guidelines* may be established where the obligor sustains undue hardship by reason of unusually high expenses in relation to exercising parenting time with a child.[67]

Suspension of the obligor's driving licence and a prospective loss of employment relating thereto do not constitute a change of circumstances that warrants variation of a child support order where the apprehended suspension of the driving licence is attributable to the obligor's default in making support payments.[68]

A court may refuse to vary a consent order for the support of an adult disabled child where the father's mandatory retirement had been within the knowledge and contemplation of the parents when they negotiated a carefully crafted agreement that gave priority to the adult child's needs over any future unfairness faced by either parent, and express provision was included whereby the means and standards of living of the parents would be taken into account in determining future child support. Judicial account may be taken of the father's substantial assets and his continued ability to earn income as a consultant, notwithstanding his retirement.[69]

On an application to vary a child support order brought pursuant to section 37 of the *Maintenance and Custody Act* (Nova Scotia),[70] a self-induced reduction of income does not justify reduction of the amount of child support previously ordered, unless the applicant establishes that the decision that led to the reduced income was reasonable in all the circumstances. The issue of reasonableness does not turn solely on an examination of the circumstances surrounding the applicant's decision; the court must also take account of the financial circumstances of the children so as to ensure that they receive a fair standard of support in accordance with the objectives set out in the *Federal Child Support Guidelines*. Coupled with the test of reasonableness applicable under section 37 of the *Maintenance and Custody Act* (Nova Scotia),[71] section 19(1)(a) of the *Federal Child Support Guidelines* empowers a court to impute income to a parent who is "intentionally under-employed." If financial consequences arising from reckless or foolhardy employment decisions would result in financial hardship to the children, a court will impute an annual income to the parent in order to protect the children's right to a reasonable standard of child support. To do otherwise would give parents a licence to deliberately reduce their incomes and thereby thwart the spirit and objective of the *Federal Child Support Guidelines*. It would also place child support payments at the whim of a less than motivated or imprudent parent who self-indulgently fails to consider the negative consequences of employment choices and their detrimental impact upon the standard of living of dependent children.[72]

---

66 *Watson v Solberg*, [2003] SJ No 333 (QB).

67 *Hutton v Hutton*, [2000] BCJ No 1274 (SC).

68 *Wiens v Wiens*, [2001] AJ No 569 (QB).

69 *Buckland v Buckland*, [2004] BCJ No 2484 (SC).

70 See now *Parenting and Support Act*, RSNS 1989, c 160, s 37.

71 *Ibid.*

72 *Peach v Peach*, [2003] NSJ No 41 (Fam Ct).

K. VARIATION OF AMOUNT OF CHILD SUPPORT MADE UNDER APPLICABLE TABLE

Pursuant to section 17(4) of the *Divorce Act* and section 14(a) of the *Federal Child Support Guidelines*, a court may vary a child support order whenever the amount of child support was determined in accordance with the applicable provincial or territorial table and any change has occurred that would result in a different child support order.[73] Such a change will occur when the obligor's annual income and consequential capacity to pay child support has increased[74] or has decreased for reasons beyond his or her control.[75] Even minor increases or decreases in the obligor's total yearly income can require a variation to the amount of child support to be paid because payment is based upon a table tied to the amount of income earned by the payor.[76] Any change that triggers a different order, whether it is a change in form, in substance, or in dollar amounts, is sufficient justification for a variation application.[77] Payment of the table amount of child support for a minor is not subject to variation merely because of the child's subsequent enrolment in boarding school.[78] The jurisdiction to vary an order for child support based on a provincial or territorial table is not confined to circumstances where the obligor's income has increased or decreased.[79] For example, a complementary provision could be included with respect to newly encountered special or extraordinary expenses, or a reconstitution of either household might justify a claim of undue hardship under sections 10(1) and 10(3) of the *Federal Child Support Guidelines*, or the residence of the obligor might change so as to trigger the application of a different provincial or territorial table under section 3(3)(a) of the Guidelines,[80] or the parenting arrangements might change or the number of children to be supported might change,[81] or the accumulation of arrears might warrant the variation of an order for periodic support into an order for lump sum support in accordance with section 11 of the Guidelines.

Section 14(a) of the *Federal Child Support Guidelines* deems that there is a change in circumstances for the purposes of section 17(4) of the *Divorce Act* if section 9 of the Guidelines is triggered[82] or a lasting change from a shared parenting arrangement occurs.[83]

A child's attainment of the provincial age of majority and attendance at an out-of-town university constitute changes of circumstances under section 14(a) of the Guidelines such as

73 *RPS v KJS*, 2014 ONSC 1385, citing *LMP v LS*, 2011 SCC 64 at paras 31–34. See also *NRG v GRG*, 2017 BCSC 478 (temporary disability; reduction of child support for fixed term); *Janmohamed v Janmohamed*, 2020 BCSC 432; *Taylor v Braund (Taylor)*, 2018 NLCA 3.

74 *Murray v Murray*, 2021 ABQB 539; *Vinagreiro v Vinagreiro*, 2022 ABKB 678; *Lee v Chung*, 2011 BCSC 404; *Levesque v Meade*, 2010 NBQB 270; *Taylor v Braund (Taylor)*, 2018 NLCA 3; *ADB v SAM*, [2006] NSJ No 252 (SC); *Khoee-Solomonescu v Solomonescu*, [2000] OJ No 743 (Div Ct).

75 *ADB v SAM*, [2006] NSJ No 252 (SC); *Guillet v Guillet*, [1999] SJ No 266 (QB); see also *Smith v Oake*, 2012 NSSC 100 (remission of arrears).

76 *Gagnon v Gagnon*, 2012 NSSC 407 at para 18, MacDonald J.

77 *Russell v Russell*, 2012 NSSC 258; *Blais v Blais*, [2001] SJ No 468 (QB).

78 *Steward v Ferguson*, 2018 BCCA 158.

79 *JAM v SAJ*, 2014 NSSC 2; *Murnaghan v Lutz*, 2014 NSSC 3.

80 *Ibid.*

81 *Ibid*; see also *Taylor v Sherlow*, 2014 ONSC 6614 at para 36.

82 *Kolada v Kolada*, [2000] AJ No 342 (QB). Compare *Kozma v Kozma*, 2012 NSSC 380.

83 *Vinagreiro v Vinagreiro*, 2022 ABKB 678.

to warrant variation of an existing child support order that provides for the applicable table amount of child support to be paid.[84]

L. VARIATION WHERE AMOUNT OF CHILD SUPPORT NOT UNDER PROVINCIAL OR TERRITORIAL TABLE

Variation of an order for child support under section 14(b) of the *Federal Child Support Guidelines*, where the amount of child support was not determined under a provincial or territorial table, may be granted when there has been a change in the condition, means, needs, or other circumstances of either spouse or former spouse or a change in the condition, means, needs, or other circumstances of any child who is entitled to support.[85] The terms "condition," "means," "needs," and "other circumstances" of either former spouse provide a wide range of relevant considerations that leave the court with an extremely broad discretionary jurisdiction to vary, rescind, or suspend a support order.[86] As Pentelechuk J of the Alberta Court of Queen's Bench observed in *Perron v Hlushko*, "a material change in circumstances under s 14(b) of the *Guidelines*, should be interpreted in a broad and contextual way. It is not limited to demonstrating a change in income, but can take into account any material change in the means or circumstances of the parties. For example, a disability or change in health of a parent or child, receipt of an inheritance, a new partner who contributes to expenses or the addition of a new dependent could all trigger the requisite change in circumstances."[87] In determining the obligor's available means, the nature and source of those means (whether salary, pension, other income, or capital) is not material.[88] Misconduct is ordinarily an irrelevant consideration.[89] Income may be imputed to a spouse in the context of an application to vary child support for the purpose of determining whether a material change of circumstances has occurred within the meaning of section 14(b) of the *Federal Child Support Guidelines*.[90]

The fairness of the original order is not subject to review in variation proceedings.[91] The onus is on the applicant to show a change in circumstances that is substantial, unforeseen, and of a continuing nature, such as would render the existing order unfair or unreasonable. Minor changes in financial circumstances, such as fluctuations in the obligor's income, will not justify a variation order.[94] The changes must be of significance and affect the overall

---

84 *Wood v Boere*, 2012 BCSC 252; *Stratton v Smith*, [2005] NJ No 101 (UFC) (application under the *Newfoundland and Labrador Child Support Guidelines*); *Shelley v Russell*, 2012 ONSC 920.

85 *Perron v Hlushko*, 2015 ABQB 595 (shared parenting); *Birks v Birks*, [2003] BCJ No 949 (SC); *TMF v AJW*, 2011 NBQB 133; *VC v JDB*, 2009 NSSC 25; *Sikler v Snow*, [2000] SJ No 271 (QB).

86 *Willick v Willick*, [1994] 3 SCR 670; see also *Perron v Hlushko*, 2015 ABQB 595 at para 8. And see Chapter 1, Section H.

87 2015 ABQB 595 at para 8.

88 *Bartlett v Bartlett* (1994), 2 RFL (4th) 202 (Nfld UFC).

89 See ss 17(6) and 15.2(5) of the *Divorce Act*; see also *Single v Single* (1986), 5 RFL (3d) 287 at 291 (NS Fam Ct); and see Chapter 3, Section K.

90 *Daku v Daku*, [1999] SJ No 330 (QB).

91 *Willick v Willick*, [1994] 3 SCR 670.

92 *Murray v Murray*, 2021 ABQB 539; *Pelley v Pelley* (1995), 14 RFL (4th) 1 (BCCA); *Hamilton v Pearce*, [2000] BCJ No 1953 (SC).

93 *Krauskopf v Pfefferle* (1993), 111 Nfld & PEIR 158 (PEITD).

94 *Willick v Willick*, [1994] 3 SCR 670.

financial picture of one or both of the spouses.[95] A frivolous application to vary may be dismissed with costs on a solicitor/client basis.[96]

A change in the financial circumstances of the obligor may justify a variation or termination of support obligations, as when the obligor subsequently has an increased ability to pay[97] or, conversely, where the obligor reaches the normal age of retirement or is forced to take early retirement with a substantial reduction in income.[98] On an application to reduce the amount of child support payable under an existing order, the applicant must satisfy the court on a balance of probabilities that his or her income has been reduced in that there is no longer any recourse to a former supplementary source of income, although the application may be dismissed without prejudice to the right to re-apply with further and better affidavit material.[99]

A material change has been defined by the Supreme Court of Canada in *Willick v Willick*[100] as being a change of such magnitude that, if the court had known of the changed circumstances at the time of the original order, it is likely that the order would have been made on different terms.[101] The change must be significant and long lasting.[102] A parent has a continuing obligation to support his or her children in spite of temporary unemployment,[103] or a fluctuating income; some degree of budgeting may be required.[104] If the change was known at the relevant time, it cannot be relied on as the basis for variation.[105] A future event that was within the contemplation of the parties when they made an agreement or that was considered by the court in making an order will not justify the variation of support when the future event occurs. This exception is narrow and requires proof that the likelihood of the future event operated on the minds of the parties or of the court when the support obligations were imposed.[106] In *Chalmers v Chalmers*,[107] Bruce J of the British Columbia Supreme

---

95 *Oldham v King* (1987), 11 RFL (3d) 75 (Man CA); *Gaudet v Gaudet* (1988), 15 RFL (3d) 65 (PEICA).
96 *Taylor v Taylor* (1989), 97 NBR (2d) 271 (QB).
97 *Anderson-Devine v Anderson*, [2002] MJ No 46 (QB); *Howlett v Rach*, [2000] SJ No 752 (QB).
98 *Strang v Strang*, [1992] 2 SCR 112; *Smyth v Smyth* (1993), 48 RFL (3d) 280 (Alta QB); *Carter v Carter* (1991), 34 RFL (3d) 1 (BCCA); *Capuska v Capuska* (1993), 46 RFL (3d) 37 (Man CA); *BB v DG*, [2004] NBJ No 197 (QB); *Blackwood v Blackwood* (1994), 7 RFL (4th) 76 (Ont Ct Gen Div); *Headon v Headon* (1981), 26 RFL (3d) 304 (Sask QB).
99 *St Pierre v St Pierre*, [1999] BCJ No 2264 (SC).
100 [1994] 3 SCR 670. See also *Walker v Walker*, 2016 ABQB 181 at para 9 wherein McCarthy J stated: "Regardless of whether [section 14](a) or (b) [of the Guidelines] applies, it now seems well established that in both instances the change must be *material* before the Court may vary the support order." And see *Leering v Leering*, 2020 BCSC 1231.
101 *Brennan v Brennan*, 2024 ABCA 50; *Meuser v Meuser*, [1998] BCJ No 2808 (CA); *MLP v MJM*, 2012 BCCA 395; *CLB v AHB*, 2013 BCCA 472; *Cook v McManus*, [2006] NBJ No 334 (QB); *Collins v Collins*, [2003] NJ No 278 (SC); *SM v JA*, 2023 NLCA 1; *Murphy v Bert*, [2007] NSJ No 543 (SC); *Cosentino v Cosentino*, 2020 ONCA 775; *Demeria v Demeria*, [1998] SJ No 898 (QB); *Rathwell v McLaughlin*, 2022 SKCA 21.
102 *Brennan v Brennan*, 2024 ABCA 50; *Birks v Birks*, [2003] BCJ No 949 (SC); *SM v JA*, 2023 NLCA 1; *Licata v Shure*, 2022 ONCA 270.
103 *NB v KJB*, [1999] BCJ No 1584 (SC).
104 *Pritchard v Christensson*, 2018 ABCA 302; *Pagani v Pagani*, [1999] BCJ No 3051 (SC).
105 *Meuser v Meuser*, [1998] BCJ No 2808 (CA); *SM v JA*, 2023 NLCA 1; *Cosentino v Cosentino*, 2020 ONCA 775.
106 *Collins v Collins*, [2003] NJ No 278 (SC).
107 2009 BCSC 517.

Court provided the following apt summary of the relevant considerations in determining whether there was a material change justifying a variation of support:

> Whether there has been such a change is governed by the test developed in *Willick v. Willick*, [1994] 3 S.C.R. 670: *L.G.* at para. 48. There are several passages in Willick that address the concept of material change and foreseeability. The relevant passages are quoted at length in paras. 49 to 51 of *L.G.* In my view, the principles derived from these passages are as follows:
>
> 1. The change must be a material one; such that if known at the time it would have likely resulted in a different order.
> 2. What is a material change will in each case be determined on the particular facts. The court should not endeavour to divide into categories those changes that are material and those that fail to satisfy this standard.
> 3. What is a sufficient change must be measured against the parties' overall financial situation.
> 4. The fact that a change was objectively foreseeable does not mean that it was contemplated by the parties and forms part of the underlying basis for the original order.
> 5. The onus rests with the applicant to prove a material change in the condition, means, needs or other circumstances warranting a review of spousal support; however, the court should maintain a flexible approach to the exercise of this discretion to ensure all of the relevant facts in a given case are considered.

And in *CAO v SJO*,[108] Johnston J of the British Columbia Supreme Court stated:

> [34] ... I conclude that what is required to warrant consideration of variation of child support under s. 17(4) of the *Divorce Act* and s. 14 of the Guidelines is a sufficient change in the payor's Guidelines income.
>
> [35] What will be sufficient will depend on the circumstances: an apparently small change can assume great importance if the income is itself modest, whereas a high-income payor may be able to sustain larger fluctuations in annual earnings.
>
> [36] This makes overall sense, as during a marriage or other relationship, the amount available to raise children would be susceptible to the ordinary vicissitudes of life: unemployment, illness interrupting income, increases in income following promotion, overtime work, etc.
>
> [37] There seems little reason to isolate the children from those normal vicissitudes after separation of the parents, so long as the vicissitudes occur naturally, and are not the product of manipulation by the payor parent.
>
> [38] Annual applications where either payor or payee wishes to explore the potential for decrease or increase can be avoided by the type of order proposed by Mr. O. in this case, that is, that he disclose his full income tax return, with all supporting documents, by June 1 each year, and his child support obligation be varied as of July 1 to reflect the income reported. I am also satisfied that costs consequences will be sufficient to discourage applications based on minor fluctuations in income.

---

108 2012 BCSC 378.

Changes in spousal incomes may be insufficient to warrant variation of a child support order granted in a shared parenting situation falling within section 9 of the *Federal Child Support Guidelines* where the wife's increased earning potential was anticipated at the time when the order was made and the husband's reduced annual income was counter-balanced by fewer expenses following his remarriage.[109] A variation of a child support order under section 17 of the *Divorce Act* may be based on either a change in the circumstances of the child or a change in the circumstances of one or both former spouses.[110] Subject to the express provisions of section 14 of the *Federal Child Support Guidelines*, the principles of *Willick v Willick* continue to apply to the variation of child support orders under the *Federal Child Support Guidelines*.[111] Pre-Guidelines caselaw dealing with proof of a material change as a prerequisite to any application to vary a child support order has no application to variation proceedings wherein the applicant seeks to vary a child support order providing for payment of the applicable table amount but the *Willick* criteria continue to be relevant in non-table cases or when the amount of support was determined on a discretionary basis under section 3(2), 4, 5, 7, 9, or 10 of the *Federal Child Support Guidelines*.[112] Regardless of which paragraph applies to a variation proceeding pursuant to section 17(4) of the *Divorce Act* and section 14 of the *Federal Child Support Guidelines*, an obligor cannot justify a reduction in the amount previously ordered on the basis of an unreasonable, self-induced reduction of his income.[113] An unforeseen reduction in the obligor's income constitutes a material change in circumstances.[114] The same is true of an unforeseen increase in the obligor's income.[115] In the absence of proof of a material change in circumstances, an application to vary a child support order must be dismissed.[116] Changes in parental incomes should be examined in relation to each other to determine whether there has been a material change to a significant degree. A father's assumption of food, shelter, and other incidental costs of an adult child may be offset by the child's ability to transfer education and tuition credits to the father for income tax purposes.[117]

In the absence of a finding of undue hardship within the meaning of section 10 of the *Federal Child Support Guidelines*, remarriage and its attendant financial obligations does not warrant variation of a pre-existing order for child support nor any reduction in the table amount of support payable in respect of the children of the second marriage. Where there are co-existing child support obligations owed to two families, the obligor cannot treat the children as if they were members of the same family and average out the child

---

109 *Birks v Birks*, [2003] BCJ No 949 (SC); see also *Walker v Walker*, 2016 ABQB 181.

110 *Bushell v Bushell*, [2000] AJ No 1499 (QB); *Bell v Bell*, [1997] BCJ No 2826 (SC); compare *CLB v AHB*, 2013 BCCA 472.

111 *Bushell v Bushell*, [2000] AJ No 1499 (QB); *Hodgson v Hodgson*, 2014 BCSC 1372; *Khoee-Solomonescu v Solomonescu*, [2000] OJ No 743 (Div Ct).

112 *McRann v McRann*, [2005] SJ No 285 (QB); see also *Gagnon v Gagnon*, 2012 NSSC 407. Compare *CLB v AHB*, 2013 BCCA 472.

113 *McRann v McRann*, [2005] SJ No 285 (QB); *Hamblin v Masniuk*, 2014 SKQB 284.

114 *Lamparski v Lamparski*, [1997] BCJ No 2730 (SC); *Leering v Leering*, 2020 BCSC 1231.

115 *Marson v Marson*, [2001] OJ No 1816 (CA).

116 *Wong v Wong*, [1997] BCJ No 2856 (SC); *Mingo v Mingo*, [1997] OJ No 4835 (Gen Div); *Koot v McLaren*, [2003] SJ No 214 (QB). See also *Varga v Varga*, [1998] AJ No 646 (QB) (judicial refusal to disturb comprehensive, mediated settlement; no change of circumstances established with the exception of return of one child to mother's residence; variation confined to dealing with that child).

117 *Khoee-Solomonescu v Solomonescu*, [2000] OJ No 743 (Div Ct).

support obligation. Support for the child or children in each family unit must be calculated independently of each other.[118]

The issue on an application to vary a support order is not at large in the same way as it is on an original application for support.[119] The jurisdiction to vary does not encompass any authority to speculate on the propriety of the order under review; there is no jurisdiction to fix *de novo* the amount of support,[120] although the court has a discretionary power under section 17(1) of the *Divorce Act* to retroactively vary or rescind an order with a consequential remission of all or part of any arrears[121] or with a consequential increase in the amount of child support payable, given a material change of circumstances since the granting of the order under review.[122] Evidence of changes of circumstances to justify variation of a child support order will generally focus on events occurring since the last order was granted, but cross-examination is not limited to recent events, if reference to earlier acts is necessary to establish the foundations of the current order.[123]

A court will not vary a support order pending an appeal unless there is evidence of changed circumstances. To do so would be tantamount to deciding the appeal on an interim basis.[124]

An applicant who seeks to vary a child support order on the ground of a material change of circumstances other than the implementation of the Guidelines should demonstrate to the court that the change is one over which he or she has no control.[125] An obligor cannot reduce an existing child support obligation by a self-imposed reduction of income.[126] It may

---

118 *Sinclair v Sinclair*, [2001] BCJ No 1000 (SC) (notice of any future application concerning child support to be given to all parties in both actions to ensure the hearing judge had all relevant information of these interrelated matters). See also *ML v RSE*, [2006] AJ No 642 (CA); *Ewing v Malette*, 2009 ABCA 128; *Meuser v Meuser*, [1998] BCJ No 2808 (CA); *WL v NDH*, 2014 NBQB 214; *Locke v Goulding*, 2012 NLCA 8. And see *Soleimani v Melendez*, 2019 ONSC 36, citing DA Rollie Thompson, "The Second Family Conundrum in Child Support" (2001) 18 *Canadian Journal of Family Law* 227–68; Elliot S Birnboim & Daniella Murynka, "Section 9 and Second Families" (2015) 93 *Canadian Bar Review* 39, 2015 CanLIIDocs 138.

119 *Story v Story* (1988), 16 RFL (3d) 216 (BCSC), aff'd (1989), 23 RFL (3d) 225 (BCCA); *Currie v Currie* (1987), 6 RFL (3d) 40 at 44 (Man QB), aff'd (1987), 10 RFL (3d) 207 (Man CA); *Lanteigne v Lanteigne* (1988), 91 NBR (2d) 275 (CA); *Fraser v Fraser* (1990), 31 RFL (3d) 322 (NBCA). Compare *Davies v Davies* (1991), 32 RFL (3d) 14 (Ont Ct Gen Div) (consent order); *Droit de la famille—913* (1990), 30 RFL (3d) 83 (Que CS) (substitution of lump sum for periodic support). But see *Willick v Willick*, [1994] 3 SCR 670.

120 *Wrobel v Wrobel* (1994), 8 RFL (4th) 403 (Alta QB); *Oakley v Oakley* (1985), 48 RFL (2d) 307 at 313 (BCCA); *Cunningham v Cunningham* (1990), 30 RFL (3d) 159 (BCCA); *Lanteigne v Lanteigne* (1988), 91 NBR (2d) 275 (CA); *Savage v Savage* (1992), 39 RFL (3d) 257 (NBCA); *Weingarden v Weingarden* (1978), 3 RFL (2d) 97 (Ont HCJ), aff'd (1979), 9 RFL (2d) 355 (Ont CA), leave to appeal to SCC refused (1979), 27 NR 179n; *Haan v Haan*, [2003] SJ No 40 (QB). Compare *Vervoost v Vervoost* (1991), 37 RFL (3d) 178 at 185 (Alta QB).

121 *Dahl v Dahl* (1995), 18 RFL (4th) 122 (Alta CA); *Ralph v Ralph* (1994), 7 RFL (4th) 238 at 243 and 248–49 (Nfld SC).

122 *Ibid.*

123 *Mosher v Mosher*, [1999] NSJ No 202 (SC).

124 *Szymanski v Szymanski* (1994), 77 OAC 252 (CA).

125 *MAA v JMA*, 2011 NBQB 298; see also *Chan v Chan*, [1999] BCJ No 929 (SC); compare *Gordon v Gordon*, [1999] OJ No 2234 (SCJ).

126 *Aziz v Aziz*, [2000] BCJ No 1134 (CA); *Donovan v Donovan*, [2000] MJ No 407 (CA) (application under *Manitoba Child Support Guidelines*); *MAA v JMA*, 2011 NBQB 298; *Hart v Neufeld*, [2004] SJ No 232 (CA). And see Section P, below in this chapter.

be otherwise if an obligor's change of employment that resulted in a reduced income was not made for selfish or illogical reasons and could prove sensible in the longer term.[127] Parents who are subject to support obligations are entitled to make decisions in relation to their careers so long as the decisions are reasonable at the time having regard to all the circumstances. The onus of proof falls on the obligor to establish that the decision was reasonable.[128] Those circumstances include the age, education, experience, skills, historical earning capacity and health of the payor, the standard of living experienced during marriage, the availability of work, the payor's freedom to relocate, the reasonableness of the career aspirations and of the motives behind any change, as well as any other obligations of the payor.[129] Where a parent has acted unreasonably in terminating his or her employment the court may give that parent "breathing space" by suspending the payment of child support for a brief period, after which ongoing child support obligations shall resume, with all arrears accruing prior thereto to be paid in full by designated monthly instalments.[130]

A reduction in the amount of a child support order may be warranted if an obligor, threatened by burnout, reduces his or her workload and thereby sustains a marked drop in income.[131]

Early retirement with a consequential reduction of income, which is attributable to ill health, may constitute a change in circumstances sufficient to warrant variation of a child support order.[132]

A change in the parenting arrangements constitutes a material change of circumstances under section 14(b) of the *Federal Child Support Guidelines*,[133] but a retroactive child support order may be deemed inappropriate where a parent was legally represented when the parenting change occurred and no claim respecting child support was made at that time.[134]

An application to reduce the amount of child support payable under the former tax-deductible regime on the basis of the obligor's current lack of income may be dismissed where the evidence warrants an imputation of income on the basis of earning capacity.[135]

Where there has been a reduction in the obligor's income but an employment severance entitlement remains to be determined, a court may endorse a short-term solution, whereby the existing order shall remain in place but payments thereunder will be reduced pending receipt of the severance package. In other circumstances, the court may enjoin the Family Responsibility Office from taking collection or enforcement proceedings while the stipulated reduced amount is being paid.[136]

---

127 *Darvill v Chorney*, [1999] SJ No 551 (QB).
128 *MAA v JMA*, 2011 NBQB 298.
129 *Kozub v Kozub*, [2002] SJ No 407 (QB).
130 *Ibid.*
131 *Chan v Chan*, [1998] BCJ No 2420 (SC).
132 *BDW v HGW*, [1999] AJ No 997 (QB); *Klotz v Klotz*, [1999] BCJ No 148 (SC).
133 *Stanford v Cole*, [1998] NJ No 300 (SC); *McBride v McBride*, [2001] NWTJ No 69 (SC).
134 *Woods v Woods*, [1998] SJ No 687 (QB).
135 *Buzon v Buzon*, [1999] AJ No 371 (QB).
136 *Elliott v Elliott*, [1998] OJ No 4827 (Gen Div).

M. VARIATION OF ORDERS PRE-DATING IMPLEMENTATION OF GUIDELINES[137]

Pursuant to sections 17(1) and 17(4) of the *Divorce Act* and section 14(c) of the *Federal Child Support Guidelines*, any order for child support that was made before 1 May 1997 may be the subject of an application to vary. The right to seek variation was necessitated by the implementation of the *Federal Child Support Guidelines* on 1 May 1997, which were accompanied by amendments to the *Income Tax Act* whereby any orders or agreements respecting child support made on or after 1 May 1997 are premised on a tax-free system.

Appellate courts in British Columbia,[138] Alberta,[139] and New Brunswick[140] have determined that implementation of the *Federal Child Support Guidelines* on 1 May 1997 does not automatically warrant variation of a child support order under section 17 of the *Divorce Act* and section 14(c) of the Guidelines, although such variation may be warranted where there has been a material change of circumstances that was not in the contemplation of the parties at the time of the order.

In contrast, appellate courts in Nova Scotia,[141] Ontario,[142] and Saskatchewan[143] have determined that, subject to the provisions of sections 15.1(5) and 17(6.2) of the *Divorce Act* which relate to agreements or orders that include special provisions that directly or indirectly benefit a child and thereby render the application of the *Federal Child Support Guidelines* inequitable, a court has no residual discretion to deviate from the Guidelines once a material change has occurred, and such a change will exist where the agreement or order pre-dated the implementation of the *Federal Child Support Guidelines* and the amendments to the *Income Tax Act* on 1 May 1997.

As of 1 November 2000, section 14 of the *Federal Child Support Guidelines* was amended with the objective of making it clear that the implementation of the *Federal Child Support Guidelines* on 1 May 1997 itself constitutes a ground on which a court shall vary a pre-Guidelines child support order to conform to the *Federal Child Support Guidelines*, except in circumstances falling within the ambit of sections 17(6.2) to (6.5) of the *Divorce Act*.

However, no amendment was made to sections 15.1 and 17 of the *Divorce Act*. The question remains, therefore, whether the aforementioned conflict of appellate rulings across Canada has been resolved by the implementation of the November 2000 amendment to

---

137 See Carol Rogerson, "Of Variation, 'Special Provisions' and 'Reasonable Arrangements' — The Effect of Prior Orders and Agreements on Child Support Determinations under the Guidelines" (available on Quicklaw, Commentary, Syrtash Collection of Family Law Articles, SFLRP/1998-012).

138 *Wang v Wang*, [1998] BCJ No 1966 (CA); *Garard v Garard*, [1998] BCJ No 2076 (CA); *Meuser v Meuser* [1998] BCJ No 2808 (CA) (s 15.1 of *Divorce Act* does not compel variation of pre-Guidelines child support agreement); *Baker v Baker*, [1999] BCJ No 1605 (CA); *Fontaine v Fontaine*, [2000] BCJ No 366 (CA); *Roberts v Beresford*, [2006] BCJ No 291 (CA).

139 *Laird v Laird*, [2000] AJ No 18 (CA); see also *Dahlgren v Hodgson*, [1998] AJ No 1501 (CA); compare *Zuk v Zuk*, [1998] AJ No 1425 (CA); *Hunt v Smolis-Hunt*, [2001] AJ No 1170 at paras 61–62 (CA); see also *Turner v Turner*, [2000] AJ No 1158 (QB) for an extensive analysis of relevant jurisprudence.

140 *Parent v Pelletier*, [1999] NBJ No 391 (CA); *Lister v Gould*, [2000] NBJ No 419 (CA).

141 *MacKay v Bucher*, [2001] NSJ No 326 (CA).

142 *Wright v Zaver*, [2002] OJ No 1098 (CA); compare *Jordan v Stewart*, 2013 ONSC 902. See also *Colucci v Colucci*, 2019 ONCA 561.

143 *Dergousoff v Schille (Dergousoff)*, [1999] SJ No 192 (CA), Cameron JA, with Tallis JA concurring; Lane JA dissenting; see also *Bachorick v Verdejo*, [1999] SJ No 450 (CA).

section 14 of the *Federal Child Support Guidelines*. In *Danchuk v Danchuk*,[144] Saunders JA of the British Columbia Court of Appeal, stated:

> While it may be that the intention in amending s. 14 of the Guidelines was to encourage a Pan-Canadian interpretation, no change has been made to s. 17 of the *Divorce Act*, the section which underpins this Court's decision in *Wang v. Wang*. I am tentatively of the view that the change to s. 14 of the Guidelines should not affect the law as it is understood in this province. However I may leave that issue to another day, as I am satisfied that this court should vary the consent order to provide for child support, in any event.

Final resolution of the conflict of appellate court opinions may have to await an appeal to the Supreme Court of Canada or specific amendment of the *Divorce Act*.[145] However, the practical significance of the conflict has substantially diminished since the implementation of the *Federal Child Support Guidelines* on 1 May 1997, because the passage of time since then will typically have brought changes in the attendant circumstances regardless of the impact of the implementation of the Guidelines.

Prior to the 1 November 2000 amendment of the *Federal Child Support Guidelines*, several courts refused to vary a pre-1 May 1997 child support order where there would be no net gain to the applicant, having regard to the deductibility of the periodic support payments from the obligor's taxable income under the pre-1 May 1997 income tax regime.[146] Other courts refused to vary a pre-1 May 1997 child support order for the purpose of accommodating the changes effectuated by the implementation of the *Federal Child Support Guidelines* and the amendments to the *Income Tax Act* on that date, where only a modest tax advantage would ensue for the obligor but a serious disadvantage would be suffered by the recipient spouse and the child.[147] It had also been held that departure from the application of the *Federal Child Support Guidelines* is not normally allowed but may be judicially endorsed where continuation of a child support order that pre-dates 1 May 1997 will produce tax savings and the parties agree to invest the savings in a fund for the children's future education.[148] In the converse situation, where the application of the Guidelines would result in a higher after-tax amount being available by way of child support, courts have not hesitated to vary a pre-existing child support order by applying the Guidelines to produce the higher net amount.[149]

144 [2001] BCJ No 755 at para 20 (CA).

145 See now *Colucci v Colucci*, 2021 SCC 24.

146 *Tremblay v Tremblay*, [1997] OJ No 3805 (Gen Div); *Parsan v Parsan*, [1997] OJ No 3918 (Gen Div); compare *Browning v Browning*, [1999] NSJ No 174 (SC).

147 *Mingo v Mingo*, [1997] OJ No 4835 (Gen Div). See also *Hamm v Hamm*, [1998] NSJ No 139 (TD) (judicial refusal to disturb child support arrangements under separation agreement that pre-dated 1 May 1997 where tax deduction/inclusion regime was more beneficial for the children by reason of the primary caregiving parent's limited income). Compare *Suian v Suian*, [2002] BCJ No 1328 (SC).

148 *Corbett v Corbett*, [1997] NSJ No 525 (TD).

149 *Good v Good*, [1998] BCJ No 2316 (SC); *Whitley v Whitley*, [1998] BCJ No 4741 (SC); *Bainbridge v Bainbridge*, [2000] BCJ No 1603 (SC); *Erickson v Erickson*, [2001] BCJ No 71 (SC).

N. ADJOURNMENTS; STAY OF VARIATION PROCEEDING

A motion to vary child support may be dismissed with leave to re-apply after proper notice has been given and appropriate documentation and income calculations have been provided.

The court may, in its discretion, refuse to entertain an application to vary a subsisting support order until accrued arrears are paid or the court is satisfied that they cannot be paid.[151] The court may decline to stay an application to vary child support pending the appli cant's payment of costs ordered against him in previous proceedings where the application to vary is not frivolous, vexatious, or an abuse of process and valid reasons may exist for the failure to pay.[152]

O. INCREASE OF SPECIAL OR EXTRAORDINARY EXPENSES

Increased expenditures relating to a child's ill health may justify an upward variation.[153] The need of a child to complete her education may result in the variation of an order, which had provided periodic support "until she reaches the age of sixteen," to reflect the continuation of the support obligation until she completes her school and university education or attains the age of twenty-one, whichever comes first.[154]

An agreement between parents that they would provide their children with a private school education may result in the court increasing the amount of child support payable by a parent.[155] However, in the absence of such an agreement, a parent cannot unilaterally send a child to private school and claim the subsequent increase in school expenses as a material change in circumstances so as to justify an increase in child support.[156]

P. REDUCTION OF CHILD SUPPORT; TERMINATION OF EMPLOYMENT

The court will not usually grant an application to reduce the child support payable under an existing order when the obligor voluntarily terminates employment, is dismissed for just cause, intentionally reduces income, pursues a less lucrative career, or returns to university to further his or her education,[157] unless the change of status and consequential loss of income is short-term and will ultimately result in an increased capacity to pay child support.

---

150 *Vogel v Vogel*, [1997] MJ No 374 (QB).

151 *Winsor v Winsor* (1994), 7 RFL (4th) 30 (Nfld SC); *Eves v Eves* (1974), 17 RFL 57 (Ont HCJ).

152 *Matsell v Young* (1994), 5 RFL (4th) 203 (Ont Prov Div).

153 *Jardine v Jardine* (1992), 119 NSR (2d) 361 (TD).

154 *McFadyen v McFadyen* (1975), 22 RFL 140 (Alta SC); see also *Hickey v Hickey* (1987), 8 RFL (3d) 416 (Nfld TD).

155 See *Segal v Brown* (1988), 54 Man R (2d) 137 (QB); *Publicover v Publicover* (1989), 92 NSR (2d) 432 (Fam Ct).

156 *Zipchen v Edwardh* (1991), 35 RFL (3d) 45 (Ont Prov Div).

157 *Cheng v Cheng* (1994), 4 RFL (4th) 442 (BCCA); *KWA v AJB*, 2012 NBQB 119; *English v English* (1995), 16 RFL (4th) 250 (Sask QB); compare *Knox v Knox* (1992), 101 Sask R 152 (QB) (support reduced while father attending university). See also *Sookorukoff v Sookorukoff*, [1998] BCJ No 2892 (SC) (student); *Ottley v Ottley*, [1998] OJ No 1734 (Gen Div); compare *Bakken v Bakken* (1995), 11 RFL (4th) 246 at 249 (Sask QB).

158 *Hynes v Tierney-Hynes* (1993), 50 RFL (3d) 279 (Man CA), leave to appeal to SCC refused (1994), 2 RFL (4th) 431 (SCC). See also *Darvill v Chorney*, [1999] SJ No 551 (QB).

A reduction in support may, however, be ordered where the obligor voluntarily changes employment in a genuine attempt to improve his or her financial prospects but the change results in a diminished ability to pay.[159] An obligor's forced retirement is no basis for reducing child support obligations where a lump sum retirement benefit is available to meet the obligation.[160] The retirement of the obligor is no basis for terminating support where the child is still in need and the obligor still has the ability to pay.[161] The obligor's prospective retirement does not warrant cancellation of support payments when there is no current reduction in earnings.[162] The court frowns upon an obligor's voluntary early retirement unless it is justified in the circumstances.[163] A voluntary *mala fides* reduction of income or termination of employment is no basis for reducing child support obligations and may result in income being attributed to the obligor.[164] However, if a change of employment is undertaken in good faith, for reasons of health, better ultimate prospects, or any other valid reason, this may be a material change of circumstances in subsequent proceedings to reduce the amount of support.[165] Severance pay may be taken into consideration on an application to vary an order for support.[166] Support in the form of medical and drug coverage obtained without additional cost from an employer may be withdrawn upon the retirement of the payor.[167] Although a *bona fide* significant decrease in the obligor's income may justify a reduction in child support payments, the onus falls on the obligor to satisfy the court that the change is real and not one of choice.[168] A mother's obligation to pay support payments may be reduced during maternity leave.[169]

A reduction in the amount of child support on the basis of impecuniosity should be done only after an exhaustive scrutiny of the payor's circumstances, to ensure that the payor has not placed other obligations before his or her obligation to the children. A court will not make an order that is impossible to perform but will aim for child support as a priority over all other obligations.[170]

---

159 *Ronan v Douglas-Walsh* (1994), 5 RFL (4th) 235 (Ont Prov Div); *Christante v Schmitz* (1993), 1 RFL (4th) 142 (Sask QB).

160 *Droit de la famille—456*, [1988] RDF 64 (CA).

161 *Hodgert v Hodgert* (1993), 47 RFL (3d) 216 (Alta CA); *Vennels v Vennels* (1993), 45 RFL (3d) 165 (BCSC).

162 *LeBlanc v LeBlanc* (1995), 14 RFL (4th) 414 (NBQB).

163 *Osterkampf v Osterkampf* (1989), 22 RFL (3d) 153 (Alta QB); *Vennels v Vennels* (1993), 45 RFL (3d) 165 (BCSC); *Bartlett v Bartlett* (1988), 86 NSR (2d) 40 (TD); *Smith v Smith* (1992), 39 RFL (3d) 442 (Ont UFC); *Droit de la famille—614*, [1989] RDF 347 (CA); *Molnar v Molnar* (1991), 35 RFL (3d) 424 (Sask QB). And see *Grainger v Grainger* (1992), 39 RFL (3d) 101 (Sask CA).

164 *Fetterley v Fetterley* (1990), 24 RFL (3d) 61 (Alta CA); *Callison v Callison* (1992), 40 RFL (3d) 451 (BCSC); *Abbott v Taylor* (1987), 11 RFL (3d) 407 (Man QB), var'd (1988), 14 RFL (3d) 9 (Man CA); *KWA v AJB*, 2012 NBQB 119; *Swallow v Swallow*, [1988] OJ No 1106 (UFC); *Droit de la famille—1134*, [1987] RDF 464 (CS); *Kyler v Kyler* (1992), 42 RFL (3d) 315 (Sask QB).

165 *Newnham v Newnham*, [1993] OJ No 3193 (Gen Div).

166 *Richard v Richard* (1994), 2 RFL (4th) 395 (NBQB).

167 *Tully v Tully* (1994), 9 RFL (4th) 131 at 137 (Ont Ct Gen Div).

168 *Reid v Reid* (1992), 40 RFL (3d) 92 (BCCA).

169 *McCaffrey v Paleolog*, 2010 BCSC 627; *Savoie v Lamarche* (1990), 71 DLR (4th) 481 (Que CA); *Zieglgansberger v Venyige*, [2003] SJ No 791 (QB).

170 *English v English* (1995), 16 RFL (4th) 250 at 257 (Sask QB), Dawson J cited with approval by MacLean J in *McInnes v McInnes*, [1997] SJ No 10 (QB), wherein child support was reduced because of the obligor's impossibility of meeting his pre-existing support obligation.

A child's refusal to visit a parent may be insufficient cause to vary child support payments.[171]

Q. EFFECT OF REMARRIAGE OR UNMARRIED COHABITATION WITH THIRD PARTY

Variation of an order respecting children of the obligor's first marriage[172] is not necessarily warranted by an order for support respecting children of the obligor's second marriage, although a court may recommend that both primary caregiving parents be given notice of any future reconsideration of support for the children of either marriage and an opportunity afforded for them to participate so that the whole circumstances can be taken into account.

In the absence of a finding of undue hardship within the meaning of section 10 of the *Federal Child Support Guidelines*,[175] the fact that the obligor has remarried or lives in an unmarried cohabitational relationship is not a material change of circumstances that justifies variation of a prior order for child support. New obligations to a second family, standing alone, cannot be relied upon to avoid pre-existing child support obligations to the first family. The needs of the children cannot be relegated to second place behind the obligor's present marital or family obligations.[176] The fact that the obligor's household enjoys a lower standard of living than that in the recipient spouse's household constitutes no basis for a finding of undue hardship within the meaning of section 10 of the Guidelines, where any hardship is attributable to the voluntary decisions of the obligor and his new wife.[177]

R. SUSPENSION OF ORDERS

Temporary suspension of a child support order has been granted for a variety of reasons. Child support payable by a mother has been suspended for a period of several months to allow her to care for her newborn child without having to resume employment during that period.[178] The enforcement of arrears of child support may be suspended pending the obligor's resumption of employment[179] or the re-establishment of his business.[180] A court may order child support payments to be suspended until the payor becomes employed or until a

---

171 *Zipchen v Edwardh* (1991), 35 RFL (3d) 45 at 52 (Ont Prov Div) (application under *Family Law Act*, RSO 1990, c F.3); compare *Law v Law* (1986), 2 RFL (3d) 458 (Ont HCJ); *Kuntz v Kuntz* (1995), 10 RFL (4th) 246 (Sask QB).

172 As to the relevance of a new spouse's income to the application of the *Federal Child Support Guidelines* see Chapter 4, Section G(21).

173 *Meuser v Meuser*, [1998] BCJ No 2808 (CA) (consent order respecting children of second marriage; potential application of s 17(6.2) of the *Divorce Act* and "undue hardship" provisions of s 10 of the *Federal Child Support Guidelines* referred to).

174 *Diminie v Diminie*, [1995] OJ No 59 (Gen Div).

175 See Chapter 7, Section G.

176 *Baker v Baker*, [1999] BCJ No 1605 (CA).

177 *Lalonde v Bailey*, [1999] BCJ No 1342 (SC).

178 *Savoie v Lamarche* (1990), 71 DLR (4th) 481 (Que CA); *Zieglgansberger v Venyige*, [2003] SJ No 791 (QB).

179 *Bakken v Bakken* (1995), 11 RFL (4th) 246 (Sask QB); see also *Freund v Dent* (1995), 14 RFL (4th) 251 (Man CA).

180 *Krueger v Krueger*, [2004] SJ No 231 (CA).

fixed date, whichever comes first, but automatic reactivation of the order may be declared subject to the obligor's right to apply to extend the period of suspension if employment has not been found by the date fixed for revival of the order.[181] If child support obligations are suspended by reason of unemployment, it may be inappropriate for a court to order automatic revival of those obligations upon the obligor's resumption of employment if it is not known when employment will be found or what income it will generate.[182]

Child support arrears do not accumulate while the order is suspended. An order for the suspension of support payments precludes any future liability arising under the original order until such time as it is reinstated.[183]

Support for an adult child may be conditionally suspended if the payee does not respond to the payor's request for information regarding changes in the adult child's circumstances relevant to the issue of support.[184]

A present inability to pay arrears of child support does not justify remission of the arrears but may justify suspension of enforcement for a designated period[185] or an order providing for periodic payments on the arrears.[186]

Judicial postponement of child support obligations may be deemed inappropriate where the obligor had failed to provide complete financial disclosure.[187]

1) Suspension of Child Support as a Sanction for Denial of Parenting Time

Before the implementation of the *Federal Child Support Guidelines* on 1 May 1997, a court could reduce, suspend, or terminate the payment of support as a result of the deliberate actions of the primary caregiving parent in frustrating court-ordered parenting time for the other parent,[188] although it would decline to do so when it could harm the child.[189] It is not clear whether this judicial discretion to terminate or suspend child support payments continues to be exercisable under sections 15.1(4) and 17(3) of the *Divorce Act* or whether it has been abrogated by section 3 of the *Federal Child Support Guidelines*.[190]

Judicial opinion remains divided on the question whether a court-ordered reduction or suspension of child support is permissible as a sanction for a primary caregiving parent's wilful refusal to allow the other parent to exercise reasonable parenting time with their child. Some courts have asserted that a primary caregiving parent's misconduct is not a valid

---

181 *Daniel v Daniel* (1991), 38 RFL (3d) 70 (BCCA) (application under *Family Relations Act*, RSBC 1979, c 121).

182 *Edwards v Edwards* (1990), 26 RFL (3d) 142 (NSTD).

183 *Dwyer v Dwyer* (1986), 4 RFL (3d) 48 (Man CA); *Fraser v Fraser* (1990), 29 RFL (3d) 83 (NS Fam Ct).

184 *Bain v Bain* (1994), 7 RFL (4th) 451 at 459 (Man QB).

185 *White v White*, [2002] NSJ No 248 (CA); *Laxton v Laxton*, [1997] PEIJ No 87 (TD); *Kulyk v Srayko*, [1997] SJ No 639 (QB).

186 *Haisman v Haisman* (1994), 7 RFL (4th) 1 (Alta CA), leave to appeal to SCC refused (1995), 15 RFL (4th) 51 (SCC); *Cederland v Cederland*, [1997] NWTJ No 59 (SC).

187 *Felgner v Felgner*, [2004] BCJ No 30 (SC).

188 *Welstead v Bainbridge* (1994), 2 RFL (4th) 419 (Ont Prov Ct); *Kuntz v Kuntz* (1995), 10 RFL (4th) 246 (Sask QB); see also Julien D Payne, *Payne on Divorce*, 4th ed (Scarborough, ON: Carswell, 1996) at 441–42.

189 *McGregor v McGregor* (1994), 148 NBR (2d) 176 at 185–86 (CA); *Welstead v Bainbridge* (1994), 2 RFL (4th) 419 (Ont Prov Ct).

190 See *Johb v Johb*, [1998] SJ No 603 (CA); but compare *Chartier v Chartier*, [1998] SCR. No 79.

reason for reducing or suspending an order for child support.[191] Other courts have asserted that child support payments can be reduced or suspended as a last resort to compel due compliance with a prior parenting order.[192] As Ryan-Froslie J (as she then was) of the Saskatchewan Court of Queen's Bench concludes in *L (DAF) v L (DAF)*, "whichever approach is adopted, the best interests of the child must be the overriding consideration."[193] And in the words of Ricchetti J of the Ontario Superior Court of Justice in *Attard v Attard*, "[t]he common thread in these cases is that while child support is absolute, it may be reduced or eliminated due to [the denial of parenting time to] the parent paying child support only in extreme or unique circumstances such as where the [primary caregiving] parent has sufficient assets and income and the children will not be deprived of appropriate support and, generally, only where the children are older."[194]

S. REMISSION OF ARREARS

1) General Review

On an application to vary or rescind an order for child support, the court may order a retroactive variation with a consequential remission of all or part of the arrears that have accumulated but only where there has been a material change of circumstances within the meaning of section 17(4) of the *Divorce Act* and section 14 of the *Federal Child Support Guidelines.*

Two most important factors on an application to remit child support arrears are the obligor's ability to pay at the time when the arrears accrued and the obligor's current ability to pay. Although the circumstances may render it inappropriate to remit the arrears, the court may conclude that the obligor should be given some breathing space by staying enforcement of the arrears for a specified period, after which time the obligor shall pay a designated monthly amount against the arrears. The general policy is that the court should be strict in enforcing child support arrears in the absence of an inability to pay when the payments became due.[195] Child support is a right of the child and arrears of child support should not be remitted simply because the defaulter lacks the present ability to pay, where there is no indication of a permanent future incapacity to pay.[196] The ability to pay is determined not only by the income of the obligor but also by the assets in his or her possession.

The test for the judicial remission of arrears of child support is whether the obligor could not pay the support when it fell due, cannot pay now, and will not be able to pay in the

191 See, for example, *Lee v Lee* (1990), 29 RFL (3d) 417 (BCCA); *Gaulton v Hynes*, [2003] NJ No 44 (SC); *King v King*, [2008] NJ No 60 (SC).

192 See, for example, *Nielsen v Nielsen*, [2000] BCJ No 879 (CA); *Paynter v Reynolds* (1997), 34 RFL (4th) 272 (PEICA); *Fernquist v Garland*, [2000] SJ No 204 (CA); see also *Hutcheon v Bissonnette*, 2016 ONSC 2785; *Fernquist v Garland*, [2004] SJ No 584 (CA); *Fernquist v Garland*, [2005] SJ No 36 (QB).

193 2003 SKQB 132 at para 16.

194 2010 ONSC 810 at para 29; see also *Starr v Starr*, [2008] OJ No 6042 (SCJ); *Hutcheon v Bissonnette*, 2016 ONSC 2785.

195 *Sequeira v Sequeira* (1992), 44 RFL (3d) 95 (BCCA).

196 *Haisman v Haisman* (1994), 7 RFL (4th) 1 (CA); *Paterson v Paterson* (1995), 16 RFL (4th) 439 (Ont Prov Div); *Stadnyk v Stadnyk*, [2004] SJ No 355 (QB).

197 *Wharton v Wharton*, [1996] AJ No 1144 (QB); *Poyntz Estate v Poyntz*, [1998] OJ No 1024 (Gen Div).

future.[198] A court may grant a partial remission of child support arrears where the obligor's income fell short of the amount previously imputed.[199]

Pursuant to provincial legislation in British Columbia and Manitoba, the obligor has the burden of establishing on a balance of probabilities that it would be grossly unfair for the court to refuse to remit all or part of the arrears.[200] Subsection 174(2) of the *Family Law Act* (BC) prescribes the following test for cancellation or reduction of arrears of a maintenance order. The court must consider the following factors:

1) the efforts of the person responsible for paying support to comply with the agreement or order respecting support,
2) the reasons why the person responsible for paying support cannot pay the arrears owing, and
3) any circumstances that the court considers relevant.[201]

What constitutes "gross unfairness" will be determined on a case-by-case basis.[202] A change in circumstances, in addition to gross unfairness, is required in order for a court to reduce or cancel child support arrears.[203] In *Luney v Luney*,[204] the British Columbia Court of Appeal stated that simply showing a change in circumstances as required for a variation in maintenance *simpliciter* is not sufficient on an application to reduce or cancel arrears and "[c]ases in which arrears have been cancelled are rare, and generally speaking, this court has continued to hold the bar of 'gross unfairness' at a high level."[205] Therefore, to reduce or cancel arrears of child support or spousal support, the payor must prove first that there has been a material change in circumstances warranting the variation, and second that it would be grossly unfair not to make a reduction or cancellation.[206]

The burden of proof will not be discharged by an obligor who wilfully fails to realize his or her earning potential.[207] An obligor cannot reduce pre-existing child support obligations by a self-induced reduction of income.[208] An obligor is not entitled to profit from a situation

---

198 *Haisman v Haisman* (1994), 7 RFL (4th) 1 (CA); *Blyth v Brooks*, [2008] AJ No 100 (CA); *Duffett v Duffett*, 2010 NLTD(F) 16; *Lavoie v Lavoie*, [2005] NWTJ No 6 (SC).

199 *JFW v PCW*, [2001] AJ No 1145 (CA).

200 See *Luney v Luney*, 2007 BCCA 567; *Dubreuil v Poloway*, 2010 BCCA 297; *Semancik v Saunders*, 2011 BCCA 264; *NDS v JAS*, 2020 BCSC 1034 (arrears under interim order); *Sekhon v Sekhon*, 2020 BCSC 1422; *Dunbar v Saunders*, 2021 BCSC 193; *Byrne v Byrne*, [2004] MJ No 315 (QB); *LJC v JCG*, 2014 MBQB 246; *Bortolussi v Cafferty*, 2016 MBQB 54, citing s 54 of *The Court of Queen's Bench Act*, CCSM c C280 and s 61(4) of *The Family Maintenance Act*, CCSM c F20; *Dingle v Dingle*, 2018 MBQB 77; *Lievaart v Smith*, 2021 MBQB 73. See also *Sawatzky v Sawatzky*, 2018 MBCA 102.

201 *Louksr v Assadbeigi*, 2010 BCSC 116.

202 *DWT v BST*, 2016 BCSC 1978.

203 *JD v YP*, 2015 BCSC 321.

204 2007 BCCA 567.

205 2007 BCCA 567 at para 43; see *CCF v DWL*, 2010 BCSC 184 at para 168; *NP v IV*, 2013 BCSC 1323; *Duffett v Duffett*, 2010 NLTD(F) 16.

206 *Dunbar v Saunders*, 2021 BCSC 193 at para 62, Armstrong J.

207 *Garcia v Rodriguez* (1997), 29 RFL (4th) 329 (BCCA); *Longstaff v Longstaff* (1993), 86 BCLR (2d) 1 (CA); *MJW v MGW*, 2012 BCSC 768; *Boe v Boe* (1996), 26 RFL (4th) 190 (Sask QB).

208 *Ellis v Ellis*, [1999] NSJ No 78 (CA); *Quintal v Quintal*, [1997] OJ No 3444 (Gen Div); *Peter v Peter*, [1999] SJ No 376 (QB). See also *Verschuren v Verschuren*, 2014 ONCA 518.

of his or her own making.[209] Although remission of part of accrued child support arrears may be deemed appropriate where enforcement would be grossly unfair to the obligor, a court may decline to abrogate arrears with mathematical precision based on the obligor's actual income where the obligor failed to avail himself of opportunities for employment for which he was qualified.[210]

The "grossly unfair" principle has been found appropriate for consideration on review and variation applications under the *Divorce Act*.[211] Although the test of gross unfairness is the statutory criterion to be applied on an application to reduce or cancel arrears of child support that have accrued under a maintenance order, identical considerations apply in cases involving the enforcement and variation of a separation agreement.[212] A judge has jurisdiction to cancel or reduce child support arrears that have accrued under a separation agreement that has been registered in the Manitoba Court of King's Bench in accordance with section 53(3.1) of *The Family Maintenance Act* (Manitoba). Where no evidence is adduced to support a finding that it would be "grossly unfair and inequitable" not to reduce or cancel the arrears, the application for a judicial remission of arrears should be dismissed.[213]

Article 644 of the *Quebec Civil Code*,[214] which limits the jurisdiction of the court to remit support arrears, has been held to be inapplicable to a support order granted in divorce proceedings by reason of the doctrine of paramountcy.[215] However, many decisions across Canada respecting the discretionary judicial jurisdiction to remit arrears have regard to provincial statutory criteria, regardless of whether the order in question was granted pursuant to provincial legislation or pursuant to the *Divorce Act*. It is inequitable to apply different criteria to the two situations, although it may be legally improper to "directly" apply provincial statutory provisions to a variation proceeding that falls subject to section 17 of the *Divorce Act*. Provincial statutory criteria may, nevertheless, be used to assist the court in the exercise of its discretion under section 17 of the *Divorce Act*.[216] Given the general language of section 17 of the *Divorce Act* and section 14 of the *Federal Child Support Guidelines* respecting variation proceedings, there may be no apparent operational conflict such as is necessary to trigger the doctrine of paramountcy.

Child support obligors cannot arbitrarily determine how and where they will advance money for the benefit of their children or selectively pay discretionary expenditures in preference to the basic necessities that are the subject of a table amount child support order. An obligor who has spent money on the children in lieu of making required payments will

---

209 *Cowan v Cowan*, [2001] AJ No 922 (QB); *Nykoliation v Nykoliation* (1989), 60 Man R (2d) 307 (QB); *Filice v Filice*, [1998] OJ No 5271 (Gen Div).

210 *Rogers v Rogers*, [1999] BCJ No 2041 (SC).

211 *MacCarthy v MacCarthy*, 2015 BCCA 496; *Warren v Warren*, 2018 BCSC 1285.

212 See *Cotey v Cotey*, [2002] BCJ No 2726 (SC); *Clayton v Crosby*, 2011 BCSC 1000; compare *Cominetti v Cominetti*, [1993] BCJ No 1486 (SC).

213 *Riddell v Levesque*, [2001] MJ No 472 (CA).

214 SQ 1991, c 64.

215 *Droit de la famille—356* (1987), 8 RFL (3d) 349 (Que CA) (Monet and L'Heureux-Dubé JJA; compare dissenting judgment of Tyndale JA).

216 *Graham v Graham*, [1999] BCJ No 2819 (SC); *Horan v Horan*, [2003] BCJ No 550 (SC); see *contra Schipper v Maher*, [2002] MJ No 319 at para 51 (QB).

217 *Stadnyk v Stadnyk*, [2004] SJ No 355 (QB).

not be permitted to set off this amount against arrears owing,[218] nor will an obligor be permitted to set off arrears against costs incurred in exercising parenting time with the children,[219] but a court may refuse to enforce arrears of child support where the spouses made alternative arrangements that yielded more substantial benefits than the court order.[220] An obligor is not entitled to discharge periodic support payments by unilaterally deciding to pay expenses associated with continued occupation of the former matrimonial home by his or her dependent spouse and children, but a court may conclude that it would be unfair to ignore the payments entirely and a partial remission of arrears may be justified.[221]

In *Earle v Earle*,[222] Martinson J of the Supreme Court of British Columbia set out the following propositions with respect to applications to reduce or cancel child support arrears:

> *Basic Principles*
>
> a. There is a heavy duty on the person asking for a reduction or a cancellation of arrears to show that there has been a significant and long lasting change in circumstances. Arrears will not be reduced or cancelled unless it is grossly unfair not to do so.
>
> b. If arrears are not reduced or cancelled, the court can order a payment plan over time if convinced the arrears cannot be paid right away.
>
> *Examples*
>
> a. Arrears will only be cancelled if the person is unable to pay now and will be unable to pay in the future.
>
> b. A reduction or a cancellation requires detailed and full financial disclosure, under oath (usually in the form of an affidavit) that at the time the payments were to be made:
>
> i. the change was significant and long lasting and
>
> ii. the change was real and not one of choice and
>
> iii. every effort was made to earn money (or more money) during the time in question, and those efforts were not successful.
>
> c. Responsibility for a second family cannot relieve the parent of his or her legal obligation to support the first family.
>
> d. Delay in enforcement is generally not a legal basis to cancel or reduce child support arrears.[223]
>
> e. Judges will not cancel arrears because the other party gets a lot of money at once. Otherwise, people would be encouraged to not pay maintenance and rewarded for not paying maintenance.

---

218 *Walker v Walker*, [1999] AJ No 828 (QB); *Haisman v Haisman* (1994), 7 RFL (4th) 1 (Alta CA); *Craig v Griffiths* (1993), 119 NSR (2d) 329 (Fam Ct).

219 *Craig v Griffiths, ibid.*

220 *Jaworsky v Jaworsky*, [1997] BCJ No 2219 (SC); see also *Bale v Bale*, [2001] OJ No 4196 (SCJ).

221 *Kazoleas v Kazoleas*, [1997] AJ No 820 (QB).

222 [1999] BCJ No 383 (SC); see also *Luney v Luney*, 2007 BCCA 567; *Ghisleri v Ghisleri*, 2007 BCCA 512; *MacCarthy v MacCarthy*, 2015 BCCA 496; *NDS v JAS*, 2020 BCSC 1034 (arrears under interim order); *Sekhon v Sekhon*, 2020 BCSC 1422; *Dunbar v Saunders*, 2021 BCSC 193; *Ottesen v Ottesen*, 2022 BCSC 405; *ADJ v FJ*, 2022 BCSC 600; *Duffettv Duffett*, 2010 NLTD(F) 16; *KB v DJB*, 2013 YKSC 6. Compare *CAK v BDK*, 2018 BCPC 404 at paras 25–29.

223 Compare *Burgie v Argent*, 2014 BCSC 364.

f. Judges will not cancel arrears because the children were looked after in spite of the nonpayment.
g. Nor will judges cancel arrears because the children no longer need the money. The children should be compensated for what they missed.
h. An agreement between parents that the maintenance for the children does not have to be paid will not be considered.[224]
i. Lack of [parenting time] between a parent and child is not a legal reason to reduce or cancel arrears.
j. Judges will not reduce or cancel arrears because other money has been spent to buy things for the children.
k. The fact that a person did not have legal advice when the order was made or during the time when the arrears added up, is not, by itself, a reason to reduce or cancel arrears.

In *Schipper v Maher,*[225] Yard J of the Manitoba Court of Queen's Bench observed that, because both parents may formulate plans on the basis of the child support order that is granted, retroactive variation of the order to a time before the other parent had notice of the variation application is inherently unfair and should be considered with considerable caution. Justice Yard concluded that only in exceptional circumstances should a court order retroactive variation of a support order where the obligation of the payor and the right of the payee is decreased. What constitutes exceptional circumstances must be determined in light of the evidence. Justice Yard listed the following seven factors as relevant when a court addresses the possible remission of child support arrears:

(1) whether the obligor is at fault for failing to recognize an obvious obligation or by trying to avoid it;
(2) whether the obligee had contributed to the obligor's current situation and in particular whether it amounted to hoarding or resting on rights so as to render retroactive remission of arrears fair;
(3) whether the change of circumstances is catastrophic;
(4) whether the important principle of respect for court orders will be negatively affected by a retroactive variation;
(5) the obligor's delay in failing to previously apply for variation should not be rewarded;
(6) whether the obligor has demonstrated that he cannot now pay and will not in the future be able to pay the arrears; and
(7) any other factor raised in and demonstrated by the evidence to have an impact on the fairness equation.

In *Haisman v Haisman,*[226] the Alberta Court of Appeal drew an important distinction between child support and spousal support arrears. It concluded that a child should not be penalized by a primary caregiving parent's delay in enforcing a child support order and the obligor should not be allowed to shift the burden of child support to the primary caregiving parent or to the public purse unless there was an inability to pay over a substantial period of

224 But see *Llewellyn v Llewellyn,* 2002 BCCA 182 at para 19; *Burgie v Argent,* 2014 BCSC 364.
225 [2002] MJ No 319 (QB).
226 (1994), 7 RFL (4th) 1 (Alta CA), leave to appeal to SCC refused (1995), 15 RFL (4th) 51 (SCC).

time during which the child support payments fell due, and this inability would have necessitated a suspension of the child support order or a reduction in the amount of the order had a timely application for variation or rescission been instituted. In the absence of some special circumstance, a judge should not vary or rescind an order for the payment of child support so as to reduce or eliminate arrears unless he or she is satisfied on a balance of probabilities that the former spouse or judgment debtor cannot then pay, and will not at any time in the future be able to pay, the arrears. A present inability to pay child support arrears does not itself justify judicial remission of the arrears, although it may justify a suspension of their enforcement for a limited term or an order for instalment payments against the arrears. In appropriate circumstances, an indefinite suspension of the enforcement of child support arrears may be ordered.[227]

Dismissal of an application to rescind arrears does not, however, constitute an absolute bar to future rescission of those same arrears, provided that there is a subsequent change of circumstances sufficient to warrant such retroactive variation of the child support order. Section 17(4) of the *Divorce Act* requires proof of a material change of circumstances before variation can be ordered, but it does not limit the scope of the variation once a material change of circumstances is found to exist. The fact that a prior application did not meet the requisite statutory threshold does not, of necessity, determine the issue of whether rescission of those same arrears is justified in the context of subsequently changed circumstances. Issue estoppel is inapplicable where a change of circumstances has occurred since the prior variation application.[228] There must be some evidence, however, that indicates that the situation has changed since the last order was made respecting the arrears. The fact that the support order has been assigned to the government so that the enforcement of the arrears will only benefit taxpayers is insufficient justification for rescission of the arrears.[229]

In determining whether to remit arrears of child support, courts in Newfoundland and Labrador, Ontario, Saskatchewan, and Yukon consider the nature of the support obligation sought to be varied, the obligor's ability to pay the arrears when they fell due, the ongoing financial capacity of the obligor, the ongoing needs of the payee and child, unreasonable and unexplained delay by the payee in enforcing the arrears, unreasonable and unexplained delay by the payor in seeking relief from the support obligation, and whether enforcement of payment will cause hardship to the payor.[230]

---

227 *Haisman v Haisman*, (1994), 7 RFL (4th) 1 (Alta CA), leave to appeal to SCC refused (1995), 15 RFL (4th) 51 (SCC); see also *Khurana v Khurana*, 2011 ABCA 261; *Kaleniuk v Kaleniuk*, 2014 ABCA 18; *Blanchard v Blanchard*, 2019 ABCA 53; *SAL v BJL*, 2019 ABCA 350; *MacCarthy v MacCarthy*, 2015 BCCA 496; *Lynch v Lundrigan*, [2004] NJ No 195 (CA); *Smith v Oake*, 2012 NSSC 100; *Wilson v Larocque*, 2016 NWTSC 26; *DiFrancesco v Couto*, [2001] OJ No 4307 (CA); *JG v MG*, [2008] PEIJ No 33 (SC); *Henry v Henry*, 2017 SKQB 337; *Matthews v Matthews*, [2007] YJ No 12 (SC).

228 *DiFrancesco v Couto*, [2001] OJ No 4307 (CA); see also *Sutherland v Sutherland*, 2023 ABCA 121; *Matheson v Matheson*, [2003] OJ No 3857 (SCJ); *Tokar-Gaber v Gaber*, [2001] SJ No 680 (QB).

229 *Finn v Finn*, [2003] OJ No 927 (SCJ).

230 *NW v RP*, 2018 ABQB 392; *Lynch v Lundrigan*, [2002] NJ No 185 (SC); *DiFrancesco v Couto*, [2001] OJ No 4307 (CA); *Cooney v Catherwood Estate*, 2016 ONSC 525 (enforcement of child support arrears against obligor's estate); *Loshney v Hankins* (1993), 48 RFL (3d) 67 (Sask QB) (wherein the court also identifies the evidence that must be adduced when remission of arrears is sought); *Frigon v Lepoudre*, [2003] SJ No 575 (QB) (enforcement of agreement); *Henry v Henry*, 2017 SKQB 337; *LT v RU*, 2023 SKKB 74; *Matthews v Matthews*, [2007] YJ No 12 (SC).

Delay alone or lack of enforcement of a child support order is not a ground for cancellation of any arrears in the absence of demonstrable prejudice to the parent in default.[231] parent cannot avoid his or her child support obligation by delay and thereby foist a disproportionate share of the child rearing expenses on the primary caregiving parent or on the taxpayer.[232] The fact that the children are no longer eligible for support does not release the obligor from the payment of child support arrears.[233] The child support obligation should be enforced in recognition of the important principle that the parents are jointly responsible for child support and this responsibility cannot be avoided by delay.[234] A remission of part of child support arrears may be justified, however, where a parent's income was far less than anticipated over a substantial period of time[235] and insofar as a part of the alleged arrears relate to a child who ceased to be a child of the marriage within the meaning of section 2(1) of the *Divorce Act*.[236] An obligor will not be entitled to a remission of arrears simply because the amount is substantial[237] or because of obligations to a second family,[238] although realism demands that the enforcement of support obligations to the first family take account of the defaulter's obligations to a second family and avoid the consequences of forcing that family to seek social assistance.[239] An obligor who has remarried and started a new family cannot seek a full remission of child support arrears, where he or she has failed to make any effort to adjust his or her lifestyle to accommodate the obligations owed to the children of the first marriage. Child support responsibilities come before the personal interests of the obligor and may well necessitate a reduced lifestyle, but that is the price that must be paid if children are in need of support and the obligor has sufficient resources to pay the amount due under the *Federal Child Support Guidelines*.[241] Child support obligations take priority over other debts[242] and the obligor's freedom to make career and lifestyle choices.[243] An obligor's misconduct in thwarting the primary caregiving parent's previous attempts to collect the amount due may result in the court denying any remission of arrears.[244] Judicial remission of child support arrears is not justified by the primary caregiving parent's refusal to allow the other parent to exercise parenting time with the child nor by an agreement to waive child support if the exercise of parenting time is not sought by the other parent. An estranged relationship or the absence of

---

231 *Meyers v Meyers* (1995), 12 RFL (4th) 170 (BCCA); *Johnston v Johnston* (1997), 26 RFL (4th) 131 (CA); *Heiden v British Columbia (Director of Maintenance Enforcement)* (1995), 19 RFL (4th) 320 (BCCA); *Cho v Cho*, [2001] OJ No 3871 (CA).

232 *Weinstein v British Columbia (Director of Maintenance Enforcement)*, [1997] BCJ No 1361 (SC); *Johnston v Johnston* (1997), 26 RFL (4th) 131 (CA).

233 *Colucci v Colucci*, 2021 SCC 24.

234 *Johnston v Johnston*, [1997] BCJ No 418 (CA).

235 *Carter v Lloyd*, [1998] NJ No 244 (SC).

236 *Bourke v Heinze*, [1997] SJ No 118 (QB), considering *Cherry v Cherry* (1996), 22 RFL (4th) 432 (BCCA); see also *Schick v Schick*, [2000] NWTJ No 12 (SC).

237 *Greve v Greve* (1987), 11 RFL (3d) 180 (Ont HCJ).

238 *Cherry v Cherry* (1996), 22 RFL (4th) 432 (BCCA); *Johnston v Johnston*, [1997] BCJ No 418 (CA); *Earle v Earle*, [1999] BCJ No 383 (SC).

239 *Doole v Doole* (1991), 32 RFL (3d) 283 (Alta QB).

240 *Kerr v Kerr* (1992), 41 RFL (3d) 264 (Ont Ct Gen Div).

241 *Crosby v Crosby*, [1998] PEIJ No 96 (SC).

242 *Kerr v Kerr* (1992), 41 RFL (3d) 264 (Ont Ct Gen Div).

243 *Blake v Blake*, [2000] OJ No 2670 (SCJ).

244 *Munro v Munro* (1987), 50 Man R (2d) 24 (QB); *Wotherspoon v Wotherspoon* (1986), 56 Sask R 162 (QB).

any relationship between the obligor and the children in respect of whom support is payable constitutes no reason for remitting arrears of child support,[245] but a court may order remission of child support arrears where the primary caregiving parent made a conscious decision to absent herself and the child from the other parent's life and thereby frustrated that parent's attempts to pay support and establish contact with the child.[246] Arrears of support for adult children attending college may be remitted if the children do not diligently pursue their studies or if they have by their behaviour withdrawn from the payor's life.[247]

Enforcement or remission of support arrears may be treated differently according to whether they are arrears of spousal support or child support. Child support arrears are less likely to be remitted or suspended because parents are not permitted to waive their child's right to support and the conduct of a parent should not prejudice the rights of the child.[248] Children should not be prejudiced by parental agreements that purport to waive child support rights and obligations[249] or trade off support and the exercise of parenting time.[250] Parents cannot agree to waive child support arrears and thereby undermine the subrogation rights of the applicable provincial ministry.[251]

An application for remission of arrears of child support may be adjourned for lack of relevant financial information and the court may issue specific directions to remedy the deficiency.[252]

Where an obligor seeks to have support arrears discharged in whole or in part, he or she must provide relevant financial statements and income tax returns, a detailed explanation why the arrears accrued, a detailed description of the hardship that would result to the payor from enforcement of the arrears, particulars of the alleged change in the payor's financial capacity, including any steps that can be taken to reverse this change, particulars of any change in the ongoing needs of the child, particulars of any lump sum or periodic payments that the payor is prepared to make in order to induce the court to reduce or discharge the outstanding arrears, and, if the payor alleges that the payee is hoarding the arrears or the payor was induced to believe that no steps would be taken to enforce the arrears, the payor must provide evidence supporting such allegations. If the payor fails to provide the information outlined above, the payor's application may be summarily dismissed.[253]

---

245 *Duke v Duke*, [1998] BCJ No 1624 (SC).

246 *Allard v Hulst*, [1998] AJ No 407 (QB); *Turecki v Turecki* (1989), 19 RFL (3d) 127 (BCCA); *Hughes v Hughes*, 2014 BCCA 196; *Jones v Anhorn*, [2000] BCJ No 614 (CA); *Yee v Yee* (1997), 30 RFL (4th) 238 (Sask QB). See also *Johnson v Mayer*, 2014 MBQB 197.

247 *Droit de la famille—1204*, [1988] RDF 430 (CS).

248 *Haisman v Haisman*, (1994) 7 RFL (4th) 1 (Alta CA), leave to appeal to SCC refused (1995), 15 RFL (4th) 51 (SCC); *Shaw v Van Louie*, [1998] BCJ No 2415 (SC); *Nash v Nash* (1989), 77 Nfld & PEIR 22 (Nfld UFC); *Grimwood v Grimwood* (1988), 68 Sask R 179 (QB); compare *Kellar v Wallbank* (1993), 142 AR 214 (QB); *Tosky v Taphorn* (1991), 36 RFL (3d) 457 (Man QB). And see *contra PMB v MLB*, 2010 NBCA 5.

249 *Earle v Earle*, [1999] BCJ No 383 (SC).

250 *Lewis v Lewis*, [2002] BCJ No 778 (SC); *Ross v Vermette*, [2007] SJ No 483 (QB).

251 *DM v Alberta (Director of Maintenance Enforcement)*, 2014 ABCA 60; *Friesen v Friesen* (1995), 16 RFL (4th) 449 (Man QB); *Frim v Brasseur*, [2001] OJ No 4384 (SCJ); compare *Williams v Williams*, [2001] AJ No 1298 (QB).

252 *Demeria v Demeria*, [1998] SJ No 898 (QB).

253 *Loshney v Hankins* (1993), 48 RFL (3d) 67 (Sask QB).

Remission of arrears may be denied where the inability to pay is due to excessive spending on the part of the obligor.[254] The fact that the recipient spouse was in receipt of governmental income assistance while the arrears were accumulating is irrelevant to determination of the issue of cancellation of arrears.[255] Arrears that accumulate during the obligor's imprisonment may not be forgiven if the obligor will be able to pay them after being released from prison.

The Saskatchewan *King's Bench Rules* do not entitle the obligor to judicial remission of arrears under a child support order merely because the order has not been served on the obligor, nor is service of the order required as a precondition to the enforcement of an order under *The Enforcement of Maintenance Orders Act, 1997* (Saskatchewan). A parent has a legal obligation to support his or her child and to make proper financial disclosure when an application for child support is pursued. A parent cannot expect arrears of support to be cancelled simply because the parent failed to provide full and complete financial information prior to the order being granted. Partial remission of the arrears may, nevertheless, be appropriate, where the income previously imputed to the parent was more than that actually earned and the parent is unable to discharge the arrears that had been allowed to accrue.[257] The fact that the obligor was unaware of his or her support obligations is a factor to consider in an application to cancel arrears but it will not necessarily be determinative. A court may exercise its discretion to cancel arrears where, had the spouse been aware of the order and had a timely application been made, the applicant would have been successful.[258] Judicial remission of child support arrears may be deemed appropriate where the obligor did not appear on the original application with the result that an artificially high order was granted. An inability to pay at the time when the order was granted and the prospect that the obligor would be financially hamstrung in the future by the contribution of the arrears may be sufficient to justify cancellation of arrears.[259]

The obligor's assignment in bankruptcy is not sufficient reason to remit arrears of spousal and child support in the absence of full and timely disclosure indicating a past, present, and future inability to pay the arrears.[260]

Full or partial remission of arrears may be granted for a variety of reasons, the most compelling of which is the obligor's inability to pay by reason of unemployment, reduction of income, or illness.[261] Where the obligor has been a recipient of Employment Insurance

---

254 *Mackie v Mackie* (1994), 96 Man R (2d) 74 (QB).

255 *Weinstein v Weinstein* (1994), 1 BCLR (3d) 174 (SC) (application under *Family Relations Act*, RSBC 1979, c 121).

256 *Mills v Mills* (1994), 130 NSR (2d) 140 at 143 (TD); see also *Michel v Desjarlais*, [1999] NWTJ No 13 (SC); compare *Saunders-Roberts v Roberts*, [2002] NWTJ No 9 (SC); *Cote v Taylor*, 2013 ONSC 5428. For a detailed review of the impact of incarceration on the remission of arrears of child support, see the judgment of Bokenfohr J of the Alberta Court of Queen's Bench in *TM v ZK*, 2021 ABQB 588 at paras 49–78.

257 *Dooley v Knight*, [2003] SJ No 211 (QB). Compare *Gray v Rizzi*, 2016 ONCA 152.

258 *Kellar v Wallbank* (1993), 142 AR 214 (QB); compare *O'Donnell v Morgan*, [2001] NBJ No 66 (QB).

259 *Duke v Hickey*, [2001] NJ No 117 (SC).

260 *Miller v Miller*, [2000] AJ No 117 (QB).

261 *Doole v Doole* (1991), 32 RFL (3d) 283 (Alta QB); *Smith v Smith* (1990), 27 RFL (3d) 32 (Man CA); *Domanski v Domanski* (1992), 83 Man R (2d) 161 (CA); *Klassen v Klassen* (1993), 44 RFL (3d) 443 (Man CA); *Stacey v Hacking* (1993), 142 NBR (2d) 99 (QB); *Pidgeon v Hickman*, [2000] NJ No 44 (SC); *Rector v Hamilton* (1989), 94 NSR (2d) 284 (Fam Ct); *Propper v Vanleeuwen*, [1999] OJ No 2297 (SCJ); *Stewart v Stewart*, [2000] SJ No 149 (QB); *Turnbull v Turnbull*, [1998] YJ No 145 (SC). See also *Bernard v Bernard* [2008] AJ No 302 (QB) (partial remission of arrears accrued during obligor's imprisonment).

benefits and welfare payments during significant periods of time during which the arrears accrued, the court may remit part of the arrears so as to avoid subjecting the obligor to a virtual and perpetual state of penury until the children attain the age of majority and even thereafter.[262] Where an obligor is unemployed and has absolutely no ability to pay child support arrears or ongoing periodic child supports, a court may give the obligor "breathing space" by granting an order freezing the arrears and suspending future payments of child support until the obligor regains employment.[263]

Although judicial opinions have differed concerning the effect of spousal reconciliation on pre-existing support obligations, resumed cohabitation will ordinarily give rise to a remission of arrears during that period of cohabitation.[264]

In fixing the amount of arrears to be paid, the court may conclude that an adult child ceased to be a "child of the marriage" eligible for support under the existing court order when that child attained the age of majority and was no longer pursuing an education, although such a child may regain the status of a "child of the marriage" who is eligible for support under the *Divorce Act* upon resuming his or her education. The onus of proving that the status has been regained falls on the parent asserting that claim.[265]

Enforcement of some or all of the arrears may be postponed with a direction for them to be discharged by future instalment payments.[266] A schedule for payment must be realistic, having regard to the potential for compliance and its sufficiency in addressing the needs of the children for whose benefit the payments are being made.[267]

Remission of child support arrears may be appropriate where spouses make adjustments that erode the relevance of the court order.[268]

Remission of arrears of child support may not be warranted, notwithstanding a child's incarceration[269] or placement in foster care,[270] where the primary caregiving parent continues to incur ongoing expenses with respect to the child. Arrears may be rescinded for periods of time when the children were taken into care by a provincial agency.[271] The Guidelines may be helpful in fixing arrears of support but should not be used to increase the arrears payable. Remission of a significant portion of child support arrears may be justified by

1) the applicant's attempt to turn his life around in recent years,
2) the applicant's modest income and lack of assets,
3) the lack of benefit to the children, if arrears are paid,

---

262 *Turnbull v Turnbull*, [1998] YJ No 145 (SC); see also *Schick v Schick*, [2000] NWTJ No 12 (SC).

263 *Tatton v Tatton*, [1998] NBJ No 310 (QB).

264 *Wolf v Wolf* (1992), 41 RFL (3d) 391 (BCSC); *Barnesky v Barnesky* (1988), 16 RFL (3d) 450 (Man QB); *Michalchuk v Michalchuk*, 2013 ONSC 5978; *Stecyk v Stecyk* (1980), 16 RFL (2d) 255 (Sask Dist Ct), aff'd (1980), 23 RFL (2d) 53 (Sask QB).

265 *Wiome v Wiome*, [2002] SJ No 615 (QB).

266 *Young v Konkle* (1993), 1 RFL (4th) 211 (Alta QB); *Beaudoin v Beaudoin* (1993), 45 RFL (3d) 412 (BCSC); *Delorme v Woodlam and Dunn* (1993), 89 Man R (2d) 16 (QB); *Moffatt v Stewart* (1994), 5 RFL (4th) 142 (Ont Prov Div).

267 *Murchison v Fitzgerald* (1995), 14 RFL (4th) 386 (PEITD).

268 *Williams v Williams*, [1998] SJ No 216 (QB).

269 *LSP v JRP*, [2002] SJ No 35 (QB).

270 *Pellissey v Skeard*, [2003] NWTJ No 5 (SC).

271 *S(JM) v M(FJ)* (2005), 15 RFL (6th) 436 (Ont Div Ct); *Nadon v Stratton*, 2011 ONSC 3248.

4) considerable delay by provincial enforcement agencies,
5) the priority of current child support needs, and
6) outstanding debts to the Canada Revenue Agency.

No useful purpose is served by imposing financial responsibilities that the applicant cannot possibly meet.[272]

Remission of child support arrears may be justified by a finding of "undue hardship" under section 10 of *Federal Child Support Guidelines* where the obligor incurs unusually high expenses in relation to exercising parenting time with the children in consequence of the necessity of seeking employment outside Canada.[273]

Fluctuations in the obligor's income while arrears accrued may be relevant but are not determinative of the question whether there should be a remission of arrears.[274]

Section 17(1) of the *Divorce Act* empowers a court to retroactively vary an order for child support, but the court may decline to so exercise its discretion where the underlying basis is referable to the delay of the applicant in pursuing a claim for overpayments previously made. Limited retroactivity may, nevertheless, be deemed appropriate where the applicant shows a material change in the parenting arrangements over the preceding few months.[275]

In *Chen v Chen*,[276] an option was judicially extended to the husband to discharge his child support arrears by a cash payment or by transfer of his taxi licence to his wife, with the right to a leaseback at an agreed monthly charge.

Arrears may be set off against the obligor's equity in the matrimonial home upon the distribution of net proceeds after sale.[277]

2) Remission of Child Support Arrears: Response of the Supreme Court of Canada in *Colucci v Colucci*

In *Colucci v Colucci*,[278] Martin J, presenting the unanimous judgment of the Supreme Court of Canada, endorsed the following principles with respect to the jurisdiction of a court to retroactively decrease an order for child support on the basis of a material change of cir cumstances within the meaning of section 17 of the *Divorce Act* and section 14 of the *Federal Child Support Guidelines*, and also the court's jurisdiction to remit arrears of child support solely on the basis of the obligor's current and prospective inability to pay the arrears:

---

272 *M v M*, [1999] OJ No 5016 (SCJ); *Cudmore v Cudmore*, [2000] PEIJ No 39 (SC) (judicial refusal to order instalment payments against child support arrears pending discharge of child-connected debt).

273 *Smith v Masellis Smith*, 1999 ABQB 767 (remission of all arrears not justified where obligor had prior ability to pay).

274 *Pellissey v Skeard*, [2003] NWTJ No 5 (SC).

275 *Tweel v Tweel*, [2000] PEIJ No 9 (SC).

276 [2000] OJ No 1176 (SCJ).

277 *Bell v Bell*, [1999] BCJ No 1999 (CA) (transfer of title to matrimonial home envisaged); *Burns v Burns* [1988] OJ No 1698 (UFC); see also *Jukosky v Jukosky* (1990), 31 RFL (3d) 117 (Ont Ct Gen Div).

278 2021 SCC 24; see also *Peters v Atchooay*, 2022 ABCA 347; *Caillier v Viray*, 2021 BCSC 2512; *AF v RR*, 2021 NBCA 37; *Currie v Currie*, 2022 NSSC 23; *Folkerts v Folkerts*, 2021 SKQB 290. And see Chapter 11, Section K(4).

[113] To summarize, where the payor applies under s. 17 of the *Divorce Act* to retroactively decrease child support, the following analysis applies:

(1) The payor must meet the threshold of establishing a past material change in circumstances. The onus is on the payor to show a material decrease in income that has some degree of continuity, and that is real and not one of choice.

(2) Once a material change in circumstances is established, a presumption arises in favour of retroactively decreasing child support to the date the payor gave the recipient effective notice, up to three years before formal notice of the application to vary. In the decrease context, effective notice requires clear communication of the change in circumstances accompanied by the disclosure of any available documentation necessary to substantiate the change and allow the recipient parent to meaningfully assess the situation.

(3) Where no effective notice is given by the payor parent, child support should generally be varied back to the date of formal notice, or a later date where the payor has delayed making complete disclosure in the course of the proceedings.[279]

(4) The court retains discretion to depart from the presumptive date of retroactivity where the result would otherwise be unfair.[280] The *D.B.S.* factors (adapted to the decrease context) guide this exercise of discretion. Those factors are: (i) whether the payor had an understandable reason for the delay in seeking a decrease; (ii) the payor's conduct; (iii) the child's circumstances; and (iv) hardship to the payor if support is not decreased (viewed in context of hardship to the child and recipient if support *is* decreased). The payor's efforts to pay what they can and to communicate and disclose income information on an ongoing basis will often be a key consideration under the factor of payor conduct.

(5) Finally, once the court has determined that support should be retroactively decreased to a particular date, the decrease must be quantified. The proper amount of support for each year since the date of retroactivity must be calculated in accordance with the *Guidelines*. . . .[281]

[132] I will now consider the scenario in which a payor who has fallen behind on payments seeks full or partial rescission of arrears under s. 17 on the basis of a current and ongoing inability to pay. . . .

[134] In this category of cases, the prior child support order or agreement corresponds with the payor's income. The arrears accurately reflect the amount of support that the payor should have paid under the *Guidelines*, after all considerations, including any claim of hardship under s. 10, have been determined. In other words, the arrears represent sums that could have been paid at the time payments came due, but were not. The payor parent's claim for rescission is thus a form of "hardship" application, in which there has been no past change in circumstances justifying a retroactive decrease in the support obligation (*Barber*, at paras. 1516; *Brown*, at para. 43).

---

279 See *Reid v Chambers*, 2022 ABKB 634; *Bilodeau v Bilodeau*, 2022 ABKB 799; *Folkerts v Folkerts*, 2021 SKQB 290.

280 See also *PJM v RMS*, 2021 BCCA 260 at para 42; *Woodrow v Lepoudre*, 2022 SKQB 143.

281 See also *Murray v Murray*, 2021 ABQB 539; *SMP v TMP*, 2022 ABQB 226; *Hinz v Davey*, 2022 BCCA 232 (jurisdiction exists under British Columbia *Family Law Act* to retroactively vary agreement with respect to child support); *Abdullahi v Warsame*, 2021 ONCJ 449; *Savage v Kaczmarek*, 2022 ONSC 1313; *Mannell v Mannell*, 2023 ONSC 4209; *LT v RU*, 2023 SKKB 74.

[135] It follows that, under this third category of cases, the payor's ongoing financial capacity is the only relevant factor. The payor must therefore provide sufficient reliable evidence to enable the court to assess their current and prospective financial circumstances, including their employment prospects and any assets, pensions, inheritances or other potential sources of future capacity to pay.

[136] Courts have taken a highly restrictive approach to the availability of rescission or suspension of child support based solely on current and ongoing inability to pay (see, e.g., *Haisman*, at paras. 26–27; *Gray*, at para. 58; *C.L.W. v. S.V.W.*, 2017 ABCA 121, at para. 30 (CanLII); *Punzo*, at para. 46; *Blanchard v. Blanchard*, 2019 ABCA 53, at para. 32 (CanLII); *S.A.L. v. B.J.L.*, 2019 ABCA 350, 31 R.F.L. (8th) 299, at para. 12; *Semancik v. Saunders*, 2011 BCCA 264, 19 B.C.L.R. (5th) 219, at para. 25; *Mayotte v. Salthouse* (1997), 1997 ABCA 145 (CanLII), 29 R.F.L. (4th) 38 (Alta. C.A.), at para. 2; *Heiden v. British Columbia (Director of Maintenance Enforcement)* (1995), 1995 CanLII 1415 (BC CA), 16 B.C.L.R. (3d) 48 (C.A.), at paras. 10 and 13). These cases demonstrate that any discretion to grant relief in this context is narrow.

[137] This strict approach to rescission and suspension of arrears based on current inability to pay is justified. The interests of the recipient and child in certainty and predictability are paramount, as the payor has failed to comply with a court order or agreement without any "excuse for non-payment of support when it came due" (*Templeton*, at para. 47). The child's interest in a fair standard of support is subverted when the payor directs support elsewhere; in such circumstances, "the child effectively subsidizes the payor's improved standard of living" (*Walsh v. Walsh* (2004), 2004 CanLII 36110 (ON CA), 69 O.R. (3d) 577 (C.A.), at para. 25, with additional reasons (2004), 2004 CanLII 24259 (ON CA), 6 R.F.L. (6th) 432). The payor parent, on the other hand, "cannot argue that the amounts claimed disrupt his/her interest in certainty and predictability" (*D.B.S.*, at para. 98).

[138] Accordingly, in this third category of cases, the payor must overcome a presumption against rescinding any part of the arrears. The presumption will only be rebutted where the payor parent establishes on a balance of probabilities that — even with a flexible payment plan — they cannot and will not ever be able to pay the arrears (*Earle*, at para. 26; *Corcios*, at para. 55; *Gray*, at para. 58). Present inability to pay does not, in itself, foreclose the prospect of future ability to pay, although it may justify a temporary suspension of arrears (*Haisman*, at para. 26). This presumption ensures rescission is a last resort available only where suspension or other creative payment options are inadequate to address the prejudice to the payor. It also encourages payors to keep up with their support obligations rather than allowing arrears to accumulate in the hopes that the courts will grant relief if the amount becomes sufficiently large. Arrears are a "valid debt that must be paid, similar to any other financial obligation", regardless of whether the quantum is significant (Bakht et al., at p. 550).

[139] While we speak of rescinding arrears, the wording of s. 17 of the *Divorce Act* makes clear that what it authorizes is rescission of the underlying court order or a term of the order which gave rise to the unmet obligations. Thus a claim to cancel arrears asks the court to set aside an existing and accurate court order, replace it with another, and forgive what is otherwise a legally enforceable debt. That child support should not attract more leniency than other debts is reinforced by the range of maintenance enforcement regimes which exist across the country to enforce compliance with child support obligations. Governments in each province and territory have established administrative Maintenance Enforcement Programs ("MEPs")

(such as Ontario's FRO) to administer child support orders and help ensure children receive the support owed to them under court orders, including by taking enforcement action such as garnishing wages and suspending drivers' licenses (see, e.g., *Family Responsibility and Support Arrears Enforcement Act, 1996*, S.O. 1996, c. 31). Further, child support arrears are not released by an order of discharge under the *Bankruptcy and Insolvency Act*, R.S.C. 1985, c. B-3, s. 178 (1)(c); these debts are prioritized even where providing a clean slate is a competing policy consideration (see *Brown*, at para. 42; *St-Jules v. St-Jules*, 2012 NSCA 97, 321 N.S.R. (2d) 133, at para. 50). Thus, s. 17 of the *Divorce Act* is not to be used to reduce or vacate arrears too readily, as this would undermine the recognition and enforcement of serious legal obligations.

[140] The court has a range of available options when faced with proven payor hardship. A court's refusal to rescind arrears does not mean the payor must pay the entire amount immediately (*Earle*, at para. 24). If the court concludes that the payor's financial circumstances will give rise to difficulties paying down arrears, the court ought to first consider whether hardship can be mitigated by ordering a temporary suspension, periodic payments, or other creative payment options (*Haisman v. Haisman* (1993), 1993 CanLII 6988 (AB QB), 7 Alta. L.R. (3d) 157 (Q.B.) ("*Haisman* (Q.B.)"), at paras. 3233, rev'd on other grounds (1994), 1994 ABCA 249 (CanLII), 157 A.R. 47 (C.A.); *Templeton*, at para. 47; *Brown*, at para. 44). MEPs may also allow the debtor to enter into a reasonable payment plan where the debtor has fallen into arrears and is struggling to keep up with payments (see, e.g., *The Family Maintenance Act*, C.C.S.M., c. F20, s. 56.2(2) and (3); J. D. Payne and M. A. Payne, *Child Support Guidelines in Canada, 2020* (2020), at p. 476). After all, blood cannot be drawn from a stone — where the payor is truly unable to make payments toward the arrears, "any enforcement options available to the support recipient and the court are of no practical benefit" (*Brown*, at para. 44).

[141] While the presumption in favour of enforcing arrears may be rebutted in "unusual circumstances" (*Gray*, at para. 53), the standard should remain a stringent one. Rescission of arrears based solely on current financial incapacity should not be ordered lightly. It is a last resort in exceptional cases, such as where the payor suffers a "catastrophic injury" (*Gray*, at para. 53, citing *Tremblay v. Daley*, 2012 ONCA 780, 23 R.F.L. (7th) 91). I agree with Ms. Colucci that the availability of rescission would otherwise become an "open invitation to intentionally avoid one's legal obligations" (*Haisman* (Q.B.), at para. 18, citing *Schmidt v. Schmidt* (1985), 1985 CanLII 3777 (MB QB), 46 R.F.L. (2d) 71 (Man. Q.B.), at p. 73; R.F., at para. 57). Simply stated, how many payors would pay in full when the amounts come due if they can expect to pay less later? The rule should not allow or encourage debtors to wait out their obligations or subvert statutory enforcement regimes that recognize child support arrears as debts to be taken seriously.[282]

T. OVERPAYMENT

As a necessary corollary to the power to order a retroactive downward variation, section 17 of the *Divorce Act* confers the power to order repayment of overpaid amounts.[283] Where there has been an overpayment of child support, the court may, in appropriate circumstances,

282 See also *Shumate v Patrick*, 2023 ABKB 98; *Stark v Tweedale*, 2021 BCSC 1133; *BJ v VL*, 2022 BCSC 1496; *JM v LC*, 2022 PESC 35; *NTG v JAMG*, 2022 SKKB 264; *LT v RU*, 2023 SKKB 74.

283 *MoazzenAhmadi v AhmadiFar*, 2021 BCCA 126 at para 75, Harris JA.

order a set-off or a repayment or otherwise make a necessary adjustment between the spouses or former spouses.[284] However, a court should not impose a financial burden on the recipient that will penalize the child,[285] nor should it excuse the conduct of a payor who overpays and knowingly does nothing about it for a substantial period of time that is likely to generate a hardship in the event of repayment.[286] Variation of a child support order may be justified by a change in the parenting arrangements resulting from the children's change of residence, but the court may decline to order that resulting overpayments be reimbursed where the recipient parent needed lengthy rehabilitation to get back on her feet and the payments received had been used for the benefit of the children.[287]

Parents who receive payments for expenses under section 7 of the *Federal Child Support Guidelines* have an obligation to terminate those payments when the expense is no longer incurred; a failure to do so warrants a reimbursement order.[288]

Section 17(1) of the *Divorce Act* empowers a court to retroactively vary an order for child support, but the court may decline to so exercise its discretion where the underlying basis is referable to the delay of the applicant in pursuing a claim for overpayments previously made. Limited retroactivity may, nevertheless, be deemed appropriate where the applicant shows a material change in the parenting arrangements over the preceding few months.[289]

A court may order reimbursement of overpayment of child support by means of an order for retroactive variation of the order, but should decline to do so when the payments were made with knowledge of the material facts.[290]

Retroactive variation of a child support order by way of an order for lump sum reim bursement of overpayments may be deemed appropriate because of the child support recipient's failure to disclose reinstatement of a provincial financial subsidy for the disabled adult child.[291]

---

284 *Willis v Willis*, 2010 ABQB 534; *Egan v Egan*, [2002] BCJ No 896 (CA); *GMW v DPW*, 2014 BCCA 282; *Moazzen-Ahmadi v Ahmadi-Far*, 2019 BCSC 1772, aff'd 2021 BCCA 126; *McLachlan v McLachlan*, 2010 MBQB 189; *Newman v Tibbetts*, [2005] NBJ No 135 (CA); *Pitcher v Pitcher*, [2005] NJ No 352 (SC) (overpayments deemed to be monies to aid younger child's stabilization between school and job); *Locke v Goulding*, 2021 NLSC 8; *Gaetz v Jakeman*, [2005] NSJ No 167 (CA) (reimbursement of overpayment denied); *Mastin v Mastin*, 2019 NSSC 248; *Wouters v Wouters*, 2013 NWTSC 9; *Smith v Smith*, 2012 ONSC 1500 (set off against ongoing child support); *Paynter v Sackville*, [2004] SJ No 422 (QB) (reimbursements of s 7 expenses for child care). Compare *Gartley v Thibert*, [2002] OJ No 3313 (SCJ) (jurisdiction to order repayment judicially questioned); see also *Hodgkinson v Hodgkinson*, 2010 SKQB 96 (reimbursement of overpayments not permissible after child ceases to qualify as a "child of the marriage"); see also *Smith v Smith*, 2015 SKQB 238. 2 And see *Edwards v Edwards*, 2018 ONSC 6869 at paras 54–55.

285 *MacKinnon v MacKinnon*, 2015 NBQB 1324; *CG v TL*, 2024 NLCA 1; *Murphy v Hancock*, 2011 NSSC 247.

286 *Fleury v Fleury*, 2009 ABCA 43; *Janes v Janes*, [2002] NJ No 151 (SC); *Stupak v Stupak*, [1997] SJ No 302 (QB); see also *Christiansen v Bachul*, [2001] AJ No 171 (QB); *H(UV) v H(MW)*, 2008 BCCA 177; *Mannell v Mannell*, 2023 ONSC 4209; *Droit de la famille — 101052*, 2010 QCCA 942.

287 *Flynn v Halleran*, [2004] NJ No 457 (SC).

288 *Harder v Harder*, [2003] SJ No 429 (QB). As to the remedies available when a recipient spouse fails to use funds received as a contribution to the payment of a child's special and extraordinary expenses for their intended purpose, see *Dorsett v Levy*, 2016 ONSC 345.

289 *Tweel v Tweel*, [2000] PEIJ No 9 (SC).

290 *Collison v Collison*, [2001] BCJ No 2080 (SC).

291 *Hanson v Hanson*, [2001] SJ No 560 (QB).

An order for child support may be reduced and backdated, with overpayments to be deducted from future payments, subject to a designated maximum monthly deduction.[292] Overpayments of support for one child may be set off against the payor's share of section 7 expenses respecting other children.[293] A court may refuse to set off an overpayment under a previous order against a current variation order for child support.[294]

A belated application for reimbursement of an alleged overpayment of child support will be dismissed where the court would be required to speculate on outdated facts.[295]

On an application by the father for reimbursement of overpayments of child support paid to the mother pursuant to a court order granted on divorce, the amount repayable pursuant to sections 8(7) and 8(8) of the *Family Responsibility and Support Arrears Enforcement Act* (Ontario) is conditioned on whether the mother held a *bona fide* belief that the adult child was entitled to ongoing support.[296]

Courts in Saskatchewan have not been particularly accommodating to applications for retroactive variation of child support orders under the *Divorce Act* that seek to recover overpayments that have accumulated over a significant period of time. It would be overly doctrinaire to state that a delay will always operate as a waiver by or an estoppel against a parent who has overpaid child support. Nonetheless, the realities of expenses involved in the raising of children usually militate against a retrospective accounting with respect to overpayments. This is especially true when the period of overpayment is a lengthy one. Apart from the difficulty of reconstructing a meaningful accounting, considerable delay in seeking reimbursement is likely to result in an unmanageable level of instant arrears that would place the payor in jeopardy and operate to the detriment of the child. Courts should also act with caution when they face an application by a parent who seeks to impose a debt or financial burden on the primary caregiving parent as a result of informal changes to parenting protocols. Sensitivity to the issue is heightened when such a financial burden would, in turn, penalize the child.[297]

Where a child support order is discharged on the basis that the payor is not the father of the child, section 44 of *The Children's Law Act, 1997* (Saskatchewan) does not confer jurisdiction on the court to order the repayment of child support previously paid. If the payor is to recover the payments made prior to the discharge of the order, he must pursue a remedy at common law, if one is available.[298]

In *Moazzen-Ahmadi v Ahmadi-Far*,[299] it was concluded that section 17 of the *Divorce Act* provides courts with the power to vary support orders both prospectively and retroactively and so they have the power to retroactively decrease support, and if further authority should be necessary, it could be found in the inherent jurisdiction of the court. It was also concluded

---

292 *Reynolds v Reynolds* (1988), 14 RFL (3d) 340 (Ont Prov Ct); see also *Purtill v Demarchi*, [1999] OJ No 5299 (SCJ) (overpayment arising from retroactive order to be invested in registered educational plan or some other form of trust fund for the children).

293 *McNulty v McNulty*, [1998] MJ No 518 (QB).

294 *Rousseau v Rousseau*, [1999] SJ No 76 (QB).

295 *Oswald v Oswald*, [2001] MJ No 73 (QB).

296 *Gartley v Thibert*, [2002] OJ No 3313 (SCJ).

297 *Lacey v Fitzgerald*, [2003] SJ No 735 (QB).

298 *Howland v Armstrong*, [2003] SJ No 621 (QB).

299 2019 BCSC 1772 at paras 40–45, aff'd 2021 BCCA 126.

that while courts may order repayment of overpaid support in appropriate circumstances, the special nature of support and the unique circumstances involved in family law require that the factors in *DBS v SRG; LJW v TAR; Henry v Henry; Hiemstra v Hiemstra,*[300] be taken into account in making any repayment order. In *Meyer v Content,*[301] Chappel J of the Ontario Superior Court of Justice concluded that a court should consider the following factors in dealing with a claim for reimbursement of overpayments of child support:

1. The amount of the overpayment;
2. The overall financial situation of the parties, including their incomes and their net worth;
3. The extent to which each party continued to support the child financially during the period of uncertainty regarding the outcome of the support dispute, and whether it was objectively reasonable for them to do so;
4. Whether an order requiring the support recipient to repay all or part of the child support overpayment would cause the recipient hardship;
5. The overall condition, means, needs and circumstances of the child of the relationship, and the extent if any to which the child's situation may impact on the level of hardship which a reimbursement order would create for the recipient;
6. Conversely, whether an order releasing the recipient from repaying the overpayment in full or in part would result in hardship for the support payor;
7. Whether there is a reasonable explanation for any delay on the part of the payor in commencing proceedings to request reimbursement;
8. Whether the support recipient has a reasonable explanation for why they continued to accept support during the time frame when the overpayment accrued;
9. Any evidence of blameworthy conduct on the part of either party relevant to the overpayment issue;
10. Whether the recipient made reasonable efforts to keep the payor apprised of changes in the child's situation which were relevant to the overpayment issue;
11. Conversely, whether the payor made reasonable efforts to keep abreast of developments in the child's life and maintain contact with the recipient so as to enable discussion and negotiation about issues involving the child;
12. The extent to which either party attempted to make efforts to resolve any concerns about overpayment with the other party or through the *Family Responsibility Office*; and
13. Evidence of any oral or written agreement between the parties during the period when the overpayment arose that sheds light on the intentions of the parties respecting child support payments during that time.

Justice Chappel acknowledged that "[n]one of these factors is determinative, and the weight if any that should be given to any factor depends on the unique facts of the case."

300 2006 SCC 37.

301 2014 ONSC 6001 at para 100; see also *Saroli v Grette*, 2022 ONSC 3560.

U. VARIATION OF CONSENT ORDERS

A consent order[302] constitutes a child support order within the meaning of sections 2(1) and 15.1(1) of the *Divorce Act* and is consequently variable both prospectively and retroactively pursuant to section 17(1)(a) of the *Divorce Act* in the event of a material change of circumstances.[303] In determining whether the conditions for variation exist, the court must be satisfied that the change of circumstances is such that, if known at the time, would likely have resulted in different terms.[304]

Although consent orders are not lightly disturbed, courts have an overriding discretion when dealing with child support to vary such orders.[305]

A consent order granted prior to the implementation of the *Federal Child Support Guidelines* on 1 May 1997 may be varied in light of a subsequent change of circumstances, notwithstanding the primary caregiving parent's purported waiver of child support for the foreseeable future.[306]

A consent order that provides higher child support than that payable under the Guidelines does not foreclose a subsequent application to reduce the amount where the obligor's ability to pay has been significantly reduced for reasons beyond his or her control.[307]

Courts are loathe to interfere with consent orders that embody a comprehensive settlement of all outstanding issues, including child support, because what is given up or accepted in one aspect has an inevitable impact on what is given up or accepted in another. A court may, nevertheless, vary the child support arrangements where the consent order has become unreasonable in light of the obligor's reduced income and a judicial refusal to vary the amount of child support payable would be grossly unfair.[308]

A consent order for child support may be set aside because of a parent's material non-disclosure of his or her financial circumstances, in which event retroactive and ongoing child support may be fixed on the basis of income imputed to that parent for unreasonable business expenses and income splitting with a new spouse.[309]

On an application to vary a consent order for child support in an amount higher than that payable under the *Federal Child Support Guidelines*, the applicant must prove a material change in circumstances that warrants variation of the order.[310] A consent order, like any other order, once made is assumed to be valid and correct unless overturned on appeal. If the payor's employment income was not used as the foundation for the consent order, changes in employment status and earnings will have limited relevance on the variation application.[311]

---

302 See Chapter 10.

303 *MKR v JAR*, 2015 NBCA 73; *Alexander v Alexander*, [1999] OJ No 3694 (SCJ).

304 *JKAW v CW*, [1999] BCJ No 2845 (SC), Warren J, citing *Willick v Willick*, [1994] 3 SCR 670 at 688, Sopinka J; *Gibson v Gibson*, [2002] OJ No 1784 (SCJ). See also *Gibson v Gibson*, 2011 ABQB 564.

305 *Newman v Thompson* (1997), 30 RFL (4th) 143 (Man CA).

306 *Todd v Morine*, [1999] NBJ No 178 (QB).

307 *Biggar v Biggar*, [1998] SJ No 570 (QB).

308 *Rogers v Rogers*, [1999] BCJ No 2041 (SC).

309 *Ziomek v Selva*, [2001] OJ No 1457 (SCJ).

310 *MLP v MJM*, 2012 BCCA 395.

311 *Empey v Groves*, [2001] BCJ No 2544 (CA) (appeal dismissed where the chamber's judge used the wrong criterion for dismissing the payor's application to vary on the basis of his reduced income, but the appellate court was not persuaded that the chambers judge erred in the result).

Variation of a consent order without need for proof of a material change of circumstances is permissible, where the order envisaged adjustment to the calculation of the obligor's income upon production of relevant financial information.[312] Rescission of a consent order for child support may be granted on proof of common mistake, misrepresentation, or some other factor that would invalidate a contract.[313]

A consent order for child support may be vitiated by fraud. Proof of fraud requires a false statement made (1) knowingly, or (2) without belief in its truth, or (3) recklessly careless whether it is true or false. Fraud must be proved strictly but the negligence of the representee affords no defence to the representor. The party alleging fraudulent misrepresentation must prove that the false statement was relied upon in order to invoke a legal remedy. Even if fraud is found, the court will refuse to rescind the consent order where the amount of child support actually paid is no less than the amount calculated as payable in light of the court's findings as to the annual income of the obligor over the years in question. In calculating the amount payable prior to the implementation of the *Federal Child Support Guidelines* on 1 May 1997 and the *Ontario Child Support Guidelines* on 1 December 1997, the court should use a means and needs analysis, but Ontario courts have never adopted the *Levesque* formula that was endorsed by the Alberta Court of Appeal in 1994, which applied a "litmus test" whereby child support would be calculated on the basis of 32 percent of the gross income of the parents in the case of a two-children family. In applying a means and needs analysis, an Ontario court may find the Guidelines instructive in examining the amount of child support payable prior to their enactment. The amounts fixed by the Guidelines should be grossed up for income tax to offset the fact that the Guidelines amounts are independent of tax. Given a judicial finding that no financial loss has been sustained in consequence of the fraudulent misrepresentation found to exist, the application to set aside the consent order for child support will be dismissed.[314]

V. VARIATION UNDER PROVINCIAL LEGISLATION

The threshold for a variation application under *The Family Maintenance Act, 1997* (Saskatchewan) is a "change of circumstances" as defined in the Guidelines, not a "material change of circumstances" as set out elsewhere in the Act.[315]

W. VARIATION PENDING APPEAL

The launching of an appeal does not preclude an application to vary a child support order in light of a material change of circumstances since the making of the order. An appellate court addresses the appropriateness of the trial judge's order at the time when it was granted; a variation proceeding should be instituted to address any material change that thereafter occurs.

312 *Egan v Egan*, [2002] BCJ No 896 (CA).

313 *Gibson v Gibson*, [2002] OJ No 1784 (SCJ).

314 *Danylkiw v Danylkiw*, [2003] OJ No 431 (SCJ).

315 *Carson v Buziak*, [1998] SJ No 229 (QB).

316 *Gordon v Solmon* (1995), 16 RFL (4th) 403 (Ont CA); *Huisman v Huisman* (1995), 17 RFL (4th) 229 (Ont Ct Gen Div).

X. TYPES OF ORDER

The types of order that may be granted in a variation proceeding and the inclusion of terms or conditions that may be incorporated therein correspond to those applicable to original applications.[317] The powers of variation, rescission, and suspension conferred by section 17 of the *Divorce Act* and section 14 of the *Federal Child Support Guidelines* are not confined to orders for unsecured periodic payments and may be exercised with respect to orders for the payment of a lump sum and orders to secure support.[318]

In a variation proceeding, a court may substitute a lump sum support order for a pre-existing order for periodic payments. Such substitution may provide an appropriate means of preventing further contentious litigation between the spouses.[319]

Y. EFFECT OF DEATH

A variation order for child support may be declared binding on the estate of the obligor.[320] The omission to include such a clause in the divorce judgment, where the separation agreement had so provided, may be sufficient to warrant a variation of the judgment to provide that the deceased parent's estate shall be bound by the order.[321]

The death of the child may constitute a material change in circumstances as required by subsection 17(4) of the *Divorce Act* to allow arrears to be remitted, insofar as they accrued after the child's death. The purpose of support is to meet ongoing expenses. If the child is no longer alive, there can be no reason for child support to continue.[322]

Section 55(1) of the *Family Law Act* (Alberta) provides that a child support order terminates on the adoption or death of the child except where the court orders otherwise. Pursuant to section 55(2) of the Act, the termination of a child support order does not affect any arrears owing under the order before it is terminated.[323]

Where a payor who has a duty to pay support under an agreement or order dies, and the agreement or order is silent about whether that duty continues after the payor's death and is a debt of his or her estate, section 171(3) of the British Columbia *Family Law Act* now allows the recipient of that support to apply for an order that the duty to pay support continues despite the death of the payor and is a debt of the estate, based on the factors in section 171(1) of the Act.[324]

---

317 *Divorce Act*, s 17(3).

318 See *Lavoie v Yawrenko* (1992), 44 RFL (3d) 89 (BCCA).

319 *Droit de la famille—913* (1990), 30 RFL (3d) 83 (Que CS).

320 *McKee v McKee* (1994), 153 AR 8 (QB); *Brickman v Brickman* (1987), 8 RFL (3d) 318 (Man QB). And see Chapter 11, Section H(7).

321 *Duplak v Duplak* (1988), 54 Man R (2d) 70 (QB); compare *Despot v Despot Estate* (1992), 42 RFL (3d) 218 (BCSC).

322 *King Estate v King* (1994), 8 RFL (4th) 380 at 391 (NBQB).

323 *Re SNL*, [2005] AJ No 1845 (QB).

324 *Bouchard v Bouchard*, 2018 BCSC 1728 at para 34, Donegan J.

Z. AUTOMATIC ANNUAL VARIATION

Sections 25.01 to 25.1(7) of the *Divorce Act* authorize the federal Minister of Justice to enter into an agreement with a province to allow for the administrative calculation and recalculation of child support as prescribed in those sections.[325]

The *Child Support Recalculation Program Regulation*, Alta Reg 287/2009, was enacted pursuant to the *Family Law Act* not the governing *Divorce Act*. However, section 25.1 of the *Divorce Act* allows Canada to enter into an agreement authorizing a provincial administrative service to recalculate child support ordered under that Act, based on updated income information. Canada and Alberta signed a section 25.1 agreement in early 2010.[326] There is nothing in the Regulation that suggests that a party is estopped from making an application to vary the calculation when new information about a payor's income comes to light. Since March 2015, Alberta's *Child Support Recalculation Program Regulation*, Alta Reg 287/2009, as amended, has imposed a requirement in Alberta for every child support order to include a reference to the support recalculation program.[327] Addressing the Alberta *Child Support Recalculation Program* in *TDM v JDM*,[328] Mandziuk J of the Alberta Court of Queen's Bench stated:

> [125] The efficacy of the CSRP was discussed by our Court of Appeal in *Pinter v Pinter*, 2016 ABCA 58:
>
> > [21] A child's entitlement to child support fluctuates with a parent's income, which led Alberta through its legislators to create the Child Support Recalculation Program. The program was conceived as an efficient, accessible, inexpensive alternative to court proceedings for families with children requiring ongoing child support recalculations (Alberta, Legislative Assembly, Hansard, 27th Leg, 1st Sess, No 27e (28 May 2008) at 1049 (Robin Campbell)). The program annually recalculates a parent's child support using the applicable guideline amounts from the parent's most recent income information: *Family Law Act, SA 2003, c F-4.5*, s 55.11.
> >
> > [22] The program has limitations and it has been recognized that it is not a suitable non-court alternative for all parties: *DPH v CAH*, 2015 ABQB 699 at paras 7-11; *JT v TT*, 2015 ABQB 648 at para 17; *Gonek v Gonek*, 2011 ABQB 166 at paras 29-30. It follows that a court's jurisdiction to recalculate a child support order under s 17 of the *Divorce Act* cannot be ousted by the program. Simply put, the Court must do whatever the program cannot: see, for example *Child Support Recalculation Program Regulation*, Alta Reg 287/2009, s 16.

---

325 See also s 26(1)(c) of the *Divorce Act* (regulation-making authority of Governor in Council). And see *Provincial Child Support Service Regulations*, SOR/2020-250.

326 *Bohn v Bohn*, 2016 ABCA 406 at paras 36–37. As to the authority of the federal Minister of Justice to enter in an agreement with a province to allow for the administrative calculation of initial child support amounts, see s 25.01 of the *Divorce Act*. See also s 26(1)(c) of the *Divorce Act* (regulation-making authority of Governor in Council). And see *Provincial Child Support Service Regulations*, SOR/2020-250.

327 See *Uba v Uba*, 2016 ABQB 19 at para 7, Veit J. As to legislative and regulatory changes respecting the recalculation of child support that came into effect in Manitoba on 1 July 2020, see *Ducharme v Burym* 2020 MBQB 160. As to Ontario, see *Child Support Guidelines*, O Reg 190/15.

328 2020 ABQB 353.

> [126] That is the situation here. The Court must do what CSRP cannot do.
>
> One of the limits of the recalculation program is that it cannot perform retroactive recalculations: *DPH v CAH* at para 9. Nor can the program award interim spousal support, or determine whether an expense is a proper s 7 expense, or whether post-secondary expenses are properly proportionately shared, all of which forms of relief were sought . . . in this case.
>
> [127] The CSRP calculations are no bar to the Court's determination of child support:
>
> There is nothing in the [*Child Support Recalculation Program*] *Regulation* that suggests that a party is estopped from making an application to vary the calculation when new information about a payor's income comes to light, as it did in this case. There is no merit to this ground of appeal. The Father acted promptly when made aware that the Corporation's income could be used to vary the appellant's Line 150 (now Line 15000) income for *Guideline* purposes (*Bohn* at para 37).
>
> [128] Therefore, the *Guideline* amounts will apply during the time periods I have identified herein (and will summarize shortly) and based on the Line 150 (now Line 15000) income of the Father for each year.

When ordering child support, the court may include specific directions for an administrative recalculation.[329] In order to avoid the necessity of future applications to vary a child support order, the court may devise a procedure that will enable the parents to recalculate child support and their respective ongoing contributions to special or extraordinary expenses under section 7 of the *Federal Child Support Guidelines*.[330]

Similar to the Alberta recalculation process described above, Newfoundland and Labrador also uses a recalculation process. The Newfoundland and Labrador process is authorized by the *Child Support Service Regulations* that describe the recalculation process, including the ability of a party to file a notice of objection. While recalculation and variation are both possible avenues to effect a change in child support payments, the recalculation process and the variation application are two distinct proceedings that coexist and do not serve the same purpose. An application for variation can be made notwithstanding a recalculation clause in a child support order, and notwithstanding that a notice of objection has been filed and a hearing held to consider the notice of objection.[331]

In *MacDonald v MacDonald*,[332] a decision of the Nova Scotia Court of Appeal, the father's base salary in 2008 had been $38,438 but he earned a total income of $72,987 because of astonishing amounts of overtime that were unlikely to be repeated. In fixing the table amount of child support payable by the father under the *Federal Child Support Guidelines*, the trial judge attributed an income of $45,000 per annum to the father. She also ordered a recalculation of child support on 15 January of each year, if the father's income for the

---

329 *CT v JL*, 2018 PESC 15; *AR v DR*, 2018 PESC 37.

330 *Andrew-Reed v Reed*, [2002] BCJ No 708 (SC).

331 *Taylor v Braund (Taylor)*, 2018 NLCA 3 at paras 70–72, O'Brien JA. See also *Silveira v McKay*, 2018 SKQB 318.

332 2010 NSCA 34; see also *Ambrose v Ambrose*, 2021 NSSC 308 at paras 20–23; *Almon v Hill*, 2022 NSSC 310.

preceding calendar year exceeded $45,000. On her appeal, the mother argued that the trial judge erred by not giving adequate consideration to the enforcement difficulties she might face with the recalculation provisions in the order for corollary relief. She further argued that the trial judge had erred by misapplying the Guidelines that require a determination of the father's income, regardless of how difficult that might be or, alternatively, in setting the father's income for 2009 at $45,000. Having admitted fresh evidence by way of correspond ence received from the Director of the Maintenance Enforcement Program indicating that the program would not enforce any recalculated amount of child support unless the parents agreed on the amount, the Nova Scotia Court of Appeal observed that the mother had other means of enforcing the recalculation provisions. Furthermore, the Maintenance Enforcement Program would enforce the court-ordered monthly payments, even if the parties were unable to agree on recalculated payments. Given the enforceability of the court-ordered payments, the availability of other means of enforcing the recalculations, albeit by resorting to the court, and the need to set a fair amount of child support, the Nova Scotia Court of Appeal was not satisfied that the trial judge erred by giving insufficient attention to the enforcement issue. Indeed, it ventured the opinion that the trial judge's foresight in proceeding as she did in the particular circumstances of this case might improve the prospect of automatic adjustments to the amount of child support without the need to resort to the court. On the second issue raised by the mother's appeal, the Nova Scotia Court of Appeal was not satisfied that the trial judge had failed to determine the father's income as required by the Guidelines or that any error of fact or law had occurred in her attributing an income of $45,000 per year to him for the purpose of fixing the amount of monthly child support. The appellate court stated that the trial judge expressly acknowledged the need to determine the father's current income at an amount that was "fair, reliable and equitable." Her reasons underlined the difficulty of making a fair determination of the father's income, given his short relevant work history, one year, and the significant role overtime played in almost doubling his base salary for 2008. Having accepted the father's unchallenged evidence as to his need and capacity to work as much overtime as possible during that year because of his extreme financial difficulties and his testimony about the uncertainty of overtime being available in the future, the Nova Scotia Court of Appeal could find no fault in the trial judge's setting the father's annual income at $45,000, comprising a base salary of $38,438 plus $6,561 for overtime, and then ordering a recalculation at the end of each year in case his income exceeded this. In its opinion, it could not be said that the trial judge failed to determine the father's income and the trial judge did not make a material error, misapprehend the evidence, or make an error of law in setting the child support as she did. For the foregoing reasons, the mother's appeal was dismissed.

Evidence;[1] Procedure;[2] Costs

A. CREDIBILITY

Where a court has serious concerns about the credibility of a party on significant disputed issues, it may reject the evidence unless there is other independent testimony or reliable documentation that provides corroboration.[3] Several criteria should be considered by a court in assessing credibility, including the reasonableness of the evidence; contradictions in the evidence (internal consistency); whether or not the witness's character has been impugned; personality and demeanour; corroboration (external consistency); self-interest; powers of observation and recollection; and capacity of expression.[4] In *Gill Tech Framing Ltd v Gill*, Ker J of the British Columbia Supreme Court set out the following important factors for resolving testimonial conflict and credibility issues:

> [27] The factors to be considered when assessing credibility were summarized by Madam Justice Dillon in *Bradshaw v. Stenner*, 2010 BCSC 1398 (CanLII) at para. 186, as follows:
>
>> Credibility involves an assessment of the trustworthiness of a witness' testimony based upon the veracity or sincerity of a witness and the accuracy of the evidence that the witness provides (*Raymond v. Bosanquet (Township)* (1919), 1919 CanLII 11 (SCC),

1 For a valuable review of the admissibility of surreptitious audio and video recordings, see *DeGiorgio v DeGiorgio*, 2020 ONSC 1674, citing Professor Martha Shaffer, "Surreptitiously Obtained Electronic Evidence in Seven Simple Steps" (2019) 38 *Canadian Family Law Quarterly* at 5. See also *Ting v Ting*, 2022 ABQB 229, aff'd 2022 ABCA 324; *KWK v VLC*, 2022 BCSC 1321; *Van Ruyven v Van Ruyven*, 2021 ONSC 5963 at paras 30–43; *DeGiorgio v DeGiorgio*, 2022 ONSC 6677; *Heimlick v Longley*, 2022 SKQB 55; *CTB v BAAB*, 2022 YKSC 15. See also *Paftali v Paftali*, 2020 ONSC 5325.

2 For an excellent review of orders relating to social media, see Justice Deborah Chappel, "Orders Referring to Social Media: The Positives and the Pitfalls", reproduced in the Proceedings of the County of Carleton Law Association, 28th Annual Institute of Family Law, Montebello, Quebec, 6–7 April 2019.

3 *AMB v MAT*, 2009 BCSC 1281 at para 111, cited with approval in *Mansoor v Mansoor*, 2012 BCSC 602.

4 *DLG v GDR*, 2012 NBQB 177; *Passarello v Passarello*, [1998] OJ No 2792 (SCJ).

5 2012 BCSC 1913, cited in *Sebok v Babits*, 2018 BCSC 585 at para 25; see also *Goodhew v Summers*, 2022 BCSC 1080; *JM v ST*, 2022 BCSC 1210; *AS v SS*, 2023 BCSC 1077.

59 S.C.R. 452, 50 D.L.R. 560 (S.C.C.)). The art of assessment involves examination of various factors such as the ability and opportunity to observe events, the firmness of his memory, the ability to resist the influence of interest to modify his recollection, whether the witness' evidence harmonizes with independent evidence that has been accepted, whether the witness changes his testimony during direct and cross-examination, whether the witness' testimony seems unreasonable, impossible, or unlikely, whether a witness has a motive to lie, and the demeanour of a witness generally (*Wallace v. Davis* (1926), 31 O.W.N. 202 (Ont. H.C.); *Faryna v. Chorny*, [1952] 2 D.L.R. 152 (B.C.C.A.) [*Faryna*]; *R. v. S.(R.D.)*, 1997 CanLII 324 (SCC), [1997] 3 S.C.R. 484 at para. 128 (S.C.C.)). Ultimately, the validity of the evidence depends on whether the evidence is consistent with the probabilities affecting the case as a whole and shown to be in existence at the time (*Faryna* at para. 356).

[28] In assessing credibility in the face of conflicting evidence, the Nova Scotia Supreme Court in *Re: Novac Estate*, 2008 NSSC 283 (CanLII) noted the following at paras. 36 and 37:

> [36] There are many tools for assessing credibility:
>
> a) The ability to consider inconsistencies and weaknesses in the witness's evidence, which includes internal inconsistencies, prior inconsistent statements, inconsistencies between the witness' testimony and the testimony of other witnesses.
>
> b) The ability to review independent evidence that confirms or contradicts the witness' testimony.
>
> c) The ability to assess whether the witness' testimony is plausible or, as stated by the British Columbia Court of Appeal in *Faryna v. Chorny*, 1951 CanLII 252 (BC CA), [1951] B.C.J. No. 152, 1951 CarswellBC 133, it is "in harmony with the preponderance of probabilities which a practical [and] informed person would readily recognize as reasonable in that place and in those conditions," but in doing so I am required not to rely on false or frail assumptions about human behavior.
>
> d) It is possible to rely upon the demeanor of the witness, including their sincerity and use of language, but it should be done with caution (*R. v. Mah*, [2002] N.S.J. No. 349, 2002 NSCA 99 (CanLII), paras. 70–75).
>
> e) Special consideration must be given to the testimony of witnesses who are parties to proceedings; it is important to consider the motive that witnesses may have to fabricate evidence. (*R. v. J.H.*, 2005 CanLII 253 (ON CA), [2005] O.J. No. 39 (Ont. C.A.), paras. 51–56).
>
> [37] There is no principle of law that requires a trier of fact to believe or disbelieve a witness's testimony in its entirety. On the contrary, a trier may believe none, part or all of a witness's evidence, and may attach different weight to different parts of a witness's evidence. (See *R. v. D.R.* 1996 CanLII 207 (SCC), [1996] 2 S.C.R. 291 at para. 93 and *R. v. J.H., supra*).

And in *McBennett v Danis*, Chappel J of the Ontario Superior Court of Justice provided the following list of relevant factors that courts variously employ in assessing credibility and the reliability of witnesses:

1. Were there inconsistencies in the witness' evidence at trial, or between what the witness stated at trial and what they said on other occasions, whether under oath or not? Inconsistencies on minor matters of detail are normal and generally do not affect the credibility of the witness, but where the inconsistency involves a material matter about which an honest witness is unlikely to be mistaken, the inconsistency can demonstrate carelessness with the truth (*R. v. G.(M.); R. v. D.A.*).
2. Was there a logical flow to the evidence?
3. Were there inconsistencies between the witness' testimony and the documentary evidence?
4. Were there inconsistencies between the witness' evidence and that of other credible witnesses?
5. Is there other independent evidence that confirms or contradicts the witness' testimony?
6. Did the witness have an interest in the outcome, or were they personally connected to either party?
7. Did the witness have a motive to deceive?
8. Did the witness have the opportunity and ability to observe the factual matters about which they testified?
9. Did they have a sufficient power of recollection to provide the court with an accurate account?
10. Were there any external suggestions made at any time that may have altered the witness' memory?
11. Did the evidence appear to be inherently improbable and implausible? In this regard, the question to consider is whether the testimony is in harmony with "the preponderance of the probabilities which a practical and informed person would readily recognize as reasonable in that place and in those conditions?".
12. Was the evidence provided in a candid and straightforward manner, or was the witness evasive, strategic, hesitant, or biased?
13. Where appropriate, was the witness capable of making concessions not favourable to their position, or were they self-serving?
14. Consideration may also be given to the demeanor of the witness, including their sincerity and use of language. However, this should be done with caution. . . . [A]n assessment of credibility based on demeanour alone is insufficient where there are many significant inconsistencies in a witness' evidence. . . . The courts have also cautioned against preferring the testimony of the better actor in court, and conversely, misinterpreting an honest witness' poor presentation as deceptive.[6]

A motions judge may be found in error by an appellate court because of a failure to order a *viva voce* hearing to resolve the issue of credibility generated by conflicting affidavits.[7] Notwithstanding the difficulties of judicially determining credibility in the face of conflicting affidavits, however, such conflicts are not an absolute bar to making findings of fact.[8] A

6 2021 ONSC 3610 at para 41.

7 *Steele v Koppanyi*, [2002] MJ No 201 (CA).

8 *Hartley v Del Pero*, 2010 ABCA 182; *D'Ambrosio v D'Ambrosio*, [2000] BCJ No 1704 (SC) (submissions sought from counsel as to whether the case should proceed on affidavit evidence or be placed on the trial list).

court is entitled to make necessary fact and credibility findings, notwithstanding conflicting affidavits, where counsel have agreed that the matter should proceed to a determination on the affidavit material already filed rather than being adjourned to await answers to interrogatories.[9] A single untruth leaves the court on guard for more.[10] An appellate court should not disturb an application judge's findings as to the husband's lack of credibility, which constitutes the basis of the judge's rejection of the husband's application to vary an existing consent order that provides for support payments in excess of the *Federal Child Support Guidelines* Where the rights of the parties are dependent on conflicting issues of credibility, the trial judge should give reasons for his decision. In the absence of such findings, an appellate court cannot properly determine the merit of the appellant's appeal and therefore the trial judgment must be set aside and a new trial ordered before another judge.[12] But as McLachlin CJ of the Supreme Court of Canada observed in *R v REM*:

> While it is useful for a judge to attempt to articulate the reasons for believing a witness and disbelieving another in general or on a particular point, the fact remains that the exercise may not be purely intellectual and may involve factors that are difficult to verbalize. Furthermore, embellishing why a particular witness's evidence is rejected may involve the judge saying unflattering things about the witness; [. . .]. In short, assessing credibility is a difficult and delicate matter that does not always lend itself to precise and complete verbalization.[13]

Credibility findings are within the domain of the trier of fact and are generally accorded deference by appellate courts.[14] It has increasingly been recognized that it is usually unreliable and often dangerous to draw a conclusion from a witness's demeanour as to the likelihood that the witness is telling the truth. Instead of focusing on the way a witness gives evidence, the court should focus on the content, consistency, and probability of the evidence itself.

B. PROOF OF PATERNITY; BLOOD TESTS AND DNA TESTS; ARTIFICIAL INSEMINATION

A husband whose wife has been artificially inseminated by an anonymous donor may be entitled to a declaration of paternity under the Ontario *Children's Law Reform Act*[16] and may be granted parenting privileges and ordered to pay child support.[17]

Where a mother is married and has acknowledged her husband as the father of the child but later seeks blood tests to confirm that another man is the father for the purpose of obtaining support, the equitable doctrines of laches and the applicant's failure to come with clean hands are irrelevant.[18]

---

9 *Schipper v Maher*, [2002] MJ No 319 (QB).
10 *Welsh v Welsh*, [1998] OJ No 4550 (Gen Div).
11 *Jacobucci v Jacobucci*, 2006 MBCA 109.
12 *Mitro v Mitro* (1978), 1 RFL (2d) 382 (Ont CA).
13 2008 SCC 51, [2008] 3 SCR 3 at para 49; see also *GRR v JES*, 2020 NBQB 154.
14 *RJ v PJ*, 2021 NBCA 28 at para 31.
15 *B-M (Children: Findings of Fact)*, [2021] EWCA Civ 1371 at para 22 (20 September 2021).
16 RSO 1990, c C12.
17 *TDL v LRL* (1994), 4 RFL (4th) 103 (Ont Ct Gen Div).
18 *D(JS) v V(WL)* (1995), 11 RFL (4th) 409 (BCCA).

Where paternity is disputed, provincial statutory provisions may empower the court to order blood tests or DNA tests.[19] It is open for a judge to draw an adverse inference from a refusal to submit to the tests, although whether such an inference should be drawn may depend on the circumstances of the particular case.[20] Provincial statutory provisions that empower a court to order blood or DNA tests and to draw an adverse inference against a party who refuses to submit to such tests do not violate sections 7, 8, or 12 of the *Canadian Charter of Rights and Freedoms*.[21]

A husband is entitled to blood tests where the evidence indicates the possibility of extramarital paternity.[22]

If paternity of a child is disputed with respect to child support or parenting, and blood tests have proved inconclusive, a court may order the parties to re-attend for DNA tests to resolve the uncertainty.[23]

A husband may be estopped from raising the issue of paternity on an application to vary interim support, notwithstanding the results of DNA tests indicating that he is not the father of the child.[24] An obligor is not entitled to contest the paternity of the child after several years had elapsed during which time child support arrears have accumulated.[25] Where child support has been ordered after a finding of paternity, in the absence of any response, the issue of paternity is not reviewable on an application to vary the child support order. The proper procedure for reopening the issue of paternity is by way of an application to set aside the default judgment as to paternity and the support order that is corollary thereto.[26] A long-standing paternity agreement may constitute no bar to an order for DNA tests to determine paternity.[27]

In a claim for child support against an alleged father, the onus of proving paternity on the balance of probabilities may not be satisfied in light of the contradictory evidence of the parties and the mother's admission of sexual relations with another man whose whereabouts are unknown. The public interest is not served by superficial determinations of paternity based on a minimum of evidence, simply to comply with the insistence of social assistance

---

19 *FJN v JK*, 2015 ABCA 353; *JCC v NNC*, 2018 ABCA 115; *TAM v MOG*, 2021 ABQB 351; *X v Y*, 2015 BCSC 1327; *DF v KG*, 2018 NSSC 65; *Re H* (1980), 9 RFL (2d) 216 (Ont HCJ). As to criteria relevant to exercise of the judicial discretion to order genetic testing for the determination of paternity, see *TS v JLW*, 2022 SKCA 35.

20 See *FJN v JK*, 2015 ABCA 353; *Fallon v Rivers* (1986), 50 RFL (2d) 30 (BCSC); *L(FA) v B(AB)* (1995), 15 RFL (4th) 107 (Man CA); *P(L) v J(W)* (1989), 99 NBR (2d) 386 (QB); *Migwans v Lovelace*, 2011 NWTSC 54; *CMM v DGC*, 2015 ONSC 1815 (application by child under *Family Law Act*, RSO 1990, c F.3). Compare *J v N* (1976), 28 RFL 234 at 235–36 (Man CA).

21 Part I of the *Constitution Act, 1982*, being Schedule B to the *Canada Act 1982* (UK), 1982, c 11 [*Charter*]. *Crow v McMynn*, [1989] BCJ No 1233 (SC); *LLDS v WGF*, [1995] OJ No 418 (Ont Ct Gen Div).

22 *C(M) v C(LA)* (1990), 24 RFL (3d) 322 (BCCA); compare *X v Y*, 2015 BCSC 1327; *Saunders v Vargas*, 2018 ONSC 1892.

23 *S(C) v L(V)* (1992), 39 RFL (3d) 294 (Ont Prov Div), aff'd (1992), 39 RFL (3d) 298 (Ont Ct Gen Div). See also *R(L) v S(L) and E(R)* (1989), 22 RFL (3d) 267 (Man CA); compare *M(BB) v M(WW)* (1994), 7 RFL (4th) 255 (Alta QB); *T(SJ) v D(S)* (1994), 94 BCLR (2d) 290 (SC); *Ketchum v Ketchum* (1987), 84 NBR (2d) 288 (CA).

24 *S(PK) v S(JS)* (1995), 13 RFL (4th) 340 (BCSC).

25 *CAS v GAP*, 2011 BCSC 1431; *GL v CE*, [2002] OJ No 905 (SCJ). Compare *Unger v Scott*, 2023 ABKB 500.

26 *Bergen v Procner*, [1998] SJ No 479 (QB).

27 *JA v EDS*, [1998] AJ No 451 (QB).

granting authorities that civil proceedings be instituted against the father. If forced to make such a claim, the mother should be furnished with sufficient resources to have necessary blood tests undertaken.[28]

Where paternity is disputed in a child support proceeding, the court may decline to draw an adverse inference against either party, either from the respondent's refusal to submit to blood tests or DNA tests or from the applicant's decision to proceed without such tests. An applicant has the onus of proving paternity on a balance of probabilities. This onus may be discharged where sexual intercourse without contraception is admitted by both parties and the child was born after the normal gestation period of approximately nine months. Judicial notice may be taken that the normal gestation period is approximately 275 days.[29]

Once a judge has decided that a "possible father" shall pay child support pursuant to section 11 of the Nova Scotia *Testators' Family Maintenance Act*,[30] the judicial discretion to deviate from the table amount specified in the *Federal Child Support Guidelines* is limited to circumstances where the father can demonstrate undue hardship within the meaning of section 10 of the Guidelines. Where the "possible father" does not dispute that he is the child's biological father, the fact that other persons stood *in loco parentis* to the child does not reduce his obligation to pay the applicable table amount of child support under the Guidelines. The mother's delay in seeking support for the child is not a barrier to an order for support because child support is the child's right and the child is not accountable for a parent's delay. Any reduction in the father's income after the trial judge's disposition should be addressed by way of a variation proceeding. The father is not entitled to complain of inadequate assistance from counsel whom he consulted before proceeding to act on his own behalf at the trial.[31]

A court may exercise its discretion and refuse to apply *res judicata* or issue estoppel where it would cause unfairness or work an injustice. Blood tests may be ordered to determine a child's paternity in the context of a child support application, notwithstanding a finding of non-paternity in a previously contested parenting dispute involving the same parties.

The issue of paternity may be revisited on a motion to vary a child support order, but not the issue of whether the obligor had demonstrated a settled intention to treat the child as a member of his family. Absent fraud or misrepresentation, the issue of "settled intention" cannot be reopened once such a finding has been made.[33]

C. WRITTEN INTERROGATORIES

On an application to vary a child support order, a court may order the use of written interrogatories where this can provide necessary information more cheaply and more quickly than traditional discovery or cross-examination on affidavit evidence.[34]

---

28 *ASM v RS*, [1999] NSJ No 128 (Fam Ct). The application was dismissed without prejudice to re-application if blood tests undertaken.

29 *NEC v CJM*, [2001] OJ No 1671 (SCJ).

30 RSNS 1989, c 465.

31 *WJA v STS*, [2001] NSJ No 151 (CA).

32 *B v J*, [2001] OJ No 2659 (SCJ); see also *Sutherland v Sutherland*, 2023 ABCA 121.

33 *Plett v Murphy*, [2003] OJ No 1673 (SCJ).

34 *Hennessey v Hennessey* (1996), 20 RFL (4th) 79 (Alta QB).

A request for written interrogatories may be rejected as premature where no affidavit of documents has been filed by the petitioner. The request may also be dismissed on the merits where the interrogatories were abusive and not totally relevant.[35]

In *Harvey v Harvey*,[36] Carr J of the Manitoba Court of Queen's Bench identified the following limitations on the use of interrogatories:

1) the party examining has no right to go on a fishing expedition by interrogating for the purpose of finding out something of which she knows nothing but that might enable her to make a case of which she had no knowledge at the time of the interrogatories;
2) the only legitimate use of interrogatories is to obtain from the party interrogated admissions of facts that it is necessary for the party interrogating to prove in order to establish her case; and if the party interrogating goes further and seeks, by her interrogatories, to get matters from the other party that it is not incumbent on her to prove, although such matters may indirectly assist her case, the interrogatories ought not to be admitted; and
3) the fact that a question may properly be put to a party on cross-examination at trial does not necessarily make the question a proper interrogatory.

D. AFFIDAVITS

An affidavit is not a statement of defence and should not be drafted in that fashion. If each affidavit recites only facts, all the necessary information will be before the court. The nature of the relief sought will appear in the pleadings and argument will be presented by counsel.[37]

A lawyer is not a party to the action and should not swear an affidavit on behalf of a party that goes to the merits of the case. Although courts have been lax in permitting lawyers to argue cases based on their own affidavits, the practice should be discouraged. A lawyer who swears an affidavit going to the merits of a case or of a motion is in the same position as a lawyer who finds himself on the witness stand; the lawyer should not be heard as both witness and counsel in the same matter.[38] A respondent's affidavit may be struck out for failure to attend an appointment for cross-examination on the affidavit.[39]

Rule 314(1) of the Alberta *Rules of Court*[40] allows for cross-examination on an affidavit. The scope of the cross-examination extends to anything relevant to the issues before the court for which the affidavit is being used. Cross-examination is not limited to the "four corners" of the affidavit and may cover all the facts relevant to the whole of the application for which the affidavit is filed. Even if a question is not relevant to the application, it may be allowed in that it questions the truth of a statement contained in the affidavit. While relevance to the pending motion is the determining factor in setting the scope of cross-examination on

35 *Palansky v Palansky* (1989), 60 Man R (2d) 141 (QB).

36 (1987), 49 Man R (2d) 245 (QB).

37 *Sutton v Sutton* (1985), 33 Man R (2d) 78 (QB); *Palansky v Palansky* (1989), 60 Man R (2d) 141 (QB) (portions of affidavit struck out).

38 *Savoie v Savoie* (1989), 101 NBR (2d) 431 (QB). See also *Lavender-Smith v Smith*, 2021 NBCA 34. For strong disapproval of the practice of affidavits being sworn by lawyers or by legal staff, see *Trombetta v Trombetta*, 2021 ONSC 4237 at para 17.

39 *Legault v Legault* (1987), 19 CPC (2d) 267 (Ont Dist Ct).

40 Alta Reg 390/1968.

an affidavit, the court also retains discretion as to whether a question on cross-examination should be answered.[41]

The contents of affidavits filed in support of an application for an interim support order are circumscribed under Rule 56A.20 of the Newfoundland and Labrador *Rules of the Supreme Court*,[42] which provides that affidavits should be confined to facts that the deponent has personal knowledge of, although hearsay evidence may be included under Rule 56A.20(2) where the source of the information is specified. The facts contained in the affidavits should be relevant to the relief sought and should not contain allegations that are unnecessary, inflammatory, or amount to an abuse of the court's process.[43]

The Saskatchewan *King's Bench Rules* provide that a deponent is to confine his or her affidavits to facts that are within the deponent's personal knowledge to avoid argument and speculation and to avoid material that is irrelevant; that may delay the trial or make it diffi cult to have a fair trial; or that is unnecessary or an abuse of the court process. They further provide that the costs of every affidavit that unnecessarily sets forth matters of hearsay or argumentative matter, or copies of or extracts from documents, must be paid by the party filing the affidavit. Where the Rules permit a deponent to state information beyond the deponent's personal knowledge, the deponent must provide the source of that information. In *Dlouhy v Dlouhy*,[44] Dawson J of the Saskatchewan Court of Queen's Bench observed how the rules respecting affidavit evidence take on particular importance in family law matters, given the emotional nature of the proceedings, and then further explained that "a deponent is not entitled to express an opinion, but is confined to deposing the facts of which he is aware." The Rules permit the court to strike out all or part of an affidavit that does not com ply with the requirements of *The King's Bench Rules*.[45] When a notice of objection is filed, a chambers judge should identify any portions of the affidavit that are to be struck, or note that none of the objections are valid.[46]

Conflicting affidavits constitute no bar to adjudication of an application to vary a child support order where the court is able to determine the facts.[47] In the words of Ottenbreit JA of the Saskatchewan Court of Appeal in *Hunchak v Anton*:

> 17 This Court has determined that a Chambers judge is entitled to deference in his or her assessment of the sufficiency of affidavit evidence or controverted affidavit evidence. Controverted evidence alone is not enough to invalidate a support order even where the order is based solely on affidavit evidence. This has most recently been stated by Herauf J.A. in *Koback v Koback*, 2013 SKCA 91, [2013] 10 WWR 491. Chambers judges are, however, expected to attempt to resolve some of the contradictions in the affidavit material or indicate why they are unable to resolve such contradictions and proceed from there. . . .

---

41 *Potter v Graham*, [2001] AJ No 1119 (QB).

42 SNL 1986, c 42, Sch D (*Judicature Act*).

43 *O v C*, [2004] NJ No 19 (SC) (interim spousal support).

44 1995 CanLII 5715 (SKQB). For a more recent detailed review of affidavit evidence under the Saskatchewan *King's Bench Rules*, see *DCI v MBI*, 2022 SKKB 265.

45 *Wongstedt v Wongstedt*, 2017 SKCA 100 at para 34, Caldwell JA.

46 *SG v KB*, 2021 SKCA 133 at para 22.

47 *Kaatz v Kaatz*, [2001] SJ No 661 (QB); compare *Mercier v Mercier*, [2005] AJ No 494 (CA). See also *Hunchak v Anton*, 2016 SKCA 44 at para 17.

19 In the absence of any serious or material conflicts in the evidence, there was no basis or need for the Chambers judge to order a *viva voce* hearing. There is also no indication that Mr. Hunchak requested there be a *viva voce* hearing. Accordingly, the Chambers judge was correct to proceed as he did on the basis of the affidavits.[48]

E. ADMISSIONS

An agreed statement of facts is in the nature of a formal admission made for the purpose of dispensing with proof at the hearing. It is ordinarily a statement of facts agreed upon by the parties as true and correct that is submitted to the court for a ruling on the law that relates to it. It is usually conclusive as to the matters admitted, with other evidence being precluded. An agreed statement of facts is binding on the parties to it and can only be altered by mutual agreement or with leave of the court, usually only given on terms. One term should generally be that the other party should be at liberty to withdraw its agreement and that the costs of such withdrawal and the necessary fresh preparation should fall on the renouncer. The discretion of the court ought to be warily exercised, normally, to defeat fiction, to help establish truth, and to relieve clients of fatal mistakes by lawyers.[49]

The court should not permit withdrawals or amendments of admitted facts unless counsel can establish, through evidence, that such admitted facts are either false or are at least a triable issue.[50]

A defendant noted in default is deemed to admit all allegations of fact in the statement of claim; no similar provision is found in the *Rules of the Ontario Court (Provincial Division) in Family Law Proceedings*.[51]

F. NOTICE; INADEQUACY OF INFORMATION; NON-ATTENDANCE

The requirement for personal service of a notice of motion may be judicially dispensed with where the respondent has actual knowledge of the contents of the notice and no prejudice is thereby caused.[52]

Where a court is unable to make a determination as to the application of the *Federal Child Support Guidelines* on the material filed, the court may direct that a pre-trial settlement conference address the issues.[53]

In proceedings to vary child and spousal support on the basis of affidavit material filed, it may be concluded that the chambers judge cannot properly assess critical issues, in which event one of the options available is the direction of a hearing where *viva voce* evidence may be called.[54]

48 2016 SKCA 44.

49 *Langton v Langton* (1987), 62 Sask R 107 (QB).

50 *Lyons v Lyons Estate* (1989), 99 NBR (2d) 220 (QB).

51 RRO 1990, Reg 199 (*Courts of Justice Act*). See *Fawcett v Hurd*, [1998] OJ No 4345 (Gen Div).

52 *Scaffidi v Scaffidi* (1998), 41 RFL (4th) 166 (Ont Ct Gen Div).

53 *O'Hara v O'Hara*, [1997] SJ No 482 (QB).

54 *Omer v Omer*, [1997] SJ No 486 (QB), applying *Zaba v Bradley* (1996), 137 Sask R 295 (CA).

A court may revisit interim orders for child support and spousal support based on an unduly optimistic imputation of income, where the obligor's non-appearance at the original hearing was not wilful. A change of circumstances need not be demonstrated when the court reconsiders the issue of child support pursuant to Rules 52(4) and (5) of the British Columbia *Supreme Court Rules*.[55]

Where a divorce petition includes a claim for child support and the respondent is given notice of the claim when served with the petition but elects not to file an answer and does not appear at trial, the judge clearly has jurisdiction to make an order for child support. Furthermore, such an order is enforceable some years later, regardless of whether the obligor was given notice that a child support order had been made against him, provided that no prejudice would thereby ensue. A spouse who fails to file an answer in divorce proceedings wherein child support is sought cannot succeed in an application to rescind arrears of support on the ground that he or she was not notified of the support order. An order for child support made at the time of the divorce judgment is enforceable, regardless of whether the obligor was notified that the order had been made.[56]

A spouse who does not contest the right to divorce but opposes a corollary claim for support is entitled to notice of the hearing. Where no such notice is given and support is ordered, an application may be made to reopen the matter and the trial judge may stay the original order and set it aside after a further hearing.[57]

In Alberta, a notice to disclose can be served to compel the disclosure of current income, assets, and other financial information. This notice can be used after a divorce has been granted in conjunction with an application to vary corollary relief. A notice to disclose may not be served simply as a means of determining whether there are any grounds to bring an application to vary support.[58] If one party has experienced a change in circumstances or has reason to believe that the other party has undergone a change in circumstances, the proper procedure is to file a notice of motion and a supporting affidavit and serve a notice to disclose with it.[59] Once a party has brought a motion to vary the amount of support, there is no need to establish a *prima facie* entitlement to variation before the party is entitled to issue a notice to disclose. The awarding of costs and the court's ability to strike out pleadings can effectively control any abuse of the process.[60] A notice to disclose must ordinarily be served more than thirty days before the date on which the motion is returnable. To allow counsel to continue to issue notices to disclose right up to the time of the hearing would be to foster and condone careless practice and would hamper reasonable settlement proposals and proper preparation of the case.[61] Financial information relating to a third party cannot be requested through a notice to disclose; it must be specifically requested by a notice of motion that explains why the information is relevant and the third person must be served with the notice of motion.

55 *Supreme Court Rules*, BC Reg 221/90; *Vivier v Luchka*, [2002] BCJ No 2827 (SC).

56 *Meyers v Meyers* (1995), 12 RFL (4th) 170 (BCCA); *Schipper v Maher*, [2002] MJ No 319 (QB).

57 *Woodman v Woodman* (1976), 26 RFL 399 (Man CA).

58 *Rosin v Rosin* (1994), 7 RFL (4th) 402 (Alta QB); *Mumby v Mumby* (1994), 7 RFL (4th) 410 (Alta QB); see also *Burke v Burke*, [2001] AJ No 1373 (QB).

59 *Mumby v Mumby* (1994), 7 RFL (4th) 410 (Alta QB).

60 *Rosin v Rosin* (1994), 8 RFL (4th) 315 (Alta QB).

61 *Paschke v Paschke* (1994), 8 RFL (4th) 341 at 346 (Alta QB).

62 *Mumby v Mumby* (1994), 7 RFL (4th) 410 (Alta QB).

A constitutional challenge of the *Federal Child Support Guidelines* on the basis that they contravene specific sections of the *Charter* may be judicially dismissed as procedurally defective where necessary parties to the action have not been served with proper notice.[63]

G. FORMAL MOTION OR APPLICATION REQUIRED; TELEPHONE APPLICATION

Where a remedy is sought, it must be contained in a motion or application.[64] A notice of motion must be filed and served before a court will address a claim for interim relief under the *Federal Child Support Guidelines*; the notice of motion for interim relief must set out the precise relief sought.[65] A motion for increased child support may be heard by way of a telephone application.[66]

H. PLEADINGS

The foundation for a successful claim before a court lies in the pleadings. They represent the judge's first contact with the case. The mindset of the judge can often be swayed by the quality of the pleadings and financial statements. Sound pleadings make for sound arguments and the appropriate marshalling of evidence; they also speak to the credibility of counsel before the court. Pleadings should be precise and succinct.

Pleadings must conform to certain standards.[67] Defective or inadequate pleadings can lead to chaotic litigation that is unnecessarily expensive and protracted. Pleadings serve the following purposes:

- they define the issues in dispute;
- they give notice to the opposing party of the case that must be met;
- they inform the court of the matters in issue;
- they provide a record of the issues raised and prevent further litigation upon matters that have already been judicially determined; and
- they define the scope of discovery.[68]

The object of pleadings is to define with clarity the issues to be determined at trial. A party must plead the facts on which he relies and not the evidence by which the facts are to be proved.[69] In the course of drafting a pleading, counsel should set forth fully but concisely all of the material facts relied on.[70]

---

63 *Aziz v Aziz*, [2000] BCJ No 1134 (CA).

64 *DesRoches v Wedge*, [2002] PEIJ No 53 (SC).

65 *Lewkoski v Lewkoski*, [1998] OJ No 894 (Gen Div).

66 *Steiger v Steiger*, [1999] AJ No 129 (QB).

67 For an excellent article on this topic, see Paul M Perell, "The Essentials of Pleading" (1995) 17 *Advocates' Quarterly* 205.

68 *Root v Root*, [2008] OJ No 2716 (SCJ), citing *Provenzano v Thunder Bay (City)*, [2008] OJ No 1884 (SCJ).

69 *Firestone v Firestone* (1975), 5 OR (2d) 659 (HCJ).

70 *Prystawik v Prystawik* (1979), 19 AR 189 (NWTSC). See also *Olson v Lazich* (1971), 4 RFL 86 (Sask QB).

The amount of child support being sought should be specified in the pleadings, although an amendment of the pleadings may be ordered to accommodate a change. In the absence of any such amendment, courts, in applying the former discretionary child support regime, would refuse to order support in amounts exceeding those claimed in the divorce petition. Under the former judicial discretionary child support regime, the British Columbia Court of Appeal ruled that, if the only application before the court is one for a reduction of the amount of support and no counterclaim has been made nor evidence led to support any increase in the amount of support, an order for increased support should not be granted.[72] A different perspective may arise under the federal and provincial guidelines. Under the Guidelines, it has been held that, where there is no element of surprise, a court may order child support in a higher amount than that set out in the notice of motion.[73] If all relevant information concerning the income of one or both parties is before the court, there appears to be no apparent reason why the court should not immediately apply the Guidelines to determine the appropriate amount of child support. Similarly, it has been held that, on an application to increase child support brought pursuant to section 96 of the British Columbia *Family Relations Act*,[74] the court may order a reduction, notwithstanding that no application for such relief has been sought by the obligor. Once the court's jurisdiction has been invoked, its jurisdiction to vary a pre-existing order is at large and must be exercised in accordance with the *Federal Child Support Guidelines*.[75] In *Phillips v Phillips*,[76] the Alberta Court of Appeal summarily rejected counsel's submission that a trial judge has no jurisdiction to order lump-sum child support when none has been sought, although the lump sum order was vacated in the absence of evidence of any shortfall from a prior interim order.

A court is not hamstrung by the inadequacy of the pleadings where a party is not taken by surprise and the issues have been otherwise addressed. A technical defence that relies upon the inadequacy of the pleadings after the issues have been addressed in affidavit materials filed on motions for interim relief or in the evidence at trial is inconsistent with contempor ary family law practice, especially when it can be dispatched by means of an amendment to the pleadings.[77] Where a child's financial or other interests are at stake, a court is unlikely to be tied by formal pleadings. In any event, several judicial decisions have extended, perhaps improperly in terms of historical foundation, the notion of *parens patriae* jurisdiction to encompass child support.

Although a court may not be fettered by the absence of pleadings, it may conclude that the issue of child support arising from a parenting change is premature until such time as the situation stabilizes and parental income becomes clarified.[78]

---

71 *Offet v Offet* (1993), 1 RFL (4th) 203 (Alta QB); *Buttoo v Buttoo* (1994), 4 RFL (4th) 36 (Ont CA); compare *Lopez v Lopez* (1993), 48 RFL (3d) 298 (Ont Ct Gen Div).

72 *Lins v Lins* (1991), 31 RFL (3d) 40 (BCCA).

73 *Lopez v Lopez*, [1998] OJ No 5370 (SC).

74 RSBC 1996, c 128.

75 *Petula v Petula*, [1998] BCJ No 2066 (SC).

76 (1995), 14 RFL (4th) 113 (Alta CA).

77 *Denesi v Neves*, [1998] OJ No 736 (Prov Div).

78 *Major v Major*, [1998] SJ No 835 (QB).

I. AMENDMENT OF PLEADINGS

A request to amend pleadings may be granted to facilitate a comprehensive resolution of all issues arising from the marriage.[79] The practice of attempting to amend pleadings in the absence of the filing of an appropriate motion or consent amendment, or in the absence of a motion on the record at the hearing is all too common and should be discouraged.[80]

In Alberta, there is a strong presumption in favour of allowing amendments to pleadings after the close of pleadings. The applicant need not show any particular reason for needing the amendment and courts should exercise their discretion to allow the amendment unless the non-moving party demonstrates an exception or compelling reason not to.[81] The Alberta *Rules of Court* empower a court to amend pleadings at any stage of the proceeding where it is necessary to determine the real issue between the parties. There are five well-identified situations where an amendment will be refused, namely,

1) where it would create serious prejudice that an order for costs could not repair;
2) where the amendment would be hopeless;
3) where the proposed amendment is not supported by a required threshold level of evidence, based on the nature of the proposed amendment;
4) where the amendment would add a new cause of action outside the limitation period for suing; and
5) where the failure to plead earlier, or the amendment itself, involves bad faith.[82]

Where an amendment of the pleadings is sought, the court should not enter into the merits of the proceeding but should determine whether a *prima facie* meritorious case exists. If the amendment reveals a plausible claim, it should be allowed.[83] Four criteria should be satisfied in order for amendments to a pleading to be allowed. They are as follows:

1) An amendment should be allowed unless it will cause injustice to the other side that cannot be compensated for by costs.
2) The material filed in support of the application must set out a *prima facie* meritorious case.
3) No amendment should be allowed if it would have been struck out if originally pleaded.
4) The proposed amendment must contain sufficient particulars to enable the other side to answer it.

In determining whether there is a *prima facie* meritorious case, the focus is on the pleadings as distinct from the underlying factual basis for the pleadings.[84]

An amendment to pleadings ought *prima facie* to be allowed, notwithstanding the lapse of time, unless the applicant is acting *mala fide* or attempting to overreach the opposite party, or unless some injury or injustice will be done to the other side by the amendment that

79 *Emery v Emery* (1987), 11 RFL (3d) 194 (Ont Dist Ct).
80 *Howe v Lorette*, 2017 NBQB 119 at para 11, Wooder J.
81 *Colenutt v Colenutt*, 2023 ABKB 562 at paras 22–25.
82 *Ibid.*
83 *Johnson v Johnson* (1998), 38 RFL (4th) 279 (Ont Ct Gen Div); *Sears v Coristine*, 2021 ONSC 7576.
84 *Cheng v Cheng*, [1993] OJ No 690 (Gen Div); see also *Fraser v Fraser*, 2017 ONSC 3774.

cannot be compensated for by costs.[85] Rule 11(3) of the Ontario *Family Law Rules* expressly provides that the court shall grant leave to amend pleadings "unless the amendment would disadvantage another party in a way for which costs or an adjournment could not compen sate."[86] Belated amendment of a notice of motion in a child-related dispute may be justified by the overriding concern that the best interests of the children merit broad investigation and by the availability of an adjournment to eliminate any element of surprise.[87]

In *Re Pearce*, Bouck J of the British Columbia Supreme Court observed:

> The trend of modern authorities in this Province seems to be that once an action or proceeding has been commenced in the appropriate court which has jurisdiction to hear the substance of the issue or issues raised by the writ or other originating document, then all amendments should be allowed which will properly result in a fair and expeditious determination of these issues. This may be qualified to the extent that if a party opposing a motion to amend so as to cure a defect, can show prejudice to him by reason of allowing the amendment, or can show that the demands of justice disentitle the applicant to the relief he is seeking then different considerations will apply. In most instances these can be provided for by either an award of costs or the granting of an adjournment, but from time to time there may be circumstances where the amendment should not be allowed and the proceedings may then have to be started again. The onus is on the party opposing the amendment to show the prejudice that he will suffer if the amendment is allowed is so great that an adjournment or an award of costs are not a sufficient compensation.
>
> The other principle that seems to be developing from the authorities is that except in extreme circumstances no person should be deprived of his common law or statutory right of action solely by the application of the Rules of Court. These Rules are enacted to provide a means whereby litigants may settle their disputes through an orderly process. From time to time solicitors err in following the appropriate Rule or form or their clients fail to adequately instruct them on the matters in issue. When this takes place amendments are necessary and it may be that the reason for the amendment is solely due to the neglect of the solicitor. While it is the duty of the court to discourage what may be called 'sloppy practice', this in my view should rarely go so far as to penalize the client of the errant solicitor. Although costs are often an inappropriate remedy, more use could be made of Order 65, Rule 11 (Marginal Rule 986) in these circumstances so that the client does not have to be the one who suffers.[88]

Similar sentiments were expressed in *Re Milner* by Dubinsky J of the Nova Scotia Supreme Court:

> I would say, generally speaking, with regard to all the Rules governing civil procedure, that our Court has taken a decidedly liberal attitude in recent years in order to enable litigants to obtain full disclosure of all aspects of the case to be met and in order to dispose of the litigation once and for all. It has been said repeatedly by judges of this and other courts "that the

85 *Jachimowicz v Jachimovicz*, [2008] NSJ No 53 (SC); *Neale v Neale* (1980), 18 RFL (2d) 211 (Ont UFC). See also *Berthin v Berthin*, 2018 BCSC 2104.

86 *Singal v Singal*, 2019 ONSC 2758; *Mio v Mio*, 2014 ONSC 2186.

87 *Bunting v Bunting* (1995), 10 RFL (4th) 231 (Alta CA).

88 (1974), 16 RFL 376 at 377 and 379–80 (BCSC).

Rules of Court are the servants not the masters of the Court, whose faculty it is to interpret those rules in the manner most likely to do justice between the parties." …

I believe, in the words of Bramwell L.J. in *Tildesley v. Harper* [(1878), 10 Ch. D. 393] at pp. 396–7, that "unless I have been satisfied that the party applying was acting *mala fide*, or that, by his blunder, he had done some injury to his opponent which could not be compensated for by costs or otherwise," I should grant leave. I should grant leave "however negligent or careless may have been the first omission, and however late the proposed amendment, if it can be made without injustice to the other side. There is no injustice if the other side can be compensated by costs."[89]

An amendment will be denied, however, where an injustice would be thereby perpetrated. Thus, in *Firestone v Firestone*, Reid J of the Ontario Supreme Court observed:

> [An] amendment that will work an injustice on the opposite party should not be allowed. This principle underlies the expressions that emerge from the decisions. They state repeatedly that by an amendment a party should not be allowed to overreach or to place another at a disadvantage that cannot be cured by costs or be seriously prejudiced or irremediably injured, or be subjected to another's *mala fides*. … The power to amend is discretionary. … I point this out because counsel for plaintiff repeatedly asserted that his client had a "right" to the amendment. While the discretion will not be exercised to cause an injustice it can nevertheless be very far-reaching. … An amendment of doubtful value should not be allowed.[90]

In order for a claim of support to be considered by the court where no such claim has been made in the divorce petition, the petition should be amended to include such a claim.[91] In *Hebert v Hebert*,[92] the wife's divorce petition included a claim for periodic support for her and the children, but no claim for a lump sum. At the divorce hearing, the wife sought a lump sum in addition to the periodic support. The court directed that an amended petition be filed and served on the respondent.

Saskatchewan *King's Bench Rule* 166 empowered a party to amend any pleading in a proceeding once without leave, at any time prior to the close of pleadings, and at any other time with the written consent of all parties. Where the requirements of this rule were not satisfied, the court might dismiss an application for child support without prejudice to the right to re-apply on proper material.[93]

89 *Re Milner* (1975), 23 RFL 86 at 91 and 95 (NSTD). See also *Farkasch v Farkasch* (1971), 4 RFL 339 (Man QB); *Van Zant v Van Zant* (1975), 24 RFL 281 (Ont HCJ).

90 *Firestone v Firestone* (1975), 20 RFL 315 at paras 7–13 (Ont HCJ). And see *Firestone v Firestone* (1975), 5 OR (2d) 659 at 660 and 662–63 (HCJ) (leave to file rejoinder after reply introduced new issues).

91 *Neaves v Neaves* (1978), 6 RFL (2d) 209 (NSCA).

92 (1976), 1 AR 452 (TD).

93 *Blondeau v Blondeau*, [1997] SJ No 617 (QB). See now *Casbohm v Winacott Spring Western Star Trucks*, 2018 SKQB 15 at paras 26–34 applying Rule 3-72(3) of *The Queen's Bench Rules* of Saskatchewan. As to amendment of a notice of appeal, see *Zelinski v Pidkowich*, 2020 SKCA 42. As to whether a claim should be struck as disclosing no reasonable cause of action, see *Kumar v Korpan*, 2020 SKQB 256 at para 17.

J. STRIKING OUT OF PLEADINGS

An application to strike out pleadings is based on the provincial rules of court and the jurisdiction of the court to prevent an abuse of its process.[94] It has been judicially asserted that the remedy of striking pleadings is extraordinary and should only be used sparingly and in limited and exceptional circumstances, and when no other remedy would suffice.[95] However, some courts have recognized a need to implement a cultural shift to promote access to justice by re-drawing the line between limiting drastic measures and applying the law robustly. In *Aslezova v Khanine*, the Ontario Court of Appeal stated that "wilful failure to comply with disclosure obligations 'must be considered egregious and exceptional,' and those who 'choose not to disclose financial information or to ignore court orders will be at risk of losing their standing in the proceedings as their claims or answers to claims may be struck.'"[97]

As stated by Linhares da Sousa J speaking for the Ontario Divisional Court in *Van v Palumbi*:

> [30] The legal principle governing the exercise of judicial discretion to strike a party's pleadings is a three-pronged test as follows:
>
> (1) Is there a triggering event justifying the striking of pleadings?;
>
> (2) Is it appropriate to strike the pleadings in the circumstances of the case?;
>
> (3) Are there other remedies in lieu of striking pleadings that might suffice?
>
> [31] These three-pronged principles are well established in the case law. (See *Kovachis v. Kovachis* (2013), 367 D.L.R. (4th) 189 (Ont. C.A.); *Chiaramonte v. Chiaramonte* (2013), 370 D.L.R. (4th) 328 (Ont. C.A.); *Purcaru v. Purcaru*, 265 O.A.C. 121 at paras. 47–48; *King v. Mongrain* (2009), 66 R.F.L. (6th) 267 (Ont. C.A.); *Haunert-Faga v. Faga* (2005), 203 O.A.C. 388 (C.A.); and *Marcoccia v. Marcoccia* (2009), 60 R.F.L. (6th) 1 (Ont. C.A.)).[98]

And as MacEachern J of the Ontario Superior Court of Justice observed in *Sakiyama v Sakiyama*:

> [9] The power to strike out a party's pleadings should be used sparingly and only in exceptional cases. In family law cases, pleadings should only be struck, and trial participation denied, in exceptional circumstances and where no other remedy would suffice.
>
> [10] In family law proceedings, wilful non-compliance of basic financial information must be considered egregious and exceptional. A party's non-compliance must be considered

---

94 *Dickie v Dickie*, [2007] 1 SCR 346; *Silver v Silver* (1980), 15 RFL (2d) 142 (Alta CA); *Armoyan v Armoyan* 2015 NSSC 191; *CMM v DGC*, 2015 ONSC 1815. For an overview of relevant Ontario caselaw, see *Peerenboom v Peerenboom*, 2018 ONSC 5796. For an excellent review of relevant principles and caselaw, see Justice Deborah Chappel, "Striking Pleadings for Disclosure Deficiencies: General Principles and Practical Tips From the Bench," County of Carleton Law Association, 32st Annual Institute of Family Law Conference, 21 April 2023, Ottawa.

95 *MR v JR*, 2018 NBCA 12 at para 33, Baird JA; *Martin v Watts*, 2020 ONCA 406; *Ferguson v Ferguson*, 2022 ONCA 543 at paras 27–33; *Parekh v Parekh*, 2022 ONSC 4700.

96 See *Peerenboom v Peerenboom*, 2018 ONSC 5796; *Soleimani v Karimi*, 2020 ONSC 6174.

97 *Aslezova v Khanine*, 2023 ONCA 153 at para 9.

98 2017 ONSC 2492 at paras 30–31; see also *Biniaminov v Biniaminov*, 2018 ONSC 5454; *Mullin v Sherlock*, 2018 ONCA 1063; *Sparr v Downing*, 2019 ONSC 6564, aff'd 2020 ONCA 793; *Soleimani v Karimi*, 2020 ONSC 6174; *Dagher v Hajj*, 2021 ONSC 2853.

in the context of the strict financial disclosure obligations repeatedly reiterated by the courts and the *Family Law Rules*.[99] Those who choose not to disclose financial information or to ignore court orders will be at risk of losing their standing in the proceedings as their claims or answers to claims may be struck.[100]

Speaking to the same issue in *Palkowski v Palkowski*,[101] Bale J of the Ontario Superior Court of Justice stated:

> [16] The Applicant's motion to strike is brought pursuant to rule 1(8) of the *Family Law Rules*:
>
> 1. (8) If a person fails to obey an order in a case or a related case, the court may deal with the failure by making any order that it considers necessary for a just determination of the matter, including,
>
> (a) an order for costs;
>
> (b) an order dismissing a claim;
>
> (c) an order striking out any application, answer, notice of motion, motion to change, response to motion to change, financial statement, affidavit, or any other document filed by a party;
>
> (d) an order that all or part of a document that was required to be provided but was not, may not be used in the case;
>
> (e) if the failure to obey was by a party, an order that the party is not entitled to any further order from the court unless the court orders otherwise;
>
> (f) an order postponing the trial or any other step in the case; and
>
> (g) on motion, a contempt order.
>
> [17] The consequences of an order striking a party's pleadings are severe:
>
> 1. (8.4) If an order is made striking out a party's application, answer, motion to change or response to motion to change in a case, the following consequences apply unless a court orders otherwise:
>
> 1. The party is not entitled to any further notice of steps in the case, except as provided by subrule 25 (13) (service of order).
> 2. The party is not entitled to participate in the case in any way.
> 3. The court may deal with the case in the party's absence.
> 4. A date may be set for an uncontested trial of the case.
>
> [18] A party's pleadings should be struck only in exceptional circumstances, where no other remedy would suffice . . .

99 See Nikki Robar & Greg Walen, "Income for Guidelines Purposes: Seven Challenging Issues for Income Determination From a Financial and Legal Perspective" (2022) 41 CFLQ 227. As to the duty of financial disclosure in family law cases, see *Kantor v Kantor*, 2023 ABCA 237, discussed in Franks & Zalev, "This Week in Family Law," 20 November 2023 (Thomson Reuters). As to financial disclosure and the availability of the tort of conspiracy to ensure that third parties, such as relatives and new partners, cannot assist a spouse in hiding income and/or assets in an attempt to defeat the other spouse's legitimate support or property claims, see *Leitch v Novac*, 2020 ONCA 257 at paras 44–47.

100 *Sakiyama v Sakiyama*, 2019 ONSC 5522 at paras 9–10; see also *MR v JR*, 2018 NBCA 12; *Lalande v Lalande*, 2023 ONCA 68.

101 2020 ONSC 24 at paras 16–22.

> [19] The adversarial structure of a proceeding should be maintained whenever possible. The remedy imposed should not go beyond that which is necessary to express the court's disapproval of the conduct in issue . . .
>
> [20] The most basic obligation in family law is the duty to disclose financial information. This requirement is immediate and ongoing. Failure to abide by this fundamental principle impedes the progress of the action, causes delay and generally acts to the disadvantage of the opposite party . . .
>
> [21] In considering a request to strike pleadings for failure to comply with disclosure obligations, the court should:
>
> 1. Consider whether substantial disclosure has been made;
> 2. Itemize the disclosure not provided;
> 3. Consider whether the breaches are willful;
> 4. Apply the principle of proportionality. Specifically, in keeping with the importance and complexity of the issues:
>   a. Consideration ought to be given to the importance or materiality of the items of disclosure not produced;
>   b. Although full and frank disclosure is necessary, exhaustive disclosure may not always be appropriate;
>   c. Courts should consider the burden that disclosure requests bring on the disclosing party, the relevance of the requested disclosure to the issues at hand, and the costs and to obtain the disclosure as compared to its importance . . .
>
> [22] A review of the appellate cases on this issue suggests that the offending party's location on the 'spectrum of compliance' should be considered; from good faith but unsuccessful efforts, to 'token' compliance, to exceptional and egregious conduct.

Courts have repeatedly cautioned against striking portions of pleadings dealing with parenting issues because courts typically require both parties' participation to make orders that are truly in the best interests of the children; where financial disclosure orders are violated, courts may strike pleadings on financial issues and permit the parenting issues to continue.[102] An enforcement order providing that the appellant's pleadings will be struck out unless she pays a designated lump sum and periodic amounts on account of monthly support arrears in addition to paying ongoing interim child and spousal support payments may be varied on appeal where compliance with the totality of the financial conditions is beyond the capacity of the bankrupt obligor.[103]

A court may order the production of specified documents coupled with a direction that failure to comply will justify an application to strike out the offending party's answer and counterpetition.[104]

---

102 *Thomas v Brereton*, 2021 ONSC 5642 at paras 25–26, Mandhane J.

103 *Higgins v Higgins*, [2006] OJ No 3913 (CA) (motion judge's order varied by the Ontario Court of Appeal to provide for striking of husband's pleadings if he failed to pay ongoing, interim periodic child and spousal support).

104 *Paul v Paul*, [2000] SJ No 780 (QB). See also *Burke v Poitras*, 2018 ONCA 1025 (settlement conference).

Pleadings that are scandalous or tend to embarrass or prejudice or delay a fair trial may be struck out, but the power to strike out such pleadings should be exercised only in plain cases.[105]

Portions of an affidavit may be struck out pursuant to BC Rule 51 as being inadmissible by virtue of the common law privilege extending to "without prejudice" settlement negotiations.[106]

Once an order is made directing the trial of an issue, any affidavits filed become pleadings. If any of the allegations contained in the material are irrelevant or tend to embarrass or delay a fair trial, they may be struck out.[107]

There is no authority under the *Divorce Act*[108] or provincial rules of court to strike out an answer or counterpetition for non-compliance with an order for costs. The respondent should not be deprived of the right to a full defence when other remedies exist to enforce obedience to an order for costs.[109]

Alberta Rule 129(1) empowers a court to strike out any pleading in an action on the ground that it discloses no cause of action. To succeed under Rule 129(1), an applicant must demonstrate that even if all the facts alleged in the statement of claim were true, the plaintiff could not succeed in his lawsuit. The burden on the applicant is a heavy one and a court should not strike out a pleading as disclosing no cause of action unless the court is satisfied beyond doubt that no cause of action exists or that no possible basis for a cause of action has been presented.[110]

On a motion to strike out a statement of claim on the basis that it discloses no reasonable cause of action, a court should not dispose of matters of law that are not fully settled by the jurisprudence, nor should the plaintiff be denied further legal recourse if there is a chance that she might succeed. The length and complexity of the issues, the novelty of the cause of action, and the potential for the defendant to present a strong defence are insufficient to disallow the plaintiff from proceeding with the case.[111]

Retroactive variation of a child support order pursuant to section 17 of the *Divorce Act* requires proof of a change in circumstances as defined in section 14 of the *Federal Child Support Guidelines*. Where nothing has changed that was not known or anticipated in the divorce judgment, the application to vary may be struck out pursuant to Rule 14.25 of the Nova Scotia *Civil Procedure Rules* on the basis that it is plain and obvious that the application discloses no reasonable cause of action.[112]

---

105 *Firestone v Firestone* (1975), 5 OR (2d) 659 at 664 (HCJ).

106 *Bartkowski v Bartkowski*, [2003] BCJ No 720 (SC).

107 *Re Paul* (1980), 28 OR (2d) 78 (HCJ).

108 RSC 1985 (2d Supp), c 3.

109 *Webber v Webber* (1970), 3 NBR (2d) 94 (CA). See also *Di Ciaula v Mastrogiacomo*, 2019 ONSC 2823.

110 *Thompson v Thompson*, [2003] AJ No 1577 (QB) (action for damages for adultery and wrongful concealment of a child's paternity). See also *PP v DD*, 2017 ONCA 180 (no action for damages available to father in fraud or negligence against mother who falsely assured him that she was using contraceptive pill). As to the situation in Saskatchewan, see *Churko v Merchant*, 2019 SKQB 307.

111 *Fein v Fein*, [2001] OJ No 4554 (SCJ) (action for damages against grandparents for the failure to support their grandchildren).

112 *Mabey v Mabey*, [2004] NSJ No 394 (SC).

An Ontario court has jurisdiction to order that a spouse's pleadings be struck by reason of a failure to answer relevant questions on an examination or because of non-compliance with prior interim orders of the court. Orders precluding a party from proceeding to have a hearing should be made sparingly, however, and this is especially so at the interim-interim stage where there has never been a hearing on the merits of the case. Balancing a need for the family to resolve pressing issues and a history of blatant non-compliance with pre-existing court orders, the court may choose to determine the amount of spousal and child support arrears to be paid and order compliance with the duly fixed arrears by means of a certified cheque payable within thirty days, with a direction that a failure to provide the cheque will entitle the wife to bring an *ex parte* motion to strike the pleadings.[113]

The answer of a respondent may be struck out for failure to attend an examination for discovery[114] or because of default under an order for interim spousal or child support.[115] An application to strike out any pleading or affidavit of a spouse for non-compliance with an order for interim support or interim disbursements should not be granted where there is an inability to pay. The sanction of striking out pleadings should not be imposed on a husband who has encountered temporary financial embarrassment by reason of general economic conditions that render him incapable of liquidating his property holdings, or finding alternative employment that would generate an income sufficient to permit the discharge of his obligations. Where the husband has discharged his financial obligations to his wife and children prior to his supervening incapacity and is willing to pay the arrears in future instalments, the court may order such payments and dismiss the wife's application to strike out his pleadings.[116]

An Ontario court may strike out a statement of claim on the basis that it discloses no cause of action because of the existence of an unanswerable defence. The issue is whether, assuming the facts to be true, the action is, nevertheless, certain to fail.[117]

A court has jurisdiction to strike the pleadings of a support defaulter under Rule 69.15(6) of the Ontario *Rules of Civil Procedure*[118] where the director is the only party entitled to enforce the order for support pursuant to sections 7(6) and 20(1) of the *Family Responsibility and Support Arrears Enforcement Act*.[119] The obligation to make payments to the director exists after filing of the order in the director's office and before steps are taken to enforce the order by deducting income at the source.[120]

---

113 *Rueter v Rueter*, [2003] OJ No 989 (SCJ); compare *Tiwana v Sandhu*, 2010 ONCA 592 at para 5.

114 *Jablonowski v Jablonowski* (1972), 8 RFL 36 (Ont HCJ).

115 *Sugar v Sugar* (1976), 23 RFL 248 (Ont CA). Compare *Underhill v Underhill* (1985), 49 CPC 237 (Ont HCJ) (the husband defaulted under support order granted pursuant to provincial statute; refusal to strike out the husband's subsequent divorce petition). And see Section R, below in this chapter. See also *Holly v Greco*, 2019 ONCA 464.

116 *Vanderschilden v Vanderschilden* (1982), 26 RFL (2d) 407 (Ont HCJ).

117 *Louie v Lastman*, [2002] OJ No 3522 (CA) (action by the former primary caregiving parent against the other parent for damages for failure to provide reasonable child support struck out where the action was brought some twenty-seven years after a settlement had been reached, by which time the children had long since attained the age of majority). For striking out of the corresponding action by the adult children against their father, see *Louie v Lastman*, [2002] OJ No 3521 (CA).

118 RRO 1990, Reg 194 (*Courts of Justice Act*).

119 SO 1996, c 31.

120 *Chickee v Chickee*, [2000] OJ No 2769 (SCJ).

K. ADJOURNMENTS

A court has the discretionary authority to allow or deny an adjournment request.[121] In *Toronto-Dominion Bank v Hylton*, Epstein JA for the Ontario Court of Appeal commented as follows on how the discretion should be exercised:

> Against the backdrop of the nature of the proceeding and the parties to the proceeding, the court should consider the evidence and strength of the evidence of the reason for the adjournment request, the history of the matter, including deliberate delay or misuse of the court process, the prejudice to the party resisting the adjournment and the consequences to the requesting party of refusing the request.[122]

Additional factors to be considered are identified in *Law Society of Upper Canada v Igbinosun* wherein Weiler JA of the Ontario Court of Appeal stated:

> A non-exhaustive list of procedural and substantive considerations in deciding whether to grant or refuse an adjournment can be derived from these cases. Factors which may support the denial of an adjournment may include a lack of compliance with prior court orders, previous adjournments that have been granted to the applicant, previous peremptory hearing dates, the desirability of having the matter decided and a finding that the applicant is seeking to manipulate the system by orchestrating delay. Factors which may favour the granting of an adjournment include the fact that the consequences of the hearing are serious, that the applicant would be prejudiced if the request were not granted, and the finding that the applicant was honestly seeking to exercise his right to counsel and had been represented in the proceeding up until the time of the adjournment request. In weighing these factors, the timeliness of the request, the applicant's reasons for being unable to proceed on the scheduled date, and the length of the requested adjournment should also be considered.[123]

And in *RN v Haulli*,[124] Johnson J of the Nunavut Court of Justice observed:

> The factors that might be considered in an adjournment application were stated at paragraph 23 of *Ludmer* quoting the Alberta Court of Queen's Bench in *Lameman v Alberta*, 2011 ABQB 40 (Can LII) at para 33, [2011] AJ No 82:
>
> 1. courts should make a just determination of the real matters in dispute and they should decide cases on their merits;
> 2. the prejudice caused by granting or denying the adjournment;
> 3. the applicant's explanation for not being ready to proceed;
> 4. the length of the adjournment the applicant is seeking and the consequent disruption of the court's schedule;
> 5. the importance of effectively enforcing previous court orders;
> 6. the proper marshaling of evidence and prosecution of complex and multifaceted actions;

---

121 *SB-B v BJS*, 2020 NBCA 9; *McCormack v Piller*, 2023 SKKB 37.

122 2010 ONCA 752 at para 38.

123 2009 ONCA 484 at para 37. See also *Embree v Embree*, 2016 NBCA 42 (spousal support); *Smart v Smart*, 2014 ONSC 4464.

124 2018 NUCJ 10 at para 23. See also *AS v SS*, 2023 BCSC 1077; *Banilevic v Cairney*, 2020 SKQB 25 at para 84; *McCormack v Piller*, 2023 SKKB 37, citing *Lameman v Alberta*, 2011 ABQB 40 at para 33.

7. whether there is a realistic expectation that the adjournment will accomplish its stated purpose;
8. the history of the proceedings, including other adjournments and delays, and at whose instance those adjournments and delays occurred;
9. where a party is seeking the adjournment to amend pleadings, how long counsel has known of the issue to which the amendment is aimed and whether counsel has had previous opportunities to amend;
10. whether the application is merely an attempt to delay the proceedings; and
11. the party that seeks the adjournment should not bear the consequences of its counsel's failures.

An adjournment may be ordered on conditions that may include court-ordered interim child support and security for costs in a disputed paternity case.[125]

Although inconvenience may result from an adjournment of the divorce proceedings under section 11(1)(b) of the *Divorce Act* on the ground that the court is not satisfied with the arrangements for child support, to proceed with an order for child support in the absence of notice would deny procedural fairness in that the spouse against whom the claim is brought is entitled to know the nature of the claim so that a full answer and defence may be given.

An application for child support may be adjourned to enable counsel to provide relevant information to the court.[127]

Where a court is unable to ascertain the spousal incomes on the material furnished, the application may be adjourned to a specified date so that the spouses can provide the court with their most recent income tax returns and updated financial statements. Upon granting the adjournment, the court may order the continuation of child support payments already being made on a voluntary basis until the matter is adjudicated.[128]

All requests for adjournment must be considered in light of the ongoing proceeding. If the request for adjournment appears to be an attempt to delay the proceeding or to unreasonably extend the time to serve and file material, a court might, in exercising its discretion, refuse to grant an adjournment.[129]

The court should deny a last-minute motion for the adjournment of an application to vary, where the sole reason put forward is the absence of the applicant's lawyer by reason of his appearance before another court and the application to vary could be handled with ease by another lawyer from the same office.[130]

A court has the discretionary jurisdiction to order an adjournment where the issue of the retroactivity of a child support order is raised belatedly; principles of natural justice demand that the obligor be given an opportunity to reply.[131]

---

125 *FJN v JK*, 2015 ABCA 353.

126 *Anderson v Anderson* (1987), 11 RFL (3d) 260 (NBCA).

127 *Kazoleas v Kazoleas*, [1997] AJ No 820 (QB); see also *MacDougall v Letilly*, [1997] SJ No 473 (QB) (variation proceeding).

128 *Carey v Carey*, [1998] BCJ No 2909 (SC).

129 *Ridley v Ridley* (1989), 37 CPC (2d) 167 (Ont HCJ).

130 *Roy v Roy* (1984), 59 NBR (2d) 410 (QB).

131 *Esligar v Esligar*, [1999] NBJ No 150 (CA).

It is proper to order an adjournment when counsel is caught by surprise and is not in a position to respond to a show cause order made on the court's own initiative.[132]

Rule 15 of the *Provincial Court (Family) Rules* (BC)[133] provide for adjournments and require a judge who has heard any evidence to finish hearing all the evidence and decide the case, unless that judge is unable to act. An appellate court may direct the adjourning judge to determine the case where an unreasonable length of time has passed since the adjournment.[134]

L. DUTY TO MAKE FULL DISCLOSURE

Lawyers must be diligent when filing a financial statement so that it reflects a budget that is a reasonable one in all the circumstances. An unrealistic budget does not reflect well on the client or the lawyer.[135] The modern approach to disclosure seeks to avoid trial by ambush. It is now incumbent on a party to disclose any document relevant to the action whether it supports or detracts from her position. Full disclosure is essential if justice is to be done.[136] Where production is objected to on the basis of privilege, the statement as to documents must identify the documents sufficiently to enable an order for their production to be enforced if the claim for privilege is unfounded. The description should contain enough detail to allow a judge, on a motion for production, to determine if a *prima facie* case has been made out for a claim of privilege. However, no details need be provided that would enable the opposite party to discover indirectly the contents of the privileged documents, as opposed to their existence and location.[137]

The failure to file a mandatory financial statement or otherwise provide relevant financial information to the other spouse may preclude an offer to settle by the delinquent party from being seriously considered and the court may draw adverse inferences respecting the delinquent's income, expenses, and assets.[138]

If a respondent fails to file the required financial statement, such failure should not be permitted to frustrate the applicant's claim and the court may allow the matter to proceed, while drawing appropriate inferences against the respondent.[139]

---

132 *Devlin v Devlin* (1994), 10 RFL (4th) 265 (Alta CA).

133 BC Reg 417/98 (*Court Rules Act*).

134 *Ward v Hanes*, [2000] BCJ No 2372 (SC).

135 *Carruthers v Carruthers* (1988), 15 RFL (3d) 321 (PEITD).

136 See Chapter 4, Section M. As to contempt and an order for a fine or special costs in British Columbia pursuant to ss 213 and 230 of the *Family Law Act*, SBC 2011, c 25, see *Reehal v Reehal*, 2020 BCSC 1635. As to provincial financial sanctions in Manitoba for non-disclosure, see *Lamontagne v Klyne* (1994), 93 Man R (2d) 79 (QB), applying s 8(2) of *The Family Maintenance Act*, CCSM c F20. For a decision-making framework in Ontario for determining the appropriate remedy for non-compliance with a court's financial disclosure order, see *Malik v Malik*, 2019 ONSC 117. As to the imposition of a fine or monetary payment under the Ontario *Family Law Rules* for a failure to make financial disclosure in the absence of a finding of contempt, see *Granofsky v Lambersky*, 2019 ONSC 3251; *Florovski v Florovski*, 2019 ONSC 5013.

137 *Schlechter v Schlechter*, [1988] SJ No 701 (QB).

138 *Payne v Payne* (1982), 31 RFL (2d) 211 (Ont UFC); see also *Almeida v Almeida* (1995), 11 RFL (4th) 131 (Alta QB); *Fabian v Fabian* (1983), 34 RFL (2d) 313 (Ont CA).

139 *Attersley v Hambleton* (1988), 12 RFL (3d) 192 (Ont Prov Ct); compare *Rivest v Rivest* (1981), 25 RFL (2d) 280 (Ont HCJ).

An application to vary or rescind a support order granted by way of corollary relief in a divorce proceeding may be stayed pending the filing of the applicant's income tax return for the preceding year.[140]

M. DISCOVERY

In the vast majority of claims that focus on child support, there will be no examinations for discovery. The parties will simply proceed to a pre-trial conference and then to a trial, if necessary.[141]

Questions are not permissible on an examination for discovery when they are, in effect, questions of law, not questions of fact.[142]

Only one examination for discovery may be had without leave of court.[143] An examination for discovery of the respondent may take place only after the answer has been delivered, or after the time for delivering it has expired or default of answer has been noted against the respondent. The entering of an appearance neither enlarges nor abridges the time within which an answer is to be made. These matters are regulated by the rules of court and the parties and their counsel do not have the power to introduce unauthorized and contradictory procedures into the practice of the court. Although the court refuses to accept or recognize an examination for discovery that contravenes the rules of court, it may give counsel the opportunity to call the court reporter who took the examination as a witness to testify as to those statements of the respondent that were admissions against his interest and heard by the court reporter.[144]

The modern trend of the law is to broaden the right to production and discovery, particularly with respect to financial disputes in matrimonial proceedings. A shareholder in a private company has the right to obtain and a positive duty to produce financial statements of the company where such production is sought by her spouse in matrimonial proceedings. Where a husband's corporations are his agents, he is not entitled to rely on the proposition that they are separate legal entities and, therefore, they must produce their books and records for discovery, even though they are not parties to the proceedings to discover the husband's financial position.[146] The court will allow the petitioner to pierce the corporate veil and compel the respondent to answer questions respecting his corporate assets where the company is the mere agent of the respondent.[147]

A husband cannot arbitrarily restrict the information that he is ordered to disclose to his wife simply by asserting possible harm arising from any leak of this information to business competitors. Accordingly, he may be ordered to open his business and corporate records to inspection by his wife's accountants and to furnish a better affidavit on production than

---

140 *Smith v Smith* (1981), 24 RFL (2d) 174 (Ont HCJ).

141 *LR v DT*, [1998] SJ No 733 (QB).

142 *Craig v Craig* (1982), 18 Man R (2d) 279 (QB).

143 *Firestone v Firestone* (1975), 20 RFL 315 (Ont HCJ).

144 *Girardin v Girardin* (1973), 15 RFL 16 (Sask QB).

145 *Hill v Hill* (1983), 34 RFL (2d) 449 (Ont HCJ); see also *Lacker v Lacker* (1982), 42 BCLR 188 (SC); *Wells v Wells* (1982), 29 CPC 186 (Ont HCJ), Master Cork.

146 *Burt v Burt* (1979), 11 RFL (2d) 143 (Ont HCJ).

147 *Lightfoot v Lightfoot* (1972), 11 RFL 242 (Ont HCJ). See also Chapter 12, Section V.

has been previously provided; such affidavit is to include a full and final disclosure of his business affairs.[148]

Failure to attend an examination for discovery does not necessarily warrant the dismissal of an application for support.[149] If counsel wishes to rely on the contents of an examination for discovery at trial, the relevant portions of the transcript should be read into the trial record.[150] An order for the production of documents will not be granted unless it is properly applied for and an opportunity to respond has been provided.[151]

N. DISCLOSURE BY THIRD PARTIES

A bank may be ordered to produce records[152] or answer interrogatories respecting a spouse's accounts, loans, and securities.[153] A wife's application to examine all the husband's business records at the various banks with which he deals in his management of various companies should be dismissed where it would be impossible for the banks to comply with an order in the absence of greater specificity and the banks would have to guess the extent of any court-ordered breach of their statutory duty of confidentiality. The dismissal of such an application may be declared to be without prejudice to a future application for similar relief at a later date when the wife has more precise information that will render it practical for the banks to comply with any appropriate order.[154] In *Purves*,[155] a husband's bank was ordered to produce records relating to a term deposit, but an order for production of all banking records was refused; costs were reserved pending determination of whether the wife's assertions had a sound foundation or she was on a fruitless "fishing expedition."

The courts must be vigilant in ensuring that custodians of financial records and financial advisers are not unduly harassed by being subpoenaed willy-nilly to attend and give evidence in interim proceedings for spousal and child support. Where the applicant has other avenues of relief available, for example, a notice to produce, and there is nothing to suggest that the respondent spouse will not provide all the information, it is improper to require the attendance of third parties for the purpose of using their evidence. Although there may be cases where the relevant information can only be obtained from strangers to the litigation, such cases are exceptional. It is an abuse of process to conduct an examination for discovery of strangers to the litigation that is nothing more than a "fishing expedition."[156]

---

148 *Graat v Graat* (1982), 29 RFL (2d) 312 (Ont HCJ).

149 *Chisholm v Chisholm* (1974), 2 OR (2d) 535 (Div Ct).

150 *MacDonald v MacDonald* (1975), 23 RFL 303 at 307 (Man QB). For limitations on the right to read discovery evidence into the trial record, see *Bowen v Hermson and Manitoba Public Insurance Corporation (Third Party)* (1983), 22 Man R (2d) 295 at 299 (QB).

151 *WPN v BJN*, [2004] BCJ No 1351 (SC).

152 *Purves v Purves* (1985), 65 BCLR 339 (SC).

153 *Little v Little* (1985), 49 CPC 169 (N.STD).

154 *Graat v Graat* (1982), 29 RFL (2d) 312 (Ont HCJ).

155 *Purves v Purves* (1985), 65 BCLR 339 (SC).

156 *Wink v Wink* (1981), 26 RFL (2d) 158 (Ont HCJ).

O. EXCLUSION OF PARTY FROM HEARING

Although the court has an inherent jurisdiction to exclude a party from the courtroom during a trial by reason of gross misconduct, contempt of court, or equally grave causes, a party is ordinarily entitled as of right to attend the trial and to hear all of the testimony.[157] Similar criteria apply to examinations for discovery and cross-examination on affidavit evidence. Since there is an inherent right to be present during the examination for discovery of any other party, the discretion to exclude a party should only be exercised where such exclusion is necessary to secure the ends of justice and the onus of proof falls on the party seeking the exclusion.[159]

P. RIGHT TO CROSS-EXAMINE AND GIVE EVIDENCE

A respondent in divorce proceedings who has filed no answer but has filed a demand of notice on the question of the amount of support and the exercise of parenting time with the children is entitled to cross-examine the petitioner and give evidence that is confined to these issues.[160] This is an established practice in Alberta.[161]

Documents to be used for purposes of cross-examination should be made available to the other party's lawyer prior to cross-examination.[162]

Pursuant to Rule 52(8) of the British Columbia *Rules of Court*, a discretion rests in the court as to whether or not to permit cross-examination on affidavits that have been filed on an application relating to child support. In exercising its discretion in accordance with proper principles, the court will consider whether there are material facts in issue, whether cross-examination is relevant to an issue that might affect the outcome of the substantive application, or whether cross-examination will serve a useful purpose in eliciting evidence that would assist in determining the application. Where there is a lack of objective evidence relating to the financial circumstances of one of the spouses, cross-examination of that party on his affidavit may be deemed appropriate in light of the interests of the child, in respect of whom the amount of support payable is disputed.[163]

Rule 56A.16(7) of the Newfoundland and Labrador *Rules of the Supreme Court*, which came into force on 1 April 2003, specifically states that a decision on an interim application is to be made "after reviewing the affidavits filed and hearing the arguments of the parties." The right to cross-examine at an interim hearing is an exception to the normal rule. Permission can be given, but the party seeking to cross-examine must satisfy the judge that there are cogent reasons for cross-examination. The scope of any cross-examination is circumscribed by the permissible contents of the affidavits filed in support of the application for interim support. Since the contents of affidavits are restricted to factual matters, so too

157 *Hemming v Hemming* (1983), 33 RFL (2d) 157 at 172 (NSCA).

158 *Wakim v Wakim*, unreported (29 May 1987) (Ont HCJ); compare *Piper v Piper* (1988), 65 OR (2d) 196 (HCJ).

159 *Kadar v Kadar*, unreported (28 July 1994) (Ont Ct Gen Div) (action for damages for sexual abuse).

160 As to the permissibility and scope of a cross-examination of a person being examined for discovery, see *King v King* (1975), 25 RFL 232 (NSTD).

161 *Lupkowski v Lupkowski* (1974), 16 RFL 105 (Alta CA).

162 *Stein v Stein* (1984), 49 CPC 99 (Ont HCJ), Master Sandler.

163 *Greenwood v Greenwood*, [1999] BCJ No 846 (SC).

is any permitted cross-examination. Cross-examination may be permitted (1) where there are major differences on relevant facts in the affidavits filed; (2) where cross-examination is necessary to challenge facts, not reasoning, deposed to by a party and those facts are critical to a proper determination of the issue in dispute; or (3) where it is necessary to elicit additional relevant information that will amplify or qualify affidavit material. Giving permission to cross-examine falls within the discretion of the hearing judge.[164]

There is no jurisdiction under the *Family Law Rules*[165] to require a party who is outside of Ontario to attend for questioning in Ontario.[166]

When a party is unrepresented at a show cause hearing dealing with support arrears, the motions judge should advise that party of the right to testify and of his or her right to cross-examine the opposite party on the affidavit evidence.[167]

Q. RIGHT TO BE HEARD; ALLEGATIONS OF JUDICIAL BIAS

Failure to give effective notice of the judicial hearing of an application for child support constitutes a fundamental breach of natural justice on the basis of which the ensuing child support order may be vacated on appeal with a direction that the matter be reheard.[168]

Judges must provide discernible reasons for their decisions and should consider submissions from counsel before reaching a decision. A failure to do so constitutes a reversible error and an appellate court may consequently order a rehearing.[169] A judgment should not be reversed on appeal simply because one party alleges judicial bias. That party must establish facts from which an apprehension of bias can be seen as reasonable. A judge's impartiality cannot be attacked on the basis of a personal perception of bias; an objective test is applied.[170] In determining whether a judge's conduct gives rise to an apprehension of bias, the test is whether a reasonable person informed as to what has taken place would be apprehensive that the complainant did not have a fair trial or whether there is any sound basis to apprehend that the judge, either consciously or unconsciously, did not bring an impartial mind to bear upon the cause.[171] A reasonable apprehension of bias may be found where the trial judge appears to have prejudged the case without hearing all the evidence, thereby denying all parties the right to an independent and impartial hearing.[172]

A court may prohibit a spouse from pursuing further applications, except by leave of court.[173] It is contrary to the best interests of children to have their parents continually litigat-

---

164 *O v C*, [2004] NJ No 19 (SC).

165 *Family Law Rules*, O Reg 114/99 (*Courts of Justice Act*).

166 *A v B*, [2007] OJ No 5555 (SCJ).

167 *Lister v Gould*, [2000] NBJ No 419 (CA).

168 *Parsons v Parsons*, [1999] NJ No 291 (CA).

169 *Morrison v Morrison*, [2005] AJ No 149 (QB); *Cabot v Mikkelson* (2004), 242 DLR (4th) 279 at para 36 (Man CA); *Nagy v Laverdiere*, [2005] SJ No 163 (CA).

170 *LeBlanc v LeBlanc* (1993), 48 RFL (3d) 457 (Man CA); *Montgomery v Montgomery*, [2000] NSJ No 1 (CA).

171 *Gurvin v Tingren* (1994), 49 BCAC 309 (private discussion of competence of lawyer with bencher of Law Society insufficient to warrant finding of bias); *Montgomery v Montgomery*, [2000] NSJ No 1 (CA), applying *R v S(RD)*, [1997] 3 SCR 484 at 502.

172 *Balazs v Balazs* (1990), 95 NSR (2d) 114 (TD); *B(JB) and B(CB) v B(JA)* (1992), 113 NSR (2d) 60 (CA).

173 *Laird v (Alberta) Maintenance Enforcement*, 2019 ABQB 12; *Peters v Keef*, 2019 ABQB 85; *TMH v PJH*, 2020 BCSC 804, citing s 221 of the BC *Family Law Act*.

ing issues of child support in the absence of any material change of circumstances. To avoid repeated and unnecessary litigation, a court may order that no further application should be made to the court before a stipulated date, unless leave to present such an application is granted by the court.[174]

Rule 37.16 of the Ontario *Rules of Civil Procedure* expressly empowers a court to prohibit a party from making further motions in a proceeding without first obtaining leave of court, where the court is satisfied that an attempt is being made to delay or add to the costs of the proceeding or otherwise abuse the process of the court by a multiplicity of frivolous or vexatious motions. The principles with respect to vexatious litigation, which are set out in *Lang Michener v Fabian*,[175] apply to motions that abuse the process of the court.[176] Mandatory legal representation is a well-established court access restriction that may be imposed where additional preliminary screening is a fair and proportionate response to abusive and damaging litigation.[177]

R. A STAY OF PROCEEDINGS FOR NON-COMPLIANCE WITH A SUBSISTING ORDER OR OTHER CAUSE

Trial or appellate proceedings may be stayed[178] pending the purging of contempt arising from non-compliance with a pre-existing order.[179] Where an objection is lodged to an application being heard until the applicant purges her contempt, the allegation of contempt must be strictly proved.[180] In *Abu-Saud v Abu-Saud*,[181] the Ontario Court of Appeal stated:

> [4] It is common ground that the court has jurisdiction to quash or dismiss an appeal in the face of non-compliance with a support order: see *Courts of Justice Act*, R.S.O. 1990, c. C.43, s. 134(3); *Dickie v. Dickie*, 2007 SCC 8, [2007] 1 S.C.R. 346, at para. 6; *Brophy v. Brophy* (2004), 2004 CanLII 25419 (ON CA), 180 O.A.C. 389 (C.A.), at para. 11; *Siddiqui v. Anwar*, 2018 ONCA 965, 22 R.F.L. (8th) 92, at para. 19. Moreover, this court has consistently refused to hear from the defaulting appellant or entertain the appeal where the record shows continuing

174 *Hamilton v Pearce*, [2000] BCJ No 1953 (SC); compare *KKS v CSS*, [2004] BCJ No 1574 (SC).

175 (1987), 59 OR (2d) 353 (HCJ). See also *Carten v Carten*, 2015 BCCA 201, citing *Lindsay v Canada (Attorney General)*, 2005 BCCA 594 at para 25; *ET v LMD*, 2019 ONSC 4071. And see Alberta, *Rules of Court*, AR 124/2010, r 3.68, online: https://albertacourts.ca/docs/default-source/qb/civil-practice-note-7---vexatious-application-proceeding-show-cause-procedure.pdf?sfvrsn=cb2fa480_6; *Laird v (Alberta Maintenance Enforcement*, 2019 ABQB 12; *Peters v Keef*, 2019 ABQB 85.

176 *Beattie v Ladouceur*, [2001] OJ No 4852 (SCJ). For broad statutory provisions in British Columbia empowering a court to prohibit a party from making further motions in a proceeding without first obtaining leave of court authority, see *Raabe v DeJong*, 2019 BCSC 1177, applying s 221 of the *Family Law Act*, SBC 2011, c 25.

177 *Peters v Keef*, 2019 ABQB 398 at para 3, citing *Unrau v National Dental Examining Board*, 2019 ABQB 283 at paras 817–20.

178 See *Vavrek v Vavrek*, 2019 ABCA 235; see also *Teixeira v Teixeira*, 2022 ONSC 6133. And see *Sharifpour v Rostami*, 2018 BCCA 458, wherein it was held that the jurisdiction to grant a stay pending appeal lies with the court that made the order.

179 *F(E) v S(JS)* (1995), 14 RFL (4th) 286 (Alta CA); *Cottick v Cottick* (1989), 23 RFL (3d) 401 (Man CA), Lyon JA, with Philp JA concurring; compare dissenting judgment of Huband JA; *Martin v Martin*, [2005] OJ No 4567 (SCJ). And see Section J, above in this chapter.

180 *Kramer v Kramer* (1986), 4 RFL (3d) 455 (BCSC).

181 2020 ONCA 824 at paras 4–5; see also *de la Fuente v Breen*, 2022 BCCA 424 at para 10.

disobedience with court orders: *Cosentino v. Cosentino*, 2017 ONCA 593, 98 R.F.L. (7th) 53, at para. 8.

[5] Quashing or dismissing an appeal for non-compliance is not automatic. Factors to be considered by the court in determining whether to exercise its discretion to quash an appeal include: the wilfulness of the breach; the amount of arrears; the excuse for the breach; and the efforts to correct the breach: *Brophy*, at paras. 9-15.

When a person disregards a court order, that person is liable to be (1) found in contempt, (2) punished by committal or attachment, and (3) refused a hearing on any application until the contempt has been purged. However, a finding of contempt or a finding of disobedience does not take away a judge's discretion to allow the disobedient party to be heard on an application. The discretion persists despite the contempt or disobedience and its exercise depends upon a consideration of such matters as whether (1) the contempt or disobedience is contumacious; (2) a refusal by the court to hear the party would do violence to the interests of the children; and (3) the contempt or disobedience, so long as it continues, impedes the course of justice in the cause by making it more difficult for the court to ascertain the truth or to enforce the orders that it may make. Whether the court has discretion to hear a party despite that party's deliberate disobedience of a court order for costs involves a consideration of the same principles that are applicable to the question of where the disobedience relates to support arrears.[182] Failure to pay the costs fixed by a consent judgment dealing with divorce and matrimonial property division does not warrant a stay of proceedings to determine unresolved issues relating to parenting and child support.[183] Nonpayment of the costs of previous proceedings constitutes no basis for a stay of subsequent proceedings where the failure to pay costs is due to inability to pay. The court should be slow to make an order for security of costs where the effect of such an order would be to bar the non-paying party from seeking variation of a previous order for corollary relief. Especially where a child is concerned, financial considerations should not be made paramount over the best interests of the child.[184]

S. DIRECTING TRIAL OF AN ISSUE

A court has jurisdiction to direct the trial of an issue where it feels that the dispute should not be decided on affidavit evidence alone.[185]

T. JOINDER AND CONSOLIDATION OF ACTIONS; ADDING OF PARTIES

Speaking to the adding of parties to litigation in *Cao v Chen*, Forth J of the Supreme Court of British Columbia stated:

---

182 *Whitehead v Ziegler* (1974), 18 RFL 357 at 359–60 (Sask QB). See also *MacKinnon v. Richards*, 2020 NSCA 44.

183 *Yakimyshyn v Yakimyshyn* (1994), 9 RFL (4th) 41 (Alta QB).

184 *Winkler v Winkler* (1990), 27 RFL (3d) 445 (Man CA).

185 *Zubot v Zubot*, [2001] AJ No 1601 (QB); *Ragot v Ragot* (1976), 30 RFL 183 (Man QB).

[50] A good summary of applicable principles for adding parties was set out in *Thomas v. Rio Tinto Alcan Inc.*, 2016 BCSC 1474:

> THE POWER TO ADD PARTIES TO THE LAWSUIT
>
> [13] Rule 6-2(7) of the *Supreme Court Civil Rules* gives the court discretion to add a person as a party to the litigation at any stage of the lawsuit. In *Alexis v. Duncan*, 2015 BCCA 135, the Court of Appeal confirmed that this subrule creates three separate and discrete circumstances in which the court may exercise its power to add a party:
>
> 1. the person ought to have been joined as a party at the outset (subrule (b)(i));
> 2. the person's participation in the proceeding is necessary to ensure that all matters in the proceeding are effectually adjudicated (subrule (b)(ii)); or
> 3. as between the person sought to be added and any party to the proceeding, there exists a question or issue relating to/connected with either the relief claimed in the proceeding or the subject matter of the proceeding and, in the opinion of the court, it would be just and convenient to determine such question or issue as between those persons (subrule (c)).
>
> [14] In *Meade v. Armstrong*, 2011 BCSC 1591, Mr. Justice Dley reviewed the relevant case law and summarized the principles governing the addition of parties to a lawsuit as follows (citations omitted):
>
> 1. A party should be added where that party's participation is necessary for the proper determination of the case;
> 2. The discretion to add parties should be generously exercised so as to enable effective adjudication upon all matters;
> 3. In exercising the discretion to add a party, the court should not concern itself as to whether the action will be successful other than to be satisfied that there may exist an issue or question between the applicant and the party being joined;
> 4. Evidence is not required in support of a joinder application. The pleadings may be sufficient to establish that there is a question to be tried between the parties;
> 5. Where an applicant relies on pleadings alone, the facts alleged, which if assumed to be true, must disclose a cause of action;
> 6. Unless there is prejudice, amendments should be granted liberally to enable the issues to be tried;
>
> (at para. 16)
>
> [15] To this list I would also add a couple of propositions which can be found in *Kitimat (District) v. Alcan Inc.*, 2006 BCCA 562 as follows:
>
> 7. Use of the word "ought" (in subrule (b)(i)) encompasses all those cases in which joining the person is a necessity and may even be broader to include situations in which joining the person may be more than mere convenience but less than a necessity.
> 8. In order to have a right of appeal under the *Court of Appeal Act*, an appellant must have been a party to the underlying lawsuit and a right to pursue such an appeal is an important component to the effectual adjudication of the issues

in question, particularly so where one or the other parties to the litigation may not wish to pursue appeal; and

9. The prime consideration in in [*sic*] determining whether a person should be a party to the litigation is the interests of justice, a consideration that is triggered when the party proposed to be added has significant interests or legal agreements that may be directly affected by the matters litigated in the action.

[51] A party seeking to be added must demonstrate a direct interest in, or that they are directly affected by, the outcome of the proceedings or that their participation is necessary for effectual adjudication. A party may be added where the applicant demonstrates a real issue between themselves and the existing parties and where the court determines that the addition of the party is just and convenient. In determining what is just and convenient, a court must consider whether the proposed party and their claim would effectively hijack the proceedings by increasing the number of parties, issues, and overall scope of the litigation with resulting costs and delays: *Gladue v. British Columbia (Attorney General)*, 2010 BCSC 788 at paras. 11 and 13.[186]

A father, who seeks to vary support orders issuing from the Provincial Court and the Supreme Court of British Columbia with respect to children born of different relationships, may be allowed to raise and join the Provincial Court proceeding with the Supreme Court proceeding in order to promote efficiency in the disposition of both applications.[187]

Issues relating to the joinder and consolidation of actions and the adding of parties often arise in the context of judicial determination of the respective child support obligations of biological or adoptive parents and of step-parents or other persons who stand in the place of parents.[188]

On an application respecting child support, there is no automatic right to add parties. Before leave to add a party will be granted, the court must be satisfied that there is no other viable remedy.[189] On an application for child support, the respondent parent's cohabitant may be joined as a party pursuant to Rule 5.03(1) of the Ontario *Rules of Civil Procedure* or Rule 7(3) of the Ontario *Family Law Rules*, where their business and personal affairs are inextricably intertwined.[190] In *Rolls v Rolls*,[191] the court refused to allow the mother to add her divorced husband's common law partner and her corporation to the father's application to reduce court-ordered child support because section 19(1) of the *Federal Child Support Guidelines* provided an alternative remedy for a failure to make proper financial disclosure, and the variation application imposed an onus on the divorced husband to prove his income and satisfy the court that it was lower than the amount previously imputed to him. The divorced husband's cross-application to add the mother's parents and their former companies was judicially perceived as retaliatory and was not justified merely because the parents had supported the mother and children in the face of the divorced husband's failure to do so.

---

186 *Cao v Chen*, 2020 BCSC 2050 at paras 50–51.
187 *Ramos v Juliano*, [2001] BCJ No 2099 (SC).
188 See Chapter 3, Section J(3).
189 *Rolls v Rolls*, [2003] AJ No 101 (QB).
190 *Coulstring v Lacroix*, [2001] OJ No 1826 (SCJ).
191 *Rolls v Rolls*, [2003] AJ No 101 (QB).

The divorced husband's application to add the biological father of two of the three children of the marriage was also rejected because the biological father's obligation had been previously established by court order and a biological father's responsibility does not extinguish the child support obligation of a step-parent standing *in loco parentis* to children. In rejecting all three of the aforementioned applications to add third parties, the court paid regard to the unnecessary complications and increased costs that would have been generated if the applications had been granted.

In *Munro v Munro*,[192] an application to consolidate an action for breach of a matrimonial property settlement and an application for retroactive child support was rejected by a majority judgment of the Alberta Court of Appeal. Speaking to the governing principles, Paperny and Bielby JJA observed:

> When faced with an application to consolidate claims, a court must weigh several relevant factors. They include the extent to which there are common claims and disputes, and the possibility that consolidation may save time and resources in pre-trial procedures and at trial. The court must also consider potential prejudice to the parties which may arise from consolidation if, for example, one action is more advanced than the other and if consolidation will result in prejudicial delay of a trial.[193]

Applying these criteria, the majority judgment found no error in principle in the decision of the chambers judge who was aware of the overlap in the factual context between the two claims but concluded that any benefit of having the claims heard together was diminished by the fundamental difference in the issues and outweighed by the prejudice that would occur if the child support application was delayed.

U. JUDICIAL RECONSIDERATION BEFORE AND AFTER FORMAL ENTRY OF JUDGMENT; REOPENING OF CASE

A court is not *functus* and may amend an order in light of "second thoughts" prior to the formal order being signed and entered.[194] The discretionary jurisdiction of a trial judge to reopen a judgment before it has been entered should be exercised sparingly. Although a reopening is often dependent on new evidence that was not previously available, the judicial discretion is not confined to this circumstance and may also be exercised where the trial judge is satisfied by the argument of counsel or on the basis of her own reconsideration of the record that the original judgment was in error because it overlooked or misconstrued material evidence or misapplied the law.[195]

---

192 2011 ABCA 279.

193 *Ibid* at para 7. For a non-exhaustive list of factors for a court to consider in determining whether to exercise its discretion to order a consolidation of proceedings, see *Beardsley v Beardsley*, 2020 ONSC 6624 at para 14.

194 *Walker v Whiting*, [1998] AJ No 1166 (QB). As to seeking leave to reopen a trial on the basis that fresh evidence has presented itself since the closing of the trial, see *Abu-Shaban v Abu-Shaaban*, 2021 ONSC 362.

195 *Sykes v Sykes* (1995), 13 RFL (4th) 273 (BCCA); *Evans v Evans*, [2004] BCJ No 986 (SC) (s 9 of the Guidelines found inapplicable); *Hopson v Hannon*, 2021 BCSC 99.

In *BJL v JRDL*,[196] Henderson J of the British Columbia Supreme Court listed the following criteria as applicable where a reconsideration of issues is sought after the pronouncement but before the entry of a judgment:

1. A trial judge has an "unfettered discretion" to reconsider an issue after pronouncement of judgment but before entry of the final order: *Clayton v. British American Securities Ltd.*, [1935] 1 D.L.R. 432 at 440; [1934] 3 W.W.R. 257 at 295 (B.C.C.A.);
2. This power must be "exercised sparingly" to avoid fraud and abuse of process: *ibid.*;
3. The underlying rationale for the unfettered discretion is to prevent a miscarriage of justice: *Clayton, supra*; *Kemp v. Wittenberg*, [1999] B.C.J. No. 810 (B.C.S.C.);
4. In general, reconsideration of an issue is not an alternative to an appeal. Reconsideration applications will not be entertained where they are motivated by tactical considerations, particularly where the argument advanced could have been advanced at trial: *Sykes v. Sykes* (1995), 6 B.C.L.R. (3d) 296 (B.C.C.A.);
5. The burden of persuasion rests with the applicant, who must show that a miscarriage of justice would probably occur unless the issue is reconsidered and decided in her favour: *Vance v. Vance* (1981), 34 B.C.L.R. 209 (B.C.S.C.);
6. An issue may be reconsidered where new, relevant evidence is adduced which was not available at the time of the original trial: *Sykes, supra*;
7. An issue may be reconsidered if the original judgment is in error because it overlooks material evidence: *Sykes, supra*;
8. An issue may be reconsidered if the original judgment is in error because it misconstrues material evidence: *Sykes, supra*.
9. An issue may be reconsidered if the original judgment is in error because it misapplies the law: *Sykes, supra*;
10. An issue may be reconsidered if the original judgment, although not in error on the day it was given, becomes erroneous because of a change in the law: *Grigg v. Berg Estate*, 2000 BCSC 858;
11. An issue may be reconsidered where there has been a change in circumstances between the date the judgment was pronounced and the time of the subsequent application, provided the change in circumstances relates to something fundamental to the original reasons for judgment: *Cheema, supra*;
12. An issue may be reconsidered where the original judgment was "so expressed as to lead to uncertainty and confusion": *Fame Construction Ltd. v. 430863 B.C. Ltd.*, [1997] B.C.J. No. 1053 (B.C.S.C.).

If counsel wish the court to reserve on the issue of costs, it is helpful if this is made clear. Counsel may, nevertheless, be entitled to reopen the issue of costs before entry of the judgment, where counsel believe that there is an opportunity to make additional submissions on costs based on pre-trial offers to settle to supplement the submissions previously made at the conclusion of the hearing relating to support under the *Federal Child Support Guidelines*.[197]

---

196 2003 BCSC 381 at para 3; see also *Mayer v Mayer Estate*, 2020 BCCA 282; *Hopson v Hannon*, 2021 BCSC 99; *FAP v LFT*, 2023 BCSC 171; *RL v TGS*, 2023 BCSC 847; *JCH v SMBH*, 2024 BCSC 54.

197 *Hershfield v Hershfield*, [2003] BCJ No 759 (SC).

The general rule is that once an order is passed and entered or otherwise perfected, the court that passed the order is *functus officio* and cannot set aside or alter the order.[198] The correction of a clerical mistake or accidental slip or omission in the formal order entered may be permitted by provincial rules of court[199] but the "slip rule" may be deemed inapplicable where fundamental changes are sought.[200]

A court may reconsider an order after formal entry where, as entered, it does not truly manifest the intention of the court or where there has been a mistake in drawing up the order.[201] BC Rule 41(2) specifically provides that the court "may at any time ... amend an order to provide for any matter which should have been but was not adjudicated upon." An order may be amended where there was an error in calculating income for the purpose of determining the amount of child support.[203]

Rule 15(14)(a) of the Ontario *Family Law Rules* permits the court to "change an order that ... was obtained by fraud." This jurisdiction to set aside or vary an order is available by way of motion rather than having to start a new case. A discrepancy between the father's admissions and declarations of income and the findings of actual receipts by the trial judge may fall short of the standard of deliberate deceit, fraud, or perjury necessary to invoke Rule 15(14)(a). Rule 15(14)(b) of the Ontario *Family Law Rules* empowers a court, on motion, to "change an order that ... contains a mistake." Rule 15(14)(b) addresses clerical mistakes or errors arising from an accidental slip or omission. Alleged substantive errors in a trial judge's reasoning or his alleged misapprehension of the evidence cannot be reviewed under Rule 15(14)(b). Such alleged errors are reviewable only by way of an appeal.[204]

The interests of justice require that all relevant and necessary financial information be placed before the court, but this principle does not permit litigants to file further material, of their own accord, after argument and before decision. Leave of court is required to file additional material. The proper procedure would be to apply under the Saskatchewan *King's Bench Rules* to reopen the case. The discretion to admit additional evidence is wide but must be exercised judicially and not capriciously. Counsel should not attempt to circumvent the rules by forwarding material directly to the court for its consideration.[205]

The Saskatchewan *King's Bench Rules* empower a court to amend its judgment in order to address calculation errors as opposed to effectuating interpretative or substantive amendments to the judgment.[206] A consent order for child support that does not reflect the true intention of the parents may be rectified or set aside pursuant to the Saskatchewan *King's Bench Rules*. A new trial is not necessary. The court has an inherent jurisdiction to rectify or

---

198 *Morice v Morice* (1972), 8 RFL 283 (Sask CA); see also *Snortheim v Snortheim* (1984), 41 RFL (2d) 334 (Alta QB) (amendment of judgment prior to entry). Compare *Russell v Russell* (1995), 16 RFL (4th) 229 (Alta QB).

199 *Dalziel v Dalziel* (1977), 3 BCLR 73 (SC); *Rankin v Rankin* (1982), 30 RFL (2d) 209 (Ont HCJ); see also *Wood v Wood* (1982), 56 NSR (2d) 217 (TD).

200 *Graham v Graham*, [1999] BCJ No 2819 (SC).

201 *Graham v Graham*, *ibid*; *Lee v Lee*, [1998] NJ No 247 (CA); *Semenchuk v Semenchuk*, [1997] SJ No 480 (QB).

202 *Graham v Graham*, [1999] BCJ No 2819 (SC).

203 *Hoggins v Bell*, [1997] AJ No 1162 (QB).

204 *Bemrose v Fetter*, [2005] OJ No 3362 (SCJ).

205 *Yurchak v Yurchak*, [2000] SJ No 287 (QB).

206 *Dearborn v Dearborn*, [2001] SJ No 276 (QB).

set aside the consent order pursuant to a motion being brought, preferably before the judge who authorized the issuance of the consent order.[207]

A trial judge's agreement that counsel should present the court with a draft order for corollary relief does not preclude the trial judge from reviewing and amending the draft order in light of new evidence adduced at a rehearing.[208] The court has an inherent jurisdiction to permit the introduction of additional evidence and, if required, to vary an order that has not previously been entered.[209]

A judge may reopen a case after giving reasons and making an endorsement but before a formal order is issued; this discretionary jurisdiction does not entitle a dissatisfied party to obtain a rehearing.[210]

In interpreting section 18 of the *Federal Child Support Guidelines* in *Hausmann v Klukas*,[211] the British Columbia Court of Appeal held that pre-tax corporate income will be assumed to be available to a parent who is obligated to pay child support unless evidence is led to the contrary. Because the father's evidence as to the needs of his company was unclear and unsubstantiated, the British Columbia Court of Appeal attributed all of the pre-tax corporate income to him. After his application for leave to appeal to the Supreme Court of Canada was dismissed, he sought to reopen the judgment of the British Columbia Court of Appeal on the basis of documentary evidence that had been available but not produced at the trial. The British Columbia Court of Appeal held that if the "new evidence" was as important as the father claimed, he should have produced it at trial, or at the very latest by way of an application to adduce new evidence at the original hearing of the appeal. The fact that he had a new counsel with a different view of the case did not justify what would amount to a rehearing of the appeal. While an appellate court has the power to reopen an appeal in appropriate circumstances, this was not one of those rare cases where a miscarriage of justice would occur if the father was denied the opportunity to reopen the appeal.[212]

V. VARIATION PROCEEDING

In Manitoba, variation applications are normally dealt with summarily, but, when there is a contested issue of fact that turns on credibility, the issue should be determined on *viva voce* evidence.[213]

In Ontario, applications to vary child support orders are frequently decided by way of motion rather than at a trial. However, where there are few substantive admissions and numerous factual issues to be resolved, the court may have no alternative but to order the application to be determined at a trial, even though the parties desire a determination without a trial.[214]

---

207 *Brandle v Brandle*, [2001] SJ No 720 (QB).
208 *Axent-Cromwell v Cromwell* (1995), 14 RFL (4th) 47 (NSCA).
209 *Alexa v Alexa* (1995), 14 RFL (4th) 93 (BCSC).
210 *Berg v Berg*, [2001] OJ No 5190 (SCJ).
211 2009 BCCA 32.
212 *Hausmann v Klukas*, 2009 BCCA 320. As to a motion for the rehearing of an appeal, see *Sydor v Keough*, 2020 MBCA 20, citing *Rémillard v Rémillard*, 2015 MBCA 42.
213 *Kollinger v Kollinger* (1995), 14 RFL (4th) 363 at para 17 (Man CA).
214 *Wynnyk v Wynnyk*, [2004] OJ No 27 (SCJ).

In Saskatchewan, variation applications are often determined on the basis of affidavit evidence alone. Whether or not a court will decide an application on affidavit evidence alone, require that the matter be set down for trial, or order a *viva voce* hearing as contemplated by the Saskatchewan *King's Bench Rules* will depend on a number of factors. These factors include the complexity of the issues to be decided, whether the affidavits conflict on contentious issues, whether the process would be significantly enhanced by cross-examination, and whether the evidence submitted by affidavit is complete and covers the various factors needed to be considered by the trier of fact. This is not an exhaustive list.[215]

W. MASTERS; REGISTRARS

In British Columbia, a court may direct a reference to the registrar for an inquiry and report concerning the determination of income or expenses for the purpose of applying the *Federal Child Support Guidelines*.[216]

A master has jurisdiction in Manitoba to deal with a motion for the production of financial information for the purpose of a child support application under the *Divorce Act*.[217]

X. COMPUTER PROGRAMS

Computer programs used to facilitate calculation of support under the *Federal Child Support Guidelines* are not infallible. They are only as reliable as the reliability of the assumptions used in the particular program.[218] Currently available computer software designed to assist in the calculation of child support under the Guidelines is based in part on certain assumptions that the designers have been required to make in the absence of judicial interpretation of the governing legislation and of the Guidelines. These assumptions must be amended on an ongoing basis to reflect developing judicial interpretation in order to ensure that the software remains reliable.[219]

Y. PLEA OF UNDUE HARDSHIP

Parties who seek special or extraordinary expenses under section 7 of the *Federal Child Support Guidelines* or who claim undue hardship within the meaning of section 10 of the Guidelines must do so by a formal notice in writing and not orally from the floor of the court when the motion is being argued.[220]

A respondent may raise a plea of undue hardship under section 10 of the *Federal Child Support Guidelines* in response to a claim for child support without filing an independent application by way of a notice of motion specifically seeking such relief. Section 10 will be properly before the court if, in response to an original application for child support or an

215 *Hannah v Warner*, [2008] SJ No 630 (QB).
216 *Yeung v Yeung*, [1999] BCJ No 2901 (SC).
217 *Buhr v Buhr*, [1997] MJ No 565 (QB).
218 *Kelly v Kelly*, [1998] AJ No 228 (QB).
219 *Kelly v Kelly*, [1998] AJ No 423 (QB).
220 *Thomson v Howard*, [1997] OJ No 4431 (Gen Div).

application to vary an existing order, the respondent informs the applicant in writing of his intention to invoke the section.[221]

Reasonable notice must be given if a party seeks to invoke the undue hardship provisions of section 10 of the *Federal Child Support Guidelines*. At the very least, counsel should identify the grounds upon which the claim will be advanced and complete and submit calculations based on financial disclosure by all members of each household.[222]

Z. PRE-TRIALS

A court may entertain a motion for a pre-trial determination of a question of law raised by the pleadings where such a determination may substantially reduce costs. No evidence is admissible on such a motion in Ontario, except by leave of the court or on consent of the parties.[223] Evidence of communications during the course of a pre-trial conference is inadmissible in Saskatchewan pursuant to the Saskatchewan *King's Bench Rules*.[224]

AA. SUMMARY JUDGMENT

On a motion to dismiss a claim by way of a summary judgment under Alberta Rule 159, the material must clearly demonstrate that the action has no reasonable prospect of success and that it does not raise a genuine issue for trial.[225]

Where there is no genuine issue for trial, an Ontario court may grant a summary judgment for divorce and for the applicable table amount of child support.[226]

Rule 16(12) of the Ontario *Family Law Rules* allows a court to decide a question of law before trial.[227] A motion for summary judgment will be dismissed where genuine issues for trial arise on both the facts and law as to whether the respondent stood in the place of a parent to the child and, if so, the extent of his child support obligation, if any.[228] Where a father's plea of undue hardship because of outstanding family debts is not unrealistic in light of his financial statement, the mother's motion for a summary judgment may be dismissed on the basis that she has failed to prove on a balance of probabilities that there is no genuine issue for trial.[229]

BB. RESCISSION OF ORDERS

Rule 59.06(2) of the Ontario *Rules of Civil Procedure* confer jurisdiction on the Ontario Superior Court of Justice to set aside or vary an order on the ground of fraud or of facts

---

221 *Brady v Brady*, [1998] BCJ No 702 (SC).
222 *BLMG v DJEG*, [1998] MJ No 278 (QB).
223 *Laczko v Laczko*, [1999] OJ No 2577 (SCJ).
224 *Foster v Amos*, 2010 SKQB 409.
225 *Thompson v Thompson*, [2003] AJ No 1577 (QB).
226 *Coulson v Farmer*, [1999] OJ No 2478 (SCJ).
227 *Budden v Briggs*, [2003] OJ No 5528 (SCJ).
228 *IG v HB*, [2003] OJ No 5285 (SCJ). For a review of relevant caselaw in Ontario, see *O'Dacre v Cross*, 2019 ONSC 2265 applying *Hryniak v Mauldin*, 2014 SCC 7.
229 *Wiltshire v Wiltshire*, [2003] OJ No 3099 (SCJ).

arising or discovered after the order is made. The Ontario *Rules of Civil Procedure* are avail able when needed as a back-up to the Ontario *Family Law Rules* by virtue of Rule 7 of the Ontario *Family Law Rules.* Where new facts have arisen or been discovered, the court has an inherent jurisdiction to prevent a miscarriage of justice by retroactively rescinding or changing an existing order.[230] As Summers J of the Ontario Superior Court of Justice observed in *Bidner v Tapp*,

> [9] It is now settled law in Ontario that rule 25(19) of the *Family Law Rules* gives a trial court jurisdiction to set aside an order. See *Gray v. Gray*, 2017 ONCA 100 (CanLII). The Rule states that the court may, on motion, change an order that,
> (a) was obtained by fraud;
> (b) contains a mistake;
> (c) needs to be changed to deal with a matter that was before the court but that it did not decide;
> (d) was made without notice; or
> (e) was made with notice, if an affected party was not present when the order was made because the notice was inadequate or the party was unable, for a reason satisfactory to the court, to be present. . . .
>
> [12] Before the court exercises its discretion to set aside a default judgment, there are certain factors to be considered. See *Mountain View Farms Ltd. v. McQueen*, 2014 ONCA 194 (CanLII) where the Ontario Court of Appeal sets out the following considerations:
> 1. Whether the Respondent moved promptly after learning of the default judgment;
> 2. Whether the Respondent has a plausible excuse or explanation for the failure to respond and comply with the Rules;
> 3. Whether the facts establish that the Respondent has an arguable case on the merits;
> 4. What is the potential prejudice to the Respondent if the default order is not set aside and what is the potential prejudice to the Applicant if the order is set aside;
> 5. What is the effect of the order made by the court on the overall integrity of the administration of justice.[231]

CC. EXPERT OPINIONS

The judgment of Cromwell J of the Supreme Court of Canada in *White Burgess Langille Inman v Abbott and Haliburton Co*[232] sets out the ground rules for the admissibility of expert opinion evidence in civil proceedings, including family law proceedings.[233] The affidavit of a chartered accountant may quite properly set out his assumptions and the factual background relied upon in formulating an opinion as to a parent's annual income, but the affidavit must not go beyond the expert's field of expertise or volunteer a legal opinion. Objection may be taken insofar as the affidavit is in the nature of a legal submission or "argument" and any

---

230 *West v West*, [2001] OJ No 2149 (SCJ) (attendant circumstances deemed insufficient to warrant judicial interference with temporary support order).

231 2017 ONSC 6846 at paras 9 and 12.

232 2015 SCC 23.

233 As to the admissibility of expert medical evidence, see *LaRoche v Lynn*, 2019 ONSC 6602.

such material may be struck from the affidavit. A court is free to accept or reject the expert's opinion in whole or in part. Where the expert has postulated his assumptions of fact and the basis on which he has come to an opinion or conclusion, it is possible for a court to give appropriate weight to the opinion without abdicating the judicial responsibility to make findings of fact on those very same assumptions. Expert opinion as to a parent's income may be presented on a motion for interim support where the parties are far apart on this issue, but in many cases the probative value of the expert opinion will be undermined by the fact that untested assumptions have been made prior to the discovery process on the basis of incomplete information. Expert opinions at the interim stage may backfire by causing the parties to become entrenched in their disparate positions. They run the risk of causing delay and excessive costs because one expert opinion may trigger another opinion on behalf of the other party. Expert evidence of a historical nature may also be of little or no relevance at the interim stage, where the court must assess the parent's expected income over the next six months or so. Although there may be cases where an expert's opinion would be helpful on an interim motion, counsel should be conscious of the limits of such evidence and cognizant of the potential objection to such evidence being received.[234]

And in *JP v British Columbia (Children and Family Development)*, Smith JA of the British Columbia Court of Appeal observed:

> [150] The test for determining the threshold admissibility of an expert's opinion is set out in *R. v. Mohan*, 1994 CanLII 80 (SCC), [1994] 2 S.C.R. 9. To be admissible, opinion evidence must be relevant and necessary; it must not be rendered inadmissible by any other exclusionary rule; and it must be offered by a properly qualified expert. Expert opinion evidence must also be fair, objective and non-partisan to be admissible: *White Burgess Langille Inman v. Abbott and Haliburton Co.*, 2015 SCC 23 (CanLII) at para. 2. If an expert is not properly qualified and is not neutral, his or her opinion has the potential to "swallow whole the fact-finding function of the court": *R. v. Abbey*, 2009 ONCA 624 (CanLII) *per* Doherty J.A. Opinion evidence that fails to meet these requirements is prejudicial to each party's right to a fair determination of the issues, lacks probative value and is therefore irrelevant, unnecessary and unhelpful.[235]

DD. JUDICIAL NOTICE

A court can take judicial notice of any fact that is "capable of immediate and accurate demonstration by resort to readily accessible sources of indisputable accuracy."[236] And it appears that this can be extended to a calculation of EI benefits by reference to an appropriate government website.[237]

234 *Picard v Picard*, [2001] OJ No 2299 (SCJ).

235 2017 BCCA 308.

236 *R v Find*, [2001] SCJ No 34 at para 48; see also *Friesen v Friesen*, 2023 SKCA 60.

237 *Cozzi v Smith*, 2015 ONSC 396 at para 25, McDermot J. As to the application of judicial notice of provincial economic conditions as they impact job prospects in the context of a child support claim involving imputed income, see *Locke v Bramwell*, 2016 NSSC 300 at paras 8–18. As to judicial notice of social science evidence, see *Friesen v Friesen*, 2023 SKCA 60 at paras 29–39.

A court is not entitled to invoke the doctrine of judicial notice to refute the documented and uncontradicted evidence of a self-employed parent as to her earning capacity in a particular field of employment.[238]

EE. DISPUTE RESOLUTION PROCESSES

The mediation process before a Dispute Resolution Officer in Alberta is privileged. The problem of having privileged information available on the court file can be addressed by a parent resubmitting financial information to the court in the form of an appendix to an affidavit. Systemic solutions to the problem might be achieved by legislative removal of the privilege or by a filing direction that segregates materials filed for the mediation process from the litigation file.[239]

An Alberta court may order the annual production of personal and corporate income tax returns to forestall future problems in determining the amount of child support to be paid, but it cannot order binding JDR (judicial dispute resolution) as part of the "formula" for dealing with future problems. Court-ordered mandatory attendance at binding JDR is inappropriate because it requires the parties to give up important substantive rights. Sufficient agreement may, nevertheless, exist between the parents about the underlying facts in dispute to allow a judge to express an opinion about the facts without ordering the trial of an issue. In that event, a special chambers application could be brought or a summary trial heard, neither of which requires a litigant to give up any substantive rights relating to appeal or review.[240]

On an application seeking a partial remission of child support arrears, a court has no jurisdiction to accept a father's proposal with respect to the payment of specified arrears where that proposal is rejected by the mother. In open court and chambers, the court's role is adjudicative; it determines the legal rights and obligations of litigants. In that role, it cannot impose a proposed settlement on either parent. Absent agreement between the parents on the facts that must support an application for cancellation of arrears, the court must order a trial of the issue where evidence will determine what facts the court will find. The proper forum in which a parent may call upon the court to exercise an advisory role is a JDR session.[241]

Litigation is not precluded by an arbitration clause in a separation agreement where the clause is not sufficiently clear and unambiguous to oust the jurisdiction of the court and the plea was raised belatedly, notwithstanding earlier opportunities to raise the issue. A court may also refuse a stay of the judicial proceeding under section 7 of the *Arbitration Act, 1991* (Ontario) where the motion to stay was brought after undue delay.[243]

238 *Dean v Brown*, [2002] NSJ No 439 (CA).
239 *Harrison v Hardy*, [2005] AJ No 1189 (QB).
240 *Yeoman v Luhtala*, [2002] AJ No 1504 (QB).
241 *Nanrhe v Nanrhe*, [2005] AJ No 1332 (QB).
242 SO 1991, c 17.
243 *Seguin v Masterson*, [2004] OJ No 2176 (SCJ).

FF. UNDERTAKINGS

Where a litigant fails to comply with undertakings, the proper procedure is for an application to be brought that asks the court to order due compliance with the undertakings. Accordingly, an appellate court may find no error of law established in a chambers judge's failure to take extant undertakings into account in granting the father's application for retroactive and prospective termination of his court-ordered child support obligation.[244]

GG. HEARSAY EVIDENCE

An issue of hearsay evidence cannot be raised on appeal if it was not raised before the chambers judge. Where there is an appeal respecting the admission of evidence in a civil proceeding, the appellant can only rely on those grounds upon which the evidence was objected to at trial.[245]

HH. SELF-REPRESENTED LITIGANTS

Self-represented litigants[246] are governed by the same legal principles, rules of evidence, and standards of procedure as those applicable to litigants who are represented by counsel.[247]

Failure to strictly comply with Rule 37.03(a) of the New Brunswick *Rules of Court*[248] is not fatal to a self-represented father's application to be credited with the overpayment of child support. The court may dispense with such compliance pursuant to Rule 2.01 where too technical an application of the rules may result in an injustice.[249]

In *Banilevic v Cairney*, Megaw J of the Saskatchewan Court of Queen's Bench stated:

> [26] The direction of Ryan-Froslie J. (as she then was) in *Bird v Bird*, 2013 SKQB 157, 419 Sask R 214 regarding self-represented litigants, is helpful:
>
> > 45) The Nova Scotia Court of Appeal in *Family and Children's Services of Cumberland County v. D.M.M., supra*, [2006] NSCA 75,29 RFL (6th) 268], at para. 25, stated the following with respect to the assistance to be offered self-represented parties:

---

244 *PEK v BWK*, [2003] AJ No 1706 (CA).

245 *Ibid.*

246 See generally Julie MacPharlane, *The National Self-Represented Litigants Project: Identifying and Meeting the Needs of Self Represented Litigants* (May 2013), online: https://representingyourselfcanada.com/wp-content/uploads/2015/07/nsrlp-srl-research-study-final-report.pdf; see also Canadian Judicial Council, *Statement of Principles on Self-represented Litigants and Accused Persons* (September 2006), online: www.cjc-ccm.gc.ca/cmslib/general/news_pub_other_PrinciplesStatement_2006_en.pdf, cited with approval in *Pintea v Johns*, 2017 SCC 23; *CAT v STB*, 2020 BCSC 593; *Bloomfield v Halfyard*, 2020 MBCA 73; *Cabana v Newfoundland and Labrador*, 2018 NLCA 52; *AD v AD*, 2018 NBCA 83; *Fraser v Ksenych*, 2022 SKCA 93; see also *Davids v Davids*, 1999 CanLII 9289 (ONCA); *Morwald-Benevides v Benevides*, 2019 ONCA 1023; *King v King*, 2021 SKQB 201 at paras 91–92, Megaw J, citing Canadian Judicial Council, *Family Law Handbook for Self-Represented Litigants*. And see *Banilevic v Cairney*, 2020 SKQB 25 in text below.

247 *Ibid.*

248 NB Reg 82-73 (*Judicature Act*).

249 *Newman v Tibbetts*, [2005] NBJ No 135 (CA).

[25] When selfrepresented parties are before the court the trial judge is expected to offer them some assistance if needed, especially in family matters. In *Murphy v. Wulkowicz* 2005 NSCA 147; [2005] N.S.J. No. 474, a family matter where both parties were unrepresented at trial, one of them complained on appeal that the trial judge helped the other one too much. MacDonald, C.J.N.S. stated:

> [37] Ms. Murphy asserts that the judge offered too much assistance to Mr. Wulkowicz as a selfrepresented litigant. I disagree. It is difficult for a judge to conduct a trial when one of the parties is selfrepresented. Two competing interests must be balanced. First the judge obviously cannot be an advocate for a party. At the same time the trial must be run as efficiently and fairly as possible. This may require the judge to offer guidance to a selfrepresented party. The appropriate balance falls within the judge's discretion. See *R. v. McGibbon* (1988), 1988 CanLII 149 (ON CA) 45 C.C.C. (3d) 334 (Ont. C.A.). In this context I conclude that the judge in guiding Mr. Wulkowicz did no more than was necessary to ensure that the trial proceeded fairly and efficiently. The judge did not act as Mr. Wulkowicz's advocate.

46) The Court went on to quote the guidelines established in *Re F.* [2001] FamCA 348, the Full Court of the Family Court of Australia, as follows:

1. A judge should ensure as far as is possible that procedural fairness is afforded to all parties whether represented or appearing in person in order to ensure a fair trial;
2. A judge should inform the litigant in person of the manner in which the trial is to proceed, the order of calling witnesses and the right which he or she has to cross examine the witnesses;
3. A judge should explain to the litigant in person any procedures relevant to the litigation;
4. A judge should generally assist the litigant in person by taking basic information from witnesses called, such as name, address and occupation;
5. If a change in the normal procedure is requested by the other parties such as the calling of witnesses out of turn the judge may, if he/she considers that there is any serious possibility of such a change causing any injustice to a litigant in person, explain to the unrepresented party the effect and perhaps the undesirability of the interposition of witnesses and his or her right to object to that course;
6. A judge may provide general advice to a litigant in person that he or she has the right to object to inadmissible evidence, and to inquire whether he or she so objects. A judge is not obliged to provide advice on each occasion that particular questions or documents arise;
7. If a question is asked, or evidence is sought to be tendered in respect of which the litigant in person has a possible claim of privilege, to inform the litigant of his or her rights;

8. A judge should attempt to clarify the substance of the submissions of the litigant in person, especially in cases where, because of garrulous or misconceived advocacy, the substantive issues are either ignored, given little attention or obfuscated. (*Neil v. Nott* (1994) 121 ALR 148 at 150);
9. Where the interests of justice and the circumstances of the case require it, a judge may:
   * draw attention to the law applied by the Court in determining issues before it;
   * question witnesses;
   * identify applications or submissions which ought to be put to the Court;
   * suggest procedural steps that may be taken by a party;
   * clarify the particulars of the orders sought by a litigant in person or the bases for such orders.

   The above list is not intended to be exhaustive and there may well be other interventions that a judge may properly make without giving rise to an apprehension of bias.

[27] At the end of the day, the court must be mindful this is the parties' litigation. They know the issues and they know the position they seek to advance before the court. And, they know the position each of them takes having been participants in the entire litigation. All of this was clear in this case as the parties voiced their positions and objections. The further comments from Ryan-Froslie J. are therefore instructive:

> 44) ... Aleta chose to represent herself in these proceedings. Whether that choice was made freely or was foisted upon her as a result of financial limitations is a subject of hot debate. Whatever the reason, in assuming the role of representing herself, Aleta assumed the responsibility for preparing and presenting her case which includes following the Rules. While great latitude is given self-represented litigants, in the final analysis a judge must maintain their neutrality. They cannot enter the fray. They can canvass the issues, explain procedure and in a general way describe what evidence may be required but they cannot tell a self-represented litigant what evidence they must call or what they need to do.[250]

Justice Pazaratz of the Ontario Superior Court of Justice, in *MAL v RHM*,[251] provided the following guidance as to orders for costs in favour of self-represented litigants:

> [9] In *Serra v. Serra*, 2009 ONCA 395 (CanLII) the Ontario Court of Appeal confirmed that costs rules are designed to foster three important principles:
>
> a. To partially indemnify successful litigants for the cost of litigation.
> b. To encourage settlement; and,
> c. To discourage and sanction inappropriate behaviour by litigants;

---

250 *Banilevic v Cairney*, 2020 SKQB 25 at paras 26–27.

251 2018 ONSC 2542 at paras 9–13; see also *Green v Whyte*, 2019 ONSC 7133; *AP v JP*, 2020 SKCA 134. Compare the conservative approach in Alberta to awarding costs to self-represented litigants: see *Lawson v Lawson*, 2020 ABQB 519.

[10] Rule 2(2) of the *Family Law Rules* adds a fourth fundamental purpose for costs: to ensure that the primary objective of the rules is met, that cases are dealt with justly. This provision needs to be read in conjunction with Rule 24 of the Rules. *Warasta v. Wahid* 2018 ONCJ 177 (CanLII), 2018 ONCJ 177 (OCJ).

[11] Most of the caselaw dealing with costs claims by self-represented litigants deals with the first of the three objectives set out in *Serra.*

a. Self-represented litigants may be awarded costs, and those costs may include an allowance for counsel fees. *Fong v. Chan*, 1999 CanLII 2052 (ON CA), (1999) 46 O.R. (3d) 330 (C.A.); *Jordan v Stewart*, 2013 ONSC 5037 (CanLII), 2013 ONSC 5037 (SCJ).
b. However, self-represented litigants — whether legally trained — are not entitled to costs calculated on the same basis as those of a litigant who retains counsel. *Pirani v Esmail*, 2014 ONCA 279 (CanLII), 2014 ONCA 279 (ON CA); *Fong v. Chan*, (supra); *Reynolds v. Higuchi*, 2014 ONSC 3375 (CanLII), 2014 ONSC 3375 (SCJ).
c. A self-represented litigant can be awarded costs for disbursements as well as the economic loss caused by having to prepare and appear to argue the case. *Fong v. Chan* (supra); *G.B. v S.A.*, 2013 ONSC 2147 (CanLII), 2013 ONSC 2147 (Divisional Ct).
d. A self-represented litigant should not recover costs for the time and effort that any litigant would have to devote to the case.
e. Costs should only be awarded to those lay litigants who can demonstrate that they devoted time and effort to do the work ordinarily done by a lawyer retained to conduct the litigation and that, as a result, they incurred an opportunity cost by foregoing remunerative activity. *Jordan v Stewart*, (supra).[252]
f. Lost wages as a result of time missed from work to prepare for or argue a case can be compensated by way of costs. *G.B. v S.A.*, (supra). But this excludes routine awards on a *per diem* basis to litigants who would ordinarily be in attendance at court in any event. *Warsh v Warsh*, 2013 ONSC 1886 (CanLII), 2013 ONSC 1886 (SCJ).
g. Compensation for the loss of time devoted to preparing and presenting the case should be moderate or reasonable. *Reynolds v. Higuchi*, (supra).
h. Once a court determines that a "counsel fee" is appropriate for a self-represented litigant, one of the biggest challenges is quantifying both the number of hours to be compensated and the appropriate hourly rate. Courts have awarded anywhere between $20.00 and $200.00 per hour for self-represented litigants, depending on the demonstrated level of skill. *Izyuk v Bilousov*, 2011 ONSC 7476 (CanLII), 2011 ONSC 7476 (SCJ). $60 per hour appears to be a commonly used figure. *Roach v. Lashley*, 2018 ONSC 2086 (CanLII), 2018 ONSC 2086 (SCJ).
i. The *Family Law Rules* do not specifically address costs claims by self-represented litigants. But all of the Rule 18 and 24 costs provisions apply equally whether litigants are represented or not.

[12] As stated, the above considerations focus on the *first* of the three costs objectives set out in Serra: "To partially indemnify successful litigants for the cost of litigation."

---

252 See *Cassidy v Cassidy*, 2019 ONSC 2774 at paras 20–24.

[13] But the remaining two objectives — "encouraging settlement" and "discouraging/sanctioning inappropriate behaviour" — are often unrelated to whether the successful party has a lawyer or not.

a. In our overburdened court system, costs is more than a question of financial reimbursement for a successful party.
b. The "risk/threat" of costs is perhaps the single most important tool our system has to ensure compliance with the *Rules*; encourage reasonable behaviour; and discourage unnecessary or inappropriate litigation.
c. All litigants should be encouraged to actively pursue settlement — whether the opposing party has counsel or not.
d. All litigants should be equally subject to sanction for inappropriate or unreasonable litigation behaviour — whether the opposing party has counsel or not.
e. All litigants should be mindful of costs implications and consequences at every step — whether the opposing party has counsel or not.
f. If we create a two-tier system — in which some litigants perceive they don't have to worry about costs because their opponent didn't hire a lawyer — we will tacitly invite wasteful, expensive and often destructive family litigation. We will lose our ability to control the process. We will fail in our responsibility to protect families from needless pain and financial burden. Our *Rules* will have no teeth.
g. At a time when our family court system is seeing ever-increasing numbers of self-represented parties, it is important to reaffirm that costs sanctions apply equally whether parties have counsel or not. No one should get a "free pass."
h. Rules 18 and 24 — and all of the "costs" jurisprudence — all try to deliver the same basic message: "Don't be unreasonable or it will cost you."
i. We have to guard against that message becoming: "Don't be unreasonable or . . . well . . . nothing will happen."

II. JUDICIAL DISCRETION OVER COSTS

Orders respecting costs in divorce and matrimonial proceedings are a matter for the exercise of discretion by the court.[253] The Ontario Court of Appeal has identified the four fundamental purposes that modern cost rules are designed to foster: (1) to partially indemnify successful litigants; (2) to encourage settlement; (3) to discourage and sanction inappropriate behaviour by litigants; and (4) to ensure that cases are dealt with justly.[254] The principle of proportionality is fundamental to any sound costs award.[255] Speaking to appropriate hourly rates for lawyers in *TG v SG*, Price J of the Ontario Superior Court of Justice observed:

253 For an insightful review of the pertinent principles that impact upon cost awards in matrimonial proceedings in Nova Scotia, see the judgment of MacDonald J in *Gagnon v Gagnon*, 2012 NSSC 137; *Leyte v Leyte*, 2020 NSSC 215; *MacLean v Miller*, 2020 NSSC 224. For an excellent review of the general principles applied in Ontario, see *Beaver v Hill*, 2018 ONSC 3352, Chappel J; and see *FK v AK and CAS of Hamilton*, 2020 ONSC 4927, Pazaratz J. See also *Rafan v Rauf*, 2021 SKQB 117.

254 *Neves v Pinto*, 2020 ONSC 5193, citing *Mattina v Mattina*, 2018 ONCA 867 at para 10.

255 *Chaulk v Andrle*, 2018 ONSC 5101, citing *Marcus v Cochrane*, 2014 ONCA 207.

[36] The "Information for the Profession" bulletin, from the Costs Sub-Committee of the Rules Committee ("the Costs Bulletin"[256]), suggests maximum hourly rates (on a partial indemnity scale) of $80.00 for law clerks, $225.00 for lawyers with less than 10 years' experience, $300.00 for lawyers with between 10 and 20 years' experience, and $350.00 for lawyers with 20 years' experience or more. These rates should be reserved for matters of the greatest complexity.[257]

As a general principle, when an appeal is allowed, the order for costs below is set aside and the appellant is awarded costs below and on appeal.[258]

The *Federal Child Support Guidelines* are easily understood and radically simplify the assessment of the amount payable. Where one parent frustrates the process by recalcitrance and obstinacy, such conduct should be reflected by an order for costs against that parent. Parents who make it difficult to resolve child support disputes in accordance with the *Federal Child Support Guidelines* should bear the costs of the proceedings that are required to resolve the issues they raise.[260] Support payors and recipients must be discouraged from raising frivolous defences to simple claims for an increase or adjustment to the applicable provincial table amount of child support. Insubstantial arguments in response to simple claims should be reflected in an order for costs against that party.[261]

While a successful party is ordinarily entitled to costs in matrimonial proceedings, especially where child support is concerned, the impact of an order for costs on the primary caregiving parent's ability to support the children should be considered.[262]

Where a paying spouse's annual income vastly exceeds $150,000 and there is a huge disparity in the ability of the respective spouses to pay the costs of litigation, the paying spouse should pay the costs of challenging the presumptive application of the provincial table amount to the assessment of child support provided that the payee spouse has not acted unreasonably and there are no offers to settle that would attract the application of Rule 18 of the Ontario *Family Law Rules*.[263]

---

256 As Price J also observed in footnote 4: "'Information for the Profession' bulletin ('the Costs Bulletin') from the Costs Sub-Committee of the Rules Committee (that the Costs Sub-Committee of the Rules Committee issued to replace the Costs Grid, which it repealed in 2005). The Costs Bulletin has advisory status only and not statutory authority, as it was not included in the Regulation that repealed the Costs Grid."

257 2019 ONSC 4662, text to footnote 4, quoted in *Cassidy v Cassidy*, 2019 ONSC 2774 at paras 20–24.

258 *Climans v Latner*, 2020 ONCA 554, citing *St Jean (Litigation Guardian of) v Cheung*, 2009 ONCA 9 at para 4.

259 *Ralph v Ralph*, [2001] NJ No 238 (SC).

260 *Carew v Ricketts*, [2003] NJ No 52 (SC).

261 *Gray v Gray*, [1998] OJ No 2278 (Gen Div); *Russell v Russell*, [1998] OJ No 3381 (Gen Div).

262 *Glad v Glad* (1994), 5 RFL (4th) 270 (Ont Ct Gen Div).

263 *Tauber v Tauber*, [2000] OJ No 3355 (CA); see also *Tauber v Tauber*, [2000] OJ No 2133 (CA); compare *Torbey v Torbey*, [2001] AJ No 1320 (QB).

JJ. COSTS ON SOLICITOR AND CLIENT BASIS; SPECIAL OR INCREASED COSTS

Solicitor and client costs are awarded in rare and exceptional cases where the actions of one of the parties are onerous as against another party.[264]

In British Columbia, a parent who deliberately misleads the court with respect to his income under the *Federal Child Support Guidelines* may be ordered to pay special costs.[265] A parent who makes resolution of the determination of child support unduly difficult may be penalized by an order for increased or special costs, but such an order may be deemed inappropriate where the conduct does not warrant rebuke.[266]

A parent's failure to comply with the disclosure provisions of Rule 70.09 of the Nova Scotia *Civil Procedure Rules* and with section 21 of the *Federal Child Support Guidelines* may trigger an order for costs as an appropriate sanction and such an order may allow costs amounting to a full indemnity.[267]

Costs may be assessed on a solicitor-and-client[268] or full-recovery basis where the obligor adamantly refuses to concede any obligation to pay child support and the delay and costs involved are totally attributable to this position.[269] A successful applicant may be awarded costs on a full-recovery basis where the respondent acts in bad faith under Rule 24(8) of the Ontario *Family Law Rules* by failing to provide full and timely financial disclosure,[270] in forcing the applicant to value the respondent's business, and in failing to pay reasonable child support and section 7 expenses while waiting for an interim motion to be determined.[271] In *Jackson v Mayerle*,[272] wherein the disputed issues ranged from property equalization, spousal support, parenting, and child support, but parenting issues dominated the trial, Pazaratz J of the Ontario Superior Court of Justice provided a detailed list of relevant Ontario caselaw in support of the following principles relating to full recovery costs awards under Rule 24 of the Ontario *Family Law Rules*:

1) Costs rules are designed to foster three important principles:
    a) To partially indemnify successful litigants for the cost of litigation.
    b) To encourage settlement; and
    c) To discourage and sanction inappropriate behaviour by litigants.
2) The assessment of costs is not a mechanical exercise. It is not just a question of adding up lawyer's dockets.

---

264 See *AL v JN*, 2017 NBCA 25 (spousal support) at para 32, citing Orkin, *The Law of Costs*, 2d ed (1987) at 2-61 and 2-62. See also *Tofin v Galbraith*, 2019 SKCA 35 (matrimonial property).

265 *Rozen v Rozen*, [2002] BCJ No 2192 (SC).

266 *Baum v Baum*, [2000] BCJ No 2565 (SC).

267 *Guillena v Guillena*, [2003] NSJ No 76 (SC).

268 As to an order that solicitor and client costs be paid personally by the respondent's lawyer, see *Dickson v Dickson*, 2011 MBQB 296.

269 *Baumann v Clatworthy* (1991), 35 RFL (3d) 200 at 213 (Ont Ct Gen Div). Compare *Buchanan v Buchanan*, [2009] OJ No 674 (SCJ). See also *Beaver v Hill*, 2018 ONCA 840.

270 See *Williams v Steinwand*, 2015 NWTSC 3.

271 *Paech v Paech*, [2004] OJ No 5067 (SCJ).

272 Paraphrasing 2016 ONSC 1556 at paras 16–108. See also *Beaver v Hill*, 2018 ONSC 3352, Chappel J.

3) The overall objective is to fix an amount that is fair and reasonable for the unsuccessful party to pay in the particular circumstances of the case, rather than an amount fixed by the actual costs incurred by the successful litigant.
4) Rules 18 and 24 of the *Family Law Rules* govern the determination of both liability for costs and the amount of costs. While these rules have not completely eliminated judicial discretion, the rules nonetheless circumscribe the broad discretion previously granted to the courts in determining costs.
5) Rules 18 and 24, and most of the caselaw focus on two words: "Success" and "Reasonableness." The latter entails two components:
   a) Reasonableness of behaviour by each party
   b) Reasonableness of the amount of costs to be awarded
6) The starting point in any costs analysis is the presumption that a successful party is entitled to costs.

Rule 18 Offers

7) To determine whether a party has been successful, the court should take into account how the order or eventual result compares to any settlement offers that were made.
8) Rule 18 deals with the formalities and consequences of offers. Rule 18(14) provides that a party who makes a written offer at least seven days before the trial, and obtains an order as favourable as or more favourable than the offer, is entitled, unless the court orders otherwise, to costs to the date that the offer was served and full recovery costs from that date.
9) Offers to settle are to be encouraged, and severable offers (or offers on specific issues) are particularly helpful to the settlement process.
10) An offer that predetermines a costs entitlement is often unhelpful. Costs are more appropriately dealt with after substantive determinations have been made. But an offer that accurately predicts the result on substantive issues and reserves costs to be determined by the court is still a valid Rule 18(14) offer.
11) To trigger full recovery costs a party must do as well or better than *all* the terms of any offer (or a severable section of an offer). The court is not required to examine each term of the offer as compared to the terms of the order and weigh with microscopic precision the equivalence of the terms. What is required is a general assessment of the overall comparability of the offer as contrasted with the order.
12) However, even if Rule 18(14) doesn't apply, Rule 18(16) allows the court to consider any written offer, the date it was made, and its terms.

Rule 24 Factors

13) Rule 24(4) provides that a successful party who has behaved unreasonably may be deprived of all or part of their costs, or ordered to pay all or part of the unsuccessful party's costs.
14) Unreasonable behaviour may be so extreme as to constitute "bad faith." Pursuant to Rule 24(8), if a party has acted in bad faith, the court shall decide costs on a full recovery basis and order the party to pay them immediately.
15) But Rule 24(8) requires a fairly high threshold of egregious behaviour, and as such a finding of bad faith is rarely made.

16) Bad faith is not synonymous with bad judgment or negligence. Rather, it implies the conscious doing of a wrong because of dishonest purpose or moral obliquity. Bad faith involves intentional duplicity, obstruction, or obfuscation.
17) There is a difference between bad faith and unreasonable behaviour. The essence of bad faith is when a person suggests their actions are aimed for one purpose when they are aimed for another purpose. It is done knowingly and intentionally. The court can determine that there shall be full indemnity for only the piece of the litigation where bad faith was demonstrated.
18) To establish bad faith the court must find some element of malice or intent to harm.
19) Bad faith can be established by the intentional failure to fulfill an agreement in order to achieve an ulterior motive or an intentional breach of court order with a view to achieving another purpose.
20) Even in the absence of bad faith, costs may be ordered on a full recovery basis and payable forthwith.
21) But even where behaviour falls short of being bad faith, where unfounded allegations significantly complicate a case or lengthen the trial process, this constitutes unreasonable behaviour relevant to the costs determination. Family law litigants are responsible and accountable for the positions they take during litigation.
22) Rule 24(6) directs the court to consider whether there was divided success, and if so, to apportion costs appropriately.
23) "Divided success" does not necessarily mean "equal success." And "some success" may not be enough to impact on costs.
    a. Rule 24(6) requires a contextual analysis.
    b. Most family court cases involve multiple issues.
    c. Not all issues are equally important, equally time-consuming, or equally expensive to determine.
    d. Comparative success can be assessed in relation to specific issues:
        i. Did a mid-point number prevail on a financial issue?
        ii. Did a compromise result on a parenting issue?
    e. Comparative success can also be assessed globally in relation to the whole of the case:
        i. How many issues were there?
        ii. How did the issues compare in terms of importance, complexity, and time expended?
        iii. Was either party predominantly successful on more of the issues?
        iv. Was either party more responsible for unnecessary legal costs being incurred?
24) Where success in a step in a case is divided, the court may exercise its discretion to apportion costs as appropriate (Rule 24(6)). The court may also in those circumstances award costs to the party who was more successful on an overall global basis.
25) Rule 24(10) establishes the general principle that the court should determine the issue of costs promptly after each step in the case. If a specific order for costs is not made at the end of a step in the case, including a conference or motion, or costs are not reserved, a judge dealing with a subsequent step or the trial judge should not generally consider the costs associated with that step when determining costs.
26) Rule 24(11) sets out additional factors to be considered in determining costs.

27) Rule 24(11)(a) directs the court to consider the importance, complexity or difficulty of the issues.
28) Rule 24(11)(c) directs the court to consider the reasonableness of the lawyers' rates. Rule 24(11)(d) directs the court to consider the time spent on the case.
29) Despite the presumptive provisions of Rule 18(14) the court still retains the discretion to award less than full recovery costs.
30) Even where the "full recovery" provisions of the Rules are triggered — either by an offer that meets Rule 18(14) requirements, or by a finding of bad faith — quantification of costs still requires an overall sense of reasonableness and fairness. The Rules do not require the court to allow the successful party to demand a blank cheque for their costs. The court retains a residual discretion to make costs awards that are proportional, fair, and reasonable in all the circumstances.
31) The costs determination must reflect proportionality to the issues argued. There should be a correlation between legal fees incurred (for which reimbursement is sought) and the importance or monetary value of the issues at stake.
32) By the same token, proportionality should not result in reduced costs where the unsuccessful party has forced a long and expensive trial.
33) The Supreme Court of Canada has recognized in *Hyrniak v Mauldin*, 2014 SCC 7 that timeliness, affordability, and proportionality are essential components of any legal system that seeks to provide true access to justice. Affordability and proportionality require that lawyers budget their time. The expenditure of a disproportionate amount of docketed time will not be sanctioned by the court.
34) Simplistically, a common theme in the "reasonable expectations" and "proportionality" analyses is that the loser should not have to reimburse the winner for excessive or unnecessarily expensive litigation behaviour that might be regarded as "overkill."
35) The size of an unsuccessful party's legal bill does not in any way dictate that the successful party's legal bill is limited to the same amount. Sometimes the winner was successful *precisely* because their lawyer put more work into the file. But at the very least the unsuccessful party's legal bill may be of assistance as a benchmark for proportionality.
36) The manner in which evidence was presented — and tested — is relevant to the consideration of proportionality and overall efficiency.
37) It is not the trial judge's place to control how counsel choose to present their case but choosing to cause or allow a trial to become protracted comes with cost consequences for both parties.
    a. The winner has to establish that they couldn't have achieved that same level of success without incurring all of their costs.
    b. The loser has to establish the winner could still have been successful, even without putting in so much time or effort.
    c. The winner can't be given a blank cheque to spend as much as they want to achieve a result.
    d. The loser will be hard-pressed to argue "you fought too hard to prove you were right."
38) Rule 24(11)(f) directs the court to consider any other relevant matter. This includes the aforementioned considerations of reasonable expectations and proportionality.

39) As well, a court must consider a party's ability to pay costs. But while a party's limited financial circumstances is a factor for the court to consider, it should not be used as a shield against *any* liability for costs and should only be taken into account regarding the quantum of costs.
40) The impact of a costs order on a party's ability to provide for a child must also be considered. But this cuts both ways:
    a. A large costs order against an unsuccessful party may affect their ability to provide for a child in their care.
    b. But inadequate reimbursement for costs may similarly impoverish a child residing in the successful party's household.

KK. FIXED COSTS

Erosion of a child support order by a judicial disposition as to costs may be avoided by fixing costs and deferring payment thereof until the last child is no longer a "child of the marriage" within the meaning of the *Divorce Act*.[273] In these circumstances, the court may order interest to accrue on unpaid costs after sixty days from the date when the payment becomes due.[274]

A court may refuse to fix significant costs in favour of a successful applicant due to complexities and uncertainties under the *Federal Child Support Guidelines*,[275] but litigants who unjustifiably refuse to accept their child support obligations under the *Divorce Act* and the Guidelines must expect to have costs ordered against them.[276]

LL. SECURITY FOR COSTS

Rule 14.67(1) of the *Alberta Rules of Court* permits a single appeal judge to order a party to provide security for costs pursuant to Part 4, Division 4 of the Rules. Rule 4.22 states that the court may order a party to provide security for payment of a costs award if the court considers it just and reasonable, taking into account all of the following:

> (a) whether it is likely the applicant for the order will be able to enforce an order or judgment against assets in Alberta;
> (b) the ability of the respondent to the application to pay the costs award;
> (c) the merits of the action in which the application is filed;
> (d) whether an order to give security for payment of a costs award would unduly prejudice the respondent's ability to continue the action; and
> (e) any other matter the Court considers appropriate.[277]

273 *Scotcher v Hampson*, [1998] OJ No 4002 (Gen Div).
274 *Ibid.*
275 *Reid-Floyd v Kelly*, [1998] NBJ No 19 (QB).
276 *Smith v Stebbings*, [1997] OJ No 5400 (Gen Div); see also *Hughes v Bourdon*, [1997] OJ No 5398 (Gen Div).
277 *Lotoski v Lotoski*, 2018 ABCA 103; *Cambareri v Cambareri*, 2019 ABCA 218; *Hicks v Gazley*, 2020 ABCA 239; *Hasham v Kanji*, 2020 ABCA 283 (interim parenting order); *Kaushal v Kaushal*, 2020 ABCA 340; *Unterschultz v Clark*, 2022 ABCA 202.

Speaking to the jurisdiction to order security for costs in *Hammond v Hammond*,[278] Gar son JA of the British Columbia Court of Appeal has observed:

> *Security for Costs of the Trial*
>
> [11] The jurisdiction to order security for the costs of the trial is found in s. 10(2)(b) of the *Court of Appeal Act*, R.S.B.C. 1996, c 77, which provides:
>
> > 10 (2) In an appeal or other matter before the court, a justice may do one or more of the following:
> >
> > (b) make an interim order to prevent prejudice to any person; …
>
> [12] The trial costs have not yet been assessed or agreed upon. In my view, on these facts it would be premature to order security for costs of the trial. I adjourn this application with liberty to renew it if appropriate.
>
> *Security for Costs of the Appeal …*
>
> [15] The jurisdiction to order security for costs of an appeal is found in s. 24(1) of the *Act*, which provides:
>
> > A justice may order that an appellant pay to or deposit with the registrar security for costs in an amount and in a form determined by the justice.
>
> [16] In *Lu v. Mao*, … 2006 BCCA 560 (Chambers) at para. 6, Ryan J.A. set out the relevant consideration:
>
> > In determining whether security for costs should be ordered, the ultimate question to be answered is whether the order would be in the interests of justice. In this regard, Madam Justice Rowles in *Ferguson v. Ferstay* … 81 B.C.L.R. (3d) 90 at para. 7; 2000 BCCA 592, (in Chambers) identified the following as relevant considerations:
> >
> > (1) appellant's financial means;
> > (2) the merits of the appeal;
> > (3) the timeliness of the application; and
> > (4) whether the costs will be readily recoverable.
>
> [17] Importantly, the burden is on the appellant to show it is in the interests of justice that the respondent's request for security for costs of an appeal should be denied: *Creative Salmon Company Ltd. v. Staniford*, 2007 BCCA 285 (CanLII) at para. 9.

In *Anderson v Bernhard*,[279] Hatch J of the Manitoba Court of Queen's Bench observed:

> [94] Rule 56.01 of the *Court of Queen's Bench Rules*, Man Reg. 553/88, gives the court discretion to order security for costs where such an order would be just. It reads as follows:

278 *Hammond v Hammond*, 2018 BCCA 399, Garson JA (in chambers). See also *AB v CD*, 2020 BCCA 57 at para 10, citing *Gardezi v Positive Living Society of British Columbia*, 2018 BCCA 84 at paras 28–33; *Bhimani v Beninteso*, 2020 BCCA 79; *Hudema v Moore*, 2021 BCCA 276; *Naimi v Yunusova*, 2022 BCCA 311.

279 *Anderson v Bernhard*, 2017 MBQB 191. For additional relevant factors, see *Garrett v Garrett*, 2024 MBKB 22 at para 18, citing *DeBono v Smith*, 1989 CanLII 7278.

56.01 The court, on motion in a proceeding may make such order for security for costs as in the particular circumstances of the case is just, including where the plaintiff or applicant,

(a) is ordinarily resident outside Manitoba;

(b) has another proceeding for the same relief pending;

(c) has failed to pay costs as ordered in the same or another proceeding;

(d) is a corporation or a nominal plaintiff, and there is good reason to believe that insufficient assets will be available in Manitoba to pay costs, if ordered to do so; or

(e) a statute requires security for costs.

[95] In the decision of *Gray et al v. Webster et al* (1998), 1998 CanLII 6168 (MB CA), 129 Man. R. (2d) 87 (C.A.), our Court of Appeal emphasized that security for costs is an extraordinary remedy, only to be ordered where justice demands it. The Court of Appeal stated:

> 32 . . . An order for security for costs should only be granted where it is essential to do so, in the interests of justice, to provide defendants with some protection for their potential costs. . . .

[96] There is a very high threshold in family law cases where a party seeks an order for security for future costs.

[97] In *Shore-Kalo v. Kalo*, 2009 MBCA 104 (CanLII), , 245 Man. R. (2d) 209, the Court of Appeal cited with approval the comments of *Winkler v. Winkler* (1990), 1990 CanLII 7968 (MB CA), 66 Man. R. (2d) 285:

> 3 . . . that decisions to order a party to post security for costs in domestic proceedings are to be exercised with extreme caution.

And in *Klefenz v Klefenz*,[280] Beveridge JA of the Nova Scotia Court of Appeal stated:

> [12] The power to order security for costs is found in *Civil Procedure Rule* 90.42:
>
> > 90.42 (1) A judge of the Court of Appeal may, on motion of a party to an appeal, at any time order security for the costs of the appeal to be given as the judge considers just.
> >
> > (2) A judge of the Court of Appeal may, on motion of a party to an appeal, dismiss or allow the appeal if an appellant or a respondent fails to give security for costs when ordered.
>
> [13] In order to exercise this discretionary power, a judge must be satisfied that "special circumstances" exist, and, even if made out, a judge may decline to order security for costs if to do so would deprive a good faith appellant from being able to prosecute an arguable appeal.
>
> [14] There are a variety of narratives that might make out "special circumstances," but the common thread is that it is unlikely the respondent will be able to collect an award of costs. As explained by Fichaud J.A. in *Williams Lake Conservation Company v. Chebucto Community Council of Halifax Regional Municipality*, 2005 NSCA 44 (CanLII), merely a

280 2018 NSCA 56; see also *Murphy v Ibrahim*, 2022 NSCA 75.

risk, without more, that an appellant may be unable to afford a costs award is insufficient to constitute "special circumstances":

> [11] Generally, a risk, without more, that the appellant may be unable to afford a costs award is insufficient to establish "special circumstances." It is usually necessary that there be evidence that, in the past, "the appellant has acted in an insolvent manner toward the respondent" which gives the respondent an objective basis to be concerned about his recovery of prospective appeal costs. The example which most often has appeared and supported an order for security is a past and continuing failure by the appellant to pay a costs award or to satisfy a money judgment: *Frost v. Herman*, at ¶ 9–10; *MacDonnell v. Campbell*, 2001 NSCA 123 (CanLII), at ¶ 4–5; *Leddicote*, at ¶ 15–16; *White* at ¶ 4–7; *Monette v. Jordan* (1997), 1997 CanLII 573 (NS CA), 163 N.S.R. (2d) 75, at ¶ 7; *Smith v. Heron*, at ¶ 15–17; *Jessome v. Walsh* at ¶ 16–19.
>
> [15] Where the claim for special circumstances is the feared inability to pay appeal costs, the appellant's financial health is naturally the focus. Where the respondent presents evidence of acts of insolvency by the appellant, particularly with regard to previous costs orders, special circumstances will not be hard to find (see for example: *Geophysical Services Inc. v. Sable Mary Seismic Inc.*, 2011 NSCA 40 (CanLII); *Branch Tree Nursery & Landscaping Ltd. v. J & P Reid Developments Ltd.*, 2006 NSCA 131 (CanLII); 2301072 *Nova Scotia Ltd. v. Lienaux*, 2007 NSCA 28 (CanLII); *Blois v. Blois*, 2013 NSCA 39 (CanLII); *Korem v. Kedmi*, 2014 NSCA 42 (CanLII); *Doncaster v. Field*, 2015 NSCA 83 (CanLII); *Ketler v. Nova Scotia (Attorney General)*, 2016 NSCA 15 (CanLII)).

Rule 24(13) of the Ontario *Family Law Rules* provides that a judge may, on motion, make an order for security for costs that is just, based on one or more of the following factors:

1. A party habitually resides outside Ontario.
2. A party has an order against the other party for costs that remains unpaid, in the same case or another case.
3. A party is a corporation and there is good reason to believe it does not have enough assets in Ontario to pay costs.
4. There is good reason to believe that the case is a waste of time or a nuisance and that the party does not have enough assets in Ontario to pay costs.
5. A statute entitles the party to security for costs.[281]

Where a husband in default of his child support obligation sought security for costs against the wife, who was seeking to enforce the support obligation, Galligan J of the Ontario Supreme Court stated:

> In any event it is unseemly indeed to require a woman who holds a foreign judgment against her husband or former husband for arrears of alimony to pay security for costs in order to seek to enforce that judgment in our courts. There is another matter that I consider most significant in this case and it is this: the endorsement also indicates that the foreign judgment is for arrears of child support. I think that it would be most unwise if this court were to permit

281 See *Fraser v Fraser*, 2017 ONSC 3774.

the requirement of security for costs to be used to prevent or hinder a mother from enforcing the obligation of a father to support his child. I do not think that such an obstacle ought to be put in her path to the assistance of the courts of this province.[282]

And in *Re Gupta and Gupta*,[283] Barnes J of the Ontario Superior Court of Justice observed:

> The Court may make an order for security for costs in circumstances where such an order is just. Such circumstances include: where the case is a waste of time or a nuisance and the party does not have enough assets in Ontario to pay for costs: *Family Law Rules*: 24(13), 24(14) and 24(15); *Rules of Civil Procedure*, R.R.O. 1990, and O. Reg. 194. Rule 56.01 and 56.02. The conduct of a party is a relevant consideration. For example, security for costs may be appropriate where the party has a low prospect of success and engaged in conduct that unnecessarily added to the cost and length of the proceeding: *Perron v Perron*, 2011 ONCA 776 (CanLII), at para. 21 to 23; or the party had deliberately accumulated the arrears: *Stelter v Stelter*, 2013 ONCA 508 (CanLII), at paras. 5 and 11.

But as the Ontario Court of Appeal pointed out in *Gauthier v Gauthier*:

> Orders for security for costs are a blunt instrument. They are not intended to act as a roadblock to genuine claims: *Izyuk v. Bilousov*, 2015 ONSC 3684 (CanLII), 62 R.F.L. (7th) 131, at para. 37. They should be used sparingly and carefully because they may well have the effect of barring a party from access to the court process for a proper review of existing orders — something, for example, to which a party is entitled respecting child support orders if there has been a change in circumstances: *Family Law Act*, R.S.O. 1990, c. F.3, s. 37(2.1).[284]

Ontario courts are cautious in ordering security in parenting cases.[285]

MM. INTERIM COSTS AND DISBURSEMENTS

An order for interim disbursements and costs is not confined to property equalization claims.[286] Such an order may be granted with respect to an application for child support where the parent against whom an order is sought has complex financial affairs. The discretion conferred by Rule 24(12) of the Ontario *Family Law Rules* is broader[287] than the equitable jurisdiction set out in *British Columbia (Minister of Forests) v Okanagan Indian Band*,[288]

282 *Mahrer v Mahrer* (1976), 26 RFL 328 at 330 (Ont HCJ).

283 2017 ONSC 6867 at para 17.

284 *Gauthier v Gauthier*, 2019 ONCA 722 at para 8.

285 *Volgemut v Decristoforo*, 2021 ONSC 3543.

286 *Kovacs v Thrasher*, 2015 ONSC 2793, [2015] OJ No 2304 (SCJ) (spousal and child support); *Parente v Parente*, 2023 ONSC 907.

287 *Biddle v Biddle*, [2005] OJ No 737 at para 55 (SCJ); *Root v Root*, [2008] OJ No 2716 (SCJ); *Sharma v Sunak*, 2011 ONSC 7670; *Peerenboom v Peerenboom*, 2018 ONSC 5118 (Div Ct); *Parente v Parente*, 2023 ONSC 907. Compare *VMH v JH*, 2020 ABCA 389 applying Rule 12.36 of the *Alberta Rules of Court*, Alta Reg 124/2010. See also *Armoyan v Armoyan*, 2015 NSSC 92 applying Rule 77.02 (1) of the *Nova Scotia Civil Procedure Rules*.

288 [2003] 3 SCR 371. See also *VLN v SRN*, 2019 ABQB 849; *Blaney v Murphy*, 2020 ABQB 196 at para 44 (interim interdependent partner support under the *Family Law Act*, Alberta); *Martin v Watts*, 2018 ONSC 6566.

wherein the Supreme Court of Canada outlined the following conditions that must be present for an interim costs or disbursements order to be granted:

1) The party seeking the order must be impecunious to the extent that, without such an order that party would be deprived of the opportunity to proceed with the case.
2) The applicant must establish a *prima facie* case of sufficient merit to warrant pursuit.
3) There must be special circumstances sufficient to satisfy the court that the case is within the narrow class of cases where this extraordinary exercise of its powers is appropriate.

It must also be established that the interim disbursements sought are reasonable given the resources of the parties and that the results sought will be of assistance to settlement dis cussions or to the trial judge.[289] Additional principles under Rule 24(12) include the levelling of the playing field and the exercise of the court's discretion to ensure "all parties can equally provide or test disclosure, make or consider offers or possibly go to trial."[290] As Rogers J of the Ontario Superior Court of Justice observed in *Stuart v Stuart*,[291]

1) The ordering of interim disbursements is discretionary.
2) A claimant must demonstrate that absent the advance of funds for interim disbursements, the claimant cannot present or analyze settlement offers or pursue entitlement.
3) It must be shown that the particular expenses are necessary.
4) The claim being advanced must be meritorious.
5) The exercise of discretion should be limited to exceptional cases.[292]
6) Interim costs in matrimonial cases may be granted to level the playing field.
7) Monies may be advanced against an equalisation payment.

And in *Fiorellino-Di Poce v Di Poce*, Akbarali J of the Ontario Superior Court of Justice observed:

> *The Legal Framework for an order for Interim Disbursements*
>
> [9] Rule 24(18) of the *Family Law Rules* O. Reg. 114/99 allows the court to "make an order that a party pay an amount of money to another party to cover part or all of the expenses of carrying on the case, including a lawyer's fees".
>
> [10] The purpose of an award for interim disbursements is "to level the playing field to ensure that meritorious claims in the family law context are not abandoned or forfeited by those who lack financial resources and, as a result, are at a significant financial disadvantage relative to the other party in the proceeding": *Morton v. Morton*, 2015 ONSC 4633 (CanLII) at para. 98.
>
> [11] Rule 24 evidences a less stringent approach in the family law context than is the case in public interest litigation. Consistent with the primary objective, r. 24 seeks to ensure the just determination of the issues between the parties, and recognizes that there may be

289 *Root v Root*, [2008] OJ No 2716 (SCJ).

290 *Agresti v Hatcher*, [2004] OJ No 910 (SCJ).

291 (2001), 24 RFL (5th) 188 at para 8 (SCJ); see also *Martin v Watts*, 2018 ONSC 6566; *Beasley v Beasley*, 2019 ONSC 1562; *Ord v Ord*, 2019 ONSC 1563; *Pizzaro v Kretschmann*, 2019 ONSC 3143; *Parente v Parente*, 2023 ONSC 907. Compare *Murphy v Murphy*, 2012 ONSC 1627. And see *Lakhoo v Lakhoo*, 2015 ABQB 357 and *Armoyan v Armoyan*, 2015 NSSC 92.

292 Compare *Haroon v Sheikh*, 2019 ONSC 3130 at para 35, citing *Romanelli v Romanelli*, 2017 ONSC 1312.

circumstances where one party cannot afford to seek justice on meritorious claims given the disparity in financial resources available to that party: *Morton,* at para. 99.

[12] On a motion seeking interim disbursements, the moving party must demonstrate:

a. The interim disbursements for which an advance payment is requested are important to matters in issue in the proceeding as a whole;

b. The disbursements are necessary and reasonable given the needs of the case and the funds available. If the disbursements are for payment of an expert, the moving party must demonstrate a clear need for the services of the expert;

c. The moving party is incapable of funding the requested amounts;

d. The claim or claims being advanced in the case must be meritorious as far as can be determined on the balance of probabilities at the time of the request for disbursements; and

e. The imposition of the payment on the responding party will not cause undue hardship to the payor: *Morton,* para. 97, citing *Stuart v. Stuart,* 2001 CanLII 28261 (ON SC), [2001] O.J. No. 5172 (S.C.), at paras. 7, 11–13.

[13] It is no longer necessary to find exceptional circumstances to order interim disbursements under the *Family Law Rules.* The order is a discretionary one. The court must ensure the primary objective of fairness under the *Family Law Rules* is met: *Ludmer v. Ludmer,* 2012 ONSC 4478 (CanLII), at para. 15.

[14] The court's discretion should be exercised to ensure that all parties can equally provide or test disclosure, make or consider offers, or possibly go to trial—in other words, to level the playing field: *Stuart,* at para. 8; *Ludmer,* at para. 16.

[15] An order for interim disbursements should not immunize a party from cost awards. The order is to allow the case to proceed fairly and should not be such that a party feels a licence to litigate: *Stuart,* para. 8; *Ludmer,* para. 16.[293]

It will be an uncommon case that will not require some level of expert assistance to value income under section 18 of the *Federal Child Support Guidelines* and a party's own interests in an incorporated or unincorporated company.[294] A court may grant an order for interim disbursements to enable a parent to engage a forensic accountant for the purpose of determining whether it is appropriate for the court to impute income to the other parent who is a minority shareholder in family-operated corporations pursuant to section 18(1)(a) of the *Federal Child Support Guidelines.* The "but for" test, which signifies that the applicant could not proceed with the litigation without an order for interim disbursements, is the appropriate criterion to apply where interim disbursements are sought.[295]

An adult child who is seeking support under the Ontario *Family Law Act*[296] and *Federal Child Support Guidelines* may be entitled to interim disbursements. Two bases exist for the exercise of such jurisdiction, namely, (1) the inherent powers of the court under section 11

293 2019 ONSC 7074; see also *Gaetano v McDadi,* 2021 ONSC 6536, citing *Samis (Guardian of) v Samis,* 2011 ONCJ 273 at para 100; *Docherty v Melo,* 2022 ONSC 5306 at paras 19–22 (spousal support).

294 *Sharma v Sunak,* 2011 ONSC 7670.

295 *Leopold v Leopold,* [2001] OJ No 3355 (SCJ); see also *Pakka v Nygard,* [2002] OJ No 3858 (SCJ).

296 RSO 1990, c F.3.

of the Ontario *Courts of Justice Act*;[297] and (2) the power conferred on the court to order costs by section 131 of the Ontario *Courts of Justice Act*.[298] Such jurisdiction may also be exercisable under section 34(1) of the Ontario *Family Law Act* whereby a court may grant an interim support order that includes a lump sum. There is no reason why this section cannot be invoked to enable a child to retain a lawyer. A court cannot order costs with respect to services provided by an agent who is not a lawyer, student-at-law, or clerk supervised by a lawyer, but it may order costs with respect to services rendered by a lawyer, even if the law yer is acting without a retainer. An adult child is not expected to deplete capital to pay legal fees. An order for interim disbursements should only be granted in exceptional cases where there appears to be a meritorious claim of substantial importance to the parties that would otherwise not be pursued.[299]

A failure to make full and timely financial disclosure is an important consideration in determining the costs of an interim application for child support.[300]

NN. PUBLIC OFFICIALS

A defendant who has failed to support family dependents may be ordered to pay costs to offset the expenditure of time by public officials who are employed to conduct proceedings for the enforcement of support orders.[301]

A court may find it inappropriate to order for costs against the Director of Maintenance Enforcement in the absence of special and unusual circumstances.[302] A court may decline to order costs against the Director of Maintenance Enforcement until the director has been given an opportunity to be heard.[303]

Section 131(1) of the *Courts of Justice Act*[304] provides no basis for an award of costs against a non-party. However, the court has inherent jurisdiction to make such an award where it is shown (1) that the non-party had status to bring the action; (2) that the plaintiff was not the true plaintiff; and (3) that the plaintiff was a "man of straw" put forward to protect the non-party from liability for costs. Costs should not be made against a non-party except in unusual and rare circumstances. It has been held that costs may be awarded against a delivery agent where the agent (1) has instigated and supported the applicant in making the application; (2) has wrongly set the court in motion; (3) has known, or ought to have known, that the appli cation was fruitless; (4) has been unsuccessful in the application; (5) was effectively identified with the application; (6) has effectively controlled the situation and the court process. The fact that the delivery agent merely assists the applicant with her unsuccessful application, in accordance with the governing legislation, will not, by itself, render the agent liable to

297 RSO 1990, c C.43.

298 See *CMM v DGC*, 2015 ONSC 1815, applying Rule 24 (12) of Ontario *Family Law Rules*, O Reg 114/99.

299 *Lynch v Lynch*, [1999] OJ No 4559 (SCJ).

300 *MacIntosh v MacIntosh*, [2003] AJ No 728 (QB).

301 *Davis v Colter* (1973), 12 RFL 84 (Sask QB); see also *Wright v Wright* (1994), 7 RFL (4th) 43 (BCSC).

302 *CAG v SG*, 2013 ABQB 12.

303 *Goudriaan v Plourde*, [2002] AJ No 272 (QB).

304 RSO 1990, c C.43.

the successful party for costs but where the delivery agent assumed a controlling role in the unsuccessful application, such conduct may attract an award of costs.[305]

The presumption that a successful party is entitled to costs does not apply to a government agency by virtue of Ontario *Family Law Act* Rule 24(2), but the court has a discretion to order costs to or against a government agency under Ontario *Family Law Act* Rule 24(3), where that agency was the largest stakeholder and took the lead in the conduct and presentation of the case.[306] In *Ontario (Director, Family Responsibility Office) v Ramsay*,[307] it was determined that the caselaw permits a court to order costs against the Family Responsibility Office in the face of special and unusual circumstance and the absence of good faith is not a necessary requirement.

It is incumbent on the Ontario Family Responsibility Office to keep up-to-date and reliable records and to respond in a timely fashion to reasonable inquiries respecting those records. An order for fixed costs against the Ontario Family Responsibility Office may be deemed appropriate for its substantial delay in responding to simple questions concerning the meaning of and justification for various entries on a statement of arrears that it provided for the purpose of a legal proceeding.[308]

The costs of an appeal respecting child support are enforceable by the Family Responsibility Office as a "support order" by virtue of section 1(1) of the *Family Responsibility and Support Arrears Enforcement Act* (Ontario).[309]

OO. ENFORCEMENT OF COSTS; BANKRUPTCY

Costs that are allocated to an order for child support will survive bankruptcy and subsequent discharge pursuant to section 178(1)(c) of the *Bankruptcy and Insolvency Act*.[310] Section 1(1)(g) of the *Family Responsibility and Support Enforcement Act*[311] provides that a "support order" includes "the payment of legal fees . . . arising in relation to support." An order for costs falls within this provision.[312] The advantages of an order under this provision are that the costs award is enforceable by the Family Responsibility Office and it is not discharged in a bankruptcy by virtue of section 178(1)(c) of the *Bankruptcy Act*.[313]

---

305 *CLE v KD*, 2010 ONSC 7072.

306 *Gauthier v Martel*, [2003] OJ No 5296 (SCJ).

307 2005 ONCJ 324. See also *Emhecht v Ontario (Family Responsibility Office)*, 2011 ONSC 2644 (SCJ).

308 *Moberg v Peterson*, [2001] OJ No 4871 (SCJ).

309 *Family Responsibility and Support Arrears Enforcement Act, 1996*, SO 1996, c 31. See *AMD v AJP*, [2003] OJ No 3 at para 17 (CA).

310 RSC 1985, c B-3. See *Madden v Dahl*, 2014 BCCA 23; *Dorey v Havens*, 2019 BCCA 47.

311 SO 1996, c 31.

312 *Sordi v Sordi*, 2011 ONCA 665.

313 RSC 1985, c B-3. See *Wildman v Wildman* (2006), 82 OR (3d) 401 at para 54 (CA); *Hatcher v Hatcher*, [2009] OJ No 3342 (SCJ).

PP. TAX DEDUCTION OF LEGAL FEES

Legal fees incurred by a recipient of child support payments in order to establish the right to child support are tax deductible, whereas payors of child support are not permitted to deduct legal fees incurred to establish their support obligations, to resist the increase of existing support obligations, to resist the payment of existing support obligations, to cause the decrease of existing support obligations, or to cause the elimination of existing support obligations. And this distinction in the treatment of payors and payees does not contravene equality rights under section 15 of the *Canadian Charter of Rights and Freedoms*.[314]

---

314 *Grenon v Canada*, 2014 TCC 265, Graham J.

CHAPTER 15

Appeals

A. DEFINITION OF "APPELLATE COURT"

Section 2(1) of the *Divorce Act* provides that "appellate court," in respect of an appeal from a court, means the court exercising appellate jurisdiction with respect to that appeal. This definition is relevant to the operation of sections 21 and 25(3) of the Act. An examination of the aforementioned provisions indicates that the determination of the appropriate appellate court and the procedure applicable on appeals has been delegated to the provinces.[1] Although section 96 of the *Constitution Act, 1867* binds both the Parliament of Canada and the provincial legislatures and precludes any appellate jurisdiction in divorce proceedings being exercised by tribunals other than those presided over by federally appointed judges, some flexibility exists for the provinces to select the appropriate appellate court in exercising their legislative jurisdiction over the administration of justice. The composition of the appellate court could also vary according to whether the appeal is in respect of an interim order or a permanent order for corollary relief.

B. GENERAL OBSERVATIONS

Section 21(1) of the *Divorce Act* confers a general right to appeal from any judgment or order, whether final or interim, made pursuant to the Act. Sections 21(2), (3), and (4), however, impose restrictions on the right of appeal, which vary according to whether the appeal relates to the judgment *qua* marital status or to interim or final corollary orders. A non-party is not entitled to appeal.

1 As to the provincial power of a trial judge to reserve or refer matters to an appellate court, see *Arnold v Arnold* (1965–69), 2 NSR 348 (CA); *Iantsis v Papatheodorou* (1971), 3 RFL 158 (Ont CA).

C. RESTRICTIONS ON STATUS APPEALS

Pursuant to sections 12(3), (4), (5), and 21(2) of the *Divorce Act*, no appeal lies from a judgment granting a divorce once the time fixed by law for instituting an appeal has expired, unless an extension of the time for appeal has been sought or granted *before* expiry of the normal period fixed by law for instituting an appeal.[2]

Although section 21(2) expressly denies any right of appeal from a judgment granting a divorce on or after the divorce takes effect pursuant to section 12, it does not preclude rescission of the divorce judgment for proper cause.[3]

D. RESTRICTIONS ON COROLLARY ORDER APPEALS

In British Columbia and Saskatchewan, it has been held that section 21 provides an automatic right to appeal corollary orders under the *Divorce Act* that prevails over any conflicting provincial legislation that requires leave to appeal.[4] In Nova Scotia, it has been held that an interim parenting or support order[5] or a consent order for corollary support granted under the *Divorce Act* requires leave to appeal to the Court of Appeal pursuant to the provisions of the *Judicature Act*.[6] In Ontario, it has been held that interim corollary orders under the *Divorce Act* require leave to appeal to the Divisional Court pursuant to section 19(1)(b) of the *Courts of Justice Act*.[7] The Ontario Court of Appeal reasoned that section 21(1) of the *Divorce Act* establishes the right to appeal an interim order but it must be read in light of section 21(6) of the *Divorce Act*, which stipulates that "an appeal under this section shall be asserted, heard and decided according to the ordinary procedure governing appeals," and having regard also to section 25, which empowers the provinces "to make rules regulating practice and procedure." And in Ontario, the "ordinary procedure" for appealing an interlocutory order is governed by section 19(1) of the *Courts of Justice Act*, which provides that "[a]n appeal lies to the Divisional Court from . . . (b) an interlocutory order of a judge of the Superior Court of Justice, with leave as provided in the rules of court." Addressing the conjoint operation of section 21 of the *Divorce Act* and section 19(1) of the *Courts of Justice Act*, the Ontario Court of Appeal determined that the doctrine of paramountcy is not engaged because there is no operational incompatibility between the federal and provincial legislative provisions. Applying the test of incompatibility set out in *Canadian Western Bank v Alberta*[8] as to whether it is impossible to comply simultaneously with both laws or whether the operation of the provincial law would frustrate the purpose of the federal legislation, the Ontario Court of Appeal observed that due compliance with both statutes is accommodated by a party seeking

2 Compare *Massicotte v Boutin*, [1969] SCR 818; *Kumpas v Kumpas*, [1970] SCR 438; *Novic v Novic*, [1983] 1 SCR 700, applying s 18(2) of the *Divorce Act*, 1968; and see current *Divorce Act*, s 21(6).

3 See Julien D Payne, *Payne on Divorce*, 4th ed (Scarborough, ON: Carswell, 1996) ch 6, "Divorce Judgments," part 1, "Effective Date of Divorce Judgment; Appeals; Rescission of Divorce Judgment."

4 *Haigh v Haigh* (1987), 15 BCLR (2d) 375 (CA); *DeFehr v DeFehr*, 2002 BCCA 577; *Kotelmach v Mattison* (1987), 11 RFL (3d) 56 (Sask CA); *Rimmer v Adshead*, 2003 SKCA 19.

5 *Charapovich v Charapovich*, 2023 NSCA 15.

6 RSNS 1989, c 240. See *Cosper v Cosper* (1995), 14 RFL (4th) 152 (NSCA).

7 *Elgner v Elgner*, 2011 ONCA 483, leave to appeal to SCC refused, [2011] SCCA No 341.

8 2007 SCC 22.

leave to appeal pursuant to section 19(2)(b) of the *Courts of Justice Act*. Pursuant to the conjoint operation of subsections 21(1) and 21(6) of the *Divorce Act*[9] and articles 29 and 511 of the *Code of Civil Procedure*,[10] an appeal from an interlocutory judgment rendered in the context of a divorce proceeding in Quebec requires leave of court, regardless of the subject matter and object of the interlocutory proceeding and whether it relates to the interpretation of a provision of the *Divorce Act*.[11] In reaching this conclusion, the Quebec Court of Appeal accepted the analysis of the Ontario Court of Appeal in *Elgner v Elgner*.[12]

Subject to section 21(4) of the *Divorce Act*, section 21(3) prohibits any appeal from an interim or final order for corollary relief, unless the appeal is instituted within thirty days after the day on which the order was made. The statutory requirements are satisfied if the appeal is filed on the thirtieth day, but the hearing is fixed for a subsequent date.[13] The Manitoba Court of Appeal has held that the time fixed by section 21(3) for filing a notice of appeal with respect to a corollary issue in divorce proceedings runs from the date of entry, not from the date of pronouncement of the order. In matters relating to corollary relief orders, it makes more sense for time to run from the date of entry and not from the date of pronouncement of the judgment because a trial judge has the privilege of varying his decision until the moment of entry so that variations in the order can and do sometimes occur at the last minute.[14] As Beard JA of the Manitoba Court of Appeal observed in *Singh v Pierpont*, "[i]t is important to note that the requirement that an order be 'entered' in the court granting the order before a notice of appeal is filed, as referred to in *Baird*, has been replaced with a requirement that an order be signed and filed in the court granting the order before an appeal is filed."[15] Cases in New Brunswick, Newfoundland and Labrador, Nova Scotia, and Prince Edward Island have proceeded on the basis that a corollary relief order is "made" when the written order is filed.[16] According to the Alberta Court of Appeal, however, the word "made" in section 21(3) refers to pronouncement, not entry.[17] The British Columbia Court of Appeal has also concluded that the time for appeal runs from the date of the oral judgment and not from the date when the reasons for judgment have been transcribed and approved.[18]

Section 21(4) of the *Divorce Act* empowers an appellate court or judge thereof to extend the time for instituting an appeal where special grounds are established and an application for such extension may be made before or after expiry of the time ordinarily applicable. It is

---

9 RSC 1985, c 3 (2d Supp).

10 RSQ, c C-25. See now Quebec *Code of Civil Procedure*, CQLR, c C-25.01, art 30.

11 *Droit de la famille — 121718*, 2012 QCCA 1229; *Droit de la famille — 123147*, 2012 QCCA 1966; *Droit de la famille — 142281*, 2014 QCCA 1692; compare *K(H) c S(D)* (1988), 18 RFL (3d) 66 (Que CA).

12 2011 ONCA 483.

13 *Novic v Novic*, [1983] 1 SCR 700.

14 *Baird v Baird*, [1977] 5 WWR 72 (Man CA); *Harvey v Harvey* (1989), 23 RFL (3d) 53 (Man CA). See also *CED v CJD*, 2020 PECA 8 (property and spousal support).

15 2015 MBCA 18 at paras 19–28.

16 *Grant v Grant*, 2011 NBCA 113; *Duffy v Duffy*, 2009 NLCA 11; *MacDonald v MacDonald*, 2010 NSCA 34.

17 *Levesque v Levesque* (1992), 41 RFL (3d) 96 (Alta CA) (extension of time for appeal granted where appeal not prejudicial to respondent and not frivolous or hopeless); *Dang v Bahramloian*, [2007] AJ No 451 (CA) (extension of time for parenting appeal denied).

18 See *Psaila v Psaila* (1984), 40 RFL (2d) 458 at 459 (BCCA); see also *Levesque v Levesque* (1992), 41 RFL (3d) 96 (Alta CA); compare *Harvey v Harvey* (1989), 23 RFL (3d) 53 (Man CA), and *Kotelmach v Mattison* (1987), 11 RFL (3d) 56 (Sask CA).

incumbent upon an applicant for an extension of time to file a notice of appeal (a) to show a *bona fide* intention to appeal while the right to appeal existed and that the failure to appeal was by reason of some special circumstances that served to excuse or justify such failure; (b) to account for the delay and to show that the other side was not so seriously prejudiced thereby as to make it unjust, having regard to the position of both parties, to disturb the judgment; (c) to show that he has not taken the benefits of the judgment from which he is seeking to appeal; and (d) to show that he would have a reasonable chance of success if allowed to prosecute the appeal.[19] Although the court should in every case consider the above requirements, it always retains an unfettered discretion to extend the time for appealing if the justice of the situation so requires. Because the court retains overriding discretion to extend the time to appeal, it is not fatal for an applicant to fail to meet all the above requirements, but it is more likely that an extension will be granted where each element is satisfied.

Where the ground for appeal is that the trial judge acted on inaccurate information, the better procedure would be to move in the Court of King's Bench for an order setting aside that part of the divorce judgment, rather than applying for an extension of time for appeal. An order extending the time for appeal can only be granted on special grounds and must be refused in the absence of a satisfactory explanation of the applicant's delay.[22] "Special grounds" within the meaning of section 21(4) of the *Divorce Act* presuppose some sufficiently compelling reason to grant an extension, such as something in the reasons why an appeal was not taken on time or something in the proceedings or about the judgment that would cause injustice if an extension were not granted. An extension may be deemed appropriate where

1) the applicant intended to appeal within the prescribed time limit, but failed to do so because of misunderstandings;
2) the applicant had an arguable case; and
3) no effective prejudice would befall the respondent except, perhaps, some difficulty in recovering the costs of the appeal if it failed.[23]

An application for an extension will not be granted where the applicant changed his or her mind or made a belated decision to appeal the disposition at trial.[24] Grounds for appellate intervention, at least in an arguable form, constitute a condition precedent to the court

---

19 *Cairns v Cairns*, [1931] 3 WWR 335 (Alta CA); *Dureab v Ben-Harhara*, 2021 ABCA 128; *Wolfe v Morrisseau*, 2021 ABCA 205; *Vey v Vey* (1984), 54 BCLR 270 (CA); *Fritschij v Bazan*, 2007 MBCA 11; *Power v Power* (1979), 24 NBR (2d) 617 (CA); *Fitzgerald v Foote*, 2003 NLCA 25; *Zenner v Zenner*, 2012 PECA 5. See also *Dixon v Cole*, 2014 NSCA 100; *CED v CJD*, 2020 PECA 8 at paras 15–17; *Patel v Whiting*, 2020 SKCA 49. As to the jurisdiction to grant a stay of an order under appeal to the Supreme Court of Canada, see *AC and JF v Alberta*, 2021 ABCA 133.

20 *Andres v Andres*, 2023 ABCA 42 at paras 17–18; *Blume v Blume*, 2023 ABCA 174.

21 *Young v Young* (1981), 17 RFL (2d) 190 (Man CA). And see Julien D Payne, *Payne on Divorce*, 4th ed (Scarborough, ON: Carswell, 1996) ch 6, "Divorce Judgments," part 1, "Effective Date of Divorce Judgment; Appeals; Rescission of Divorce Judgment."

22 Compare *MacIsaac v Seffern*, [1969] RP 183 (Que CA), applying s 17(4) of the *Divorce Act*, 1968; see also *Stewart v Stewart* (1990), 30 RFL (3d) 67 (Alta CA); *Andronyk v Cox* (1984), 57 BCLR 69 (CA).

23 *Wood v Wood*, [2001] SJ No 2 (CA).

24 *Psaila v Psaila* (1984), 40 RFL (2d) 458 at 460 (BCCA).

granting an extension of time within which to appeal.[25] A mistake of counsel concerning the period within which the notice of appeal shall be filed may not constitute special grounds for an extension of the time for appeal.[26] Similarly, an application for an order extending the time for appeal may not be favourably entertained where the prospective appellant failed to consult newly appointed counsel until after expiry of the statutorily designated period.[27] Where a spouse has changed lawyers and the new lawyer has deferred filing notice of appeal pending receipt of the reasons for judgment, an extension of the time for appeal has been granted.[28] A spouse has also been granted an extension of the time for appeal where he intended to appeal within the prescribed time but was late in instructing his solicitors to do so because he was out of the province and honestly believed that he had more time to file an appeal and it appeared at least arguable that the support order sought to be appealed was so excessive as to warrant a reduction. An application to extend the time for appeal will be dismissed in the absence of effective material in support of the application.

The factors that should influence a court in deciding whether to exercise its discretion to extend the time for filing a notice of appeal are not applicable with the same force or in the same way in deciding whether the court should exercise the discretion to extend the time for filing a factum embodying a notice of cross-appeal. The time limit for giving notice of the cross-appeal is set by reference to the time of filing the appellant's factum. Extensions of time for filing factums are given on much more flexible principles than those applicable to extensions of time for filing notices of appeal.[29]

An appeal may not be made concerning an evidential ruling made in the course of a trial until the final adjudication has been rendered. To permit appeals from interlocutory decisions concerning admissibility of evidence creates delay and confusion and the issue raised may ultimately be a moot point.[30]

Where a parent unilaterally reduces the amount of child support, thereby breaching a court order, an appellate court may, in the absence of a convincing explanation of the impossibility of compliance, refuse to hear the appeal.[31]

E. ROLE AND POWERS OF APPELLATE COURT

Section 21(5) of the *Divorce Act* expressly empowers an appellate court to

a) dismiss the appeal, or
b) allow the appeal and

---

25 *Power v Power* (1979), 24 NBR (2d) 617 (CA); *Fraser v Fraser* (1979), 30 NSR (2d) 289 (CA); *Re Beliveau and Director, Legal Aid, Hamilton, Ontario* (1972), 6 RFL 1 (Ont CA).

26 See *Labelle v Robitaille*, [1970] RP 144 (Que CA); compare *Levesque v Levesque* (1992), 41 RFL (3d) 96 (Alta CA); *Vey v Vey* (1984), 54 BCLR 270 (CA); *Re Saskatchewan Registration No 76-07-017181* (1985), 47 RFL (2d) 334 (BCCA). Compare *Dixon v Cole*, 2014 NSCA 100.

27 See *Botsis v Mourelatos*, [1970] RP 191 (Que CA).

28 *Wur v Wur* (1975), 17 RFL 251 (Man CA).

29 *Newson v Newson* (1980), 18 BCLR 203 (CA).

30 *Children's Aid Society of Halifax v H(LT)* (1989), 19 RFL (2d) 171 (NSCA).

31 *Elensky v Elensky* (1993), 50 RFL (3d) 231 (BCCA).

i) render the appropriate judgment or corollary order that should have been made,[32]
ii) order a new hearing where this is necessary to avoid a substantial wrong or miscar riage of justice or to bring forth additional information.[33]

Where a refusal to grant child care expenses under section 7(1)(a) of the Guidelines is reversed on appeal, the appellate court may conclude that it is impractical to remit the issue of the amount to the trial judge because of the costs involved. In that event, the appellate court may leave it open to the parties to agree upon the appropriate amount in light of cur rent financial information available to them, while ordering that a fixed monthly sum shall be paid in the absence of agreement.

Appellate courts should not overturn support orders, unless there is an error of princi ple, a significant misapprehension of the evidence, or unless the order is clearly wrong.[34] is not for the appellate court to intervene by substituting its own evaluative judgment for that of the trial judge.[35] An appellate court is not precluded from identifying errors in the trial judge's findings of fact where those findings are sufficiently palpable and important and have a sufficiently decisive effect that they warrant appellate intervention and review. It is not sufficient, however, to identify errors in the details of the findings of fact made by the judge of first instance, if the overall characterization of the effect of the facts is correct in law.[37] Insofar as the *Federal Child Support Guidelines* are mandatory and not permissive, an appellate court is required to intervene where the trial judge made an error of law in not addressing the issues according to the Guidelines.[38] The exercise of discretion by a Master on a question of fact should not be disturbed on appeal unless it was "clearly wrong," but a judge sitting on appeal on a point of law from a Master has a conventional appellate jurisdiction in which the legal issue may be argued and decided on the merits.[39]

---

32 *Kubel v Kubel* (1995), 15 RFL (4th) 356 (Alta CA); *Jens v Jens*, 2008 BCCA 392; *Perfanick v Panciera*, [2001] MJ No 528 (CA); *Williams v Williams*, [1999] NJ No 254 (CA); *Wedsworth v Wedsworth*, [2000] NSJ No 306 (CA); *R v R*, [2002] OJ No 1095 (CA); *Wilson v Grassick* (1994), 2 RFL (4th) 291 (Sask CA).

33 *Brill v Brill* (1995), 10 RFL (4th) 372 (Alta CA); *Kits v Kits*, [2001] BCJ No 898 (CA) (terms of order under appeal to continue in force pending rehearing); *Cabot v Mikkelson*, [2004] MJ No 240 (CA); *Lister v Gould*, [2000] NBJ No 419 (CA); *King v King* (1994), 2 RFL (4th) 407 (Nfld CA); *Gorham v Gor ham* (1994), 132 NSR (2d) 396 (CA); *Wunsche v Wunsche* (1994), 70 OAC 380 (CA); *Rist v Rist*, [2000] SJ No 637 (CA).

34 *Hickey v Hickey*, [1999] 2 SCR 518; *DBS v SRG; LJW v TAR; Henry v Henry; and Hiemstra v Hiemstra*, 2006 SCC 37; *Michel v Graydon*, 2020 SCC 24 at para 30; *Barendregt v Grebliunas*, 2022 SCC 22; *BJT v JD*, 2022 SCC 24; *Kreke v Alansari*, 2021 SCC 50; *Peters v Atchooay*, 2022 ABCA 347; *Santelli v Trinetti* 2019 BCCA 319; *Smederovac v Eichkorn*, 2020 MBCA 57; *Kamer v Ptashnik*, 2020 MBCA 70; *MLB v WRP*, 2019 NBCA 63; *CM v GM*, 2020 NBCA 17; *Bowes v Bowes*, 2021 NLCA 10; *Joudrey v Reynolds*, 2020 NSCA 60; *Thomson v Pitchuck*, 2020 NSCA 65; *Hendriks v Hendriks*, 2022 ONCA 165; *Zhao v Xiao*, 2023 ONCA 453; *Lavallée v Trevors*, 2019 PECA 10; *Granquist v Lemond*, 2022 SKCA 90.

35 *Willick v Willick*, [1994] 3 SCR 670 at 692, Sopinka J; *Hill v Hill*, [2002] BCJ No 672 (CA); *Scott v Scott* [2004] NBJ No 468 (CA); *Green v Green*, [2005] NJ No 165 (CA); *Wedsworth v Wedsworth*, [2000] NSJ No 306 (CA); *Lacosse v Lacosse*, [2005] OJ No 4720 (CA); *Hamel v Hamel*, [2001] SJ No 692 (CA).

36 *Blyth v Brooks*, [2008] AJ No 100 (CA); *Hawco v Myers*, [2005] NJ No 378 (CA).

37 *Marinangeli v Marinangeli*, [2003] OJ No 2819 (CA) (trial judge's misapprehension of certain facts found insufficient to warrant appellate intervention).

38 *Zuk v Zuk*, [1998] AJ No 1425 (CA).

39 *Maynard v Maynard*, [1999] BCJ No 325 (SC).

While disapproving the procedure, an appellate court may find no reversible error in the trial judge's decision not to allow evidence on all issues in dispute.[40]

An appeal may be allowed in part where the evidence before the trial court was insufficiently clear with respect to expenses sought pursuant to section 7 of the Guidelines.[41]

Where the passage of time has been too great or the appellant seeks to demonstrate a change of circumstances subsequent to the making of the order, variation proceedings may be a more appropriate avenue of recourse than the appellate court.[42] An appellate court may take into account a change of circumstances since the making of an order where a failure to consider the change would lead the appellate court to make an order that would inevitably be varied on a fresh application.[43]

The launching of an appeal does not preclude an application to vary a subsisting order on the basis of a change that has occurred since the granting of the order.[44]

F. INTERIM ORDERS

As stated in Chapter 11, appellate courts have endorsed a general policy of not disturbing interim orders and are very reluctant to interfere with interim support orders, unless there is an obvious error or patent injustice that must be immediately corrected.[45]

G. DENIAL OF APPEAL; MOTION TO DISMISS APPEAL; REINSTATEMENT OF APPEAL

A spouse, who is in default under a support order, may be denied an audience in the Court of Appeal while he or she remains in contempt.[46] In *Abu-Saud v Abu-Saud*,[47] the Ontario Court of Appeal stated:

> [4] It is common ground that the court has jurisdiction to quash or dismiss an appeal in the face of non-compliance with a support order: see *Courts of Justice Act*, R.S.O. 1990, c. C.43, s. 134(3); *Dickie v. Dickie*, 2007 SCC 8, [2007] 1 S.C.R. 346, at para. 6; *Brophy v. Brophy* (2004), 2004 CanLII 25419 (ON CA), 180 O.A.C. 389 (C.A.), at para. 11; *Siddiqui v. Anwar*, 2018 ONCA 965, 22 R.F.L. (8th) 92, at para. 19. Moreover, this court has consistently refused to hear from the defaulting appellant or entertain the appeal where the record shows continuing

---

40 *Ryba v Schoenroth*, [1999] SJ No 201 (CA).

41 *Wesolowski v Wesolowski*, [1999] AJ No 183 (CA).

42 *Nash v Nash*, [1975] 2 SCR 507; *Berry v Murray* (1983), 30 RFL (2d) 310 (BCCA); *Milinkovic v Milinkovic* (1991), 37 RFL (3d) 97 (Ont CA); *Thompson v Thompson* (1988), 11 RFL (3d) 422 (Sask CA). See also *Grohmann v Grohmann* (1991), 37 RFL (3d) 71 (BCCA), wherein Southin JA observed that "the [appellate] court, generally, should only exercise original jurisdiction where it has been shown that the judgment below was erroneous. If that is not shown, then it does seem to me that subsequent events are for a fresh application below."

43 *LeBlanc v LeBlanc* (1993), 48 RFL (3d) 457 (Man CA).

44 *Re Seaman* (1977), 28 RFL 275 (Ont HCJ).

45 See Chapter 11, Section B(18).

46 *Cyr v Cassista* (1986), 50 RFL (2d) 33 (NBCA); *Ainslie v O'Neill*, 2018 ONCA 858, citing *Dickie v Dickie*, 2007 SCC 8; *Abu-Saud v Abu-Saud*, 2020 ONCA 314. And see text to footnote 47.

47 2020 ONCA 824 at paras 4–5.

disobedience with court orders: *Cosentino v. Cosentino*, 2017 ONCA 593, 98 R.F.L. (7th) 53, at para. 8.

[5] Quashing or dismissing an appeal for non-compliance is not automatic. Factors to be considered by the court in determining whether to exercise its discretion to quash an appeal include: the wilfulness of the breach; the amount of arrears; the excuse for the breach; and the efforts to correct the breach: *Brophy*, at paras. 9-15.

It is the practice of the British Columbia Court of Appeal not to hear appeals unless a convincing explanation is given for non-compliance with a subsisting court order.[48] An exception may be admitted where the interests of justice require the appellate court to make a ruling on an unsettled question in order to avoid the expense of further litigation.[49]

Where the effluxion of time before the appeal is heard renders it appropriate, the appellate court may remit the issues of spousal and child support to the trial court for a new hearing on up-to-date evidence. Pending the resolution of the matter in the trial court, the appellate court may order interim periodic spousal and child support, but may also direct that the interim order is purely a stopgap measure and that it should not be taken as a guide to the proper order for the trial judge to make.[50]

An appellant who complies with the Rules of Court can pursue an appeal notwithstanding delay and the alleged impracticality of the appeal. It is only when an appeal is clearly moot or hopeless that it will be summarily dismissed. The normal remedy for improbable appeals lies in costs.[51]

An order to restore an appeal struck from the list is discretionary. Where the appeal appears to have been struck through the inadvertence of counsel and the matter is dealt with fairly, quickly, and responsibly thereafter, an order may be granted restoring the appeal to the list, unless the appeal is found to lack merit and the onus of proving this falls on the party who opposes the restoration application.[52]

H. EFFECT OF APPEAL

When an appeal is successful, the decision of the appellate court stands in the place of the order or judgment appealed from and takes effect from the date of the original order or judgment.[53] Where the successful appeal involves the right to or amount of child support, the appellate court has jurisdiction under section 21 of the *Divorce Act* to direct that its judgment shall take effect only from the date of the decision, but such an exceptional course of action can only be justified where there are circumstances that render it unjust to do otherwise.

48 *Hokhold v Gerbrandt*, 2015 BCCA 268.

49 *Kowalewich v Kowalewich*, [2001] BCJ No 1406 (CA) (successful appellant denied costs by reason of his failure to pay money owing under court orders, which produced a financial strain on the respondent's resources).

50 *Forbes v Forbes* (1994), 5 RFL (4th) 79 (BCCA).

51 *Starko v Starko* (1991), 33 RFL (3d) 277 (Alta CA).

52 *Kieser v Kieser*, [2003] AJ No 611 (CA).

53 *Dennis v Wilson*, [1998] OJ No 4854 (CA).

54 *Prewada v Prewada* (1993), 48 RFL (3d) 190 (Man CA); see also *Metzner v Metzner*, [2000] BCJ No 104 (CA); *King v King* (1994), 115 Nfld & PEIR 56 (Nfld CA).

I. STAY OF ORDER PENDING APPEAL

Orders for child support should not be stayed pending appeal unless the respondent would be unduly prejudiced and suffer irreparable harm if a stay were not granted.[55]

A fairly heavy burden falls on the applicant who seeks to prevent the other party from immediately realizing his or her entitlement under the order. A three-stage test will be applied. First, a preliminary assessment must be made of the merits of the case to ensure that there is an arguable issue raised on the appeal. Second, it must be determined whether the applicant would suffer irreparable harm if a stay is refused. Third, an assessment must be made as to which of the parties would suffer greater harm from the granting or refusal of a stay pending the outcome of the appeal. If the applicant fails to meet these criteria, she must satisfy the court that there are exceptional circumstances that would make it fit and just that the stay be granted. A partial stay of the child support order may be deemed appropriate to the circumstances of the appeal.[56]

In British Columbia, jurisdiction to entertain an application to stay execution of a support order pending determination of an appeal vests in a single justice, who must undertake a preliminary assessment of the merits of the case, but a final determination of whether the appeal should be granted or dismissed can only be made by the panel of justices who hear the appeal.[57]

J. ABSENCE OR DELAY OF REASONS FOR JUDGMENT

An appeal is from the formal order, not the reasons, and if the formal order reaches a correct conclusion in light of the evidence and the law, the appeal must be dismissed.[58] While it is not an error, in itself, for a trial judge to give a judgment without indicating the findings of fact and without giving the reasons for a support award, it is highly desirable for a trial judge to give reasons in order to facilitate an appellate court's task of determining whether the trial judge's conclusions are supported by the evidence or whether they disclose an error in principle.

The absence of reasons for judgment places the appellate court under a serious disability. If they are not volunteered, counsel proposing to appeal should request the judge to give reasons for judgment to facilitate the appeal.[59]

---

55 *Armstrong v Armstrong* (1992), 40 RFL (3d) 438 (Ont CA); *Zenner v Zenner* (1991), 32 RFL (3d) 11 (PEICA); *CED v CJD*, 2020 PECA 8; see also *Ciachurski v Ciachurski* (1994), 47 BCAC 208 (CA); *JL v EB*, 2021 CanLII 40689 (NBCA); *Brooks-Gualtieri v Gualtieri*, [1998] OJ No 5591 (Gen Div) (arrears of child support; stay refused). Compare *Hoar v Hoar* (1992), 39 RFL (3d) 125 (Ont CA) (application under *Family Law Act*, RSO 1990, c F.3).

56 *Armstrong v Armstrong*, [1998] BCJ No 2309 (CA); *Green v Green*, 2022 NSCA 30; *MacNeil v Yeadon*, 2022 NSCA 32; *Tauber v Tauber*, [1999] OJ No 713 (CA) (appropriate amount of child support pending appeal fixed at $11,000; differential between this amount and higher amount ordered by trial court to be deposited in interest-bearing trust account); *Spadacini Kelava v Kelava*, 2021 ONCA 345. See also *N v F*, 2021 ONCA 688 (stay granted pending outcome of application for leave to appeal to the Supreme Court of Canada). And see *JL v TT*, 2023 SKCA 43.

57 *Zak v Zak*, 2021 ABCA 131 (stay of interim parenting order); *Armstrong v Armstrong*, [1998] BCJ No 2309 (CA).

58 *Stricker v Stricker* (1994), 4 RFL (4th) 29 (Alta CA); *Razutis v Garrett*, [1999] BCJ No 1505 (CA).

59 *Bacon v Stonehouse* (1990), 25 RFL (3d) 71 (Ont Div Ct); compare *Voortman v Voortman* (1994), 4 RFL (4th) 250 (Ont CA).

A litigant is entitled to adequate, albeit not perfect, reasons for decisions made by a motion judge, even though these judges frequently have heavy daily dockets that require them to quickly decide urgent issues in the face of conflicting and incomplete evidence. A motion judge must give reasons for her decision so that a party can give informed consider ation to the advisability of an appeal and interested members of the public can satisfy them selves whether or not justice has been done. The need for reasons is based on the following three rationales:

1) public confidence in the administration of justice;
2) the right of the losing party to know the reasons for having lost; and
3) to make the right of appeal meaningful.

The adequacy of reasons must be determined by a functional approach that applies the aforementioned rationales. Where the table amount of child support is ordered for adult children pursuing post-secondary education, an explanation of the specific amount is not required. But where a judge exercises his discretion to fix support for the children under sec tion 3(2)(b) of the *Federal Child Support Guidelines*, reasons for the amount ordered must be provided. The amount of support ordered pursuant to section 3(2)(b) cannot be determined without findings of fact relating to "the condition, means, needs and other circumstances of the child[ren] and the financial ability of each parent to contribute to the support of the child[ren]." Where a motion judge has neither articulated the law nor the evidence relied upon in fixing the amount of support ordered under section 3(2)(b) of the *Federal Child Support Guidelines* and the record does not enable an appellate court to make the requisite findings, the appellate court has no alternative except to remit the matter for a fresh hearing with an appropriately enhanced record.[60]

Justice may sometimes be better served by an announcement of the disposition of the issues as soon as the deliberation process is completed, but before full written reasons can be made available to the parties. The filing of a notice of appeal after the disposition has been announced does not preclude the appellate court from considering the reasons for judgment that are subsequently released.[61]

K. FRESH EVIDENCE

The following principles govern the admission of fresh evidence before an appellate court:

1) the evidence should generally not be admitted if by due diligence it could have been adduced at trial;
2) the evidence must be relevant in the sense that it bears upon a decisive or potentially decisive issue at the trial;
3) the evidence must be credible in the sense that it was reasonably capable of belief; and
4) the evidence must be such that if believed, it could reasonably be expected to have affected the result at trial.[62]

---

60 *Bodnar v Blackman*, [2006] OJ No 3675 (CA).

61 *Crocker v Sipus* (1992), 41 RFL (3d) 19 at 24 (Ont CA).

62 *Palmer v The Queen*, 1979 CanLII 8 (SCC), [1980] 1 SCR 759; *GPJK v CAK*, 2023 MBCA 55.

When the best interests of a child are at stake, this test is applied in a somewhat more flexible manner.[63] In addition, the above criteria are not necessarily applied, or applied with the same rigour, when the evidence is offered for a different purpose, such as when it is not directed at a finding made at trial but instead challenges the very validity of the trial process.[64]

There is no material difference between new evidence and fresh evidence. The former is evidence that was not in existence at the time of trial but has arisen as a result of events or matters that transpired subsequent to trial. The latter is evidence that existed at the time of the trial but was not adduced at that time. The aforementioned four principles that were set out in *Palmer v The Queen* apply to the admission of all additional evidence tendered on appeal for the purpose of reviewing the decision below. A flexible approach to Palmer in cases involving the welfare of children must not permit what is in substance a disguised application to vary.[65]

The tender of computer generated tables, which are merely mathematical tools enabling the court to undertake complicated calculations, does not offend the "fresh evidence" rule that customarily applies to appeals.[66]

A judge is not *functus officio* where a formal order reflecting her reasons for judgment has not been entered. Where the Crown seeks reconsideration of a prior judicial remission of arrears based on the finding that the husband was unaware of his wife's receipt of social assistance, the Crown is not exempted from meeting the requirements of the "fresh evidence rule" simply because the court could have unilaterally relied upon the Provincial Court order on file to which neither party made reference in the original application. The fresh evidence rule is not rendered inapplicable because previously untendered evidence was available on the court file.[67]

L. APPEALS TO THE SUPREME COURT OF CANADA

Section 18 of the *Divorce Act*, 1968[68] specifically provided for appeals to the Supreme Court of Canada. No similar provision is included in the current *Divorce Act*. Accordingly, appeals to the Supreme Court of Canada now fall subject to the relevant provisions of the *Supreme Court Act*.[69]

Leave to appeal to the Supreme Court of Canada may be granted by a provincial appellate court in those rare cases in which an issue is raised of such obvious and compelling importance that the litigation calls for the attention of the country's highest court without regard to competing demands for the court's attention.[70]

---

63 *House v Pritchard*, 2021 BCCA 122; *Bors v Bors*, 2021 ONCA 513; *SWBM v CSM*, 2021 SKCA 64 at para 29; *AMD v MRM*, 2021 SKCA 71 at para 34.

64 *CH v SF*, 2021 SKCA 24 at para 18.

65 *Barendregt v Grebliunas*, 2022 SCC 22 at paras 55 and 90; see also *Ting v Ting*, 2022 ABCA 324; *LDB v ANH*, 2023 BCCA 480; *GPJK v CAK*, 2023 MBCA 55; *KM v RV*, 2022 NBCA 71 at para 32; *Peterson c Brine*, 2023 CanLII 47814 (NBCA); *Friesen v Friesen*, 2023 SKCA 60.

66 *Meuser v Meuser*, [1998] BCJ No 2808 (CA).

67 *Williams v Williams*, [2001] AJ No 1558 (QB).

68 SC 1967–68, c 24.

69 RSC 1985, c S-26. Compare *Pelech v Pelech*, [1987] 1 SCR 801.

70 *Chartier v Chartier*, [1997] MJ No 574 (CA), applying *Ashmead v British Columbia*, [1992] 6 WWR 763 (BCCA).

Table of Cases

A v B (2007), 52 RFL (6th) 271, [2007] OJ No 5555 (SCJ) 554, 622
A(DR) v M(RM) (1997), 30 RFL (4th) 269, [1997] OJ No 6365 (Gen Div) 107
AA v CA, 2012 BCSC 1419 226
AA v JA, 2023 NBKB 210 .... 340, 342, 374, 378, 494
Aalbers v Aalbers, 2017 SKCA 43 .... 183, 239
Aamodt v Aamodt, [2000] BCJ No 1912 (SC) 98
Aaston v Alm, [2000] SJ No 383, [2000] 10 WWR 676 (QB) 48
AB v CD, 2020 BCCA 57 647
AB v MH, 2018 SKQB 317 .... 171, 183
Abbott v Abbott, 2014 NLTD(F) 2 .... 200, 349, 356
Abbott v Crane, [2004] NJ No 292, 9 RFL (6th) 1 (UFC) 280
Abbott v Meadus, 2014 NBQB 18 340
Abbott v Taylor (1987), 11 RFL (3d) 407 (Man QB), var'd (1988), 14 RFL (3d) 9 (Man CA) 570
ABC v XYZ, [2004] AJ No 1231, 9 RFL (6th) 7 (QB) 10
Abdellatif v Abdellatif, 2015 SKQB 396 556
Abdullahi v Warsame, 2021 ONCJ 449 .... 498, 584
Abear v Abear, [1998] BCJ No 2894 (SC) 208, 362
Abell v Abell, [2003] SJ No 576, 43 RFL (5th) 252 (QB) 30
Abelman v Abelman, 2017 ONSC 1810 125
Abelson v Mitra, [2008] BCJ No 1672, 2008 BCSC 1197 .... 285, 306
Abu-Saud v Abu-Saud, 2020 ONCA 824 .... 623–24, 662–63
Abu-Shaban v Abu-Shaaban, 2021 ONSC 362 627
Abulnaga v Jamshidian, [2002] BCJ No 535 (SC) 304
Abumatar v Hamda, 2021 ONSC 2165 .... 196, 489, 500, 503
AC and JF v Alberta, 2021 ABCA 13 659
ACG v WLG, 2020 SKQB 43 .... 121, 179, 415, 455
Achkewich v Achkewich, [1998] AJ No 383, 220 AR 385 (QB) 56, 59
Ackland v Brooks, [2001] BCJ No 1733, 19 RFL (5th) 7 (SC) 332
Acorn v DeRoche, [1997] PEIJ No 82, 155 Nfld & PEIR 325 (SCTD) 2, 306, 333
ACS v CJS, 2021 BCSC 1193 .... 145, 499
AD v AD, 2018 NBCA 83 .... 493, 636
AD v ME, 2022 NBKB 249 .... 193, 194
AD v TD, [1998] QJ No 724, [1998] RDF 353 (CS) 14

Adams v Adams, [1998] NBJ No 15, [1998] NBR (2d) (Supp) No 7 (QB) ... 26, 30
Adams v Adams, [2000] AJ No 247, 5 RFL (5th) 9 (QB) ... 182
Adams v Adams, 2011 ABQB 576 ... 185, 347, 348, 354, 355
Adams v Loov, [1998] AJ No 666, 40 RFL (4th) 222 (QB) ... 380, 383, 387
Adams v Mustard, [2002] OJ No 3363 (SCJ) ... 427
Adamson v Adamson, [1998] BCJ No 2697, 44 RFL (4th) 74 (CA) ... 412
ADB v SAM, [2006] NSJ No 252, 2006 NSSC 201 ... 216, 242, 558, 560
Addison v Schneider, [1999] MJ No 300, 49 RFL (4th) 181 (QB) ... 333, 509
Adie v Adie (1994), 7 RFL (4th) 54, [1994] NSJ No 395 (SCTD) ... 16
ADJ v FJ, 2022 BCSC 600 ... 123, 128, 416, 425, 576
ADJ v TDP, 2017 BCSC 2360 ... 339, 340
Adler v Jonas, [1998] BCJ No 2062, 48 RFL (4th) 218 (SC) ... 107
Adubofuor v Ontario (Director, Family Responsibility Office), [2001] OJ No 708 (CA) ... 527
AE v AE, 2021 ONSC 8189 ... 279, 285
AEC v GBH, [1998] NSJ No 580 (Fam Ct) ... 362
AEF v LAF, 2011 PESC 23 ... 277
AEL v JDL, [2002] AJ No 441, 26 RFL (5th) 385 (QB) ... 43
AF v RR, 2021 NBCA 37 ... 489, 497, 499, 583
AG v BR, [2005] BCJ No 127, 2005 BCSC 96 ... 195
AG v LS, [2006] AJ No 1308, 2006 ABCA 311 ... 12, 24
Agioritis v Agioritis, 2011 SKQB 257 ... 335
Agnew v Agnew (1994), 93 Man R (2d) 243 (QB) ... 481
Agresti v Hatcher, [2004] OJ No 910, [2004] OTC 225 (SCJ) ... 253, 651
AHB v CLB, 2019 BCCA 349 ... 264, 357
Ahenkora v Ahenkora, [1999] BCJ No 1770 (SC) ... 462
Ainslie v O'Neill, 2018 ONCA 858 ... 662
AJB v JM, 2020 BCSC 242 ... 162
AJK v SLM, [2003] OJ No 2180, 42 RFL (5th) 48 (SCJ) ... 307
AJL v JTB, 2020 ABQB 649 ... 148, 317, 420
Aker v Howard, [1998] OJ No 5562 (Gen Div) ... 395, 437, 480
Aker v Howard, [1999] OJ No 651 (Gen Div) ... 388, 404
Akert v Akert, [2000] SJ No 269, 2000 SKQB 185 ... 36
Akkawi v Habli, 2017 ONSC 6124 ... 162, 196
Aksugyuk v Aksugyuk (1975), 17 RFL 224, 53 DLR (3d) 156 (NWTSC) ... 85
AL v JN, 2017 NBCA 25 ... 214, 642
AL v JT, 2010 NBQB 419 ... 270
AL v OG, [2000] QJ No 912 (CS) ... 452, 459
Alansari v Kreke, 2020 SKCA 122, rev'd on appeal to Supreme Court of Canada, 2021 SCC 50, leave to appeal to SCC granted 2021 CanLII 52020 (SCC) ... 661
Alberding v Alberding (1989), 74 Sask R 208, [1989] SJ No 688 (CA) ... 516
Albinet v Albinet, [2003] MJ No 44, 33 RFL (5th) 275 (CA) ... 168, 483
Aleixandre v Aleixandre (1984), 43 RFL (2d) 245 (Ont HCJ) ... 551
Alexa v Alexa (1995), 14 RFL (4th) 93, [1995] BCJ No 723 (SC) ... 630
Alexander v Alexander, [1999] OJ No 3694 (SCJ) ... 159, 218, 336, 460, 484, 590
Alexander v Alexander, 2010 BCSC 1674 ... 216
Alfaro v Alfaro, [1999] AJ No 1062, 3 RFL (5th) 1 (QB) ... 244, 372
Alford v Che-Alford, [1999] OJ No 4206 (SCJ) ... 462, 466
Algner v Algner, [2008] SJ No 182, 2008 SKQB 132 ... 196, 197, 199, 202
Ali v McCurdy, 2022 MBQB 36 ... 245
Ali v Williams-Cespedes, 2015 ONSC 3560 ... 214
Allaire v Allaire, [2003] OJ No 1069, 35 RFL (5th) 256 (CA) ... 163
Allard v Allard, [1999] OJ No 3535 (SCJ) ... 82
Allard v Hulst, [1998] AJ No 407 (QB) ... 580

Allen v Allen (1991), 32 RFL (3d) 160 (Ont CA) 521, 540
Allen v Allen (1994), 9 RFL (4th) 48, [1994] BCJ No 2418 (SC) 274, 487
Allen v Allen, 1999 CanLII 6749 (BCSC) 85
Allen v Allen, [2000] BCJ No 2474 (SC) 441, 455
Allen v Allen, [2002] AJ No 133 (QB) 207, 208
Allen v Allen. See also TA v RCA.
Allooloo v Allooloo, [1999] NWTJ No 48 (SC) 56
ALM v NJO, 2015 BCSC 70 .... 344, 354, 355, 356
Alma v Zachary, [2005] AJ No 772, 2005 ABQB 468 473
Almeida v Almeida (1995), 11 RFL (4th) 131, [1995] AJ No 143 (QB) 262, 618
Almeida v Malek-Gilani, 2018 ONSC 5699 .... 68, 216
Almon v Hill, 2022 NSSC 310 .... 196, 594
Alonzo v Alonzo, [2000] BCJ No 2389 (SC) 113, 325
Alpugan v Baykan, 2014 ABCA 152 429
Alsafouti v Alsafouti, [2005] OJ No 4079 (SCJ) 527
ALY v LMY, [2001] AJ No 506, 17 RFL (5th) 233 (QB) 287, 291, 314, 452
AM c RB, 2019 NBBR 170 495
AM v GM, 2018 BCSC 942 .... 280, 328
AMB v MAT, 2009 BCSC 1281 596
Ambrose v Ambrose, 2021 NSSC 308 594
AMD v AJP (2003), 35 RFL (5th) 323, [2003] OJ No 3 (CA) 207, 654
AMD v AJP. See also Drygala v Pauli.
AMD v MRM, 2021 SKCA 71 666
Ames v Ames, [1999] BCJ No 1816 (SC) 235, 356
Amos v Fischer, [2006] SJ No 72, 2006 SKQB 53 350
Amos v Fischer, 2013 SKQB 49 349
AMT v RDC, 2012 SKQB 85 127
AMW v BW, 2018 ABQB 518 .... 124, 130
Andela v Jovetic, 2011 ONSC 892 95
Andersen v Andersen, [1997] BCJ No 2496, 32 RFL (4th) 177 (SC) 54, 124, 193
Anderson v Anderson (1987), 11 RFL (3d) 260, [1987] NBJ No 1050 (CA) 617
Anderson v Anderson, [1993] SJ No 342 (QB) 472
Anderson v Anderson, [2000] AJ No 752 (QB) 457
Anderson v Anderson, [2000] BCJ No 522, 5 RFL (5th) 235 (SC) 342
Anderson v Anderson, [2005] MJ No 243, 2005 MBQB 133 .... 216, 299
Anderson v Anderson, 2010 ABQB 763 194
Anderson v Bernhard, 2017 MBQB 191 647–48
Anderson v Wilkins, [2002] OJ No 2724 (SCJ) 473
Anderson-Devine v Anderson, [2002] MJ No 46, 162 Man R (2d) 74 (QB), var'd [2002] MJ No 484 (CA) 373, 438, 562
Anderson-Devine v Anderson, 2002 MBCA 166 429
Andrada v Garcia, [1998] BCJ No 2980 (Prov Ct) 391
Andreassen v Andreassen, 2016 BCSC 1196 214
Andres v Andres, [1999] MJ No 103 (sub nom Cornelius v Andres) (1999), 170 DLR (4th) 254 (CA) 124, 149, 226
Andres v Andres, 2023 ABCA 42 659
Andrew-Reed v Reed, [2002] BCJ No 708 (SC) 594
Andrews v Andrews (1986), 60 Nfld & PEIR 20, [1986] PEIJ No 66 (CA) 22
Andrews v Andrews (1992), 38 RFL (3d) 200, 88 DLR (4th) 426 (Sask CA) 85
Andrews v Andrews, [1999] OJ No 3578, 50 RFL (4th) 1 (CA) 147, 156, 316, 318, 319, 407, 410
Andrews v Andrews, [2000] OJ No 4060, [2000] OTC 753 (SCJ) 512
Andrews v Andrews, 531 NE2d 219 (Ind Ct App 1988) 314

Andries v Andries, [1997] MJ No 301, 119 Man R (2d) 224 (QB), var'd [1998] MJ No 196, 159 DLR (4th) 665 (CA) 282, 294, 300, 314
Anger v Anger, [2004] OJ No 3422, [2004] OTC 744 (UFC) 330
ANH v LDG, 2018 BCSC 2012 .... 173, 183
ANH v MKC, 2010 NBQB 120 405
Anthony v Anthony, 2009 NSSC 343 .... 113, 216
Antonio v Shaw, 2010 ABCA 141 251
Antonishyn v Boucher, 2011 SKQB 147 12
Anwender-Rempel v Rempel, [2004] SJ No 646, 253 Sask R 314 (QB) 212
AP v JP, 2020 SKCA 134 638
Appu v Appu, 2014 ONSC 19 .... 122, 123, 223
Aquila v Aquila, 2016 MBCA 33 .... 55, 79, 83
Aquilina v Winn, 2016 ONSC 4530 163
Aquilini v Aquilini, 2019 BCSC 1146 425
AR v DR, 2018 PESC 37 594
Arcinas v Stanley, [1999] BCJ No 1388, 49 RFL (4th) 157 (SC) 9
Arif v Arif, [2005] AJ No 1559, 2005 ABCA 378 260
ARJ v ZSH, 2021 BCSC 274 .... 124, 196
Arlt v Arlt, [2003] SJ No 713, 243 Sask R 110 (QB) 218
Arlt v Arlt, 2014 ONSC 2173 .... 340, 343
Armaz v Van Erp, [2000] OJ No 1544, 7 RFL (5th) 1 (SCJ) 27, 314
Armoyan v Armoyan, 2015 NSSC 191 611
Armoyan v Armoyan, 2015 NSSC 92 .... 650, 651
Armstrong v Armstrong (1992), 40 RFL (3d) 438, [1992] OJ No 536 (CA) 664
Armstrong v Armstrong, [1998] BCJ No 2309 (CA) 647, 664
Armstrong v Armstrong, [1999] OJ No 2614 (SCJ) 75, 470
Armstrong v Armstrong, [2004] BCJ No 1678, 5 RFL (6th) 42 (SC) 541
Armstrong v Armstrong, 2010 BCSC 1686 .... 3, 256, 356
Armstrong v Armstrong, 2012 BCCA 166 247
Arnault v Arnault, 2022 ABQB 176 .... 49, 491
Arnett v Arnett, 2018 BCSC 1982 210
Arnold v Arnold (1965–69), 2 NSR 348 (CA) 656
Arnold v Washburn, [2001] OJ No 4996, 20 RFL (5th) 236 (CA) 134, 136, 137, 329
Arsenault v Arsenault, [1998] NBJ No 401, [1998] NBR (2d) (Supp) No 82 (QB) 74
AS v SS, 2023 BCSC 1077 .... 596, 616
Asadoorian v Asadoorian, [1997] OJ No 3115, 37 RFL (4th) 197 (Gen Div) 119, 507
Aschenbrenner v Aschenbrenner, [2000] BCJ No 1950 (SC) 336
Ash v Summat, [2003] BCJ No 2027, 44 RFL (5th) 4 (SC) 400, 403
Ashlie v Ashlie, 2010 BCSC 1101 76
Ashman v Ashman, [2009] OJ No 3310 (SCJ) 81
Ashmead v British Columbia, [1992] 6 WWR 763 (BCCA) 667
ASL v LSL, 2020 NBCA 15 .... 347, 348, 349
Aslezova v Khanine, 2023 ONCA 153 611
ASM v RS (1999), 48 RFL (4th) 145, [1999] NSJ No 128 (Fam Ct) 601
Asre v Asre, 2011 BCSC 1232 528
Asselstine v Asselstine, unreported, 14 February 1972 (Ont CA) 448
Assinck v Assinck, [1998] OJ No 875 (Gen Div) 14
AT v CMK, [1999] QJ No 2530 (CS) 42
Atkinson v Atkinson (1994), 124 Nfld & PEIR 271 (PEITD) 481
Attard v Attard, 2010 ONSC 810 573
Atte v Atte, 2021 BCSC 133 .... 338, 357
Attersley v Hambleton (1988), 12 RFL (3d) 192, [1988] OJ No 2380 (Prov Ct) 618
Attwood v Sharma, [2000] OJ No 1129, 6 RFL (5th) 23 (SCJ) 31

Aubert v Cipriani, 2015 ONSC 6103 .... 50, 61, 84
Auckland v McKnight, [1999] SJ No 652 (QB) 221, 336
Aucoin v Aucoin, [2002] PEIJ No 13, 210 Nfld & PEIR 112 (SC) 329
Auer v Auer, 2015 ABQB 67 .... 117, 246, 248
Auer v Auer, 2022 ABCA 375 .... 5, 8, 13, 20, 491, 494
Augaitis v Augaitis, [1998] OJ No 1795, 40 RFL (4th) 341 (Gen Div) 154, 164
Aukstuolyte v Balchun, [2005] OJ No 3363 (SCJ) 309
Aulatjut v Aulatjut, [1997] NWTJ No 125 (SC) 384
Auld v Auld (1994), 5 RFL (4th) 132, 123 Nfld & PEIR 43 (PEITD) 52, 81
Austin v Austin, [2007] OJ No 4283 (SCJ) 129, 130
AVR v MJA, 2016 SKQB 272 .... 113, 155, 192
AWH v CGS, [2007] NSJ No 262, 2007 NSSC 181 .... 34, 53, 325
Axent-Cromwell v Cromwell (1995), 14 RFL (4th) 47, [1995] NSJ No 158 (CA) 630
Azimi v Mirzaei, [2007] OJ No 5007, 2007 ONCA 901 538
Aziz v Aziz, [2000] BCJ No 1134, 2000 BCCA 358 .... 565, 606
Azougarh v Maliakkal, 2010 ONCJ 610 .... 92, 99, 105, 109

B (LD) v S (RN), 2019 PESC 44 .... 340, 342, 344
B-JG v BD, 2023 NBKB 30 .... 202, 340
B-M (Children: Findings of Fact), [2021] EWCA Civ 1371 (20 September 2021) 599
B(JB) and B(CB) v B(JA) (1992), 113 NSR (2d) 60, [1992] NSJ No 200 (CA) 622
B(R) v B(M) (1989), 19 RFL (3d) 92 (Ont HCJ) 448
Babcock v Babcock, [1999] OJ No 391 (Prov Div) 427
Baberakubona v Kanso, 2014 ONSC 697 206
Babich v Babich, 2015 SKQB 22 .... 130, 148, 157
Bablitz v Bablitz (1994), 10 RFL (4th) 84, [1994] BCJ No 2678 (CA) 211
Babyak v Antosh (1990), 26 RFL (3d) 280, [1990] SJ No 184 (QB) 212
BAC v DLC, [2003] BCJ No 1303 (SC) 224, 319, 386
Bachorick v Verdejo, [1999] SJ No 450, 180 Sask R 89 (CA) 423, 482, 567
Bachynski v Cale, 2019 SKQB 176 35
Bacon v Bacon (1991), 33 RFL (3d) 170 (Sask CA) 459
Bacon v Stonehouse (1990), 25 RFL (3d) 71 (Ont Div Ct) 664
Badakhshan v Moradi (1993), 127 NSR (2d) 75, [1993] NSJ No 534 (Fam Ct) 20
Badley v Badley, [2000] NSJ No 443 (SC) 305
Badry v Badry, [2004] BCJ No 2432, 2004 BCSC 1528 372
Baerg v Baerg, [1997] SJ No 808, 162 Sask R 194 (QB) 164, 308
Bagu v Bagu, [2004] SJ No 279, 2004 SKQB 185 .... 109, 219
Bahnman v Bahnman, [1999] SJ No 888, 188 Sask R 152 (QB) 395
Bailey v Bailey (1982), 26 RFL (2d) 209 (Ont CA) 478
Bailey v Bailey, 2012 ONSC 2486 271
Bain v Bain (1994), 7 RFL (4th) 451, [1994] MJ No 422 (QB) 60, 572
Bainbridge v Bainbridge, [2000] BCJ No 1603 (SC) 568
Bains v Bains, 2008 ABQB 319, [2008] AJ No 941 538
Baird v Baird, [1977] 5 WWR 72 (Man CA) 658
Bak v Dobell, 2007 ONCA 304 .... 122, 156, 191, 192, 214, 218, 219
Bakay v Bakay, [2000] SJ No 781 (QB) 557
Baker v Baker (1990), 27 RFL (3d) 76, [1990] BCJ No 747 (CA) 202
Baker v Baker (1994), 2 RFL (4th) 147 (Alta QB) 78
Baker v Baker, [1999] BCJ No 1605 (CA) 567, 571
Baker v Peterson, [2001] NSJ No 52, 13 RFL (5th) 8 (SC) 37, 555
Bakes v Kelly (1995), 15 RFL (4th) 361 (BCCA) 537
Bakken v Bakken (1995), 11 RFL (4th) 246, [1995] SJ No 132 (QB) 220, 569, 571
Bakken v Bakken, [1999] SJ No 559, 184 Sask R 148 (QB) 181, 305

Bakshi v Bakshi, 2011 ONSC 3557 275
Balaski v Balaski, [1999] SJ No 259, 45 RFL (4th) 114 (QB) 224, 228
Balazs v Balazs (1990), 95 NSR (2d) 114, [1990] NSJ No 38 (TD) 622
Balcom v Balcom, [1999] NSJ No 458 (QB) 427
Baldini v Baldini, [1999] BCJ No 1426, 46 RFL (4th) 407 (SC) 212, 466
Bale v Bale, [2001] OJ No 4196 (SCJ) 536, 576
Ball v Ball, [1998] SJ No 572, 170 Sask R 192 (QB) 344, 363
Ball v Broger, 2010 ONCJ 557, [2010] OJ No 5824 .... 82, 94
Ball v Murray, 2008 NLTD 176, [2008] NJ No 328 .... 86, 90
Ballanger v Ballanger, 2020 ONCA 626 496
Banfield v Banfield, 2012 NSSC 68 318
Banilevic v Cairney, 2020 SKQB 25 .... 616, 636–38
Baram v Bakshy, [2000] OJ No 2349 (SCJ) 312
Barber v Barber (1995), 18 RFL (4th) 282, [1995] NJ No 387 (SCTD) 38
Barber v Barber, 2011 SKQB 131 .... 372, 379
Barendregt v Grebliunas, 2022 SCC 22 .... 661, 666
Bari v Nassr, 2015 ONSC 4318 57
Barker v Barker, [1952] P 184 (Eng CA) 467, 469
Barker v Barker, [1999] BCJ No 2020 (SC) 337, 427
Barker v Barker, [2002] BCJ No 1193, 27 RFL (5th) 231 (CA) 189
Barker v Barker, [2005] BCJ No 687, 15 RFL (6th) 43, 2005 BCCA 177 .... 204, 205, 308, 328, 330
Barkhouse v Wile, 2014 NSCA 11 .... 538, 539
Barnes v Bates, 2014 CarswellBC 1410 (BCSC) 326
Barnes v Carmount, 2011 ONSC 3925 .... 342, 343, 344
Barnesky v Barnesky (1988), 16 RFL (3d) 450 (Man QB) 478, 582
Barnett v Barnett, [2001] PEIJ No 71, 20 RFL (5th) 8 (SC) 325
Barnsley v Barnsley, [1998] OJ No 5332, 43 RFL (4th) 290 (Gen Div) 212, 487
Baron v Baron (1990), 29 RFL (3d) 37 (Man QB) 477–78
Barrett v Mychasiw, [2001] OJ No 2023 (SCJ) 14, 21
Barry (Wilson) v Wilson (1990), 29 RFL (3d) 42, [1990] NBJ No 902 (QB) 468
Barry v Davis, 2021 BCSC 546 222
Barry v Rogers, [2001] NJ No 123, 202 Nfld & PEIR 212 (SC) 242
Barry v Rogers, [2002] NJ No 115, 213 Nfld & PEIR 239 (SC) 558
Bartkowski v Bartkowski, [2003] BCJ No 720, 37 RFL (5th) 242, 2003 BCSC 490 .... 190, 614
Bartlett v Bartlett (1988), 86 NSR (2d) 40 (TD) 570
Bartlett v Bartlett (1994), 2 RFL (4th) 202 (Nfld UFC) 561
Bartole v Parker, [2006] SJ No 349, 2006 SKQB 216 219
BAS v GDS, [2000] AJ No 192 (QB) 462
Baskin v Rogers, 2010 NWTSC 73 104
Basque v Basque (1988), 89 NBR (2d) 214 (QB) 556
Bassett v Magee, 2020 BCSC 1994 .... 372, 379
Basso v Reesor, 2015 SKQB 329 .... 359, 360
Bast v Dyck, [1997] SJ No 174, 28 RFL (4th) 131 (QB) 81
Bates v Bates (1995), 10 RFL (4th) 261, [1995] AJ No 135 (CA) 52
Bates v Bates (2000), 49 OR (3d) 1, [2000] OJ No 2269, 5 RFL (5th) 259 (CA) 12, 15, 378
Bates v Welcher, [2001] MJ No 93, 17 RFL (5th) 25, 2001 MBCA 33 .... 9, 10, 266, 267, 270
Bauer v Bauer, [2009] OJ No 135 (SCJ) 58
Bauer v Noonan, 2005 SKQB 427, [2005] SJ No 616, 20 RFL (6th) 20 (QB) 323, 336
Baum v Baum, [1999] BCJ No 3025 (SC) 436
Baum v Baum, [2000] BCJ No 2565, 13 RFL (5th) 258, 2000 BCSC 1835 .... 263, 297, 300, 642
Baumann v Clatworthy (1991), 35 RFL (3d) 200, [1991] OJ No 1211 (Gen Div) 642
Bayliss v Bayliss, [2000] MJ No 52 (QB) 211
Bayrack v The Queen, 2019 TCC 53 365

BB v DG, [2004] NBJ No 197, 2004 NBQB 188 ... 562
BBW-B v DMB, 2005 SKQB 462 ... 285
BC v AM, 2014 NBQB 77 ... 14
BC v DU, [1997] BCJ No 2431 (SC) ... 486
BC v MC, 2011 NBQB 285 ... 201, 466
BD v LDB, [2003] BCJ No 648 (CA) ... 471
BDD v GTS, 2021 BCSC 1010 ... 158, 456
BDW v HGW, [1999] AJ No 997, 251 AR 343 (QB) ... 212, 566
Beach v Tolstoy, 2015 ONSC 7248 ... 113, 147, 316
Bear v Thomson, 2013 SKQB 270, var'd 2014 SKCA 111 ... 297, 306, 329, 330
Beardsley v Beardsley, 2020 ONSC 6624 ... 627
Beasley v Beasley, 2019 ONSC 1562 ... 651
Beattie v Ladouceur (1995), 13 RFL (4th) 435 (Ont Ct Gen Div) ... 517
Beattie v Ladouceur (2001), 23 RFL (5th) 33, [2001] OJ No 4852 (SCJ) ... 534, 623
Beattie v Ladouceur, [2002] OJ No 5501 (SCJ) ... 468, 531
Beatty v Beatty, [1997] BCJ No 995, 28 RFL (4th) 211 (CA) ... 22, 107
Beatty v Beatty, [2000] OJ No 1755 (SCJ) ... 407
Beaudoin v Beaudoin (1993), 45 RFL (3d) 412 (BCSC) ... 582
Beaudoin v Stevens, 2023 ONSC 4401 ... 193, 194, 218, 275, 347
Beaudry v Beaudry, 2010 ABQB 119 ... 145, 227
Beaudry-Fortin v Fortin, [2001] BCJ No 1880 (SC) ... 206
Beauregard v Beauregard (1991), 38 RFL (3d) 407 (Man QB) ... 545
Beaver v Hill, 2018 ONCA 840 ... 642
Beaver v Hill, 2018 ONSC 3352 ... 640, 642
Beavis v Beavis, 2014 BCSC 422 ... 540
Bebenek v Bebenek (1979), 11 RFL (2d) 137 (Ont CA) ... 478
Beck v Weisgerber, [1999] SJ No 560 (QB) ... 158
Beckman v Hanna, 2017 SKQB 80 ... 474
Bedard v Bedard, [2003] OJ No 862, 36 RFL (5th) 10 (SCJ) ... 383, 391
Bedi v Bedi, [2004] OJ No 2207, 13 RFL (6th) 40 (SCJ) ... 170
Beeching v Beeching, [1998] SJ No 355, 40 RFL (4th) 15, 169 Sask R 18 (QB) ... 180–81, 187
Beeler v Beeler, [1997] SJ No 612, 32 RFL (4th) 397 (QB) ... 387
Beggair v Nixon, [2006] NWTJ No 26, 2006 NWTSC 22 ... 350
Beilstein v Beilstein, [1999] NWTJ No 34, 47 RFL (4th) 242 (SC) ... 192, 208, 223, 230, 456, 457
Beisel v Henderson, [2004] SJ No 413, 250 Sask R 272 (QB) ... 201, 206, 280, 316, 378
Beissner v Matheusik, 2015 BCCA 308 ... 61, 65, 196, 199, 240
Bekeros v Bekeros (1989), 19 RFL (3d) 432, [1989] OJ No 547 (UFC) ... 211
Belanger v Belanger, [2005] OJ No 3033, 17 RFL (6th) 235 (SCJ) ... 83
Belansky v Belansky, [2009] OJ No 5480 (SCJ) ... 393
Beliveau and Director, Legal Aid, Hamilton, Ontario (Re) (1972), 6 RFL 1 (Ont CA) ... 660
Bell v Bell, [1997] BCJ No 2826 (SC) ... 408, 564
Bell v Bell, 1999 BCCA 497, [1999] BCJ No 1999, 1 RFL (5th) 1 (SC) ... 163, 164, 583
Bell v Bell, [2006] OJ No 2843 (SCJ) ... 448
Bell v Bell, 2011 BCSC 212 ... 26, 27, 134, 137
Bell v Glynn, [2000] BCJ No 1505 (SC) ... 136
Bell-Angus v Angus, [2000] OJ No 2074, 8 RFL (5th) 13 (SCJ) ... 296, 319
Bellingham v Bellingham, [2003] MJ No 348, 178 Man R (2d) 60 (QB) ... 431, 434
Belliveau v Arsenault-Dawson, [2001] PEIJ No 114, 207 Nfld & PEIR 139 (SC) ... 374
Bellman v Bellman, [1999] BCJ No 1196, 46 RFL (4th) 414 (SC) ... 312
Belof v Belof (1972), 9 RFL 60 (Sask QB) ... 458
Belot v Connelly, 2013 MBQB 98 ... 152, 153, 164, 166, 358
Belway v Canada, 2015 TCC 249 ... 366
Bembridge v Bembridge, 2009 NSSC 158 ... 179, 188

Bemrose v Fetter, [2005] OJ No 3362 (SCJ) ... 629
Ben-Ami v Ben-Ami, [2001] OJ No 5109, 23 RFL (5th) 75 (SCJ) ... 376, 401
Beninger v Beninger, [2005] BCJ No 1781, 2005 BCSC 1154 ... 291, 316
Beninger v Beninger, 2007 BCSC 1306, [2007] BCJ No 1913, aff'd 2009 BCCA 145 ... 288
Beninger v Beninger, 2010 BCSC 1509 ... 58
Bennett v Bennett (1997), 34 RFL (4th) 290, [1997] OJ No 4768 (Gen Div) ... 116
Bennett v Bennett, [1999] SJ No 728 (QB) ... 300, 317
Bennett v Bonatsos, 2014 ONSC 1048 ... 223, 241, 300, 301
Benoit v Benoit, [2000] OJ No 1019 (SCJ) ... 449
Benoit v Benoit, 2019 MBCA 106 ... 458
Benson v Benson (1987), 8 RFL (3d) 32 (Nfld CA) ... 508
Berg v Berg, [2000] SJ No 118 (QB) ... 474
Berg v Berg, [2001] OJ No 5190 (SCJ) ... 630
Bergen v Procner, [1998] SJ No 479, (sub nom B(TL) v P(R)) 41 RFL (4th) 202 (QB) ... 600
Berger v Berger, 2016 ONCA 884 ... 61
Bergman-Illnik v Illnik (1997), [1997] NWTJ No 93, [1998] NWTR 131 (SC) ... 292, 331, 333, 335, 379
Berki v Berki, [1999] OJ No 843 (Gen Div) ... 260, 468
Bernard v Bernard, [2008] AJ No 302, 2008 ABQB 190 ... 581
Bernardin v Bernardin, 2020 BCSC 807 ... 279, 357
Berry v Berry, 2002 BCCA 151 ... 263
Berry v Murray (1983), 30 RFL (2d) 310 (BCCA) ... 662
Berta v Berta, 2019 ONCA 218 ... 538
Berthin v Berthin, 2018 BCSC 2104 ... 609
Beruschi v Muller, 2021 BCSC 78 ... 280, 316
Best (Guardian ad litem) v Young, [1999] BCJ No 280 (SC) ... 545
Best v Combden, [1998] NJ No 74 (SC) ... 481
Best v MacKay, 2021 NSSC 124 ... 492, 494
Betts v Chisholm, 2023 ABCA 55 ... 49
Beutler v Maki, [2005] SJ No 562 (QB) ... 53
Bexon v McCorriston, 2019 ONSC 6060 ... 343
Bezanson v Bezanson, 2021 NSSC 126 ... 253, 254
Bezanson v Falle, [1998] OJ No 5392 (CA) ... 464
BFC v DGW, [2001] BCJ No 1509 (SC) ... 474
BFL v KRL, 2018 PESC 1 ... 82
BGM v PGM, 2013 ABQB 67 ... 42
BGMS v JEB, 2018 BCSC 1628 ... 238
Bhandari v Bhandari, [2002] OJ No 658 (SCJ) ... 118, 169
Bhatthal v Bhatthal (1990), 28 RFL (3d) 152 (Alta QB) ... 466
Bhimani v Beninteso, 2020 BCCA 79 ... 647
Bhoi v Bhoi, [2001] OJ No 4864, 23 RFL (5th) 255 (SCJ) ... 147
Bhopal v Bhopal, [1997] BCJ No 1746 (SC) ... 182
Bhullar v Bhullar, [2001] OJ No 3034, [2001] OTC 589 (SCJ) ... 95, 220
Bhupal v Bhupal, 2013 ONSC 60 ... 318
Bially v Bially, [1997] SJ No 352, 28 RFL (4th) 418 (QB) ... 293, 308, 333
Biamonte v Biamonte (1998), 36 RFL (4th) 349, [1998] OJ No 541 (Gen Div) ... 219
Bickerton v Bickerton, [2004] BCJ No 2635, 2004 BCSC 1632 ... 58
Biddle v Biddle (2005), 13 RFL (6th) 63, [2005] OJ No 737 (SCJ) ... 189, 274, 456, 457, 650
Bidner v Tapp, 2017 ONSC 6846 ... 633
Biggar v Biggar, [1998] SJ No 570, 170 Sask R 315 (QB) ... 431, 590
Billark v Billark (1996), 36 RFL (4th) 361 (Ont Ct Gen Div) ... 344, 346
Billett v Billett, 2013 SKQB 269 ... 114
Billingsley v Billingsley, 2010 ONSC 3381 ... 204
Bilodeau v Bilodeau, 2022 ABKB 799 ... 498, 584

Binczak v Binczak (1992), 44 RFL (3d) 122 (Ont Ct Gen Div) 472
Bindig v Wilchynski, [2002] SJ No 377 (QB) 528
Biniaminov v Biniaminov, 2018 ONSC 5454 611
Birch v Birch, 2010 ONSC 2915 62
Bird v Ritcey, [2004] NSJ No 514, 228 NSR (2d) 269 (SC) 45, 58
Birks v Birks, [2003] BCJ No 949 (SC) 561, 562, 564
Birnie v Birnie, 2018 SKQB 87 ..... 180, 183
Birnie v Birnie, 2019 SKQB 303 ..... 39, 148
Birss v Birss, [2000] OJ No 3692, 12 RFL (5th) 9 (Div Ct) 12, 374, 378, 392, 508
Bishop v Bishop, [2001] SJ No 47 (QB) 161
Bishop v Bishop, 2017 MBQB 97 ..... 194, 218, 327, 328
Bitterman v Weaver, [2002] NBJ No 42, [2002] NBR (2d) (Supp) No 1 (QB) 58
BJ v VL, 2022 BCSC 1496 586
BJG v DLG, 2010 YKSC 33 ..... 260–61, 392
BJG v KRG, [2001] AJ No 1310 (QB) 450
BJL v DBL, 2018 SKQB 213 419
BJL v JRDL, 2003 BCSC 381 611
BJM v KFB, [2003] BCJ No 581, 38 RFL (5th) 130 (SC) 205
Bjornson v Bjornson (1970), 2 RFL 414 (BCCA) 112
BJT v JD, 2022 SCC 24 661
BKWR v NVR, 2023 NBKB 17 86
Black v Black (1995), 19 RFL (4th) 442 (BCCA) 116, 427, 510
Blackburn v Rose, [1999] OJ No 4361, 2 RFL (5th) 340 (SCJ) 247, 259
Blacklock v Tkacz, 2021 ONCA 630 478
Blackwood v Blackwood (1994), 7 RFL (4th) 76 (Ont Ct Gen Div) 562
Blagaich v Blagaich (2007), 43 RFL (6th) 350, [2007] OJ No 3399 (SCJ) 444
Blain-Hughes v Blain (1998), 39 RFL (4th) 327 (sub nom Hughes v Blain) [1998] OJ No 3011 (Gen Div) 445
Blaine v Sanders, [2000] MJ No 149, 144 Man R (2d) 300 (QB) 188, 221, 314
Blair v Blair, [1997] OJ No 4949, 34 RFL (4th) 370 (Gen Div) 73, 74, 440
Blair v Callow (1998), 41 RFL (4th) 44, [1998] BCJ No 1345 (SC) 359
Blais v Blais, [2001] SJ No 468, 20 RFL (5th) 17 (QB) 166, 208, 560
Blake v Blake (1994), 121 Nfld & PEIR 263, [1994] NJ No 145 (SCTD) 46
Blake v Blake, [2000] OJ No 2670, 8 RFL (5th) 233 (SCJ) 22, 579
Blanchard v Blanchard, 2019 ABCA 53 ..... 35, 371, 578, 585
Blanchard v Kemp, [2000] MJ No 506, 11 RFL (5th) 20 (CA) 188
Blanchard v Maxwell, 2022 MBQB 113 199
Bland v Bland, [1999] AJ No 344, 48 RFL (4th) 250, 1999 ABQB 236 ..... 158, 286, 293, 331, 542
Blaney v Murphy, 2020 ABQB 196 650
Blaschuk v Bridgewater, [2005] OJ No 3324, 18 RFL (6th) 271 (SCJ) 56, 57
Bledin v Bledin, 2021 ONSC 3815 ..... 121, 155
Bleoo v Bleoo, 2011 ABQB 16 347
BLGR v LMR, [1998] SJ No 583 (QB) 427, 433
BLMG v DJEG (1998), 127 Man R (2d) 311, [1998] MJ No 278 (QB) 230, 632
Block v Baltimore, [2000] MJ No 132, 5 RFL (5th) 18 (QB) 51, 260
Block v Block, 2018 BCSC 716 510
Block v Block, 2020 BCSC 1694 ..... 132, 166, 167
Blondeau v Blondeau, [1997] SJ No 617 (QB) 610
Blonski v Blonski, 2010 ONSC 2552 77
Bloomfield v Halfyard, 2020 MBCA 73 636
BLP v DAP, 2014 ABQB 89 49
BLS v EJS, 2014 BCSC 1549 53–54
BLS v JMS, 2010 BCSC 1319 215

Blume v Blume, 2023 ABCA 174 659
Blumer v Blumer, 2004 BCSC 314 238
Blumer v Dancey, 2010 ONSC 5707 154
Blumes v Blumes, [1998] AJ No 346, 221 AR 129 (QB) 293, 542
Blyth v Brooks (2008), 47 RFL (6th) 297, [2008] AJ No 100 (CA) 574, 661
BM v ALG, 2014 NSSC 443 .... 74, 213, 216
BM v KR, 2022 NBCA 50 .... 455, 505
BM v PM, 2019 SKQB 36 ....47, 66, 72, 113, 123
BMD v CND, 2010 BCSC 1785 .... 170, 178
BMH v LH, [1997] MJ No 493 (QB).... 11
BNM v PJM, 2017 SKQB 331....128, 193, 282, 341, 343, 359
Bobyn v Bobyn, 2014 BCSC 1441 35
Bocaneala v Bocaneala, 2014 NSSC 450 .... 280, 300
Bodine-Shah v Shah, 2014 BCCA 191....217, 280, 282
Bodman v Bodman, [1998] MJ No 62, 38 RFL (4th) 210 (QB)....264
Bodnar v Blackman (2006), 32 RFL (6th) 236, [2006] OJ No 3675 (CA) 665
Bodner v Huckerby, 2013 SKQB 89 87
Bodor v Bodor (1988), 12 RFL (3d) 425, [1988] AJ No 147 (QB)....16, 17
Boe v Boe (1996), 26 RFL (4th) 190 (Sask QB)....574
Bohn v Bohn, 2016 ABCA 406 ....129, 145, 593
Boissy v Boissy, [2004] OJ No 3400 (SCJ) 123, 142
Boisvert v Boisvert, [2000] AJ No 1393, 280 AR 63 (QB) 34, 35
Boivin v Smith, 2013 ONCJ 426....99, 100
Bola v Bola, 2014 BCSC 861 53
Bolen v Bolen, 2010 SKQB 202....538
Bolingbroke v Bolingbroke, [2001] AJ No 53, 285 AR 396 (QB)....507
Bolleter v Livingstone, 2015 NWTSC 47....347
Bolton v Bolton, 2022 ABQB 277....343
Bombier v Bombier (1984), 42 RFL (2d) 93, [1984] OJ No 2207 (Master) 22
Bond v Bond (2007), 44 RFL (6th) 28, [2007] OJ No 3677 (Div Ct) 77
Boniface v Boniface, [2007] BCJ No 2303, 2007 BCSC 1543 136
Boon v Boon, 2022 BCSC 1444....152
Booth v Booth, [2000] BCJ No 2544 (SC)....151
Booth v Vucetic (1989), 19 RFL (3d) 240, [1989] OJ No 176 (Fam Ct) 381
Boppart v Boppart, [1999] BCJ No 555 (SC)....375
Bordin v Bordin, 2015 ONSC 3730....230
Borland v Borland, 2019 SKQB 220....54
Bors v Bors, 2021 ONCA 513....666
Bort v Derworiz, [1998] SJ No 177, 37 RFL (4th) 220 (QB)....244
Bortolussi v Cafferty, 2016 MBQB 54....574
Borutski v Jabbour, [2000] OJ No 5173 (SCJ)....345
Bose v Bose, 2023 NSSC 269 539
Boser v Boser, [2001] SJ No 347 (QB)....188
Boser v Boser (2003), 47 RFL (5th) 259, [2003] SJ No 714, 2003 SKQB 477 ....122, 178, 188
Bosgra v Squires, [2001] NWTJ No 78 (SC)....373, 386, 391, 400
Bosse v Bosse (1996), 19 RFL (4th) 54, [1996] NBJ No 33 (QB) 55, 427
Boston v Boston, [2001] 2 SCR 413, 17 RFL (5th) 4....429
Botha v Botha, [2000] AJ No 1533, 283 AR 201 (QB) 228
Botsis v Mourelatos, [1970] RP 191 (Que CA)....660
Bouchard v Bouchard, 2018 BCSC 1728....478, 542, 592
Bouchard v Sgovio, 2021 ONCA 709 530
Boucher v Boucher, [1997] NBJ No 43, [1997] NBR (2d) (Supp) No 2 (QB)....386

Boucher v Kennedy, [1998] OJ No 1612, 60 OTC 137 (Gen Div), aff'd [1999] OJ No 3407, 124 OAC 151 (CA) 531
Boudreau v Jarvie, [2001] OJ No 381 (SCJ) 537
Boudreau v Marchand, 2012 NSCA 79 348
Boundford v Jacobs, [2006] NJ No 199, 2006 NLTD 115 52
Bourgon v Paquette, [2004] OJ No 3236, 7 RFL (6th) 8 (SCJ) 449
Bourke v Heinze, [1997] SJ No 118 (QB) 579
Bourque v Janzen, 2012 SKQB 458 26
Bourque v Phillips, [2000] NBJ No 13, 223 NBR (2d) 242 (SC) 395
Boutin v Boutin, 2022 ONSC 3239 530
Boutin v Boutin, 2022 ONSC 4776 530
Boutin v Boutin, 2023 SKCA 41 ..... 117–118, 124, 128
Bouzane v Martin, 2014 BCSC 1690 ..... 102, 167, 384
Bowen v Bowen, [2001] OJ No 480 (SCJ) 187
Bowen v Hermson and Manitoba Public Insurance Corporation (Third Party) (1983), 22 Man R (2d) 295, [1983] MJ No 406 (QB) 620
Bowering v Bowering, [1998] NJ No 305, 171 Nfld & PEIR 50 (SC) 333
Bowering v Bowering, [2001] SJ No 657 (QB) 229
Bowers v Bowers, [2000] BCJ No 1108 (SC) 296, 311
Bowes v Bowes, 2021 NLCA 10 ..... 124, 192, 193, 196, 200, 201, 205, 661
Bowes v Mattie, [2003] NBJ No 68 (QB) 540
Boyda v Boyda, [1998] AJ No 279, 220 AR 86 (QB) 487, 507
Boyer v Bradley (1995), 15 RFL (4th) 33, [1995] OJ No 1670 (Gen Div) 25, 555
Boykiw v Boykiw, 2013 BCSC 1107 135
Boyko v Boyko, 2010 SKQB 247 ..... 98, 305
Boyko v Fitzgerald, 2022 BCSC 614 347
Boylan v MacLean, 2018 NSSC 15 ..... 166, 281, 483, 487
Boyle v Boyle, [1998] OJ No 3783, 41 RFL (4th) 388 (Gen Div) 108
Boznick v Boznick (1993), 45 RFL (3d) 354 (BCSC) 448
BP v AT, 2013 NBQB 309 ..... 86, 87
BPE v AE, 2016 BCCA 335 ..... 347, 348, 357
BRAA v RVA, [1998] NSJ No 579 (Fam Ct) 294
Bradley v Brooks, 2015 NLTD(F) 34 ..... 279, 288
Bradley v Zaba (1996), 137 Sask R 295, 22 RFL (4th) 52, [1996] SJ No 5 (CA) 49, 51, 322
Bradshaw v Bradshaw, 2011 BCSC 1103 ..... 425, 429
Bradshaw v Davidson, [1999] OJ No 1391 (Gen Div) 345
Brady v Brady, [1998] BCJ No 702 (SC) 632
Bragg v Bragg, [2000] NJ No 14, 2 RFL (5th) 344 (UFC) 81
Braich v Braich, [1997] BCJ No 1764 (SC) 413, 414, 467
Branch v Branch, [2003] NBJ No 50, 256 NBR (2d) 262 (QB) 158, 371
Brandle v Brandle, [2001] SJ No 720, 2001 SKQB 522 630
Brandner v Brandner, [2002] BCJ No 1398, 170 BCAC 186 (CA) 84
Brandt v Brandt, [2003] NJ No 168, 42 RFL (5th) 257 (CA) 371
Brar v Brar, 2021 BCSC 748 497
Bray-Long v Long, [2000] NSJ No 10, 3 RFL (5th) 341 (SC) 260
Brear v Brear, 2019 ABCA 419 79
Brennan v Brennan, 2010 ABQB 221 36
Brennan v Brennan, 2024 ABCA 50 562
Brett v Brett, [1999] OJ No 1384, 44 OR (3d) 61 (CA) 487, 488
Briard v Briard, 2010 BCCA 431 ..... 38, 40, 41, 42, 244
Brickman v Brickman (1987), 8 RFL (3d) 318 (Man QB) 592
Briggs v Kasdorf, 2020 BCSC 1702 ..... 66, 348, 419
Brill v Brill (1995), 10 RFL (4th) 372, [1995] AJ No 155 (CA) 661

Brink v Young, 2011 ONSC 4955 385
British Columbia (Director of Maintenance Enforcement) v CJH, [2002] BCJ No 1373 (Prov Ct) 207
British Columbia (Director of Maintenance Enforcement) v Fults (1991), 38 RFL (3d) 80 (BCSC) 514
British Columbia (Director of Maintenance Enforcement) v IWA Forest Industry Pension Plan (Trustees of) (1991), 37 RFL (3d) 266 (BCCA) 518
British Columbia (Director of Maintenance Enforcement) v Lagore, [1993] BCJ No 899 (Prov Ct) 536
British Columbia (Director of Maintenance Enforcement) v McLeod (1994), 88 BCLR (2d) 222 (SC) 533
British Columbia (Minister under the BC Benefits (Income Assistance) Act) v Dent, [2000] BCJ No 2035, 80 BCLR (3d) 338 (SC) 28
British Columbia (Public Trustee) v Price (1989), 21 RFL (3d) 51 (BCSC), rev'd (1990), 25 RFL (3d) 113 (BCCA) 514
Broaders v Broaders, 2014 NLTD(F) 13 .... 82, 112
Brock v Sorger, 2015 ONSC 7478 30
Brockie v Brockie (1987), 5 RFL (3d) 440, [1987] MJ No 56 (QB), aff'd (1987), 8 RFL (3d) 302, [1987] MJ No 295 (CA) 16, 17, 307
Brockman v Ofukany, [1998] SJ No 650, 41 RFL (4th) 426 (QB) 76
Broder v Broder (1994), 93 Man R (2d) 259, [1994] MJ No 760 (QB) 408
Brodland v Brodland, [1997] SJ No 688, 34 RFL (4th) 79 (QB) 342
Brokop v Stepenoff, [1999] SJ No 574, 184 Sask R 153 (QB) 181, 220
Bromm v Bromm, 2010 SKQB 85 .... 430, 432
Brooke v Hertz, 2008 SKQB 461 .... 50, 51, 52, 300
Brooks-Gualtieri v Gualtieri, [1998] OJ No 5591 (Gen Div) 543, 664
Brophy v Brophy, [2002] OJ No 3658, 32 RFL (5th) 1 (SCJ) 179, 623, 662
Brost v Brost, [2004] YJ No 104, 2004 YKSC 57 429
Brosteneants v Brosteneants, [1999] OJ No 819, 45 RFL (4th) 122 (Gen Div) 123, 325
Brougham v Brougham, 2009 BCSC 897 340
Brouse v Brouse, [1999] OJ No 1834 (Gen Div) 391
Brown v Brown (1993), 45 RFL (3d) 444, [1993] BCJ No 994 (SC) 59
Brown v Brown, [1997] NBJ No 287 (QB) 145
Brown v Brown, [2002] OJ No 862, 26 RFL (5th) 240 (CA) 240
Brown v Brown, [2003] OJ No 4988, 47 RFL (5th) 272 (SCJ) 427
Brown v Brown, 2012 NBCA 11 .... 152, 165
Brown v Brown, 2014 BCCA 152 .... 124, 129, 132, 165, 166
Brown v Brown, 2020 BCCA 53 .... 4, 365, 366
Brown v Canada (Attorney General), 2019 YKSC 21 20
Brown v Hudon (2004), 267 Sask R 53, [2004] SJ No 437, 2004 SKQB 294 .... 283, 305
Brown v Pierce, 2018 PECA 23 156
Brown v Rowe, 2016 ONSC 5153 40
Browning v Browning, [1999] NSJ No 174 (SC) 568
Brubaker v Brubaker, [1999] AJ No 879, 1999 ABQB 549 345
Bruce v Kelly, [2001] PEIJ No 53, 2001 PESCTD 48 30
Bruce v Kelly, [2002] PEIJ No 43, 30 RFL (5th) 42 (SCTD) 74
Bruehler v Bruehler (1985), 49 RFL (2d) 44, [1985] BCJ No 1958 (CA) 78
BSW v WFW, 2023 BCSC 1925 361
Buchanan v Buchanan, [2009] OJ No 674 (SCJ) 642
Bucholtz v Smith, [2001] BCJ No 1872 (SC) 181, 182, 483
Buckhold v Buckhold, [2006] BCJ No 2755, 2006 BCCA 472 61
Buckingham v Buckingham, 2013 ABQB 155 .... 155, 497
Buckland v Buckland, [2004] BCJ No 2484, 2004 BCSC 1466 559

Buckley v Blackwood, 2019 ONSC 6918 ... 287
Buckley v Holden (1991), 32 RFL (3d) 182, [1991] BCJ No 174 (SC) ... 244
Budden v Briggs, [2003] OJ No 5528, 50 RFL (5th) 263 (SCJ) ... 108, 632
Budden v Budden, [2001] BCJ No 269, 16 RFL (5th) 256 (SC) ... 81
Budden v Combden, [1999] NJ No 199 (SC) ... 285, 287, 288, 295, 305, 312, 507
Budyk v Sol, [1998] MJ No 252, 40 RFL (4th) 348 (CA) ... 55, 142
Buhler v Buhler, 2012 SKQB 366 ... 357, 510
Buhr v Buhr (1997), 124 Man R (2d) 89, [1997] MJ No 565 (QB) ... 251, 264, 631
Buick v Buick (1988), 12 RFL (3d) 402, [1988] OJ No 897 (Dist Ct) ... 16
Buller v Rosen, [2003] BCJ No 1686, 2003 BCSC 1107 (SC) ... 47
Bundus v Bundus, [1999] SJ No 715 (QB) ... 75, 77
Bunting v Bunting (1995), 10 RFL (4th) 231, [1995] AJ No 55 (CA) ... 609
Burbank v Garbutt, 2012 BCSC 190 ... 542, 544
Burgess v Burgess (1995), 24 OR (2d) 547, 16 RFL (4th) 388 (CA) ... 487
Burgess v Burgess, 2013 NLTD(F) 27 ... 558
Burgess v Burgess, 2016 NLCA 11 ... 147, 351, 359
Burgie v Argent, 2014 BCSC 364 ... 576, 577
Burhoe v Goff, [1999] NBJ No 296, 50 RFL (4th) 218 (QB) ... 240, 243
Burisch v Gosal, 2007 ONCA 569, [2007] OJ No 3120 ... 194
Burke v Burke, [2001] AJ No 1373, 2001 ABQB 880 ... 605
Burke v Burke, [2003] BCJ No 2324, 2003 BCSC 1564 ... 274
Burke v Poitras, 2018 ONCA 1025 ... 613
Burke v Poitras, 2020 ONSC 3162 ... 163, 217, 218
Burley v Burley, 2009 ONCA 2, [2009] OJ No 23 ... 295, 552
Burnett v Burnett, [1999] OJ No 3063 (SCJ) ... 463
Burns v Burns (1994), 158 AR 153, [1994] AJ No 576 (QB) ... 89
Burns v Burns, [1988] OJ No 1698 (UFC) ... 583
Burns v Burns, [1998] OJ No 2602, 40 RFL (4th) 32 (Gen Div) ... 360, 431
Burry v Burry, 2011 NLTD(F) 49 ... 462
Burt v Burt (1979), 11 RFL (2d) 143, [1979] OJ No 4478 (HCJ) ... 619
Burt v Burt, [1998] AJ No 1228, 236 AR 127 (QB) ... 289
Burton v Burton (1982), 27 RFL (2d) 170 (BCCA) ... 552
Burton v Burton, [1997] NSJ No 560, 158 DLR (4th) 174 (TD) ... 319
Burton v Burton, [1998] SJ No 61 (QB) ... 542
Bury v Beaton, 2012 NSSC 37 ... 61, 62
Burzminski v Burzminski (Lewis). See Burzminski v Burzminski.
Burzminski v Burzminski, 2010 SKCA 16 ... 26, 27, 45, 51, 73
Bushell v Bushell, [2000] AJ No 1499, 280 AR 119 (QB) ... 192, 557, 564
Butilkin v Butilkin, [1972] OJ No 280 (CA) ... 452
Butler v Butler (1980), 27 Nfld & PEIR 1, [1980] NJ No 154 (UFC) ... 16, 17
Butler v Butler, [1999] OJ No 940 (Gen Div) ... 220
Button v Button, [1999] NJ No 130, 48 RFL (4th) 258 (UFC) ... 387
Buttoo v Buttoo (1994), 4 RFL (4th) 36, [1994] OJ No 636 (CA) ... 607
Butzelaar v Butzelaar, [1998] SJ No 741, 174 Sask R 125 (QB) ... 14, 98
Buzon v Buzon, [1999] AJ No 371, 48 RFL (4th) 263 (QB) ... 28, 77, 244, 566
BW v JG, 2014 NLCA 5 ... 494
Byrne v Byrne, [1999] BCJ No 1087 (SC) ... 385
Byrne v Byrne, [2004] MJ No 315, 2004 MBQB 190 ... 574

C v S, 2010 NBQB 252 ... 124, 179, 184, 192, 218, 223
C(M) v C(LA) (1990), 24 RFL (3d) 322, [1990] BCJ No 134 (CA) ... 600
C(NS) v C(D), 2011 NBQB 229 ... 305
C(S) v W(R) (1996), 23 RFL (4th) 7, [1996] BCJ No 1415 (CA) ... 11

CA v SF, [1997] QJ No 3989 (CS)....380
CAB v MSCS, 2006 BCSC 1393, [2006] BCJ No 2136....148
Cabana v Newfoundland and Labrador, 2018 NLCA 52....636
Cabernel v Cabernel, [1997] MJ No 375 (QB)....217, 293
Cabot v Mikkelson (2004), 242 DLR (4th) 279, 2004 MBCA 107, [2004] MJ No 240....338, 344, 346, 368, 489, 622, 661
Caccamo v Kenny, [1998] OJ No 4123, 76 OTC 286 (Gen Div)....230
Cador v Chichak, [2000] AJ No 24, 2000 ABCA 10....55
CAE v MD, 2011 NBCA 17....404
CAG v DJG, [1998] SJ No 796 (QB)....159
CAG v SG, 2012 ABQB 529, supplementary reasons 2013 ABQB 12....653
Cahill v Weaver, [2005] AJ No 1121, 2005 ABQB 618....362, 373
Cail v Cail, [2003] NBJ No 179 (QB)....520
Caillier v Viray, 2021 BCSC 2512....499, 583
Caine v Ferguson, 2012 ONCJ 139....195
Cairns v Cairns, [1931] 3 WWR 335 (Alta CA)....659
CAK v BDK, 2018 BCPC 404....576
CAL v DEL, 2019 BCSC 1483....155
Calcada v Ferreira, [2002] BCJ No 1802, 2002 BCSC 1153....292, 316
Caldwell v Caldwell, 2011 BCSC 1019....338
Caldwell v Simms (1995), 11 RFL (4th) 28 (BCSC)....535
Callahan v Brett, [2000] NJ No 354, 197 Nfld & PEIR 29 (SC)....79, 151, 215, 243
Callahan v Callahan, [2002] NJ No 117 (SC)....61, 74
Callison v Callison (1992), 40 RFL (3d) 451 (BCSC)....570
Callwood v Purdy, 2021 ONSC 5815....372, 374
Calogeracos v Canada, [2008] TCJ No 297, 2008 TCC 389....365
Calogheros v Calogheros, [2001] BCJ No 2391 (SC)....302
Calver v Calver, 2013 ABQB 469, var'd 2014 ABCA 63....127, 128, 496
Calvy v Calvy, 2012 NBCA 47....470
CAM v JC, 2021 PESC 41....361
CAM v TCH, 2016 BCSC 1756....153
CAM v TCH, 2023 BCSC 1283....498, 504
Cambareri v Cambareri, 2019 ABCA 218....646
Cameron v Cameron, [1998] BCJ No 3046 (SC)....534
Cameron v Cameron, [1999] PEIJ No 62 (SC)....538, 543
Cameron-Masson v Masson, [1997] NSJ No 207 (Fam Ct)....251, 299, 407
Camirand v Beaulne (1998), 160 DLR (4th) 749, [1998] OJ No 2163 (Gen Div)....374, 375, 378, 380, 392, 393, 403, 405
Campbell v Campbell (1989), 79 Nfld & PEIR 179 (PEITD)....536
Campbell v Campbell, [1997] BCJ No 2 (SC)....464
Campbell v Campbell, [1998] SJ No 180, 37 RFL (4th) 228 (QB)....466
Campbell v Campbell, 2012 NSCA 86....148, 153
Campbell v Campbell, 2014 MBCA 104....199, 211
Campbell v Campbell, 2016 MBQB 57....200, 243, 372, 379
Campbell v Campbell, 2022 ONSC 5816....47
Campbell v Chapple, [2004] NWTJ No 42, 2004 NWTSC 47....25
Campbell v Martijn, [1998] PEIJ No 33, 40 RFL (4th) 41 (SC)....330, 332
Campbell v McRudden, [2001] BCJ No 676, 88 BCLR (3d) 274 (SC)....488
CAMT v APGT, 2011 BCSC 1456....50
Canada v Canada-Somers (2008) 51 RFL (6th) 262, 2008 MBCA 59, [2008] MJ No 164....62, 300, 378, 416
Canadian Western Bank v Alberta, 2007 SCC 22....657
Cane v Newman, [1998] OJ No 1776 (Gen Div)....433, 434

Cane v Newman, [1998] OJ No 2116, 68 OTC 237 (Gen Div) 486
Canuel v Canuel, [1997] BCJ No 1654, 33 RFL (4th) 195 (CA) 211
Cao v Chen, 2020 BCSC 2050 624–26
CAO v SJO, 2012 BCSC 378 563
Capuska v Capuska (1993), 46 RFL (3d) 37 (Man CA) 562
Caravello v Wickett, 2011 ONSC 3702 .... 62, 524, 525
Carbonneau v Carbonneau, [1998] SJ No 82 (QB) 74
Carew v Ricketts, [2003] NJ No 52, 223 Nfld & PEIR 262, 2003 NLSCUFC 4 .... 163, 641
Carey v Carey, [1998] BCJ No 2909 (SC) 617
Carey v Laiken, 2015 SCC 17 .... 529, 530
Carmichael v Carmichael (1992), 43 RFL (3d) 145 (NSCA) 478
Carmichael v Douglas, [2008] SJ No 474, 2008 SKQB 320 .... 280, 283, 287, 292
Carmichael v Kiggins, 2010 ABQB 78 .... 58, 496
Carnegie v Carnegie, 2008 MBQB 249, [2008] MJ No 333 348
Carpenter v March, 2012 NLTD(F) 11 .... 39, 44
Carpentier v British Columbia (Director of Family Maintenance Enforcement), 2017 BCSC 250 542
Carrier v Carrier, 2008 SKQB 439, [2008] SJ No 684 52
Carroll v Richardson, 2014 NSSC 293 281
Carrothers v Carrothers, [1997] BCJ No 1535 (SC) 333
Carruthers v Carruthers (1988), 15 RFL (3d) 321, [1988] PEIJ No 69 (TD) 618
Carruthers v Carruthers, 2015 BCSC 104 279
Carson v Buziak, [1998] SJ No 229 (QB) 207, 591
Carten v Carten, 2015 BCCA 201 623
Carter v Carter (1991), 34 RFL (3d) 1 (BCCA) 562
Carter v Lloyd, [1998] NJ No 244 (SC) 579
Carter v Sprague, [1999] NSJ No 2 (Fam Ct) 309
Carty v Jones (1995), 15 RFL (4th) 367, [1995] OJ No 1827 (Prov Div) 262
Carvell v Carvell, [1969] 2 OR 513 (CA) 457
Carver v Carver, [2001] PEIJ No 130, 210 Nfld & PEIR 34 (SC) 344, 356
Carwick v Carwick (1972), 6 RFL 286, [1972] OJ No 355 (CA) 112
Cary v Cary, [1999] SJ No 569, 186 Sask R 311 (QB) 221
CAS v GAP, 2011 BCSC 1431 600
Casals v Casals, [2006] OJ No 5602 (SCJ) 318
Casbohm v Winacott Spring Western Star Trucks, 2018 SKQB 15 610
Casey v Casey, [2000] NBJ No 102, [2000] NBR (2d) (Supp) No 20 (QB) 288, 289
Casey v Casey, [2004] NBJ No 434, 281 NBR (2d) 225 (QB) 385, 396
Casey v Chute, 2010 NSFC 8 90
Cassar-Fleming v Fleming (1996), 20 RFL (4th) 201, [1996] OJ No 675 (Gen Div) 89, 102
Cassidy v Cassidy, 2019 ONSC 2774 .... 639, 641
CAT v STB, 2020 BCSC 593 636
Caterini v Zaccaria, 2010 ONSC 6473 .... 112, 113, 215
Catizzone v Cowell, 2016 ONSC 5297 505
CAV v LCM, 2020 NSSC 168 200
Cavanagh v Cassidy, [2000] OJ No 1658 (SCJ) 468
Cavanagh v Wagner, 2020 ONSC 7444 497
Cavanaugh v Cavanaugh, [2001] NSJ No 312 (SC) 164
Cavanaugh v Glass, [2001] OJ No 457, 14 RFL (5th) 251 (SCJ) 325, 485
Cavanaugh v Ziegler, [1998] AJ No 1423, 228 AR 283, 43 RFL (4th) 40 (CA) 10, 13, 487
CAW v KCS, 2018 BCSC 298 47
Cawker v Cawker (1994), 7 RFL (4th) 282 (BCSC) 540
CC v KK, 2020 PESC 16 .... 49, 66, 494
CC v MR, 2013 NBQB 330 .... 113, 114

CC v RT, 2021 PESC 2 492
CCF v DWL, 2010 BCSC 184 574
CCR v TAR, 2016 BCSC 519 210
Cecotka v Cecotka, [2000] AJ No 7 (QB) 401
CED v CJD, 2020 PECA 8....................658, 659, 664
Cederland v Cederland, [1997] NWTJ No 59 (SC) 572
Cennon v Cennon, [1999] SJ No 504 (QB)....................49, 113, 487, 507
CERB v L Estate, [2004] MJ No 83, 182 Man R (2d) 148 (QB)....................479
Cervi v McDonald, 2021 ONSC 1843....................60, 84, 278, 321, 322, 323
CG v TL, 2024 NLCA 1 ....39, 42, 508, 587
CGG v CHG, [2001] AJ No 1410 (QB) 476
CGL v DKL, 2016 ABQB 71....................226
CGR v JLR, 2020 BCSC 842....................392
CH v SF, 2021 SKCA 24....................666
Chace v Chace, [1998] PEIJ No 64, 166 Nfld & PEIR 287 (TD) 192
Chadwick v Canada, 2013 FCA 181....................2
Chalifoux v Chalifoux, 2008 ABCA 70, [2008] AJ No 174....................216, 484
Chalmers Estate v Chalmers (1990), 27 RFL (3d) 54 (Alta QB)....................478, 552
Chalmers v Chalmers, [1997] AJ No 433 (QB)....................49
Chalmers v Chalmers, 2009 BCSC 517 562
Chamanlall v Chamanlall, [2006] OJ No 251 (SCJ) 460
Chambers v Chambers, [1998] NWTJ No 54, 40 RFL (4th) 351 (SC) 129, 158
Chambers v Chambers (2004), 9 RFL (6th) 62, [2004] MJ No 397, 2004 MBQB 239....................328
Champagne v Champagne, [2001] SJ No 290, 16 RFL (5th) 67 (QB) 289
Champion v Champion (1994), 2 RFL (4th) 455, [1994] PEIJ No 18,
    115 Nfld & PEIR 175 (TD) 21, 481
Champion v Champion, [2001] PEIJ No 129 (SC) 385
Chan v Chan, [1998] BCJ No 2420 (SC)....................566
Chan v Chan, [1999] BCJ No 1155 (SC)....................438
Chan v Chan, [1999] BCJ No 929 (SC)....................565
Chan-Henry v Liu, 2018 BCSC 2140 119
Chan-Henry v Liu, 2021 BCCA 318 166
Chapman v Chapman, [1998] BCJ No 2401 (SC) 268
Chapman v Summer, 2010 BCCA 237 ....174, 187
Chapple v Campbell, [2005] MJ No 323, 19 RFL (6th) 252 (QB)....................27, 69, 70
Chaput v Chaput, [1997] OJ No 4924 (Gen Div) 306
Charan v Charan, 2018 BCSC 1537 ....86, 93
Charapovich v Charapovich, 2023 NSCA 15....................657
Charbonneau v Charboneau, 2010 ONSC 3883....................34
Charles v Charles, [1999] BCJ No 395 (SC)....................192
Charles v Charles, [2005] BCJ No 117, 2005 BCSC 42 252
Charlton v Dodman, [2000] SJ No 821, 13 RFL (5th) 353 (QB)....................378
Chartier v Chartier (1998), [1998] SCJ No 79, [1999] 1 SCR 242,
    43 RFL (4th) 1 ....34, 49,
    86, 87, 88–89, 92, 96, 97, 99, 100, 104, 108, 109, 110, 112, 116, 426, 572
Chartier v Chartier, [1997] MJ No 574 (CA) 666
Chatman v Chatman, 2014 BCSC 430....................544
Chatwin v Falbo, [1998] BCJ No 2862 (Prov Ct)....................395
Chaulk v Andrle, 2018 ONSC 5101 640
Chaulk v Avery, 2009 NLTD 185....................34, 35, 80, 81
Chekowski v Howland, 2013 ABCA 299....................175, 234
Chen v Chen, [2000] OJ No 1176, 5 RFL (5th) 288 (SCJ) 219, 583
Chen v Ma, 2022 MBQB 114....................301

Cheng v Cheng, [1993] OJ No 690 (Gen Div) 569, 608
Cheng v Cheng (1996), 21 RFL (4th) 58, [1996] OJ No 910 (CA) 93
Cheng v Liu, 2017 ONCA 104 19, 21, 23
Cheng v Sze, 2020 ONSC 937 194
Cherewyk v Cherewyk, 2018 MBCA 13 347, 455, 457, 458, 554
Cherneski v Rathwell, 2013 SKCA 133 414, 416, 417, 426, 558
Cherneski v Rathwell, 2014 SKQB 399 422
Chernyakhovsky v Chernyakhovsky, [2005] OJ No 944 (SCJ) 274, 306, 309
Cherry v Cherry (1996), 22 RFL (4th) 432 (BCCA) 579
Cherry v Cherry, [2004] OJ No 2881, [2004] OTC 595 (SCJ) 202, 579
Chertow v Chertow, 2005 CanLII 13911 (Ont CA) 505
Chester v Chester, [2001] AJ No 1475 (QB) 486
Chevalier v Chevalier (1993), 128 NSR (2d) 112, [1993] NSJ No 513 (TD) 16
Chiaramonte v Chiaramonte, 2012 ONSC 6886 461
Chiasson v Doucet, 2014 NBCA 49 191, 195
Chickee v Chickee, [2000] OJ No 2769 (SCJ) 339, 615
Chin v Chow, [1998] BCJ No 1278 (SC) 123
Chisholm v Chisholm (1974), 2 OR (2d) 535, [1974] OJ No 1818 (Div Ct) 620
Cho v Cho (2001), 56 OR (3d) 150, [2001] OJ No 3871 (CA) 579
Chomitzky v Beckstead, 2012 SKQB 376 510
Chong v Donnelly, 2021 ONSC 5263 316
Chopek v McKenzie, 2015 MBQB 207 128
Chou v Chao (1996) 21 RFL (4th) 45, [1996] BCJ No 378 (SC) 467
CHR v EBC, [1997] AJ No 561 (QB) 8
Chrintz v Chrintz, [1998] OJ No 3289, 41 RFL (4th) 219 (Gen Div) 414
Christante v Schmitz (1993), 1 RFL (4th) 142 (Sask QB) 570
Christiansen v Bachul, [2001] AJ No 171 (QB) 587
Church v Chafe, 2010 NLTD(F) 31 367
Church v Church, 2021 MBQB 20 196, 215
Churko v Merchant, 2019 SKQB 307 614
Chutter v Chutter, 2016 BCSC 2407 58, 425
Chyz v Prystupa, [2008] SJ No 580, 2008 SKQB 347 75, 76
Ciachurski v Ciachurski (1994), 47 BCAC 208 664
Ciardullo v Ciardullo (1995), 15 RFL (4th) 121, [1995] BCJ No 1311 (SC) 49, 51, 59, 114
Cipriano v Hampton, 2015 ONSC 349 213
Cisecki v Cisecki, 2011 ONSC 1343 455
CJB v ECB, [2003] NSJ No 362, 218 NSR (2d) 5 (Fam Ct) 309
CJD v CED, 2020 PESC 21 408, 409
CJD v RIJ, 2018 ABQB 287 529
CJI v VMW, [2000] OJ No 4292, 13 RFL (5th) 399 (SCJ) 313
CJT v GAT, 2012 ABQB 193 280
CJT v GAT, 2019 ABQB 851 295, 322
CL v SF, 2009 NBQB 129 293
Clark v Clark (1971), 4 RFL 27 (Ont SC) 476
Clark v Clark, [1997] NBJ No 432, [1997] NBR (2d) (Supp) No 121 (QB) 69
Clark v Clark, [1998] BCJ No 1934 (SC) 270
Clark v Clark, [2006] OJ No 233 (SCJ) 484
Clark v Clark, 2012 BCCA 297 134
Clark v Clark, 2012 ONSC 1026 280
Clark v Leska, 2014 ONSC 268 360
Clark v Taylor, [2004] NWTJ No 5, 2004 NWTSC 9 31
Clark v Vanderhoeven, 2011 ONSC 2286 555
Clarke v Babensee, 2009 BCCA 122, [2009] BCJ No 533 366

Clarke v Clarke, [1998] BCJ No 2370 (SC) 105, 110
Clarke v Clarke, 2014 BCSC 824 278, 279, 290
Clarke v Dowe, 2016 ONSC 4773 340
Clarke v Gale, 2009 NSSC 170 477, 478
Claughton v Bokenfohr, 2018 ABQB 1053 222
Claxton v Jones, [1999] BCJ No 3086 (Prov Ct) 338, 357
Clayton v Crosby, 2011 BCSC 1000 575
CLB v AHB, 2013 BCCA 472 354, 355, 362, 557, 562, 564
CLB v BTC, [2006] BCJ No 3112 (SC) 79
CLC v BTC, 2012 BCSC 736 112
CLD v RJB, 2019 ABQB 852 51, 54
CLE v BMR, 2010 ABCA 187 159, 236, 316, 317, 328, 329, 378, 385
CLE v KD, 2010 ONSC 7072 654
Cleasby v Cleasby, 2013 SKQB 67 365–66
Clegg v Downing, [2004] AJ No 1511, 2004 ABQB 955 330, 331, 510
Clewlow v Clewlow, [2004] OJ No 3468, [2004] OTC 757 (SCJ) 82
Climans v Latner, 2020 ONCA 554 641
Clink v Leydier, [2007] MJ No 482, 2007 MBQB 321 286, 307
CLL v SWJ, 2013 BCSC 917 415
Close v Close, [1997] OJ No 3288, 33 RFL (4th) 210 (Gen Div) 160
Close v Close (1999), 50 RFL (4th) 342, [1999] NBJ No 300 (QB) 31
Cloutier v Cloutier, 2012 ABQB 336 28
CLY v DGY, 2013 ONSC 6550 215
CM v GM, 2019 NBQB 182 40
CM v GM, 2020 NBCA 17 42, 44, 64, 67, 661
CM v PM, 2019 NSSC 250 483
CMC v GWC, [1998] BCJ No 2344 (SC) 107
CMM v DGC, 2014 ONSC 567 28
CMM v DGC, 2015 ONSC 1815 218–19, 426, 600, 611, 653
CMM v DGC, 2015 ONSC 2447 29
CMMR v RWAR, 2011 NBQB 159 191
CMP v PEP, [1999] AJ No 1478, 257 AR 36 (QB) 73, 229
CMR v LFR, 2019 BCCA 371 113
CNC v WJM, 2018 PESC 45 86, 87
CNG v SMR (2007), 38 RFL (6th) 137, [2007] BCJ No 1251, 2007 BCSC 822 510
Coadic v Coadic (2005), 237 NSR (2d) 362, [2005] NSJ No 415, 2005 NSSC 291 151, 200, 215
Coady v Coady, [1999] OJ No 2305 (SCJ) 464, 508
Coates v Watson, 2017 ONCJ 454 37
Coathup v Coathup, [2000] OJ No 289 (SCJ) 468
Cochrane v D'Andrea, [2005] OJ No 1536 (SCJ) 264, 298
Cochrane v Zarins, [1998] BCJ No 756, 36 RFL (4th) 434 (SC) 319
Code v McLeod, 2023 BCSC 1686 146, 184
Coe v Coe, [1999] BCJ No 1373 (SC) 394
Coghill v Coghill, [2006] OJ No 2602 (SCJ) 53, 61, 64, 66, 72, 76, 134, 136, 157, 158, 159
Cohen v Cohen (1995), 11 RFL (4th) 1, [1995] BCJ No 528 (CA) 469, 470
Colbourne v Colbourne, 2014 ABQB 547 311, 312
Cole v Cole, [2000] NSJ No 74, 183 NSR (2d) 176 (SC) 218, 273, 275
Cole v Cole, [2005] OJ No 5191 (SCJ) 202
Cole v Cole, [2008] NSJ No 263, 54 RFL (6th) 396, 2008 NSSC 189 54
Cole v Cole, 2010 BCSC 1330 238
Cole v Cole, 2016 BCSC 716 65
Cole v Jerome, 2017 NWTSC 28 372, 373
Cole v McNeil, [2001] NBJ No 37, [2001] NBR (2d) (Supp) No 20 (QB) 228

Colenutt v Colenutt, 2023 ABKB 562....608
Coles v Coles, [2002] BCJ No 1142 (SC)....358
Coley v Coley (1981), 20 RFL (2d) 327 (Man CA)....457
Colizza v Arnot, [2000] MJ No 176, 6 RFL (5th) 100 (CA)....318
Colizza v Arnot, [2007] MJ No 499, 2008 MBCA 17....270
Collinge v Collinge, [2004] BCJ No 1707, 2004 BCSC 1108....453
Collins v Collins, [1998] AJ No 417, 221 AR 111 (QB)....48, 487
Collins v Collins, [2003] NJ No 278, 46 RFL (5th) 354 (SC)....557, 562
Collins v Collins, 2008 NLUFC 31, [2008] NJ No 296....89, 99, 102
Collins v Collins, 2010 NLTD(F) 15....62
Collison v Collison, [2001] BCJ No 2080 (SC)....522, 587
Colonval v Munson, [1998] BCJ No 1178 (SC)....26
Colter v Colter, 2015 NSSC 2....552
Colucci v Colucci, 2019 ONCA 561....567
Colucci v Colucci, 2021 SCC 24....5, 7, 9, 239–40, 489, 490, 492, 493, 494, 497, 500, 503, 505, 506, 507, 522, 545, 568, 579, 583
Comeau v Comeau, [1997] NSJ No 409 (TD)....59, 319
Comeau v Newman, 2021 NBQB 197....26, 74, 378
Cominetti v Cominetti, [1993] BCJ No 1486 (SC)....575
Connell v Connell, [2006] PEIJ No 12 (SCTD)....457
Connelly v McGouran, [2006] OJ No 993, 207 OAC 368 (CA)....242
Connors v Connors, [1999] BCJ No 2793 (SC)....439
Conron v Conron, [1999] OJ No 38 (Gen Div)....462
Contino v Leonelli-Contino, [2005] SCJ No 65, [2005] 3 SCR 217....15, 338, 347, 351, 362, 367, 368, 370, 405
Conway v Conway, 2011 ABCA 137....348, 350
Cook v Ballantyne, 2022 SKQB 172....364
Cook v Cook (1980), 30 Nfld & PEIR 42, 120 DLR (3d) 216 (Nfld TD)....24
Cook v Cook, [2000] NSJ No 19, 182 NSR (2d) 299, 3 RFL (5th) 373 (SC)....87, 88, 89, 90
Cook v Cook, [2007] SJ No 332, 2007 SKQB 222....428
Cook v Cook, 2016 NBQB 55....62, 78, 279, 314
Cook v Kilduff, [2000] SJ No 482 11 RFL (5th) 48 (QB)....98, 104
Cook v McManus, [2006] NBJ No 334, 2006 NBQB 138....184, 185, 186, 188, 222, 223, 562
Cooke v Cooke, 2011 BCCA 444....346
Cooling v Noye, [1999] PEIJ No 46 (SC)....15
Cooney v Catherwood Estate, 2016 ONSC 525....542, 543, 578
Cooper v Cooper, [2002] SJ No 226 (QB)....408
Cooper v Cooper, [2004] OJ No 5096, [2004] OTC 1106 (SCJ)....454
Coppens v Cal, [1998] SJ No 871, 175 Sask R 1 (QB)....207, 308
Corbett v Corbett, [1997] NSJ No 525 (TD)....568
Corbett v Lanteigne, [1998] BCJ No 2207 (SC)....231
Corbett v McEachren, 2017 NSSC 108....372
Corby v Corby, 2015 ONSC 2700....76, 323
Corder v Corder, 2009 BCSC 915....434
Corey v Corey, 2010 NBQB 112....290
Corkum v Clarke, [2000] NSJ No 285 (Fam Ct)....288, 290, 312, 314
Corkum v Corkum (1988), 14 RFL (3d) 275 (Ont HCJ)....476
Cornborough v Cornborough, [1997] BCJ No 1981 (SC)....163
Cornelissen v Cornelissen, [2002] BCJ No 1459 (SC), var'd 2003 BCCA 666, [2003] BCJ No 2714, 46 RFL (5th) 366....162, 318, 483
Cornelius v Andres, [1998] MJ No 86, 36 RFL (4th) 436 (QB)....413
Cornish v Cornish, [2001] NJ No 116, 200 Nfld & PEIR 350 (SC)....253
Correia v Correia, [2002] MJ No 248, 2002 MBQB 172....283, 284, 286, 327

Corsano v Simms, [2002] NSJ No 440, 33 RFL (5th) 301 (CA)....72
Cosentino v Cosentino, 2020 ONCA 775....562, 624, 663
Cosper v Cosper (1995), 14 RFL (4th) 152 (NSCA)....657
Costa v Perkins, 2012 ONSC 3165 (Div Ct)....374, 378, 494
Costa v Petipas (2006), 258 Nfld & PEIR 234, [2006] PEIJ No 39 (SC)....338, 347, 348, 349, 350, 356, 359
Cote v Cote, [1995] OJ No 807 (Ct J)....94
Cote v Taylor, 2013 ONSC 5428....204, 581
Cotey v Cotey, [2002] BCJ No 2726 (SC)....538, 575
Cotton v Cotton (1966), 60 DLR (2d) 117 (BCCA)....466
Cougan v Piche, [2004] SJ No 587, 10 RFL (6th) 22, 2004 SKQB 391....30
Coulson v Farmer (1999), 50 RFL (4th) 345, [1999] OJ No 2478 (SCJ)....632
Coulstring v Lacroix, [2001] OJ No 1826 (SCJ)....626
Courchesne v Charlebois, [1998] OJ No 2656 (Prov Ct)....231
Courchesne v Courchesne, [2004] OJ No 442 (SCJ)....205
Court v McQuaid, [2005] PEIJ No 24, 246 Nfld & PEIR 43 (SC)....558
Coutts v Coutts (1995), 14 RFL (4th) 234, [1995] SJ No 258 (QB)....20
Couture v Ferguson, [2003] OJ No 942, 37 RFL (5th) 289 (SCJ)....109
Cove v Cove, 2010 NSSC 407....476
Covin v Covin, 2021 NBQB 228....12, 316, 317
Covington v Covington, [1999] AJ No 5 (QB)....187
Cowan v Cowan, [2001] AJ No 669 (QB)....321
Cowan v Cowan, [2001] AJ No 922 (QB)....575
Cowan v Cowan, 2018 ONSC 2495....198, 200
Cox v Cox, [1998] AJ No 1282 (QB)....467
Cox v Cox, [1999] NJ No 242, 181 Nfld & PEIR 212 (UFC)....97, 116, 331
Cozzi v Smith, 2015 ONSC 396....634
CPB v Canada, 2013 TCC 118....366
CPZ v TMZ, [2005] AJ No 1209, 2005 ABQB 206....506
CR v IA, [2001] OJ No 1053 (SCJ)....296
Craig v Craig (1982), 18 Man R (2d) 279, [1982] MJ No 382 (QB)....619
Craig v Niro, 2022 ONSC 5178....77, 286, 320, 329
Cram v Cram, [1999] BCJ No 2518 (SC)....79, 335, 481
Crawford v Crawford, [1998] OJ No 3894 (Prov Div)....30
Crawford v Crawford, [1998] OJ No 885, 67 OTC 308 (Gen Div)....48, 148
Crawford v Crawford, [1998] SJ No 322 (QB)....229
Crawford v Crawford, [1999] NBJ No 173, 45 RFL (4th) 211 (CA)....40
Crawford v Crawford, [1999] SJ No 238 (QB)....217
Crawley v Tobin, [1998] NJ No 293, 42 RFL (4th) 327 (SC)....310
CRB v KJM, 2023 NBKB 224....342, 343, 345
CRC v DAJC, 2020 ABCA 143....214, 218, 321
CRE v KLE, 2011 BCSC 291....136
Creaser v Creaser, [2002] NSJ No 542 (SC)....168
CRHE v FGE, [2004] BCJ No 1057, 1 RFL (6th) 173, 2004 BCCA 297, aff'g [2003] BCJ No 2129, 2003 BCSC 1401....315, 357, 367
Crick v Crick, [1997] BCJ No 2222, 43 BCLR (3d) 251 (SC)....7, 344, 381–82
Crisp v Crisp, 2012 ONSC 521....73, 251
CRL v SLL, 2019 BCSC 2103....42
Crocker v Sipus (1992), 41 RFL (3d) 19 (Ont CA)....665
Croft v Foote, 2023 NLCA 36....153, 312
Crofton v Sturko, [1998] BCJ No 38 (SC)....343, 344
Croissant v Croissant, 2022 SKCA 5....179, 183
Croll v Croll, [2003] BCJ No 2937, 2003 BCSC 1912....316

Crook v Crook (1992), 42 RFL (3d) 297 (NSTD) 455
Crosbie v Crosbie, 2012 ONCA 516 .... 218, 540
Crosby v Crosby, [1998] PEIJ No 96 (SC) 579
Crosby v Crosby, [2002] SJ No 164, 26 RFL (5th) 20 (QB) 483
Cross v Batters, 2016 SKCA 71 ....413, 414, 415, 474
Cross v Cross, [1997] BCJ No 1741 (SC) 251, 316, 345, 374
Cross v Thompson, 2019 MBQB 44....239
Crossley v Vorell, 2021 BCSC 2484.... 122, 136, 243
Crow v McMynn, [1989] BCJ No 1233 (SC)....600
Crowdis v Crowdis, [2003] SJ No 371, 235 Sask R 201 (QB).... 82, 290, 301
CRP v NDP, 2023 NBKB 197 .... 124, 151, 188, 191, 232, 233–34
Csecs v Csecs, [2001] OJ No 1424 (SCJ) 287, 469
CSH v EMH, 2013 ABQB 660....431
CSW v TDS, 2023 SKKB 182.... 291, 359
CT v JL, 2018 PESC 15 594
CTB v BAAB, 2022 YKSC 15....596
CTG v RRG, 2016 SKQB 387....432, 447, 453, 456
CU v MR, [1997] QJ No 3289 (CS) 56
CU v MR, [1998] QJ No 3443 (CS) 56
Cuddie v Cuddie, [1998] BCJ No 159 (SC) 402
Cuddy v Cuddy, [1999] OJ No 1399, 45 RFL (4th) 131 (SCJ) 508
Cudmore v Cudmore, [2000] PEIJ No 39 (SC).... 296, 583
Cui v Liwanpo, 2022 ONSC 4549....86
Cunha v Cunha (1994), 99 BCLR 93 (SC).... 463, 493
Cunningham v Cunningham (1990), 30 RFL (3d) 159 (BCCA).... 557, 565
Cunningham v Seveny, 2017 ABCA 4 ....145, 146, 222, 249
Currie v Currie (1987), 6 RFL (3d) 40 (Man QB), aff'd (1987), 10 RFL (3d) 207 (Man CA)....565
Currie v Currie, [1999] OJ No 2170 (SCJ)....481, 483, 484
Currie v Currie, 2022 NSSC 23 ....239, 497, 583
Currie-Johnson v Johnson, 2015 SKQB 315 100
Cusack v Cusack, [1999] PEIJ No 90 (SC).... 35, 409
Cusick v Squire, [1999] NJ No 206, 178 Nfld & PEIR 351 (SC) 343
Cutmiski v Aubert, [1998] SJ No 825 (QB)....389
CWT v KAT, 2013 ABQB 678.... 372, 385
CYD v JRD, [2005] BCJ No 2596, 2005 BCSC 1635 509
CYJ v RJ, 2022 BCSC 1901 208
Cyr v Cassista (1986), 50 RFL (2d) 33 (NBCA) 662

D (DE) v J (QR), 2019 PESC 39.... 281, 295
D'Ambrosio v D'Ambrosio, [2000] BCJ No 1704, 2000 BCSC 1252....537, 544, 598
D'Entremont v D'Entremont, [2001] NSJ No 586 (SC)....408
D'Ovidio v Clement, 2013 ONSC 5002....76
D'Urzo v D'Urzo, [2002] OJ No 2415, 30 RFL (5th) 277 (SCJ)....343
D(GA) v D(G) (1995), 11 RFL (4th) 270, [1995] AJ No 325 (QB) 211, 527, 535
D(J) v J(J) (1998), 42 RFL (4th) 335 (Ont Prov Div)....445
D(JS) v V(WL) (1995), 11 RFL (4th) 409, [1995] BCJ No 653 (CA) 599
Da Silva v Da Silva, [2004] OJ No 1976, 5 RFL (6th) 274 (SCJ) 4, 436
Da Silva v Kelly, 2022 ONSC 1402....40
da Silva v Moreira, 2020 ONSC 5167 65
DA v SA, 2017 SKQB 108.... 340, 343
DA(R)A v DJR, [2008] PEIJ No 20, 2008 PESCTD 21 329
Dagenais v Blais, 2010 ABQB 324....47

Dagg v Chenier, 2014 ONSC 336 .... 353, 355, 359, 360
Dagg v Pereira, [2000] OJ No 4450, 12 RFL (5th) 325 (SCJ) 31
Dagher v Hajj, 2021 ONSC 2853 611
Dahl v Dahl (1995), 178 AR 119, 18 RFL (4th) 122, [1995] AJ No 1075 (CA) 486, 487, 507, 565
Dahler v Dahler, [2002] OJ No 2671 (SCJ) 555
Dahlgren v Hodgson, [1998] AJ No 1501, 43 RFL (4th) 176 (CA) 151, 215, 484, 567
Daicar-Gendron v Gendron, [2004] BCJ No 2005, 35 BCLR (4th) 326 (SC) 58
Daku v Daku, [1999] SJ No 330 (QB) 211, 227, 561
Dalep v Dalep (1987), 11 RFL (3d) 359, [1987] BCJ No 2138 (SC) 114
Dalgleish v Dalgleish, [2003] OJ No 2918 (SCJ) 195, 325, 466
Dalke v Dalke, 2012 BCSC 173 114
Dalton v Clements, 2016 NSSC 38 201
Dalton v Craig, [2002] OJ No 4686, 33 RFL (5th) 63 (CA) 235
Dalziel v Dalziel (1977), 3 BCLR 73, [1977] BCJ No 308 (SC) 629
Damphouse v Damphouse, 2020 ABQB 101 .... 49, 66, 286, 506
Danchuk v Danchuk, [2001] BCJ No 755, 2001 BCCA 291 .... 430, 436, 437, 557, 568
Dand v Ady, 2014 SKQB 101 .... 130, 177
Dang v Bahramloian, [2007] AJ No 451, 2007 ABCA 142 658
Daniel v Daniel (1991), 38 RFL (3d) 70 (BCCA) 572
Daniel v Daniel, 2022 SKKB 279 .... 426, 430, 432
Daniel-DeFreitas v Francis, 2012 ONSC 515 .... 199, 204, 300
Daniels v Daniels, 2010 MBQB 46, var'd 2011 MBCA 94 .... 522, 523
Daniels v Lakes (1987), 11 RFL (3d) 159 (BCCA) 543
Danylkiw v Danylkiw, [2003] OJ No 431 (SCJ) 591
Danyluk v Danyluk (2008), 55 RFL (6th) 141, [2008] AJ No 509, 2008 ABQB 276 27
Darbyson v Darbyson, [1998] OJ No 2173 (Gen Div) 434
Darel v Darel, [2002] AJ No 1200, 322 AR 398 (QB) 255
Darlington v Darlington, [1997] BCJ No 2534, 32 RFL (4th) 406 (CA) 49, 50, 97
Darlington v Moore, 2013 NSSC 103 .... 122, 216
Darvill v Chorney, [1999] SJ No 551 (QB) 566, 569
DAT v SLP, 2018 NBQB 135 .... 127, 151, 215, 455, 495
Davari v Namazi, [1999] BCJ No 116 (SC) 466, 536
Davids v Davids, [1998] OJ No 2859, 66 OTC 321 (Gen Div) 55, 56, 59, 219, 413, 470, 485
Davids v Davids, 1999 CanLII 9289 (ONCA) 636
Davidson v Davidson, [1998] AJ No 1040, 42 RFL (4th) 154 (QB) 437
Davie v Davie, [1998] BCJ No 1691 (SC) 235, 433
Davies v Davies (1991), 32 RFL (3d) 14 (Ont Ct Gen Div) 565
Davis v Colter (1973), 12 RFL 84, [1973] SJ No 145 (QB) 653
Davis v Davis, [1999] BCJ No 1832 (SC) 70, 279, 323, 326, 336, 476
Davis v Davis, [2000] NSJ No 86 (SC) 408
Davis v Davis, 2013 NBQB 115 .... 12, 410, 414, 415, 416
Davis v Davis, 2016 NLTD(F) 2 376
Davis v Davis, 2022 NSSC 212 216
DAW v WMZ, [2000] OJ No 2391, 7 RFL (5th) 212 (SCJ) 111, 426, 427
Day v Day (1994), 129 NSR (2d) 169, [1994] NSJ No 83 (TD) 15, 17, 468
Day v Weir, 2014 ONSC 5975 85
Daye v Ekkebus, [2008] BCJ No 529, 2008 BCSC 362 56
DB v HMB, 2019 NLSC 105 .... 196, 376
DBB v DMB, 2017 SKCA 59 .... 12, 34, 38, 39, 40, 42, 43, 51, 79, 199, 475
DBC v RMW, [2004] AJ No 1559, 12 RFL (6th) 14 (QB) 522
DBF v BF, 2017 ABCA 272 538
DBS v SRG, [2005] AJ No 2, 7 RFL (6th) 373 (CA) 10, 489

DBS v SRG; LJW v TAR; Henry v Henry; Hiemstra v Hiemstra, [2006] 2 SCR 231, 2006 SCC 37, [2006] SCJ No 37 .... 6, 34, 300, 425, 486, 487, 489, 490, 491, 492, 493, 494, 495, 496, 497, 500, 507, 509, 589, 661
DC v PC, 2017 PESC 26 261
DCC v DWC, 2022 CarswellNB 645 (KB) 204, 205
DCD v RJPC, 2014 BCSC 2420 .... 86, 93
DCI v MBI, 2022 SKKB 265 603
DDG v GNG, 2019 MBQB 98 114
DDM v JMM, 2023 BCSC 1834 498
DDR v KTR, 2019 BCSC 1805 510
De Beck v De Beck, 2012 BCCA 465 .... 63, 65, 83
de Goede v de Goede, [1999] BCJ No 330 (SC) 135, 136, 345
de Goede v de Goede, [2000] BCJ No 5 (SC) 157
De Grandis v De Grandis (1990), 28 RFL (3d) 45 (BCSC) 458
de la Fuente v Breen, 2021 BCSC 2000 183
de la Fuente v Breen, 2022 BCCA 424 623
de Oliviera v Kohlfurst, [1999] OJ No 3504 (Ct J) 301
de Rooy v Bergstrom, 2010 BCCA 5 .... 432, 434
DE v LE, 2014 NBCA 67 129
Deagnon v Folk, 2009 SKQB 499 356
Deale v Deale (1995), 15 RFL (4th) 95 (BCSC) 466
Dean v Barrett, [2004] AJ No 183, 2004 ABCA 76 396
Dean v Brown, [2002] NSJ No 439, 2002 NSCA 124 635
Dean v Dean, [1997] OJ No 3224 (Gen Div) 488
Dean v Friesen, [1999] SJ No 15 (QB) 404
Dean v Friesen, [1999] SJ No 424, 50 RFL (4th) 363 (QB) 224, 228, 394
Deane v Deane (1995), 14 RFL (4th) 55, [1995] OJ No 1150 (Gen Div) 388
Deans v Deans, 2010 ABQB 17 .... 462, 464
Dearborn v Dearborn, [2001] SJ No 276, 2001 SKQB 86 629
DeBono v Smith, 1989 CanLII 7278 647
Debora v Debora (2006), 33 RFL (6th) 252, [2006] OJ No 4826 (CA) 541
DeBora v DeBora, [2003] OJ No 575 (SCJ) 31
Decaen v Decaen, 2013 ONCA 218 .... 58, 163
Dedoscenco v Beauchamp, [2005] BCJ No 1053, 2005 BCSC 692 .... 151, 215
DeFehr v DeFehr, 2002 BCCA 577 657
Degagne v Sargeant, [1999] AJ No 506, 232 AR 355 (CA) 72, 74
DeGiorgio v DeGiorgio, 2020 ONSC 1674 596
DeGiorgio v DeGiorgio, 2022 ONSC 6677 596
Deimuth v Fortin, [2003] MJ No 60, 37 RFL (5th) 69 (QB) 95
Deiter v Sampson, [2002] OJ No 4160, 31 RFL (5th) 296 (SCJ), aff'd [2004] OJ No 904, 50 RFL (5th) 338 (CA) 441, 443
Del Puppo v Del Puppo, [1999] BCJ No 1722 (SC) 2
Delaney v Delaney (1995), 11 RFL (4th) 155, [1995] BCJ No 307 (CA) 22
Delaney v Delaney, [1997] BCJ No 1675 (SC) 235
Delaney v Delaney, 2014 NLTD(F) 28 .... 162, 277, 359, 360
Delargy v Ciolfi, [1999] BCJ No 1335 (SC) 99
Delichte v Rogers, 2013 MBCA 106 .... 282, 295
Delichte v Rogers, 2018 MBQB 75 .... 145, 146, 283, 295
Delorey v Callahan, 2009 NSSC 387 88
Delorme v Woodlam and Dunn (1993), 89 Man R (2d) 16 (QB) 582
Demeria v Demeria, [1998] SJ No 898 (QB) 562, 580
Demers v Moar, [2004] AJ No 1331, 6 RFL (6th) 240, 2004 ABCA 380 210
Demonte v Demonte, [1998] BCJ No 1041 (SC) 435

Denesi v Neves (1998), 36 RFL (4th) 154, [1998] OJ No 736 (Gen Div) 485, 487, 607
Deng v Zhang, 2022 BCCA 271 ....49, 497
Denis v Denis, 2012 SKQB 49...453
Dennett v Dennett, [1998] AJ No 440, 225 AR 50 (QB)..342, 345, 354, 363
Dennis v Wilson, [1998] OJ No 4854, 42 RFL (4th) 131 (CA)..663
Depace v Michienzi, [2000] OJ No 453, 5 RFL (5th) 40 (SCJ)..................................... 211, 235, 259
Depeel v Abramyk, [1997] SJ No 749, 174 Sask R 56 (QB)...80
Dergousoff v Schille (Dergousoff), [1999] SJ No 192, 48 RFL (4th) 1 (CA) 567
Derkach v Derkach (1989), 22 RFL (3d) 423, [1989] MJ No 489 (QB)...80
Desjardines v Desjardines (1991), 31 RFL (3d) 449 (Alta QB) 508
Desjardins v Bouey, 2013 ABQB 714.. 340, 342
Desjardins v Desjardins, [1999] MJ No 70, 44 RFL (4th) 93 (CA)..409
Despot v Despot Estate (1992), 42 RFL (3d) 218 (BCSC) 478, 534, 592
Desrochers v Desrochers, [1998] MJ No 379 (QB)..225, 227
Desrochers v Desrochers, [2004] BCJ No 1465, 2004 BCSC 930 202
DesRoches v Wedge, [2002] PEIJ No 53, 2002 PESCTD 39 606
Desrosiers v Pastuck, 2016 NSSC 308...145, 187
Destine v Cloutier, 2022 ABCA 331 .... 146, 348, 492
Deveau v Groskopf, [2000] SJ No 281, 192 Sask R 227 (QB)... 384, 385, 395
Devlin v Devlin (1994), 10 RFL (4th) 265, [1994] AJ No 1012 (CA)...618
Dewan v Dewan, 2012 ONSC 503...217
DeWolfe v McMillan, 2011 NSSC 301.. 147, 166
Dey v Malhotra, 2013 ONSC 2469..263
DF v KG, 2018 NSSC 65 600
DGS v HAS, 2019 ABQB 887 494
DH v DW, [1992] OJ No 1737 (Gen Div) 11
Dhein v Pratt, 2016 BCSC 857...505
Di Ciaula v Mastrogiacomo, 2019 ONSC 2823..614
DI v SD, [2003] YJ No 74, 2003 YKSC 33...356
DI v SI, 2011 BCSC 1788.. 316, 318, 351
Dias v Dias, 2015 ONSC 7512 230
Dick v Dick (1993), 46 RFL (3d) 219, [1993] OJ No 140 (Gen Div) 16
Dick v Knoblauch, [1998] SJ No 631, 171 Sask R 146 (QB) 383
Dickie v Dickie, [2007] 1 SCR 346, [2007] SCJ No 8, 2007 SCC 8........................... 531, 552, 611, 623, 662
Dickinson v Dickinson, [1998] OJ No 4815 (Gen Div).. 311, 414, 469, 470, 540
Dicks v Dicks, [2000] OJ No 3964 (SCJ)... 427, 534
Dicks v Dicks, [2001] NSJ No 302, 196 NSR (2d) 53 (SC) 31
Dickson v Dickson, 2009 MBQB 274 ....124, 125, 152, 414
Dickson v Dickson, 2011 MBQB 296 642
Diehl v Diehl, [1998] AJ No 1303, 238 AR 363 (QB) 307
Dietz v Dietz, [1998] SJ No 197 (QB)..412
Difede v Difede, [2007] OJ No 622 (SCJ) 152
DiFrancesco v Couto, [2001] OJ No 4307 (CA) 578
Dillon v Dillon, [2005] NSJ No 548, 2005 NSCA 166...153, 159, 350, 353
Diminie v Diminie, [1995] OJ No 59, 10 RFL (4th) 193 (Gen Div)..383, 571
Dingle v Dingle, 2018 MBQB 77 574
Dinn v Dinn, 2011 NLTD(F) 19...520
Diotallevi v Diotallevi (1982), 27 RFL (2d) 400, 37 OR (2d) 106 (HCJ) 55
DiPasquale v DiPasquale, [1998] NWTJ No 58 (SC)... 330, 332
Dixon v Cole, 2014 NSCA 100 .... 659, 660
Dixon v Dixon (1995), 13 RFL (4th) 160, [1995] AJ No 342 (QB)... 25, 550, 555
Dixon v Dixon, [1997] AJ No 692, 222 AR 1 (QB) 293
Dixon v Fleming, [2000] OJ No 1218, 6 RFL (5th) 124 (SCJ) 244, 373, 385

DJE v PAE, 2014 ABCA 403 .... 316, 333
DL v EC, 2023 ONCA 494 85
DL v FK, [1998] NWTJ No 42 (SC) 10
DL v GSL, [2001] OJ No 2824, [2001] OTC 529 (SCJ) 223, 454
DL v MB, 2010 NBQB 33 54
DL v ML, 2012 NBQB 382 .... 209, 404
DLA v JTA, [1999] AJ No 312, 45 RFL (4th) 1 (QB) 219, 507
DLB v PJB, [2005] AJ No 207, 2005 ABQB 113 259
DLC v FMC, 2011 BCCA 444 346
DLD v RAG, 2010 BCSC 1080 374
DLG v GDR, 2012 NBQB 177 596
DLM v JAM, 2008 NBCA 2, [2008] NBJ No 9 .... 192, 194, 196, 199
Dlouhy v Dlouhy, 1995 CanLII 5715 (SKQB) 603
DLP v SJ, 2010 NSSC 107 296
DM v Alberta (Director of Maintenance Enforcement), 2014 ABCA 60 580
DMA v MS, [2008] NBJ No 498, 2009 NBQB 4 484
DMCT v LKS, 2008 NSCA 61, 54 RFL (6th) 13 134
DMD v RLD, 2015 BCSC 2332 100
DMES v WLS, [2003] MJ No 185, 174 Man R (2d) 297 (QB) 193
DMH v CMM, 2011 SKQB 104 38
DMR v AR, [2006] BCJ No 42, 2006 BCSC 38 55
DN v CR, [1999] SJ No 403 (QB) 228
DNL v CNS, 2013 BCSC 858 .... 120, 193, 219
Dobson v Dobson, [2005] SJ No 686, 2005 SKQB 477 .... 187, 232
Docherty v Melo, 2022 ONSC 5306 652
Doe v Alberta, [2005] AJ No 1719, 21 RFL (6th) 327 (QB) 445
Doe v Alberta, 2007 ABCA 50, [2007] AJ No 138 .... 93, 426, 506
Doerksen v Houlahan, 2012 MBQB 110 .... 49, 455, 488
Doherty v Decoff, [2007] NSJ No 263, 2007 NSSC 183 496
Doherty v Doherty, [2001] OJ No 2400, 19 RFL (5th) 46 (SCJ) 285, 332
Dolsen v Lariviere, 2015 SKQB 127 100
Domanski v Domanski (1992), 83 Man R (2d) 161 (CA) 581
Domzalska v Desjardins, 2017 ABQB 177 389
Donald v Brown, [2005] SJ No 692, 2005 SKQB 450 (QB) 71
Doncaster v Doncaster (1991), 31 RFL (3d) 235, [1991] SJ No 100 (QB) 17
Donovan v Canada, [2005] TCJ No 494, 2005 TCC 667 365
Donovan v Donovan, 2000 MBCA 80, [2000] MJ No 407, 9 RFL (5th) 306, 150 Man R (2d) 116 (CA) 196, 199, 207, 208, 565
Donovan v Lee, [2002] MJ No 226, 164 Man R (2d) 299 (QB) 210, 557
Dool v Dool, [1997] OJ No 1256 (Gen Div) 465
Doole v Doole (1991), 32 RFL (3d) 283 (Alta QB) 579, 581
Dooley v Dooley, [2000] NSJ No 252, 186 NSR (2d) 388 (SC) 242
Dooley v Knight, [2003] SJ No 211 (QB) 581
Dopson v Cameron, [2001] OJ No 3024 (SCJ) 511
Dorey v Dorey, 2011 ABCA 192 50
Dorey v Havens, 2019 BCCA 47 .... 279, 654
Dorge v Dorge, 2012 MBQB 97 379
Dorion v Merkley, 2014 ONSC 1777 223
Dorman v Dorman, [2001] BCJ No 1635 (SC) 206, 223
Dornick v Dornick, [1999] BCJ No 2498, 1 RFL (5th) 37 (CA) 159, 221
Dorsett v Levy, 2016 ONSC 345 587
Dort v Dort, 2009 NSSC 372 74
Dostie v Poapst, 2014 ONSC 6959 320

Doucet v Doucet, 2020 BCSC 1218 155
Doucet v Lau, [2005] AJ No 1809, 2005 ABQB 963 510
Dougan v Clark, [2003] PEIJ No 87, 229 Nfld & PEIR 228 (SC) 374, 405
Dougherty v Humbel, [2000] BCJ No 2323, 2000 BCSC 1673 40
Dougherty v Jepson, [2002] OJ No 1349, [2002] OTC 226 (SCJ) 254
Douglas v Campbell, [2006] NSJ No 350, 2006 NSSC 266 .... 49, 57
Douglas v Douglas, 2013 ONCJ 242 27
Douglas v Faucher, 2014 ONSC 4045 .... 373, 453
Douglas v Ward, [2006] SJ No 57, 2006 SKQB 29 395
Dove v MacIntyre, 2021 NSSC 1 .... 50, 56, 84
Dovicin v Dovicin, [2002] OJ No 5339, 29 RFL (5th) 281 (SCJ) 92, 98
Dowden v Dowden (1980), 29 Nfld & PEIR 165, [1980] NJ No 128 (TD) 25
Dowe v Dowe, [2001] NSJ No 313 (SC) 214
Dowling v Dowling, [2005] OJ No 2682 (Div Ct) 362
Doyle v Doyle, [2006] BCJ No 523, 2006 BCCA 128 361
DR v EPR, 2014 BCSC 1912 493
Dragun v Dragun, [1984] 6 WWR 171 (Man QB) 533
Dram v Foster, 2009 MBCA 125 461
DRC v JEM, 2022 SKQB 26 528
Dreger v Dreger, [2000] SJ No 11 (QB) 228
Dring v Gheyle, 2018 BCCA 435 49
Droit de la famille — 092181, 2009 QCCS 4122 6
Droit de la famille — 101016, 2010 QCCA 926 295
Droit de la famille — 101052, 2010 QCCA 942 587
Droit de la famille — 1118, [1988] RDF 308 (Que CS) 388
Droit de la famille — 1134, [1987] RDF 464 (Que CS) 570
Droit de la famille — 1204, [1988] RDF 430 (Que CS) 580
Droit de la famille — 121718, 2012 QCCA 1229 658
Droit de la famille — 1231, [1989] RDF 189 (Que CS) 456
Droit de la famille — 123147, 2012 QCCA 1966 658
Droit de la famille — 1271, [1989] RDF 592 (Que CS) 550, 556
Droit de la famille — 1275, 2012 QCCA 87 196
Droit de la famille — 133554, 2013 QCCA 2176 196
Droit de la famille — 139, 2013 QCCA 15 6
Droit de la famille — 142281, 2014 QCCA 1692 .... 458, 658
Droit de la famille — 152697, 2015 QCCA 1738 145
Droit de la famille — 191160, 2019 QCCA 1098 283
Droit de la famille — 19819, 2019 QCCA 830 42
Droit de la famille — 1991, 2019 QCCA 137 214
Droit de la famille — 3148, [2000] RJQ 2339, (sub nom OM v AK)
[2000] QJ No 3224 (CS) 6, 15, 416, 424, 482,
Droit de la famille — 324, [1987] RJQ 149 (CS) 478
Droit de la famille — 356 (1987), 8 RFL (3d) 349 (Que CA) 575
Droit de la famille — 456, [1988] RDF 64 (Que CA) 570
Droit de la famille — 541, [1988] RDF 484 (Que CA) 550
Droit de la famille — 614, [1989] RDF 347 (Que CA) 570
Droit de la famille — 620, [1989] RDF 224, JE 89-513 (Que CA) 17
Droit de la famille — 913 (1990), 30 RFL (3d) 83 (Que CS) 565, 592
Drover v Drover, 2020 NLCA 9 200
Drozdzik v Drozdzik (1992), 39 RFL (3d) 138 (BCCA) 457
Drygala v Pauli, [2002] OJ No 3731, 29 RFL (5th) 293 (CA) 195, 196, 201, 208
Drygala v Pauli. See also AMD v AJP.
DS v EPS, 2011 BCSC 1102 216

DS v JSR, 2014 NBQB 111 159
DS v WDG, 2016 BCSC 1345 34
DSS v NMG, 2012 PESC 12 426
Dubreuil v Poloway, 2010 BCCA 297 574
Ducharme v Burym, 2020 MBQB 160 593
Ducharme v Ducharme, 2019 MBQB 72 200
Dudka v Dudka, [1997] NSJ No 526 (TD) 335
Dueck v Dueck, 2006 SKQB 417, [2006] SJ No 578 .... 516, 526
Dufault v Dufault, 2009 BCSC 1220 81
Duffee v Scott, [2003] SJ No 212 (QB) 401
Duffett v Duffett, 2010 NLTD(F) 16 .... 557, 574
Duffield v Duffield, [1998] BCJ No 184 (SC) 435
Duffus v Frempong-Manso, 2015 ONSC 7051 176
Duffy v Boisvert, 2017 BCSC 500 93
Duffy v Duffy, [1999] OJ No 3663 (Gen Div) 462
Duffy v Duffy, 2009 NLCA 11 658
Duffy v Duffy, 2009 NLCA 48 .... 196, 200, 201, 208
Duhnych v Duhnych, [2004] OJ No 2655, 4 RFL (6th) 278 (SCJ) 472, 528
Duke v Duke, [1998] BCJ No 1624 (SC) 580
Duke v Hickey, [2001] NJ No 117 (SC) 581
Duleba v Sorge, 2018 ONSC 6022 271
Dumas v Dumas (1992), 41 RFL (3d) 204, [1992] OJ No 1295 (Gen Div) 555
Dumas v Dumas (1992), 43 RFL (3d) 260 (Alta QB) 439
Dumont v Dumont (1987), 86 NBR (2d) 183 (QB) 457
Dumont v Dumont, 2017 BCSC 668 35
Dunbar v Saunders, 2021 BCSC 193 .... 202, 574, 576
Duncan v Duncan (1992), 40 RFL (3d) 358 (Alta QB) 476
Duncan v Duncan, [1999] BCJ No 2201 (CA) 432, 434
Duncan v Duncan, [1999] NBJ No 144, 211 NBR (2d) 174 (QB) 22
Duncan v Mokelki, [2008] SJ No 663, 2008 SKQB 442 14
Dungey v Dungey, 2020 SKCA 138 183
Dunham v Dunham, [1998] OJ No 4758 (Gen Div) 151, 187, 219, 243
Dunleavy v Comeau, 2019 ONSC 4535 .... 86, 94, 216
Dunn v Dunn (1995), 14 RFL (4th) 50, [1995] NSJ No 276 (TD) 381
Dunn v Dunn, 2011 ONSC 6899 14
Dunn v Dunn, 2013 NLTD(F) 7 .... 75, 76, 323, 325
Dunnett v Dunnett, 2018 BCCA 262 166
Dunsdon v Dunsdon (1978), 5 RFL (2d) 89 (Ont CA) 557
Duplak v Duplak (1988), 54 Man R (2d) 70 (QB) 592
Dupont v Dupont (1993), 47 RFL (3d) 273 (BCSC) 456
Durant v Durant, [2001] NSJ No 10 (SC) 211, 472
Dureab v Ben-Harhara, 2021 ABCA 128 659
Durocher v Klementovich, 2013 ABCA 115 455
Durose v Durose, [1996] BCJ No 420 (SC) 49
Durso v Mascherin, 2013 ONSC 6522 75
Dusseault v Dolfo and McGarry, [1998] BCJ No 1209 (Prov Ct) 104
Dutrisac v Ulm, [2000] BCJ No 178 (CA) 94, 99, 100
DWM v MAB, 2012 NBQB 146 .... 47, 50, 56
DWS v NMJC, 2017 YKSC 60 494
DWT v BST, 2016 BCSC 1978 574
Dwyer v Dwyer (1986), 4 RFL (3d) 48 (Man CA) 572
Dyck v Bell, 2015 BCCA 520 .... 350, 359, 360, 361
Dyck v Dyck (1979), 1 Sask R 43, [1979] SJ No 562 (QB) 112

Dyck v Dyck, 2008 MBCA 135, [2008] MJ No 403 ... 170, 184
Dyck v Highton, [2003] SJ No 600, 45 RFL (5th) 322 (QB) ... 20, 216, 243, 380, 396, 454
Dyczek v Dyczek, [1986] OJ No 1085 (CA) ... 471
Dykman v Dykman, 2011 BCSC 883 ... 112
DYP v NPT, 2015 NBQB 67 ... 153, 161, 223

Eadie v Eadie, [1998] NBJ No 352 (QB) ... 385
EAG v DLG, 2010 YKSC 23 ... 170
EAL v HMG, 2010 BCSC 892 ... 14
EAM v SHM, 2018 PESC 19 ... 65
Earle v Earle, [1999] BCJ No 383 (SC) ... 557, 576, 579, 580
Earles v Earles, [2006] BCJ No 346, 2006 BCSC 221 ... 291
Easton v Coxhead, 2018 ONSC 4784 ... 49, 51, 56, 62, 70, 76, 147
Easton v McAvoy, [2005] OJ No 5479 (Ct J) ... 353
Ebrahim v Ebrahim, [1997] BCJ No 2039 (SC) ... 293, 317, 331
ECH v WEH, [2003] BCJ No 715 (SC) ... 305
Eckert v Eckert, 2018 MBQB 117 ... 370, 374, 376
Edden v Foley, 2024 ABKB 48 ... 470
Edgar v Edgar, 2012 ONCA 646 ... 408, 539
EDM v JCDM, [2007] BCJ No 2644, 2007 BCSC 1781 ... 329, 330
Edwards v Edwards (1975), 21 RFL 121 (Ont HCJ) ... 557
Edwards v Edwards (1990), 26 RFL (3d) 142 (NSTD) ... 572
Edwards v Edwards (1994), 133 NSR (2d) 8, 5 RFL (4th) 321, [1994] NSJ No 361 (CA) ... 255, 264
Edwards v Edwards (1994), 97 BCLR (2d) 177, 7 RFL (4th) 105, [1994] BCJ No 1654 (SC) ... 21
Edwards v Edwards (1997), 31 RFL (4th) 320, [1997] AJ No 899 (CA) ... 24, 150
Edwards v Edwards, [2001] PEIJ No 51 (SC) ... 386
Edwards v Edwards, [2002] AJ No 24, 309 AR 364 (QB) ... 288
Edwards v Edwards, 2015 NLTD(G) 165 ... 49
Edwards v Edwards, 2018 ONSC 6869 ... 63, 587
Edwards v Edwards, 2021 ONSC 1550 ... 35, 49, 60, 83, 84
Edwards v Watt (1993), 123 NSR (2d) 210, [1993] NSJ No 622 (TD) ... 81
EG v DG, 2022 ABCA 129 ... 338
Egan v Egan, [2002] BCJ No 896, 26 RFL (5th) 288 (SC) ... 227, 228, 587, 591
EGP v SLP, 2009 BCSC 1221, [2009] BCJ No 1019 ... 359
Ekland v Sangsari (1996), 24 RFL (4th) 119, [1996] BCJ No 1705 (CA) ... 23
EKR v GAW (1997), 122 Man R (2d) 120, 32 RFL (4th) 202, [1997] MJ No 501 (QB) ... 241, 283, 296
El Gahwas v Ghremida, 2020 SKQB 311 ... 54, 57, 417
El Himili v Benmoussa, 2022 ONSC 5311 ... 194
El Ouazzani v Chabini, 2022 ONSC 5773 ... 286, 287, 333
EL v ML, 2021 BCSC 835 ... 157
Elensky v Elensky (1993), 50 RFL (3d) 231 (BCCA) ... 263, 660
Elfar v Elfar, 2012 ABCA 375 ... 162
Elgaard v Elgaard (1986), 1 RFL (3d) 256 (BCSC) ... 466
Elgner v Elgner, 2011 ONCA 483, leave to appeal to SCC refused, [2011] SCCA No 341 ... 657, 658
Elhert v Sailer, 2023 ABCA 371 ... 155, 221, 267
Elias v Elias, 2018 CarswellOnt 10816 ... 326
Elliott v Elliott, [1998] OJ No 4827, 42 RFL (4th) 341 (Gen Div) ... 566
Elliott v Elliott, 2010 ABQB 789 ... 208, 496
Elliott v MacAskill, [2005] NSJ No 479, 21 RFL (6th) 270 (Fam Ct) ... 353, 367
Elliott v Melnyk, 2014 NSSC 446 ... 382
Ellis v Carpenter, [1999] OJ No 934 (Gen Div) ... 231
Ellis v Ellis, [1997] PEIJ No 119, 158 Nfld & PEIR 193 (SC) ... 336, 345

Ellis v Ellis, [1999] NSJ No 78 (CA) 372, 374, 574
Ellis v Ellis, 1999 CanLII 4274 (NSCA) 389
Embree v Embree, 2016 NBCA 42 616
Emery v Emery (1987), 11 RFL (3d) 194, [1987] OJ No 2302 (Dist Ct) 608
Emhecht v Ontario (Family Responsibility Office), 2011 ONSC 2644 .... 525, 654
EMLF v SLS, 2009 BCSC 1242 93
Emmerson v Emmerson, 2017 ONCA 917 .... 484, 505
EMO v WRO, [2003] BCJ No 661, 37 RFL (5th) 401, 2003 BCCA 191 126
Empey v Groves, [2001] BCJ No 2544 (CA) 590
Emslie v Emslie, 2015 ABQB 581 166
Engebretson v Pellettieri, [1998] SJ No 411 (QB) 288, 291
Englar v Englar (1978), 2 RFL (2d) 237 (Ont CA) 486
English v English (1995), 16 RFL (4th) 250, [1995] SJ No 417 (QB) 569, 570
Enman v Enman, [2000] PEIJ No 48, 189 Nfld & PEIR 1 (SC) 260, 305, 488
Ennis v Ennis, [1999] AJ No 352, 45 RFL (4th) 323 (QB) var'd (2000), 281 AR 161, [2000] AJ No 75, 5 RFL (5th) 302 (CA) 152, 217, 289, 294, 296, 507
Epp v Robertson, [1998] SJ No 684, 171 Sask R 315 (QB) 388, 432, 433, 434
Erb v Erb, [2003] OJ No 1527, 41 RFL (5th) 49 (SCJ) 84, 92
Erdman v Erdman, 2024 BCSC 119 .... 64, 66, 77
Erickson v Erickson, [1999] NSJ No 159, 47 RFL (4th) 326 (SC) 70
Erickson v Erickson, [2001] BCJ No 71 (SC) 305, 432, 568
Erickson v Erickson, [2007] NSJ No 483, 2007 NSSC 333 47
Erikson v Cabeza, [2002] BCJ No 286, 25 RFL (5th) 282 (SC) 460, 462
Esligar v Esligar (1999), 45 RFL (4th) 258, [1999] NBJ No 150 (CA) 127, 508, 617
Espersen v Espersen, 2017 BCSC 1206 162
Estey v Estey, [1999] NSJ No 226, 178 NSR (2d) 87 (SC) 337
Estrela v Estrela, [1997] OJ No 2916, 43 OTC 265 (Gen Div) 182, 308
ET v LMD, 2019 ONSC 4071 623
Etchegary v Etchegary (1990), 81 Nfld & PEIR 189 (Nfld UFC) 538
Etemadi v Maali, 2021 BCSC 1003 252
Ethier v Skrudland, 2011 SKCA 17 .... 35, 46, 79, 80, 516
Etienne v Etienne, [2002] OJ No 4220 (SCJ) 73
Evanow v Lannon, 2018 BCCA 208 .... 52, 125, 136, 170
Evans v Evans (1992), 41 RFL (3d) 400 (Nfld TD) 478
Evans v Evans, [1987] BCJ No 67, 6 RFL (3d) 166 (SC) 22
Evans v Evans, [1998] SJ No 91, 35 RFL (4th) 158 (QB) 323
Evans v Evans, [1999] BCJ No 2919 (SC) 475
Evans v Evans, [2004] BCJ No 986, 2004 BCSC 658 .... 342, 627
Evans v Evans, 2023 ONSC 3919 .... 120, 122, 196, 223, 497
Evans v Gravely, [2000] OJ No 4748, 14 RFL (5th) 74 (SCJ) 343, 357
Everill v Everill, [2005] NSJ No 37, 229 NSR (2d) 198 (SC) 66, 202, 260
Eves v Eves (1974), 17 RFL 57 (Ont HCJ) 569
EW v MMP, [1997] QJ No 3474 (CS) 474
Ewan v Emrick, [2000] SJ No 742, 200 Sask R 305 (QB) 97
Ewaniw v Ewaniw, [1998] AJ No 704, 41 RFL (4th) 94 (QB) 384, 386, 476
Ewing v Ewing (1987), 7 RFL (3d) 168, 56 Sask R 260 (CA) 255
Ewing v Ewing (2007), 36 RFL (6th) 249, [2007] AJ No 217, 2007 ABCA 72 170
Ewing v Ewing, 2009 ABCA 227 .... 8, 166, 418, 420–21
Ewing v Malette, [2009] AJ No 346, 2009 ABCA 128 .... 12, 565
EZ v PZ, 2017 BCSC 375 85

F v F, [1967] 2 All ER 660 469

F v V, [2002] OJ No 3900 (SCJ)....468
F (ML) v B (IE), 2021 ONSC 3522....72, 76
F(RL) v F(S) (1996), 26 RFL (4th) 392, [1996] OJ No 4178 (Gen Div)....89
FA v NA, 2018 NBQB 215....157
Fabian v Fabian (1983), 34 RFL (2d) 313, [1983] OJ No 78 (CA)....618
Fair v Jones, [1999] NWTJ No 17, 44 RFL (4th) 399 (SC)....47, 49, 85
Falbo v Falbo, [1998] BCJ No 1497 (SC)....408
Fallis v Garcia (2008), 55 RFL (6th) 441, [2008] OJ No 2099 (SCJ)....492
Fallon v Rivers (1986), 50 RFL (2d) 30, [1986] BCJ No 3089 (SC)....600
FAP v LFT, 2023 BCSC 171....628
Farah v Ontario (Director, Family Responsibility Office), 2018 ONCJ 829....528
Farden v Farden (1993), 48 RFL (3d) 60, [1993] BCJ No 1315 (SC)....40, 49, 50, 97, 112, 114, 115
Farkasch v Farkasch (1971), 4 RFL 339, [1971] MJ No 129 (QB)....610
Farmer v Conway, [1998] NSJ No 536, 175 NSR (2d) 143 (TD)....336
Farnell v Farnell, [2002] NSJ No 491, 209 NSR (2d) 361 (SC)....211
Farnsworth v Chang, 2014 ONSC 1871....122
Farooq v Farooq, 2023 ONSC 3679....194
Farrus v Farrus, [2000] AJ No 680, 267 AR 103 (QB)....54
Fatima v Canada, 2012 TCC 49....4
Faulkner v Faulkner, [1997] AJ No 730 (QB)....30
Fauth v Fauth, [2002] AJ No 580, 314 AR 248 (QB)....210
Favero v Favero, 2013 ONSC 4216....166, 191
Fawcett v Hurd, [1998] OJ No 4345, 80 OTC 398 (Gen Div)....195, 604
Fawcett-Kennett v Kennett, 2016 SKQB 111....157, 161
FB v LB, [2000] OJ No 3833 (SCJ)....11
FDM v EGM, 2023 ABCA 100....152
Fearon v Tzeng Fearon, 2021 ONSC 7545....47, 74, 75, 323
Fedorovich v Fedorovich (1974), 15 RFL 386 (Alta TD)....458
Fedortchouk v Boubnoy, 2018 NSSC 66....281, 360, 474, 494, 510
Fedoruk v Jamieson, [2002] BCJ No 503 (SC)....243, 244, 440
Fedorychka v Fedorychka (1985), 44 RFL (2d) 458 (Sask UFC)....517
Fein v Fein, [2001] OJ No 4554, [2001] OTC 837, 21 RFL (5th) 24 (SCJ)....93, 485, 614
Feinstat v Feinstat, 2012 ONSC 5339....468
Felgner v Felgner, [2004] BCJ No 30, 2004 BCSC 6....572
Felts v Silvestre, 2021 BCSC 523....40, 166, 492
Fenster v Fenster, 2011 ONSC 3852....389
Ferguson v Ferguson (1970), 1 RFL 387, [1970] MJ No 116 (QB)....54
Ferguson v Ferguson (1983), 33 RFL (2d) 322, [1983] NBJ No 8 (QB)....22
Ferguson v Ferguson, [1999] AJ No 1107 (QB)....427
Ferguson v Ferguson, [2005] PEIJ No 22, 12 RFL (6th) 304, 2005 PESCTD 16....342, 343, 344
Ferguson v Ferguson, 2022 ONCA 543....622
Ferguson v Thorne (2007), 38 RFL (6th) 252, [2007] NBJ No 45, 2007 NBQB 66....283
Fergusson v Kurylo, [2005] SJ No 166 (QB)....58, 72
Fernbach v Fernbach, [2004] OJ No 1188 (SCJ)....543
Fernquist v Garland, [2000] SJ No 204, 6 RFL (5th) 146 (CA)....573
Fernquist v Garland, [2004] SJ No 584, 10 RFL (6th) 332 (CA)....573
Fernquist v Garland, [2005] SJ No 36, 12 RFL (6th) 315 (QB)....573
Fernquist v Garland, [2005] SJ No 747, 22 RFL (6th) 371 (QB)....51, 64, 65, 76, 112, 114
Ferris v Longhurst, 2014 SKQB 294....348
Ferster v Ferster, [2002] BCJ No 172, 24 RFL (5th) 20 (SC)....359
Fetterley v Fetterley (1989), 24 RFL (3d) 61 (Alta CA)....570
Feucht-Fender v Hepworth, [2000] SJ No 620 (QB)....167
Feuchter v Feuchter, [2000] BCJ No 248 (SC)....537

Ffrench v Ffrench, [2001] NSJ No 82, 17 RFL (5th) 70 (CA) 206
Ffrench v Williams, 2016 ONCJ 105 198
Fibiger v Fibiger, [1998] BCJ No 187, 38 RFL (4th) 258 (SC) 160
Fibke v Fibke, [1999] AJ No 172, 48 RFL (4th) 288 (QB) 8, 207
Fidyk v Hutchison, 2013 SKQB 27 134, 135, 162, 343, 345
Fielding v Fielding, [1999] OJ No 2072, 45 RFL (4th) 29 (Gen Div) 254
Filice v Filice, [1998] OJ No 5271 (Gen Div) 575
Fillier v Bubley, [1997] AJ No 1285 (QB) 535
Finch v Finch, 2014 BCSC 2144 312
Fincham v Fincham, 2017 ONSC 4279 82, 112, 200, 206
Finlay v Finlay, 2004 NBQB 138, [2004] NBJ No 448 460
Finn v Finn, [2003] OJ No 927 (SCJ) 578
Finn v Levine, [1997] OJ No 2201, 31 OTC 192 (Gen Div) 323
Finney v Finney, [1998] BCJ No 1848 (SC) 431
Finnie v Rae (1977), 16 OR (2d) 54 (HCJ) 478
Fiorellino-Di Poce v Di Poce, 2019 ONSC 7074 651–52
Fiorino v Fiorino, 2013 ONSC 2445 113
Firestone v Firestone (1975), 20 RFL 315, [1975] OJ No 2190 (HCJ) 610, 619
Firestone v Firestone (1975), 5 OR (2d) 659 (HCJ) 606, 610, 614
Firkola v Firkola, 2017 SKQB 31 76, 323
Fisher v Fisher (1990), 28 RFL (3d) 324 (Ont HCJ) 451
Fisher v Fisher, [2001] OJ No 5477, [2001] OTC 976 (SCJ) 279, 354, 356
Fisher v Gerrard, [1998] SJ No 688, 174 Sask R 163 (QB) 320
Fisher v Green, [2003] OJ No 2745 (SCJ) 260
Fisher v Heron, [1997] PEIJ No 77, 157 Nfld & PEIR 42 (TD) 292, 293, 432
Fisher v Pade, [2001] BCJ No 1469, 2001 BCSC 1049 316
Fisher v Rogers, 2012 ONSC 669 82, 203
Fitzell v Weisbrod, [2005] OJ No 791, 11 RFL (6th) 239 (SCJ) 478, 543
Fitzgerald v Foote, 2003 NLCA 25 659
Fitzgerald v Gerlich, [2003] OJ No 1946, 40 RFL (5th) 84 (SCJ) 316
Fitzpatrick v Fitzpatrick, [2000] NJ No 62 (UFC) 335
FJN v JK, 2015 ABCA 353 600, 617
FJN v JK, 2019 ABCA 305, leave to appeal to SCC denied 2020 CanLII 8218 (SCC) 280, 282, 286, 455
FK v AK and CAS of Hamilton, 2020 ONSC 4927 640
Flanagan v Heal, [1998] SJ No 805, 174 Sask R 311 (QB) 151, 383
Flasch v Flasch (2007), 308 Sask R 112, [2007] SJ No 653 (QB) 342
Fleming v Boyachek, 2011 SKCA 11 76, 323
Fleming v Spence, 2023 ABCA 315 492, 497
Flemming v Flemming, [2009] OJ No 566 (Div Ct) 63
Fletcher v Bourgeois, [2004] NSJ No 164, 3 RFL (6th) 363 (SC) 536
Fletcher v Keilty, [2003] NBJ No 10, 2003 NBQB 12, aff'd [2004] NBJ No 152, 49 RFL (5th) 29 (CA) 367
Fleury v Fleury, [2000] OJ No 3021 (Ct J) 401
Fleury v Fleury, 2009 ABCA 43, [2009] AJ No 105 219, 587
Flick v Flick, 2011 BCSC 264 351
Flikerski v Flikerski, [2001] OJ No 2964, 20 RFL (5th) 47 (SCJ) 59
Florovski v Florovski, 2019 ONSC 5013 618
Floyd v Rodger, 2023 MBKB 3 500
Flynn v Daoust, 2012 MBQB 295 43
Flynn v Halleran, [2004] NJ No 457, 241 Nfld & PEIR 1 (SC) 587
FM v TH, 2016 NBCA 29 300, 340, 474
Folkerts v Folkerts, 2021 SKQB 290 497, 498, 499, 583, 584

Fong v Charbonneau (2005), 194 Man R (2d) 45, [2005] MJ No 124, 2005 MBQB 92 .... 260, 283
Fong v Fong, 2010 MBQB 5 192
Fong v Fong, 2011 BCSC 42 205
Fonseca v Fonseca, [1998] BCJ No 2772 (SC) 432
Fontaine v Andall, [1998] SJ No 510, 169 Sask R 291 (QB) 386, 387, 397, 398
Fontaine v Fontaine, [2000] BCJ No 366, 4 RFL (5th) 217 (CA) 2, 567
Forbes v Forbes (1994), 2 RFL (4th) 121, [1994] SJ No 726 (QB) 99
Forbes v Forbes (1994), 5 RFL (4th) 79, [1994] BCJ No 2487 (CA) 663
Forester v Odjick, 2021 BCSC 789 .... 124, 147
Forrest v Aerin, 2022 BCCA 184 .... 43, 49, 83
Forrest v Forrest, [2006] NSJ No 136, 2006 NSSC 112, ... 378
Forrester v Forrester, [1997] OJ No 3437, 46 OTC 159 (Gen Div) 307
Fortune v Fortune (1987), 51 Man R (2d) 127, [1987] MJ No 404 (QB) 24
Forward v Martin, [1999] NBJ No 433, 217 NBR (2d) 61 (QB) 182
Forzley v Forzley, [1997] BCJ No 2881, 34 RFL (4th) 105 (SC) 307
Foss v Foss (1991), 31 RFL (3d) 367 (Sask CA) 458
Foss v Foss, 2011 NSSC 115 .... 350, 358, 368
Foster v Amos, 2010 SKQB 409 .... 112, 300, 323, 325, 326, 632
Foster v Foster, [1994] NBJ No 167, 146 NBR (2d) 235 (QB) 22
Foster v Foster, [2000] OJ No 4006 (SCJ) 73
Foster v Sauvé, 2019 BCSC 1656 .... 132, 136, 342
Fournier v Fournier, [1997] BCJ No 2299 (SC) 85
Fournier v Labranche, 2019 ONSC 4651 166
Fournier v Meyers, 2014 SKQB 283 75
Fournier v Phelan, [2000] OJ No 2638 (Div Ct) 439
Fox v Fox (2007), 319 NBR (2d) 97, 2007 NBQB 243 356
Francis v Baker, [1998] OJ No 924, 38 OR (3d) 481, 34 RFL (4th) 317 (CA), aff'd [1999] SCJ No 52, [1999] 3 SCR 250, 50 RFL (4th) 228 .... 8, 67, 68, 276, 413, 414, 415, 417, 419, 420, 422–23
Francis v Filion, [2003] OJ No 1138, [2003] OTC 258 (SCJ) 126, 152, 466
Francis v Francis, [1999] AJ No 1190 (QB) 158, 164
Francis v Isadore-Francis, 2010 NSSC 208 556
Francis v McLeod (1998), 30 BCLR (2d) 163 (SC) 534
Franke v Franke, 2012 SKQB 204 426
Fransoo v Fransoo, [2001] SJ No 121, 14 RFL (5th) 303 (QB) 333, 337, 488
Fraser v Canada, 2010 TCC 23, [2010] TCJ No 9 5
Fraser v Fraser (1979), 30 NSR (2d) 289 (CA) 660
Fraser v Fraser (1990), 29 RFL (3d) 83 (NS Fam Ct) 572
Fraser v Fraser (1990), 31 RFL (3d) 322 (NBCA) 565
Fraser v Fraser, [2001] OJ No 3765 (SCJ) 241, 337
Fraser v Fraser, 2011 BCSC 1852 165
Fraser v Fraser, 2012 ONSC 685, var'd 2013 ONCA 715 .... 152, 153, 155, 202, 207
Fraser v Fraser, 2017 ONSC 3774 .... 608, 649
Fraser v Gallant, [2004] PEIJ No 5, 2004 PESCTD 5 .... 150, 337
Fraser v Jones (1995), 17 RFL (4th) 218, [1995] SJ No 659 (QB) 50, 114
Fraser v Ksenych, 2022 SKCA 93 636
Fraser v Lewandowski, [1999] OJ No 1457, 45 RFL (4th) 262 (Gen Div) 546
French v MacKenzie, [2003] OJ No 1786, 38 RFL (5th) 81 (SCJ) 21
Frerichs v Frerichs, [1998] AJ No 388, 226 AR 208 (QB) 164
Freund v Dent (1995), 14 RFL (4th) 251, [1995] MJ No 584 (CA) 571
Frey v Frey, [1987] SJ No 322, 8 RFL (3d) 154 (CA) 552, 553
Friday v Friday, 2013 ONSC 1931 .... 34, 72, 83
Friedman v Friedman, 2018 MBQB 91 266

Friedt v Fraser, [2002] SJ No 150, 26 RFL (5th) 80 (QB) ... 258
Friesen v Braun, 2020 SKQB 253 ... 50, 112
Friesen v Friesen (1995), 16 RFL (4th) 449, [1995] MJ No 684 (QB) ... 242, 580
Friesen v Friesen, 2020 ABQB 103 ... 86, 96
Friesen v Friesen, 2021 BCSC 2447 ... 221, 222
Friesen v Friesen, 2023 SKCA 60 ... 634, 666
Friesen v Lague, [2001] SJ No 125 (QB) ... 311
Friesen v The Queen, 2022 TCC 53 ... 5, 126, 364–65
Frigon v Blanchard, 2014 MBQB 212 ... 216
Frigon v Lepoudre, [2003] SJ No 575, 45 RFL (5th) 189 (QB) ... 538, 543, 578
Frim v Brasseur, [2001] OJ No 4384 (SCJ) ... 35, 580
Fritschij v Bazan, 2007 MBCA 11 ... 659
Froese v Froese, 2010 MBQB 156 ... 123
Froom v Froom, [2005] OJ No 507, 11 RFL (6th) 254 (CA) ... 340, 341, 346
Frost v Frost, [2000] OJ No 1600 (SCJ) ... 362
Frydrysek v Frydrysek, [1998] BCJ No 394 (SC) ... 409, 413
Fuhrman v Fuhrman (1980), 19 RFL (2d) 404 (Alta QB), var'd (1981), 32 RFL (2d) 129 (Alta CA) ... 476
Fulcher v Fulcher, 2012 ONSC 3721 ... 510
Fuller v Fuller, [2000] OJ No 4726 (Ct J) ... 219
Fung v Lin, [2001] OJ No 456, 16 RFL (5th) 83 (SCJ) ... 167, 419
Fung-Sunter v Fabian, [1998] BCJ No 861, 38 RFL (4th) 266 (SC) ... 2
Furlan v The Queen, 2018 TCC 25 ... 364
Fuzi v Fuzi, [1999] BCJ No 2263 (SC) ... 121, 164, 447

G(G) v H(J) (1996), 22 RFL (4th) 69, [1996] NWTJ No 18 (SC) ... 111, 427
G(JD) v G(SL), 2017 MBCA 117 ... 538
Gaetano v McDadi, 2021 ONSC 6536 ... 652
Gaetz v Gaetz, [2001] NSJ No 131, 15 RFL (5th) 73 (CA) ... 374, 392, 393
Gaetz v Jakeman, [2005] NSJ No 167, 13 RFL (6th) 367 (CA) ... 587
Gagnier v Gagnier, [2002] OJ No 2183 (SCJ) ... 50, 77, 123, 165
Gagnon v Gagnon, 2011 NSSC 486 ... 157
Gagnon v Gagnon, 2012 NSSC 137 ... 640
Gagnon v Gagnon, 2012 NSSC 407 ... 43, 45, 79, 560, 564
Gagnon v Petke, [2008] BCJ No 879, 2008 BCSC 610 ... 134, 137
Gal v Gal, [2002] OJ No 2937 (Div Ct) ... 19
Galan v Galan (1990), 25 RFL (3d) 225 (Man CA) ... 551–52
Galbraith v Galbraith, 2014 NSSC 337 ... 50
Galbraith v Galbraith, 2018 SKQB 157 ... 39, 496
Gale v Dawson, 2015 BCSC 1795 ... 439
Gallant v Houde, 2017 BCCA 391 ... 199
Galliford v Galliford, [1998] BCJ No 268 (SC) ... 299, 371, 409
Galloway v Galloway, [2008] BCJ No 94, 2008 BCSC 83 ... 143
Galloway v Galloway, 2022 BCSC 10 ... 334
Galpin v Galpin, 2018 BCSC 1572 ... 202
Gamey v Gamey, [2000] MJ No 304, 147 Man R (2d) 140 (QB) ... 42
Gannon v Gannon, 2014 NSSC 113 ... 126, 364
Garard v Garard, [1998] BCJ No 2076 (CA) ... 433, 437, 567
Garbers v Garbers (1993), 48 RFL (3d) 217, [1993] OJ No 1470 (UFC) ... 25, 535, 552
Garcia v Rodriguez (1997), 29 RFL (4th) 329, [1997] BCJ No 1281 (CA) ... 212, 574
Gard v Gard, 2013 MBQB 128 ... 327, 328
Gardezi v Positive Living Society of British Columbia, 2018 BCCA 84 ... 647
Gardiner v Gardiner (2007), 257 NSR (2d) 390, [2007] NSJ No 367 (SC) ... 338, 339

Garinger v Thompson, [2006] SJ No 36, 2006 SKQB 41 .... 35, 80
Garm v Straker, 2011 BCSC 1104 351
Garnet v Garnet, 2013 ONSC 6389 530
Garrett v Garrett, 2024 MBKB 22 647
Garrett-Rempel v Garrett-Rempel, [2000] BCJ No 1771, 2000 BCSC 1275 .... 135, 161, 427, 432, 489
Garrow v Garrow, [1997] BCJ No 1818 (SC) 54
Gartley v Thibert, [2002] OJ No 3313 (SCJ) 587, 588
Gartman v Hancheroff, 2015 BCSC 160 127
Gartner v Gartner (1978), 5 RFL (2d) 270, [1978] NSJ No 23 (SC) 78
Gaspers v Gaspers, 2008 SKCA 94 .... 281, 316, 328
Gass v Garland, [2003] PEIJ No 126, 233 Nfld & PEIR 32 (SC) 343, 344
Gaudet v Gaudet (1988), 15 RFL (3d) 65 (PEICA) 562
Gaulton v Hynes, [2003] NJ No 44, 36 RFL (5th) 114 (SC) 573
Gauthier v Gauthier, 2019 ONCA 722 650
Gauthier v Gauthier, 2022 BCCA 193 .... 495, 502
Gauthier v Hart, 2011 ONSC 815 .... 338, 339, 341, 345
Gauthier v Martel, [2003] OJ No 5296 (SCJ) 654
Gavigan v Gavigan (1990), 30 RFL (3d) 314, [1990] AJ No 1057 (QB) 89, 90
GC v DC, 2010 NBQB 81 262
GD c GD, [2003] QJ No 10303 (CS) 80
Geboers v Geboers, 2018 BCSC 181 .... 50, 84
Geddes v Svendsen, [1997] NSJ No 565, 164 NSR (2d) 318 (Fam Ct) 81
Gee v Ng, [1997] SJ No 350 (QB) 463
Geherman v Geherman, [2004] AJ No 1254, 2004 ABQB 785 473
Georgelin v Bingham, 2011 BCSC 47 .... 342, 358
Geran v Geran, 2011 SKCA 55 .... 49, 50, 63, 65, 66, 69, 71, 75, 83, 84
Gero v Joseph, [1999] AJ No 1658 (QB) 306, 309
Gershon v Shulson, [1998] SJ No 811 (QB) 412
Gervais v Tongue, [2000] OJ No 529, 4 RFL (5th) 224 (SCJ) 81, 549
Gervasio v Gervasio, [1999] OJ No 1366, 45 RFL (4th) 342 (Gen Div) 148
GES v FC, 2012 NBQB 165 .... 56, 68
GF v EF, [1999] AJ No 1104, 251 AR 371 (Prov Ct (Fam Div)) 47
GF v JACF, 2016 NBCA 21 .... 156, 193, 295, 347, 350, 470
GFW v JLR, 2012 BCCA 245 .... 26, 28, 493
GG v JTG, 2013 ABQB 726 .... 25, 26, 426
Ghent v Busse, 2016 ONSC 5282 210
Ghisleri v Ghisleri, 2007 BCCA 512, [2007] BCJ No 2356 576
Ghosn v Ghosn, [2006] NSJ No 33, 2006 NSSC 2 .... 125, 136, 219, 414
Ghremida v Elgahwas, 2023 SKCA 23 .... 26, 54, 410, 413, 482
Giammarco v Moccia, [2005] OJ No 5506 (SCJ) 325
Giao v McCready, [2005] NSJ No 50, 229 NSR (2d) 322 (SC) 150, 446
Gibb v Gibb, [1987] OJ No 982 (HCJ) 455
Gibb v Gibb, [2005] BCJ No 2730 (SC) 228, 447
Gibillini v Gibillini, [1998] OJ No 2860 (Gen Div) 308
Gibney v Gibney, [1998] BCJ No 632 (SC) 461
Gibson v Gibson, [2002] OJ No 1784 (SCJ) 167, 322, 590, 591
Gibson v Gibson, [2008] SJ No 373, 2008 SKQB 248 302
Gibson v Gibson, 2011 ABQB 564 .... 122, 590
Gibson v Gibson, 2011 ONSC 4406 .... 125, 147, 260
Giene v Giene (1998), 234 AR 355, [1998] AJ No 1305 (QB) 158, 184, 342, 343, 356
Giesbrecht v Storos, 2017 SKQB 40 207
Giles v Villeneuve, [1998] OJ No 4492, 43 RFL (4th) 61 (Gen Div) 243, 292, 301, 312
Gilkinson v Nichols, 2023 ONSC 1504 .... 39, 84, 456

Gill Tech Framing Ltd v Gill, 2012 BCSC 1913 596
Gillespie v Gormley, [2002] NBJ No 344, 251 NBR (2d) 359 (QB), rev'd [2003] NBJ No 369, 43 RFL (5th) 331, 2003 NBCA 72 ..... 290, 378, 380, 392, 394, 395
Gillie v Ritchie, [2001] NSJ No 440 (SC) 126, 242, 302
Gilroy v Gilroy, [2003] SJ No 250 (CA) 43
Giorno v Giorno (1992), 39 RFL (3d) 345, [1992] NSJ No 94 (CA) 49
Girardin v Girardin (1973), 15 RFL 16, [1973] SJ No 255 (QB) 619
GJL v MJL, 2017 BCSC 688 ..... 347, 357
GKD v CSD, 2021 BCSC 367 ..... 460, 462, 463
GL v CE (2002), 25 RFL (5th) 323, [2002] OJ No 905 (SCJ) 600
GL v KH, 2020 SKQB 167 ..... 216, 385
Glad v Glad (1994), 5 RFL (4th) 270, [1994] OJ No 4002 (Gen Div) 641
Glaspy v Glaspy, 2011 NBCA 101 26
Glen v Glen (1997), 34 RFL (4th) 105, [1997] BCJ No 2806 (SC) 62, 71
Glenn v Glenn, 2018 BCSC 2 ..... 38, 285
GMS v DBS, [1999] NJ No 278, 181 Nfld & PEIR 304 (UFC) 313, 387
GMW v DPW, 2014 BCCA 282 587
GNP v LAG, 2001 NSSC 165, 210 DLR (4th) 753 ..... 85, 102
Gobeil v Gobeil, [2007] MJ No 19, 2007 MBCA 4 429
Gobeille v Savard, [1975] CA 94 (Que) 448
Godfrey-Smith v Godfrey-Smith, [1997] NSJ No 544, 165 NSR (2d) 245 (TD) 333
Godin v Stone, 2022 ABQB 86 214
Goerlitz v Paquette, [1998] AJ No 491, 221 AR 182 (QB) 253
Goett v Goett, 2013 ABCA 216 ..... 183, 184, 190, 249
Gold v Romhanyi, 2006 BCSC 443 290
Goldstein v Canada, 2013 TCC 165 ..... 4, 5
Gomes v Gomes (1985), 47 RFL (2d) 83, [1985] BCJ No 2683 (SC) 22
Gonek v Gonek, 2011 ABQB 166 ..... 521, 593
Good v Good, [1998] BCJ No 2316 (SC) 568
Goodfellow v Goodfellow (1982), 38 OR (2d) 54 (SC) 448
Goodhew v Summers, 2022 BCSC 1080 596
Goodwin v Goodwin, [2002] SJ No 45, 24 RFL (5th) 28 (QB) 147, 295
Gordashko v Boston, [2009] AJ No 404, 2009 ABQB 229 496
Gordinier-Regan v Regan, 2011 NSSC 297 ..... 315, 316, 318, 447
Gordon v Gordon, [1999] OJ No 2234 (SCJ) 565
Gordon v Norris, 2018 BCSC 188 ..... 194, 201
Gordon v Solmon (1995), 16 RFL (4th) 403, [1995] OJ No 2681 (CA) 30, 551, 591
Gordon-Tennant v Gordon-Tennant, [1997] OJ No 3436 (Gen Div) 2
Gore-Hickman v Gore-Hickman, [1999] SJ No 30, 44 RFL (4th) 425, 187 Sask R 45 (QB) 251
Gore-Hickman v Gore-Hickman, [1999] SJ No 503, 177 DLR (4th) 222 (QB) 345, 346, 438
Gorgichuk v Gorgichuk, [1997] SJ No 211, 154 Sask R 273 (QB) 148
Gorham v Gorham (1994), 132 NSR (2d) 396 (CA) 661
Gormley v Gormley, [1999] PEIJ No 83, 181 Nfld & PEIR 204 (SC) 306
Gosse v Sorensen-Gosse, 2011 NLCA 58 ..... 170, 173184, 187, 188, 227, 339
Gossen v Gossen, [2003] NSJ No 113, 213 NSR (2d) 217 (SC) 173, 186, 223, 227
Gottinger v Runge, 2018 SKQB 343 ..... 264, 347, 348, 351, 357
Goudie v Buchanan, [2001] NJ No 187, 19 RFL (5th) 280 (UFC) 209, 379
Goudriaan v Plourde, [2002] AJ No 272, 2002 ABQB 227 ..... 477, 653
Gould v Gould, 2013 SKCA 34 420
Goulding v Goulding, 2016 NLCA 6 494
Goulding v Keck, 2014 ABCA 138 ..... 425, 492, 494, 509
Goulet v Racher, [2002] BCJ No 2430, 32 RFL (5th) 341 (SC) 211
Goundrey-Beskau v Beskau, 2015 BCSC 168 ..... 84, 426

GPJK v CAK, 2023 MBCA 55 ... 665, 666
GR v TR, [2005] BCJ No 1496, 2005 BCSC 969 ... 333
Graat v Graat (1982), 29 RFL (2d) 312, [1982] OJ No 2488 (HCJ) ... 620
Graham v Bruto, [2007] OJ No 656 (SCJ) ... 525
Graham v Graham, [1998] BCJ No 185 (SC) ... 467
Graham v Graham, [1998] BCJ No 2436 (SC) ... 42
Graham v Graham, [1999] BCJ No 2819 (SC) ... 575, 629
Graham v Graham, 2008 MBQB 25 ... 282
Graham v Graham, 2013 MBCA 66 ... 348, 358
Graham v Tomlinson, 2010 SKCA 101 ... 453
Grail v Grail (1990), 27 RFL (3d) 317 (Ont Master), aff'd (1990), 30 RFL (3d) 454 (Ont Ct Gen Div) ... 78, 447, 477
Grainger v Grainger (1992), 39 RFL (3d) 101 (Sask CA) ... 570
Gran v Gran, [1997] SJ No 330 (QB) ... 211
Granofsky v Lambersky, 2019 ONSC 3251 ... 618
Granquist v Lemond, 2022 SKCA 90 ... 430, 432, 433, 661
Grant v Grant, [2001] NSJ No 100, 16 RFL (5th) 91 (SC) ... 4, 136
Grant v Grant, 2011 NBCA 113 ... 658
Grant v Wolansky (1994), 4 RFL (4th) 365, [1994] AJ No 566 (QB) ... 220, 530, 535
Granter v Tricco, 2018 ONSC 6906 ... 360
Graveline v Graveline, 2024 ABCA 31 ... 458
Graves v Eager (2002), 29 RFL (5th) 313, [2002] OJ No 3878 (CA) ... 223
Graves v Graves, [2003] BCJ No 2240 (SC) ... 534
Gray v Gray, [1997] OJ No 4652, 33 RFL (4th) 273 (Gen Div) ... 276
Gray v Gray, [1998] OJ No 2175, 78 OTC 125 (Gen Div) ... 160
Gray v Gray, [1998] OJ No 2278 (Gen Div) ... 641
Gray v Gray, [1998] OJ No 2291, 68 OTC 217 (Gen Div) ... 330, 524
Gray v Gray, [2002] MJ No 274, 29 RFL (5th) 320 (QB) ... 232
Gray v Gray, 2014 ONCA 659 ... 409
Gray v Metcalf, 2011 ABQB 773 ... 389
Gray v Ransom, 2011 SKQB 139 ... 464
Gray v Rizzi, 2016 ONCA 152 ... 239, 556, 581
Greco v Greco, [2000] OJ No 3594 (SCJ) ... 458
Green v Green (1995), 11 RFL (4th) 207, [1995] AJ No 57 (QB) ... 386
Green v Green, [2000] BCJ No 1001, 6 RFL (5th) 197 (CA) ... 338, 342, 355, 363,
Green v Green, [2005] NJ No 165 (CA) ... 49, 50, 51, 70, 113, 158, 374, 661
Green v Green, 2011 ABQB 476 ... 91, 94
Green v Green, 2022 NSCA 30 ... 664
Green v Whyte, 2019 ONSC 7133 ... 638
Greene v Greene, 2010 BCCA 595 ... 389, 435
Greenham v Woodfine Greenham, 2015 NLTD(F) 2 ... 58, 64, 71
Greenslade v Porter, [2004] NJ No 184, 3 RFL (6th) 41 (UFC) ... 310, 314
Greenwood v Greenwood, [1998] BCJ No 729, 37 RFL (4th) 422 (SC) ... 303, 309, 320, 334, 463, 481
Greenwood v Greenwood, [1999] BCJ No 2093, 2 RFL (5th) 190 (SC) ... 318, 481
Greenwood v Greenwood, [1999] BCJ No 846 (SC) ... 254, 621
Gregorash v Comuzzi, [1999] OJ No 1856 (SCJ) ... 452, 453
Grenier v Imbeault, 2018 ONSC 6467 ... 204
Grenon v Canada, 2014 TCC 265 ... 655
Gresham v Gresham (1988), 14 RFL (3d) 446 (Sask CA) ... 551
Greve v Greve (1987), 11 RFL (3d) 180 (Ont HCJ) ... 579
Grey v McNeil, [1997] NSJ No 87 (TD) ... 477
Griffeth v Griffeth, [2001] SJ No 742, 2001 SKQB 540 ... 289
Griffin v Griffin, [1999] BCJ No 397 (SC) ... 119, 151

Griffith v Wolfram, [1998] BCJ No 2970 (Prov Ct) 242
Griffiths v Griffiths, [1999] AJ No 283, 45 RFL (4th) 353 (QB) 375
Grimes v Grimes, [2002] AJ No 981, 2002 ABQB 704 40
Grimwood v Grimwood (1988), 68 Sask R 179 (QB) 580
Gritti v Gritti, [2001] OJ No 1363, 17 RFL (5th) 75 (SCJ) 409
Grohmann v Grohmann (1990), 67 DLR (4th) 597 (BCSC), aff'd (1991), 37 RFL (3d) 71 (BCCA) 662
Gron v Gron, 2021 BCSC 1375 63
Grose v Grose, 2016 SKQB 339 453
Grossi v Grossi, [2005] BCJ No 125, 10 RFL (6th) 28 (CA) 163, 188
GRR v JES, 2020 NBQB 154 119, 296, 348, 349, 599
Grzelak v Grzelak, [1997] OJ No 4838 (Gen Div) 436
GTF v KLF, 2009 YKSC 72 49
GTW v AMK, [2006] BCJ No 124, 2006 BCPC 22 23
Guarino v Guarino, [1999] OJ No 4836 (SCJ) 118
Guenette v Morrisey, 2019 ONSC 4326 371
Guenther v Guenther, 2016 SKQB 322 170, 174, 180, 187
Guhl v Guhl, [2008] SJ No 818, 2008 SKQB 520 56
Guidry v Guidry (1994), 153 NBR (2d) 125, [1994] NBJ No 426 (QB) 89
Guignard v Guignard, [2009] OJ No 2267 (SCJ) 235
Guillena v Guillena, [2003] NSJ No 76, 212 NSR (2d) 101, 2003 NSSF 6 511, 642
Guillet v Guillet, [1999] SJ No 266 (QB) 332, 560
Guinn v Descoteau, 2013 BCSC 1408 100
Guiotto v Guiotto, [2001] BCJ No 1032, 18 RFL (5th) 84 (SC) 25
Gunn v Gunn (1994), 10 RFL (4th) 197 (Man CA) 386
Guptill v Guptill (1987), 11 RFL (3d) 278 (NSCA) 455
Gursky v Gursky, [2008] SJ No 388, 2008 SKQB 253 130
Gurvin v Tingren (1994), 49 BCAC 309, [1994] BCJ No 2119 622
Guy v Guy (1975), 22 RFL 82 (Ont HCJ) 458
Guy v Tulloch, [2004] OJ No 2197, 5 RFL (6th) 293 (SCJ) 205

H v J, 2017 NBQB 69 279
H(CA) v N(BD) (1987), 10 RFL (3d) 317 (Ont Fam Ct), aff'd (1987), 11 RFL (3d) 429 (Ont Dist Ct) 534
H(UV) v H(MW), 2008 BCCA 177, [2008] BCJ No 717 96, 98, 99, 100, 110, 111, 508, 587
Haan v Haan, [2003] SJ No 40 (QB) 565
Haavisto v Haavisto, 2008 SKQB 446, [2008] SJ No 681 516
Haber v Nicolle, 2011 BCSC 210 425
Hachey v Dempster, [2003] NBJ No 124, 261 NBR (2d) 61 (QB) 90
Hackett v Hackett, [2001] NJ No 317 (SC) 161, 168, 204, 211
Hagen v Rankin, [2002] SJ No 15, 24 RFL (5th) 38 (CA) 66, 69, 71, 75
Haggerty v Haggerty, 2023 ONSC 377 222
Hahn v Hahn, [2001] AJ No 571, 17 RFL (5th) 330 (QB) 386
Haig v Whitmore, 2015 ABQB 267 153
Haigh v Haigh (1987), 15 BCLR (2d) 375, [1987] BCJ No 1541 (CA) 657
Haigh v Haigh (1987), 9 RFL (3d) 301, [1987] BCJ No 1767 (CA) 459
Haimanot v Haimanot, [2002] SJ No 12 (CA) 123, 124
Haisman v Haisman (1994), 7 RFL (4th) 1, [1994] AJ No 553, 22 Alta LR (3d) 356 (CA), leave to appeal to SCC refused (1995), 15 RFL (4th) 51 (SCC) 28, 493, 540, 572, 573, 574, 576, 577, 578, 580, 586
Haist v Haist, 2010 ONSC 1283 57, 61
HAK v TJW, 2011 SKQB 68 8, 295
HAK v TJW, 2013 SKQB 70 355, 357

Hall v Becker, 2009 BCSC 1607 ... 102
Hall v Cooper, [1994] OJ No 696, 3 RFL (4th) 29 (Gen Div) ... 538
Hall v Galbraith, 2023 ONSC 2161 ... 319
Hall v Hall, [1997] BCJ No 1191, 30 RFL (4th) 333 (SC) ... 342, 363, 431
Hall v Hall, [1999] OJ No 453, 91 OTC 230 (Gen Div) ... 212, 474
Hall v Hall, [2006] AJ No 563, 2006 ABQB 329 ... 215, 230, 320
Hall v Zaidel, 2017 BCSC 2045 ... 342
Hallworth v Hallworth (1987), 14 BCLR (2d) 209, [1987] BCJ No 1176 (SC) ... 203
Hama v Werbes, [1998] BCJ No 2682 (SC) ... 409, 471
Hama v Werbes, [1999] BCJ No 2558, 2 RFL (5th) 203 (SC) ... 456, 457
Hama v Werbes, [2000] BCJ No 1556 (SC) ... 457, 466
Hamam v Mantello, 2020 ONSC 4948 ... 346, 355
Hamblin v Masniuk, 2014 SKQB 284 ... 564
Hamdan v Hamdan, 2012 NBQB 331 ... 46, 52, 54
Hamel v Hamel, [2001] SJ No 692, 213 Sask R 197, 2001 SKCA 115 (CA) ... 52, 97, 115, 661
Hamel-Smith v Gonsalves, [2000] AJ No 430, 5 RFL (5th) 368 (QB) ... 112
Hamelin v Bratlien, 2011 BCSC 708 ... 210
Hamilton v Hamilton, [1999] NBJ No 297 (QB) ... 212
Hamilton v Hamilton, 2010 BCSC 844 ... 81, 280
Hamilton v Hamilton, 2010 NSSC 198 ... 129
Hamilton v Pearce, [2000] BCJ No 1953, 11 RFL (5th) 114, 2000 BCSC 1432 ... 561, 623
Hamilton v Pearce, [2001] BCJ No 1546, 2001 BCSC 1092 ... 558
Hamm v Hamm, [1998] NSJ No 139 (TD) ... 338, 343, 568
Hammond v Hammond, 2018 BCCA 399 ... 647
Hammond v Maloney, 2008 NLUFC 37, [2008] NJ No 386 ... 436
Hamoline v Hamoline, 2014 SKQB 316 ... 74
Hamonic v Gronvold, [1999] SJ No 32 (QB) ... 337
Hamonic v Gronvold, [2003] SJ No 847, 1 RFL (6th) 246 (QB) ... 520
Handy v Handy, [1999] BCJ No 6 (SC) ... 338, 433
Haney v Haney, [2005] OJ No 2329, [2005] OTC 441 (SCJ) ... 339, 355
Hanmore v Hanmore, [2000] AJ No 171, 4 RFL (5th) 348 (CA) ... 372, 374, 378, 392, 393
Hann v Elms, 2016 NLTD(F) 15 ... 170, 184
Hannah v Warner, [2008] SJ No 630, 2008 SKQB 372 ... 631
Hannigan v Hannigan, [1998] BCJ No 3177 (SC) ... 279
Hannigan v Hannigan, [2003] BCJ No 2278, 2003 BCSC 1504 ... 46, 52
Hanrahan-Cox v Cox, 2011 NSSC 182, reconsideration allowed 2011 NSSC 256 ... 124, 142, 318
Hansen v Hansen (1995), 13 RFL (4th) 335, [1995] OJ No 1139 (Gen Div) ... 25, 263, 555
Hansen v Hansen, [1998] OJ No 4982, 82 OTC 340 (Gen Div) ... 393
Hansen v Roy, [2009] OJ No 282 (SCJ) ... 62
Hansford v Hansford (1973), 9 RFL 233, 30 DLR (3d) 392 (Ont HCJ) ... 25
Hanson v Hanson, [1999] BCJ No 2532 (SC) ... 199, 201, 204, 449
Hanson v Hanson, [2001] SJ No 560, 21 RFL (5th) 279 (QB) ... 45, 587
Hanson v Hanson, [2003] SJ No 514, 43 RFL (5th) 109 (QB) ... 41
Hanson v Hanson, 2019 SKCA 102 ... 430, 432, 433, 496
Hansvall v Hansvall, [1997] SJ No 782, 160 Sask R 201 (QB) ... 158, 292, 312, 380, 381, 391, 403
HAP v DBC, 2015 YKSC 4 ... 63, 235
Haq v Haq, [2003] OJ No 4687 (SCJ) ... 219, 456
Haras v Camp, 2018 ONSC 3456 ... 123
Hardayal v Asrula, 2018 ONSC 6948 ... 280
Harder v Canada, 2016 CarswellNat 4358 (TCC [Informal Procedure]) ... 366
Harder v Harder, [2000] BCJ No 467, 2000 BCSC 347 ... 294, 295, 381
Harder v Harder, [2003] SJ No 429, 41 RFL (5th) 69, 2003 SKQB 286 ... 60, 558, 587
Hardy v Hardy, [1998] BCJ No 1182, 55 BCLR (3d) 300 (SC) ... 94

Hardy-Generoux v Generoux, [2001] PEIJ No 52, 202 Nfld & PEIR 226 (SCTD) ... 396
Hare v Kendall, [1997] NSJ No 310, 161 NSR (2d) 157 (TD) ... 30, 241, 388
Hargrove v Holliday, 2010 ABQB 70 ... 509
Hari v Hari, 2013 ONSC 5562 ... 102
Haroon v Sheikh, 2019 ONSC 3130 ... 651
Harras v Lhotka, 2016 BCCA 246 ... 162, 163
Harrington v Harrington (1981), 22 RFL (2d) 40, 33 OR (2d) 150, 123 DLR (3d) 689 (CA) ... 42, 244, 476
Harris v Gilbert (1992), 39 RFL (3d) 458 (Ont Ct Gen Div) ... 556
Harris v Harris (1978), 90 DLR (3d) 699 (BCSC) ... 25, 555
Harris v Harris (1982), 37 OR (2d) 552 (UFC) ... 450
Harris v Harris, [1999] AJ No 484, 48 RFL (4th) 341 (QB) ... 152
Harris v Harris, [2006] NSJ No 257 ... 45
Harris v Mayo, [2001] OJ No 4751 (SCJ) ... 483, 527
Harrison v Falkenham, 2017 NSSC 139 ... 361
Harrison v Hardy, [2005] AJ No 1189, 2005 ABQB 693 ... 635
Harrison v Harrison, [2001] OJ No 470, 14 RFL (5th) 321 (SCJ) ... 355
Harrison v Harrison, 2020 BCSC 1203 ... 407
Harrison v Vargek, [2002] MJ No 155, 28 RFL (5th) 176 (QB) ... 47, 48, 84
Hart v Hart, [1997] SJ No 692 (QB) ... 308
Hart v Neufeld, [2004] SJ No 232, 2004 SKCA 49 ... 565
Hart v Pownall, 2020 MBQB 168 ... 553
Hart v Talbot, 2010 NSSC 311 ... 386
Hartley v Del Pero, 2010 ABCA 182 ... 218, 598
Hartshorne v Hartshorne, 2010 BCCA 327 ... 40, 42, 60, 492
Harvey v Armbruster, 2014 SKQB 363 ... 362
Harvey v Harvey (1987), 49 Man R (2d) 245, [1987] MJ No 179 (QB) ... 602
Harvey v Harvey (1989), 23 RFL (3d) 53 (Man CA) ... 658
Harvey v Sturk, 2016 ONSC 4669 ... 372, 392
Hasham v Kanji, 2020 ABCA 283 ... 646
Hatcher v Hatcher, [2009] OJ No 3342 (SCJ) ... 654
Hatfield v Hatfield, [2000] NSJ No 211 (SC) ... 296
Hathaway v Hathaway, 2014 BCCA 310, aff'g 2013 BCSC 752 ... 418, 419, 422
Hatt v Heather, 2021 ABQB 878 ... 504, 510
Hauff v Hauff (1994), 5 RFL (4th) 419, [1994] MJ No 287 (CA) ... 255
Hauger v Hauger, [2000] AJ No 753, 9 RFL (5th) 46 (QB) ... 182, 225
Hausmann v Klukas, 2009 BCCA 32, supplementary reasons 2009 BCCA 320 ... 173, 183, 184, 188, 630
Hawco v Myers, [2005] NJ No 378, 22 RFL (6th) 17 (CA) ... 35, 159, 661
Hawkins v Hawkins, 2019 ONSC 7149 ... 199, 286
Haxton v Haxton, [2002] NSJ No 229, 204 NSR (2d) 223 (SC) ... 31
Hayden v Hayden, 2011 ABQB 731 ... 117
Haynes v Canada, 2013 TCC 84 ... 365
HB v AB, 2010 ABCA 279 ... 429
HB v JB, 2019 ABQB 321 ... 425
HBC v CEM, [2001] NSJ No 263, 196 NSR (2d) 115 (Fam Ct) ... 264, 265, 298
HBC v CEM (2002), 208 NSR (2d) 97 (Fam Ct) ... 66
HC v PN, [2013] SCCA No 113 ... 6
Head v Head, 2010 SKQB 25 ... 58
Headon v Headon (1981), 26 RFL (3d) 304 (Sask QB) ... 562
Heard v Heard, 2014 ONCA 196 ... 219
Hearn v Bacque (2006), 29 RFL (6th) 339, [2006] OJ No 2385 (SCJ) ... 85, 87, 88, 211
Hebert v Hebert (1976), 1 AR 452, [1976] AJ No 400 (TD) ... 610

Hebert v Klebeck, [2005] SJ No 775, 273 Sask R 296 (QB)....................382
Hebert v Orsini, 2010 ABQB 309....................264
Hedderson v Kearsey, [1998] NJ No 62, 162 Nfld & PEIR 271 (SC)....................332, 383
Heidel v Heidel, 2013 SKQB 8....................150
Heiden v British Columbia (Director of Maintenance Enforcement) (1995), 19 RFL (4th) 320 (BCCA)....................579, 585
Heigh v Rubidge, 2010 SKCA 80....................347, 366
Heimlick v Longley, 2022 SKQB 55....................596
Hein v Hein, 2009 SKQB 23, [2009] SJ No 156....................202
Heisler v Heisler, 2012 BCSC 753....................530
Helle-Wort v Brisson, [2001] YJ No 113, 22 RFL (5th) 104 (SC)....................129
Hellinckx v Large, [1998] BCJ No 1462 (SC)....................313
Hemming v Hemming (1983), 33 RFL (2d) 157, [1983] NSJ No 420 (CA)....................621
Hemond v Galano, 2013 ONSC 6929....................348, 487
Hemsworth v Hemsworth, 2002 BCSC 648....................163
Henderson v Bal, 2014 BCSC 1347....................102
Henderson v Henderson, [1999] BCJ No 2938 (SC)....................85
Henderson v Henderson, 2021 NBQB 88....................184, 270
Henderson v Micetich, 2021 ABCA 103....................371, 487, 489, 491, 492, 493, 494
Henderson-Jorgensen v Henderson-Jorgensen, 2013 ABQB 213, aff'd 2013 ABCA 328....................145, 204
Hendrickson v Hendrickson, [2005] NSJ No 395, 237 NSR (2d) 89 (SC)....................164, 170, 179, 306
Hendriks v Hendriks, 2022 ONCA 165....................661
Hennenfent v Loftsgard, 2015 SKQB 289....................328, 453
Hennessey v Hennessey (1992), 122 NSR (2d) 220 (TD)....................557
Hennessey v Hennessey (1996), 20 RFL (4th) 79, [1996] AJ No 3 (QB)....................601
Henry v Henry, [2005] AJ No 4, 7 RFL (6th) 275 (CA)....................489
Henry v Henry, 2017 SKQB 337....................578
Henry v Henry. See also DBS v SRG; LJW v TAR; Henry v Henry; Hiemstra v Hiemstra.
Heppner v Jylli, 2010 BCSC 1020....................484
Herbert v Herbert, [1999] AJ No 1241, 254 AR 173 (QB)....................160, 163, 387
Hernon v Renaud, [1999] BCJ No 2509 (SC)....................466
Herriot v Herriot, [2003] BCJ No 1274, 2003 BCSC 838....................323
Hersey v Hersey (1993), 47 RFL (3d) 117, 135 NBR (2d) 67 (CA)....................264
Hershfield v Hershfield, [2003] BCJ No 759, 2003 BCSC 509....................628
Heschel v Heschel (1991), 119 AR 35 (QB)....................456
Hesse v Hesse, 2010 ABQB 314....................232
Hesson v Hesson, [2000] SJ No 257, 193 Sask R 315 (QB)....................170, 178, 181
Heubach v Heubach, 2011 ONSC 1057....................54
Heuft v Bramwell, 2021 ABQB 642....................191, 193, 493
Hewett v Hewett, 2016 BCSC 2429....................460
Hewitt v Rogers, 2018 ONSC 1384....................216
Hickey v Gaulton, 2013 NLTD(G) 156....................126
Hickey v Hickey (1987), 8 RFL (3d) 416 (Nfld TD)....................569
Hickey v Hickey (1994), 2 RFL (4th) 65 (NSCA)....................458
Hickey v Hickey, [1999] SCJ No 9, [1999] 2 SCR 518....................661
Hicks v Gazley, 2020 ABCA 239....................646
Hickson v Canada, [2001] TCJ No 344, [2001] 3 CTC 2174....................4
Hiebert v Hiebert (2007), 48 RFL (6th) 121, [2007] SJ No 569, 2007 SKQB 381....................47, 63
Hiemstra v Hiemstra (2005), 13 RFL (6th) 169, [2005] AJ No 287, 2005 ABQB 192....................283, 286
Hiemstra v Hiemstra, [2005] AJ No 27, 13 RFL (6th) 166 (CA)....................489
Hiemstra v Hiemstra. See also DBS v SRG; LJW v TAR; Henry v Henry; Hiemstra v Hiemstra.
Higgins v Higgins, [2001] OJ No 3011, 19 RFL (5th) 300 (SCJ)....................69, 71

Higgins v Higgins, [2006] OJ No 3913 (CA) ... 613
Hilborn v Hilborn, [2007] OJ No 3068 (SCJ) ... 407
Hilchie v Hilchie, [1997] NSJ No 353 (Fam Ct) ... 2
Hildebrandt v Rossmo, [1997] SJ No 630 (QB) ... 49
Hill v Davis, [2005] NSJ No 274, 235 NSR (2d) 227 (CA) ... 39, 40, 45, 243
Hill v Davis, [2006] NSJ No 331, 31 RFL (6th) 326 (SC) ... 10, 41, 42, 51, 56
Hill v Hill (1983), 34 RFL (2d) 449, [1983] OJ No 2192 (HCJ) ... 619
Hill v Hill (1990), 29 RFL (3d) 386 (Sask QB) ... 478
Hill v Hill, [1999] SJ No 145, 48 RFL (4th) 110 (QB) ... 222
Hill v Hill, [2002] BCJ No 672 (CA) ... 661
Hill v Ilnicki, [2000] AJ No 1219, 13 RFL (5th) 73 (QB) ... 387
Hill v Monkhouse, [1998] SJ No 278 (QB) ... 165
Hilliard v Johnston, 2010 ONSC 5819 ... 349
Hillier v Hillier, [2003] PEIJ No 58 (SC) ... 484
Hillock v Hillock, [2001] OJ No 3837, 21 RFL (5th) 295 (SCJ) ... 32, 60, 465
Hinds v Jacobs, 2018 SKQB 51 ... 405, 494
Hinkson v Hinkson, [1998] SJ No 568 (QB) ... 291
Hinz v Davey, 2022 BCCA 232 ... 490, 498, 584
Hiscock v Hiscock, 2014 NLTD(F) 14 ... 102, 116, 280, 328
Hiscocks v Marshman (1991), 34 RFL 12 (Ont Gen Div) ... 550
Hitchens v Hitchens, [2004] OJ No 2019, 2 RFL (6th) 63 (SCJ) ... 213
HJ v PJ, 2020 BCSC 378 ... 505
HK v SK, [2002] NSJ No 475 (SC) ... 483
Hladun v Hladun, [2002] SJ No 476, 222 Sask R 141 (QB) ... 335
HM-T v DRGM, 2023 NBKB 180 ... 264, 349, 357
HMS v MH, 2019 SKQB 311 ... 161
Hnidy v Hnidy, 2017 SKCA 44 ... 46, 47, 496
HNML v CPJL, 2010 SKQB 456 ... 43, 45
Hoar v Hoar (1992), 39 RFL (3d) 125 (Ont CA) ... 664
Hobbs v Hobbs, 2008 ONCA 598 ... 530
Hodder v Hodder, [2007] NJ No 402, 2007 NLTD 202 ... 87
Hodge v Jones, 2011 ONSC 2363 ... 158, 352, 558
Hodgert v Hodgert (1993), 47 RFL (3d) 216 (Alta CA) ... 570
Hodgkinson v Hodgkinson, 2010 SKQB 96 ... 587
Hodgkinson v Hodgkinson, 2011 BCSC 634 ... 184, 188
Hodgson v Hodgson, 2014 BCSC 1372 ... 61, 564
Hofsteede v Hofsteede, [2006] OJ No 304 (SCJ) ... 359, 360
Hogan v Matthew, [2005] SJ No 684, 272 Sask R 9 (QB) ... 209
Hoggins v Bell, [1997] AJ No 1162 (QB) ... 629
Hohl v Hohl, 2021 ONSC 2182 ... 271
Hojnik v Hojnik, 2010 ABCA 192 ... 65, 69
Hokhold v Gerbrandt, 2012 BCSC 1683 ... 260
Hokhold v Gerbrandt, 2015 BCCA 268 ... 663
Hokhold v Gerbrandt, 2018 BCSC 183 ... 530
Holbrook v Canada, [2007] FCJ No 145, 2007 FCA 145, 361 NR 258 ... 2
Holeman v Holeman, [2006] MJ No 456, 2006 MBQB 278 ... 282, 316
Holizki v Reeves, [1997] SJ No 746, 34 RFL (4th) 414 (QB) ... 56
Holland v Holland, [2007] AJ No 1350, 2007 ABQB 720 ... 49
Hollenbach v Hollenbach, [2000] BCJ No 2316, 10 RFL (5th) 280 (CA) ... 181, 414, 418, 422
Hollett v Vessey, [2005] NSJ No 538, 240 NSR (2d) 21 (SC) ... 222, 384
Holly v Greco, 2019 ONCA 464 ... 615
Holman v Bignell, [2000] OJ No 3405 (SCJ) ... 336
Holmes v Holmes (1991), 96 Nfld & PEIR 281, [1991] PEIJ No 86 (TD) ... 81

Holtby v Holtby, [1997] OJ No 2237, 30 RFL (4th) 70 (Gen Div) 124, 157, 251, 388
Holtskog v Holtskog, [1999] SJ No 304 (CA) 376
Holtzman v Holtzman, 2011 SKQB 10 326
Holtzman v Holtzman, 2012 SKQB 74, reconsideration allowed 2013 SKQB 408 ....140, 145, 262, 401
Homann v Briscoe, 2020 NSSC 52 ....33, 34, 286
Homenuk v Homenuk, [1999] SJ No 263, 48 RFL (4th) 114 (QB) 228
Homier v Paquette, 2011 ONSC 3319 315
Hommel v Hommel (1985), 71 NSR (2d) 85, [1985] NSJ No 449 (TD) 20
Homsi v Zaya, 2009 ONCA 322 193
Hookey v Smith, [1998] NJ No 238 (SC) 394
Hoover v Hoover (1997), [1998] NWTR 209, [1997] NWTJ No 43 (SC) 7, 280, 290, 316, 378, 380
Hopson v Hannon, 2021 BCSC 99 ....627, 628
Horan v Horan, [2003] BCJ No 550 (SC) 575
Horbas v Horbas, 2020 MBCA 34 ....193, 199, 200, 425
Horne v Horne (1989), 19 RFL (3d) 399 (BCSC) 452
Horner v Horner, [2004] OJ No 4268, 6 RFL (6th) 140 (CA) 259, 336
Horning v Horning, [2000] BCJ No 189 (SC) 165
Hornoi v Cornejo-Bilawchuk, [2004] SJ No 230, 2004 SKCA 47 555
Horowitz v Nightingale, 2015 ONSC 190 153
Horton v Horton, [1999] OJ No 4855 (SCJ) 127, 241
Horvath v Horvath, [2000] MJ No 428, 2000 MBCA 93 83
Hosseini v Assadbeigi, [1998] BCJ No 1642 (SC) 467
Hosseini v Kazemi, 2010 BCSC 666 316
Hosseini v Kazemi, 2021 BCSC 1938 ....61, 63
Houghton v Houghton, [2000] MJ No 298, 7 RFL (5th) 330 (QB) 204
Hourie v Anderson, [1998] SJ No 754 (QB) 259, 374
House v Pritchard, 2021 BCCA 122 ....295, 666
Hovey v Hanson, 2021 NSSC 89 ....491, 493, 494
How v How, 2010 MBCA 11 261
Howard v Cox, 2017 ABCA 111 492
Howard v Howard, 2020 ABQB 292 ....132, 166
Howe v Howe, 2013 SKQB 74 ....129, 130
Howe v Lorette, 2017 NBQB 119 ....279, 282, 608
Howe v Tremblay (2007), 44 RFL (6th) 140, [2007] OJ No 4043 (SCJ) 167
Howland v Armstrong, [2003] SJ No 621, 47 RFL (5th) 100 (QB) 588
Howlett v Howlett, [2004] OJ No 3566, [2004] OTC 768 (SCJ) 98
Howlett v Rach, [2000] SJ No 752, 201 Sask R 90 (QB) 294, 562
Hoyer v Hoyer (1982), 30 RFL (2d) 261 (BCCA) 472
Hrabluik v Hrabluik, [1999] MJ No 472, 1 RFL (5th) 294 (QB) 79, 488
Hradowy v Hradowy, 2011 MBQB 64 ....114, 229, 274
Hrechka v Andries, [2003] MJ No 114, 38 RFL (5th) 246 (QB) 81, 112, 113
Hryhoriw v D'Lugos, [1997] SJ No 636, 161 Sask R 161 (QB) 10, 193
Hryhoriw v Hryhoriw (1973), 9 RFL 287 (Sask QB) 452
Hryhoruk v Hryhoruk, [1994] BCJ No 103, 2 RFL (4th) 140 (CA) 93
Hryniak v Mauldin, 2014 SCC 7 632
HS v PW, 2016 NLCA 67 ....7, 12, 15, 338, 342
HS v PW, 2018 NLSC 65 35
Hsieh v Lui, 2017 BCCA 51 ....304, 505
HT v SS, 2010 NBQB 312 ....159, 160
Huber v Huber, [1999] OJ No 4400, [1999] OTC 31 (SCJ) 24
Huber v Yaroshko, [2000] SJ No 201 (QB) 225
Hubic v Hubic, [1997] SJ No 491, 157 Sask R 150 (QB) 354, 358
Hudema v Moore, 2021 BCCA 276 647

Hudson v Klassen, [2005] SJ No 167, 13 RFL (6th) 349, 2005 SKQB 123 .... 298, 334
Hudson v Markwart, [2003] SJ No 264, 233 Sask R 31 (QB) 228
Huggins v Huggins, [1999] NSJ No 494 (SC) 260
Hughes (Re) (1959), 28 WWR 170 (Sask Dist Ct) 477
Hughes v Alfano, [2006] BCJ No 133, 2006 BCSC 109 354
Hughes v Bourdon, [1997] OJ No 4263, 66 OTC 144 (Gen Div) 395, 646
Hughes v Hughes, [1997] NBJ No 261, 30 RFL (4th) 179 (QB) 322
Hughes v Hughes, [1997] NSJ No 445, 35 RFL (4th) 185 (CA) 6
Hughes v Hughes, 2014 BCCA 196 .... 112, 580
Huisman v Huisman (1995), 17 RFL (4th) 229 (Ont Ct Gen Div) 591
Hull v Kornilov, 2024 BCSC 82 .... 372, 374, 375, 378, 385
Hulley v Carroll (2007), 47 RFL (6th) 159, [2007] OJ No 4820 (SCJ) 330
Hunchak v Anton, 2016 SKCA 44 .... 63, 603–4
Hunt v Hunt (1994), 94 Man R (2d) 81 (QB) 457
Hunt v Quinn, [1998] BCJ No 2234 (SC) 299
Hunt v Smolis-Hunt, 2001 ABCA 229, [2001] AJ No 1170, 286 AR 248, 20 RFL (5th) 409 (CA) 197, 408, 459, 460, 486, 555, 567
Hunter v Hunter, [1998] OJ No 1527, 37 RFL (4th) 260 (Gen Div) 160
Hunter v Hunter, [2001] NWTJ No 62, 2001 NWTSC 70 .... 243, 413
Hurst v Hurst, [1999] AJ No 165 (QB) 212
Hussain v Saunders, 2021 NSSC 166 .... 348, 355
Hutcheon v Bissonnette, 2016 ONSC 2785 573
Hutchings v Hutchings, [1999] BCJ No 2897 (CA) 436, 464
Hutchinson v Hutchinson, [1996] MJ No 549 (QB) 46
Hutchison v Gretzinger (2007), 48 RFL (6th) 167, [2007] OJ No 5058 (SCJ) 202, 205
Hutton v Hutton, [2000] BCJ No 1274 (SC) 559
Hyatt v Ralph, 2015 ONSC 580 85
Hyde v Hyde, [1948] P 198 469
Hyde v Lang (1996), 22 RFL (4th) 317, [1996] OJ No 1696 (Gen Div) 116
Hynes v Tierney-Hynes (1993), 50 RFL (3d) 279 (Man CA), leave to appeal to SCC refused (1994), 2 RFL (4th) 431 (SCC) 569

Iantsis v Papatheodorou (1971), 3 RFL 158 (Ont CA) 656
IC v MC, 2023 NSSC 170 199
Iddon v Iddon, [2006] OJ No 237 (SCJ) 285, 320
IE v SG, 2017 SKQB 257 419
IG v HB, [2003] OJ No 5285 (SCJ) 632
IG v LG, [2000] AJ No 113 (QB) 202
IJ v TS, 2015 NBQB 86 550
Inglis v Birkbeck, [2000] SJ No 227, 7 RFL (5th) 114 (QB) 336
Inglis v Inglis, [2001] BCJ No 411 (SC) 468
Innocente v Innocente, 2014 ONSC 7082 .... 553, 554
Inns v Inns, [1999] OJ No 4209 (SCJ) 474
Ireland v McMillan, [1997] MJ No 496, 127 Man R (2d) 276 (QB) 263
Ironstand v Ironstand (1999), 45 RFL (4th) 159, [1999] SJ No 250 (QB) 126, 403
Irvine v Beausoleil, 2020 SKQB 281 .... 207, 341
Irving v Irving (1994), 153 AR 337, [1994] AJ No 310 (QB) 16
Iselmoe v Iselmoe, [2003] OJ No 4076 (SCJ) 158
Ivan v Leblanc, 2012 ONSC 4445 478
Ivany v Ivany (1996), 24 RFL (4th) 289, [1996] NJ No 266 (SC) 48, 54
Izyuk v Bilousov, 2011 ONSC 7476 .... 538, 639, 650

J v N (1976), 28 RFL 234, [1976] MJ No 126 (CA) 600
JA v EDS, [1998] AJ No 451, 1998 ABQB 124 600
JAA v SRA, [1999] BCJ No 634, 45 RFL (4th) 165 (CA) 112, 396
Jaasma v Jaasma, [1999] AJ No 1186, 3 RFL (5th) 74 (QB) 189
JABD v RAB, 2012 PESC 6 .... 64, 378, 395
Jablonowski v Jablonowski (1972), 8 RFL 36, [1972] OJ No 1869 (HCJ) 615
Jacklin v Daigle, 2020 NSSC 248 556
Jackman v Tarrant, [2000] NJ No 250, 194 Nfld & PEIR 325 (Prov Ct) 303
Jackson v Holloway, [1997] SJ No 691, 35 RFL (4th) 272 (QB) 311, 374, 379, 380, 382, 383, 393, 403, 461
Jackson v Jackson, [1973] SCR 205, 8 RFL 172 ....20, 38, 47, 54, 515
Jackson v Jackson, 2021 ONSC 2614 ....60, 65
Jackson v Jackson, 2023 SKCA 70 .... 388, 392
Jackson v Mayerle, 2016 ONSC 1556 642
Jacobson v Jacobson, 2011 SKQB 402 447
Jacobucci v Jacobucci, 2006 MBCA 109, [2006] MJ No 322 599
Jacques v Jacques, [1997] SJ No 265 (QB) 391
JAF v PU, 2019 YKSC 68 338
Jaggs v Jaggs, 2018 BCSC 1578 ....456, 457
Jahan v Chowdhury, 2016 ONCJ 503 195
Jahn-Cartwright v Cartwright, 2010 ONSC 923 .... 64, 143
Jakob v Jakob, 2010 BCCA 136 163
JAL v AAJ, 2020 YKSC 7 195
JAM v JPM, 2019 BCSC 654 282
JAM v SAJ, 2014 NSSC 2 .... 34, 560
James v Belosowsky, 2012 SKQB 316 163
James v James, [1998] OJ No 1301 (Gen Div) 164
James v James, 2022 BCSC 1402 42
Jamieson v Jamieson (1995), 14 RFL (4th) 354, [1995] NBJ No 342 (CA) 56, 57, 58
Jamieson v Loureiro, 2010 BCCA 52 538
Jamieson v Loureiro, 2011 BCSC 1251 .... 538, 539
Janes v Janes, [1999] AJ No 610, 245 AR 315 (QB) 98, 103, 104
Janes v Janes, [2002] NJ No 151 (SC) 587
Janfield v Foote, [1999] AJ No 1355, 254 AR 124 (QB) 11
Jang v Jang, [2001] AJ No 563, 17 RFL (5th) 370 (QB) 143
Janiten v Moran, 2019 ABCA 380 239
Janmohamed v Janmohamed, 2014 BCSC 107 456
Janmohamed v Janmohamed, 2020 BCSC 432 ....113, 218, 560
Jaques v Marlin, [1995] OJ No 596, 11 RFL (4th) 224 (UFC) 388
Jarbeau v Pelletier, [1998] OJ No 3029 (Prov Div) 123
Jardine v Jardine (1992), 119 NSR (2d) 361 (TD) 569
Jarocki v Rice, [2003] SJ No 178 (QB) 342, 343
Jarvis v Parker (2008), 51 RFL (6th) 125, [2008] SJ No 47 (QB) 188
Jarzebinski v Jarzebinski, [2004] OJ No 4595, [2004] OTC 979 (SCJ) 49
Jaworsky v Jaworsky, [1997] BCJ No 2219 (SC) 576
Jay v Jay, [2003] PEIJ No 1 (TD) 427
JB v DM, 2014 ONSC 7410 .... 289, 325
JC v AAG, 2020 BCSC 1485 .... 146, 222
JC v CS, 2009 PESC 8 328
JC v KS, [2003] QJ No 4113 (CA) 465
JC v MC, 2014 NBQB 161 ....330, 350, 351, 359, 360, 364
JC v SAW, 2008 YKSC 95 .... 280, 286, 297
JC v SAW, 2013 YKSC 1 61

JCC v NNC, 2018 ABCA 115 600
JCH v SMBH, 2024 BCSC 54 .... 540, 628
JCM v MJM, 2018 NBCA 42 .... 237, 300, 347
JCR v JJR, 2006 BCSC 1422 53
JCW v JKRW, 2024 BCSC 139 .... 35, 41, 63, 83
JD v YP, 2015 BCSC 321 .... 241, 574
JDF v GEW, [2007] NSJ No 116, 2007 NSFC 15 382
JDF v HMF, [2001] NSJ No 456, 198 NSR (2d) 244, 2001 NSFC 17 29
JDG v JAB, 2012 NSSC 20 496
JDG v JJV, 2016 BCSC 2389 .... 136, 137, 465, 466
JDG v SLG. See G(JD) v G(SL).
JDK v CEM, 2009 MBQB 175 228
Jeannotte v Jeannotte, [2004] SJ No 445, 252 Sask R 69 (QB) 426
Jeans v Jeans, [2000] NJ No 42, 5 RFL (5th) 398 (UFC) 307, 371, 378, 379, 380
Jebb-Waples v Waples, 2014 ABQB 26 .... 340, 342
Jefic v Jefic (Grujicic), 2022 ONSC 7240 40
JEH v PLH, 2014 BCSC 125 .... 251, 252
Jellis v Jellis, 2016 BCSC 2270 .... 351, 354, 355
Jenkins v Quinn, [2005] PEIJ No 75, 2005 PESCTD 59 260
Jens v Jens, 2008 BCCA 392, [2008] BCJ No 1886 651
Jensen v Jensen, 2018 BCSC 283 .... 39, 42, 64, 187
Jensen v Siagris, [1998] BCJ No 743 (SC) 315
JET v CDT, [2001] AJ No 1054, 21 RFL (5th) 418 (QB) 129
JF v GF, 2016 NBQB 46 .... 196, 241, 338
JFW v PCW, [2001] AJ No 1145 (CA) 260, 483, 574
JG v MG, [2008] PEIJ No 33, 2008 PESCTD 30 .... 543, 544, 578
JG v T-LG, 2020 ONSC 5217 .... 258, 554
JGT v TN, [2001] AJ No 1426, 25 RFL (5th) 208 (QB) 242, 416
Jhanji v Canada, 2014 TCC 126 4
Jivraj v Jivraj, 2010 ONSC 4949 25
JJ v AM, 2011 NBQB 368 .... 374, 380, 391
JJDC v SLC, [1996] OJ No 3501, 25 RFL (4th) 288 (Gen Div) 82
JJR v JFM, 2013 NBQB 253 156
JK v DK, 2010 NBQB 23 .... 153, 193
JK v SD, [1999] QJ No 4155 (CS) 51, 114
JKAW v CW, [1999] BCJ No 2845 (SC) 590
JL v AA, 2013 NBQB 121 .... 292, 506
JL v EB, 2021 CanLII 40689 (NBCA) 664
JL v TT, 2023 SKCA 43 664
JLL v VLL, 2017 NBQB 76 .... 14, 45, 49
JLP v TRP, 2019 SKQB 293 157
JLT v JDNT, 2011 BCSC 855 320
JLT v KLH, 2011 BCSC 560 34
JM v GKM, [2001] NBJ No 227, [2001] NBR (2d) (Supp) No 57 (QB) 305
JM v KB, 2012 NBQB 243 .... 157, 160, 161
JM v LC, 2022 PESC 35 .... 491, 497, 586
JM v ST, 2022 BCSC 1210 596
JMD v RMJD, 2011 BCSC 1295 .... 165, 166
JMG v FG, [2001] OJ No 3010, 19 RFL (5th) 105 (SCJ) 320
JMG v LDG, 2016 ONSC 3042 487
JO v MMM, 2010 BCSC 1237 264
Jochimski v Jochimski (1994), 2 BCLR (3d) 191 (SC) 448
Joe-Joe v Joe-Joe, 2023 ABKB 551 279

Joffres v Joffres, 2014 BCSC 1778 .... 56, 468, 478
Johal v Johal, 2013 BCSC 1592 361
Johannson v Haaranen, 2018 ABQB 554 .... 426, 486
Johb v Johb, [1998] SJ No 603, 40 RFL (4th) 379 (CA) 110, 112, 572
Johnson v Barker, 2017 NSCA 53 .... 180, 188, 195
Johnson v Bradford, [1999] AJ No 678 (QB) 357
Johnson v Checkowy, [1997] SJ No 451, 157 Sask R 71 (QB) 164, 219
Johnson v Downey, 2021 NSSC 2 .... 375, 392
Johnson v Johnson (1982), 27 RFL (2d) 10 (BCSC) 220
Johnson v Johnson (1998), 38 RFL (4th) 279, [1998] OJ No 1120 (Gen Div) 105, 608
Johnson v Johnson, [1998] BCJ No 1080 (SC) 70, 72, 303, 322
Johnson v Johnson, [1999] BCJ No 1064 (SC) 470, 476
Johnson v Johnson, [2000] BCJ No 2065, 2000 BCSC 1504 .... 217, 230
Johnson v Johnson, [2002] OJ No 3298, [2002] OTC 624 (SCJ) 27
Johnson v Johnson, [2004] OJ No 3567, 9 RFL (6th) 380 (SCJ) 51
Johnson v Johnson, 2011 BCCA 190 .... 237, 349, 357, 358, 557
Johnson v Johnson, 2012 SKCA 87 .... 219, 228, 229
Johnson v Mayer, 2014 MBQB 197 580
Johnson v Punga, [1998] SJ No 633 (QB) 301, 308
Johnston v Johnston, [1997] BCJ No 418, (1997) 26 RFL (4th) 131 (CA) 543, 579
Johnston v Johnston, [1998] NSJ No 177 (TD) 433
Johnston v Johnston, [2004] AJ No 333, 49 RFL (5th) 82 (QB) 216, 288
Johnstone v Johnstone, [1998] OJ No 5337, 86 OTC 1 (Gen Div) 358
Jon v Jon, 2011 NSSC 419 247
Jonasson v Evans, [1997] SJ No 71, 27 RFL (4th) 319 (QB) 81
Jonasson v Jonasson, [1998] BCJ No 726, 37 RFL (4th) 266 (SC) 56, 58, 59, 84
Jones v Anhorn, [2000] BCJ No 614 (CA) 580
Jones v Chappell, 2009 ABQB 728 392
Jones v Jones (1994), 4 RFL (4th) 293 (Sask QB) 149
Jones v Jones, [2001] SJ No 199 (QB) 462, 538
Jones v Jones, [2005] SJ No 284, 15 RFL (6th) 215 (QB) 243
Jones v Jones, 2012 SKQB 59 .... 415, 416
Jones v Jones, 2017 SKCA 46 414
Jordan v Bolt, [2004] NJ No 417, 10 RFL (6th) 54 (SC) 324
Jordan v Jordan, [2005] SJ No 168, 12 RFL (6th) 382 (QB), 2005 SKQB 129 .... 62, 128
Jordan v La Russa, 2021 ONSC 7049 22
Jordan v Stewart, 2013 ONSC 902 .... 65, 567, 639
Jordan v Stewart, 2014 ONSC 5797 271
Jorgenson v Jorgenson, [2003] NSJ No 292, 43 RFL (5th) 386 (SC) 41
Joudrey v Reynolds, 2020 NSCA 60 661
Joyce v Joyce (1987), 8 RFL (3d) 164 (NBQB) 476
JP v JAP, 2010 ABQB 53 496
JR v CR, [2005] NSJ No 502, 2005 NSSC 336 .... 226, 305
JR v NR, 2017 BCSC 455 151
JRB v SCB, 2011 BCSC 1683 359
JS v AB, 2010 NBQB 429 .... 482, 483
JSG v MFG, 2011 MBQB 177 .... 328, 356, 454
JT (KD) (In re), 16 Fam L Rep (BNA) 1046 (NY Fam Ct 1989) 423
JT v CT, 2013 BCSC 28 83
JT v KC, 2011 BCSC 1723 181
JT v TK, 2018 NSSC 42 236
JTD v JPD, 2012 BCSC 343 486
Juffs v Investors Group Financial Services Inc, [2005] OJ No 3872 (SCJ) 480

Jukosky v Jukosky (1990), 31 RFL (3d) 117 (Ont Ct Gen Div) ... 542, 583
Julien v Julien, 2021 ONSC 8435 ... 86
Juneau v Latreille, 2011 ONSC 6424 ... 82, 94
Jungaro v Wannamaker (1990), 26 RFL (3d) 292 (Sask CA) ... 540
JWF v JAT (2003), 216 NSR (2d) 232, [2003] NSJ No 226 (Fam Ct) ... 77

K(H) c S(D) (1988), 18 RFL (3d) 66 (Que CA) ... 658
KA v TD, [2008] AJ No 600, 2008 ABQB 222 ... 296
Kaatz v Kaatz, [2001] SJ No 661, 212 Sask R 62, 2001 SKQB 480 ... 603
KAB v PDM, 2023 BCSC 1156 ... 119, 245, 252
KAC v JDEC, 2020 BCSC 1373 ... 347
Kadar v Kadar, unreported (28 July 1994) (Ont Ct Gen Div) ... 621
Kaderly v Kaderly, [1997] PEIJ No 74 (TD) ... 119, 388, 407, 425
KAF v JLF. See Fincham v Fincham.
Kaiswatum-Thomson v Thomson, [2004] SJ No 406, 2004 SKCA 95 ... 216
KAL v KJL, 2017 BCSC 651 ... 199, 214, 460, 465
Kalchuk v Kalchuk, [2000] AJ No 813 (QB) ... 194, 213
Kaleniuk v Kaleniuk, 2014 ABCA 18 ... 578
Kallen v Michaud, 2010 MBQB 151 ... 34
Kamer v Ptashnik, 2020 MBCA 70 ... 661
KAMR v WHG, 2014 BCSC 103 ... 158, 159, 331, 484
Kantor v Kantor, 2023 ABCA 237 ... 262, 612
KAP v KAMP, 2012 BCSC 811 ... 468
Kapell v Richter, [1997] SJ No 796 (QB) ... 299, 463
Kapogianes v Kapogianes, [2000] OJ No 2572, 10 RFL (5th) 63 (SCJ) ... 77, 408
Kapounek v Brown, [2000] OJ No 1301, 7 RFL (5th) 144 (SCJ) ... 52
Karhoffer v Karhoffer, [2002] BCJ No 2550 (SC) ... 70
Karisik v Chow, 2010 BCCA 548 ... 226
Karol v Karol, [2005] SJ No 349, 264 Sask R 290 (QB) ... 82
Kaser v Kaser, 2023 ABKB 6 ... 197
Kasper v Mundy (1993), 81 BCLR (2d) 256, [1993] BCJ No 1314 (SC) ... 28
Kasprzyk v Burks, [2005] OJ No 289, 15 RFL (6th) 221 (SCJ) ... 21
Kaszas v Guinta, [2001] OJ No 2572, 20 RFL (5th) 88 (SCJ) ... 109
Katerynych v Hamel, [2004] SJ No 329, 248 Sask R 272 (QB) ... 62, 235
Katz v Katz, 2014 ONCA 606, 377 DLR (4th) 264 ... 465, 468, 478
Katzer v Egeland, [1997] SJ No 672, 33 RFL (4th) 416 (QB) ... 10
Kaul v Hart, 2012 ONSC 7186 ... 359
Kaupp v Kaupp, [2008] AJ No 668, 2008 ABQB 372 ... 243, 264, 401, 405
Kaur v Khurana, 2022 BCSC 1613 ... 374
Kaushal v Kaushal, 2020 ABCA 340 ... 646
Kaushal v Kaushal, 2023 ABCA 155 ... 193, 262
Kavanagh v Kavanagh, [1999] NJ No 358, 3 RFL (5th) 96 (UFC) ... 56, 231, 321, 336
KAW v MEW, 2020 ABCA 277 ... 171, 172, 482, 494, 507
Kawalewich v Kawalewich, [1997] BCJ No 1419, 19 RFL (5th) 330 (SC) ... 219
Kawaluk v Kawaluk (1995), 17 RFL (4th) 185 (Man CA) ... 487
Kazmierczak v Kazmierczak, [2001] AJ No 955 (QB) ... 511
Kazoleas v Kazoleas, [1997] AJ No 820 (QB) ... 26, 576, 617
KB v DJB, 2013 YKSC 6 ... 576
KB v MA, 2019 NBQB 90 ... 157, 373
KD v SD, 2022 BCSC 1299 ... 495
Keast v Keast, 2016 SKQB 124 ... 359
Keefe v Randall, [2005] NSJ No 264, 234 NSR (2d) 219 (SC) ... 6
Keen v Keen (1990), 30 RFL (3d) 172, [1990] SJ No 588 (QB) ... 38

Keenleyside v Keenleyside (1996), 140 Sask R 31 (QB) 149
Kehl v Innes (1988), 88 NSR (2d) 259 (Fam Ct) 524
Kehler v Kehler, [2001] AJ No 1048, 290 AR 393 (QB) 371
Keighley v Keighley, [1998] BCJ No 2845 (SC) 487
KEK v LEL, 2010 MBQB 266 ..... 316, 327
Kelland v Stanley, 2013 NLTD(F) 40 ..... 152, 153, 484
Kellar v Wallbank (1993), 142 AR 214 (QB) 580, 581
Keller v Black, [2000] OJ No 79, 182 DLR (4th) 690 (SCJ) 307
Keller v MacDonald, [1998] AJ No 1294, 167 DLR (4th) 334, 229 AR 106 (QB) 10, 308, 314
Kelly v Kelly, [1998] AJ No 228, 1998 ABQB 73, 38 RFL (4th) 444, supplementary reasons [1998] AJ No 423, 1998 ABQB 220 ..... 302, 631
Kelly v Kelly, 2011 BCCA 173 ..... 374, 378, 384, 392
Kelly v Kelly, 2013 ONSC 6733 ..... 129, 519
Kelly v Kingston, [2000] PEIJ No 22, 5 RFL (5th) 71 (SC) 374, 375, 381, 391
Kelly v Lyle, [2001] YJ No 90 (SC) 219
Kelly v Lyle, [2002] YJ No 116 (SC) 476
Kelly v White, [2002] OJ No 5397, [2002] OTC 1073 (SCJ) 241
Kelly v Wright, 2014 ONSC 6285 343
Kempkes v Kempkes, [2000] BCJ No 1018 (SC) 385
Kendry v Cathcart, [2001] OJ No 277, 14 RFL (5th) 333 (SCJ) 124, 134, 185, 290, 337
Kennedy v Kennedy, [1997] NSJ No 450 (Fam Ct) 306, 380
Kennedy v Kennedy, [2006] BCJ No 509 (SC) 353
Kennedy v Kennedy, 2022 BCSC 256 497
Kennedy v Sinclair, [2001] OJ No 1837, 18 RFL (5th) 91 (SCJ) 208
Kennedy-Dalton v Dalton, [2000] NJ No 41 (UFC) 313, 322
Kennedy-Dowell v Dowell, [2002] NSJ No 123, 28 RFL (5th) 187 (SC) 375, 380, 385
Kenney v Kenney, [2000] AJ No 333 (QB) 313
Kenning v Kenning (1995), 11 RFL (4th) 216, [1995] BCJ No 25 (SC) 408
Kent v Kent, 2010 NLUFC 5, rev'd 2010 NLCA 53 ..... 265, 297
Keogan v Weekes, [2004] SJ No 583, 2004 SKCA 122 156
Keogan v Weekes, [2005] SJ No 170, 13 RFL (6th) 203 (QB) 552, 555
Keogh v Keogh, [2008] NJ No 228, 2008 NLUFC 2 462
Keown v Procee, 2014 ONSC 7314 170
Kereluk v Kereluk, [2004] OJ No 4337, 9 RFL (6th) 385 (SCJ) 213
Kerr v Baranow and Vanasse v Seguin, 2011 SCC 10, [2011] 1 SCR 269 ..... 487, 488
Kerr v Erland, 2014 ONSC 3555 222
Kerr v Kerr (1975), 20 RFL 312 (Man QB) 476
Kerr v Kerr (1992), 41 RFL (3d) 264 (Ont Ct Gen Div) 579
Kerr v Kerr, [1997] MJ No 6 (QB) 487
Kerr v Kerr, [2002] BCJ No 1468, 29 RFL (5th) 360 (SC) 370
Kerr v Pickering, 2013 ONSC 317 ..... 340, 351
Ketchum v Ketchum (1987), 84 NBR (2d) 288, [1987] NBJ No 1044 (CA) 600
KF v TB, 2012 NBQB 144 110
Khairzad v McFarlane, 2015 ONSC 7148 347
Khan v Khan, 2022 ABCA 370 197
KHM v JMF, 2014 BCPC 246 ..... 105, 106
Khoee-Solomonescu v Solomonescu, [1997] OJ No 4876 (Gen Div) 50, 51, 114, 316, 336
Khoee-Solomonescu v Solomonescu, [2000] OJ No 743 (Div Ct) 290, 560, 564
Khoury v Khoury (1994), 149 NBR (2d) 1, [1994] NBJ No 188 (QB) 55
KHP v RP, [1997] BCJ No 1166 (SC) 386
Khullar v Khullar, [1999] AJ No 1260 (QB) 461
Khurana v Khurana, 2011 ABCA 261 578
Kidder v Lackten, [2003] SJ No 729, 2003 SKCA 110 258

Kidson v Techentin (1994), 129 NSR (2d) 228, [1994] NSJ No 177 (FamCt) ... 54, 220
Kielesinski v Kielesinski, 2011 BCSC 538 ... 368
Kieser v Kieser, [2003] AJ No 611 (CA) ... 663
Kilrea v Kilrea, [1998] OJ No 3677, 75 OTC 269 (Gen Div) ... 291, 475
Kimber v Nikkari, [2000] SJ No 326, 8 RFL (5th) 125 (QB) ... 362
Kimmerly v Henschel, 2016 ABQB 540 ... 372, 374
Kinasewich v Kinasewich, [1997] AJ No 1220 (QB) ... 333
Kinasewich v Kinasewich, [2000] AJ No 267 (QB) ... 556, 558
Kinasewich v Kinasewich, [2001] AJ No 1185, 301 AR 244 (QB) ... 170, 178, 182
Kincaid v Arsenault, [2002] OJ No 1516, [2002] OTC 270 (SCJ) ... 91
King Estate v King (1994), 8 RFL (4th) 380 (NBQB) ... 592
King v King (1975), 25 RFL 232, [1975] NSJ No 28 (TD) ... 621
King v King (1994), 115 Nfld & PEIR 56, 2 RFL (4th) 407 (Nfld CA) ... 661, 663
King v King, [1998] NJ No 283 (SC) ... 427
King v King, [2004] SJ No 527, 2004 SKQB 342 ... 126
King v King, [2008] NJ No 60, 2008 NLUFC 3 ... 573
King v King, 2021 SKQB 201 ... 171, 224, 636
King v McSymytz, 2015 SKQB 224 ... 359
King v Sutherland, [2004] OJ No 3569, [2004] OTC 770 (SCJ) ... 44
Kingston v Kelly, [1999] PEIJ No 52 (SC) ... 311, 316
Kirk v Kirk, [2001] BCJ No 773 (SC) ... 287
Kirkpatrick v Bellvau, [2000] BCJ No 2481 (SC) ... 242, 358
Kirkpatrick v Kendall, [1997] SJ No 212, 154 Sask R 266 (QB) ... 52
Kits v Kits, [2001] BCJ No 898 (CA) ... 661
KJ v VP, 2008 SKQB 489, [2008] SJ No 772 ... 75
KJK v PBK, [2002] BCJ No 2114 (SC) ... 522, 527
KJP v BSJG, 2024 BCSC 167 ... 147, 213, 510
KK v AK, 2012 NBQB 276 ... 100
KKS v JSS, 2019 BCSC 136 ... 55, 79, 112, 280
Klassen v Klassen (1993), 44 RFL (3d) 443 (Man CA) ... 581
Klassen v Morrow, [2002] AJ No 909, 30 RFL (5th) 347 (CA) ... 338
Klaudi v Klaudi (1990), 25 RFL (3d) 134, [1990] OJ No 282 (HCJ) ... 17
KLB v SWB, 2021 BCSC 1437 ... 86, 97
Klefenz v Klefenz, 2018 NSCA 56 ... 648
Klein v Klein, 2019 SKQB 268 ... 203
Klein v Martin, 2010 MBQB 159 ... 362
Klette v Leland, 2014 SKCA 122 ... 40, 42, 68, 240, 413, 414, 420
KLH v SH, 2018 ABQB 41 ... 414
Klimm v Klimm, 2018 BCSC 5 ... 297
KLK v EJGK, 2010 BCSC 1437 ... 156
Kloc v Wozniak, 2013 ONCJ 363 ... 285, 287
Kloczko v Kloczko (1991), 36 RFL (3d) 424 (Sask QB) ... 531
Klotz v Klotz, [1999] BCJ No 148, 44 RFL (4th) 236 (SC) ... 52, 566
KLS v JES, 2010 ABQB 410 ... 431
Kluczny v Kluczny, [1999] AJ No 1420, 253 AR 398 (QB) ... 56, 72
KLW v LPW, 2012 NBQB 91 ... 311, 468
KM v RV, 2022 NBCA 71 ... 666
KM v SW, 2014 BCSC 2240 ... 127
KMB v JY, [1999] BCJ No 280 (SC) ... 242
KMH v MRN, [2001] NSJ No 262, 2001 NSFC 10 ... 32
KMR v IWR, 2020 ABQB 77 ... 79, 347
Kneller v Kneller, [2004] BCJ No 2439, 2004 BCSC 1527 ... 307
KNH v JPB, 2019 ABQB 511 ... 47, 113

Knight v Frobel, 2018 ONSC 3651 295
Knott (Jacob) v Jacob (1986), 2 RFL (3d) 255, [1986] OJ No 1696 (Prov Ct) 23
Knowles v Green, 2014 NSSC 290 300
Knox v Knox (1992), 101 Sask R 152 (QB) 569
KO v CO, [1999] SJ No 29 (QB) 336, 337
Koback v Koback, 2013 SKCA 91 .... 300, 494, 603
Koch v Koch, 2010 BCSC 1722, var'd 2012 BCCA 378 210
Kochar v Kochar, 2014 ONSC 3220 196
Koenen v Koenen, [2001] AJ No 223, 15 RFL (5th) 101 (CA) 194, 267
Koester v Koester, [2003] OJ No 5406, 50 RFL (5th) 78 (SCJ) 158, 179
Koester v Koester, 2014 NSSC 367 156
Kofoed v Fichter, [1997] SJ No 558, 32 RFL (4th) 1 (QB), aff'd [1998] SJ No 338, 39 RFL (4th) 348 (CA) 298, 328, 329
Kohan v Kohan, 2016 ABCA 125 .... 46, 47
Kohlman v Bergeron, 2015 ABCA 410 .... 124, 169
Kolada v Kolada, [1999] AJ No 376, 48 RFL (4th) 370 (QB) 111, 470
Kolada v Kolada, [1999] AJ No 609, 6 RFL (5th) 288 (QB) 202, 343, 346
Kolada v Kolada, [2000] AJ No 342 (QB) 560
Kolisnyk v Loscerbo, 2010 MBCA 1 .... 347, 367, 368
Kollinger v Kollinger (1995), 14 RFL (4th) 363, [1995] MJ No 676 (CA) 16, 630
Kolt v Kolt, 2009 ABQB 305 342
Komori v Malins (1996), 24 RFL (4th) 1 (BCCA) 460, 462
Kondics v Kondics, 2017 ABQB 493 178
Koot v McLaren, [2003] SJ No 214 (QB) 436, 564
Kopp v Burke, 2014 MBQB 247 201
Kopp v Kopp, 2010 BCSC 1663, var'd 2012 BCCA 140 .... 170, 187, 426
Korem v Kedmi, 2017 NSSC 184 649
Koren v Blum, [2000] PEIJ No 121, 11 RFL (5th) 132 (CA) 9, 223, 224, 226, 228
Korkola v Korkola, [2009] OJ No 343 (SCJ) 146
Korman v Korman, 2015 ONCA 578 .... 191, 214, 316, 319
Koronkiewicz v Gottselig, [2006] SJ No 339, 2006 SKQB 245 229
Kosior v Kosior, 2013 SKQB 42 .... 170, 183
Kosolofski v Kosolofski, 2016 SKCA 106 207
Kosowan v Vanderstap, 2016 SKCA 149 .... 44, 497
Kotelmach v Mattison (1987), 11 RFL (3d) 56 (Sask CA) 657, 658
Kotylak v Kotylak, [1999] SJ No 430 (QB) 99
Koval v Brinton, 2010 NSCA 78 .... 389, 405
Kovich v Kreut, [1998] BCJ No 2586 (SC) 52, 216, 239
Kowalewich v Kowalewich, [1999] BCJ No 1715 (SC) 220
Kowalewich v Kowalewich (2001), 19 RFL (5th) 330, [2001] BCJ No 1406, 2001 BCCA 450 .... 122, 170, 171, 173, 185, 187, 663
Kowalski v Kowalski, [1997] OJ No 4050 (Gen Div) 231
Kowalski v Kowalski, [2008] AJ No 257, 2008 ABQB 163 136
Koyama v Leigh, [1998] BCJ No 279, 36 RFL (4th) 64 (CA) 470
Koyama v Leigh, [1998] BCJ No 2127 (SC) 470
Kozak v Moore, 2020 SKQB 22 .... 69, 71, 426, 453
Kozma v Kozma, 2012 NSSC 380 560
Kozub v Kozub, [2002] SJ No 407, 29 RFL (5th) 88 (QB) 407, 566
Kramchynsky v Kramchynsky, 2013 MBQB 56 .... 315, 320
Kramer v Kramer (1986), 4 RFL (3d) 455, [1986] BCJ No 883 (SC) 623
Kramer v Kramer, [1999] MJ No 338 (QB) 306, 307, 375
Krammer (Ackerman) v Ackerman, 2020 SKQB 280 .... 135, 170, 171, 281, 349, 350
Krammer v Ackerman, 2020 SKQB 207 263

Krangle (Guardian ad litem of) v Brisco, [2000] BCJ No 465, 184 DLR (4th) 251 (CA), rev'd [2002] 1 SCR 205 41
Krause v Bougrine, 2022 ONCA 161 19
Krauskopf v Pfefferle (1993), 111 Nfld & PEIR 158 (PEITD) 561
Krawczyk v Krawczyk, [1998] OJ No 2526, 67 OTC 244 (Gen Div) 293
Kreke v Alansari, 2021 SCC 50 661
Kretchmer v Baran, 2010 SKQB 63 96
Kretschmer v Terrigno, 2012 ABCA 345 ..... 217, 218
Krill v Krill, [2000] AJ No 163, 4 RFL (5th) 249 (QB) 323
Krislock v Krislock, [1997] SJ No 698, 34 RFL (4th) 420 (QB) 142, 292, 294, 302, 313, 318, 333
Kroupa v Stoneham, 2011 ONSC 5824 425–26
Krueger v Krueger, [2004] SJ No 231, 2004 SKCA 48 571
Krueger v Tunison, [1999] SJ No 482, 183 Sask R 255 (QB) 46, 52, 72, 77
Krupa v Krupa, 2010 BCSC 1400 ..... 56, 72, 165
Krzak v Erixon, 2008 SKQB 468, [2008] SJ No 735 ..... 76, 167, 228
Kubel v Kubel (1995), 15 RFL (4th) 356 (Alta CA) 661
Kuehn (Re) (1976), 2 BCLR 97, 29 RFL 72 (SC) 25, 555
Kuffner v Kuffner, 2012 SKQB 427 112
Kulchyski v Kulchyski, [1996] OJ No 992, 22 RFL (4th) 261 (Gen Div) 23
Kuling v Kuling, [2004] SJ No 520, 10 RFL (6th) 391 (QB) 428
Kulyk v Srayko, [1997] SJ No 639 (QB) 572
Kumar v Korpan, 2020 SKQB 256 610
Kumpas v Kumpas, [1970] SCR 438 657
Kunkel v Kunkel (1994), 2 RFL (4th) 1, 111 DLR (4th) 457 (Alta CA) 20
Kuntz v Chow, [1998] SJ No 23 (QB) 438
Kuntz v Kuntz (1995), 10 RFL (4th) 246 (Sask QB) 571, 572
Kuntz v Kuntz, [1998] SJ No 743, 173 Sask R 149 (QB) 145
Kusnir v Kusnir, [2001] OJ No 3491, 21 RFL (5th) 90 (Ct J) 45, 48, 55, 59, 62, 73, 301, 321
Kuznecov v Kuznecov, [2006] BCJ No 1155, 2006 BCSC 748 ..... 215, 216, 230, 252, 268
KV v TE, [2004] BCJ No 792, 19 RFL (6th) 442 (SC) 218, 462
KW v GW, 2022 NBKB 236 193
KW v LH, 2018 BCCA 204 184
KWA v AJB, 2012 NBQB 119 ..... 569, 570
KWF v EW, [2000] OJ No 147 (SCJ) 395
Kyle v Kyle, [1998] SJ No 55, 37 RFL (4th) 286 (QB) 127
Kyler v Kyler (1992), 42 RFL (3d) 315 (Sask QB) 570
Kyung v Bowman, [1999] BCJ No 1305 (SC) 229

L (DAF) v L (DAF), 2003 SKQB 132 573
L'Heureux v L'Heureux, [1999] SJ No 437 (QB) 299, 305, 318, 455
L(FA) v B(AB) (1995), 15 RFL (4th) 107, [1995] MJ No 229 (CA) 600
L(GM) v L(VA) (1993), 127 NSR (2d) 66 (Fam Ct) 533
LAB v MLB, 2012 BCSC 1066 355
Labatte v Labatte, 2022 ONSC 4787 ..... 326, 483
Labelle v Robitaille, [1970] RP 144 (Que CA) 660
Labine v Fenske, [2000] AJ No 122 (QB) 527
Labrecque v Labrecque, 2012 SKQB 320 550
Labrecque v Labrecque, 2014 SKCA 59 ..... 150, 184
Lacey v Fitzgerald, [2003] SJ No 735, 240 Sask R 313 (QB) 588
Lachapelle v Vezina, [2000] OJ No 3171, 11 RFL (5th) 328 (SCJ) 119
Lacker v Lacker (1982), 42 BCLR 188, [1982] BCJ No 1514 (SC) 619
Lackie v Lackie, [1998] OJ No 888 (Gen Div) 409, 507
Lacosse v Lacosse, [2005] OJ No 4720, 204 OAC 133 (CA) 661

Lacroix v D'Aoust, 2011 ONSC 5586 .... 75, 219
Laczko v Laczko (1999), 50 RFL (4th) 406, [1999] OJ No 2577 (SCJ) 468, 632
Ladissa v Ladissa, [2005] OJ No 276, 11 RFL (6th) 50 (CA) 35
Ladouceur v Dupuis, 2020 ONSC 8048 235
LAF v CPM, 2015 BCSC 281 297
Laflamme v Laflamme, [1998] AJ No 292, 38 RFL (4th) 335 (QB) 193
Lafleur v Donoghue, [2005] OJ No 5416 (SCJ) 81, 396
Lafontaine v Lafontaine, 2011 ONSC 1833 147
Laframboise v Laframboise, 2015 ONSC 1752 .... 85, 86
Lafrance v Latimer, 2010 ONSC 1117 (Div Ct) 493
Lafrentz v Palmer, 2021 BCSC 1332 .... 194, 447
Lahanky v Lahanky, 2011 NBQB 220 .... 414, 456
Lahanky v Lahanky, 2011 NBQB 84 .... 188, 253, 257
Laird v (Alberta) Maintenance Enforcement, 2019 ABQB 12 .... 622, 623
Laird v Laird, [2000] AJ No 18 (CA) 567
LAK v AAW, [2005] AJ No 1140, 2005 ABQB 657 .... 158, 229
Lake v Lake (1988), 11 RFL (3d) 234 (NSCA) 515
Lake v Lake, [2004] NBJ No 61, 2004 NBQB 74 368
Lakhoo v Lakhoo, 2015 ABQB 357 651
Lakusta v Hrytsay, [1998] AJ No 969, 233 AR 368 (QB) 11
Lalande v Lalande, 2023 ONCA 68 612
Lalonde v Bailey, [1999] BCJ No 1342 (SC) 571
Lalonde v Lalonde, 2016 ABQB 600 50
Lalonde v Potier, 2013 ONSC 1513 361
LAM v SCM, 2020 BCSC 67 .... 280, 281, 328
Lamarche v Crevier, [2000] OJ No 45, 4 RFL (5th) 88 (SCJ) 97
Lamb v Copeland, 2015 ONSC 3547 .... 91, 100
Lamb v Hoffman, [2000] NSJ No 156 (SC) 416
Lambright v Brown, [2003] BCJ No 2612, 45 RFL (5th) 209 (CA) 426, 557
Lameman v Alberta, 2011 ABQB 40 616
Lamontagne v Culham, 2013 SKQB 96, aff'd 2013 SKCA 100 .... 210, 453
Lamontagne v Klyne (1994), 93 Man R (2d) 79, [1994] MJ No 14 (QB) 618
Lamparski v Lamparski, [1997] BCJ No 2730 (SC) 564
Landry v Landry (1980), 31 NBR (2d) 16 (QB) 476
Landry v Landry, 2012 ONSC 7187 .... 151, 215
Lane v Hustings-Lane, [2005] NJ No 379, 253 Nfld & PEIR 45 (SC) 354
Lang Michener v Fabian (1987), 59 OR (2d) 353, [1987] OJ No 355 (HCJ) 623
Lang v Racine, [1998] NSJ No 584 (SC) 386
Langevin v Langevin (1955), 10 RFL (4th) 229 (Alta CA) 458
Langstaff v Langstaff, [1999] BCJ No 327 (SC) 470
Langton v Langton (1987), 62 Sask R 107, [1987] SJ No 591 (QB) 604
Lanteigne v Lanteigne (1988), 91 NBR (2d) 275 (CA) 565
Laprise v Laprise, 2023 ONSC 6195 491
Lapshinoff v Allen, 2017 ONSC 1023 .... 554, 555
LARA v DSB, 2009 YKSC 74 374
Laramie v Laramie, 2018 ONSC 4740 .... 39, 42, 63
Laraque v Allooloo, [1999] NWTJ No 49, 48 RFL (4th) 381 (SC) 392, 484
Lariviere v Kelleher, [1999] OJ No 1824 (SCJ) 545
Lariviere v Lariviere, [2001] AJ No 251, 2001 ABQB 155 56
Larkin v Jamieson, [2000] PEIJ No 65, 193 Nfld & PEIR 22 (SC) 372, 373, 380, 397, 412
LaRoche v Lynn, 2019 ONSC 6602 633
Larocque v Larocque, 2011 SKQB 140 123
Laroque v Misling, [1998] NWTJ No 18 (SC) 36

Larosa v Larosa, [2003] MJ No 203, 175 Man R (2d) 72 (QB) 325, 488
Larson v Boje, [1999] AJ No 682 (QB) 507
Laskosky v Laskosky, [1999] AJ No 131 (QB) 301, 306, 309, 538
Latimer v Latimer (1979), 24 OR (2d) 134 (HCJ) 203
Latreille v Bard, 2021 ONSC 1290 530
LAU v LLL, 2016 PESC 3, var'd 2016 PECA 15 113, 143, 300, 301
Laughlin v Cormier, [1997] PEIJ No 80, 155 Nfld & PEIR 289 (TD) 485, 507
Laurain v Clarke, 2011 ONSC 7195 156
Laurie v Barre, 2009 MBQB 284 80
Laurie v Laurie, 2002 BCCA 317 326
Laurie v Laurie, [2004] MJ No 87, 2004 MBQB 59 327
Laushway v Messervey & Sobeys Group Inc, 2014 NSCA 7 253
Lavallée v Trevors, 2019 PECA 10 661
Lavdovsky v Lavdovsky, [1998] BCJ No 1952 (SC) 70, 325
Lavender-Smith v Smith, 2021 NBCA 34 602
Lavergne v Lavergne, 2007 ABCA 169, [2007] AJ No 580 157, 159, 484
Lavie v Lavie, 2018 ONCA 10 196
Lavoie v Lavoie (Lillos), 2011 ABQB 781 370
Lavoie v Lavoie, [2005] NWTJ No 6, 2005 NWTSC 7 574
Lavoie v Lavoie, 2024 ABCA 85 196, 198, 201
Lavoie v Wills, [2000] AJ No 1359, 13 RFL (5th) 93 (QB) 163, 165, 219, 260, 288, 334, 357, 363
Lavoie v Yawrenko (1992), 44 RFL (3d) 89 (BCCA) 550, 592
Law v Law (1986), 2 RFL (3d) 458, [1986] OJ No 2513 (HCJ) 112, 571
LAW v MRE, 2009 BCSC 490, [2009] BCJ No 728 294, 308
Lawless v Asaro, [2003] OJ No 2522, 39 RFL (5th) 129 (SCJ) 84
Lawrence v Mortensen, [2000] OJ No 1578, 8 RFL (5th) 133 (SCJ) 50–51
Lawson v Lawson, 2020 ABQB 519 638
Laxton v Laxton, [1997] PEIJ No 87 (TD) 572
LB v PAV, [2008] AJ No 1174, 2008 ABQB 623 72, 75
LB v PE, 2021 ONCJ 114 489
LBL v SB, 2010 NBQB 339 493
LBM v RDE, 2016 YKSC 4 86
LC v ROC, [2007] AJ No 513, 2007 ABCA 158 342
LCB v RJS, [1999] BCJ No 1427 (SC) 209
LCR v IJER, 2019 SKQB 229 35, 475, 494
LCT v RK, 2017 BCCA 64 372, 378
LDB v ANH, 2023 BCCA 480 666
LDB v CWG, [1997] SJ No 626 (QB) 9
LDF v SJF, 2010 BCSC 1055 351
LDW v KDM, 2011 ABQB 384 152, 335, 337
Le Bourdais v Le Bourdais, [1998] BCJ No 2488, 42 RFL (4th) 64 (SC) 209, 255
Le Page v Porter, [2000] OJ No 2574, 7 RFL (5th) 335 (SCJ) 247
Le v Nguyen, 2022 ONSC 6265 191
Leask v Leask (1975), 24 RFL 275 (BCSC) 451
Leavitt v Leavitt, [1999] BCJ No 648 (SC) 357
LeBlanc (Re) (1986), 77 NSR (2d) 49 (TD) 514
LeBlanc v LeBlanc (1982), 42 NBR (2d) 639 (CA) 26
LeBlanc v LeBlanc (1993), 48 RFL (3d) 457, [1993] MJ No 295 (CA) 508, 622, 662
LeBlanc v LeBlanc (1995), 14 RFL (4th) 414 (NBQB) 570
LeBlanc v LeBlanc, 2015 NBQB 164 113, 154
Lebouthillier v Manning, 2014 ONSC 4081 389
Lebrun v Lebrun, [1999] OJ No 3393 (SCJ) 384
Lecompte v Jensen, 2011 ONSC 3223 302

Lecreux v Lecreux, [1987] NSJ No 293 (Co Ct) 517
Lee v Chung, 2011 BCSC 404 .... 75, 326, 327, 560
Lee v Lee (1990), 29 RFL (3d) 417, [1990] BCJ No 2277 (CA) 112, 573
Lee v Lee, [1998] NJ No 247, 43 RFL (4th) 339 (CA) 157, 159, 474, 629
Lee v Lee, 2009 NSSC 121 .... 56, 64
Lee v Taggart, 2015 BCSC 1959 338
Lee-Broomes v Broomes, 2012 ONSC 2195 297
Leering v Leering, 2020 BCSC 1231 .... 562, 564
Lees (Bankruptcy of), 2002 BCSC 570 534
Leet v Beach, 2010 NSSC 433 .... 134, 153
Leet v Leet (1994), 131 NSR (2d) 19, [1994] NSJ No 144 (TD) 211
Leet v Leet, [2002] NBJ No 87, 25 RFL (5th) 302 (QB) 235
Legault v Legault (1987), 19 CPC (2d) 267, [1987] OJ No 2336 (Dist Ct) 602
Leger v Allain, [2002] NBJ No 189 (QB) 557, 558
Leger v Leger (1994), 146 NBR (2d) 32 (QB) 533
Leger v Leger, [2000] NBJ No 52, [2000] NBR (2d) (Supp) No 2 (QB) 134, 413
Legere v Legere, [2001] NSJ No 173 (SC) 208
Leibel v Davis, [2001] SJ No 208, 15 RFL (5th) 379 (QB) 245, 301
Leigh v Leigh (1976), 26 RFL 282 (Ont HCJ) 455
Leinburd v Leinburd, [2003] MJ No 456, 49 RFL (5th) 102 (QB) 270
Leis v Leis, [2002] OJ No 4306 (SCJ) 454
Leis v Leis, 2014 ABCA 36 .... 47, 65, 67, 129
Leitch v Novac, 2020 ONCA 257 .... 185, 262, 612
Lekakis v Lekakis, 2023 BCSC 376 340
Leland v Klette, 2013 SKQB 277 .... 143, 468
LEM v DMI, 2019 BCSC 796 .... 39, 42
Lemay c Longpré, 2014 ONCS 5107 497
Lemire v Lemire, 2016 BCSC 2340 .... 152, 153, 165, 497
Lenko v Lenko, 2011 BCSC 28 152
Lennox v Frender (1990), 27 RFL (3d) 181, [1990] BCJ No 1591 (CA) 318
Lenz v Lenz, [2008] SJ No 130, 2008 SKQB 96 300
Leonard v Leonard (1996), 29 RFL (4th) 237, [1996] NWTJ No 113 (SC) 80, 83
Leontowicz v Leontowicz, 2020 ABCA 324 .... 457, 458
Leopold v Leopold, [2001] OJ No 3355 (SCJ) 652
Lepage v Lepage, [1999] SJ No 174, 179 Sask R 34 (QB) 135, 152, 342, 343, 408, 414
Lepage v Lepage, [2006] SJ No 16, 2006 SKQB 18 555
LePine v LePine, 2015 ONSC 7341 58
Lepp v Lepp, 2008 BCSC 448, [2008] BCJ No 640 410
Lerner v Lerner, 2013 BCSC 239 .... 43, 65
Lesko v Lesko, 2021 ONCA 369 162
Leskun v Leskun, [2006] 1 SCR 920, 34 RFL (6th) 1, 2006 SCC 25 .... 16, 74, 284, 294, 475, 493
Lessard v Lessard, [1999] AJ No 525 (QB) 465
Lessard v Mahoney, 2019 BCSC 551 530
Lesser v Lesser (1985), 44 RFL (2d) 255 (Ont HCJ), aff'd (1985), 51 OR (2d) 100 (CA) 479, 552
Letoria v Canada, 2015 TCC 221 366
Leung v Lee, 2004 BCSC 234 302
Levasseur v Ellis, [2004] NSJ No 248, 223 NSR (2d) 298 (SC) 217
Leveille v Lemieux, [2002] OJ No 3422, [2002] OTC 641 (SCJ) 206
Levesque v Comeau, [1970] SCR 1010, 16 DLR (3d) 425 204
Levesque v Levesque (1992), 41 RFL (3d) 96 (Alta CA) 658, 660
Levesque v Levesque (1994), 4 RFL (4th) 375, 116 DLR (4th) 314 (Alta CA) 25, 149, 276, 293, 388
Levesque v Levesque, [1999] OJ No 3056 (SCJ) 306
Levesque v Levesque, [2001] MJ No 43, 154 Man R (2d) 89 (QB) 206

Levesque v Levesque, [2003] SJ No 848, 244 Sask R 178 (QB) ... 243
Levesque v Meade, 2010 NBQB 270 ... 121, 140, 160, 295, 317, 545
Lewcock v Natali-Lewcock, [2001] OJ No 2051 (SCJ) ... 87
Lewi v Lewi (2006), 28 RFL (6th) 250, [2006] OJ No 1847 (CA) ... 47, 63, 65, 66, 71, 74, 75, 323
Lewis v Adesanya, 2014 ONCJ 326 ... 505
Lewis v Carlson-Lewis, [2001] SJ No 117 (QB) ... 334
Lewis v Correia, 2014 ABQB 314 ... 114
Lewis v Lewis (1987), 11 RFL (3d) 402 (Alta QB) ... 109
Lewis v Lewis, [2000] AJ No 556, 264 AR 90 (QB) ... 334
Lewis v Lewis, [2002] BCJ No 778 (SC) ... 580
Lewkoski v Lewkoski, [1998] OJ No 1736, 40 RFL (4th) 86 (Gen Div) ... 21
Lewkoski v Lewkoski, [1998] OJ No 894 (Gen Div) ... 606
Leyte v Leyte, 2020 NSSC 215 ... 640
LF v CGC, 2014 BCSC 1069 ... 216
LF v RB, 2021 BCSC 464 ... 49, 66, 291, 549
LFF v KG, [2004] AJ No 493, 3 RFL (6th) 314 (QB) ... 325
LFR(H) v RBH, 2021 NBQB 50 ... 185, 255, 270
LG v RG, 2013 BCSC 983 ... 112
LGP v JRH, [2003] NSJ No 218, 40 RFL (5th) 346 (SC) ... 90
LHG v CBG, [1998] AJ No 542, 222 AR 113 (QB) ... 212
LHMK v BPK, 2012 BCSC 435 ... 260, 291, 295, 297, 298, 299, 316, 317, 318, 321
Li v Wong, 2010 ABCA 296 ... 218
Li v Wu, 2020 ONSC 7329 ... 89, 94
Licata v Shure, 2022 ONCA 270 ... 562
Lickfold v Robichaud, [2008] OJ No 4117 (SCJ) ... 356
Lidster v Lidster, [2000] BCJ No 1017 (SC) ... 60
Lidstone v Lidstone (1993), 46 RFL (3d) 203 (NSCA) ... 475
Lidstone v Lidstone, [2001] PEIJ No 118, 207 Nfld & PEIR 142 (SC) ... 324
Lidstone v Lidstone, [2003] PEIJ No 77 (SC) ... 405
Liggett v Doucet, 2021 ONSC 3886 ... 117
Lightfoot v Lightfoot (1972), 11 RFL 242, [1972] OJ No 2039 (HCJ) ... 619
Lightle v Kotar, 2014 BCCA 69 ... 129
Lindholm v Lindholm, [1999] BCJ No 1704, 71 BCLR (3d) 118 (SC) ... 12
Lindsay v Canada (Attorney General), 2005 BCCA 594 ... 623
Lindsay v Lindsay (1992), 38 RFL (3d) 12 (Ont Prov Div) ... 532
Lins v Lins (1991), 31 RFL (3d) 40, [1991] BCJ No 372 (CA) ... 607
LIP v LHB, 2013 MBQB 37 ... 80, 82
Lipskaya v Guo, 2020 BCSC 209 ... 467
Liscio v Avram, [2009] OJ No 3406 (SCJ) ... 322
Liscio v Liscio, [2009] OJ No 3406 (SCJ) ... 322
Lisevich v Lisevich, [1998] AJ No 777, 20 RFL (4th) 435 (QB) ... 43
Lisitza v Herle (Lisitza), 2022 SKQB 71 ... 147, 148
Lisko v Lisko, 2016 SKQB 38 ... 152
Lister v Gould, [2000] NBJ No 419, 2000 NBCA 33 ... 567, 622, 661
Little v Little (1985), 49 CPC 169, [1985] NSJ No 114 (TD) ... 620
Livermore v Livermore (1992), 43 RFL (3d) 163 (Ont Ct Gen Div) ... 478
Livingston v King, 2022 BCSC 1906 ... 181, 495, 499
Livingston v Trainor, [2002] PEIJ No 46 (SC) ... 157
Livingstone v Livingstone, [1999] BCJ No 996 (CA) ... 481
LJC v JCG, 2014 MBQB 246 ... 574
LJL v LRS, 2013 SKQB 168 ... 150
LJM v GSM, [2006] NBJ No 202, 2006 NBQB 176 ... 316, 322
LJW v TAR, [2005] AJ No 3, 9 RFL (6th) 232 (CA) ... 489

LJW v TAR. See also DBS v SRG; LJW v TAR; Henry v Henry; Hiemstra v Hiemstra.
LKB v JG, 2023 NBQB 90 ... 198
LKF (Re), [1998] BCJ No 3186 (Prov Ct) ... 93
LKF (Re), [1999] BCJ No 819 (Prov Ct) ... 93
LL v GB, 2008 ABQB 536, aff'd 2009 ABCA 356 ... 291
LL v MC, 2013 ONSC 1801 ... 338, 343, 345
LLDS v WGF (1995), 11 RFL (4th) 145, [1995] OJ No 418 (Gen Div) ... 600
Llewellyn v Llewellyn, [2002] BCJ No 542, 26 RFL (5th) 389, 2002 BCCA 182 ... 142, 210, 388, 577
LLF v JD, [2004] NSJ No 466, 228 NSR (2d) 187 (Fam Ct) ... 401
LLL v BAL, 2010 BCSC 301 ... 165, 416
LLM v DRM, 2022 BSSC 143 ... 35, 497
LM v TM, 2012 NBQB 238 ... 328, 329, 331, 333
LMA v PH, 2014 ONSC 1707 ... 96, 97, 98, 100, 101, 103, 494
LMG v REG, 2020 ONSC 2825 ... 42, 43
LMH v GDH, 2011 BCCA 443 ... 263
LMK v JMK, 2015 MBQB 1 ... 222, 226
LMP v LS, 2011 SCC 64 ... 560
LN v NL, [2002] OJ No 1082 (SCJ) ... 92
LN v TMN, 2015 NBQB 155 ... 78
Lo v Lo, 2011 ONSC 7663 ... 58, 193, 195, 220
Lobo v Lobo, [1999] AJ No 113, 45 RFL (4th) 366 (QB) ... 192, 212, 299, 462, 487
Locke v Bramwell, 2016 NSSC 300 ... 194, 372, 634
Locke v Goulding, 2012 NLCA 8 ... 12, 15, 370, 371, 372, 373, 374, 376, 378, 379, 392, 393, 394, 396, 401, 404, 494, 565
Locke v Goulding, 2021 NLSC 8 ... 38, 39, 44, 587
Lockerby v Lockerby, 2010 NSSC 282 ... 311
Lockerby v Lockerby, 2017 NSCA 26 ... 83
Loehr v Loehr, 2023 BCSC 2229 ... 132, 152
Loesch v Walji, 2008 BCCA 214, [2008] BCJ No 897 ... 458, 459
Loewen v Traill, [1998] BCJ No 466, 36 RFL (4th) 231 (SC) ... 307, 475
Lonergan v Lonergan, [1998] BCJ No 150 (SC) ... 467
Lonergan v Lonergan, 2011 ONSC 1410 ... 156
Long v Long (1993), 1 RFL (4th) 110 (Alta QB) ... 468
Long v Long, [2001] BCJ No 2943, 2001 BCSC 996 ... 41
Long v Sun, 2019 BCSC 2129 ... 447
Longhurst v Longhurst, [2004] BCJ No 1637, 2004 BCSC 1017 ... 35
Longlitz v Longlitz, 2012 BCSC 130 ... 27, 61
Longstaff v Longstaff (1993), 86 BCLR (2d) 1 (CA) ... 574
Loosdrecht v Loosdrecht, [1998] BCJ No 1629 (SC) ... 380, 403
Lopatynski v Lopatynski, [1998] AJ No 1312 (QB) ... 363
Lopez v Lopez (1993), 48 RFL (3d) 298, [1993] OJ No 1927 (Gen Div) ... 452, 607
Lopez v Lopez, [1998] OJ No 5370 (Gen Div) ... 450, 650
Loran v Loran, [2007] SJ No 371, 2007 SKQB 253 ... 308
Loran v Loran, 2009 SKQB 514 ... 134
Loscerbo v Loscerbo (2008), 57 RFL (6th) 186, [2008] MJ No 246, 2008 MBQB 183 ... 210, 358
Loshney v Hankins (1993), 48 RFL (3d) 67 (Sask QB) ... 578, 580
Lotoski v Lotoski, 2018 ABCA 103 ... 646
Lotten v Lotten, [2003] SJ No 831, 2003 SKQB 542 ... 211
Loughran v Loughran, [2000] NSJ No 41, 182 NSR (2d) 143 (SC) ... 116, 308
Louie v Lastman, [2001] OJ No 1888 (SCJ), aff'd (2002), 61 OR (3d) 449, [2002] OJ No 3521 (CA) ... 511, 615
Louie v Lastman, [2002] OJ No 3522, 29 RFL (5th) 108 (CA) ... 615
Louisseize v Louisseize, [1999] OJ No 5000 (SCJ) ... 322, 395

Louksr v Assadbeigi, 2010 BCSC 116 ... 522, 574
Lovett v Lovett (1982), 26 RFL (2d) 194 (Ont Co Ct), subsequent proceedings (1983), 31 RFL (2d) 109 (Ont HCJ) ... 22
Low v Robinson, [2000] AJ No 96, 4 RFL (5th) 368 (QB) ... 307
Lowe v Lowe, [2006] OJ No 128 (SCJ) ... 204, 353
Lozinski v Lozinski, 2017 BCCA 280 ... 216, 348
LP v SP, 2022 NSSC 197 ... 348, 357
LPH v JMR, 2021 BCSC 1282 ... 142, 490, 491, 506
LPS v MSF, 2015 NBCA 23 ... 65, 67
LR v DT (1998), 178 Sask R 115, [1998] SJ No 733 (QB) ... 147, 619
LRC v JMC, 2008 BCSC 408 ... 364
LRP v BJP, 2013 ABQB 685 ... 55
LRR v EM, 2018 NBCA 2 ... 538
LRS v SSD, 2020 ABCA 206 ... 213, 242, 313
LS v EP, [1999] BCJ No 1451, 50 RFL (4th) 302, 1999 BCCA 393 ... 489, 507
LSP v JRP, [2002] SJ No 35, 25 RFL (5th) 150 (QB) ... 127, 241, 454, 582
LT v RU, 2023 SKKB 74 ... 578, 584, 586
LTG v WH and MH (1989), 89 NSR (2d) 67, [1989] NSJ No 511 (Fam Ct) ... 112
Lu v Sun, [2004] NSJ No 459, 2004 NSSF 108, var'd [2005] NSJ No 314, 17 RFL (6th) 57 (CA) ... 26, 61, 62, 489
Lu v Yao, 2019 BCSC 652 ... 35
Lucas v Evans (1994), 135 NSR (2d) 367, [1994] NSJ No 610 (Fam Ct) ... 242
Lucas v Gallant, [2000] AJ No 457, 263 AR 80 (QB) ... 394
Lucia v Martin, [1998] BCJ No 1798 (SC) ... 7
Lucier v Lucier, [1999] BCJ No 402 (SC) ... 104
Luckett v Luckett, [2002] SJ No 232, 218 Sask R 153 (QB) ... 123
Ludlow v Harkins, 2014 NLTD(G) 23 ... 347, 348, 354, 355
Ludmer v Ludmer, 2014 ONCA 827 ... 143, 152, 153, 165, 221–22, 295, 652
Luedke v Luedke, [2004] BCJ No 1157, 10 RFL (6th) 74 (CA) ... 126, 223, 227, 325, 358, 362
Lundrigan v Lundrigan, 2009 NLUFC 28 ... 288
Luney v Luney, 2007 BCCA 567, [2007] BCJ No 2483 ... 574, 576
Lupkowski v Lupkowski (1974), 16 RFL 105, [1974] AJ No 252 (CA) ... 621
Lussier v Lussier, [2001] OJ No 169 (Ct J) ... 340
Lussier v Lussier, 2012 MBQB 274 ... 457
Lussier v Ritchie, 2023 BCSC 1817 ... 132, 153
Lutz v Lutz, 2014 SKQB 146 ... 160
Lutz v Sequeira, [2000] SJ No 460, 195 Sask R 87 (QB) ... 388, 432, 437
LW v FW, 2022 BCSC 642 ... 426
LWH v SC, 2012 NBQB 2 ... 389
Lygouriatis v Gohm, 2006 SKQB 448, [2006] SJ No 609 ... 449
Lynch v Lundrigan, [2002] NJ No 185 (SC), aff'd [2004] NJ No 195, 5 RFL (6th) 126 (CA) ... 578
Lynch v Lynch (1999), 1 RFL (5th) 309, [1999] OJ No 4559 (SCJ) ... 29, 653
Lynch v Segal (2006), 33 RFL (6th) 279, [2006] OJ No 5014 (CA) ... 469, 541
Lyons v Lyons Estate (1989), 99 NBR (2d) 220, [1989] NBJ No 617 (QB) ... 604
Lyons v Lyons, 2022 SKQB 70 ... 196
Lyttle v Bourget, [1999] NSJ No 298, 178 NSR (2d) 1 (SC) ... 221, 293, 293, 317, 320, 407
Lyttle v Lyttle (1992), 41 RFL (3d) 422, [1992] OJ No 1608 (Gen Div) ... 22, 25

M v M, [1999] OJ No 5016 (SCJ) ... 583
M(BB) v M(WW) (1994), 7 RFL (4th) 255, [1994] AJ No 579 (QB) ... 541, 600
M(CF) v M(MF) (1996), 23 RFL (4th) 55, [1996] NBJ No 282 (QB) ... 11, 89, 92, 96
M(CS) v L(WS), 2015 CarswellBC 2674 ... 326
M(DE) v S(HJ) (1996), 25 RFL (4th) 264, [1996] SJ No 411 (QB) ... 93, 95, 107

MA v FA, 2013 BCSC 1077 82
MA v FHA, 2011 BCSC 1047 .... 280, 557
MA v NM, 2021 ONSC 5468 .... 262, 346, 348, 349, 355
Ma v Xu, 2023 ABKB 346 198
MAA v JMA, 2011 NBQB 298 .... 204, 205, 206, 208, 565, 566
MAB v HIL, 2010 YKSC 8 .... 201, 206
MAB v TLB, [2002] NSJ No 192, 204 NSR (2d) 118 (Fam Ct) 90
Mabbett v Mabbett, [1999] NSJ No 125, 48 RFL (4th) 157 (SC) 142, 412
Mabey v Mabey, [2004] NSJ No 394, 2004 NSSF 92 614
MacAlister v MacAlister, [1997] YJ No 62 (SC) 557
MacArthur v Demers, [1998] OJ No 5868, 166 DLR (4th) 172 (Gen Div) 99, 101–2, 110, 449, 451
MacBeth v MacBeth, [1998] AJ No 195 (QB) 487
MacCarthy v MacCarthy, 2015 BCCA 496 .... 497, 505, 575, 576, 578
MacDiarmid v MacDiarmid, 2014 NBQB 12 143
MacDonald v Brodoff, 2020 ABCA 246 .... 347, 348, 349, 350, 351, 353
MacDonald v Frampton (1987), 78 NSR (2d) 258 (Fam Ct) 556
MacDonald v Keddy-Smith (1990), 30 RFL (3d) 461 (NS Fam Ct) 477
MacDonald v MacDonald (1975), 23 RFL 303, [1975] MJ No 245 (QB) 620
MacDonald v MacDonald, [1997] AJ No 1262, 57 Alta LR (3d) 195, 209 AR 178 (CA) 147, 148
MacDonald v MacDonald, [1997] OJ No 4250 (CA) 462
MacDonald v MacDonald, [2001] NSJ No 498, 198 NSR (2d) 216 (SC) 53, 323
MacDonald v MacDonald, [2002] BCJ No 121, 22 RFL (5th) 356 (CA) .... xxv, 414, 418
MacDonald v MacDonald, [2002] BCJ No 2320, 33 RFL (5th) 119 (SC) 418
MacDonald v MacDonald, 2010 NSCA 34 .... 201, 594, 658
MacDonald v MacDonald, 2016 NSSC 290 193
MacDonald v Moutter, [2000] BCJ No 2114 (SC) 449
MacDonald v Pink, 2011 NSSC 421 .... 200, 281, 286
MacDonald v Rasmussen, [2000] SJ No 660, 198 Sask R 1 (QB) 61, 71, 84, 481
MacDonald v Seguin, 2011 NSSC 337 380
MacDonald v Simpson, [1998] OJ No 1045 (Gen Div) 437
MacDougall v Letilly, [1997] SJ No 473 (QB) 617
MacDougall v MacDougall, [2005] NSJ No 129, 19 RFL (6th) 103 (SC) 230
MacDuff v MacDuff (1994), 97 Man R (2d) 188, [1994] MJ No 543 (CA) 242
MacEachern v Hardy, 2010 NSSC 246 .... 372, 391
MacEachern v MacEachern, [1999] NSJ No 62, 174 NSR (2d) 331 (TD) 330
MacEachern v MacLeod, 2014 NSSC 238 .... 27, 63
Maceus-Agyckum v Agyckum, [2005] OJ No 1306 (SCJ) 212
MacFarlane v MacFarlane (1987), 83 NBR (2d) 306 (CA) 557
MacFarlane v MacFarlane, [1999] BCJ No 3008 (SC) 379
MacGillivary v Ross, [2008] NSJ No 506, 2008 NSSC 339 .... 201, 203
MacGregor v MacGregor, [1998] PEIJ No 102 (TD) 540
Mach v Mach, 2021 BCSC 1655 119
MacInnes v MacInnes (1993), 122 NSR (2d) 329 (Fam Ct) 518
MacIntosh v MacIntosh, [2003] AJ No 728, 40 RFL (5th) 200, 2003 ABQB 498 .... 452, 653
MacIntyre v MacIntyre, [2001] PEIJ No 39 (SC) 163
MacIsaac v Seffern, [1969] RP 183 (Que CA) 659
MacKay v Bucher, [2001] NSJ No 326, 2001 NSCA 120 .... 430, 440, 441, 567
Mackechnie v Mackechnie, [1998] BCJ No 2096 (SC) 518
MacKenzie v MacKenzie, [1998] BCJ No 2416 (SC) 309
MacKenzie v MacKenzie, 2022 PESC 20 497
Mackie v Mackie (1994), 96 Man R (2d) 74 (QB) 581
MacKinnon v Duffy, [2000] OJ No 2948 (SCJ) 540
MacKinnon v MacKinnon, [2005] OJ No 1552, 75 OR (3d) 175 (CA) 280, 487, 505

MacKinnon v MacKinnon, 2015 NBQB 1324 .... 303, 587
MacKinnon v Marshall, [1998] NSJ No 537 (Fam Ct) 260, 398
MacLachlan v MacLachlan, 2020 SKQB 117 .... 150, 170, 178
Maclean v Jackson (1996), 24 RFL (4th) 134 (PEITD) 544
MacLean v Miller, 2020 NSSC 224 640
MacLean v Mio, 2019 BCSC 375 .... 33, 34
MacLellan v MacLellan, [1998] NSJ No 349 (TD) 299, 310, 312, 330, 333
MacLennan v MacLennan, [2003] NSJ No 15, 35 RFL (5th) 384 (CA) 35, 49, 50, 58, 62
MacLennan v MacLennan, 2021 SKCA 132 .... 35, 64, 121, 347, 348, 416
MacLeod v Druhan, [1997] NSJ No 573, 34 RFL (4th) 206 (Fam Ct) 337
Maclurcan v Maclurcan (1897), 77 LT 474 (Eng CA) 469
MacMillan v Layden, [2002] NJ No 156, 214 Nfld & PEIR 227 (SC) 54
MacMinn v MacMinn (1995), 17 RFL (4th) 88 (Alta CA) 488, 507
MacNaught v MacNaught, [1998] PEIJ No 27, 37 RFL (4th) 79 (TD) 231, 338, 342, 354, 363
MacNeil v Garney-MacNeil, 2012 ONSC 3332 216
MacNeil v MacNeil, [2000] NWTJ No 4, 4 RFL (5th) 273 (SC) 156, 342, 383, 384
MacNeil v MacNeil, 2012 NSSC 345 61
MacNeil v MacNeil, 2013 ONSC 7012 .... 292, 331, 332,
MacNeil v Yeadon, 2022 NSCA 32 664
MacNeil v Yeadon, 2022 NSCA 79 499
MacNutt v MacNutt, [2008] BCJ No 1831, 2008 BCSC 1290 98
MacPhail v MacPhail, [2000] PEIJ No 41 (SC) 389
MacPherson v MacPherson, [2005] OJ No 3448 (SCJ) 69, 73, 321
Madden v Dahl, 2014 BCCA 23 654
Madi v King, 2023 ONCA 443 191
MAF v WAF, [1998] SJ No 224, 165 Sask R 313 (QB) 363
Magee v Faveri, [2007] OJ No 4826 (SCJ) 285, 333, 356
Magee v Magee, [1997] SJ No 468, 159 Sask R 223 (QB) 124, 144
Maginley v Maginley, [2003] NSJ No 35, 212 NSR (2d) 62 (SC) 318
Magionas v Magionas (1988), 12 RFL (3d) 194 (NSCA) 455
Magne v Magne (1990), 26 RFL (3d) 364, [1990] MJ No 274 (QB) 39
Magnes v Magnes, [1997] SJ No 407 (QB) 322
Magotiaux v Magotiaux, 2016 SKQB 406 113
Mahannah v Mahannah, 2012 BCSC 403 210
Maher v Maher, [2001] BCJ No 1912 (SC) 87, 89
Mahrer v Mahrer (1976), 26 RFL 328, [1976] OJ No 265 (HCJ) 650
Mainwaring v Alberta, [1998] AJ No 105, 48 RFL (4th) 171 (QB) 32
Major v Major, [1998] SJ No 835, 175 Sask R 34 (QB) 96, 607
MAK v KAB, [2000] PEIJ No 8, 187 Nfld & PEIR 224 (SC) 192, 208
Maka v Maka, 2015 ONSC 3480 .... 406, 510
Makdissi v Masson, 2017 ONSC 6498 56
MAL v RHM, 2018 ONSC 2542 638
Malbeuf v Malbeuf, [1999] SJ No 635, 185 Sask R 267 (QB) 244, 445
Malboeuf v Belter, 2018 ONSC 6516 468
Malboeuf v Hanna, 2018 ONSC 6562 468
Malcolm v Chabot, [2004] SJ No 817, 258 Sask R 312 (QB) 60
Malik v Malik, 2019 ONSC 117 618
Malinowski v Malinowski, 2010 SKQB 27 453
Maloney v Maloney, [2003] OJ No 5828 (Div Ct) 319
Maloney-Chumney v Maloney-Chumney, [1999] NBJ No 108, 210 NBR (2d) 223 (QB) 395
MAM v DLL, 2018 BCSC 2114 .... 134, 256
Mancuso v Mancuso (1991), 35 RFL (3d) 265 (Ont Prov Div) 517
Manis v Manis, [2000] OJ No 4539, [2000] OTC 880 (SCJ) 130

Manley v Lund, 2009 BCSC 903 ... 534
Mann v Mann, 2009 BCCA 181 ... 506
Mannell v Mannell, 2023 ONSC 4209 ... 498, 584, 587
Mansoor v Mansoor, 2012 BCSC 602 ... 193, 194, 273, 459, 596
Mansour v Hassan, 2023 ONSC 2054 ... 203
Manuele v O'Connell, 2012 NSSC 271 ... 259, 430
Manzoni v Manzoni (1987), 67 Nfld & PEIR 339 (Nfld TD) ... 514
Marcella v Marcella, 2016 SKQB 407 ... 126, 144, 313
Marchak v Fleury (1995), 15 RFL (4th) 458, [1995] MJ No 263 (CA) ... 293
Marchand v Boon, [2004] SJ No 76, 243 Sask R 296 (QB) ... 258
Marcus v Cochrane, 2014 ONCA 207 ... 640
Mardanisamani v Farshad, 2022 SKQB 160 ... 289, 295
Marinangeli v Marinangeli (2003), 66 OR (3d) 40,
[2003] OJ No 2819, 38 RFL (5th) 307 (CA) ... 133, 134, 138, 138, 259, 260, 489, 661
Marino v Marino, 2008 BCSC 1402, [2008] BCJ No 1996 ... 203
Marks v Marks, 2000 ABQB, [2000] AJ No 1247 ... 4
Marquez v Zapiola, 2013 BCCA 433 ... 143
Marquis v Marquis, 2013 SKQB 76 ... 150
Marriage of Stamberg (Re), 218 Ill App 3d 333, 578 NE2d 261 (1991) ... 423
Marsh v Jashewski, 2011 ONSC 3793 ... 43, 64
Marsh v Marsh, [2006] BCJ No 615, 2006 BCCA 144 ... 35
Marshall v Marshall, [1998] NSJ No 311 (SC) ... 27
Marshall v Marshall, [2000] AJ No 347, 2000 ABQB 170 ... 56
Marshall v Marshall, [2007] NSJ No 552, 2008 NSSC 11 ... 201
Marsland v Gibb, [2000] BCJ No 558, 5 RFL (5th) 40, 2000 BCSC 471 ... 50, 112, 114
Marson v Marson, [2001] OJ No 1816 (CA) ... 564
Martel v Martel, [2000] SJ No 322, 6 RFL (5th) 342 (QB) ... 311
Martel v Martel, [2001] OJ No 759 (Ct J) ... 124, 400
Martell v Height (1994), 3 RFL (4th) 104, [1994] NSJ No 120 (CA) ... 48, 56, 57, 58
Martens v Martens, [2009] SJ No 180, 2009 SKQB 116 ... 14
Marthinsen v Marthinsen, 2020 BCSC 619 ... 35, 113
Martin v Martin (1988), 14 RFL (3d) 388 (BCCA) ... 550
Martin v Martin, [1997] NJ No 61 (TD), aff'd [1998] NJ No 323, 42 RFL (4th) 251 (CA) ... 112, 477
Martin v Martin, [1999] OJ No 813, 44 RFL (4th) 125 (Gen Div) ... 434
Martin v Martin, [2005] OJ No 4567 (SCJ) ... 623
Martin v Martin (2007), 46 RFL (6th) 286, [2007] MJ No 449, 2007 MBQB 296 ... 347, 349, 350, 353, 354, 355, 368
Martin v Sansome, 2014 ONCA 14 ... 511
Martin v Schaeffer, [2001] SJ No 210 (QB) ... 484
Martin v Watts, 2018 ONSC 6566 ... 650, 651
Martin v Watts, 2020 ONCA 406 ... 611
Martindale v Martindale (1990), 30 RFL (3d) 229 (Man CA) ... 455
Martinez v Olson, [1998] AJ No 1137 (QB) ... 345
Martinuk v Graham, 2015 ONSC 6769 ... 511
Marud v Marud, [1999] SJ No 478, 2 RFL (5th) 113 (QB) ... 36, 93
Marunic v Liberty, 2014 ONSC 957 ... 286
Marzetti v Marzetti (1994), 5 RFL (4th) 1 (SCC) ... 517
Mascarenhas v Mascarenhas, [1999] OJ No 37, 44 RFL (4th) 131 (Gen Div),
aff'd (2000), 18 RFL (5th) 148 (Ont Div Ct) ... 22, 134, 241, 297
Mask v Mask (2008), 55 RFL (6th) 98, [2008] OJ No 423 (SCJ) ... 153
Maskell v Maskell, [1999] NSJ No 424 (SC) ... 473, 538
Mason v Mason, [2006] NSJ No 227, 2006 NSSC 171 ... 362
Mason v Mason, 2013 ONSC 5974 ... 155

Mason v Mason, 2016 ONCA 725 .... 162, 183
Massicotte v Boutin, [1969] SCR 818 657
Massingham-Pearce v Konkulus (1995), 13 RFL (4th) 313, [1995] AJ No 404 (QB) 20
Massler v Massler, [1999] AJ No 206, 1999 ABQB 155 .... 317, 333
Mastin v Mastin, 2019 NSSC 248 .... 62, 64, 218, 280, 510, 587
Matechuk v Kopp (Yaworenko), 2020 SKQB 196 .... 34, 36, 134, 157, 166, 314, 430
Matheson v Matheson, [2003] OJ No 3857, 48 RFL (5th) 283 (SCJ) 43, 578
Mathusz v Carew, 2011 NLTD(F) 28 .... 27, 63, 216, 243
Matsell v Young (1994), 5 RFL (4th) 203 (Ont Prov Div) 569
Mattes v Mattes, [1997] NSJ No 191 (TD) 463
Matthews v Hancock, [1998] SJ No 617, 42 RFL (4th) 72 (QB) 401
Matthews v Matthews (1988), 11 RFL (3d) 431, [1988] NJ No 407 (SCTD) 38, 78
Matthews v Matthews (1990), 96 NSR (2d) 376, [1990] NSJ No 147 (TD), var'd (1991), 34 RFL 201, [1991] NSJ No 334 (CA) 381
Matthews v Matthews, [2007] YJ No 12, 2007 YKSC 11 578
Mattila v Liski, [1997] SJ No 495 (QB) 253
Mattina v Mattina, 2018 ONCA 867 640
Matty v Rammasoot, 2014 ABQB 2 24
Matwichuk v Stephenson, [2007] BCJ No 2347, 2007 BCSC 1589 64
Matwijiw v Matwijiw, [2004] OJ No 1887 (SCJ) 51
Maultsaid v Blair, 2009 BCCA 102, [2009] BCJ No 467 .... 340, 342, 343, 344
Maurier v Maurier, 2022 ABKB 856 134
Mavridis v Mavridis, [1999] BCJ No 1935 (SC) 305, 344
MAW v PCW, 2014 ABQB 703 134
Maxwell v Brandel, [1998] BCJ No 1327 (SC) 242
May-Rutter v Crisp, [2002] OJ No 2689, 29 RFL (5th) 402 (Div Ct) 244
Mayer v Mayer Estate, 2020 BCCA 282 628
Mayer v Mayer, [1999] OJ No 5286 (SCJ) 485
Mayer v Mayer, [2001] NSJ No 404 (SC) 472
Mayer v Mayer, 2013 ONSC 7099 .... 102, 106, 180, 183, 349
Maynard v Maynard, [1999] BCJ No 325, 45 RFL (4th) 395 (SC) 193, 297, 301, 661
Mayo v O'Connell, [1998] NJ No 239, 42 RFL (4th) 193 (SC) 380, 387, 391
Mayson-Blacklaws v Blacklaws, 2011 SKQB 334 453
MB v FA, 2011 MBQB 7 113
MB v NS, [2001] QJ No 3039 (CS) 59, 525
MB v SBB, 2018 ONSC 4893 214
MC v JO, 2017 NBCA 15 .... 124, 129, 130, 184, 270, 277, 494
McAdam v McAdam (1994), 8 RFL (4th) 252, [1994] MJ No 514 (QB) 79
McAfee v McAfee, [1998] BCJ No 413 (SC) 164
McArthur v Kyle (1994), 113 DLR (4th) 263 (Ont Ct Gen Div) 551
McArthur v McArthur, [1998] AJ No 1522, 44 RFL (4th) 241 (QB) 57
McArthur v McArthur, [1999] BCJ No 1239 (SC) 380
McBean v McBean, 2019 ABCA 1 509
McBennett v Danis, 2021 ONSC 3610 .... 124, 196, 239, 597
McBride v McBride, [2001] NWTJ No 69, 2001 NWTSC 59 .... 98, 104, 359, 566
McCabe v MacInnis, [2000] PEIJ No 61, 193 Nfld & PEIR 1 (SC) 46, 52, 83
McCaffrey v Dalla Longa, [2008] AJ No 335, 2008 ABQB 183 .... 124, 125, 127, 128
McCaffrey v Paleolog, 2010 BCSC 627, rev'd 2011 BCCA 378 .... 210, 570
McCain v McCain, 2021 ONSC 7744 .... 499, 504
McCallum v McCallum, [1999] AJ No 1548 (QB) 536
McCargar v McCargar, [1997] AJ No 678 (QB) 113, 475
McCarty v McCarty, 2016 ABQB 91 483
McClement v McClement, 2017 BCCA 416 .... 63, 66

McConkey v McConkey, 2022 ONSC 4600 ... 447, 452
McConnell v McConnell (1975), 11 NBR (2d) 19, [1975] NBJ No 79 (CA) ... 446, 469
McConnell v McConnell, [2002] SJ No 117, 25 RFL (5th) 341 (QB) ... 77
McConnell v McConnell, 2015 ONSC 2243 ... 326
McCormack v Piller, 2023 SKKB 37 ... 616
McCoy v Hucker, [1998] OJ No 2831, 75 OTC 12 (Gen Div) ... 299, 315
McCrae v McCrae, [2005] OJ No 50, [2005] OTC 11 (SCJ) ... 60
McCrate v McCrate, 2019 NSSC 167 ... 497
McCrea v McCrea, [1999] BCJ No 1514, 1 RFL (5th) 320 (SC) ... 309, 325, 540
McCurdy v Morisette, [1999] BCJ No 2292 (SC) ... 296, 357, 362
McDermott v McDermott, [2006] BCJ No 1380, 2006 BCSC 929 ... 385
McDonald v Gross, [1998] SJ No 301, 167 Sask R 97 (QB) ... 161
McDonald v McDonald (Mombourquette), 2023 NSSC 153 ... 253
McDonald v McDonald, [1998] BCJ No 3150 (SC) ... 400
McDonald v McDonald, [2001] BCJ No 2570, 22 RFL (5th) 135, 2001 BCCA 702 ... 284, 320
McDonald v McDonald, [2008] BCJ No 1694, 2008 BCSC 1203 ... 497
McEachern v McEachern (1994), 5 RFL (4th) 115 (Ont Ct Gen Div) ... 450
McEachern v McEachern, [1998] SJ No 507 (QB) ... 317
McElravey v Healey, 2019 SKQB 157 ... 496
McFadyen v McFadyen (1975), 22 RFL 140 (Alta SC) ... 569
McFarland v McFarland (1995), 18 RFL (4th) 59 (Ont Ct Gen Div) ... 94
McGill v McGill (1994), 8 RFL (4th) 84 (Sask QB) ... 517
McGowan v McGowan, [1998] SJ No 662, 173 Sask R 27 (QB) ... 212
McGowan v McGowan, [2003] SJ No 515, 42 RFL (5th) 420 (QB) ... 192
McGrath v McGrath (1998), 86 NSR (2d) 35 (TD) ... 481
McGrath v McGrath, [2001] BCJ No 1555 (SC) ... 4, 428, 436
McGrath v McGrath, [2006] NJ No 201, 2006 NLUFC 32 ... 338, 343, 345
McGregor v McGregor (1994), 3 RFL (4th) 343, 148 NBR (2d) 176, [1994] NBJ No 220 (CA) ... 54, 56, 112, 572
McGuire v Bator, 2022 ONCA 431 ... 86
McIllwraith v McIllwraith, [1999] NBJ No 129 (QB) ... 432, 439
McIndoe v McIndoe (1966), 57 WWR 577 (Sask QB) ... 458
McInnes v McInnes, [1997] SJ No 10 (QB) ... 570
McInnes v Young, [1998] NWTJ No 91 (SC) ... 457
McIntosh v McIntosh (1985), 46 RFL (2d) 249, [1985] BCJ No 2682 (SC) ... 204
McIntosh v McIntosh (1996), 19 RFL (4th) 46 (Man QB) ... 463
McIntosh v McIntosh, 2007 BCSC 1331 ... 407
McIntyre v Veinot, 2016 NSSC 8 ... 148, 200
McIver v McIver, [1998] AJ No 1012, 231 AR 376 (QB) ... 414
McIver v McIver, 2010 ABCA 155 ... 42
McIvor v McIvor, [1997] BCJ No 1666, 41 BCLR (3d) 77 (SC) ... 31
McKee v McKee (1994), 153 AR 8 (QB) ... 592
McKenna v McKenna, 2015 ONSC 3309 ... 193, 195, 219
McKenzie v McKenzie, 2014 BCCA 381 ... 124
McKenzie v Perestrelo, 2014 BCCA 161 ... 147, 148, 153, 165, 216
McKenzie v Petrie, [2003] BCJ No 808 (SC) ... 302
McKerracher v McKerracher, [1997] BCJ No 2257 (SC) ... 363
McKinley v McKinley, 2011 NBQB 260 ... 27, 30
McKinnon v McKinnon, [1998] AJ No 85, 217 AR 342 (QB) ... 48
McLachlan v McLachlan, [2002] BCJ No 386, 2002 BCSC 291 ... 243
McLachlan v McLachlan, 2010 MBQB 189 ... 587
McLaren v McLaren, [1998] BCJ No 2485 (SC) ... 291
McLarty v Ontario (Director, Family Responsibility Office), [2001] OJ No 707 (CA) ... 527

McLaughlin v McLaughlin, [1998] BCJ No 2514, 44 RFL (4th) 148 (CA)....301, 306, 327, 328
McLaughlin v McLaughlin, [1999] BCJ No 485, 44 RFL (4th) 176 (CA)....462
McLaughlin v McLaughlin, [2004] SJ No 716, 260 Sask R 114 (QB)....112, 355
McLean v McLean, [1997] OJ No 5315, 50 OTC 18 (Gen Div)....54, 409
McLean v McLean, 2013 ABQB 700....114, 291
McLean v Rice, [2005] OJ No 576 (SCJ)....394
McLean v Vassel, [2004] OJ No 3036, 4 RFL (6th) 63 (SCJ)....216
McLellan v McLellan, [1999] NBJ No 348 (QB)....220
McLellan v McLellan, 2020 NSSC 161....136, 173, 180
McLeod v McLeod (1993), 45 RFL (3d) 181, [1993] NSJ No 603 (Fam Ct)....456
McLeod v McLeod, [2002] BCJ No 1817, 2002 BCSC 1154 (SC)....221
McLeod v McLeod, 2013 BCCA 552....429, 465
McMahon v Hodgson, [2002] OJ No 555, 25 RFL (5th) 102 (SCJ)....228
McMahon v Sharaput, 2011 ONSC 3399....389
McMaster-Pereira v Pereira, 2021 ONCA 547....465, 499, 504–5
McNaughton v Murray, [2002] SJ No 223 (QB)....449
McNeil v McNeil, 2013 NBCA 65....134, 137, 166
McNulty v McNulty, [1998] MJ No 518, 133 Man R (2d) 297 (QB)....211, 588
McPhee v McPhee, [1999] BCJ No 337 (SC)....394
McPhee v Thomas, 2010 NSSC 367....378
McRann v McRann, [2005] SJ No 285, 263 Sask R 139 (QB)....555, 564
McVeetors v McVeetors (1995), 43 RFL (2d) 113 (Ont CA)....538
MD v PD, 2023 NBKB 202....35, 279, 280
MDA v MS, [2008] NBJ No 498, 2009 NBQB 4....10, 170, 179, 259, 416, 419, 508
MDG v GDG, 2013 ABCA 49....86
MDL v CR, [2004] SJ No 326, 5 RFL (6th) 361 (QB)....15, 300, 302, 310, 311
MDL v CR, 2020 SKCA 44....280, 283, 289, 295, 296, 315, 316, 317, 332, 333, 474
Meade v Meade, [2002] OJ No 3155, 31 RFL (5th) 88 (SCJ)....251
Meakin v Meakin, [1999] SJ No 649, 1999 SKQB 68....291
MEC v DEJ, [2009] BCJ No 766, 2009 BCSC 519....460
Meggerson v Geisbrect, [2006] SJ No 79, 2006 SKQB 45....156
Mehling v Mehling, 2008 MBCA 66, [2008] MJ No 172....340, 341
Mehlsen v Mehlsen, 2012 SKCA 55....143
Meier v Sirman, 2023 ABKB 704....279, 285, 342
Meister v Meister, [1998] SJ No 849 (QB)....47
MEKF v FF, 2015 BCSC 621....510
MEL v BGL, 2012 BCSC 1841....389, 466
MEL v PRH, 2018 NBQB 224....67, 68, 426
Melik v Ducholke, [2004] AJ No 1190, 2004 ABQB 757....451
Mellway v Mellway, [2004] MJ No 300, 4 RFL (6th) 70 (CA)....486
Melnychuk v Melnychuk (1995), 16 RFL (4th) 366, [1995] SJ No 444 (QB)....16
Melnyk v Glynn, 2012 BCSC 219....286
Meloche v Kales (1997), 35 OR (3d) 688, [1997] OJ No 6335 (Gen Div)....342
Melwood v Melwood, [1998] AJ No 1435, 240 AR 135 (Prov Ct)....22
Menegaldo v Menegaldo, 2012 ONSC 2915....58, 68–69, 76, 77, 112, 296, 300
Merasty v Merasty, [2000] SJ No 341, 7 RFL (5th) 373, 194 Sask R 91 (QB)....81, 217, 310
Mercer v Canada, [2007] TCJ No 13, 2007 TCC 43....474
Mercer v Rosenau, 2013 NLTD(F) 18, leave to appeal refused, 2013 NLCA 64....419
Mercier v Mercier, [2005] AJ No 494, 2005 ABCA 117....603
Merrifield v Merrifield, 2021 SKCA 85....121, 170, 171, 174, 183, 194, 233, 418, 422, 457, 458

Merritt v Merritt, [1999] OJ No 1732, 98 OTC 321 (SCJ) 12, 74, 135, 169, 188, 240
Merritt v Merritt, 2010 ONSC 4959 .... 166, 421
Mertler v Kardynal, [1997] SJ No 720, 35 RFL (4th) 72 (QB) 362
Messier v Baines, [1997] SJ No 627, 161 Sask R 132 (QB) 392, 395
Messier v Robillard, [1999] NJ No 368, 188 Nfld & PEIR 129 (SC) 476, 539
Meszen v Meszen, 2021 ONSC 224 286
Metzner v Metzner, [1997] BCJ No 2903 (SC), rev'd [1999] BCJ No 1607 (CA) 344
Metzner v Metzner, [2000] BCJ No 104 (CA) 663
Metzner v Metzner, [2000] BCJ No 1693, 9 RFL (5th) 162 (CA) 414, 419
Meuser v Meuser, [1998] BCJ No 1614, 40 RFL (4th) 295 (SC),
var'd [1998] BCJ No 2808, 43 RFL (4th) 140 (CA) 12, 119, 333, 562, 565, 567, 571, 666
Meyer v Content, 2014 ONSC 6001 .... 65, 589
Meyers v Meyers (1995), 12 RFL (4th) 170, [1995] BCJ No 636 (CA) 579, 605
MF v MW, 2011 NSFC 2 147
MG v AF, [2003] BCJ No 1196, 38 RFL (5th) 86 (SC) 32
MGH v KLDH, 2020 NBCA 46 .... 1, 4, 136, 221, 348, 350, 425, 425, 432
MH v AB, 2019 SKCA 135,
leave to appeal to SCC denied 2020 CanLII 36067 (SCC) 121, 129, 130, 215
MHG v DJG, [2006] BCJ No 275, 2006 BCSC 214 .... 124, 158, 288
MHR v JM, 2011 BCSC 1622 104
Miceli v Miceli, [1998] OJ No 5460, 83 OTC 297 (Gen Div) 314, 468, 489
Michalchuk v Michalchuk, 2013 ONSC 5978 .... 477, 582
Michalezski v Michalezski, [2002] AJ No 501 (QB) 483
Michaud v Kasali, 2021 ONSC 6847(Div Ct) 239, 240
Michaud v Michaud, [2003] AJ No 1601, 2003 ABQB 1055 .... 313, 314,
Michaud v Michaud, [2005] AJ No 1093, 2005 ABQB 630 506
Michaud v Michaud, [2005] AJ No 1095, 2005 ABQB 634 .... 112, 163, 494
Michel v Desjarlais, [1999] NWTJ No 13 (SC) 581
Michel v Graydon, 2020 SCC 24 .... 489, 490, 491,
492, 493, 494, 496, 497, 500, 501, 502, 505, 661
Michie v Michie, [1997] SJ No 668, 36 RFL (4th) 90 (QB) 46, 70
Mickey v Mickey, [1998] BCJ No 1805 (SC) 458
Middleton v MacPherson, [1997] AJ No 614, 29 RFL (4th) 334 (QB) 276, 278, 290,
298, 301, 313, 317, 318, 331, 345, 346, 358, 370, 371, 401, 404, 439
Midena v Collette, [2000] OJ No 4429 (Ct J) 29, 53, 60, 213
Mierins v Mierins (1973), 9 RFL 396, [1973] 1 OR 421 (Ont SC) 25
Miglin v Miglin, [2003] 1 SCR 303, 34 RFL (5th) 255 429
Migwans v Lovelace, 2011 NWTSC 54 .... 126, 361, 600
Milanovich v Joldzic-Milanovich, [1997] AJ No 754 (QB) 295
Mildren v Mildren, 2013 ONSC 1435 .... 223, 251
Milinkovic v Milinkovic (1991), 37 RFL (3d) 97 (Ont CA) 662
Millar v Millar, [1998] BCJ No 2489 (SC) 207
Millar v Millar, [2001] BCJ No 1803 (SC) 87
Millar v Millar, 2007 SKQB 25 497
Miller v Hayduk, [1998] SJ No 465 (QB) 332
Miller v Joynt, 2007 ABCA 214, 48 RFL (6th) 256, [2007] AJ No 959 .... 170, 173, 180, 184, 185
Miller v McClement, [1997] SJ No 761, 35 RFL (4th) 83 (QB) 74, 291
Miller v Miller (1988), 13 RFL (3d) 80, [1988] OJ No 556 (HCJ) 89
Miller v Miller (1992), 42 RFL (3d) 278 (Sask CA) 557
Miller v Miller (1994), 4 RFL (4th) 33 (NSCA) 457
Miller v Miller, [1997] BCJ No 1322 (SC) 293
Miller v Miller, [2000] AJ No 117 (QB) 581
Miller v Miller, 2019 NSSC 28 26

Miller v Miller, 2021 NSSC 152 361
Miller v Mitchell, 2013 ONSC 7021 25
Miller v Pchajek, [2005] SJ No 29, 13 RFL (6th) 234 (CA) 449
Miller v Ufoegbune, [2000] OJ No 3979, 11 RFL (5th) 347 (SCJ) 11, 375
Miller v Volk, [2009] OJ No 3297 (SCJ) 350, 351
Miller v White, 2018 PECA 11 .... 30, 428, 430, 439, 447, 453, 458
Miller v White, 2022 PESC 4 .... 118, 126, 156
Mills v Mills (1994), 130 NSR (2d) 140 (TD) 581
Mills v Mills, [1997] BCJ No 2258 (SC) 297
Mills v Mills, [1999] SJ No 177, 48 RFL (4th) 184 (QB) 71, 453
Millward v Millward, [2003] OJ No 1517, [2003] OTC 312 (SCJ) 90, 102, 103
Milner, Re (1975), 23 RFL 86, [1975] NSJ No 409 (TD) 609–10
Milton v Milton, 2008 NBCA 87 470
Min v Soe, [2008] OJ No 927 (SCJ) 379
Miner v Miner, [2004] OJ No 488, 2 RFL (6th) 105 (SCJ), aff'd [2004] OJ No 3303, 6 RFL (6th) 356 (CA) 118, 178, 189, 253
Mingo v Mingo, [1997] OJ No 4835 (Gen Div) 564, 568
Minish v Timmons, 2021 ONSC 7622 .... 47, 65, 75, 322
Minski v Minski, [2002] SJ No 773, 229 Sask R 87 (QB) 57, 216
Minthorn v Minthorn, [1992] OJ No 1233 (Gen Div) 214
Minuk v Minuk, [1999] MJ No 188, 137 Man R (2d) 115 (QB) 257
Mio v Mio, 2014 ONSC 2186 609
Mirzahi v Sana, 2022 ABQB 313 .... 38, 48, 49, 50, 60, 84
Misner v Misner, 2010 ONSC 2284 42
Mistry v Mistry, 2019 ONSC 193 323
Mitansky v Mitansky, [2000] AJ No 179, 258 AR 188 (QB) 203
Mitchell v Hill, [2000] MJ No 228, 7 RFL (5th) 393 (QB) 212
Mitchell v Mitchell (1993), 129 NSR (2d) 351 (TD) 448
Mitchell v Mitchell, [1998] SJ No 404, 41 RFL (4th) 181 (QB) 93, 96
Mitchell v Mitchell, [2002] OJ No 2504, 30 RFL (5th) 365 (SCJ) 153
Mitchell v Mitchell, 2011 ONSC 7015 26
Mitro v Mitro (1978), 1 RFL (2d) 382, [1978] OJ No 2 (CA) 599
MJB v WPB, [1999] MJ No 314, 139 Man R (2d) 288 (QB) 244, 483
MJB v WPB, [2004] MJ No 123, 2 RFL (6th) 35 (QB) 126, 243, 290, 445, 519
MJD v JPD, [2001] BCJ No 107 (SC) 537
MJM v ADEM, 2012 NBQB 71 .... 386, 396
MJM v CM, 2013 NBQB 228 305
MJW v BJW, [2006] AJ No 7, 2006 ABQB 19 184
MJW v MGW, 2012 BCSC 768 574
MK v RAS, [2004] BCJ No 2930, 2004 BCSC 1798 .... 155, 156, 235
MKR v JAR, 2015 NBCA 73 .... 157, 259, 426, 590
ML v BH, 2012 NBQB 233 218
ML v LAL, 2015 NBQB 150 .... 157, 158, 159, 250
ML v RSE, [2006] AJ No 642, 2006 ABCA 178 .... 12, 565
ML v SP, 2015 NBQB 249 .... 243, 350, 355, 357
MLB v WRP, 2019 NBCA 63 661
MLG v KGG, 2021 BCSC 682 .... 414, 419, 429
MLH v DWH, [2003] AJ No 992 (QB) 541
MLO v DGO, 2023 MBKB 171 407
MLP v MJM, 2012 BCCA 395 .... 562, 590
MLR v SLR, 2020 ABQB 444 .... 159, 161, 510
MLS v BJM, 2011 SKQB 163 382
MM v AM, 2008 NBQB 305 .... 163, 349

MM v MS, 2021 NBQB 183 ... 199
MMA v SAT, 2016 NBQB 109 ... 291
MMG v KJT, 2006 SKQB 41 ... 36
MMK v PRM, [2000] OJ No 2361 (SCJ) ... 538
MML v PMF, [2005] SJ No 514, 268 Sask R 159 (QB) ... 86, 99
MN v CGF, 2019 BCSC 1406 ... 374, 392
MN v NP, [1999] QJ No 5524 (CS) ... 24
Moazzen-Ahmadi v Ahmadi-Far, 2019 BCSC 1772, aff'd 2021 BCCA 126 ... 587, 588–89
Moberg v Peterson (2001), 25 RFL (5th) 133, [2001] OJ No 4871 (SCJ) ... 654
Mobin v Stephens, 2013 ONCJ 53 ... 156
Moen v Ropchan, 2021 ABQB 777 ... 498, 499
Moffatt v Stewart (1994), 5 RFL (4th) 142 (Ont Prov Ct) ... 582
Moge v Moge, [1992] 3 SCR 813, 43 RFL (3d) 345 ... 15, 304, 307, 411
Mohamed v Martone, 2019 BCSC 38 ... 65
Mohammed v Murtaza, 2010 BCSC 177 ... 28
Mohamud v Abdullahi, 2023 ABKB 371 ... 198
Mohr v Baxter, [1999] OJ No 1541 (Prov Div) ... 23, 110
Mol v Mol, [1997] OJ No 4060, 40 OTC 1 (Gen Div) ... 344
Molloy v Molloy, [2001] YJ No 142, 23 RFL (5th) 307, 2001 YKSC 548 ... 52, 81
Molnar v Bruton, 2013 SKQB 301 ... 88, 204
Molnar v Molnar (1991), 35 RFL (3d) 424 (Sask QB) ... 570
Monaghan v Monaghan, [2002] OJ No 4168, 14 RFL (3d) 308 (SCJ) ... 56
Monahan-Joudrey v Joudrey, 2012 ONSC 5984 ... 193, 222, 335
Mondoux v Mondoux (1994), 152 NBR (2d) 259, [1994] NBJ No 375 (QB) ... 52
Monette v Jordan, [1997] NSJ No 337, 163 NSR (2d) 70 (TD) ... 220, 253, 649
Mongrain v Mongrain (1986), 1 RFL (3d) 330, [1986] OJ No 2511 (HCJ) ... 22, 477
Monilaws v Monilaws, 2022 ABKB 652 ... 504
Moniz v Deschamps, 2010 ONSC 598 ... 349
Monkhouse v Monkhouse (1987), 10 RFL (3d) 445, [1987] SJ No 686 (QB) ... 456
Monkman v Beaulieu, [2003] MJ No 24, 33 RFL (5th) 169 (CA) ... 94
Monkman v Monkman, 2013 SKQB 80 ... 125
Monney v Monney, [1999] MJ No 17, 44 RFL (4th) 264 (QB) ... 434
Montalbetti v Montalbetti, [2000] BCJ No 1834 (CA) ... 558
Montalto v Montalto, 2011 ABQB 574 ... 35, 38, 51, 63, 64, 77
Montgomery v Jones, 2015 ONSC 4540 ... 262
Montgomery v Montgomery, [2000] NSJ No 1, 3 RFL (5th) 126, 2000 NSCA 2 ... 196, 209, 622
Moody v Holden, 2015 NLTD(F) 45 ... 199, 348
Moore v Fernandes, [2001] OJ No 5192 (SCJ) ... 447
Moore-Orlowski v Johnston, [2006] SJ No 389, 2006 SKQB 279 ... 114
Moores v McLellan, 2018 CarswellNB 48 ... 392
Moors v Moors, 2013 ABQB 740 ... 414, 420
Morden v Kelly, 2019 ONSC 4620 ... 40, 42
More v Shurygalo, 2010 SKQB 203 ... 134, 162, 165, 180, 224, 227
Moreau v Fliesen, [2008] BCJ No 1925, 2008 BCSC 1358 ... 349
Moreau v Moreau, [2004] AJ No 1296, 2004 ABQB 660 ... 260
Moreton v Inthavixay, 2020 ONSC 4881 ... 156, 194, 348, 354
Morgan v Morgan, [2000] BCJ No 431, 2000 BCSC 371 ... 216, 237
Morgan v Morgan, [2006] BCJ No 1795, 30 RFL (6th) 413, 2006 BCSC 1197 ... 27, 322
Morgan v Morgan, [2006] NJ No 9, 22 RFL (6th) 419 (SC) ... 311
Morice v Morice (1972), 8 RFL 283, [1972] SJ No 336 (CA) ... 629
Morin v Matheson, 2018 SKCA 9 ... 520
Morissette v Ball, [2000] OJ No 73 (SCJ), var'd [2000] OJ No 4307 (CA) ... 57, 58
Morley v Morley, [1999] SJ No 31, 44 RFL (4th) 442 (QB) ... 184, 290, 316

Morrison v Morrison, [2001] YJ No 521 (SC) 437, 438, 443
Morrison v Morrison, [2005] AJ No 149, 2005 ABCA 72 622
Morrissey v Morrissey, 2015 PECA 16 .... 122, 157, 158, 159, 193, 194, 339
Morton v May, [2004] NBJ No 254, 3 RFL (6th) 95 (QB) 90
Mortson v Kminkova, 2021 ABQB 476 .... 214, 492, 493, 494
Morwald-Benevides v Benevides, 2015 ONSC 7290 24
Morwald-Benevides v Benevides, 2019 ONCA 1023 636
Mosey v Mosey, [1956] P 26 469
Mosher v Martin, [1998] NJ No 180, 166 Nfld & PEIR 97 (SC) 342
Mosher v Mosher, [1999] NSJ No 202, 47 RFL (4th) 445 (SC) 473, 565
Mosher v Turner (1990), 26 RFL (3d) 230 (NSTD) 536
Moshuk v Moshuk, 2010 ABQB 540 .... 261, 521
Moss v Moss, [1997] NJ No 299, 159 Nfld & PEIR 1 (SC) 74, 182, 291, 312, 313, 318, 325
Motuzas v Yarnell, [1997] MJ No 520, 37 RFL (4th) 305 (QB) 86
Motyka v Motyka, [2001] BCJ No 52, 2001 BCCA 18 .... 212, 219, 273, 507
Moulson v Graves, [2002] OJ No 2582 (SCJ) 126, 151
Moutal v Moutal, [1997] BCJ No 2463 (SC) 531
Moynihan v Nakano, 2022 BCSC 2186 86
MPM v ACM, 2022 BCSC 122 .... 468, 505
MPT v RWT, 2008 YKSC 94 359
MR v JR, 2018 NBCA 12 .... 152, 273, 279, 283, 510, 552, 611, 612
MR v SRR, [2000] BCJ No 1954 (SC) 80
Mraovic v Mraovic, [2003] MJ No 457, 50 RFL (5th) 364 (QB) 94
Ms M v Mr B, [2000] AJ No 1497 (QB) 536
MS v CS, 2009 NBCA 66 .... 86, 100
MS v DMA, 2011 NBQB 79 75
MS v EJS, 2017 BCSC 564 .... 151, 215
MS v JC, 2010 PESC 50 .... 370, 371, 391, 393
MS v KS, 2019 BCSC 1458 510
MSB v LMB, 2012 BCPC 520 204
MSD obo NC v AL, 2022 NBQB 21 .... 12, 279, 291, 317, 326, 329, 330, 331, 378
MT v BC, [2001] BCJ No 2791 (Prov Ct) 440
MT v JS, 2020 BCSC 203, var'd 2023 BCCA 64 .... 62, 66, 123, 145, 146, 162, 163, 177183, 184, 222, 223
MTP v TP, 2019 NBQB 80 .... 157, 158, 159
Mudrinic v Mudrinic (1978), 6 RFL (2d) 326 (Ont HCJ) 448
Mudronja v Mudronja, 2020 ONCA 569 .... 124, 142, 299, 540
Muirhead v Muirhead (1995), 14 RFL (4th) 276, [1995] BCJ No 1088 (CA) 16
Muise v Fox, 2011 NSSC 258 349
Muise v Fox, 2013 NSSC 349 328
Mulders v Mulders, 2014 NWTSC 50 .... 49, 56, 67
Mullen v Mullen, [1998] NBJ No 338, 204 NBR (2d) 351 (QB) 243
Mullin v Mullin (1989), 24 RFL (3d) 1 (PEICA) 476
Mullin v Sherlock, 2018 ONCA 1063 611
Mullins v Mullins (1995), 12 RFL (4th) 461 (Nfld UFC) 449
Mullins v Mullins, 2016 ABQB 226 .... 122, 124, 126, 215, 243, 297, 300
Mumby v Mumby (1994), 7 RFL (4th) 410 (Alta QB) 605
Mundle v Mundle, [2001] NSJ No 111, 14 RFL (5th) 364 (SC) 300, 301
Munn v Munn, [1999] OJ No 738, 44 RFL (4th) 179 (CA) 142
Munro v Munro (1987), 50 Man R (2d) 24 (QB) 579
Munro v Munro, 2011 ABCA 279 627
Murchison v Fitzgerald (1995), 14 RFL (4th) 386 (PEITD) 582
Murdoch-Woods v Zywina, 2011 ONSC 705 148

Murnaghan v Lutz, 2014 NSSC 3 ... 560
Murphy v Bert, [2007] NSJ No 543, 2007 NSSC 376 ... 372, 562
Murphy v Hancock, 2011 NSSC 247 ... 587
Murphy v Howes, 2021 NSSC 354 ... 134, 166, 223, 229
Murphy v Ibrahim, 2022 NSCA 75 ... 648
Murphy v Laurence, [2002] OJ No 1368 (SCJ) ... 93
Murphy v Murphy, [1998] NJ No 304, 171 Nfld & PEIR 122 (SC) ... 296, 301
Murphy v Murphy, [1999] BCJ No 318 (SC) ... 340
Murphy v Murphy, [2000] BCJ No 1253, 8 RFL (5th) 338 (SC) ... 120
Murphy v Murphy, 2007 BCCA 500, [2007] BCJ No 2258 ... 557
Murphy v Murphy, 2012 ONSC 1627 ... 360, 361, 651
Murray v Murray (1981), 10 Sask R 151, [1981] SJ No 1303 (QB) ... 594
Murray v Murray (1991), 35 RFL (3d) 449, [1991] AJ No 721 (QB) ... 306
Murray v Murray, [1997] SJ No 175, 155 Sask R 127 (QB) ... 81
Murray v Murray, 2021 ABQB 539 ... 126, 145, 498, 560, 561, 584
Muslake v Muslake (1987), 6 RFL (3d) 280 (Ont UFC) ... 480
MV v DV, [2005] NBJ No 505, 2005 NBQB 412 ... 25, 26, 50, 51, 52, 113, 114, 321
MWDP v MAG, 2019 NBQB 62 ... 145, 163, 348
MWM v HLM, 2010 NBCA 86 ... 192
Myers v Myers, [2000] NSJ No 367, 189 NSR (2d) 214 (SC) ... 127, 215, 330
Myers v Myers, [2010] NJ No 329 (UFC) ... 291
Myers v Myers, 2013 ONSC 170 ... 216
Myke v Myke, [2000] OJ No 2056, [2000] OTC 397 (SCJ) ... 289, 292, 302
Myketiak v Myketiak, [2001] SJ No 85, 13 RFL (5th) 431 (CA) ... 229
Myles v Armstrong, 2011 NBQB 61 ... 122, 156
Mylrea v Benoit, [2003] OJ No 2921, 42 RFL (5th) 82 (SCJ) ... 152, 482

N v F, 2021 ONCA 688 ... 664
NA v CMW, [2003] OJ No 1780, 39 RFL (5th) 1 (SCJ) ... 93
Nadalin v Canada, 2012 TCC 48 ... 5
Nadeau v Mitchell, [1997] OJ No 2833, 36 OTC 34 (Gen Div) ... 321
Nadon v Stratton, 2011 ONSC 3248 ... 582
Nafar-Ross v Raahemi, 2018 ONSC 3054 ... 49, 58, 113
Nagy v Laverdiere, [2005] SJ No 163, 2005 SKCA 39 ... 622
Nagy v Tittemore, [1997] SJ No 810, 162 Sask R 54 (QB) ... 375
Naidoo v Naidoo, [2004] OJ No 1458, 2 RFL (6th) 362 (SCJ) ... 217
Nakazawa v Klassen, [2005] BCJ No 1847, 2005 BCSC 1196 ... 306, 309
Nand v Nand, 2011 ABQB 324 ... 466
Nanrhe v Nanrhe, [2005] AJ No 1332, 2005 ABQB 722 ... 635
Nash v Nash, [1975] 2 SCR 507, 16 RFL 295 ... 466, 662
Nash v Nash (1989), 77 Nfld & PEIR 22 (Nfld UFC) ... 580
Nataros v Nataros, [1998] BCJ No 1417, 40 RFL (4th) 308 (SC) ... 307, 317, 330, 407
Natywary v Natywary, [2003] OJ No 5628 (Div Ct) ... 205, 295
NB v KJB, [1999] BCJ No 1584 (SC) ... 562
NCL v AJL, [2001] NWTJ No 102 (SC) ... 386
Nderitu v Kamoji, 2017 ONSC 2617 ... 340, 343
NDS v JAS, 2020 BCSC 1034 ... 83, 204, 574, 576
Neale v Neale (1980), 18 RFL (2d) 211, [1980] OJ No 2009 (UFC) ... 609
Neaves v Neaves (1978), 6 RFL (2d) 209, [1978] NSJ No 25 (CA) ... 610
NEC v CJM, [2001] OJ No 1671 (SCJ) ... 601
Necemer v Necemer, [1999] BCJ No 3023, 4 RFL (5th) 409 (SC) ... 97
Neil v Neil, [2002] OJ No 3003, [2002] OTC 544 (SCJ) ... 37, 87
Neil v Neil, [2003] NJ No 146, 227 Nfld & PEIR 255 (SC) ... 355

Neilly v Neilly, 2019 ABCA 504 123
Nein v Nein (1991), 36 RFL (3d) 417 (Sask QB) 457
Nelson v Nelson, [1999] AJ No 242, 44 RFL (4th) 365 (QB) 104, 105, 264
Nelson v Nelson, [2005] NSJ No 18, 14 RFL (6th) 26 (SC) 52, 83
Nesbitt v Nesbitt, [2001] MJ No 291, 19 RFL (5th) 359 (CA) 9, 170, 184
Ness v Ness, [1999] BCJ No 262, 43 RFL (4th) 363 (CA) 344
Neufeld v Neufeld, [2001] BCJ No 1682, 2001 BCSC 1197 202
Neufeld v Neufeld, [2003] OJ No 5382, 180 OAC 197 (Div Ct) 322
Neves v Pinto, 2020 ONSC 5193 640
New Brunswick (Minister of Income Assistance) v Hodnett, [1995] NBJ No 323, 14 RFL (4th) 138 (QB) 11
Newman v Bogan, 2010 NWTSC 69 .... 112, 374, 378, 392
Newman v Newman, [1998] NJ No 269, 171 Nfld & PEIR 138 (UFC) 321
Newman v Thompson (1997), 30 RFL (4th) 143, [1997] MJ No 447 (CA) 55, 56, 57, 241, 590
Newman v Tibbetts, [2004] NBJ No 72, 272 NBR (2d) 337 (QB), rev'd [2005] NBJ No 135, 16 RFL (6th) 318 (CA) 46, 291, 317, 587, 636
Newnham v Newnham, [1993] OJ No 3193 (Gen Div) 570
Newson v Newson (1980), 18 BCLR 203 (CA) 660
Newson v Newson (1998), 115 BCAC 151 (CA) 449
Nguetsop v Nguetsop, 2014 MBQB 131 299
NH v JH, 2017 ONSC 6607 359
Nichol v Johnson, [2003] SJ No 736, 49 RFL (5th) 385 (QB) 134, 163, 228
Nicholauson v Nicholauson, 2019 SKQB 287 .... 102, 228
Nicholl v Nicholl, 2020 BCCA 173 .... 65, 429
Nicolson v Prekaski, [2004] SJ No 714, 2004 SKQB 479 445
Nielsen v Nielsen, [2000] BCJ No 879, 6 RFL (5th) 379 (CA) 573
Nielsen v Nielsen, 2006 BCCA 436, [2006] BCJ No 2629 15
Nielsen v Nielsen, 2007 BCCA 604, [2007] BCJ No 2599 237
Ninham v Ninham, [1997] OJ No 2667, 29 RFL (4th) 41 (Gen Div) 193, 213
Nishnik v Smith, [1997] SJ No 812, 162 Sask R 200 (QB) 374, 375, 405
Nitchie v Nitchie, [1999] BCJ No 2865 (SC) 536
Nitchie v Nitchie, 2014 BCSC 468 .... 49, 54
Nitkin v Nitkin, [2006] OJ No 2769 (SCJ) 49, 51, 330
Nixon v Nixon, 2014 SKQB 264 .... 302, 330, 366
Njegovan v Melnuk, [2000] MJ No 409 (QB) 417, 507
NK v RE, 2021 NSSC 13 200
Nkwazi v Nkwazi, [1998] SJ No 571, 171 Sask R 120 (QB) 217, 322
Nkwazi v Nkwazi, 2014 SKCA 61 .... 39, 62
NMM v NSM, [2004] BCJ No 642, 2004 BCSC 346 .... 285, 316, 454
NMPH v LLH, [2006] BCJ No 67, 2006 BCSC 62 .... 345, 383
NNN v DEB, 2023 BCSC 1538 511
Noble v Boone, 2010 NLTD 65 .... 408, 539
Noel v Earle (1986), 3 RFL (3d) 387 (Ont Dist Ct) 524
Noel v Noel, [2001] MJ No 441 (CA) 396
Noiles v Noiles, [2007] NBJ No 393, 2007 NBQB 350 314
Nolan v Nolan, [2005] BCJ No 2864, 2005 BCSC 1807 44
Nolte v Nolte, [2001] SJ No 362, 208 Sask R 88 (QB) 43, 413
Nordeen v Nordeen, 2013 BCCA 178 35
Norlander v Norlander (1989), 21 RFL (3d) 317, [1989] SJ No 361 (QB) 408
Nova Scotia (Community Services) v EL, 2020 NSSC 193 457
Nova Scotia (Director of Maintenance Enforcement) v Stuckless, [2003] NSJ No 296 (SC) 532
Novic v Novic, [1983] 1 SCR 700, 36 RFL (2d) 337 .... 657, 658
NP v IV, 2013 BCSC 1323 .... 34, 99, 574

NP v MCP, 2012 BCSC 1843 .... 124, 358
NRG v GRG, 2017 BCSC 478 560
NS v RC, 2009 BCSC 1676 301
NSC v DC, 2011 NBQB 229 .... 280, 298, 556
NTG v JAMG, 2022 SKKB 264 .... 528, 586
Nugent v Nugent, [2004] AJ No 1161, 2004 ABQB 741 546
Nugent v Nugent, 2011 NLTD(F) 4 .... 30, 237
Nunn v McLeod, [1999] SJ No 168 (QB) 46, 52
NW v MV, 2023 NBKB 160 .... 349, 357
NW v RP, 2018 ABQB 392 578
Nyereyogona v Schofield, 2021 ABQB 662 492
Nygren v Johnson, 2011 SKQB 12 322
Nykiforuk v Richmond, 2007 SKQB 433 .... 177, 180
Nykoliation v Nykoliation (1989), 60 Man R (2d) 307 (QB) 575
Nykolyshyn v Dalton, 2022 ABKB 860 326
Nykvist v Nykvist, [2004] MJ No 411, 10 RFL (6th) 107 (CA) 256
NZ v OZ, 2015 BCSC 2130 .... 315, 316, 317, 318

O v C, [2004] NJ No 19, 2004 NLSCTD 7 .... 603, 622
O'Brien v O'Brien, [1999] NWTJ No 56 (SC) 127, 128, 312
O'Brien v O'Brien, 2011 NBQB 179 .... 124, 143
O'Connell v McIndoe, [2000] BCJ No 1311, 8 RFL (5th) 326 (SC) 50
O'Connor v Merlo, 2020 ONSC 2531 201
O'Connor v O'Connor, [1999] OJ No 362, 75 OTC 296 (Gen Div) 98, 396, 545
O'Connor v O'Connor, 2022 ONSC 3482 324
O'Dacre v Cross, 2019 ONSC 2265 632
O'Dell v Kraugh, [1999] SJ No 51, [1999] 2 CTC 289 (QB) 127
O'Donnell v Morgan, [2001] NBJ No 66 (QB) 581
O'Donnell v O'Donnell, 2011 NBQB 56 .... 51, 112
O'Hara v O'Hara, [1995] NBJ No 291, 15 RFL (4th) 408 (QB) 102
O'Hara v O'Hara (1997), 33 RFL (4th) 37, [1997] SJ No 482 (QB) 371, 604
O'Kane v Lillqvist-O'Kane, 2022 ABKB 661 135
O'Kane v O'Kane, 2013 ONSC 1617 43
O'Keefe v Clarke, [1994] NJ No 444, 7 RFL (4th) 398, 122 Nfld & PEIR 178 (UFC) 56
O'Neill v O'Neill (2007), 39 RFL (6th) 72, [2007] OJ No 1706 (SCJ) 184, 469
O'Regan v O'Regan (2001), 194 NSR (2d) 257, [2001] NSJ No 219 (SC) 126
O'Riordon v O'Riordon (1987), 11 RFL (3d) 52 (BCCA) 466
O'Sanlou v O'Sanlou, [1998] BCJ No 684 (SC) 439
OAAF v AAF, [2001] OJ No 2032 (Ct J) 557
Oakley v Oakley (1985), 48 RFL (2d) 307 (BCCA) 565
Oates v Oates, [2004] OJ No 2984, [2004] OTC 626 (SCJ) 57, 324
Ochitwa v Canada, 2014 TCC 263 365
Oczkowski v New, 2011 ONSC 3932 .... 26, 27
Odermatt v Odermatt, [1998] BCJ No 55 (SC) 307, 321
Offet v Offet (1993), 1 RFL (4th) 203, [1993] AJ No 1029 (QB) 607
Ogonowski v Ogonowska, [2001] OJ No 335 (SCJ) 488
Ohayon v Ohayon, [1969] OJ No 381 (HCJ) 451
Ohlmann v Ohlmann, [2005] AJ No 140, 14 RFL (6th) 64 (QB) 125, 312
Olaitan v MacDougall, 2014 PECA 5 .... 279, 280, 291, 292, 300, 305, 405
Olaveson v Olaveson (2007), 40 RFL (6th) 327, [2007] OJ No 2431 (SCJ) 297, 329, 330
Olchowecki v Olchowecki, [2005] SJ No 192, 2005 SKQB 144 .... 121–22, 189
Oldham v King (1987), 11 RFL (3d) 75 (Man QB) 524, 562
Oleksiewicz v Oleksiewicz, 2017 BCSC 228 .... 38, 51, 113

Olesen v Olesen, [1999] AJ No 494 (QB) ... 509
Oliver v Oliver, [1998] AJ No 340 (QB) ... 412
Ollinger v Ollinger, [1999] SJ No 218 (QB) ... 451
Ollinger v Ollinger, 2006 SKQB 433, [2006] SJ No 658 ... 97, 114
Ollivier v Zarins, [2003] BCJ No 298, 2003 BCSC 191 ... 212, 209, 297
Olsen v Olsen, [1997] SJ No 476, 159 Sask R 67 (QB) ... 475
Olson v Lazich (1971), 4 RFL 86, [1971] SJ No 22 (QB) ... 606
Olson v Olson, [2003] AJ No 230, 320 AR 379, 36 RFL (5th) 196 (CA) ... 47, 49
Olszewski v Willick, 2009 SKCA 133 ... 49
Olszewski v Willick, 2010 SKQB 289 ... 116, 421
OM v AK, [2000] QJ No 3224, 9 RFL (5th) 111 (CS) ... 6, 15, 424, 482
Omah-Maharajh v Howard, [1998] AJ No 173, 215 AR 159 (QB) ... 146, 148, 229, 310, 331, 332, 385, 403, 413, 437, 481
Omer v Omer, [1997] SJ No 486 (QB) ... 604
Ontario (Director of Support & Custody Enforcement) v Glover (1987), 11 RFL (3d) 58 (Ont Fam Ct) ... 524
Ontario (Director of Support & Custody Enforcement) v McIntyre (1987), 11 RFL (3d) 89 (Ont Fam Ct) ... 524
Ontario (Director of Support & Custody Enforcement) v Sarsfield (1988), 15 RFL (3d) 192 (Ont Fam Ct) ... 514
Ontario (Director of Support & Custody Enforcement) v Thomas (1990), 27 RFL (3d) 135 (Ont Dist Ct) ... 519
Ontario (Director, Family Responsibility Office) v Hay, [2002] OJ No 1335 (Ct J) ... 518
Ontario (Director, Family Responsibility Office) v Pennell, [2002] OJ No 1816 (Ct J) ... 527, 532
Ontario (Director, Family Responsibility Office) v Ramsay, 2005 ONCJ 324 ... 654
Ontario (Director, Family Support Plan) v Freyseng (1994), 4 RFL (4th) 454 (Ont Prov Div) ... 519
Ord v Ord, 2019 ONSC 1563 ... 651
Ormerod v Ormerod (1990), 27 RFL (3d) 225 (Ont UFC) ... 466
Orring v Orring, [2006] BCJ No 1520, 2006 BCSC 990 ... 315
Orser v Grant, [2000] OJ No 1429 (SCJ) ... 215, 217
Orser v Grant, [2000] OJ No 5493 (SCJ) ... 264, 270
Orth v Orth, [1999] SJ No 886, 176 Sask R 192 (QB) ... 356
Ortynski v Ortynski, 2014 BCSC 73 ... 348, 351
Osborne v Osborne (1973), 14 RFL 61 (Sask QB), var'd (1974), 23 RFL 358 (Sask CA) ... 16
Oshanek v Oshanek, [1999] AJ No 680 (QB) ... 470
Osiowy v Osiowy, [1998] SJ No 573 (QB) ... 310
Osman v ElKadi, 2015 ONSC 1124 ... 50, 152
Osmar v Osmar, [2000] OJ No 2060 (SCJ) ... 222, 378, 443, 509
Ostafie v Ostafie, [2001] SJ No 149, 15 RFL (5th) 419 (QB) ... 375
Ostapchuk v Ostapchuk, [2003] OJ No 1733, 38 RFL (5th) 172 (CA) ... 143, 144
Osterkampf v Osterkampf (1989), 22 RFL (3d) 153 (Alta QB) ... 570
Osterlund-Lenahan v Lenahan, 2014 ONSC 7074 ... 21, 56
Ostlund v Ostlund, [2000] BCJ No 1158 (SC), var'd [2003] BCJ No 661 (CA) ... 163, 319
Ostrovskaia v Ostrovsky, [2001] OJ No 640, 14 RFL (5th) 405 (SCJ) ... 221
Oswald v Oswald, [2001] MJ No 73, 17 RFL (5th) 127 (QB) ... 48, 62, 147, 158, 588
Ottesen v Ottesen, 2022 BCSC 405 ... 576
Ottley v Ottley, [1998] OJ No 1734 (Gen Div) ... 569
Otto v Between, [1996] OJ No 4786 (Gen Div) ... 25, 439
Ouellette v Ouellette, 2012 BCCA 145 ... 163, 191
Ouellette v Uddin, 2018 ONSC 4520 ... 230, 485
Owen v Owen, 2011 BCSC 1284 ... 26
Owen v Owen, 2015 ONSC 4002 ... 152
Oxby v Oxby (1987), 11 RFL (3d) 369 (Sask QB) ... 534

P v H, 2022 CarswellOnt 3203 (SCJ)....554
P(L) v J(W) (1989), 99 NBR (2d) 386, [1989] NBJ No 619 (QB)....600
PA v FA, [1997] BCJ No 1566 (SC)....253
Pace v Barry, 2019 ONSC 1739....384, 392
Paddon v Paddon, [2006] NBJ No 1, 2006 NBQB 3....340
Paech v Paech (2004), 12 RFL (6th) 127, [2004] OJ No 5067 (SCJ)....642
Paftali v Paftali, 2020 ONSC 5325....596
Pagani v Pagani, [1999] BCJ No 3051 (SC)....562
PAH v RBH, [2001] OJ No 5748 (SCJ)....93
Pakka v Nygard, [2001] OJ No 2934 (SCJ)....530
Pakka v Nygard, [2002] OJ No 3858, 61 OR (3d) 328 (SCJ)....169, 277, 418, 451, 652
Pakozdi v Pakozdi, 2016 BCSC 2428....34
Palansky v Palansky (1989), 60 Man R (2d) 141, [1989] MJ No 384 (QB)....602
Pallot v Pallot, 2010 BCSC 1146....163, 179, 185, 233
Palmer v Palmer, [1998] BCJ No 2092 (SC)....75, 76
Pamma v Pamma, [1999] BCJ No 2252 (SC)....218
Pangborn v Elash, [1999] SJ No 786 (QB)....94
Paniccia v Butcher, [2003] OJ No 1880 (SCJ)....205
Paradon v Ratzlaff, 2019 SKQB 86....384, 385
Parekh v Parekh, 2022 ONSC 4700....611
Parent v Pelletier, [1999] NBJ No 391 (CA)....567
Parente v Parente, 2023 ONSC 907....650, 651
Parham v Jiang, 2013 ONSC 6003....218
Park v Park, [1999] OJ No 5078....15, 337
Park v Thompson, [2005] OJ No 1695, 2005 CanLII 14132 (CA)....65, 72, 285, 305, 329
Park v Walsh, [2003] NJ No 63, 223 Nfld & PEIR 116 (SC)....368
Parker v Parker, [2003] NSJ No 139, 214 NSR (2d) 57 (SC)....391
Parker v Tinline, 2012 SKQB 313....23
Parker v Wagner, [2002] OJ No 1581 (SCJ)....92
Parkes v Mones, [2001] SJ No 777, 23 RFL (5th) 320 (QB)....202
Parkinson v Parkinson, [1973] 3 OR 293, 11 RFL 128, [1973] OJ No 2018 (CA)....552
Parkinson v Parkinson (1974), 16 RFL 135 (Ont HCJ)....459
Parks v Parks, [2000] OJ No 2863 (SCJ)....219
Parmar v Canada, [2007] TCJ No 465, 2007 TCC 660....4
Parniak v Parniak, [1999] MJ No 37 (QB)....467
Parr v Lavallee (1992), 42 RFL (3d) 58, [1992] OJ No 1377 (Gen Div)....555
Parsalidis v Parsalidis, 2012 ONSC 2963....466
Parsan v Parsan, [1997] OJ No 3918 (Gen Div)....568
Parsons v Clarke, [2002] NJ No 162 (SC)....213, 231
Parsons v Parsons (1994), 9 RFL (4th) 437, [1994] AJ No 852 (QB)....79
Parsons v Parsons (1999), 181 Nfld & PEIR 337, [1999] NJ No 291 (CA)....622
Paschke v Paschke (1994), 8 RFL (4th) 341, [1994] AJ No 665 (QB)....605
Pascual v Pascual, 2018 ONSC 5412....539
Pasquali v Cox, 2017 ONSC 7654....258
Passarello v Passarello, [1998] OJ No 2792, 64 OTC 118 (Gen Div)....38, 596
Pastway v Pastway, [1999] OJ No 2525, 49 RFL (4th) 375 (SCJ)....253, 254
Pastway v Pastway, [2000] OJ No 3062, 2 CPC (5th) 18 (SCJ)....254, 270
Patel v Whiting, 2020 SKCA 49....659
Paternity of Tukker MO (Re), 544 NW2d 417 (1996)....423
Paterson v Paterson (1995), 16 RFL (4th) 439 (Ont Prov Div)....573
Paton (Bushko) v Bushko, [1999] SJ No 49 (QB)....301
Patrick v Patrick, [1999] BCJ No 1245 (SC)....209, 217, 337
Paul v Dennis, 2012 NSSC 366....216, 275

Paul v Paul, [2000] SJ No 780, 2000 SKQB 575 .... 532, 613
Paul, Re (1980), 28 OR (2d) 78 (HCJ) 614
Pauli v Pauli, [2001] OJ No 150 (SCJ) 207
Pawliuk v Pawliuk, [1999] SJ No 268, 181 Sask R 212 (QB) 545
Pawlus v Pawlus, [2004] OJ No 5706 (SCJ) 241, 451
Payne v Payne (1982), 31 RFL (2d) 211, [1982] OJ No 1071 (UFC) 618
Paynter v Reynolds (1997), 34 RFL (4th) 272, [1997] PEIJ No 114 (CA) 573
Paynter v Sackville, 2004 SKQB 258, [2004] SJ No 422, 250 Sask R 313 (QB) 510, 587
PC v SV, 2022 ABKB 644 81
PCJR v DCR, [2003] BCJ No 792, 38 RFL (5th) 408 (CA) 222, 510
PD v CD, 2011 NBQB 239 257
PDR v JER, [2005] NBJ No 51, 17 RFL (6th) 151 (QB) 148
Peach v Peach, [2003] NSJ No 41, 212 NSR (2d) 96 (Fam Ct) 212, 559
Peacock v Peacock, [1999] NBJ No 313, 215 NBR (2d) 39 (QB) 87, 98
Pearce v Pearce, [1999] BCJ No 2278, 1 RFL (5th) 402 (SC) 55, 383, 488
Pearce, Re (1974), 16 RFL 376, [1974] BCJ No 259 (SC) 609
Pearse v Pearse, 2010 BCSC 117 .... 46, 299
Pearson v Pearson (1990), 25 RFL (3d) 79 (NBQB) 551
Pearson v Pearson (1995), 16 RFL (4th) 75 (Man QB) 477, 540
Pearson v Pearson, [2002] SJ No 10, 214 Sask R 181 (QB) 343
Pearson v Pearson, [2003] SCCA No 75 343
Pearson v Pearson, [2004] SJ No 539, 2004 SKQB 348 122
Peck v Peck, [1998] NSJ No 286 (TD) 375
Pederson v Pederson, [2001] BCJ No 2252 (SC) 427, 438
Peerenboom v Peerenboom, 2018 ONSC 5118 (Div Ct) 650
Peerenboom v Peerenboom, 2018 ONSC 5796 611
PEK v BWK, [2003] AJ No 1706, 348 AR 77, 2004 ABCA 135 636
Pela v Pela, [1998] SJ No 804, 174 Sask R 249 (QB) 212, 381
Pele-Tolaini v Tolaini, 2010 ABCA 223 251
Pelech v Pelech, [1987] 1 SCR 801, 7 RFL (3d) 225 666
Pellegrini v Tkach, 2023 SKCA 85 .... 196, 197, 199
Pelletier v Kakakaway, [2002] SJ No 448, 2002 SKCA 94 .... 126, 391, 403
Pelletier v Lukasik, [1999] OJ No 2649 (SCJ) 253
Pelletier v Richard, 2021 NBQB 77 .... 38, 41, 497, 510
Pelley v Pelley (1995), 14 RFL (4th) 1 (BCCA) 557, 561
Pellissey v Skeard, [2003] NWTJ No 5 (SC) 582, 583
Peltz v Peltz, [2000] OJ No 3778, [2000] OTC 732 (SCJ) 144
Penn v Penn, 2014 ONSC 6321 .... 56, 57, 58
Penner v Danbrook (1992), 39 RFL (3d) 286 (Sask CA), leave to appeal to SCC refused (1993), 44 RFL (3d) 85n (SCC) 36
Penner v Penner, [1998] MJ No 353 (QB) 190, 217, 342, 363
Penner v Penner, [1999] MJ No 88, 44 RFL (4th) 294 (QB) 344, 357
Penney v Boland, [1999] NJ No 71, 175 Nfld & PEIR 1 (UFC) 13, 62, 230, 240, 481
Penney v Penney, [2001] NJ No 85, 16 RFL (5th) 388 (SC) 235
Pentland v Pentland, [1998] OJ No 2678, 71 OTC 233 (Gen Div) 230
Pepin v Jung, [1997] OJ No 4604, 65 OTC 351 (Gen Div) 285, 333
Pepin v Jung, [2003] OJ No 1779, 39 RFL (5th) 383 (SCJ) 51, 113
PER v CAR, 2018 BCSC 339 .... 38, 40, 41
Perdue v Perdue, 2014 NBQB 262 .... 129, 132
Peregrym v Peregrym, 2011 ABQB 558 389
Pereverzoff v Pereverzoff, 2017 BCSC 687 .... 326, 483, 505
Perez v Chiris, 2021 ONSC 101 .... 76, 491, 494
Perfanick v Panciera, [2001] MJ No 528, 22 RFL (5th) 178 (CA) 661

Perlman v Canada, 2010 TCC 658 4
Perovic v Nagtzaam, [2001] OJ No 3462, 21 RFL (5th) 387 (Ct J) 29, 83, 93, 102
Perrier v Daigle, 2012 NSSC 54 152
Perrin v Canada, 2010 TCC 331 365
Perron v Hlushko, 2015 ABQB 595 .... 129, 241, 355, 561
Perry v Perry, [1997] BCJ No 1567 (SC) 211
Peter v Peter, [1999] SJ No 376 (QB) 574
Peters v Atchooay, 2022 ABCA 347 .... 193, 197–98, 205, 206, 209, 215, 216, 235, 347, 348, 351, 353, 583, 661
Peters v Evenson, [2003] BCJ No 948 (SC) 155
Peters v Graham, [2001] NSJ No 452, 210 DLR (4th) 753 (SC) 85
Peters v Keef, 2019 ABQB 85 .... 622, 623
Peters v Keef, 2019 ABQB 398 623
Peters v Peters, [1999] SJ No 392 (QB) 202, 334
Peters v Peters, [2002] NSJ No 413 (SC) 69, 407, 409
Peterson c Brine, 2023 CanLII 47814 (NBCA) 666
Peterson v Farrer (2010), 360 NBR (2d) 341, [2010] NBJ No 189 (QB) 49
Peterson v Horan (2006), 29 RFL (6th) 241, [2006] SJ No 333, 2006 SKCA 61 .... 151, 215, 243, 244, 430, 433, 445
Peterson v Peterson, [2001] AJ No 1044, 298 AR 195 (QB) 187
Peterson v Peterson, 2011 SKQB 365 .... 51, 475, 556
Peterson v Peterson, 2019 SKCA 76 159
Petipas v Petipas, [2000] NSJ No 133 (SC) 301
Petrocco v Von Michalofski, [1998] OJ No 200, 36 RFL (4th) 278 (Gen Div) 413
Petroczi v Petroczi, 2011 BCSC 1223 .... 538, 539
Petterson v Petterson, 2010 SKQB 418 .... 226, 341
Petula v Petula, [1998] BCJ No 2066 (SC) 607
PG v DDG, 2017 BCSC 724 .... 27, 65
PGB v JLT, [2000] AJ No 1408, 282 AR 186 (QB) 36
Phelan v Verni, 2013 ONSC 2893 .... 94, 374
PHH v NRY, 2015 BCSC 320 .... 27, 117
Philibert v Webber, 2011 BCSC 623 .... 378, 382
Phillipchuk v Phillipchuk, [1999] AJ No 438 (QB) 71
Phillips v Bourque, [2000] NBJ No 13, 223 NBR (2d) 242 (QB) 392
Phillips v Delaney, [2001] PEIJ No 86, 21 RFL (5th) 171 (SC) 165
Phillips v Phillips (1985), 43 RFL (2d) 462 (BCCA) 458
Phillips v Phillips (1995), 14 RFL (4th) 113, [1995] AJ No 668 (CA) 211, 607
Phillips v Phillips, [1997] BCJ No 2376, 32 RFL (4th) 218 (SC) 142
Phillips v Phillips, [2002] OJ No 717, 25 RFL (5th) 367 (SCJ) 297
Phillips v Phillips, [2005] SJ No 350, 266 Sask R 154 (QB) 44
Phillips v Saunders, 2020 BCCA 265 162–63
Phiroz v Mottiar (1995), 16 RFL (4th) 353 (Ont Prov Div) 543
Picard v Picard (2001), 18 RFL (5th) 352, [2001] OJ No 2299 (SCJ) 634
Picco v Picco, [2000] NJ No 64, 187 Nfld & PEIR 88 (UFC) 158, 425, 437, 510
Picken v Picken (1991), 37 RFL (3d) 250, [1991] MJ No 638 (QB) 381
Pidgeon v Hickman, [2000] NJ No 44 (SC) 581
Pietrus v Preston, [1999] SJ No 34, 176 Sask R 316 (QB) 213
Pigeon v Pigeon, [2000] AJ No 1515 (QB) 543
Piller v Piller, [1998] NJ No 179, 165 Nfld & PEIR 314 (SC) 332
Pilotte v Pilotte, 2013 NSSC 24 .... 320, 332
Pink v Pink (1991), 31 RFL (3d) 233, [1991] MJ No 86 (CA) 46, 508
Pintea v Johns, 2017 SCC 23 .... 529, 636
Pinter v Pinter, 2016 ABCA 58 593

Piper v Piper (1988), 65 OR (2d) 196, [1988] OJ No 683 (HCJ)....621
Piper v Piper, 2010 BCSC 1718....156, 193
Pircio v Sarno, [2003] BCJ No 977, 2003 BCSC 411....46
Pitcher v Pitcher, [2002] NJ No 358 (UFC)....126, 296, 308, 329, 405
Pitcher v Pitcher, [2005] NJ No 352, 21 RFL (6th) 399 (SC)....587
Pitcher v Pitcher, 2013 NLTD(F) 11....39, 42, 80
Pitt v Mouland, 2015 NWTSC 4....87, 94
Pitt v Pitt, [1997] BCJ No 1528 (SC)....134, 240, 473
Pitt v Tee, 2016 NWTSC 40....152, 153
Pitura v Pitura, [1999] NWTJ No 70 (SC)....337
Piwek v Jagiello, 2011 ABCA 303....286, 293, 297
Pizzaro v Kretschmann, 2019 ONSC 3143....651
PJD v WKW, 2019 BCSC 1188....295
PJM v RMS, 2021 BCCA 260....498, 584
PKC v JRR, 2014 BCSC 932....163
PKM v JDM, 2019 BCSC 625....418
Plante v Plante, [1998] AJ No 1206 (QB)....336
PLC v CG, 2020 ABQB 211....8
Plese v Herjavec, 2018 ONSC 7749....124
Plester v Plester, [1997] BCJ No 1862 (SC)....276
Plester v Plester, [1998] BCJ No 2438, 56 BCLR (3d) 352 (SC)....414, 415
Plett v Murphy (2003), 38 RFL (5th) 387, [2003] OJ No 1673 (SCJ)....601
Plett v Plett, [2002] BCJ No 2078 (SC)....454
Plett v Plett, 2009 BCSC 227, [2009] BCJ No 326....124, 134
Plett v Plett, 2010 BCSC 758....296
Plimmer v Burke, 2019 ONSC 1915....538
Ploughman v Ploughman (1989), 78 Nfld & PEIR 170, [1989] NJ No 267 (TD)....244
Plourde v Morin, [2005] NSJ No 505, 2005 NSSC 332....349, 366
Plowman v Plowman (1995), 16 RFL (4th) 82, [1995] OJ No 2204 (Gen Div)....262, 293
PM v DJT, [1999] OJ No 4955 (SCJ)....412
PMB v MLB, 2010 NBCA 5....580
PMJ v ADJ, [2003] BCJ No 1144, 38 RFL (5th) 99 (CA)....292
PML v BGL, [2003] AJ No 1401, 2003 ABQB 937....289
PMR v MHR, 2011 BCSC 1621....135
PMZ v DJT, 2023 BCSC 1444....459, 460
Podruchny v Evans, 2018 SKQB 262....130, 453
Poff v Fenel, [1998] SJ No 608, 173 Sask R 275 (QB)....149–50, 193, 225, 228
Pohlod v Bielajew, [1998] OJ No 1770, 38 RFL (4th) 35, 62 OTC 49 (Gen Div)....113, 116, 318
Pohlod v Bielajew, [1998] OJ No 3345 (Gen Div)....318
Polack v Sterling, 2010 ABQB 122....382
Politis v Politis, 2018 ONSC 323....265, 272
Pollitt v Pollitt, 2010 ONSC 1617....165, 215
Pollock v Rioux, [2004] NBJ No 467, 11 RFL (6th) 330, 2004 NBCA 98....37, 63, 65, 66, 67, 68, 321, 384
Polson v Polson, [2000] BCJ No 2050, 2000 BCSC 1477....31
Pomerleau v Agopsowicz, [1999] OJ No 1967 (SCJ)....260
Pomozova v Mann, 2010 ONCA 212....136, 148, 216
Pomroy v Greene, [2000] NJ No 38, 188 Nfld & PEIR 186 (UFC)....14
Pongor v Pongor (1976), 27 RFL 109 (Ont CA)....476
Pontius v Murray, 2011 SKCA 121....196
Poohkay v Poohkay (1997), 33 RFL (4th) 140, [1997] AJ No 1182 (CA)....81
Poohkay v Thomlison, 2022 ABQB 282....360, 361
Pope v Janes, 2014 NLTD(F) 27....325, 511

Pope v Pope (1995), 12 RFL (4th) 391, [1995] NJ No 77 (UFC) 28
Porter v Porter, [1998] NSJ No 426 (SC) 489
Pothier v Pothier, [2001] NSJ No 489 (SC) 81
Potter v Graham, [2001] AJ No 1119, 2001 ABQB 736 603
Potter v Graham, [2004] AJ No 1133, 2004 ABQB 532 27, 31, 221, 301, 318, 319, 540
Potzus v Potzus, 2017 SKCA 15 162, 170, 171, 173, 183, 184, 185, 188, 189, 415, 418, 419, 420, 458
Potzus v Potzus, 2018 SKQB 55 170, 469, 541
Poultney v Poultney, 2011 SKQB 420 447
Pound v Pound (1987), 6 RFL (3d) 231, [1987] BCJ No 109 (CA) 80
Poursadeghian v Hashemi-Dahaj, 2010 BCCA 453 218, 247, 258
Pousette v Janssen, 2023 BCCA 176, supp reasons 2023 BCCA 272 191, 216, 218, 241
Pousette v Pousette (1993), 46 RFL (3d) 152 (BCSC) 552
Powell v Powell, 2019 BCSC 303 426
Power v Hunt, [2000] NJ No 315, 196 Nfld & PEIR 149 (UFC) 71
Power v Power (1979), 24 NBR (2d) 617 (CA) 659, 660
Power v Power, 2020 NSSC 379 531
Poyntz Estate v Poyntz, [1998] OJ No 1024, 37 RFL (4th) 134 (Gen Div) 54, 542, 544, 573
Pozzolo v Pozzolo, 2020 BCCA 281 335, 336
PP v DD, 2017 ONCA 180 85, 614
Praetzel v Porter, 2022 NWTSC 19 372, 384, 385
Premi v Khodeir (2009), 73 RFL (6th) 292, [2009] OJ No 3365 (SCJ) 5, 8, 13, 19, 20
Prescesky v Prescesky, 2015 SKCA 111 456, 553–52
Prescott-Russell Services for Children and Adults v G(N) (2007), 82 OR (3d) 686 (CA) 530
Preston v Preston (1981), 22 RFL (2d) 137 (Sask QB) 551
Pretty v Pretty, 2011 NSSC 296 200–1, 335, 372, 378, 384
Prewada v Prewada (1993), 48 RFL (3d) 190 (Man CA) 508, 663
Price v Holman-Price, 2014 NLTD(F) 30 65, 334
Price v Price (1994), 5 RFL (4th) 383 (BCSC) 466
Prichichi v Prichichi, [2005] OJ No 1979, 14 RFL (6th) 425 (SCJ) 21
Prime v Prime, 2021 SKQB 130 347, 351, 353, 355, 356, 359
Primeau v Primeau (1986), 2 RFL (3d) 113, [1986] OJ No 2515 (HCJ) 111
Primrose v Hanlon, [2000] BCJ No 82, 3 RFL (5th) 269 (SC) 193
Prince Edward Island (Director of Maintenance Enforcement) v Callaghan (1991), 32 RFL (3d) 117 (PEICA) 551
Prince Edward Island (Director of Maintenance Enforcement) v Campbell, [1990] PEIJ No 141, 30 RFL (3d) 76 (CA) 520
Prince Edward Island (Director of Maintenance Enforcement) v Moase, [2001] PEIJ No 117 (SC) 533
Prince Edward Island (Director of Maintenance Enforcement) v Skinner, [2000] PEIJ No 29 (TD) 144
Prince v Soenen, 2015 MBQB 31 83, 151, 215
Pritchard v Christensson, 2018 ABCA 302 562
Prittie v Dorey, 2010 BCSC 1923 35
PRM v BJM, 2012 BCSC 1795 62
Proctor v Klammer, 2023 ONSC 5279 (Div Ct) 62
Proctor v Proctor (1979), 26 OR 394, 14 RFL (2d) 385 (Div Ct), aff'd (1980), 28 OR (2d) 776 (CA) 203
Propp v Dobson, [1998] SJ No 703 (QB) 362, 363
Propper v Vanleeuwen, [1999] OJ No 2297 (SCJ) 581
Proulx v Proulx, [2002] AJ No 163 (QB) 535
Proulx v Proulx, [2009] OJ No 1680 (SCJ) 87, 229

Proulx v Zigart, [1998] AJ No 545 (QB)....489
Provenzano v Thunder Bay (City), [2008] OJ No 1884 (SCJ)....606
Provost v Marsden, 2009 NSSC 365....482
Provost v Marsden, 2010 NSSC 162....295, 301
Prowse-Myers v Myers, [2004] SJ No 212, 2 RFL (6th) 408 (QB)....89
PRR v JCG, 2013 NBQB 405....49, 100
Prystawik v Prystawik (1979), 19 AR 189, [1979] NWTJ No 17 (SC)....606
Psaila v Psaila (1984), 40 RFL (2d) 458 (BCCA)....658, 659
Psaila v Psaila (1987), 10 BCLR (2d) 336, 6 RFL (3d) 141 (CA)....557
PT v IT, [2004] NJ No 98, 2004 NLSCUFC 9....344
PT v RB, [2004] AJ No 803, 361 AR 163 (CA)....10
Publicover v Publicover (1989), 92 NSR (2d) 432 (Fam Ct)....569
Purdue v Purdue, 2014 NBQB 262....152
Purewal v Purewal, 2011 BCSC 169....462
Purse v Purse (1987), 50 Man R (2d) 9 (QB)....448
Purtill v Demarchi, [1999] OJ No 5299 (SCJ)....588
Purves v Purves (1985), 65 BCLR 339, [1985] BCJ No 225 (SC)....620
Putnam v Putnam, 2010 NSSC 115....228
PW v CM, 2021 NSSC 127....239
Pye v Pye, [1995] BCJ No 1315, 15 RFL (4th) 76 (SC)....104, 105
Pyper v Neville (1995), 14 RFL (4th) 262, [1995] SJ No 308, 132 Sask R 300 (QB)....149, 386

Qaraan v Qaraan, 2014 ONCA 401....122
QP v QN, 2017 BCSC 400....204
Quercia v Francioni, 2011 ONSC 6844....340, 426
Quinn v Keiper, [2005] OJ No 5034, 23 RFL (6th) 226 (SCJ)....255, 471
Quinn v Quinn, [1999] BCJ No 2099 (SC)....99
Quintal v Quintal, [1997] OJ No 3444, 38 OTC 68 (Gen Div)....193, 211, 574
Quinton v Kehler, 2020 BCCA 254....171, 172–73, 174, 468
Quiquero v Quiquero, 2016 ONSC 6696....162, 163

R v Find, [2001] SCJ No 34....634
R v R, [2000] OJ No 2830, 10 RFL (5th) 88 (SCJ), var'd [2002] OJ No 1095, 24 RFL (5th) 96 (CA)....221, 410, 418, 422, 661
R v REM, 2008 SCC 51, [2008] 3 SCR 3....599
R v S(RD), [1997] 3 SCR 484, [1997] SCJ No 84....622
R(L) v S(L) and E(R) (1989), 22 RFL (3d) 267, [1989] MJ No 444 (CA)....600
Raabe v DeJong, 2019 BCSC 1177....623
Racette v Gamauf, [1997] PEIJ No 123, 35 RFL (4th) 357 (TD)....331, 333, 371, 372
Racicot v Racicot, [2003] OJ No 4666, 47 RFL (5th) 384 (SCJ)....44
Radford v Radford, 2010 SKQB 157....62, 71
Rae v Rae (1983), 37 RFL (2d) 16 (Ont HCJ)....524
Rafan v Rauf, 2020 SKQB 107....201
Rafan v Rauf, 2021 SKQB 117....640
Raftus v Raftus (1998), 166 NSR (2d) 179, 159 DLR (4th) 264, 37 RFL (4th) 59, [1998] NSJ No 119 (CA)....282, 305, 331
Ragot v Ragot (1976), 30 RFL 183, [1976] MJ No 205 (QB)....624
Raiku v Kokkinis, [2000] BCJ No 1703 (SC)....260
Rainer v Rainer, [2000] AJ No 918 (QB)....235
Rainey v Rainey, [2003] BCJ No 481, 2003 BCSC 327....49
Rains v Rains, [1997] OJ No 2516 (Gen Div)....211, 313, 473
Ralph v Brockerville, [2000] NJ No 289 (Prov Ct)....512
Ralph v Ralph (1994), 7 RFL (4th) 238, [1994] NJ No 267 (SC)....565

Ralph v Ralph (2001), 205 Nfld & PEIR 145, [2001] NJ No 238 (SC) 127, 223, 641
Ramachala (Holland) v Holland, 2020 ABQB 432 .... 129, 156, 338, 339, 340, 351, 549
Ramlochan v Ramlochan, 2010 ONSC 4323 195–96
Ramos v Juliano, [2001] BCJ No 2099, 2001 BCSC 1422 626
Ramsay v Mackintosh, 2013 ABQB 80 179
Rana v Rana, 2020 BCSC 1232 239
Rana v Rana, 2024 BCSC 49 199
Rankin v Rankin (1982), 30 RFL (2d) 209, [1982] OJ No 950 (HCJ) 629
Ransom v Coulter, 2014 NWTSC 55 .... 340, 341–42, 343, 345
Rapoport v Rapoport, 2011 ONSC 4456 151
Rarick v Rarick, [2000] AJ No 429 (QB) 532
Rasmussen v MacDonald, [1997] SJ No 667, 34 RFL (4th) 451 (QB) 159, 160, 250
Ratajczak v Ratajczak, 2010 ONSC 4286 .... 347, 357
Rathwell v McLaughlin, 2022 SKCA 21 562
Rattenbury v Rattenbury, [2000] BCJ No 889, 2000 BCSC 722 231
Rausch v Rausch, [2004] SJ No 171, 248 Sask R 85 (QB) 407
RAV v SMIV (2007), 48 RFL (6th) 413, [2007] BCJ No 2808, 2007 BCSC 1896 .... 98, 102, 103
Rawluk-Harness v Harness, 2014 ONSC 2531 129
Rayes v Dominguez-Cortes, 2015 ONSC 3693 .... 295, 296
Raymond-Theoret v Smith, 2011 ONSC 7215 .... 162, 208, 317
Raynor v Raynor, [1997] NSJ No 411, 163 NSR (2d) 117 (TD) 315, 373
Razavi v Aavani, [1998] BCJ No 1885 (SC) 207
Razutis v Garrett, [1999] BCJ No 1505, 48 RFL (4th) 452 (CA) 486, 507, 664
RBK v AMK, [1997] SJ No 599 (QB) 412
RBN v MJN, [2002] NSJ No 530 (SC) 389
RC v AL, 2021 NSFC 01 196
RC v CW, [2003] OJ No 3755, 49 RFL (5th) 11 (SCJ) 85
RC v DRC, 2019 BCSC 1218 505
RCT v AKT, 2023 BCSC 654 510
RDM v EEK, [2002] NSJ No 332, 28 RFL (5th) 374, 2002 NSFC 12 29
RDO v CJO, [2003] BCJ No 1179, 40 RFL (5th) 329 (SC) 372
Re Gupta and Gupta, 2017 ONSC 6867 650
Re Wiley and Wiley (1919), 49 DLR 643 (Ont HC) 477
Reardon v Smith, [1999] NSJ No 403, 1 RFL (5th) 83 (CA) 475, 507
Rebenchuk v Rebenchuk, [2005] MJ No 201, 17 RFL (6th) 171 (QB) 46
Rebenchuk v Rebenchuk (2007), 35 RFL (6th) 239, 2007 MBCA 22 .... 35, 49, 50, 51, 52, 53, 54, 56, 62, 63, 64, 65, 66, 72, 75, 76, 77, 113, 115, 301, 322
Reber v Reber, 2002 BCSC 884, [2002] BCJ No 1281 (SC) 126, 348, 355, 358
Rector v Hamilton (1989), 94 NSR (2d) 284 (Fam Ct) 581
Reddin v Reddin (1990), 80 Nfld & PEIR 181 (PEITD), aff'd (1992), 94 Nfld & PEIR 328 (PEICA) 478
Redlick v Redlick, 2013 BCSC 1155 .... 152, 383
Reed v Smith (1988), 86 NSR (2d) 72 (CA) 90
Reeder v Leach, [2001] SJ No 757, 215 Sask R 14 (QB) 289
Reehal v Reehal, 2020 BCSC 1635 618
Reeves v Reeves, [2003] PEIJ No 50, 226 Nfld & PEIR 225 (SC) 486
REG v TWJG, 2011 SKQB 269 .... 142, 174, 178, 187, 220, 422–23
Regaudie v Thomas, [2002] OJ No 2231, 29 RFL (5th) 153 (SCJ) 326
Rego v Santos, 2015 ONCA 540 .... 538, 539
Reich v Sager, [1997] BCJ No 2850, 33 RFL (4th) 101 (CA), rev'g [1995] BCJ No 2620, 20 RFL 4th 24 (SC) 99
Reid v Catalano, [2008] OJ No 912 (SCJ) 467
Reid v Chambers, 2022 ABKB 634 .... 239, 498, 584

Reid v Faubert, 2019 NSCA 42 .... 9, 14, 173, 180, 188, 371, 372, 374, 378, 397, 403
Reid v Reid (1992), 40 RFL (3d) 92 (BCCA) 570
Reid v Reid, 2017 BCCA 73 .... 162, 419, 425, 429
Reid v Reid, 2018 NLSC 33 .... 173, 179
Reid-Floyd v Kelly, [1998] NBJ No 19, [1998] NBR (2d) (Supp) No 4 (QB) 477, 646
Reidy v Reidy, [2005] OJ No 5152 (SCJ) 81
Reis v Thompson, [2009] AJ No 264, 2009 ABQB 156 .... 100, 103, 107, 110
Reiss v Reiss, [2001] SJ No 37, 201 Sask R 277 (QB) 36, 108
Reiter v Reiter, [1997] BCJ No 2835, 36 RFL (4th) 102 (SC) 380, 397, 404
REL v MLSB, 2008 BCSC 663, [2008] BCJ No 969 41
Rémillard v Rémillard, 2014 MBCA 101 .... 15, 40, 42, 414, 415, 419, 420
Rémillard v Rémillard, 2015 MBCA 42 630
Renpenning v Renpenning (1992), 103 Sask R 23 (QB) 457
Renshi v Renshi, 2022 BCSC 1942 .... 350, 425
REQ v GJK, 2019 BCSC 1116 .... 348, 468
Resch v Resch (1995), 12 RFL (4th) 410 (Man CA) 449
Reyes v Rollo, [2001] OJ No 5110, 24 RFL (5th) 120 (SCJ) 23, 275, 296, 297, 322, 555
Reyher v Reyher (1993), 48 RFL (3d) 111, [1993] MJ No 264 (QB) 408
Reynolds v Andrew, [2008] SJ No 532, 2008 SKQB 352 216
Reynolds v Reynolds (1988), 14 RFL (3d) 340 (Ont Prov Ct) 588
Reynolds v Reynolds, [1999] SJ No 7 (QB) 160, 330
RF v JM, 2017 SKQB 51 389
Rhynold v Van der Linden, 2007 NSCA 72, [2007] NSJ No 255 483
Rhys-Williams v Rhys-Williams, 2023 BCSC 16 191
Riad v Riad, [2002] AJ No 1338, 317 AR 201, 10 Alta LR (4th) 207 (CA) 14, 240
Ribeiro v Li (1996), 22 RFL (4th) 459 (Ont Ct Gen Div) 489
Richard v Holmes, 2020 ONSC 6485 .... 117, 152, 153
Richard v Richard (1994), 2 RFL (4th) 395 (NBQB) 540, 570
Richard v Richard, [1999] SJ No 348 (QB) 2
Richards v Richards, [1998] BCJ No 2657 (SC) 358
Richardson v Richardson, [1987] 1 SCR 857, 7 RFL (3d) 304, [1987] SCJ No 30 .... 3, 26, 89, 425, 426
Richardson v Richardson, [1997] OJ No 2795 (Gen Div) 336, 463
Richardson v Richardson, [2002] OJ No 2463 (SCJ) 48, 448
Richardson v Richardson, 2013 BCCA 378 .... 136, 227
Richardson v Richardson, 2016 SKQB 356 .... 219, 307
Richardson's Will Trusts v Llewellyn-Evans' Trustees, [1958] Ch 504 469
Richer v Freeland, 2019 ONSC 6840 .... 283, 329
Richter v Vahamaki (2000), 8 RFL (5th) 194, [2000] OJ No 5282 (SCJ) 296, 393, 408
Riddell v Blackburn, [2003] SJ No 53, 230 Sask R 18 (QB) 45, 244
Riddell v Levesque, [2001] MJ No 472 (CA) 575
Riddell v Riddell, 2013 MBQB 4 429
Rideout v Woodman, 2016 NSSC 205 .... 36, 204
Ridgeway v Ridgeway, [2000] PEIJ No 4 (SC) 524
Ridley v Ridley (1989), 37 CPC (2d) 167, [1989] OJ No 1121 (HCJ) 550, 617
Rieder v Jenei, [2006] BCJ No 176, 2006 BCSC 153 27
Riel v Holland, [2003] OJ No 3901, 42 RFL (5th) 120 (CA) 129–30, 182, 196, 217, 221, 222, 230, 466
Riley v Riley, [2009] SJ No 142, 2009 SKQB 98 58
Rimmer v Adshead, 2003 SKCA 19 657
Rintaluhta v Rintaluhta (1987), 11 RFL (3d) 397 (Ont Dist Ct) 524
Ripley v Ripley (1991), 30 RFL (3d) 41, [1991] BCJ No 4 (CA) 39, 468

Ripulone v Smith, 2018 ABCA 167 249
Risdale v Risdale, [1999] AJ No 1517 (QB) 538
Risen v Risen, [1998] OJ No 3184, 78 OTC 189 (Gen Div) 192
Rist v Rist, [2000] SJ No 637 (CA) 661
Ritchie v Ritchie, [2003] SJ No 326, 40 RFL (5th) 352 (CA) 81, 82
Ritchie v Solonick, [1999] YJ No 66 (SC) 156, 157, 159, 372, 390
Rivard v Rivard, [2004] AJ No 589, 2004 ABQB 390 .... 259, 275, 556
Rivest v Rivest (1981), 25 RFL (2d) 280, [1981] OJ No 2424 (HCJ) 618
Rivett v Bylund, [1998] OJ No 325, 40 RFL (4th) 416 (Gen Div) 319
RJ v PJ, 2021 NBCA 28 599
RJC v RJJ, [2006] BCJ No 2150, 2006 BCSC 1422 53
RJM v EM, 2015 BCSC 414 .... 34, 50, 389
RJO v ACO, [2000] BCJ No 2562 (SC) 358
RL v BI, [1997] QJ No 4450 (CS) 31, 294, 316
RL v TGS, 2023 BCSC 847 628
RLS v DCM, [2003] BCJ No 1030, 2003 BCSC 692 388
RLS v MNR, [2005] BCJ No 52, 37 BCLR (4th) 355 (SC) 98
RM v AM, 2018 BCSC 318 66
RM v NM, 2014 BCSC 1755 .... 468, 478
RM v PM, [2000] NJ No 180, 8 RFL (5th) 320 (SC) 87
RN v Haulli, 2018 NUCJ 10 616–17
Robbins v Robbins (1975), 20 RFL 327, [1975] SJ No 84 (QB) 22
Robbins v Robbins (1986), 43 Man R (2d) 53, [1986] MJ No 401 (QB) 29, 551
Robblee v Reid, [2003] OJ No 429, 34 RFL (5th) 142 (SCJ) 369
Roberts v Beresford, [2006] BCJ No 291, 22 RFL (6th) 243 (CA) 567
Roberts v Roberts, [2000] OJ No 3234 (SCJ) 163
Roberts v Roberts, 2011 ONSC 7130 .... 125, 224, 229
Robertson v Hibbs, [1997] BCJ No 1305 (SC) 81
Robertson v Vega Soto, 2019 BCSC 1140 348
Robichaud v Robichaud (1988), 17 RFL (3d) 285, [1988] BCJ No 2427 (CA) 15
Robichaud v Robichaud (1992), 124 NBR (2d) 332, [1992] NBJ No 403 (QB) 15, 16
Robinson v Domin, [1998] BCJ No 1145, 39 RFL (4th) 92 (SC) 105, 110
Robinson v Robinson (1989), 22 RFL (3d) 10, [1989] OJ No 1495 (HCJ) 318
Robinson v Robinson (1994), 5 RFL (4th) 72 (Ont Ct Gen Div) 541
Robski v Robski, [1997] NSJ No 444, 166 NSR (2d) 161 (SC) 311, 477, 483
Robski v Robski, [2001] NSJ No 454, 198 NSR (2d) 290 (SC) 293, 307, 538
Roby v Canada, [2001] TCJ No 801 4
Roby v Roby, [2003] OJ No 4408, 48 RFL (5th) 389 (SCJ) 466
Rockwell v Rockwell, [1998] BCJ No 3240 (SC) 304
Rodbard v Rodbard (1993), 45 RFL (3d) 451 (Ont Ct Gen Div) 477
Roemer v Roemer, [2003] SJ No 499 (QB) 384
Rogers v Lowe, [2001] BCJ No 2329 (SC) 458
Rogers v Rogers (1962), 3 FLR 398 (NSWSC) 17
Rogers v Rogers, [1999] BCJ No 2041 (SC) 575, 590
Rogge v Rogge (1991), 37 RFL (3d) 108, [1991] MJ No 555 (QB) 51
Rolinger v Rolinger, 2021 ABQB 474 .... 170, 249, 254, 457
Rollins v Kutash (1982), 26 RFL (2d) 444 (Alta Prov Ct) 536, 537
Rolls v Rolls, [2003] AJ No 101, 2003 ABQB 15 626–27
Rolls v Whittaker-Rolls, 2010 MBQB 12 .... 349, 357
Romanelli v Romanelli, 2017 ONSC 1312 651
Romanyshyn v Romanyshyn, [2000] BCJ No 328, 2000 BCSC 231 40
Ronan v Douglas-Walsh (1994), 5 RFL (4th) 235 (Ont Prov Div) 570

Rondeau v Kirby, [2003] NSJ No 436, 49 RFL (5th) 189 (SC), aff'd [2004] NSJ No 143 (CA) 148, 165, 202, 409, 474
Rooker v Rooker, 2017 ABCA 17, leave to appeal refused 2017 CanLII 71233 (SCC) 216
Rooney v Rooney, [2003] NJ No 227, 230 Nfld & PEIR 183 (SC) 485
Root v Root, [2008] OJ No 2716 (SCJ) 606, 650, 651
Roote v Thompson, [2005] OJ No 5590 (SCJ) 216
Ropchan v Moen, 2022 ABKB 811 206
Rosati v Dellapenta, [1997] OJ No 5047, 35 RFL (4th) 102 (Gen Div) 358, 363
Roseberry v Roseberry, 2015 ABQB 75 .... 222, 256, 506
Rosenberg v Rosenberg (1987), 11 RFL (3d) 126 (Ont HCJ) 313, 463
Rosenberg v Rosenberg, [2003] OJ No 2962, 42 RFL (5th) 440 (SCJ) 51, 114
Roshau v Roshau, [1997] BCJ No 2589 (SC) 428
Rosin v Rosin (1994), 7 RFL (4th) 402, [1994] AJ No 650 (QB) 605
Rosin v Rosin (1994), 8 RFL (4th) 315, [1994] AJ No 663 (QB) 605
Ross v Dunphy, 2009 NBQB 281 .... 53, 76, 83, 144, 322
Ross v Ross (1995), 16 RFL (4th) 1, [1995] NBJ No 463 (CA) 16
Ross v Ross, [1997] NSJ No 444 (TD) 477
Ross v Ross, [2001] MJ No 317, 22 RFL (5th) 426 (QB) 104
Ross v Ross, [2001] NSJ No 184, 17 RFL (5th) 422 (CA) 374, 392
Ross v Vermette, [2007] SJ No 483, 2007 SKQB 272 580
Ross v Welsh, 2009 SKQB 483 497
Rossiter-Forrest v Forrest (1994), 129 NSR (2d) 130 (TD) 468
Roszko v Roszko, [2000] AJ No 920, 269 AR 399 (QB) 213
Rotella v Rotella, [2006] OJ No 208 (SCJ) 61
Roth v Gallagher, [2003] BCJ No 260 (SC) 368
Roth v Roth, 2010 ONSC 2532 .... 75, 297, 323
Rothenburg v Rothenburg, [2003] OJ No 1551 (SCJ) 82
Rothgiesser v Rothgiesser (2000), 46 OR (3d) 577, [2000] OJ No 33 (CA) 20
Rotondi v Rotondi, 2014 ONSC 1520 .... 60, 83
Rousseau v Rousseau, [1999] SJ No 76, 181 Sask R 144 (QB) 588
Rowsell v Rowsell, [2000] NJ No 254, 195 Nfld & PEIR 207 (SC) 104
Roy v Roy (1984), 59 NBR (2d) 410, [1984] NBJ No 373 (QB) 614
Roy v Roy, [1999] SJ No 680 (QB) 223
Royer v Peters, 2021 ONSC 1637 .... 347, 352
Royko v Royko, [2008] SJ No 155 (QB) 65
Rozen v Rozen, [2001] BCJ No 1633, 2001 BCSC 1173, rev'd [2002] BCJ No 2192, 2002 BCCA 537 .... 27, 213, 434, 436, 509, 642
Rozzi v Ontario (Director, Family Responsibility Office), [2003] OJ No 1723 (Ct J) 528
RPS v KJS, 2014 ONSC 1385 .... 320, 323, 560
RR v DLK, [2005] OJ No 5591, 21 RFL (6th) 178 (SCJ) 85
RRH v BK, 2011 BCSC 948 470
RS v TS (2005), 21 RFL (6th) 411, [2005] NBJ No 448 (QB) 159, 160, 235
RSAO v RB, [2005] YJ No 49, 2005 YKSC 20 37
RSW v ATW, [1997] BCJ No 3065 (SC) 481
RTC v NMC, 2021 BCSC 2273 201
Ruck v Ruck, 2016 NSSC 45 .... 295, 300
Rudachyk v Rudachyk, [1999] SJ No 312, 47 RFL (4th) 363 (CA) 151, 181, 188, 224, 227, 232, 233
Rudulier v Rudulier, [1999] SJ No 366, 182 Sask R 23 (QB) 63, 97, 186, 312
Ruecker v Ruecker, [1998] SJ No 408, 170 Sask R 90 (QB) 187
Ruel v Ruel, [2006] AJ No 621, 2006 ABCA 170 389
Ruel v The Queen, 2017 TCC 93 365
Rueter v Rueter, [2003] OJ No 989 (SCJ) 615
Ruffell v Ruffell, 2021 ABCA 39 145

Ruffolo v David, 2016 ONSC 754 ... 239, 556
Ruiterman v Ruiterman (1994), 5 RFL (4th) 192, [1994] BCJ No 1453 (SC) ... 21
Rumpel v Wills, 2010 SKQB 397 ... 52, 316
Rumpf v Rumpf, 2000 SKQB 510, [2000] SJ No 878 ... 526
Rupert v Rupert, [1999] NBJ No 5, 207 NBR (2d) 177 (QB) ... 408
Rush v Rush, [2002] PEIJ No 29, 27 RFL (5th) 151 (SC) ... 228, 285, 300, 468
Russell v Russell (1995), 16 RFL (4th) 229, [1995] AJ No 762 (QB) ... 629
Russell v Russell, [1998] OJ No 2234, 68 OTC 288 (Gen Div) ... 374, 380, 383, 393, 394, 396
Russell v Russell, [1998] OJ No 3381, 74 OTC 159 (Gen Div) ... 641
Russell v Russell, [2002] BCJ No 1983, 2002 BCSC 1233 ... 124
Russell v Russell, [2005] SJ No 423, 270 Sask R 118 (QB) ... 534
Russell v Russell, 2011 MBQB 274 ... 193, 214
Russell v Russell, 2012 NSSC 258 ... 4, 279, 285, 286–87, 326, 331, 560
Russell v Ullett Russell, 2021 ABQB 769 ... 214, 347
Rust v Rust, [2003] SJ No 394, 42 RFL (5th) 161 (CA) ... 259
Ruttan v Ruttan, [1982] 1 SCR 690, [1982] SCJ No 35 ... 515, 516
RWG v SIG, [2002] SJ No 231, 26 RFL (5th) 307 (QB), var'd (sub nom Gilroy v Gilroy) [2003] SJ No 250 (CA) ... 43, 49, 250, 419
RWL v LB, 2012 BCSC 457 ... 13
RY v CSY, [2001] BCJ No 1570 (SC) ... 483
Ryan v Pitchers, 2019 ABQB 19 ... 37
Ryan v Ryan, 2010 ABQB 672 ... 312
Ryan v Ryan, 2010 NSCA 2 ... 46
Ryba v Schoenroth, [1999] SJ No 201, 47 RFL (4th) 381 (CA) ... 662
Ryckman v Camick, 2020 ONSC 5429 ... 528
Ryder v Kent, 2016 NLTD(F) 1 ... 156, 157
Rykert v Rykert, [2000] OJ No 4453 (SCJ) ... 469
RYW v DWW, 2013 BCSC 472 ... 57, 58

S v A, 2023 ONSC 4719 ... 538
S CA v S CO, 2022 NBBR 238 ... 46, 47, 48, 49
S v S, [1999] BCJ No 1043 (SC) ... 31
S v S, [2007] NBJ No 422, 2007 NBQB 360 ... 486
S(C) v L(V) (1992), 39 RFL (3d) 294, [1992] OJ No 1632 (Prov Div), aff'd (1992), 39 RFL (3d) 298, [1992] OJ No 3776 (Gen Div) ... 600
S(JM) v M(FJ) (2005), 15 RFL (6th) 436 (Ont Div Ct) ... 582
S(PK) v S(JS) (1995), 13 RFL (4th) 340, [1995] BCJ No 784 (SC) ... 600
S(T) v P(T) (1996), 23 RFL (4th) 333, [1996] NJ No 145 (Prov Ct) ... 23, 28
SA v EA, 2010 NBQB 61 ... 129
SAB v CDB. See Blumer v Blumer.
Saby v MacIntosh, [2002] BCJ No 1813, 2002 BCSC 1144 ... 370, 371
SAC v MAB, [2002] NSJ No 128, 203 NSR (2d) 15 (Fam Ct) ... 270
SAC v SEC, 2015 MBQB 61 ... 192, 205
Saccary v Spencer, 2022 BCSC 1151 ... 80
Sackney v Ficko, [1999] SJ No 27, 182 Sask R 299 (QB) ... 229
Sacrey v Sacrey, [2008] NJ No 392 (UFC) ... 72
SAD v MA, 2019 NBQB 85 ... 40, 42, 217, 230, 244
Sadkowski v Harrison-Sadkowski, [2008] OJ No 1013, 2008 ONCJ 115 ... 360
Sage v Sage, 2014 ONSC 1330 ... 305, 309
Sagl v Sagl, [1997] OJ No 2837 (Gen Div) ... 317
SAH v KAH, 2022 NBCA 17 ... 338, 348, 349
SAJM v DDM, [1999] MJ No 118, 45 RFL (4th) 301 (CA) ... 2, 410
Sakiyama v Sakiyama, 2019 ONSC 5522 ... 611–12,

SAL v BJL, 2019 ABCA 350 .... 538, 578
SAL v KH, 2011 SKQB 397 .... 93, 96
Salehi v Tawoosi, 2016 ONSC 540 214
Salo v Boguist, [1998] OJ No 5786, 88 OTC 307 (Gen Div) 333
Salvadori v Kebede, [1998] BCJ No 1819 (SC) 387, 414
SAM v JAB, 2023 BCSC 2110 .... 49, 155
Samis (Guardian of) v Samis, 2011 ONCJ 273 652
Sampson v Sampson, [1997] OJ No 5356 (Gen Div) 507
Sampson v Sampson, [1998] AJ No 1214 (QB) 373, 394, 412
Sampson v Sampson, [1999] NSJ No 104 (TD), var'd [1999] NSJ No 379 (CA) 127, 472
Samson v Samson, [2003] NJ No 289, 49 RFL (5th) 202 (SC) 73, 75
SAN v JMS, 2011 BCSC 963 162
Sanders v Sliede, [2009] OJ No 1657 (SCJ) 288
Sanderson v Pennycook, 2013 NWTSC 48 493
Sandhals v Lorette, [2001] BCJ No 34 (SC) 99
Sandor v Sandor, [2004] OJ No 2741, 4 RFL (6th) 161 (SCJ) 81
Sankey v Aydt, [2004] SJ No 673, 12 RFL (6th) 460 (QB) 449
Santelli v Trinetti, 2018 BCSC 300 459–60
Santelli v Trinetti, 2019 BCCA 319 .... 279, 459, 661
Santos v Potter, 2010 SKQB 115 .... 127, 379, 385
Saper v Silverman, [2002] MJ No 215, 2002 MBCA 73 52
Sapergia v Larner (1995), 15 RFL (4th) 389, [1995] SJ No 407 (QB) 46
Sapergia v Sapergia, [1998] SJ No 877, 179 Sask R 9 (QB) 52
Sappier v Francis, 2013 NBQB 168 34
Sarafinchin v Sarafinchin, [2000] OJ No 2855, 189 DLR (4th) 741 (SCJ) 145, 217, 221, 230, 254, 416, 417
Sarchfield v Sarchfield (1989), 103 NBR (2d) 81, [1989] NBJ No 1069 (QB), rev'd (1990), 109 NBR (2d) 335, [1990] NBJ No 852 (CA) 202a
Saroli v Grette, 2022 ONSC 3560 589
Sarro v Sarro, 2011 BCSC 1010 .... 125, 136, 414
Saskatchewan (Director of Maintenance Enforcement) v Gerbrandt, [2003] SJ No 569, 45 RFL (5th) 456 (CA) 515
Saskatchewan Registration No 76-07-017181 (Re) (1985), 47 RFL (2d) 334 (BCCA) 660
Saunders v Saunders (1988), 18 RFL (3d) 298 (NBQB) 115, 536
Saunders v Saunders, 2011 NSCA 81 241
Saunders v Saunders, 2020 ABCA 226 .... 124, 142
Saunders v Vargas, 2018 ONSC 1892 .... 85, 60
Saunders-Roberts v Roberts, [2002] NWTJ No 9, 2002 NWTSC 11 .... 201, 204, 581
Sauve v Watson, 2021 ONSC 4188 448
Savage v Kaczmarek, 2022 ONSC 1313 .... 498, 584
Savage v Savage (1992), 39 RFL (3d) 257 (NBCA) 565
Savage v Savage, [1997] AJ No 1244 (QB) 291, 294
Savoie v Lamarche (1990), 71 DLR (4th) 481 (Que CA) 570, 571
Savoie v Savoie (1989), 101 NBR (2d) 431, [1989] NBJ No 931 (QB) 602
Sawatzky v Sawatzky, 2018 MBCA 102 574
Sawma v Zeidan, 2018 ONSC 4319 146
Sayong v Aindow, [1999] NWTJ No 43 (SC) 337
SB v RB, [2000] QJ No 3298 (CS) 25, 73, 323
SB-B v BJS, 2020 NBCA 9 616
SC v ASC, 2011 MBCA 70 538
SC v SH, 2016 NLCA 43 344
Scaffidi v Scaffidi (1998), 41 RFL (4th) 166, [1998] OJ No 3584 (Gen Div) 540, 604
Scammell v Davies, [1999] SJ No 298 (QB) 385, 386

Schaan v Schaan, [2000] BCJ No 61, 2000 BCSC 55 337
Schaefer v Schaefer, 2014 SKQB 8 220
Schaff v Schaff (1997), 30 RFL (4th) 63, [1997] BCJ No 1398 (CA) 21, 23
Scharf v Scharf, [1998] OJ No 199, 40 RFL (4th) 422 (Gen Div) 311, 336, 370, 380, 381
Schellenberg v Schellenberg, [2001] MJ No 233, 158 Man R (2d) 242 (QB) 356
Schenkeveld v Schenkeveld, [2002] MJ No 69, 23 RFL (5th) 352 (CA) 235, 378, 392
Schick v Schick, [1997] SJ No 447 (QB) 408
Schick v Schick, [2000] NWTJ No 12, 6 RFL (5th) 421 (SC) 208, 357, 475, 579, 582
Schick v Schick, 2008 ABCA 196, [2008] AJ No 556 .... 134, 138, 165, 298, 347, 354, 356
Schill v Schill, 2012 ONSC 3503 .... 300, 314
Schindle v Schindle, [2001] MJ No 564, 21 RFL (5th) 188 (CA) 196, 240
Schipper v Maher, [2002] MJ No 319, 31 RFL (5th) 152, 2002 MBQB 225 .... 2, 575, 577, 599, 605
Schlechter v Schlechter (1988), 73 Sask R 13, [1988] SJ No 701 (QB) 618
Schlichting v Gauld, [1999] BCJ No 928 (SC) 458
Schluessel v Schluessel, [1999] AJ No 1555, 282 AR 190 (QB) 220, 393
Schmid v Smith, [1999] OJ No 3062, 1 RFL (5th) 447 (SCJ) 143, 207, 299, 301, 337, 371, 380, 385, 391, 410, 461
Schneider v Owers, 2022 BCSC 787 538
Schnell v Schnell (2001), 21 RFL (5th) 197, [2001] SJ No 704, 2001 SKCA 123 .... 122, 161, 168, 240
Schnell v Schnell, [1988] 3 WWR 447 (Man QB) 533
Schoff v Schoff, 2020 SKQB 290 231
Scholes v Scholes, [2003] OJ No 3432 (SCJ) 194
Schom-Moffatt v Moffatt, [1997] BCJ No 2055 (SC) 211
Schorath v Schorath, [2000] AJ No 1050 (QB) 544
Schryver v Schryver, 2013 ONSC 3082 431
Schultz v Schultz (1994), 3 RFL (4th) 422 (Ont Ct Gen Div) 449
Schultz v Schultz, [1998] AJ No 245 (QB) 81
Schwark v Schwark, [2000] SJ No 489, 195 Sask R 108 (QB) 225, 287, 317
Scorgie v Scorgie, [2006] OJ No 225 (SCJ) 460
Scory v Scory, [1999] SJ No 644, 1 RFL (5th) 276 (CA) 147, 467
Scotcher v Hampson (1998), 43 RFL (4th) 132, [1998] OJ No 4002 (Gen Div) 646
Scott v Chenier, 2015 ONSC 7866 .... 126, 157, 158, 159
Scott v Scott, [1999] SJ No 659 (QB) 456, 528
Scott v Scott, [2000] BCJ No 1147, 2000 BCSC 844 372
Scott v Scott, [2002] OJ No 1418 (SCJ) 309
Scott v Scott, [2004] NBJ No 468, 10 RFL (6th) 135, 2004 NBCA 99 .... 40, 146, 170, 661
Scott v Scott, [2006] AJ No 1740, 2006 ABCA 296 222
Scott v Scott (2006), 31 RFL (6th) 454, [2006] BCJ No 1701 (SC) 348, 362
Scott v The King, 2022 TCC 131 365
SDB v PW, [1998] NSJ No 565, 47 RFL (4th) 228 (Fam Ct) 63, 322
SDH v ARH, 2019 ABQB 212 384
SDM v KFM, [2004] BCJ No 67, 2004 BCSC 59 196
SDP v LMT, 2016 SKQB 48 96
Sea v He, 2022 BCSC 2169 278
Seabrook v Major, [2005] OJ No 3085, 15 RFL (6th) 436 (Div Ct) 83
Seaman (Re) (1977), 28 RFL 275 (Ont HCJ) 662
Sears v Coristine, 2021 ONSC 7576 608
Seaton v Zheng, 2013 ONSC 4469 214
SEB v JTM, 2019 NBQB 76 .... 156, 497, 505
Sebok v Babits, 2018 BCSC 585 596
Seburn v Seburn, [2001] OJ No 1467 (SCJ) 54
Secours v Secours, [2001] AJ No 956 (QB) 543
See v See, [1999] OJ No 698, 44 RFL (4th) 306 (Gen Div) 230

Seeley v McKay, [1998] OJ No 2857, 72 OTC 211 (Gen Div) ... 427
Segal v Brown (1988), 54 Man R (2d) 137 (QB) ... 569
Segal v Segal (1988), 14 RFL (3d) 453, [1988] MJ No 264 (QB) ... 94
Segall v Fellinger, [1998] SJ No 253 (QB) ... 194, 306
Segat v Segat, 2015 ONCA 16 ... 460, 538
Seguin v Masterson (2004), 5 RFL (6th) 425, [2004] OJ No 2176 (SCJ) ... 359, 635
SEH v SRM, [1999] BCJ No 1458 (SC) ... 93, 335
Seidlikoski v Hall, [1998] SJ No 297, 40 RFL (4th) 427 (QB) ... 273
Seiferling v Langmaier, [1998] SJ No 84, 36 RFL (4th) 296 (QB) ... 315
Sekhon v Sekhon, 2020 BCSC 1422 ... 574, 576
Selberis v Selberis, [1994] BCJ No 1336, 5 RFL (4th) 110 (SC) ... 242
Selig v Smith, 2008 NSCA 54, [2008] NSJ No 250 ... 52, 59, 75, 76, 322, 510, 511
Seltsas v Seltsas, [2008] OJ No 4948 (SCJ) ... 318
SEM v JJR, 2013 ONSC 86 ... 398
Semancik v Saunders, 2011 BCCA 264 ... 76, 323, 510, 574, 585
Semenchuk v Semenchuk (1997), 157 Sask R 319, [1997] SJ No 480 (QB) ... 629
Semeschuk v Biletski, [2004] SJ No 200, 2004 SKQB 98 ... 382
Senos v Karcz, 2014 ONCA 459 ... 40, 41, 42
Sequeira v Sequeira (1992), 44 RFL (3d) 95 (BCCA) ... 573
SER v JS, 2020 ABQB 267 ... 249–50, 253, 301, 308
Sevier v Sevier, [2003] BCJ No 1540, 42 RFL (5th) 174 (SC) ... 210
SG v KB, 2021 SKCA 133 ... 603
SG v KG, 2012 BCSC 1937 ... 416
SGS v CLS, [2004] OJ No 2177, [2004] OTC 442 (SCJ) ... 155
SGW v JDF, 2023 BCSC 1851 ... 199
SHA v WDA, [2002] BCJ No 1007, 28 RFL (5th) 1 (SC) ... 299
Shambrook v Shambrook, [2003] BCJ No 548, 2003 BCSC 386 ... 301
Shamli v Shamli, [2004] OJ No 4999 (SCJ) ... 274
Shankman v Shankman, [2001] OJ No 3798 (SCJ) ... 319
Sharf v Sharf, [2000] OJ No 4052 (SCJ) ... 279, 312
Sharifpour v Rostami, 2018 BCCA 458 ... 623
Sharma v Sharma, 2022 MBQB 27 ... 34, 36, 47, 49, 62, 63, 74, 83, 84, 113
Sharma v Sunak, 2011 ONSC 7670 ... 650, 652
Sharpe v Sharpe, [2001] MJ No 406, 158 Man R (2d) 312 (QB) ... 9, 257
Sharpe v Sharpe, [2004] MJ No 56, 180 Man R (2d) 305 (CA) ... 414
Sharpley v Sharpley, [2005] OJ No 5697, 21 RFL (6th) 443 (Ct J) ... 275, 531
Shaw v Arndt, 2016 BCCA 78 ... 101, 113
Shaw v Przybylski, 2014 ABQB 667 ... 129
Shaw v Shaw, [1997] MJ No 400, 120 Man R (2d) 310 (QB) ... 135, 145, 221, 222
Shaw v Shaw, [2002] OJ No 2782 (SCJ) ... 127, 146, 356
Shaw v Van Louie, [1998] BCJ No 2415 (SC) ... 533, 580
Shears v Gould, 2014 NLCA 2 ... 493
Sheffiel-Lambros v Sheffiel, [2005] OJ No 697, [2005] OTC 148 (SCJ) ... 32
Shelleby v Shelleby, [1997] OJ No 2608 (Gen Div) ... 182
Shelley v Russell, 2012 ONSC 920 ... 34, 50, 54, 561
Shelly v Shelly, [2004] OJ No 743, [2004] OTC 205 (SCJ) ... 466
Shen v Tong, 2013 BCCA 519 ... 101
Shentow v Bewsh, [1998] OJ No 3142 (Gen Div) ... 291, 407
Shepherdson v Shepherdson, [2008] OJ No 4703 (SCJ) ... 170
Sheppard v Sheppard (1992), 44 RFL (3d) 1, [1992] NJ No 355 (CA) ... 211
Sheridan v Cupido, 2018 ONSC 5817 ... 204
Sherlock v Sherlock, [1998] BCJ No 116, 36 RFL (4th) 301 (SC) ... 27
Sherlock v Sherlock, [1999] BCJ No 1856 (SC) ... 27, 52

Sherlow v Zubko, [1999] AJ No 644, 76 Alta LR (3d) 202, 50 RFL (4th) 160, 1999 ABQB 435 .... 34, 35, 62, 71, 143, 299
Shewchuk v Canada, [2000] TCJ No 398, [2000] 3 CTC 2738 .... 300, 365
Shields v Shields, [2006] AJ No 569, 2006 ABQB 368 .... 165, 167, 429
Shiels v Shiels, [1997] BCJ No 1924, 27 RFL (4th) 332 (SC) 7
Shinkarik v Shinkarik (1993), 87 Man R (2d) 39 (QB) 462
Shipka v Shipka, [2001] AJ No 213, 288 AR 106 (QB) 163, 305
Shipowick v Shipowick, 2016 MBQB 124 .... 39, 550
Shirley v Shirley, 2007 ABCA 281 91
Shock v Shock, 2019 BCSC 2179 .... 166, 205, 212, 459
Shoukri v Mishriki, 2012 ONSC 7336 359
Shumate v Patrick, 2023 ABKB 98 .... 198, 497, 586
SIB v MDB, 2009 ABQB 612 77
Sich v Sich, 2014 SKQB 174 219
Sidhu v Chima, 2020 BCSC 768 .... 49, 113, 425, 426
Siemieniuk v Siemieniuk (1976), 7 RFL (2d) 90 (Ont CA) 459
Sigurdson v Sigurdson (1980), 7 Sask R 422 (UFC) 212
Sikler v Snow, [2000] SJ No 271 (QB) 304, 561
Sills v Sills, [2002] OJ No 3679 (SCJ) 510
Silveira v McKay, 2018 SKQB 318 594
Silver v Silver (1980), 15 RFL (2d) 142, [1980] AJ No 45 (CA) 611
Silver v Silver (1990), 30 RFL (3d) 211, [1990] MJ No 623 (CA) 257
Silverman v Silverman (1987), 10 RFL (3d) 37 (NS Fam Ct) 508
Simard v Simard, [2000] SJ No 539, 199 Sask R 258 (CA) 322
Simmonds v Turner, [2005] NSJ No 460, 2005 NSSC 315 507
Simmons v Wilcox, [2001] OJ No 2923, 21 RFL (5th) 218 (SCJ) 62, 296
Simms v Simms, [1997] BCJ No 1553 (SC) 475
Simon v Adey, 2012 NBCA 63 .... 65, 66
Simon v Simon, [1997] OJ No 4145, 33 RFL (4th) 310 (Gen Div), rev'd [1999] OJ No 4492, 46 OR (3d) 349, 1 RFL (5th) 119 (CA) 276, 416, 423, 482
Simon v Simon (2000), 1 RFL (5th) 119 (Ont CA) 484
Simons v Simons, [1999] OJ No 1437, 47 RFL (4th) 60 (SCJ) 427
Simpkin v Hasson, 2016 NSSC 82 241
Simpson v Bettenson, 2014 ABCA 21 .... 191, 218
Simpson v Lockman, 2012 MBQB 216 38
Simpson v Palma, [1998] SJ No 581, 171 Sask R 89 (QB) 70, 225, 297
Simpson v Simpson, [1997] BCJ No 2885 (SC) 440
Simpson v Simpson, [1999] PEIJ No 73, 179 Nfld & PEIR 227 (SCTD) 363
Simpson v Simpson, [2004] OJ No 2564 (SCJ) 127
Simpson v Trowsdale, 2007 PESCTD 3, [2007] PEIJ No 7 .... 280, 329
Sinclair v McAuley, 2012 MBCA 86 478
Sinclair v Sinclair, [2001] BCJ No 1000, 2001 BCSC 716 565
Singal v Singal, 2019 ONSC 2758 609
Singh v Pierpont, 2015 MBCA 18 658
Singh v Singh, [1997] BCJ No 1550, 30 RFL (4th) 307 (SC) 105
Single v Single (1986), 5 RFL (3d) 287 (NS Fam Ct) 561
Sipos v Sipos, [2007] OJ No 711, 2007 ONCA 126 243
Sirdevan v Sirdevan, 2010 ONSC 2375, [2009] OJ No 3796 .... 342, 351, 420
SJB v RDBB, 2019 ABQB 624 .... 143, 459
SJP v CAP, 2010 BCSC 1426 328
Skemer v Skemer, 2016 BCSC 1199 552
Skiba v Skiba, [2000] OJ No 76 (SCJ) 301
Skinner v Cullen, 2009 NSSC 200 95

Skolney v Herman, [2008] SJ No 73, 2008 SKQB 55 ....23, 25
Skormorowski v Bernier, 2009 SKQB 55, [2009] SJ No 125 486
Skorulski v Zupan, 2012 MBQB 98.................... 372, 396
Skotnicki v Cayen, 2019 ONSC 4831....................426
SKS v AAS, 2023 BCSC 1777....................299
SLA v BAA, 2013 NBQB 372....................101
Slade v Slade, [2001] NJ No 5, 13 RFL (5th) 187 (CA) 279, 338, 350, 362
Slater v Slater, 2010 NSSC 353 192
Slattery v Slattery (1993), 48 RFL (3d) 38, [1993] BCJ No 1294 (SC) 21, 22
SLD v WAD, 2020 BCSC 690.................... 124, 183
SLD v WAD, 2021 BCSC 942....................166
Sleiman v Sleiman, [2003] OJ No 588 (SCJ) 463, 485–86
SLF v JWF, 2016 ABQB 635....................49, 53
SLH v AWH, 2020 YKSC 12 459
SLL v DBL, 2022 SKKB 277 ....86, 94, 96, 99
Sloat v Sloat (1981), 25 RFL (2d) 378 (BCSC) 535
Sloat v Sloat (1990), 102 NBR (2d) 390, [1990] NBJ No 37 (QB).................... 89, 90
Sloggett v Sloggett (1989), 19 RFL (3d) 148, [1989] OJ No 3011 (HCJ)....................219
SLS v RJP, 2023 MBKB 69 86
SM v JA, 2023 NLCA 1.................... 193, 562
SM v PEN, [2003] QJ No 14125, [2003] RDF 925 (CS) 316
SM v RP, [1998] QJ No 4119 (CS)....................98, 305, 372
SM-M v SM, 2022 NSSC 256.................... 199, 359, 361
Small v Small, 2020 BCSC 707 511
SMC v DLH, [2008] PEIJ No 34, 2008 PESCTD 32....................104
SME v JAE, 2020 BCSC 332....................136
Smederovac v Eichkorn, 2020 MBCA 57....................347, 348, 349, 355, 661
Smellie v Smellie (1987), 8 RFL (3d) 135 (Man QB)....................530
SMF v BWF, 2019 ABQB 806 492
Smith v Gulka, 2020 ABQB 32 494
Smith v Helppi, 2011 NSCA 65....................196, 199, 204
Smith v Hookey, [1999] NJ No 243, 179 Nfld & PEIR 205 (UFC) 127, 380, 391, 392
Smith v Masellis Smith, 1999 ABQB 767....................583
Smith v Oake, 2012 NSSC 100 .... 560, 578
Smith v Reynolds, 2020 ONSC 4459 378
Smith v Smith (1981), 24 RFL (2d) 174, [1981] OJ No 2431 (HCJ) 619
Smith v Smith (1986), 4 RFL (3d) 210, [1986] OJ No 1757 (Prov Ct)....................30
Smith v Smith (1987), 12 RFL (3d) 50, [1987] BCJ No 2498 (SC)....................78
Smith v Smith (1989), 22 RFL (3d) 173 (Ont HCJ), additional reasons (1989), 22 RFL (3d) 393 (Ont HCJ)....................477
Smith v Smith (1990), 27 RFL (3d) 32, 71 DLR (4th) 612 (Man CA) 56, 58, 581
Smith v Smith (1992), 39 RFL (3d) 442 (Ont UFC) 570
Smith v Smith (1998), 36 RFL (4th) 419, [1998] OJ No 617 (Gen Div)....................409
Smith v Smith, [1997] AJ No 1265 (QB)....................211
Smith v Smith, [1997] OJ No 4833, 48 OTC 316 (Gen Div)....................292
Smith v Smith, [1999] AJ No 1180, 1999 ABQB 767.................... 371, 386
Smith v Smith, [1999] BCJ No 1399 (SC).................... 452, 458
Smith v Smith, [1999] MJ No 74, 135 Man R (2d) 62 (QB) 216, 230
Smith v Smith, [2000] BCJ No 206, 2000 BCSC 177 23
Smith v Smith, [2001] AJ No 1420, 22 RFL (5th) 213 (CA).................... 229, 455
Smith v Smith, [2001] NSJ No 8 (SC)....................462
Smith v Smith, [2001] NSJ No 87 (SC)....................543
Smith v Smith, [2005] BCJ No 480 (SC)....................412

Smith v Smith, 2008 SKCA 141, [2008] SJ No 689 ....80, 515
Smith v Smith, 2010 SKQB 2 .... 52, 54
Smith v Smith, 2011 NSSC 269 ....349, 356, 362, 483, 557
Smith v Smith, 2012 ONSC 1500....587
Smith v Smith, 2013 ONCJ 657....123
Smith v Smith, 2014 NSSC 15 .... 223, 295
Smith v Smith, 2015 SKQB 238....496, 587
Smith v Smith, 2016 ONSC 4622....285, 287
Smith v Smith, 2020 ABQB 775 34
Smith v Stebbings, [1997] OJ No 5400, 67 OTC 378 (Gen Div) 646
SMM v DPG, [2003] YJ No 98, 2003 YKSC 41.... 151, 215
SMM v KCM, [2005] BCJ No 1197, 2005 BCSC 763....158
Smola v Roger, [2002] OJ No 1254, [2002] OTC 207 (SCJ) 288
SMP v TMP, 2022 ABQB 226 .... 498, 584
SMR v ELM, 2019 BCPC 236 204
SMS v SMU, 2021 BCSC 93....122
Smyth v Smyth (1993), 48 RFL (3d) 280 (Alta QB)....562
Sneddon v Sneddon (1993), 46 RFL (3d) 373, [1993] AJ No 261 (QB)....409
SNL (Re) (2005), [2005] AJ No 1845, 2006 ABQB 9.... 36, 592
Snortheim v Snortheim (1984), 41 RFL (2d) 334, [1984] AJ No 2610 (QB) 629
Snow v Snow, 2013 ABQB 146 .... 96, 104
Snow v Wilcox, [1999] NSJ No 453, 3 RFL (5th) 171 (CA).... 118, 134, 145, 148, 221, 229, 245, 255, 557
Snyder v Snyder (1973), 12 RFL 335 (Ont Fam Ct)....477
Snyder v Snyder, [1999] NBJ No 32 (QB) 336
Sobczak v Evraire, 2013 ONSC 1249....123, 162, 239
Sochowski v Sochowski, 2020 ABCA 59....447
Soderberg v Soderberg, [1998] NWTJ No 128, 42 RFL (4th) 403 (SC) 357
Sodhi v Sodhi, 2014 BCSC 1622....326
Soleimani v Karimi, 2020 ONSC 6174 611
Soleimani v Melendez, 2019 ONSC 36 .... 12, 283, 284, 287, 392, 565
Sollis v Sollis, [2003] BCJ No 1643, 2003 BCSC 1078....30
Solomon v Solomon, [2001] OJ No 2996 (SCJ)....217
Solonenko v Stice, [1998] SJ No 291 (QB) 362
Song v Canada, 2009 FCA 278 4
Sonne v Wurzer, 2011 BCSC 609....342
Sookorukoff v Sookorukoff, [1998] BCJ No 2892 (SC) 207, 569
Sordi v Sordi, 2011 ONCA 665 654
Sorensen v Kelly, [2003] BCJ No 950 (SC)....344
Sorya v Parmar, 2012 BCSC 129 213
Sosnowski v Sosnowski, [2000] BCJ No 1883 (SC)....313
Soucie v Soucie, 2010 BCSC 1783....260
Souhaibb v Javed, 2023 BCSC 584 ....19, 21
Souliere v Leclair, [1998] OJ No 1393, 38 RFL (4th) 68 (Gen Div) 321, 401
South v South, [1998] BCJ No 962 (SC)....389
SP v BM, 2013 BCSC 1825....156
SP v RP, 2010 ONSC 2247, [2010] OJ No 1642, var'd 2011 ONCA 336....60, 216
Spadacini Kelava v Kelava, 2021 ONCA 345....664
Spanier v Spanier, [1998] BCJ No 452, 40 RFL (4th) 329 (SC).... 147, 309
Sparr v Downing, 2019 ONSC 6564, aff'd 2020 ONCA 793 611
Speakman v Willis, [2003] BCJ No 1465 (SC)....297
Speirs v Speirs, 2011 ONSC 3712 .... 312, 488
Spence v Boyd, [1999] BCJ No 2612 (SC) 93

Spencer v Irvine, [1999] OJ No 1493 (SCJ) 444
Sperker v Sperker (1994), 2 RFL (4th) 243, [1994] NSJ No 8 (CA) 299
Spettigue v Varcoe, 2011 ONSC 6618 258
Spezowska v Reed, [1998] AJ No 730 (QB) 221
Spiess v Spiess, 2021 ABQB 961 ..... 356, 357
Spiring v Spiring, [2002] MJ No 424, 31 RFL (5th) 433 (QB) 161, 239
Sporer v Sporer, [2000] OJ No 2413 (SCJ) 375
Spring v Spring (1987), 61 OR (2d) 743 (UFC) 98
Spring v Spring, 2022 ABCA 19 210
Sproule v Sproule (1986), 2 RFL (3d) 54, [1986] NSJ No 192 (CA) 78
Spry v Shetler, 2021 ONSC 603 ..... 100, 101, 103
Squires v Crouch, 2016 ONCA 774 323
Squires v Severs, [2000] BCJ No 1083 (SC) 98, 103
SR v BE, 2011 BCSC 1586 ..... 214, 345, 356
SRM v NGTM, 2014 BCSC 442 416
SRM v NGTM, 2020 BCSC 468 347
SS v DS, 2010 NSCA 74 458
SS v DS, 2013 NSSC 384 385
SS v JG, 2021 NSSC 228 ..... 126, 300
SS v PS, 2012 ABCA 163 ..... 85, 91, 98
SSG v SKG, 2022 ABCA 379 475
St Amour v St Amour, [1997] NSJ No 363 (TD) 14, 321
St Arnaud v St Arnaud, [1998] BCJ No 3155 (SC) 313
St Jean (Litigation Guardian of) v Cheung, 2009 ONCA 9 641
St Mars v St Mars, [1997] SJ No 700, 160 Sask R 221 (QB) 402
St Pierre v St Pierre, [1999] BCJ No 2264 (SC) 562
Stacey v Hacking (1993), 142 NBR (2d) 99 (QB) 581
Stadnyk v Stadnyk, [2004] SJ No 355, 4 RFL (6th) 198 (QB) 202, 573, 575
Stafford c Stafford, 2023 NBCA 39 195
Stamp v McIntosh, [1998] AJ No 429, 49 RFL (4th) 416 (QB) 219
Stanbridge v Stanbridge, [1998] BCJ No 193 (SC) 182, 334
Stanford v Cole, [1998] NJ No 300, 43 RFL (4th) 237 (SC) 156, 566
Stang v Stang, [2002] AJ No 106, 2002 ABQB 99 ..... 190, 267, 268
Stanghi v Stanghi, [2001] OJ No 1892 (CA) 557, 558
Stannard v Stannard (1991), 34 RFL (3d) 249, [1991] AJ No 679 (QB) 456, 457
Stanton v Solby, [1999] BCJ No 1348, 49 RFL (4th) 422 (SC) 290
Staples v Callender, 2010 NSCA 49 ..... 142, 201, 328, 452
Staples v Callender, 2020 NSSC 365 ..... 295, 405
Stark v Tweedale, 2021 BCSC 1133 ..... 499, 586
Starko v Starko (1991), 33 RFL (3d) 277 (Alta CA) 663
Starling v Starling, 2016 SKQB 112 ..... 151, 155, 215, 216
Starr v Starr, [2008] OJ No 6042 (SCJ) 539, 573
Stasiewski v Stasiewski, 2007 BCCA 205 155
Stebner v Stebner, [2005] AJ No 1556, 2005 ABQB 839, supplementary reasons [2005] AJ No 1625, 2005 ABQB 871 ..... 485, 522, 526
Stebner v Stebner, [2005] AJ No 392, 17 RFL (6th) 363 (QB) 80, 486
Stecyk v Stecyk (1980), 16 RFL (2d) 255 (Sask Dist Ct), aff'd (1980), 23 RFL (2d) 53 (Sask QB) 477, 582
Steele v Koppanyi, [2002] MJ No 201, 2002 MBCA 60 ..... 196, 284, 319, 392, 598
Steeves v English, [2004] AJ No 632, 6 RFL (6th) 125 (CA) 147, 152, 162, 298
Stefanovic v Stefanovic (1990), 30 RFL (3d) 201 (BCCA) 536
Steidinger v Morrell, 2013 MBQB 143 ..... 39, 44
Steiger v Steiger, [1999] AJ No 129, 1999 ABQB 74 ..... 318, 606

Stein v Stein (1975), 10 Nfld & PEIR 358 (Nfld TD) ... 476
Stein v Stein (1984), 49 CPC 99, [1984] OJ No 2276 (HCJ) ... 621
Stein v Stein, [2001] NSJ No 550 (SC) ... 161, 168
Steinhuebl v Steinhuebl (1970), 2 RFL 317 (Ont CA) ... 452
Stelter v Klingspohn, [1999] BCJ No 2926 (SC) ... 319
Stelter v Stelter, 2012 SKCA 117 ... 162, 170, 650
Stenhouse v Stenhouse, 2011 ABQB 530 ... 113
Stephan v Cunningham, 2016 ABCA 177 ... 75, 76
Stephen v Stephen, [1999] SJ No 479, 183 Sask R 161 (QB) ... 124, 187, 455
Stephens v Stephens, 2019 SKQB 114 ... 49, 113
Stere v Stere; Herron, Third Party (1980), 30 OR (2d) 200, 19 RFL (2d) 434 (HCJ) ... 98, 105, 110, 111
Stevens v Boulerice, [1999] OJ No 1568, 49 RFL (4th) 425 (SCJ) ... 152, 212, 277
Stevens v Stevens, [1999] AJ No 1550, 257 AR 183 (QB) ... 165, 337
Stevens v Stevens, 2012 BCSC 1698 ... 163, 216
Stevenson v Perry, [2005] BCJ No 1664, 2005 BCSC 1089 ... 98
Stevenson v Smit, 2014 ONCA 521 ... 557
Stevenson v Stevenson, [1999] BCJ No 324 (SC) ... 383
Stevenson v The Queen, 2018 TCC 176 ... 365
Steward v Ferguson, 2012 BCSC 279 ... 164, 347, 416
Steward v Ferguson, 2018 BCCA 158 ... 13, 560
Stewart v Stewart (1990), 30 RFL (3d) 67 (Alta CA) ... 659
Stewart v Stewart, [2000] SJ No 149 (QB) ... 124, 581
Stewart v Stewart, [2004] AJ No 362, 2004 ABQB 241 ... 142
Stewart v Stewart, [2004] MJ No 272, 2004 MBQB 162 ... 162
Stewart v Stewart (2006), 28 RFL (6th) 193, [2006] MJ No 190 (QB), aff'd 2007 MBCA 66, [2007] MJ No 178 ... 346, 348, 350
Stewart v Stewart, 2009 BCSC 917 ... 126
Stiver v Mercer, [2000] OJ No 568 (SCJ) ... 211, 212
Stoate v Stoate, [2005] OJ No 1655, 17 RFL (6th) 408 (SCJ) ... 209
Stocchero v Stocchero (1997), 29 RFL (4th) 223, [1997] AJ No 628 (CA) ... 83
Stockall v Stockall, 2020 ABQB 229 ... 34, 188, 221, 348, 349
Stoddard v Randall (1985), 72 NSR (2d) 99 (Fam Ct) ... 517
Stokes v Stokes, [1999] OJ No 5192 (SCJ) ... 240, 408, 409
Stokes v Stokes, [2002] NJ No 249, 217 Nfld & PEIR 81 (SC) ... 126, 539
Stones v Stones, [2002] BCJ No 2521, 216 DLR (4th) 252 (SC) ... 326
Storey v Simmons, 2013 ABQB 168 ... 151, 155, 215, 216
Story v Story (1988), 16 RFL (3d) 216 (BCSC), aff'd (1989), 23 RFL (3d) 225 (BCCA) ... 565
Strand v Strand (1995), 12 RFL (4th) 188, [1995] SJ No 192 (QB) ... 46
Strand v Strand, [1999] AJ No 545, 50 RFL (4th) 174 (QB) ... 459, 466
Strang v Strang, [1992] 2 SCR 112, 39 RFL (3d) 233 ... 16, 294, 562
Stratton (Guardian ad litem of) v Gullage, [2001] NJ No 332 (Prov Ct) ... 29
Stratton v Smith, [2005] NJ No 101, 2005 NLUFC 9 ... 142, 561
Stricker v Stricker (1994), 4 RFL (4th) 29 (Alta CA) ... 664
Strickland v Strickland (1991), 32 RFL (3d) 179, [1991] NSJ No 61 (CA) ... 22
Strickland v Strickland, [1998] OJ No 5869 (Gen Div) ... 331
Strickland v Strickland, [1999] OJ No 2293 (SCJ) ... 333
Stromquist v Stromquist, 2020 BCSC 1556 ... 128
Strong v Strong (1987), 5 RFL (3d) 209, [1987] OJ No 1331 (HCJ) ... 22
Struck v Struck, 2018 BCSC 44 ... 538
Stuart v Multan, 2006 MBQB 238 ... 322
Stuart v Stuart (2001), 24 RFL (5th) 188 (Ont SCJ) ... 651, 652
Studzinski v Studzinski, 2020 ONSC 2540 ... 193, 217, 218, 262, 460
Stupak v Stupak, [1997] SJ No 302, 155 Sask R 286 (QB) ... 157, 587

Suchanek v Suchanek, 2010 BCSC 1271 309
Suen v Dunn, 2018 NSSC 17 497
Sugar v Sugar (1976), 23 RFL 248, [1976] OJ No 2117 (CA) 450, 455, 615
Suian v Suian, [2002] BCJ No 1328, 29 RFL (5th) 234 (SC) 370, 568
Sukhram v Sukhram (1987), 6 RFL (3d) 200 (Man QB) 530
Sullivan v Struck, 2015 BCCA 521 .... 86, 88, 96, 119, 218, 483
Sullivan v Struck, 2018 BCCA 256 100
Sullivan v Sullivan (1986), 2 RFL (3d) 251, [1986] OJ No 1896 (Dist Ct) 29
Sullivan v Sullivan, [1999] OJ No 3973, 50 RFL (4th) 326 (Div Ct) 48, 449
Sundararajan v Periasamy, 2021 SKQB 148 76
Surette v Surette, [2000] OJ No 675 (SCJ) 30, 488, 538, 543
Sutcliffe v Sutcliffe, [2001] AJ No 629 (QB) 147, 336
Sutherland v Schlamp, 2014 SKQB 34 .... 52, 100
Sutherland v Sutherland, [1998] BCJ No 342 (SC) 386
Sutherland v Sutherland, 2023 ABCA 121 .... 427, 455, 457, 578, 601
Sutton v Sutton (1985), 33 Man R (2d) 78, [1985] MJ No 314 (QB) 602
Sutton v Sutton, [1999] BCJ No 1933 (SC) 387, 393
Sveinbjornson v Deurbrouck, [1998] SJ No 853 (QB) 112
Swain v Montanaro, 2016 ONSC 4295 .... 371, 372, 379
Swaine v Swaine, [1996] NSJ No 553 (TD) 97
Swainson v Swainson, [2001] YJ No 129 (SC) 4
Swallow v Swallow, [1988] OJ No 1106 (UFC) 570
Swan v Swan, 2024 SKCA 2 228
Swannie v Swannie (1989), 75 Nfld & PEIR 284 (Nfld TD) 477
Swanson v Swanson, [2004] OJ No 5266, [2004] OTC 1149 (SCJ) 195, 462
SWBM v CSM, 2021 SKCA 64 666
Sweeney v Sweeney, 2016 ABQB 131 .... 173, 190
Sweeney v Sweeney, 2018 ONSC 6499 199
Sweet v Sweet (1971), 4 RFL 254 (Ont SC) 476
Sweezey v Sweezey, 2016 ABQB 131 .... 178, 222, 254
Swerid v Swerid (1994), 94 Man R (2d) 86 (QB) 481, 542
Swerid v Swerid, 2022 MBQB 94 .... 63, 113, 115
Swift v Swift, [1998] OJ No 501 (Gen Div) 401
Swindler v Belanger, [2005] SJ No 709 (CA) 88, 96
Switzer v Switzer (1969), 1 RFL 262 (Alta CA) 469
Sydor v Keough, 2019 MBCA 119 183
Sydor v Keough, 2020 MBCA 20 630
Sydor v Sydor, 2011 MBQB 38 352
Sykes v Sykes (1995), 13 RFL (4th) 273, [1995] BCJ No 821 (CA) 627
Symonds v Symonds, 2009 NSSC 26, [2009] NSJ No 40 75
Symons v Taylor, [2000] OJ No 2703, 10 RFL (5th) 443 (SCJ) 33, 99
Sypher v Sypher (1986), 2 RFL (3d) 413 (Ont CA) 459
Syvitski v Syvitski (1988), 86 NSR (2d) 248, [1988] NSJ No 578 (Fam Ct) 219
Szitas v Szitas, 2012 ONSC 1548 .... 40, 112, 122, 193, 223, 226, 229, 558
Szymanski v Szymanski (1994), 77 OAC 252 (CA) 565

T(SJ) v D(S) (1994), 94 BCLR (2d) 290, [1994] BCJ No 1454 (SC) 600
Taccone v Taccone, 2023 ONSC 1646 .... 338, 340, 342
Tack v Fournier, [1998] MJ No 596, 135 Man R (2d) 123 (QB) 14, 296, 297, 374, 375, 383, 403
Tadayon v Mohtashami, 2015 ONCA 777 540
TAF v JSM, [1999] BCJ No 1576 (SC) 313
TAF v MWB, 2013 MBQB 213 .... 13, 295
Tagseth v Tagseth, 2016 SKQB 66 113

Taillefer v Taillefer, 2013 ONSC 6105 129
Taillon v Taillon, [2005] OJ No 1116 (SCJ) 363, 464
Tait v Barker, 2016 MBQB 148 .... 165, 166
Takach v Rose, [2001] BCJ No 865, 2001 BCSC 640 307
TAL v SDB, 2018 ABQB 589 .... 191, 219
Tallman v Tomke, [1997] AJ No 682, 204 AR 119 (QB) 299, 306, 313, 377
TAM v MOG, 2021 ABQB 351 600
Tamke v Tamke, [2001] SJ No 791 (QB) 165, 227, 449
Tang v Tang, [1998] BCJ No 2890 (SC) 305, 309
Tanner v Simpson, [1997] NWTJ No 22 (SC) 386, 391, 391
Tanner v Simpson, [1999] NWTJ No 71 (SC) 336, 382, 385, 391, 402
TAP v JTP, 2009 BCSC 970 319
TAP v JTP, 2014 BCSC 2265 39
Taplin v Laurie (1992), 41 RFL (3d) 197 (Man CA) 476
Tapper v Connolly, [2002] NJ No 83, 26 RFL (5th) 199 (SC) 202, 219, 296
Tapping v Hetherington, [1998] BCJ No 2907 (CA) 557
Tapson v Tapson (1969), 2 RFL 305, [1970] 1 OR 521 (CA) 25
Tarapaski v Tarapaski, 2009 ABCA 365 193
Tarrant v Tarrant, [2005] NJ No 212, 250 Nfld & PEIR 117 (SC) 81
Tataryn v Kriese, 2024 BCSC 75 162
Tatlock v Lays, [2001] AJ No 962 (QB) 210
Tatton v Tatton, [1998] NBJ No 310 (QB) 582
Tauber v Tauber, [1999] OJ No 359, 43 OR (3d) 42 (Gen Div) 7, 437
Tauber v Tauber, [1999] OJ No 713 (CA) 664
Tauber v Tauber (2000), 48 OR (3d) 577, [2000] OJ No 2133 (CA) 641
Tauber v Tauber (2000), 51 OR (3d) 81, [2000] OJ No 3355 (CA) 641
Tauber v Tauber, [2001] OJ No 3259, 18 RFL (5th) 384 (SCJ)
aff'd (2003), 64 OR (3d) 229 (CA) 157, 159, 187, 232, 233, 418, 459
Taylor v Braund (Taylor), 2018 NLCA 3 .... 560, 594
Taylor v Hitchman, 2013 ONCJ 655 222
Taylor v Sherlow, 2014 ONSC 6614 .... 122, 291, 560
Taylor v Taylor (1989), 97 NBR (2d) 271 (QB) 562
Taylor v Taylor, [1999] SJ No 541, 184 Sask R 300 (QB) 386
Taylor v Taylor, [1999] SJ No 732, 191 Sask R 315 (QB) 78
Taylor v Taylor, [2002] NJ No 52, 210 Nfld & PEIR 157 (SC) 71
Taylor v Taylor, [2009] AJ No 22, 2009 ABQB 7 202
TBT v LCG, [2004] AJ No 289, 2004 ABQB 193 195
TC v AJ, 2021 BCSC 1696 .... 124, 169
TDB v LNU, 2010 NBQB 408 538
TDL v LRL (1994), 4 RFL (4th) 103, [1994] OJ No 896 (Gen Div) 599
TDM v JDM, 2020 ABQB 353 .... 49, 593
TDO v RGO, [2000] BCJ No 524, 6 RFL (5th) 389 (SC) 98, 436
Tedham v Tedham, [2003] BCJ No 2554, 44 RFL (5th) 204 (CA) 492
Teitler v Dale, 2017 ONSC 248 214
Teixeira v Teixeira, 2022 ONSC 6133 623
Teja v Dhanda, 2009 BCCA 198 183
Templeton v Nuttall, 2018 ONSC 815 196
Terracol v Terracol, 2010 ONSC 6442 .... 210, 237
Terracol v Terracol, 2012 ONSC 2801 201
Terry v Francis, [2004] NSJ No 366, 11 RFL (6th) 159 (CA) 275
Terry v Terry Estate (1994), 1 BCLR (3d) 299 (SC) 478
TG v SG, 2019 ONSC 4662 .... 81, 640–41
TH v JH, 2016 NBQB 6 353

Thackeray v Sellstead, [2001] SJ No 248 (QB) 483
Theriault v Theriault, [1994] AJ No 187, 2 RFL (4th) 157 (CA) 109–10
Thibaudeau v Canada (Minister of National Revenue), [1995] 2 SCR 627, 124 DLR (4th) 449, 182 NR 1 2
Thistle v Thompson, [2000] NJ No 57 (SC) 412
Thomas v Brereton, 2021 ONSC 5642 613
Thomas v Thomas, 2012 NSSC 440 35
Thomas v Thomas, 2014 ABQB 481 453
Thomas v Thomas, 2019 NLCA 32 228
Thompson v Bear. See Bear v Thompson.
Thompson v Ducharme, [2004] MJ No 129, 1 RFL (6th) 401 (CA) 35
Thompson v Gilchrist, 2012 ONSC 4137 519
Thompson v Gordon, 2009 SKQB 323 389
Thompson v Scullion, [2000] NBJ No 209, 7 RFL (5th) 440 (QB) 147
Thompson v Thompson (1988), 11 RFL (3d) 422 (Sask CA) 662
Thompson v Thompson (1988), 13 RFL (3d) 372, [1988] OJ No 333 (Div Ct) 52
Thompson v Thompson (1988), 16 RFL (3d) 415 (Ont HCJ) 532
Thompson v Thompson, [1998] NSJ No 501, 172 NSR (2d) 50 (SC) 27
Thompson v Thompson, [1999] SJ No 317, 49 RFL (4th) 350 (QB) 325, 481
Thompson v Thompson, [2003] AJ No 1577 (QB) 614, 632
Thompson v Thompson, 2010 MBQB 7 81
Thompson v Thompson, 2013 ONSC 5500 .... 175–76, 179, 184, 188, 359, 360
Thomson v Howard (1997), 33 RFL (4th) 45, [1997] OJ No 4431 (Gen Div) 291, 332, 486, 631
Thomson v Pitchuck, 2020 NSCA 65 661
Thorp v Thorp, [2002] BCJ No 2826 (SC) 79
Thorvaldson v Vanin (1996), 25 RFL (4th) 273, [1996] SJ No 746 (QB) 104, 105
Tibbo v Bush, [2000] NSJ No 352, 189 NSR (2d) 203 (Fam Ct) 151
Tice v Tice, [1998] SJ No 742, 173 Sask R 281 (QB) 145
Tidball v Tidball, [1999] OJ No 904, 45 RFL (4th) 437 (Gen Div) 224
Tillmanns v Tillmanns, 2014 ONSC 6773 196
TIM v TLM, [2003] BCJ No 2902, 1 RFL (6th) 266 (SC) 448
Timoshchenko v Timoshchenko, 2012 ABQB 200 .... 14, 24
Ting v Ting, 2022 ABQB 229, aff'd 2022 ABCA 324 .... 596, 666
Tingley v Tingley (1993), 49 RFL (3d) 87, [1993] NBJ No 424 (QB) 42
Titchener v Titchener (1991), 31 RFL (3d) 173 (BCSC) 449
Titova v Titov, 2012 ONCA 864 .... 280, 285–86
Tiwana v Sandhu, 2010 ONCA 592 615
TK v RJHA, 2015 BCCA 8 196
Tkachuk v Bigras, [1997] OJ No 5453 (Gen Div) 311, 471, 474
TLB v RB, 2010 BCSC 710 .... 125, 190
TLK v DNK, [1999] SJ No 401, 182 Sask R 318 (QB) 228
TLR v RWR, [2006] BCJ No 409, 2006 BCSC 292 359
TLS v DJM, 2009 NSSC 79, [2009] NSJ No 100 .... 284, 286, 319
TM v DM, 2014 NBQB 132 .... 158, 164, 335, 475
TM v ZK, 2021 ABQB 588 .... 503–4, 581
TMD v JPG, 2018 NBCA 15 .... 300, 473, 495
TMF v AJW, 2011 NBQB 133 561
TMH v PJH, 2020 BCSC 804 .... 258, 622
TMR v SMS, 2019 NBQB 40 .... 65, 66, 67, 68, 279, 324
Tobias v Meadley, 2011 BCCA 472 .... 28, 493
Tobias v Tobias, [2000] AJ No 346, 2000 ABQB 172 .... 27, 322, 488
Tobin v Tobin, 2019 NSSC 314 216
Tochor v Kerr, 2011 SKQB 42 259

Todd v Morine, [1999] NBJ No 178 (QB) 590
Toews v Toews, [1998] MJ No 346, 130 Man R (2d) 173 (QB) 392, 402, 403
Tofin v Galbraith, 2019 SKCA 35 642
Tokar-Gaber v Gaber, [2001] SJ No 680 (QB) 578
Tookenay v Laframboise, 2015 ONSC 2898 155
Tooth v Knott, [1998] AJ No 1395 (QB) 337, 338, 345
Torbey v Torbey, [2001] AJ No 1320, 2001 ABQB 830 543, 641
Toronchuk v Wainwright, 2021 ABQB 862 494
Torrone v Torrone, 2010 ONSC 661 343, 349
Torti v Torti, [2001] OJ No 1827 (SCJ) 302, 452
Tosky v Taphorn (1991), 36 RFL (3d) 457 (Man QB) 580
Tougher v Tougher, [1999] AJ No 848 (QB) 263
Tracey v Clarke, [1998] NJ No 236, 169 Nfld & PEIR 137 (SC) 27
Tran v Tran, 2013 NSSC 280 335, 337
Trang v Trang, 2013 ONSC 1980 192, 239, 240, 556
Travis v Travis, 2010 SKCA 83 12
Trebilcock v Trebilcock, 2012 ONCA 452 461
Trecroce v Chorney, 2023 ONSC 96 48, 62
Trefry v Sweeney (1995), 15 RFL (4th) 309, [1995] NSJ No 615 (Fam Ct), aff'd (1995), 15 RFL (4th) 315 (NSTD) 256
Trehearne v Trehearne, [2000] AJ No 1632, 2000 ABQB 991 408
Tremaine v Tremaine, [1997] AJ No 379 (QB) 160, 391
Tremblay v Tremblay [1997] OJ No 3805 (Gen Div) 568
Tremblay v Tremblay, 2016 ONSC 588 179
Trembley v Daley, 2012 ONCA 780 570, 586
Trevisanutto v Crnkovic, [2005] OJ No 2276, [2005] OTC 478 (SCJ) 61
Trevors v Jenkins, 2011 NBCA 61 156, 162, 532, 558
Trick v Trick, [2003] OJ No 1263, 39 RFL (5th) 418 (SCJ) 209
Trick v Trick, 2006 CanLII 22926, (2006), 31 RFL (6th) 237, [2006] OJ No 2737 (CA) 519
Troisi v Gillen, 2013 ONCJ 677 259
Trombetta v Trombetta, 2021 ONSC 4237 602
Trottier v Bradley, [1999] MJ No 227, 49 RFL (4th) 432 (CA) 51
TRS v DGS, [2001] AJ No 1311, 305 AR 97 (QB) 21
Trueman v Trueman, [2000] AJ No 1301, 273 AR 334 (QB) 184, 224, 225, 227, 285, 286, 287, 289, 330, 331, 332
Trueman v Trueman, [2001] AJ No 1272, 305 AR 100 (QB) 47
TS v GC, 2013 NBQB 358 49
TS v JLW, 2022 SKCA 35 600
Tsaros v Ontario (Director, Family Responsibility Office), 2012 ONSC 2449 524
Tschudi v Tschudi, 2010 BCCA 170 262
Tse v Fiddis, 2009 BCSC 1579 223
TTB v PHD, 2014 NBQB 164 26, 46, 47, 50, 54
Tu v Tu, [2000] OJ No 1336 (SCJ) 525
Tubbs v Phillips, [2000] SJ No 282, 192 Sask R 241 (QB) 312, 316
Tucesku v Tucesku, 2015 NSSC 281 142, 389
Tucker v Tucker, 2019 SKQB 317 129, 130, 188
Tuesday v Daniels, [2002] MJ No 316, 165 Man R (2d) 216 (QB) 395
Tughan v Tughan, [2003] OJ No 2656, 39 RFL (5th) 227 (SCJ) 80
Tully v Tully (1994), 9 RFL (4th) 131 (Ont Ct Gen Div) 570
Turcotte v Turcotte (1996), 22 RFL (4th) 364, [1996] OJ No 1327 (Gen Div) 383
Turecki v Turecki (1989), 19 RFL (3d) 127, [1989] BCJ No 267 (CA) 112, 580
Turk v Turk (2008), 50 RFL (6th) 211, [2008] OJ No 397 (SCJ) 414
Turnbull v Turnbull, [1998] YJ No 145 (SC) 581, 582

Turner v Ansell, 2012 ONSC 2598 .... 240, 243
Turner v Turner, [1998] BCJ No 2615 (CA) 472
Turner v Turner, [2000] AJ No 1158 (QB) 567
Turner v Yerxa, [2002] NBJ No 199, 30 RFL (5th) 446 (QB) 372
Turple v Turple, 2011 NSSC 150 .... 30, 31, 291
Tusnady v Tusnady, 2010 BCSC 1310 .... 53, 58, 75
Tutty v Tutty, [2005] NSJ No 514, 2005 NSSC 338 .... 372, 384, 396, 436
Tuz, (Re) (1975), 25 RFL 87, 11 OR (2d) 617 (CA) 22
TVC v MLH, 2015 ABQB 668 356
TW v SL, 2017 SKQB 45 85
Twaddle v Twaddle (1995), 46 RFL (2d) 337, [1985] NSJ No 316 (CA) 112
Tweel v Tweel (1994), 7 RFL (4th) 204, [1994] PEIJ No 83 (SCTD) 21
Tweel v Tweel, [2000] PEIJ No 9, 186 Nfld & PEIR 99 (SC) 135, 157, 325, 344, 345, 362, 583, 587
Tybring v Tybring, [2003] NWTJ No 81, 2003 NWTSC 67 204
Tynan v Moses, [2002] BCJ No 197, 25 RFL (5th) 445 (SC) 205
Tyndall v Tyndall, 2022 ONSC 131 .... 240, 493

Uba v Uba, 2016 ABQB 19 593
Udaipaul v Kissoon, [2005] OJ No 5535 (SCJ) 262
Udalaya v Amfoubalela, 2018 PECA 16 86
Uhrich-Cormier v Cormier, [2000] SJ No 595, 11 RFL (5th) 434 (QB) 374, 383, 389
Ulsen v Keating, 2014 SKQB 364 260
Underhill v Underhill (1985), 49 CPC 237, [1985] OJ No 1610 (HCJ) 615
Underwood v Underwood (1994), 113 DLR (4th) 571, [1994] OJ No 707 (Gen Div) 16
Unger v Scott, 2023 ABKB 500 .... 85, 600
Unrau v National Dental Examining Board, 2019 ABQB 283 623
Unterschultz v Clark, 2022 ABCA 202 646
Uriu v Rivadeneyra, 2017 ONSC 7457 538
Urquhart v Loane, 2016 PECA 15 .... 51, 63, 65, 73, 113
Urquhart v Loane. See also LAU v LLL.
Ursel v Ursel, 2014 BCSC 1219 185
Usova v Harrison, 2010 BCSC 723 .... 166, 478
Uto v Szemok, [2005] BCJ No 1417, 2005 BCSC 912 412
UVH v MWH, 2008 BCCA 177 493

Validen v Validen (1990), 30 RFL (3d) 163 (Man QB) 456
Vallis v Vallis, [1998] NSJ No 342, 170 NSR (2d) 116 (TD) 260
Van Bilsen v Van Bilsen, [2003] OJ No 4657, 48 RFL (5th) 448 (SCJ) 279
Van Boekel v Van Boekel, 2020 ONSC 5265 .... 166, 167, 222, 228, 239, 549
Van Der Voort v Keating, [2006] NSJ No 9, 239 NSR (2d) 392 (SC) 62, 66, 81
Van Deventer v Van Deventer (2000), 3 RFL (5th) 300, [2000] BCJ No 37, 2000 BCCA 9 .... 220, 319
Van Dusen v Van Dusen, 2010 ONSC 220 468
Van Gool v Van Gool, [1998] BCJ No 2513, 113 BCAC 200 .... 196, 199, 201, 208, 211, 372, 374, 378, 392, 393, 394, 508
Van Gool v Van Gool (1999), 44 RFL (4th) 331, [1999] BCJ No 683 (CA) 210
Van Harten v Van Harten, [1998] OJ No 1299, 59 OTC 299 (Gen Div) 42, 244, 312
Van Ruyven v Van Ruyven, 2021 ONSC 5963 596
Van Vroenhoven v Van Vroenhoven, [2009] OJ No 995 (SCJ) 72, 217
Van Wynsberghe v Van Wynsberghe, [1997] OJ No 2566 (Gen Div) 46, 52, 299
Van Zant v Van Zant (1975), 24 RFL 281, [1975] OJ No 1710 (HCJ) 610
Van Zyderveld v Van Zyderveld, [1977] 1 SCR 714, 23 RFL 200 467
Vance v Kovacs, [2005] NBJ No 540, 295 NBR (2d) 165 (QB) 190
Vanderschilden v Vanderschilden (1982), 26 RFL (2d) 407 (Ont HCJ) 615

Vandervort v Brettler (1989), 22 RFL (3d) 160, [1989] OJ No 1579 (HCJ) 318
Vanos v Vanos, 2010 ONCA 876 505
VanSickle v VanSickle, 2012 ONSC 7340 ....46, 67, 482
Vantomme v Vantomme, 2014 SKQB 227 ....49, 56, 57, 59, 113, 279
Varcoe v Varcoe, [2001] OJ No 229 (SCJ) 393, 408
Vardy v Vardy, 2015 NLTD(F) 36 323
Vardy v Vardy, 2019 NSSC 285 372
Varga v Varga, [1998] AJ No 646 (QB) 427, 564
Varga v Varga, [2009] BCJ No 626, 2009 BCSC 416 ....86, 111
Varga v Varga, 2013 SKQB 22 ....374, 392
Vargas v Berryman, 2010 BCSC 542 ....343, 351
Vaughan v Vaughan, 2014 NBCA 6 216
Vavrek v Vavrek, 2019 ABCA 235 ....146, 623
VAW v MEH, 2003 SKQB 255, var'd 2004 SKCA 104 546
VAW v RL, [2004] OJ No 3418, 7 RFL (6th) 444 (SCJ) 454
VB (Next friend of) v DB, [1998] OJ No 4814 (Gen Div) 24
VB v KB, 2013 SKQB 412 467
VC v JDB, [2009] NSJ No 37, 2009 NSSC 25 ....242, 279, 561
VC v PR, 2016 NBQB 90 ....156, 183, 192
Vecchioli v Vecchioli, [1999] AJ No 799, 1999 ABQB 532 ....333, 543
Vegh v Canada, 2012 TCC 95 4
Veinotte v Veinotte, [1999] NSJ No 327 (Fam Ct) 31
Veltkamp v Veltkamp, [1998] SJ No 34, 162 Sask R 77 (QB) 384
Venco v Lie, 2009 BCSC 831 462
Vennels v Vennels (1993), 45 RFL (3d) 165 (BCSC) 570
Verhey v Verhey, 2017 ONSC 2216 196
Verones v Canada, 2012 TCC 291 365
Verones v Canada, 2013 FCA 69 365
Verschuren v Verschuren, 2014 ONCA 518 574
Vervoost v Vervoost (1991), 37 RFL (3d) 178, [1991] AJ No 1050 (QB) 565
Verwey v Verwey, 2007 MBCA 102, 41 RFL (6th) 29, [2007] MJ No 309 ....170, 184, 217
Veskovic v Nielsen, 2022 SKCA 134 ....121, 155, 190, 191, 245, 255, 270
Vetro v Vetro, 2017 ONSC 7294 ....519, 520
Veugelers v Yeoh, [1999] OJ No 3962 (SCJ) 354
Vey v Vey (1979), 11 BCLR 193, 97 DLR (3d) 76 (CA) 293
Vey v Vey (1984), 54 BCLR 270 (CA) 659, 660
Vezina v Vezina, [2006] SJ No 105, 2006 SKCA 27 ....116, 557
Vickers v Vickers, [2001] NSJ No 218, 18 RFL (5th) 431 (CA) 243, 507
Vidal v Dunn, 2018 ONSC 2801 290
Villeneuve v Lafferty, [1999] NWTJ No 128 (SC) 452
Vinagreiro v Vinagreiro, 2022 ABKB 678 ....499, 550, 560
Vincent v Tremblett, [1998] NJ No 292 (SC) 148
Vincent v Vincent, 2012 BCCA 186 ....133, 134, 170, 188, 215, 234, 414
Vinderskov v Vinderskov, [2002] BCJ No 2428, 33 RFL (5th) 229 (CA) 387
Virc v Blair, 2016 ONSC 49 414
Virc v Blair, 2017 ONCA 849 519
Visnjic v Visnjic, [2000] OJ No 1018, 7 RFL (5th) 195 (SCJ) 206
Vitagliano v Di Stavalo, [2001] OJ No 1138, 17 RFL (5th) 194 (SCJ) 147
Vivier v Luchka, [2002] BCJ No 2827, 2002 BCSC 1718 605
Vivier v Vivier, [1997] MJ No 414, 120 Man R (2d) 231 (QB) 211
VKG v IG, 2023 ONSC 6329 ....191, 217, 241
Vlahovic v Vlahovic (1991), 37 RFL (3d) 247, [1991] BCJ No 3718 (CA) 16
Vlasveld v Vlasveld, [1999] BCJ No 1084 (SC) 464

Vlek v Graff, 2013 BCSC 1906 .... 338, 347, 349
VLM v RDM, 2010 NBQB 412 85
VLN v SRN, 2019 ABQB 849 .... 447, 650
VMH v JH, 2020 ABCA 389 650
VMH v JH, 2020 ABQB 156 .... 35, 113
VOE v LLE, 2018 ABQB 940 178
Vogel v Vogel, [1997] MJ No 374 (QB) 569
Vokey v Vokey (1991), 35 RFL (3d) 458, [1991] MJ No 510 (QB) 49
Volgemut v Decristoforo, 2021 ONSC 3543 650
Volken v Volken, [2001] BCJ No 1344, 19 RFL (5th) 205 (SC) 31, 188
Vollmer v Vollmer, [1998] OJ No 5389, 43 RFL (4th) 254 (Gen Div) 273, 277
Vollmershausen v Vollmershausen, 2013 ONSC 4273 .... 304, 305
Von Hessert v Von Hessert (1986), 3 RFL (3d) 27 (Sask CA) 467
Vongrad v Vongrad, [2005] AJ No 632, 2005 ABQB 52 103
Voortman v Voortman (1994), 4 RFL (4th) 250 (Ont CA) 664
Vorlicek v Soares, [1999] BCJ No 3083 (Prov Ct) 518
Voth v Voth, [2004] MJ No 137, 3 RFL (6th) 228 (QB) 227, 230
VS v DMS, 2016 BCSC 1346 .... 25, 28, 34
VSJ v LJG, [2004] OJ No 2238, 5 RFL (6th) 319 (SCJ) 127

W(CSJ) v W(BH) (1996), 24 RFL (4th) 432 (NSCA) 427
W(EG) v P(ME) (1996), 25 RFL (4th) 270, [1996] MJ No 405 (CA) 107
Wadden v Wadden, [2000] BCJ No 1287, 9 RFL (5th) 425 (SC) 243
Wade v Wade, 2016 ONSC 1056 176
Waese v Bojman, [2001] OJ No 2009, 19 RFL (5th) 220 (SCJ) 151, 164, 232, 233
WAF v WF, 2011 NBQB 319 90
Wagener v Wagener (1988), 17 RFL (3d) 308, [1988] MJ No 486 (QB) 478
Wahl v Wahl, 2000 ABQB 10, [2000] AJ No 29, 2 RFL (5th) 307 (QB) 25, 47, 48, 51, 54, 66, 72, 97, 114, 322
Wainman v Clairmont, [2004] NSJ No 69, 2 RFL (6th) 435 (SC) 379
Wait v Wait, [2000] BCJ No 1282, 7 RFL (5th) 446 (CA) 306, 308, 320
Waite v Clements, [2002] PEIJ No 8, 26 RFL (5th) 221 (SC) 392, 394
Wakeford v Wakeford, 2011 ABQB 106 27
Wakeman v Wakeman, 2021 BCSC 1095 456
Wakim v Wakim, unreported (29 May 1987) (Ont HCJ) 621
Walgren v Walgren, [2002] BCJ No 881, 26 RFL (5th) 226 (SC) 216
Walkeden v Zemlak, [1997] SJ No 601 (QB) 480
Walker v Gardner, [2000] PEIJ No 99 (SC) 480
Walker v Rutledge, [2002] OJ No 4521, [2002] OTC 925 (SCJ) 142, 386
Walker v Walker, [1999] AJ No 828, 1 RFL (5th) 180 (QB) 385, 576
Walker v Walker, [2001] AJ No 553, 17 RFL (5th) 225 (CA) 213,
Walker v Walker, 2016 ABQB 181 .... 558, 562, 564
Walker v Walker, 2019 ABQB 385 241
Walker v Walker, 2019 SKCA 96 .... 170, 183, 184, 191
Walker v Walker, 2024 ONSC 198 .... 125, 136, 138–42
Walker v Whiting (1998), 235 AR 58, [1998] AJ No 1166 (QB) 627
Walker-Bodnarek v Bodnarek, [2005] SJ No 658, 271 Sask R 151 (QB) 104, 333
Wall v Eeles, [2006] BCJ No 142, 2006 BCSC 115 312
Wallace v Wallace, [1998] BCJ No 203 (SC) 434
Wallace v Wallace, [1998] BCJ No 2086 (SC) 148, 451
Wallace v Wallace, [2002] BCJ No 1558 (SC) 313
Wallberg v Wallberg (1994), 8 RFL (4th) 372, [1994] BCJ No 2202 (CA) 16
Waller v Waller, [1998] OJ No 5387 (Gen Div) 332, 336, 345, 507

Walling v Holosney, 2011 BCSC 104 348
Walliser v Pouliot, [2005] SJ No 580, 270 Sask R 66 (QB) 148, 158
Walls v Walls, [1998] NBJ No 246, [1998] NBR (2d) (Supp) No 49 (QB) 27
Walls v Walls, 2014 BCSC 586 122
Walpole v Walpole, 2012 ONSC 2731 204
Walsh v Walsh (1988), 16 RFL (3d) 1, [1988] NBJ No 611 (CA) 81
Walsh v Walsh, [1996] OJ No 3970, 20 OTC 77 (Gen Div) 388
Walsh v Walsh, [1999] NJ No 12 (UFC) 543
Walsh v Walsh, [2004] OJ No 254, 46 RFL (5th) 455 (CA) 259, 554, 585
Walsh v Walsh, [2006] NJ No 33, 2006 NLUFC 7 .... 143, 144, 283, 290, 300, 312, 317, 339, 342
Walsh v Walsh, [2008] OJ No 98 (SCJ) 538, 539
Wambolt v Wambolt, [2008] NBJ No 63, 2008 NBQB 27 63
Wang v Wang, [1997] BCJ No 1678, 41 BCLR (3d) 375 (SC),
aff'd [1998] BCJ No 1966, 39 RFL (4th) 426 (CA) 429, 432, 567
Wang v Wang, [2003] BCJ No 2211, 2003 BCSC 1451 190
Wanstall v Walker, [1998] BCJ No 1808 (SC) 294, 308, 316, 319
Warbinek v Canada, 2008 DTC 6674, [2008] FCJ No 1317, 2008 FCA 276 2
Ward v Hanes, [2000] BCJ No 2372, 2000 BCSC 1656 .... 28, 618
Ward v Murphy, 2022 NSCA 20 .... 176–77, 184, 191
Ward v Murphy, 2023 NSSC 370 .... 135, 171, 215, 498
Ward v Spear, [1999] OJ No 1795, 46 RFL (4th) 396 (Prov Div) 22
Ward v Ward (1988), 13 RFL (3d) 259 (Ont HCJ), rev'd in part (1990),
26 RFL (3d) 149 (Ont CA) 476
Ward v Ward, [1998] AJ No 63 (QB) 481
Ward v Ward, [1999] OJ No 458, 44 RFL (4th) 340 (Gen Div) 159, 292
Ward v Ward, [2001] BCJ No 1206, 19 RFL (5th) 232 (SC) 216
Ward v Ward, [2001] BCJ No 206 241
Ward v Ward, 2015 ONSC 6221 .... 316, 328
Warren v Baird, 2015 ABQB 479 166
Warren v Warren, [1998] NBJ No 315, 203 NBR (2d) 356 (QB) 402
Warren v Warren, [2001] NJ No 262 (SC) 439
Warren v Warren, 2018 BCSC 1285 575
Warren v Warren, 2021 ABQB 213 .... 123, 124, 152, 166
Warsh v Warsh, 2012 ONSC 6903 .... 55, 58, 112
Warsh v Warsh, 2013 ONSC 1886 639
Wasney v Wasney, [1999] OJ No 3389 (SCJ) 469, 536
Wasuita v Wasuita, [1998] AJ No 695, 224 AR 145 (QB) 148, 217
Watch v Watch, [1999] SJ No 490, 182 Sask R 237 (QB) 93
Waterman v Waterman (1995), 16 RFL (4th) 10, [1995] NJ No 295 (CA) 16, 507
Watkin v Hall, [1998] MJ No 310, 130 Man R (2d) 90 (QB) 194
Watson v Solberg, [2003] SJ No 333 (QB) 559
Watson v Watson, [1998] MJ No 356 (QB) 544
Watson v Watson, [2006] BCJ No 329, 2006 BCSC 256 .... 217, 274
Watts v Willie, [2004] BCJ No 1824 (SC) 72
Watts v Willie, [2004] BCJ No 2482, 8 RFL (6th) 456, 2004 BCCA 600 .... 199, 208
Waugh v Waugh, 2010 BCSC 110 .... 350, 362
Wawzonek v Page, 2015 ONSC 4374 113
WB v JV, [1999] OJ No 3489 (SCJ) 528
Webb v Webb, [1999] OJ No 507, 92 OTC 257 (Gen Div) 434
Webber v Webber (1970), 3 NBR (2d) 94, [1970] NBJ No 115 (CA) 614
Weber v Merritt, 2018 ONSC 3086 271
Weber v Weber, 2020 ONSC 4098 .... 39, 549
Webster v Lusty (1992), 44 RFL (3d) 56 (Man CA) 459

Webster v Webster, 2014 BCSC 730 128–29
Wedge v McKenna, [1997] PEIJ No 75, 155 Nfld & PEIR 294 (TD) 145, 437
Wedgwood v Wedgwood (1988), 69 Nfld & PEIR 134 (Nfld UFC) 448
Wedsworth v Wedsworth, [2000] NSJ No 209, 185 NSR (2d) 215 (SC), var'd [2000] NSJ No 306, 2000 NSCA 108 12 RFL (5th) 232 (CA) 126, 212, 306, 661
Wedsworth v Wedsworth, [2001] NSJ No 239, 19 RFL (5th) 455 (CA) 555
Wehrhahn v Murphy, 2014 ABCA 194 159
Weibe v Oviatt, [1998] SJ No 303, 40 RFL (4th) 338 (QB) 212
Weichholz v Weichholz (1987), 81 AR 236, [1987] AJ No 331 (QB) 89, 90
Weinert v Weinert, [2005] OJ No 584 (SCJ) 104
Weingarden v Weingarden (1978), 3 RFL (2d) 97 (Ont HCJ), aff'd (1979), 9 RFL (2d) 355 (Ont CA), leave to appeal to SCC refused (1979), 27 NR 179n 565
Weinstein v British Columbia (Director of Maintenance Enforcement), [1997] BCJ No 1361 (SC) 579
Weinstein v Weinstein (1994), 1 BCLR (3d)174 (SC), rev'd (1995), 15 RFL (4th) 353 (BCCA) 551, 581
Weir v Landry, [2003] PEIJ No 116, 2003 PESCTD 97 358
Weismiller v Jolkowski, [2000] OJ No 1775, 7 RFL (5th) 453 (SCJ) 358
Wellman v Gilcash, [2003] NBJ No 214 (CA) 459
Wells v Watson, [2000] BCJ No 1638 (SC) 320
Wells v Wells (1982), 29 CPC 186, [1982] OJ No 2269 (HCJ) 619
Welner v Welner (1984), 64 NSR (2d) 72, 38 RFL (2d) 323 (Fam Ct) 112
Welsh v Welsh, [1998] OJ No 4550, 79 OTC 81 (Gen Div) 38, 48, 54, 63, 244, 313, 540, 599
Welstead v Bainbridge (1994), 2 RFL (4th) 419, [1994] OJ No 352 (Prov Ct) 112, 572
Weniuk v Weniuk (1986), 3 RFL (3d) 110 (FCTD) 517
Werden v Werden, [2005] OJ No 5257 (Sup Ct) 457
Werenka v Werenka, 2021 ABQB 1023 .... 76, 323
Werenka v Werenka, 2021 ABQB 789 .... 42, 143
Wesemann v Wesemann, [1999] BCJ No 1387, 49 RFL (4th) 435 (SC) 27, 63, 64, 65, 67
Wesolowski v Wesolowski, [1999] AJ No 183 (CA) 662
West v West, [2001] OJ No 2149, [2001] OTC 422, 18 RFL (5th) 440 (SCJ) 194, 209, 633
Westcott v Westcott, [1997] OJ No 3060 (Gen Div) 52, 142, 182
Westergard v Buttress, 2012 BCCA 38 60
Wetsch v Kuski, 2017 SKCA 77 .... 64, 122, 134, 166, 348, 349, 351, 405, 494
WG v SG, 2014 ONSC 3258 485
Whalen v Canada, [2001] TCJ No 81, 16 RFL (5th) 432 302
Whalen v Whalen, [2000] OJ No 2658 (SCJ) 408
Whalen v Whalen, 2010 NSSC 432 345
Wharry v Wharry, 2016 ONCA 930 .... 455, 511
Wharton v Wharton, [1996] AJ No 1144 (QB) 573
Whelan v Whelan, [2005] NJ No 134 (CA) 552
White Burgess Langille Inman v Abbott and Haliburton Co, 2015 SCC 23 .... 633, 634
White v Rushton, [1998] BCJ No 1227, 38 RFL (4th) 454 (SC) 375
White v White, [1998] BCJ No 2635 (SC) 480
White v White, [2000] BCJ No 516 (SC) 373
White v White, [2001] NSJ No 558 (SC), aff'd [2002] NSJ No 248, 27 RFL (5th) 462 (CA) 208, 537, 572
White v White, [2002] AJ No 1049 (QB) 467
White v White, 2015 NSCA 52 .... 142, 156, 157, 194, 200, 212, 235
Whitehead v Whitehead, [1999] BCJ No 1783 (SC) 485
Whitehead v Ziegler (1974), 18 RFL 357, [1974] SJ No 240 (QB) 624
Whitley v Whitley, [1997] BCJ No 3116 (SC) 63, 72, 241, 279
Whitley v Whitley, [1998] BCJ No 4741 (SC) 568

Whittall v Whittall (1987), 19 BCLR (2d) 202 (SC) ... 466
Whittle v Clements, [1998] NJ No 140 (UFC) ... 144
Whittleton v Whittleton, [2003] AJ No 746 (QC), 2003 ABQB 513 ... 127
Widdis v Widdis, [2000] SJ No 614, 198 Sask R 15 (QB) ... 88, 98, 449
Wiebe v Treissman, 2017 BCSC 1523 ... 256
Wieland v Wieland (1994), 3 RFL (4th) 56, [1994] OJ No 518 (Gen Div) ... 81
Wiens v Wiens, [2001] AJ No 569 (QB) ... 559
Wiewiora v Wiewiora, 2014 MBQB 218 ... 76, 323
Wigmore v Wigmore, [2004] PEIJ No 49, 7 RFL (6th) 219 (TD) ... 35
Wilbur v MacMurray (1991), 38 RFL (3d) 74, [1991] NBJ No 1101 (QB) ... 112
Wilde v Wilde, [1998] AJ No 430, 221 AR 140 (QB) ... 313
Wildeman v Wildeman, 2014 ABQB 732 ... 249, 277, 425
Wildman v Wildman (2006), 82 OR (3d) 401, [2006] OJ No 3966 (CA) ... 469, 541, 654
Wilk v Martin-Wilk, 2023 SKCA 64 ... 158
Wilk v Re, [1997] AJ No 732 (QB) ... 322
Wilkins v Wilkins, [1998] NBJ No 325, 204 NBR (2d) 70 (QB) ... 27, 70, 72
Will v Thauberger Estate (1991), 34 RFL (3d) 432 (Sask QB), var'd (1991), 38 RFL (3d) 68 (Sask CA) ... 478, 479
Willcock v Terrell, [1879] 3 Ex D 323 (CA) ... 523
Willford v Schaffer, [2003] SJ No 840, 2003 SKQB 554 ... 309, 342
Williams v Ontario (Family Responsibility Office, Director), [1999] OJ No 5051 (SCJ) ... 528
Williams v Smith, [2001] AJ No 248 (QB) ... 400
Williams v Steinwand, 2014 NWTSC 74, supplementary reasons 2015 NWTSC 3 ... 280, 286, 327, 374, 385, 642
Williams v Steinwand, 2017 NWTSC 50 ... 14, 147
Williams v Wallace, 2017 ABQB 421 ... 52, 56
Williams v Williams (1995), 18 RFL (4th) 129, [1995] OJ No 4336 (Div Ct) ... 244
Williams v Williams, [1997] BCJ No 2091 (SC) ... 2
Williams v Williams, [1997] NWTJ No 49, 32 RFL (4th) 23 (SC) ... 13, 145, 148, 212, 259, 371, 385, 386, 387, 396
Williams v Williams, [1998] SJ No 216 (QB) ... 582
Williams v Williams, [1999] NJ No 254 (CA) ... 661
Williams v Williams, [2000] NJ No 317, 196 Nfld & PEIR 343 (UFC) ... 260
Williams v Williams, [2001] AJ No 1298 (QB) ... 580
Williams v Williams, [2001] AJ No 1558 (QB) ... 666
Williams v Williams, [2007] NJ No 257, 2007 NLUFC 20 ... 202
Williams v Williams, 2011 SKCA 84 ... 473
Williams v Williams, 2013 ONSC 220 ... 554
Williamson v Rezonja, 2014 ONCJ 72 ... 319
Williamson v Williamson (1991), 31 RFL (3d) 378, [1991] NBJ No 24 (QB) ... 94, 99, 109
Williamson v Williamson, 2016 ONSC 1180 ... 262
Willick v Willick, [1994] 3 SCR 670, 6 RFL (4th) 161 ... 15, 304, 411, 423, 441, 443, 561, 562, 563, 563, 564, 565, 590, 661
Willie v Willie, [2000] SJ No 750, 2000 SKQB 482 ... 48, 463
Willis v Nagy, 2023 BCSC 1493 ... 40
Willis v Willis, 2010 ABQB 534 ... 158, 484, 587
Willms v Willms, 2019 BCSC 1944 ... 40, 42
Willms v Willms, 2020 BCCA 51 ... 407
Willock v Willock, [2005] BCJ No 2664, 2005 BCSC 1697 ... 47
Wilson v Daffern, [1998] BCJ No 2899 (SC) ... 427
Wilson v Eronchi, [2000] NWTJ No 3, 4 RFL (5th) 146 (SC) ... 9, 459, 462, 463, 472
Wilson v Grassick (1994), 2 RFL (4th) 291 (Sask CA) ... 661
Wilson v Larocque, 2016 NWTSC 26 ... 578

Wilson v Wilson (1963), 46 WWR 217 (Man QB) 544
Wilson v Wilson, 1983 CanLII 1165 (Ont Ct J) 477
Wilson v Wilson, [1998] SJ No 236, [1998] 8 WWR 493, 165 Sask R 241 (QB) 223, 224, 556
Wilson v Wilson, [1999] BCJ No 2458 (SC) 290, 296, 310, 438
Wilson v Wilson, [2004] BCJ No 116, 2004 BCSC 88 407
Wilson v Wilson, 2011 ONCJ 103 223
Wilson v Wilson Estate, [1998] BCJ No 2516, 43 RFL (4th) 153 (SC) 479
Wiltshire v Wiltshire, [2003] OJ No 3099 (SCJ) 632
Wink v Wink (1981), 26 RFL (2d) 158, [1981] OJ No 2421 (HCJ) 620
Winkler v Winkler (1990), 27 RFL (3d) 445, [1990] MJ No 341 (CA) 624, 648
Winnipeg Child and Family Services (Northwest Area) v G(DF), [1997] 3 SCR 925, 31 RFL (4th) 165, [1997] SCJ No 96 29
Winofsky v Winofsky, 2012 BCSC 433 45
Winram v Cassidy (1991), 37 RFL (3d) 230 (Man CA) 550
Winseck v Winseck (2008), 235 OAC 38 (Div Ct) 284
Winsemann v Donaldson, [2007] BCJ No 1936, 2007 BCSC 1322 64
Winsor v Winsor (1994), 7 RFL (4th) 30 (Nfld SC) 569
Winsor v Winsor, 2017 NLCA 54 .... 48, 49
Winstanley v Winstanley, 2016 MBCA 17 .... 63, 75, 115, 297
Winterburn v Evanchuk, [1999] OJ No 5968 (Ct J) 556
Wiome v Wiome, [2002] SJ No 615, 2002 SKQB 402 582
Wionzek v Magyar, 2013 SKQB 194 .... 63, 65
Wishart v Wishart (1990), 29 RFL (3d) 68, [1990] BCJ No 2300 (SC) 219
Wishlow v Bingham (2000), 261 AR 299, 10 RFL (5th) 229, [2000] AJ No 809 (CA) 507
Wislesky v Wislesky, [1999] OJ No 1220, 47 RFL (4th) 208 (Gen Div) 382, 388, 466
Witt v Johnson, 2022 ABQB 105 457
Wittke v Wittke (1974), 16 RFL 349, [1974] SJ No 20 (QB) 16
WJA v STS, [2001] NSJ No 151, 15 RFL (5th) 449, 2001 NSCA 69 .... 99, 108, 111, 397, 601
WK v VLC, 2022 BCSC 1321 596
WL v NDH, 2014 NBQB 214 .... 12, 374, 405, 506, 565
WL v RW, [2005] NBJ No 470, 290 NBR (2d) 306 (QB) 280, 288, 329, 330
WLG v ACG, 2021 SKCA 112 .... 118, 163, 183, 191, 456
Wlodarczyk v Wlodarczyk, [2002] BCJ No 1940 (SC) 394
WM v DO, [1999] AJ No 1338, 3 RFL (5th) 249 (QB) 405
Wojcichowsky v Wojcichowsky, 2009 SKQB 89, [2009] SJ No 124 448
Wolbaum v Royal, [1998] SJ No 235, 166 Sask R 60 (QB) 207
Wolf v Wolf (1992), 41 RFL (3d) 391, 41 RFL (3d) 391 (BCSC) 478, 582
Wolfe v Morrisseau, 2021 ABCA 205 659
Wolfson v Wolfson, 2021 NSSC 260 .... 135, 171, 180, 183, 184, 346, 349, 354, 355, 362
Wolkowski v Doroshenko, [2002] SJ No 170, 27 RFL (5th) 214 (QB) 456
Woloshyn v Woloshyn, [2000] MJ No 53 (QB) 517
Wong v Wong (1990), 27 RFL (3d) 215, [1990] OJ No 1062 (CA) 211
Wong v Wong, [1997] BCJ No 2856 (SC) 564
Wong v Wong, 2012 NSSC 430 204
Wongstedt v Wongstedt, 2017 SKCA 100 603
Wood v Boere, 2012 BCSC 252 .... 476, 561
Wood v Wood (1971), 5 RFL 82 (Ont SC) 476
Wood v Wood (1982), 56 NSR (2d) 217, [1982] NSJ No 31 (TD) 629
Wood v Wood, [1997] BCJ No 1501 (SC) 43
Wood v Wood, [2001] SJ No 2 (CA) 659
Wood v Wood, [2005] BCJ No 910, 2005 BCSC 614 80
Woode v Woode, [2002] SJ No 55, 26 RFL (5th) 232 (QB) 309, 312

Woodford v Horne, 2015 NSSC 208 ... 117
Woodford v MacDonald, 2014 NSCA 31 ... 349, 350, 357
Woodland v Kirkham, 2021 ONSC 8194 ... 491, 492, 494, 511
Woodman v Woodman (1976), 26 RFL 399, [1976] MJ No 37 (CA) ... 605
Woodrow v Lepoudre, 2022 SKQB 143 ... 88, 98, 99, 100, 104, 105, 295, 498, 584
Woods v Woods, [1998] SJ No 687, 42 RFL (4th) 123 (QB) ... 72, 73, 566
Woodward v Woodward, 2016 SKQB 301 ... 148, 150
Woolgar v Woolgar (1995), 10 RFL (4th) 309, [1995] NJ No 188 (UFC) ... 262
Woolhouse v Jarosz, [1998] SJ No 62, 162 Sask R 314 (QB) ... 403
Woolsey v Redman, [2003] SJ No 823, 1 RFL (6th) 422 (QB) ... 102
Woroniuk v Woroniuk, 2011 MBQB 268 ... 452, 454
Worrall v Worrall (1991), 38 RFL (3d) 435 (Ont Ct Gen Div) ... 486
Wotherspoon v Wotherspoon (1986), 56 Sask R 162 (QB) ... 579
Wotton v Banks, [2001] PEIJ No 22, 15 RFL (5th) 225 (SC) ... 165, 483
Wouters v Wouters, [2001] SJ No 232, 16 RFL (5th) 438, 2001 SKQB 142 ... 359, 453
Wouters v Wouters, [2002] SJ No 520 (QB), var'd [2005] SJ No 340, 19 RFL (6th) 235 (CA) ... 366, 540
Wouters v Wouters, 2008 NWTSC 61, [2008] NWTJ No 61 ... 35
Wouters v Wouters, 2013 NWTSC 9 ... 35, 587
WPN v BJN, [2004] BCJ No 1351 (SC) ... 620
WPN v BJN, [2005] BCJ No 12, 2005 BCCA 7 ... 50, 52, 56, 58, 62, 63, 65, 66, 72, 322
WRA (Next friend of) v GFA, [2001] AJ No 1472, 100 Alta LR (3d) 59 (QB) ... 10
Wright v Canada (Attorney General) (1988), 13 RFL (3d) 343 (Ont Div Ct) ... 528
Wright v Wright (1994), 7 RFL (4th) 43, [1994] BCJ No 1233 (SC) ... 653
Wright v Wright (1996), 141 Sask R 44 (CA) ... 266
Wright v Wright, [1998] AJ No 1167 (QB) ... 307
Wright v Wright, [2002] BCJ No 458 (SC) ... 336
Wright v Zaver, [2002] OJ No 1098, 24 RFL (5th) 207 (CA) ... 100, 110, 429, 430, 440, 441, 442, 567
Wrightsell v Wrightsell (1973), 11 RFL 271 (Ont SC) ... 476
Wrobel v Wrobel (1994), 8 RFL (4th) 403 (Alta QB) ... 565
Wundele v Wundele (1994), 8 RFL (4th) 325, [1994] BCJ No 2514 (CA) ... 220, 472
Wunsche v Wunsche (1994), 70 OAC 380 (CA) ... 661
Wur v Wur (1975), 17 RFL 251 (Man CA) ... 660
Wurmlinger v Cyca, [2003] SJ No 247, 231 Sask R 282 (QB) ... 314, 317
Wuzinski v Wuzinski (1987), 10 RFL (3d) 420, [1987] MJ No 496 (QB) ... 85, 89
Wyndels v Minuk, 2019 MBQB 96 ... 226
Wynnyk v Wynnyk, [2004] OJ No 27 (SCJ) ... 630

X v Y, 2015 BCSC 1327 ... 600
X(RL) v X(JF), [2002] BCJ No 1889 (SC) ... 213, 372, 537, 540
Xu v Chu, 2019 BCCA 414 ... 213

Yagelniski v Yagelniski, [1999] SJ No 35 (QB) ... 119
Yakimitz v Chorkwa, 2013 ABQB 443 ... 340
Yakimyshyn v Yakimyshyn (1994), 9 RFL (4th) 41, [1994] AJ No 859 (QB) ... 627
Yar v Yar, 2015 ONSC 151 ... 202
Yaschuk v Logan, [1992] NSJ No 99, 39 RFL (3d) 417 (CA) ... 54, 56
Yaskiel v Canada, [2005] TCJ No 600, [2006] 1 CTC 2483 ... 303
Yee v Yee (1997), 30 RFL (4th) 238 (Sask QB) ... 580
Yenovkian v Gulian, 2019 ONSC 7279 ... 470
Yensen v Yensen, [2003] BCJ No 2086, 2003 BCSC 1372 ... 285
Yeo v Yeo, [1998] PEIJ No 100, 43 RFL (4th) 408 (TD) ... 182, 330, 332
Yeo v Yeo, [1998] PEIJ No 97, 42 RFL (4th) 418 (CA) ... 552, 553

Yeoman v Luhtala, [2002] AJ No 1504, 2002 ABQB 1045 .... 168, 635
Yeung v Silva, 2016 BCSC 1682 196
Yeung v Yeung, [1999] BCJ No 2901 (SC) 631
Yhard v Mulvihill, 2017 NSSC 101 .... 194, 201
YHB v JPB, 2014 BCSC 618 52
Yi v Yung (1994), 52 BCAC 1, [1994] BCJ No 3217 256
YL v GL, 2020 BCSC 808 .... 181, 191
Youle v Galloway, 2018 SKQB 211 .... 26, 76, 323
Young v Hubbert (1987), 8 RFL (3d) 453 (FCTD) 513
Young v Konkle (1993), 1 RFL (4th) 211 (Alta QB) 582
Young v Marshall, 2018 NSSC 211 216
Young v Rodgers, [2000] OJ No 4564 (SCJ) 52, 165, 544
Young v Vincent, [1997] NSJ No 163 (TD) 293, 311, 473
Young v Young (1981), 17 RFL (2d) 190 (Man CA) 659
Young v Young, [1998] BCJ No 1120 (SC) 334
Young v Young, [1998] BCJ No 453, 39 RFL (4th) 110 (SC) 119, 435
Young v Young, [1999] NSJ No 63, 49 RFL (4th) 455 (SC) 43, 242, 409
Young v Young, [2000] NBJ No 93, 7 RFL (5th) 228 (CA) 287
Young v Young, 2012 BCSC 1727 75
Yovcheva v Hristov, 2019 ONSC 1007 .... 145, 162
Yovcheva v Hristov, 2022 ONSC 5284 338
Yunger v Zolty, 2011 ONSC 5943 298
Yurchak v Yurchak, [2000] SJ No 287, 192 Sask R 312, 2000 SKQB 213 629
Yurchuk v Yurchuk (1976), 2 AR 277 (CA) 476

Zaba v Bradley (1996), 137 Sask R 295, 18 RFL (4th) 1, [1996] SJ No 5 (CA) 75, 604
Zaba v Bradley (1996), 140 Sask R 297, 22 RFL (4th) 52 (QB) 75
Zacks v Zacks, [1973] SCR 891, 10 RFL 53 20
Zadegan v Zadegan, [2003] OJ No 5282, 2 RFL (6th) 445 (SCJ) 530
Zadera v Zadera, 2023 BCSC 1880 145
Zak v Zak, 2021 ABCA 131 664
ZAM v AVT, 2018 ABQB 319 157
Zarins v Cochrane, [1999] BCJ No 2876 (SC) 549
ZAS v TS, 2022 BCSC 435 447
Zdan v Zdan, [2001] MJ No 444, supplementary reasons [2001] MJ No 450, 22 RFL (5th) 220 (QB) 9, 454, 487
ZDD v RCG, 2004 BCSC 1239 327
Zdyb v Zdyb, 2017 ABQB 44 .... 146, 222
Zeeper v Zeeper, [2000] AJ No 309, 264 AR 97 (QB) 274
Zeggelaar v Zeggelaar, 2024 NSSC 34 .... 213, 218
Zehr v MacConnell, 2012 NWTSC 80 .... 301, 307
Zelinski v Pidkowich, 2020 SKCA 42 610
Zemliak v Zemliak (1992), 40 RFL (3d) 181 (Man CA) 448
Zenner v Zenner (1991), 32 RFL (3d) 11 (PEICA) 664
Zenner v Zenner, 2012 PECA 5 659
Zeyha v Canada (Attorney General), [2004] SJ No 721, 11 RFL (6th) 465 (CA) 20
Zhang v Lin, 2010 ABQB 420 56
Zhao v Xiao, 2023 ONCA 453, leave to appeal to SCC denied 2023 CanLII 115636 (SCC) 295, 432, 661
Zheng v Yang, 2020 MBQB 146 214
Zho v Chen, [2000] OJ No 4520, 11 RFL (5th) 231 (SCJ) 296
Zieglgansberger v Venyige, [2003] SJ No 791, 1 RFL (6th) 462 (QB) 210, 570, 571
Zien v Woida, [2003] BCJ No 1864, 43 RFL (5th) 241 (SC) 36

Zigiris v Foustanellas, 2016 ONSC 7528 280
Zilic v Zilic, 2019 BCSC 1482 162
Zilic v Zilic, 2021 BCCA 107 299
Ziomek v Selva, [2001] OJ No 1457 (SCJ) 590
Zipchen v Edwardh (1991), 35 RFL (3d) 45, [1991] OJ No 1243 (Prov Div) 569, 571
Zivot v Tobey, 2009 MBQB 269 384
Zorn v Zorn, [1998] BCJ No 3014 (SC) 401, 402
Zsiak v Bell, [1998] BCJ No 2233 (SC) 306
Zubek v Nizol, 2011 BCSC 776 .... 125, 394
Zubot v Zubot, [2001] AJ No 1601, 2001 ABQB 1079 624
Zuk v Zuk, [1998] AJ No 1425 (CA) 567, 661
Zuniga v Zuniga, 2021 BCSC 1625 493

About the Authors

Julien D Payne, CM, KC, LLD, LSM, FRSC, one of Canada's pre-eminent family law specialists, has been called the architect of the Unified Family Court and no-fault divorce. He has taught family law at the Universities of Alberta, Western Ontario, Ottawa, and Saskatchewan, and written extensively about family law and family dispute resolution. Julien D Payne is the author of *Payne on Divorce,* 4th ed, 1996 (Carswell) and the co-author of *Canadian Family Law* (Irwin Law). His writings have been cited more than 2,000 times by trial courts and appellate courts in Canada, including by the Supreme Court of Canada. He was awarded the Law Society Medal by the Law Society of Upper Canada in 2002 and was made a member of the Order of Canada in 2004.

Marilyn A Payne is an experienced author and the founding editor of the looseleaf service, *Payne's Divorce and Family Law Digest,* 1980–1999 (Richard de Boo). She is the co-author of *Canadian Family Law* (Irwin Law).

Printed and bound by CPI Group (UK) Ltd, Croydon, CR0 4YY
15/09/2026
14962405-0002